March 6–9, 2017
Vienna, Austria

Association for
Computing Machinery

Advancing Computing as a Science & Profession

HRI'17

Proceedings of the 2017 ACM/IEEE International Conference on Human-Robot Interaction

Sponsored by:

ACM SIGCHI, ACM SIGAI, & IEEE RAS

In-cooperation with:

AAAI & HFES

Association for
Computing Machinery

Advancing Computing as a Science & Profession

The Association for Computing Machinery
2 Penn Plaza, Suite 701
New York, New York 10121-0701

Notice to Past Authors of ACM-Published Articles
ACM intends to create a complete electronic archive of all articles and/or other material previously published by ACM. If you have written a work that has been previously published by ACM in any journal or conference proceedings prior to 1978, or any SIG Newsletter at any time, and you do NOT want this work to appear in the ACM Digital Library, please inform permissions@acm.org, stating the title of the work, the author(s), and where and when published.

ISBN: 978-1-4503-4336-7 (Digital)

ISBN: 978-1-4503-5445-5 (Print)

Additional copies may be ordered prepaid from:

ACM Order Department
PO Box 30777
New York, NY 10087-0777, USA

Phone: 1-800-342-6626 (USA and Canada)
+1-212-626-0500 (Global)
Fax: +1-212-944-1318
E-mail: acmhelp@acm.org
Hours of Operation: 8:30 am – 4:30 pm ET

Printed in the USA

HRI'17 Chairs' Welcome

We are excited to welcome you to the Twelfth Annual ACM/IEEE International Conference on Human-Robot Interaction (HRI 2017). The HRI Conference is a highly selective, single track, international meeting showcasing the best research in human-robot interaction, with roots in and broad participation from various communities of scholars, including but not limited to robotics, human-computer interaction, artificial intelligence, engineering, social and behavioral sciences, and design.

The theme of this year's conference is "Smart Interaction," following our host city Vienna's ongoing "Smart City" initiative. Designed with increasingly intelligent capabilities, robots must utilize such intelligence also in their interactions with people to improve the effectiveness, naturalness, and intuitiveness of these interactions as well as their moral and ethical consequences. Achieving intelligence in interaction requires the multidisciplinary convergence of technical, social, and design perspectives. To represent this multidisciplinarity, we solicited and reviewed papers under four submission themes: "Human-Robot Interaction User Studies," "Technical Advances in Human-Robot Interaction," "Human-Robot Interaction Design," and "Theory and Methods in Human-Robot Interaction." Each submission theme was overseen by a dedicated theme chair and reviewed by a dedicated group of program committee members, who worked together with the program chairs to define and apply review criteria appropriate to each of the four contribution types.

The conference attracted 211 submissions from 38 unique countries from Asia-Pacific, Europe, the Middle East, and North America. Each full paper was aligned with a theme-appropriate subcommittee, and subsequently reviewed through a double-blind process, which was followed by a rebuttal phase, and shepherding where found appropriate by the program committee. As a result of the review process, the program committee selected 51 (24.2%) of the submissions for presentation as full papers at the conference. As the conference is jointly sponsored by IEEE and ACM, papers are archived in both the ACM Digital Library and the IEEE Xplore.

Along with the full papers, the conference program and proceedings include the Late Breaking Reports, Videos, Demos, and an alt.HRI section. Out of 144 total submissions, 142 (98.6%) Late Breaking Reports (LBRs) were accepted and will be presented as posters at the conference. A new peer-review process ensured that authors of LBR submissions received detailed feedback on their work. Sixteen (80.0%) short videos were accepted for presentation during a dedicated video session from 20 submissions. The program also includes 12 demos of robot systems that participants will have an opportunity to interact with during the conference. We continue to include an alt.HRI session in this year's program, consisting of 4 papers (selected out of 19 submissions) that push the boundaries of thought and practice in the field. This year, we have reintroduced the Student Design Competition event to encourage student participation in the conference and enrich the program with novel ideas and insights developed by student teams. Finally, we have the pleasure of presenting three inspiring keynote speakers who will discuss topics relevant to HRI: Dr. Cynthia Breazeal from the MIT Media Lab and Jibo Inc. in the USA, Dr. Lucia Jacobs from the University of California, Berkeley in the USA, and Dr. Danica Kragic from the Royal Institute of Technology (KTH) in Sweden. HRI 2017 was made possible through the significant volunteer efforts of the organizing committee, program committee, reviewers, and the steering committee. We thank the keynote speakers, financial supporters, and international reviewers for their support and participation. The conference is sponsored by ACM SIGCHI, ACM SIGART, IEEE Robotics and Automation Society, and is in cooperation with AAAI and HFES.

We also want to commend and thank the authors who submitted papers, videos, and demos to HRI 2017, and whose efforts make HRI an exciting field and vibrant community. We hope you will enjoy the conference content, seeing old friends and making new ones, and your visit to Vienna, Austria.

Bilge Mutlu
HRI'17 General Co-Chair
University of Wisconsin–Madison, USA

Manfred Tscheligi
HRI'17 General Co-Chair
University of Salzburg, Austria

James E. Young
HRI'17 Program Co-Chair
University of Manitoba, Canada

Astrid Weiss
HRI'17 Program Co-Chair
Vienna University of Technology, Austria

Table of Contents

Session 3: Robots in Education

Session Chair: Tony Belpaeme *(Plymouth University)*

Session 4: Personal Factors in HRI

Session Chair: Kerstin Dautenhahn *(University of Hertfordshire)*

Session 5: New Methodologies and Techniques

Session Chair: Paul Baxter *(University of Lincoln)*

Keynote 2

Session 6: Robots and People Adapting to Each Other

Session Chair: Anca Dragan *(University of California Berkeley)*

Keynote 3

Session 7: New Techniques for Remotley Controlling Robots

Session Chair: Aaron Steinfeld *(Carnegie Mellon University)*

HRI 2017 Organization

General Chairs

Bilge Mutlu, University of Wisconsin–Madison, USA
Manfred Tscheligi, University of Salzburg, Austria

Program Chairs

Astrid Weiss, Vienna University of Technology, Austria
James E. Young, University of Manitoba, Canada

Finance Chairs

David Feil-Seifer, University of Nevada, Reno, USA
Angelika Peer, University of Bristol, UK

Local Arrangements Chair

Markus Vincze, Vienna University of Technology, Austria

Publications Chairs

Frank Broz, Heriot-Watt University, UK
Yugo Takeuchi, Shizuoka University, Japan

Late Breaking Papers Chairs

Hirotaka Osawa, University of Tsukuba, Japan
Laurel Riek, University of California, San Diego, USA

Workshop/Tutorial Chairs

Guy Hoffman, Cornell University, USA
Friederike Eyssel, Bielefeld University, USA

Video & Demonstrations Chairs

Jun Kato, AIST, Japan
Dan Szafir, University of Colorado Boulder, USA

Industrial Relations & Fundraising Chairs

Aaron Steinfeld, Carnegie Mellon University, USA
Daisuke Sakamoto, University of Tokyo, Japan
Dirk Wollherr, Technical University of Munich, Germany

Registration Chairs

Maha Salem, University of Hertfordshire, UK
Jakub Zlotwoski, University of Canterbury, UK

Publicity Chairs

Sonia Chernova, Georgia Institute of Technology, USA
Nicole Mirnig, University of Salzburg, Austria
Masahiro Shiomi, ATR, Japan

Web/Design Chairs

Manuel Giuliani, University of Salzburg, Austria
Marc Hanheide, University of Lincoln, UK

Student Research Competition Chairs

Sonya S. Kwak, Ewha Womans University, South Korea
Nagisa Munekata, Hokkaido University, Japan
David Sirkin, Stanford University, USA

altHRI Chair

Heather Knight, Stanford University, USA
Séverin Lemaignan, Plymouth University, UK

Student Volunteer Chairs

Markus Bajones, Vienna University of Technology, Austria
Stela Seo, University of Manitoba, Canada

HRI Pioneers Chairs

Sarah Strohkorb, Yale University, USA
Markus Bajones, Vienna University of Technology, Austria

Program Committee

Human-Robot Interaction User Studies

Tony Belpaeme, *Theme Co-chair*
Takayuki Kanda, *Theme Co-chair*
Frank Broz
Dylan Glas
Iolanda Leite
Lilia Moshkina
Hideyuki Nakanishi
Tatsuya Nomura
Astrid Rosenthal von der Pütten
Selma Sabanovic
Maha Salem
Brian Scassellati
Aaron Steinfeld
Fumihide Takana
Greg Trafton
Alan Wagner
Agnieszka Wykowska
Holly Yanco

Technical Advances in Human-Robot Interaction

Candace Sidner, *Theme Chair*
Henny Admoni
Maya Cakmak
Marc Hanheide
Bradley Hayes
Severin Lemaignan
Yukie Nagai
Mark Neerincx
Laurel Riek
Masahiro Shiomi
Adriana Tapus

Human-Robot Interaction Design

Guy Hoffman, *Theme Co-chair*
Malte Jung, *Theme Co-chair*
Sonya S. Kwak

Min Kyung Lee
Mohammad Obaid

Hirotaka Osawa
Daisuke Sakamoto

Theory and Methods in Human-Robot Interaction

Kerstin Fischer, *Theme Chair*
Christoph Bartneck
Paul Baxter
Hatice Gunes
Megan Strait
Mary-Anne Williams
Solace Shen

Steering Committee

Co-chairs

Sagerer Gerhard, Bielefeld University, Germany
Jeonghye Han, Cheongju National University of Education, South Korea

Members

Ana Maria Paiva, Technical University of Lisbon, Portugal
Angelika Peer, University of Bristol, UK
Astrid Weiss, Vienna University of Technology, Austria
Bilge Mutlu, University of Wisconsin–Madison, USA
Christoph Bartneck, University of Canterbury, New Zealand
Cindy Bethel, Mississippi State University, USA
David Feil-Seifer, University of Nevada, USA
Hirotaka Osawa, University of Tsukuba, Japan
James Young, University of Manitoba, Canada
Kerstin Fischer, University of Southern Denmark, Denmark
Laurel Riek, UC San Diego, USA
Manfred Tscheligi, University of Salzburg, Austria
Maya Cakmak, University of Washington, USA
Odest Jenkins, Brown University, USA
Sonia Chernova, Georgia Institute of Technology, USA
Sara Kiesler, Carnegie Mellon University, USA
Sonya Kwak, Ewha Womans University, Korea
Selma Sabanovic, Indiana University, USA
Takayuki Kanda, ATR, Japan
Yukie Nagai, Osaka University, Japan

HRI 2017 Reviewers

Yomna Abdelrahman
Andre T Pereira
Roxana Agrigoroaie
Reza Ahmadzadeh
Baris Akgun
Samir Aknine
Jason Alexander
John Y Aloimonos
Ragaad AlTarawneh
Patricia Alves-Oliveria
Amir Aly
Farshid Amirabdollahian
Rajen A Anderson
Sean Andrist
Marvin Andujar
Thomas A Arnold
Maria V aus der Wieschen
Ruth Aylett
Wilma Bainbridge
Rebecca Balebako
Jimmy Baraglia
Emilia Barakova
Wolmet Barendregt
Pablo B Barros
Angelo Basteris
Mehmet A Baytas
Jenay M Beer
Momotaz B Begum
Tony Belpaeme
Eduardo Benitez Sandoval
Kirsten Bergmann
Jasmin Bernotat
Jonas Beskow
Cindy L Bethel
Nadia Bianchi-Berthouze
Francesco Biondi
Andreas Bischof
Laura Boccanfuso
Andrea B Bonarini
Adrian B Boteanu
Federico Botella
Paul Bremner
Joost Broekens
Magdalena B Bugajska
John-John Cabibihan
David Cameron
Lola Canamero
Stefan P Carmien
Elizabeth J Carter
Ginevra Castellano
Alvaro Castro-Gonzalez
Jessica R Cauchard
Lawrence Cavedon
Oya Celiktutan
Elizabeth Cha
Darren Chan
Wan-ling Chang
Vicky Charisi
Debaleena Chattopadhyay
Yevgen Chebotar
Jessie Y Chen
Jing Chen
EunJeong Cheon
Sonia C Chernova
Pauline Chevalier
Jung Ju Choi
Dimitris C Chrysostomou
Eunki Chung
Adrian Clark
Jesse Clark
David Cohen
Mark Colton
Jonathan Connell
Filipa Correia
Celine Coutrix
Jacob W Crandall
Chris S Crawford
Raymond Cuijpers
Gabriel Culbertson
Andreea Danielescu
Kate Darling
Daniel Davison
Maartje M de Graaf
Joachim de Greeff
Asaf Degani
Virginie Demulier
Nick DePalma
Sandra D Devin
Joao Dias
Christian Dondrup
Afsaneh Doryab
Brittany Duncan
Sabrina Eimler
Sarah Elliott
Friederike Eyssel
David Feil-Seifer
François Ferland
Roland Fernandez
Francesco Ferrise
Naomi Fitter
Tesca Fitzgerald
Frank Foerster
Mary Ellen Foster
Andrea E Frank
Marlena R Fraune
Steve E Funke
Fei Gao
Denise Y Geiskkovitch
Michael Genesereth
Michele Geronazzo
Manuel Giuliani
Matthew Gombolay
Pablo Gomez Esteban
Paulo Goncalves
Barbara Gonsior
Michael A Goodrich
Goren Gordon
Anders Green
Cindy Grimm
Dylan Hadfield-Menell
Nur Al-huda Hamdan
Musad Haque
David A Harley
Anthony Harrison
Nick Hawes
Cory J Hayes
Laura V Herlant
Laura Hiatt
Koen H Hindriks
Martin Hitz
Larua Hoffmann
Patrick Holthaus
Thomas Howard
Ayanna Howard
Sandy H Huang
Lixiao Huang
Justin Huang
Chien-Ming Huang
Eva Hudlicka
Shah R Humayoun
Zhiyu Huo
Inseok Hwang
Takamasa Iio
Michita Imai

Luca Iocchi
Tariq Iqbal
Bahar Irfan
Carlos T Ishi
Alexis Jacq
Krithika Jagannath
Shervin J Javdani
Lars Jensen
Lars C Jensen
Elizabeth A Jochum
Wafa Johal
Benjamin Johnston
Michiel Joosse
Wendy Ju
Hyunggu Jung
Merel M Jung
Jasmin Kajopoulos
Santosh K Kalwar
Mitsuhiro Kamezaki
Hyemee Kang
Yamini Karanam
Daphne E Karreman
Deneth Karunarathne
Jun Kato
Kerstin S Keil
James Kennedy
Mohamed Khamis
Piyush Khandelwal
Jun San Kim
EunHo Kim
Min-Gyu Kim
Yunkyung Kim
Nathan K Kirchner
David S Kirk
Franziska Kirstein
Andrey Kiselev
Hedvig Kjellstr テカ m
Ross A Knepper
Heather Knight
Okan Koc
Tomoko Koda
Takanori Komatsu
Jacqueline K Westlund
Annica Kristoffersson
Klas Kronander
Dennis Krupke
Katherine J Kuchenbecker
Benjamin Kuipers
Özge Kumoğlu
Yoshinori Kuno
Lars Kunze
Pablo Lanillos
Hee Rin Lee
Grégoire Lefebvre
Hagen Lehmann
Q. Vera Liao
kuochin l lien
Angelica Lim
Changsong Liu
Sara Ljungblad
Rosemarijn Looije
Tamara Lorenz
Stephanie Lowry
Zhihan Lu
Paul K Luff
Bruce M MacDonald
Karl MacDorman
Allan MacLean
Joseph Maguire
Christian Mai
Maxim Makatchev
Bertram F Malle
Olivier M Mangin
Nikolas Martelaro
Eric Martinson
Samuel Mascarenhas
Sean McGlynn
Timothy S McNerney
Ross A Mead
Timothy M Merritt
Alexander Meschtscherjakov
Michael Yip
Chulhong Min
James Minogue
Nicole Mirnig
Dipendra K Misra
Anahita Mohseni-Kabir
Alberto Montebelli
Maryam Moosaei
Vivian G Motti
Christos Mousas
Oscar Mozos
Omar Mubin
Alexander Muir
Sasanka Nagavalli
Mikio Nakano
Priya Narayanan
Daniele Nardi
Oliver Niebuhr
Scott Niekum
Stefanos Nikolaidis
Diana Nowacka
Tania R Nunez
Ioana Ocnarescu
Michio Okada
Jahna Otterbacher
Maike Paetzel
Fotios Papadopoulos
Chung Hyuk Park
Hae Won Park
Sujit PB
Angelika Peer
Claudia Perez D'Arpino
Jairo Perez Osorio
Christopher Peters
Sofia Petisca
Jennifer A. Piatt
Karola Pitsch
Rui Prada
Parinya Punpongsanon
Irene Rae
Aditi Ramachandran
Photchara Ratsamee
Paula Raymond
Francesco R Rea
Daniel J Rea
Natalia Reich-Stiebert
Tiago Ribeiro
Michael Richardson
Ingmar Riedel-Kruse
Paul Robinette
Andrzej Romanowski
Silvia Rossi
Thijs J Roumen
Matthew Rueben
Peter Ruijten
Sidharth Sahdev
Benjamin I Salem
Satoru Satake
Yann Savoye
Kristin Schaefer
Lars Schillingmann
Thomas Schmiedel
Stefan Schneegass
Alessandra Sciutti
Yasaman S Sefidgar
Johanna Seibt
Emmanuel Senft
Stela H Seo
Ehud Sharlin
Mahni Shayganfar
Wen Shen
Jaeeun Shim
Elaine Short
Candace L Sidner
David Sirkin

Daniel Sjölie
Gabriel Skantze
Bill Smart
Katrin Solveig Lohan
Viraj Srivastava
Aaron St. Clair
Frank Steinicke
Charlene Stokes
Brett Stoll
Sarah Strohkorb
Bener Suay
Yuta Sugiura
Hidenobu Sumioka
Ming Sun
S. Shyam Sundar
Harry Surden
Katelyn Swift-Spong
Daniel Szafir
Bernard M Hart
Kazuki Takashima
Haodan Tan
John C Tang
Angelique M Taylor
Hamish Tennent
Kazunori Terada
Konstantinos Theofilis
James Tompkin
Meg Tonkin
Ilaria Torre
Peter T Trautman
Manfred Tscheligi
Katherine Tsui
Umair ul Hassan
Daniel Ullman
Vaibhav V Unhelkar
Burcu Urgen
Jan Van den Bergh
Jasper van der Waa
Giovanna Varni
Radu-Daniel Vatavu
Eduardo E Veas
Marjo Virnes
Evgenios Vlachos
Angeleki S Vlachostergiou
Jered Vroon
Marynel Vázquez
Sven Wachsmuth
Petra Wagner
Bruce N Walker
Aaron Walsman
Matthew W Walter
Michael L Walters
Ning Wang
Dakuo Wang
Yue Wang
Xiying Wang
Yi Wang
Eva W Wiese
Andrew Williams
Tom Williams
Jason Wilson
Donghee Yvette Wohn
Robert H Wortham
Paweł Woźniak
Sebastian Wrede
Britta Wrede
Zining Yang
Qian Yang
Sang Ho Yoon
Yuichiro Yoshikawa
Zahoor Zafrulla
Cristina Zaga
Xiaorong Zhang
Zhengchen Zhang
Yanxia Zhang
Xuan Zhao
Kevin Zish
Jakub Zlotowski
Ayberk Özgür

HRI 2017 Sponsors & Supporters

Sponsors

In Cooperation with

Supporters

Gold Supporters

Silver Supporters

Bronze Supporters

Social Robots: From Research to Commercialization

Cynthia Breazeal
MIT Media Lab
20 Ames Street, E15-449
Cambridge, MA 02139
cynthiab@media.mit.edu

ABSTRACT
The fields of Social Robotics and Human-Robot Interaction are undergoing rapid growth, motivated by important societal challenges facing the general public such as aging in place, healthcare, education, manufacturing, transportation, and much more. Such applications motivate the development of ever more intelligent and capable autonomous robots and technologies that can work collaboratively with people in human environments. In the consumer marketplace, intelligent conversational technologies are entering the home at a surprising rate as Internet of Things devices are enabled by AI-based SDKs. Affordable social robots are also poised to enter the market as mass consumer products and 3rd party developer platforms.

The importance of developing and understanding the beneficial and longitudinal impact of such technologies on daily life never been more relevant. This keynote presentation highlights a number of provocative research findings from the Personal Robots Group at the MIT Media Lab along these themes. We develop social robots and apply them as a new kind of scientific tool to understand human behavior. We then use these insights to design and develop social robots that can longitudinally engage people to enhance quality of life outcomes. In this presentation, we highlight relevant work in healthcare and early childhood education.

Research in social robotics builds a critical foundation for real world applications. Social robots can be viewed as a new medium for content that is capable of humanized engagement. As such, social robots are a highly differentiated and compelling platform for 3rd party content and app developers. The entrepreneurial journey of bringing a social robot consumer product to market in the USA will also be discussed in the context of Jibo, Inc.

CCS Concepts/ACM Classifiers
• Human-Centered Computing; Applied Computing

Author Keywords
Social Robotics; Entrepreneurism; Healthcare; Education; Long-Term Interaction

BIOGRAPHY
Dr. Cynthia Breazeal is an Associate Professor of Media Arts and Sciences at the Massachusetts Institute of Technology where she founded and directs the Personal Robots Group at the Media Lab. She is also founder and Chief Scientist of Jibo, Inc. She is a pioneer of Social Robotics and Human-Robot Interaction. Her recent work investigates the impact of social robots on helping people of all ages to achieve personal goals that contribute to quality of life in domains such as education, health, wellbeing, empathy, and social connection via telepresence. Her work balances technical innovation and design with understanding the human psychology of engaging with social robots to maximize beneficial outcomes. She has authored the book Designing Sociable Robots, has published over 150 peer-reviewed articles She is an award-winning innovator, designer, and entrepreneur. She did her graduate work at the MIT Artificial Intelligence Lab, and received her doctorate in 2000 in Electrical Engineering and Computer Science from the Massachusetts Institute of Technology.

HRI'17, March 6–9, 2017, Vienna, Austria.
ACM ISBN 978-1-4503-4336-7/17/03.
http://dx.doi.org/10.1145/2909824.3020258

REFERENCES
1. robotic.media.mit.edu
2. www.jibo.com

Expressing Emotions through Color, Sound, and Vibration with an Appearance-Constrained Social Robot

Sichao Song
The Graduate University for Advanced Studies (SOKENDAI)
Department of Informatics
2-1-2 Hitotsubashi, Chiyoda, Tokyo, Japan
sichaos@nii.ac.jp

Seiji Yamada
National Institute of Informatics
2-1-2 Hitotsubashi, Chiyoda, Tokyo, Japan
seiji@nii.ac.jp

ABSTRACT

Many researchers are now dedicating their efforts to studying interactive modalities such as facial expressions, natural language, and gestures. This phenomenon makes communication between robots and individuals become more natural. However, many robots currently in use are appearance constrained and not able to perform facial expressions and gestures. In addition, although humanoid-oriented techniques are promising, they are time and cost consuming, which leads to many technical difficulties in most research studies. To increase interactive efficiency and decrease costs, we alternatively focus on three interaction modalities and their combinations, namely color, sound, and vibration. We conduct a structured study to evaluate the effects of the three modalities on a human's emotional perception towards our simple-shaped robot "Maru." Our findings offer insights into human-robot affective interactions, which can be particularly useful for appearance-constrained social robots. The contribution of this work is not so much the explicit parameter settings but rather deepening the understanding of how to express emotions through the simple modalities of color, sound, and vibration while providing a set of recommended expressions that HRI researchers and practitioners could readily employ.

Keywords

Color; sound; vibration; emotional expression of a robot; multi-modality interaction; human-agent interaction (HAI).

1. INTRODUCTION

As Cynthia Breazeal [2] claimed, robots are actually a really intriguing social technology and have the ability to "push our social buttons." People respond to social media (robots in particular) similar to how they respond to people, especially if the robots communicate with people using the same body language and other nonverbal cues that people use. Thus, more and more researchers are now dedicating their efforts to studying human-like robots. Unfortunately, such robots are high cost and technically difficult to design. To date, a range of robots currently in use for applications such as search and rescue and domestic purposes (cleaning robots) are not designed to be anthropomorphic, meaning that their abilities in affective expression are highly restricted [7, 6, 33]. While such robots may not require rich expressivity, they do need to have certain abilities to show affection. [6, 7] addressed such an issue. For example, victims may perceive a rescue robot as "creepy" so that such a robot needs to convey affect to reduce their intense emotions. There is a significant challenge in finding what other effective interactive modalities these appearance-constrained robots can employ to support affective human-robot interaction.

To tackle such limitations and make interaction design simple, low cost, and intuitive, we probe three modalities: color, sound, and vibration. Previous studies have shown their impact on a person's perception [21, 36, 34]. However, few papers have comprehensively evaluated the effect of these modalities in scenarios involving affective communication with a social robot. Thus, this leads our research question as to how the three modalities affect a human's emotional perceptions through expressions.

In this work, we work through a structured process to reach our design. We survey a number of pieces of literature to form our fundamental assumptions, and further build our prototypical social robot "Maru" for an experiment. On the basis of the results, we recommend a set of nine expressions that can well express affection.

2. RELATED WORK

Affective communication for social robots has been discussed intensively in recent years. Various robots are now designed, from humanoids to androids, to be able to establish interactions with humans [3, 1, 16]. They have been intensively studied in various scenarios such as education [35, 14], autism therapy [5, 11], guidance [18], and driving support [17, 25]. For such social robots, natural language has been considered to be a significant interactive modality. However, the current state-of-the-art in natural language and related technologies is still far from satisfying [37]. Previous research has shown that over 80% of human communication is encoded in facial expressions and body movements [32]. Hence, non-verbal cues are viewed as essential affective communication methods [7]. For instance,

HRI '17, March 06-09, 2017, Vienna, Austria

DOI: http://dx.doi.org/10.1145/2909824.3020239

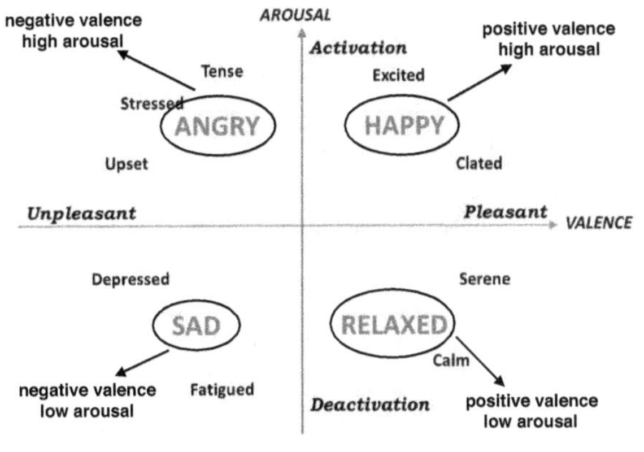

Figure 1: The circumplex model of affect.

facial expressions have been a popular mechanism for showing affection with robots as well as body movement [9, 8, 24, 31], posture [9, 8, 24, 31], and orientation [9, 8, 10, 28].

Although such interaction methods are natural and effective, they are limited by the embodiment of robots. As many currently-in-use robots are appearance-constrained, they do not have the abilities to provide social cues through modalities such as facial expression, gesture, and gaze [7, 6]. Thus, it is important to explore other interactive modalities that are simple, low cost, but intuitive.

Three alternative modalities, namely color, sound, and vibration, have also been investigated particularly in HCI and psychology. For instance, a number of studies on the role of color and light [23, 22, 26, 27, 34, 15] have been carried out; a handful of studies, particularly on semantic-free utterances (SFU), have explored the design of sounds that allow emotion and intent expressions with machines [19, 21, 20, 37]; Vibration feedback has mostly been studied as an auxiliary means to support the communication of emotions [30, 36, 4]. However, no previous work discussed affective interaction through combinations of the three modalities. Such multi-modal approaches are important since there are currently no sound principles for expressing particular emotions though single modalities.

Particularly, [13] investigated different light behaviors (for a single LED) as a means to convey a system's states to a user. Our approach is adapted and improved from their well-structured design process.

3. EXPRESSION DESIGN

The circumplex model of affect [29] is used to map emotions onto a valence-arousal space (see Figure 1). In this model, emotions can be represented at levels of valence and arousal. It can offer benefits to maximize diversity if we focus on four emotions, relaxed, happy, sad, and angry, since each emotion can be mapped onto a different quadrant of the valence-arousal space. Specifically, relaxed is of positive and low arousal, happy is of positive and high arousal, sad is of negative and low arousal, and angry is of negative and high arousal. Most emotions in the same quadrant are similar to each other but quite different from other quadrants. For instance, calm and serene are close to relaxed but distinct from happy. Therefore, we say that the four emotions can still represent participants' perceptions to the greatest extent without introducing additional complexity if more emotions are introduced. The remaining parameters regarding color, sound, and vibration modalities are selected on the basis of this model.

3.1 Meta-Analysis

We first surveyed a number of related pieces of literature to decide on a set of basic expressions that represent the mappings between each single modality and the emotions. Further, mixed-modality expressions were built upon these basic expressions.

3.1.1 Color

According to [1], green elicits the feeling of excitement, and red was stated as being tiring and depressive. Similarly, [26] supports the idea that the color green attained the most positive emotion, and [22] claims that a strong color (especially red) puts the brain into a highly excited state and might induce a bad mood. Moreover, [27] reviews various studies on mapping emotional states onto colors. The studies suggest that white means peaceful, blue means depressed, and red means angry.

We found that mappings between emotional states and colors are conflictive on the basis of the above studies, which means that different authors may suggest different relationships between emotions and colors. Nevertheless, we selected the mappings that were supported by most researchers.

3.1.2 Sound

Affective sounds, especially non-linguistic utterances (NLUs), are weighted much. For example, [19] suggests that, when beep sounds with upward slopes (increasing intonation) are presented from a computer, people perceive the computer's attitude as showing "disagreement" regardless of the duration of the beeps and that, when slower downward slopes (decreasing intonation) with a longer duration are presented, the computer's attitude is interpreted as "hesitation". Basically, "disagreement" can be interpreted as an emotion consisting of negative affection and a high level of arousal, while "hesitation" consists of a negative emotion with a low level of arousal. As a result, we claim that both suggestions also hold if "disagreement" and "hesitation" are replaced by the emotions "angry" and "sad."

3.1.3 Vibration

Vibration is mostly investigated as an auxiliary modality for conveying affection in various HCI related studies. To our knowledge, no study uses single vibration modalities to communicate affection. [30] and [36] infer that levels of vibration intensity are associated with different emotions. Hence, we decided to associate relaxed with a mildly intense vibration, happy with highly intense vibration (lower than that for angry), sad with low intense vibration, and angry with a highly intense vibration.

3.2 Pre-Design Session

We asked a panel of five researchers (members of our research group; one female) to discuss the selection of emotional expressions. None of them were familiar with our project before joining the session. The design session lasted for about 30 minutes. We asked them to comment on the parameters we currently decided on and give suggestions on expressing relaxed and happy through sound modality.

To be specific, we started by asking the researchers if they

Table 1: Assumptions of mappings between single modality and emotion, forming 12 basic expressions.

Emotion	Color(c)		Sound(s)		Vibration(v)	
relaxed	white	c1	flat beep sound	s1	mildly intense vibration	v1
happy	green	c2	flat beep sound (louder than s1)	s2	highly intense vibration (lower than v4)	v2
sad	blue	c3	falling beep sound	s3	low intense vibration	v3
angry	red	c4	rising beep sound	s4	highly intense vibration	v4

Table 2: List of all 28 candidate expressions; 1 - 12 are basic expressions, 13 - 28 are mixed-modality expressions.

1	c1	15	cs3
2	c2	16	cs4
3	c3	17	cv1
4	c4	18	cv2
5	s1	19	cv3
6	s2	20	cv4
7	s3	21	vs1
8	s4	22	vs2
9	v1	23	vs3
10	v2	24	vs4
11	v3	25	cvs1
12	v4	26	cvs2
13	cs1	27	cvs3
14	cs2	28	cvs4

were satisfied with our basic expressions. Although the researchers are all agreed with the mappings, they mentioned the possibility that some participants might not take these mappings as a ground truth. Thus, we decided to treat the basic expressions as assumptions but not as true relationships that are accepted by everyone. The researchers also suggested using a flat beep sound to express both relaxed and happy emotions. To differentiate between the two, the beep sound associated with happy was made louder since happy is of higher arousal than relaxation.

3.3 Candidate Expressions

Our set of candidate expressions consisted of basic expressions (expressions through one single modality) and mixed-modality expressions (expressions through multiple modalities). Table 1 shows 12 basic expressions. Each of them was assigned with a unique code, for example a white color expression was assigned with "c1," and a falling beep sound was assigned with "s3." On the basis of them, we further designed 16 mixed-modality expressions. Specifically, each mixed-modality expression was a combination of two or three basic expressions from the same emotion category. Their names were decided by mixing codes of combined modalities followed by a number indicating which emotion category of the basic expressions they belonged to. For instance, cvs1 is a mixed-modality expression that consists of three basic expressions, c1, s1, and v1. Table 2 demonstrates all the candidate expressions, where Nos. 1 to 12 are basic expressions, and Nos. 13 to 28 are mixed-modality expressions.

3.4 Assumptions

We made assumptions to design our set of candidate expressions. On the basis of a survey of related literature, we first assumed a set of basic mappings between single modalities and emotions. Further, we assumed that valid mixed-modality expressions should be combinations of basic expressions from the same emotion categories. The benefit of doing so was that the size of our design space was significantly reduced. We cut down the number of candidate expressions from the original number of 124 (allowing any combination of modalities) to the current number of 28.

We are aware of the bias we introduce when such assumptions are made. However, since we do not take our assumptions as a ground truth for the participants, we claim that our results are minimally affected by the bias.

3.5 Maru the Robot

We built Maru as a prototypical social robot to carry out the user experiment. We applied a minimumal design and intentionally made Maru's embodiment and appearance simple while still having the attribute of anthropomorphism. Maru is made of two pieces of hollow, semi-spherical Styrofoam. Four LEDs (white, green, blue, and red) are assembled behind each of its eyes. In addition, a speaker is used to generate beep sound cues, and a vibration motor is attached to the inner body to produce vibration cues. An Arduino UNO board is programmed to control the robot. Figure 2 shows Maru and how it expresses emotions through the three modalities of color, sound, and vibration and their combinations.

4. EXPERIMENT

Twenty-four Japanese in total (12 males, 12 females) ranging from 20 to 39 years old (M = 29.09, SD = 5.90) were recruited for the experiment. All of them were native Japanese speakers with a certain amount of knowledge on English. In

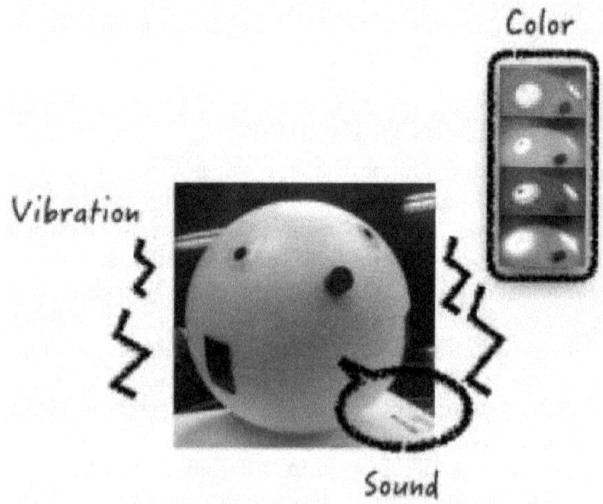

Figure 2: Maru and its expressions made through color, sound, and vibration.

addition, none of them had experience in using or working with a robot.

4.1 Procedure

Maru was placed in front of the participants at a distance of about 50 cm (see Figure 3). The Arduino UNO board inside its body controlled all of its expressions. Before the experiment started, the experimenter briefly explained the purpose and setting of the study. The participants were required to complete a short pre-questionnaire consisting of demographic information and questions regarding experience with robots. After finishing the pre-questionnaire, the experimenter started the experiment. In total, 28 trials were conducted for each participant, where in each trial, Maru repeatedly performed a single expression (1-second-long expression followed by a 1-second pause; all modalities were synchronized) from the candidate set.

The expressions were randomized across participants. Each trial lasted for 10 seconds, and between each two trials, the participants had a 20-second pause to select one emotion out of the four (relaxed, happy, sad, and angry) that they believed Maru had just expressed. After all the trials were completed, the experimenter ended the experiment and thanked the participants.

5. RESULTS

We summarized the answers from all 24 participants. Figure 4 provides an overview of the experimental results. For each candidate expression, the selection rate (SR), indicating how many participants perceived an expression as a particular emotion, was counted with regard to each of the four emotion categories. Because the total number of participants was 24 in this experiment, the value of the selection rate ranges from 0 to 24. For instance, c2 has a SR of 0 regarding the emotion of anger as no participant perceived c2 as angry when Maru expressed it, but it has SRs of 11, 11, and 2 with regard to relaxed, happy, and sad, respectively.

In addition to the SRs, we gathered participants' subjective comments on our expression design through open questions in post-questionnaires. We believed that feedback from users would also be essential to our selection of expressions.

5.1 Criteria for Selecting Expressions

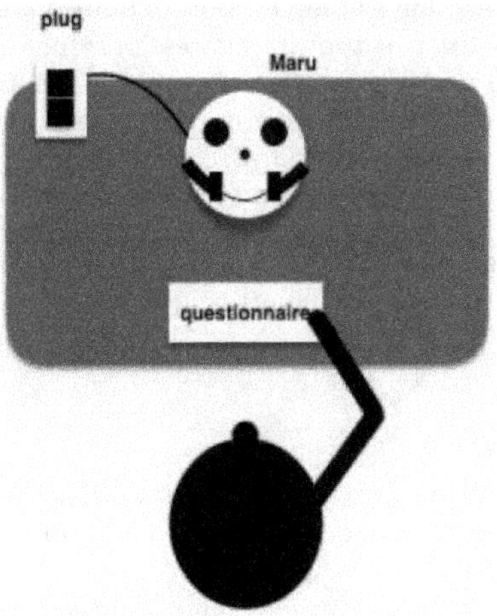

Figure 3: Experiment setting.

We analyzed the candidate expressions with regard to the four emotions separately. For the evaluation, we first introduced two criteria to select good expressions: (1) an expression must have a strong interpretation regarding an emotion (selection rate in the top quartile, or in other words, above the third quartile), and (2) an expression must be iconic, meaning that it has only one dominant perception among the four emotions. For instance, an expression is ambiguous and not desirable if the participants perceive it as more than one emotion.We assessed the iconic-ness for each candidate expression that meets criteria (1). To evaluate, we used one-sample tests of proportions with a multinomial test. For each test that was significant, we further conducted post-hoc multinomial tests with Bonferroni correction for multiple comparisons. Because of the four emotion categories, the hypothesized probability that each emotion would be chosen at random regarding an expression was set to one-fourth (25%, which is the probability of a random guess).

After a selection based on the two criteria, we discarded expressions that were not in line with the participants' comments. The reason for doing so is that we believe that the collected comments reveal the participants' perceptions of our design. For example, the participants expressed their opinions through open questions such as "How do you think of the robot expressing emotions through color/sound/vibration." Twenty-three out of the 24 participants answered the open questions. In Table 3, we summarize the representative viewpoints that were given by at least three participants. Nine expressions (Figure 4, shaded area) were selected as our recommended set of emotion expressions made through color, sound, and vibration. We now describe them with regard to each emotion category respectively.

5.1.1 Relaxed

We recommend c1 for expressing a relaxed emotion. It also has the highest selection rate in the relaxed category (see Figure 5). Although both cv1 and cs2 also met criteria (1) and (2), they were discarded because of the participants' comments (d) and (f) (see Table 3).

A multinomial test indicated a significance difference in c1 ($p<0.01$). Post-hoc tests with Bonferroni correction suggest that the result for relaxed was significant [see Table 4 and Figure 9(a), significantly above 25%, $p<0.001$], while results for the other three emotions were not (happy: n.s.; sad:

Table 3: Summary of representative comments from participants. Numbers in parenthesis indicate number of participants who gave comments.

a	It was difficult to recognize the happy emotion.(7)
b	Color is the most important modality for expressing affection.(8)
c	Using vibration alone was confusing.(4)
d	Vibration conveys negative emotions, and a highly intense vibration especially conveys angry.(6)
e	Rising/falling sounds were easily recognized as angry/sad, but flat sounds were difficult to interpret.(7)
f	It was difficult to recognize the relaxed emotion when sound was used.(3)
g	Using multiple modalities is better understandable than using a single modality alone.(6)

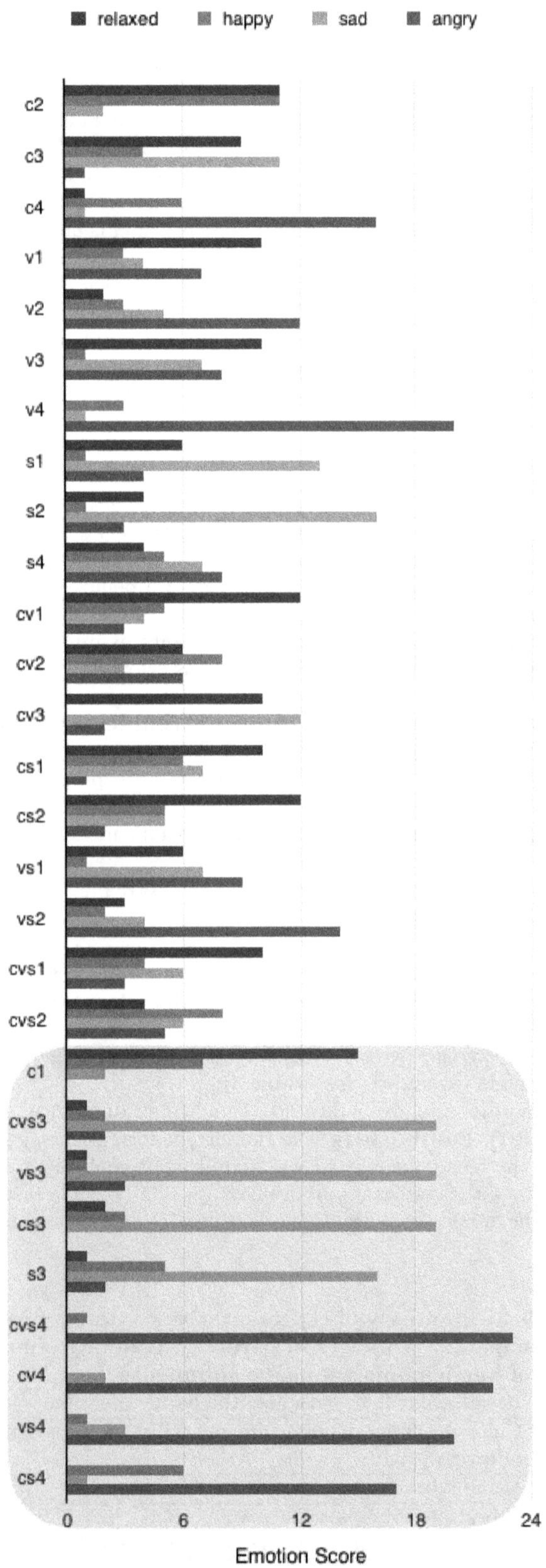

Figure 4: Overview of our results. Selection rate (SR), ranging from 0 to 24, indicates how many participants mapped expressions onto emotions; shaded area shows nine recommended expressions.

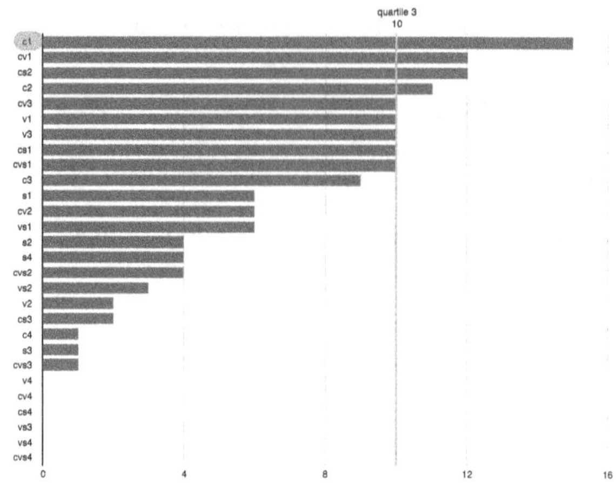

Figure 5: Selection rates (SR) for relaxed emotion category.

Table 4: Post-hoc tests with Bonferroni correction on c1; see Figure 9(a).

	p(relaxed)	p(happy)	p(sad)	p(angry)
c1	p<0.001, significantly **above** 25%	n.s.	n.s.	p<0.01, significantly under 25%

n.s.; angry: significantly under 25%, p<0.01). In addition, the selection of c1 met our assumptions as we assumed the mapping between the color white and relaxed emotion (see Table 1).

5.1.2 *Happy*

No expressions met our selection criteria in the happy category (see Figure 6). Although the four expressions had SRs above the third quartile, post-hoc tests showed that none of the four expressions were iconic [see Table 5 and Figure 9(b)]. This meets comment (a) suggesting the difficulty of recognizing the happy emotion.

5.1.3 *Sad*

We recommend cvs3, vs3, cs3 and s3 for expressing a sad emotion. They had the top five selection rates in the sad category except for s2 (see Figure 7). We conducted multinomial tests for the top six expressions that met criteria (1). Table 6 and Figure 9(c) show the results of post-hoc tests with Bonferroni correction, indicating that all the six expressions also met criteria (2).

We further discarded s2 and s1 because of comment (e). All of the remaining four expressions formed our recommend expressions for sad, which consist of basic expressions that are mapped to the sad emotion (c3: blue color; v3: low intense vibration; s3: falling beep sound). This also met our assumptions.

5.1.4 *Angry*

Four expressions, cvs4, cv4, vs4, and cs4, are recommended for expressing an angry emotion. These are the top five scores in the angry category except for v4 (see Figure 8). Similar with the sad category, all of the top six expressions were iconic in the angry category [see Table 7 and Figure 9(d)].

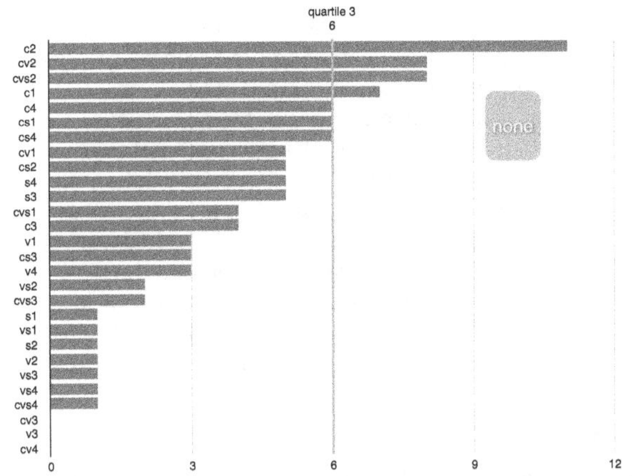

Figure 6: Selection rates for happy emotion category.

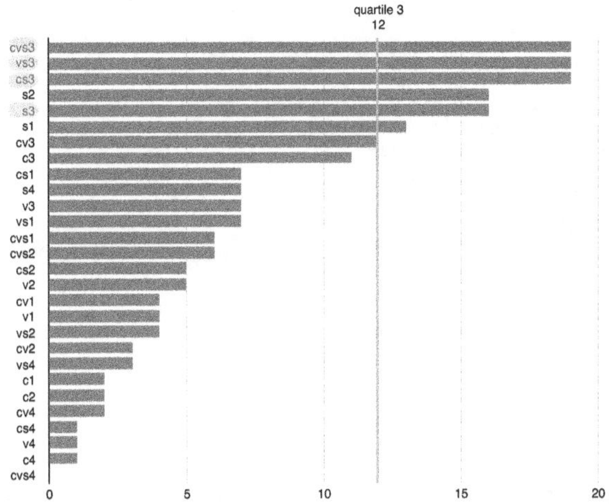

Figure 7: Selection rates for sad emotion category.

Table 5: Post-hoc tests with Bonferroni correction on c1; see Figure 9(b).

	p(relaxed)	p(happy)	p(sad)	p(angry)
c2	n.s.	n.s.	n.s.	$p<0.05$, significantly under 25%
cv2	n.s.	n.s.	n.s.	n.s.
cvs2	n.s.	n.s.	n.s.	n.s.
c1	$p<0.001$, significantly above 25%	n.s.	n.s.	$p<0.05$, significantly under 25%

Further, we discarded v4 and c4 because of comments (c) and (g). All of the four recommended expressions consisted of basic expressions that were mapped to the angry emotion (c4: red color; v4: highly intense vibration; s4: rising beep sound), which again met our assumptions.

6. DISCUSSION

On the basis of our analysis results, we recommend a set of nine emotional expressions that can well convey affection (see Figure 4, shaded area). For a relaxed emotion (positive valence and low arousal), we suggest c1. For sad (negative valence and low arousal), we suggest four expressions, cvs3, vs3, cs3, and s3. For angry (negative valence and high arousal), we suggest four expressions, cvs4, cv4, vs4, and cs4. Unfortunately, we did not find any good expressions for happy (positive valence and high arousal) emotion. A possible reason may be that the assumptions we made for the happy category are inadequate. It is also possible as we find that people tend to perceive highly intensive expressions as negative emotion rather than positive emotions.

We conclude from our findings that expressions made though the three modalities are capable of conveying various emotions. In particular, the color modality, among the three, was found to be the most important for communicating affection. Sound and vibration are considered to show a certain bias toward some emotions. On the basis of our findings, we offer six suggestions as general design guidelines:

I. It is better to use expressions that contain color modality;

II. When expressing sadness, a falling sound is strongly recommended;

Table 6: Post-hoc tests with Bonferroni correction on cvs3, vs3, cs3, and s3; see Figure 9(c).

	p(relaxed)	p(happy)	p(sad)	p(angry)
cvs3	$p<0.05$, significantly under 25%	n.s.	$p<0.001$, significantly **above** 25%	n.s.
vs3	$p<0.01$, significantly under 25%	$p<0.01$, significantly under 25%	$p<0.001$, significantly **above** 25%	n.s.
cs3	n.s.	n.s.	$p<0.001$, significantly **above** 25%	$p<0.01$, significantly under 25%
s3	$p<0.05$, significantly under 25%	n.s.	$p<0.001$, significantly **above** 25%	n.s.

III. When expressing anger, a rising sound and highly intense vibration are strongly recommended;

IV. Use multiple modalities rather than a single modality, if possible;

V. It is better not to use vibrations for positive emotions.

VI. It is much easier to express negative expressions rather than positive expressions.

For each emotion, we selected all of the expressions that met our criteria rather than pick only the best one. This is because there might not be one best expression that holds for everyone. Instead, we offer a set of good expressions so that variety and flexibility are promised. A practical issue could be of the various designs of robotic platforms. A robot may not be able to perform expressions through all the three modalities, especially vibration. Thus, for designers who would apply our findings to their projects, we suggest that they start with choosing the expressions that have the highest selection rates while meeting their hardware configurations and that they further adjust their choices on the basis of the performance.

Our assumptions on basic mappings between each single modality and emotion formed our set of basic expressions, on the basis of which we further designed the mixed-modality expressions. Noticeably, we never made these assumptions as a ground truth for the participants. In other words, we

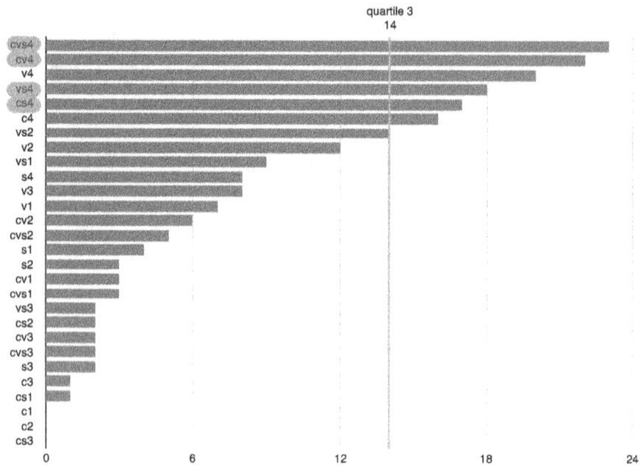

Figure 8: Selection rates for angry emotion category.

Table 7: Post-hoc tests with Bonferroni correction on cvs4, cv4, vs4, and cs4; see Figure 9(d).

	p(relaxed)	p(happy)	p(sad)	p(angry)
cvs4	p<0.01, significantly under 25% 25%	p<0.05, significantly under 25% 25%	p<0.01, significantly under 25%	p<0.001, significantly **above** 25%
cv4	p<0.01, significantly under 25%	p<0.01, significantly under 25%	n.s.	p<0.001, significantly **above** 25%
vs4	p<0.01, significantly under 25%	n.s.	n.s.	p<0.001, significantly **above** 25%
cs4	p<0.01, significantly under 25%	n.s.	n.s.	p<0.001, significantly **above** 25%

did not interpret if the participants correctly recognized an expression. In fact, our purpose for introducing assumptions to the design process was to reduce the size of our design space (we successfully cut down the number of candidate expressions from 124 to 28). We only wanted to find the expressions that can well convey emotions. As the selected expressions all met the assumptions we made, we believe that the bias caused by these assumptions was not strong enough to affect the experimental results. Thus, we claim that our design process was appropriate and our recommendation of the expressions is valid.

The generality of our results may be restricted due to the design of our robot Maru. Maru was built to have two eyes to gain the attribute of anthropomorphism, and LEDs are attached behind the eyes. As a result, expression through color modality is achieved by Maru "blinking" in the eyes. There is thus the possibility that our results (particularly expressions with regard to color modality) depend on the face-like appearance of the robot. However, because of humans' intrinsic mechanism of anthropomorphizing things [12], we say that the generality of our findings is minimally affected.

This work can be further explored. For example, we restricted our set of candidate expressions to avoid too large a design space. We made our assumptions on the mappings between single modalities and emotions, and we further designed mixed-modality expressions on the basis of these assumptions. As a result, many other combinations of modalities are out of discussion. How expressions through those conflicting modalities affect a human's emotional perceptions is unknown. Further exploration may reveal an interesting phenomenon.

When we evaluated our candidate expressions, we only considered the combinations of basic parameters (color for color modality, pitch variation for sound modality, and level of intensity for vibration modality). However, explicit values of such parameters have not been studied thoroughly. In addition, many other parameters such as duration could also affect people's emotional perceptions towards the expressions. Thus, it is important to further explore the setting of parameters on the basis of our current findings.

7. CONCLUSION

In this paper, we discussed our research on how to express emotions with a social robot through three modalities: color, sound, and vibration. We worked through a structured design process to carefully select a set of expressions that can well convey emotions. Our study began with a broad literature survey followed by a pre-design session. This resulted in a set of 28 candidate expressions that consist of one or multiple modalities. The results suggest, in total, nine best expressions that can well convey relaxed, sad, and angry emotions, while no expression can be recommended for the happy emotion. We claim that our findings possess good diversity, as each of the four emotions was mapped onto a particular quadrant of a valence-arousal space (the circumplex model).

Although most current studies on affective communication are focused on interaction modalities such as facial expressions, natural language, and body gestures, their limitations cannot be ignored. They in general suffer from high cost and technical difficulties. In addition, many of the present robots are designed without the capability to make natural interactions, especially through facial expressions and human-like body gestures. The three modalities, in comparison, have the advantage of being simple, low cost, and intuitive. This paper suggests multi-modal approaches for affective communication for an appearance-constrained robot, for instance, a rescue and search robot or a domestic-use cleaning robot. We believe that designers in HRI as well as other related fields will find our results beneficial.

8. ACKNOWLEDGMENTS

This study was partially supported by JSPS KAKENHI "Cognitive Interaction Design" (No.26118005). The authors would like to thank Yushan Pan for his valuable suggestions to this work.

9. REFERENCES

[1] https://www.ted.com/talks/cynthia_breazeal_the_rise_of_personal_robots, 2008 (accessed September 3, 2016).

[2] https://www.ted.com/talks/cynthia_breazeal_the_rise_of_personal_robots, 2010 (accessed September 7, 2016).

[3] https://www.ald.softbankrobotics.com/en/cool-robots/nao, accessed September 6, 2016.

[4] F. Arafsha, K. M. Alam, and A. El Saddik. Design and development of a user centric affective haptic jacket. *Multimedia Tools and Applications*, 74(9):3035–3052, 2015.

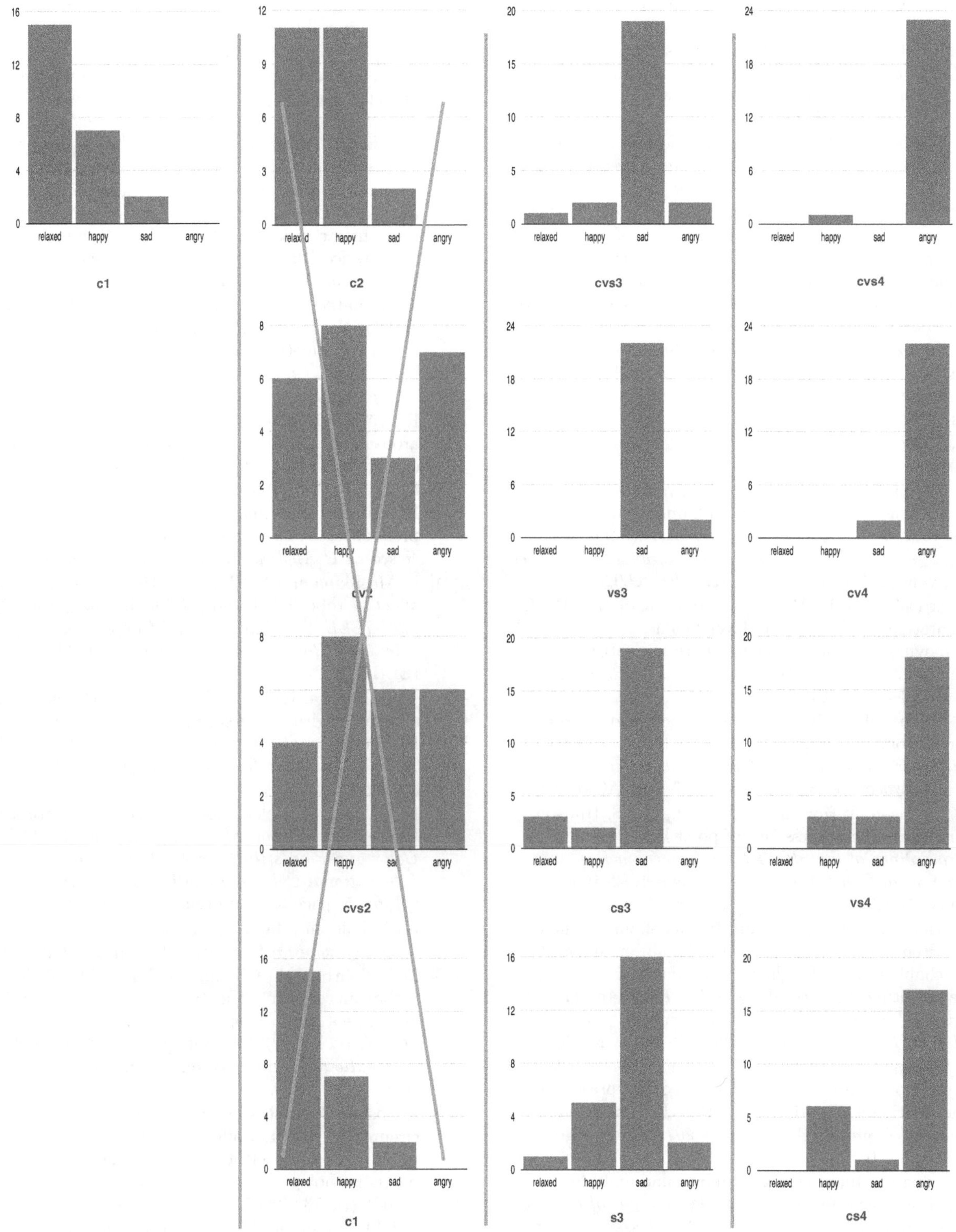

(a) relaxed (b) happy (c) sad (d) angry

Figure 9: Selection rates vs. emotions regarding each expression. All expressions except for four under happy emotion category are recommended.

[5] M. Begum, R. W. Serna, D. Kontak, J. Allspaw, J. Kuczynski, H. A. Yanco, and J. Suarez. Measuring the efficacy of robots in autism therapy: How informative are standard hri metrics'. In *Proceedings of the Tenth Annual ACM/IEEE International Conference on Human-Robot Interaction*, pages 335–342. ACM, 2015.

[6] C. L. Bethel and R. R. Murphy. Affective expression in appearance constrained robots. In *Proceedings of the 1st ACM SIGCHI/SIGART conference on Human-robot interaction*, pages 327–328. ACM, 2006.

[7] C. L. Bethel and R. R. Murphy. Survey of non-facial/non-verbal affective expressions for appearance-constrained robots. *IEEE Transactions on Systems, Man, and Cybernetics, Part C (Applications and Reviews)*, 38(1):83–92, 2008.

[8] C. Breazeal. Social interactions in hri: the robot view. *IEEE Transactions on Systems, Man, and Cybernetics, Part C (Applications and Reviews)*, 34(2):181–186, 2004.

[9] C. L. Breazeal. *Designing sociable robots.* MIT press, 2004.

[10] A. Bruce, I. Nourbakhsh, and R. Simmons. The role of expressiveness and attention in human-robot interaction. In *Robotics and Automation, 2002. Proceedings. ICRA'02. IEEE International Conference on*, volume 4, pages 4138–4142. IEEE, 2002.

[11] P. S. Dehkordi, H. Moradi, M. Mahmoudi, and H. R. Pouretemad. The design, development, and deployment of roboparrot for screening autistic children. *International Journal of Social Robotics*, 7(4):513–522, 2015.

[12] S. R. Fussell, S. Kiesler, L. D. Setlock, and V. Yew. How people anthropomorphize robots. In *Proceedings of the 3rd ACM/IEEE international conference on Human robot interaction*, pages 145–152. ACM, 2008.

[13] C. Harrison, J. Horstman, G. Hsieh, and S. Hudson. Unlocking the expressivity of point lights. In *Proceedings of the SIGCHI Conference on Human Factors in Computing Systems*, pages 1683–1692. ACM, 2012.

[14] D. Hood, S. Lemaignan, and P. Dillenbourg. When children teach a robot to write: An autonomous teachable humanoid which uses simulated handwriting. In *Proceedings of the Tenth Annual ACM/IEEE International Conference on Human-Robot Interaction*, pages 83–90. ACM, 2015.

[15] I. Infantino, G. Pilato, R. Rizzo, and F. Vella. I feel blue: Robots and humans sharing color representation for emotional cognitive interaction. In *Biologically Inspired Cognitive Architectures 2012*, pages 161–166. Springer, 2013.

[16] H. Ishiguro. Interactive humanoids and androids as ideal interfaces for humans. In *Proceedings of the 11th international conference on Intelligent user interfaces*, pages 2–9. ACM, 2006.

[17] N. Karatas, S. Yoshikawa, and M. Okada. Namida: Sociable driving agents with multiparty conversation. In *Proceedings of the Fourth International Conference on Human Agent Interaction*, pages 35–42. ACM, 2016.

[18] Y. Kato, T. Kanda, and H. Ishiguro. May i help you?: Design of human-like polite approaching behavior. In *Proceedings of the Tenth Annual ACM/IEEE International Conference on Human-Robot Interaction*, pages 35–42. ACM, 2015.

[19] T. Komatsu. Toward making humans empathize with artificial agents by means of subtle expressions. In *International Conference on Affective Computing and Intelligent Interaction*, pages 458–465. Springer, 2005.

[20] T. Komatsu and S. Yamada. How does the agents' appearance affect users' interpretation of the agents' attitudes: Experimental investigation on expressing the same artificial sounds from agents with different appearances. *Intl. Journal of Human–Computer Interaction*, 27(3):260–279, 2011.

[21] T. Komatsu, S. Yamada, K. Kobayashi, K. Funakoshi, and M. Nakano. Artificial subtle expressions: intuitive notification methodology of artifacts. In *Proceedings of the SIGCHI Conference on Human Factors in Computing Systems*, pages 1941–1944. ACM, 2010.

[22] R. Küller, B. Mikellides, and J. Janssens. Color, arousal, and performance?a comparison of three experiments. *Color Research & Application*, 34(2):141–152, 2009.

[23] B. Manav. Color-emotion associations and color preferences: A case study for residences. *Color Research & Application*, 32(2):144–150, 2007.

[24] L. Moshkina and R. C. Arkin. Human perspective on affective robotic behavior: A longitudinal study. In *2005 IEEE/RSJ International Conference on Intelligent Robots and Systems*, pages 1444–1451. IEEE, 2005.

[25] Y. Nakagawa, K. Park, H. Ueda, and H. Ono. Driving assistance with conversation robot for elderly drivers. In *International Conference on Universal Access in Human-Computer Interaction*, pages 750–761. Springer, 2014.

[26] K. Naz and H. Helen. Color-emotion associations: Past experience and personal preference. In *AIC 2004 Color and Paints, Interim Meeting of the International Color Association, Proceedings*, volume 5, page 31. Jose Luis Caivano, 2004.

[27] N. A. Nijdam. Mapping emotion to color. *Book Mapping emotion to color?(2009)*, pages 2–9, 2009.

[28] I. R. Nourbakhsh, C. Kunz, and T. Willeke. The mobot museum robot installations: A five year experiment. In *Intelligent Robots and Systems, 2003.(IROS 2003). Proceedings. 2003 IEEE/RSJ International Conference on*, volume 4, pages 3636–3641. IEEE, 2003.

[29] J. Posner, J. A. Russell, and B. S. Peterson. The circumplex model of affect: An integrative approach to affective neuroscience, cognitive development, and psychopathology. *Development and psychopathology*, 17(03):715–734, 2005.

[30] S. U. Réhman and L. Liu. Vibrotactile emotions on a mobile phone. In *Signal Image Technology and Internet Based Systems, 2008. SITIS'08. IEEE International Conference on*, pages 239–243. IEEE, 2008.

[31] M. Scheeff, J. Pinto, K. Rahardja, S. Snibbe, and R. Tow. Experiences with sparky, a social robot. In

Socially Intelligent Agents, pages 173–180. Springer, 2002.

[32] J. Scheirer and R. Picard. Affective objects. *MIT Media lab Technical Rep.*, 524, 2000.

[33] A. Singh and J. E. Young. A dog tail for utility robots: exploring affective properties of tail movement. In *IFIP Conference on Human-Computer Interaction*, pages 403–419. Springer, 2013.

[34] M. V. Sokolova and A. Fernández-Caballero. A review on the role of color and light in affective computing. *Applied Sciences*, 5(3):275–293, 2015.

[35] F. Tanaka and S. Matsuzoe. Children teach a care-receiving robot to promote their learning: Field experiments in a classroom for vocabulary learning. *Journal of Human-Robot Interaction*, 1(1), 2012.

[36] S. ur Réhman and L. Liu. ifeeling: Vibrotactile rendering of human emotions on mobile phones. In *Mobile multimedia processing*, pages 1–20. Springer, 2010.

[37] S. Yilmazyildiz, R. Read, T. Belpeame, and W. Verhelst. Review of semantic-free utterances in social human–robot interaction. *International Journal of Human-Computer Interaction*, 32(1):63–85, 2016.

Making Noise Intentional: A Study of Servo Sound Perception

Dylan Moore*, Hamish Tennent**, Nikolas Martelaro*, & Wendy Ju*

* Center for Design Research
Stanford University
Stanford, CA 94305
{djmoore3, nikmart, wendyju}@stanford.edu

** Department of Information Science
Cornell University
Ithaca, NY 14853
ht353@cornell.edu

ABSTRACT

How do sounds shape interaction with robots? The present study explores aural impressions associated with servo motors commonly used to prototype robotic motion. This exploratory analysis constructs a framework to objectively and subjectively characterize sound using acoustic analyses and novice evaluators on Amazon Mechanical Turk. Participants evaluated unfamiliar sounds through pairwise comparison, resulting in subjective ratings of servo motor sounds. In this study, subjective measures of sound correlated well internally, but correlated weakly with objective measures. Moreover, qualitative commentary offered by participants suggests both anthropomorphic associations with sounds as well as negative impressions of the sounds overall. We conclude with a roadmap for exploration into the field of consequential sonic interaction design.

CCS Concepts

•**Human-centered computing → Empirical studies in interaction design;** *Systems and tools for interaction design;* Interface design prototyping;

Keywords

Sonic interaction design; Consequential sound; Acoustics

1. INTRODUCTION

In Hollywood, robots are designed to only emit sound that enhances the viewer's experience and give characters expressiveness in their communication, such as R2D2. While these synthesized sounds can be carefully designed for specific purposes, such as expressing emotion [34], real-world roboticists must deal with the sound generated by mechanical actuation. Inherent to all moving robots, though often not designed, these sounds can have significant impacts on human-robot interaction (HRI). For example, one reason Boston Dynamic's LS3 pack-mule robot has not been integrated into military patrols is that it is "too loud," possibly endangering troops by giving up their position [38].

HRI '17, March 06-09, 2017, Vienna, Austria

© 2017 ACM. ISBN 978-1-4503-4336-7/17/03...$15.00

DOI: http://dx.doi.org/10.1145/2909824.3020238

When designing new robots to be so closely integrated with everyday life, engineers and designers have to compete with what Langeveld et al. describe as both *intentional* and *consequential* sounds [15]. That is, there are purposeful sounds designed into the robot *intentionally* and sounds which are created by the mechanical components of the robot as a *consequence* of their mechanical motion, both of which forge an impression through interaction. While there has been research exploring robot speech and non-linguistic utterances, there is a lack of attention spent on how consequential sound influences interaction.

The aesthetics of the sounds produced by actuators are generally not foremost in the minds of roboticists as they specify parts or first enable motion in a robot's design. Actuation components such as motors, pneumatics, or hydraulics are chosen for kinematic and control properties. It is only after a prototype is assembled that a robot's overall sonic profile can be recorded and characterized. But at this stage, little can be done to change it. The few machine design guidelines that do address sound generally focus on characterizing or eliminating it, not its impact on perception.

How do people perceive robot motor sounds? We intend to give designers tools to understand, discuss, and design for sounds early in the design process to make noise associated with mechanical motion more intentional and communicative. Objective measures of sound are easy to calculate and should, in theory, correlate with subjective preferences. Through this quantification process, we begin to parse the nature of positive, neutral, and negative sounds. Going forward, we will use this methodology to analyze more complex sounds, including entire products, to better understand the full picture of how sounds influence perception of robots.

2. BACKGROUND

2.1 Perception and Interaction

As more everyday products become mechanically actuated, we are seeing the effects of consequential sound on people's perception and interaction with these products. Ju [14] discusses how the hum of automatic doors preparing to open subtly initiates introductions to unsuspecting passersby. Norman discusses sounds' emotional association with everyday products including expensive car doors, melodious kettles that whistle chords when the water is boiling, and the Segway gearbox, which "sounds exactly two musical octaves apart" when moving, making "music, not noise" [26, p. 120].

In research however, studies of intentional and consequential sounds currently operate independently of one another. Robotics research has yet to find a way to better understand and control auditory emissions. The emerging field of Sonic Interaction Design seeks to shape the human-object relationship by means of sound [35] but is currently focusing on controlling the intentional sounds and discounting the consequential. This is due in no small part to the perception of consequential sound being hard to quantifiably characterize and tune [2].

Perhaps the largest variable in any study of sound is that peoples' perception of sound is "based on a relative evaluation of the sound compared to the expected sound of the product, and is often not based on technical merit or even the reality" [31, p. 989]. It is difficult for users to articulate the expectation that drives a positive, neutral, or negative reaction to any given sound. In addition, Blauert and Jekosch [2, p. 750] argue that sound processing itself is colored by "non-auditory senses, prior knowledge, and association to actions and emotions." This may explain anthropomorphism of sound such as Read and Belpaeme's finding that children ascribe emotion to non-linguistic utterances of robots such as "clicks, whirrs, and beeps" [33].

In attempting to articulate these metaphysical interactions and expectations, researchers adapt vocabulary from other domains. For example, brightness of sound and brightness of color are strongly correlated [22], as well as color and abstract metaphor in visual interactions, such as darker colors being congruent with "heavy" [5, 19]. This parallels research demonstrating interactions between the various senses. For instance, spectral manipulation of sounds (similar to adjusting an audio equalizer) made potato chips seem fresher when eaten [42] and hands drier when rubbed together [13]. Similarly, Fenko et al. [9] explored the interaction of visual and auditory *noisiness*, described as "irrelevant or superfluous information or activity," on products through subjective ratings of combinations of sonic and visual patterns. They found the effect of noisiness to be more pronounced when increased through auditory rather than visual channels, finding a positive correlation between noisiness and annoyance and a negative correlation between noisiness and pleasantness.

Thus, sonic impressions formed by consequential robotic sound likely translate to visual or tactile domains. Though quantitatively gauging this impression through objective measures remains elusive.

2.2 Product Sound Design

According to Lyon [21], sounds emitted by consumer products can be described by four main dimensions:

1. *Strength:* loudness of sound
2. *Annoyance:* roughness or noisiness of sound
3. *Amenity:* regularity or pleasantness of sound
4. *Information content:* identification, performance, or condition conveyed by sound

These dimensions combine to form the overall *acceptability* of a sound. But this acceptability is also subject to context and biases (e.g., a friendly neighbor mowing their lawn vs. an unfriendly motorcyclist speeding in a quiet neighborhood).

For now, we explore Lyon's latter three dimensions, keeping strength constant, as it is easily a confounding variable for the others and highly variable in real world contexts. It is worth noting that reducing the strength of sound does not necessarily enhance one's experience. A silent food mixer failed on the market because it was not perceived to have any power [7]. The auto and motorcycle industries are highly aware of this principle; manufacturers such as BMW play engine sounds through car speakers to increase the perceived performance of the engine [12] and the roaring sound of the Harley Davidson motorcycle defines the brand [24]. On a smaller scale, increasing an electric toothbrush's loudness correlates with less pleasant and more rough ratings of the experience [42]. All in all, while strength of sound is an important factor, annoyance, amenity, and information are stronger areas for exploration and designers' direct influence.

Norman notes that while sound "is a potent vehicle for expression" it also "propagates through space, reaching everyone within range," [26, p. 121] which can lead to varied reactions to the same stimulus. In one study of air conditioning noises, one group of participants' preference varied with loudness, while another group's preference varied with tonal characteristics [43]. Other studies found the background noise provided a mask for other distracting sounds [9].

Thus, amenity and annoyance are truly in the ear of the beholder – one person's amenity may be another's annoyance. Undesirable sounds "produce anxiety, elicit negative emotional states, and thereby reduce the effectiveness of all of us" [26, p. 122]. Conversely, desirable sounds that are soothing or playful have a positive impact on mood and perception.

The information sound conveys may represent "ergonomics, safety, emotions, hedonics, psychoacoustics, and other attributes depending on product's design" [27, p. 11], and can be quantified and qualified in a number of ways through both objective and subjective measures. Sound is an important channel of communication in industrial settings [37]. For example it it is well known that car mechanics rely on engine sounds to diagnose mechanical problems [25]. In addition, information communicated by consequential sound can be manipulated, such as the audibly perceived temperature of water while being poured [10].

2.3 Characterizing Sound

Our inquiry can be broken down by distinguishing a sound's *emission* (i.e., recording and analyzing the source of the sound) from a sound's *immission* (i.e., the sound heard by a listener). Sound emission is fairly consistent across different environments while sound immission can be influenced by the surrounding environment, such as when listening to a sound inside or outside [6]. In addition, interpretation of noise immission is influenced by individual predispositions such as personality, mood, culture, and distance from source [2]. Studying emission can be done quickly with a microphone and software packages, while studying immission requires human evaluation, which is time consuming and often expensive. Given these many variables, we chose to explore sound both objectively through acoustic measurement and subjectively through users' opinions with the goal of testing for correlations between subjective preference and objective measure.

To chart this path, we draw from a long history of acoustics that has analyzed, characterized, and replicated sounds, mostly focused on harmonic sounds such as musical instruments.

2.3.1 Objective Measures of Sound

The most widely applied characterization of sound is through the Fourier Transform, an example of which can be

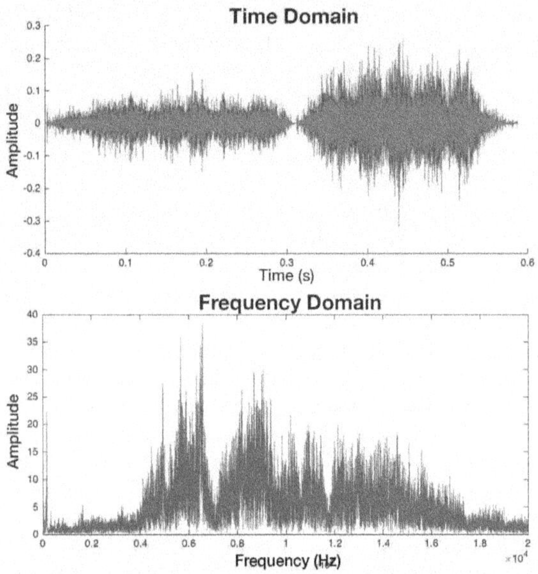

Figure 1: Wave form (time domain) to Fourier transform (frequency domain) of the DGServo S06NF sound.

seen in Figure 1. Fourier Transforms convert a waveform from the time domain to the frequency domain thereby identifying the various frequencies that contribute to a sound's timbre [40]. This is analogous to breaking down white light into its component light frequencies using a spectrograph. Exploring sound within the frequency domain enables the easy calculation of a variety of quantitative descriptors of the overall spectrum [30]. Section 3.3.2 describes a selection used in this study.

Various composite models of these quantitative metrics have claimed to estimate sensory perception. For instance, models estimate roughness [32], sensory pleasantness [44], and unbiased annoyance [8]. Audio tools such as the MIR Toolbox [17] implement these models to provide easy characterizations of sounds in MATLAB. However, the resemblance of these measures to subjective judgment is uncertain.

One interesting note is that noises with strong tonal centers receive a "tonal penalty" from customers [8]. That is, spectra with pronounced frequency peaks should be preferred less by consumers. For this reason, some believe the sensory pleasantness model, which gives tonal noises a bonus, to be flawed [8]. We verify this claim in Section 4.3.

2.3.2 Subjective Measures of Sound

To determine subjective preference, standard practice in product sound design testing is evaluation by juries of consumers, known as *sound quality assessment.* Juries evaluate sounds either through pairwise comparison of two sounds on a given dimension or rating of one sound at a time along a scale or semantic differential. In the past, jurors have rated sounds on a number of different criteria, including but not limited to, acceptability, loudness, power, annoyance, effectiveness, pleasantness, noisiness, gentleness, spaciousness, brightness, and clarity [20, 9, 4].

Wessel [45] used pairwise ratings of perceived contrast in recordings of musical instruments to explore musical timbre. Multi-dimensional scaling converts differentiation of sound into two or more dimensional plots of the sample set. With these plots, researchers can perform post hoc analyses of the set to label the axes on which the multidimensional scaling found the sounds were differentiated (e.g., in [45], the sounds were differentiated along the dimensions of "brighter" and "more bite"). This is an ideal tool when one does not know the characteristics on which sounds may be differentiated, but is also prone to wide interpretation of the results.

3. METHODOLOGY

To begin exploring the consequential robot sound space, we chose to narrow our focus to a diverse range of servomotors. We chose servos as a starting point for our inquiry into sound immissions as they are a fundamental building block of robotics prototyping and are often used by designers and researchers to quickly test out physical motion design. We made the decision to conduct a purely acoustic-driven study without overlaying the context of robots or human-robot interaction, driven by our lack of finding an existing body of work to build on. Our goal was to create a baseline understanding of the acoustic elements of servo motors and how they are perceived before introducing a context-driven inquiry. We recorded the servos making simple sweeps, analyzed these recordings with a variety of acoustic measures, and then evaluated them through pairwise comparisons on Amazon Mechanical Turk. We then performed exploratory analysis to check for correlations between objective measures and subjective preference and test acoustic models of sensory experience. Figure 2 shows an overview of our methodology.

3.1 Servo Selection

For the purposes of the study we wanted to explore different taxonomies of servo motors that designers, HRI researchers, and other professionals prototyping robotic systems would use. We bought servo motors available from popular distribution websites such as Adafruit and Sparkfun, as well as others, to form a representative sample in terms of different characteristics such as price, speed and size. A total of 20 servos included micro, high torque, continuous, and regular servo motors, and ranged in price from \$3.50 to \$79.99. A complete list of servos used for comparison is in Table 6.

3.2 Recording Procedure

To generate recordings, we connected each servo to a power supply and controlled them with a 490 *Hz* PWM signal using

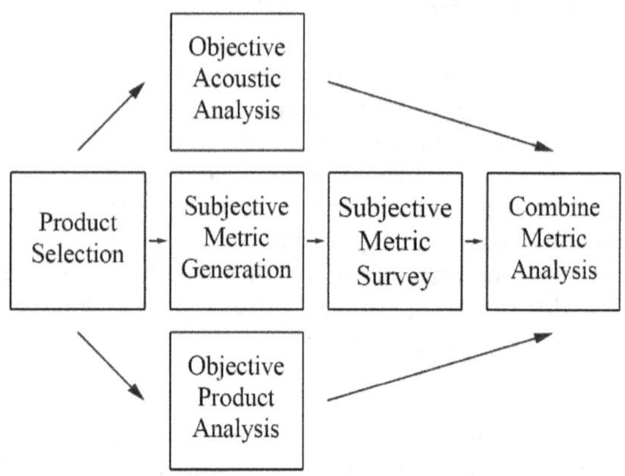

Figure 2: Timeline of the project process

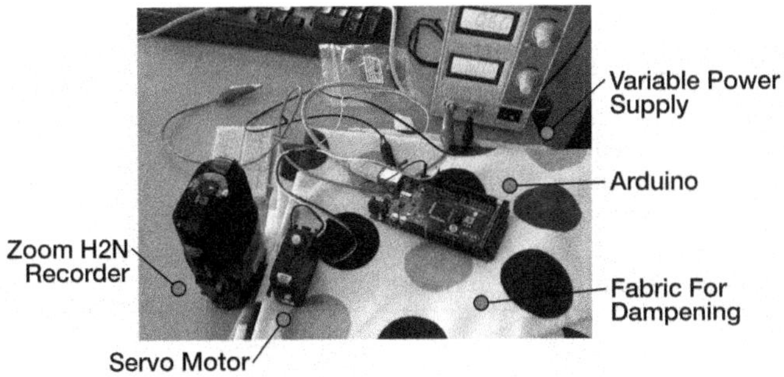

Figure 3: Recording setup.

an Arduino microcontroller, as shown in Figure 3. The motors were placed on a small cloth to minimize resonance with the table the recording setup was on. Each servo moved through an unloaded 180 degree sweep. For the continuous rotation servo motors, we programmed a similar back and forth with 2 seconds in each direction. This ensured sounds were roughly equivalent, although with differences in speeds, clips ranged from 0.5 sec to 5 seconds. To record, we used a Zoom H2N microphone in an acoustically isolated sound mixing studio. After recording all sounds, we normalized the volume in each clip and cropped them to isolate sound during the $0° \rightarrow 180° \rightarrow 0°$ sweep. The sounds used for the acoustic analysis and survey are available in the attached video figure.

3.3 Measures

3.3.1 Objective Acoustic Measures

We analyzed the sound clips with a range of established acoustic measures that characterize sound using the MIR[1] and HUtear[2] Toolboxes available with MATLAB. While more measures were explored (see complete list in Table 1) the measures that gave appreciably varying values across our set of sounds were:

- *Centroid*: the mean frequency or "center of mass" of the frequency spectrum, strongly correlated with perceptual brightness of sound.
- *Spread*: the spread of a spectrum around its centroid (analogous to standard deviation around the mean).
- *Roughness*: a measure of sensory dissonance caused by sinusoidal frequencies close in frequency, computed across all possible pairs of peaks.[3]
- *Irregularity*: the degree of variation among successive peaks of a spectrum.
- *Zerocrossing*: the number of times a signal's amplitude changes sign across time, a proxy for noisiness of a signal.
- *Sensory pleasantness*: a quantitative combination of acoustic metrics estimating pleasantness of a sound.
- *Unbiased annoyance*: a quantitative combination of acoustic metrics estimating annoyance of a sound.

See [16, 30] for more detailed descriptions of these metrics.

[1]https://www.jyu.fi/hum/laitokset/musiikki/en/research/coe/materials/mirtoolbox
[2]http://legacy.spa.aalto.fi/software/HUTear/
[3]For example, two piano notes very close to each other sounded together will clash and generate a harsher sound than two notes farther apart.

Table 1: Objective measures, product specifications, and subjective measures explored.

Acoustic	Product	Subjective
Roughness	Price	Precision
Centroid	Volume	Strength
Flatness	Weight	Pleasantness
Kurtosis	Speed	Expensiveness
Entropy	Torque	Roughness
Spread		Annoyance
Skewness		Preference
Irregularity		
Zerocrossing		
Unbiased Annoyance		
Sensory Pleasantness		

3.3.2 Objective Product Measures

Product specifications such as cost, weight, speed, and volume also factored into our analysis. These measures allowed us to compare subjective qualities of the sound directly with objective product and acoustic measures to see if there was consensus in categories such as perceived cost, quality, or strength of the servo motor.

3.3.3 Subjective Perceptual Measures

In identifying useful subjective characteristics for designers, we applied prior scales from product sound design and HRI. We also utilized brainstorming methods similar to those used by Lenz et al. [18], Spadafora et al. [41], and Sirkin et al. [39] to generate a number of descriptors to articulate the subjective quality of the sound. As participants listened to a few sounds, they wrote down words that came to mind. We grouped this set of descriptors and identified emergent groups and themes such as "weak" to "strong" and "not functional" to "responsive." We compared these themes to descriptors previously used in HRI, sound design, and objective models described in Section 3.3.1 to reduce the list to a select group.

This piloting process was necessary as many existing HRI metrics (e.g. Godspeed [1]) are not directly applicable to the sound domain. Seven subjective qualities were chosen from matching the themes among descriptors from the pilot study conducted with 15 people from our research lab with prior descriptors and metrics in product sound design perception and acoustics [21, 29]. This list combines purely subjective measures (*precise* and *preference*) as well as subjective analogs of objective measures (*rough, strong, pleasant, annoying, and expensive*). These subjective dimensions are of interest to designers as they are key indicators of a sound's acceptability within a space [20]. The sound's perceived strength and cost are also of interest for their influence on visual perception.

3.4 Pairwise Comparison Survey Format

Following previous work in sound design (see Sec. 2.2) we collected subjective preference ratings through pairwise evaluation of sounds. This method minimizes cognitive load for amateur judges who most likely have neither evaluated sounds nor are intimately familiar with servo motors.

For the participant rating system, we applied an adaptation of the Analytic Hierarchy Process [36] made by Pang and Seepersad [28] for crowdsourcing evaluation of design concepts. Each page of the survey displayed a pair of sounds, which participants could listen to as many times as they

Table 2: Participant demographics (N=379)

Gender		Age		Electronics Assembly Experience		Familiarity with Robots	
Female	48%	<24	9.8%	None at all	72.6%	Not familiar at all	9.2%
Male	51%	25-44	70.2%	Limited Experience	24.5%	Only from pop culture (movies/tv, etc.)	66.8%
Other	1%	45-54	12.4%	Extensive Experience	2.9%	Encountered them in real life	20.1%
		>55	7.7%			Repeated exposure to robots and robotic systems	2.4%
						Built and worked on/with robots	1.6%

desired. Below each pair was a table with the seven subjective descriptors listed on the left with radio buttons allowing participants to select their choice for each rating. Participants gave their opinion on how well the sound matched the descriptor. Choices and point values assigned to each choice are listed in Table 3.

3.5 Survey Design

The survey was setup using the Qualtrics online platform. Before listening to any sounds, participants were asked to listen to a pair of test sounds and adjust their headphones so that they could clearly hear them. Upon calibration they were then asked to not make any adjustment to the volume or device they were listening with. After the instructions, Qualtrics displayed 10 pairs of sounds to each participant ensuring that each participant saw a random sampling of the 380 questions and that each of the 380 were presented equally.

Context is an important factor in interpreting sound, but to create a baseline relationship between objective and subjective measures, we chose to not prime subjects with a specific idea of what the sound was being used for, only saying they are "short motor sounds." Moreover, given the crowdsourced platform, we had no control over the environment in which participants took the study, and acknowledge these as sources of variability in the data.

3.6 Participants

Participants were $N = 379$ workers on Amazon Mechanical Turk (AMT), all from the United States with previous ratings of 95% or higher and paid $1.00 for the estimated 10 minute task. AMT responses have been shown to correlate well with laboratory data and allow for quick data collection and study iterations [23, 3]. Any worker whose completed time was less than 2 minutes (the minimum time researchers believed the task could be legitimately completed) were planned to be removed, but none were below this threshold. There were a total of 380 possible pairs evaluated, and each was evaluated 10 times. The order of the pairs was reversed for completeness (i.e., sounds 1 vs. 2 and 2 vs. 1 were both presented). Average time to complete the survey was 8.6 minutes, with a minimum of 2.4 and a maximum of 24.8. Lastly, we collected demographic information such as age, any hearing loss, and experience with electronics. In a final feedback box, workers could comment on the survey. Participants were diverse with respect to age, gender, and experience with robotics and electronics, but most rated they were not very familiar with the sounds they heard. All reported having normal hearing without the need for hearing aids.

We chose AMT as a way to prototype a large-scale pairwise comparison exploratory research methodology with consequential sounds. First, we wanted to test the validity of our metrics for consequential sound. Second, we wondered if lay people could differentiate the sounds at all. Third, we wondered how effective the pairwise comparison method would be at large scale. Genuine data to answer these questions was collected quickly and relatively inexpensively. In addition, as few explicit guidelines inform consequential sound design in HRI, the subjective experience of the user is most important, and is easily gathered from a diverse audience online.

Table 3: Pairwise comparison question choices and point value assignments

Choices	Point value
Definitely A	+2 for A
Probably A	+1 for A
No Preference/Can't tell	0 points assigned
Probably B	+1 for B
Definitely B	+2 for B

3.7 Converting Raw Score to Normalized Score

We designed the survey to gather 10 responses per question, however due to small technical issues with AMT and Qualtrics, not all pairs were seen the exact same number of times. Therefore some scores had a lower theoretical score maximum. Scores of servos heard less were scaled up using the following formula:

$$\frac{Raw\ Score}{No.\,of\ times\ heard} * Max\ times\ sound\ heard\ in\ category \tag{1}$$

This correction resulted in less than 5% increase of scores across all subjective ratings, and did not significantly impact the results.

After correcting for the number of times seen, the scores were normalized setting the servo with the highest rating in a given metric to be 100.

$$\frac{Corrected\,Score}{Max\,Corrected\,Score\,in\,Metric} * 100 \tag{2}$$

The theoretical minimum is 0 if a servo received no points in any comparison. This procedure makes the ratings more digestible as the raw scores are only useful as a comparative relationship from one servo to another.

4. RESULTS

4.1 Subjective Measures Summary

The results of the pairwise ranking produced well distributed scores, indicating a hierarchy resulting from the set of 20 servo sounds. As expected, nearly all subjective measures interrelate strongly, indicating internal consistency among the ratings of participants.

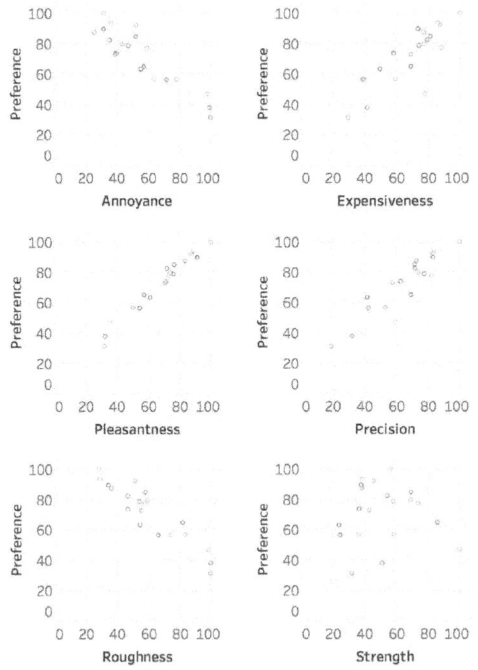

Figure 4: Interrelation of subjective measures.

Preference correlated positively with precise, $r(18) = .91$, $p < .001$, pleasant, $r(18) = .98$, $p < .001$, and negatively with roughness, $r(18) = -.92$, $p < .001$, and annoyance $r(18) = -.90$, $p < .001$. As expected, there was a strong correlation between rough and annoying sounds $r(18) = .94$, $p < .001$. Strength had the most variability, only marginally correlating with expensive, $r(18) = .49$, $p = .029$. Table 6 shows the normalized subjective ratings of all sounds. Strong correlations are shown between preference and other metrics in Figure 4, and additional correlations are in Figure 5.

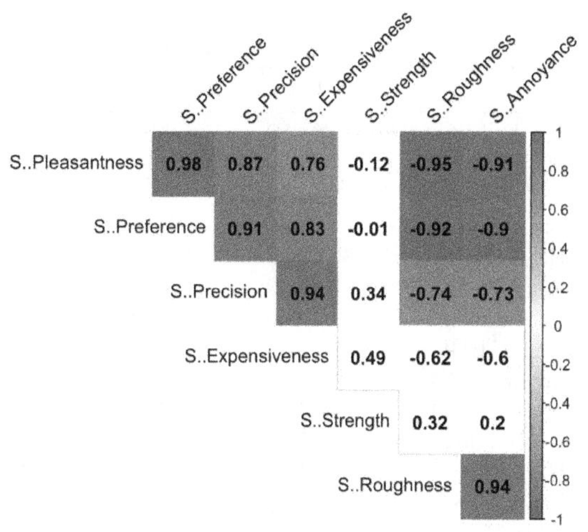

Figure 5: Correlation between subjective measures. Colored squares are significant at $\alpha = .05$ (Bonferroni corrected).

Table 4: Summary of objective acoustic measures.

Measure	*M*	*SD*
Centroid [*Hz*]	10754.23	1244.16
Spread [*Hz*]	4387.24	353.45
Roughness	781.23	359.36
Flatness	0.57	0.06
Kurtosis	2.73	0.39
Entropy	0.96	0.01
Skewness	-0.02	0.21
Irregularity	0.44	0.41
Inharmonicity	0.50	0.01
Zerocrossing	9819.45	1264.34
Sensory Pleasantness	18.40	24.97
Unbiased Annoyance	512.23	86.97

4.2 Objective Measures Summary

Mean values of objective acoustic measures for servo sounds are presented in Table 4. The data set represented a wide range of characteristics. Notably the spectral centroid of the set is quite high ($M = 10754$ *Hz*, $SD = 1244$ *Hz*) at about twice the fundamental frequency of the highest note on a grand piano. This indicates that servo noise is dominated by high frequencies and is spread out across the audible frequency spectrum, as indicated by the large mean spread ($M = 4387$ *Hz*, $SD = 353$ *Hz*). Some measures did not demonstrate strong differences across the set, such as inharmonicity ($M = .50$, $SD = .01$) or entropy ($M = .96$, $SD = .01$). As many of these metrics are designed to analyze harmonic sounds, it is not surprising that they do not show variation across a set of noises.

4.3 Comparing Objective Characteristics and Subjective Measures

Somewhat surprisingly, we found little correlation between objective characteristics and subjective ratings in our data set. Moreover, there was little significant correlation between subjective measures and objective specifications. The only noticeable correlations are between spectral centroid and subjective strength, $r(18) = -.60$, $p < .01$, and servo weight, $r(18) = -.72$, $p < .001$. Intuition suggests that price and subjective expensiveness would be somewhat correlated, but this is not supported by the data, $r(18) = -.11$, $p = .65$.

Moreover, the data set showed little relationship between the compound sensory models described in Section 2.3.1 purported to predict aesthetic value of roughness, sensory pleasantness, and annoyance, as shown in Table 5. No correlation was found when categorizing the servo motors into gear material, although some manufacturers reported simply "plastic," others went as far as to list specific materials. While material properties may play a role, the sample size for each (plastic, etc.) is too small to draw significant conclusions.

4.4 Ordering Effects

The net point differential (i.e., points for A vs points for B in any given pair) was examined to determine if ratings

Table 5: Comparison of objective acoustic and subjective measures.

Comparison	r	p
Acoutic Roughness vs. Sub. Roughness	-0.23	0.33
Sensory Pleasantness vs. Sub. Pleasantness	0.18	0.46
Unbiased Annoyance vs. Sub. Annoyance	0.32	0.17

Table 6: Normalized scores of subjective measures sorted by servo price

Name	Price	Precision	Strength	Pleasantness	Expensiveness	Roughness	Annoyance	Preference
Towerpro DG 9G	$3.50	82.8	45.6	87.9	87.5	51.7	52.5	92.0
HXT500 Micro	$3.64	19.2	31.9	32.1	29.7	99.9	100.0	31.2
A0900	$8.95	83.1	38.0	91.3	73.6	34.7	31.6	89.5
Batan S1123	$9.95	72.6	38.3	83.5	76.9	36.4	25.6	87.2
Hitec HS-322HD	$9.99	62.9	36.5	71.6	58.4	46.9	40.0	73.6
SpringRC SM-S3317SR	$9.99	59.7	100.0	35.7	78.0	98.6	98.1	46.7
DGServo S05NF	$10.95	42.9	36.1	50.7	39.7	74.6	63.9	56.5
FeeTech FS5103R	$11.95	53.1	58.6	50.2	59.3	83.4	78.3	56.6
Towerpro MG92B	$11.95	42.5	24.7	54.7	39.0	66.4	71.9	56.4
Towerpro SG5010	$12.00	82.4	73.7	72.7	88.6	57.7	59.2	77.3
Feetech FS5106B	$12.95	77.5	58.1	76.2	74.0	54.5	47.4	78.6
Hitec HS-425BB	$12.95	57.6	43.2	71.0	69.0	55.3	39.0	72.6
SpringRC SM-S4304R	$13.95	71.6	69.2	76.5	81.3	58.2	52.1	84.8
Batan B2122	$14.95	100.0	56.4	100.0	100.0	28.6	31.8	100.0
DGServo S06NF	$24.74	71.5	54.4	72.0	79.4	46.8	35.6	82.4
Hitec HS-35HD	$24.95	83.5	38.5	87.9	85.8	29.3	36.5	93.3
OSEPP LS-8101F	$25.99	32.2	51.1	32.7	41.8	100.0	99.2	37.9
Hitec HS-625MG	$31.95	69.2	86.1	57.4	69.1	81.9	57.4	64.8
Hitec HS-805BB	$39.95	73.6	69.2	74.4	76.8	59.5	43.5	79.6
Hitec HSR-8498HB	$79.99	41.6	23.8	61.4	49.6	54.5	55.3	63.2

are consistent independent of order. That is, given a pairing A and B, is Sound A vs. Sound B rated differently than Sound B vs. Sound A. Consistency was lower than expected, as indicated by Cronbach's Alpha between all pairs for each metric ranging from 0.39 to 0.66.

However, no systemic bias towards the first or second sounds presented arose in analysis, which could be a result of a small sample size (approximately 10 per pair) or influence of other factors such as varying individual preference. It is important to note we could not verify that the sounds were listened to in the presented order.

4.5 Qualitative Commentary

While participants left positive comments about the survey, many left very negative comments about the sounds themselves, which offer interesting reflections on the study.

A number of participants commented on their displeasure of the sounds they were hearing including comments such as, "*Sound B is horrible. Please don't use that noise for anything ever,*" and, "*Sound A is the sound of robot nightmares.*" At the end of the survey, one participant wrote, "*all the sounds were not very pleasant.*" As mentioned early on, this could be a factor of expectation, with some commenting "*B sounds like a more realistic sound, like one I would hear in daily life. A sounds made up almost.*"

In addition, some participants anthropomorphized sounds as in, "*B sounds more professional, like a robot I can trust,*" and, "*B gives the impression that the machine is working very hard*" which suggest consequential sounds also convey personality just as intentional sounds do. One person also commented "*Sound B is too flat. It has no personality.*" In addition, people related sounds to products or experiences they knew, the most notable of these were razors, cameras, the dentist, robots, nails on a chalkboard, and insects.

Finally, there were many comments on the participants' inability to pick favorites between the two sounds, and they often used the subjective measures as the only way of differentiating between them. One person wrote that they sound "*very, very close to me and it's hard to tell them apart, but 'A' sounds just a teeny bit rougher.*" This highlights the challenge in evaluating sound while emphasizing the importance of gathering subjective judgments in accessible ways such as pairwise comparisons.

5. DISCUSSION

This study was motivated by the observation that the sounds robots make are likely influencing perception. Given this hypothesis, one would hope for a correlation between acoustical properties of servo sounds and subjective experience. On the whole, we did not find this, reinforcing the notion that there is significant difference between immission of sound experienced and the sound emissions created by the device [6].

It was expected that spectral centroid would correlate better with subjective ratings, as it has in other domains [11]. However, centroid's correlation with perceived strength is interesting, suggesting that higher frequency sounds are indicative of weaker sounding motors. Strength itself did not correlate well with other variables, perhaps suggesting that perceived strength is not necessarily highly valued, or is more context dependent than our data can identify.

Perhaps most surprising of all was that previously developed compound models of roughness, pleasantness, and annoyance did not significantly correlate with their subjective counterparts. While these quick calculations are tempting to designers wanting to design for sound on their robots, at least in our sample, they are not predictive of subjective experience of servo motor sound.

However, from the variability of the data, and lack of correlation with objective measures, it is clear that the subjective ratings are far from universal, and there are likely many contextual and cultural factors that influence what people hear and the qualia associated with the experience.

Servos that scored highest in subjective ratings were not the most expensive. In particular, the sound of the Batan

B2122 was scored to be the most precise, pleasant, expensive, and preferred, as well as the least rough and almost the least annoying. The A0900 rates similarly. These servos are $14.95 and $8.95 respectively. The most expensive servo tested was the Hitec HSR-8498HB, at $79.99, and did not fare well in any ratings. However, one of the the least expensive servos rated, the HXT500 Micro at $3.64, sounded the least precise and the most annoying, while the cheapest servo tested, the Towerpro DG 9G fared well overall. The SpringRC SM-S3317SR was rated as the strongest sounding, but also was one of the least pleasant sounding, which indicates that some see strength in rougher sounds. Overall, these examples speak to the variability present across different price ranges, and should provide useful guidance for designers when buying motors for their robots.

However, while these data highlight the best servos in each subjective measure, the qualitative data still suggest that the general opinion of servo sounds is not positive. These data only tease out the lesser evils of servo sounds, rather than identifying sounds people would actually like to hear. It is valuable to collect such information from lay users with little electronics or robotics experience (96% never having repeated exposure or worked on robots).

Methodologically, the pairwise comparison method easily collected information from users, who did not report difficulty completing the task. We also found, at least with our sample, preference is not irrespective of presentation order, so future studies should be sure to cover all pairs.

6. LIMITATIONS AND FUTURE WORK

Our sample of servos did not include larger industrial servos, which have different acoustic properties. The servos were unloaded and we did not account for varying servo speed, as is likely a variable in real-world usage, leaving both for future study. We also had no control over the external environment or audio playback hardware through which people evaluated the sounds on AMT, which adds variability to the data. Moreover, we provided no specific context in which the sounds would be heard (e.g., specifying a residential or industrial setting), and in the comments it was clear that certain unexpected associations arose that may have influenced evaluation of the sounds. Now that we have a baseline to start with, future research can apply various primes to participants to gauge the difference in reaction to the same stimuli.

One limitation of the acoustic analysis is that we evaluated the sound clips as a whole, not looking at different parts of the sounds separately. For instance, transients (the onset of a sound) are the primary means we differentiate musical instruments, so they may play a role in our interpretation of servo sound. This is due in part to the Fourier Transform of a sound's transients being very different from the steady state sound. Future work should further break down sounds into smaller pieces to determine if there are certain segments of a sound that convey more meaning than others.

Going forward, we aim to apply this methodology to explore more complicated sounds with the goal of identifying how subjective impressions formed by sounds translate to visual or tactile perception and interaction. Part of this exploration involves understanding the expectation users hold as they interact with robots for the first time. Read and Belpaeme highlight this difficulty, saying that "film and animation have long presented robots in a light that far exceeds the true technological state-of-the-art and can lead to naive users having drastically incorrect expectations of the real technology" [34, p. 34]. Lastly, most robots are not comprised of single servos, and we aim to study more complex sounds that result from multiple components working in concert.

We also hope this vein of research motivates attention to the consequential sounds robots make and produces a methodology for roboticists to deliberately design for it in their systems. Many robots, like those mentioned in our introduction, generate sounds that are not very pleasant on the ear, and we are making steps towards demonstrating that these sounds have a potentially negative impact on perception. These studies will ground the present study's implications on the interpretation of consequential sound.

7. CONCLUSIONS

This work provides a roadmap for exploration into the field of consequential sonic interaction design, contributing tools to future researchers studying the effect of sound on the overall perception of robots. We believe an understanding of consequential sound can enhance the design of intentional sound. Subjective measures of servo sounds interrelated well, although we found no resounding themes connecting objective and subjective measures. However we see potential in this methodology to start a larger conversation around subjective experience of consequential sound creation. Through capturing sound of the most readily available servo motors and juxtaposing the most agreed upon acoustic measures with the most alluring mathematical models of subjective preference, we show that the subjective experience from a user's standpoint is as of yet difficult to relate to acoustic measurement. In other words, noise emission does not necessarily correlate with noise immission.

This should be of note to engineers, designers, and roboticists looking to prototype and test interactions. A designer might naively assume that by simply paying more for a higher quality servo, they would get a sound which could be considered more "pleasant" or "expensive." Our data show these factors do not correlate. Moreover, given the overall negative opinions reflected by participants about the sounds, it follows that people creating prototypes and testing human-robot interaction must be conscious of the fact that the servo motor sound could in fact be tarnishing peoples' perception of the presented device. However, more research is needed to connect characteristics of sound to specific perceptions.

8. ACKNOWLEDGMENTS

Thank you to Matt Wright at the Center for Computer Research in Music and Acoustics for his guidance on acoustical metrics as well as Marco Spadafora for his help in determining aesthetic measures to evaluate. We also thank Abhijeet Agnihotri for calculation of the objective aesthetics models. Lastly, thank you to everyone at the Center for Design Research who lent a hand to this project along the way. This research was supported by Stanford MediaX and the Center for Design Research Affiliate Fund.

9. REFERENCES

[1] C. Bartneck, D. Kulic, E. Croft, and S. Zoghbi. Measurement instruments for the anthropomorphism, animacy, likeability, perceived intelligence, and

perceived safety of robots. *International Journal of Social Robotics*, 1(1):71–81, 2009.

[2] J. Blauert and U. Jekosch. Sound-Quality Evaluation - A Multi-Layered Problem. *Acta Acustica united with Acustica*, 83:747–753, 1997.

[3] K. Chen, C. Wu, Y. Chang, and C. Lei. Crowdsourceable QoE evalutation framework for multimedia content. In *MM*, pages 491–500, Beijing, China, 2009.

[4] S. Choisel and F. Wickelmaier. Evaluation of multichannel reproduced sound: scaling auditory attributes underlying listener preference. *The Journal of the Acoustical Society of America*, 121(1):388–400, 2007.

[5] B. Colombo, N. Bartesaghi, L. Simonelli, and A. Antonietti. The combined effects of neurostimulation and priming on creative thinking. A preliminary tDCS study on dorsolateral prefrontal cortex. *Frontiers in human neuroscience*, 9(July):403, 2015.

[6] N. A. o. E. Committee on Technology for a Quieter America. *Technology for a Quieter America*, volume 59. National Academies Press, 2010.

[7] D. Cox. The sorting rule model of the consumer product evaluation process. *Risk taking and information handling in consumer behavior*, pages 324–369, 1967.

[8] H. Fastl. Psychoacoustics and Sound Quality Hugo. In J. Blauert, editor, *Communication Acoustics*, pages 139–162. Springer, 2005.

[9] A. Fenko, H. N. J. Schifferstein, and P. Hekkert. Noisy products: Does appearance matter? *International Journal of Design*, 5(3):77–87, 2011.

[10] A. Golan and A. Fenko. Toward a Sustainable Faucet Design: Effects of Sound and Vision on Perception of Running Water. *Environment and Behavior*, 47(1):85–101, 2013.

[11] J. M. Grey and J. Gordon. Perceptual effects of spectral modifications on musical timbres. *The Journal of the Acoustical Society of America*, 63(5):1493, 1978.

[12] D. Hartwell. America's best-selling cars and trucks are built on lies: The rise of fake engine noise, 1 2015.

[13] V. Jousmäki and R. Hari. Parchment-skin illusion: sound-biased touch. *Current biology*, 8(6):R190, 1998.

[14] W. Ju. The Design of Implicit Interactions. *Synthesis Lectures on Human-Centered Informatics*, 8(2):1–93, 2015.

[15] L. Langeveld, René van Egmond, R. Jansen, and E. Özcan. Product sound design: Intentional and consequential sounds. *Advances in Industrial Design Engineering*, 2013.

[16] O. Lartillot, P. Toiviainen, and T. Eerola. A Matlab Toolbox for Music Information Retrieval. In C. Preisach, H. Burkhardt, L. Schmidt-Thieme, and R. Decker, editors, *Data Analysis, Machine Learning and Applications, Studies in Classification, Data Analysis, and Knowledge Organization*. Springer-Verlag, 2008.

[17] O. Lartillot and P. Toivianinen. A Matlab Toolbox for Musical Feature Extraction From Audio. In *International Conference on Digital Audio Effects*, Bordeaux, 2007.

[18] E. Lenz, S. Diefenbach, and M. Hassenzahl. Exploring Relationships Between Interaction Attributes and Experience. In *DPPI 2013*, pages 126–135, Newcastle upon Tyne, UK, 2013.

[19] D. Löffler, L. Artl, T. Toriizuka, R. Tscharn, and J. Hurtienne. Substituting Color for Haptic Attributes in Conceptual Metaphors for Tangible Interaction Design. In *TEI*, pages 118–125, Eindhoven, The Netherlands, 2016.

[20] R. H. Lyon. *Designing for Product Sound Quality*. CRC Press, 2000.

[21] R. H. Lyon. Product sound quality: From perception to design. *Sound and Vibration*, 37(3):18–23, 2003.

[22] L. Marks. On Associations of Light and Sound : The Mediation of Brightness, Pitch, and Loudness. *American Journal of Psychology*, 87(1):173–188, 1974.

[23] W. Mason and S. Suri. Conducting behavioral research on AmazonâĂŹs Mechanical Turk. *Behavior Research Methods*, 44(1):1–23, 2012.

[24] T. O. M. Murphy. The Music of Sound–Exhaust analysis goes scientific, 1999.

[25] K. Nakamura. Car mechanic training course and acoustic technique education. *Internoise 2014*, pages 1–8, 2014.

[26] D. N. Norman. *Emotional Design - Why we love (or hate) everyday things*. Basic Books, 2005.

[27] E. Özcan and R. Van Egmond. Product sound design and application: Overview. *5th Conference on Design and Emotion 2006*, (August), 2006.

[28] M. A. Pang. *An Empirical Study of the Effects of Priming on Crowdsourced Evaluations of Design Concepts*. PhD thesis, The University of Texas at Austin, 2016.

[29] T. H. Pedersen. *The Semantic Space of Sounds*, volume 1. 2008.

[30] G. Peeters. A large set of audio features for sound description. Technical Report 0, 2004.

[31] G. Pietila and T. C. Lim. Intelligent systems approaches to product sound quality evaluations - A review. *Applied Acoustics*, 73(10):987–1002, 2012.

[32] R. Plomp and W. J. M. Levelt. Tonal Consonance and Critical Bandwidth. *The Journal of the Acoustical Society of America*, 38(4):548–560, 1965.

[33] R. Read and T. Belpaeme. How to use non-linguistic utterances to convey emotion in child-robot interaction. *Human-Robot Interaction (HRI), 2012 7th ACM/IEEE International Conference on*, pages 219–220, 2012.

[34] R. Read and T. Belpaeme. People Interpret Robotic Non-linguistic Utterances Categorically. *International Journal of Social Robotics*, 8(1):31–50, 2016.

[35] D. Rocchesso and S. Serafin. Sonic Interaction Design. *International Journal of Human Computer Studies*, 67(11):905–906, 2009.

[36] T. L. Saaty. A scaling model for priorities in hierarchical structures. *Journal of Mathematical psychology*, 15:213–281, 1977.

[37] A. Sauppé and B. Mutlu. The Social Impact of a Robot Co-Worker in Industrial Settings. *Proceedings of the 33rd Annual ACM Conference on Human Factors in Computing Systems - CHI '15*, pages 3613–3622, 2015.

[38] H. H. Seck. Marine Corps Shelves Futuristic

Robo-Mule Due to Noise Concerns, Dec. 2015.

[39] D. Sirkin, B. Mok, S. Yang, R. Maheshwari, and W. Ju. Design thinking research: Making design thinking foundational. In H. Plattner, C. Meinel, and L. Leifer, editors, *Design Thinking Research: Understanding Innovation*, pages 93–108. 2016.

[40] J. Smith. *Mathematics of the discrete Fourier transform (DFT): with audio applications.* W3K Publishing, 2008.

[41] M. Spadafora, V. Chahuneau, N. Martelaro, D. Sirkin, and W. Ju. Designing the Behavior of Interactive Objects. In *TEI '16*, pages 70–77, Eindhoven, The Netherlands, 2016.

[42] C. Spence and M. Zampini. Auditory contributions to multisensory product perception. *Acta Acustica united with Acustica*, 92(6):1009–1025, 2006.

[43] P. Susini, S. McAdams, S. Winsberg, I. Perry, S. Vieillard, and X. Rodet. Characterizing the sound quality of air-conditioning noise. *Applied Acoustics*, 65(8):763–790, 2004.

[44] E. Terhardt. Wohlklang und Lärm aus psychophysikalischer Sicht. In A. Schick and K. Walcher, editors, *Ergebnisse des 3. Oldenburger Symposions zur Psychologischen Akustik.*, pages 403–409. P Lang AG, Bern, 1984.

[45] D. Wessel. Timbre Space as a Musical Control Structure. *Computer Music Journal*, 3(2):45–52, 1979.

Expressive Robot Motion Timing

Allan Zhou
UC Berkeley

Dylan Hadfield-Menell
UC Berkeley

Anusha Nagabandi
UC Berkeley

Anca D. Dragan
UC Berkeley

ABSTRACT

Our goal is to enable robots to *time* their motion in a way that is purposefully expressive of their internal states, making them more transparent to people. We start by investigating what types of states motion timing is capable of expressing, focusing on robot manipulation and keeping the path constant while systematically varying the timing. We find that users naturally pick up on certain properties of the robot (like confidence), of the motion (like naturalness), or of the task (like the weight of the object that the robot is carrying). We then conduct a hypothesis-driven experiment to tease out the directions and magnitudes of these effects, and use our findings to develop candidate mathematical models for how users make these inferences from the timing. We find a strong correlation between the models and real user data, suggesting that robots can leverage these models to autonomously optimize the timing of their motion to be expressive.

Keywords

motion timing; expressive motion; human cognitive models

1. INTRODUCTION

Robot motion trajectories have two components. There is a kinematic component, which is the geometric path through the robot's configurations space – a sequence of configurations that the robot will traverse. But there is also a timing component – a function that assigns a time stamp to each configuration along the path, dictating *how* the robot will traverse the configuration sequence.

Robotics motion planners for manipulation tend to focus on the path [18, 19, 33, 27], with few exceptions *explicitly* incorporating timing, for instance to improve efficiency or conservative obstacle avoidance [5, 4]. Most commonly, timing is an after-thought in robotics, left to the controller to assign post-hoc.

And yet, timing is crucial in *HRI*. Imagine seeing a robot arm carry a cup smoothly across the table, like in the top image in Fig.1. Now, imagine seeing a different arm pausing

HRI '17, March 6–9, 2017, Vienna, Austria.

ISBN 978-1-4503-4336-7/17/03. . . $15.00

DOI: http://dx.doi.org/10.1145/2909824.3020221

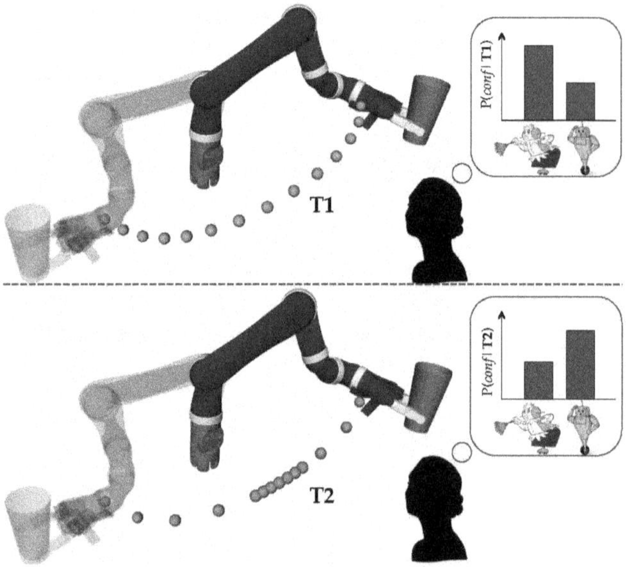

Figure 1: Different timings of the same motion convey different things about the robot. We find effects on perceived confidence, naturalness, even the perceived weight of the object being manipulated. We develop mathematical models for these perceptions that correlate with user data and enable robots to optimize their timing for expressiveness.

and restarting, slowing down and then speeding back up, like in the bottom image. The path might be the same, but the difference in timing might make us think very differently about the robots and about what they are doing. We might think that the second robot is less capable, or maybe that its task is more difficult. Perhaps it doesn't have as much payload, perhaps the cup is heavier, or perhaps it does not know what to do:

> *The timing of a path affects how observers perceive the robot and the task that it is performing.*

Studies have already shown that the average velocity and changes in velocity of motion affect perceptions of expressed emotion [7], intent [10], elation [2], animacy [32], arousal and dominance [25], and energy [3]. When it comes to robot motion, human observers will interpret the timing regardless of whether the robot is planning to express anything or not. Our goal is to give robots control over what their timing inadvertently expresses:

> *Robots should leverage timing to be more expressive of their internal states.*

Techniques from animation can be useful in improving robot expressiveness [29, 24], and animated characters have long taken advantage of timing, both for making motion more natural (e.g. ease-in ease-out is one of the 12 animation principles [31]), and more expressive [23, 25]. This made timing a center of focus in the graphics community, developing automated tools for assigning timing to a path. Most tools still leave the *animator* in control of the timing, but simplify the assignment process (e.g. by allowing the animator to "act out" the timing of a motion with something like a pen and tablet [30]). Other tools *align* timing to a different trajectory or an external event like a beat [17, 14]. Others yet *re-time* a particular motion to satisfy new constraints (like finishing faster) while maintaining physical *realism* [21].

Overall, although realistic timing can be automated, even virtual characters still rely on an external expert when it comes to *expressive* timing – be it on an animator or on an artist's trajectory. Robots, on the other hand, can't afford to rely on experts for every motion they need to perform. They plan their motion autonomously, and have to autonomously decide on how to time it.

Our focus is on enabling robots to produce expressive timing. Two questions remain in this area. First, there is the question of what timing *can* express in the first place – prior work looked at effects on perceived emotional state, but are there also effects on function-related properties? Second, there is the synthesis question – how can we enable robots to autonomously *generate* timing *from scratch* that is purposefully expressive, rather than efficient or physically realistic. We take a step in this direction by analyzing motion timing during manipulation, from an open ended study, to hypothesis-driven experiments, to candidate mathematical models that capture human timing-based inferences.

We make three contributions:

Exploring the possible effects of timing. So far, studies focusing on timing mainly looked for effects on perceived emotional state. We designed and conducted a study to identify what types of variables timing influences more broadly. Rather than biasing users with questionnaires that already suggest how the timing should be interpreted, we used simple open-ended questions. We systematically manipulated timing across three axes inspired by prior work in a factorial design, and asked users to characterize the robot and the task. We clustered their responses to identify common interpretations, and uncovered robot competence, confidence, disposition, along with (unsurprisingly) motion naturalness, and a manipulation-specific characteristic of the task: the weight of the object being manipulated by the robot. This list of variables by no means comprise the entirety of timing effects, nor is it as specific as we would ultimately desire. It does, however, provide us with a rich set of dependent measures for more in-depth analysis.

Experiments that test these effects. Only after identifying candidate dependent variables based on open-ended questions did we put these effects to the test. We conducted a hypothesis-driven experiment to understand the magnitude and directionality for each. Some of our findings support intuition, like the robot being perceived as less confident if it pauses during the motion. Others are quite surprising. For instance, when the robot is carrying an object, we found that people estimated that object to have approximately the same weight regardless of whether or not the timing had pauses or speed changes. Overall, pausing had a much stronger effect than speed.

Mathematical models and evaluation. Our experiment shows *what* effects timing has, but not *why*. For robots to generate their timing autonomously in different situations, they need a mechanism for generalizing these findings. We attempt such a mechanism for three of the dependent variables. We introduce mathematical models for the inferences that humans make from motion timing. We take a Bayesian inference approach, in which the timing serves as an observation to the human about the states that they can't observe, like the robot's confidence or the object's weight. We show strong correlations between these models and the real user data. The models are constructive, in the sense that robots can use them to optimize their timing to be expressive.

Overall, this paper shows how several timing features interact to affect perceptions of the robot and task, and uses these findings to introduce optimization criteria that correlate with the user data and that robots could use to autonomously *time* motion in a way that is expressive (e.g. of the robot's confidence). We look forward to future work on further analysis and refinement of these criteria to ensure generality across settings, as well as further exploration of effects that are more difficult to model, such as how timing influences the robot's perceived disposition.

2. NOTATION

A trajectory in our experiment consists of two components: the sequence of of way point configurations that the robot moves through, and the time at which the robot reaches each way point. We use q_i to represent the ith robot configuration. T_i is the time that the robot reaches the ith configuration. We assume that trajectories begin at time 0. T_N is the total duration of the trajectory (i.e., the time at which the robot reaches the final configuration).

We will usually be interested in the speed the robot travels over the course of its trajectory. We use

$$v_i = \frac{q_{i+1} - q_i}{T_{i+1} - T_i}$$

to represent this velocity (in radians per second). We use

$$v_i^{EE} = \frac{\phi(q_{i+1}) - \phi(q_i)}{T_{i+1} - T_i}$$

where ϕ is the robot's forward kinematics function, to represent the velocity of the end effector (in meters per second).

To summarize:

q: A sequence of robot configurations that represents the kinematic component (path) of a trajectory.
q_i: The ith robot configuration in the trajectory.
T: A sequence of time stamps that represents the timing component of a trajectory.
T_i: The time when the robot reaches q_i.
T_N: The total time taken by the trajectory.
v_i: The velocity of the robot from q_i to q_{i+1}.
v_i^{EE}: The end effector velocity of the robot from q_i to q_{i+1}.

3. EXPLORATORY STUDY

We start with a study that builds on prior work to find what kinds of effects timing can have on what people infer about the robot during a manipulation task. Our goal with this study is to find the different dimensions of perception that timing affects, i.e. the dependent measures we should test – is it energy, elation, dominance, or something different? We need to avoid biasing the users towards a particular interpretation, so we ask the users open-ended questions and use their responses to form hypotheses for our next experiment.

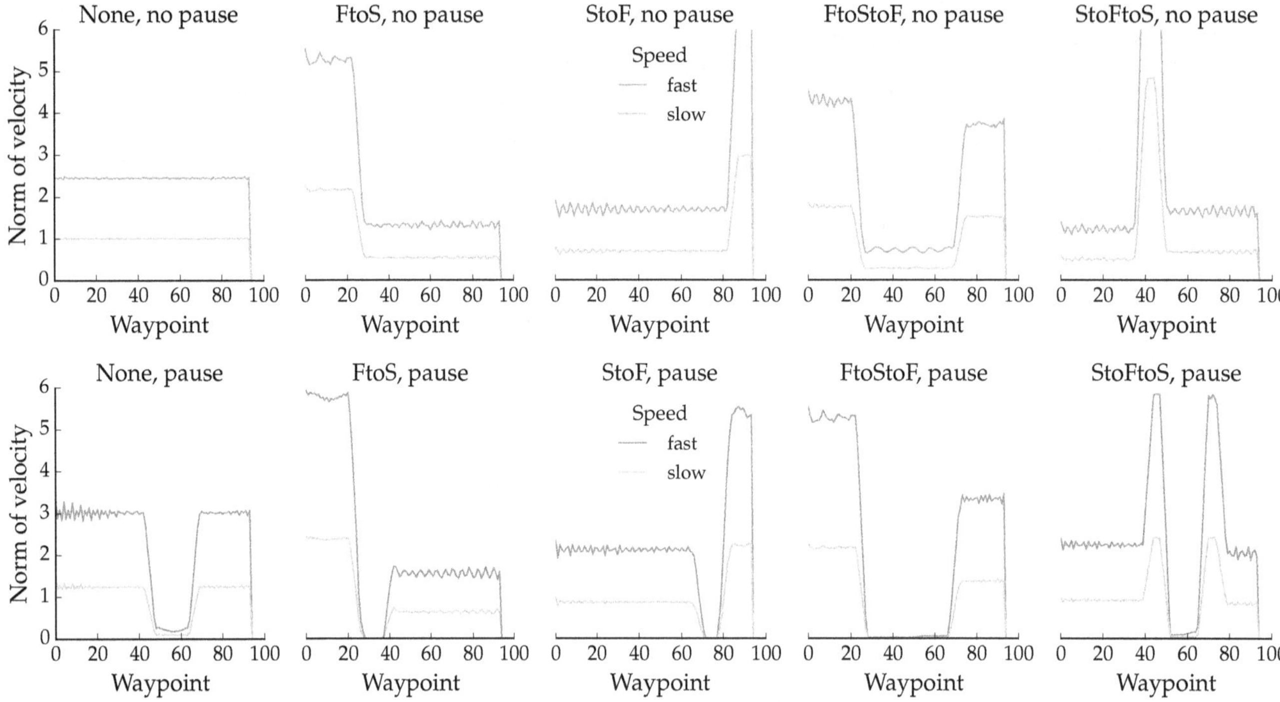

Figure 2: Norm of the robot's configuration space velocity v_i for each way point configuration q_i in each of our 20 conditions. Each column is a different speed change pattern, with the top row representing the conditions without a pause and the bottom representing the conditions with a pause, where we see the velocity go to 0. Each plot contains both the slow motion (lighter color) and its fast counterpart (darker color).

3.1 Study Design

Robot Task. We used a Kinova 6DOF Mico arm (Fig.1) in our study. We chose one of the most common interactive manipulation tasks for the robot: a handover [6, 28, 20, 22]. The robot carried an object (a cup) from a table to a handover configuration (see Fig.1).

Manipulated Factors. The biggest challenge in studying the effects of timing on people's perceptions is identifying which timing variations to test. A simple answer would be to randomly sample timings, which would uniformly cover the space of all timings. However, they would almost uniformly be interpreted in the same way – as erratic and unnatural. Instead, we decided to *systematically* generate timings by manipulating several factors.

Our first factor is overall ***speed***. Previous studies found that overall robot speed has effects on perceptions [2, 25]. We use 2 levels for this factor: *slow* and *fast*.

Our second factor is ***change in speed***. In studies on abstract characters and human motion, changes in speed have been shown to affect perceived animacy [32], emotion content [7], and energy [3]. Here, we considered 0, 1, and 2 changes, leading to a total of 5 levels for this factor: *none* (no change), *StoF* (starting to go faster), *FtoS* (slowing down), *StoFtoS* (faster, then slower), and *FtoStoF* (slower, than faster). Fig.2 (top) shows the magnitude of the velocity v_i across the trajectory way points for each of these patterns, and for both the overall slow and the overall fast levels.

Finally, we also explore an edge case of change in speed: coming to a full stop. Our third factor is thus ***pause***, with 2 levels: either the robot pauses or it does not. The pausing variants are at the bottom of Fig.2, and they differ in that the velocity goes to 0 for a portion of the trajectory.

We used a 2 by 5 by 2 factorial design, leading to a total of 20 conditions, each corresponding to a different timing $\mathbf{T}$ for a path $\mathbf{q}$ (shown in Fig.2).

Dependent Measures. We asked users to describe how the robot moved the cup, what adjectives they would use to characterize the robot, and what they think is in the cup.

Subject Allocation. We wanted a within-subjects design to enable users to see multiple possible timings and have bases for comparisons, as they would if they would interact with the robot on a longer term. However, we had 20 conditions, making within-subjects infeasible. We opted for a randomized assignment, where each participant evaluated 8 randomly sampled conditions. There were a total of 61 participants (63% male and 37% female, median age = 36) all from the United States and recruited through Amazon's Mechanical Turk platform. All had a minimum approval rating of 95% on Mechanical Turk.

3.2 Analysis

We started by computing word counts for each question. Fig.3 shows the word cloud that this induced for the question of describing the robot, and identifying what the robot is carrying.[1] We then clustered the words into equivalence classes for easier analysis, ignoring words that appear fewer than 3 times in the data.

Adjectives. Two of the most common adjectives used to describe the robot were literal: *slow* and *fast* (or quick, speedy, rapid, efficient), giving rise to two of our clusters. But beyond those, many users described the motion as smooth, natural, predictable, or fluid, which formed the *natural* cluster with the highest word count (left histogram in Fig.3). The counterparts were also present (unnatural, jerky, robotic, mechanical, uneven, awkward), forming the *unnatural* cluster. And finally, users described the robot as careful, cautious,

[1] We quickly realized that when asked to describe how the robot moved the cup, users quite literally described what the robot did (e.g. "move the cup slowly away from the table"), and we are not including the analysis for that question.

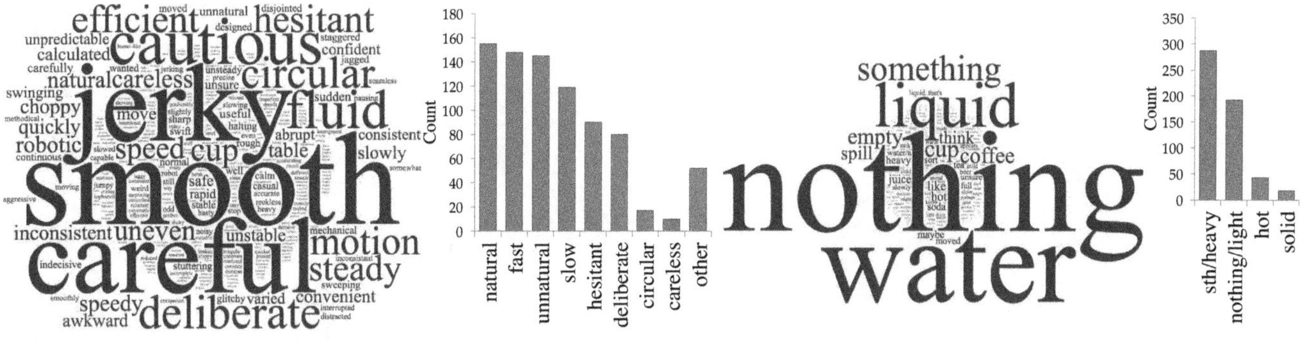

Figure 3: Words that participants in the exploratory study used to characterize the robot (left) and what it was carrying (right). The histograms cluster words into equivalence classes. We use these classes to devise the 5 dependent measures for our experiment, 4 of which are perceptions of the robot and its motion: competence, confidence, disposition, and naturalness. The other dependent measure is functional, the perceived weight of the object in the handover.

deliberate, hesitant, indecisive, calculated. We split these into two clusters: one that suggests low confidence but high ability, like *deliberate*, and one that suggests low confidence and low ability, like *hesitant*. The exact split of these is difficult to determine, so the relative counts for deliberate and hesitant should be taken with a grain of salt. The sum of the two, however, is important, and is larger than any of our other clusters, suggesting the importance of timing in perceptions of competence/confidence. Their counterpart, *careless*, is also present. The histogram plots clusters with more than 10 entries, and groups the remaining words into "other".

Based on these clusters, we see that motion timing might affect perceived motion ***naturalness***, but also two important other variables: perceived ***competence*** and perceived ***confidence***. Confidence alone is not sufficient, because it doesn't enable us to differentiate between hesitation and deliberation. But taken together, these two variables can help represent our clusters. Surprisingly, none of the descriptions directly related to arousal, dominance, energy (with the exception of the word "aggressive"). Previous studies found effects when directly measuring these, but they do not seem to specifically occur when users aren't directly asked about them. However, the adjectives that participants used could be interpreted as suggesting higher or lower values for these variables, and we capture them with a broader term: perceived ***disposition*** (with positive or negative values).

Object. For what the robot was carrying, the most common words were "water" and "nothing". While this is not surprising, their difference is important: the cup is heavier when it has something inside. Participants provided many other options, and we differentiated them between standard (e.g. something, water, soda, etc.), options that mentioned hot liquids (e.g. coffee), and solids that cannot be spilled, e.g. (jell-o, or even metal). Hot contents and solid contents were uncommon (right histogram) and not generalizable far beyond open containers, so we identify one variable here: perceived ***weight*** of the object that the robot is carrying.

4. EXPERIMENTS ON TIMING EFFECTS

We designed our experiments based on the findings from the exploratory study. The word counts already suggest certain effects, e.g. that slower motion tends to be more often described as careful or cautious or deliberate than fast motion (all three appear in top 15 words for slow and do not for fast).

However, we noticed that the difference remains the same when considering changes in speed and when not. Because of this and because changes in speed and pauses are related, we decided to separate into two experiments rather than testing all possible interactions: a first one focusing on speed and pauses, and a second focusing on the speed change patterns.

4.1 Speed, Pauses, and Their Interaction

4.1.1 Experiment Design

Manipulated Factors. In this experiment, we manipulate the ***speed*** and ***pause*** factors as we did in Sec. 3.1.

Dependent Measures. We use the measures we identified in the previous section. We measure perceived ***competence, confidence, disposition, naturalness***, and ***weight*** using 7-point scales.

For each dependent measure, the scales were labeled at either end and in the very middle. For example, the disposition scale was labeled "very negative", "neither positive nor negative", and "very positive" on the leftmost, middle, and rightmost options, respectively. We chose to label the scales in this fashion instead of having participants mark their agreement with a statement (as is typical in Likert scales) such as "The robot's disposition is positive." We did so because disagreeing with that statement does not necessarily mean the same thing as the robot having a "very negative" disposition: disagreeing with positive does not imply agreeing with negative. This is important because here, we are just as interested in whether timing can cause the perception of negative disposition as we are in whether timing can cause the perception of a positive one.

Subject Allocation. The experiment was within-subjects, every participant saw each of the 4 conditions. There were a total of 40 participants (80% male and 20% female, median age = 29). As in the exploratory study, all participants were from the United States and were recruited through Amazon's Mechanical Turk, with a minimum approval rating of 95%.

Hypotheses. We state generic and intuitive hypotheses, motivated in part by prior work findings when it comes to disposition and weight, and extrapolating to confidence and competence. However, the devil is in the details, and as we will see in the analysis, not all factors will have their anticipated effects, nor the effect sizes will be the same. Our mathematical models will leverage these details.

We hypothesize that faster motion is more positively perceived (it has already been shown before to positively affect disposition-related perceptions [3], and this could extrapolate), and makes objects look lighter (known from animating dropping objects [23]):

H1. *Increasing speed positively affects perceived competence,*

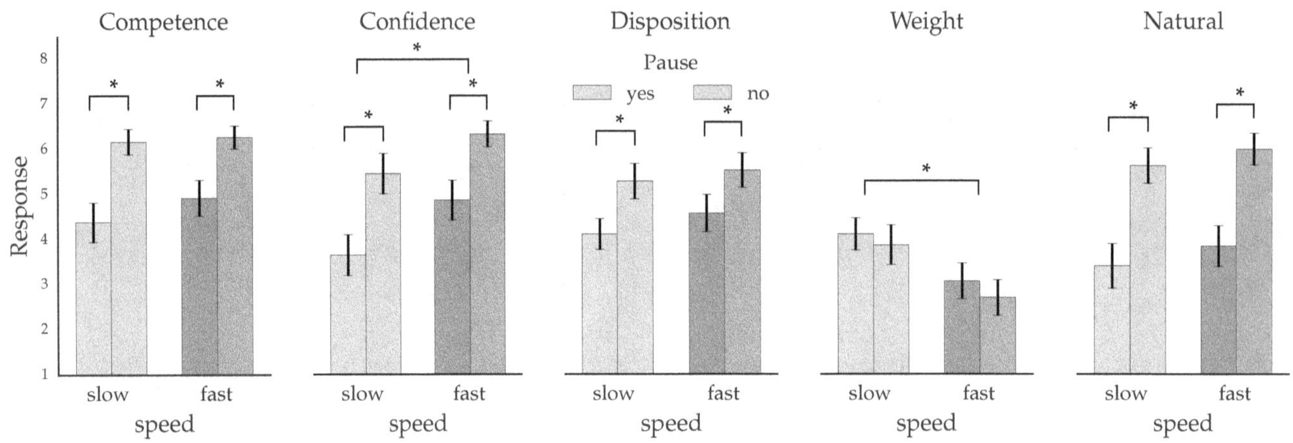

Figure 4: Our first hypothesis-driven experiment measured the effect of overall speed and pausing and their interaction. Speed significantly affected perceived confidence and weight. Pausing significantly affected perception of every property *except* weight.

confidence, disposition, naturalness, and negatively affects perceived weight.

In contrast, pausing (incorporating infinitesimally slow motion) should have the opposite effect:

H2. *Pausing negatively affects perceived competence, confidence, disposition, naturalness, and positively affects perceived weight.*

4.1.2 Analysis

We first performed a multivariate analysis on the data, and found that the different items were not highly correlated (we computed item reliability, and found Cronbach's $\alpha = .67$), so we proceeded with separate analyses for each.

We used a factorial repeated measures ANOVA with speed and pause as factors for each dependent measure. Fig.4 plots the results.

Competence. We found a significant main effect for ***pause*** ($F(1,163) = 65.81$, $p < .0001$), and no other effects (main or interaction). Pausing made the robot seem *less* competent. Surprisingly, moving faster made the robot seem only ever-so-slightly more competent, suggesting that it is not overall efficiency that matters for perceived competence.

Confidence. ***Pausing*** made the robot seem significantly *less* confident ($F(1,163) = 45.60$, $p < .0001$). But unlike for competence, higher ***speed*** made the robot seem significantly *more* confident ($F(1,163) = 10.79$, $p = 0013$), but resulted in a smaller mean difference than pausing. The interaction effect was not significant.

Disposition. ***Pausing*** resulted in a more *negative* disposition ($F(1,163) = 24.08$, $p < .0001$). Surprisingly, speed did not have a significant effect, though moving faster did result in a sightly more positive perception, in line with prior work [3].

Naturalness. Again, we found that ***pausing*** has a significant main *negative* effect ($F(1,163) = 68.01$, $p < .0001$). Pausing made the motion less natural, intuitively because it is not as smooth, or because it does not match what a person would expect the robot to do. Speed had a very marginal positive effect ($F(1,163) = 1.85$, $p = .1766$), though perhaps looking at other values for overall speed would lead to the motion becoming less natural.

Weight. In the case of weight, it was ***speed*** that had a significant *negative* effect ($F(1,163) = 19.97$, $p < .0001$), with moving faster resulting in the object being perceived as lighter. This is in line with animation advice for animating objects dropping, and physically it makes sense that objects that drop faster are lighter. But seeing this effect on a robot is important because *the object is no longer free, but rather being moved by an agent.* The robot does not need to move any different when the object is heavier, and yet people do make inferences on weight based on how the robot moves. Surprisingly, pausing did not affect weight, even though pausing did make the robot seem less confident and competent, which could suggest that it is carrying something heavier.

Summary. Overall, the effects we *did* find were intuitive: pausing negatively affected competence, confidence, disposition, and naturalness, while speed positively affects confidence and negatively affects weight. Participant comments suggested that pauses make the robot look like it is "planning" – it is uncertain about something or trying to locate something. We build on this uncertainty idea in our model in the next section.

It is the effects that we did *not* find that were surprising. For instance, speed did not seem to influence perceived competence, but influenced perceived confidence. Pausing did not seem to influence perceived weight. Of course, not finding an effect does not mean it is not there, but here the means suggest a small effect size, if at all. We dig deeper into these findings in our model section.

4.2 Speed Change Patterns

4.2.1 Experiment Design

Manipulated Factors. We manipulated ***speed changes*** as in Sec. 3.1, using the levels for 1 and 2 changes (previous experiment already evaluated 0 changes).

Dependent Measures. We used the same measures as in Sec. 4.1.

Subject Allocation. There were 40 participants (59% male and 41% female, median age = 37), selected and allocated as in 4.1.

Hypothesis. We hypothesize that changes in speed will make the robot seem more hesitant and have a negative disposition, but make the object look heavier:

H3. *More changes in speed have a negative effect on perceived competence, confidence, disposition, naturalness, and a positive effect on perceived weight.*

Which kind of changes (e.g. *StoF* vs *FtoS*) have which effect remains to be determined.

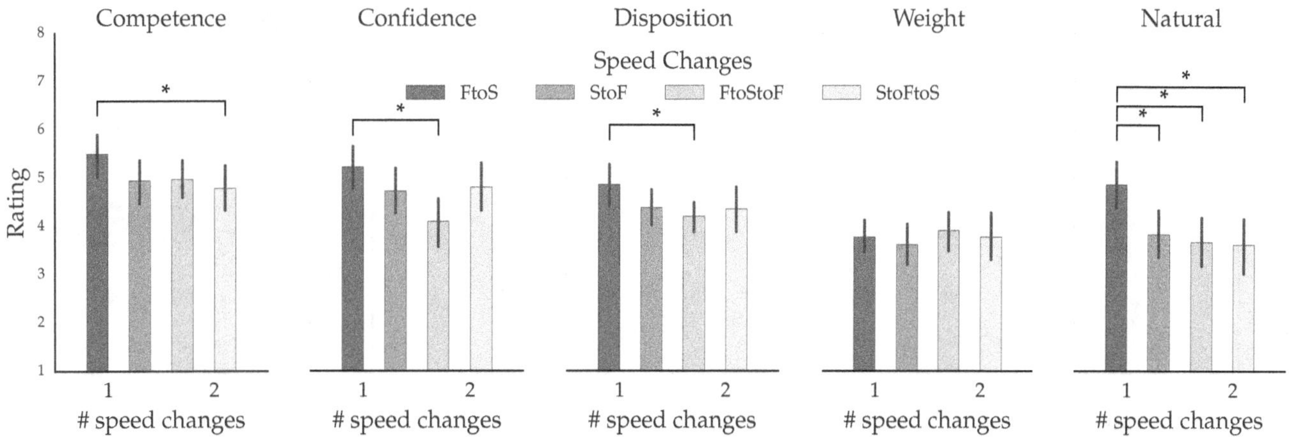

Figure 5: Our second hypothesis-driven experiment measured the effect of speed changes on competence, confidence, disposition, weight, and naturalness. Fast-to-Slow was the highest rated pattern for every property except weight.

4.2.2 Analysis

Number of Speed Changes. We first analyzed the effects that the number of speed changes has, combining data from this experiment with data from the former. A regression analysis shows, in line with our hypothesis, that having ***more changes*** significantly *decreases* perceived competence ($F(1,163) = 21.30$, $p < .0001$), confidence ($F(1,192) = 12.24$,$p = 0.006$), disposition ($F(1,163) = 14.59$, $p = .0002$), and naturalness ($F(1,163) = 37.23$, $p < .0001$). It does *not*, however, significantly affect perceived weight, and in fact the slope on the linear fit is very close to 0, namely .02. This is consistent with our finding that pausing did not significantly affect perceived weight, but counter-intuitive nonetheless.

Speed Change Patterns. Aside from number of changes, the actual pattern is interesting as well – does it make a difference, for instance, if the robot starts slower and accelerates, or starts faster and decelerates? We ran a repeated measures ANOVA for each dependent measure, and found a significant effect for every case but perceived weight, so we followed up with Tukey HSD. The results are plotted in Fig.5.

For competence, we found that *FtoS* was the best option, significantly better than *StoFtoS*, the worst option ($p = .0372$). This was similar for confidence, but here the worst option was *FtoStoF*. Disposition had the same result as confidence. For naturalness, *FtoS* was better than every other option, all with $p < .03$.

Summary. Overall, more speed changes negatively impacted all perceptions but weight. Slowing down was the most positively perceived speed change of all. At least for manipulation tasks, if the robot is going to change speed, slowing down will make it seem more competent, confident, and natural compared to speeding up or even speeding up and then slowing back down. This is somewhat surprising, but likely has to do with the notion of reaching a goal that the robot needs to do something with, like handing over the bottle or picking it up. Indeed, participants did often comment in this condition that the robot is changing speed to hand the object over more smoothly.

Surprisingly, speed changes had no effect (close to 0 slope) on perceived weight, even though intuitively the ability to change speed could indicate a lighter object, and the need to change speed could indicate a heavier object. Neither option seemed to be the case.

5. CANDIDATE MATHEMATICAL MODELS FOR TIMING-BASED HUMAN INFERENCES

Our findings inform us about the effects of motion timing, but they are only *descriptive* and not *constructive*: the robot can't use them to time its motion automatically in order to express what it wants. All the robot can do now is compare the specific timings we explored and predict what users will infer based on them. But what it needs instead is to be able to predict how *any* timing will be interpreted.

We take an inferential approach to enabling generalization in this section. We construct models of the inferences that people make from robot motion timing based on our findings so far, and show how they correlate with the real user data. Armed with such models, the robot can *simulate* what a new timing $\mathbf{T}$ would convey to a person, given a path, and even *optimize* its timing to purposefully convey something.

5.1 General Formulation

We start with a general approach, and then fill in the details for confidence, weight, and naturalness.

We will model people's inference on some hidden robot or task state θ (e.g., the robot's confidence) given timing $\mathbf{T}$ and path $\mathbf{q}$ as evidence. Thus, we model people as estimating $P(\theta|\mathbf{T},\mathbf{q})$ via Bayesian inference from an observation model $P(\mathbf{T}|\mathbf{q},\theta)$. If the robot can approximate the person's $P(\theta|\mathbf{T},\mathbf{q})$, then it knows what $\mathbf{T}$ conveys about θ.

To model $P(\mathbf{T}|\mathbf{q},\theta)$, we suppose that the person expects the timing to be based on some criterion, with different hidden variables leading to different criteria. We use $C(\mathbf{T};\mathbf{q},\theta)$ to represent the criterion for a timing given a θ value (e.g., a weight or a confidence value) and a path $\mathbf{q}$. Given θ and $\mathbf{q}$, the probability of a trajectory timing is

$$P(\mathbf{T}|\mathbf{q},\theta) \propto e^{-\lambda C(\mathbf{T};\mathbf{q},\theta)} \tag{1}$$

Such a formulation has been used for paths and general actions in an MDP in [8, 1, 11, 12].

In our experiments, the users observe timed trajectories and infer θ. To get this from our model, we apply Bayes' rule to compute

$$P(\theta|\mathbf{T},\mathbf{q}) \propto P(\mathbf{T}|\theta,\mathbf{q})P(\theta|\mathbf{q}) \tag{2}$$

Note that given this probability distribution, the robot can also search for a timing for its path that maximizes the probability of a particular θ, e.g. $\max_{\mathbf{T}} P(\theta_1|\mathbf{T},\mathbf{q})$.

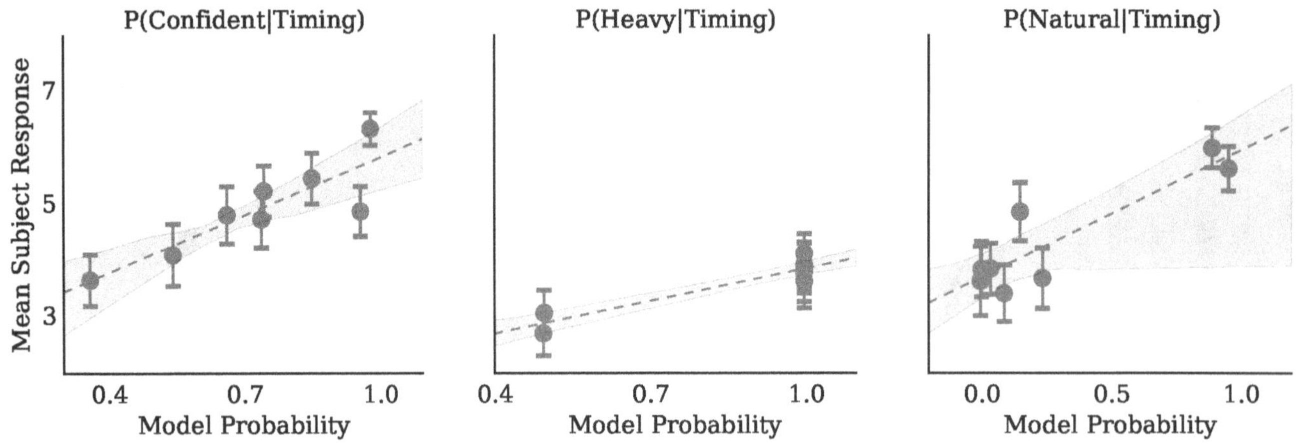

Figure 6: Correlation between our model predictions and real user data. We varied the timing of the trajectories across 8 different conditions (described in Section 4) and the plots above have one data point per condition. The x-coordinate of each data point is the best model's prediction for that condition and the y-coordinate is the mean subject response, with a 95% confidence interval. We also show a 95% confidence interval on the regression. We see that higher probability for the robot being confident, the object being heavy, and the motion being natural usually does imply a higher rating along these criteria from the users. This suggests that the models are good candidates for capturing the inferences that people make, enabling robots to predict what their timing will convey. We also test how well the models can fit random data as opposed to real user data to check that they actually approximate the inferences that people make and not just overfitting.

Model Evaluation and Parameter Selection. Next, we consider what C can be for confidence, weight, and naturalness. We will evaluate these models by measuring the correlation between the model prediction, for a given trajectory timing, with the mean subject response for that timing. Our models include some free parameters (e.g., λ in (1)) that we fit to the data by doing a grid search and selecting the parameters that correlate best with the data.

This means that there are two possible explanations for a high correlation: either the model actually explains people's inferences, or it is complex enough that it can overfit to any data. Thus, we have a confound. To address it, we run the same procedure on randomly generated synthetic data: if we get a high correlation with random data, then it is likely that our model has overfit. On the other hand, a low correlation with random synthetic data suggests that our model *does actually help explain* the predictions that users made.

5.2 Confidence

Model. We observed that high speed led to an increase in perceived confidence and pausing led to a decrease in perceived confidence. We propose that a mathematical model for confidence can be the precision (i.e., inverse variance) in the robot's belief state.

We thus model the observer as assuming, for simplicity, that the robot's belief state is a Gaussian $\mathcal{N}(\mu, \sigma^2)$ with initial precision

$$\tau_0 = \frac{1}{\sigma_0^2}$$

where high τ_0 corresponds to high confidence and vice versa.

The robot gets observations at a constant rate over the course of the trajectory. Our observer expects the robot to use a different timing depending on the confidence – intuitively, if it starts with low precision, it needs to get more observations than if it starts with high precision. More concretely, the timing that the observer will expect for an initial precision, τ_0, is related to the cost C that the observer expects the robot to optimize when timing motion. We propose that C should target high final precision τ_f, while trading off with being efficient on the task:

$$C(\mathbf{T}; \mathbf{q}, \tau_0) = kT_N + \frac{1}{\tau_f} \quad (3)$$

If the robot moves faster, it gets fewer observations so its final precision is lower. k controls the relative importance of speed versus precision. If each of these observations has Gaussian noise with precision τ_{obs}, then the robot's belief state updates with a Kalman filter [16]. The precision at the end of the trajectory is thus

$$\tau_f = n_{obs}\tau_{obs} + \tau_0 \quad (4)$$

where n_{obs} is the number of observations the robot gets during the trajectory.

This first model attempt explains the interaction between speed and perceived confidence, but can not explain the interaction with pauses; paused trajectories in our experiment still have the same overall duration, so the effect we found for pausing can not be explained by the current model.

To account for pauses, we further suppose that the quality of each observation depends on the robot's velocity. If the robot is not moving, then it gets observations with precision τ_{obs}. As the robot speeds up, the precision of its observations decreases. This gives us the following formula for τ_f:

$$\tau_f = \tau_0 + \sum_i (T_{i+1} - T_i) \frac{\tau_{obs}}{1 + r\,\|v_i\|}. \quad (5)$$

Recall that T_i is the time the robot reaches configuration q_i and v_i is the corresponding velocity. r governs how quickly the observation precision falls off as the robot speeds up.

The inference task is to determine the value of τ_0, given a timed trajectory. We consider two possible values for τ_0: $\tau_0 = 1$ represents "high confidence" and $\tau_0 = 0.5$ represents "low confidence."

Evaluation. We used grid search to fit r, k and λ. For each parameter we consider 10 values between 10^{-2} and 10^2, evenly distributed in log space. The best fit parameters were $r = 10^2, k = 0.6, \lambda = 12.9$. The corresponding correlation is 0.86. The average best-fit correlation with random data was

0.3. Fig.6 (left) plots the confidence model's output versus the mean student ratings for confidence.

5.3 Weight

Model. Previous work has shown that humans make inferences about the weights of objects based on their motions and that their perceptions can be modelled as Bayesian inference with a simplified physics model [26, 13]. However, this work focused on objects in free fall and collisions, while we are interested in objects being moved by a different entity, namely the robot. We found that human inferences about weight depend primarily on the speed of the object. A higher speed led users to infer that the held object was lighter.

It is tempting to apply a model where trajectories trade off between, e.g., energy for the robot (sum of squared torques on its joints) and the duration of the trajectory. This would lead to the appropriate inference with respect to speed; a higher weight means that the same torque results in a lower speed. However a sum of squared torques cost does not give a good explanation of the impact speed changes or pauses had on the inferred weight. A robot minimizing sum of squared torques will pay a higher penalty to pause with a heavy object, so pausing would change the inferred weight in this model.

As an alternative, we model the robot as attempting to control the overall *momentum* of the object it is holding. In this model, the robot is not minimizing the effort it expends to move the object, but rather it minimizes the amount of effort it would take to bring the object to a halt. The overall cost function trades off between duration and the sum of momentums across the trajectory:

$$C(\mathbf{T};\mathbf{q},m) = kT_N + m\sum_i \left\| v_i^{EE} \right\| \tag{6}$$

where m is the mass of the object being held, T_N is the duration, and v_i^{EE} is the velocity of the end effector. In this model, the inferred mass of the object will depend on the average velocity of the object and does not have any dependence on speed changes that occur during the trajectory. This is in contrast to cost functions that minimize the sum of squared torques or the kinetic energy of the object.

The inference task is to determine m, given a timed trajectory. We considered two physically plausible values of m: $m = 0.5$kg represents a light mass and $m = 0.8$kg represents a heavy mass.

Evaluation. We used grid search to fit k and λ. For each parameter we considered 10 values between 10^{-2} and 10^{2}, evenly distributed in log space. The best fit parameters were $k = 4.6, \lambda = 35.9$. The corresponding correlation is 0.93. The average best-fit correlation with random data was 0.18. Fig.6 (center) plots the confidence model's output versus the mean student ratings for confidence.

5.4 Naturalness

Model. Our model for naturalness is the simplest of the three. Natural human arm motions can be modeled as minimizing an objective function defined as the magnitude of jerk integrated over the motion [9]. In the case of robot-human handovers (the task used in our experiment), it has been shown that minimum jerk motions lead to faster reaction times from the human [15].

The cost function for naturalness inference is therefore a tradeoff between the duration of the trajectory (as before) and the sum of squared jerks along the trajectory:

$$C(\mathbf{T};\mathbf{q},k) = kT_N + \sum_i ||J_i||^2 \tag{7}$$

where k is the naturalness parameter that governs how natural the trajectory should be in comparison to its duration. J_i is the jerk associated with the ith we can express this in terms of stepwise velocities as

$$J_i = v_{i+1} + v_{i-1} - 2v_i \tag{8}$$

The inference task is to determine k given a trajectory timing. We suppose that k can take on two possible value k_{high} and k_{low} that we fit to the data.

Evaluation. We used grid search to fit k_{high}, k_{low}, and λ. We considered 10 values between 10^{-2} and 10^{2}, evenly distributed in log space. During the grid search, we enforced the constraint that $k_{high} > k_{low}$. The best fit was $k_{high} = 100, k_{low} = 1.66, \lambda = 4.64$. The corresponding correlation was 0.90. The average best-fit correlation with random data was 0.29. Fig.6 (right) plots the naturalness model's output versus the mean student ratings for naturalness.

6. DISCUSSION

Summary. We already knew from prior work that timing is important, and expected to see effects on perceptions of non-functional properties of the robot, like disposition and naturalness. More exciting is that we have also found effects on perceptions of functional properties as well, like competence, capability, and carried object weight.

We introduced mathematical models for some of these perceptions, whose predictions strongly correlated with the perceptions of actual users. These contribute to enabling robots to anticipate what their timing will convey, as well as to optimize their timing, given a path, to purposefully convey that they are not confident, that they are handing the person over a heavy object, or to simply produce more natural or predictable motion.

Limitations and Future Work. Despite these promising results supporting the importance of timing and bringing us closer to autonomous expressive timing, we have just scratched the surface of this deep area of research. Timing is complex and multi-faceted, and we have only studied three factors that contribute to timing: speed, changes of speed (in particular ways), and pausing (at particular times).

Our models for weight, confidence, and naturalness help generalize to new timings outside of the conditions in our study. But more investigation is needed to put each model to the test with novel timing situations, new paths, new robots, and new tasks. Further, the fact that the current models correlate with the data we collected does not necessarily imply that they produce useful timings when optimized. Performing the timing generation and adjusting the models accordingly is our main direction of future work.

Finally, for each of our current models we defined a timing cost function based on some physical or informational quantity (e.g., momentum in the weight cost or precision in the confidence cost). Doing the analogous for effects like disposition is a significant future challenge, because such quantities are hard to directly relate to concrete physical properties.

7. ACKNOWLEDGMENTS

This work is supported by The Center for Information Technology Research in the Interest of Society, Berkeley DeepDrive, and the Center for Human-Compatible AI.

8. REFERENCES

[1] Chris L Baker, Rebecca Saxe, and Joshua B Tenenbaum. Action understanding as inverse planning. *Cognition*, 113(3):329–349, 2009.

[2] Cindy L Bethel and Robin R Murphy. Survey of non-facial/non-verbal affective expressions for appearance-constrained robots. *IEEE Transactions on Systems, Man, and Cybernetics, Part C (Applications and Reviews)*, 38(1):83–92, 2008.

[3] Philip W Blythe, Peter M Todd, and Geoffrey F Miller. How motion reveals intention: Categorizing social interactions. 1999.

[4] James E Bobrow, Steven Dubowsky, and JS Gibson. Time-optimal control of robotic manipulators along specified paths. *The international journal of robotics research*, 4(3):3–17, 1985.

[5] Arunkumar Byravan, Byron Boots, Siddhartha S Srinivasa, and Dieter Fox. Space-time functional gradient optimization for motion planning. In *2014 IEEE International Conference on Robotics and Automation (ICRA)*, pages 6499–6506. IEEE, 2014.

[6] Maya Cakmak, Siddhartha S Srinivasa, Min Kyung Lee, Sara Kiesler, and Jodi Forlizzi. Using spatial and temporal contrast for fluent robot-human hand-overs. In *Proceedings of the 6th international conference on Human-robot interaction*, pages 489–496. ACM, 2011.

[7] Antonio Camurri, Ingrid Lagerlöf, and Gualtiero Volpe. Recognizing emotion from dance movement: comparison of spectator recognition and automated techniques. *International journal of human-computer studies*, 59(1):213–225, 2003.

[8] Anca D Dragan, Kenton CT Lee, and Siddhartha S Srinivasa. Legibility and predictability of robot motion. In *2013 8th ACM/IEEE International Conference on Human-Robot Interaction (HRI)*, pages 301–308. IEEE, 2013.

[9] Tamar Flash and Neville Hogan. The coordination of arm movements: an experimentally confirmed mathematical model. *The journal of Neuroscience*, 5(7):1688–1703, 1985.

[10] Michael J Gielniak and Andrea L Thomaz. Generating anticipation in robot motion. In *2011 RO-MAN*, pages 449–454. IEEE, 2011.

[11] Noah D Goodman and Andreas Stuhlmüller. Knowledge and implicature: Modeling language understanding as social cognition. *Topics in cognitive science*, 5(1):173–184, 2013.

[12] Thomas L Griffiths, Charles Kemp, and Joshua B Tenenbaum. Bayesian models of cognition. 2008.

[13] Jessica B Hamrick, Peter W Battaglia, Thomas L Griffiths, and Joshua B Tenenbaum. Inferring mass in complex scenes by mental simulation. *Cognition*, 157:61–76, 2016.

[14] Eugene Hsu, Kari Pulli, and Jovan Popović. Style translation for human motion. In *ACM Transactions on Graphics (TOG)*, volume 24, pages 1082–1089. ACM, 2005.

[15] Markus Huber, Claus Lenz, Markus Rickert, Alois Knoll, Thomas Brandt, and Stefan Glasauer. Human preferences in industrial human-robot interactions. In *Proceedings of the International Workshop on Cognition for Technical Systems*, pages 4749–4754, 2008.

[16] Rudolph Emil Kalman. A new approach to linear filtering and prediction problems. *Transactions of the ASME–Journal of Basic Engineering*, 82(Series D):35–45, 1960.

[17] Tae-hoon Kim, Sang Il Park, and Sung Yong Shin. Rhythmic-motion synthesis based on motion-beat analysis. In *ACM SIGGRAPH 2003 Papers*, SIGGRAPH '03, pages 392–401, New York, NY, USA, 2003. ACM.

[18] Steven M LaValle. Rapidly-exploring random trees: A new tool for path planning. 1998.

[19] Steven M LaValle and James J Kuffner. Randomized kinodynamic planning. *The International Journal of Robotics Research*, 20(5):378–400, 2001.

[20] Jim Mainprice, E Akin Sisbot, Léonard Jaillet, Juan Cortés, Rachid Alami, and Thierry Siméon. Planning human-aware motions using a sampling-based costmap planner. In *Robotics and Automation (ICRA), 2011 IEEE International Conference on*, pages 5012–5017. IEEE, 2011.

[21] James McCann, Nancy S Pollard, and Siddhartha Srinivasa. Physics-based motion retiming. In *Proceedings of the 2006 ACM SIGGRAPH/Eurographics symposium on Computer animation*, pages 205–214. Eurographics Association, 2006.

[22] AJung Moon, Daniel M Troniak, Brian Gleeson, Matthew KXJ Pan, Minhua Zheng, Benjamin A Blumer, Karon MacLean, and Elizabeth A Croft. Meet me where i'm gazing: how shared attention gaze affects human-robot handover timing. In *Proceedings of the 2014 ACM/IEEE international conference on Human-robot interaction*, pages 334–341. ACM, 2014.

[23] G Scott Owen. Timing and motion. https://www.siggraph.org/education/materials/HyperGraph/animation/character_animation/principles/timing.htm, 1999.

[24] Tiago Ribeiro and Ana Paiva. The illusion of robotic life: principles and practices of animation for robots. In *Proceedings of the seventh annual ACM/IEEE international conference on Human-Robot Interaction*, pages 383–390. ACM, 2012.

[25] Martin Saerbeck and Christoph Bartneck. Perception of affect elicited by robot motion. In *Proceedings of the 5th ACM/IEEE international conference on Human-robot interaction*, pages 53–60. IEEE Press, 2010.

[26] Adam N Sanborn, Vikash K Mansinghka, Thomas L Griffiths, et al. A bayesian framework for modeling intuitive dynamics. In *Proceedings of the 31st annual conference of the cognitive science society*, 2009.

[27] John Schulman, Jonathan Ho, Alex X Lee, Ibrahim Awwal, Henry Bradlow, and Pieter Abbeel. Finding locally optimal, collision-free trajectories with sequential convex optimization. In *Robotics: science and systems*, volume 9, pages 1–10. Citeseer, 2013.

[28] Kyle Wayne Strabala, Min Kyung Lee, Anca Diana Dragan, Jodi Lee Forlizzi, Siddhartha Srinivasa, Maya Cakmak, and Vincenzo Micelli. Towards seamless human-robot handovers. *Journal of Human-Robot Interaction*, 2(1):112–132, 2013.

[29] Leila Takayama, Doug Dooley, and Wendy Ju. Expressing thought: improving robot readability with animation principles. In *Proceedings of the 6th international conference on Human-robot interaction*, pages 69–76. ACM, 2011.

[30] S. C. L. Terra and R. A. Metoyer. Performance timing for keyframe animation. In *Proceedings of the 2004 ACM SIGGRAPH/Eurographics Symposium on Computer Animation*, SCA '04, pages 253–258, Aire-la-Ville,

Switzerland, Switzerland, 2004. Eurographics Association.

[31] Frank Thomas, Ollie Johnston, and Walton Rawls. *Disney animation: The illusion of life*, volume 4. Abbeville Press New York, 1981.

[32] Patrice D Tremoulet and Jacob Feldman. Perception of animacy from the motion of a single object. *Perception*, 29(8):943–951, 2000.

[33] Matt Zucker, Nathan Ratliff, Anca D Dragan, Mihail Pivtoraiko, Matthew Klingensmith, Christopher M Dellin, J Andrew Bagnell, and Siddhartha S Srinivasa. Chomp: Covariant hamiltonian optimization for motion planning. *The International Journal of Robotics Research*, 32(9-10):1164–1193, 2013.

Using Facially Expressive Robots to Calibrate Clinical Pain Perception

Maryam Moosaei[1], Sumit K. Das[2], Dan O. Popa[2], Laurel D. Riek[3]

[1]Computer Science and Engineering, University of Notre Dame, USA
[2]Electrical & Computer Engineering, University of Louisville, USA
[3]Computer Science and Engineering, University of California, San Diego, USA

ABSTRACT

In this paper, we introduce a novel application of social robotics in healthcare: high fidelity, facially expressive, robotic patient simulators (RPSs), and explore their usage within a clinical experimental context. Current commercially-available RPSs, the most commonly used humanoid robots worldwide, are substantially limited in their usability and fidelity due to the fact that they lack one of the most important clinical interaction and diagnostic tools: an expressive face. Using autonomous facial synthesis techniques, we synthesized pain both on a humanoid robot and comparable virtual avatar. We conducted an experiment with 51 clinicians and 51 laypersons (n = 102), to explore differences in pain perception across the two groups, and also to explore the effects of embodiment (robot or avatar) on pain perception. Our results suggest that clinicians have lower overall accuracy in detecting synthesized pain in comparison to lay participants. We also found that all participants are overall less accurate detecting pain from a humanoid robot in comparison to a comparable virtual avatar, lending support to other recent findings in the HRI community. This research ultimately reveals new insights into the use of RPSs as a training tool for calibrating clinicians' pain detection skills.

CCS Concepts

•Computer systems organization → Robotics; •Social and professional topics → *Medical technologies;* **•Applied computing →** Health informatics;

Keywords

patient simulation; facial expressions; emotion; social robots; humanoid robots; affective communication; non-verbal communication; human robot interaction; medical technologies; health informatics

1. INTRODUCTION

Robots are becoming more common in our daily lives, and soon robots and people will be interacting proximately [50]. There is a desire among robotics researchers and designers to enable robots to communicate quickly and effectively with humans. While there are ongoing questions within the Human Robot Interaction (HRI) community about the most appropriate form of communication between robots and people and the degree of anthropomorphism robots should employ, nonverbal communication is an exceptionally efficient means for communication which people are adept at perceiving [52, 50, 12, 1, 56, 69]. Therefore, it is worth exploring both how to enable robots to express nonverbal behaviors, and explore how successfully they are perceived by people.

People employ multiple kinds of nonverbal signals when communicating with each other, including: changing the prosody of their voice, performing gestures, shifting their posture, signaling attention with their eyes or head direction, and creating facial expressions. Across all of these communication modalities, the face is the most spontaneous channel for the rapid communication of social and emotional displays. It can be used to convey not only basic emotions such as fear, sadness, and disgust, but also complex cognitive mental states, such as confusion, contemplation, and nostalgia [53, 4]. Facial expressions can also be used to enhance conversation, show empathy, and acknowledge the actions of others [6].

Thus, employing human-like facial expressions may allow robots to communicate and interact with humans more effectively in some domains [36]. Several applications for facially expressive robots and virtual avatars bridge the fields of entertainment, education, community healthcare, and neurorehabilitation. Our work focuses on a specific medical application of facially expressive robots: robotic patient simulators (RPS). RPSs are the most frequent application of humanoid robots. They are human-sized robots that can breathe, bleed, react to medication, and convey hundreds of different biosignals (see Fig. 1). RPSs enable clinical learners to safely practice clinical skills without the fear of harming real patients, and can include: patient communication, patient condition assessment, and procedural practice. RPS usage can help reduce preventable medical errors, which kill approximately 400,000 people per year in hospitals alone, and are the third leading cause of death in the United States [28, 15].

Although commonly used in clinical education, one capability of RPSs is in need of attention: enabling face-to-face interactions between RPSs and learners. Despite the importance of patients' facial expressions in making diagnostic decisions, commercially available robotic patient simulators are not currently equipped with expressive faces. They have static faces that cannot express any visual pathological signs or distress. Therefore, clinicians can fall into the incorrect habit of not paying attention to a patient's face, which can result in them going down an incorrect diagnostic path.

Almost all areas of healthcare include face-to-face interaction [40] and healthcare providers who are skilled at detecting communication cues have improved outcomes, better patient satisfaction,

HRI '17, March 06-09, 2017, Vienna, Austria

DOI: http://dx.doi.org/10.1145/2909824.3020216

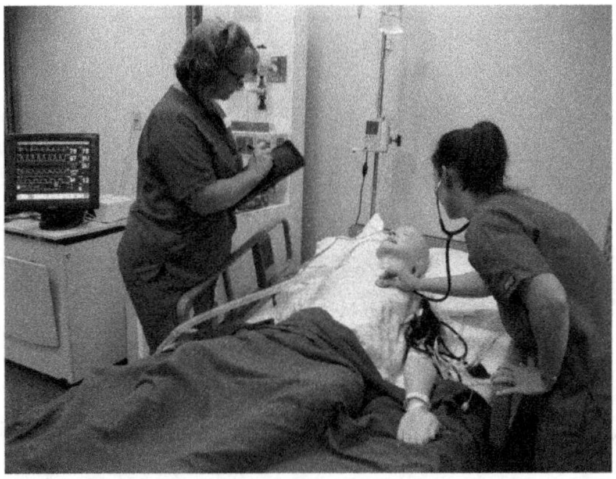

Figure 1: Clinicians practice their bedside procedural skills using RPS systems. These systems can breathe, bleed, respond to medications, and speak, but they have static faces. Our work explores building expressive RPS systems.

and experience fewer malpractice lawsuits [14, 3]. Research shows that communication errors are the cause of 70% of essential events and 75% of them results in patient's death [34].

Our work focuses on making RPSs more realistic by enabling them to convey realistic, clinically-relevant, patient-driven facial expressions to clinical trainees. We are designing a new type of RPSs with a wider range of expressivity, including the ability to express pain, neurological impairment, and other pathologies in its face. By developing expressive RPSs, our work serves as a next-generation educational tool for clinical learners to practice face-to-face communication, diagnosis, and treatment with patients in simulation. As the application of robots in healthcare continues to grow [49], expressive robots are another tool that can aid the clinical workforce by considerably improving the realism and fidelity of patient simulation.

In this paper, we focus on RPS pain synthesis, and clinician recognition. Clinicians need to both visually (and verbally) assess the amount of pain patients are experiencing in order to make treatment decisions. However, research suggests that clinicians are likely to both underestimate the intensity of patients' self-reported pain [47], and they are also likely to overall interpret facial expressions with less accuracy than laypersons [21]. Some researchers have hypothesized this is due to the decline in empathy as clinicians progress through their training [27]. Unfortunately, ignoring patients' emotional needs can lead to incorrect diagnostic decisions, poorer health outcomes, and reduced patient satisfaction [70, 30].

Fortunately, training can be effective in improving clinicians' ability to detect patient facial expressions [23, 11]. Thus, RPSs may prove to be an excellent training tool to facilitate this learning process. Certainly this effect has been shown to be true in the virtual space (c.f. [20]); however, it is difficult to use virtual simulations *in situ* at the bedside, where clinicians must visually assess patient faces while simultaneously conduct physical exams [29, 41]. Furthermore, augmented reality and projected displays are unfortunately ill-suited to most hospital simulation domains due to space and power issues [22], and can cause physical barriers between the patient and clinician. Thus, perhaps physically-embodied, expressive RPS systems may be an effective educational intervention for patient facial expression decoding.

In previous work, Moosaei et al. introduced a new method for patient-driven pain synthesis [42], and tested how well synthesized expressions of pain were perceived using a virtual patient simulator [41]. This study replicated an experiment by Riva et al. [55], who used manual Facial Action Coding System (FACS)-animation to synthesize pain on virtual avatars. Moosaei et al. found that participants are able to accurately distinguish pain from commonly conflated expressions (anger and disgust), and also showed that automatic, patient-driven pain synthesis is a viable alternative to laborious key-frame animation synthesis techniques.

While this was an interesting finding, we were curious to know if the results might change if the expression synthesis was conducted on a humanoid robot (in comparison to a matched virtual avatar). Furthermore, we were curious if there might be differences between clinicians and non-clinicians in their ability to accurately classify and perceive painful facial expression intensity.

Thus, we have three main research questions. First, are people more accurate in detecting pain expressed on a humanoid robot compared to a comparable virtual avatar? While other researchers in the HRI community have explored the robot vs. avatar question with somewhat conflicting results ([7, 9, 33]), the work has often been conducted on zoomorphic or other non-anthropomorphic platforms, and usually just focused on the six basic emotions. Both our application space (high-fidelity patient simulation) and our intended user population necessitates a higher-degree-of-freedom (DOF), human-like, facially expressive robot, and also necessitates the synthesis of more nuanced, varied-intensity expressions (such as pain, neurological impairment, etc).

Second, does having a clinical background affect synthesized pain detection accuracy? The literature suggests that clinicians might have lower accuracy in overall facial expression detection compared to laypersons [21]. Additionally, other researchers have found that clinicians tend to miss emotional cues and signs of distress in patients [43, 35, 23]. Based on these findings, we predict that clinicians will be overall less accurate in detecting synthesized painful facial expressions compared to lay participants.

Third, do participants with a clinical background perceive pain intensity on robots and avatars differently than lay participants do? Some researchers have shown that clinical experience with patients results in underestimating patients' pain [47, 17, 48]. Based on these findings, we predict that the clinical trend toward an underestimation bias will also be present when rating intensity of synthesized pain (e.g., they will not be as good as laypersons).

We address these research questions through an experiment in which participants perceived the expression of and the intensity of synthesized facial expressions (pain, anger, disgust) depicted on either a humanoid robot or its virtual model. We describe our methodology in Section 3, results in Section 4, and contextualize our findings for both the HRI and clinical education communities in Section 5.

2. BACKGROUND

Facial expressions of pain are important nonverbal communication signals, particularly in healthcare [25, 47]. Communicating pain via facial expressions is important because it signals to clinicians that a patient might need medical attention. While self-reporting is the main method of assessing pain, there are issues with this method. The most critical issue is that self-report cannot be used for children or patients with communication challenges such as patients with cognitive impairments or unconscious patients. In such cases, an observer must visually assess patients' pain. However, there are differences between how clinicians and how patients conceptualize pain (clinicians are substantially impaired at pain perception), which leads to problems when making diagnostic decisions for these patients [47, 66, 2, 39].

Prkachin et al. compared pain assessment by three methods, including: self-reporting, observer judgment, and FACS-coded facial actions among patients with shoulder injuries [46]. The results suggested that when the pain is severe, all three ratings are highly correlated. In contrast, when the pain is submaximal, observer judgment is not correlated with the other two methods. Prkachin et al. showed that observers tend to underestimate pain and the greater amount of clinical experience with patients increases this underestimation [46, 47]. This underestimation is important when critical decisions need to be made about the patients. Therefore, research on nonverbal cues of pain has important medical implications and there is a need in the clinical community to improve learners' skills in assessing pain.

While, a fair number of studies are available on automatic pain detection [2], there are only a few on automatic pain synthesis on virtual avatars [55, 41], and, to our knowledge, none on patient-driven facial expression synthesis on physical robots. Moreover, none of these synthesis studies included clinicians as participants, despite the fact that clinicians perceive pain differently (worse) than lay people. Thus, in our work, we decided to explore pain facial expression synthesis on a humanoid robot in addition to its virtual model, and included both lay participants and clinicians in our study to explore if a clinical education affects pain perception.

This work builds on work by Moosaei et al., which extended the state-of-the-art in facial expression synthesis by employing models of patients to automatically synthesizing pain on virtual avatars [41]. The researchers used a CLM-based face tracker [5] to extract 66 feature points frame-by-frame from videos from two facial expression data sets: the McMaster-UNBC Pain Archive [38] and the MMI database [45]. They then mapped the extracted feature points to control points of a virtual avatar in Source SDK, and conducted a perceptual experiment. The researchers had several notable and relevant findings. First, they found that participants had higher accuracy in detecting pain compared with anger and disgust using naturalistic performance-driven synthesis. Second, they found that there is no significant relation between an avatar's gender and pain detection accuracy. Finally, they showed that realistic pain synthesis on virtual avatars is comparable with manual pain synthesis, and is even arithmetically better [41].

3. METHODOLOGY

We used performance-driven synthesis to map facial expressions of pain, anger, and disgust onto both a humanoid robot and a comparable avatar, employing techniques similar to those described by Moosaei et al. [42, 41]. We applied a Constrained Local Model (CLM)-based face tracker to realistic source videos acquired from the Binghamton Pittsburgh 4D Spontaneous Expression Database (BP4D-Spontaneous) [68].

Our stimuli creation process included three steps. First, using a CLM-based face tracker [5], we extracted 66 feature points frame by frame from each source video. Second, for each source video we mapped the extracted feature points to servo motors of Philip K. Dick (PKD) [24, 26] (a humanoid robot from Hanson Robotics which resembles the late science fiction author) and control points of a modified virtual character from Steam Source SDK. We mapped the five source videos of the three expressions (pain, anger, and disgust) to two embodiments (PKD and avatar) resulting in 30 stimuli videos. Finally, to decide which stimuli videos to included in the main study, we ran a pilot study. This resulted in 18 stimuli videos.

Figure 2: Sample frames from the BP4D database. From left to right: disgust, happiness, pain, anger.

3.1 Source video acquisition

The BP4D-Spontaneous is a fully labeled database of realistic expressions [68]. Figure 2 shows some sample frames from this database. The authors designed an activity for naturally eliciting eight facial expressions (happiness, sadness, surprise, embarrassment, fear, pain, anger, and disgust.) from people, across 41 participants (23 women, 18 men). The first task was to talk to the experimenter and listen to a joke to evoke happiness or amusement. Participants watched a documentary video about a real emergency situation which triggered sadness. Participants experienced surprise by suddenly being exposed to a loud siren. Embarrassment was triggered by playing a game in which the subjects improvised a silly song. Participants played a game with danger of physical injury which stimulated fear. Pain was experienced when the participants submerged their hands in ice water. Subjects were insulted by the experimenter to stimulate anger. Last, subjects smelled an unpleasant odor to evoke disgust.

The researchers captured both 2D and 3D videos for each task. At the frame level, each video has metadata including manually annotated facial action units (FACS AUs), automatically tracked head poses, and 2D/3D facial features. In 3D feature tracking, 83 feature points were tracked using a method which involved fitting a multi-frame constrained 3D temporal deformable shape model (3D-TDSM). For 2D feature tracking, researchers used a CLM-based tracker to automatically track 49 feature points frame by frame in each of the videos.

All the 2D tracked videos were reviewed offline and labelled as "Good tracking," "Multiple errors," "Jawline off," "Occlusion," and "Face out of frame." The researchers chose a tracking score for each frame and the frame was reported as lost-track if the score was lower than a threshold.

At the sequence level, each video has participants' self report ratings and observer ratings. After each task, participants labeled the intensity of their emotions using a 6-point Likert-type scale (0-5). The participants experienced more than one emotion for each task. However, the results showed that for all the expressions except anger, the intended emotion was the one most frequently labeled by the participants.

In the subjective experiment, five naive observers were asked to watch all the videos and label each video with two expressions for all the tasks. Each observer was also asked to label their confidence level of each choice using a 3-point scale indicating high, moderate, and low confidence. Their results showed that the intended emotion for each task was most frequently labeled by observers.

Since participants' self reports and observer ratings of each expression's intensity were not released with the database, we analyzed the labeled action units to decide which source videos we should include in our experiment. Five action units were released with the database: AU 6,10,12,14, and 17. For pain videos, we computed the average intensity of AU6 and AU10 across all the frames of the video and chose the five videos that had the highest average intensity across all their frames. We chose AU6 and AU10 because they are important in expressing pain [46]. Since AU10 is important in expressing disgust, we computed the average intensity of AU10 across all the frames of each disgust source video and chose the five videos that had highest average intensity across all their frames.

For expressing anger, AU4 would have been ideal to use, but it was not available in the database. Therefore, we asked two naive observers to watch anger videos one by one and rated their perceived intensities using a Discrete Visual Analogue Scale (DVAS), which ranged from "none" to "very intense." We chose the five anger videos that had the highest average intensities across the two observers.

3.2 Feature extraction

For tracking facial features, we used a CLM-based face tracker to track 66 facial feature points frame by frame from each source video. Constrained Local Models are person-independent, shape-based tracking techniques that do not require any manual labeling of a performer's face [5, 16, 18]. There are also several extensions of CLM-based tracking approaches [18]; we used one developed by Baltrusitus et al. [5], which is robust to light variations and head-pose rotations.

CLM-based models have been mostly used in the literature for face tracking, or expression detection, not for synthesis [5, 16]. In our work, we used this technique to synthesize facial expressions of pain, anger, and disgust on a humanoid robot and its virtual avatar model.

3.3 Humanoid robot

We used Philip K. Dick (PKD), a humanoid robot modeled after the famous science fiction writer Philip K. Dick, who authored many well-known novels such as *The man in the high castle* and *A scanner darkly*. The robot was built by Hanson Robotics [26], and is an expressive robot with 24 DOFs on its face, head, neck. It has a Frubber skin, which is a flesh-like rubber that gives PKD a very realistic appearance [59, 19]. This spongy material used to make PKD's skin can be stretched to mimic human-like facial expressions. PKD has 24 servomotors, which enables it to express a wide range of facial expressions, as well as head and eye movements [24]. These servo motors are connected to the skin through tethers which push and pull the skin to create facial expressions. Figure 3 (right) shows PKD's face.

3.4 Avatar model creation

To ensure a fair comparison of pain detection accuracy between the robot and the avatar, we created a similar virtual model of the robot PKD. This was to mitigate appearance difference effects. To generate the avatar, we first extracted a base avatar model, "Breen", from Source SDK [62], which enables FACS-based virtual character animation. We then used GCFScape to extract textures from the model, and used VTFEdit to convert the textures to modifiable TARGA files (a raster graphic file format). We then had an artist use Adobe Photoshop to modify Breen's texture to look like PKD. This included enlarging the jaw-line, cheekbones, and chin. Figure 3 shows the final avatar model side-by-side with PKD.

3.5 Stimuli creation and labeling

We initially created 30 stimuli videos. We had two types of embodiments (robot and avatar), three expression types (pain, anger, and disgust), and five videos of each expression. In our work, we used the 66 CLM facial feature points that were tracked frame by frame from each of the 15 videos from the BP4D-Spontaneous database. We used these feature points as the raw features in our

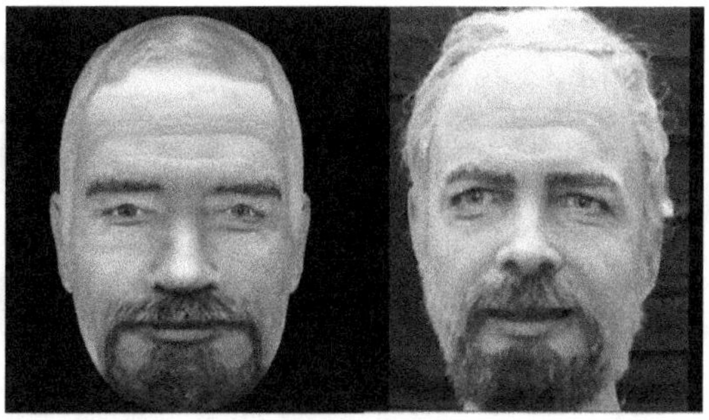

Figure 3: Left: the created avatar model similar to PKD, right: PKD robot.

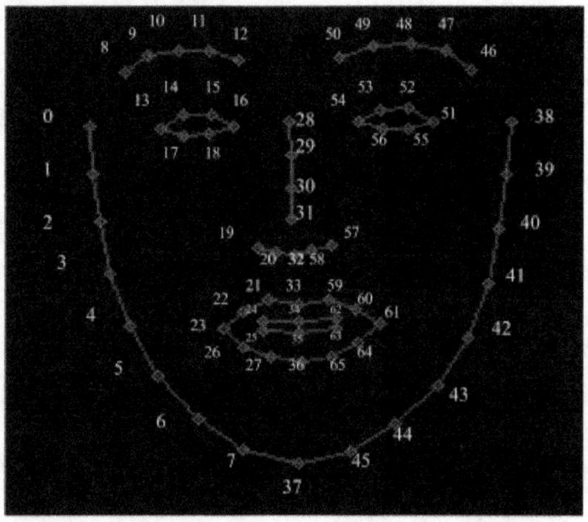

Figure 4: The CLM-based face tracker extracts 66 facial features.

work. We first removed rotation, translation, and scaling based on the eye corner positions. Then, we measured the distance of each of the 66 CLM feature points to the tip of the nose as a reference point and saved the 66 distances in a vector.

The tip of the nose stays static regardless of the expression one is expressing. In-plane rotations and translations do not affect distances of facial points to the tip of the nose. Therefore, any changes in the distance of a facial point to the tip of the nose means a change in facial expression is occurring. In each frame, we kept track of the changes each facial point had to the tip of the nose. We then mapped these changes to servo motors of the PKD robot and control points of its virtual model. We performed this in three steps.

First, for each of the PKD's servo motors and each of the avatar's control points we found a group of one or multiple CLM facial points whose movement would affect that motor or control point. For example, as PKD has two motors to control each of its eyebrows, one to control its inner eyebrow and another to control its outer eyebrow. However, as figure 4 shows, our face tracker tracks five points on each of the eyebrows (e.g. 46, 47, 48, 49, 50 for the left eyebrow). Therefore, we considered a group of points (48, 49, 50) for the left inner eyebrow and a group of points (46, 47, 48) for the left outer eyebrow. If a performer moves her left inner eyebrow (e.g. in anger expression), the distance of these three facial points (48, 49, 50) to the tip of the nose (32) decreases.

Second, for each servo motor or control point, we averaged the movements of all the points in that group to calculate only one number as the command for that motor or control point.

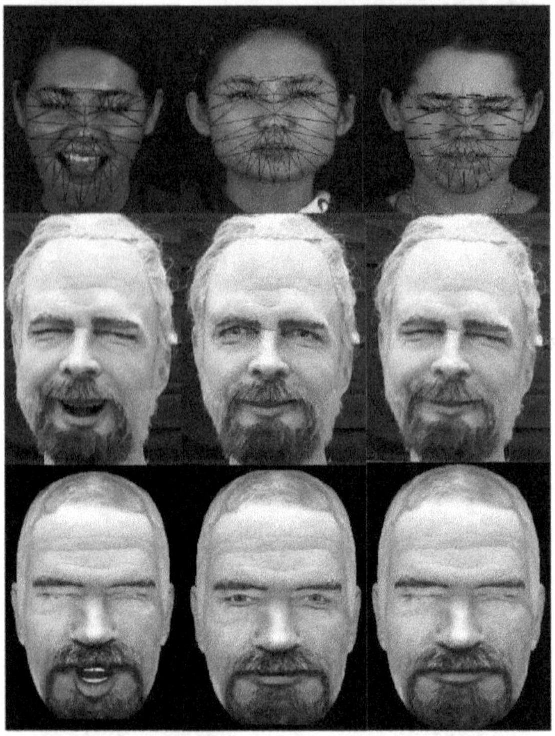

Figure 5: Sample frames from the stimuli videos and their corresponding source videos, with CLM meshes. From left to right: pain, anger, disgust. From top to bottom: source videos, PKD robot, and avatar.

Servo motors of PKD and control points of the avatar have a different actuation range of values compared with feature points. Therefore, in the third step we created a conversion between these values. We found the minimum, maximum, and default values of each group of CLM facial points, each servo motor, and each control point. We then used linear interpolation to map movements of each group of CLM facial points to each servo motor of PKD or control point of the avatar.

We recorded PKD and its virtual model expressing each of the 15 source videos. After generating the 30 raw stimuli videos, we processed them before running our study. Stimuli videos had different lengths because their source videos from BP4D-Spontaneous database had different lengths. We cropped the videos to be three seconds long to ensure consistency. We added two seconds of a black screen with a white crosshair to the beginning of each video to prepare participants for the stimulus video. Then, a facial expression on PKD or the virtual character was presented for three seconds, followed by a black screen. Figure 5 shows example frames of the created stimuli videos.

3.6 Pilot study

We ran an online pilot study to determine which stimuli videos should be included in our main study and to establish their ground truth labels, following established methods in the literature [52, 41]. 20 participants were recruited via Amazon Mturk (12 female and 8 male). Participants were all native English speakers, and aged between 23 to 46 years old (mean age 35.6 years old).

Participants were asked to watch each video once, and label the expression they perceived and its intensity. The expression labels were semi-forced choice: *pain, anger, disgust*, and *none of the above*. We employed this paradigm to align with the methodological labeling approach proposed by Tottenham et al. [61]. They suggested that a semi-forced choice method is less strict than a forced choice method [57], and that it is easier to interpret findings in the semi-forced choice paradigm compared with a free-choice paradigm.

For labeling the intensity of perceived expression in each video, we used a 6-point DVAS. We decided to have an even number of choices (0 to 5) for intensity, because otherwise participants tend to always pick the middle if there are an odd number of choices. Zero was associated with none and five was associated with very intense.

We calculated the accuracy of each of our videos across our participants, and chose the three best videos of each expression that had the highest average accuracy across the two embodiments (robot and avatar).

We had average accuracies of 82%, 65%, and 67% for pain, 62%, 35%, and 32% for anger, and 27%, 25%, and 17% for disgust. We were not surprised by the low detection accuracies for disgust, since it is known to be a poorly distinguishable facial expression in the literature [8, 7, 10]. One reason for low detection accuracies for anger was that the source videos came from a naturalistic dataset (BP4D) and therefore had very low intensities.

Zhang et al. designed an activity for simulating different natural expressions including anger and disgust in their participants [68]. Therefore, the naturally stimulated anger videos had very low intensity compared to an acted dataset such as the one we used in our previous work [41]. Naturalistic anger source videos were hard to recognize due to their very low intensity. However, since our research questions were focused on pain, we decided to continue with the study and include anger and disgust in addition to pain to make sure we do not ask participants to only watch and label only one type of expression (pain).

3.7 Main experiment

Following the pilot study, we selected three videos of each expression to use in our main experiment, resulting in a total of 18 stimuli videos. The videos were prepared and presented in the same format as our pilot and randomized accordingly. Participants were asked to select a semi-forced choice expression label (pain, anger, disgust, none of the above) and expression intensity (on a 6-point DVAS scale).

Our main experiment was a video-based study. In HRI, these studies are commonly employed in order to include a larger number of participants [65], and to reach a more diverse audience. In video-based HRI studies, participants typically view videos of human-robot interactions and answer questions about them. In our work, instead of watching a human and robot interact, participants watched a robot or its avatar model expressing pain, anger, and disgust, and were asked to label the perceived expression and its intensity.

While some researchers argue that video-based studies are not suitable for answering some research questions considering that participants do not actually interact with the robot, other HRI research findings suggest that video-based studies have comparable results to live studies [63, 32, 67, 31, 44]. For example, Kidd did not find any significant differences between subjects' ratings of personality traits for live and video-based studies of an interaction with a robotic head [31]. Furthermore, Kiesler et al. studied the subjective perception of live and recorded agents (robots and avatars) and found the results were similar [32].

As more interaction is involved between robot and participant in a study, the less suitable a video-based study would be because of

Table 1: Frequencies and percentages of hits and errors in the main study.

	Overall		Avatar		Robot	
	Clinician	Non-clinician	Clinician	Non-clinician	Clinician	Non-clinician
Pain						
Total number of responses	306	306	153	153	153	153
Correct answers	158 (51.63%)	205 (66.99%)	85 (54.48%)	127 (83%)	73 (47.71%)	78 (50.98%)
Judged as anger	68 (22.22%)	15 (4.90%)	35 (22.43%)	9 (5.88%)	33 (21.56%)	6 (3.92%)
Judged as disgust	52 (16.99%)	35 (11.43%)	26 (16.66%)	10 (6.53%)	26 (16.99%)	25 (16.33%)
Judged as none of the above	28 (9.15%)	51 (16.66%)	7 (4.48%)	7 (4.57%)	21 (13.72%)	44 (28.75%)
Anger						
Total number of responses	306	306	153	153	153	153
Correct answers	89 (29.08%)	104 (33.98%)	51 (33.33%)	69 (45.09%)	38 (24.83%)	35 (22.87%)
Judged as pain	89 (29.08%)	57 (18.62%)	26 (16.99%)	18 (11.76%)	63 (41.17%)	39 (25.49%)
Judged as disgust	67 (21.89%)	70 (22.87%)	34 (22.22%)	18 (11.76%)	33 (21.56%)	52 (33.98%)
Judged as none of the above	61 (19.93%)	75 (24.50%)	42 (27.45%)	48 (31.37%)	19 (12.41%)	27 (17.64%)
Disgust						
Total number of responses	306	306	153	153	153	153
Correct answers	73 (23.85%)	73 (23.85%)	30 (19.60%)	18 (11.76%)	43 (28.10%)	55 (35.94%)
Judged as pain	101 (33.00%)	98 (32.02%)	53 (34.64%)	62 (40.52%)	48 (31.37%)	36 (23.52%)
Judged as anger	71 (23.20%)	47 (15.35%)	33 (21.56%)	25 (16.33%)	38 (24.83%)	22 (14.37%)
Judged as none of the above	61 (19.93%)	88 (28.75%)	37 (24.18%)	48 (31.37%)	24 (15.68%)	40 (26.14%)

the increased importance of aspects of embodiment [63]. Because our work is focused on how people *perceive* robot expressions, with a particular focus on validating our synthesis algorithms and also on their affect on clinical trainees, we hoped to still gain valuable findings about visual pain perception on an RPS at this stage of our research program. Furthermore, we aimed to recruit a large number of interprofessional clinicians from across the United States which would have been very challenging if we wanted to bring all of them to our lab. In the future, we do plan to replicate with a live study.

We recruited 102 participants for our experiment, 51 clinicians and 51 non-clinicians. We recruited clinicians by sending an advertisement email to over a dozen different medical and nursing schools across the United States. The clinicians were from multidisciplinary backgrounds, 37% were registered nurses (RNs), 41% were physicians, and the rest included pharmacists, medical technicians, clinical researchers, and therapists (approximately 20%).

Lay participants were recruited via Amazon Mturk. Participants were eligible only if they did not participate in our previous studies, were over 18, and were native English speakers. Additionally, each participant completed a demographic questionnaire at the beginning of the study. In this questionnaire, participants were asked if they ever received a clinical education, or if they ever held a clinical related job. If they answered affirmatively, they were unable to continue the study. Overall, participant ages ranged from 19-64 (mean age = 33.6 years) and they were of mixed heritage, and were all native English speakers. In terms of gender, the clinicians were 39% male, and the non-clinicians were 54% male.

Each participant watched the 18 videos (6 pain, 6 anger, and 6 disgust) in a random order. Nine videos were from the robot and nine were from the avatar. Participants were asked to watch each video once and label the expression that they perceived and its intensity. Expressions were semi-forced choice: pain, anger, disgust, and none of the above. For labeling the intensity of perceived expression in each video, we used a 6-point DVAS (0 (none) to 5 (very intense)).

The results from the main experiment are described in the subsequent sections. We measured accuracy (correct or incorrect) across our three independent variables (embodiment type, educational background, and expression type). We describe the statistical details of our analysis below.

4. RESULTS

4.1 Regression method

To answer the first and second research questions, we used binary logistic regression. We had accuracy as the one dependant variable derived from the expression classification task (i.e. classification of the expressions as pain, anger, or disgust). Accuracy is based on the ground truth that we gained from our pilot studies. We had three independent categorical variables: expression with three levels (pain, anger, and disgust), embodiment type with two levels (robot and avatar), and clinical education background with two levels (clinician and non-clinician).

The dependent variable was analyzed using a within-subjects binary logistic regression since the only dependant variable was binary (1: accurate, 0: inaccurate). In the following analyses, significant effects are those with p-values <.05. Table 1 shows the details regarding the exact number of errors that participants made in the classification of 18 videos. In this classification, we considered an answer correct if the participant's label matched with the source video label. The percentage of correct classifications was computed across each of the three expressions types within each embodiment and each education background : 3 *(Expression: pain, anger, or disgust)* $\times$ 2 *(Embodiment: robot or avatar)* $\times$ 2 *(Background: clinician or non-clinician).*

The three independent variables (expression, embodiment type, and clinical education background) were significant predictors for the dependent variable (see Table 3). We compared the full model with three predictors (expression, embodiment, and background) with the restricted model with just a constant factor. The results of the analysis of the full model with three predictors (independent variables) suggest a significant effect of the set of predictors on the correct identification rate as the dependant variable.

The Wald test in Table 3 shows the degree to which each expression affected accuracy. While the chi-square value in Table 2 shows that the predictors together have a significant effect on the model, the Wald test is the significant test for each individual predictor. Table 3 shows the effect of each individual independent variable on the classification rate. The standardized Beta value represents the weight that each predictor has in the final model. Negative weight shows a negative relation. Since the regression was run with pain

Table 2: Omnibus Tests of Model Coefficients. $\chi^2(4) = 198.035$, p <.001. Combined predictors have a significant effect on the model.

		Chi-square	df	Sig.
Step 1	Step	198.035	4	0.000
	Block	198.035	4	0.000
	Model	198.035	4	0.000

as the reference value, it does not have a Beta value. The Wald test suggests that all the three expressions are significant predictors for accuracy, ($p < .001$). Medical background is also a significant predictor for accuracy, $W = 8.92, p < .05$. Embodiment type is a significant predictor for accuracy as well, $W = 8.33, p < .05$.

4.2 Multi-Factor ANOVA

Our third research question explored the effect of a clinical education background on the perceived intensity of pain. To answer this question, we ran a multi-factor ANOVA. We had one dependent variable in this test, intensity, which was a scalar variable between 0 and 5. We had two categorical independent variables, clinical education background with two levels (clinician and non-clinician), and embodiment type with two levels (robot and avatar).

Table 4 shows that a clinical background is not a significant predictor for the perceived intensity. Therefore, we found that there is no significant difference between clinicians and non-clinicians in overall pain intensity perception.

However, Table 4 shows that embodiment type is a significant predictor for perceived pain intensity. Therefore, we found that participants tend to perceive a lower intensity of pain expressed by a robot compared to its similar avatar.

5. DISCUSSION

We synthesized naturalistic painful facial expressions on a humanoid robot and its virtual model, and answered different research questions regarding their perception. This work explores new applications of social robots in patient simulation, and gives some insights on how simulator type (avatar or robot) or educational background (clinician or non-clinician) may affect perception of pain.

We found support for our first research question, which supports earlier findings in the literature, that clinicians are less accurate than laypersons in decoding pain [21, 23, 43, 35, 27, 17]. Our work showed that this effect is found regardless of simulation embodiment (robot or virtual character), which suggests even the novelty of the embodiment is not sufficient to incur improved decoding skills. However, since training has been shown to help mitigate these clinical habituation effects, expressive, interactive RPSs may be useful in the medical education curriculum to be used alongside procedural skills training. For example, rather than having infrequent and contextless patient empathy training sessions [58], clinical learners could be continually learning pain decoding skills as they practice other critical care skills on patient simulators (e.g., performing physical exams, assessing patient state, etc.).

Some of these applications have recently been explored in the HRI community. For example, using robots for a range of health communication interventions to empower people with facial masking or facial movement disorders (e.g., Parkinson's disease, cerebral palsy, dystonia) when interacting with their clinicians [13, 54, 60, 51]. We are in fact currently exploring masked synthesis on RPSs in our research, and believe these kinds of interventions could also be useful in a clinical education context to help with destigmatization and to improve provider empathy.

We did not find support for our prediction that participants with a clinical education background tend to miss lower levels of pain intensity compared to laypersons. This is in contrast to findings by Prkachin et al. [47, 17, 48] who showed that clinicians tend to vastly underestimate patient pain intensity compared to laypersons. One reason for this finding could involve the type of pain studied. Prior work has focused on chronic pain perception by clinicians; however, we employed acute pain models in our work. Further work is needed to explore this finding; preferably longitudinally *in situ* in clinic.

It also may be interesting to explore if clinicians underestimate pain intensity on expressive RPSs when patient history is provided to the clinical learner. It is well documented that clinicians underestimate expressed pain in patients who exhibit risky lifestyle behaviors (e.g., drug use), those that come from low socio-economic strata, culturally-underrepresented minorities, older adults, and women. Lok et al. [64] recently showed that clinicians can achieve self-awareness of their pain perception biases within this context, which suggests that there may be a place for RPS training programs to help mitigate these effects.

We also found that all participants (clinicians or laypersons) are more accurate in detecting pain from a virtual avatar compared to a similar robot, and able to perceive higher pain intensities on the avatar. These results lend support to some recent findings in the HRI community. For example, Bennett and Sabanovic [9] found that detection accuracy is higher for facial expressions on an avatar compared to a physical robot. Also, Li et al. [37] found that when a human lecturer giving a presentation was replaced with an expressive virtual avatar, knowledge recall was higher than when the lecturer was replaced by an expressive social robot.

Bennett and Sabanovic argued that the higher detection accuracy finding for virtual avatars might be because it is easier to maintain FACS fidelity on an avatar compared to a physical robot [9]. This may also be true for our findings, however, we conducted dozens of small pilot studies to ensure FACS similarity and fidelity between the robot and the virtual character. However, it is possible subtle expressivity differences existed between the two embodiments that were too subtle to detect. We plan to conduct additional follow-on studies to further explore this idea.

This finding relates to a limitation of our work, which was that PKD did not have any range of motion nor wrinkles around the nose area or cheeks. Therefore we could not map AU9 or AU10, which are both important for expressing pain and disgust [46]. (We also disabled these degrees of freedom in the virtual avatar to ensure a fair comparison). Adding these action units to both the robot and avatar could help improve overall detection accuracy and intensity perception.

In the development of our own robot, we have used these findings to improve its design. For example, it is now clear to us that AU9, AU10, and AU4 are critical action units to have on our robot. Upon its completion, we plan to experimentally explore the implications of these AUs, and also replicate this experiment to see if our results differ.

Another reason for low detection accuracies of some facial expressions may be because our videos came from a naturalistic dataset (BP4D). It is well understood in the affective computing community that naturally evoked emotions overall have far lower intensities compared to acted datasets (such as the MMI corpus [45]).

It is worth noting that the recognition rate itself is not the key finding with regards to the path to applicability - it is the significant difference in accuracy between clinicians (51%) and non-clinicians (67%). This result provides direct support to other findings in the clinical literature that as clinicians progress through their training

Table 3: Independent variables in the regression equation and their individual effects on the classification task.

		B	S.E	Wald	df	Sig.	Exp(B)	95% C.I.for EXP(B)	
								Lower	Upper
Step 1	Embodiment	-0.294	0.102	8.337	1	0.004	0.745	0.610	0.910
	Education background	-0.304	0.102	8.928	1	0.003	0.738	0.604	0.901
	Pain			172.874	2	0.000			
	Anger	1.553	0.126	151.089	1	0.000	4.727	3.690	6.056
	Disgust	0.381	0.129	8.683	1	0.003	1.464	1.136	1.886
	Constant	-0.873	0.116	56.372	1	0.000	.418		

Table 4: Univariate Analysis of Variance (tests of between subjects effects). Embodiment had a significant effect on perceived intensity. Having a clinical education background did not have a significant effect on the perceived intensity.

	Sum of squares	df	Mean square	F	Sig.
Corrected model	56.660	3	18.88	11.49	0.000
Intercept	5568.16	1	5568.16	3388.23	0.000
Embodiment	45.02	1	45.02	27.39	0.000
Education background	3.16	1	3.16	1.92	0.16
Embodiment * Education background	8.47	1	8.47	5.15	0.02
Error	999.17	608	1.64		
Total	6624.00	612			
Corrected total	1055.83	611			

they lose their expression decoding abilities, which affects how well they can provide care. This research offers a new paradigm for training that may enable clinicians to overcome these decoding deficits through repeated interactions and exposure. Expressive RPSs are perfect for providing such training.

Despite their high clinical relevance, commercially available RPSs do not currently support human-like face-to-face interactions with learners. However, this is problematic as clinicians need to learn how to start reading patient facial expressions from their very first day of training, and continue to hone their facial expression decoding skills throughout their training. These face-to-face communication skills should not be kept separate from other beside training skills (e.g., taking vital signs, inserting IV lines), but rather should be well-ingrained into the simulation curriculum in a manner that maintains simulation fidelity.

Our work has implications for the HRI community because it explores a novel application of facially expressive robots in healthcare which is using these robots as expressive patient mannequins. We also explored how synthesizing facial expressions on robotic patient simulators can make their interactions with clinical learners more realistic. Our work can help design more effective social robots for healthcare applications by studying how these robots are perceived by different groups, and how different factors, such as physical embodiment or educational background, can affect perception of these robots.

The clinical community can benefit from our work because we are developing new training tools for clinical learners to help them improve their skills in reading patients' faces. Our results supported findings by other researchers that compared to lay participants, clinicians have a lower accuracy in detecting pain in patients. However, to the best of our knowledge our work is the first to replicate these findings through simulation with an expressive robot instead of a real patient. Considering that both robotic patient mannequins and virtual avatars can be used as part of a training tool for improving learners' skill in decoding visual signals of illness and pain in patients, our results can help clinical professionals understand how choosing different simulation systems (virtual or robotic) can affect perception of expressions.

6. ACKNOWLEDGEMENT

This material is based upon work supported by the National Science Foundation under Grant No. IIS-1253935 and Grant No. IIP-1534124. The authors also would like to thank Dr. Roya Ghiassedin for providing input for the statistical methods used in Section 4 of this paper.

7. REFERENCES

[1] S. Andrist, X. Z. Tan, M. Gleicher, and B. Mutlu. Conversational gaze aversion for humanlike robots. *Proceedings of the 2014 ACM/IEEE international Conference on Human-Robot Interaction*, pages 25–32, 2014.

[2] A. B. Ashraf, S. Lucey, J. F. Cohn, T. Chen, Z. Ambadar, K. M. Prkachin, and P. E. Solomon. The painful face–pain expression recognition using active appearance models. *Image and Vision Computing*, 27(12):1788–1796, 2009.

[3] A. L. Back and et al. Efficacy of communication skills training for giving bad news and discussing transitions to palliative care. *Archives of Internal Medicine*, 167(5), 2007.

[4] T. Baltrušaitis, L. D. Riek, and P. Robinson. Synthesizing expressions using facial feature point tracking: how emotion is conveyed. In *Proceedings of the 3rd ACM international workshop on Affective interaction in natural environments*, pages 27–32, 2010.

[5] T. Baltrusaitis, P. Robinson, and L. Morency. 3D constrained local model for rigid and non-rigid facial tracking. In *IEEE Conference on Computer Vision and Pattern Recognition (CVPR)*, pages 2610–2617, 2012.

[6] S. Baron-Cohen, A. Cox, G. Baird, J. Swettenham, N. Nightingale, K. Morgan, A. Drew, and T. Charman. Psychological markers in the detection of autism in infancy in a large population. *The British Journal of Psychiatry*, 168(2):158–163, 1996.

[7] C. Bartneck, J. Reichenbach, and v. A. Breemen. In your face, robot! the influence of a character's embodiment on how users perceive its emotional expressions. In *Proceedings of the Design and Emotion*, pages 32–51, 2004.

[8] D. Bazo, R. Vaidyanathan, A. Lentz, and C. Melhuish. Design and testing of a hybrid expressive face for a humanoid robot. In *IEEE/RSJ International Conference on Intelligent Robots and Systems (IROS)*, 2010.

[9] C. C. Bennett and S. Šabanović. Deriving minimal features for human-like facial expressions in robotic faces. *International Journal of Social Robotics*, 6(3):367–381, 2014.

[10] K. Berns and J. Hirth. Control of facial expressions of the humanoid robot head roman. In *IEEE/RSJ International Conference on Intelligent Robots and Systems (IROS)*, 2006.

[11] D. Blanch-Hartigan, S. A. Andrzejewski, and K. M. Hill. The effectiveness of training to improve person perception accuracy: a meta-analysis. *Basic and Applied Social Psychology*, 34(6):483–498, 2012.

[12] C. Breazeal, C. D. Kidd, A. L. Thomaz, G. Hoffman, and M. Berlin. Effects of nonverbal communication on efficiency and robustness in human-robot teamwork. In *IEEE/RSJ International Conference on Intelligent Robots and Systems*, pages 708–713, 2005.

[13] P. Briggs, M. Scheutz, and L. Tickle-Degnen. Are robots ready for administering health status surveys': First results from an hri study with subjects with parkinson's disease. In *Proceedings of the Tenth Annual ACM/IEEE International Conference on Human-Robot Interaction*, pages 327–334, 2015.

[14] J. Brown. How clinical communication has become a core part of medical education in the UK. *Medical Education*, 42(3), 2008.

[15] A. J. Card. Patient safety: this is public health. *Journal of Healthcare Risk Management*, 34(1):6–12, 2014.

[16] S. W. Chew, P. Lucey, S. Lucey, J. Saragih, J. F. Cohn, and S. Sridharan. Person-independent facial expression detection using constrained local models. In *IEEE International Conference on Automatic Face and Gesture Recognition*, 2011.

[17] K. D. Craig. The social communication model of pain. *Canadian Psychology/Psychologie canadienne*, 50(1):22, 2009.

[18] D. Cristinacce and T. F. Cootes. Feature detection and tracking with constrained local models. In *British Machine Vision Conference (BMVC)*, volume 17, pages 929–938, 2006.

[19] S. K. Das. Realistic interaction with social robots via facial expressions and neck-eye coordination. Master's thesis, The University of Texas at Arlington, USA, 2015.

[20] A. Foster, N. Chaudhary, T. Kim, J. L. Waller, J. Wong, M. Borish, A. Cordar, B. Lok, and P. F. Buckley. Using virtual patients to teach empathy: A randomized controlled study to enhance medical students' empathic communication. *Simulation in Healthcare*, 11(3):181–189, 2016.

[21] A. J. Giannini, J. D. Giannini, and R. K. Bowman. Measurement of nonverbal receptive abilities in medical students. *Perceptual and Motor Skills*, 90(3c):1145–1150, 2000.

[22] M. J. Gonzales, J. M. Henry, A. W. Calhoun, and L. D. Riek. Visual task: A collaborative cognitive aid for acute care resuscitation. *10th EAI International Conference on Pervasive Computing Technologies for Healthcare (Pervasive Health)*, pages 1–8, 2016.

[23] P. Gulbrandsen, B. F. Jensen, A. Finset, and D. Blanch-Hartigan. Long-term effect of communication training on the relationship between physicians' self-efficacy and performance. *Patient Education and Counseling*, 91(2):180–185, 2013.

[24] A. Habib, S. K. Das, I.-C. Bogdan, D. Hanson, and D. O. Popa. Learning human-like facial expressions for android phillip k. dick. In *IEEE International Conference on Automation Science and Engineering (CASE)*, pages 1159–1165, 2014.

[25] T. Hadjistavropoulos, K. D. Craig, and S. Fuchs-Lacelle. Social influences and the communication of pain. *Pain: Psychological Perspectives*, 2004.

[26] D. Hanson. Exploring the aesthetic range for humanoid robots. In *Proceedings of the ICCS/CogSci-2006 Long Symposium: Toward Social Mechanisms of Android Science*, pages 39–42. Citeseer.

[27] M. Hojat, M. J. Vergare, K. Maxwell, G. Brainard, S. K. Herrine, G. A. Isenberg, J. Veloski, and J. S. Gonnella. The devil is in the third year: a longitudinal study of erosion of empathy in medical school. *Academic Medicine*, 84(9):1182–1191, 2009.

[28] J. T. James. A new, evidence-based estimate of patient harms associated with hospital care. *Journal of patient safety*, 9(3), 2013.

[29] A. Janiw, L. Woodrick, and L. Riek. Patient situational awareness support appears to fall with advancing levels of nursing student education (submission# 968). *Simulation in Healthcare*, 8(6):345, 2013.

[30] J. Jansen, J. C. van Weert, J. de Groot, S. van Dulmen, T. J. Heeren, and J. M. Bensing. Emotional and informational patient cues: the impact of nurses' responses on recall. *Patient Education and Counseling*, 79(2):218–224, 2010.

[31] C. D. Kidd. Phd thesis:sociable robots: The role of presence and task in human-robot interaction. *Citeseer*, 2003.

[32] S. Kiesler, A. Powers, S. R. Fussell, and C. Torrey. Anthropomorphic interactions with a robot and robot-like agent. *Social Cognition*, 26(2):169, 2008.

[33] T. Kishi, T. Otani, N. Endo, P. Kryczka, K. Hashimoto, K. Nakata, and A. Takanishi. Development of expressive robotic head for bipedal humanoid robot. In *IEEE/RSJ International Conference on Intelligent Robots and Systems (IROS)*, pages 4584–4589, 2012.

[34] M. Leonard. The human factor: the critical importance of effective teamwork and communication in providing safe care. *Quality and Safety in Health Care*, 13, 2004.

[35] W. Levinson, R. Gorawara-Bhat, and J. Lamb. A study of patient clues and physician responses in primary care and surgical settings. *Jama*, 284(8):1021–1027, 2000.

[36] A. Li, M. Florendo, L. Miller, H. Ishiguro, and A. P. Saygin. Robot form and motion influences social attention. In *ACM/IEEE International Conference on Human-Robot Interaction*, 2015.

[37] J. Li, R. Kizilcec, J. Bailenson, and W. Ju. Social robots and virtual agents as lecturers for video instruction. *Computers in Human Behavior*, 55:1222–1230, 2016.

[38] P. Lucey, J. F. Cohn, K. M. Prkachin, P. E. Solomon, and I. Matthews. Painful data: The unbc-mcmaster shoulder pain expression archive database. In *IEEE International Conference on Automatic Face & Gesture Recognition*, 2011.

[39] P. Lucey and et al. Automatically detecting pain using facial actions. In *3rd International Conference on Affective Computing and Intelligent Interaction (ACII)*, 2009.

[40] L. R. Martin and H. S. Friedman. Nonverbal communication and health care. *Applications of Nonverbal Communication*, 2005.

[41] M. Moosaei, M. J. Gonzales, and L. D. Riek. Naturalistic pain synthesis for virtual patients. *International Conference on Intelligent Virtual Agents (IVA)*, pages 295–309, 2014.

[42] M. Moosaei, C. J. Hayes, and L. D. Riek. Performing facial expression synthesis on robot faces: A real-time software system. *In Proceedings of the 4th International AISB Symposium on New Frontiers in Human-Robot Interaction*, 2015.

[43] D. S. Morse, E. A. Edwardsen, and H. S. Gordon. Missed opportunities for interval empathy in lung cancer communication. *Archives of Internal Medicine*, 168(17):1853–1858, 2008.

[44] A. Paiva, J. Dias, D. Sobral, R. Aylett, P. Sobreperez, S. Woods, C. Zoll, and L. Hall. Caring for agents and agents that care: Building empathic relations with synthetic agents. In *Proceedings of the Third International Joint Conference on Autonomous Agents and Multiagent Systems-Volume 1*, pages 194–201, 2004.

[45] M. Pantic, M. Valstar, R. Rademaker, and L. Maat. Web-based database for facial expression analysis. In *IEEE International Conference on Multimedia and Expo (ICME)*, 2005.

[46] K. M. Prkachin, S. Berzins, and S. R. Mercer. Encoding and decoding of pain expressions: a judgement study. *Pain*, 58(2), 1994.

[47] K. M. Prkachin and K. D. Craig. Expressing pain: The communication and interpretation of facial pain signals. *Journal of Nonverbal Behavior*, 19(4), 1995.

[48] K. M. Prkachin, P. E. Solomon, and J. Ross. Underestimation of pain by health-care providers: towards a model of the process of inferring pain in others. *Canadian Journal of Nursing Research (CJNR)*, 39(2):88–106, 2007.

[49] L. Riek. Healthcare robotics. *Communications of the ACM, in review*.

[50] L. D. Riek. The social co-robotics problem space: Six key challenges. *Proceedings of Robotics Challenges and Vision (RCV)*, 2013.

[51] L. D. Riek. Robotics technology in mental health care. *Artificial Intelligence in Behavioral and Mental Health Care*, pages 185–203, 2015.

[52] L. D. Riek, T.-C. Rabinowitch, P. Bremner, A. G. Pipe, M. Fraser, and P. Robinson. Cooperative gestures: Effective signaling for humanoid robots. In *5th ACM/IEEE International Conference on Human-Robot Interaction (HRI)*, pages 61–68, 2010.

[53] L. D. Riek and P. Robinson. Real-time empathy: Facial mimicry on a robot. In *Workshop on Affective Interaction in Natural Environments (AFFINE) at the International ACM Conference on Multimodal Interfaces (ICMI 08)*, 2008.

[54] L. D. Riek and P. Robinson. Using robots to help people habituate to visible disabilities. In *IEEE International Conference on Rehabilitation Robotics*, pages 1–8, 2011.

[55] P. Riva, S. Sacchi, L. Montali, and A. Frigerio. Gender effects in pain detection: Speed and accuracy in decoding female and male pain expressions. *European Journal of Pain*, 2011.

[56] K. Ruhland, C. E. Peters, S. Andrist, J. B. Badler, N. I. Badler, M. Gleicher, B. Mutlu, and R. McDonnell. A review of eye gaze in virtual agents, social robotics and hci: Behaviour generation, user interaction and perception. *Computer Graphics Forum*, 34(6):299–326, 2015.

[57] J. A. Russell. Is there universal recognition of emotion from facial expressions? a review of the cross-cultural studies. *Psychological bulletin*, 115(1), 1994.

[58] J. M. Satterfield and E. Hughes. Emotion skills training for medical students: a systematic review. *Medical education*, 41(10):935–941, 2007.

[59] Y. Tadesse, S. Priya, H. Stephanou, D. Popa, and D. Hanson. Piezoelectric actuation and sensing for facial robotics. *Ferroelectrics*, 345(1):13–25, 2006.

[60] L. Tickle-Degnen, M. Scheutz, and R. C. Arkin. Collaborative robots in rehabilitation for social self-management of health. *Proceedings of RESNA 2014*, 2014.

[61] N. Tottenham and et al. The nimstim set of facial expressions: judgments from untrained research participants. *Psychiatry Research*, 168(3), 2009.

[62] Valve Software: Source SDK. source.valvesoftware.com/sourcesdk.php.

[63] M. L. Walters, M. Lohse, M. Hanheide, B. Wrede, D. S. Syrdal, K. L. Koay, A. Green, H. Hüttenrauch, K. Dautenhahn, G. Sagerer, et al. Evaluating the robot personality and verbal behavior of domestic robots using video-based studies. *Advanced Robotics*, 25(18):2233–2254, 2011.

[64] L. D. Wandner, J. E. Letzen, C. A. Torres, B. Lok, and M. E. Robinson. Using virtual human technology to provide immediate feedback about participants' use of demographic cues and knowledge of their cue use. *The Journal of Pain*, 15(11):1141 – 1147, 2014.

[65] A. Weiss. Creating service robots for and with people: A user-centered reflection on the interdisciplinary research field of human-robot interaction. In *15th Annual STS Conference Graz, Critical Issues in Science, Technology, and Society Studies*, 2016.

[66] A. C. d. C. Williams, H. T. O. Davies, and Y. Chadury. Simple pain rating scales hide complex idiosyncratic meanings. *Pain*, 85(3), 2000.

[67] S. N. Woods, M. L. Walters, K. L. Koay, and K. Dautenhahn. Methodological issues in hri: A comparison of live and video-based methods in robot to human approach direction trials. In *The 15th IEEE International Symposium on Robot and Human Interactive Communication (ROMAN)*, pages 51–58, 2006.

[68] X. Zhang, L. Yin, J. F. Cohn, S. Canavan, M. Reale, A. Horowitz, P. Liu, and J. M. Girard. BP4D-spontaneous: a high-resolution spontaneous 3D dynamic facial expression database. *Image and Vision Computing*, 32(10):692–706, 2014.

[69] R. Zhao, T. Sinha, A. Black, and J. Cassell. Socially-aware virtual agents: Automatically assessing dyadic rapport from temporal patterns of behavior. In *16th International Conference on Intelligent Virtual Agents*, 2016.

[70] C. Zimmermann, L. Del Piccolo, and A. Finset. Cues and concerns by patients in medical consultations: a literature review. *Psychological bulletin*, 133(3):438, 2007.

Towards Robot Autonomy in Group Conversations: Understanding the Effects of Body Orientation and Gaze

Marynel Vázquez [1], Elizabeth J. Carter [2], Braden McDorman [2],
Jodi Forlizzi [2,3], Aaron Steinfeld [1], Scott E. Hudson [2,3]

[1]Robotics Institute
Carnegie Mellon University
Pittsburgh, PA
{marynel,steinfeld}
@cmu.edu

[2]Disney Research Pittsburgh
4720 Forbes Avenue
Pittsburgh, PA
{liz.carter,braden.mcdorman}
@disneyresearch.com

[3]HCI Institute
Carnegie Mellon University
Pittsburgh, PA
{scott.hudson,forlizzi}
@cs.cmu.edu

ABSTRACT

We conducted a 2×2 between-subjects experiment to examine the effects of two orientation and two gaze behaviors during group conversations for a mobile, low degree-of-freedom robot. For this experiment, we designed a novel protocol to induce changes in the robot's group and study different social contexts. In addition, we implemented a perception system to track participants and control the robot's orientation and gaze with little human intervention. The results showed that the gaze behaviors under consideration affected the participants' perception of the robot's motion and that its motion affected human perception of its gaze. This mutual dependency implies that robot gaze and body motion must be designed and controlled jointly, rather than independently of each other. Moreover, the orientation behaviors that we studied led to similar feelings of inclusion and sense of belonging to the robot's group, suggesting that both can be primitives for more complex orientation behaviors.

Keywords

Social Human-Robot Interaction; Robot Motion; Gaze

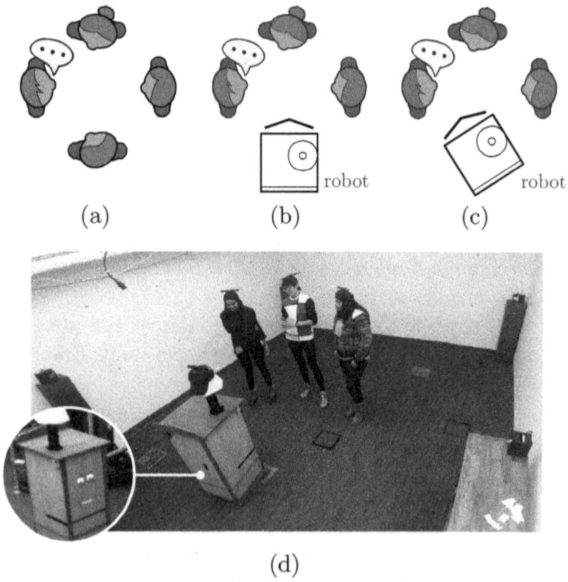

Figure 1: (a) Group conversation. (b) One member is a robot and it orients towards the group center. (c) The robot orients towards the speaker. (d) HRI experiment where we tested these orientation behaviors along with two gaze behaviors.

1. INTRODUCTION

The idea that robots will interact around and with human groups has recently motivated significant research efforts within Human-Robot Interaction (HRI). For example, algorithms for group detection [34, 66, 47] and engagement classification [33] have been developed. Planning for navigation has begun to consider the social costs of crossing between group members [48, 13]. Experimental evidence further suggests that people establish similar spatial arrangements with robots as they do with people during free-standing group conversations [53, 76]. People position and orient themselves to maximize their opportunities to monitor each other as well as maintain their group as a spatially distinct unit from other nearby interactions. These spatial arrangements are known as *F-Formations* [29] and often emerge as a circle during conversations among multiple people (Fig. 1(a)).

Although we know that a robot's body orientation may induce reconfigurations of dyadic F-formations [31], little is known about its effects during conversations with more people. How should robots orient themselves with respect to a group during a conversation? At first glance, one may think that a robot should mimic human behavior and orient its body towards the middle of the group (Fig. 1(b)). This approach was previously proposed by Althaus and colleagues [5] and was associated with more positive perceptions of the behavior of a telepresence robot [69]. However, this strategy is not the only reasonable one for mobile, low degree-of-freedom (DoF) robots. For robots with a fixed head, such as FROG [18], SPENCER [64], or the CoBots [68], it may be better to orient towards the focus of attention of the conversation, e.g., the speaker, as illustrated in Fig. 1(c). This behavior could convey attentiveness to the interaction and make users perceive the robot as more active or responsive.

HRI '17, March 06–09, 2017, Vienna, Austria

ISBN 978-1-4503-4336-7/17/03...$15.00

DOI: http://dx.doi.org/10.1145/2909824.3020207

To further our understanding of robot positioning during group conversations, we conducted an experiment in which a mobile robot interacted with small groups of people (Fig. 1(d)) while we manipulated its orientation and gaze behaviors. Gaze was manipulated because the robot that we used has a fixed head, but the direction of its eyes could still communicate mental states and attention [7, 2]. We expected gaze to affect the perception of the orientation of the robot.

Another contribution of this paper is a new protocol for studying group interactions in the context of HRI. In this protocol, the robot asks the participants to help it solve a problem in a brainstorming session in the laboratory. Even though this is not a public setting, our design makes the interaction naturalistic. Participants are free to move in the environment as desired and, periodically, are induced to leave the robot's conversational group to document their ideas. This dynamic creates a variety of group formations on a frequent basis, thereby generating numerous instances for studying multi-party interactions. For example, groups with one to four people emerged during our experiment as a result of the flow of the activity. In addition, the proposed brainstorming protocol does not require us to provide the participants with specific instructions on their roles. This property leads to increased interaction time during experiments in contrast to a prior role-playing game protocol that was used to study group interactions with a social robot [65].

The body and gaze behaviors of the robot were controlled automatically by a multi-modal perception system during most of the the brainstorming activity. This system relied on several off-the-shelf sensors and data fusion techniques to (1) track the users and the robot, (2) detect conversational groups by reasoning about spatial behavior, and (3) detect the current speaker in the environment. Although the core components of this system were developed previously, their integration is valuable. First, it allowed us to run parts of the experiment in an automated fashion. Second, it allowed us to collect a corpus of human spatial behavior with and around our robot, which we are using to develop more complex perception capabilities and evaluate group detection methods. We describe our system and its limitations for future replication and adaptation efforts.

2. RELATED WORK

Proxemics. Many factors can influence how people use physical spaces during interactions [22]. In HRI, these factors include social norms, familiarity among the interactants, users' personal characteristics, mutual gaze, a robot's voice and height, and the direction from which a robot approaches users [41, 61, 70, 73, 72, 71].

Proxemics have been used as a cue to estimate users' engagement level with robots [39, 40, 51, 54, 26]. For example, Michalowski and colleagues [39] proposed an engagement model based on spatial information and head pose. Satake and colleagues [51] used motion to estimate if users would accept interacting with a robot. In this work, we used position and body orientation features to detect F-formations [66] and infer who was conversing with our mobile platform.

Initiating interactions. Different strategies and motion controllers have been developed to appropriately approach users and initiate interactions [5, 27, 49, 51, 53]. In particular, the controller of Althaus and colleagues [5] reduced the speed of the robot as it approached a group of users. This controller also adjusted the robot's orientation towards the middle of the group. In our experiment, a wizard teleoperated our robot at the beginning of the interaction to achieve a similar result and orient the mobile platform towards the participants. Once the brainstorming activity started, the wizard switched to automatic orientation control, as further explained in Sections 3 and 4.

Robot orientation. The middle orientation behavior that we studied in our experiment was proposed earlier for social navigation [5]. Karreman and colleagues [26] implemented this behavior on a museum guide robot that gave short tours to visitors. Turning the robot towards visitors led to increased interest in the platform in contrast to turning towards points of interest, like art pieces. There is also evidence that suggests that orienting a telepresence robot towards the center of a group makes people comfortable [69].

Social gaze. There is significant work in social eye gaze for human-computer and human-robot interaction [50, 2]. Related to our work, Garau and colleagues [20] found that synchronizing an avatar's head and eye animations with turn-taking patterns could improve its communication with humans in comparison to a random gaze behavior in which its head and eye animations were unrelated to conversational flow. As in our experiment, random gaze behaviors were also used in prior efforts to study robot gaze. For example, Yoshikawa and colleagues [75] compared a random gaze behavior versus three other gaze behaviors on a Robovie-R2 platform. Their experiment suggests that responsive robot gaze, e.g., gaze that communicates shared attention, induces stronger feelings of being looked at on users in comparison to non-responsive gaze. In addition, Skantze and colleagues [58] studied a random gaze behavior versus a human-inspired gaze behavior on a Furhat robot. This robot has back-projected eyes like the platform used in this work.

Other research has focused on analyzing gaze duration and frequency. For example, prior work [1] suggests that short, frequent fixations by a robot can give an observer stronger feelings of being looked at versus longer, less frequent stares. Also, a robot that looks towards users more often may be perceived as more extroverted than to one that looks more towards the task space [6]. Note that gaze can also influence people's roles in a conversation with a robot [30, 43] and their attitudes towards these machines [25]. Some gaze behaviors may work better than others, depending on the type of conversation [14].

Sense of groupness. Several efforts within HRI have investigated how much people perceive themselves as part of a group [23, 37, 43, 46]. Similar to prior work, we follow the approach of Mutlu and colleagues [43] to measure interpersonal closeness to our robot with the "Inclusion of Other in Self" (IOS) scale [8]. We use the survey by Williams and colleagues [74] to measure feelings of groupness and ostracism.

Multi-modal perception. Our perception system was inspired by work in multi-modal sensing [32, 10, 28, 56, 57, 63, 11, 44] and is an alternative to other approaches meant to enable human-robot interactions in controlled settings. In particular, our system estimates users' positions and body orientations by fusing ultra wide-band tracking information and skeleton data output by a Kinect. Even though prior work used ultra wide-band localization systems to track people [21, 9] or the Kinect to enable interactions [38, 3, 77, 24], we are the first to fuse these types of data for HRI to the best of our knowledge. The fusion offers key advantages: operation beyond the Kinect's range, better occlusion handling, and simple user identification.

Our perception system also builds on advances in localization [62] and human spatial analysis [29, 15, 66]. While recent efforts to detect social interactions based on spatial behavior have focused on analyzing users only [36, 34, 47], we opt to jointly reason about the users' and our robot's spatial configurations in a unified perspective.

3. ORIENTATION AND GAZE BEHAVIORS

We studied two orientation and two gaze behaviors during group conversations with the furniture platform Chester [67]. This robot has a differential drive base, a fixed face, and back-projected eyes, as shown in Fig. 1(d). Even though the robot's design led to specific decisions for the orientation and gaze behaviors, they can be easily adapted to other mobile platforms with expressive eyes. We detail our implementation to facilitate future explorations in this direction.

For the following explanations, assume that the robot has started a conversation and we know its position $\mathbf{r} = [r_x\ r_y]^T$ and orientation ρ (yaw angle) on the ground. Assume that we also know the position $\mathbf{p}^i$, the lower body orientation, and the velocity of any person i near the robot, so that we can detect its conversational group by reasoning about F-formations (e.g., using [15, 52, 66]). Finally, assume that we know who is speaking in the robot's conversation. Data collection methods are later described in Sec. 3.3.

3.1 Body Orientation Behaviors

For any member i in the robot's conversation, let $\mathbf{u}^i = [u_x^i\ u_y^i]^T = \mathbf{p}^i - \mathbf{r}$ be the direction from the robot to this person, and $\gamma^i = \text{atan2}(u_y^i, u_x^i)$ the corresponding angle. We used this angle to orient the robot as described below.

3.1.1 *Middle Orientation Behavior (MO)*

The robot oriented towards the middle of its conversational group G using the *mean direction* $\bar{\theta}$ of all γ^i [19]:

$$\bar{\theta} = \text{atan2}\left(\sum_{i\in G}\sin(\gamma^i), \sum_{i\in G}\cos(\gamma^i)\right) \quad (1)$$

3.1.2 *Attentive Orientation Behavior (AO)*

If the robot was speaking, it biased its orientation towards its addressee; otherwise, it biased its orientation towards the current speaker in its conversational group. Let γ^i be the orientation towards the speaker or the addressee, and $\bar{\theta}$ be the middle orientation in the group, as in eq. (1). At any given time, the orientation $\hat{\rho}$ of the robot was set as follows:

$$\hat{\rho} = \begin{cases} \bar{\theta} - \tau & \text{if minAngDiff}(\gamma^i, \bar{\theta}) < -\tau \\ \bar{\theta} + \tau & \text{if minAngDiff}(\gamma^i, \bar{\theta}) > \tau \\ \gamma_i & \text{otherwise} \end{cases} \quad (2)$$

where minAngDiff returns the signed minimum difference between two angles, and τ is a parameter that controls how much the robot rotates away from the middle orientation $\bar{\theta}$ (Fig. 2). In particular, we set $\tau = 60°$ for our robot so that it would not turn its back to group members to its side.

If the robot was not addressing anyone and nobody had spoken for a significant time (10 seconds), the platform's orientation was set towards the middle direction as in the MO behavior. This also happened when the robot conversed with a single user, given that $\hat{\rho}$ in eq. (2) became $\bar{\theta}$.

3.2 Gaze Behaviors

We tested simple gaze behaviors to complement the effects of our orientation manipulation. These behaviors serve as a baseline for future investigations on the relationship between body motion and complex gaze patterns, e.g., involving discourse structure or fixations on the environment [12, 42].

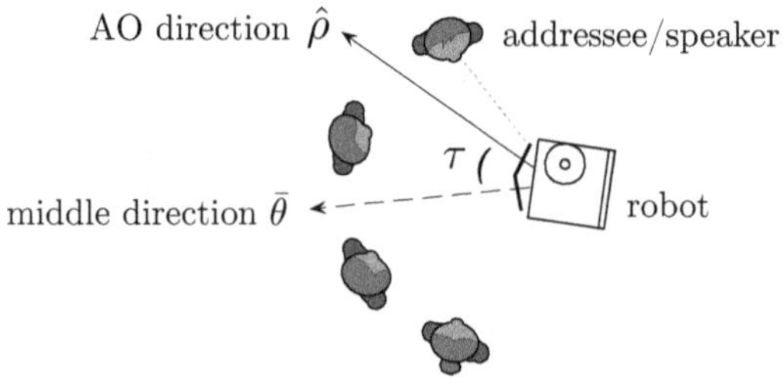

Figure 2: Geometric relations for the AO behavior. The $\wedge$ mark denotes the robot's front. The middle direction corresponds to eq. (1) and $\hat{\rho}$, τ to eq. (2).

Gaze was calibrated using a projective mapping from 3D world coordinates to 2D pupil positions. The mapping was used for both pupils of the robot, making their lines of sight parallel. While this constraint prevented vergence eye movements, it worked well in practice because the robot's eyes look cartoonish and have a slight curvature. This design makes users forgiving of gaze patterns that do not fully mimic human gaze and induces the Mona Lisa gaze effect [4]: users perceive mutual gaze more often than intended.

3.2.1 *Random Gaze Behavior (RG)*

The robot executed several pre-defined eye animations that helped communicate ideas while it spoke (Fig. 3). For example, referential gaze was used at times with verbal utterances to convey spatial information. When no pre-defined animation was scheduled for the eyes, they blinked occasionally or their pupils moved randomly at small intervals.

Figure 3: Left to right: eyes look up and to the right of the robot, look forward, and squint.

Our specific implementation of eye blinks was inspired by human blinking activity [16]. The duration of inter-blink intervals followed a normal distribution $\mathcal{N}(5.2, 3^2)$ in seconds.

Gaze shifts were scheduled by sampling time intervals in seconds from the uniform distribution $Unif(1.8, 3)$. When the timer triggered and no blink was set to occur, the pupils moved a small amount horizontally (d_x) and vertically (d_y), based on the size of the eyes:

$$d_x = eye\_width * \epsilon_1 \text{ and } d_y = eye\_height * \epsilon_2$$

with ϵ_1 and ϵ_2 sampled uniformly in a small interval. Any displacement (d_x, d_y) that rendered the pupils outside the limits of the eyes was considered invalid and was re-computed by sampling new values. Furthermore, we prevented Chester from fixating significantly downwards, towards the ground, so that it would not look extremely introverted.

3.2.2 *Attentive Gaze Behavior (AG)*

The robot used the same blinking pattern and pre-defined eye animations as in RG. When no animation was scheduled, the robot attempted to establish mutual gaze with the person who was the focus of attention. That is, the person that the robot addressed in particular, the current speaker if the robot was quiet, or anybody who moved with a speed of at least 0.5 m/s in the group when everybody was silent.

Once the robot gazed towards someone, gaze shifts were sampled as often as in RG but were biased towards the head of the focus of attention. If $\mathbf{q}$ is the 3D position of the head, then the new, biased positions for the pupils were set as:

(x,y) = lookAt($\mathbf{q}$) `// pupils position towards` q
$r \sim Unif(0, 1)$
if $r < 0.2$ **then** `// add noise` 20% `of the time`
    $x = x + eye\_width * \alpha_1$ with $\alpha_1 \sim \mathcal{N}(0, \sigma^2)$
    $y = y + eye\_height * \alpha_2$ with $\alpha_2 \sim \mathcal{N}(0, \sigma^2)$

where lookAt returned the 2D location of the pupils that made the robot look towards the desired direction, and σ controlled the amount of variation in gaze shifts. After 10 seconds of silence and no significant motion in the group, gaze shifts continued without the bias as in RG.

3.3 Multi-Modal Perception System

We implemented a real-time system to control the robot's orientation and gaze based on human behavior, as well as to collect data during the experiment. The system required instrumenting the environment with ultra wide-band (UWB) localization beacons[1] and a Kinect. Each participant wore an instrumented baseball cap with two UWB radio beacons for tracking and identification, as shown in Fig. 1(d). The robot also wore a cap to make it look like the participants.

3.3.1 System Components

Figure 4 shows the main components of the system. Grey boxes denote modules that ran on the robot; the rest executed on external computers. The boxes with thicker edges correspond to modules that were in charge of the manipulated behaviors. Note that the robot's speech was controlled by a hidden operator, as detailed in Sec. 4.1.

The system processed data as follows. First, the position of the UWB beacons carried by the participants was smoothed with a Kalman filter ("Filter" module in Fig. 4). The smoothed values were then aggregated to estimate the position and orientation of each hat ("Hat Pose" module) and fused with the skeleton output of a Kinect ("User Tracker" module). This fusion step output estimates of the position and orientation of each participant, taking advantage of both sensing modalities. The Kinect reduced localization error, which ranged up to 30 cm on average for the hats. The UWB data provided continuous tracking information throughout the environment as well as participants' identities.

[1]We used DWUSB sensors by Ciholas, Inc.

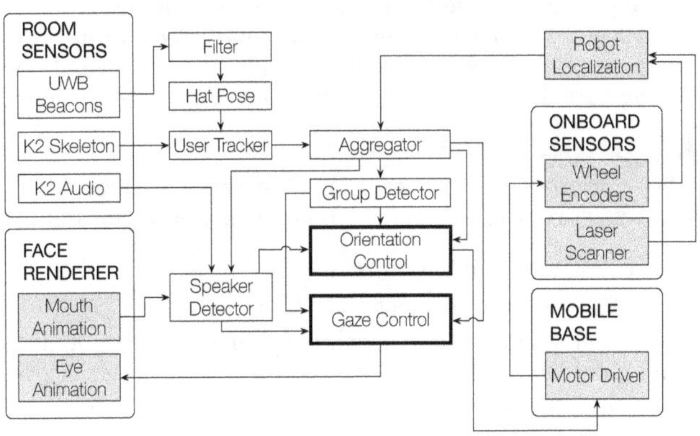

Figure 4: The system used to control the body orientation and gaze of the robot. "UWB" stands for ultra wide-band and "K2" stands for Kinect v2.

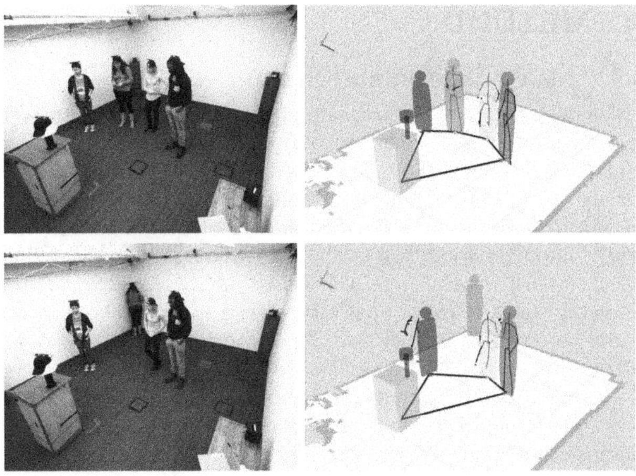

Figure 5: Experiment (left) and outputs of our perception system (right). A Kinect in the left corner of the room output skeleton data (shown in black near the participants). Colored markers denote participants' pose as output by the "User Tracker" module. The black lines on the ground connect the estimated members of the robot's conversational group.

While users were localized, the "Robot Localization" module estimated Chester's pose using an on-board laser scanner and a map of the environment [62]. The "Aggregator" program then grouped all this localization information and passed it to the "Group Detector" and "Speaker Detector" modules. The former module reasoned about conversational groups based on F-formations, as in [66] and illustrated in Fig. 5. The latter module was in charge of identifying the current speaker based on the interactants' positions, sound detections (output by "K2 Audio"), and information from Chester's dialog engine ("Mouth Animation" module). If Chester's mouth was moving, the robot was identified as the current speaker. Otherwise, the speaker was the person closest to the Kinect's audio beam (within 1 m) or nobody when no sound was localized.

Finally, the locations of the participants, the conversational groups, and the identity of the speaker were sent to the "Orientation Control" and "Gaze Control" modules. These programs output motion and gaze commands for the robot.

3.3.2 Limitations

Our system is a practical contribution of this work because it can enable human-robot interactions with little human intervention. However, it does not solve all perception problems in HRI, e.g., because it requires instrumentation and this may be impossible or undesirable in some cases.

Two types of errors due to shortcomings of the underlying technologies were the main factors that influenced the system's performance. First, tracking errors were common at the edges of the room due to the Kinect's limited range and field of view as well as a noticeable bias that affected UWB localization in these regions. As discussed in Sec. 4.6, these errors rarely affected group detection and the robot's orientation during the experiment because the participants were usually in the middle of the space. Second, sound localization errors were typically caused by simultaneous speech. These events were also infrequent in our experiment as interactants respected turn-taking.

4. METHOD

4.1 Study Design and Setup

We designed a 2 × 2 between-subjects experiment to test orientation (middle vs. attentive) and gaze (random vs. attentive) behaviors. The experiment followed a *Wizard with Oz* arrangement [59] in which the manipulated behaviors were autonomous, but the sequencing of events within the study and the robot's speech were managed by a hidden operator or "wizard". In a few instances, the wizard also re-configured the robot spatially with respect to the participants, as detailed in Sec. 4.6. The experiment was approved by our Institutional Review Board.

During the experiment, the robot led and participated in a brainstorming session with a small group of participants. Each session was performed under one of four conditions:

MO+RG condition. The robot oriented towards the middle of its conversational group and randomized its gaze.

AO+RG condition. The robot biased its orientation towards the focus of attention and randomized its gaze.

MO+AG condition. The robot oriented towards the middle and tried to establish mutual gaze with the person who was the focus of attention.

AO+AG condition. The robot biased its orientation and gaze towards the focus of attention.

Given these conditions, we hypothesized that:

H1. The gaze behaviors would affect the perception of the robot's motion, with AG increasing perceived naturalness.

H2. For the AO behavior, participants would find the robot more attentive and responsive than MO.

H3. The AO behavior would make the participants feel like the robot was more of a part of their group than MO.

H4. The AO+AG condition would lead to reduced feelings of ostracism or increased feelings of inclusion compared to MO+RG.

The experiment was conducted in a room with a free space of 4.4 × 4.4 meters (Fig. 1(d)). A table was placed adjacent to a wall for the participants to write down the brainstormed ideas on slips of paper. These slips then had to be deposited in different boxes in the room, according to the author.

The room was equipped with a UWB sensor network, a Kinect v2 and four RGB cameras near the ceiling. The UWB sensors and the Kinect were used to localize the participants, identify them, and detect speakers, as described in Sec. 3.3. The cameras recorded the interaction from multiple views and allowed the wizard to monitor the experiment remotely.

4.2 Participants

We recruited 20 groups (5 per condition) of 3 or 4 people using a participant pool, word of mouth, and fliers. The participants were at least 18 years of age, fluent in English, and had grown up in the U.S. The last restriction was imposed to reduce the effects of cultural biases in spatial behavior.

Table 1 shows details of the 69 participants that interacted with our robot. In general, most participants were university students, and their average age was 24.8 years old (SE = 1.0). In 7 sessions, two or more participants knew each other.

Before the interaction, the participants indicated how often they used a computer and their familiarity with robots on a 7 point Likert responding format (1 being lowest). Most participants used computers daily (M = 6.97, SE = 0.02) but were not very familiar with robots (M = 3.38, SE = 0.20).

Table 1: Participant characteristics per condition. "G", "F", "M", and "P" are used to abbreviate groups, female, male, and participants, respectively.

Condition	#G	#F	#M	#P	Age (Std Err)
MO+RG	5	8	10	18	22.2 (0.8)
MO+AG	5	9	9	18	23.5 (0.8)
AO+RG	5	11	5	16	24.4 (1.3)
AO+AG	5	9	8	17	29.3 (3.6)

4.3 Procedure

First, an experimenter gave a colored badge to each participant for identification purposes and administered a demographics survey. She then asked the participants to wear instrumented baseball caps with UWB beacons, and explained that each of them had a box in the room with their same color identifier. The experimenter introduced the robot, gave it an instrumented cap to make it look like the participants, and stepped away. The robot opened its eyes, and started a semi-scripted conversation with three phases:

1. *Introduction.* Chester presented itself to the group. The robot explained that the laboratory wanted to retire him, but people might keep him around if they found him useful. Chester encouraged the participants to think of how it could help in the lab and explained its sensors and capabilities. To facilitate brainstorming, the robot provided a first example and explained how it delivered souvenirs to lab visitors in the past. Chester then opened the floor to new ideas.

2. *Brainstorming.* The robot encouraged the group to brainstorm tasks that it could do in the lab for 6 min. Chester replied favorably to useful ideas and requested that authors write them on a slip of paper and deposit the slip in their corresponding box. The robot also asked for more details or discouraged unrealistic and complicated tasks. When people ran out of ideas, Chester provided more suggestions.

3. *Closing.* Chester asked a participant to count the ideas in the boxes and write the color of the box on each slip to help keep track of them. Meanwhile, the robot asked other people about their favorite ideas and gave his opinion. Chester thanked everybody for helping and said good-bye.

Finally, the experimenter adminstered a post-test survey, paid the participants, and debriefed them about the wizard. During debriefing, the experimenter also explained that the requests to deposit paper slips on boxes were an excuse to induce people to leave the robot's conversation and re-enter in natural ways. These requests were motivated by our prior experience, where we found that we had little chance of observing varied spatial behaviors without a task like this one.

4.4 Dependent Measures

We considered subjective and objective measures. The post-test survey asked people about their impressions of:

- the robot's motion and gaze;
- closeness to the robot using the IOS scale [8];
- the robot's and the participants' feelings of belongingness and ostracism in the brainstorming group [74];
- Chester with respect to a set of attributes, e.g., perceived intelligence, responsiveness, and entertainment value;
- Chester's ability to lead the brainstorming session and whether it should be decommissioned; and
- any unusual behavior for the robot [55].

Objective measures included the distance that the participants kept from the robot, the participants' membership in the robot's conversational group, and the number of paper slips collected during the brainstorming activity.

4.5 Pilot Sessions

Before starting the experiment, we recruited 35 people to conduct two types of pilot sessions. First, we ran 3 human-only sessions to evaluate the dynamics of the brainstorming activity and collect example tasks for the robot. Second, we ran 8 human-robot pilot sessions to test the Chester's dialog and the manipulated behaviors. During these sessions, we also simplified the wizard's teleoperation interface and the protocol of the experiment to avoid confusing procedures.

We considered studying a random orientation behavior for our robot as a baseline. However, the pilot sessions quickly showed that people are highly sensitive to inappropriate or unexpected orientations. These motions often halted interactions because people did not know how to interpret them.

4.6 Confirmation of Autonomy and Behaviors

The robot moved autonomously for most of the interaction as defined by the experimental condition. The exceptions were (1) when the robot started conversing, (2) when it said good-bye, and (3) during a handful of situations due to technical difficulties. In the first case, the wizard reconfigured the robot to show that it could move and tacitly induce an F-formation. In the second, the wizard moved Chester away to end the interaction. In the third, the wizard corrected for slight undesired changes in the robot's orientation, e.g., because of people-tracking failures in our perception system. During the brainstorming phase – the main part of the experiment – sporadic reconfigurations of this sort happened in 16 sessions out of 20. In these sessions, total teleoperation time while brainstorming was 9.37 sec on average (SE = 2.04), which represented only 2.4% of the duration of this phase (M = 383.53 sec, SE = 5.43, N = 16). REstricted or REsidual Maximum Likelihood (REML) analyses [45, 60] on the number of teleoperation events and teleoperation time while brainstorming showed no significant differences for the effects of Orientation (Attentive, Middle) and Gaze (Attentive, Random).

To confirm that the robot oriented as expected during the brainstorming phase, two coders annotated the members of the robot's conversation.[2] Using this ground truth and the logs from our perception system, we then computed the *ideal* middle orientation of the robot at 1 Hz. As expected, the absolute angular difference between the robot's orientation and this ideal middle direction was smaller for MO (M = 7.04°, SE = 0.12, N = 3686) than for AO (M = 14.33°, SE = 0.27, N = 3644). Note that these differences were induced in part by the robot's motion planner and a small bias in the robot's orientation towards the table in the room. The planner prevented Chester from jittering by ignoring turns of 5° or less. The bias (1.63° on average) was generated by occasional user tracking errors that made Chester believe that some people were still conversing with it when they left to write paper slips. Interestingly, the motion induced by these errors was interpreted as though Chester was checking that participants were following its instructions.

We transcribed when people spoke in the robot's group and its specific addressees in 2 sessions per condition. We then used the data to check when Chester adjusted its orientation towards these people. As expected, the robot turned more towards these foci of attention with AO (47% of 280 annotated events) than with MO (25% of 319). The robot did not move in many cases because the target was within 5° of its orientation (22% of the events for AO; 21% for MO).

We also inspected Chester's eye fixations during the experiment to confirm that the gaze behaviors worked as expected. As can be seen in Fig. 6, the positions of the pupils were less concentrated for RG than for AG because the robot tried to establish mutual gaze with the focus of attention in the latter case. Also, the robot had a tendency to look forward because several of our pre-defined eye animations positioned the pupils towards the middle of the eyes.

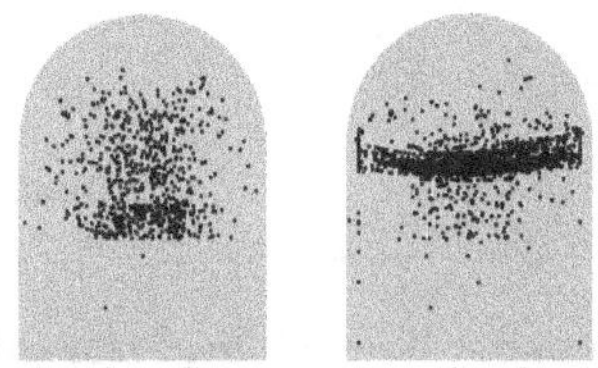

Figure 6: Chester's eye fixations in the 20 sessions of the experiment.

5. RESULTS

We first analyse survey results and the spatial behavior of the participants around our robot. Then, we discuss the implications of our findings in terms of our hypotheses.

5.1 Survey Results

We ran REML analyses to evaluate survey responses. Unless noted, analyses used Participant as a random effect nested by Session, and Orientation (Attentive, Middle), Gaze (Attentive, Random), and Gender as main effects. Student's t-tests and Tukey HSD tests (with significance thresholds of $p < 0.05$) were used for post-hoc analyses of two sample and multiple pair-wise comparisons, respectively. Ratings were on 7-point Likert responding formats and responses were grouped only when Cronbach's alpha was above 0.7.

Robot's gaze. In general, Chester's gaze looked natural to the participants (M = 4.93, SE = 0.16). They did not feel like Chester was staring at them (M = 2.91, SE = 0.17) nor avoiding looking at them (M = 2.01, SE = 0.12). These results had no significant main effects.

The robot's orientation led to significant differences on how much the participants felt that Chester looked at them ($F[1, 68] = 7.47$, $p < 0.01$). As shown in Fig. 7, the AO behavior (M = 4.72, SE = 0.18) had significantly higher ratings than the MO behavior (M = 4.11, SE = 0.15) in this respect. The fact that the results were not significantly different for Gaze may be explained by the Mona Lisa gaze effect and the tendency of the robot to look forward.

Robot's motion. Gaze had a significant effect on the ratings for "Chester's motion looked natural during the interaction" ($F[1, 68] = 4.08$, $p = 0.05$). As shown in Fig. 8, the AG behavior elicited significantly higher agreement with the statement relative to RG (M = 4.71, SE = 0.28 vs. M = 4.00, SE = 0.23). No significant differences were found for "Chester's motion was distracting" (M = 2.03, SE = 0.13), "I felt confident that the robot was not going to hit me" (M = 6.42, SE = 0.18), nor "Chester's motion made me anxious" (M = 1.57, SE = 0.12).

[2]Inter-coder reliability was computed for 4 sessions (20%). Two annotations were misaligned; Cohen's kappa for the other 75 annotations was 1.0, indicating perfect reliability.

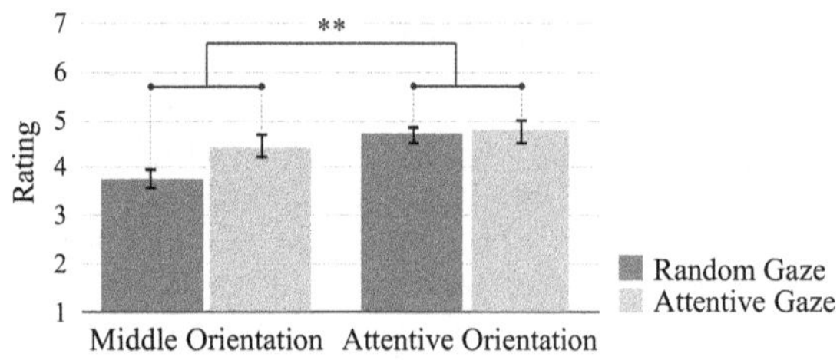

Figure 7: Ratings for how much the participants felt that Chester looked at them. (**) denotes $p < 0.01$.

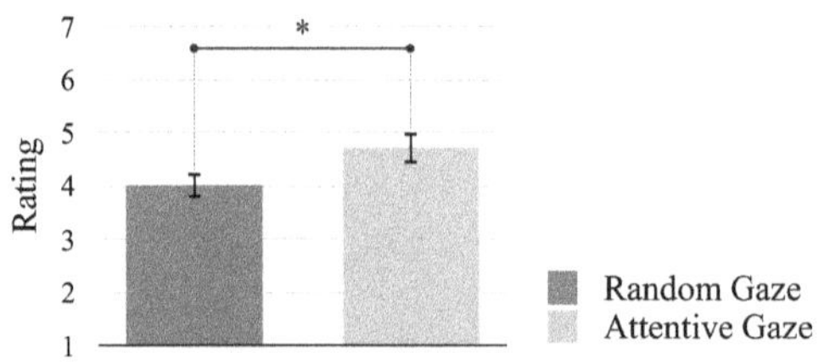

Figure 8: Ratings for how natural the robot's motion looked based on its gaze. (*) denotes $p < 0.05$.

Robot's attentiveness. Participants rated how much they thought that Chester paid attention to what they said (M = 5.33, SE = 0.16) and to what the other participants said (M = 5.48, SE = 0.14). A REML analysis with Participant as random effect nested by Session, and Orientation, Gaze, Gender, and Speaker (Me, Others) as main effects showed significant differences for the interaction between Orientation and Gender only (F[3, 66] = 4.94, p = 0.03). The post-hoc test then showed no significant pair-wise differences, but the tendency was interesting: male participants thought that the robot paid more attention with AO than with MO (M = 5.73, SE = 0.20 vs. M = 4.92, SE = 0.25).

Inclusion and ostracism: IOS scale [8] ratings indicated that the participants did not feel close to Chester (M = 2.57, SE = 0.14). However, they thought that both they (M = 5.03, SE = 0.17) and the robot (M = 5.33, SE = 0.19) belonged to the brainstorming group.

We found low perceptions of being ignored or excluded by the robot (M = 1.57, SE = 0.12) or the other participants (M = 1.42, SE = 0.09). REML analyses for these results resulted in no significant differences, but Orientation was close for the former (p = 0.06). The trend suggested that MO could lead to higher feelings of ostracism from the robot than AO (M = 1.77, SE = 0.17 vs. M = 1.33, SE = 0.14).

Other perceptions of the robot. The participants generally thought that Chester was a good leader for the brainstorming activity (M = 5.00, SE = 0.17) and had significantly different impressions of how much the robot and the other participants liked them (F[1, 68] = 4.98, p = 0.03). In particular, the participants thought that the robot liked them significantly more than did the other people in the experiment (M = 5.16, SE = 0.14 vs. M = 4.93, SE = 0.13).

Chester was not perceived as anti-social (M = 1.58, SE = 0.09). The only trend in this respect (p = 0.06) suggested that RG could make the robot look more anti-social than AG (M = 1.76, SE = 0.16 vs. M = 1.4, SE = 0.09).

Table 2 shows a factor analysis on a series of additional attributes for the robot. Factor I was associated with interactivity, Factor II with competence, and Factor III with

Table 2: Ratings for the factors resulting from factor analysis. Machine-like was reversed (R) for the analysis and for computing Chronbach's alpha.

Attribute	Mean (SE)	Cronbach's α	Factor
Responsive Interactive	5.33 (0.11)	0.786	I
Useful Knowledgeable Intelligent Competent	4.62 (0.13)	0.791	II
Entertaining Funny	5.47 (0.15)	0.846	III
Lifelike Machine-like (R)	4.14 (0.18) 4.20 (0.15)	0.623	-

entertainment. These factors explained 18.3%, 26.4%, and 20.3% of the variance, respectively. Their ratings were positive in general with no significant main effects of condition.

Only 8 participants of 69 indicated that Chester should be decommissioned in the post-survey. Their responses were typically associated with the robot's usefulness (e.g., *"I can't see a practical use for it, but the robot was entertaining"*).

Interaction: In general, the interaction with Chester was enjoyable (M = 5.45, SE = 0.14). Desire to brainstorm for longer was correlated with the number of paper slips written per session (r(67) = 0.48, p< 0.01), which tended to be just a few, or ten or more. This result motivated a REML analysis on the ratings for wanting to brainstorm for longer with Slip Count (1 if ten or more slips, 0 otherwise), Orientation, Gaze, and Gender as main effects, and Participant as random effect within Session. Not surprisingly, Slip Count had a significant effect (F[1, 68] = 15.09, p< 0.01). Ratings in sessions with many slips were significantly higher than the rest (M = 4.65, SE = 0.28 vs. M = 3.00, SE = 0.24). Also, the interaction between Gender and Slip Count was significant (F[3, 66] = 6.78, p= 0.01). Male participants wanted to brainstorm significantly more when there were at least ten slips (M = 5.27, SE = 0.37) than in other cases (M = 2.53, SE = 0.30). Female ratings were more uniform and neutral.

Note that the robot did not use a balancing criteria to ask people for ideas during the brainstorming activity. A REML analysis on the number of ideas proposed by the participants did not result in any significant differences for the main effects of Orientation, Gaze, and Gender, suggesting that this aspect of the protocol did not generate a confound. Moreover, all but one of the 69 participants proposed ideas. The only person that stayed quiet during the brainstorming phase took part in the activity towards the end, when the robot asked him to count the number of slips in the boxes.

5.2 Human Spatial Behavior

We analyzed proxemics during the brainstorming phase, when the participants often moved to write ideas at the table. For the analyses, we used the spatial information output by our perception system (sampled at 1Hz) and the group membership annotations described in Sec. 4.6.

When the participants conversed with the robot in the brainstorming phase, their average separation from Chester was typical of social encounters (M = 2.15m, SE = 0.04, N = 69) [22]. Because people often adjusted their position as they became familiar with the robot and the activity, we decided to further analyze proxemics during the last minute of the brainstorming part of the experiment. We performed a REML analysis on the distance between the robot and the participants during this period, considering Orientation, Gaze, and Gender as main effects and Participant as random effect nested by Session. Gaze was significant ($F[1,68] = 5.67$, $p = 0.02$): participants stood significantly farther away from the robot with RG (M = 2.29, SE=0.05) than with AG (M = 2.09, SE = 0.06). The interaction between Gaze and Orientation was also significant ($F[3,66] = 4.27$, $p = 0.04$). The members of the robot's group were significantly farther away from it with MO+RG than with MO+AG (M = 2.40, SE=0.07 vs. M = 2.03, SE=0.10), as shown in Fig. 9.

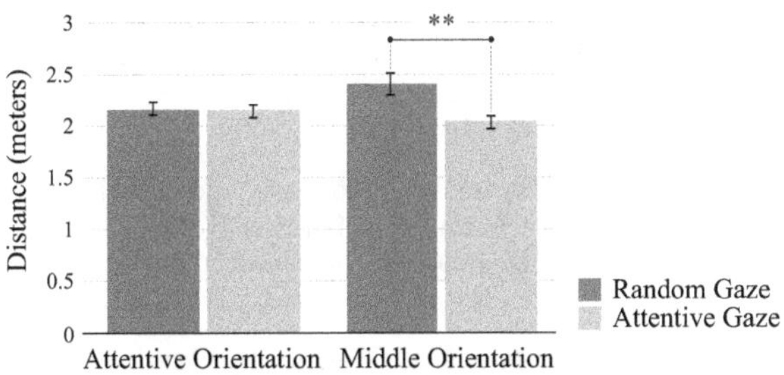

Figure 9: Distance to Chester during the last minute of brainstorming. (**) denotes $p < 0.01$.

Throughout the experiment, we observed qualitatively circular or side by side spatial arrangements. In a few cases in which the robot engaged in a dyadic interaction and it was not oriented as expected, participants proactively changed their positions to stand in front of it. These efforts to establish appropriate spatial arrangements suggest that people may be willing to collaborate with robots to establish F-formations and adapt to unforeseen circumstances.

5.3 Hypotheses Support and Implications

Attentive Gaze made the participants think that Chester's motion looked more natural in comparison to Random Gaze. This result supported our first hypothesis (H1) and is related to prior findings on the influence of gaze on the perception of a robot's head motion [35]. Furthermore, the orientation behaviors also affected the perception of the robot's gaze. With Attentive Orientation, the participants perceived that the robot looked at them more. These outcomes suggest that robot gaze and body motion should be designed and controlled jointly, rather than independently of each other.

We expected the Attentive Orientation behavior to make the robot seem more attentive and responsive than the Middle Orientation behavior (H2). While we did not find that the robot's orientation altered how responsive it looked, the participants thought that the robot gazed at them more with AO than with MO, as mentioned before. There was also a trend that suggested that male participants thought that the robot paid more attention to what people said with AO.

Opinions on how close the participants felt to the robot and whether they perceived it as part of their group were not significantly affected by the orientation behaviors, as hypothesized in H3. Interestingly, the distance between the participants and the robot varied significantly with MO based on the robot's gaze, but did not vary as much with AO. This finding might indicate more subtle effects of the manipulation than can be gleaned from questionnaires. Also, the lack of support opens up possibilities for developing more complex orientation behaviors and fulfilling other non-social tasks during multi-party interactions. Given that both MO and AO were acceptable and did not affect the perception that the robot was part of the group, both behaviors could be used by robots depending on other factors besides the interaction. For example, robots could switch between MO and AO to reduce uncertainty about the environment.

In terms of H4, the AO+AG condition did not reduce feelings of ostracism or increase feelings of inclusion relative to MO+RG. Nonetheless, there was a trend that suggested that MO could lead to higher feelings of ostracism than AO. This finding should be explored further in future research.

Finally, we learned an important lesson from the pilot sessions: people are sensitive to inappropriate or unexpected robot orientations. If users do not understand why a robot moves, interactions can easily be disrupted. This outcome is related to prior work on legible and predictable motion [17].

6. DISCUSSION

Limitations. Our work was limited in several ways. First, Chester's dialog was scripted and, thus, it could not respond appropriately in all circumstances. Second, the physical appearance and capabilities of our robot could have influenced our results and biased some aspects of the design of the behaviors under consideration. For example, the differential drive base of the robot constrained the complexity of its spatial behavior and, in turn, this could have affected the perception of its motion. Third, the perception system that we implemented for the experiment required instrumentation. While this system enabled autonomous robot behaviors, we are now interested in shifting towards on-board computation. This includes improving robots' capabilities so that they can reason about social contexts using on-board sensors only and, therefore, interact more casually.

Methodology. Overall, the perception of the brainstorming activity used in the experiment was positive. The protocol successfully created opportunities for changes in conversation group size, which allowed us to study the behaviors under consideration in different social contexts. In the future, this protocol could be used to study turn-taking patterns and collaboration in HRI. Similar to social games [65], brainstorming activities are customizable (e.g., the topic of the conversation can be easily adapted) and can be conducted with groups of strangers. In contrast, brainstorming sessions are less adversarial and do not require teaching very specific instructions.

Findings. The gaze of the robot affected the participants' perception of its motion and its motion affected the perception of its gaze. This dependency implies that robots should reason about and control their gaze and body motion jointly. Furthermore, some trends implied that the Attentive Orientation could be preferred over the Middle Orientation (e.g., AO could make the robot look more attentive and less antisocial). However, these behaviors led to similar feelings of inclusion and belonging to the group, suggesting that both AO and MO could be used as primitives for more complex orientation behaviors.

The implications of these findings are particularly important for mobile and low DoF robots, like ours, that engage in multi-party interactions, e.g., during social gatherings, or as they travel in human environments. In these circumstances, appropriate orientation and gaze behaviors can lead to more effective human-robot communication and user adoption.

7. ACKNOWLEDGMENTS

We thank Disney Research for continued support of this research effort, as well as Peter Carr and Alanson Sample for helping us set up the perception system used in this work.

References

[1] H. Admoni, B. Hayes, D. Feil-Seifer, D. Ullman, and B. Scassellati. Are You Looking at Me?: Perception of Robot Attention is Mediated by Gaze Type and Group Size. In *Proc. of the 8th ACM/IEEE Int'l Conf. on Human-robot Interaction*, HRI, 2013.

[2] H. Admoni and B. Scassellati. Social Eye Gaze in Human-Robot Interaction: A Review, 2017. Online access: hennyadmoni.com/documents/jhri17.pdf.

[3] S. Al Moubayed, J. Beskow, G. Skantze, and B. Granström. *Cognitive Behavioural Systems: COST 2102 International Training School, Revised Selected Papers*, chapter Furhat: A Back-Projected Human-Like Robot Head for Multiparty Human-Machine Interaction, pages 114–130. Springer Berlin Heidelberg, 2012.

[4] S. Al Moubayed, J. Edlund, and J. Beskow. Taming Mona Lisa: Communicating Gaze Faithfully in 2D and 3D Facial Projections. *ACM Trans. on Interactive Intelligent Systems*, 1(2):25, 2012.

[5] P. Althaus, H. Ishiguro, T. Kanda, T. Miyashita, and H. Christensen. Navigation for human-robot interaction tasks. In *Proc. of the 2004 IEEE Int'l Conf. on Robotics and Automation*, ICRA, 2004.

[6] S. Andrist, B. Mutlu, and A. Tapus. Look Like Me: Matching Robot Personality via Gaze to Increase Motivation. In *Proc. of the 33rd Annual ACM Conf. on Human Factors in Computing Systems*, CHI, 2015.

[7] M. Argyle. *Bodily Communication*. University paperbacks. Methuen, 1988.

[8] A. Aron, E. N. Aron, and D. Smollan. Inclusion of Other in the Self Scale and the structure of interpersonal closeness. *Journal of personality and social psychology*, 63(4):596, 1992.

[9] B. Bodt, R. Camden, H. Scott, A. Jacoff, T. Hong, T. Chang, R. Norcross, T. Downs, and A. Virts. Performance Measurements for Evaluating Static and Dynamic Multiple Human Detection and Tracking Systems in Unstructured Environments. In *Proc. of the 9th Workshop on Performance Metrics for Intelligent Systems*, PerMIS, 2009.

[10] H.-J. Böhme, T. Wilhelm, J. Key, C. Schauer, C. Schröter, H.-M. Groß, and T. Hempel. An approach to multi-modal human-machine interaction for intelligent service robots. *Robotics and Autonomous Systems*, 44(1):83 – 96, 2003.

[11] D. Bohus and E. Horvitz. Dialog in the Open World: Platform and Applications. In *Proc. of the 2009 Int'l Conf. on Multimodal Interfaces*, ICMI-MLMI, 2009.

[12] J. Cassell, O. E. Torres, and S. Prevost. Turn taking versus discourse structure. In *Machine conversations*, pages 143–153. Springer, 1999.

[13] I. Chatterjee. A low-cost, human-inspired perception approach for dense moving crowd navigation. Master's thesis, Robotics Institute, Carnegie Mellon University, August 2016.

[14] J. J. Choi, Y. Kim, and S. S. Kwak. Have You Ever Lied?: The Impacts of Gaze Avoidance on People's Perception of a Robot. In *Proc. of the 8th ACM/IEEE Int'l Conf. on Human-robot Interaction*, HRI, 2013.

[15] M. Cristani, L. Bazzani, G. Paggetti, A. Fossati, D. Tosato, A. Del Bue, G. Menegaz, and V. Murino. Social Interaction Discovery by Statistical Analysis of F-Formations. In *Proc. of the British Machine Vision Conf.*, BMVC, 2011.

[16] M. J. Doughty. Consideration of three types of spontaneous eyeblink activity in normal humans: during reading and video display terminal use, in primary gaze, and while in conversation. *Optometry & Vision Science*, 78(10):712–725, 2001.

[17] A. Dragan, S. Bauman, J. Forlizzi, and S. Srinivasa. Effects of Robot Motion on Human-Robot Collaboration. In *Proc. of the 10th ACM/IEEE Int'l Conf. on Human-Robot Interaction*, HRI, 2015.

[18] V. Evers, N. Menezes, L. Merino, D. Gavrila, F. Nabais, M. Pantic, P. Alvito, and D. Karreman. The Development and Real-world Deployment of FROG, the Fun Robotic Outdoor Guide. In *Proc. of the 9th ACM/IEEE Int'l Conf. on Human-robot Interaction*, HRI, 2014.

[19] N. Fisher. *Statistical Analysis of Circular Data*. Cambridge University Press, 1995.

[20] M. Garau, M. Slater, S. Bee, and M. A. Sasse. The Impact of Eye Gaze on Communication Using Humanoid Avatars. In *Proc. of the SIGCHI Conf. on Human Factors in Computing Systems*, CHI, 2001.

[21] A. Godil, R. Bostelman, K. Saidi, W. Shackleford, G. Cheok, M. Shneier, and T. Hong. 3D Ground-Truth Systems for Object/Human Recognition and Tracking. In *Proc. of the IEEE Conf. on Computer Vision and Pattern Recognition (CVPR) Workshops*, 2013.

[22] E. T. Hall. *The Hidden Dimension*. Doubleday, 1966.

[23] Z. Henkel, C. Bethel, R. Murphy, and V. Srinivasan. Evaluation of Proxemic Scaling Functions for Social Robotics. *IEEE Transactions on Human-Machine Systems*, 44(3):374–385, 2014.

[24] C.-M. Huang, M. Cakmak, and B. Mutlu. Adaptive Coordination Strategies for Human-Robot Handovers. In *Proc. of Robotics: Science and Systems*, R:SS, 2015.

[25] D. Karreman, G. Bradford, B. Van Dijk, M. Lohse, and V. Evers. What happens when a robot favors someone? How a tour guide robot uses gaze behavior to address multiple persons while storytelling about art. In *Proc. of the 8th ACM/IEEE Int'l Conf. on Human-Robot Interaction*, HRI, 2013.

[26] D. E. Karreman, G. D. Ludden, E. M. van Dijk, and V. Evers. How can a tour guide robot's orientation influence visitors' orientation and formations? In *Proc. of the 4th Int'l Symposium on New Frontiers in Human-Robot Interaction*, 2015.

[27] Y. Kato, T. Kanda, and H. Ishiguro. May I Help You?: Design of Human-like Polite Approaching Behavior. In *Proc. of the 10th ACM/IEEE Int'l Conf. on Human-Robot Interaction*, HRI, 2015.

[28] M. Katzenmaier, R. Stiefelhagen, and T. Schultz. Identifying the Addressee in Human-human-robot Interactions Based on Head Pose and Speech. In *Proc. of the 6th Int'l Conf. on Multimodal Interfaces*, ICMI, 2004.

[29] A. Kendon. *Conducting Interaction: Patterns of Behavior in Focused Encounters.* Cambridge UP, 1990.

[30] N. Kirchner, A. Alempijevic, and G. Dissanayake. Nonverbal Robot-group Interaction Using an Imitated Gaze Cue. In *Proc. of the 6th Int'l Conf. on Human-robot Interaction*, HRI, 2011.

[31] H. Kuzuoka, Y. Suzuki, J. Yamashita, and K. Yamazaki. Reconfiguring Spatial Formation Arrangement by Robot Body Orientation. In *Proc. of the 5th ACM/IEEE Int'l Conf. on Human-robot Interaction*, HRI, 2010.

[32] S. Lang, M. Kleinehagenbrock, S. Hohenner, J. Fritsch, G. A. Fink, and G. Sagerer. Providing the Basis for Human-robot-interaction: A Multi-modal Attention System for a Mobile Robot. In *Proc. of the 5th Int'l Conf. on Multimodal Interfaces*, ICMI, 2003.

[33] I. Leite, M. McCoy, D. Ullman, N. Salomons, and B. Scassellati. Comparing Models of Disengagement in Individual and Group Interactions. In *Proc. of the 10th Annual ACM/IEEE Int'l Conf. on Human-Robot Interaction*, HRI, 2015.

[34] T. Linder and K. Arras. Multi-model hypothesis tracking of groups of people in RGB-D data. In *Proc. of the 17th Int'l Conf. on Information Fusion*, FUSION, 2014.

[35] C. Liu, C. T. Ishi, H. Ishiguro, and N. Hagita. Generation of Nodding, Head Tilting and Eye Gazing for Human-robot Dialogue Interaction. In *Proc. of the 7th ACM/IEEE Int'l Conf. on Human-Robot Interaction*, HRI, 2012.

[36] M. Luber and K. O. Arras. Multi-Hypothesis Social Grouping and Tracking for Mobile Robots. In *Proc. of Robotics: Science and Systems*, R:SS, 2013.

[37] Y. Matsuyama, I. Akiba, S. Fujie, and T. Kobayashi. Four-participant group conversation: A facilitation robot controlling engagement density as the fourth participant. *Computer Speech & Language*, 33(1):1 – 24, 2015.

[38] R. Mead, A. Atrash, and M. J. Mataric. Recognition of Spatial Dynamics for Predicting Social Interaction. In *Proc. of the 6th Int'l Conf. on Human-Robot Interaction Extended Abstracts*, HRI EA, 2011.

[39] M. P. Michalowski, S. Sabanovic, and R. Simmons. A Spatial Model of Engagement for a Social Robot. In *Proc. of the 9th Int'l Workshop on Advanced Motion Control*, AMC, 2006.

[40] S. Muller, S. Hellbach, E. Schaffernicht, A. Ober, A. Scheidig, and H.-M. Gross. Whom to talk to? Estimating user interest from movement trajectories. In *Proc. of the 17th IEEE Int'l Symposium on Robot and Human Interactive Communication*, RO-MAN, 2008.

[41] J. Mumm and B. Mutlu. Human-robot Proxemics: Physical and Psychological Distancing in Human-robot Interaction. In *Proc. of the 6th Int'l Conf. on Human-robot Interaction*, HRI, 2011.

[42] B. Mutlu, J. Forlizzi, and J. Hodgins. A Storytelling Robot: Modeling and Evaluation of Human-like Gaze Behavior. In *Proc. of the 2006 6th IEEE-RAS Int'l Conf. on Humanoid Robots*, Humanoids, 2006.

[43] B. Mutlu, T. Shiwa, T. Kanda, H. Ishiguro, and N. Hagita. Footing in human-robot conversations: How robots might shape participant roles using gaze cues. In *Proc. of the 4th ACM/IEEE Int'l Conf. on Human-Robot Interaction*, HRI, 2009.

[44] M. A. Nicolaou, H. Gunes, and M. Pantic. Continuous Prediction of Spontaneous Affect from Multiple Cues and Modalities in Valence-Arousal Space. *IEEE Trans. on Affective Computing*, 2(2):92–105, 2011.

[45] H. D. Patterson and R. Thompson. Maximum likelihood estimation of components of variance. In *Proc. of the 8th Int'l Conf. on Biochem.*, 1974.

[46] I. Rae. Using Robot-mediated Communication to Improve Remote Collaboration. In *Proc. of CHI'13 Extended Abstracts on Human Factors in Computing Systems*, CHI EA, 2013.

[47] O. A. I. Ramírez, G. Varni, M. Andries, M. Chetouani, and R. Chatila. Modeling the dynamics of individual behaviors for group detection in crowds using low-level features. In *Proc. of the 2016 IEEE Int'l Symposium on Robot and Human Interactive Communication*, RO-MAN, 2016.

[48] J. Rios-Martinez, A. Spalanzani, and C. Laugier. Understanding human interaction for probabilistic autonomous navigation using Risk-RRT approach. In *Proc. of the 2011 IEEE/RSJ Int'l Conf. on Intelligent Robots and Systems*, IROS, 2011.

[49] V. Rousseau, F. Ferland, D. Létourneau, and F. Michaud. Sorry to interrupt, but may I have your attention? Preliminary design and evaluation of autonomous engagement in HRI. *Journal of Human-Robot Interaction*, 2(3):41–61, 2013.

[50] K. Ruhland, S. Andrist, J. Badler, C. Peters, N. Badler, M. Gleicher, B. Mutlu, and R. Mcdonnell. Look me in the eyes: A survey of eye and gaze animation for virtual agents and artificial systems. In *Eurographics 2014 - State of the Art Reports*, 2014.

[51] S. Satake, T. Kanda, D. Glas, M. Imai, H. Ishiguro, and N. Hagita. How to approach humans? - strategies for social robots to initiate interaction. In *Proc. of the 4th ACM/IEEE Int'l Conf. on Human-Robot Interaction*, HRI, 2009.

[52] F. Setti, C. Russell, C. Bassetti, and M. Cristani. F-formation Detection: Individuating Free-standing Conversational Groups in Images. *CoRR*, abs/1409.2702, 2014.

[53] C. Shi, M. Shimada, T. Kanda, H. Ishiguro, and N. Hagita. Spatial Formation Model for Initiating Conversation. In *Proc. of Robotics: Science and Systems*, R:SS, 2011.

[54] M. Shiomi, T. Kanda, H. Ishiguro, and N. Hagita. A Larger Audience, Please!: Encouraging People to Listen to a Guide Robot. In *Proc. of the 5th ACM/IEEE Int'l Conf. on Human-Robot Interaction*, HRI, 2010.

[55] E. Short, J. Hart, M. Vu, and B. Scassellati. No fair!! An interaction with a cheating robot. In *Proc. of the 5th ACM/IEEE Int'l Conf. on Human-Robot Interaction*, HRI, 2010.

[56] C. Sidner, C. Lee, C. Kidds, N. Lesh, and C. Rich. Explorations in Engagement for Humans and Robots. *Artificial Intelligence*, 2005.

[57] C. L. Sidner, C. Lee, L.-P. Morency, and C. Forlines. The Effect of Head-nod Recognition in Human-Robot Conversation. In *Proc. of the 1st ACM Conf. on Human-Robot Interaction*, HRI, 2006.

[58] G. Skantze, A. Hjalmarsson, and C. Oertel. Exploring the effects of gaze and pauses in situated human-robot interaction. In *Proc. of the 14th Annual Meeting of Special Interest Group on Doscourse and Dialogue*, SIGDial, 2013.

[59] A. Steinfeld, O. C. Jenkins, and B. Scassellati. The Oz of Wizard: Simulating the human for interaction research. In *Proc. of the 4th ACM/IEEE Int'l Conf. on Human-Robot Interaction*, HRI, 2009.

[60] W. W. Stroup. *Generalized Linear Mixed Models: Modern Concepts, Methods and Applications*. CRC Press, 2012.

[61] L. Takayama and C. Pantofaru. Influences on Proxemic Behaviors in Human-Robot Interaction. In *Proc. of the 2009 IEEE/RSJ Int'l Conf. on Intelligent Robots and Systems*, IROS, 2009.

[62] S. Thrun, W. Burgard, and D. Fox. *Probabilistic Robotics*. Intelligent Robotics and Autonomous Agents. MIT Press, 2005.

[63] J. G. Trafton, M. D. Bugajska, B. R. Fransen, and R. M. Ratwani. Integrating vision and audition within a cognitive architecture to track conversations. In *Proc. of the 2008 3rd ACM/IEEE Int'l Conf. on Human-Robot Interaction*, HRI, 2008.

[64] R. Triebel, K. Arras, R. Alami, L. Beyer, S. Breuers, R. Chatila, M. Chetouani, D. Cremers, V. Evers, M. Fiore, H. Hung, O. A. I. Ramírez, M. Joosse, H. Khambhaita, T. Kucner, B. Leibe, A. J. Lilienthal, T. Linder, M. Lohse, M. Magnusson, B. Okal, L. Palmieri, U. Rafi, M. van Rooij, and L. Zhang. SPENCER: A Socially Aware Service Robot for Passenger Guidance and Help in Busy Airports. In *Proc. of the 10th Conf. on Field and Service Robotics*, FSR, 2015.

[65] M. Vázquez, E. J. Carter, J. A. Vaz, J. Forlizzi, A. Steinfeld, and S. E. Hudson. Social Group Interactions in a Role-Playing Game. In *Proc. of the 10th ACM/IEEE Int'l Conf. on Human-Robot Interaction Extended Abstracts*, HRI EA, 2015.

[66] M. Vázquez, A. Steinfeld, and S. E. Hudson. Parallel Detection of Conversational Groups of Free-Standing People and Tracking of their Lower-Body Orientation. In *Proc. of the 2015 IEEE/RSJ Int'l Conf. on Intelligent Robots and Systems*, IROS, 2015.

[67] M. Vázquez, A. Steinfeld, S. E. Hudson, and J. Forlizzi. Spatial and Other Social Engagement Cues in a Child-robot Interaction: Effects of a Sidekick. In *Proceedings of the 2014 ACM/IEEE Int'l Conf. on Human-robot Interaction*, HRI, 2014.

[68] M. M. Veloso, J. Biswas, B. Coltin, and S. Rosenthal. CoBots: Robust Symbiotic Autonomous Mobile Service Robots. In *Proc. of the 24th Int'l Joint Conf. on Artificial Intelligence*, IJCAI, 2015.

[69] J. Vroon, M. Joosse, M. Lohse, J. Kolkmeier, J. Kim, K. Truong, G. Englebienne, D. Heylen, and V. Evers. Dynamics of social positioning patterns in group-robot interactions. In *Proc. of the 2015 24th IEEE Int'l Symposium on Robot and Human Interactive Communication*, RO-MAN, 2015.

[70] M. Walters, K. Dautenhahn, K. Koay, C. Kaouri, R. Boekhorst, C. Nehaniv, I. Werry, and D. Lee. Close encounters: spatial distances between people and a robot of mechanistic appearance. In *Proc. of the 5th IEEE-RAS Int'l Conf. on Humanoid Robots*, 2005.

[71] M. Walters, D. Syrdal, K. Koay, K. Dautenhahn, and R. te Boekhorst. Human approach distances to a mechanical-looking robot with different robot voice styles. In *Proc. of the 17th IEEE Int'l Symposium on Robot and Human Interactive Communication*, RO-MAN, 2008.

[72] M. L. Walters, K. Dautenhahn, R. te Boekhorst, K. L. Koay, C. Kaouri, S. Woods, C. Nehaniv, D. Lee, and I. Werry. The influence of subjects' personality traits on personal spatial zones in a human-robot interaction experiment. In *Proc. of the IEEE International Workshop on Robot and Human Interactive Communication*, RO-MAN, 2005.

[73] M. L. Walters, K. Dautenhahn, R. Te Boekhorst, K. L. Koay, D. S. Syrdal, and C. L. Nehaniv. An empirical framework for human-robot proxemics. *Procs of New Frontiers in Human-Robot Interaction*, 2009.

[74] K. D. Williams, C. K. Cheung, and W. Choi. Cyberostracism: effects of being ignored over the Internet. *J. of Personality and Social Psychology*, 79(5):748, 2000.

[75] Y. Yoshikawa, K. Shinozawa, H. Ishiguro, N. Hagita, and T. Miyamoto. Responsive robot gaze to interaction partner. In *Proc. of Robotics: Science and Systems*, R:SS, 2006.

[76] M. A. Yousuf, Y. Kobayashi, Y. Kuno, A. Yamazaki, and K. Yamazaki. Development of a Mobile Museum Guide Robot That Can Configure Spatial Formation with Visitors. In *Intelligent Computing Technology*, volume 7389 of *Lecture Notes in Comput. Sci.* 2012.

[77] Z. Yumak, J. Ren, N. M. Thalmann, and J. Yuan. Tracking and Fusion for Multiparty Interaction with a Virtual Character and a Social Robot. In *SIGGRAPH Asia 2014*, SA, pages 3:1–3:7, 2014.

Transgazer: Improving Impression by Switching Direct and Averted Gaze Using Optical Illusion

Yuki Kinoshita [1], Masanori Yokoyama [2], Shigeo Yoshida [1]
Takayoshi Mochizuki[2], Tomohiro Yamada [2],
Takuji Narumi [1], Tomohiro Tanikawa[1], Michitaka Hirose[1]
[1]Cyber Interface Laboratory, The University of Tokyo.
[2]NTT Organization of Service Evolution Laboratories, NTT Corporation.
[1]{kino, shigeodayo, narumi, tani, hirose}@cyber.t.u-tokyo.ac.jp,
[2]{yokoyama.masanori, mochizuki.takayoshi, yamada.tomohiro}@lab.ntt.co.jp

ABSTRACT

To effectively utilize gaze in one-to-many communication, robots must direct and avert their gaze with appropriate timing. However, few studies have focused on this aspect of communication because of the difficulty in detecting the position of many gaze recipients and directing appropriate gazes to each. This paper proposes a system of robotic eyes that can send averted or direct gazes simultaneously to multiple recipients by switching between convex and hollow eye shapes, which we call Transgazer. Using Transgazer, we experimentally confirm that hollow eyes can direct a gaze more broadly whereas convex eyes can convey gaze direction more correctly. In our main experiment, Transgazer uses both eye types while giving lectures to two participants without precisely retrieving the gaze recipients' directions. Transgazer allows robots to gaze appropriately and enhances one-to-many communication, improving the audience's impression of the speaker.

Keywords

direct gaze; averted gaze; reverse perspective; hollow-face; gaze cone; one-to-many communication

1. INTRODUCTION

One-to-many communication between robots and humans is promising among various applications, such as education (e.g. between a teacher and students), advertisement (e.g. between a shopkeeper and customers), and entertainment (e.g. a museum guide and visitors, or a mascot costume and visitors). In those scenarios, it is important for robots that communicate with multiple people, to utilize not only verbal information but also nonverbal information (e.g. facial expressions, body movement, proximate, and eye gaze).

Nonverbal information enriches the transmission of nonlogical and intuitive information. Many researchers have been studying the usage of robots for expressing nonverbal information in order to improve the communication quality between robots and humans [7, 35].

HRI '17, March 06-09, 2017, Vienna, Austria
© 2017 ACM. ISBN 978-1-4503-4336-7/17/03...$15.00
DOI: http://dx.doi.org/10.1145/2909824.3020235

Gaze cues are among the main indicators of nonverbal information in one-to-many communication. They serve several positive functions in one-to-many communication [3] and are effective for a wide range of gaze recipients. There are two types of eye gaze: direct and averted. A direct gaze is that wherein the eyes are directed toward the recipients; it promotes eye contact that leads to several positive effects, such as impression formation and turn-taking. An averted gaze is that wherein the eye direction is elsewhere; it can be used to drive and guide the observers' attention to a target [13]. Direct gaze is that wherein the eye direction towards the receivers. It promotes an eye-contact that has several positive effects, such as impression formation and turn-taking. These gaze effects are commonly used during nonverbal communication.

These gaze effects are common in nonverbal communication. However, their utilization is difficult in one-to-many communication, especially for large crowds. The duration of the direct gaze to each person decreases as the number of people increases, as sending a direct gaze to each person at the same time is impossible. Thus, gaze effects on each person decrease for large crowds in one-to-many communication, whether the sender of the gaze is a human or robot. Previous studies have focused on methods for accurately imitating or conveying human gaze [1]. In contrast, our study aims to solve the problems of one-to-many communication described above. We propose sending direct and averted gazes to multiple people simultaneously by changing the shape of the robot's eyes.

We develop a prototype system, called Transgazer, to demonstrate this concept. Transgazer utilizes two types of eyes: hollow and convex. Transgazer can direct its gaze to multiple people simultaneously using hollow eyes, which produce an optical illusion for the audience. The convex eyes can be used to direct the audience's attention to another recipient. Transgazer can immediately switch between hollow and convex eyes to change the range of gaze directions (called the gaze cone [15]) in which an audience member perceives being looked at. Transgazer can use the effects of both direct and averted gazes on different people in a given scenario.

In this study, we demonstrate that Transgazer can achieve direct and averted gazes by using two types of eyes. First, we test Transgazer's convex and hollow eyes' accuracy in conveying gaze direction and their gaze cones. These tests confirm that convex eyes can convey gaze direction accurately and that hollow eyes have a broader gaze cone than convex eyes.

Then, we show that we can make use of both eyes' effects as the audience members form their impression of the speaker. Using both eye types generated good impressions from two listeners simultaneously: direct gaze with hollow eyes improved the audience members' impression of Transgazer and averted gaze with convex eyes regulated the impression of several listeners.

2. RELATED WORK

This section describes previous work on gaze effects and robots that make use of them. In addition, we introduce some optical illusions related to our concept in this section.

2.1 Functions of Eye Gaze

Gaze is a powerful nonverbal cue that yields numerous positive effects in human interactions. Both the head and eyeball directions can convey gaze direction, although eyeball direction is especially important. The human eye has a strong contrast between the iris and sclera. Kobayashi et al. suggest that human eyes evolved such colors for effective communication and social interaction [26]. They further suggest that the human eye has been used positively for communication since ancient times. Eye gaze is a main communication tool for conveying information between people.

Gaze effects, which may be classified into those resulting from averted and direct gaze directions, are based on function [3], and neurological mechanisms [16]. The two types of eye gaze are fundamentally different. We focus on gaze effects related to one-to-many communication.

An averted gaze can convey gaze direction or instruct an interlocutor to adopt the same gaze direction as the sender. In general, an averted gaze reveals an individual's focus of attention and point of reference. The main effects of an averted gaze are gaze cueing and impression regulation. A gaze shift or continued staring by the sender causes the recipients' gazes to move in response [10]. Conversely, averted gaze can be used to regulate social interaction [11], adjusting intimacy and avoiding the bad impression formed because of a very long direct gaze [36]. Continuous gaze conditions do not produce a more favorable evaluation of the gaze sender [9]; recipients feel that too much direct gazing is inappropriate [25, 36]. In addition, an averted gaze can create an impression: looking down induces a "warm" impression in audience members and looking up is thought to be "strong" [42].

A direct gaze signals that the gazer is looking at the perceiver, produces mutual gaze, and regulates social impression and social interaction. Direct gaze influences evaluations of attraction, attentiveness, competence, social skills, credibility, and dominance [24] and can also promote social interaction, inducing responses from recipients [4]. Further, direct gaze can immediately heighten arousal [30], which leads to improvements in receivers' recall [32], and promotes joint attention [34].

2.2 Gaze Applications

Two-dimensional agents cannot convey gaze direction to the real world, but three-dimensional agents can direct their very accurately [1]. Therefore, robots that can alter their gaze have been actively developed.

Many robots focus on the effects of an averted gaze. Imai et al. show that robots can induce joint attention [18]. Robots can influence people's decisions in a game by shifting their eyes, even when the participants do not report seeing those cues [29]. Uno et al. used a museum guide robot to show that robots can use averted gaze to direct the attention of its listeners [27]. Kim made a robot called DONA that roams freely and solicits donations by joint attention [22].

Many studies have also focused on direct gaze effects. Mutlu et al. found that participants recalled a story told by a humanoid robot significantly better when the robot directed its gaze at them more [28], Bee et al. found that robots can initiate communication [5], and Mutlu et al. demonstrated that a robot can use gaze cues to regulate position in human-robot conversations [29]. These studies indicate that robots are effective for enhancing communication.

2.3 Gaze Perception in Optical Illusions

Gamer and Hecht found that subjective criteria for being engaged in a mutual gaze are surprisingly liberal, and that mutual gaze occurs when an observer looks at or in the direction of the eyes of another person [15]. They designated the range of gaze directions perceived as a mutual gaze as the gaze cone. When an optical illusion was perceived as a direct gaze, the resulting brain response was similar to that produced by a real direct gaze [6].

Two types of optical illusion can widen the gaze cone: the Mona Lisa effect and the Hollow Face illusion.

The Mona Lisa effect is an effect in which a flat face (such as in a painting) can appear to follow a moving viewer. The gaze cone was found to be slightly wider in pictures compared to that in three-dimensional images and physical heads [15]. This optical illusion occurs because humans use iris eccentricity–the relative position of the irises within the portion of the sclera visible through the eyes of the gazer–as a cue for gaze direction [2, 39].

The Hollow Face (or Hollow Mask) illusion is an optical illusion in which a hollow mask is perceived as a convex face and appears to move as if following a moving observer [17]. This illusion is an example of a reverse perspective illusion, in which a hollow shape can be perceived as a normal convex shape [40, 41].

However, hollow faces cannot convey specifics of gaze direction. There has not yet been any research that has made use of the Hollow Face illusion in communication, as far as we found. In this study, we utilize the Hollow Face illusion for our robots' eyes, to improve human-robot communication.

3. CONCEPT: CHANGING EYE SHAPE FOR CONTROLLING THE BROADNESS OF GAZE CONE

We present the concept that robotic eyes can control the broadness of their gaze cone by changing their shape. Three types of eye shape (convex, flat, and hollow or concave) are perceived differently.

Convex eyes have the same shape as human eyes and have the narrowest gaze cone, producing a gaze similar to that of humans.

Flat and hollow eyes have broad gaze cones and can send a direct gaze to more recipients than convex eyes can. Further, the hollow eyes produce a broader gaze cone than flat eyes. Therefore, we can narrow or broaden the gaze cone by controlling eye concavity.

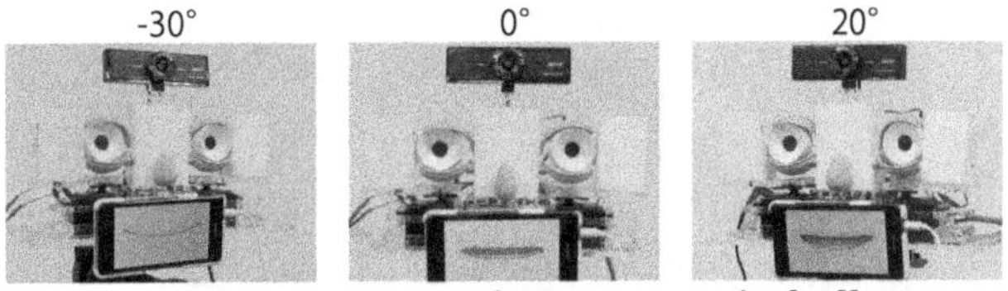

Figure 1: Appearance of Transgazer's hollow eyes from different angles.

3.1 Expected Merits and Applications

We expect that our concept can benefit both the sender and recipients in one-to-many communication. For the sender, it can reduce the burden of sending a direct gaze to many people. For the merits of recipients, each recipient can perceive a more appropriate gaze and its effects.

3.1.1 Merits for the Sender

Changing eye shape reduces the costs of achieving eye contact with many recipients. Several studies have investigated the difficulties in achieving eye contact [8].

To send a direct gaze, robots needed to correctly determine a recipient's face and gaze position because the gaze cone of a convex eye is very narrow.

In contrast, hollow eyes can be perceived to produce eye contact even when not oriented to the recipient's precise gaze direction. Therefore, robots do not need to detect and allocate a direct gaze to each recipient's face precisely.

3.1.2 Merits for Recipients

Our concept can be used to send more appropriate gazes to every recipient and use gaze effects to obtain more targets. For example, it can use the effect of direct gaze to regulate the impression it produces for more recipients by altering the amount of direct or averted gaze used [21]. By using convex and hollow eyes, it becomes easier to control these variables. The convex eyes can prevent robots from orienting a direct gaze toward a specific recipient for too long a duration.

We are confident that direct gaze's function can be used to reach each audience member for an appropriate time simultaneously. For example, direct gaze can emphasize words in speech and improve recall. In addition, when the hollow eyes induce responses from recipients, they can produce a greater response when the sender wants to observe recipients' reactions.

We can also use the effects of an averted gaze at the appropriate time. Joint attention by human and robots with three-dimensional eyes can be induced only by convex eyes. However, direct gaze can better promote it by attracting the recipients' attention [34]. Thus, there is a possibility that hollow eyes can improve joint attention.

4. IMPLEMENTATION: TRANSGAZER

We implemented Transgazer to demonstrate above concept. Transgazer has two types of eyes: convex and hollow. Transgazer controls its gaze cone by switching between convex and hollow eye shapes. Transgazer can thus use different eye types depending on its intended purpose. The convex eyes can send a direct gaze to one person or an averted gaze that indicates its gaze direction to recipients. The hollow eyes can send a direct gaze and eye contact to many recipients simultaneously. The appearance of Transgazer is shown in Fig. 1.

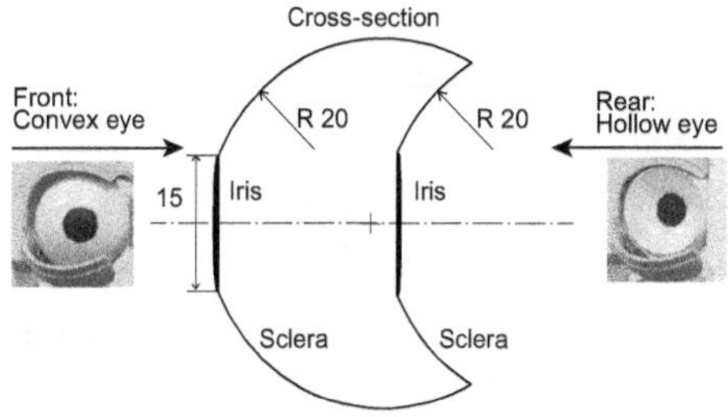

Figure 2: Shape of a Transgazer's eye.

Transgazer contains two reversible eyes and two eyelids. In addition, it can attach a mouth module and a standard webcam. Transgazer was operated through serial communication between an Arduino board and a computer. The operation program was written in JavaScript. It also can be operated via a prewritten gaze movement command file, which includes operation commands such as the eye types, gaze direction, and execution time.

4.1 Eyes

Transgazer has two reversible eyes. Each eye has a convex front and a hollow back. Transgazer can switch between having convex and hollow eyes by rotating the eyes 180°. Fig. 2 shows a side view of Transgazer's eyes, which can be rotated by panning and tilting. By rotating the convex eyes, it can change its gaze direction. By rotating the hollow eyes, it can change the area of its gaze cone. The hollow eyes can send direct gaze by roughly matching their direction to the center of recipients.

To achieve high contrast, the eyeballs' pupils and irises were painted black and the sclera were painted white. Each eyeball's diameter was 40mm larger than human eyes, making Transgazer easy to see even from a distance. In addition, we used a matte surface for the hollow eyes to make them indistinguishable from the convex eyes.

4.2 Eyelids

Upper and lower gray eyelids were attached to Transgazer's eyes. The eyelids hide the eyes when changing eye types (Fig. 3). To ensure that the observers feel that Transgazer's gaze direction changes naturally, it is necessary to make the switching of eye shapes invisible to the observer. We assumed that we would be able to apply the flicker paradigm when switching eye shapes to make it inconspicuous and induce change blindness [33].

The flicker paradigm is a key concept in perceptual psychology; when a brief blank is shown during alternating displays (such as during a blink) a striking failure of perception is induced. Identifying changes, even significant ones, becomes extremely difficult. We use blinking to produce change blindness, especially when Transgazer changes from convex to hollow eyes, because this eye rotation process stands out more than that for the change from hollow to convex.

The total time required for changing eye type from convex to hollow was minimized to about 400 ms on average for natural movement, which is very near to the duration of a human blink (between 100–400 ms [37]). This blink during changing eye type is natural for the oculomotor system as well. Blinks very often occur almost simultaneously with the onset of eye and gaze movements, particularly large ones (greater than 30° [12]).

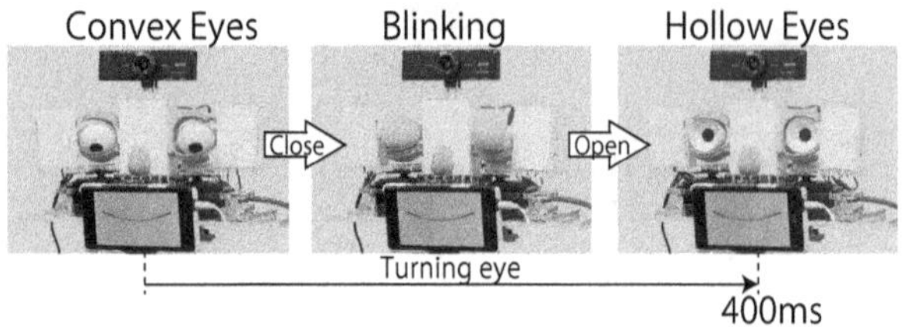

Figure 3: Process of changing the eye from convex to hollow.

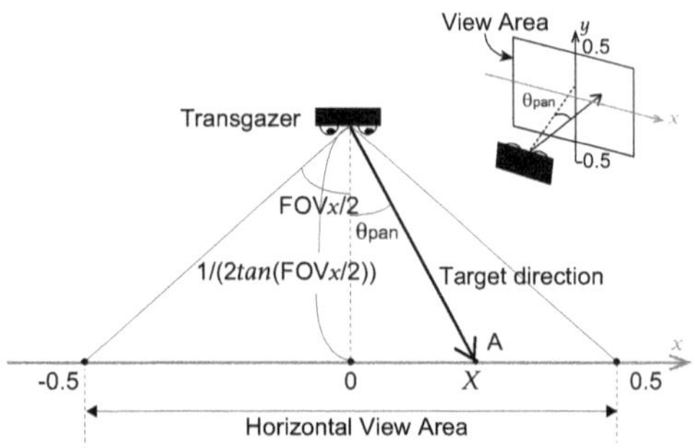

Figure 4: Variable definition for calculating the target direction from Transgazer.

4.3 Calculation of Eyes' Direction

Transgazer calculates the rotation angle of the eyes (θ_{pan}, θ_{tilt}) from the coordinate of freely-selected position (point A in Fig. 4) in a webcam image. The webcam image is normalized between -0.5 and 0.5 both horizontally and vertically. Point A, the target point for eye rotation, is (X, Y) in this coordinate system. FOV_x is the horizontal field-of-view angle of the camera. The pan angle θ_{pan} (and the tilt angle θ_{tilt}) can be computed by the following expression.

$$\theta_{pan} = \mathrm{arctan2}\{\frac{1}{2\tan\frac{FOV_x}{2}}, X\}$$

4.4 Mouth

Transgazer has a removable mouth module. This mouth module lip-syncs to Transgazer's voice in real time during speech, causing recipients to recognize the voice as Transgazer's. The mouth was displayed on a Sony Xperia screen. This program was built with the OVRLipSync for Unity framework [31].

5. EVALUATION OF CONVEYING ACCURACY AND BROADNESS OF GAZE CONE

In order to evaluate the effects of Transgazer's convex and hollow eyes, we measured the broadness of the gaze cone and the accuracy of conveying gaze direction for each eye. The purpose of the measurements in this section is to show the effects of both eye types and support the concept of using the effects of both averted and direct gazes. To prevent participants' gaze perception from being affected by the mouth module (Section 4.4), it was not attached to the Transgazer in the experiments in this section.

5.1 Accuracy of Conveyance of Gaze Direction

We measured the accuracy with which convex and hollow eyes can convey gaze direction to assess the role of convex eyes. We expect that convex eyes can convey gaze direction more correctly than hollow eyes. We recruited ten participants (10 males; 21 to 25 years of age; normal or corrected-to-normal vision; no autism spectrum disorders).

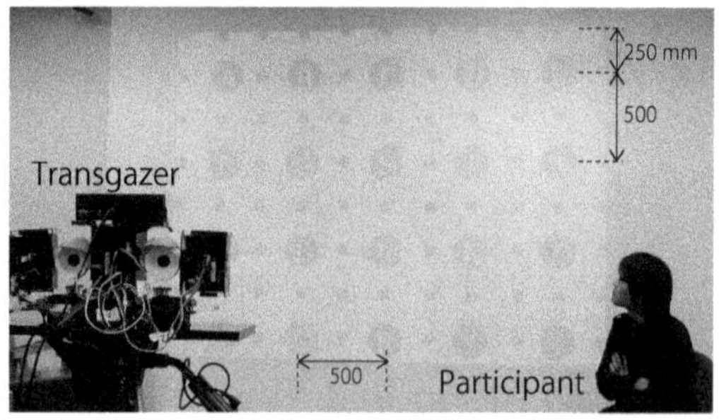

Figure 5: Experimental conditions described in Section 5.1. Transgazer faces the screen, so this figure shows the back side of Transgazer.

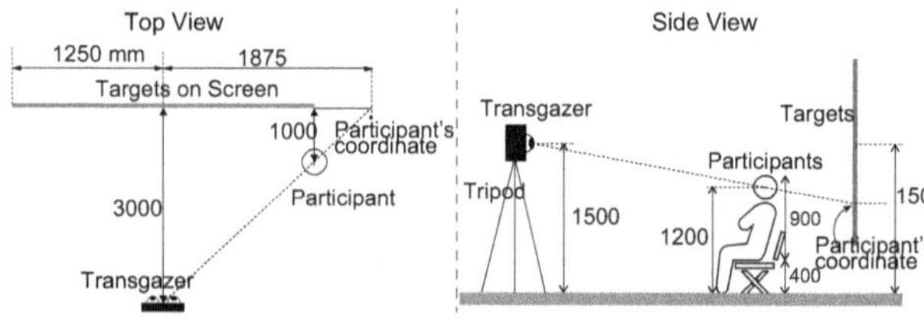

Figure 6: Top and side views of the experiment detailed in Section 5.1.

Transgazer faced a screen on which target characters were projected (Fig. 5). Each participant tried to figure out which character Transgazer was looking at. Participants were permitted to turn their head and upper body freely and to look at Transgazer and the screen in turn.

The following steps were conducted for two conditions: convex and hollow eyes. 1) Transgazer looked at the target character projected on the screen. 2) Participants attempted to determine which character Transgazer was looking at. 3) Participants responded with the characters they perceived Transgazer to be looking at. 4) Steps 1 through 3 were repeated for 25 targets. The characters order was randomly assigned.

5.1.1 Result and Discussion

Figs. 7 and 8 show the average coordinates that the participants selected and the actual target positions. The positive and negative X and Y error bars show standard errors. Some participants answered that Transgazer looked at them, even though they knew that Transgazer turned its eyes to one of targets on the screen. Therefore, we calculated this position by substituting its coordinate for the intersection point of the screen and an extended line from Transgazer to the participant's eyes (participant's coordinate is shown in Figs. 6 to 8).

The gaze direction was perceived near to the actual target position for convex eyes (Fig. 7) and near to the participant for hollow eyes (Fig. 8). The total difference between Transgazer's gazing target and the participants' selection target (Fig. 9) was significantly different between convex eye and hollow eye conditions in a *t*-test ($p = 0.010$ Fig. 9), supporting our hypothesis that the convex eyes can indicate Transgazer's gaze direction to observers more correctly than hollow eyes.

Interestingly, we can see that the answers O and T in the convex eye condition (Fig. 7) is very near to the participant coordinate, perhaps because the convex eyes cause stronger

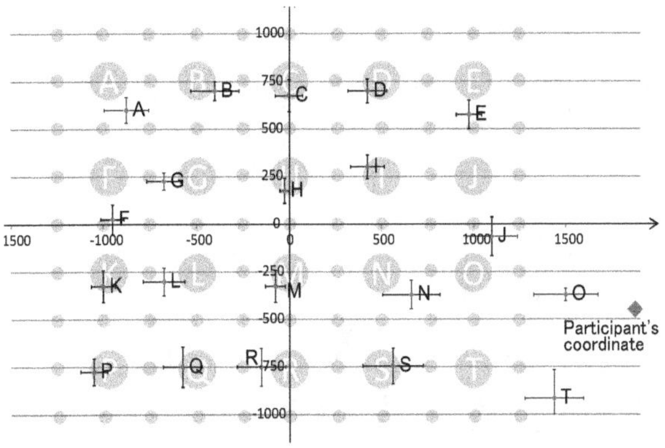

Figure 7: Average position that participants selected in the convex eye condition.

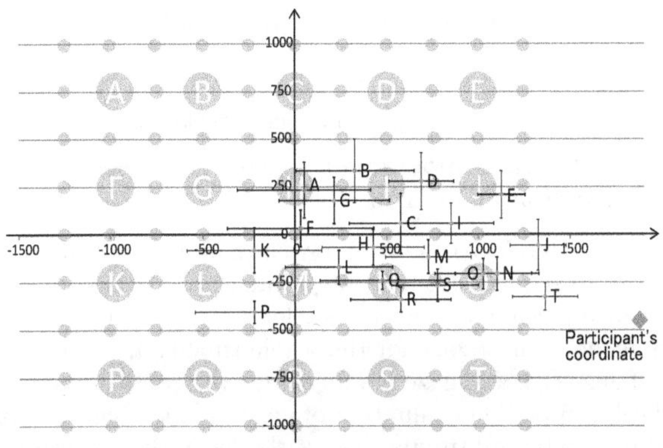

Figure 8: Average position that participants selected in the hollow eye condition.

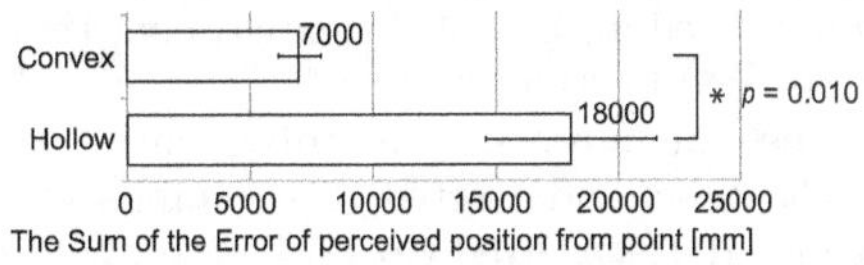

Figure 9: The average of each target's error for the convex and hollow eye conditions.

feelings of eye contact than the hollow eyes when the gaze direction is near to the observers.

5.2 Gaze Cone Broadness

We measured how broadly the convex and hollow eyes are perceived as making eye contact to assess the role of hollow eyes. We hypothesize that hollow eyes seem to be making eye contact more broadly than convex eyes. We recruited eleven participants (11 males; 21 to 31 years of age; normal or corrected-to-normal vision; no autism spectrum disorders). Transgazer's eyes were fixed forward.

Participants looked at Transgazer from every marked position in Fig. 10. They determined whether they felt Transgazer was making eye contact with them at that position. Participants sat on a chair whose height was adjusted the chair height to make the participants' eyes level with Transgazer's. They looked at Transgazer at the marked positions, 1.5m from Transgazer, and were asked whether they felt looked at.

The following steps were conducted for the convex and hollow eye conditions. 1) Participants responded with a three-step evaluation (0: felt looked at by both eyes, 0.5: looked at by only one, 1: looked at by neither eye). 2) Participants then looked away from Transgazer and moved to

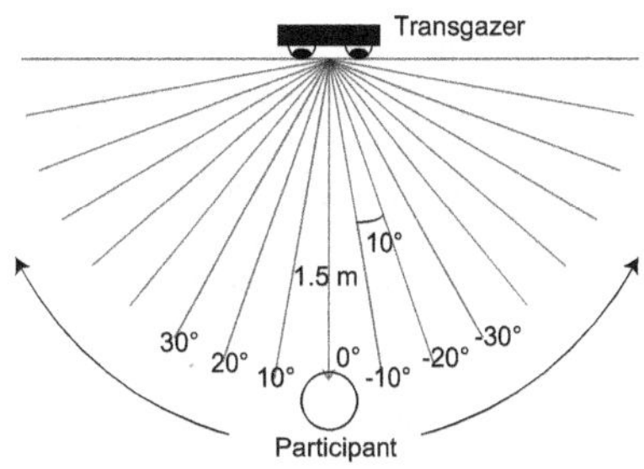

Figure 10: Top view of the experimental setup for measuring gaze cone broadness.

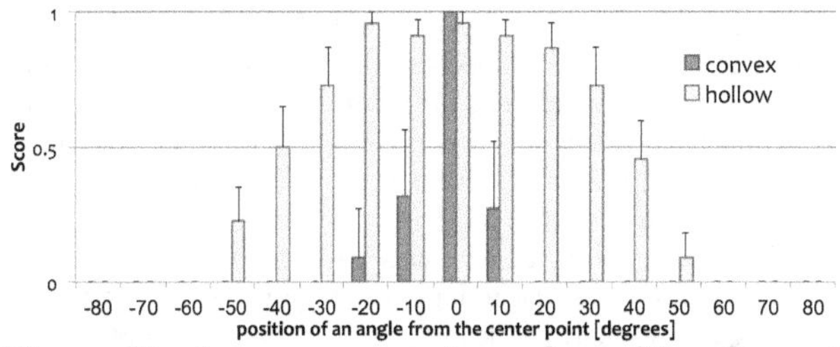

Figure 11: Average scores in each position for each eye type.

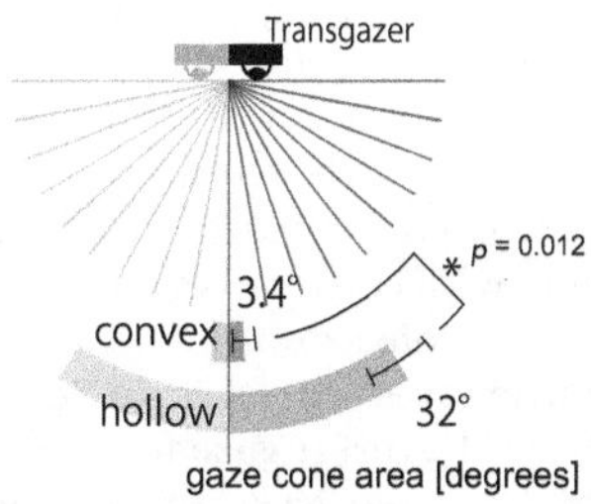

Figure 12: Average of gaze cone broadness for each eye type.

the next position (10° counterclockwise). 3) Steps 1 through 2 were repeated until participants did not feel looked at by either eye. 4) Participants return to the point in front of Transgazer and repeated steps 1 through 3 for the clockwise direction.

5.2.1 *Result*

Fig. 11 shows the average scores at each angle of position. Fig. 12 shows the average of the maximum angle that each participant felt eye contacting (the broadness of gaze cone). The maximum angle was the last position each participant evaluated as 1 point (looked by both eyes) or 0.5 points (looked by only one eye) at step 4). When participants answered 0.5 points, 5 degrees was subtracted to adjust and evaluate the small sense of eye contact. A Welch's paired t-test was conducted to compare the eye contact area of the convex and hollow eye conditions. There was a significant difference in the scores for convex eyes (M = 3.4°, SD=11); $p = 0.012$ (Fig. 12). The result of the gaze cone measurement shows that hollow eyes have a broader gaze cone than the convex eyes.

6. EXPERIMENT: IMPRESSION IMPROVEMENT

The main study of this paper explores improvement of the participants' impression of Transgazer by regulating the amount of each gaze type during a lecture. Impression improvement is the main effect of eye contact and has a wide range of uses in many applications. Most research on gaze effects in communication concentrates on methods for improving the impression of gaze recipients. To give a good impression to observers, the eyes needs to use both direct and averted gazes at the proper rate for many recipients. The purpose of this experiment is to ensure that Transgazer can improve its impression using an averted gaze with convex eyes and a direct gaze with hollow eyes. We examined whether Transgazer can produce a good impression for two recipients simultaneously.

6.1 Study Design

Transgazer delivered a seven-minute lecture about a cooking method to two listeners simultaneously using the prerecorded voice of a 59-year-old man. The participants did not know that the voice was recorded and were told that the voice was real-time. Transgazer moved its eyes based on one of three conditions during the lecture (Section 6.2). A within-participants design was used for this study. Our experiment involved one independent manipulated variable, type of gaze, with three levels, each of which is defined as follows.

Each participant receives gaze as below in each condition.
Convex eyes with Direct and Averted gaze (CDA): direct gaze for 50% of the total lecture time with convex eyes and averted gaze for 50% of the lecture with convex eyes.
Convex eyes with Averted gaze only (CA): direct gaze for 0% of the lecture with convex eyes and averted gaze for 100% of the lecture with convex eyes.
Mixture of convex eyes with Averted gaze and hollow eyes with direct gaze (M): direct gaze for 50% of the lecture with hollow eyes and averted gaze for 50% of the lecture with convex eyes.

Our experimental arrangement setup bears a close resemblance to the one proposed by Mutlu et al [28]. Participants were sat in positions ±20° from the Transgazer's front and 3.5 m (public distance) from Transgazer (Fig. 13). They were told not to speak or move their position during the lecture. A video camera was set below Transgazer and recorded to ensure that the participants were looking at Transgazer during the lecture.

The experiment was conducted as follows: 1) Participants sat in the prescribed position. 2) The participants heard a lecture from Transgazer. 3) Participants filled out a questionnaire about the lecture and the speaker. 4) Participants took a 3-minute break. 5) Steps 1 through 4 were repeated for four sets. 6) Participants filled out a final questionnaire about the whole experiment.

The first set of four sets was a trial section to exclude errors caused by procedures that are unfamiliar to the participants. The other three sets, one for each gaze condition, were for real measurement. Three conditions were assigned to each participant in these three lecture (Fig. 13). For each lecture, Transgazer sent gaze directions at timing decided by the gaze model described in Section 6.2.

The mouth expression was unified to a smile during this experiment because the impression of mutual gaze differs with facial expression [19].

6.2 Gaze Movement

A gaze model based on Fukayama's gaze movement model was used in this experiment [14]. Fukayama's model focuses on the timing of direct or averted gazes. We applied

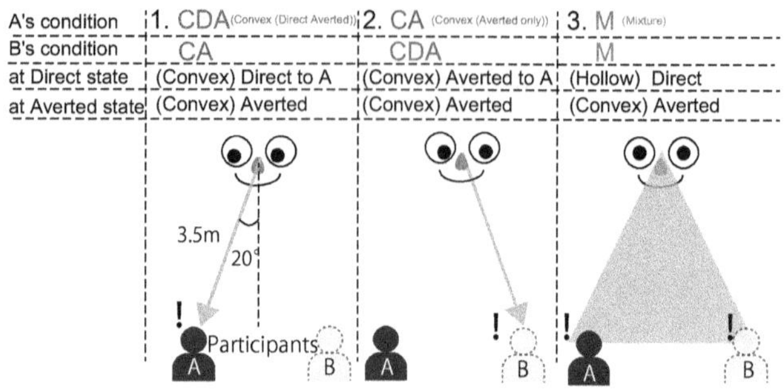

Figure 13: Conditions and the way Transgazer send gaze in three lectures.

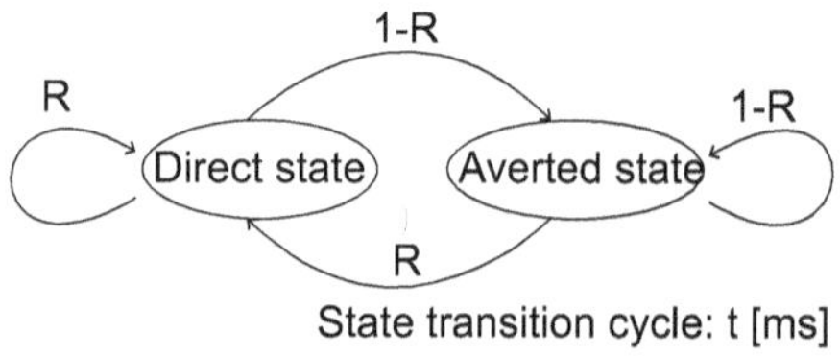

Figure 14: Gaze movement state model referred to the Fukayama et al [14].

Fukayama's model to one-to-many communication with Transgazer. This model outputs gaze points that are derived from three gaze parameters, which is effective for impression formation: amount of gaze for the whole time (R), mean duration of gaze (L), and gaze points while averted. It is apposite to check impression evaluation of gaze independently of the lecture content and timing. The variables in this experiment were set as follows.
The amount of gaze (R): $R = 50$ %. In Fig. 14, the averted state is used for half of the experiment time and the direct state is used for the other half of the time. R was set to 50 % because the impression improved when Transgazer's eyes sent 50 % direct and averted gazes, compared with 0 % direct gaze and 100 % averted gaze [14] or 100 % direct gaze and 0 % averted gaze [43].
Mean duration of gaze (L): $L = 2$ [sec], set based on the mean duration of humans' direct gaze in a previous study [20].
The state transition cycle (t): $t = (1 - R)L$ [ms].

This model moves as a two-state specialized Markov model shown in Fig. 14. In the direct gaze state, Transgazer uses a direct gaze on one of the participants (1, 2 of Fig. 13) or both participants (3 of Fig. 13). Participants were under three different gaze conditions: CDA, CA, and M.

In the direct state, Transgazer sent the gaze shown in Fig. 13 in each condition. When Transgazer sent a direct gaze with hollow eyes in condition M (3 of Fig. 13), Transgazer turned its hollow eyes to its front, orienting the hollow eyes to the center point between A and B so that they do not direct to the exact position of the participants.

- **CDA & CA**: Transgazer gives a participant eye contact (CDA) and does not give another participant eye contact at all (CA) with convex eyes. (i.e., when participant A is assigned as CDA, participant B is assigned as CA and vice versa, as in 1 and 2 of Fig. 13).
- **M**: Transgazer gives eye contact with hollow eyes to Participants A and B.

In the averted state, Transgazer sent an averted gaze to both participants by gazing at a point chosen randomly from the lower area between the two participants with convex eyes. We unified the averted gaze to looking down because looking down and looking up induce different impressions [14].

6.3 Measurements

A survey was conducted using the Likert method to quantify the participants' impressions of Transgazer. Participants were asked to rate the speaker (Transgazer) by circling one of seven points along each dimension. We adopted nine pairs classified into three groups, as follows.

- **Competence**: "strong" – "weak" and 'unassured" – "assured".
- **Like**: "cold" – "warms", "considerate" – "inconsiderate" and "attractive" – "unattractive".
- **Mutual interests**: "attentive" – "inattentive", "the duration of eye contact" (long – short) and "the frequency of eye contact" (frequent – rare).

Adjective factors (all except duration and frequency) were chosen in reference to past social psychology studies and Fukayama's research [14] so that we can compare the result with previous work that used the gaze model we referenced. We added two questions about the duration and frequency with which they perceived Transgazer's mutual gaze to check that the observer perceived the hollow eyes' gaze as a direct gaze.

6.4 Hypotheses

We hypothesized that Transgazer can yield higher ratings by sending a direct gaze for half of the lecture time and an averted gaze for the other half. We assumed that the rating increased in conditions CDA and M, in which Transgazer sent a direct gaze to the participant and an averted gaze in the direct state, and that the rating decreased in condition CA, in which Transgazer sent only an averted gaze the whole time. The mean would become CDA > CA, M > CA, CDA = M if the hypothesis was true.

6.5 Participants

Twelve people in 6 pairs participated in this experiment. The participants were twelve students (10 male, 2 female; 21 to 24 years of age; native Japanese speakers; no autism spectrum disorders; normal hearing; normal or corrected-to-normal vision). They took part as listeners in the study.

6.6 Results

We could see one participant slept during the lecture by checking the video of the experiment. This participant's data were eliminated from the following analysis. The other participants looked at and listened to Transgazer and did not averted their gaze from Transgazer significantly during the whole lecture.

A one-way ANOVA for repeated measures was conducted to compare the effect of gaze type on speaker impression for each factor. An analysis of variance showed that the effect of gaze type on all factors mentioned in the hypothesis were significant (Strong: $F(2,11) = 9.461$, $p < 0.001$, Assured: $F(2,11) = 4.987$, $p = 0.014$, Warm: $F(2,11) = 18.3$, $p < 0.001$, Considerate: $F(2,11) = 20.04$, $p < 0.001$, Attractive: $F(2,11) = 8.96$, $p < 0.001$, Attentive: $F(2,11) = 41.67$, $p < 0.001$, Duration of mutual gaze: $F(2,11) = 117.6$, $p < 0.001$, Frequency of mutual gaze: $F(2,11) = 112.3$, $p < 0.001$).

A paired Holm multiple comparison test was conducted with each factor to see if the direct gaze with convex and hollow eyes is more effective than the averted gaze with convex eyes. A p-value less than 0.05 was considered statistically significant. Fig. 15 shows the results of the Holm multiple comparison test, indicating the ratings in impression measures of each adjective. Each dot shows the score of a participant.

The factors that met the significance level of 5% between direct gaze with both eyes (CDA and M) and CA were "strong", "warm", "attractive", "attentive", "duration" and "frequency". The Assure factor met the 5% significance level only between CDA and CA, not between CA and M. However, the Considerate factor met the 10% significance level between CDA and M. In addition, the average evaluation value of CDA was a little higher than that of M for all factors, even if there was no significant difference.

A Pearson product-moment correlation coefficient was computed to assess the relationship between the rating factors and the rating of duration or between the rating factors and frequency of eye contact. There was a positive correlation between the variables ($p < 0.01$). Table 1 summarizes these results. Overall, there was a strong, positive correlation between the rating factors and duration or frequency. There was a moderate correlation in strong, assured and attractive factors. There was a high correlation in warm, considerate and attentive factors.

On the questionnaire, all participants answered that they had no prior interactions with the lecture. One participant pointed out that he noticed the eye turning and felt odd with the way the eyes changed. Even so, he rated the direct gaze with hollow eyes higher than the averted gaze with convex eyes in all factors.

6.7 Discussion

A significant difference was seen between the convex and hollow eyes' direct gazes in most impression factors. The results showed that Transgazer could use the effect of averted and direct gazes by using both eye types for two recipients simultaneously. The hollow eyes' gaze could improve the impression of speaker, and the convex eyes could regulate impression in simple speech conditions. We also conclude that Transgazer can improve the impression of the speaker without setting the precise direction of the recipients. It is assumed that the hollow eyes can use this effect for all person in the gaze cone, not only at the $\pm 20°$ position.

About CDA and CA, it showed that Transgazer can improve all impression factors investigated in this research. It is the same result compared with the result of previous research [14].

On the other hand, according to the assured and considerate factors, which suggested that there is a difference between direct gaze with convex and with hollow eyes, possibly because the perception of the hollow eyes has bigger distribution than that of the convex eyes, so there is a bigger individual difference in hollow eyes than convex eyes. Another reason might be that hollow gazes were perceived as weaker than those of convex eyes even if the duration and frequency were perceived as almost the same. From a correlative value, we can see the relation between evaluation values and subjectivity of the participant; the evaluation value affected by the amount of the direct gaze the participants felt subjectively. Highly rated values (considerate, warm, attentive) were strongly influenced by the amount of gaze perceived.

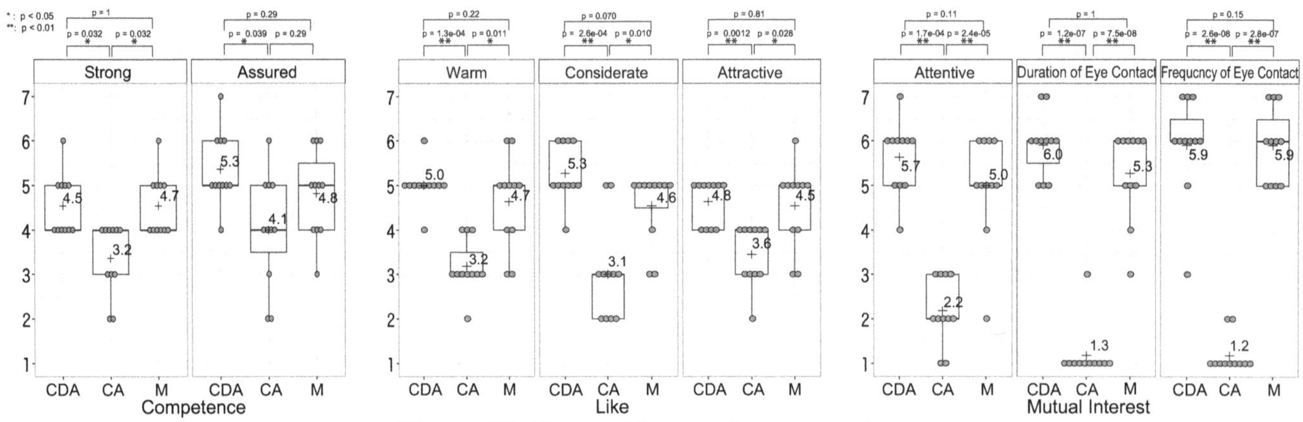

Figure 15: Score of impression on speaker

Table 1: Correlation coefficient between the rating factors and the amount of eye contact receivers felt. (* $p < 0.05$)

	Strong	Assured	Warm	Considerate	Attractive	Attentitive
`Duration`	0.59 *	0.50 *	0.68 *	0.73 *	0.55 *	0.83 *
`Frequency`	0.59 *	0.46 *	0.75 *	0.69 *	0.59 *	0.90 *

There are several of limitations in the results here. First, the gender of the participants was almost entirely limited to male. Therefore, we cannot conclude that the results hold for female or mixed-gender participants.

Second, our results might not be generalizable beyond the current cultural context. We recruited only Japanese students in our experiment. Most Japanese people have positive feelings about robots, which could affect our results positively. In addition to this, Japanese people tend to send less direct gaze during conversations compared to people from other culture [3]. Other cultural differences, such as age and organization, might affect our results.

Third, the effect when the number of participants increases was not considered because we conducted experiments on pairs of people. As Transgazer is designed to be used in situations where the audience does not interact with each other, as in presentations and lectures, we assumed that the interaction dynamics would not change.

Fourth, the position of participants' seats were limited to 20° on both sides. No participants mentioned social messages of eyes, like mocking, even when they received a sidelong glance in our experiments. However, we need further experimentation to determine whether the participants feel unintended social signals at more slanted angles.

Fifth, we did not consider head movement at this time to test the effect of only eye movement.

7. CONCLUSIONS AND FUTURE WORK

This paper has presented a system that allows robots to control their gaze cone by changing eye shape and use the effect of direct and averted gazes for multiple recipients. Using this concept, robots can send an averted or direct gaze to many recipients simultaneously, resulting in more appropriate gazes for each person involved in one-to-many communication. We have described the advantage of this concept: It can use direct and averted gaze effects to receivers broader, and it save costs to achieve eye contact with many receivers on by one. To apply this concept, we have developed a system called Transgazer, which can alternate between convex and hollow eye shapes. We have designed a method to make the change of eye type inconspicuous and to determine eye gaze direction without depth sensors. First, we confirmed that convex eyes can convey gaze direction more accurately, whereas hollow eyes can make eye contact with observers in a wider range of angles. Next, we showed that recipients' impressions of Transgazer improved when it utilized both eye types.

Further study is required for both the system and practical aspects of this work. On the system side, further study of how head movement influences the hollow eye effect is needed. On the practical side, further study is required to determine the effects of each gaze type on the improvement of impression in speech, as in the application example in Section 3.

We also consider the application of this system for telepresence requiring one-to-many communication, such as lectures and speeches. Recently, "Transcendent Telepresence", which enhances positive psychological effects and suppresses negative effects by modifying the information transmitted via telecommunication has been proposed [23, 38]. In telepresence, reducing the speakers' burden is a very important factor. The concept explored in this paper can be applied to telepresence for both speaker- and listener-oriented communication, and realize remote communication that is superior to face-to-face communication.

We believe that this concept will improve one-to-many communication and make a significant contribution to the future of human-robot communication.

8. REFERENCES

[1] S. Al Moubayed, J. Edlund, and J. Beskow. Taming mona lisa: communicating gaze faithfully in 2d and 3d facial projections. *ACM Transactions on Interactive Intelligent Systems*, 1(2):25, 2012.

[2] S. M. Anstis, J. W. Mayhew, and T. Morley. The perception of where a face or television'portrait'is looking. *The American journal of psychology*, 82(4):474–489, 1969.

[3] M. Argyle and M. Cook. *Gaze and mutual gaze.* Cambridge U Press, 1976.

[4] J. B. Bavelas, L. Coates, and T. Johnson. Listener responses as a collaborative process: The role of gaze. *Journal of Communication*, 52(3):566–580, 2002.

[5] N. Bee, E. André, and S. Tober. Breaking the ice in human-agent communication: Eye-gaze based initiation of contact with an embodied conversational agent. In *International Workshop on Intelligent Virtual Agents*, pages 229–242. Springer, 2009.

[6] E. Boyarskaya, A. Sebastian, T. Bauermann, H. Hecht, and O. Tüscher. The mona lisa effect: Neural correlates of centered and off-centered gaze. *Human brain mapping*, 36(2):619–632, 2015.

[7] C. Breazeal, C. D. Kidd, A. L. Thomaz, G. Hoffman, and M. Berlin. Effects of nonverbal communication on efficiency and robustness in human-robot teamwork. In *2005 IEEE/RSJ International Conference on Intelligent Robots and Systems*, pages 708–713. IEEE, 2005.

[8] C. Breazeal and B. Scassellati. A context-dependent attention system for a social robot. *rn*, 255:3, 1999.

[9] M. Cook and J. SMITH. The role of gaze in impression formation. *British journal of social and clinical psychology*, 14(1):19–25, 1975.

[10] J. Driver IV, G. Davis, P. Ricciardelli, P. Kidd, E. Maxwell, and S. Baron-Cohen. Gaze perception triggers reflexive visuospatial orienting. *Visual cognition*, 6(5):509–540, 1999.

[11] N. J. Emery. The eyes have it: the neuroethology, function and evolution of social gaze. *Neuroscience & Biobehavioral Reviews*, 24(6):581–604, 2000.

[12] C. Evinger, K. A. Manning, J. J. Pellegrini, M. A. Basso, A. S. Powers, and P. A. Sibony. Not looking while leaping: the linkage of blinking and saccadic gaze shifts. *Experimental brain research*, 100(2):337–344, 1994.

[13] A. Frischen, A. P. Bayliss, and S. P. Tipper. Gaze cueing of attention: visual attention, social cognition, and individual differences. *Psychological bulletin*, 133(4):694, 2007.

[14] A. Fukayama, T. Ohno, N. Mukawa, M. Sawaki, and N. Hagita. Messages embedded in gaze of interface agents—impression management with agent's gaze. In *Proceedings of the SIGCHI conference on Human factors in computing systems*, pages 41–48. ACM, 2002.

[15] M. Gamer and H. Hecht. Are you looking at me? measuring the cone of gaze. *Journal of Experimental Psychology: Human Perception and Performance*, 33(3):705, 2007.

[16] N. George and L. Conty. Facing the gaze of others. *Neurophysiologie Clinique/Clinical Neurophysiology*, 38(3):197–207, 2008.

[17] R. L. Gregory. *The intelligent eye.* ERIC, 1970.

[18] M. Imai, T. Ono, and H. Ishiguro. Physical relation and expression: Joint attention for human-robot interaction. *IEEE Transactions on Industrial Electronics*, 50(4):636–643, 2003.

[19] B. C. Jones, L. M. DeBruine, A. C. Little, C. A. Conway, and D. R. Feinberg. Integrating gaze direction and expression in preferences for attractive faces. *Psychological Science*, 17(7):588–591, 2006.

[20] A. Kendon. Some functions of gaze-direction in social interaction. *Acta psychologica*, 26:22–63, 1967.

[21] A. Kendon and M. Cook. The consistency of gaze patterns in social interaction. *British Journal of Psychology*, 60(4):481–494, 1969.

[22] M. Kim. Robotic fundraiser. http://www.minsukim.net/Robotic-Fundraiser, 2011.

[23] Y. Kinoshita, M. Yokoyama, K. Suzuki, T. Mochizuki, T. Yamada, S. Sakurai, T. Narumi, T. Tanikawa, and M. Hirose. Transcendent telepresence: tele-communication better than face to face interaction. In *International Conference on Distributed, Ambient, and Pervasive Interactions*, pages 429–438. Springer, 2016.

[24] C. L. Kleinke. Gaze and eye contact: a research review. *Psychological bulletin*, 100(1):78, 1986.

[25] C. L. Kleinke and P. D. Pohlen. Affective and emotional responses as a function of other person's gaze and cooperativeness in a two-person game. *Journal of Personality and Social Psychology*, 17(3):308, 1971.

[26] H. Kobayashi and S. Kohshima. Unique morphology of the human eye and its adaptive meaning: comparative studies on external morphology of the primate eye. *Journal of human evolution*, 40(5):419–435, 2001.

[27] Y. Kuno, K. Sadazuka, M. Kawashima, K. Yamazaki, A. Yamazaki, and H. Kuzuoka. Museum guide robot based on sociological interaction analysis. In *Proceedings of the SIGCHI conference on Human factors in computing systems*, pages 1191–1194. ACM, 2007.

[28] B. Mutlu, J. Forlizzi, and J. Hodgins. A storytelling robot: Modeling and evaluation of human-like gaze behavior. In *2006 6th IEEE-RAS International Conference on Humanoid Robots*, pages 518–523. IEEE, 2006.

[29] B. Mutlu, T. Shiwa, T. Kanda, H. Ishiguro, and N. Hagita. Footing in human-robot conversations: how robots might shape participant roles using gaze cues. In *Proceedings of the 4th ACM/IEEE international conference on Human robot interaction*, pages 61–68. ACM, 2009.

[30] K. Nichols and B. Champness. Eye gaze and the gsr. *Journal of Experimental Social Psychology*, 7(6):623–626, 1971.

[31] Oculus. Oculus ovrlipsync for unity 5 v1.0.1-beta. https://developer3.oculus.com/downloads/.

[32] J. P. Otteson and C. R. Otteson. Effect of teacher's gaze on children's story recall. *Perceptual and Motor Skills*, 1980.

[33] R. A. Rensink, J. K. O'Regan, and J. J. Clark. To see or not to see: The need for attention to perceive changes in scenes. *Psychological science*, 8(5):368–373, 1997.

[34] D. N. Saito, H. C. Tanabe, K. Izuma, M. J. Hayashi, Y. Morito, H. Komeda, H. Uchiyama, H. Kosaka, H. Okazawa, Y. Fujibayashi, et al. "stay tuned": inter-individual neural synchronization during mutual gaze and joint attention. *Frontiers in integrative neuroscience*, 4:127, 2010.

[35] D. Sakamoto, T. Kanda, T. Ono, H. Ishiguro, and N. Hagita. Android as a telecommunication medium

with a human-like presence. In *Human-Robot Interaction (HRI), 2007 2nd ACM/IEEE International Conference on*, pages 193–200. IEEE, 2007.

[36] L. Scherwitz and R. Helmreich. Interactive effects of eye contact and verbal content on interpersonal attraction in dyads. *Journal of Personality and Social Psychology*, 25(1):6, 1973.

[37] H. R. Schiffman. *Sensation and perception: An integrated approach* . John Wiley & Sons, 1990.

[38] K. Suzuki, M. Yokoyama, Y. Kionshita, T. Mochizuki, T. Yamada, S. Sakurai, T. Narumi, T. Tanikawa, and M. Hirose. Gender-impression modification enhances the effect of mediated social touch between persons of the same gender. *Augmented Human Research*, 1(1):2, 2016.

[39] D. Todorović. Geometrical basis of perception of gaze direction. *Vision research*, 46(21):3549–3562, 2006.

[40] N. J. Wade and P. Hughes. Fooling the eyes: trompe l'oeil and reverse perspective. *Perception*, 28(9):1115–1119, 1999.

[41] J. E. W. Wallin. *Optical illusions of reversible perspective: A volume of historical and experimental researches.* The author, 1905.

[42] P. H. Waxer. Nonverbal cues for anxiety: An examination of emotional leakage. *Journal of abnormal psychology*, 86(3):306, 1977.

[43] Y. Yoshikawa, K. Shinozawa, H. Ishiguro, N. Hagita, and T. Miyamoto. Responsive robot gaze to interaction partner. In *Robotics: Science and systems*, 2006.

Persistent Lexical Entrainment in HRI

Jürgen Brandstetter
HITLabNZ
juergen.brandstetter
@pg.canterbury.ac.nz

Clay Beckner
NZILBB
clayton.beckner
@canterbury.ac.nz

Eduardo Benitez Sandoval
HITLabNZ
eduardo.sandoval
@pg.canterbury.ac.nz

Christoph Bartneck
HITLabNZ
christoph.bartneck
@canterbury.ac.nz

Keywords

HRI; Persuasive Robotics; Lexical Entrainment

ABSTRACT

In this study, we set out to ask three questions. First, does lexical entrainment with a robot interlocutor persist after an interaction? Second, how does the influence of social robots on humans compare with the influence of humans on each other? Finally, what role is played by personality traits in lexical entrainment to robots, and how does this compare with the role of personality in entrainment to other humans?

Our experiment shows that first, robots can indeed prompt lexical entrainment that persists after an interaction is over. This finding is interesting since it demonstrates that speakers can be linguistically influenced by a robot, in a way that is not merely motivated by a desire to be understood. Second, we find similarities between lexical entrainment to the robot peer and lexical entrainment to a human peer, although the effects are stronger when the peer is human. Third, we find that whether the peer is a robot or a human, similar personality traits contribute to lexical entrainment. In both peer conditions, participants who score higher on "Openness to experience" are more likely to adopt less conventional terminology.

1. INTRODUCTION

It is known from numerous studies that when people talk, they influence each other's speech patterns, that is, speakers converge on similar linguistic features [1, 11, 14, 25, 26, 35, 36]. Convergent phenomena are known to occur with respect to pronunciations, speech rate, and sentence structure, among other domains. In the current study, we are particularly interested in word choice. Even though in a conversation, speakers have a wide range of words to choose from to refer to the same entity, once one speaker chooses a particular reference term, his or her interlocutors tend to follow suit by using the same term [11, 13]. The tendency for speakers to imitate one another's vocabulary choices is known as **lexical entrainment**.

A variety of studies have shown evidence that people adjust their speech when interacting with machines, including robots and speech recognition systems [4, 10, 27]. However, it is important to note that, in general, speakers may have various reasons for adjusting their speech. For instance, speakers may shift their language output toward that of interlocutors they hold in high regard [16], suggesting that convergence is motivated by a desire for social solidarity or prestige. On the other hand, speakers may adjust their speech simply to make it easier for their interlocutor to understand. Note that speakers might be especially motivated by the second mechanism – easing comprehensibility – if they have a poor opinion of their interlocutor's language abilities. Such considerations cause people to make particular adjustments when addressing a non-native language speaker, such as speaking slower and louder, and using simplified vocabulary and grammar [5, 12, 28, 32].

Indeed, Branigan et al. [8] observe that much of the existing research on linguistic accommodation to machines may, in fact, represent this latter kind of speech shift – motivated by an attempt to be understood by a device that is far from an expert in one's native language. Such could be the case with previous robot research by Iio et al. [17, 18]. In that study, lexical entrainment is measured only during the course of interaction with a robot interlocutor. For purposes of facilitating communication (and completing the assigned experimental task), it is only natural to switch to terms the robot already uses. If switches are made solely for immediate, practical purposes, they may very well not persist beyond the limited scope of interactions with a robot. In contrast, it is known that the effects of human-to-human interactions can be extended to new conversation partners, and they play a role in language change over time [13].

In this study, we thus test carefully for both similarities and differences between human-robot lexical entrainment and human-human lexical entrainment. We set out to investigate lexical entrainment to robots, such that we can rule out mere communicative facilitation, in contrast with previous research [17, 18]. Thus, in our experimental design, we measure lexical entrainment effects which linger after the interaction phase is completed. Moreover, we will compare our lexical entrainment results with a robot peer against a

HRI '17, March 06-09, 2017, Vienna, Austria

DOI: http://dx.doi.org/10.1145/2909824.3020257

control condition, in which a human actor takes the place of the robot.

It is anticipated that it may be challenging to observe shifts in word choice which are not motivated by communicative facilitation. We note, for instance, that in previous research based on Solomon Asch's conformity studies, participants failed to converge to robots in their choice of English past tenses when there was no communicative incentive to do so [3, 7]. Thus, in an attempt to maximize the influence of robots, we ask participants to engage in a collaborative exercise with robots, to observe if this setup will encourage them to accept the robots as social peers. The collaborative exercise is based on a navigation task that requires interaction and teamwork. In this task, the participant and the robot have to help each other navigate on a field, such that one team member needs to move on the field, while the partner has the required map.

Our collaborative exercise is designed to encourage the participant to develop a sense of in-group belonging with his/her partner (whether robot or human). We prompted each participant/peer pairing to be competitive against other teams performing the tasks, with respect to the amount of time required to finish. This team-building approach creates a situation where the the participant and robot/actor are part of the same in-group, and define themselves against competitor out-groups [22]. The social effects of in-groups are well-documented; individuals are known to trust in-group members more than out-group members [24, p. 695] [29, p. 335]. Furthermore, the effect of in-group/out-group membership can be observed between humans and robots[22]. People are more likely to favour answers from their own in-group than from the out-group. The effect of in- and out-groups can also be found in linguistic settings [34]. Unger et. al. find that participants in an in-group will mimic their interlocutors more than if the interlocutor is from an out-group.

1.1 Research questions

The aim of our study is to see whether social robots can influence human language beyond the time of interaction. Furthermore, we want to see how social robots compare to humans in the same task. With this in mind we built the interaction so as to test the following research questions:

1. Is it possible for a social robot to prompt lexical entrainment that persists even after the interaction with the robot is complete?
2. Does the influence of social robots to humans align with the influence of humans on each other? Is the effect stronger in one condition compared to the other?
3. What role is played by personality traits in lexical entrainment to robots, and how does this compare in lexical entrainment to other humans?

2. STIMULUS SELECTION

Before we could start experimenting with lexical entrainment, we had to find image stimuli on which to influence and test the participants. Since the items need to be used as visual reference points, we obtained highly imageable words from the MRC Psycholinguistic Database [37]. We chose ninety-nine items from the MRC list, and sought corresponding images to serve as simple, schematic prompts that would be visible within a complex map grid. We collected icon images using the www.flaticon.com database, limiting our results to images which are licensed under the Creative Commons Licence or Flaticon Basic License. Example images appear within the map layout of Fig. 2. The next step was to generate a list of possible terms for each of the ninety-nine items. To do so, in a pilot study we asked twelve volunteers to generate as many words as possible for all ninety-nine icons. For each icon we sorted the responses to determine which terms are most likely understandable by future participants.

The final step was to finalize a set of eighty icons to be used in the experiment. During this selection process we avoided the inclusion of any icons that overlapped in their candidate terms to avoid cross-item priming effects. For example, both a work boot and a deck shoe might prompt "shoe", and thus one of these icons would be disqualified. An illustration of an icon plus example candidate terms can be seen in Table 1.

Ultimately, the eighty selected icons are split into two halves: 40 items are designated as distractor items, and 40 are designated as stimulus items. For the distractor items, it will be the participant's job to provide directions to his or her navigation partner. For the stimulus items, it will be the navigation partner's job to direct the participant; it is thus on these items that peer influence will be exerted. Distractor items are used to distract the participant from the real experiment, and to give him/her the impression of a reciprocal collaboration.

The baseline naming study discussed above was used to establish an "Expected Term List" for the 80 icons used in the experiment, containing all the words that volunteers used as names for the items. This list is used as a database during the experiment, to allow for smooth interactions in response to participants' verbal responses. Moreover, based on the Expected Term List, for each of the 40 stimulus icons, we selected two top candidates (the "Preferred Pair") as options available to the participant's (robot/actor) peer, to influence the participant over the course of the experiment.

Icon	Candidate Term
	• Alligator • Crocodile • ...
	• Soldier • Terrorist • ...

Table 1: Excerpt of icons plus terms from the Expected Term List

3. EXPERIMENTAL SETUP

The basic experimental design follows a pre-/main-/post-task setup. In the pre-task, we recorded what the participant named the items we presented to them, and used this information to customize the influence exerted during the main task. In the main, collaborative task, the robot/actor peer introduces new words for some of the items, i.e., in selected instances, the peer's terms differ from the participant's pre-task terms. Finally, in the post-task, we again record what the participant calls the same icons. The influence of the main task on the post-task is then analyzed.

As an important element of this experiment design, we wanted to see how robot influence compares to human influence. Thus, some participants were paired with a robot partner – a robot with a synthesized female voice, which we introduced as "Helen". Participants in a different condition were paired with a female actor (also named "Helen"). Our goal was to keep the two conditions as similar as possible, thus limiting the change only to body shape (robot vs. human), but using the same voice in each case. This, of course, created the problem of having to provide an excuse for why the actor has a synthesized voice. We made a decision to tell the participant that they are in a control condition, and that it was necessary to use the same, artificial voice that we were using with a different group of participants.

Figure 1: Shows a successful and non-successful robot influence comparing between the pre- and post-tasks.

The context in which participants are tested is a map navigation task. The general form of this task works as follows: the two participants have both a map, in which stimulus icons designate individual navigation points on the map. There is only one correct route to navigate from one side of the map to the other. To make it a collaborative task, the two participants hold each other's map, such that teamwork is required to navigate successfully. The goal is to see if a newly introduced term from one participant is picked up by the other.

To control what the robot/actor does and says during the experiment we use a hidden operator, in a Wizard-of-Oz paradigm. The operator's job is to control what the robot/actor says during the experiment and to record the participant's selections. To make sure conditions are comparable to each other, the operator has to strictly follow a predefined script.

3.1 Implementation

This section is intended to give, first, an overview of how the navigation task is implemented from the participant's perspective, and second, how this task is implemented from the operator's perspective. Moreover, it will give an overview of how the experiment's scenario is presented to the participant as a collaborative task.

3.1.1 Map task: The participant's job

In the navigation task, each participant (also the actor/robot) sees a map on a screen in front of them with a virtual avatar representing either themselves or the partner. The map itself is composed of hexagonal tiles with stimulus icons on them. Some of these tiles are yellow bordered, indicating that this is a safe path/tile to step on (see Figure 2). The goal is to navigate the avatar from tile to tile (step by step) by only stepping on the yellow bordered tiles.

Figure 2: Excerpt of the game board. The yellow bordered hexagon field show the correct path. The red arrow highlights the avatar which represents the participant or robot/actor.

Since we have two different types of tasks (pre-/post-task and main-task), the way to move the avatar on the map is slightly different. The difference depends on if the participant is alone in the room or is collaborating with the robot/actor. For the pre-/post-task the participant will see his/her own avatar on the map and will also see his/her own correct path. For the main-task, the participant will see his/her own avatar on a map without the correct path, and – on a different map – the partner's avatar, with the correct path highlighted.

The actions the participant has to take for the two types of tasks work as follows. In the pre-/post-task the participant is presented with a marked map; no navigational partner is present, so for each response, the participant merely says aloud the name of the icon on the next highlighted hexagon. In the main-task the participant and the robot/actor take turns. If it is the participant's turn to move, the robot/actor will tell the participant what icon to move to next. In this case the participant will use the computer mouse to click on the map space with the appropriate icon. If it is the robot's/actor's turn to move, the participant will tell the robot/actor what icon to move to next. Turn by turn, each participant and robot/actor character will move closer to the end of the map until the task is over.

3.1.2 Map task: The operator's job

While the participant works through the pre-/main-/post-tasks the operator's job is to perform the speech-to-text recognition that enters participant responses, and to initiate system responses at context-appropriate times. The specific responses of the robot/actor are determined by the participant's pre-task answers and a pre-set script, as described below in Section 3.5.

While entering participant responses, the operator has available a set of likely names for each item (the "Expected Term List") to allow the experiment to proceed smoothly. During the pre-/post-task, as the participant provides the name of each item, the operator simply clicks on the appropriate term from the Expected Term List. If the participant uses a term not on the list, the operator simply records it as "OTHER."

During the main, collaborative task, the actions the operator take are slightly different, as follows. If the participant uses a word from the Expected Term List, the operator will click this term's button, which will prompt the robot/actor to move to the appropriate icon on the map. Additionally, the robot/actor will say "I'll move to the [word]". In case the word is not in the list, but it is a correct term for the given icon, the operator can click on the OTHER button. This will also make the robot/actor move forward but will prompt the robot to say "OK".

3.1.3 Scenario

Linguistic research shows that social connection is needed to influence language [33], and passive exposure to speech (especially robot speech) may be insufficient to change behaviour [3, 7]. Thus, we set out to devise a collaborative experimental task which would foster a sense of social connection with a partner. Moreover, we encouraged the sense that the participant and their robot (or actor) peer formed an in-group, and could be contrasted against out-groups (see Section 1).

Toward this end, we presented participants with the map described above, and described the following scenario: *Both of you are lost in the middle of the Forest of Random Things. You have to navigate across the landscape to reach the edge. You need to follow the yellow bordered tiles, as you did in the previous task. It is important to only step on the yellow bordered tiles, and not on the other tiles.*

You and your partner must collaborate by telling each other which hexagon to travel to next. The trick is that each of you has the map that your partner needs. You must help each other navigate, and have to take turns. You can only take one step before the other one can take a step. For this task, you will use your mouse to click on the tile that your partner tells you to move to, rather than moving your own character, and the same applies to your partner.

You and your partner are a team, and you are competing against other teams who will be doing the same task. The goal is to be faster than other teams. Try not to make mistakes, so you can travel to the end of the map faster than other teams.

3.2 Procedure

The series of tasks for an experiment participant proceed as follows. (See Figure 3). First, the participant is welcomed by the operator into the experimental room where s/he is asked to take a seat. At this stage, the operator gives a short introduction about the general tasks and asks the participant to sign the consent form. Next, the operator start a tutorial level of the pre-task. After the participant becomes familiar with the setup and knows how to use the speech-to-text system to navigate around the map, the operator loads the pre-task. During the pre-task the operator moves to his/her desk where s/he is invisible to the participant and waits until the participant finishes the pre-task. Next, the operator asks the participant to fill out a demographic survey and complete a personality test, while the operator brings in the robot/actor. Before the robot/actor and participant proceed to the main-task, the operator will introduce them to a scenario (see above). After that the operator loads the main-task tutorial, so the robot/actor and the participant can practice the task. As soon as they are ready, the operator loads the main-task. After about ten minutes, the main-task is over and the operator will leave

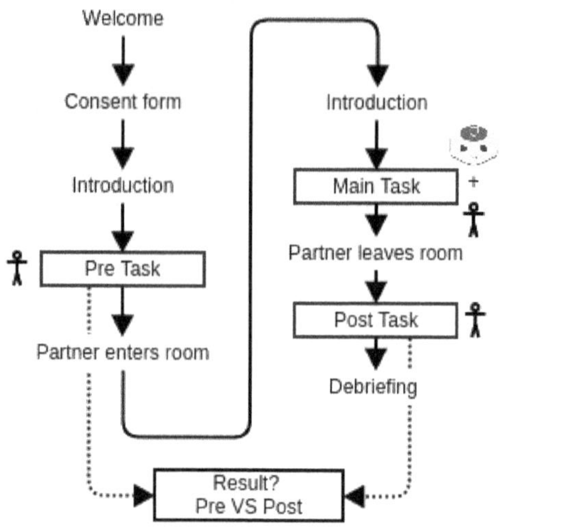

Figure 3: The experimental procedure a participant will go through.

the room with the robot/actor. After the operator comes back, he/she loads the post-task and asks the participant to finish it. At the end, the participant gets debriefed and received $10.

3.3 Apparatus

The apparatus consists of a table with two monitors on it, an Aldebaran NAO robot or actor, a microphone and an extra computer. The computer was used to control the recording, run the map system and to start/control the experimental conditions. The participant and the robot/actor are positioned opposite to each other. The angle of the monitors is set in a way that the participant and the robot/actor can see one another's faces; however, their monitor displays are not visible to each other.

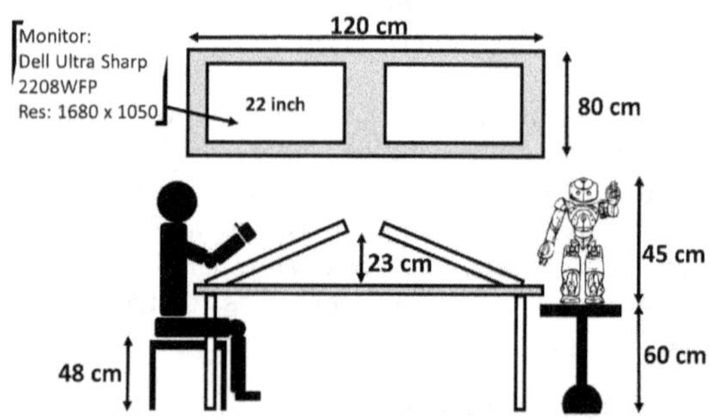

Figure 4: Schematic depiction of the physical setup with accurate physical dimensions.

3.4 Participants

Forty participants were recruited at the University of Canterbury, including students and staff. Subjects received a voucher in the amount of $10 NZD for participating. All participants were native New Zealand English speakers. The average age of our participants was 23.7 years, whereas the oldest was 45 years and the youngest was 18 years. 55% of the participants reported themselves as male and 45% of the participants reported themselves as female. Out of the 40 participants, 20 were assigned to the robot-peer condition and 20 to the human-peer condition.

3.5 Map task: The computer's job

The responses generated by the robot/actor are based on a script in which we define the behaviour the robot/actor should have. This behaviour comes partially from the pre-task, which establishes what term the participant used at the beginning of the experiment, and partially from an individual initialization, which defines (a) the random pre-assignment of influence strategies for each item (explained below), and (b) the random sequence of stimulus items. Please refer to table 2 for an excerpt from one set of random initial conditions. This same setting would be implemented with two different participants: one in the robot peer condition, and a matched participant in the human peer condition.

The influence strategies are designed so as to be variable for each participant: on some items, the navigation term used by robot/actor should CHANGE from the participant's pre-task term. On other items, the navigation term should MATCH the pre-task term. The balancing of CHANGE and MATCH robot behaviours (20 items of each, for each individual condition) is intended to allow for statistical comparisons of behaviours under different circumstances, that is, when new terms are introduced by the peer, and when they are not. Moreover, matching the participant's pre-task term some of the time avoids making the peer's vocabulary manipulation too obvious.

Since responses in the experiment are open-ended, it is impossible to anticipate every response by participants, and matching (or systematically changing from) these responses is potentially quite complex. On the other hand, in many cases the same responses are volunteered by a large number of participants. We elected to draw on our experiment's pilot study (see Section 2) to provide the robot/actor a repertoire of two possible terms to choose from (the "Preferred Pair"). This more controlled approach was felt to be preferable to presenting participants with an open-ended set of prompts. The CHANGE/MATCH designations were thus implemented as follows. If, on a particular experiment run, an item is designated as a MATCH, and the participant's pre-task answer is in the Preferred Pair (e.g., "crocodile"), the robot's/actor's navigation term is also "crocodile"). If the item was designated as a CHANGE, the robot/actor will answer with the other item from the pair ("alligator"). If the participant's pre-task answer is not one of the Preferred Pair items, it is necessary to choose at random one of the Preferred Pair items for the robot's response. Note that this approach means that some items originally designated as MATCH items, are effectively treated as CHANGE items. However, this approach still results in the robot/actor matching the participant's original selection approximately one-third of the time.

4. RESULTS

4.1 Peer condition comparisons: Matching specified targets

To study the effects of peer influence on post-task responses, we designated a semi-arbitrary set of response terms as "targets". In the present analysis, we label as the "target" the less likely of the two available peer responses, as determined by the pre-task (across all participants). [1] The analysis thus measures, as its dependent variable, whether or not the participant's post-task response was the target response.

Table 3 shows raw numbers of how often, in each peer condition, the participant already matched the target of interest at the pre-task stage. In the human-peer condition, participants' pre-task answers matched the target 10.31% of the time, compared with 12.10% for participants in the robot-peer condition. Calculating an average (by participant) target-matching score for the pre-task reveals that there are no significant differences between the two peer conditions; ($t(35.16) = -1.240$, $p = .22$).

Moreover, the peer influence during the navigation phase is also matched across the two peer conditions. That is, there are no cross-condition differences in how often the (robot, human) peer matched the target. The raw counts are shown in Table 4. In sum, robot peers matched the target items 50.03% of time, compared with 49.49% of human peers. Analysis of the average target-matching score (grouped by participant, but focusing on the peer's behaviour) reveals that there are no significant differences between the two peer conditions in the navigation phase: ($t(37.50) = 0.234$, $p = .82$).

Since the tendency to match target items – in the pre-task as well as the navigation phase – is matched across the two peer conditions, we are justified in making comparisons across these peer conditions in the post-task results.

Indeed, differences are evident between the post-task responses between the robot and human peer conditions. Table 5 shows the raw numbers of post-task matches to the target items, by condition. In the robot peer condition, participants matched the target 24.04% of the time in the post-task, as compared with 32.07% of the time in the human peer condition. Comparing participant-specific average target-match scores shows that there is a significant difference in the post-task ($t(36.30) = 2.532$, $p = .016$).

4.2 Analysis 1: Effect of the navigation peer, and differences by peer condition

The foregoing analyses shows that there are broad differences in behaviours between the human and robot peer conditions. However, we now perform more fine-grained analyses to explore the experiment dynamics in detail. First, we use logistic mixed-effects regression to investigate whether (a) a significant difference exists in post-task responses between human and robot conditions, as suggested above, and (b) whether, in *both* conditions, the influence of the navigation partner is, in fact, significant.

In our regression modeling, we include several predictors as categorical variables. First, as a between-subjects variable, we note the PEER CONDITION (robot or human). As an additional variable, we note whether the participant's preferred response (during the pre-task) matched the target. Inclusion of this predictor (PRE-TASK_ MATCH_ TARGET) is necessary to account for the fact that some pre-task responses already match the target (see Table 3). Finally,

[1] Note that the present analysis also works in a separate analysis, if the more likely response is chosen as the designated target.The designation of one target vs. another is not essential.

item	Navigator	PreferredTerm1	PreferredTerm2	change
thief	robot	robber	thief	CHANGE
axe	participant	NA-distractor	NA-distractor	NA-distractor
dog	robot	dog	wolf	MATCH

Table 2: An excerpt of an input setting file for one participant.

	human condition	robot condition
does not match target	696	684
matches target	80	94
TOTAL	776	778

Table 3: Breakdown of matches to target term: subject's answer during pre-task.

	human condition	robot condition
does not match target	388	393
matches target	388	385
TOTAL	776	778

Table 4: Breakdown of matches to target term: peer choice during interaction (main task).

the variable PEER_ MATCH_ TARGET notes whether the peer (whether robot or human) matched the target term during the collaborative task (see Table 4). This variable is the crucial indicator of the presence or absence of influence by the peer. The dependent variable is a TRUE or FALSE variable, corresponding to whether the participant used the target word during post-task responses.

We performed logistic mixed-effects regression, incorporating random intercepts for participants and items [19]. The model also incorporates random slopes: for each participant, the slope is allowed to vary for PRE-TASK_MATCH_ TARGET and PEER_MATCH_TARGET, and for each item, the slope is allowed to vary for PEER CONDITION. The resulting model is summarised in Table 6.

The model indicates the following. First, matching the target in the pre-task (PRE-TASK_MATCH_TARGET) is a significant predictor of matching in the post-task. If a participant was already using the target word in the pre-task, he or she is likely to continue doing so in the post-task. This result is unsurprising, but it represents a factor that needed to be controlled to verify influence of the peer.

Secondly, as a general main effect, the peer's use of the target term in the navigation phase (PEER_MATCH_TARGET) is a significant predictor of matching the target during the post-task. Thus, in both conditions, the robot or actor's choice of the target terms was likely to prompt use of this term by the participant, after the peer interaction was completed. This main effect provides evidence of significant influence by the partner, in *both* robot and human conditions.

	human condition	robot condition
does not match target	528	591
matches target	248	187
TOTAL	776	778

Table 5: Breakdown of matches to target term: subject's answer during post-task.

Thirdly, the influence of the navigation partner is stronger overall in the human condition, compared with the robot condition. This is evident from the interaction between PEER CONDITION and PEER_MATCH_TARGET. This interaction is shown in the effect plot of Figure 5. Note that the peer condition (robot or human) is not significant as a main effect in this model. This is not surprising because the data for this model includes both cases where the peer did, and cases where the peer did not, introduce a new term during the navigation task. The difference between conditions is evident only when the peer could have conceivably prompted a switch to the target item, i.e., from the PEER CONDITION and PEER_ MATCH_ TARGET interaction.

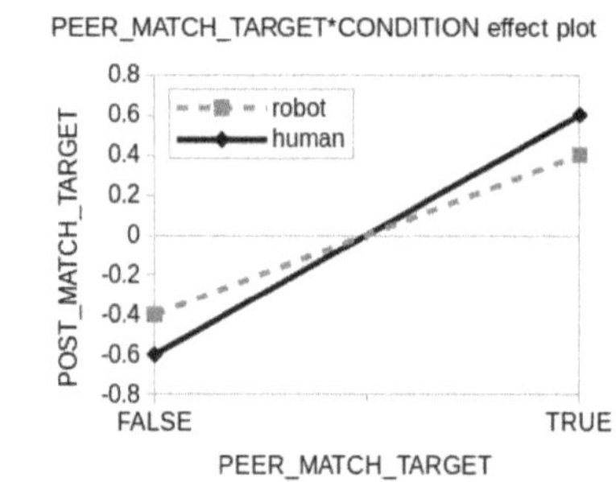

Figure 5: Interaction plot from the model in Table 6

4.3 Peer condition comparisons: Switching to peer's term

The foregoing analyses examine all participant responses in the post-task, including cases where the peer did not exert any relevant influence on word choice (that is, because the participant was already using the same term in the pre-task, and thus could not switch). We may perform even finer-grained analyses by focusing only on responses where the participant had a meaningful opportunity to change to the peer's word choice.

Thus we may ask: focusing on instances where the peer introduces a term that is new to the participant, how often does the participant switch to the new term? We consider this question, first of all, as an average measure for each participant. This measure is summarized in Figure 6, which shows density plots of participant aggregates (grouped by peer condition). This plot shows that overall, clearly it is more likely for participants who are paired with a human to switch terms, as compared to participants paired with a robot peer. In the human-peer condition, participants switch to their peer's term on 61.12% of all opportunities to do so (across participants, SD = 20.53). By comparison, participants switch 38.92% of the time to a robot peer's term (SD = 18.65). This difference is statistically significant ($t(37.65) = 3.58$, $p < .001$). However, it is notewor-

	Estimate	Std.Error	z value	pval
(Intercept)	-5.04	0.59	-8.51	< .001
PRE-TASK_MATCH_TARGET	3.15	0.48	6.62	< .001
PEER_CONDITION = robot	0.84	0.63	1.34	0.18
PEER_MATCH_TARGET	5.23	0.69	7.57	< .001
CONDITION =robot* PEER_MATCH_TARGET	-1.83	0.82	-2.22	0.03

Table 6: Regression model summary.

thy that much cross-participant variation exists within each condition, and a considerable overlap exists across the two conditions; see the double-shaded region in the middle of the density plot. That is, there are some participants in the robot-peer condition who switch terms more often than some participants in the human-peer condition.

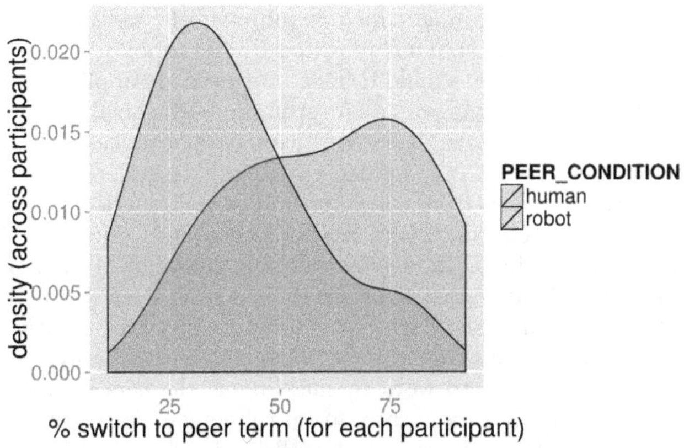

Figure 6: Cross-participant tendencies to switch to peer's term

4.4 Analysis 2: Switching terms, term likelihood, and personality traits

Next, we perform additional regression analyses, focusing only on the subset of the data where the participant had the opportunity to shift to the peer's term. In this analysis, the dependent variable is a TRUE vs. FALSE response, indicating whether or not the participant switched to a new term introduced by the peer.

In this model, as one predictor, we again have the PEER CONDITION (robot vs. human). Secondly, we have the PRIOR PROBABILITY of the word introduced by the peer. This measure represents how likely a particular word is as a response to a particular image, as indicated by a population of task participants. Specifically, to quantify the prior probability of a term, we calculate how often this particular response was offered by 58 participants in a pre-task. (This group consists of the 40 individuals in the current study, plus 18 from a separate pilot study). Thus, for instance, for an icon of a coffee cup, the prior probability of the word "cup" is .379, since this proportion of 58 respondents volunteered "cup". For the same image, the word "mug" has a prior probability of .121. We predict that prior probability of a term will give some indication of how appropriate, and how accessible, a particular label is for a given picture. Responses that, in the population as a whole, are more probable in the pre-task should be easier to prompt via peer influence as individuals' responses in the post-task.

As additional predictors, from the Big-Five personality traits [23], we investigated the influence of two traits in the task: Agreeableness, and Openness to experience. These two traits are chosen since there are theoretical motivations for a link between self-reported personality measures and tendencies to imitate other social agents. "Openness", as an element of the Big-Five, is said to encompass a range of linked personality traits, including curiosity and (most relevantly for the present experiment) an affinity for variety and novel experiences [23]. Previous research has shown that participants who are more "open" are more likely to imitate linguistic behaviours of their interlocutors [2]. "Agreeableness" on the other hand, describes how cooperative/compliant a person is, compared to quarrelsome/distrustful [20]. To acquire the Big-Five personality values we chose the TIPI test [15]. This test is a simple, fast and valid assessment system for the Big-Five which is not only used in the psychology community but also by other robotics researchers [30].

We performed logistic mixed-effects regression, including random intercepts for participants (random slope for PRIOR PROBABILITY) and items (random slope for PEER CONDITION and OPENNESS). The best-fitting model is summarised in Table 7. Agreeableness of the participant was not found to be significant, and it is thus excluded from the model. However, there were significant effects for PEER CONDITION, PRIOR PROBABILITY, and the participant's OPENNESS.

In this model, we first note that PEER CONDITION predicts switching; participants who have interacted with a human peer are more likely to switch terms than participants who interacted with a robot. Note that, in this model, peer condition is significant as a main effect (not just as an interaction), since in this dataset, we have restricted our focus to items where a peer-influenced switch could take place.

Secondly, we note that PRIOR PROBABILITY predicts participants' tendency to switch terms. Participants are more likely to adopt a word which has a high prior probability of use. However, note that in the model, this PRIOR PROBABILITY effect does not interact with PEER CONDITION. This suggests that the same kind of influence may be at work in the robot condition and the human condition; participants are more swayed by responses that are highly common (and thus presumably highly suitable) responses.

Finally, we note that the "openness" of the participant does not, as a main effect, predict the tendency to switch to the peer's term. However, this personality trait does interact with PRIOR PROBABILITY in a sensible way. This interaction can be visualised in the effect plot in Figure 7. This plot shows that participants who are less "open" to new experiences tend to carefully adhere to PRIOR PROBABILITY with respect to degree of influence; high-probability re-

	Estimate	Std.Error	z value	pval
(Intercept)	0.55	0.30	1.86	0.06
PEER_CONDITION = robot	-1.21	0.37	-3.315	< .001
PRIOR_PROBABILITY (item)	2.59	0.51	5.13	< .001
OPENNESS (participant)	0.25	0.18	1.36	0.18
PRIOR_PROB * OPENNESS	-0.94	0.42	-2.23	0.03

Table 7: Regression model summary: Tendency to switch to peer's term.

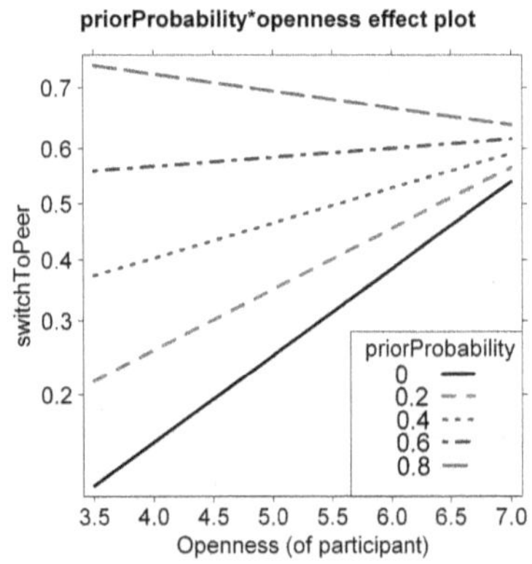

Figure 7: Interaction plot for subject personality*item predictability

sponses are likely to trigger a switch, but low-probability responses are unlikely. However, participants who score higher on OPENNESS are more likely to adopt all kinds of words introduced by their peer; such participants switch to low-probability terms in addition to high-probability ones. Interestingly, there is no interaction with PEER CONDITION; the personality trait seems to operate similarly whether the navigation peer was a human or a robot.

5. CONCLUSION & IMPLICATIONS

In this work, our aim is to see if a social robot can influence the word choice of a human interlocutor. We developed an experimental design in which the robot/actor and the human have to help each other proceed on a virtual game board. Moreover, to show to what extent the robot can influence the human, we created a pre-/main-/post-task experiment. By comparing the pre- and post-task we can study the influence of the robot. Furthermore, we are interested on how a social robot compares with a human actor.

Regarding the questions asked in the introduction section, whether social robots prompt lexical entrainment and whether it persists, the answer is yes. The current experiment proves that participants will shift their word choices to be more similar to those of robot interlocutors. This result supports previous lexical entrainment findings in a different context [17, 18], but extends such findings further. The current study measured effects separately from interactive tasks, and the entrainment is thus not merely for communicative ease. It is important to note that the timescale between the interaction with the robot and the measurement was about 30 minutes. Whether this short-term persistence also leads to long-term persistence is not yet tested by us. However, studies by Garrod et al.[13] support the notion that continued exposure and cooperation can lead to changes, and shared linguistic conventions, in a network of agents.

Looking at the influence of the robot compared to the actor, we can say that the lexical entrainment is similar under both conditions. However, as expected the robot's influence on humans was significantly weaker than the actor's (human-human). The reason why this could be is that robots might have a lower social status than humans. Furthermore, humans might include more subtle and unrecognised cues which were not repeated by the robot.

At this point, we should think about possible implications of persistent language change prompted by social robots. This is especially the case when we look at the sheer numbers of robots in development. We can consider, for instance, indicators from sales per unit, where service robots already overtook industrial robots. An overall purchase of 2.3 million units on industrial robots in the year 2011, compared to 2.5 million units of service robots is already a reality [38]. Second, the development can be observed in areas where robots are planned to be introduced, like classrooms, as help in offices, to work in sales, or as cleaners at home [6, 9, 21, 31]. If, in any case, social robots gain traction like service robots, and are used for all kinds of social interaction, they might have enough "power" to affect the language of a whole population. This effect is particular interesting to study when institutions, for example Apple or Google, provide the speech system for the robots. Any change such an institution makes on their speech system will most likely take immediate effect on all robots via updates. That means that whoever provides the future speech systems for robots, might hold the key for future language development in their hands.

6. RECOGNITIONS

This project was made possible through the support of a Sub-award under a grant to Northwestern University from the John Templeton Foundation (Award ID 36617). The opinions expressed in this publication are those of the author(s) and do not necessarily reflect the views of the John Templeton Foundation. Beckner was also supported by a Rutherford Discovery Fellowship awarded to the NZILBB.

This project was approved by the University Canterbury Ethics Committee: HEC APPLICATION 2015 / 17 / LR-PS and the Northwestern University Ethics Committee: STU00200941. A special thanks goes to the actor Latifah Almanea and to the research assistant Alia Hope-Wilson. We also want to thank the HITLabNZ for the material and facilities as well as supporting Brandstetter.

7. REFERENCES

[1] C. Abrego-Collier, J. Grove, M. Sonderegger, and A. C. L. Yu. Effects of speaker evaluation on phonetic

convergence. In *Proc. Int. Congress of the Phonetic Sciences, Hong Kong*, 2011.

[2] C. Alan, C. Abrego-Collier, and M. Sonderegger. Phonetic imitation from an individual-difference perspective: Subjective attitude, personality and 'autistic' traits. *PloS one*, 8(9):e74746, 2013.

[3] C. Beckner, P. Racz, J. Hay, J. Brandstetter, and C. Bartneck. Participants Conform to Humans but Not to Humanoid Robots in an English Past Tense Formation Task. *Journal of Language and Social Psychology*, 35(2), Apr. 2016.

[4] L. Bell, J. Gustafson, and M. Heldner. Prosodic adaptation in human-computer interaction. In *Proceedings of ICPHS*, volume 3, pages 833–836, 2003.

[5] H. Bortfeld and S. E. Brennan. Use and acquisition of idiomatic expressions in referring by native and non-native speakers. *Discourse Processes*, 23(2):119–147, 1997.

[6] J. Brandstetter and N. Liebman. Fidgebot : Working Out while Working. In *Proceedings of the Tenth Annual ACM/IEEE International Conference on Human-Robot Interaction Extended Abstracts*, volume 02-05-Marc, pages 149–150, 2015.

[7] J. Brandstetter, P. Racz, C. Beckner, E. B. Sandoval, J. Hay, and C. Bartneck. A peer pressure experiment: Recreation of the Asch conformity experiment with robots. In *2014 IEEE/RSJ International Conference on Intelligent Robots and Systems*, pages 1335–1340. IEEE, Sept. 2014.

[8] H. P. Branigan, M. J. Pickering, J. Pearson, and J. F. McLean. Linguistic alignment between people and computers. *Journal of Pragmatics*, 42:2355–2368, 2010.

[9] C. L. Breazeal. *Designing sociable robots.* MIT Press, 2004.

[10] S. E. Brennan. Lexical entrainment in spontaneous dialog. *Proceedings of ISSD*, 96:41–44, 1996.

[11] S. E. Brennan and H. H. Clark. Conceptual pacts and lexical choice in conversation. *Journal of Experimental Psychology: Learning, Memory, and Cognition*, 22(6):1482, 1996.

[12] C. A. Ferguson. Toward a characterization of English foreigner talk. *Anthropological linguistics*, 17:1–14, 1975.

[13] S. Garrod and G. Doherty. Conversation, co-ordination and convention: An empirical investigation of how groups establish linguistic conventions. *Cognition*, 53(3):181–215, 1994.

[14] S. Garrod and M. J. Pickering. Joint action, interactive alignment, and dialog. *Topics in Cognitive Science*, 1(2):292–304, 2009.

[15] S. D. Gosling, P. J. Rentfrow, and W. B. Swann. A very brief measure of the Big-Five personality domains. *Journal of Research in Personality*, 37:504–528, 2003.

[16] S. W. Gregory Jr and S. Webster. A nonverbal signal in voices of interview partners effectively predicts communication accommodation and social status perceptions. *Journal of Personality and Social Psychology*, 70(6):1231, 1996.

[17] T. Iio, M. Shiomi, K. Shinozawa, T. Miyashita, T. Akimoto, and N. Hagita. Lexical entrainment in human-robot interaction: Can robots entrain human vocabulary? In *2009 IEEE/RSJ International Conference on Intelligent Robots and Systems*, pages 3727–3734. IEEE, Oct. 2009.

[18] T. Iio, M. Shiomi, K. Shinozawa, K. Shimohara, M. Miki, and N. Hagita. Lexical Entrainment in Human Robot Interaction. *International Journal of Social Robotics*, 7(2):253–263, apr 2015.

[19] T. F. Jaeger. Categorical data analysis: Away from ANOVAs (transformation or not) and towards logit mixed models. *Journal of memory and language*, 59(4):434–446, 2008.

[20] L. A. Jensen-Campbell and W. G. Graziano. Agreeableness as a moderator of interpersonal conflict. *Journal of personality*, 69(2):323–362, 2001.

[21] T. Kanda, T. Hirano, D. Eaton, and H. Ishiguro. Interactive robots as social partners and peer tutors for children: A field trial. *Human-computer interaction*, 19(1):61–84, 2004.

[22] D. Kuchenbrandt, F. Eyssel, S. Bobinger, and M. Neufeld. When a Robot's Group Membership Matters. *International Journal of Social Robotics*, 5(3):409–417, Aug. 2013.

[23] R. R. McCrae and O. P. John. An introduction to the five-factor model and its applications. *Journal of personality*, 60(2):175–215, 1992.

[24] D. Myers. *Social Psychology.* McGraw-Hill Medical Publishing, 10th edition, 2010.

[25] M. Natale. Convergence of mean vocal intensity in dyadic communication as a function of social desirability. *Journal of Personality and Social Psychology*, 32(5):790, 1975.

[26] M. Natale. Social desirability as related to convergence of temporal speech patterns. *Perceptual and Motor Skills*, 40(3):827–830, 1975.

[27] S. Oviatt, C. Darves, and R. Coulston. Toward adaptive conversational interfaces: Modeling speech convergence with animated personas. *ACM Transactions on Computer-Human Interaction (TOCHI)*, 11(3):300–328, 2004.

[28] S. Ross and I. M. Shortreed. Japanese foreigner talk: Convergence or divergence. *Journal of Asian Pacific Communication*, 1(1):135–45, 1990.

[29] C. A. Sanderson. *Social Psychology.* Wiley, 1st edition, 2009.

[30] E. B. Sandoval, J. Brandstetter, M. Obaid, and C. Bartneck. Reciprocity in Human-Robot Interaction: A Quantitative Approach Through the Prisoner's Dilemma and the Ultimatum Game. *International Journal of Social Robotics*, 8(2):303–317, 2016.

[31] G. Shaw-Garlock. Looking forward to sociable robots. *International Journal of Social Robotics*, 1(3):249–260, 2009.

[32] C. L. Smith. Prosodic accommodation by French speakers to a non-native interlocutor. In *Proceedings of the XVIth International Congress of Phonetic Sciences*, pages 313–348, 2007.

[33] J. Stuart-Smith, G. Pryce, C. Timmins, and B. Gunter. Television can also be a factor in language change: Evidence from an urban dialect. *Language*, 89(3):501–536, Sept. 2013.

[34] L. Unger. The Social Role of Linguistic Alignment with In-Group and Out-Group Members. Master's thesis, The University of Edinburgh, Nov. 2010.

[35] J. Webb. Interview synchrony: An investigation of two speech rate measures in an automated standardized interview. In A. Siegman and B. Pope, editors, *Studies in dyadic communication: Proceedings of a research conference on the interview*, pages 115–133. Pergamon, New York, 1970.

[36] E. J. Weiner and W. Labov. Constraints on the agentless passive. *Journal of linguistics*, 19(1):29–58, 1983.

[37] M. Wilson. MRC psycholinguistic database: Machine-usable dictionary, version 2.00. *Behavior Research Methods, Instruments, & Computers*, 20(1):6–10, 1988.

[38] Worldrobotics.org. World Robotics - Industrial Robots 2012 Executive Summary. Technical report, 2012.

Conversational Bootstrapping and Other Tricks of a Concierge Robot

Shang Guo
IBM Watson Research Center
1101 Kitchawan Rd,
Yorktown Heights, NY 10598, USA
sguo@us.ibm.com

Jonathan Lenchner
IBM Research Africa
Langata Rd,
Nairobi 00100, Kenya
jonathan.lenchner@ke.ibm.com

Jonathan Connell
IBM Watson Research Center
1101 Kitchawan Rd,
Yorktown Heights, NY 10598, USA
jconnell@us.ibm.com

Mishal Dholakia
IBM Watson Research Center
1101 Kitchawan Rd,
Yorktown Heights, NY 10598, USA
mdholak@us.ibm.com

Hidemasa Muta
IBM Research Australia
204 Lygon St,
Carlton, Victoria 30503, Australia
mutahide@au.ibm.com

ABSTRACT
We describe the effective use of online learning to enhance the conversational capabilities of a concierge robot that we have been developing over the last two years. The robot was designed to interact naturally with visitors and uses a speech recognition system in conjunction with a natural language classifier. The online learning component monitors interactions and collects explicit and implicit user feedback from a conversation and feeds it back to the classifier in the form of new class instances and adjusted threshold values for triggering the classes. In addition, it enables a trusted master to teach it new question-answer pairs via question-answer paraphrasing, and solicits help with maintaining question-answer-class relationships when needed, obviating the need for explicit programming. The system has been completely implemented and demonstrated using the SoftBank Robotics [34] humanoid robots Pepper and NAO, and the telepresence robot known as Double from Double Robotics [4].

Keywords
Spoken dialog systems; text classification; online learning; conversational agents; human-robot interaction; concierge robots

1. INTRODUCTION
A number of intelligent computer dialog systems create virtual agents and bots that combine voice recognition, some aspect of natural language understanding, and integrated dialog tools to provide automated customer engagements. The human-computer interaction in the dialog system is achieved by communicating with an avatar (a 2D or 3D anthropomorphic, speech-enabled interface) or a physical robot. These systems are designed to serve in capacities such as automated sales agents, information kiosks, and query portals.

A nagging problem with such systems is that customers are always finding new ways to ask questions, thus breaking the system. That is, the system knows the answer; it just does not understand the question. Many such dialog systems depend on voice recognition, however quality is often poor, especially in noisy environments and for people with heavy accents, where the speech recognition system might drop or mangle words or even whole phrases. Furthermore, the dialog systems typically feed the transcriptions into text classification systems that do not robustly accommodate such mis-transcriptions. While better training of the classifier can ameliorate such effects, classifier training often has to be performed by experts.

In this paper we provide an interesting way to incorporate online learning into the classification task. One part of the system judges when to directly respond to an utterance as opposed to asking for clarification. Another part of the system collects new class instances as they are encountered in the field, distinguishing those that the robot accurately classifies, which are used to reinforce the robot's knowledge base (training data), from another group that are frequently encountered but stump the robot. This latter group is passed back to the system development team or to a Mechanical Turk for answering and subsequent adding to the training data. In addition, the system also lets one or more trusted masters teach it new question/answer pairs via paraphrasing and soliciting help with maintaining question-answer-class relationships when needed, allowing for broadening of the robot's topic coverage through conversation, without the need for explicit programming.

The remainder of this paper is structured as follows: in the next section we review related work. Following that we describe the architecture of the system. We then give a detailed account of the learning mechanisms of the system and follow that with a description of our experiments and associated results. We finish up with a summary discussion and mention of some recently started follow-on work.

2. RELATED WORK
As speech recognition and robot technology improve, humanoid robots are beginning to take the place of humans for some daily tasks requiring verbal interaction. Concierge or "greeter" robots at hotels [35] and retail facilities [3] provide some examples. These interactive conversational agents present a variety of challenges including achieving "naturalness" of interaction, and the possession of a sufficiently robust base of knowledge to be able to carry on a satisfactory conversation. Early intelligent dialog systems acted on declarative knowledge to process data and respond to humans. The development of a learning framework

HRI '17, March 06-09, 2017, Vienna, Austria
 ISBN 978-1-4503-4336-7/17/03…$15.00
DOI: http://dx.doi.org/10.1145/2909824.3020232

relied on explicitly defined rules. Declarative knowledge, in the form of rules, governed the information retrieval and context selection tasks [15]. Typically, these rules were predefined. Questions were compared against rules to trigger actions, answer questions and execute selected movement or other behaviors. Such implemented systems include, for example, a guide in a shopping mall [20], a comic humanoid robot, ZOEI [1], a museum guide [2], and a robotic receptionist [10]. Within the rule-based system, the user's input had to be matched to templates in the rules. This template-based matching greatly limited the ways in which humans could ask questions. If the human's question did not follow the template of any rules, the robot would not be able to answer the question, or run a contextually appropriate movement.

As natural language processing (NLP) has become more mature, greater interest has surfaced in using NLP for reasoning about human speech. Using various methods of machine learning a variety of systems have been devised that create a classification model which better understands the questions, or other utterances, and maps the questions/utterances to relevant categories, each category (a.k.a. "class") of which may call for the same response [19, 30]. There are two fundamentally different approaches to question classification: those that are rule-based and those that are learning-based. Rule based approaches try to match the question with handcrafted rules [14, 28]. These approaches however, suffer from the need to define more and more rules [23]. Furthermore, while rule-based approaches may perform well on particular datasets, they may perform quite poorly on new datasets and consequently it is difficult to scale them. Li and Roth [23] provide an example that shows some of the difficulties encountered by rule-based approaches.

Learning-based approaches on the other hand, perform classification by extracting features from the questions or other utterances and training a classifier using these features. The trained classifier is then used to predict class labels for new incoming utterances. Many successful learning-based classification approaches have been proposed [30]. Most recent work on question classification uses supervised learning where the training set consists of labeled questions or other utterances. Supervised methods mainly differ in the classification model and the features that are extracted from the utterances. The choice of classifier highly influences the final question classifier system. Different classifiers have been tried, including support vector machines [12, 13, 25, 32], maximum entropy models [25, 28], and others. In addition, there are hybrid approaches that combine rule-based and learning based approaches [13, 21, 32].

Apart from text classification, the bulk of the previous work on learning in dialog systems has to do with learning in the context of a very constrained dialog, e.g., the case of purchasing a ticket to board a train. The system may know that you want to purchase a train ticket (e.g. because you have come to a machine labeled as such in a train station) and the system offers you the option of proceeding through speech. Such constrained dialog systems, with a clear set of states that the dialog may be in, and a well-defined goal (e.g. selling the user a ticket that best matches their constraints and objectives) can be modeled as POMDPs (Partially Observable Markov Decision Processes) and are amenable to reinforcement learning. This idea was first described by Levin, Pieraccini and Eckert in [22] and has been picked up by various subsequent authors, including [27, 33].

As an alternative to text classification based systems, some authors have tried to use more sophisticated linguistic frameworks, especially for command and control of the physical actions of robots and dialog revolving around such physical actions. Eppe, Trott, and Feldman [6] describe the use of a so-called "embodied construction grammar" to systematically construct concepts about a robot's physical grounding, a notion first explored in [7, 8]. In [4], Connell et al. describe an extensible (spoken) language interface, ELI, for a robot's manipulation of physical objects. Finally Marge and Rudnicky [24] discuss use of language to recover from situated grounding problems. If it is understood that the purpose of dialog with a robot is to guide its physical actions, this context becomes a strong constraint on the universe of discourse.

Although our methods of learning in the context of a fairly generic natural language classification problem appear to be new, there have been successful applications of machine learning for specialized natural language classification tasks, e.g. for classifying mail as spam [11], for assisting with the filing of email into folders [31], and various others.

We note that although our language learning system is more generic than has been typically seen in prior work, it is not completely generic. Our robot has a designated area of expertise. It is a "concierge robot" for a research Exploratorium inside a larger research lab. Its language model is tuned to words it expects to hear frequently in this context and its text classification model is geared around answering questions about the Exploratorium and the greater research lab, and not more general questions, or questions involving esoteric factual knowledge of the sort possessed by the Watson Jeopardy!-playing system [9], though such questions are occasionally asked.

3. ARCHITECTURE

Our system starts by receiving an acoustic signal from a user via a detached, dedicated, microphone or via the microphone on a smartphone using a specially created app. The robot provides feedback to the user by nodding its head, blinking its eyes, and in some instances saying "yes." This raw speech is transferred to the cloud-based Watson Speech-to-Text (STT) service [16], which returns a text string. On the Pepper robot, this string is also displayed to the user via a chest-mounted tablet. Some of the architectural details of the system are depicted in Figure 1.

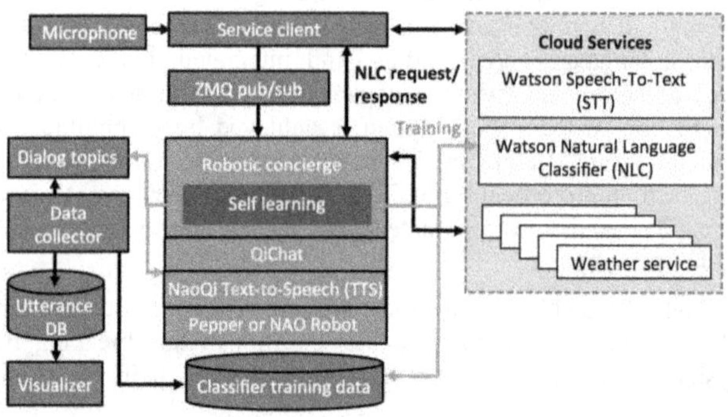

Figure 1: Robot Dialog Architecture for the SoftBank Pepper and NAO Robots. The Dialog Architecture for the Double Robot is similar.

Initially our robot was called "Rosie" and this name also served as a special attention word, required in most utterances directed at the robot. The purpose of using an attention word is to filter out background noise or incidental utterances that are not intended for the robot. Interestingly, we eventually renamed the robot "Jessica" because there were too many possible mis-transcriptions of "Rosie" (e.g. "Ross he", "Go see", "Woe is he", etc.), and the name "Jessica" does not suffer from this problem.

There are three basic forms in which the attention word is used: 1. as the only word in an utterance, followed by a question in another utterance; 2. at the beginning of an utterance, but allowing 0-3 other words prior to it; 3. at the end of a question. For instance, the following are valid forms:

> "Jessica, <pause> where is the bathroom?" → form 1: two separate utterances
> "Jessica, where is the bathroom?" → form 2
> "Where is the bathroom, Jessica?" → form 3

We also set a preliminary threshold for further processing depending on whether the attention word is spotted and a couple of other factors, such as the confidence scores returned from the Speech-to-Text service indicating how likely the transcription is correct. (These are distinct confidences from those returned by the Natural Language Classifier, to be discussed next.)

1. The attention word is spotted, threshold = 0.0
2. No attention word, utterance has multiple words, threshold = 0.3
3. No attention word, utterance has only a single word, threshold = 0.5

The idea of these thresholds is that without an attention word we need to have some noticeable level of confidence in order to embark on further processing, and all the more so if the utterance contains just a single word. The single words "Yes" and "No" are frequently valid responses, which, when valid, will trigger confidences above 0.5. However, single word utterances are often spurious noises or words heard that are not meant for the robot.

Once a transcribed utterance is received from the STT service, the transcription is passed to the Watson Natural Language Classifier (NLC) [16], which has been trained for the specific context in which the robot operates – a research Exploratorium, called the "ThinkLab" within our larger research institution. The NLC clusters those utterances that essentially say or ask the same thing into a single class. The rationale is that, if any of these utterances is heard, the same response should be given. For example, "Where is the bathroom?" and "Can you direct me to the restroom?" are both associated with the single class bathroom_location because they are essentially different ways of asking the same thing. It is the job of the NLC, when presented with the textual representation of an utterance, to return a set of confidence values between 0 and 1 reflecting how well the utterance matches each of the trained classes that it knows about.

Generally (though with a variety of caveats that we shall explain in subsequent sections), what the system does is look for the class with the highest confidence above a minimum threshold, and then return the response associated with that class. There can be several response phrases associated with each request class, in which case the agent chooses from among the available responses, either randomly, or sequentially (in other words, the first time an answer from the answer class is requested the first answer is given, the second time the second answer is given, and so on, eventually cycling back to the first answer). Certain classes have more complicated response templates where variable information can be filled in. This happens with time or weather queries like "What time is it?" or "What is the temperature outside?", as well as for such questions as "Who am I?" In such cases the system consults an outside service. For example, in the latter case, a face recognition service is queried to help generate a substring to complete the template. The SoftBank robots' built-in QiChat dialog service manages this question/utterance, or question/utterance class to response mapping. The Watson Dialog Service manages these mappings on the Double robot.

After an answer is formulated, it is passed to a Text-to-Speech (TTS) system to generate an appropriate audio output. For the SoftBank robots we have been using the built-in NaoQi Text-to-Speech service, while for the Double we use the Watson Text-to-Speech service [18]. In addition, there are a few request classes that do not follow this path, particularly requests to sing and dance. In these cases, particular sound and animation routines on the robot are activated instead.

The dialog system described in this paper does not have to run on a robot. However, our particular robot does make use of its physicality and knowledge of where it is situated, which is not always at the same location, in the following four ways: (i) The robot always tries to look at the person that it believes is talking to it, even when in a crowd of people. (ii) The robot uses face recognition to know when a "trusted master" is speaking to it, or to greet a person it has seen before who has provided their name in response to being asked. (iii) The robot uses a variety of different mannerisms to (a) indicate that it has heard what you've said, (b) that it has understood what you've said, and (c) that it is trying to come up with an answer in the case where it expects some delay in processing before it can provide an answer. In case (a) it typically changes the color of its eyes; in case (b) it will nod its head up and down, and in case (c) it may briefly say "hmm" or "ahhh." Finally, (iv) the robot always knows where it is in the rather large ThinkLab in which it is situated (details of its localization technique, making use of a grid of ceiling-mounted ultrasound emitters and onboard microphones, are interesting but beyond the scope of the paper), along with what direction it is facing. As a result it is able to answer certain relative location questions, such as "Where is the closest restroom?" and point in the appropriate direction.

4. LEARNING

Beyond the basic functionality described, the robot is also able to improve its performance by soliciting and responding to feedback from the user. The feedback is mediated by a self-learning module, which works in conjunction with the STT and NLC systems. The self-learning module collects explicit and implicit user feedback from a conversation and relays it to the classifier in the form of new class instances and adjusted threshold values for triggering the classes. In addition, it enables a trusted master to teach the system new question/answer pairs via question-answer paraphrasing and clarifying the relationship of question-answer pairs to existing and possibly new classes, obviating the need for explicit programming.

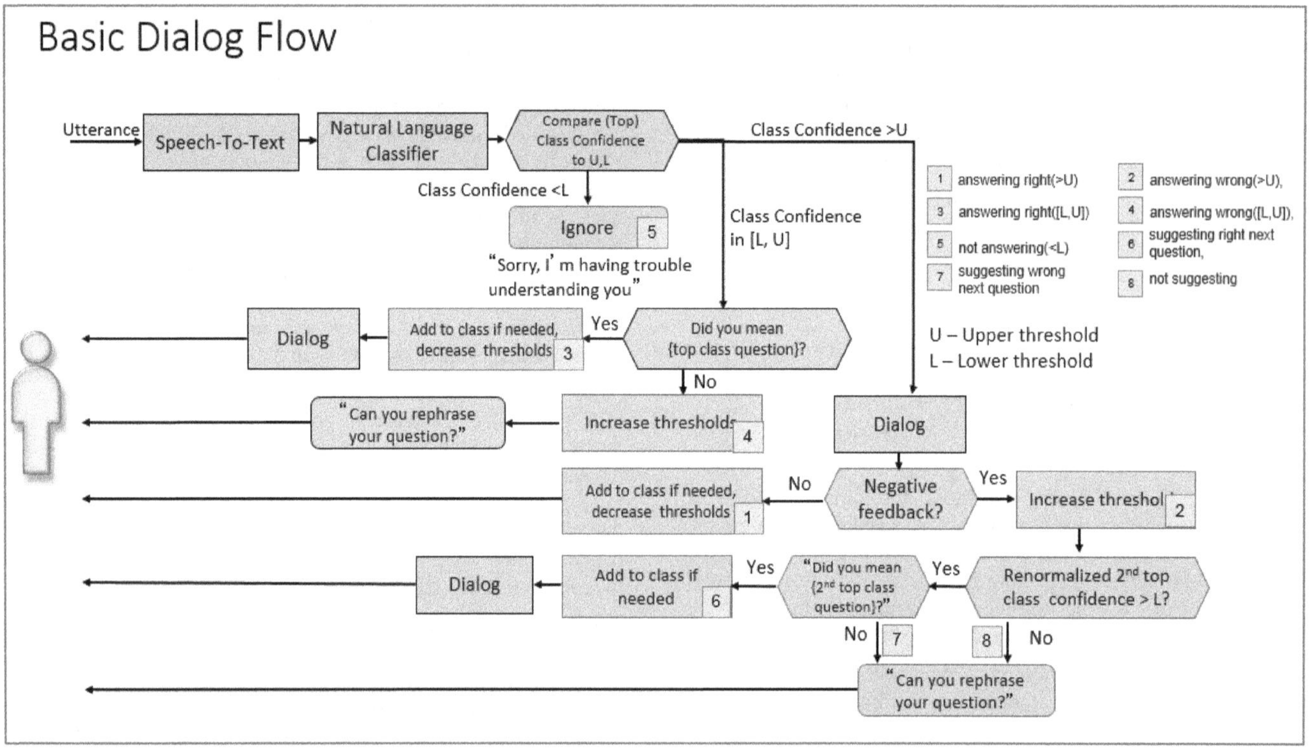

Figure 2: The basic dialog flow showing how an utterance gets processed and its effect on learning.

The system uses an upper threshold U and a lower threshold L to decide when to respond directly and, on the other hand, when less certain, when to request confirmation of its understanding of a user request. When the NLC returns a top class confidence above the upper threshold U, the robot assumes it is right and answers. When the confidence is between the upper and lower thresholds, it instead asks a confirmatory question of the form "Did you mean ...?" where "..." is the so-called prototype instance for the class (by convention, the first instance listed in the training dataset). When the confidence is below the lower threshold the system assumes it does not know how to answer the question with its current knowledge. Figure 2 gives a detailed account of all the possible ways an utterance can be handled by the system. The case where the class confidence is less than L corresponds to box 5. We shall return to this case a bit later, but after the robot *does* answer a question, the user may give feedback regarding their satisfaction with the answer provided. If the feedback is negative, e.g. "No, Jessica, that is not what I meant", the robot will suggest the class it is next most confident in, again by asking "Did you mean...?", as long as the classifier's confidence, after renormalizing its confidence levels, is above the lower threshold L. For most new users we instruct them to give the robot such explicit negative feedback when the robot gives either an incorrect or inappropriate response. In Figure 2 the boxes marked "Dialog" refer either to the QiChat dialog service for the SoftBank robots, or the Watson Dialog Service for the Double robot – in either case the result is to map from a question class believed or known to be correct to a spoken response.

The system maintains separate U and L thresholds for each class and they are automatically adjusted based on either (i) directly volunteered feedback, (ii) the user's response to a confirmation request, or (iii) the user's implicit feedback. If feedback is negative, meaning that the user realizes the answer is wrong and tells the robot so, the system nudges thresholds up by an amount Δ. Likewise, if feedback is positive or no feedback is received (e.g., the user does not feel the need to make a correction), the system nudges the thresholds down by Δ. In general, the Δ we use is a decreasing function of the total number of times, N, the particular class is essayed (i.e. the robot answered based on this class, either correctly or incorrectly). A multiplicative factor of $1/\log(N)$ allows the system to move the thresholds quickly at the beginning, but then resist transitory changes later on.

Not only are the class thresholds changed, but troublesome utterances can be marked for further processing, for example when the same utterance is received several times but the robot does not know how to respond to it – these utterances are sent to our development team or to a Mechanical Turk for possible addition to the training set (where they become additional instances of existing classes or sometimes new classes). Referring again to Figure 2, in cases 3 and 6, the utterances are added to the classes to automatically broaden them. Although these utterances were classified correcly, it can be annoying to the human to have to confirm them. After adding the new training examples, the classifier should return a higher confidence for the same question and so answer it directly without requesting confirmation.

If the confidence in the top class is below L, the robot does not just respond "I don't know" but, instead, seeks more informative feedback. One of the methods it uses is to ask the user to rephrase their original question. If this is then recognized successfully, the original confusing utterance is added to the class associated with the rephrased question. To make this concrete, let us look at an example:

> Human: I need to powder my nose. (non-recognized question)
>
> Robot: Can you rephrase the question?
>
> Human: Where is the bathroom. (class bathroom_location is returned from NLC-QUESTION)
>
> Robot: The bathroom is in aisle 13.

In this conversation, the system adds the non-recognized question ("I need to powder my nose") to the class bathroom_location in the NLC-QUESTION training data.

Just like humans, robots can also acquire new skills through social interactions. In our case, the robot can learn new questions and new answers from conversation. Part of this ability stems from an extension to the classifier system. Not only do we aggregate similar queries into a single question class, in this way maintaining a question classifier, but we also aggregate similar answers into answer classes and maintain an independent answer classifier. Figure 3 depicts how these two types of classifiers, the new NLC-ANSWER, and the original NLC-QUESTION, are integrated.

When working with a recognized trusted teacher, if the robot does not understand the question being asked (step (1) in Figure 3 – the question is not recognized to be in NLC-QUESTION), it can choose to solicit an explicit answer (step (2)). If the given answer gets a high top class confidence back from the answer classifeier, NLC-ANSWER (step (3)), the robot finds the corresponding class or classes from NLC-QUESTION that call out that answer class. The robot then asks the trusted teacher if the question asked is actually the same as that from any of the known corresponding question classes (step (4)). If the teacher says that it is, then the question can now be answered and the original question utterance is added to the NLC-QUESTION training data. On the other hand if the question from the trusted master is not the same as that from any NLC-QUESTION class, then a new class is created to accommodate the question.

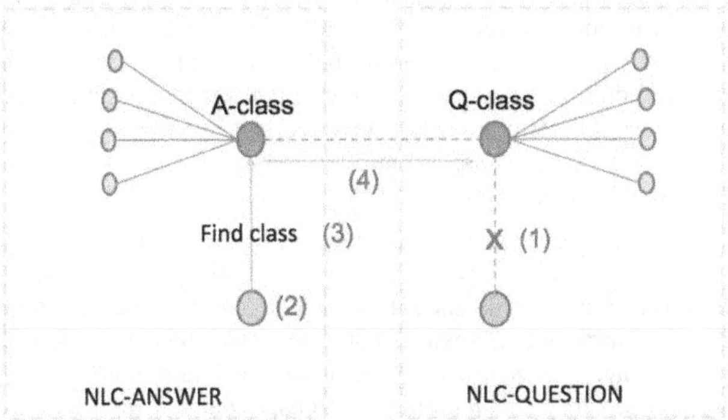

Figure 3: Interaction with a trusted teacher: leveraging the special answer classifier (NLC-ANSWER), to learn new question-answer pairs that can either be used to create a new question class, or to place the new question in an existing question class.

Below is a sample interaction with a teacher:

> Human: I need to wash my hands. (non-recognized question)
>
> Robot: Sorry, I don't know the answer. If you know the answer to the question you just asked, please suggest how I can answer it the next time by saying the words "the answer is" followed by your suggested answer.
>
> Human: The answer is "the bathroom is in aisle 13." (class bathroom_location is returned from NLC-ANSWER)
>
> Robot: Got it. Can you confirm to me that the question you asked is essentially equivalent to "Where is the closest restroom?"
>
> Human: Yes, that is correct.

Here we have the class bathroom_location returned from NLC-ANSWER. Since there is a relationship between the class in NLC-ANSWER and the companion class in NLC-QUESTION, the class bathroom_location in NLC-QUESTION is found through the class of NLC-ANSWER. The robot asks for confirmation that the question asked is equivalent to the prototype question it knows about for the bathroom_location class. The system then adds the non-recognized question ("I need to wash my hands") to the class bathroom_location in the NLC-QUESTION training data.

At first blush it seems that as long as the answers to two distinct questions are the same, that we should be OK with merging the questions into a single class. However, there are two reasons for not doing this. The first reason is that if the questions are sufficiently different, the merged class will have two distinct centroids and confidences in this class may not be what one would naturally expect. The second problem is best illustrated with an example. Suppose we have two question classes represented by the prototypical questions "Where is the closest bathroom?" and "Where is the closest stairway?" Moreover, suppose each question has an answer "Between aisles 9 and 10." In fact bathrooms and stairways happen to be located together in most parts of our building. Now imagine what would happen if we were to merge the two question classes. Since only one of the questions can serve as the prototype, suppose we take the prototype to be "Where is the closest bathroom?" but someone with a bit of an accent asks "Where is the closest stairway?" In this case imagine that the system returns the bimodal class as the top class, but with confidence that is between its lower and upper thresholds, L and U. It will now ask "Did you mean 'Where is the closest bathroom?'" A newcomer to our research center will certainly not recognize the equivalence between the questions 'Where is the closest bathroom?' and the question asked, 'Where is the closest stairway?'

The next case is a bit different. When the provided answer is not recognizable (the confidence of the answer is lower than L from NLC-ANSWER), the robot creates a new class for the question and a linked new class for the answer. It then adds the question and its answer into the NLC-QUESTION and NLC-ANSWER training sets, respectively. Again, we limit this action so that it may occur only when the robot is interacting with a trusted master. For our robots, we use a face recognition service coupled with a user profile to determine whether a particular individual is trusted.

Suppose the conversation proceeds as follows:

> Human: I need some cash. (non-recognized question)
>
> Robot: Sorry, I don't know the answer. If you know the answer to the question you just asked, please suggest how I can answer it the next time by saying the words 'the answer is' followed by your suggested answer.
>
> Human: The answer is the ATM is in aisle 20. (non-recognized answer)
>
> Robot: Got it.

In this conversation, the system extracts keywords and composes a class name ATM_aisle. Then it adds the new class and sample question "I need some cash" to the NLC-QUESTION training data. Simultaneously, it adds the answer "The ATM is in aisle 20" to the response list as well as to the training data for the associated NLC-ANSWER class.

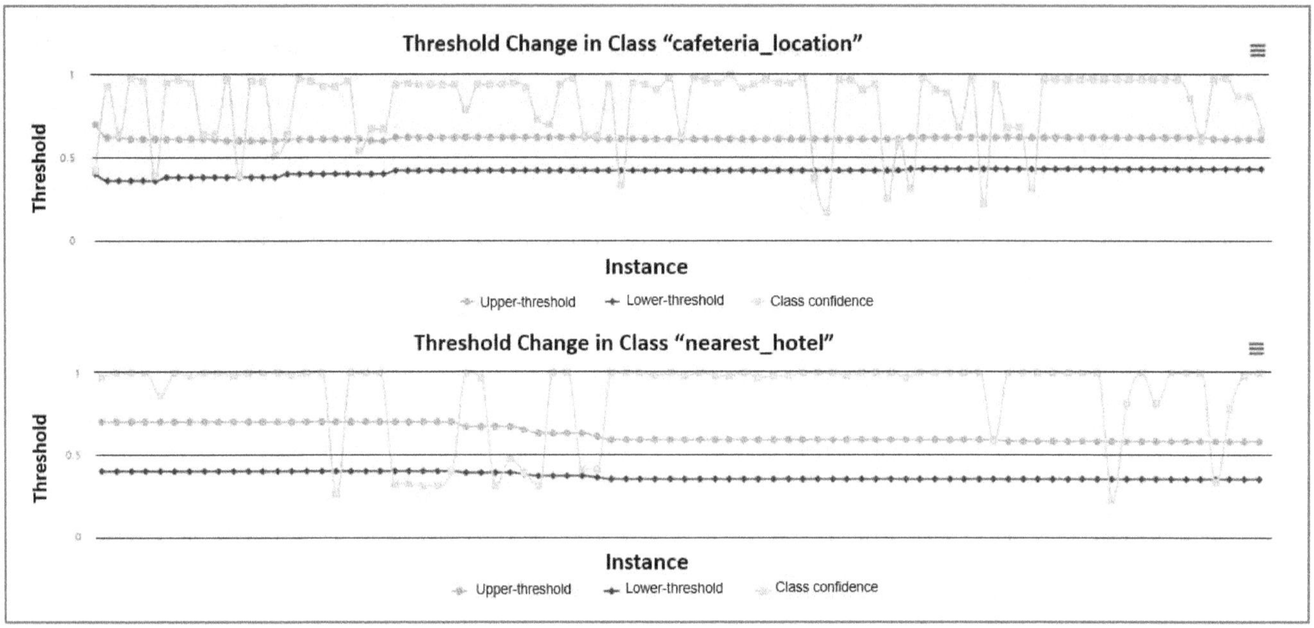

Figure 4: A trace of how upper and lower thresholds change over time for two common classes.

A final way the system learns is by aggregating questions that it hears, which include an appropriate attention word, but that it does not understand (i.e. that it believes do not match anything in NLC-QUESTION), into a separate set of classes. We call this additional set of classes the NLC-QUESTION-ORPHAN set. When the classifier hears a new question that is associated with an existing entry in NLC-QUESTION-ORPHAN at a confidence that exceeds the average upper confidence in NLC-QUESTION, the questions are merged into a common class. Once such a class has been accessed a number of times beyond a given threshold, the class is sent out for answering, either by members of our development team, or by one of our volunteer Mechanical Turkers. The answer received is then fed back into NLC-ANSWER and the question class is moved from NLC-QUESTION-ORPHAN to NLC-QUESTION. If the questions are deemed to not all be members of a common class, that fact too is fed back, with the class members split into separate NLC-QUESTION-ORPHAN classes (or NLC-QUESTION classes if answers are provided).

5. EXPERIMENTS

We have described two methods for enhancing the performance of a response-based robot dialog system: threshold tuning and extra example harvesting. To determine whether these mechanisms really improve performance we designed a user study involving 16 participants. We first asked each subject to generate 10 free-form questions for the robot. Next, we showed them a list of the names of 42 categories (class names) that the robot could respond to. We then requested that they ask an additional 15 questions about some selection of these topics. The subjects used a desktop microphone when speaking and their inputs were transcribed by the Watson STT service using its built-in language model (in other words, a language model not tuned to this application).

It should be noted that these samples are not all unique. For instance, when asking about the location of the bathroom, many users say the exact same thing: "Where are the restrooms?" However, in other cases the form of a given question is rarely the same from user to user. Finally, transcriptions are very often not perfect, particularly for "out-of-vocabulary" words like "ThinkLab" (the name of our Exploratorium), which was variously transcribed as "think laugh", "thing club", "pink lab", "thick cloud", etc.

In total, 638 transcribed utterances were collected (some study participants were overly-enthusiastic), of which 422 corresponded to known request categories. The collection was then used to test the performance of the system before and after training had occurred during the course of regular demos that are given at our lab. The full system has 191 categories, not just the 42 presented to the study participants. Note that none of the user study data was used in the prior training of the system.

To evaluate system performance, we chose to tabulate events that are annoying to the user. There are essentially three different varieties of such annoyance. First, it is annoying when the robot directly blurts out an answer, but it misunderstood the question. For instance, when asked "Where are the bathrooms?" it may proudly declare "This building was constructed in 1961," which is the answer associated with another question class. We use the label "wrong" for such unconfirmed, incorrect responses. Another annoyance is when the robot fails to provide any response, or complains that it does not understand when in fact the question should have been recognized as belonging to one of its known question classes. We label such errors as "none". Finally, although it can help eliminate the other two types of errors, constantly being asked "Did you mean …" by the robot can be tiresome. We call this category of annoying response "confirm".

Ideally one would want the lowest possible "wrong", "none", and "confirm" counts. Unfortunately, there is a tradeoff between these categories. For instance, forcing there to be no "confirm" events would inevitably boost the number of "wrong" and "none" events. Therefore, to rank various systems we assign a penalty to each type of annoyance. The most severe "wrong" events have a multiplier of 5, the not as bad "none" events have a weight of 3, and the merely irksome "confirm" events are penalized by a factor of 2. This generates an overall demerit score for each system.

To demonstrate that threshold tuning has an effect, and that different thresholds are needed for each class, Figure 4 shows two examples. Here we show the evolution of the upper and lower thresholds during a series of regular demos in our lab. As can be seen, particularly when the most likely class has a low confidence, the thresholds change over time. However, in the two cases shown, they move in different directions and end up at different values. In fact, after training with 3186 (pre-experimental) utterances we found that L ranged from 0.34 to 0.7, and U varied from 0.53 to 0.86.

To quantify the effects the changed thresholds have, we ran the 638 utterances from the user study through the system. For comparison, we also fixed all thresholds to initial values of U = 0.7 and L = 0.4 and tested the same set of queries. The results are shown in table 1, along with the score for each system. In all cases, lower scores are better. Here it can be seen that after tuning the system generated 15 more hard errors (wrong + none) but asked for 31 fewer confirmations. Using the weights we assigned previously, the trained system has a slightly lower score than the initial system and thus, overall, is marginally better.

Because the shift was not very dramatic, we felt compelled to determine whether our initial choice of weights had just been fortuitous. In fact, we find the average class thresholds to be L = 0.42 +/- 0.04 and U = 0.69 +/- 0.04 after training. But what if we had started further from these near-ideal values? To explore this question without requiring the robot to have extensive additional experience, we tried various other combinations of uniform, fixed thresholds. As can be seen from the table, none of these alternatives systems was better than the tuned version. Thus, assuming that the tuning will eventually converge to something close to 0.7 and 0.4, learning can help correct for initially bad guesses. Interestingly, it can also be seen that the base classifier performance is limited. No matter where the L threshold is set, there are 27 unanswered questions. Similarly, no matter what value the U threshold assumes, there are always 38 incorrectly answered questions. Thus the minimum score possible is 271 (with no confirmations).

Table 1: The effect of adjusting the L and U thresholds on various error measures.

system	none (x3)	confirm (x2)	wrong (x5)	score
tuned per class	58	140	58	744
fixed 0.7, 0.4	50	171	51	747
fixed 0.7, 0.3	27	231	51	798
fixed 0.8, 0.4	50	208	38	756
fixed 0.8, 0.3	27	268	38	807

Table 2: The effect of increased training data on system performance.

amount of data	avg. training	correct	none	confirm	wrong	score
<= 2 examples	1.85	64% (408)	116	154	59	951
<= 4 examples	2.94	73% (466)	70	155	68	860
all examples	3.97	89% (577)	50	171	51	747

Our system also solicits new variations on the way questions can be asked. These are then added as additional training data for the topic classifier. While initially starting with only 1 or 2 sample utterances per class, some classes eventually have as many as 16 samples. To demonstrate the effect of increased training data, we started with the final system that has an average of 3.97 training examples per class. We then artificially reduced the data to only 2 or 4 examples per class (although some classes did not have even this much data) by randomly removing some training samples. After this, the classifier was retrained and all 638 utterances from the user study data were processed by the resulting system.

Table 2 shows that the number of requests for which an appropriate response was given. Here, if the question falls outside the scope of the classifier categories, a correct response is considered to be "I don't understand that". Furthermore, whether or not a confirmation is requested from the user, if the final category acted on matches the ground truth for the utterance, this is considered a correct response. For completeness we have reported the same metrics as for the threshold adjustment study.

As expected, automatically accumulating more training data yields better performance. And, not only does the system generate more "correct" responses, it's annoying-ness index ("score") also decreases. However, notice that training with all examples results in a better system than one in which the number of training examples has been capped at 4. This more-training-data benefit is despite the fact that the average number of training examples per class in nearly 4 in the final system, and demonstrates that some classes are harder and hence need more training data than others. Just setting a simple goal of 4 examples per class is not sufficient to yield optimal performance.

6. CONCLUDING REMARKS

We have presented new techniques for what we call "conversational bootstrapping," or systematically improving the text classification and dialog capabilities of a speaking robot using active learning. We have described an utterance/response methodology that uses two confidence thresholds to give the robot the ability to confirm requests when it has an intermediate level of certainty about its response, as opposed to more standard dialog methodologies that are based on a single threshold and use that threshold to either respond or not respond to a given user utterance. We have also described techniques for systematically adding new training examples to question classes and for dynamically modifying class confidence thresholds. We have evaluated these techniques through a series of experiments that bear out the increased utility of the two confidence threshold approach as well as our approach to learning.

In addition, we have introduced a method for learning from a trusted master that enables the system to learn new question/utterance classes. This technique makes use of backward inferencing, to allow the robot to tie human-supplied answers to questions that it may already know about, via an answer classifier. In addition, we have presented a method for the systematic resolution of new but repeatedly encountered question/utterance classes using Mechanical Turkers.

An obvious question is why the system should use different thresholds for different classes, rather than maintaining upper and lower confidence thresholds that are the same for all classes. To appreciate why we have taken this approach, note that as time goes on the classes are essayed and accumulate more instances at different rates. If both the upper and lower thresholds are very high the robot is essentially only answering at all if it is extremely confident in its understanding of the question, thus in the exploitation versus exploration tradeoff it is purely exploiting. On the other hand, if the lower threshold is extremely low it is tolerating a healthy amount of exploration. In general, the more class instances one has the higher the thresholds should become – arguing clearly for separate thresholds per class. An additional wrinkle is that sometimes there are several wildly different ways of asking the same question and this mixture of words tends to lead to mistaken classifications until many correct (and incorrect) class instances are seen for the given class.

In recent months we have begun to explore ways to go beyond response-based dialog. We are experimenting with ways to initiate a conversation with someone who seems hesitant to talk, or push forward in what seems to be a stalled conversation. The robot also has a sizable collection of jokes, and motivated by the work of Addo and Ahmed [1], we are investigating the role of context and audience appropriate humor.

Another approach to pushing beyond response-based dialog is to try to inject reinforcement learning into the dialog model. In the somewhat open-ended dialog use case of the concierge robot discussed in this paper, the robot does not have a clear goal and hence there is no way to measure progress toward a goal. In a variation on the current work however, one could model the concepts discussed as a series of entities, relations and confidences associated with those relations. A goal for such a robot could be to establish as much clarity as possible about what is being discussed. An aspect of clarity may be to understand who the humans are, as well as what their interests, motivations and goals are. Priors about a person's interests, motivations and goals may be obtained from a company's organizational chart, by crawling the web, and from prior conversations. Thus in the pursuit of clarity the robot could assimilate the satisfying of users goals, to the extent that they might be knowable, and in this way make the problem somewhat amenable to reinforcement learning.

7. REFERENCES

[1] Addo, I. and Ahamed, S. 2014. Applying affective feedback to reinforcement learning in ZOEI, a comic humanoid robot, *23rd IEEE International Symposium on Robot and Human Interactive Communication*, 423-428.

[2] Burgard, W., Cremers, A., Fox, D., Hähnel, D., Lakemeyer, G., Schulz, D., Steiner, W., and Thrun S. 1998. The interactive museum tour-guide robot, Proc. *of 15th National Conference on Artificial Intelligence, 11-18.*

[3] CNBC, 2016. *Lowe's introduces LoweBot, a new autonomous in-store robot*, DOI=http://www.cnbc.com/2016/08/30/lowes-introduces-lowebot-a-new-autonomous-in-store-robot.html, August 30, 2016.

[4] Connell, J., Marcharat, E, Pankanti, S., Kudoh, M., and Nishiyama R. 2012. An Extensible Language Interface for Robot Manipulation, *Proc. Artificial General Intelligence Conf., Lecture Notes in Computer Science*, 7716: 21-30.

[5] Double Robotics, 2016. *Double Robot.* DOI= http://www.doublerobotics.com.

[6] Eppe, M., Trott, S., and Feldman J. 2016. Exploiting deep semantics and compositionality of natural language for Human-Robot-Interaction, *Proc. of the 2016 International Conference on Intelligent Robots and Systems.*

[7] Feldman, J., Bryant, J. E., and Dodge, E. 2009. Embodied Construction Grammar, *Oxford Handbook of Computational Linguistics*, Oxford University Press, 38-111.

[8] Feldman, J., Dodge, E., and Bryant, J. E. 2009. A neural theory of language and embodied construction grammar, *Oxford Handbook of Linguistic Analysis*, 111-138.

[9] Ferrucci, D., Brown, E., Chu-Carroll, J., Fan, J., Gondek, D., Kalyanpur, A., Lally, A., Murdock, J. W., Nyberg, E., Prager, J., Schlaefer, N., and Welty, C. 2010. Building Watson: An Overview of the DeepQA Project, *AI Magazine*, 31(3): 59-79.

[10] Gockley, R., Forlizzi, J., and Simmons, R. 2006. Interactions with a Moody Robot, *Proc. of the 1st ACM SIGCHI/SIGART Conference on Human-Robot Interaction*, 186-193.

[11] Guzella, T. and Caminhas, W. 2009. A review of machine learning techniques in spam filtering, *Expert Systems with Applications*, 36: 10206-10222.

[12] Huang, Z., Thint, M., and Qin, Z. 2008. Question classification using head words and their hypernyms, *Proc. of the Conference on Empirical Methods in Natural Language Processing,* 927–936.

[13] Huang, Z., Thint, M., and Celikyilmaz, A. 2009. Investigation of question classifier in question answering, *Proc. of the 2009 Conference on Empirical Methods in Natural Language Processing*, 543–550.

[14] Hull, D. A. 1999. Xerox TREC-8 question answering track report, *Proc of the 8th Text Retrieval Conference.*

[15] Hung, V., Elvir, M., Gonzales, A., and DeMara, R. 2009. Towards a Method for Evaluating Naturalness in Conversational Dialog Systems, *2009 IEEE International Conference on Systems, Man, and Cybernetics*, 1236-1241.

[16] IBM. 2016. *Watson Natural Language Classifier*, DOI=http://www.ibm.com/watson/developercloud/doc/nl-classifier/.

[17] IBM. 2016. *Watson Speech-To-Text service*, DOI=http://www.ibm.com/watson/developercloud/doc/speech-to-text/input.shtml.

[18] IBM. 2016. *Watson Text-To-Speech service*, DOI= https://www.ibm.com/watson/developercloud/text-to-speech.html.

[19] Joachims, T. 2005. Text categorization with support vector machines: learning with many relevant features, *Lecture Notes in Computer Science*, vol. 1398: 137-142.

[20] Kanda, T., Shiomi, M., Miyashita, Z., Ishiguro, H., and Hagita, N. 2009. An Affective Guide Robot in a Shopping Mall, *4th ACM/IEEE International Conference on Human-Robot Interaction*, 173-180.

[21] Kumar S., Singh, S., and Joshi, B. P. 2010. A semantic approach for question classification using WordNet and Wikipedia, *Pattern Recognition Letters*, 31:1935–1943.

[22] Levin, E., Pieraccini, R., and Eckert, W. 1997. Learning dialogue strategies within the Markov Decision Process Framework, Proc. *IEEE Workshop on Automatic Speech Recognition and Understanding.*

[23] Li, X. and Roth. D. 2004. Learning question classifiers: The role of semantic information, *Proc. of the International Conference on Computational Linguistics*, 556–562.

[24] Marge, M., and Rudnicky, A. I. 2015. Miscommunication Recovery in Physically Situated Dialogue, *Proc. of the 16th Annual Meeting of the Special Interest Group on Discourse and Dialogue.*

[25] Metzler, D. and Croft, W. B. 2005. Analysis of statistical question classification for fact-based questions, *Information Retrieval*, 8:481–504.

[26] Nguyen, M., Nguyen, T., and Shimazu, A. 2007. Subtree mining for question classification problem, *Proc. of the 20th*

international joint conference on Artificial intelligence, 1695–1700.

[27] Pietquin, O. and Dutoit, T. 2006. A probabilistic framework for dialog simulation and optimal strategy learning, *IEEE Transactions on Audio, Speech and Language Processing*, 14(2): 589–599.

[28] Prager, J., Radev, D., Brown, E., and Coden, A. 1999. The use of predictive annotation for question answering in TREC-8, *Proc. of the 8th Text Retrieval Conference*, 399–411.

[29] Roth, D. 1998. Learning to resolve natural language ambiguities: a unified approach, *Proc. of the Fifteenth International Conference on Artificial intelligence/Innovative applications of artificial intelligence, AAAI '98*, 806–813.

[30] Sebastini, F. 2002. Machine learning in automated text categorization, *ACM Computing Surveys*, 34(1): 1-47.

[31] Segal, R. and Kephart, J. 2000. Incremental Learning in SwiftFile, *Proc. of the Seventh International Conference on Machine Learning.*

[32] Silva, J., Coheur, L., Mendes, A., and Wichert, A. 2011. From symbolic to sub-symbolic information in question classification, *Artificial Intelligence Review*, 35(2):137–154.

[33] Singh, S., Kearns, M., Litman, D., and Walker, M. 1999. Reinforcement Learning for Spoken Dialogue Systems, *Neural Information Processing Systems (NIPS-99).*

[34] SoftBank Robotics, 2016. *Pepper and NAO robots.* DOI= https://www.ald.softbankrobotics.com/en.

[35] USA Today, 2016. *Introducing Connie, Hilton's new robot concierge,* DOI=http://www.usatoday.com/story/travel/roadwarriorvoices/2016/03/09/introducing-connie-hiltons-new-robot-concierge/81525924/, March 14, 2016.

Child Speech Recognition in Human-Robot Interaction: Evaluations and Recommendations

James Kennedy*
Plymouth University, U.K.

Séverin Lemaignan
Plymouth University, U.K.

Caroline Montassier
INSA Rouen, France

Pauline Lavalade
Université Pierre et Marie Curie, France

Bahar Irfan
Plymouth University, U.K.

Fotios Papadopoulos
Plymouth University, U.K.

Emmanuel Senft
Plymouth University, U.K.

Tony Belpaeme
Plymouth University, U.K.
Ghent University, Belgium

ABSTRACT

An increasing number of human-robot interaction (HRI) studies are now taking place in applied settings with children. These interactions often hinge on verbal interaction to effectively achieve their goals. Great advances have been made in adult speech recognition and it is often assumed that these advances will carry over to the HRI domain and to interactions with children. In this paper, we evaluate a number of automatic speech recognition (ASR) engines under a variety of conditions, inspired by real-world social HRI conditions. Using the data collected we demonstrate that there is still much work to be done in ASR for child speech, with interactions relying solely on this modality still out of reach. However, we also make recommendations for child-robot interaction design in order to maximise the capability that does currently exist.

Keywords

Child-Robot Interaction; Automatic Speech Recognition; Verbal Interaction; Interaction Design Recommendations

1. INTRODUCTION

Child-robot interaction is moving out of lab and into 'the wild', contributing to domains such as health-care [2], education [15, 25], and entertainment [20]. An increasing amount is being understood about how to design interactions from a nonverbal behaviour perspective [13, 14], but many of these domains hinge on effective verbal communication. This includes not only appropriate speech production by robots, but transcribing and understanding speech from young users as well. A prerequisite to this interpretation of speech is having a sufficiently accurate transcription of what is being said.

*Corresponding author: james.kennedy@plymouth.ac.uk

HRI '17, March 06 - 09, 2017, Vienna, Austria

ISBN 978-1-4503-4336-7/17/03...$15.00

DOI: http://dx.doi.org/10.1145/2909824.3020229

For this reason, high-quality Automatic Speech Recognition (ASR) is a vital component for producing autonomous human-robot interaction. ASR engines have undergone significant improvements in recent years, particularly following the introduction of new techniques such as deep learning [26]. However, these engines are commonly evaluated against standardised datasets of adult speech [23]. One might naively assume that these improvements will also translate to child speech, and will cope relatively well with noisy (i.e., real-world) environments, such as those experienced in applied HRI. However, this is often observed to not be the case, cf. [19].

In this paper we seek to evaluate the state-of-the-art in speech recognition for child speech, and to test ASR engines in settings inspired by real-world child-robot interactions. We record a variety of pre-determined phrases and spontaneous speech from a number of children speaking English using multiple microphones. We separate recordings by whether they are comparatively clean, or contain noise from the real-world environment. Through consideration of the results, we highlight the limitations of ASR for child speech, and also make a number of interaction design recommendations to maximise the efficacy of the technology currently available.

2. BACKGROUND

Speech recognition has undergone significant advances, building on or moving on from the use of Hidden Markov Models (HMM) towards using deep neural networks (DNN). DNNs have been shown to outperform older HMM based approaches by some margin against standard benchmarks [12]. For example, in a Google speech recognition task a deep neural network reduced the Word Error Rate (WER) to 12.3%, a 23% relative improvement on the previous state-of-the-art [12].

However, these benchmarks are based on adult speech corpora, such as the TIMIT corpus [17]. It has been noted by other researchers that there is a lack of corpora for children's speech, leading to a lack of training data and a lack of benchmarking for children's speech recognition models [5, 9, 11]. It is commonly assumed that the recent improvements observed in adult speech recognition mean that child speech recognition improved at the same pace, and recognising children's utterances can be achieved with a similar degree of success. However, anecdotal evidence suggests that this is not the case; Lehman et al. [19] state that recognition of children's speech "remains an unsolved problem", calling for research to be undertaken to understand more about the limitations of ASR for children to ease interaction design.

Children's speech is fundamentally different from adult speech: the most marked difference being the higher pitched voice, due to children having a shorter, immature vocal tract. In addition, spontaneous child speech is marked by a higher number of disfluencies and, especially in younger children, language utterances are often ungrammatical (e.g., "The boy *putted* the frog in the box"). As such, typical ASR engines, which are trained on adult speech, struggle to correctly recognise children's speech [8, 24]. An added complexity is caused by the ongoing development of the vocal apparatus and language performance in children: an ASR engine trained for one age group is unlikely to perform well for another age group.

There have been various attempts to remedy this, from adapting adult-trained ASR engines to the spectral characteristics of children's speech [18, 22], to training ASR engines on child speech corpora [6, 8, 10], or combinations of both. For example, Liao et al. [21] have used spoken search instructions from YouTube Kids to train DNNs with some success, resulting in a WER between 10 and 20%. In [24] vocal-tract length normalisation (VTLN) and DNN are used in combination, and when trained on read speech of children aged between 7 and 13 years, result in a WER of approximately 10%. It should be noted that these results are achieved in limited domains, such as spoken search instructions, read speech, or number recognition [22]. Also, the circumstances in which the speech is recorded are typically more controlled than interactions encountered in HRI, where ambient noise, distance and orientation to the microphone, and language use are more variable.

Whilst children's speech recognition in general is a challenge, HRI brings further complexities due to factors such as robot motor noise, robot fan noise, placement and orientation of microphones, and so on. Many researchers adopt interaction approaches that do not rely on verbal interaction due to the unreliability of child ASR, particularly in 'wild' environments. Wizard of Oz (WoZ) approaches have proven popular to substitute for sub-optimal speech recognition and natural language interaction, but when autonomy is important, WoZ is impractical and the use of mediating interfaces to substitute for linguistic interaction has proven successful. Touchscreens, for example, can serve as interaction devices, they provide a focus for the interaction while constraining the unfolding interaction [1]. However, if we wish the field to continue to progress into real-world environments, then it is unrealistic to exclude verbal interaction due to the prevalence of this communication channel in natural interaction.

3. RESEARCH QUESTIONS

The previous section highlights that the current performance of ASR for child speech remains unclear. We wish to address this by exploring different variables in the context of child speech, such as the type of microphone, the physical location of the speaker relative to a robot, and the ASR engine. These variables motivate a set of research questions presented below, all in the context of child speech. Their evaluation will be conducted with the aim of producing evidenced guidelines for designing verbal human-robot interactions with children.

Figure 1: Equipment layout for recording children in a school. The Aldebaran NAO is turned on (but not moving) and records to a USB memory card. The studio microphone and portable microphone record simultaneously.

Q1 Do external microphones produce better results than robot-mounted microphones?

Q2 How can physical interaction setups be optimised for ASR?

Q3 Is there a benefit to using cloud-based or off-board ASR engines compared to a stock robot ASR engine?

Q4 What is the impact of 'real-world' noise on speech recognition in an HRI inspired scenario?

4. METHODOLOGY

In order to address the research questions posed in the previous section, a data collection and testing procedure was designed. At the time of writing, no corpus of child speech suitable for the intended analysis was publicly available. As such, there is a need for the collection of this data; the procedure for this will be outlined here.

4.1 Participants

A total of 11 children took part in our study, with an average age M=4.9, SD=0.3; 5F/6M. The age group is motivated by the many large-scale initiatives in the US, Europe and Japan exploring linguistic interactions in HRI [2, 3, 19, 20, 25], and the fact that this age group is preliterate, so cannot interact using text interfaces. All children had age-appropriate competency in speaking English at school. All participants gave consent to take part in the study, with the children's parents providing additional consent for participation, and recording and using the audio data. The children were rewarded after the study with a presentation of social robots.

4.2 Data Collection

In order to collect a variety of speech utterances, three different categories were devised: single word utterances, multi-word utterances, and spontaneous speech. The single word and multi-word utterances were collected by repeating after an experimenter. This was done to prevent any issues with child reading ability. Spontaneous speech was collected through retelling a picture book, 'Frog, Where Are You?' by Mercer Mayer, which is a common stimulus for this activity in language development studies [4]. The single word utterances were numbers from 1 to 10, and the multi-word utterances were based on spatial relationships between two nouns, for example, 'the horse is in the stable'. Five sentences of this style were used; the full set can be downloaded from [16].

The English speech from children was collected at a primary school in the U.K. This served two purposes: firstly, to conduct the collection in an environment in which the children are comfortable, and secondly, to collect data with background noise from a real-world environment commonly used in HRI studies, e.g., [15]. An Aldebaran NAO (hardware version 5.0 running the NaoQi 2.1.4 software) was used as the robotic platform. This was selected as it is a commonly used platform for research with children, as well as for its microphone array and commercial-standard speech recognition engine (provided by Nuance). The robot would record directly from the microphones to a USB memory stick. Simultaneously, a studio grade microphone (Rode NT1-A) and a portable microphone (Zoom H1) were also recording. The studio microphone was placed above the robot and the portable microphone just in front of the robot (Fig. 1).

4.3 Data Processing

Encoding and Segmentation.

All audio files were recorded in lossless WAV format (minimum sampling rate of 44kHz). The audio files from each of the three microphones were synchronised in a single Audacity project. The audio files were then split to extract segments containing the speech under consideration. These segments were exported as lossless WAV files, resulting in 16 files per microphone (48 in total) per child. The spontaneous speech was transcribed and split into sentences. This produced a total of 222 spontaneous speech utterances of various lengths ($M = 7.8$ words per utterance, $SD = 2.6$). The full dataset (audio files and transcripts) is available online at [16].

Noisy vs. Clean Audio Recordings.

As the recordings of children in English were collected during the course of a school day, there is a range of background noise. To study the impact of noise on ASR performance, it is desirable to separate the recordings into those that have minimal background noise ('clean' recordings) and those that have marked background noise ('noisy' recordings). Some noise is unavoidable, or would be present in any HRI scenario, such as robot fan noise, so these were considered 'clean'. Other noise, such as birds outside, other children shouting from the adjacent room, doors closing, or coughing would be considered 'noisy'. This means that the clean recordings are not noise-free like those from a studio environment, but are a realistic representation of a minimal practical noise level in a 'wild' HRI scenario, thereby allowing us to evaluate recognition accuracy with greater veracity.

To appropriately categorise the recordings as clean or noisy, each one was independently listened to by 3 human coders with the guidance from above as to what is considered clean vs. noisy. Overall agreement levels between coders was good, with Fleiss $\kappa = .74$ (95% CI [.65,.84]) for the fixed utterances and $\kappa = .68$ (95% CI [.60,.75]) for the spontaneous

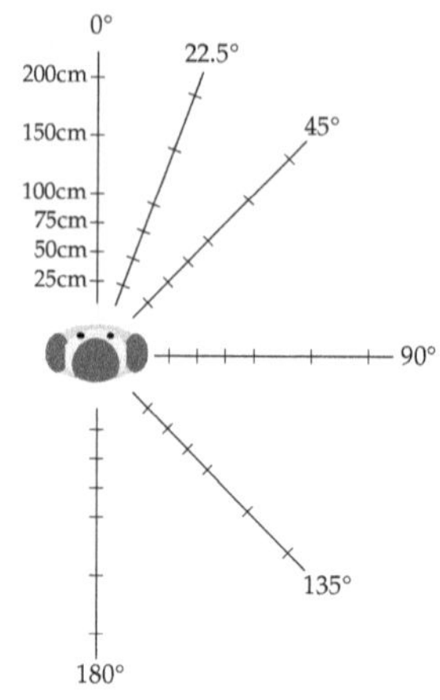

Figure 2: Locations at which speech it played to the NAO to explore how the physical layout of interactions may influence speech recognition rates.

utterances. A recording was categorised as noisy or clean if all 3 coders agreed it was respectively noisy or clean. Where there was any disagreement between coders, the recordings were omitted from analysis of noise impact (59 fixed and 54 spontaneous utterances were excluded). This resulted in 80 noisy recordings, and 37 clean recordings being analysed from the fixed utterances set and 83 clean/85 noisy recordings from the spontaneous utterances set. For some children, the NAO recording failed due to technical difficulties. Therefore, when comparing across microphones, the fixed utterance selection is reduced to 29 clean recordings and 60 noisy recordings.

Manipulation of the Sound Location.

To evaluate the impact of distance and angle on speech recognition, it was necessary to vary the distance between the robot and child, while at the same time keeping the speech utterances constant. As children struggle to exactly reproduce speech acts and over 500 utterances are needed to be recognised, we used pre-recorded speech played through an audio reference speaker (the PreSonus Eris E5) placed at different locations around the robot. In order to match the original volume levels, a calibration process was used where a recording would be played and re-recorded at the original distance between the child and the robot. The audio signal amplitudes between the original and recorded file were then compared. The speaker volume was iteratively revised until the amplitudes matched. This volume was then maintained as the speaker was moved to different distances and angles from the robot, while always facing the robot (to address, at least in part, Q2 from Sec. 3); see Fig. 2 for a diagram of these positions.

4.4 Measures

For recognition cases where a *multiple choice* grammar is used (i.e., the list of possible utterances is entirely predefined, and the recognition engine's task is to pick the correct one), the recognition percentage is used as the metric. Each word or sentence correctly recognised adds 1; the final sum is divided by the number of tested words or sentences. All Confidence Intervals calculated for the recognition percentage include continuity correction using the Wilson procedure. We use the same metric when using template-based grammars (Sec. 5.2.1).

For the cases in which an open grammar is used, we use the Levenshtein distance as a metric at the *letter* level. This decision was made as it reduces punishment for small errors in recognition, which would typically not be of concern for HRI scenarios. For example, when using the Levenshtein distance at the word level (as with Word Error Rate), if the word 'robots' is returned for an input utterance of 'robot', this would be scored as completely unrecognised. At the letter level, this would score a Levenshtein distance of 1, as only a single letter needs to be inserted, deleted or substituted (in this example, the letter 's') to get the correct result. To compare between utterances, normalisation by the number of letters in the utterance is then required to compensate for longer inputs incurring greater possibility of higher Levenshtein distances.

5. RESULTS

This section will break down the results and analysis such that the research questions are addressed. The results are split into two main subsections concerning: 1) technical implementation details, and 2) general ASR performance. The intention is to then provide a practical guide for getting the best performance from ASR in HRI scenarios, as well as an indication of the performance level that can be expected more generally for child speech under different circumstances.

5.1 Technical Best Practices

Throughout this subsection, the ASR engine will remain constant so that other variables can be explored. In this case, the ASR engine used is the one that comes as default on the Aldebaran NAO, provided by Nuance (VoCon 4.7). A grammar is provided to this engine, consisting of numbers (as described in Sec. 4.2) and single word utterances. Longer utterances, along with open grammar and spontaneous speech will be explored in the subsequent subsection.

5.1.1 Type of microphone

Upon observation of the results it became clear that the robot-mounted microphone was vastly outperforming the portable and studio microphones. When visually comparing the waveforms, there was a noticeable difference in recorded amplitude between the NAO signal and the other two microphones. This was despite the standalone microphone input gains being adjusted to maximise the signal (whilst preventing peak clipping). To increase the signal amplitude whilst maintaining the signal-to-noise ratio, the files were normalised. This normalisation step made a significant difference to the results of the speech recognition. For the portable microphone, the recognition percentage after normalisation (70%, 95% CI [59%,79%]) was significantly improved compared to before normalisation (2%, 95% CI [0%,9%]); Wilcoxon signed-rank test[1] $Z = -7.483, p < .001, r = 0.67$. A similar improvement was observed for the studio microphone when comparing before (5%, 95% CI [2%,12%]) and after (81%, 95% CI [70%,88%]) normalisation; $Z = -7.937, p < .001, r = 0.71$ (Fig. 3). This suggests that the NAO microphones are tuned to maximise the speech level, and if

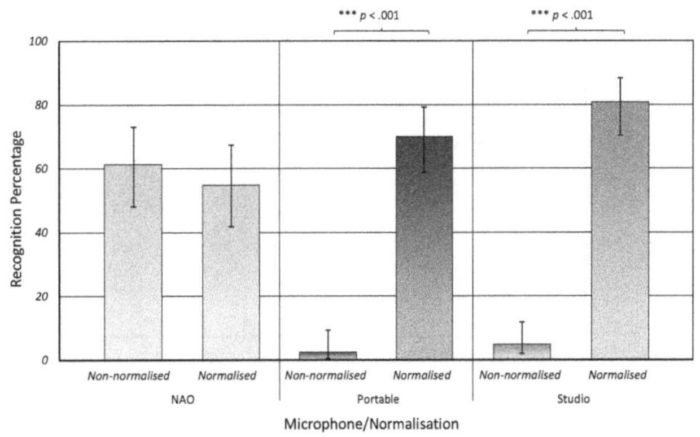

Figure 3: A comparison of recognition percentage of English words and short sentences spoken by children, split by microphone before and after normalisation. * indicates significance at the p<.001 level. The recognition is much improved for the portable and studio microphones following normalisation.**

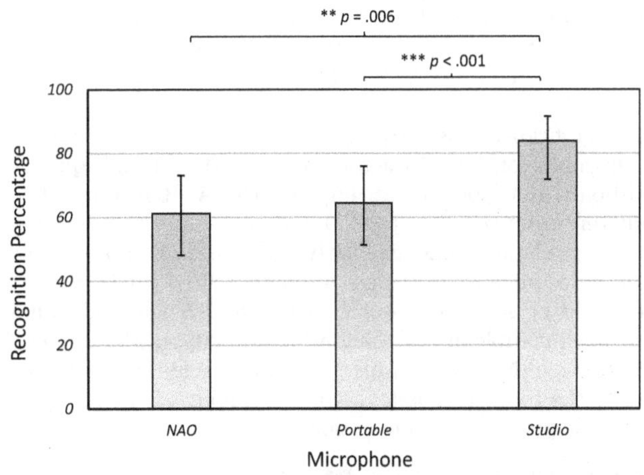

Figure 4: Recognition percentage of numbers spoken by children, split by microphone type (62 utterances). * indicates significance at the p<.001 level, ** indicates significance at the p<.01 level. The studio microphone provides the best ASR performance, but the difference between on- and lower quality off-board microphones is relatively small.**

external microphones are to be used, then normalisation of the recordings should be considered a vital step in processing prior to sending to an ASR engine. Therefore, for the remainder of the analysis here, only normalised files are used for the studio and portable microphones.

In exploring Q1, it is observed that the differences between microphones is smaller than may have been expected. The NAO microphones are mounted in the head of the robot near a cooling fan which produces a large amount of background noise. It could therefore be hypothesised that the ASR performance would greatly increase by using an off-board microphone, and that using a higher-quality microphone would improve this further. Using Friedman's test, a significant difference at the $p < .05$ level is found between the NAO (61%, 95% CI [48%,73%]), portable (65%, 95% CI [51%,76%]), and studio (84%, 95% CI [72%,92%]) micro-

[1]Due to the recognition being binary on single word inputs, the resulting distributions are non-normal, so non-parametric tests are used for significance testing.

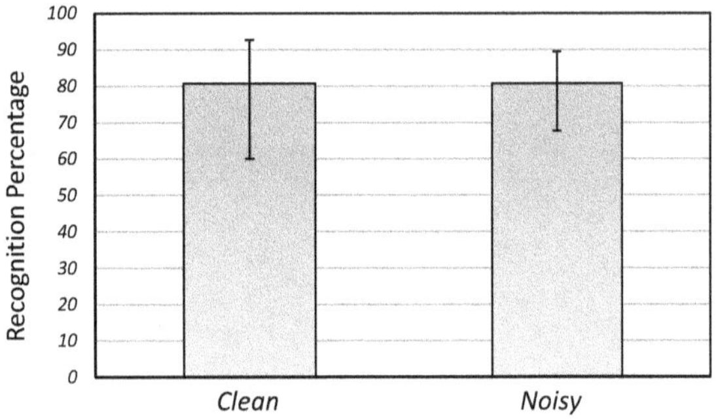

Figure 5: Recognition percentage of single word utterances spoken by children, split by background noise level (83 total utterances). Noise level does not have a significant effect on the recognition rate.

phones; $\chi^2(2) = 9.829, p = .007$. Post-hoc Wilcoxon signed-rank pairwise comparisons with Bonferroni correction reveal a statistically significant difference between the portable and studio microphones ($Z = -3.207, p < .001, r = 0.29$; Fig. 4), and between the NAO and studio microphones ($Z = -2.746, p = .006, r = 0.24$). Differences between the portable and NAO microphones ($Z = -0.365, p = .715, r = 0.03$) were not significant. This suggests that there is no intrinsic value to using an off-board microphone, but that a high quality off-board microphone can improve the ASR results. The difference between the robot microphone and the external studio grade microphone is fairly substantial, with a recognition percentage improvement of around 20%point ($r = 0.28$). It would be scenario specific as to whether the additional technical complexity of using a high-quality external microphone would be worth this gain, and indeed, in scenarios where the robot is mobile, use of a studio grade microphone may not be a practicable option.

5.1.2 Clean vs. Noisy Recording Environment

Splitting the files by whether they were judged to be clean or noisy (as described in Sec. 4.3), it was observed that the noise did not appear to have a significant impact on the results of the ASR. Using the studio microphone (i.e., the best performing microphone) for the number utterances, a Mann-Whitney U test reveals no significant difference between clean (81%, 95% CI [60%,93%]) and noisy (81%, 95% CI [68%,90%]) speech; $U = 740.5, p = .994, r = 0.00$ (Fig. 5). The apparent robustness of the ASR engine to noise is of particular benefit to HRI researchers given the increasingly 'real-world' application of robots, where background noise is often near impossible (nor desirable) to prevent.

However, this does not mean that noise does not play a role in recognition rates. In this instance, the ASR engine is restricted in its grammar; the effect of noise in open grammar situations is explored in the next subsection. Additionally, when the distance of the sound source to the microphone is varied, background noise becomes a greater factor.

5.1.3 Sound Source Location

Measurements were made as in Fig. 2 using the built in NAO microphone, with the replayed audio from the studio microphone (as described in Sec. 4.3). Due to the number of data points this generates (540 per child), the findings in full will not be produced here, but to get a high-level picture

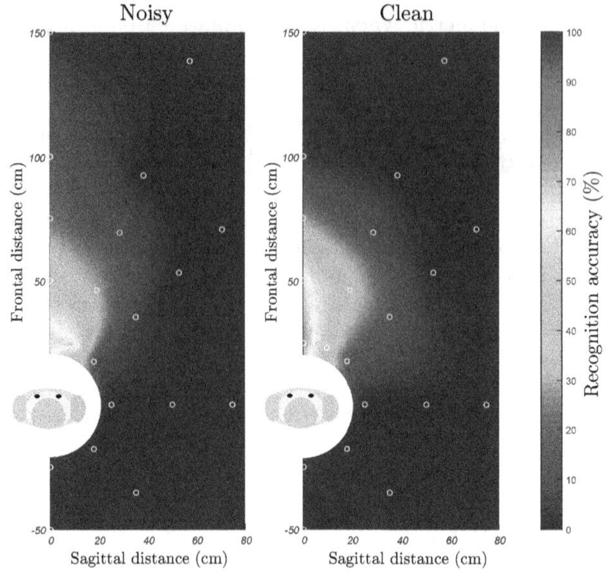

Figure 6: Interpolated heatmap of recognition percentage as a function of distance and orientation to the robot. Interpolation has been performed based on the measurements made at the small white circles. On the *left* is the heatmap for the noisy audio, whereas the *right* is for clean audio. The clean audio is better recognised at further distances from the robot, however, in both cases, recognition accuracy is 0% to the side and behind the robot.

of how the distance and orientation influences recognition rates, a heatmap can be seen in Fig. 6.

Two observations can be made from this data that have particular relevance for HRI researchers. The first is the platform-specific observation that with the NAO robot (currently one of the most widely used research platforms for social HRI) the utterance recognition rate drops dramatically once the sound source reaches a 45 degree angle to the robot head, and becomes 0 once it reaches 90 degrees. The implication of this is that when using the NAO, it is vital to rotate the head to look at the sound source in order to have the possibility of recognising the speech. This is of course dependent on the current default software implementation; four channels of audio exist, but for ASR only the front two are used, and so a workaround could be created for this. The second, broader observation, is that the background noise and distance seem to influence recognition rates when combined. Fig. 5 shows how little impact noise has when the files

Distance (cm)	Clean % [95% CI]	Noisy % [95% CI]
25	73 [52,88]	77 [64,87]
50	65 [44,82]	44 [31,58]
75	27 [12,48]	23 [13,36]
100	4 [0,22]	18 [9,30]

Table 1: ASR recognition rates for children counting from one to ten. Recordings were played frontally at different distances from the robot. Note how recognition falls sharply with distance when the speech contains noise.

are fed directly into the robot ASR, but when combined with distance, there is a marked difference beyond 50cm. Table 1 shows the measurements for the first metre directly in front of the robot; at 25cm the difference between clean and noisy files are minimal, however at 50cm, the difference is more pronounced, with recognition rates dropping fast.

5.2 ASR Performance with Children

The previous subsection addressed variables in achieving a maximal possible speech recognition percentage through modifying the technical implementation, such as different microphones, distances to a robot, orientation to a robot, and background noise levels. This subsection will provide a complementary focus on exploring the current expected performance of ASR with children under different speech and ASR engine conditions. This will include a comparison of differing length utterances, spontaneous utterances, and different ASR engines with varying grammar specifications. For all analyses in this section, the studio microphone signal is used to provide the best quality sound input to the speech engines (and provide a theoretical maximal performance).

5.2.1 Impact of Providing a Grammar

Tests on child speech in the previous subsection were performed with single word utterances, with a grammar consisting of only those utterances. This kind of multiple choice is relatively straightforward, and this carries over to slightly longer utterances too. We compare the recognition rate of the fixed multi-word utterances (34 spatial relation sentences as described in Sec. 4.2) under 3 conditions using the built-in NAO ASR: 1) with a fixed grammar containing the complete utterances, e.g., "one" or "the dog is on the shed" (i.e., multiple choice), 2) with a template grammar for the sentences (as seen in Fig. 8), and 3) with an open grammar. This progressively reduces the prior knowledge the ASR engine has about what utterances to expect. The full mix of noisy and clean utterances were used as there was no observed significant correlation in any of the three conditions between ASR confidence level and noise condition, nor between noise condition and resulting recognition rates. The grammar condition has a significant impact on the recognition percentage; Friedman's test $\chi^2(2) = 39.92, p < .001$. Post-hoc Wilcoxon signed-rank pairwise comparisons with Bonferroni correction reveal a statistically significant difference between the multiple choice (74%, 95% CI [55%,86%]) and template grammars (53%, 95% CI [35%,70%]); $Z = -2.646, p = .008, r = 0.32$. The template grammar in turn offers a significant improvement over the open grammar (0%, 95% [0%,13%]); $Z = -4.243, p < .001, r = 0.51$ (Fig. 7).

5.2.2 Comparison of ASR Engines

Finally, we look at how different ASR engines perform, under identical recording conditions. We compare the Google Speech API (as found in the Chrome web browser for instance), the Microsoft Speech API (as found in the Bing search engine), CMU PocketSphinx, and the NAO-embedded Nuance VoCon 4.7 engine; studies were run in August 2016. The audio samples are those recorded with the studio microphone; they include native and non-native speakers as well as noisy and clean samples; they include both the fixed sentences and the spontaneous speech; no grammar is provided to the engine (i.e., open grammar).

As performing recognition with an open grammar is a much harder challenge for recognition engines, the recognition percentage alone is no longer a sufficient measurement to compare between performance of ASR engines due to the very low number of exact utterance recognitions across all engines. Instead we use the Levenshtein distance (LD) at the letter level. As the utterance length for the spontaneous speech is also variable, the Levenshtein distance is normalised by utterance length (as per Sec. 4.4). This provides a value between 0 and 1, where 0 means the returned transcription matches the actual utterance, and 1 means not a single letter was correct. Values in between indicate the proportion of letters that would have to be changed to get the correct response, therefore lower scores are better. Table 2 provides one recognition example with the corresponding Levenshtein distances.

While the LD provides a good indication of how close the result is from the input utterance, the examples in Table 2

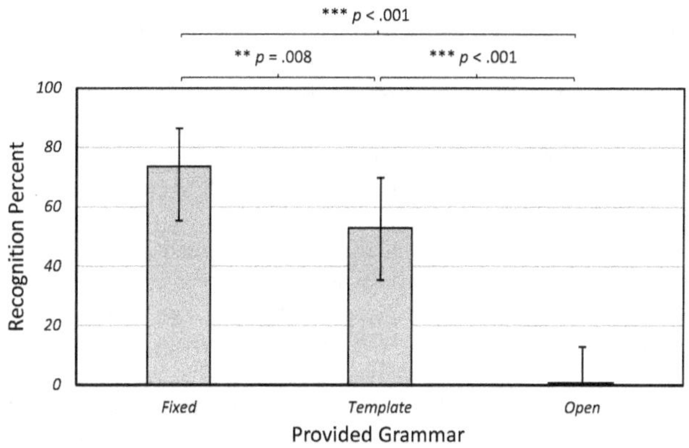

Figure 7: Recognition percentage when providing a fixed grammar, a template grammar, and an open grammar on short utterances. The fixed 'multiple choice' grammar produces the best recognition, followed by a template. The open grammar, on average, recognises almost no sentences correctly.

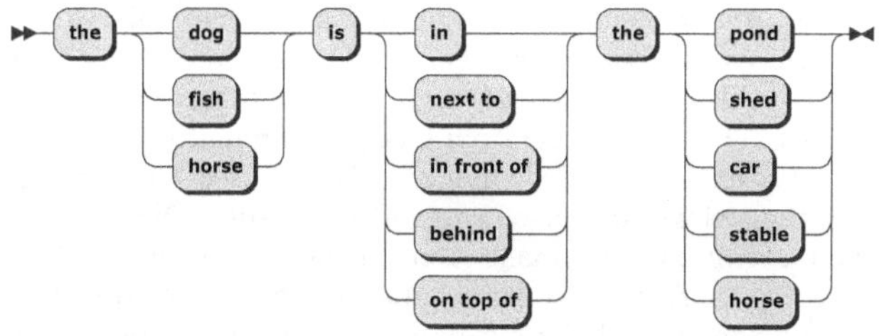

Figure 8: Template for the grammar provided to the ASR for the fixed utterances. 75 different sentences can be generated from this grammar.

Google API	*then the wraps looks at the dog*	[LD=0.17]
Microsoft API	*rat look at dogs*	[LD=0.48]
PocketSphinx	*look i personally*	[LD=0.83]

Table 2: Recognition results and Levenshtein distance for three ASR engines on the input utterance "then the rat looked at the dog". The NAO-embedded Nuance engine did not return any result.

evidence that this metric does not necessarily reflect *semantic* closeness. In this particular case, the Bing result "rat look at dogs" is semantically closer to the original utterance than the other answers. For this reason, we assess recognition performance in open grammar using a combination of three metrics: 1) the Levenshtein distance; 2) raw accuracy (i.e., the number of exact matches between the original utterance and the ASR result); 3) a manually-assessed 'relaxed' accuracy. The utterance would be considered accurate in the 'relaxed' category if small grammatical errors are present, but not semantic errors. Grammatical errors can include pluralisation, removal of repetitions, or small article changes ('the' instead of 'a'). For example, if an input utterance of "and then he found the dog" returned the result "and then he found a dog", this would be considered accurate, however "and then he found the frog" would produce a similar LD, but the semantics have changed, so this would not be included in the relaxed accuracy category.

Table 3 shows that when the input utterance set is changed to use spontaneous speech, the average normalised LD does not change much for any of the ASR engines. Nor do the LD rates change much when only clean spontaneous speech is used, providing further evidence for the minimal impact of noise as established in Sec. 5.1.2. However, there is a marked difference between Google and the other recognition engines. The average LD from Google is around half that of the other engines, and the number of recognised sentences in both the strict and relaxed categories is substantially higher. The recognition performance remains however generally low: using relaxed rules, the currently best performing ASR engine (Google Speech API) for our data recognises only about 18% of a corpus of 222 child utterances (utterances have a mean length of $M = 7.8$ words, $SD = 2.6$).

To help decide whether or not the results returned from Google would actually be usable in autonomous HRI scenarios, it is necessary to determine when the utterance is correctly recognised. This is typically indicated through the *confidence value* returned by the recognition engine. To further explore this, we assess the number recognition percentage at different thresholds within the confidence level (Fig. 9). A total of 101 results from the 222 passed to the recogniser returned a confidence level (a confidence value is not returned when the uncertainty of the ASR engine is too high). To achieve just below 50% semantically correct recognition accuracy, the confidence threshold could be set to 0.8, which would only include 36 utterances. While a clear improvement over the 18% previously achieved when not taking into consideration the confidence value, a 50% recognition rate is arguably not sufficient for a smooth child-robot verbal interaction, and would still require the system to reject nearly 2/3 of the child utterances.

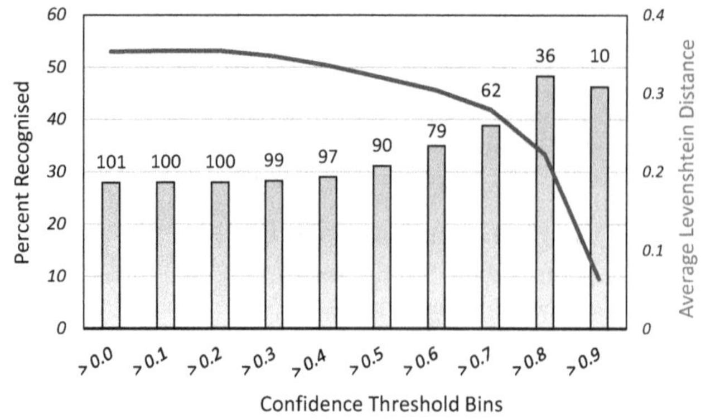

Figure 9: Histogram of recognition percentage (using the relaxed, manually coded criteria) for spontaneous speech grouped by confidence levels (indicated by the number above each bar) returned by Google ASR. The average Levenshtein Distance is also shown on the secondary axis. Recognition increases with higher confidence ranges, but few utterances have a high confidence.

6. DISCUSSION

Our results show that, at the time of writing, automatic speech recognition still does not work reliably with children, and should not be relied upon for autonomous child-robot interaction.

Speech segmentation is one aspect that we did not investigate. The segmentation of speech units and rejecting non-speech parts is an important factor in speech recognition. For example, noise can be mistakenly recognised by ASR engines as speech, or a pause in the middle of a sentence might interrupt the segmentation. Existing solutions (like a beep sound indicating when to talk) are not ideal for children of this age. Our manual segmentation likely leads to better results than would be expected with automatic segmentation.

We did not analyse if gender had an effect on ASR due to the age of the children used in the study. It has been shown that there are no significant differences in the vocal tract between genders at the age under consideration (5-6 years old) [7], so we do not expect differing performance based on gender.

Mitigation strategies for poor ASR performance depend on the ASR engine. We have specifically investigated the use of constrained grammar with the NAO's Nuance engine; and the use of the recognition confidence with the Google ASR. While severely constraining the interaction scope, none of these techniques were found to provide satisfactory results. In our most favourable test case (children speaking numbers from one to ten in front of the robot, at about 25cm; the robot having an explicit 'multiple choice' grammar), the ASR would return an incorrect result in one of four cases, and could not provide any meaningful confidence value. This result is disappointing, particularly when considering that interactions based on 'multiple choice' are difficult to rely on with children, as they tend not to remember and/or comply to the given set of recognisable utterances.

Template-based grammars (or 'slot-filling' grammars) where the general structure of the sentence is known beforehand, and only a limited set of options are available to fill the 'gaps' are a potentially interesting middle-ground between 'multiple choice' grammars and open speech. However, we show that in our test case (grammar depicted in Fig. 8), the correct utterance was recognised in only 50% of the cases, again without any useful confidence value.

In the realm of open grammars, the Google Speech API returned the most accurate results by a large margin. When run on grammatically correct, regular sentences (the ones generated from the grammar depicted in Fig. 8), it reaches 38% accuracy in recognition when minor grammatical differences are allowed. This result, while likely not yet usable in today's applications, is promising. However, when looking

	Google		Bing		Sphinx		Nuance	
	M LD [95%CI]	*% rec.*	*M* LD [95%CI]	*% rec.*	*M* LD [95%CI]	*% rec.*	*M* LD [95%CI]	*% rec.*
fixed (n=34)	**0.34** [0.24,0.44]	*11.8* *[38]*	0.64 [0.56,0.71]	*0* *[0]*	0.68 [0.64,0.73]	*0* *[0]*	0.76 [0.73,0.80]	*0* *[0]*
spontaneous (n=222)	**0.39** [0.36,0.43]	*6.8* *[17.6]*	0.64 [0.61,0.67]	*0.5* *[2.4]*	0.80 [0.77,0.84]	*0* *[0]*	0.80 [0.78,0.82]	*0* *[0]*
spontaneous clean only (n=83)	**0.40** [0.35,0.45]	*6.0* *[16.9]*	0.63 [0.58,0.68]	*1.2* *[1.2]*	0.78 [0.72,0.85]	*0* *[0]*	0.78 [0.75,0.81]	*0* *[0]*

Table 3: Comparison between four ASR engines using fixed, all spontaneous, and clean spontaneous speech utterances as input. Mean average normalised Levenshtein Distance (*M* LD) indicates how good the transcription is. *% rec* indicates the percentage of results that are an exact match for the original utterance, with the values in square brackets *[ ]* indicating matches with 'relaxed' accuracy.

at children's spontaneous speech, the recognition rate drops sharply (to around 18% of successful recognition). This difference can be explained by the numerous disfluencies and grammatical errors found in natural child speech. To provide an example, a relatively typical utterance from our data was "and... and the frog didn't went to sleep". The utterance has a repetition and disfluency at the start, and is followed by grammatically incorrect content. This is, in our opinion, the real challenge that automatic child speech recognition faces: the need to account for the child-specific language issues, beyond the mere differences between the acoustic models of adults vs. children. This is a challenge not only for speech-to-text, but as well for later stages of the verbal interaction, like speech understanding and dialogue management.

Our results allow us to make a number of recommendations for designing child-robot interaction scenarios that include verbal interaction. Most of these are also applicable to adult settings and would be expected to contribute to a smoother interaction.

- Constrain the interaction by leading the child to a limited set of responses. This typically works well for older children, but carries the risk of making the interaction stale.
- Use additional input/output devices. A touchscreen has been found to be a particularly effective substitute for linguistic input [1, 14], but also other devices -such as haptic devices- should be considered.
- Place the young user in the optimal location for ASR. The location and orientation relative to the microphone (and robot) has a profound impact on ASR performance (Sec. 5.1.3). A cushion, stool or chair can help children sit in the optimal location.
- Constrain the grammar of the ASR. While not all ASR engines allow for this (cf. Bing), some will allow constraints or "hints" on what is recognised. This proves to be valuable in constrained interaction settings, for example, when listening only for numbers between 1 and 10 (Sec. 5.2.1).
- Background noise appears to be less of an issue than initially anticipated. It appears that the current ASR engines have effective noise cancelling mechanisms in place. Nevertheless, "the less noise, the better" remains true, particularly when interacting at a distance from the robot (Sec's 5.1.2 & 5.1.3).
- A lack of ASR performance does not mean that the robot should not produce speech, as speech has been found to be particularly effective to engage children.

We opted to evaluate the ASR capabilities of the Aldebaran NAO platform, as it is the most commonly used robot in commercial and academic HRI. While the NAO system under performs for child speech, some performance could be gained through using a high-quality external microphone and cloud-based ASR, with Google as clear favourite.

7. CONCLUSION

Language is perhaps the most important modality in human-to-human interaction and as such, functional natural language interaction forms a formidable prize in human-machine interaction. Speech recognition is the entry point to this and while there has been steady progress in speaker-independent adult speech recognition, the same progress is currently lacking from children's speech recognition. For various reasons -pitch characteristics of children's voices, speech disfluencies, and unsteady developmental changes- child speech recognition is expected to require a multi-pronged approach and recognition performance in unconstrained domains is currently too low to be practical.

This has a profound impact on the interaction between children and technology, especially where pre-literacy children are concerned, typically ages 6 and younger. As they have no means of entering input other than by speaking to the device, the interaction with pre-literacy children stands or falls with good speech recognition.

Our results show that natural language interactions with children are not yet practicable. Today, building rich and natural interactions between robots and children still requires a complex alchemy: a careful design of the interaction that leads the responses of the young user in such a way that restrictive ASR grammars are acceptable, the understanding and production of rich non-verbal communication cues like gaze, and a judicious use of supporting technology such as touchscreens.

8. ACKNOWLEDGEMENTS

This work has been supported by the EU H2020 L2TOR project (grant 688014), the EU FP7 DREAM project (grant 611391), and the EU H2020 Marie Sklodowska-Curie Actions project DoRoThy (grant 657227).

9. REFERENCES

[1] P. Baxter, R. Wood, and T. Belpaeme. A touchscreen-based 'sandtray' to facilitate, mediate and contextualise human-robot social interaction. In *Proceedings of the 7th annual ACM/IEEE international conference on Human-Robot Interaction*, pages 105–106. ACM, 2012.

[2] T. Belpaeme, P. Baxter, R. Read, R. Wood, H. Cuayáhuitl, B. Kiefer, S. Racioppa, I. Kruijff-Korbayová, G. Athanasopoulos, V. Enescu, R. Looije, M. Neerincx, Y. Demiris, R. Ros-Espinoza, A. Beck, L. Cañamero, A. Hiolle, M. Lewis, I. Baroni, M. Nalin, P. Cosi, G. Paci, F. Tesser, G. Sommavilla, and R. Humbert. Multimodal Child-Robot Interaction: Building Social Bonds. *Journal of Human-Robot Interaction*, 1(2):33–53, 2012.

[3] T. Belpaeme, J. Kennedy, P. Baxter, P. Vogt, E. E. Krahmer, S. Kopp, K. Bergmann, P. Leseman, A. C. Küntay, T. Göksun, A. K. Pandey, R. Gelin, P. Koudelkova, and T. Deblieck. L2TOR - second language tutoring using social robots. In *Proceedings of the 1st International Workshop on Educational Robots*, Paris, France, 2015.

[4] R. A. Berman and D. I. Slobin. *Relating events in narrative: A crosslinguistic developmental study.* Psychology Press, 2013.

[5] P. Cosi, M. Nicolao, G. Paci, G. Sommavilla, and F. Tesser. Comparing open source ASR toolkits on Italian children speech. In *Proceedings of the Workshop on Child Computer Interaction*, 2014.

[6] S. Fernando, R. K. Moore, D. Cameron, E. C. Collins, A. Millings, A. J. Sharkey, and T. J. Prescott. Automatic recognition of child speech for robotic applications in noisy environments. *arXiv preprint*, arXiv:1611.02695, 2016.

[7] W. T. Fitch and J. Giedd. Morphology and development of the human vocal tract: A study using magnetic resonance imaging. *The Journal of the Acoustical Society of America*, 106(3):1511–1522, 1999.

[8] M. Gerosa, D. Giuliani, S. Narayanan, and A. Potamianos. A review of ASR technologies for children's speech. In *Proceedings of the 2nd Workshop on Child, Computer and Interaction*, pages 7:1–7:8. ACM, 2009.

[9] P. Grill and J. Tučková. Speech databases of typical children and children with SLI. *PloS one*, 11(3):e0150365, 2016.

[10] A. Hagen, B. Pellom, and R. Cole. Children's speech recognition with application to interactive books and tutors. In *Proceedings of the IEEE Workshop on Automatic Speech Recognition and Understanding, 2003*, pages 186–191. IEEE, 2003.

[11] A. Hämäläinen, S. Candeias, H. Cho, H. Meinedo, A. Abad, T. Pellegrini, M. Tjalve, I. Trancoso, and M. Sales Dias. Correlating ASR errors with developmental changes in speech production: A study of 3-10-year-old European Portuguese children's speech. In *Proceedings of the Workshop on Child Computer Interaction*, 2014.

[12] G. Hinton, L. Deng, D. Yu, G. E. Dahl, A.-r. Mohamed, N. Jaitly, A. Senior, V. Vanhoucke, P. Nguyen, T. N. Sainath, et al. Deep neural networks for acoustic modeling in speech recognition: The shared views of four research groups. *IEEE Signal Processing Magazine*, 29(6):82–97, 2012.

[13] C.-M. Huang, S. Andrist, A. Sauppé, and B. Mutlu. Using gaze patterns to predict task intent in collaboration. *Frontiers in Psychology*, 6, 2015.

[14] J. Kennedy, P. Baxter, and T. Belpaeme. Nonverbal Immediacy as a Characterisation of Social Behaviour for Human-Robot Interaction. *International Journal of Social Robotics*, in press.

[15] J. Kennedy, P. Baxter, E. Senft, and T. Belpaeme. Social Robot Tutoring for Child Second Language Learning. In *Proceedings of the 11th ACM/IEEE International Conference on Human-Robot Interaction*, pages 67–74. ACM, 2016.

[16] J. Kennedy, S. Lemaignan, C. Montassier, P. Lavalade, B. Irfan, F. Papadopoulos, E. Senft, and T. Belpaeme. Children speech recording (English, spontaneous speech + pre-defined sentences). Data set, 2016. http://doi.org/10.5281/zenodo.200495.

[17] L. F. Lamel, R. H. Kassel, and S. Seneff. Speech database development: Design and analysis of the acoustic-phonetic corpus. In *Speech Input/Output Assessment and Speech Databases*, 1989.

[18] L. Lee and R. Rose. A frequency warping approach to speaker normalization. *IEEE Transactions on Speech and Audio Processing*, 6(1):49–60, Jan 1998.

[19] J. F. Lehman. Robo fashion world: a multimodal corpus of multi-child human-computer interaction. In *Proceedings of the 2014 Workshop on Understanding and Modeling Multiparty, Multimodal Interactions*, pages 15–20. ACM, 2014.

[20] I. Leite, H. Hajishirzi, S. Andrist, and J. Lehman. Managing chaos: models of turn-taking in character-multichild interactions. In *Proceedings of the 15th ACM International Conference on Multimodal Interaction*, pages 43–50. ACM, 2013.

[21] H. Liao, G. Pundak, O. Siohan, M. Carroll, N. Coccaro, Q.-M. Jiang, T. N. Sainath, A. Senior, F. Beaufays, and M. Bacchiani. Large vocabulary automatic speech recognition for children. In *Proceedings of Interspeech*, 2015.

[22] A. Potamianos and S. Narayanan. Robust recognition of children's speech. *IEEE Transactions on Speech and Audio Processing*, 11(6):603–616, 2003.

[23] M. L. Seltzer, D. Yu, and Y. Wang. An investigation of deep neural networks for noise robust speech recognition. In *Proccedings of the IEEE International Conference on Acoustics, Speech and Signal Processing*, pages 7398–7402. IEEE, 2013.

[24] R. Serizel and D. Giuliani. Deep-neural network approaches for speech recognition with heterogeneous groups of speakers including children. *Natural Language Engineering*, 1:1–26, 2016.

[25] F. Tanaka, K. Isshiki, F. Takahashi, M. Uekusa, R. Sei, and K. Hayashi. Pepper learns together with children: Development of an educational application. In *Proceedings of the IEEE-RAS 15th International Conference on Humanoid Robots*, HUMANOIDS 2015, pages 270–275. IEEE, 2015.

[26] D. Yu and L. Deng. *Automatic Speech Recognition: A Deep Learning Approach.* Springer, 2015.

Creating Prosodic Synchrony for a Robot Co-player in a Speech-controlled Game for Children

Najmeh Sadoughi[1,2], André Pereira[1], Rishub Jain[1,3], Iolanda Leite[1], Jill Fain Lehman[1]
1. Disney Research, Pittsburgh, USA
2. University of Texas at Dallas, Texas, USA
3. Carnegie Mellon University, Pittsburgh, USA
nxs137130@utdallas.edu

ABSTRACT

Synchrony is an essential aspect of human-human interactions. In previous work, we have seen how synchrony manifests in low-level acoustic phenomena like fundamental frequency, loudness, and the duration of keywords during the play of child-child pairs in a fast-paced, cooperative, language-based game. The correlation between the increase in such low-level synchrony and increase in enjoyment of the game suggests that a similar dynamic between child and robot co-players might also improve the child's experience. We report an approach to creating on-line acoustic synchrony by using a *dynamic Bayesian network* learned from prior recordings of child-child play to select from a predefined space of robot speech in response to real-time measurement of the child's prosodic features. Data were collected from 40 new children, each playing the game with both a synchronizing and non-synchronizing version of the robot. Results show a significant order effect: although all children grew to enjoy the game more over time, those that began with the synchronous robot maintained their own synchrony to it and achieved higher engagement compared with those that did not.

1. INTRODUCTION

Human-human interaction is more than just exchanging messages explicitly. There are other para-linguistic cues that facilitate the interaction by creating a sense of rapport and bonding between the interlocutors. Among these cues are nonverbal behaviors such as gestures, postures, and prosody [3, 13]. Studies have shown that there are subtle cues of synchrony between prosodic features of speech from both parties in a conversation [13, 15, 25], and that coordination between dyads is associated with a positive effect on engagement, even very early in life [9,17]. The positive effect of synchrony on interactions between people suggests that we might make human-robot interaction more natural and engaging by incorporating similar mechanisms in a robot partner and making it responsive not only to the content, but also the para-verbal behavior of the user.

We explore this possibility in the context of a simple, language-based video game called *Mole Madness* (MM). Previous work examining the behavior of child-child and child-robot co-players in MM showed two related phenomena. Chaspari et al. [6] investigated children's level of engagement during game play with each other[1]. It was found that the association of speech features between the two children - including fundamental frequency (F0), loudness, and word duration - was stronger during the times that the children were judged to be highly engaged in the game. When the analysis was extended to child-robot play with the same set of children [7], there was no coordination of prosodic features and lower engagement scores overall.

The work reported here tests the hypothesis that children's experience with the robot can be improved by better approximating the synchrony found in more engaged child-child pairs. In particular, we use the data from children studied in [6] to train a *dynamic Bayesian network* (DBN) that captures the strong correlations for F0 and loudness. The model is used during gameplay to select the robot's prosodic features adaptively, based on the child's values. Although rate of keyword speech did not reach statistical significance in [7], the trend in the data was strong enough to suggest adding that type of verbal synchrony to the robot's behavior as well. Our proposed system uses a k nearest-neighbor approach in the multi-dimensional space of F0, loudness, and repetition to choose an utterance for the robot when a game action is required. In an experiment with a new set of children, each child played multiple game levels with both synchronizing and non-synchronizing versions of the robot, with order of condition counterbalanced across children. The results showed both the dyadic nature of synchronization and its profound effects. Children who played with the synchronizing version of the robot first maintained their prosodic synchrony to it even when it stopped maintaining its prosodic and verbal synchrony to them, and in this order engagement rose steadily across the session. In contrast, children who began with the non-synchronizing robot co-player never reached the same level of engagement over time, despite the robot's eventual adoption of synchronous speech.

After reviewing related work by others (Section 2), we describe prior work with *Mole Madness* in detail, both to explain the properties of the data we used to train our robot's

[1]Technically, the scales measure child's degree of willingness to continue to play, as judged by adults with extensive experience with young children.

HRI '17, March 06 - 09, 2017, Vienna, Austria

ISBN 978-1-4503-4336-7/17/03...$15.00

DOI: http://dx.doi.org/10.1145/2909824.3020244

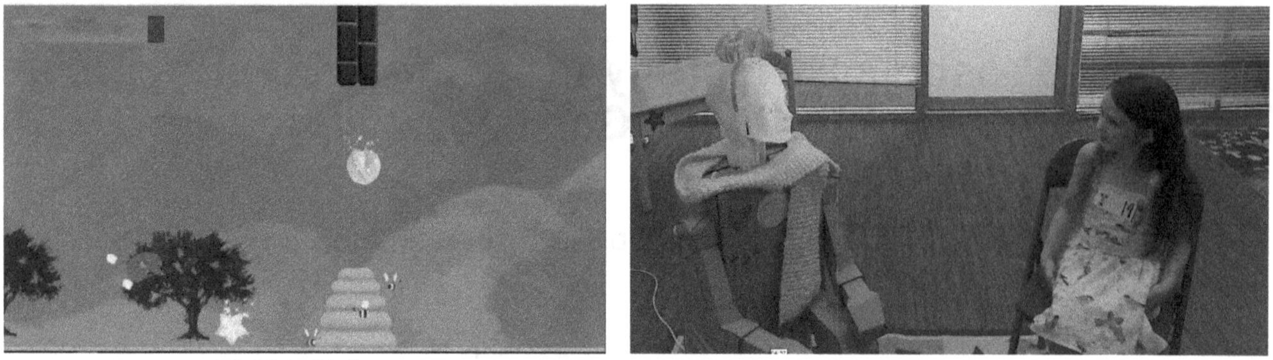

(a) *Mole Madness* (b) Sammy-Child play

Figure 1: Snapshots of the game and participants.

new adaptive behavior and to create a baseline for analyzing synchrony (Section 3). We then turn to the method for training (Section 4), describe deployment of the models in a real-time adaptive implementation (Section 5), and present results from a new set of child co-players (Section 6).

2. RELATED WORK

Several authors have investigated synchrony between prosodic features of interactants and its effects on conversation. De Looze et al. [15] studied the relationship between mimicry of prosodic speech features and the level of involvement of people in a conversation. Mimicry strength was measured by correlations among several features throughout the conversation, and their results showed that level of involvement is positively correlated with the coordination of speakers' prosodic cues. Suzuki and Katagiri [25] conducted a similar experiment to see whether humans entrain to prosodic features while communicating with a computer. They manipulated prosodic features of the speech generated by the computer such as loudness and pause duration, and observed the user's response. The results indicated that users entrain to some extent to the speech provided to them, e.g., they produced louder sounds as the volume from the computer increased. Our approach extends this work not only by exploring other speech related features such as F0, but also by using a robot instead of disembodied computer-generated speech, and by examining the phenomena in interactions with children.

Most HRI studies about synchrony have been focused on rhythmic adaptation [4]. Michalowski and colleagues [18], for example, studied the effects of the synchronous and non-synchronous behaviors of a Keepon robot that was able to dance in coordination with music and children's movements. They found that children's interaction with the robot was positively affected by the robot's responsiveness to their actions. In a more recent laboratory study using the same robot [19], the authors found contradictory results when measuring children's retention (i.e., willingness to continue interacting with the robot) while dancing with a synchronous robot and a non-synchronous one. The authors attribute the mixed results to limitations in their rhythmic perception system, and discuss the challenges of measuring children's engagement in playful interactions. In the same line of research, Avrunin et al. [2] investigated people's impressions of agency and life-likeness of dancing robots. In their study, adult participants judged videos of dancing robots with regard to dance quality, life-likeness and entertainment value. While life-like motion was considered more entertaining, the results suggest that perfect synchrony (i.e., robot movement always matching the sound) is less life-like than a situation in which the robots are not always in sync. More recently, Hoffman and Vanunu [11] conducted a study where participants listened to music in the presence of a robot that was moving in sync with the music, off beat, or not moving at all. Despite not being aware of the beat precision, participants interacting with the synchronizing robot rated the songs more positively, and provided higher ratings in perception traits like human-likeness and similarity.

Another related area is psycho-motor alignment, wherein research typically focuses on the temporal relations between the actions of two or more agents (humans or robots) performing an activity together. In this domain, Prepin and Gaussier [22] proposed an architecture that enables a robot to move its arms in synchrony to the arms of a human user. The convergence of their reinforcement learning algorithm is a sign that the robot successfully learned to synchronize its movements to those of the user. Iqbal et al. [12] investigated psycho-motor entrainment in the context of human-robot teamwork. They presented an event-based model to enable robots to measure synchronous motion between humans, with the ultimate goal of enabling fluid joint action between robots and groups of people. Using data collected from mobile robots sensing pairs of humans marching synchronously and non-synchronously, the authors showed that their model can accurately detect synchronous motion. We use a method that is analogous to theirs but in a different modality and with continuous phenomena.

3. UNDERSTANDING SYNCHRONY IN MM

Our work extends previous results with children playing the same game. Indeed, the method for building a synchronizing version of the robot co-player, Sammy, relies on data collected during those earlier studies, and the non-synchronizing play observed in those games establishes a baseline against which to evaluate our results. In this section we review the prior work in detail to clearly distinguish both what is new and why.

3.1 The Game

Mole Madness (MM) is a speech-controlled, interactive

side-scroller in which two players move a mole through its environment, avoiding obstacles and gaining rewards [14]. Effective play requires coordinated use of the keywords "go" and "jump," which control horizontal and vertical motion, respectively (see Figure 1(a)). Each participant is responsible for one keyword/direction at a time, but switches roles between levels. The game is designed to be easy to learn by children as young as four, but still fast-paced enough to be fun for children who are nine or ten.

MM can be played by two children (CC), or by a child and Sammy (SC), a back-projected robot head designed by Furhat Robotics [1] that has been set in a cardboard body to sit next to the child in a more peer-like way (Figure 1(b)). An overall architecture controls the multiple parallel processes for the game, the robot, and the custom word spotter that performs keyword recognition. The game is programmed in Unity3D, and Sammy plays by accessing an A^* search algorithm that returns a go/jump decision based on the next move along an optimal path. Sammy's vocal space of utterances consists mainly of a set of pre-recorded keyword files that vary with respect to prosodic features, durations, and frequency, although the robot also has some social speech that can be deployed at various points in the environment when gameplay allows.

3.2 Data Set 2015

Although MM has been used and reported on across many data collections, the data set that forms the basis of the models described in Section 4 (hereafter, DS15) reflects play by 86 children (51.16% girls), ages four through nine, in 2015. Children in DS15 played MM first in child-child pairs, then one-on-one with Sammy, producing 43 CC games with a mean duration of 355 seconds, and 85 SC games (one of the children did not play with the robot) with a mean duration of 216 seconds. Data was recorded by two high resolution cameras and a high-precision, omni-directional microphone. Instances of "go," "jump," and non-keyword social speech were segmented and annotated by hand.

3.3 Analysis of Synchrony in DS15

Windowing. Following Chaspari et al., we examine the correlation between speech and prosodic features over 10-second window intervals (see Figure 2(a)). Using the human annotations for the keywords "go" and "jump," acoustic features for loudness and F0 are extracted using openSMILE [8], separately for each keyword. Because the system uses only one microphone, we exclude portions of the segment where the annotations indicate voice overlap in order to avoid cross-participant contamination of the values.[2] If a window contains multiple instances of the same keyword, the values of each feature are averaged across the 10-sec interval. We also derive an additional feature that encodes separately for each keyword the number of times that keyword was uttered in the segment (a point we will return to in Section 4). Pearson correlation (r) tests between the features extracted for each player in the same window of

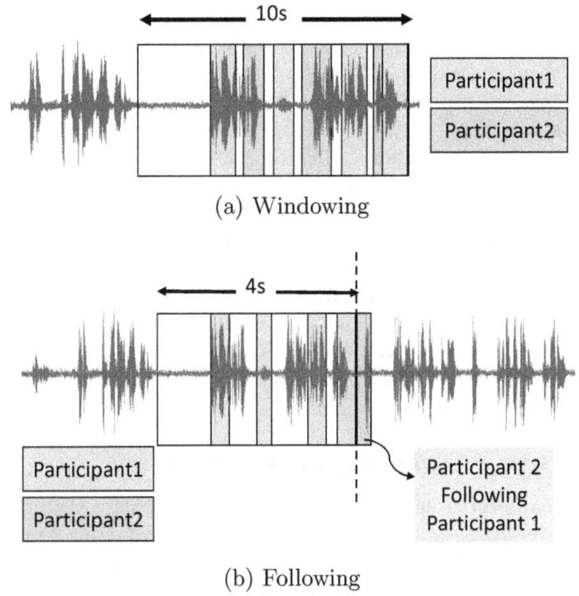

(a) Windowing

(b) Following

Figure 2: Two strategies for analyzing the amount of synchrony between participants. In (a), average values for prosodic features are computed separately for each player's non-overlapping speech within a ten second window and correlation is computed for windowed pairs. In (b), the influence is assumed to be limited to the duration of the echoic buffer and the segment containing a non-overlapped instance of player 2's keyword is paired with all of player 1's non-overlapped speech in the previous four seconds.

analysis showed higher correlation percentages in the CC sessions ($r_{F0}\,(11486) = 61.66, p < 0.001$, $r_{loudness}\,(11486) = 67.34, p < 0.001$, $r_{\#keywords}\,(11486) = 56.28, p < 0.001$)[3] than in the SC games ($r_{F0}\,(18177) = 5.69, p < 0.001$, $r_{loudness}$ $(18177) = 13.40, p < 0.001$, $r_{\#keywords}\,(18177) = 14.26$, $p < 0.001$). Considering that Sammy's keywords were randomly selected from a small pool of pre-recorded keywords, the lower correlation values in the SC pairs are not surprising.

Following. An alternative way to analyze synchrony constrains player 1's influence on the prosodic features of player 2's keyword to the duration of player 2's auditory short-term memory [5]. Under this method, depicted in Figure 2(b), we produce paired values for each non-overlapping keyword with the average values for non-overlapping instances of the other keyword in the prior four seconds. Such pairs implicitly define two different "follow" relations: the subset of instances in which player 1 follows player 2 and the subset of instances in which player 2 follows player 1. Thus we can separately compute correlations when child follows child from the CC sessions and when child follows Sammy and Sammy follows child from the SC sessions of D15. We find that correlations between pairs of segments where Sammy follows the child ($r_{F0}\,(5656) = 0.019, p = 0.24$ and $r_{loudness}\,(5656) = 10.63, p < 0.001$) and where the child follows Sammy ($r_{F0}\,(6962) = 4.35, p < 0.001$ and $r_{loudness}$

[2]The custom word spotter avoids the problem of sound localization by explicitly modeling keyword overlap. Because children are assigned one keyword on each level and moving the mole requires cooperative use of both commands, it is almost always the case that different keywords belong to different voices. The small number of occasions when a child usurps the other player's role in the excitement do add some noise to data.

[3]The Pearson correlations are reported as r(#instances), p-value.

(6962) $= 15.60, p < 0.001$) are lower than when the two children are following each other (r_{F0} (6098) $= 46.44, p < 0.001$ and $r_{loudness}$ (6098) $= 52.90, p < 0.001$).

These results indicate that Sammy's vocal behavior was not synchronous with the child during the game, especially in terms of F0. Although the analysis shows a positive correlation of 10.63 when Sammy follows the child, this value is much smaller than the average correlation value when a child follows another child ($r = 46.44$), and may be the result of low variability in the loudness of Sammy's small set of pre-recorded keywords. Note that the correlations derived from the *following* method show the same overall trends as the correlations derived from *windowing* but give us a more cognitively-motivated approach to understanding the child's behavior in response to Sammy's.

4. SYNCHRONIZING SAMMY

Because greater engagement was seen in child-child pairs who were in sync, we consider their verbal behaviors to be a model of how Sammy should behave as a peer co-player with the goal of creating an enjoyable game experience. Thus, we take advantage of the child-child data in D15 to synthesize more synchronized verbal behaviors for Sammy. The process has two phases: building the entrainment model that captures the strong correlation of acoustic features in the CC sessions and deploying the model in real-time play.

4.1 Modeling Entrainment

We chose to model the children's coordination with a dynamic Bayesian network (DBN) learned from the child-child sessions in the DS15 corpus. DBNs are a type of statistical model that has been shown to be able to capture the strong correlations between time series. DBNs also learn the possible dependencies between consecutive frames as their transition probabilities, and have been used in the past to generate head movements synchronized with speech prosodic features [16,23,24].

The relationship Sammy's Bayesian graph must capture can be seen in Figure 3. The nodes $F0_{c1}$, L_{c1}, $F0_{c2}$, and L_{c2} represent observed continuous variables for F0 and Loudness of two children playing together, which are modeled by Gaussian distributions. The two nodes affiliated with c2 are only observed during training, and are synthesized by the model during testing and play. The nodes $H_{c1,c2}$ are discrete variables representing the hidden states. The hidden states model the possible joint configurations between the prosodic features of the first and second child. For instance, if high F0 in one child is usually accompanied with high F0 in the other child, the hidden states learn this association. These discrete variables are trained to capture the correlation between the input modalities, and exploit that during synthesis.

For the model, we assume that the transition probabilities follow a Markov property of order one, i.e., they depend only on one previous time step. We choose a one second time step for responsiveness; this step size allows Sammy to adapt, close to real time, to changes that are happening with the features of the child. Although children may only be sensitive to prosodic features in the prior four seconds of speech, Sammy does not need to have that limitation. More importantly, by extending the window for computing features to 10 seconds, as was done in the windowing analysis, we increase the number of training instances available to the model from the DS15 corpus. For instances where there are no keywords from the other player even in the previous ten seconds, we use a fixed F0 and loudness based on the speaking child's averages in DS15.

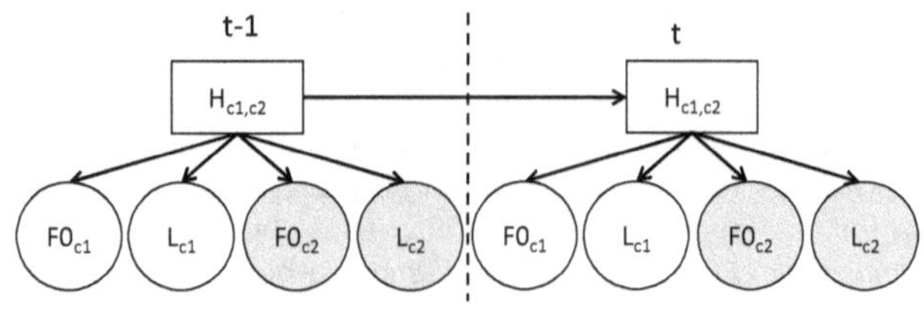

Figure 3: The Bayesian graph of the model for entrainment, where L is loudness, and the subscripts c1 and c2 refer to the first and second child.

The DBN comprises the prior probabilities of the hidden states, the transition probabilities between the states, and the observation probabilities given each hidden state. We optimize all these parameters using an Expectation Maximization algorithm (EM). To use the EM algorithm, we first derive the probabilities of the states given the observed sequences, by running the forward-backward algorithm [16,20] (E-step). Next, we maximize the likelihood of the model by updating all the parameters (M-step). The details of training a DBN are provided in [20].

Note that, during testing, we do not have access to the future data, and therefore, we run only the forward algorithm [20]. Given the observation vector until time t, the forward path gives us $\alpha_{i,t}$, which is the probability of the ith hidden state ($\alpha_{i,t} \triangleq P(H_{c1,c2_t} = i|y_{1:t})$). Given a sequence of features for one of the players, the following equations calculate the expected values of the features for the other player (in our case, the robot), where $\mu_{F0_{i,2}}$, and $\mu_{L_{i,2}}$ are the mean of the F0 and loudness for the ith hidden state for the second player.

$$\begin{aligned} E\left[F0_{c2,t}\middle|\, F0_{c1,1:t}, L_{c1,1:t}\right] &= \sum_{i=1}^{n} \alpha_{i,t} \times \mu_{F0_{i,2}} \\ E\left[L_{c2,t}\middle|\, F0_{c1,1:t}, L_{c1,1:t}\right] &= \sum_{i=1}^{n} \alpha_{i,t} \times \mu_{L_{i,2}} \end{aligned} \quad (1)$$

During testing with the entrainment model, we provide the DBN with F0 and loudness of the first child, and get the predicted values for F0 and loudness for the second child (which is Sammy), but there is no guarantee that Sammy's sound files have an instance of the keyword with values that exactly match the predictions.

4.1.1 Optimizing the model on DS15

Using the entrainment model, we aim to capture the strong correlation which is demonstrated in D15 recordings between children in the CC sessions. Utilizing this correlation will allow us to generate prosodic features for Sammy which are synchronous to the child. Overall, we used 11486 (10-s) windows for predicting child1 from child2, and because Sammy can be in either role, concatenated them with the same data reflecting child2 predicting child1. Therefore, we used 22972 samples for training in total.

Since the aim of this model is to predict the verbal features, we measure the R-squared between the predicted fea-

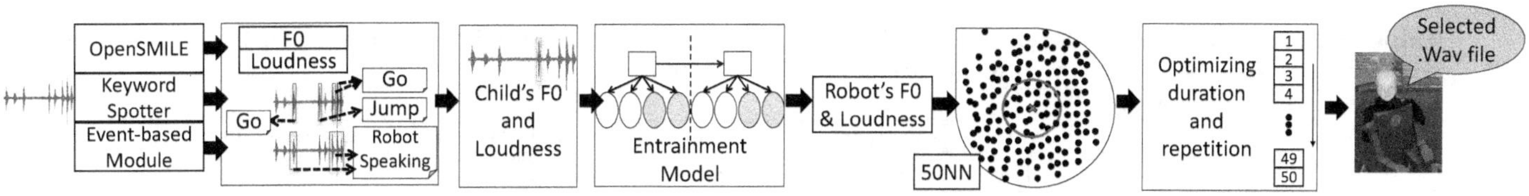

Figure 4: Overview of the real-time system.

tures and the original ones. We use the average of the R-squared for the two features as the metric to find the optimal number of states ($R^2_{o,p}$) by running a *Leave One Pair Out* (LOPO) cross validation – in every loop we use one fold for testing, one fold for validation, and the remaining 41 folds for training. The LOPO cross validation metrics are given in Table 1, where $r_{o,p}$ is the Pearson correlation between the original and predicted features, $r_{o_{c1},p_{c2}}$ is the Pearson correlation between the original feature for the first child, and the predicted feature for the second child. The result shows that our entrainment model is able to capture the high correlation displayed in the data. The average of the chosen number of states across folds is $[15.6] = 16$. Thus, the model trained with all the data, to be used by Sammy in real-time play, uses 16 states.

4.2 On-line adaptation for keywords

The entrainment model outputs, in real-time, an estimation of the F0 and loudness that the robot should approximate in its own speech in order to behave in synchrony with the child. This section describes the implementation details that enable the robot to perceive the child's prosodic features in real-time and make its own keyword selection based on the entrainment model. An overview of this pipeline is shown in Figure 4.

The first step of the process consists of segmenting children's speech and excluding the overlapping segments where the child and the robot are speaking in parallel. This is done by combining information from an event-based module that keeps track of when the robot begins and finishes speaking and a real-time keyword spotter that recognizes the keywords "go" and "jump" with 89% accuracy [10]. For the recognized keyword segments not belonging to Sammy, the system then extracts F0 and loudness in real time with the port-audio version of OpenSMILE [8]. Whenever Sammy receives a request from the game module to issue a game keyword, the system uses the most up to date F0 and loudness values extracted from the child's speech segments (recall that we use a 10-s window cache) as the input for the entrainment model, which in turn outputs the robot's desired F0 and loudness.

The next step is to select a sound file with the most similar features to the ones given by the entrainment model. The

Table 1: Evaluation metrics on the predicted F0 and loudness with the entrainment model of 86 children.

Metric	F0 [%]	Loudness [%]
$R^2_{o,p}$	46.31	42.26
$r_{o,p}$	69.53	66.24
$r_{o_{c1},p_{c2}}$	95.33	89.30

robot has available a pool of pre-recorded keyword samples, including 1923 samples for "jump" and 1600 samples for "go" with different volumes, F0 levels, and keyword durations (e.g., elongated and rapid keywords). From this pool, we select the 50 nearest neighbors of the features predicted by the entrainment model and create a list of candidate audio files.

We then sort the 50 candidate audio files according to how close their total duration is to the duration of the child's speech segment, because in the child-child data we observed that the children's total duration of keywords was correlated with each other ($r = 47.46\%$ and their average distance $= 1.062$). Finally, we select from the ordered list the top file that has not been used in the past 20 seconds in order to ensure variability in the choices the child hears. In the unlikely situation that all the keyword files from the 50 NN have been played in the past 20 seconds, we ignore this rule and play the best fit.

5. EVALUATION

To evaluate the impact of the entrainment model during real-time game play, we invited a new group of children (hereafter, DS16) to play *Mole Madness* who had never played the game before. In a repeated-measures design, each child played with two different versions of Sammy: *synchronizing* and *non-synchronizing*. The two versions differ in the algorithm for selecting the sound file for the robot's speech when the game module issues a go/jump command. In the synchronizing version, the system chooses a sound file from the 50 nearest neighbors according to the process described in the previous section; in the non-synchronizing version, Sammy's sound file is randomly selected from all possible files **other than** the 50 nearest neighbors. We counterbalanced the order of conditions across participants: children who started by playing with the synchronizing version of the robot and then switched to the non-synchronizing version are labeled as being in the **SN** condition, while children who played with the non-synchronizing version of Sammy first are labeled as **NS**.

5.1 Participants

We recruited 40 new children (50% girls) via postings in physical and online community boards. The children's ages ranged from 4 to 10 years old ($M = 6.73$ years, $SD = 1.72$). Twenty-one of the children were assigned to the SN condition ($M = 7.07$ years, $SD = 1.73$) and the rest (19) to the NS condition ($M = 6.36$ years, $SD = 1.69$). Both conditions were gender-balanced.

5.2 Procedure

To put the children at ease, an experimenter began the session by introducing the child to Sammy and letting him/her

Table 2: **Percentage of correlation achieved using entrainment (Sammy follows child) in DS16. Values marked with asterisks are statistically different from zero ($p < 0.001$)**

	Condition	SN		NS		–	
	Robot behavior	Synch.	Non-Synch.	Non-synch.	Synch.	All Synch.	All Non-synch.
	#Samples	474	634	482	435	909	1116
r [%]	F0	66.25*	6.31	3.14	68.08*	66.99*	5.06
r [%]	Loudness	36.39*	-0.00	5.69	33.90*	32.17*	-2.43

Table 3: Percentage of correlation for the child following Sammy in DS16. Values marked with asterisk are statistically different from zero ($p < 0.01$)

	Condition	SN		NS		–	
	Robot behavior	Synch.	Non-Synch.	Non-synch.	Synch.	All Synch.	All Non-synch.
	#Samples	681	793	661	648	1329	1454
r [%]	F0	40.38*	9.53*	5.80	23.35*	32.57*	8.01*
r [%]	Loudness	32.72*	14.04*	2.30	20.75*	27.27*	9.02*

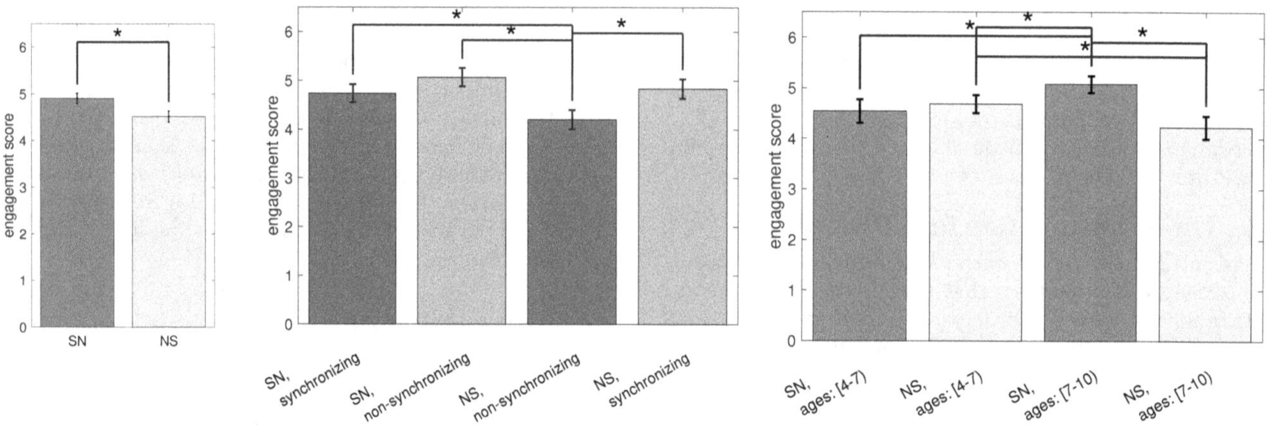

(a) (b) (c)

Figure 5: Engagement scores of children in DS16 from multiple views. Asterisks denote significance ($p < 0.05$).

personalize the robot's appearance using a variety of accessories. Next, the child watched a brief video tutorial about how to play the game, then was told by the experimenter that Sammy had two different ways to play the game and together they would play both.

Each child played a total of four levels of the game, alternating between the "go" and "jump" roles. Depending on the experimental condition to which the child was assigned, Sammy played the first two levels using the synchronizing or non-synchronizing version, then after a short break, switched to the other mode for the third and fourth levels. To ensure the same difficulty in both conditions, the first two levels were exactly the same as the last two but had different backgrounds to make the repetition of the levels less conspicuous to the child. Data from these sessions were recorded by two high-resolution cameras and a high-definition microphone for future analysis.

5.3 Results and Discussion

We analyzed the recordings in DS16 to explore possible effects of the robot's synchronizing and non-synchronizing behaviors. We first calculated the amount of synchrony that we actually created in the robot when it played with the children. Next, we measured the amount of synchrony elicited from the children by different versions of Sammy. Finally, we investigated the relationships among the children's engagement scores, the versions of Sammy (synchronizing vs. non-synchronizing), the order of the games (first two rounds vs. second two rounds), and the age of the children.

5.3.1 Analysis of Synchrony in DS16

We replicated the *Following* methodology described in Section 3.3 to analyze the audio data collected in the D1S6 experiment and compared it with the DS15 results. F0 and loudness were extracted for all of the non-overlapping keywords from both Sammy and the child and paired in a similar manner as in Section 3.3. We then sorted the keyword pairs into two groups: Sammy follows Child and Child follows Sammy. The Pearson correlation (r) percentages, organized by experimental condition and robot's behavior, are displayed in Tables 2 and 3[4].

The results for the instances in Table 2, where Sammy follows the child, serve as a basic assessment of the online entrainment method in real play. While the synchronizing games show significant high correlations for both F0

[4]The results for the 10-s *Windowing* method revealed exactly the same trends as the ones we report for *Following*.

and loudness, the correlations are not significant for either prosodic feature in the non-synchronizing games. As mentioned previously, we cannot guarantee "perfect synchrony" unless we synthesize the voice or have available a large enough number of sound files that the robot can always find a perfect match for every combination of features. Nevertheless, these results indicate that our method was successful.

The most interesting results, however, are the degree of correlation for the instances of the child following Sammy, shown in Table 3. When children played with the synchronizing version of the robot, our features of interest were significantly positively correlated, regardless of the order that children were assigned (SN or NS). However, the patterns for the non-synchronizing games are more complex: when children began by playing with the non-synchronizing version of Sammy (NS condition), the prosodic features of the child and the robot are not significantly correlated in those non-synchronizing levels, but when they started by playing with the synchronizing version of Sammy (SN condition) and then switched to the non-synchronizing version, significant positive correlations in those non-synchronizing levels remained. These results suggest that children maintain their prosodic synchrony with the robot for some time even after the robot stops synchronizing its prosody with them.

5.3.2 *Analysis of Engagement*

We asked three annotators with extensive experience in behavioral analysis (including coding more than 100 children in MM in previous years) to judge the children's levels of engagement during the game. The annotators were blind to our research questions. They were asked to watch videos of the DS16 MM sessions with only the child visible and segment the video according to a seven-point scale describing the child's willingness to continue to play. Four of the scale's ratings were labeled; 1 as *ready to do something else*, 3 as *could take it or leave it*, 5 as *very much into the game* and 7 as *can't drag him/her away*, while ratings 2, 4, and 6 were unlabeled. One level could have multiple annotations with different ratings; thus, to derive the level's engagement score, we performed a weighted average of the ratings given by an annotator based on the duration of the ratings in the entire game. Because each child played four levels of the game, annotation of DS16 produced 4 engagement scores×40 children×3 annotators.

The Cronbach's alpha between the ratings given by the three annotators is 0.79. Note that randomly selecting one of the coders when their agreement is high or averaging the ratings of multiple coders are both valid approaches for analyzing behavioral data. Despite the high agreement between DS16 coders, our past experience with engagement coding revealed that often coders use the full range of the coding scale differently. Therefore, similar to the previous studies with MM [6, 7], we analyzed the results for each annotator separately and found the same trends for all three coders. Hence, we present the results for one coder in the remainder of the section to avoid redundancy.

Overall, children in the SN group had significantly higher engagement scores ($M = 4.90, SD = 0.73$) than children in the NS group ($M = 4.52, SD = 0.67$), $t(158) = -3.4316, p < 0.001$ (see Figure 5(a)). Given that the only difference between the two conditions was the order in which children played with the two versions of the robot, we further investigated these results by conducting a two-way ANOVA considering the version of Sammy (synchronizing vs. non-synchronizing) collapsed across conditions, and the order of the games (first two rounds vs. second two rounds) as within-subjects factor. The analysis of variance showed a significant main effect for order, $F(1, 156) = 21.086, p < 0.001$, but no significant main effect for the version of the robot (synchronizing vs. non-synchronizing), $F(1, 156) = 2.06, p = 0.51$. We also found a significant interaction effect between robot version and the order of the rounds, $F(1, 156) = 13.307, p < 0.001$. As depicted in Figure 5(b), while children who began playing with the synchronizing version of Sammy sustained their engagement levels when switching to the non-synchronizing games, children who began playing with the non-synchronizing version of Sammy showed lower engagement when playing in this mode and ended their session in a less engaged state. This result strengthens the findings obtained in the prosodic feature correlation showing that when first exposed to a synchronizing robot, children maintain their behavior for some time even when they then interact with a non-adaptive robot.

Finally, since previous research on child developmental theory suggests that language interactions can be affected by age differences [21], we looked at potential age effects in our data. We divided children into two age groups based on their developmental stage [21]: less than 7 years old, and greater than or equal to 7 years old. We have 19 children in the younger age group and 21 children in the older age group. The average engagement scores in these four conditions is given in Figure 5(c). A two-way ANOVA revealed significant differences in engagement between the NS and SN experimental groups, $F(1, 156) = 10.209, p = 0.0017$, and a significant interaction effect between condition and age, $F(1, 156) = 17.766, p < 0.0001$. Pairwise comparisons revealed a significant age difference between SN and NS conditions among the older age group ($p < 0.0001$), but no significant differences for the younger children ($p = 0.892$).

6. CONCLUSION

In this paper, we proposed a framework to create synchronous verbal behavior for a social robot, Sammy, playing a fast-paced, speech-based game with a child. Analysis of the gameplay of 86 children in 2015 showed a strong correlation between the acoustic characteristics of children playing in pairs. Using the data from those children, we built a DBN model that learns the joint representation of prosodic speech features in those child-child pairs. In real-time play of the game with Sammy as co-player, we measure the prosodic speech features and keyword duration from the child, use the DBN to predict synchronous prosodic values for Sammy, and select the nearest match for the prosodic features and keyword duration from a large but fixed space of possible utterances. To test the performance of the method, we recorded data from 40 new children, each of whom played with both a synchronizing and non-synchronizing version of Sammy, balanced for order. We analyzed their gameplay with subjective and objective metrics, both of which show that the the order of conditions matters. Objectively, children who started with the synchronizing version of Sammy showed more synchronous behavior, even in the non-synchronizing levels, compared to the children who started with the non-synchronizing version. Subjectively, children who started with the synchronizing version ended the session with higher engagement levels compared with those that started with the non-synchronizing version of the robot. Moreover, the results showed an age effect, demonstrating that most of the engagement result was due to differences in the older children under the two order conditions. It remains for future work to see whether entrainment of the same paralinguistic features in other interaction scenarios will produce the same patterns of behavior and enjoyment.

7. REFERENCES

[1] S. Al Moubayed, J. Beskow, G. Skantze, and B. Granström. Furhat: A Back-Projected Human-Like robot head for multiparty Human-Machine interaction. In *Cognitive Behavioural Systems*, Lecture Notes in Computer Science, pages 114–130. Springer Berlin Heidelberg, 2012.

[2] E. Avrunin, J. Hart, A. Douglas, and B. Scassellati. Effects related to synchrony and repertoire in perceptions of robot dance. In *Proceedings of the 6th international conference on Human-robot interaction (HRI)*, pages 93–100. ACM, 2011.

[3] W. S. Condon and W. D. Ogston. Sound film analysis of normal and pathological behavior patterns. *The Journal of Nervous and Mental Disease*, 143(4):338–347, 1966.

[4] C. Crick, M. Munz, and B. Scassellati. Synchronization in social tasks: Robotic drumming. In *The 15th IEEE International Symposium on Robot and Human Interactive Communication (RO-MAN)*, pages 97–102. IEEE, 2006.

[5] C. J. Darwin, M. T. Turvey, and R. G. Crowder. An auditory analogue of the sperling partial report procedure: Evidence for brief auditory storage. *Cognitive Psychology*, 3(2):255–267, April 1972.

[6] T. C. et al. Exploring children's verbal and acoustic synchrony: Towards promoting engagement in speech-controlled robot-companion games. In *Proceedings of the 1st Workshop on Modeling INTERPERsonal SynchrONy And infLuence*, pages 21–24, Seattle, November 2015.

[7] T. C. et al. An acoustic analysis of child-child and child-robot interactions for understanding engagement during speech-controlled computergames. In *Proceedings of INTERSPEECH. 2016*, pages –, San Francisco, September 2016.

[8] F. Eyben, M. Wöllmer, and B. Schuller. OpenSMILE: the Munich versatile and fast open-source audio feature extractor. In *ACM International conference on Multimedia (MM 2010)*, pages 1459–1462, Florence, Italy, October 2010.

[9] R. Feldman. Parent–infant synchrony biological foundations and developmental outcomes. *Current directions in psychological science*, 16(6):340–345, 2007.

[10] A. for blind review. pages –, September 2016.

[11] G. Hoffman and K. Vanunu. Effects of robotic companionship on music enjoyment and agent perception. In *The 8th ACM/IEEE International Conference on Human-Robot Interaction (HRI)*, pages 317–324. ACM/IEEE, 2013.

[12] T. Iqbal, M. J. Gonzales, and L. D. Riek. Joint action perception to enable fluent human-robot teamwork. In *Robot and Human Interactive Communication (RO-MAN), 2015 24th IEEE International Symposium on*, pages 400–406, Japan, September 2015.

[13] A. Jakkam and C. Busso. A multimodal analysis of synchrony during dyadic interaction using a metric based on sequential pattern mining. In *IEEE International Conference on Acoustics, Speech and Signal Processing (ICASSP 2016)*, pages 6085–6089, Shanghai, China, March 2016.

[14] J. F. Lehman and S. Al Moubayed. Mole madness–a multi-child, fast-paced, speech-controlled game. In *Proceedings of AAAI Symposium on Turn-taking and Coordination in Human-Machine Interaction. Stanford, CA*, 2015.

[15] C. D. Looze, C. Oertel, S. Rauzy, and N. Campbell. Measuring dynamics of mimicry by means of prosodic cues in conversational speech. In *International Conference on Phonetic Sciences (ICPhS). Hong Kong*, pages 1294–1297, 2011.

[16] S. Mariooryad and C. Busso. Generating human-like behaviors using joint, speech-driven models for conversational agents. *IEEE Transactions on Audio, Speech and Language Processing*, 20(8):2329–2340, October 2012.

[17] A. N. Meltzoff and W. Prinz. *The imitative mind: Development, evolution and brain bases*, volume 6. Cambridge University Press, 2002.

[18] M. P. Michalowski, S. Sabanovic, and H. Kozima. A dancing robot for rhythmic social interaction. In *Human-Robot Interaction (HRI), 2007 2nd ACM/IEEE International Conference on*, pages 89–96, Washington DC, USA, March 2007.

[19] M. P. Michalowski, R. Simmons, and H. Kozima. Rhythmic attention in child-robot dance play. In *The 18th IEEE International Symposium on Robot and Human Interactive Communication (RO-MAN)*, pages 816–821, 2009.

[20] K. Murphy. *Dynamic Bayesian Networks: Representation, Inference and Learning.* PhD thesis, University of California Berkely, Fall 2002.

[21] J. Piaget. *The moral judgement of the child.* Simon and Schuster, 1997.

[22] K. Prepin and P. Gaussier. How an agent can detect and use synchrony parameter of its own interaction with a human? In *Development of Multimodal Interfaces: Active Listening and Synchrony*, pages 50–65. 2010.

[23] N. Sadoughi and C. Busso. Retrieving target gestures toward speech driven animation with meaningful behaviors. In *International conference on Multimodal interaction (ICMI 2015)*, pages 115–122, Seattle, WA, USA, November 2015.

[24] N. Sadoughi, Y. Liu, and C. Busso. Speech-driven animation constrained by appropriate discourse functions. In *International conference on multimodal interaction (ICMI 2014)*, pages 148–155, Istanbul, Turkey, November 2014.

[25] N. Suzuki and Y. Katagiri. Prosodic alignment in human-computer interaction. *Connection Science*, 19(2):131–141, June 2007.

Telling Stories to Robots: The Effect of Backchanneling on a Child's Storytelling *

Hae Won Park, Mirko Gelsomini†, Jin Joo Lee, and Cynthia Breazeal
Personal Robots Group, MIT Media Lab
20 Ames Street, E15-468, Cambridge, MA 02139 USA
{haewon, gelso, jinjoo, cynthiab}@media.mit.edu

ABSTRACT

While there has been a growing body of work in child-robot interaction, we still have very little knowledge regarding young children's speaking and listening dynamics and how a robot companion should decode these behaviors and encode its own in a way children can understand. In developing a backchannel prediction model based on observed nonverbal behaviors of 4–6 year-old children, we investigate the effects of an attentive listening robot on a child's storytelling. We provide an extensive analysis of young children's nonverbal behavior with respect to how they encode and decode listener responses and speaker cues. Through a collected video corpus of peer-to-peer storytelling interactions, we identify attention-related listener behaviors as well as speaker cues that prompt opportunities for listener backchannels. Based on our findings, we developed a backchannel opportunity prediction (BOP) model that detects four main speaker cue events based on prosodic features in a child's speech. This rule-based model is capable of accurately predicting backchanneling opportunities in our corpora. We further evaluate this model in a human-subjects experiment where children told stories to an audience of two robots, each with a different backchanneling strategy. We find that our BOP model produces contingent backchannel responses that conveys an increased perception of an attentive listener, and children prefer telling stories to the BOP model robot.

1. INTRODUCTION

Social robots have great potential to support children's education as peer learning companions. As a physically embodied technology, social robots can leverage our social means of communication (e.g., speech, gestures, gaze, and

*A teaser video of the research can be viewed from the following URL: `https://goo.gl/HMEfnt`

†Mirko Gelsomini was also affiliated with Politecnico di Milano, Italy at the time this research was conducted.

HRI '17, March 06-09, 2017, Vienna, Austria

DOI: http://dx.doi.org/10.1145/2909824.3020245

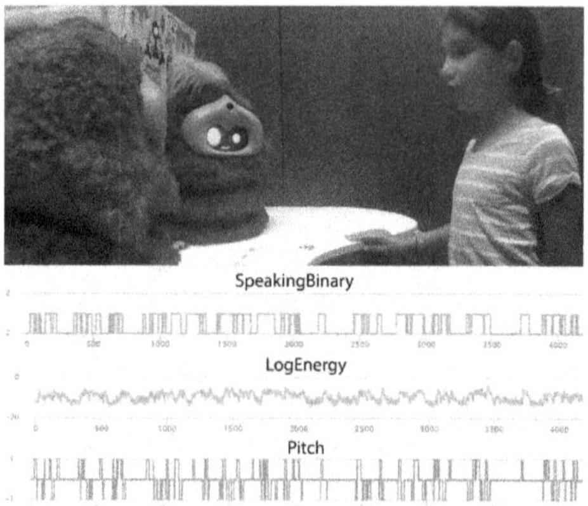

Figure 1: We investigate the effects of an attentive listening robot on a child's storytelling behavior. The robot detects nonverbal prosodic cues from the storyteller's speech to provide backchannel feedback to signal engagement.

facial expressions) to engage with us in more natural, intuitive, and interpersonal ways. They combine the general benefits of technology such as scalability, customization, easy content deployment with student-paced, adaptive software. Prior research has shown that young children will not only treat social robots as companions and guides [15, 29], but will also readily learn new information from them [19, 31] where a robot's perceived credibility as an educator is impacted by how socially contingent it behaves [3]. Beyond academic learning, peer-modeled robot companions have demonstrated to be social influencers that can positively impact a child's attitude by fostering curiosity or a growth mindset [24, 10] and teach positive interpersonal skills [23, 22]. In modeling children more holistically, researchers have found that incorporating the emotional experience of learners can personalize their engagement during educational activities [11] as well as lead to more accurate assessments of student performance [30].

Given this potential, we aim to study how a peer-like social robot can successfully foster the development of early language skills of preschoolers and kindergarteners. Storytelling and other forms of conversational activity are key to children's language development and are a mutually regulated activity between speaker and listener. In this paper, we specifically focus on one of the key dynamics in storytelling activities – the back-and-forth process of speaker cues and listener backchannels (BC) that encourages both parties to stay engaged in the activity and enables long-term interaction. Speakers elicit feedback from listeners through subtle nonverbal cues, and listeners respond nonverbally to communicate that the listener is paying attention and following along. We hypothesize that a social robot that contingently backchannels will be perceived as an attentive listener by child storytellers and will affect their storytelling behavior (Figure 1).

In this work, we offer the following contributions. First, we provide quantitative analyses of kindergarten children's (ages between 4–6) backchanneling response behavior. While adults' BC behavior has been widely studied including cultural diversities [37], it is seldom studied how children develop and produce (encode) speaker cues as a storyteller to request feedback from the listener and how they understand (decode) those signals as a listener. Here, we specifically present analyses on young children's nonverbal behavior in a storytelling context. Namely, we 1) identify backchanneling behaviors that indicate the engagement state of the listener, 2) identify speaker cues that child listeners acknowledge and respond to, and 3) characterize the bidirectionality of nonverbal behaviors (i.e., can children decode what they encode?) (Section 3). Secondly, we 1) define a robot listener's action space based on the identified child listener's backchanneling behaviors and 2) design a backchanneling opportunity prediction (BOP) model around the identified child speaker cues (Section 4). To the best of our knowledge, we pioneer the development of a computational backchanneling model based on children voices and behaviors. Finally, we evaluate the proposed BOP model on a social robot listener to respond appropriately and reciprocally to a child as he/she tells a story. We find that children do perceive the contingent backchanneling robot as an attentive listener and stay engaged by directing their storytelling to the contingent robot versus the non-contingent robot. (Section 6 & 7).

2. RELATED WORK

2.1 Backchannel (BC) behavior

In this work, we focus on the use of nonverbal listener response behaviors, typically referred to as backchannels (BC), including gestures such as gaze locking and nodding, and non-lexical utterances such as *yeah, ok, uh huh, mhmm.* Backchanneling is a listener response that serves cognitive functions indicating the state of engagement, understanding (or lack thereof), repair or clarification of the message, and sentence completion [7, 6]. There is surprisingly limited amount of work that reports on young children's BC behavior and the effects of BC on their language development. In [25], the positive effects of BC behaviors on children's language learning is reported. Twenty preschoolers (mean age 3.7) were randomly assigned to either an intervention or control group. During an year-long intervention, parents of the intervention group were asked to encourage their child's narratives through providing backchanneling responses, which resulted in longer narratives and improved vocabulary learning immediately after the session terminated. Children in the intervention group showed significant improvements in overall narrative skills. In particular, they produced more context-setting descriptions about where and especially when the described events took place. In [28], it is also reported that 4-year olds' narratives are influenced by adult listeners' behaviors. According to the authors' observations, children try to create more complex narratives when the adult listener appears more attentive. Also when the adult listener is more attentive, children tend to try harder to re-attract their attention when they are momentarily distracted.

While the above works provide some insights into how young children's narratives can be improved by adult listener's BC responses, it lacks important details of children's encoding (how children develop and produce speaker cues to request feedback from the listener) and decoding (how children understand and detect speaker cues as a listener) abilities. Learning what speaker cues and listener responses children in preschools and kindergartens can perceive and produce is necessary when developing an appropriate BC model. As such, we conducted a data collection of peer-to-peer storytelling interactions between kindergarten children and identified key speaker cues and prosodic features that prompt listener backchannels. This analysis is provided in Section /refsec:cb.

2.2 Computational models of BC

Backchannels are elicited by a variety of speaker verbal and nonverbal cues, and its contingent timing makes for a significant technical challenge. Without having to necessarily attend to the content of speech, approaches have been successful in detecting prosodic features (e.g. voice activity detection (VAD), energy, and pitch) in realtime to determine appropriate backchannel opportunities [18, 20, 21].

Ward and Tsukahara [34] suggest that an important prosodic cue is a region of low pitch located toward the end of an utterance. Their model was produced manually through an analysis of English and Japanese conversational data. Truong et al. [26] consider features from the speaker's speech along with gaze cues to determine the placement of BCs. They found that the number, timing, and type of BC has a significant effect on how human-like BC behavior is perceived. Morency et al. [18] present a realtime multimodal BC prediction system. They automatically select features from speech and gaze and train conditional random fields to model sequential probabilities. Other studies have used decision trees [20] based on pitch and power features, and others have used hidden Markov models [21] where state transitions correspond to changes in prosodic context.

All these prior approaches have design their computational models based on observed adult behaviors and trained on the adult voices. As a first work that attempts to develop a BC model specifically targeted at 4–6 year-old children, we propose a model comparable to Ward and Tsukahara's [34] and Truong et al.'s [26] with children storytelling and listening datasets.

3. NONVERBAL BEHAVIORS OF CHILDREN

3.1 Data Collection

Eighteen participants of typical development were recruited from a single kindergarten (K2) classroom in a local public elementary school. The average age was 5.22 years-old (SD=0.44) with a 61:39 male:female ratio. Each child participated in at least three rounds of storytelling with different partners and storybooks over a span of five weeks (58 episodes in total). In each session, a pair of students take turns narrating their story to the other; each turn generating a storytelling episode. Three time-synchronized cameras

Behavior	N	Mean Freq	Mean Dur	%Pop	Linear Regression Model: Main Effect	Freq Term	Dur Term
Gaze Partner	284	4.95	2.02	100	$F(2, 223) = 23.66$, $p^* = 4.80e^{-10}$	$B = 2.19$, $p^* = 1.55e^{-06}$	$B = 1.48$, $p = 0.02$
Lean Toward	124	2.14	7.97	100	$F(2, 204) = 12.98$, $p^* = 4.92e^{-06}$	$B = 0.91$, $p^* = 8.55\ e^{-05}$	$B = 0.29$, $p = 0.17$
Brow Raise	103	1.78	2.32	100	$F(2, 170) = 5.04$, $p^* = 7.49e^{-03}$	$B = 0.70$, $p^* = 0.02$	$B = -1.75$, $p^* = 4.28e^{-03}$
Smile	189	3.26	6.55	94	$F(2, 202) = 7.14$, $p^* = 1.01e^{-03}$	$B = 0.29$, $p = 0.31$	$B = 0.71$, $p^* = 5.59e^{-03}$
Nod	18	0.31	1.13	39	$F(2, 43) = 2.24$, $p = 0.11$	$B = 1.37$, $p = 0.28$	$B = -0.40$, $p = 0.97$
Utterance	18	0.31	0.88	50	$F(2, 51) = 3.35$, $p^* = 0.04$	$B = 1.33$, $p = 0.12$	$B = 1.51$, $p = 0.86$

Table 1: Descriptive Statistics and the Linear Regression Model for Listener Responses. N is the total occurrences found in the dataset. The Mean Frequency is the average number of occurrences in a storytelling episode (i.e., N/58). The Mean Duration is the average duration of the emitted behavior in seconds. %Pop refers to the proportion of the population (18 participants) that demonstrated a single instance of the behavior across the repeated interactions. The linear regression model predicts a child's level of listening (coded as -1 or 1) based on the normalized duration and frequency rate of the observed behavior.

captured the frontal-view of each participant along with a bird's eye view.

For each storytelling episode, the nonverbal behaviors of both the listener and storyteller as well as the listeners' attentive state were manually coded using video-annotation software ELAN[1] with a custom developed template. Four coders marked the onset and offset times for the occurring nonverbal behaviors and achieved moderate levels of agreement (Fleiss' $\kappa = 0.55$). Three additional coders were recruited to simulate themselves being a listener and to mark the moments when they wanted to BC to the audio recording of the child storyteller. After this simulation, coders reviewed the audio snippets surrounding these moments to further categorize the type of speaker cues perceived: pitch, energy, pause, filled pause, a long contiguous utterance (or wordy), and other. We followed the Parasocial Consensus approach from [14] to build consensus of when backchannel opportunities occurred. More specifically, each of our three coders' registered backchannel times were added as a 'vote' on a consensus timeline with a duration of one second around the central moment. An area in the timeline with more than two total votes was counted as a valid backchannel moment.

3.2 Analysis of Listener Behavior

To identify attention-related nonverbal behaviors, we examined the ability of the frequency and duration of behaviors to predict whether a child is listening or not. Based on the annotations of the listener's mental state, the storytelling episodes were split into segments where the child was listening and not listening. For each nonverbal behavior, a linear regression analysis was performed to predict a child's level of listening based on the normalized duration and frequency rate of the behavior observed in each segment. As shown in Table 1, partner gazes, leaning toward, smiles, and utterances significantly predict a listener's mental state. Interestingly, the frequency of brow raises holds a significant positive relationship, while its duration holds a significant negative relationship. Nods have a positive relationship to the child listening, but their rare occurrences in this population make it difficult to evaluate as significant.

3.3 Analysis of Speaker Cues

To identify the speaker cues that child-listeners acknowledge and respond to, we first examined the ability of speaker cues to predict the likelihood of a positive response from the listener. From our storytelling episodes, we extract observational pairs of the type of cue generated by the speaker and whether a positive response was observed from the listener within 3 seconds. Based on our prior analysis on attention-related behaviors, the onset of a partner gaze, lean toward, smile, utterance, brow raise, and nod were considered to be positive responses to a cue. A logistic regression was performed to ascertain the effects of the individual speaker cues on the likelihood that a listener would respond. Based on the Wald Chi-square statistic, the overall logistic regression model was statistically significant, $\chi^2(6) = 40.69$, $p = 3.33e^{-07}$. As shown in Table 2, the speaker cues—gaze, pitch, and wordy—have the ability to elicit a positive re-

Variables	N	Mean Freq	Logistic Regression Model: B	tStat	Sig.
Intercept	—	—	-1.00	-5.01	$^*p=7.98e^{-07}$
Gaze	218	3.76	1.08	5.62	$^*p=3.47e^{-08}$
Pitch	175	3.02	0.43	2.53	*p=0.01
Pause	156	2.69	0.09	0.54	p=0.59
Energy	61	1.05	0.14	0.66	p=0.51
FilledP	37	0.64	0.23	0.81	p=0.42
Wordy	18	0.31	0.70	2.06	*p=0.04

Table 2: Descriptive Statistics and the Logistic Regression Model for Individual Speaker Cues. N is the total occurrences found in the dataset. The Mean Frequency is the average number of occurrences in a storytelling episode (i.e., N/58). The logistic regression model predicts the likelihood of a positive response from the listener based on the type of emitted speaker cue.

[1]https://tla.mpi.nl/tools/tla-tools/elan/

1 Cue	N	Rate	Sig.	2 Cues	N	Rate	Sig.	2+ Cues	N	Rate	Sig.
G.....	218	0.70	$p^*=2.74e^{-09}$	.CP...	80	0.55	p=0.22	GC.E..	17	0.94	$p^*=1.37e^{-04}$
.C....	175	0.57	$p^*=4.80e^{-02}$	.C.E..	50	0.66	$p^*=0.02$	GCP...	16	0.88	$p^*=2.09e^{-03}$
..P...	156	0.48	p=0.34	GC....	41	0.88	$p^*=3.92e^{-07}$	.CPE..	14	0.64	p=0.21
...E..	61	0.57	p=0.15	..P.F.	26	0.50	p=0.58	.CP..W	6	0.67	p=0.34
....F.	37	0.46	p=0.37	G.P...	21	0.86	$p^*=7.45e^{-04}$	GCPE..	5	1.00	$p^*=3.12e^{-02}$
.....W	18	0.72	$p^*=4.81e^{-02}$	..PE..	20	0.50	p=0.59				
				.C...W	12	0.75	p=0.07				
				.C..F.	10	0.20	p=0.05				

Table 3: Descriptive Statistics and the Binomial Test for Combinations of Speaker Cues. The most frequently observed cue combinations specified through the presence of the cue's symbolic letter. G:Gaze C:Pitch: P:Pause E:Energy F:Filled Pause W:Wordy. A dot represents the absence of that cue. N is the total occurrences of the cue combination found in the data set. The one-sided binomial tests whether the cue combination elicits a response rate that is greater than the expected chance rate of 0.5.

sponse from the young listeners. As expected, some of the speaker cues (energy, pause, and filled pause) taken alone did not offer significant predictive ability when examined in isolation. However, young children have been previously observed to respond more often in greater cue contexts where two or more cues are co-occurring [13].

Our next analysis examined the ability of cue combinations to predict the likelihood of a positive response from the listener. Speaker cues were considered to be co-occurring if they are within 1.3 seconds of each other (empirically determined). The aforementioned observational pairs were merged based on this criteria. The likelihood of observing a combination of cues is much smaller than individual cues, resulting in a sample size. Rather than performing a logistic regression, we use the binomial exact test to see whether the response rate of a cue combination is greater than an expected rate of 0.5. As shown in Table 3, the one-sided binomial test indicates that the response rate of the co-occurring cues Pitch-Energy, Gaze-Pitch, Gaze-Pause, Gaze-Pitch-Energy, Gaze-Pitch-Pause, and Gaze-Pitch-Pause-Energy is higher than chance.

3.4 Analysis of Mirrored Encoding-Decoding

Traditionally, nonverbal communication research has been divided into the encoding and decoding of nonverbal behaviors with little research on the differences or similarity between the two processes. With one notable exception, in the field of developmental psychology, 12-month-old infants were found to more likely succeed in producing communicative pointing gestures if they also demonstrated their comprehension of an adult's pointing intention [2]. With some evidence of the bidirectional understanding of communicative nonverbal behavior, we pose the question of whether children understand the function of cues both in the role of the communicator (the storyteller) and recipient (the listener). To support our assumption of a mirrored process when decoding and encoding nonverbal behaviors, we examine the correlation between the frequency a child produces a certain speaker cue as the storyteller and the frequency the child responds to that particular cue when in the role of a listener. Looking only at the set of cue contexts, a strong positive correlation exists between the frequency in which a child exhibits and responds to a particular cue, $r(160)^2 = 0.56$, $p = 5.26e^{-15}$. The more frequent a child expressed a speaker cue, the more frequent that child demonstrated a response to the same cue.

4. BACKCHANNEL OPPORTUNITY PREDICTION (BOP) MODEL

In the following sections, we present a rule-based method to predicting BC opportunities. We first formulate these rules by consulting children's speaker-cue analyses from Section 3.3. The four combinations of features we model are: wordy & pause, long pause, pitch & pause, and energy & pause. We used 71% of Dataset 1 (i.e., from Section 3.1) to develop these rules, and tested the BC models on the remaining 29% of Dataset 1 and another dataset collected from a different kindergarten class (Dataset 2). Our work combines prior approaches to BC modeling, in detecting cues such as wordy utterances [12], long pauses [5], pitch [35, 33, 34], changes in energy [32], and extends them to better correspondence to our corpus of children's prosodic features.

Wordy Model (Figure 2(a)): This model predicts BC opportunity based on inter-pausal units, $IPUs$. An IPU is a maximal sequence of words surrounded by a pause of duration W_PAUSE. A turn of duration W_SPEAK is defined as a maximal sequence of IPUs from a speaker, such that between any two adjacent IPUs, the silence is not greater than the value of SIL. The BC opportunity is predicted when the following conditions are met:

```
P1 a pause of W_PAUSE (800ms) length,
P2 preceded by at least W_SPEAK (1.5s) of speech,
P3 given that no BC triggered within BC_RATE (1.3s).
```

Long Pause Model (Figure 2(b)): This model predicts BC opportunities based on detecting a long pause LP_PAUSE that is preceded by a speech LP_SPEAK.

```
P1 a pause of LP_PAUSE (1.7s) length,
P2 preceded by at least LP_SPEAK (1.0s) of speech,
P3 given that no BC triggered within BC_RATE (1.3s).
```

Pitch Model (Figure 2(c)): This model predicts BC opportunities by detecting, after a certain amount of speech, a falling or rising pitch change that is followed by a pause.

```
P1 a pause of P&P_PAUSE (400ms),
P2 preceded by at least P&P_SPEAK (1.0s) of speech,
P3 where the last P&P_LENGTH (300ms),
P4 contain a rising/falling pitch of at least
     P&P_SLOPE rise/drop (25%).
P5 given that no BC triggered within BC_RATE (1.3s).
```

Energy Model (Figure 2(d)): This model predicts BC

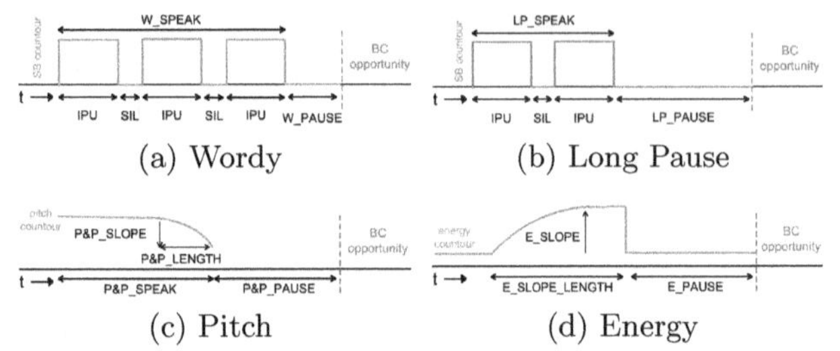

(a) Wordy (b) Long Pause

(c) Pitch (d) Energy

Figure 2: Four rule-based models were developed to detect prosodic speaker cues that collectively make up our backchannel opportunity prediction (BOP) model. Model parameters were trained and tested against children storytelling dataset.

opportunities similar to the Pitch model but detects for energy changes.

```
P1 a pause of E_PAUSE (300ms),
P2 preceded by at least E_SLOPE_LENGTH (500ms) of
     speech,
P3 contain a rising/falling energy of at least
     E_SLOPE rise/drop (30%).
P4 given that no BC triggered within BC_RATE (1.3s).
```

Model thresholds were selected by incrementing/decrementing values at steps of 100ms and trying various combinations to determine best fit using Dataset 1.

4.1 Speaking Binary Classifier

Much of the BOP model depends on accurately knowing the start and stop of speech events. A speaking binary (SB) classifier detects voicing activity from the speaker's acoustic features. We used openSMILE [8], an open-source audio-feature-extraction software[2], and applied a low-pass filter and an energy-based check to their voice activity detector (VAD). We implemented a low-pass filter that weighs the previous value of VAD, $VAD(t-1)$, higher than the current value $VAD(t)$ and applied a step function with a cut-off value of 0.9 for an SB decision. More specifically:

$$VAD(t) = 0.8 \cdot VAD(t-1) + 0.2 \cdot VAD(t), \quad (1)$$

$$\text{then, } SB(t) = \begin{cases} 1, & \text{if } VAD(t) > 0.9 \\ 0, & \text{otherwise.} \end{cases} \quad (2)$$

We reduced false-positives from the SB signal due to background noise using a simple energy-based check. During moments when SB reports no voicing activity, we sample the energy signal to establish a rolling average of the environment's noise level. So when a voice is believed to be detected, we also check to see if the current energy level is above this established minimum. We do not apply this discounting until at least 700ms into the detection process to form a reasonable baseline. Figure 3 illustrates how with each step we improve on openSMILE's VAD detector and get closer to the ground truth. Using Dataset 1, we found that our SB classifier achieves a precision of 96.8% and recall of 87.5%.

4.2 BOP Model Evaluation

We evaluated the performance of our BOP model on the remaining 29% of Dataset 1 and on a new dataset. The second dataset consists of 128 episode of 17 children (age $M = 4.88$, $SD = 0.49$, 59% female) telling a story to a robot rather than a peer [16]. We again had coders simulate being a listener to annotate BC opportunities. Using Dataset 1 and Dataset 2, we measured the BOP model's performance by comparing the cue label and BC timestamp to the coders' ground truth. We measured the performance as a function of precision which emphasizes false-positives. We prioritized avoiding inappropriate BC responses over missing a BC opportunity, which would be emphasized through false-negatives if we used a recall measure. The evaluation results are presented in Table 4.

[2]https://github.com/naxingyu/opensmile

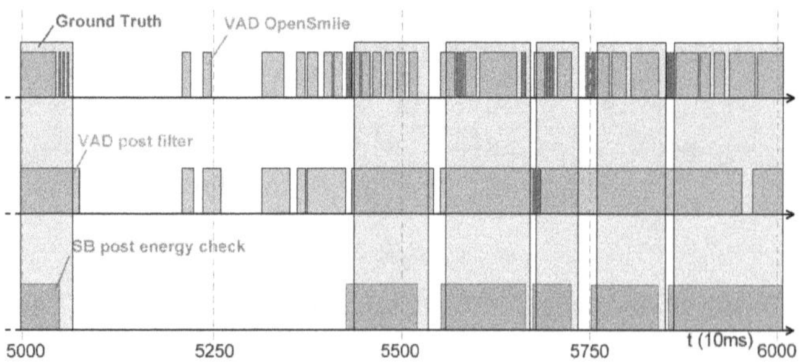

Figure 3: Identifying voice activities. The ground truth (transparent black) from human coders is compared to voice activity detection from openSMILE (VAD, blue), VAD after applying a low-pass filter (VAD post-filter, orange), and a speaking binary classifier after performing a energy-based check to filter background noise (SB, green).

Table 4: Performance of the BOP model to detect speaker cues in two different datasets. Precision is measured against the ground truth of coders.

	Dataset 1				Dataset 2
	Wordy	Long Pause	Pitch & Pause	Energy	Overall
MEAN	89.5%	78.3%	61.1%	67.3%	84.9%
STD	7.4%	8.3%	13.8%	13.2%	9.4%

5. SYSTEM DESCRIPTION

5.1 Robot Platform

Tega is an expressive social robot designed for long-term deployment in homes and schools to support children's early education [36]. An Android smart-phone mounted in the head is used to graphically display the robot's animated face as well as perform computational tasks such as sensor processing, data collection, wireless communications, decision making, and motor control. Tega expresses full-bodied animations using five degrees-of-freedom: head tilt up/down, waist tilt left/right, waist lean forward/back, body extension up/down, and body twist left/right.

5.2 System Architecture for Autonomous Interaction

For our human-subject experiment, we developed a system architecture to support a fully autonomous human-robot interaction (see Figure 4). Each module publishes its own states or computed results over the Robot Operating System (ROS) [27] network and subscribes to messages that

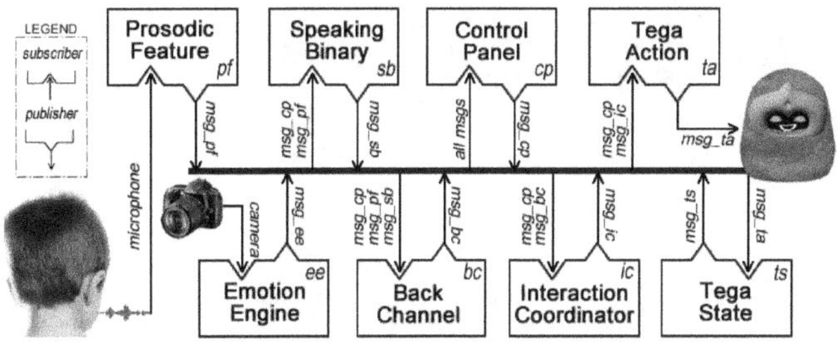

Figure 4: Realtime system architecture to support a backchanneling robot listener.

are input to their process. Using a high-quality microphone, we extracted speakers' prosodic features in realtime using openSMILE (*pf*) to determine speaking binaries(*sb*) and predict backchannel (*bc*) opportunities with our BOP model. These modules publish messages to maintain our interaction controller (*ic*) which coordinates robot behavior based on past and present events (i.e., Tega action (*ta*) and state(*ts*)). Camera images are fed into our emotion engine (*ee*) to capture the participant's head orientation and facial affect features for post-study analyses. Information such as this as well as all messages published are recorded in our logging module (control panel (*cp*)).

6. HUMAN-SUBJECTS EXPERIMENT

Through a human-subjects experiment in which children told stories to an audience of two robots with contingent and non-contingent backchanneling strategies, we investigate the effects of an attentive listening robot on a child's storytelling.

6.1 Hypotheses

We hypothesize that children will prefer to engage with the more attentive and contingent BOP robot. We demonstrate this preference through both behavior-based and subjective measures:

- **H1**: Children will direct their storytelling more toward the contingent BOP robot.
- **H2**: Non-contingent BC responses from a robot will interrupt children's storytelling.
- **H3**: Children will perceive the contingent BOP robot as more attentive and interested in their story.

6.2 Participants

Twenty-three children (age $M = 6.13$, $SD = 1.36$; 43.5% female) were recruited through a local parents' mailing-list. All children interacted with both the contingent and non-contingent robots at the same time. Such study design, a comparison study that presents two stimuli concurrently, is a popular method utilized in studying child language acquisition through social interaction [17] as well as children's vocabulary learning with a robot companion [4] and studying users' perception of a robotic agent's verbal and nonverbal feedback in a dialogue interaction [9].

6.3 Experimental Conditions

After a short introduction to the robots, participants were brought to the experimental room and was asked to tell stories to the two robots (Figure 5). One of the robots provided contingent BC feedback using the BOP model. The other robot provided random non-contingent BC feedback with a set frequency.

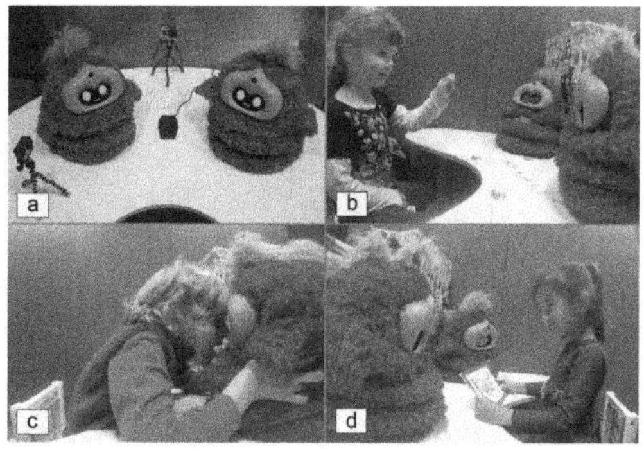

Figure 5: (a) Experimental room setup with two identically looking Tegas each representing the contingent and non-contingent condition. (b-c) Participants are engaged in storytelling with the robots. (d) a child is presenting a sticker to the more attentive robot.

- **Contingent Robot:** The behavior of the contingent robot closely mirrored that of the child listener's. Using the analyses on child listener reponses in Table 1, we developed twenty combinations of facial and body expressions that represent BC responses — gazing, leaning forward, nodding, smiling, eye-widening to emulate eyebrow movement, and short utterances [3]. When a BC opportunity is detected, the robot adapted its level of expressiveness depending on the speaker's energy level. For instance, when high energy level is detected at an energy event, the robot plays large excited motion.
- **Non-contingent Robot:** The non-contingent robot used the same set of animated nonverbal behaviors as the contingent robot but gazed at the speaker randomly and did not adapt its expressiveness to the speaker's energy level. However, the overall expressiveness of the behavior was matched in realtime to the contingent robot. This robot triggered animations and gaze behavior every 5.53 ± 1.5 seconds, which is the average frequency children produces BC response in our storytelling dataset.

To prevent any bias in the study results, we carefully controlled the robots' appearance and behavior. The robots looked identical, used the same name, and the expressivity level of the behaviors was matched between conditions. The placement of the robots was counter-balanced — in 45% of the sessions, the contingent robot was placed on the left side and 55% of the sessions on the right.

6.4 Study Protocol

The study procedure had three phases: a story brainstorming, a storytelling session with robots, and a post survey. The story brainstorming session took place in the waiting area while other phases were conducted in the study room with the robots.

6.4.1 Story brainstorming

At the time of study enrollment, parents were asked to provide information on what story their child likes to tell.

[3]Please refer to the trailer video for examples of these behaviors.

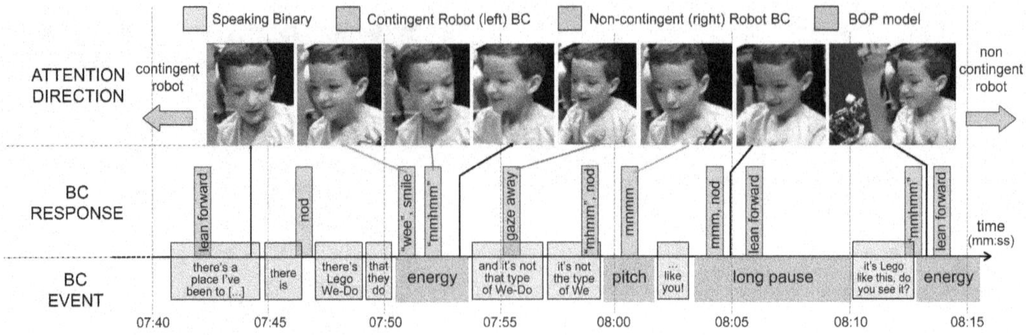

Figure 6: A snippet of a study session depicting the *backchannel events*, two robots' *backchannel responses*, and a child's *attention* towards the robots. The orange bar shows the contingent behavior of the BOP robot, and the blue bar shows a static frequency BC response of the non-contingent robot. The child significantly gazed more towards the contingent robot (on his left side) when storytelling.

Using this information, the experimenter engaged the child in a story brainstorming session. The experimenter asked about the child's experience over the breaks or used graphic books to help children who had difficulty in creating a story of their own. Afterwards, the experimenter provided the following backstory:

> *We have a problem. The two Tegas you were supposed to meet today are baby Tegas. They fell asleep and I can't wake them up. But their favorite activity is listening to children's stories! Maybe if you tell them you're here to tell them stories, they might wake up! Would you like to come try?*

This session successfully prepared children for the following phase, and only one child refused to tell stories to the robots.

6.4.2 Storytelling interaction with robots

Participants were brought to the study room with two sleeping Tegas on a table. The child was asked to sit on a chair in the center of the table, and the parents were invited to observe the session from a chair three feet behind the child. Children initiated the interaction by either gently rubbing, greeting, or telling Tegas that they were here to tell stories. Tegas "woke up" yawning at random intervals and started backchanneling as the participant told his/her story. When the child indicated he/she was done, the robots fell back asleep before the post survey began in order to prevent the child from feeling bad about making comments on Tegas' behaviors.

6.4.3 Post survey

The post survey consisted of questionnaires asking the likeability of the robots (how much did you like Tegas?), enjoyability of the storytelling task (how much did you like telling stories to Tegas?), and the level of interest each robot showed toward the story (how much do you think this Tega enjoyed your story?) in a 5-point Likert scale based on smileyometer. Participants were then asked to give a sticker to the robot they thought to be the better listener and was more interested in their story. The experimenter further asked the reasons behind their answers.

7. RESULTS AND DISCUSSION

Among 23 participants, we were able to analyze data from 20 children (age $M = 6.25$, $SD = 1.33$; 45% female). One 4-year-old did not want to tell a story and withdrew from the study. We excluded two participants' data because the frontal view camera was out of focus, and we could not extract gaze-orientation data from the videos. The average length of children's stories was 10.77 ± 4.12 minutes. We found no statistical significance in the number of BC feedback provided and the level of expressiveness of the BC motions (categorized as small or large) between the contingent and non-contingent robots, thereby we can safely assume that the expressiveness of both robots was similar. Figure 6 presents a snippet of one of the study sessions.

We evaluated whether the contingency of a robot's BC response affects children's storytelling behavior by analyzing children's gaze patterns, affective reactions toward each robot, and post-survey answers.

7.1 Children direct their storytelling more toward the contingent robot

We analyzed children's gaze pattern using the yaw data of the head orientation. We also correlated this data with speaking binary to understand which robot the child attends to while telling a story.

The overall gaze direction during the entire interaction showed insignificance between the two robots measured as a fraction of each session length (contingent: $M = 0.359$, $SD = 0.070$, non-contingent: $M = 0.396$, $SD = 0.076$; $t(38) = 1.598$, $p = 0.118$). However, children significantly gazed more at the contingent robot when telling a story (SB=1) (contingent: $M = 0.185$, $SD = 0.076$, non-contingent: $M = 0.146$, $SD = 0.040$; $t(38) = 2.031$, $p = 0.049$). This confirms our main hypothesis **H1**. Also, when no speech event was detected (SB=0) children gazed more at the non-contingent robot (contingent: $M = 0.174$, $SD = 0.031$, non-contingent: $M = 0.250$, $SD = 0.053$; $t(38) = 5.523$, $p < 0.01$). An inspection of the videos suggests that the non-contingent robot's random feedback interrupts the child's speech prompting a momentary gazing reaction (Figure 7).

7.2 Children are distracted by the non-contingent robot

To better understand the affective content of participants' facial expressions, we used Affdex, a commercially available automated affect recognition software [1]. It extracts 15 physical expressions from facial features that are used as predictors to calculate the likelihood of an exhibited emotion as well as to estimate the degree of valence (positive and negative emotion) and expressiveness (intensity of an expression).

Although no significant difference was found in positive affect between the two conditions, an analysis of expres-

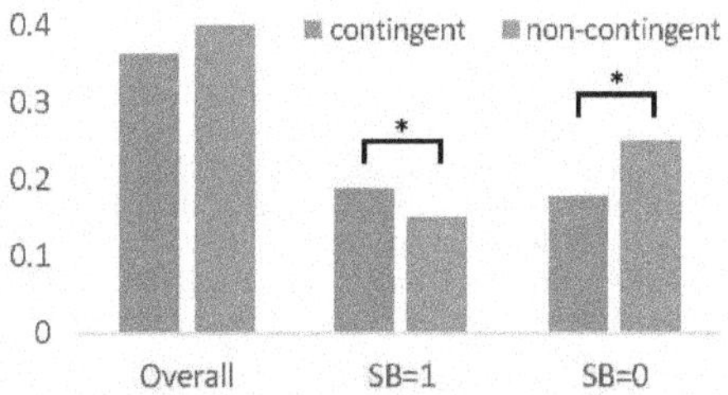

Figure 7: An average fraction of gaze length over the entire length of a session. Children gazed significantly more at the contingent robot ($p < 0.05$) when telling a story ($SB = 1$).

siveness (continuous scale of [0,100]) showed that children were more calm towards the contingent robot (contingent: $M = 56.42$, $SD = 19.23$, non-contingent: $M = 76.34$, $SD = 24.35$; $t(38) = 2.871$, $p < 0.01$). Children expressed emotions with higher valence towards the non-contingent robot, which children described the robot as "'funny", "made me laugh", and "shy." Analysis revealed high correlation between expressiveness and pauses from storytelling (SB=0) ([SB=0: $M = 67.83$, $SD = 19.21$];[SB=1: $M = 54.25$, $SD = 12.38$]; $t(38) = 2.658$, $p = 0.012$), consistently suggesting that children paused from storytelling and reacted affectively to the non-contingent robot making random feedback (Figure 8).

The analyses of the participants' gaze behavior and affect response consistently suggest that the non-contingent robot distracts children from telling a story, supporting our second hypothesis, **H2**.

7.3 Children perceive the contingent robot more attentive

From the 5-point Likert-scale survey, our analysis revealed a high degree of likeability towards Tegas ($M = 4.70$, $SD = 0.66$) and enjoyability of telling a story to Tegas ($M = 4.50$, $SD = 0.69$). When asked about the robots' perspective, most children answered both Tegas enjoyed their story, and no difference was observed between the two conditions (contingent: $M = 4.63$, $SD = 0.60$; non-contingent: $M = 4.53$, $SD = 0.61$). Fisher's exact test revealed that there is no statistical significance between which side the contingent robot was placed versus the robot child indicated as a better listener.

Based on the sticker test, 15 out of 20 children selected the contingent robot as the more attentive listener than the non-contingent robot (p=0.0038). Children who chose the non-contingent robot as the more attentive listener reported that the robot "made large motions" ($N = 1$), "seemed very happy/excited" ($N = 2$), and "made less 'mmm' sound" ($N = 4$).

We particularly find the last reason interesting, since as observed in Section 3.2, only 50% of child listeners use short utterances like 'mmm' as backchannel feedback. This observation in conjunction with how children decode what they encode from Section 3.4, we can assume that a possible reason behind why these children did not choose the contingent robot is because they perceived the backchannel utterances as interruptive and distracting rather than as a signal of an attentive listener (since they themselves do not use the signal in a similar way).

In summary, subjective analysis on children's questionnaire responses supports our last hypothesis **H3**, that children would perceive the contingent BOP robot as more attentive and interested in their story.

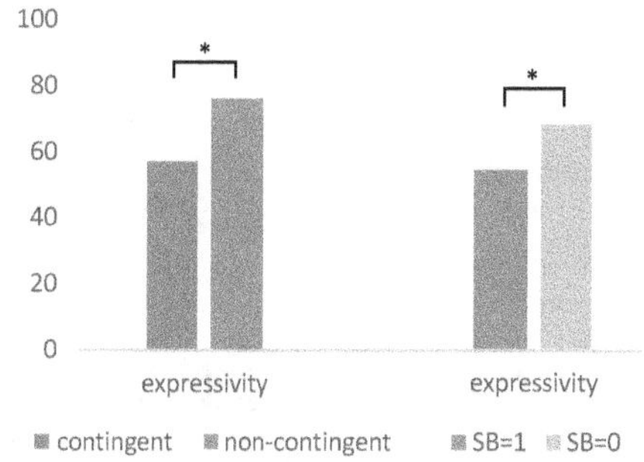

Figure 8: Level of expressivity is shown in scale [0,100]. Children's facial expressivity significantly increases toward the non-contingent robot. Correlation analysis reveals that children tend to be more calm when telling a story ($SB = 1$).

8. CONCLUSION

Our work has addressed the challenge of developing a backchannel prediction model based on observed child nonverbal behaviors as well as evaluating its effects when utilized as a listening robot. We began by first understanding the demonstrated nonverbal behaviors of children in a storytelling context. We identified backchannel behaviors—partner gazes, leaning toward, smiles, utterances, brow raises, and nods—that indicate a positive engagement state of the listener. We identified speaker cues—gaze, pitch, word, energy, pauses taken singly and in combinations—that children listeners acknowledge and respond to. We characterized the bidirectionality of nonverbal behaviors in that children understand the function of nonverbal behaviors both in the role of the communicator and recipient. Children can decode nonverbal behaviors they encode. Based on our findings, we developed a rule-based backchannel opportunity prediction (BOP) model capable of accurately predicting backchanneling opportunities.

Our aim was to evaluate two crucial questions that motivate the design and development of social robot learning companions that can successfully foster early language skills of preschoolers and kindergarteners. Can a social robot generate backchannel behaviors that children perceive as attentiveness? Is contingency of agent feedback crucial toward creating these perceptions? Our study suggests that contingency matters as it leads children to appropriately direct their storytelling to their audience and also contributes to the perception of an attentive audience.

9. ACKNOWLEDGMENTS

We thank professors Stephanie Gottwald, David DeSteno, and Paul Harris for their feedback in this research. We also thank Aradhana Adhikari, Katharine Brush, Raina Hall, Emily Holding, Sean Ko, Yiyu Li, Madelyn Payne, Jose Salas, Matthew Sears, and Michal Shlapentokh-Rothman for annotating videos and helping conduct the user studies. This work was supported by the National Science Foundation (grant IIS-1523118), Dolores Zohrab Liebmann Fellowship, and William Asbjornsen Albert Memorial Fellowship.

10. REFERENCES

[1] Affectiva. Emotion recognition software and analysis, 2016.

[2] T. Behne, U. Liszkowski, M. Carpenter, and M. Tomasello. Twelve-month-olds' comprehension and production of pointing. *British Journal of Developmental Psychology*, 30(3):359–375, 2012.

[3] C. Breazeal, K. Dautenhahn, and T. Kanda. Social robotics. In *Springer Handbook of Robotics*, pages 1935–1972. Springer, 2016.

[4] C. Breazeal, P. L. Harris, D. DeSteno, K. Westlund, M. Jacqueline, L. Dickens, and S. Jeong. Young children treat robots as informants. *Topics in cognitive science*, 2016.

[5] N. Cathcart, J. Carletta, and E. Klein. A shallow model of backchannel continuers in spoken dialogue. In *Proceedings of the tenth conference on European chapter of the Association for Computational Linguistics-Volume 1*, pages 51–58. Association for Computational Linguistics, 2003.

[6] H. H. Clark and S. E. Brennan. Grounding in communication. *Perspectives on socially shared cognition*, 13(1991):127–149, 1991.

[7] A. R. Dennis and S. T. Kinney. Testing media richness theory in the new media: The effects of cues, feedback, and task equivocality. *Information systems research*, 9(3):256–274, 1998.

[8] F. Eyben, F. Weninger, F. Gross, and B. Schuller. Recent developments in opensmile, the munich open-source multimedia feature extractor. In *Proceedings of the 21st ACM international conference on Multimedia*, pages 835–838. ACM, 2013.

[9] S. Fujie, K. Fukushima, and T. Kobayashi. A conversation robot with back-channel feedback function based on linguistic and nonlinguistic information. In *Proc. ICARA Int. Conference on Autonomous Robots and Agents*, pages 379–384, 2004.

[10] G. Gordon, C. Breazeal, and S. Engel. Can children catch curiosity from a social robot? In *Proceedings of the Tenth Annual ACM/IEEE International Conference on Human-Robot Interaction*, pages 91–98. ACM, 2015.

[11] G. Gordon, S. Spaulding, J. K. Westlund, J. J. Lee, L. Plummer, M. Martinez, M. Das, and C. Breazeal. Affective Personalization of a Social Robot Tutor for Children's Second Language Skills. In *Thirtieth AAAI Conference on Artificial Intelligence*, 2016.

[12] A. Gravano and J. Hirschberg. Backchannel-inviting cues in task-oriented dialogue. In *INTERSPEECH*, pages 1019–1022, 2009.

[13] L. J. Hess and J. R. Johnston. Acquisition of back channel listener responses to adequate messages. *Discourse Processes*, 11(3):319–335, 1988.

[14] L. Huang, L.-P. Morency, and J. Gratch. Parasocial consensus sampling: Combining multiple perspectives to learn virtual human behavior. In *Proceedings of the 9th International Conference on Autonomous Agents and Multiagent Systems: volume 1-Volume 1*, pages 1265–1272. International Foundation for Autonomous Agents and Multiagent Systems, 2010.

[15] P. H. Kahn Jr, T. Kanda, H. Ishiguro, N. G. Freier, R. L. Severson, B. T. Gill, J. H. Ruckert, and S. Shen. "Robovie, you'll have to go into the closet now": Children's social and moral relationships with a humanoid robot. *Developmental psychology*, 48(2):303, 2012.

[16] J. Kory and C. Breazeal. Storytelling with robots: Learning companions for preschool children's language development. In *The 23rd IEEE International Symposium on Robot and Human Interactive Communication*, pages 643–648. IEEE, 2014.

[17] P. K. Kuhl. Is speech learning 'gated' by the social brain? *Developmental science*, 10(1):110–120, 2007.

[18] L.-P. Morency, I. de Kok, and J. Gratch. A probabilistic multimodal approach for predicting listener backchannels. *Autonomous Agents and Multi-Agent Systems*, 20(1):70–84, 2010.

[19] J. Movellan, M. Eckhardt, M. Virnes, and A. Rodriguez. Sociable robot improves toddler vocabulary skills. In *Proceedings of the 4th ACM/IEEE international conference on Human robot interaction*, pages 307–308, 2009.

[20] H. Noguchi and Y. Den. Prosody-based detection of the context of backchannel responses. In *ICSLP*, 1998.

[21] Y. Okato, K. Kato, M. Kamamoto, and S. Itahashi. Insertion of interjectory response based on prosodic information. In *Interactive Voice Technology for Telecommunications Applications, 1996. Proceedings., Third IEEE Workshop on*, pages 85–88. IEEE, 1996.

[22] H. W. Park and A. M. Howard. Understanding a child's play for robot interaction by sequencing play primitives using hidden markov models. In *Robotics and Automation (ICRA), 2010 IEEE International Conference on*, pages 170–177. IEEE, 2010.

[23] H. W. Park and A. M. Howard. Retrieving experience: Interactive instance-based learning methods for building robot companions. In *2015 IEEE International Conference on Robotics and Automation (ICRA)*, pages 6140–6145. IEEE, 2015.

[24] H. W. Park, R. Rosenberg-Kima, M. Rosenberg, G. Gordon, and C. Breazeal. Growing growth mindset with a social robot peer. In *Proceedings of the 12th ACM/IEEE international conference on Human robot interaction*. ACM, 2017.

[25] C. Peterson, B. Jesso, and A. McCabe. Encouraging narratives in preschoolers: An intervention study. *Journal of child language*, 26(01):49–67, 1999.

[26] R. Poppe, K. P. Truong, D. Reidsma, and D. Heylen. Backchannel strategies for artificial listeners. In *International Conference on Intelligent Virtual Agents*, pages 146–158. Springer, 2010.

[27] M. Quigley, K. Conley, B. Gerkey, J. Faust, T. Foote, J. Leibs, R. Wheeler, and A. Y. Ng. Ros: an open-source robot operating system. In *ICRA workshop on open source software*, volume 3, page 5. Kobe, Japan, 2009.

[28] M. Shatz and R. Gelman. The development of communication skills: Modifications in the speech of young children as a function of listener. *Monographs of the society for research in child development*, pages 1–38, 1973.

[29] M. Shiomi, T. Kanda, I. Howley, K. Hayashi, and N. Hagita. Can a social robot stimulate science curiosity in classrooms? *International Journal of Social Robotics*, 7(5):641–652, 2015.

[30] S. Spaulding, G. Gordon, and C. Breazeal. Affect-Aware Student Models for Robot Tutors. In *Proceedings of the 2016 International Conference on Autonomous Agents & Multiagent Systems*, pages 864–872. International Foundation for Autonomous Agents and Multiagent Systems, 2016.

[31] F. Tanaka and S. Matsuzoe. Children teach a care-receiving robot to promote their learning: Field experiments in a classroom for vocabulary learning. *Journal of Human-Robot Interaction*, 1(1), 2012.

[32] K. P. Truong, R. Poppe, I. de Kok, and D. Heylen. A multimodal analysis of vocal and visual backchannels in spontaneous dialogs. 2011.

[33] K. P. Truong, R. Poppe, and D. Heylen. A rule-based backchannel prediction model using pitch and pause information. 2010.

[34] N. Ward. Using prosodic clues to decide when to produce back-channel utterances. In *Spoken Language, 1996. ICSLP 96. Proceedings., Fourth International Conference on*, volume 3, pages 1728–1731. IEEE, 1996.

[35] N. Ward and W. Tsukahara. Prosodic features which cue back-channel responses in english and japanese. *Journal of pragmatics*, 32(8):1177–1207, 2000.

[36] J. K. Westlund, J. J. Lee, L. Plummer, F. Faridi, J. Gray, M. Berlin, H. Quintus-Bosz, R. Hartmann, M. Hess, S. Dyer, and others. Tega: A Social Robot. In *2016 11th ACM/IEEE International Conference on Human-Robot Interaction (HRI)*, pages 561–561. IEEE, 2016.

[37] S. White. Backchannels across cultures: A study of americans and japanese. *Language in society*, 18(01):59–76, 1989.

Navigational Instruction Generation as Inverse Reinforcement Learning with Neural Machine Translation

Andrea F Daniele
TTI-Chicago
afdaniele@ttic.edu

Mohit Bansal
UNC Chapel Hill
mbansal@cs.unc.edu

Matthew R Walter
TTI-Chicago
mwalter@ttic.edu

ABSTRACT

Modern robotics applications that involve human-robot interaction require robots to be able to communicate with humans seamlessly and effectively. Natural language provides a flexible and efficient medium through which robots can exchange information with their human partners. Significant advancements have been made in developing robots capable of interpreting free-form instructions, but less attention has been devoted to endowing robots with the ability to generate natural language. We propose a model that enables robots to generate natural language instructions that allow humans to navigate a priori unknown environments. We first decide which information to share with the user according to their preferences, using a policy trained from human demonstrations via inverse reinforcement learning. We then "translate" this information into a natural language instruction using a neural sequence-to-sequence model that learns to generate free-form instructions from natural language corpora. We evaluate our method on a benchmark route instruction dataset and achieve a BLEU score of 72.18% compared to human-generated reference instructions. We additionally conduct navigation experiments with human participants demonstrating that our method generates instructions that people follow as accurately and easily as those produced by humans.

Input: map and path

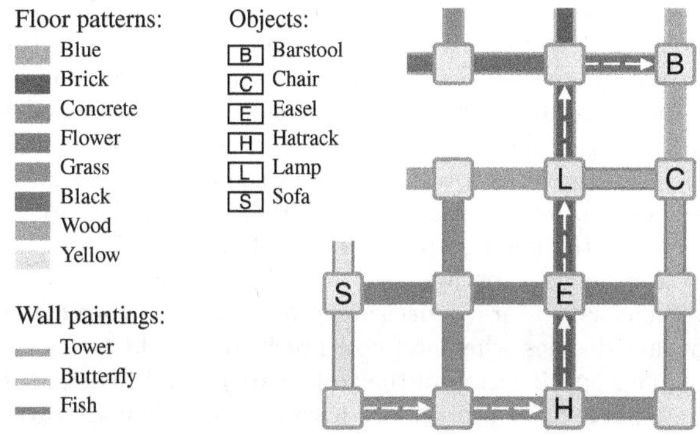

Output: route instruction

"turn to face the grass hallway. walk forward twice. face the easel. move until you see black floor to your right. face the stool. move to the stool"

Figure 1: An example route instruction that our framework generates for the shown map and path.

1. INTRODUCTION

Robots are increasingly being used as our partners, working with and alongside people, whether it is serving as assistants in our homes [60], transporting cargo in warehouses [11], helping students with language learning in the classroom [28], and acting as guides in public spaces [23]. In order for humans and robots to work together effectively, robots must be able to communicate with their human partners to convey information, establish a shared understanding of their collaborative task, or to coordinate their efforts [21, 17, 50, 49]. Natural language provides an efficient, flexible medium through which humans and robots can exchange information. Consider, for example, a search-and-rescue operation carried out by a human-robot team. The human may first issue spoken commands (e.g., "Search the rooms at the end of the hallway") that direct one or more robots to navigate throughout the building searching for occupants [40, 54, 41]. In this process, the robot may engage the user in dialogue to resolve any ambiguity in the task (e.g., to clarify which hallway the user was referring to) [55, 15, 47, 56, 24]. The user's ability to trust their robotic partners is also integral to effective collaboration [20], and a robot's ability to generate natural language explanations of its progress (e.g., "I have inspected two rooms") and decision-making processes have been shown to help establish trust [16, 2, 61].

In this paper, we specifically consider the surrogate problem of synthesizing natural language route instructions and describe a method that generates free-form directions that people can accurately and efficiently follow in environments unknown to them a priori (Fig. 1). This problem has previously been considered by the robotics community [44, 18, 45] and is important for human-robot collaborative tasks, such as search-and-rescue, exploration, and surveillance [33], and for robotic assistants, such as those that serve as guides in

HRI '17, March 06 - 09, 2017, Vienna, Austria

ISBN 978-1-4503-4336-7/17/03...$15.00

DOI: http://dx.doi.org/10.1145/2909824.3020241

museums, offices, and other public spaces. More generally, the problem is relevant beyond human-robot interaction to the broader domain of indoor navigation. There are two primary challenges to generating effective, natural language route instructions, which are characteristic of the more general problem of free-form generation.

The first challenge is *content selection*, the problem of deciding what and how much information to convey to the user as part of the directions. In general, the more detailed an instruction is, the less ambiguous it is. However, verbose instructions can be unnatural and hard for followers to remember and, thus, ineffective. Consequently, it is important to balance the value of including particular information as part of a route instruction with the cost that comes with increasing the level of detail. Further, not all information is equally informative. Existing commercial navigational solutions typically rely on a set of hand-crafted rules that consider only street names and metric distances as valid candidates, the latter of which requires that follower's keep track of their progress. In contrast, studies have shown that people prefer route instructions that reference physical, salient landmarks in the environment [59]. However, no standard exists with regards to what and how these landmarks should be selected, as these depend on the nature of the environment and the demographics of the follower [62, 27].

We propose a method that models this content selection problem as a Markov decision process with a learned policy that decides what and how much to include in a formal language specification of the task (path). We learn this policy via inverse reinforcement learning from demonstrations of route instructions provided by humans. This avoids the need for hand-crafted selection rules, and allows our method to automatically adapt to the preferences and communication style of the target populations and to simultaneously choose to convey information that minimizes the ambiguity of the instruction while avoiding verbosity.

The second challenge is *surface realization*, which is the task of synthesizing a natural language sentence that refers to the selected content. Existing solutions rely on sentence templates, generating sentences by populating manually defined fields (e.g., "turn ⟨direction⟩") and then serializing these sentences in a turn-by-turn fashion. As expected, the use of such templates reduces coherence across sentences and limits the ability to adapt to different domains (e.g., from outdoor to indoor navigation). Additionally, while the output is technically correct, the resulting sentences tend to be rigid and unnatural. Studies show that language generated by a robot is most effective when it emulates the communication style that people use [57].

We address the surface realization problem through a neural sequence-to-sequence model that "translates" a formal language specification of the selected command into a natural language sentence. Our model takes the form of an encoder-aligner-decoder architecture that first encodes the formal path specification with a recurrent neural network using long short-term memory (LSTM-RNN) [25]. The model then decodes (translates) the resulting abstraction of the input into a natural language sentence (word sequence), using an alignment mechanism to further refine the selected information and associate output words with the corresponding elements in the input formal specification. The use of LSTMs as the hidden units enables our model to capture the long-term dependencies that exist among the selected information and among the words in the resulting instruction. We train our surface realization model on instruction corpora, enabling our method to generate free-form directions that emulate the style of human instructions, without templates, specialized features, or linguistic resources.

We evaluate our method on the benchmark SAIL dataset of human-generated route instructions [39]. Instructions generated with our method achieve a sentence-level BLEU score of 72.18%, indicating their similarity with the reference set of human-provided instructions. We perform a series of ablations and visualizations to better understand the contributions of the primary components of our model. We additionally conduct human evaluation experiments that demonstrate that our method generates instructions that people are able to follow as efficiently and accurately as those generated by humans.

The paper presents what is, to the best of our knowledge, the first framework that generates natural language instructions that reflect the preferences and rhetorical style of humans. We achieve this firstly via a decision process that learns to emulate human content selection preferences from demonstrations; and secondly through a neural machine translation model that learns to express this content via natural language. Human experiments reveal that our method produces instructions that are as accurate, effective, and usable as those generated by humans.

2. RELATED WORK

Existing research related to the generation of route instructions spans the fields of robotics, natural language processing, cognitive science, and psychology. Early work in this area focuses on understanding the way in which humans generate natural language route instructions [62, 1, 38] and the properties that make "good" instructions easier for people to follow [36, 48, 59]. These studies have shown that people prefer to give directions as a sequence of turn-by-turn instructions and that they favor physical objects and locations as intuitive landmarks.

Based on these studies, much of the existing research on generating route instructions involves the use of hand-crafted rules that are designed to emulate the manner in which people compose navigation instructions [51, 13]. Look et al. [36] compose route instructions using a set of templates and application rules engineered based upon a corpus of human-generated route instructions. Look [37] improves upon this work by incorporating human cognitive spatial models to generate high-level route overviews that augment turn-by-turn directions. Similarly, Dale et al. [14] analyze a dataset of route instructions composed by people to derive a set of hand-designed rules that mimic the content and style of human directions. Goeddel and Olson [18] describe a particle filter-based method that employs a generative model of direction following to produce templated instructions that maximize the likelihood of reaching the desired destination. Meanwhile, Morales Saiki et al. [44] propose a system that enables robots to provide route instructions using a combination of language and pointing gestures. Unlike our approach, their method is limited to paths with no more than three direction changes and employs four generation templates, limiting the content and structure of the instructions.

The challenge with instruction generation systems that rely upon hand-crafted rules is that it is difficult to design a policy that generalizes to a wide variety of scenarios and followers, whose preferences vary depending on such factors as their cultural background [27] and gender [62]. Cuayáhuitl et al. [12] seek to improve upon this using reinforcement learning with hand-crafted reward functions that model the length of the instructions and the likelihood that they will confuse a follower. They then learn a policy that reasons both over the best route and the corresponding navigational instructions. However, this approach still requires that domain experts define the reward functions and specify model parameters. In contrast, Oswald et al. [45] model the problem of deciding what to include in the instruction (i.e., the content selection problem) as a Markov decision process and learn a policy from a human-generated navigation corpus using maximum entropy inverse reinforcement learning. Given the content identified by the policy, their framework does not perform surface realization, and instead generates instructions by matching the selected content with the nearest match in a database of human-generated instructions. Our method also uses inverse reinforcement learning for content selection, but unlike their system, our method also learns to perform surface realization directly from corpora, thus generating newly-composed natural language instructions.

Relatedly, much attention has been paid recently to the "inverse" problem of learning to follow (i.e., execute) natural language route instructions. Statistical methods primarily formulate the problem of converting instructions to actions as either a semantic parsing task [40, 9, 4] or as a symbol grounding problem [31, 54, 34, 26, 10]. Alternatively, Mei et al. [41] translate free-form instructions to action sequences in an end-to-end fashion using an encoder-aligner-decoder.

Meanwhile, selective generation considers the more general problem of converting a rich database to a natural language utterance, with existing methods generally focusing on the individual problems of content selection and surface realization. Barzilay and Lee [7] perform content selection on collections of unannotated documents for the sake of text summarization. Barzilay and Lapata [6] formulate content selection as a collective classification problem, simultaneously optimizing local label assignments and their pairwise relations. Liang et al. [35] consider the related problem of aligning elements of a database to textual description clauses. They propose a generative semi-Markov model that simultaneously segments text into utterances and aligns each utterance with its corresponding entry in the database. Meanwhile, Walker et al. [58] perform surface realization via sentence planners that can be trained to generate sentences for dialogue and context planning. Wong and Mooney [63] effectively invert a semantic parser to generate natural language sentences from formal meaning representations using synchronous context-free grammars. Rather than consider individual sub-problems, recent work focuses on solving selective generation via a single framework [8, 29, 3, 32, 42]. Angeli et al. [3] model content selection and surface realization as local decision problems via log-linear models and employ templates for generation. Mei et al. [42] formulate selective generation as an end-to-end learning problem and propose a recurrent neural network encoder-aligner-decoder model that jointly learns to perform content selection and surface realization from database-text pairs. Unlike our method, they do not reason over the correctness or unambiguity of the summaries, nor do they attempt to model human content selection preferences.

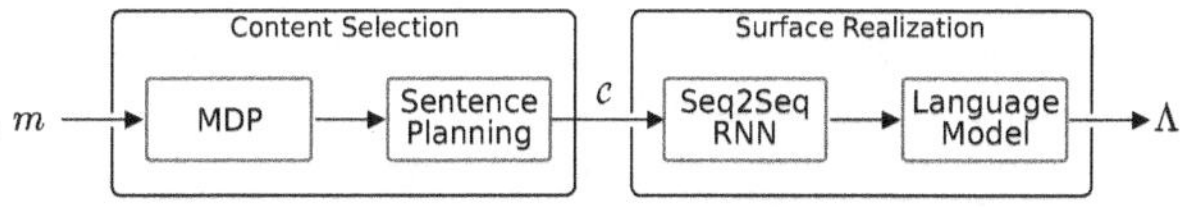

Figure 2: Our method generates natural language instructions for a given map and path.

3. TASK DEFINITION

We consider the problem of generating natural language instructions that allow humans to navigate environments that are unknown to them a priori. The given map m takes the form of a hybrid metric-topologic-semantic representation (Fig. 1) that encodes the position of and connectivity between a dense set of locations in the environment (e.g., intersections) and the position and type of objects and environment features (e.g., floor patterns). The path p is a sequence of poses (i.e., position and orientation) that corresponds to the minimum distance route from a given initial pose to a desired goal pose. We split the path according to changes in direction, representing the path $p = (p_1, p_2, \ldots p_M)$ as a sequence of intermediate segments p_i.

Training data comes in the form of tuples $(m^{(i)}, p^{(i)}, \Lambda^{(i)})$ for $i = 1, 2, \ldots, n$ drawn from human demonstrations, where $m^{(i)}$ is a map of the environment, $\Lambda^{(i)}$ is a human-generated natural language route instruction, and $p^{(i)}$ is the path that a different human took when following the instructions. At test time, we consider only the map and path pair as known and hold out the human-generated instruction for evaluation. The dataset that we use for training, validation, and testing comes from the benchmark SAIL corpus [39].

4. MODEL

Given a map and a path, our framework (Fig. 2) performs content selection to decide what information to share with the human follower and subsequently performs surface realization to generate a natural language instruction according to this selected content. Our method learns to perform content selection and surface realization from human demonstrations, so as to produce instructions that are similar to those generated by humans.

Our framework only assumes knowledge of the user's pose and can be readily implemented on a mobile robot or body-worn device that provides natural language guidance as the user navigates, re-planning and issuing corrections as necessary. By maintaining probabilistic models of information content and ambiguity, our method is amenable to incorporating user feedback (e.g., utterances and gaze) to revise the information shared with the user (e.g., referencing landmarks based upon gaze). By using inverse reinforcement learning, our method can also adapt the content selection policy based on feedback to better learn user preferences.

4.1 Compound Action Specifications

In order to bridge the gap between the low-level nature of the input paths and the natural language output, we encode paths using an intermediate logic-based formal language. Specifically, we use the Compound Action Specification (CAS) representation [39], which provides a formal abstraction of navigation commands for hybrid metric-topologic-semantic maps. The CAS language consists of five *actions* (i.e., Travel, Turn, Face, Verify, and Find), each of which is associated with a number of *attributes* (e.g., Travel.distance, Turn.direction) that together define specific commands. We distinguish between CAS *structures*, which are instructions with the attributes left empty (e.g., *Turn(direction=**None**)*) thereby defining a class of instructions, and CAS *commands*, which correspond to instantiated instructions with the attributes set to particular values (e.g., *Turn(direction=**Left**)*). For each English instruction $\Lambda^{(i)}$ in the dataset, we generate the corresponding CAS command $c^{(i)}$ using the MARCO architecture [39]. For a complete description of the CAS language, see MacMahon et al. [39].

4.2 Content Selection

There are many ways in which one can compose a CAS representation of a desired path, both in terms of the type of information that is conveyed (e.g., referencing distances vs. physical landmarks), as well as the specific references to use (e.g., different objects provide candidate landmarks). Humans exhibit common preferences in terms of the type of information that is shared (e.g., favoring visible landmarks over distances) [59], yet the specific nature of this information depends upon the environment and the followers' demographics [62, 27]. Our goal is to learn these preferences from a dataset of instructions generated by humans.

4.2.1 MDP with Inverse Reinforcement Learning

In similar fashion to Oswald et al. [45], we formulate the content selection problem as a Markov decision process (MDP) with the goal of then identifying an information selection policy that maximizes long-term cumulative reward consistent with human preferences (Fig. 2). However, this reward function is unknown a priori and is generally difficult to define. We assume that humans optimize a common reward function when composing instructions and employ inverse reinforcement learning (IRL) to learn a policy that mimics the preferences that humans exhibit based upon a set of human demonstrations.

An MDP is defined by the tuple (S, A, R, P, γ), where S is a set of states, A is a set of actions, $R(s, a, s') \in \mathbb{R}$ is the reward received when executing action $a \in A$ in state $s \in S$ and transitioning to state $s' \in S$, $P(s'|a, s)$ is the probability of transitioning from state s to state s' when executing action a, and $\gamma \in (0, 1]$ is the discount factor. The policy $\pi(a|s)$ corresponds to a distribution over actions given the current state. In the case of the route instruction domain, the state s defines the user's pose and path in the context of the map of the environment. We represent the state in terms of 14 *context* features that express characteristics such as changes in orientation and position, the relative location of objects, and nearby environment features (e.g., different floor colors). We encode the state s as a 14-dimensional binary vector that indicates which context features are active for that state. In this way, the state space S is spanned by all possible instantiations of context features. Meanwhile, the action space corresponds to the space of different CAS structures (i.e., without instantiated attributes) that can be used to define the path.

We seek a policy $\pi(a|s)$ that maximizes expected cumulative reward. However, the reward function that defines the value of particular characteristics of the instruction is unknown and difficult to define. For that reason, we frame the task as an inverse reinforcement learning problem using human-provided route instructions as demonstrations of the optimal policy. Specifically, we learn a policy using the maximum entropy formulation of IRL [64], which models user actions as a distribution over paths parameterized as a log-linear model $P(a; \theta) \propto e^{-\theta^\top \xi(a)}$, where $\xi(a)$ is a feature vector defined over actions and θ is a parameter vector. We consider 9 instruction features (*properties*) that include features expressing the number of landmarks included in the instruction, the frame of reference that is used, and the complexity of the command. The feature vector $\xi(a)$ then takes the form of a 9-dimensional binary vector. The Supplementary Material presents the full set of context and property features used to parameterize the states and actions. Maximum entropy IRL then solves for the distribution as

$$\begin{aligned} P(a; \theta^*) &= \arg\max_{\theta} P(a; \theta) \log P(a; \theta) \\ \text{s.t. } \xi_g &= \mathbb{E}[\xi(a)], \end{aligned} \tag{1}$$

where ξ_g denotes the features from the demonstrations and the expectation is taken over the action distribution. For further details regarding maximum entropy IRL, we refer the reader to Ziebart et al. [64].

The policy defines a distribution over CAS structure compositions (i.e., using the *Verify* action vs. the *Turn* action) in terms of their feature encoding. We perform inference over this policy to identify the maximum a posteriori property vector $\xi(a^*) = \arg\max_{\xi} \pi$. As there is no way to invert the feature mapping, we then match this vector $\xi(a^*)$ to a database of CAS structures formed from our training set. Rather than choosing the nearest match, which may result in an inconsistent CAS structure, we retrieve the k_c nearest neighbors from the database using a weighted distance in terms of mutual information [45] that expresses the importance of different CAS features based upon the context. As several of these may be valid, we employ spectral clustering using the similarity of the CAS strings to identify a set of candidate CAS structures $\mathcal{C}_s$.

4.2.2 Sentence Planning

Given the set of candidate CAS structures $\mathcal{C}_s$, our method next chooses the attribute values such that the final CAS commands are both valid and not ambiguous. We express the likelihood that a command $c \in \mathcal{C}_s$ is a valid representation of a particular path p defined on a map m as

$$P(c|p, m) = \frac{\delta(c|p, m)}{\sum_{j=1}^{K} \delta(c|\hat{p}_j, m)}. \tag{2}$$

The index j iterates over all possible paths that have the same starting pose as path p. We define $\delta(c \mid p, m)$ as

$$\delta(c|p, m) = \begin{cases} 1 & \text{if } \eta(c) = \phi(c, p, m) \\ 0 & \text{otherwise} \end{cases}$$

where $\eta(c)$ is the number of attributes defined in the command c, and $\phi(c, p, m)$ is the number of attributes in the command c that are valid relative to the path p and map m.

For each candidate CAS structure $c \in \mathcal{C}_s$, we generate multiple CAS commands by iterating over the possible attributes values. We evaluate the correctness and ambiguity of each configuration according to Equation 2. A command is deemed valid if its likelihood is greater than a threshold P_t. Since the number of possible configurations for a structure increases exponentially with respect to the number of attributes, we assign attributes using greedy search. The iteration is constrained to use only objects and properties of

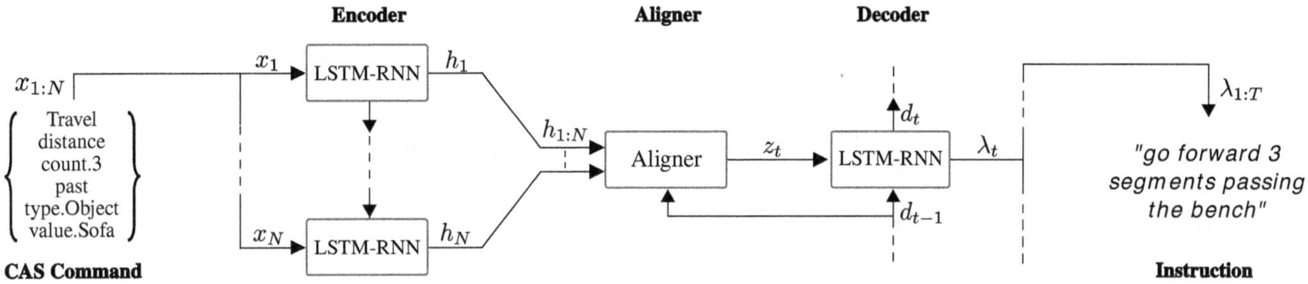

Figure 3: Our encoder-aligner-decoder model for surface realization.

the environment visible to the follower. The result is a set $\mathcal{C}$ of valid CAS commands.

4.3 Surface Realization

Having identified a set of CAS commands suitable to the given path, our method then proceeds to generate the corresponding natural language route instruction. We formulate this problem as one of "translating" the instruction specification in the formal CAS language into its natural language equivalent.[1] We perform this translation using an encoder-aligner-decoder model (Fig. 3) that enables our framework to generate natural language instructions by learning from examples of human-generated instructions, without the need for specialized features, resources, or templates.

4.3.1 Sequence-to-Sequence Model

We formulate the problem of generating natural language route instructions as inference over a probabilistic model $P(\lambda_{1:T}|x_{1:N})$, where $\lambda_{1:T} = (\lambda_1, \lambda_2, \ldots, \lambda_T)$ is the sequence of words in the instruction and $x_{1:N} = (x_1, x_2, \ldots x_N)$ is the sequence of tokens in the CAS command. The CAS sequence includes a token for each action (e.g., *Turn*, *Travel*) and a set of tokens with the form *attribute.value* for each attribute-value pair; for example, *Turn(direction=Right)* is represented by the sequence (*Turn*, *direction.Right*). Generating an instruction sequence then corresponds to inference over this model.

$$\lambda^*_{1:T} = \arg\max_{\lambda_{1:T}} P(\lambda_{1:T}|x_{1:N}) \tag{3a}$$

$$= \arg\max_{\lambda_{1:T}} \prod_{t=1}^{T} P(\lambda_t|\lambda_{1:t-1}, x_{1:N}) \tag{3b}$$

We formulate this task as a sequence-to-sequence learning problem, whereby we use a recurrent neural network (RNN) to first encode the input CAS command

$$h_j = f(x_j, h_{j-1}) \tag{4a}$$

$$z_t = b(h_1, h_2, \ldots h_N), \tag{4b}$$

where h_j is the encoder hidden state for CAS token j, and f and b are nonlinear functions that we define later. An aligner computes the context vector z_t that encodes the language instruction at time $t \in \{1, \ldots, T\}$. An RNN decodes the context vector z_t to arrive at the desired likelihood (Eqn. 3)

$$P(\lambda_t|\lambda_{1:t-1}, x_{1:N}) = g(d_{t-1}, z_t), \tag{5}$$

where d_{t-1} is the decoder hidden state at time $t-1$, and g is a nonlinear function.

Encoder Our encoder (Fig. 3) takes as input the sequence of tokens in the CAS command $x_{1:N}$. We transform each token x_i into a k_e−dimensional binary vector using a word embedding representation [43]. We feed this sequence into an RNN encoder that employs LSTMs as the recurrent unit due to their ability to learn long-term dependencies among the instruction sequences without being prone to vanishing or exploding gradients. The LSTM-RNN encoder summarizes the relationship between elements of the CAS command and yields a sequence of hidden states $h_{1:N} = (h_1, h_2, \ldots, h_N)$, where h_j encodes CAS words up to and including x_j. In practice, we reverse the input sequence before feeding it into the neural encoder, which has been demonstrated to improve performance for other neural translation tasks [53].

Our encoder is similar to that of Graves et al. [19]

$$\begin{pmatrix} i^e_j \\ f^e_j \\ o^e_j \\ g^e_j \end{pmatrix} = \begin{pmatrix} \sigma \\ \sigma \\ \sigma \\ \tanh \end{pmatrix} T^e \begin{pmatrix} x_j \\ h_{j-1} \end{pmatrix} \tag{6a}$$

$$c^e_j = f^e_j \odot c^e_{j-1} + i^e_j \odot g^e_j \tag{6b}$$

$$h_j = o^e_j \odot \tanh(c^e_j) \tag{6c}$$

where T^e is an affine transformation, σ is the logistic sigmoid that restricts its input to $[0,1]$, i^e_j, f^e_j, and o^e_j are the input, output, and forget gates of the LSTM, respectively, and c^e_j is the memory cell activation vector (the Supplementary Material provides a visualization of an LSTM unit). The memory cell c^e_j summarizes the LSTM's previous memory c^e_{j-1} and the current input, which are modulated by the forget and input gates, respectively.

Aligner Having encoded the input CAS command into a sequence of hidden annotations $h_{1:N}$, the decoder then seeks to generate a natural language instruction as a sequence of words. We employ an alignment mechanism [5] (Fig. 3) that permits our model to match and focus on particular elements of the CAS sequence that are salient to the current word in the output instruction. We compute the context vector as

$$z_t = \sum_j \alpha_{tj} h_j. \tag{7}$$

The weight α_{tj} associated with the j-th hidden state is

$$\alpha_{tj} = \exp(\beta_{tj}) / \sum_k \exp(\beta_{tk}), \tag{8}$$

[1]Related work [40, 4, 41] similarly models the inverse task of language understanding as a machine translation problem.

where the alignment term $\beta_{tj} = f(d_{t-1}, h_j)$ expresses the degree to which the CAS element at position j and those around it match the output at time t. The term d_{t-1} represents the decoder hidden state at the previous time step. The alignment is modeled as a one-layer neural perceptron

$$\beta_{tj} = v^\top \tanh(W d_{t-1} + V h_j), \tag{9}$$

where v, W, and V are learned parameters.

Decoder Our model employs an LSTM decoder (Fig. 3) that takes as input the context vector z_t and the decoder hidden state at the previous time step d_{t-1}, and outputs the conditional probability distribution $P_{\lambda,t} = P(\lambda_t | \lambda_{1:t-1}, x_{1:N})$ over the next token as a deep output layer

$$\begin{pmatrix} i_t^d \\ f_t^d \\ o_t^d \\ g_t^d \end{pmatrix} = \begin{pmatrix} \sigma \\ \sigma \\ \sigma \\ \tanh \end{pmatrix} T^d \begin{pmatrix} d_{t-1} \\ z_t \end{pmatrix} \tag{10a}$$

$$c_t^d = f_t^d \odot c_{t-1}^d + i_t^d \odot g_t^d \tag{10b}$$

$$d_t = o_t^d \odot \tanh(c_t^d) \tag{10c}$$

$$q_t = L_0(L_d d_t + L_z z_t) \tag{10d}$$

$$P_{\lambda,t} = \mathrm{softmax}(q_t) \tag{10e}$$

where L_0, L_d, and L_z are parameters to be learned.

Training We train our encoder-aligner-decoder model so as to predict the natural language instruction $\lambda_{1:T}^*$ for a given input sequence $x_{1:N}$ using a training set of human-generated reference instructions. We use the negative log-likelihood of the reference instructions at each time step t as our loss function.

Inference Given a CAS command represented as a sequence of tokens $x_{1:N}$, we generate a route instruction as the sequence of maximum a posteriori words $\lambda_{1:T}^*$ under our learned model (Eqn. 3). We use beam search to perform approximate inference, but have empirically found greedy search to often perform better.[2] For that reason, we generate candidates using both greedy and beam search.

4.3.2 Language Model

The inference procedure results in multiple candidate instructions for a given segment, and additional candidates may exist when there are multiple CAS specifications. We rank these candidate instructions using a language model (LM) trained on large amounts of English data. We formulate this LM as an LSTM-RNN [52] that assigns a perplexity score to each of the corresponding instructions.

Given the CAS specifications for a segmented path $p = (p_1, p_2, \ldots p_M)$, we generate the final instruction Λ by sequencing the M sentences $\{\Lambda_1^*, \ldots, \Lambda_M^*\}$ (i.e., one for each path segment)

$$\Lambda_i^* = \arg\min_{\Lambda_{ij}} L(\Lambda_{ij}), \tag{11}$$

where Λ_{ij} is the j-th candidate for the i-th segment and $L(\Lambda_{ij})$ is the perplexity score assigned by the language model to the sentence Λ_{ij}.

[2]This phenomenon has been observed by others [3, 42], and we attribute it to training the model in a greedy fashion.

5. EXPERIMENTAL SETUP

5.1 Dataset

We train and evaluate our system using the publicly available SAIL route instruction dataset collected by MacMahon et al. [39]. We use the original data without correcting typos or wrong instructions (e.g., confusing "left" and "right"). The dataset consists of 3213 demonstrations arranged in 706 paragraphs produced by 6 instructors for 126 different paths throughout 3 virtual environments, where each demonstration provides a map-path-command tuple $(m^{(i)}, p^{(i)}, \Lambda^{(i)})$. We partition the dataset into separate training (70%), validation (10%), and test (20%) sets. We utilize command-instruction pairs $(c^{(i)}, \Lambda^{(i)})$ from the training, validation and test sets for training, hyper-parameter tuning, and testing of our encoder-aligner-decoder model, respectively. We use path-command pairs $(p^{(i)}, c^{(i)})$ from the training set for IRL and pairs from the validation set to tune the hyper-parameters of the content selection model. Finally, we use path-instruction pairs $(p^{(i)}, \Lambda^{(i)})$ from the test set for evaluations with human participants.

5.1.1 Data Augmentation

The SAIL dataset is significantly smaller than those typically used to train neural sequence-to-sequence models. In order to overcome this scarcity, we augment the original dataset using a set of rules. We use the augmented dataset to train the neural encoder-aligner-decoder model and the original dataset to train the content selection model. The Supplementary Material provides further details.

5.2 Implementation Details

We implement and test the proposed model using the following values for the system parameters: $k_c = 100$, $P_t = 0.99$, $k_e = 128$, and $L_t = 95.0$. The encoder-aligner-decoder consists of 2 layers for the encoder and decoder with 128 LSTM units per layer. The language model similarly includes a 2-layer recurrent neural network with 128 LSTM units per layer. The size of the CAS and natural (English) language vocabularies is 88 and 435, respectively, based upon the SAIL dataset. All parameters are chosen based on the performance on the validation set. We train our model using Adam [30] for optimization. At test time, we perform approximate inference using a beam width of two. Our method requires an average of 33 s (16 s without beam search) to generate instructions for a path of 9 movements on a laptop with an Intel Core i7 CPU (2.0 GHz) and 8 GB of RAM.

5.3 Automatic Evaluation

To the best of our knowledge, we are the first to use the SAIL dataset for the purposes of generating route instructions. Consequently, we evaluate our method by comparing our generated instructions with a reference set of human-generated commands from the SAIL dataset using the BLEU score (a 4-gram matching-based precision) [46]. For each command-instruction pair $(c^{(i)}, \Lambda^{(i)})$ in the validation set, we first feed the command $c^{(i)}$, into our model to obtain the generated instruction Λ^*, and secondly use $\Lambda^{(i)}$ and Λ^* as the reference and hypothesis, respectively, to compute the BLEU score. We consider the average BLEU score at the individual sentence (macro-average precision) and the full-corpus (micro-average precision) levels.

5.4 Human Evaluation

The use of BLEU score indicates the similarity between instructions generated via our method and those produced by humans, but it does not provide a complete measure of the quality of the instructions (e.g., instructions that are correct but different in prose will receive a low BLEU score). In an effort to further evaluate the accuracy and usability of our method, we conducted a set of human evaluation experiments in which we asked 42 novice participants on Amazon Mechanical Turk (21 females and 21 males, ages 18–64, all native English speakers) to follow natural language route instructions chosen randomly from two equal-sized sets of instructions generated by our method and by humans for 50 distinct paths of various lengths. The paths and corresponding human-generated instructions were randomly sampled from the SAIL test set. Given a route instruction, human participants were asked to navigate to the best of their ability using their keyboard within a first-person, three-dimensional virtual world representative of the three environments from the SAIL corpus. The Supplementary Material provides an example of the participants' field of view while following route instructions. After attempting to follow each instruction, each participant was given a survey comprised of eight questions, three requesting demographic information and five requesting feedback on their experience and the quality of the instructions that they followed. We collected data for a total of 441 experiments (227 using human annotated instructions and 214 using machine-generated instructions). The system randomly assigned the experiments to discourage the participants from learning the environments or becoming familiar with the style of a particular instructor. No participants experienced the same scenario with both human annotated and machine-generated instructions. The Supplementary Material provides further details regarding the experimental procedure.

6. RESULTS

We evaluate the performance of our architecture by scoring the generated instructions using the 4-gram BLEU score commonly used as an automatic evaluation mechanism for machine translation. Comparing to the human-generated instructions, our method achieves sentence- and corpus-level BLEU scores of 74.67% and 60.10%, respectively, on the validation set. On the test set, the method achieves sentence- and corpus-level BLEU scores of 72.18% and 45.39%, respectively. Figure 1 shows an example of a route instruction generated by our system for a given map and path.

6.1 Aligner Ablation

Our model employs an aligner in order to learn to focus on particular CAS tokens that are salient to words in the output instruction. We evaluate the contribution of the aligner by implementing and training an alternative model in which the last encoder hidden state is fed to the decoder.

	Full Model	No Aligner
sentence-level BLEU	**74.67**	74.40
corpus-level BLEU	**60.10**	57.40

Table 1: Aligner ablation results.

Table 1 compares the performance of the two models on

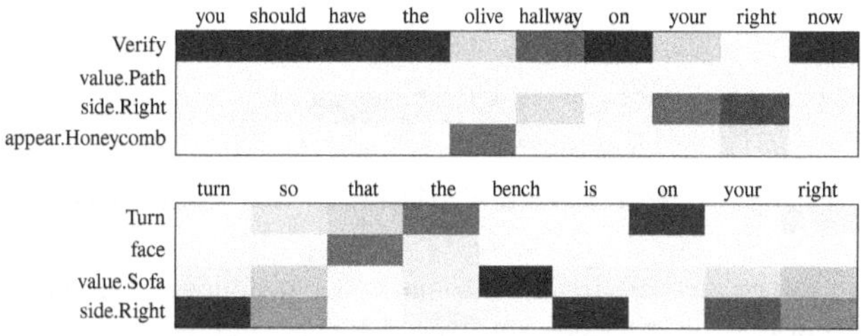

Figure 4: Alignment visualization for two pairs of CAS and natural language instructions.

the original validation set. The inclusion of an aligner results in a slight increase in the BLEU score of the generated instructions relative to the human-provided references, and is also useful as a means of visualizing the inner workings of our model (as discussed later). Additionally, we empirically find that the aligner improves our model's ability to learn the association between CAS elements and words in the output, thereby yielding better instructions.

6.2 Language Model Ablation

Our method employs a language model to rank instructions generated for the different candidate CAS commands with different beam width settings. In practice, the language model, trained on large amounts of English data, helps to remove grammatically incorrect sentences produced by the sequence-to-sequence model, which is only trained on the smaller pairwise dataset. Table 2 presents two instruction candidates generated by our encoder-aligner-decoder model for two CAS commands. Our language model successfully assigns high perplexity to the incorrect instructions, with the chosen instruction being grammatically correct.

LM-score	Candidate
105.00	"so so a straight chair to your left"
27.65	"turn so that the chair is on your left side"
101.00	"keep going till the blue flor id on your left"
11.00	"move until you see blue floor to your right"

Table 2: Language model ablation outputs.

6.3 Aligner Visualization

Figure 4 presents heat maps that visualize the alignment between a CAS command that serves as input for surface realization (rows) and the generated instruction (columns) for two different scenarios drawn from the SAIL validation set. The visualizations demonstrate that our method learns to align elements of the formal CAS command with their corresponding words in the generated instruction. For example, the network learns the association between the honeycomb textured floor and its color (top); that "bench" refers to sofa objects (bottom); and that the phrase "you should have" indicates a verification action (top).

6.4 Human Evaluation

We evaluate the accuracy with which human participants followed the natural language instructions in terms of the Manhattan distance d between the desired destination (i.e., the last pose of the target path) and the participant's location when s/he finished the scenario. Figure 5 compares the

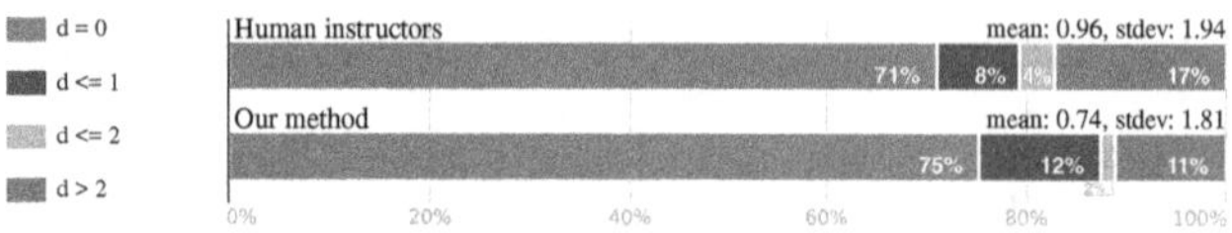

Figure 5: Participants' distances from the goal.

accuracy of the participants' paths when following human-generated instructions with those corresponding to instructions that our method produced. We report the fraction of times that participants finished within different distances from the goal.[3] The results demonstrate that participants reached the desired position 4% more often when following instructions generated using our method compared to the human instruction baseline. When they didn't reach the destination, participants reached a location within one vertex away 8% more often given our instructions. Meanwhile our method yields a failure rate ($d > 2$) that is 6% lower, though the difference is not statistically significant, as confirmed by a p-value of 0.131 relative to a standard significance level of 0.05. Of scenarios in which participants reached the destination, the total time required to interpret and follow our method's instructions is 9.52 s less than those generated by humans.

Figure 6 presents the participants' responses to the survey questions that query their experience following the instructions. By using IRL to learn a content selection policy for constructing CAS structures, our method generates instructions that convey enough information to follow the command and were rated as providing too little information 15% less frequently than the human-generated baseline (Fig. 6(a)). Meanwhile, participants felt that our instructions were easier to follow (Fig. 6(b)) than the human-generated baselines (72% vs. 52% rated as "easy" or "very easy" for our method vs. the baseline). Participants were more confident in their ability to follow our method's instructions (Fig. 6(c)) and felt that they had to backtrack less often (Fig. 6(d)). Meanwhile, both types of instructions were confused equally often as being machine-generated (Fig. 6(e)), however participants were less sure of who generated our instructions.

Figure 7 compares the paths that participants took when following our instructions with those that they took given the reference human-generated directions for one scenario. In particular, five participants failed to reach the destination when provided with the human-generated instruction. Two of the participants went directly to location 1, two participants navigated to location 2, and one participant went to location 2 before backtracking and taking a right to location 1. We attribute the failures to the ambiguity in the human-generated instruction that references "fish walled areas," which could correspond to most of the hallways in this portion of the map (as denoted by the pink-colored lines). On the other hand, each of the five participants followed the intended path (shown in green) and reached the goal when following the instruction generated using our method.

7. CONCLUSION

We presented a model for natural language generation in the context of providing indoor route instructions that exploits a structured approach to produce unambiguous, easy to follow and grammatically correct human-like route instructions. Currently, our model generates natural language route instructions for the shortest path to the goal. However, there are situations in which a longer path may afford instructions that are more straightforward [48] or that increase the likelihood of reaching the destination [22]. Another interesting direction for future work would be to integrate a model of instruction followers [41] with our architecture in an effort to learn to generate instructions that are easier to follow. Such an approach would permit training the model in a reinforcement learning setting, directly optimizing over task performance.

[3]We note that the $d = 0$ accuracy for the human-generated instructions is consistent with that reported elsewhere [9].

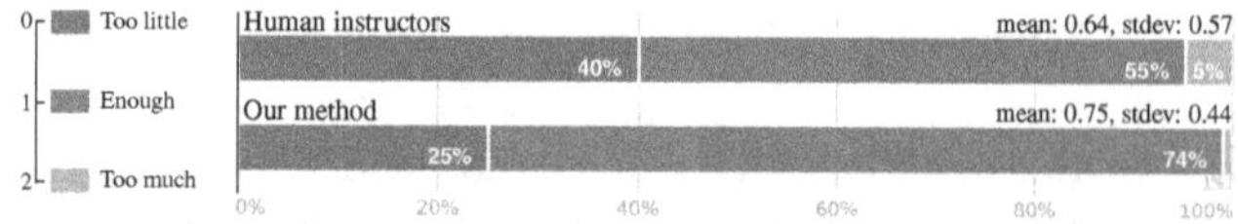

(a) "Define the amount of information provided" (p-value: 0.041)

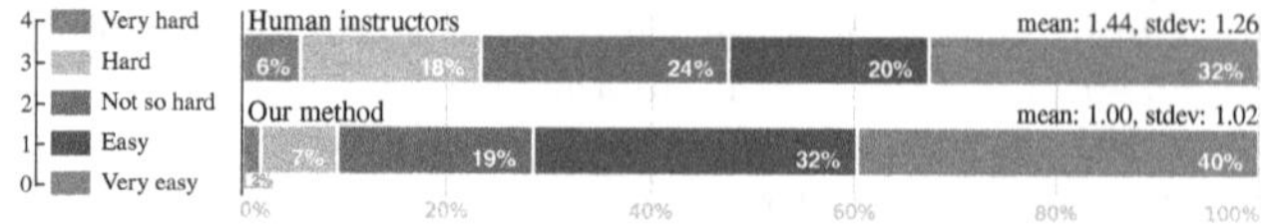

(b) "Evaluate the task in terms of difficulty" (p-value: 0.007)

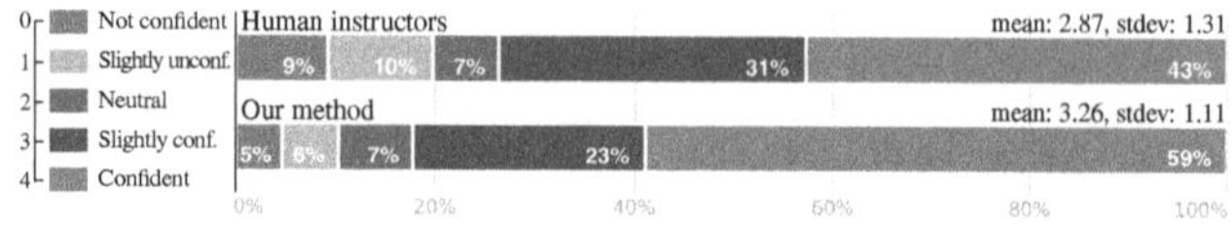

(c) "Your confidence about the path just followed" (p-value: 0.002)

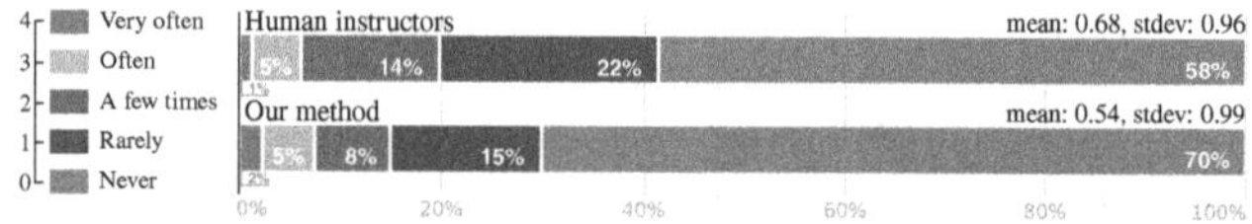

(d) "How many times did you have to backtrack?" (p-value: 0.155)

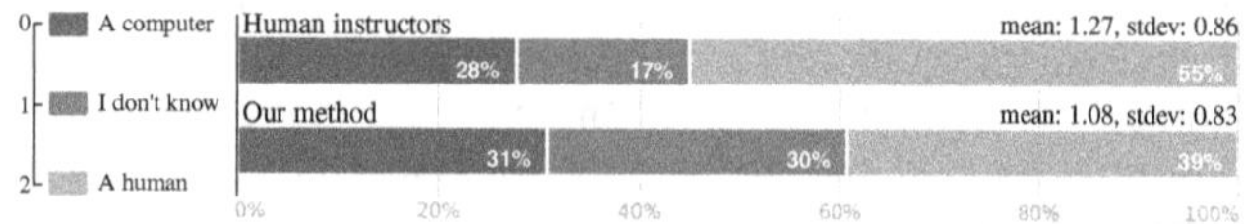

(e) "Who do you think generated the instructions?" (p-value: 0.036)

Figure 6: Participants' survey response statistics.

Map and Path

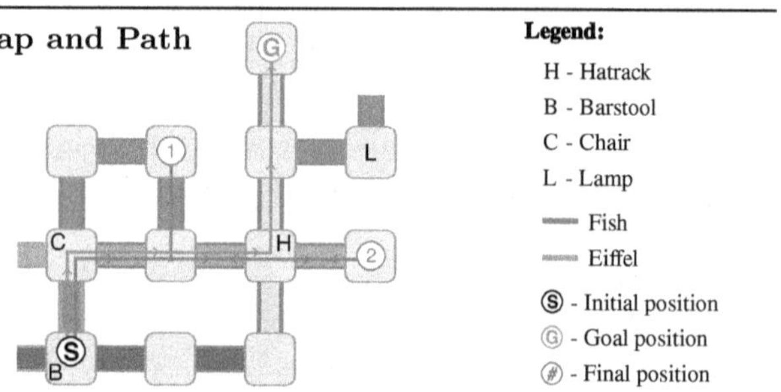

Instructions

Human: "head toward the blue floored hallway. make a right on it. go down till you see the fish walled areas. make a left in the fish walled hallway and go to the very end"

Our's: "turn to face the white hallway. walk forward once. turn right. walk forward twice. turn left. move to the wall"

Figure 7: Paths followed by five participants given human-generated (red) and our (green) directions.

References

[1] G. L. Allen. From knowledge to words to wayfinding: Issues in the production and comprehension of route directions. In *Proc. Int'l Conf. on Spatial Information Theory (COSIT)*, pages 363–372, 1997.

[2] S. Andrist, E. Spannan, and B. Mutlu. Rhetorical robots: Making robots more effective speakers using linguistic cues of expertise. In *Proc. ACM/IEEE Int'l. Conf. on Human-Robot Interaction (HRI)*, pages 341–348, Tokyo, Japan, March 2013.

[3] G. Angeli, P. Liang, and D. Klein. A simple domain-independent probabilistic approach to generation. In *Proc. Conf. on Empirical Methods in Natural Language Processing (EMNLP)*, pages 502–512, 2010.

[4] Y. Artzi and L. Zettlemoyer. Weakly supervised learning of semantic parsers for mapping instructions to actions. *Trans. Assoc. for Computational Linguistics*, 1:49–62, 2013.

[5] D. Bahdanau, K. Cho, and Y. Bengio. Neural machine translation by jointly learning to align and translate. *CoRR*, abs/1409.0473, 2014.

[6] R. Barzilay and M. Lapata. Collective content selection for concept-to-text generation. In *Proc. Human Language Technology Conf. and the Conf. on Empirical Methods in Natural Language Processing (HLT/EMNLP)*, pages 331–338, 2005.

[7] R. Barzilay and L. Lee. Catching the drift: Probabilistic content models, with applications to generation and summarization. *arXiv preprint cs/0405039*, 2004.

[8] D. L. Chen and R. J. Mooney. Learning to sportscast: a test of grounded language acquisition. In *Proc. Int'l Conf. on Machine Learning (ICML)*, pages 128–135, 2008.

[9] D. L. Chen and R. J. Mooney. Learning to interpret natural language navigation instructions from observations. In *Proc. Nat'l Conf. on Artificial Intelligence (AAAI)*, pages 859–865, San Francisco, CA, August 2011.

[10] I. Chung, O. Propp, M. R. Walter, and T. M. Howard. On the performance of hierarchical distributed correspondence graphs for efficient symbol grounding of robot instructions. In *Proc. IEEE/RSJ Int'l Conf. on Intelligent Robots and Systems (IROS)*, Hamburg, Germany, October 2015.

[11] A. Correa, M. R. Walter, L. Fletcher, J. Glass, S. Teller, and R. Davis. Multimodal interaction with an autonomous forklift. In *Proc. ACM/IEEE Int'l. Conf. on Human-Robot Interaction (HRI)*, pages 243–250, Osaka, Japan, March 2010.

[12] H. Cuayáhuitl, N. Dethlefs, L. Frommberger, K.-F. Richter, and J. Bateman. Generating adaptive route instructions using hierarchical reinforcement learning. In *Proc. Int'l Conf. on Spatial Cognition*, pages 319–334, 2010.

[13] A. C. Curry, D. Gkatzia, and V. Rieser. Generating and evaluating landmark-based navigation instructions in virtual environments. In *Proc. Europ. Workshop on Natural Language Generation (ENLG)*, pages 90–94, Brighton, UK, September 2015.

[14] R. Dale, S. Geldof, and J.-P. Prost. Using natural language generation in automatic route. *J. Research and Practice in Information Technology*, 37(1):89, 2005.

[15] R. Deits, S. Tellex, P. Thaker, D. Simeonov, T. Kollar, and N. Roy. Clarifying commands with information-theoretic human-robot dialog. *J. of Human-Robot Interaction*, 2(2): 58–79, 2013.

[16] M. T. Dzindolet, S. A. Peterson, R. A. Pomranky, L. G. Pierce, and H. P. Beck. The role of trust in automation reliance. *Int'l J. of Human-Computer Studies*, 58(6):697–718, June 2003.

[17] T. Fong, C. Thorpe, and C. Baur. Collaboration, dialogue, and human-robot interaction. In *Int'l Symp. of Robotics Research (ISRR)*, Lorne, Victoria, Autralia, November 2001.

[18] R. Goeddel and E. Olson. DART: A particle-based method for generating easy-to-follow directions. In *Proc. IEEE/RSJ Int'l Conf. on Intelligent Robots and Systems (IROS)*, pages 1213–1219, 2012.

[19] A. Graves, M. Abdel-rahman, and G. Hinton. Speech recognition with deep recurrent neural networks. In *Proc. IEEE Int'l Conf. on Acoustics, Speech and Signal Processing (ICASSP)*, pages 6645–6649, 2013.

[20] V. Groom and C. Nass. Can robots be teammates?: Benchmarks in human-robot teams. *Interaction Studies*, 8(3):483–500, 2007.

[21] B. J. Grosz. Collaborative systems. *AI Magazine*, 17(2): 67–85, 1996.

[22] S. Haque, L. Kulik, and A. Klippel. Algorithms for reliable navigation and wayfinding. In *Spatial Cognition V Reasoning, Action, Interaction*, pages 308–326. 2006.

[23] K. Hayaski, D. Sakamoto, T. Kanda, M. Shiomi, S. Koizumi, H. Ishiguru, T. Ogasawara, and N. Hagita. Humanoid robots as a passive-social medium: A field experiment at a train station. In *Proc. ACM/IEEE Int'l. Conf. on Human-Robot Interaction (HRI)*, pages 137–144, Arlington, VA, March 2007.

[24] S. Hemachandra and M. Walter. Information-theoretic dialog to improve spatial-semantic representations. In *Proc. IEEE/RSJ Int'l Conf. on Intelligent Robots and Systems (IROS)*, Hamburg, Germany, October 2015.

[25] S. Hochreiter and J. Schmidhuber. Long short-term memory. *Neural Computation*, 9(8):1735–1780, 1997. .

[26] T. Howard, S. Tellex, and N. Roy. A natural language planner interface for mobile manipulators. In *Proc. IEEE Int'l Conf. on Robotics and Automation (ICRA)*, 2014.

[27] A. M. Hund, M. Schmettow, and M. L. Noordzij. The impact of culture and recipient perspective on direction giving in the service of wayfinding. *J. of Environmental Psychology*, 32(4): 327–336, 2012.

[28] T. Kanda, T. Hirano, D. Eaton, and H. Ishiguro. Interactive robots as social partners and peer tutors for children: A field trial. *J. Human-Computer Interaction*, 19(1):61–84, June 2004.

[29] J. Kim and R. J. Mooney. Generative alignment and semantic parsing for learning from ambiguous supervision. In *Proc. Int'l Conf. on Computational Linguistics*, pages 543–551, 2010.

[30] D. Kingma and J. Ba. Adam: A method for stochastic optimization. *arXiv preprint arXiv:1412.6980*, 2014.

[31] T. Kollar, S. Tellex, D. Roy, and N. Roy. Toward understanding natural language directions. In *Proc. ACM/IEEE Int'l. Conf. on Human-Robot Interaction (HRI)*, pages 259–266, 2010.

[32] I. Konstas and M. Lapata. Unsupervised concept-to-text generation with hypergraphs. In *Proc. Conf. of the North American Chapter of the Assoc. for Computational Linguistics (NAACL)*, pages 752–761, 2012.

[33] L. Kunze, K. Kumar, and N. Hawes. Indirect object search based on qualitative spatial relations. In *Proc. IEEE Int'l Conf. on Robotics and Automation (ICRA)*, 2014.

[34] C. Landsiedel, R. D. Nijs, K. KÃijhnlenz, D. Wollherr, and M. Buss. Route description interpretation on automatically labeled robot maps. In *Proc. IEEE Int'l Conf. on Robotics and Automation (ICRA)*, 2013.

[35] P. Liang, M. I. Jordan, and D. Klein. Learning semantic correspondences with less supervision. In *Proc. Assoc. for Computational Linguistics (ACL)*, pages 91–99, 2009.

[36] G. Look, B. Kottahachchi, R. Laddaga, and H. Shrobe. A location representation for generating descriptive walking directions. In *Proc. Int'l Conf. on Intelligent User Interfaces (IUI)*, pages 122–129, 2005.

[37] G. W. K. Look. *Cognitively-inspired direction giving.* PhD thesis, Massachusetts Institute of Technology, 2008.

[38] K. L. Lovelace, M. Hegarty, and D. R. Montello. Elements of good route directions in familiar and unfamiliar environments. In *Int'l Conf. on Spatial Information Theory*, pages 65–82, 1999.

[39] M. MacMahon, B. Stankiewicz, and B. Kuipers. Walk the talk: Connecting language, knowledge, and action in route instructions. In *Proc. Nat'l Conf. on Artificial Intelligence (AAAI)*, 2006.

[40] C. Matuszek, D. Fox, and K. Koscher. Following directions using statistical machine translation. In *Proc. ACM/IEEE Int'l. Conf. on Human-Robot Interaction (HRI)*, pages 251–258, Osaka, Japan, March 2010.

[41] H. Mei, M. Bansal, and M. R. Walter. Listen, attend, and walk: Neural mapping of navigational instructions to action sequences. In *Proc. Nat'l Conf. on Artificial Intelligence (AAAI)*, 2016.

[42] H. Mei, M. Bansal, and M. R. Walter. What to talk about and how? Selective generation using lstms with coarse-to-fine alignment. In *Proc. Conf. of the North American Chapter of the Assoc. for Computational Linguistics (NAACL)*, 2016.

[43] T. Mikolov and J. Dean. Distributed representations of words and phrases and their compositionality. In *Advances in neural information processing systems*, 2013.

[44] L. Y. Morales Saiki, S. Satake, T. Kanda, and N. Hagita. Modeling environments from a route perspective. In *Proc. ACM/IEEE Int'l. Conf. on Human-Robot Interaction (HRI)*, pages 441–448. ACM, 2011.

[45] S. Oswald, H. Kretzschmar, W. Burgard, and C. Stachniss. Learning to give route directions from human demonstrations. In *Proc. IEEE Int'l Conf. on Robotics and Automation (ICRA)*, pages 3303–3308, 2014.

[46] K. Papineni, S. Roukos, T. Ward, and W.-J. Zhu. BLEU: A method for automatic evaluation of machine translation. In *Proc. Assoc. for Computational Linguistics (ACL)*, pages 311–318, 2002.

[47] V. Raman, C. Lignos, C. Finucane, K. C. T. Lee, M. Marcus, and H. Kress-Gazit. Sorry dave, I'm afraid I can't do that: Explaining unachievable robot tasks using natural language. In *Proc. Robotics: Science and Systems (RSS)*, Berlin, Germany, June 2013. .

[48] K.-F. Richter and M. Duckham. Simplest instructions: Finding easy-to-describe routes for navigation. In *Geographic information science*, pages 274–289. 2008.

[49] A. Sauppé and B. Mutlu. Effective task training strategies for human and robot instructors. *Autonomous Robots*, 39 (3):313–329, October 2015.

[50] A. St. Clair and M. Matarić. How robot verbal feedback can improve team performance in human-robot task collaborations. In *Proc. ACM/IEEE Int'l. Conf. on Human-Robot Interaction (HRI)*, pages 213–220, Portland, OR, March 2015.

[51] K. Striegnitz, A. Denis, A. Gargett, K. Garoufi, A. Koller, and M. Theune. Report on the second challenge on generating instructions in virtual environments (GIVE-2.5). In *Proc. Europ. Workshop on Natural Language Generation (ENGL)*, pages 270–279, September 2011.

[52] M. Sundermeyer, R. Schlüter, and H. Ney. LSTM neural networks for language modeling. In *Proc. of Interspeech*, pages 194–197, 2012.

[53] I. Sutskever, O. Vinyals, and Q. V. Le. Sequence to sequence learning with neural networks. *CoRR*, abs/1409.3215, 2014.

[54] S. Tellex, T. Kollar, S. Dickerson, M. R. Walter, A. G. Banerjee, S. Teller, and N. Roy. Understanding natural language commands for robotic navigation and mobile manipulation. In *Proc. Nat'l Conf. on Artificial Intelligence (AAAI)*, pages 1507–1514, San Francisco, CA, August 2011.

[55] S. Tellex, P. Thaker, R. Deits, D. Simeonov, T. Kollar, and N. Roy. Toward information theoretic human-robot dialog. In *Proc. Robotics: Science and Systems (RSS)*, Sydney, Australia, July 2012.

[56] S. Tellex, R. Knepper, A. Li, D. Rus, and N. Roy. Asking for help using inverse semantics. In *Proc. Robotics: Science and Systems (RSS)*, Berkeley, CA, July 2014.

[57] C. Torrey, S. R. Fussell, and S. Kiesler. How a robot should give advice. In *Proc. ACM/IEEE Int'l. Conf. on Human-Robot Interaction (HRI)*, pages 275–282, Tokyo, Japan, March 2013.

[58] M. A. Walker, O. Rambow, and M. Rogati. SPoT: A trainable sentence planner. In *Proc. Conf. of the North American Chapter of the Assoc. for Computational Linguistics (NAACL)*, Pittsburgh, PA, June 2001.

[59] D. Waller and Y. Lippa. Landmarks as beacons and associative cues: their role in route learning. *Memory & Cognition*, 35(5):910–924, 2007.

[60] M. L. Walters, K. Dautenhahn, S. N. Woods, and K. L. Koay. Robotic etiquette: Results from user studies involving a fetch and carry task. In *Proc. ACM/IEEE Int'l. Conf. on Human-Robot Interaction (HRI)*, pages 317–324, Arlington, VA, March 2007.

[61] N. Wang, D. V. Pynadath, and S. G. Hill. Trust calibration within a human-robot team: Comparing automatically generated explanations. In *Proc. ACM/IEEE Int'l. Conf. on Human-Robot Interaction (HRI)*, Christchurch, New Zealand, March 2016.

[62] S. L. Ward, N. Newcombe, and W. F. Overton. Turn left at the church, or three miles north: A study of direction giving and sex differences. *Environment Behavior*, 18(2):192–213, 1986.

[63] Y. W. Wong and R. J. Mooney. Generation by inverting a semantic parser that uses statistical machine translation. In *Proc. Conf. of the North American Chapter of the Assoc. for Computational Linguistics – Human Language Technologies (NAACL HLT)*, pages 172–179, 2007.

[64] B. D. Ziebart, A. Maas, J. A. Bagnell, and A. K. Dey. Maximum entropy inverse reinforcement learning. In *Proc. Nat'l Conf. on Artificial Intelligence (AAAI)*, pages 1433–1438, Chicago, IL, July 2008.

Cellulo: Versatile Handheld Robots for Education

Ayberk Özgür[1], Séverin Lemaignan[1,2,3], Wafa Johal[1,2], Maria Beltran[2], Manon Briod[2], Léa Pereyre[2], Francesco Mondada[2], Pierre Dillenbourg[1]
[1]CHILI, [2]LSRO, EPFL, Switzerland
{firstname.lastname}@epfl.ch
[3]Centre for Robotics and Neural Systems, Plymouth University, U.K.
severin.lemaignan@plymouth.ac.uk

ABSTRACT

In this article, we present *Cellulo*, a novel robotic platform that investigates the intersection of three ideas for robotics in education: designing the robots to be versatile and generic tools; blending robots into the classroom by designing them to be pervasive objects and by creating tight interactions with (already pervasive) paper; and finally considering the practical constraints of real classrooms at every stage of the design. Our platform results from these considerations and builds on a unique combination of technologies: groups of handheld haptic-enabled robots, tablets and activity sheets printed on regular paper. The robots feature holonomic motion, haptic feedback capability and high accuracy localization through a microdot pattern overlaid on top of the activity sheets, while remaining affordable (robots cost about €125 at the prototype stage) and classroom-friendly. We present the platform and report on our first interaction studies, involving about 230 children.

Keywords

Human-Robot Interaction; Robots for Learning; Haptic Interfaces; Tangible Robots

1. INTRODUCTION

The adoption of educational robots in schools is a potential key contribution to education, but is limited by several factors: Price, integration within the existing curriculum and disciplines, actual contribution to the learning of the material, teachers' ethical concerns and fears of additional workload, the complexity of the system and difficult logistics in the classroom, among others. As a result, research in robotics for education has mainly focused on certain subjects in specific teaching situations: custom robotic platforms to teach programming and other closely related Science, Technology, Engineering and Mathematics (STEM) concepts; and studies that create rich social interactions for tutoring or peer-learning of specific topics such as language and writing. To overcome these limitations and open new perspectives, we investigate a novel approach where the robotic education platform is designed to be *ubiquitous*, *versatile* and *practical*.

HRI '17, March 06 - 09, 2017, Vienna, Austria

ISBN 978-1-4503-4336-7/17/03...$15.00

DOI: http://dx.doi.org/10.1145/2909824.3020247

The design of a *ubiquitous* platform follows the analogy of "pen and paper": a set of pervasive yet unremarkable tools that blend into the daily learning routine. This is achieved by designing devices to be reliable (they must be trusted to work at any time), readily replaceable, and intuitive to use. These design goals translate into desirable qualities for an ubiquitous educative robot: a small size; a plain and sturdy appearance; a low price point; a limited set of simple affordances. Besides, to be readily replaceable, the device should not elicit strong affective bonding i.e. it should not be uniquely associated to one child, it should not call for personalization, and it should not elicit projected agency. This contrasts with certain branches of research in educational robotics where children's engagement is often sought through social bonding, and therefore, social robots.

A *versatile* system should be designed so as to be applicable to a broad range of learning scenarios, instead of as a specialized tool bound to the teaching of a particular subject. It should be easy and natural for the teachers to imagine the role and added value of the robots when creating new teaching activities in different disciplines. This implies that the robots' hardware, appearance and interaction modalities must not imply or be constrained to specific use cases.

Finally, a *practical* teaching tool must be flexible yet reliable as they are meant to be used intensively by pupils; the fragile hardware and complex software typically found in robotics do not effectively support uninterrupted learning and teaching in such scenarios. In order to gain field acceptance in the classrooms, educative robots must critically represent a net educative gain and must not incur higher workload for the teachers. Time-consuming initialization, configuration or calibration of the robots, as well as any software manipulation that would prevent the teacher to focus on the classroom for a non-trivial amount of time, should be avoided. As such, designing a robot to be practical in the classroom environment requires carefully designed ergonomics to achieve a simple and robust user experience for both the pupils and the teachers.

The Cellulo project explores the intersection of these three, partially conflicting, design goals. Our approach builds on *groups of small, low-cost, haptic-enabled tangible robots*, as seen in the concepts pictured in Figure 1. Each robot has a plain and minimalist appearance, and the robots collectively operate on large sheets of printed paper representing a learning activity. The robots can autonomously move and interact with the activity sheet; interact with each other; be

Figure 1: Concept Cellulo activities: *Left:* Robots simulate planets orbiting the sun. The learners can move the planets to alter their orbits or even attempt to remove the sun. *Right:* Robots represent atoms with Brownian motion. The learners can directly interact with atoms to change their temperature or add/remove atoms to experiment with conditions under which molecules form and break down.

held by the learner or teacher to interact with the activity; and provide planar haptic feedback. In addition, all robots are wirelessly connected to tablets (or smartphones) that coordinate the activity and the robots, and optionally provide additional dynamic content or input to the activity.

In this article, we present the design of the Cellulo platform and two preliminary field studies that do not yet aim to show clear learning gains but rather to demonstrate the Cellulo's potential as an educative tool by illustrating its capabilities. After discussing the related work in Section 2, we describe the developed technologies that allow to fulfill the aforementioned requirements in Section 3. Then, we present the field studies co-developed with designers in Section 4. Finally, we give our outlook and future plans for Cellulo in Section 5.

2. RELATED WORK

Cellulo draws inspiration from – and in return, contributes to – several fields: educational robotics, clearly, but also *manipulatives* seen in Tangible User Interfaces (TUI).

Educational robotics.

The application domain for educative robots is split between robots used in programming, robotics, or other closely related STEM subjects where robots occur as a natural and suitable tool; or robots used in other disciplines, not necessarily technical or even scientific.

Many studies have been conducted studying robots in STEM, like [22, 8, 1, 13, 21]. [2, 11] provide reviews of both the studies and the devices used for this purpose. In terms of robots, individual programmable mobile robots (often with a differential drive for locomotion) and programmable robotic construction kits are the two major choices for teaching robotics, programming and related STEM subjects.

In the case of robots used for non-programming related curricula, the learning scenarios reported in the literature usually involve robots that possess social qualities (*i.e.* social robots) and often adopt the role of a tutor or peer; humanoid robots are unsurprisingly often found in such scenarios where social aspects of interaction are exploited for learning. [10, 7, 15, 3, 23, 12] are examples where the teaching of such topics is explored; [14] is a rare example that uses a non-social robot to teach an artificial vocabulary (where the goal is ultimately to interact with robots).

In this regard, the Cellulo project investigates the design and use of robots in education where it is not to be perceived as a robot (*i.e.* not programmed or constructed) or a social tutor/peer; but as an "on-demand" support tool for teachers the be used in a multitude of teaching domains.

Manipulatives.

Manipulatives are physical objects specifically designed to foster learning. Cellulo, being based on robotic devices, is an extension of digital manipulatives (introduced in [20]). [24] proposes a classification of manipulatives into *Froebel Manipulatives* (*FiMs*, manipulatives to model the world) and *Montessori Manipulatives* (*MiMs*, manipulatives to model abstract structures). We believe that Cellulo, whose design does not enforce any application case, can be equally used as *FiMs* (*e.g.* concepts in Figure 1) or as *MiMs* (*e.g.* points on a cartesian plane in a geometry activity).

Manipulatives that are accurately 2D-localized in (x,y,θ) have been studied before; our design, which includes an open-source implementation of a localization technique developed in the context of handwriting recognition [19], achieves similar performances as [17] for a fraction of the cost. Besides, as each robot localizes itself independently, it is scalable and does not require the deployment of an external apparatus.

Being based on paper, our approach is especially well-suited for the classroom compared to techniques involving special hardware (typically, a table-top AR environment like [17]). Beyond its evident advantages in terms of costs and scalability, paper integrates smoothly into classroom ecosystems. It matches several principles for minimizing classroom orchestration load, such as flexibility and minimalism ([4]).

Using tangible interfaces to teach has been extensively explored and numerous applications have been developed covering various domains (see [4] for a review). Our approach is novel in that our manipulatives are robots and can move by themselves. As highlighted in the concepts (Figure 1) and further discussed hereafter, we believe this opens a new venue of research by bridging Educational HRI and TUIs.

Table 1: Cost of the Cellulo robot prototype.

Component	Cost (€)
Processor (*PIC32MZ1024ECG064*)	8.51
Localization subsystem [9]	17.24
Locomotion subsystem [16]	49.77
Communication (*RN42*)	12.12
UI subsystem (*TLC5947*, *AT42QT1070*)	7.36
Battery & charging & protection	8.86
Other (terminal, resistor, capacitor *etc.*)	8.77
Housing (53.3g PLA) & fastening	1.91
PCB manufacturing	11.39
Total	**125.93**

3. PLATFORM DESIGN

3.1 Overview

Our platform, pictured in Figure 1 in two concept activities, is composed of low-cost mobile robots that operate on printed sheets of paper, overlaid with a microdot pattern that enables self-localization. These sheets are printable in regular home/office printers or in printing houses and their length is not bounded (in our experiments, we used paper playgrounds up to 1m×2.4m). The robots are designed to be small, sturdy, low-cost and simple to operate; all robots are connected wirelessly to a mobile device (a tablet or smartphone) that runs the activity and orchestration logic.

The current Cellulo robot is the result of two design iterations (Figure 2), and it includes: self-localization on the activity sheet; holonomic motion; 6 capacitive touch buttons (independently back-illuminated in full RGB) and wireless Bluetooth communication. All the components found in the robot can be seen in Table 1 along with their costs at the prototype stage. Below, we detail the design of the various subsystems involving the robot and the paper, and how they come together to form the Cellulo platform.

3.2 Localization & Role of the Paper

In order to achieve complex, swarm-like robot motions in the classroom environment, we require fast and accurate localization of many robots in a way that is straightforward to deploy and store away, and is robust against kidnapping and occlusions due to childrens' manipulations. Our method, described in detail in [9], uses a dense, deterministic and well-defined optical microdot pattern printable on regular office printers, with enough x, y space to cover over 170 million km^2 with unique patterns. The robots, equipped with a downward facing camera and a low-cost microcontroller, decode a $\sim$1cm^2 region on the printed activity sheet to obtain their own 3DOF pose (x, y, θ) at about 93Hz. This method offers global and absolute localization with $\sim$0.27mm and $\sim$1.5° accuracy without the need for any calibration. Moreover, there is no limitation on the number of robots that can be localized since the entire algorithm runs onboard the robot. The physical placement of the camera beneath the robot and the hardware design (global shutter sensor, high framerate) allows any manipulation to be performed on the robot without any adverse effect to localization performance, instant recovery from kidnapping, and perfect robustness against external illumination conditions.

The interactions between the robots, the learners and the activities rely partly on this paper-supported localization mechanism. From the larger perspective, the activity itself is printed on large paper sheets that can feature any desired graphical elements. This capacity allows the definition of "active zones": arbitrary-defined areas of the activity sheet that are associated with specific robot behaviors (*e.g.* green zones that deactivate the robots in Figure 1, left; red and blue reactor zones that dictate different pressure/temperature conditions in Figure 1, right). The raw robot positions are also used, *e.g.* for onboard closed-loop motion control (including haptic feedback) and, on the external controller, for multi-robot formation control.

From another perspective, absolute global localization-enabled paper opens up further possibilities, similar to the ones discussed in [6], in addressing usability concerns in the classroom. Smaller paper sheets (possibly down to A4 or A5) can be overlaid with unique patterns for each learner and the teacher; other functional sheets can also be designed to affect the flow of the activities, behaviors of the robots or host subtasks within activities. These can be freely passed around and used on any flat surface without the requirement of any other device than the robot, potentially "making the educational workflow tangible".

3.3 Locomotion & Haptics

The Cellulo robot is capable of holonomic motion by virtue of the permanent-magnet assisted omnidirectional ball drive, previously presented in [16] (Figure 2b). Holonomic motion is a significant improvement over differential drive motion found in nearly every educational mobile robot, as it allows the robot to start moving in any direction; change the direction of motion near-instantaneously; preserve a high level of motion freedom in cluttered environments like multi-robot formations; and finally be moved in any direction without damage when forcibly manipulated by the learner. The drive also offers mechanical robustness against intensive user manipulation and potential mishandling, while remaining compact enough to fit inside a handheld device with low cost and (almost exclusively) off-the-shelf components.

We have as well to address the integration of a haptics controller to a traditional motion controller that allows the robot to *move* and *be moved at the same time.* This requires a hybrid motion controller that appropriately combines different sources of commanded motor outputs depending on the activity logic, where these sources might be: (i) drive velocities for the robot to move independently from one pose to another, (ii) tactile or kinesthetic haptic feedback in the form of force/torque output to the learner's hand, (iii) drive velocities to assist the learner to move the robot from one pose to another in order to overcome the natural impedance of the robot on the activity sheets due to the natural friction of the blocked wheels. The development and evaluation of such a controller is currently in progress.

3.4 Software Design & Orchestration

The Cellulo platform is designed to be activity-driven rather than driven by the capabilities of the platform itself. An *activity* is the combination of the paper elements, the robots with particular interaction modalities and the tablet(s) that run(s) the activity-specific software. As such, the role of the robots and paper depends on the design of each particular learning activity.

The most basic element of an activity is composed of the

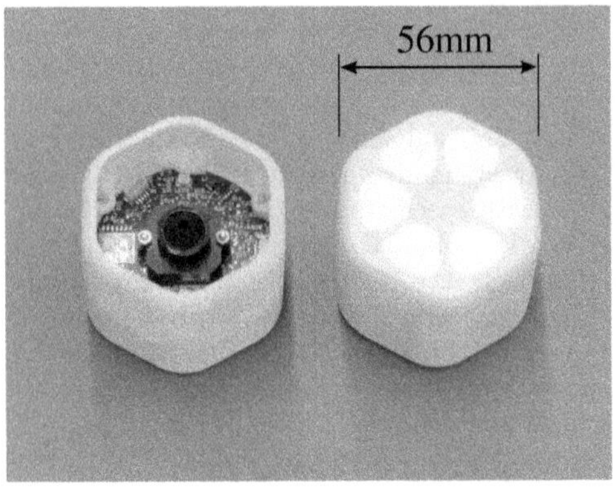

(a) 1st revision: localization and illuminated touch buttons implemented. On the left: upside down robot with exposed optical system.

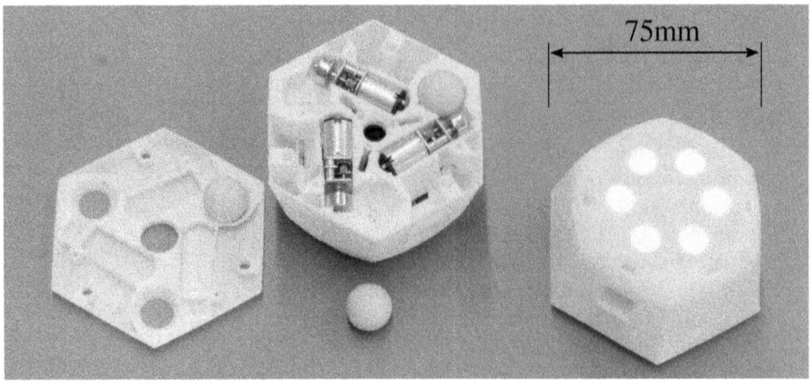

(b) 2nd revision: locomotion added, ergonomy and appearance refined. On the left: upside down robot with open housing exposing locomotion components and optical system in the center. Two ball wheels out of sockets for visibility.

Figure 2: Two major revisions of the Cellulo robot design. 1-to-1 scale preserved between the images.

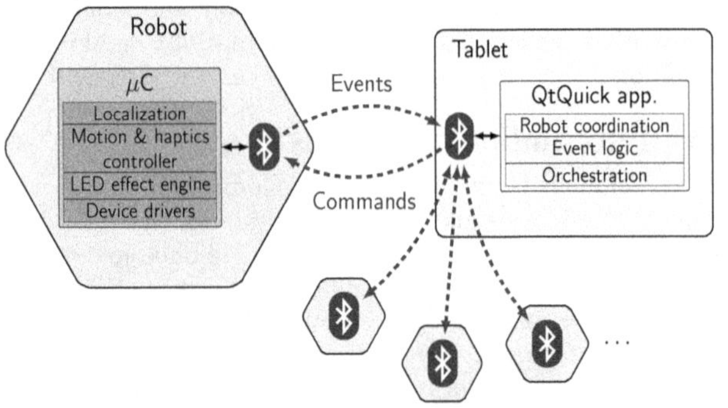

Figure 3: Software architecture of the most basic element of a Cellulo activity. Multiple robots are connected through Bluetooth to a mobile tablet where the activity logic and orchestration software resides.

activity sheet, hereafter called the *playground*, the robots that operate on the playground and the tablet. The robots run latency or bandwidth-sensitive software components onboard within the single-threaded bare-metal firmware written in C, such as the motion/haptics controller, image processing for localization and the LED effect engine. Each robot is connected through a Bluetooth 2.1 Serial Port Profile (SPP) channel to the tablet that runs a *QtQuick* application to coordinate the activity, as well as host graphical input/output elements such as buttons and often illustrations required by the activity. The architecture of these core elements can be seen in Figure 3.

From a software development and deployment point of view, QtQuick allows rapid development of the activity software using Qt Modeling Language (QML, JSON-like declarative language) with Javascript and supports deployment to many platforms and devices. In addition, any performance-sensitive components can be developed in C++ as native back-end plugins to be loaded and interfaced from within QML/Javascript. This allows us to deploy our applications to consumer mobile devices (running iOS or Android) that we develop and test on desktop computers (running Linux, Windows or Mac OS) while seamlessly using hardware resources (such as Bluetooth SPP sockets).

The paper elements, including the playground, are exported and transported as PDF files at the end of their graphics design phase. With external tools that we developed, we overlay the microdot pattern with any desired origin coordinate on these sheets. We can define the active zones with a simple custom authoring tool that operates on these PDFs and exports the zones in JSON format which are then loaded into our mobile applications. The dotted PDFs are easily printed on any platform or sent to printing houses with poster printing facilities if they are in larger sizes. It is useful to note that this workflow design, while alleviating development by providing correct tools, does not facilitate educational content creation and an education professional must be present to design the didactic sequence.

One tablet, as depicted in Figure 3, can orchestrate an activity with a maximum of 7 robots (due to Bluetooth limitations). Classroom-wide activities might require more robots. In such cases, more tablets (or other Bluetooth controllers, like smartphones) are required. For such scenarios, we envision the possibility for the teacher to have a "master" tablet connected to the pupils' tablets over WiFi, and allowing him/her to monitor, start, pause, control, record activities at the whole classroom level. This teacher-centric approach would support the classroom orchestration by the teacher, and address some of the issues raised in [5]. This is left as future work.

4. EXPLORATORY STUDIES

4.1 Interaction Space

The platform design opens up numerous possibilities in terms of educative interactions with the activities. We investigate this interaction design space along three dimensions:

- *Passive – Autonomous robots*: at one end, the robots are passive and manually moved by the children (pure *tangible* devices); at the other end, they are entirely autonomous and the children do not manipulate them.
- *Independent robots – Multi-robot environment.* "Independent robots" act independently and unknown to other robots (it may as well be an interaction with a single robot); "Multi-robot environment" refers to

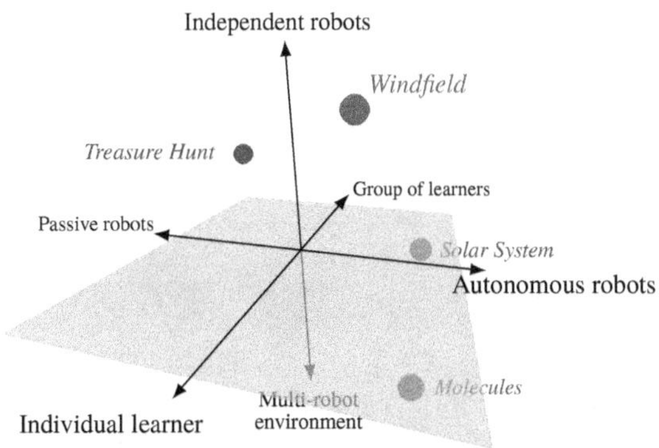

Figure 4: Three dimensions of Cellulo interaction envisioned so far. The two colored dots represent the two reported studies. The two gray dots represent the two concept activities depicted in Figure 1.

activities where the interactions between robots are numerous and essential.

- *Individual learner – Group of learners.* This dimension represents the learning process from the students' perspective: individual or collective.

Importantly, these dimensions are not binary: learning activities might be located anywhere in this 3 dimensional interaction space, as depicted in Figure 4. We present in the following sections two exploratory studies that probe two points in this space: the "Treasure Hunt" (Section 4.2) game, and the "Windfield" activity (Section 4.3).

These two studies played a key role in the platform design process as real-world testbeds for our prototypes. The technical performance of the prototypes as well as their acceptance by the children during these studies is reported along with our observations regarding the emergent interactions with the Cellulo platform.

4.2 Treasure Hunt study

4.2.1 Activity Design

In this study, the robots are used as tangible items (*i.e. passive robots*) by a group of children. Each child is given their own robot to interact with the activity (Figure 5). We used the robots resulting from the first design iteration (Figure 2a). This instance used robots with the localization component and illuminated touch buttons as well as a 1m×2.4m playground and the mobile application with playful graphics and instructions running on the tablet. The children completed three consecutive tasks, some of which had collaborative aspects, in order to eventually let their pirate characters reach a treasure chest.

The activity was designed to explore various interactions (seen in Figure 6) enabled by the Cellulo platform in a playful situation where specific learning outcomes were not targeted. The goals of this study were first to assess the usability and reliability of the pattern-based localization system when manipulated by children "in the wild"; second, to evaluate the combination of robots, paper and tablet over a range of interaction modalities in terms of legibility and intuitiveness.

The activity was run with a total of 85 children (11 to 14 years old) with no prior experience with Cellulo. The children were split into 14 groups of 5 (each child has one

Figure 5: Treasure Hunt activity, exploring *passive* and mostly *independent* robots in a *group* activity.

robot and the tablet is shared) or 6 (5 children have one robot each and one child operates the tablet and reads the instructions). After a brief introduction, the children were instructed to follow the indications on the tablet and no further instructions were given by the experimenters. The game lasted around 12min (M=11min 47s, SD=1min 47s, min=9min 19s, max=15min 32s), and the children were invited to replay it if they wished (replay data not included in discussion).

Each child was first assigned one pirate character, represented by his/her robot and one character card (Figure 6b). Four tasks were then completed sequentially:

Task 1: Reproduce a sequence of 6 flashing LEDs by tapping the corresponding buttons (performed by all 5 children in parallel, each had random sequence); interaction pictured in Figure 6c;

Task 2: Scan the playground for the hidden key to the treasure chest, avoiding false positives (performed by all 5 children in parallel, children would spontaneously coordinate to explore different regions of the playground); interaction in Figure 6d;

Task 3: Spin the robot to pull up the treasure chest from the well (performed by the first child in each group), with the interaction in Figure 6e, similar to [18];

Task 4: Move the robot along the paths on the planks and rocks on the playground (4 paths performed sequentially by the remaining 4 children, the correct paths to follow were drawn on the back of the character cards); interaction in Figure 6f.

Before each task, the robots had to be placed on specific areas on the playground marked with "A","B" and "C" (as in Figure 6a). The activity on the tablet would wait until the five robots are correctly placed to start the next task. This simple multi-robot behavior enabled effective synchronization points amongst the group of children.

4.2.2 Results & Discussion

The localization subsystem was observed to have mostly satisfactory performance in terms of accuracy and responsiveness. No performance decrease could be observed after

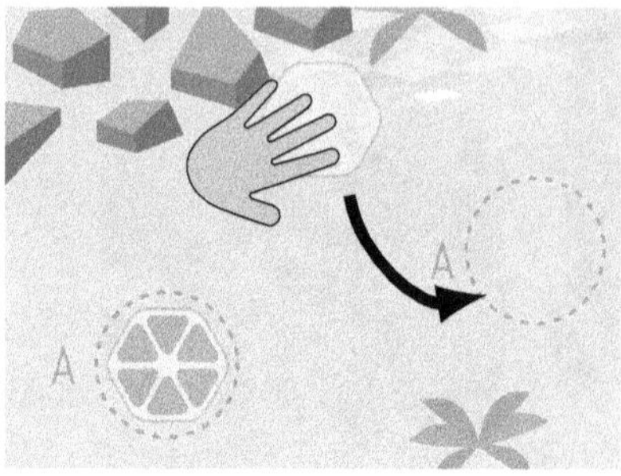

(a) *Positionning:* Placing the robots in active zones to trigger events.

(b) *Role Assignment:* Placing the robots on character cards; correct assignment lights the robot in green.

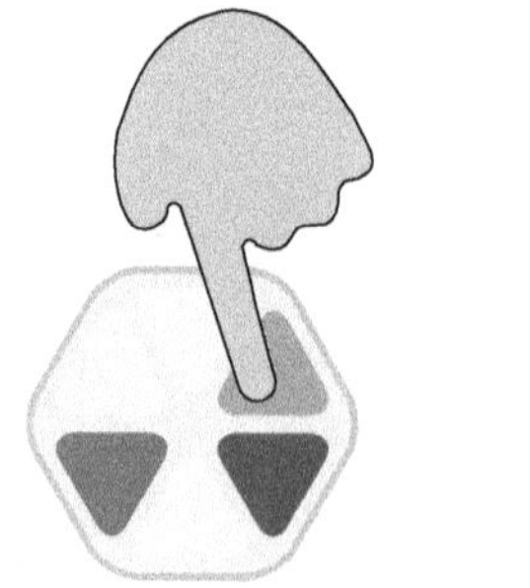

(c) *Touch:* Pressing the illuminated capacitive touch keys on the robot, *e.g.* in a pre-defined sequence.

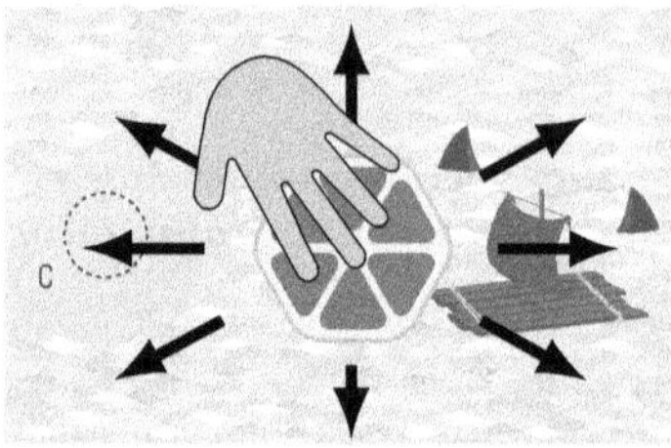

(d) *Scan:* Moving the robot on the playground to find a hidden target; as the robot gets closer to the target, the color progressively changes from the "coldest" to the "warmest".

(e) *Spin:* Turning the robot in place to change a continuous value; an animation on the tablet tied to this value accompanies the interaction.

(f) *Follow the path:* Moving the robot through the path illustrated on an auxiliary sheet without leaving the path.

Figure 6: Interaction methods used in Treasure Hunt.

Table 2: Treasure Hunt task completion times, $N =$ 14 groups, all values in seconds.

	M (SD)	Min	Max
Task 1: Touch sequence	131.1 (35.4)	85	199
Task 2: Scan	125.2 (51.6)	47	222
Task 3: Spin	13.6 (4.3)	5	21
Task 4: Follow path	162.9 (37.4)	114	224

slight progressive wear on the playground print during one day of intensive use. Three activities were run in parallel in the same room, with 3 groups on 3 tablets and 15 robots; none of the Bluetooth connections dropped at any time but slight delays were observed, which may have been caused by wireless interference from other Bluetooth devices or from the many Wi-Fi routers present on the experiment site.

The children interacting for the first time with the robot (even though some were at first reluctant to interact with the unknown technology) were observed to quickly understand that the robots "knew where they are" and the proposed interactions were easily picked up. Importantly, the constantly changing role of the robot (from a pirate character, to a pad to enter a code – Figure 6c, to a metal detector – Figure 6d, to a well handle – Figure 6e) was well accepted by the children, the tasks were all completed by all groups without any assistance (Table 2 provides the mean completion times for each of the tasks). This suggests that our goal of designing a versatile device was successfully attained in this scenario.

During the touch key sequence task (which is essentially a memory task), children who completed their sequence were generally observed to aid those who were still struggling with theirs, resulting in a cooperative aspect that naturally emerged. Likewise, the scan task naturally fostered collaboration amongst the children to effectively "scan" the various parts of the large playground.

The spin task was explained only by a depiction of the robot with two circular arrows (similar to Figure6e) on the back of the character card. The interaction mechanism was picked up surprisingly fast (14 seconds on average to complete the task, as fast as 5 seconds for one group).

The "follow the path" task was completed by each child in about 40 seconds on average, and the completion was observed to be delayed by both children's mistakes caused by misperceiving the paths on the character cards and by occasional localization errors due to excessive contrast on some playground graphics.

At a higher level, the main results of the first study are: (i) Children easily engage with tangible activities with printed graphics on paper; (ii) A variety of roles can be ascribed to small robots with an unremarkable, anonymous design; children easily accept and engage in such role assignment.

The next study explores how using an active, mobile robot instead of a passive one impacts the interaction design.

4.3 Windfield study

4.3.1 Activity Design

The second activity is a learning game, and explores a different point in the interaction design space: single robots are used as haptic devices by individual children (Figure 8a). The robots use the locomotion module developed during

Figure 7: Screen capture of the Windfield activity application running on the tablet. Position of the balloon is synchronized with the position of the robot on the real map. Low and high pressure areas are represented in blue and red respectively.

(a) Child finding a high pressure point south of Paris.

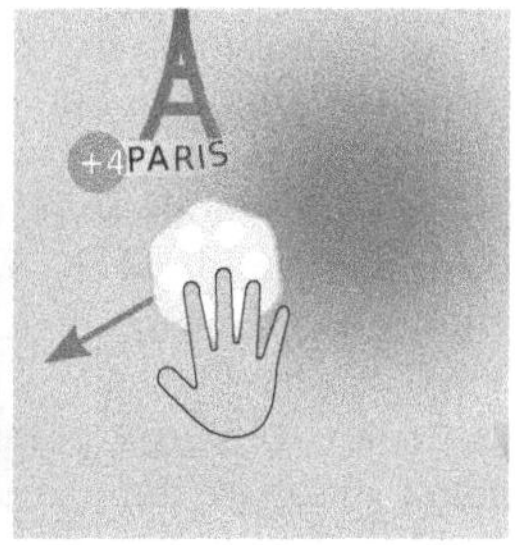

(b) *Active scan*: Scanning the playground with the robot that applies haptic feedback. The arrow shows the robot's haptic output, representing the wind caused by the (invisible) pressure points.

Figure 8: Haptic interaction in Windfield.

the second design iteration (Figure 2b), and a preliminary haptic feedback controller to convey the force generated by the winds resulting from atmospheric pressure differences.

The activity is designed to take place on the geographical map of Europe (printed on a 0.66m × 1.7m playground) where multiple atmospheric pressure points (high and low) are placed. Following their real physical counterparts, these points affect the pressure over the entire activity area and their effects diminish with distance. Given all pressure points and their positions, atmospheric pressure values are calculated over a grid spanning the entire playground (resulting in a simplified Finite Element Analysis-like method). These values are then used to calculate the pressure gradient on a given position, which dictates the intensity and direction of the wind on that position (additional factors that affect the wind such as the Coriolis effect are not considered).

The robots play the role of "hot air balloons" that can be placed on any desired position on the playground and convey the force of the wind with haptic feedback while being grasped, as illustrated in Figure 8b. This is achieved by mapping the wind velocity in the global playground frame to the motor outputs in the local robot frame through inverse kinematics. This velocity output then results in a force output when the robot is grasped and blocked in place.

Two high and two low pressure points are randomly placed on the playground, and must be discovered by the children using haptic feedback. The children explore the playground by moving the robot on various locations and "feel" how the wind blows there. By following the winds, they can locate the pressure points. They indicate their guesses by dragging and dropping the corresponding icons on the tablet (where the playground and the location of their hot air balloon is displayed), as seen in Figure 7. Prior to the activity start, the participants are told what the activity is about and what the robots are standing for. The atmospheric pressure points and how they "blow wind outwards" and "suck winds inwards" are also introduced. After playing the game, the learners are expected to gain the knowledge that: (i) the wind blows from high to low pressure; (ii) the strength of the wind diminishes with increasing distance from pressure points.

4.3.2 Results & Discussion

We ran the study during two open-door events on two consecutive days for more than 6 hours in total. The two events attracted about fifteen thousand attendees, most of which were children accompanied by their parents. The attendees came to our booths at their discretion and stayed as much as they wanted. Under these circumstances, with 3 activities running in parallel on 3 separate playgrounds, we estimate that about 150 children ranging from 5 to 14 years old interacted with our activity non-trivially (*i.e.* excluding children who were just looking and were manipulating the robots/tablets aimlessly and leaving) attempting to find the hidden pressure points for durations ranging from 2min to 15min (Figure 8a). Due to uncontrolled conditions, we report hereafter qualitative observations about the interactions.

Children engaged easily with the activity: they did not show reluctance to manipulate the robots. The haptic modality of conveying a planar force was generally well-received, most children were able to tell where in which direction the robot was pushing their hand when asked. In addition, there were multiple questions like *"Where can we buy these [robots]?"*, *"Are you giving these [robots] away?"*, *"Can we take this [playground sheet] with us?"* that suggest that the platform was approachable and attractive. In a few instances, the parents did not let their children approach the activity due to the presence of a tablet; these children were presumably being raised in a "mobile device-free" manner until a certain age. This needs to be accounted for in the adoption process of our platform, and remediation (like a tablet-free mode of operation) may be sought after.

From a hardware design perspective, force/torque sensors on the grasped surface are in principle required to control the force feedback in a closed loop. Since these are not present on our current robots, we detect grasps by the touch buttons on the top surface and disable the haptic feedback when the robot is not grasped. This requires the learners to grasp the robot from the top, and causes side grasps and top grasps where the palm does not touch the robot surface to remain undetected. In addition, this does not guarantee the actual transmission of forces to the learner's hand, resulting in approximate force feedback which occasionally results in the robot's motion due to weak grasps.

From an interaction point of view, the effectiveness of the *active scan* (Figure 8b) interaction was observed to depend on the directionality of the force: Low pressure points are almost always found before high pressure points since 'following the wind' naturally leads the robot to one of the sink holes, *i.e.* a low pressure point. On the contrary, high pressure points are more difficult to find as they push the robots away and require the exploration of the surrounding area to be uncovered. In that sense, the design of a haptic-enabled activity requires care.

From the learning perspective, the age group of the participants had a clear impact on their performance. Children under 11-12 years old (the majority of our participants) often could not find the high pressure points. The ones that did find them were still not able to give satisfactory answers to questions like "What do you think the wind is doing?" or "How do you think wind is connected to the pressure points?". Youngest participants (5-6 years old) were observed to have difficulties reaching over the far side of the playground and grasping the robot; this prevented them from properly interacting with the activity and underlines that the expected manipulations of the robots and physical size of the playground must be adjusted to the target age group.

Participants over 11-12 years old were generally able to understand that pressure points acted in all directions by scanning around the points and finding them. Some children exhaustively searched and found all pressure points by spending an abundant time in the activity. Some were able to provide answers to the questions like "It seems to blow from these high points to these low points.", often pointing at the pressure points on the playground itself. This indicates that children were able to transfer their findings from the tablet to the physical playground, and suggest – at least for older children – that the combination paper, robot, tablet can be perceived as a single, multi-modal, educational tool.

At higher-level, the 'Windfield' study confirms the educational potential of the complete platform: it demonstrates a set of rich interactions between paper (the printed activity playground), robots (autonomous, self-localizing mobile devices offering haptic interaction) and an active pupil. This combination enables the child to physically experience a complex and invisible phenomenon (the interplay of the atmospheric pressures) in a natural and playful manner.

5. CONCLUSION

5.1 Summary

This article's main contributions are two-fold: First, we detailed the design and implementation of a novel tangible robotic device that takes into account the constraints of real and unsupervised use in classrooms; to the best of our knowledge, building such an educative platform that combines mobile robots with paper-based tangible and haptic interactivity has not been attempted before. Our design process was driven by the classroom environment and the teachers' constraints (including ease of use, low disturbance, reliability), and led to the development of a small, low-cost and robust wireless robot (*i.e. practical*) that is aimed to blend in the classroom ecosystem through its rich interactions with the traditional and pervasive paper (*i.e. ubiquitous*). In that sense, it seeks to expand (rather than replace) current teaching practices through a multitude of activities that cover a variety of disciplines (*i.e. versatile*).

Second, we presented two exploratory studies, *Treasure Hunt* and *Windfield*, ran in ecological environments that showed the feasibility to combine robots with augmented paper sheets, to easily deploy the robots and to engage the children in these sample activities. They contained very different sets of interaction affordances utilizing both active and passive robot behaviors, and were well received by the children. Although the activities were not designed to measure clear learning gains, they are highly useful in communicating the versatility, practicality and ubiquity potential of the platform to education professionals, with whom we are now beginning to actively collaborate.

The interaction design space created by the Cellulo platform is large: building upon these two studies, we have proposed an initial formalization of this design space, along three dimensions: level of autonomy of the robot; number of robots; number of interacting pupils. Within this space, we have experimented with and identified a range of interaction patterns that combine the robots and the paper playground.

5.2 From Here to Adoption - Future Work

As we conclude these initial stages of design and testing, we acknowledge that we still have many tasks to accomplish in order to prove the potential of the Cellulo platform. For one, the haptic interaction component was designed up to now in a shallow manner, and requires more work to be adequately useful. Our current work involves the proper design of this component and explicit testing of the usability of this joint control paradigm that is *moving vs. being moved* through concrete manipulation measures.

From the educational perspective, the design process of activities should naturally involve teachers (to conceive the learning scenarios), interaction designers (to propose interaction patterns), graphic designers (to produce the visuals on paper and tablet) and software engineers (to implement the applications running the activities). The studies presented in this article were focused on exploring natural interactions with Cellulo robots rather than creating actual educative content; as such, they were co-developed by an interaction designer, a graphic designer and educational researchers who developed the software. Our current and future work involves the design of educational activities with the guidance of teachers, who are in fact also meant to be one of the main users of our platform. With these, we will aim to show that Cellulo is effective for the actual learning of multiple subjects within a real curriculum.

Following this, we plan to focus our research on the integration of Cellulo in classrooms as part of standard learning curricula (as conceptualized in Figure 1), building on co-design techniques with education professionals to ensure suitability and foster acceptance. Finally, we aim to test this integration with focused deployment studies where we will measure our platform's practicality and overall acceptance in the long term.

6. ACKNOWLEDGEMENTS

This work has been partially supported by the Swiss National Science Foundation through the National Centre of Competence in Research Robotics, Gebert Rüf Stiftung and the EU H2020 Marie Sklodowska-Curie Actions project DoRoThy (grant 657227).

7. REFERENCES

[1] T. Balch, J. Summet, D. Blank, D. Kumar, M. Guzdial, K. O'Hara, D. Walker, M. Sweat, G. Gupta, S. Tansley, J. Jackson, M. Gupta, M. N. Muhammad, S. Prashad, N. Eilbert, and A. Gavin. Designing Personal Robots for Education: Hardware, Software, and Curriculum. *IEEE Pervasive Computing*, 7(2):5–9, 2008.

[2] F. B. V. Benitti. Exploring the educational potential of robotics in schools: A systematic review. *Computers & Education*, 58(3):978–988, 2012.

[3] C.-W. Chang, J.-H. Lee, P.-Y. Chao, C.-Y. Wang, and G.-D. Chen. Exploring the Possibility of Using Humanoid Robots as Instructional Tools for Teaching a Second Language in Primary School. *Educational Technology & Society*, 13(2):13–24, 2010.

[4] S. Cuendet, Q. Bonnard, S. Do-Lenh, and P. Dillenbourg. Designing augmented reality for the classroom. *Computers & Education*, 68:557–569, 2013.

[5] P. Dillenbourg and P. Jermann. *New Science of Learning: Cognition, Computers and Collaboration in Education*, chapter Technology for Classroom Orchestration, pages 525–552. 2010.

[6] P. Dillenbourg, G. Zufferey, H. Alavi, P. Jermann, S. Do-Lenh, Q. Bonnard, S. Cuendet, and F. Kaplan. Classroom Orchestration: The Third Circle of Usability. In *Connecting Computer-Supported Collaborative Learning to Policy and Practice: CSCL2011 Conference Proceedings*, volume 1, pages 510–517, 2011.

[7] J. Han and D. Kim. r-Learning Services for Elementary School Students with a Teaching Assistant Robot. In *Proceedings of the 2009 4th ACM/IEEE International Conference on Human-Robot Interaction (HRI)*, pages 255–256, 2009.

[8] K. Highfield, J. Mulligan, and J. Hedberg. Early mathematics learning through exploration with programmable toys. In *Proceedings of the Joint Meeting of PME 32 and PME-NA*, pages 169–176, 2008.

[9] L. O. Hostettler, A. Özgür, S. Lemaignan, P. Dillenbourg, and F. Mondada. Real-Time High-Accuracy 2D Localization with Structured Patterns. In *Proceedings of the 2016 IEEE International Conference on Robotics and Automation (ICRA)*, pages 4536–4543, 2016.

[10] T. Kanda, T. Hirano, D. Eaton, and H. Ishiguro. Interactive Robots as Social Partners and Peer Tutors for Children: A Field Trial. *Human-Computer Interaction*, 19(1):61–84, 2004.

[11] M. E. Karim, S. Lemaignan, and F. Mondada. A review: Can robots reshape K-12 STEM education? In *Proceedings of the 2015 IEEE International Workshop on Advanced Robotics and its Social Impacts (ARSO)*, pages 1–8, 2015.

[12] S. Lemaignan, A. Jacq, D. Hood, F. Garcia, A. Paiva, and P. Dillenbourg. Learning by Teaching a Robot: The Case of Handwriting. *IEEE Robotics Automation Magazine*, 23(2):56–66, 2016.

[13] F. Mondada, M. Bonani, X. Raemy, J. Pugh, C. Cianci, A. Klaptocz, S. Magnenat, J.-C. Zufferey, D. Floreano, and A. Martinoli. The e-puck, a Robot Designed for Education in Engineering. In *Proceedings of the 9th Conference on Autonomous Robot Systems and Competitions*, volume 1, pages 59–65, 2009.

[14] O. Mubin, C. Bartneck, L. Feijs, H. H. van Huysduynen, J. Hu, and J. Muelver. Improving Speech Recognition with the Robot Interaction Language. *Disruptive Science and Technology*, 1(2):79–88, 2012.

[15] S. Y. Okita, V. Ng-Thow-Hing, and R. Sarvadevabhatla. Learning Together: ASIMO Developing an Interactive Learning Partnership with Children. In *Proceedings of the IEEE International Symposium on Robot and Human Interactive Communication (RO-MAN)*, pages 1125–1130, 2009.

[16] A. Özgür, W. Johal, and P. Dillenbourg. Permanent Magnet-Assisted Omnidirectional Ball Drive. In *Proceedings of the 2016 IEEE/RSJ International Conference on Intelligent Robots and Systems (IROS)*, 2016.

[17] J. Patten, H. Ishii, J. Hines, and G. Pangaro. Sensetable: A Wireless Object Tracking Platform for Tangible User Interfaces. In *Proceedings of the SIGCHI Conference on Human Factors in Computing Systems*, CHI '01, pages 253–260, 2001.

[18] E. W. Pedersen and K. Hornbæk. Tangible Bots: Interaction with Active Tangibles in Tabletop Interfaces. In *Proceedings of the SIGCHI Conference on Human Factors in Computing Systems (CHI)*, pages 2975–2984, 2011.

[19] M. P. Pettersson. Method and Device for Decoding a Position-Coding Pattern, Dec. 5 2006. US Patent 7,145,556.

[20] M. Resnick, F. Martin, R. Berg, R. Borovoy, V. Colella, K. Kramer, and B. Silverman. Digital Manipulatives: New Toys to Think with. In *Proceedings of the SIGCHI Conference on Human Factors in Computing Systems*, CHI '98, pages 281–287, 1998.

[21] F. Riedo, P. Rétornaz, L. Bergeron, N. Nyffeler, and F. Mondada. A Two Years Informal Learning Experience Using the Thymio Robot. In *Advances in Autonomous Mini Robots*, pages 37–48. Springer, 2012.

[22] E. Schweikardt and M. D. Gross. roBlocks: A Robotic Construction Kit for Mathematics and Science Education. In *Proceedings of the 8th International Conference on Multimodal Interfaces*, pages 72–75, 2006.

[23] F. Tanaka and S. Matsuzoe. Children Teach a Care-Receiving Robot to Promote Their Learning: Field Experiments in a Classroom for Vocabulary Learning. *Journal of Human-Robot Interaction*, 1(1), 2012.

[24] O. Zuckerman, S. Arida, and M. Resnick. Extending Tangible Interfaces for Education: Digital Montessori-inspired Manipulatives. In *Proceedings of the SIGCHI Conference on Human Factors in Computing Systems*, CHI '05, pages 859–868, 2005.

Adaptive Robot Language Tutoring Based on Bayesian Knowledge Tracing and Predictive Decision-Making

Thorsten Schodde
CITEC, Bielefeld University
Bielefeld, Germany
tschodde@techfak.uni-bielefeld.de

Kirsten Bergmann
CITEC, Bielefeld University
Bielefeld, Germany
kirsten.bergmann@uni-bielefeld.de

Stefan Kopp
CITEC, Bielefeld University
Bielefeld, Germany
skopp@techfak.uni-bielefeld.de

ABSTRACT

In this paper, we present an approach to adaptive language tutoring in child-robot interaction. The approach is based on a dynamic probabilistic model that represents the interrelations between the learner's skills, her observed behaviour in tutoring interaction, and the tutoring action taken by the system. Being implemented in a robot language tutor, the model enables the robot tutor to trace the learner's knowledge and to decide which skill to teach next and how to address it in a game-like tutoring interaction. Results of an evaluation study are discussed demonstrating how participants in the adaptive tutoring condition successfully learned foreign language words.

CCS Concepts

•Computing methodologies → Probabilistic reasoning; Cognitive robotics; •Applied computing → Interactive learning environments; •Human-centered computing → *Empirical studies in HCI;*

Keywords

Language tutoring; Education; Assistive robotics; Bayesian Knowledge Tracing; Decision making

1. INTRODUCTION

The use of robots for educational purposes has increasingly moved into focus in recent years. This is due to two major developments. First, robots became cheaper and more robust so that applications in everyday environments are now conceivable. In particular, technology has matured up to a point where intuitive interaction using natural language or gesture has become feasible. Second, the need for second language learning becomes increasingly important, and empirical evidence has demonstrated that learning with and from a physically present, interactive robot can be more effective than learning from classical on-screen media [14, 15, 20, 22]. In fact, recent research showed that performance can increase up to 50% [17]. It can, hence, be assumed that tutoring using social robots is qualitatively different from alternative digital tutoring technologies. Nowadays, first practical applications can be found, e.g. in nursery where toy robots teach the alphabet to kids in a very simple way. More generally, findings from a variety of settings seem to suggest that robots can help small children to develop in an educational setting [10, 18, 24, 27].

In the L2TOR project[1], we investigate in how far a social robot can support children at pre-school age with respect to second language learning. Learning a language is a very complex task. It involves not only acquiring vocabulary, but also learning prosodic features, syntactical structures, semantic meanings as well as situation-dependent language use. Yet, it has been argued that social robots can create the interactive environment and motivational experience needed to learn languages [19].

One of the most important aspects in tutoring is the robot's ability to keep track of the knowledge state, i.e. the learned and not-yet-learned skills, of the child interacting with it. This information is indispensable to enable a personalized tutoring interaction and to optimize the learning experience for the child [27]. The tutor has to structure the tutoring interaction, choose the skills to be trained, adjust the difficulty of the learning tasks appropriately and has to adapt its verbal and non-verbal behaviour.

The importance of personalized adjustments in the robot's behaviour has been substantiated in recent research showing that participants who received personalized lessons from a robot (based on heuristic skill assessment) outperformed others who received a non-personalized training [22]. Suboptimal robot behaviour (e.g. too much, too distracting, mismatching or in other ways inappropriate) can even hamper learning [17]. In this paper we present an integrated approach for tracing the knowledge of the learner during a L2 learning interaction together with a strategic adaptation of tutoring actions.

In the following, we discuss related work in Section 2. In Section 3 an extension of Bayesian Knowledge Tracing is presented as well as a model to select the next tutoring actions based on the predicted effects they may have on the learner's knowledge state. This model has been implemented in a robot that provides language tutoring in a game-like fashion. Section 4 introduces the empirical basis for this scenario and observational studies on language tutoring in kindergarten. Section 5 presents an evaluation study carried out with this robot and Section 6 discusses the results.

HRI '17, March 06 - 09, 2017, Vienna, Austria

ISBN 978-1-4503-4336-7/17/03...$15.00

DOI: http://dx.doi.org/10.1145/2909824.3020222

[1]http://www.l2tor.eu

2. RELATED WORK

Numerous studies have investigated the effects of social robots in tutoring scenarios. Empirical evidence demonstrates that learning with and from a physically present, interactive robot can be more effective than learning from classical on-screen media [14, 15, 20], and that robots can help children to develop in educational settings [10, 18, 24, 27]. However, at the same time, it is found that suboptimal behaviour of the robot can hamper learning [17]. Thus, a crucial ingredient for successful robot tutoring is the ability to provide personalized lessons [22] and to adapt in appropriate ways to the needs of the learner. The key question is when and how to adapt robot tutoring, according to which adaptation strategies, and based on what features of the state of learner or the tutoring interaction.

2.1 Approaches to Adaptive Tutoring

In the realm of Intelligent Tutoring System (ITS), dedicated *pedagogical modules* are employed for planning an optimal path through the curriculum by using an internal model of the learner's present knowledge state (cf. [8]). Cakmak and Lopes [3], for example, proposed a teaching algorithm that selects the most informative demonstrations for the learner. This learning agent makes use of Inverse Reinforcement Learning (IRL) to reduce the learner's hypothesis space of possible reward functions as fast as possible. In an evaluation, the authors showed that a learner trained with non-optimal selected expert demonstrations require significantly more demonstrations to achieve a similar performance as the optimally taught learner. This system, however, is designed for a sequential decision task in which no uncertainty about the learner's knowledge/skill exists. This assumption does not hold for the domain of L2 learning where the learner's current state of knowledge can, at best, be inferred from observed behaviour. Another important limitation of this approach is a lack of flexibility as no adaptation towards students' individual needs is considered.

Addressing especially the issue of adaptation towards students' individual needs, Partial Observable Markov Decision Processes (POMDPs) have been employed as basis for the pedagogical module of an ITS. Rafferty et al. [25], for instance, proposed different algorithms for planning an action-policy based on a POMDP and compared these against two different random and a maximum information gain (MIG) choice. They showed that even a simple action-policy based on a POMDP can achieve a significant faster skill learning than choosing actions randomly. But compared to the simple MIG algorithm, no significant difference was observed. Only with increasing skill space the MIG algorithm seems not to be sufficient anymore. A likely explanation for this finding is that the knowledge tracing model is insufficient. In addition, finding a good policy based on a POMDP is often computational intractable.

Clement et al. [4] compared two algorithms choosing the next skill and action in a tutoring interaction against a lesson given by a human expert. Both algorithms based on prior knowledge, e.g. the impact of actions on the learning gain or the difficulty of different types of tasks, which had been annotated by experts beforehand. The algorithms differed with regard to the adaptation method and the amount of additional knowledge stored besides the prior. The authors showed that even if the ITS does not make use of an internal model to store beliefs about the child's knowledge state regarding a specific skill, the use of their algorithm can lead to a higher learning gain compared to an expert lesson. Furthermore their second proposed algorithm, which additionally stores information about the knowledge state of the child, performed even better. Clement et al. concluded that extending their system with a more complex model for tracing the knowledge state of a student might lead to a higher learning.

An often criticized issue in this line of research is the lack of an effective *knowledge-tracing* method in the pedagogical module of an ITS that could be profitable for the learning interaction, e.g. by increasing the students' learning gain. Hence, we review research on knowledge tracing methods in the following.

2.2 Knowledge Tracing

Knowledge tracing aims to model learners' mastery of the knowledge being tutored. An often used approach is *Bayesian Knowledge Tracing* (BKT). BKT is a specific type of *Dynamic Bayesian Networks* (DBN), or more precisely, of Hidden Markov Models consisting of observed and latent variables. The latent variables represent the 'skills' and are classically assumed to be binary. That is, a skill is represented to be mastered or not. Generally, separate BKT networks are used for each skill to be learned [5]. Belief update is based on the observation of an answer to a given task testing a specific skill. The observed answer is binary too. Further, BKT models have two types of parameters: The emission probability and the transition probability. The emission probabilities are given by the 'guess probability' $p(guess)$, the probability of answering correctly without knowing the skill, and the 'slip probability' $p(slip)$ of answering wrongly although knowing the skill. In contrast, the transition probabilities are given by $p(t)$, the skill transition from unknown to known, and $p(f)$ the probability of forgetting a previously known skill. Often $p(f)$ is assumed to be zero.

Spaulding et al. [29] recently adopted BKT to trace the language-reading skill of children in robot-based language tutoring. They proposed the 'Affective BKT model', which is characterized by two further observable variables called 'smile' and 'engagement' to take into account the affective state of the child. This model structure allows emotions to influence the belief-state of each skill as they are included in every belief-update. The authors showed that the affective state of the children can be successfully integrated into BKT and that this approach outperforms traditional models for tracing the knowledge state in learning situations [29].

Another modification of BKT was published by Käser et al. [16]. Instead of using a dedicated BKT for every skill, they defined one comprehensive DBN to trace the knowledge on all skills to be learned. This enables to trace the knowledge on each skill individually and, in addition, to represent and reason with skill inter-dependencies. This allows for searching some kind of order in which skills may be learned best. The authors could demonstrate that this more detailed model outperforms other traditional models of knowledge tracing, including the normal BKT, with regard to the accuracy of the skill belief [16].

Finally, Gordon et al. [11] recently presented a so-called 'active learner model' to trace the word-reading skills of small children. This model does not work on the basis of BKT but employs a simple distance metric to approximate the conditional probability $p(w_2|w_1)$ of whether the child can read a word w_2 if it already knows the word w_1. Their evaluation showed that their system is able to adapt to users of different age and to trace their reading knowledge up to a certain extent [11].

In this paper we present an expandable model based on BKT for knowledge tracing that, in contrast to the systems reviewed above [16, 29], allows for the simulation of actions and decision-making in teaching interactions.

3. ADAPTIVE LANGUAGE TUTORING

As a basis for our approach to adaptive language tutoring, we adopt the Bayesian Knowledge Tracing model [5] which has been successfully employed in other work and was shown to be easily extensible. However, we modify and extend the BKT model in order to enable predictive decision-making based on the represented beliefs about the learner's knowledge state. In this section, we first introduce our version of BKT and then present the approach for decision-making.

3.1 Bayesian Knowledge Tracing

The traditional approach to BKT uses only one latent variable S to represent the skill belief and one observable variable O for the user's answer. This suffices to represent if a skill is mastered or not, and how probable it would be that the user will answer correctly. Also, this information can be used to choose the next skill to learn, e.g. the skill which has the lowest belief probability of having been mastered. However, this model does not include information about how a skill can be addressed for teaching. In consequence, there is no possibility to take possible actions and their influence on the update of skill beliefs into account. We thus add a decision node A for actions to the Bayesian network (see Figure 1). This node not only influences the possible observation but also the belief update in the next time step. Further, we use a latent variable S that can attain six discrete values for each skill, corresponding to six bins for the belief state (0%, 20%, 40%, 60%, 80%, 100%). This allows for a more detailed model of the impact of tutoring actions on the possible observations and skills. Moreover, it becomes possible to better quantify the robot's uncertainty about the learner's skill.

With these changes, especially the conditional probability table $p(O^t|S^t)$ and the additional influence of the action A^t on the observable (now $p(O^t|S^t, A^t)$), the classical BKT update function, which was based on simple assumptions about guessing $p(guess)$ and slipping $p(slip)$ during the answer process, cannot be applied anymore. Instead, we apply a normal Bayesian update rule for the conditioning of skill beliefs including a transition probability $p(S_i^{t+1}|s_k, O^t, A^t)$ where s_k identifies a bin of the skill S_i^t. As a simplification we substitute this probability with $p(S^{t+1}|s_k)$:

$$\begin{aligned} p(S_i^{t+1}) &:= p(S_i^{t+1}|O^t, A^t) \\ &= \sum_{s_k \in S_i^t} [p(S_i^{t+1}|s_k, O^t, A^t) \cdot p(s_k|O^t, A^t)] \\ &\approx \sum_{s_k \in S_i^t} [\frac{p(O^t|s_k, A^t) \cdot p(A^t|s_k) \cdot p(s_k)}{p(O^t, A^t)} \cdot p(S_i^{t+1}|s_k)] \end{aligned}$$

3.2 Predictive Decision-Making

The extended BKT model is used to decide which tutoring action the robot should take next. At first, the skill to

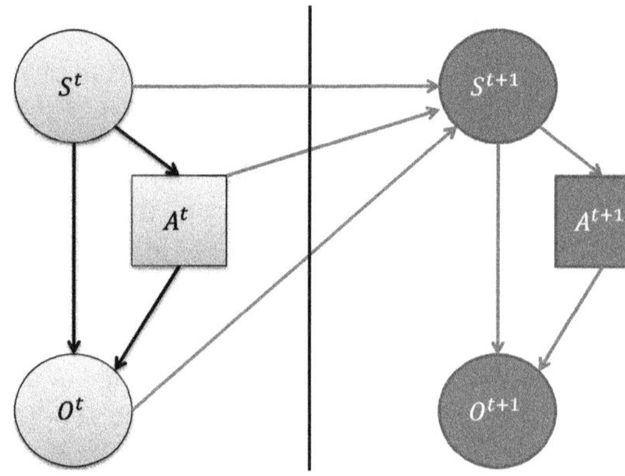

Figure 1: Dynamic Bayesian Network for BKT: The action node A^t predicts the observation O^t and influences the belief update of S^t for the next time step $t+1$.

address with the next tutoring action is chosen. For this, the Kullback-Leibler divergence (KLD) between the current skill belief and the desired skill belief is used, the latter being a maximally certain belief in a maximally high skill of the learner:

$$next\_skill = \underset{\forall S_i^t \in \mathbb{S}}{\operatorname{argmin}}[\alpha(S_i^t) \cdot KLD(p(S_i^t), p(S_{opt}))]$$

$\mathbb{S}$ represents the set of all skills that can be addressed, which consists of all words to be taught to the user. $p(S_{opt})$ is the desired belief for each skill, which means 99.999% of probability mass in the last bin (100%). The factor $\alpha(S_i^t)$ has been added for each skill to regulate the skill occurrence frequency. It is decreased each time the skill is addressed, and it is increased if another skill is being practised. In this way, the skill-selection algorithm takes care of the maximization of each skill belief as well as the balancing of all skills.

After the skill has been chosen, the next step is to decide with which tutoring action this should be done. Here, we consider abstract tasks as tutoring actions. These tasks will have to be mapped onto concrete exercises or pedagogical acts at a later stage in the robot control architecture (see Section 4). For simplicity, we distinguish between tutoring actions according to the difficulty (easy, medium or hard) of the task that addresses the corresponding skill. Finding the best action a_l for a given skill S_i^t is thus a minimization problem of the following form:

$$next\_action = \underset{\forall a_l \in A^t}{\operatorname{argmin}}[\alpha(a_l) \cdot KLD(p(S_i^{t+1}), p(S_{opt}))]$$

where

$$\begin{aligned} p(S_i^{t+1}) &:= p(S_i^{t+1}|a_l) \\ &= \sum_{s_k \in S_i^t} \sum_{o_j \in O^t} p(S_i^{t+1}|o_j, s_k, a_l) \cdot p(o_j, s_k|a_l) \\ &\approx \sum_{s_k \in S_i^t} p(s_k|a_l) \sum_{o_j \in O^t} p(S_i^{t+1}|s_k) \cdot p(o_j|s_k, a_l) \end{aligned}$$

with

$$p(o_j, s_k|a_l) = p(o_j|s_k, a_l) \cdot p(s_k|a_l)$$

Here, $p(S_i^{t+1})$ could be seen as predicting the effect of applying the current action a_l to the skill S_i, where we again substitute the transition probability $p(S_i^{t+1}|o_j, s_k, a_l)$ with $p(S_i^{t+1}|s_k)$ regarding simplicity. In addition, here again the skill belief is compared with $p(S_{opt})$ which represents the desired tutor belief state for each skill. The factor $\alpha(a_l)$ provides a more detailed selection of the "best" action. This way, the model will select an easy task if the skill is believed to be low, a hard task if it is high, and medium in-between. The goal of this strategy is to create a feeling of flow which can lead to better learning results [2, 7, 12]. Thus, it strives not to overburden the learner with too difficult tasks nor to bore him with too easy tasks, both of which may lead to frustration and thus hamper the learning [9, 13].

4. ROBOT LANGUAGE TUTORING

The adaptive model as described in the previous section has been brought to application in a child-robot second language (L2) tutoring game on the basis of empirical data from adult-child language tutoring interactions.

4.1 Empirical Basis

To design a tutoring interaction that matches children's needs, we decided to design the interaction on an empirical basis of language tutoring data. We collected video recordings of language tutoring games as they take place in kindergartens. Given that 1:1 interactions of educator and child can hardly be realized in kindergartens, the games typically involve one educator and a small group of children. Data of four language tutoring games have been collected: reading a picture book together with children in an interactive manner; card game "I spy with my little eye"; card game "I'm giving you a present"; and a rhyming game. The children were between four and six years of age. The data collected comprises round about 681 min of video data. These video data have been transcribed and annotated with regard to the following categories:

- **Dialogue acts**: Utterances are classified due to the underlying intention based on the DAMSL annotation scheme [6].
- **Children's mistakes**: Types of language errors the children made, e.g. wrong plural form, missing articles, wrong syntax, etc.
- **Educator's speech repair**: Pedagogical acts used to correct the errors, e.g. reformulation, corrected repetition, etc.
- **Nonverbal behaviour**: Nods, smiles, gestures etc. used by the educators.

On the basis of these annotations, we identified some overall patterns to inform the detailed design of the robot's behaviour. These fall basically into two categories, (i) overall interaction structure and (ii) feedback behaviour by the educators.

4.1.1 Overall Interaction Structure

A common pattern in all language tutoring games under investigation was the following basic course of actions:

1. **Opening:** Marks the beginning of the interaction and should mitigate the children's timidity as well as it should motivate the child.
2. **Game Setup:** This step is used to prepare the game by explaining the task and clarify the necessary terms.
3. **Test run:** A test run of the game is conducted to test whether the instructions have been understood and to practice the game flow.
4. **Game:** Here, the main interaction game takes place. Every move is accompanied by the educator's feedback and motivations to continue.
5. **Closing:** Marks the end of the learning interaction. Additionally, it is used to ensure motivation for future interactions by acknowledge the participation, joint singing a goodbye song and an outlook on what's going to happen next time.

4.1.2 Educator's Feedback Behaviour

In addition, we analysed the educators' behaviour when providing children with feedback. An important and common pattern is that language errors are almost never corrected explicitly. Instead, feedback is always provided in a positive way, falling into one of the following categories with the percentage of their occurrence given in squared brackets: (i) **praising the child** for a correct utterance whereby praise is often combined with a repetition of the correct word [13%] (ii) **implicit correction** in case of an error made by the child: repetition of the word as if correct (e.g. correct pronunciation, with article, plural form, etc.) [54%], (iii) **correct recasting of a sentence**, e.g. after syntax errors [32%], (iv) **moving on to next task**, e.g. when the child's message is unclear due to incomprehensible pronunciation [1%]. All kinds of educators' feedback behaviour is typically accompanied by looking at the child, smiling and nodding.

4.2 Game Setup

We have chosen the game "I spy with my little eye..." as a paradigm for our child-robot language tutoring game. The robot – in the role of a tutor, assisting the child in learning novel L2 vocabularies – is acting as 'the spy'. The child-robot setting is further enriched with a tablet PC on which objects are displayed (see Figure 2). In addition, the tablet's touch-screen displays three buttons to enable further user input in terms of 'yes' and 'no' answers as well as the option to let the robot repeat its previous statement.

A basic move of the game is structured as follows: It starts with a set of objects being displayed on the tablet screen and the robot saying "I spy with my little eye, something that is ...", followed by a foreign language word that refers to a property of one of the items on the screen. The child's task is now to respond by selecting the object referred to via touch input on the tablet. The robot's feedback behaviour in response to a correct or false answer is realized on the basis of our empirical data (see Section 4.1.2). That is, the robot responds to correct answers by praising the learner as well as repeating the L2 word and the corresponding L1 translation. In case of a false guess by the child, the robot explains the correct meaning of the to-be-learned word one more time. In addition, the wrongly chosen object as well as the actually correct object are both displayed on the tablet screen and the child is asked to select the correct object. The overall game structure is framed by the other elements making up typical language tutoring games in adult-child interaction (see Section 4.1.1).

Figure 2: Experimental setup (left) with a participant sitting in front of a tablet displaying the graphical user interface (right). The robot *Nao* stands next to the tablet slightly rotated towards the user.

4.3 Technical Realization

We employed the Nao robot[2] for our language tutoring game. It is standing in a bit more than 90 degrees rotated, to the right of the participant. In addition a Microsoft Surface Pro 4[3] tablet PC is used to catch the user input and to display the graphical user interface realized via a HTML website. For the implementation of the interaction and dialogue structure, the state-chart based dialogue-manager IrisTK has been used [28]. NAOqi[4] has been applied as middleware between the robot, the graphical user interface, the dialogue manager, and our developed adaptive tutoring model. NAOqi is shipped with each Nao robot and allows to communicate via a simple event system between various programming-languages (Python, Java, C++, JScript).

5. EVALUATION STUDY

To assess the effects of our adaptive model on L2 word learning, we set up an evaluation study based on the language tutoring game described in the previous section. The major objective behind this study was to evaluate the effects of the adaptive model on learners' performance. We used the Nao robot to deliver all task information and direct feedback to the learner. This enables us to test the model within the desired final setting, including the effects of a robot's presence in the tutoring interaction. Given that children show a high degree of inter-individual variation and might further need child-specific adaptations of, for instance, synthesized speech to enable them to understand what the robot says, we decided to conduct this first study with adult learners.

We employed a between-subjects design with a manipulation of training type: Participants learned L2 vocabulary items either with the fully adaptive model, or in a random control condition. In the adaptive condition, the skill to be taught and the action to address the skill were chosen by the model as described in Section 3. In our language tutoring game, skill relates to the foreign language words and action refers to the specific task used in the game (target word, objects displayed). The difficulty of the actions/tasks in this study were implemented by using less or more distractor objects that were shown together with the correct object on the screen. For instance, an easy task consisted of two distractor objects, whereas a hard task had four distractors. Distractors were chosen with respect to the skill beliefs of the user, with the set of objects mainly consisting of items for which the L2 words were still/mostly unknown by the learner.

As shown by Craig et al. [7], better learning performance is to be expected when learners have to expend the right amount of cognitive effort (i.e. not too hard or too easy tasks). Accordingly, while learning with our model in the adaptive condition, no hard tasks are shown until the system believes the user to have basic knowledge on all skills. Then, the system will increase task difficulty (as determined by the adaptive tutoring model) by adding distractor objects. Note, however, that at a certain point the user will know too many skills/words so that finding a distractor set (i.e. task difficulty) that cannot be sorted out by exclusion becomes impossible. In the control condition, all skills are taught in a random order and always with 'medium' task difficulty.

Participants' performance was assessed with two measures: (1) we tracked learners' response behaviour over the course of the training to investigate the progress of learning, (2) we conducted a post-test on the taught vocabulary in the form of both L1-to-L2 translations and L2-to-L1 translations to assess participants' state of knowledge subsequent to the intervention.

5.1 Materials

The training materials for the study comprised German–'Vimmi' word pairs. Vimmi is an artificial language created for experimental purposes [23] that aims to avoid associations with other known words or languages. The Vimmi items are created according to Italian phonotactic rules. Ten items have been chosen: four colour terms, four shape-encoding terms and two terms describing size (see Table 1).

5.2 Procedure

Upon entering the lab, participants were randomly assigned to one of the two experimental conditions. They were informed that they take part in an experiment on foreign language learning and were asked to sign an informed consent form. They also filled out a questionnaire that covered personal information like age and nationality as well as a personal estimation of language learning skills in general and memorization ability for L2 vocabulary.

[2]https://www.ald.softbankrobotics.com/en/cool-robots/nao

[3]https://www.microsoft.com/surface/en-gb/devices/surface-pro-4

[4]http://doc.aldebaran.com/2-1/naoqi/

N	German	Vimmi	English translation
1	blau	bati	blue
2	grün	uteli	green
3	gelb	dirube	yellow
4	rot	fesuti	red
5	rund	beropuga	round
6	dreieckig	pewo	triangular
7	quadratisch	tanedila	square
8	rechteckig	paltra	rectangular
9	klein	kiale	small
10	groß	ilado	big

Table 1: The 10 words from Vimmi to be learned in the evaluation study with its corresponding translation in German as well as English for comprehension purposes.

Next, a list of the to-be-learned Vimmi items were presented to the participants for 30 seconds. This was to enable participants to practice the items right from the first game interaction on. Then, the learning interaction with the Nao robot began. After introducing itself, the robot explained the "I spy with my little eye"-game and started a test-run with the participants. Once this test run was finished and the participants agreed that (s)he understood the game, the main interaction consisting of a total of 30 trials (game moves) began. Each trial addressed one vocabulary item as described in Section 4.2. That is, the robot asked for one of the objects displayed on the tablet screen, whereby the question was in L1 (German) for the most part, except for the referring, to-be-learned word in L2 (Vimmi). After 30 trials, the game was finished, the Nao robot thanked the participants and said goodbye.

Subsequent to the interaction with the robot, participants' learning performance was assessed with a post-test. In an interview with the experimenter, they had to translate the ten to-be-learned vocabulary items from German to Vimmi and likewise from Vimmi to German (both in randomized order). The whole interaction and the vocabulary-post-test at the end of the study were recorded with an external camera. Also the system decisions taken during the interaction and the probability distributions for each updated skill belief were logged.

5.3 Participants

A total of 40 participants (20 per condition) with an average age of 24.13 ($SD = 3.82$) took part in this study (16 males and 24 females). All participants had very good command of the German language and normal or corrected sight. All of them were paid or received credits for their participation.

5.4 Results

5.4.1 Learning Progress During Training

In order to assess the learners' progress during training, we compared the number of correct responses addressing the initial quarter of the tutoring game (first seven items) against the final quarter (last seven items). When an item occurred repeatedly within the initial quarter, the first occurrence has been taken into account. When an item occurred repeatedly within the final quarter, the last occurrence has been considered.

	Adaptive (A)		Control (C)		A, C	
	M	SD	M	SD	M	SD
F7	3.75	1.37	4.00	1.17	3.88	1.27
L7	6.90	0.31	5.15	1.69	6.03	1.49
F7, L7	5.33	0.69	4.58	1.12		

Table 2: Means (M) and standard deviations (SD) of correct answers for the initial quarter of the training interaction (first seven items – F7) and the final quarter (last seven items – L7) in each condition, as well as the inter-model (A, C) and intra-model (F7, L7) means and standard deviations.

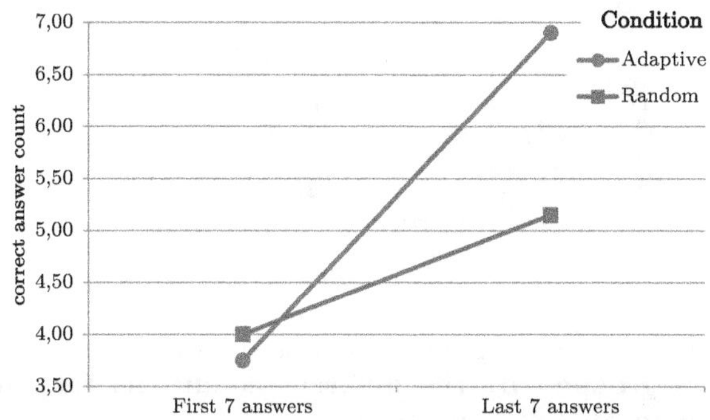

Figure 3: Mean numbers of correct answers at the beginning (first 7) and end (last 7) of the interaction in the different conditions.

A mixed-design ANOVA with training phase (initial, final) as a within-subjects factor and training type (adaptive-model-based, control) as between-subjects factor has been conducted. Results are summarized in Table 2 and Figure 3. Not surprisingly, there was a main effect of training phase at a significant level ($F(1, 38) = 66.85, p < .001, \eta^2 = .64$): Learners' performance was significantly better in the final phase as compared to the initial phase. In the first quarter of training, participants achieved a mean of 3.88 ($SD = 1.27$) correct responses, whereas in the final quarter, a mean of 6.03 ($SD = 1.49$) items was selected correctly. More interestingly, there was also a main effect of training type ($F(1, 38) = 6.52, p = .02, \eta^2 = .15$) such that participants who learned in the adaptive condition had a higher score of correct answers ($M = 5.33, SD = .69$) as compared to learners in the control condition with an average of $M = 4.58$ ($SD = 1.12$) correct answers. Finally, the interaction between training phase and training type was also significant ($F(1, 38) = 14.46, p = .001, \eta^2 = .28$) indicating that the benefit of adaptive-model-based training develops over time (see Figure 3). While participants' response behaviour in the first quarter of training was similar across conditions, a benefit of training with the adaptive model became evident in the final quarter. At this stage of training, participants in the adaptive model condition achieved a mean of $M = 6.9$ ($SD = .31$) correct responses, whereas participants in the control condition achieved a mean of $M = 5.15$ ($SD = 1.69$) correct responses.

	Adaptive (A)		Control (C)	
	M	SD	M	SD
German-to-Vimmi	3.95	2.56	3.35	1.98
Vimmi-to-German	7.05	2.56	6.85	2.48

Table 3: Results of both post-tests (German-to-Vimmi and Vimmi-to-German): Means (M) and standard deviation (SD) of correct answers grouped by the experimental conditions.

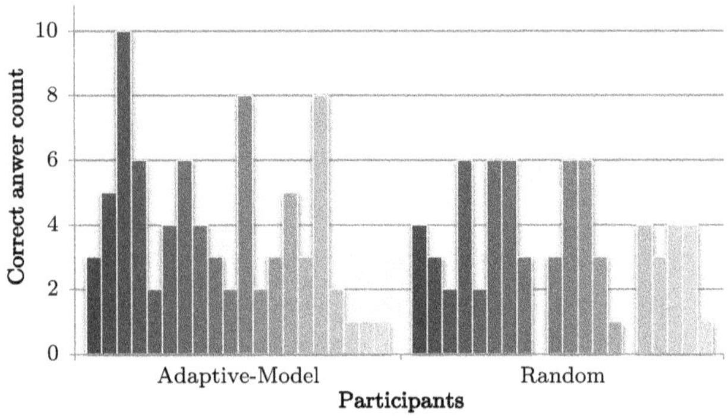

Figure 4: Participant-wise amount of correct answers grouped by the different conditions for the German-to-Vimmi post-test.

5.4.2 *Post-Test*

Participants' learning performance subsequent to the intervention has been measured with two translation tests (L2-to-L1 and L1-to-L2). Results are summarized in Table 3. Paired-samples t-tests were conducted to compare the number of correctly recalled words after training with the adaptive model as compared to training in the control condition. For the German-to-Vimmi translation, there was no significant main effect ($T(38) = .25, p = .80$). Participants who trained with the adaptive-model recalled a mean of 3.95 ($SD = 2.56$) out of ten words correctly, while participants in the control condition recalled a mean of 3.35 ($SD = 1.98$) words. Likewise, there was no significant main effect ($T(38) = .83, p = .41$) for the Vimmi-to-German translation task. Participants' performance after learning with the adaptive model amounted to a mean of 7.05 ($SD = 2.56$) correct items, participants' performance in the control condition to a mean of 6.85 ($SD = 2.48$) correct items.

Although no main effect of training type emerged in the post-test, some details might nevertheless be worth mentioning. In the German-to-Vimmi post-test, a maximum of ten correct responses was achieved by participants in the adaptive-model condition, whereas the maximum on the control condition were six correct answers. Moreover, there were two participants in the control condition who did not manage to perform any German-to-Vimmi translation correctly. In the adaptive-model condition, all participants achieved at least one correct response (see Figure 4).

6. CONCLUSION

In this paper we have presented a novel approach to personalize language tutoring in human-robot interaction. This adaptive tutoring is enabled through a model of how tutors mentalize about learners – by keeping track of their knowledge state and by selecting the next tutoring actions based on their likely effects on the learner. This is realized via an extended model that combines Bayesian Knowledge Tracing (of the learned) with tutoring actions (of the tutor) in one causal probabilistic model. This allows, for selecting skills and actions based on notions of optimality – here the desired learner's knowledge state as well as optimal task difficulty – to achieve this for a given skill. This model has been implemented into a robot language tutoring game and tested in a first evaluation study.

The analysis of participants' response behaviour over the course of training has clearly shown that participants learned the L2 words during the human-robot interaction. Importantly, they learned more successfully with our adaptive model as compared to a randomized training. That is, the repeated trials addressing still unknown items as chosen by the adaptive model (until the belief state about these words equalled that of known items) outperformed the tutoring of the same material (same number of trials and items) but in randomized order. In the post-test, however, there was no significant difference across experimental conditions, despite a trend towards better performance in the adaptive model conditions over the controls.

Different explanations may account for this inconsistent finding. One potential explanation could be that the way how responses were prompted was not identical in training sessions and post-test. In the training sessions, participants saw pictures reflecting the meaning of the to-be-learned words whereas in the post-test they just received a linguistic cue in form of a word they had to translate. It might be that repeated trials as they were particularly supported for difficult-to-remember items by the adaptive model, led to stronger associations between linguistic and imagistic materials. This might have caused a stronger decline of correct responses for participants who trained with the adaptive model as opposed to those in the control condition. An alternative explanation could be that test results measured immediately after the training session are subject to strong inter-individual differences among learners. This is the reason why studies on vocabulary learning usually range over repeated sessions spread over several days (cf. 1). A typical pattern is that significant results emerge after two or three sessions/days and/or in the long-term (measured several weeks after training took place). So it might well be that further training sessions or delayed tests might result in a post-test performance that matches the picture of the during-session performance.

One might argue that the performance of our adaptive model is comparable to the vocabulary learning technique of *spaced repetition* as implemented, for instance, in the Leitner system [21]. In this system flashcards are sorted into groups according to how well the learner knows each one. Learners try to recall items written on a flashcard. If they succeed, the card is sent to the next group. If they fail, the card is sent back to the first group. Each succeeding group has a longer period of time before the learner is required to revisit the cards. This way all items, that are hard to remember for the learner will be repeated more often. In contrast to such spaced repetition systems, our model is more flexible as it can vary the difficulty of the tasks by providing more or less distractor items. In addition, we plan a more comprehensive action space of the model to account for motivating actions where necessary or adaptations in the robot's verbal or non-verbal behaviour.

Overall, results from the evaluation study are, at least, in parts very promising: learners' performance during training was significantly improved by personalized robot tutoring based on the adaptive model. Nevertheless, the fact that this positive effect did not hold in the post-test, inter alia, marks a starting point for further refinements of the model: Training stimuli should be designed such that they match the way language learners need to apply them best possible. That is, when the aim is to enable people to translate words from one language to another, training stimuli should provide cues for this process of mapping linguistic materials on each other. Moreover, a further study with more learning sessions (e.g. over several days as common in many vocabulary studies) should be conducted. Regarding the model itself, we plan to incorporate skill-interdependencies as well as to take the affective user state into account, too. Both kind of extensions have been shown to improve learning [16, 29]. Additionally, the model can (and is meant to) provide a basis for exploiting the full potential of an embodied tutoring agent. Regarding this, we plan to advance the model such that the robot's verbal and non-verbal communicative behaviour is adapted to the learner's state of knowledge and progress. Specifically, we aim to enable dynamic adaption of (i) embodied behaviour such as iconic gesture use to be known to support vocabulary acquisition as a function of individual differences across children (cf. [26]); (ii) the robot's synthetic voice to enhance comprehensibility and prosodic focusing of content when needed; and (iii) the robot's socio-emotional behaviour depending on the learners' current level of motivation or engagement. Further, as the long-term goal of our work is to enable robot-supported language learning for pre-school children, another important goal is to make children-specific adaptations to the language game and test it in child-robot interaction studies.

7. ACKNOWLEDGEMENTS

This work was supported by the L2TOR (www.l2tor.eu) project supported by the EU Horizon 2020 Program, grant number: 688014, and by the Cluster of Excellence Cognitive Interaction Technology 'CITEC' (EXC 277) at Bielefeld University, funded by the German Research Foundation (DFG).

8. REFERENCES

[1] K. Bergmann and M. Macedonia. *A Virtual Agent as Vocabulary Trainer: Iconic Gestures Help to Improve Learners' Memory Performance*, pages 139–148. Springer Berlin Heidelberg, Berlin, Heidelberg, 2013.

[2] D. E. Berlyne. Conflict, arousal, and curiosity. 1960.

[3] M. Cakmak and M. Lopes. Algorithmic and human teaching of sequential decision tasks. In *AAAI Conference on Artificial Intelligence (AAAI-12)*, 2012.

[4] B. Clement, D. Roy, P.-Y. Oudeyer, and M. Lopes. Multi-armed bandits for intelligent tutoring systems. *arXiv preprint arXiv:1310.3174*, 2013.

[5] A. T. Corbett and J. R. Anderson. Knowledge tracing: Modeling the acquisition of procedural knowledge. *User modeling and user-adapted interaction*, 4(4):253–278, 1994.

[6] M. G. Core and J. Allen. Coding dialogs with the damsl annotation scheme. In *AAAI fall symposium on communicative action in humans and machines*, volume 56. Boston, MA, 1997.

[7] S. Craig, A. Graesser, J. Sullins, and B. Gholson. Affect and learning: An exploratory look into the role of affect in learning with autotutor. *Journal of Educational Media*, 29(3):241–250, 2004.

[8] C. Dede. A review and synthesis of recent research in intelligent computer-assisted instruction. *International Journal of Man-Machine Studies*, 24(4):329–353, 1986.

[9] S. Engeser and F. Rheinberg. Flow, performance and moderators of challenge-skill balance. *Motivation and Emotion*, 32(3):158–172, 2008.

[10] M. Fridin. Storytelling by a kindergarten social assistive robot: A tool for constructive learning in preschool education. *Comput. Educ.*, 70:53–64, Jan 2014.

[11] G. Gordon and C. Breazeal. Bayesian active learning-based robot tutor for children's word-reading skills. In *Proceedings of the Twenty-Ninth AAAI Conference on Artificial Intelligence*, AAAI'15, pages 1343–1349. AAAI Press, 2015.

[12] J. Gottlieb, P.-Y. Oudeyer, M. Lopes, and A. Baranes. Information-seeking, curiosity, and attention: computational and neural mechanisms. *Trends in cognitive sciences*, 17(11):585–593, 2013.

[13] M. J. Habgood and S. E. Ainsworth. Motivating children to learn effectively: Exploring the value of intrinsic integration in educational games. *The Journal of the Learning Sciences*, 20(2):169–206, 2011.

[14] J. Han, M. Jo, S. Park, and S. Kim. The educational use of home robots for children. In *ROMAN 2005. IEEE International Workshop on Robot and Human Interactive Communication, 2005.*, pages 378–383, Aug 2005.

[15] E. ja Hyun, S. yeon Kim, S. Jang, and S. Park. Comparative study of effects of language instruction program using intelligence robot and multimedia on linguistic ability of young children. In *RO-MAN 2008 - The 17th IEEE International Symposium on Robot and Human Interactive Communication*, pages 187–192, Aug 2008.

[16] T. Käser, S. Klingler, A. G. Schwing, and M. Gross. *Beyond Knowledge Tracing: Modeling Skill Topologies with Bayesian Networks*, pages 188–198. Springer International Publishing, Cham, 2014.

[17] J. Kennedy, P. Baxter, and T. Belpaeme. The robot who tried too hard: Social behaviour of a robot tutor can negatively affect child learning. In *Proceedings of the Tenth Annual ACM/IEEE International Conference on Human-Robot Interaction*, HRI '15, pages 67–74, New York, NY, USA, 2015. ACM.

[18] J. Kory and C. Breazeal. Storytelling with robots: Learning companions for preschool children's language development. In *The 23rd IEEE International Symposium on Robot and Human Interactive Communication*, pages 643–648, Aug 2014.

[19] J. Kory Westlund, G. Gordon, S. Spaulding, J. Lee, L. Plummer, M. Martinez, M. Das, and C. Breazeal. Learning a second language with a socially assistive robot. In *The 1st International Conference on Social Robots in Therapy and Education*, 2015.

[20] H. Kose-Bagci, E. Ferrari, K. Dautenhahn, D. S. Syrdal, and C. L. Nehaniv. Effects of embodiment and gestures on social interaction in drumming games with a humanoid robot. *Advanced Robotics*, 23(14):1951–1996, 2009.

[21] S. Leitner. So lernt man lernen: Der weg zum erfolg [learning to learn: The road to success]. *Freiburg: Herder*, 1972.

[22] D. Leyzberg, S. Spaulding, M. Toneva, and B. Scassellati. The physical presence of a robot tutor increases cognitive learning gains. In *CogSci*. Citeseer, 2012.

[23] M. Macedonia, K. Müller, and A. D. Friederici. Neural correlates of high performance in foreign language vocabulary learning. *Mind, Brain, and Education*, 4(3):125–134, 2010.

[24] J. R. Movellan, M. Eckhardt, M. Virnes, and A. Rodriguez. Sociable robot improves toddler vocabulary skills. In *Human-Robot Interaction (HRI), 2009 4th ACM/IEEE International Conference on*, pages 307–308, March 2009.

[25] A. N. Rafferty, E. Brunskill, T. L. Griffiths, and P. Shafto. Faster teaching via pomdp planning. *Cognitive Science*, 2015.

[26] M. L. Rowe, R. D. Silverman, and B. E. Mullan. The role of pictures and gestures as nonverbal aids in preschoolers' word learning in a novel language. *Contemporary Educational Psychology*, 38(2):109–117, 2013.

[27] M. Saerbeck, T. Schut, C. Bartneck, and M. D. Janse. Expressive robots in education: Varying the degree of social supportive behavior of a robotic tutor. In *Proceedings of the SIGCHI Conference on Human Factors in Computing Systems*, CHI '10, pages 1613–1622, New York, NY, USA, 2010. ACM.

[28] G. Skantze and S. Al Moubayed. Iristk: A statechart-based toolkit for multi-party face-to-face interaction. In *Proceedings of the 14th ACM International Conference on Multimodal Interaction*, ICMI '12, pages 69–76, New York, NY, USA, 2012. ACM.

[29] S. Spaulding, G. Gordon, and C. Breazeal. Affect-aware student models for robot tutors. In *Proceedings of the 2016 International Conference on Autonomous Agents & Multiagent Systems*, AAMAS '16, pages 864–872, Richland, SC, 2016. International Foundation for Autonomous Agents and Multiagent Systems.

Growing Growth Mindset with a Social Robot Peer

Hae Won Park
Personal Robots Group
MIT Media Lab
haewon@media.mit.edu

Rinat Rosenberg-Kima
Curiosity Lab
Tel Aviv University, Israel
rinat.rosenberg.kima@gmail.com

Maor Rosenberg
Curiosity Lab
Tel Aviv University, Israel
maor.rosenberg@cs.tau.ac.il

Goren Gordon
Curiosity Lab
Tel Aviv University, Israel
goren@gorengordon.com

Cynthia Breazeal
Personal Robots Group
MIT Media Lab
cynthiab@media.mit.edu

ABSTRACT

Mindset has been shown to have a large impact on people's academic, social, and work achievements. A *growth mindset*, i.e., the belief that success comes from effort and perseverance, is a better indicator of higher achievements as compared to a *fixed mindset*, i.e., the belief that things are set and cannot be changed. Interventions aimed at promoting a growth mindset in children range from teaching about the brain's ability to learn and change, to playing computer games that grant brain points for effort rather than success. This work explores a novel paradigm to foster a growth mindset in young children where they play a puzzle solving game with a peer-like social robot. The social robot is fully autonomous and programmed with behaviors suggestive of it having either a growth mindset or a neutral mindset as it plays puzzle games with the child. We measure the mindset of children before and after interacting with the peer-like robot, in addition to measuring their problem solving behavior when faced with a challenging puzzle. We found that children who played with a growth mindset robot 1) self-reported having a stronger growth mindset and 2) tried harder during a challenging task, as compared to children who played with the neutral mindset robot. These results suggest that interacting with peer-like social robot with a growth mindset can promote the same mindset in children.

Keywords

early childhood education, mindset, perseverance, grit, child-robot interaction, cognitive architecture, social robots

1. INTRODUCTION

Psychologists have shown that beliefs about the malleability of human attributes such as intelligence can have strong effects on motivation, reaction to challenge or failure, and academic achievement [4, 12, 17]. Mindset, according to Dweck [8, 33], dictates how people perceive their own and other people's capabilities, behaviors and attitudes. People with a *fixed mindset* think that nothing can be changed – that capabilities are fixed and cannot be improved. People with a *growth mindset* believe that achievements are dictated by effort and resilience to failure, often referred to as grit [7]. It has been shown that people with a growth mindset have higher academic, social, and work achievements [4, 30, 33].

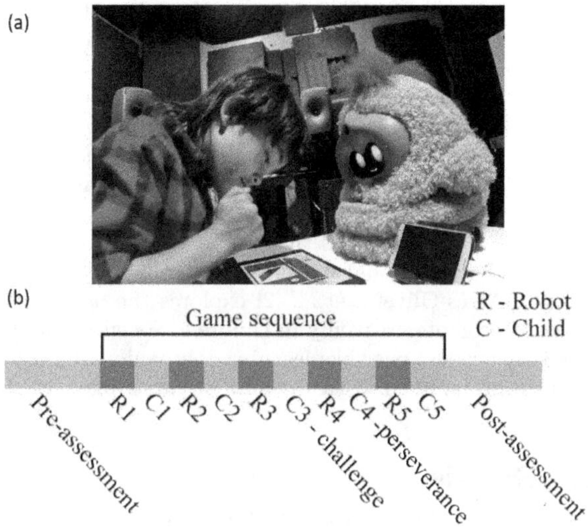

Figure 1: (a) Experimental setup including Tega, tablet and child; (b) sequence of the experiment and sequence of the puzzle solving turns between the robot and the child over 5 rounds.

1.1 Background & Related Work

Several intervention strategies have been developed to promote a growth mindset, especially in children [22, 4, 3, 12, 19]. In [24], an educational online game was developed and demonstrated to encourage the growth mindset by incentivizing effort, use of strategy, and incremental progress through a "brain points" score system.

Both laboratory and classroom studies have shown that mindset can be changed through careful intervention, often involving social interaction [8, 16, 4, 22, 19]. For instance, directly teaching students that intelligence is malleable has been shown to improve classroom motivation and achievement compared to a control group [4]. Praising children for

HRI '17, March 06-09, 2017, Vienna, Austria
© 2017 ACM. ISBN 978-1-4503-4336-7/17/03...$15.00
DOI: http://dx.doi.org/10.1145/2909824.3020213

their strategy or effort as they solve problems (rather than praising their talent) produces a growth mindset, higher motivation, and task persistence [22, 19]. These interventions not only change people's attitudes, they also positively impact achievements [9]. Unfortunately, praising children in a way that reinforces a fixed mindset can have negative consequences. Gunderson et al. [16] have confirmed the role of praise in mindset, showing that the type of praise parents give to young children predicts the child's mindset five years later.

These kinds of adult-child interventions are important. However, peer-to-peer interactions can also have an important influence on children's attitudes and behaviors. The impact of peer influence on children's mindset, however, has yet to be studied in a methodological way.

Social robots as educational companions for children have been recently explored in a growing breadth of scenarios including vocabulary acquisition [21, 31], second-language learning, mathematics, computational thinking, and social skills [27, 26]. The interaction skills of such robots have been found to impact children's behavior and learning in important ways. It has been shown that children treat robots as informants [6] and positively respond to personalization of affective, verbal and nonverbal behaviors [15].

Especially noteworthy is that social robots can promote higher level motivational attributes and cognitive skills. For example, Alves-Oliveira et al. [2] explores the use of social robots to promote creativity in children. Social robots portrayed as curious, peer-like learning companions have been shown to promote curiosity in children via co-play [14, 13].

1.2 Overview

In this paper, we investigate whether social robots, framed as peers, can promote a growth mindset in children. To address this question, we first developed an expressive cognitive architecture that combines problem solving with mindset driven expressiveness. We use this architecture to generate the behaviors of a child friendly social robot that are indicative of having either a neutral or growth mindset. We then designed and conducted a novel study in which children played spatial puzzle solving games with either a growth or neutral mindset robot. The robot was introduced to each child as a playmate and had a similar puzzle-solving skill level as the child.

We developed a suite of novel apps for this purpose including a Tangram game app and two pre/post assessment activity apps to measure mindset and spatial skill [5, 28]. The child and robot take turns selecting which puzzles to try and solve under time pressure. In the growth mindset condition (GROWTH), the robot selects the more challenging tangrams to solve and makes growth mindset related comments about its own and the child's abilities and efforts throughout the session. In contrast, in control condition (NEUTRAL), the robot selects similar difficulty level tangrams as the child and makes neutral comments, mainly factual statements about the success or failure of the task. Towards the end of the session, a particularly challenging, time limited tangram puzzle is used to confront children with failure. After this, another challenging tangram, but with no time limit, was used to assess children's perseverance. Children's answers and behaviors during these activities were measured and analyzed to determine how each condition influenced children's mindset as expressed through their beliefs and actions.

1.3 Contributions

This paper presents a first of its kind growth mindset intervention study using an autonomous robotic agent. Specifically, we offer the following contributions. We developed novel assessment apps for measuring children's spatial reasoning skills and mindset. These shall be made open source[1]. Second, we designed and conducted a novel study to explore the effect of peer-like interaction on children's mindset. It is also the first study to investigate the effect of a peer-like social robot on chidren's mindset. Finally, our results support our main hypothesis, namely, that interacting with a peer-like robot that expresses a growth mindset has a positive impact on children's mindset as expressed through their communicated beliefs and task-based behaviors in the face of challenge.

2. SYSTEM DESCRIPTION

The system is composed of *Tega* as a social robot platform, an *expressive cognitive architecture* that supports problem solving as well as generating mindset driven robot behaviors, and a *tablet* as a shared space for presenting child-robot interaction tasks such as the *Tangram puzzle app* (Figure 1(a)). Data exchange takes place over the network in which each module publishes its states and actions and subscribes to others' messages. The Robot Operating System (ROS) [29] handles the synchronization of these messages.

2.1 Robot Platform

Tega is an appealing, expressive, child friendly robot, designed for long-term deployment in various educational settings such as children's homes, schools, and therapeutic centers [32, 15]. It is a size of a teddy bear (about 11 inches tall) and is brightly colored with a plush exterior. It has five degrees of freedom to perform a wide range of expressive movements: head tilt up/down, waist tilt left/right, waist lean forward/back, body extension up/down, and body twist left/right. The robot has an efficient battery-powered system that can run for up to six hours before needing to be recharged. An Android smartphone mounted in the head is used to graphically display the robot's animated face as well as perform computational tasks such as sensor processing, data collection, wifi communications, decision making, and motor control. The robot's electronic design extends the smartphone's ability with on-board speakers and an additional high-definition camera with a wide field of view.

Tega is a peer-like social robot. A *peer* is a group of people in similar ages that influences each other's language, behavior, and beliefs through interaction. Tega's peer attributes include child-like high pitched voice, exaggerated body and facial expressions, as well as its intrinsic tangram solver that mimics the thought process of a child in terms of spatial reasoning and speed. With its peer attributes, Tega is able to engage in taking turns solving a puzzle with a child while encouraging each other. Combined with the expressive cognitive architecture presented in the following section, Tega can reason about the child's cognitive states and express its

[1]The assessment apps will be made available with documentation in June 2017 in the following link: https://github.com/CuriosityLabTAU

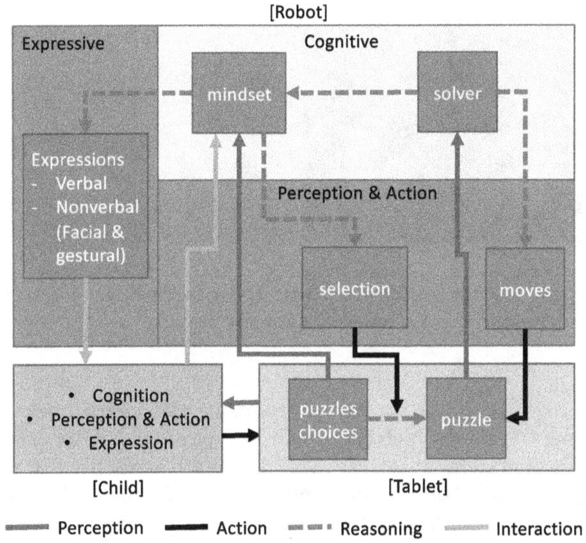

Figure 2: The expressive cognitive architecture that combines problem solving with mindset driven expressiveness. The modules within the robot are computational mental models mimicking those of the child's.

(a) Tangram selection: "I will choose this one because it looks challenging"

(b) Child win: "You worked hard and succeeded! Yay!"

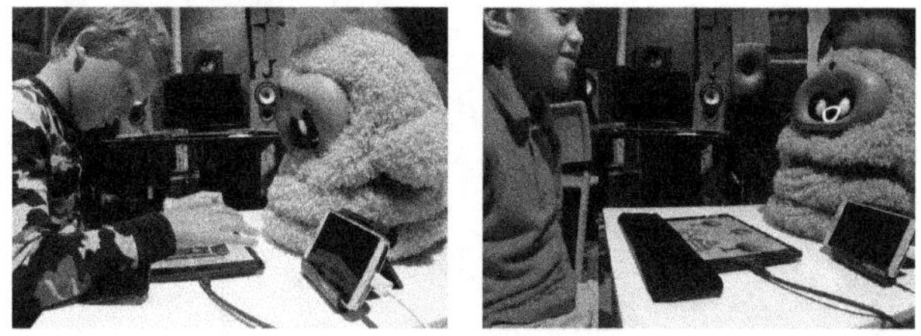

(c) Perseverance task: "you are working hard to solve this puzzle"

(d) Game end: "We worked hard and succeeded!"

Figure 3: Utilizing its expressive cognitive architecture, Tega expresses its mindset in various stages of the interaction through verbal and nonverbal behavior.

growth mindset mental model through a set of verbal and nonverbal behaviors.

2.2 Expressive Cognitive Architecture

The expressive cognitive architecture bridges an algorithm for solving tangram puzzles to generating robot's mindset dependent expressive behaviors. The idea is that, within a context of tangram puzzle solving, we are creating a computational mental model of a child's cognitive processes (mindset and puzzle solver), perception and action (puzzle selection and making moves), and expressiveness (verbal and nonverbal behavior based on the mindset state). This mental model is then applied to Tega for it to generate tangram solving and mindset oriented expressive behaviors. With such a model, a robot can not only act more peer-like, but can also help foster a growth oriented mindset in children by setting an example. For instance, by selecting a more challenging puzzle and demonstrating that one can also learn by failing, a child may overcome her fear of making mistakes. As depicted in Figure 2, the mindset module is triggered by the information flow from the surrounding modules and the environment: the child, tablet, and the solver. Using this information, the mindset module creates an assumption of the task and the child's states. It also generates its next set of actions, such as commanding the expression-generation module to produce robot behavior or making a puzzle selection based on its mindset. The modules exist within the robot enabling it as an autonomous agent. Hence, in the tablet's perspective, the child and the robot are just individual players.

During its turn, the robot solves a tangram puzzle and performs actions on the tablet game using a neural network solver. The tangram solving algorithm is a neural network model following Oflazer's connectionist approach [23]. Each tangram piece, represented combinatorially by its position and rotation on a puzzle grid, is mapped to a node in the network. Their inhibitory connectivity represents physical constraints, such as uniqueness of pieces and their non-overlap in possible solutions. The nodes are then excited by their relative overlap with the input tangram silhouette, akin to how humans mentally align tangram pieces to the silhouette when first confronted with a puzzle. A relaxation search algorithm is performed according to the Bolzman machine model [1], converging to the puzzle solution. The active nodes for each search iteration are then serialized to produce a sequence of moves toward a solution. This serialization step is analogous to the thought process of a person when confronted with a new puzzle.

The expression-generation module takes the state of the task as an input to generate the robot's nonverbal and verbal behaviors. Throughout the session, this module generates expressive behaviors, coordinating the robot's physical movements, facial expressions, and vocalizations so that the robot can produce behavior during its own and the child's play. In the growth mindset configuration, the robot detects the state of a child's effort and provides comments and encouragements on the child's perseverance and willingness to take on challenges, as depicted in Figure 3. In the neutral mindset configuration, the robot simply acknowledges and provides factual comments on the success or failure of itself and the child's. Details on robot's speech examples are presented in Section 3.4.

2.3 Tablet Shared Workspace

Recently tablets have been extensively used as a shared human-robot interaction space, due to it's inviting interface both for the person (touchscreen) and the robot (wireless communication) [25]. The tablet is an Android device with a 10-inch screen. The following three apps were installed on the tablet: the main Tangram app and two apps corresponding to digitized assessment activities to measure mind-

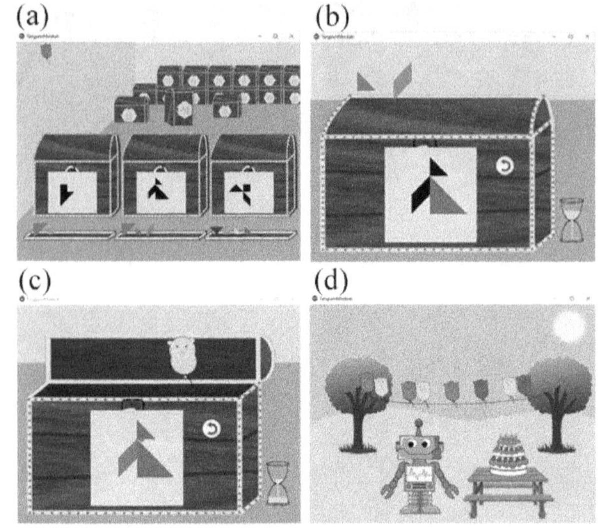

Figure 4: Screenshots from the Tangram App: (a) tangram selection room, (b) solving a tangram puzzle, (c) puzzle solved, (d) party screen.

set and spatial skill. The tablet also performs data collection, recording how children and robot play with these apps. For instance, in the tangram app, the states of the tangram game, touch events, hourglass events, tangram piece locations, number of attempts and timestamps, player turns, and puzzle selections are logged.

2.4 Tangram Treasure App

The tangram app is designed as a game where the objective is to collect balloons to decorate a birthday party. To get a balloon, the player needs to unlock treasure boxes, each holding a balloon inside. To unlock a treasure box, the player needs to solve a tangram puzzle depicted as a silhouette on the outside of the box.

Each round, three tangram puzzles are generated to produce three distinct levels of difficulty. The difficulty level of a puzzle is determined by the number of pieces and the total length of joint piece edges. At the beginning of each turn, the player first selects one out of three treasure boxes, ordered by difficulty, with the left being the easiest and the right the most difficult (Figure 4(a)). Upon selecting a treasure box, the player needs to unlock it by solving the tangram puzzle in less than 2 minutes (Figure 4(b)). Otherwise, the treasure box remains locked with the balloon inside. If the player solves the tangram puzzle, the treasure box is unlocked and one balloon is gained (Figure 4(c)).

If the player succeeds at solving any of the puzzles, the difficulty level of the next round increases by one. If the player fails, the difficulty level remains the same, unless this happens on the easiest puzzle. In this case, the difficulty level for the next round decreases by one. By proceeding in this way, the goal is to challenge the child while maintaining a level matched to her performance.

The game ends with the party scene with all the acquired balloons decorating the scene (Figure 4(d)).

2.5 Mindset Assessment App

Our mindset assessment app probes children's beliefs about their own mindset through introducing two characters and asking the child which character they agree with more over a series of statements they make. The statements used in the app are based on Dweck's mindset questionnaires [8], and the age adjusted statements are adopted from [18]. Two characters appear on the screen, Buffy and Fluffy, accompanied by the following instructions by the app: "This is Buffy, and this is Fluffy. They are siblings. Buffy and Fluffy really like school, and they want to know if you like school, too! Buffy and Fluffy want to know more about what you like or don't like about school. They will tell you about how they feel, and then I want you to pick whether you are more like Buffy, or more like Fluffy. Okay? Are you ready to play?" (Figure 5(a)).

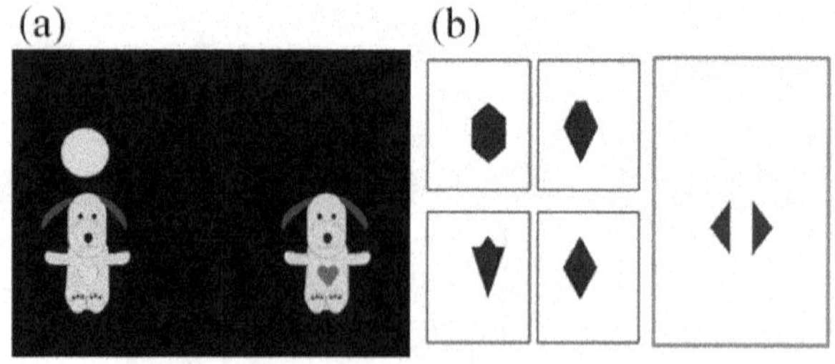

Figure 5: Screenshots from: (a) mindset assessment app, (b) spatial skill assessment app.

Buffy and Fluffy each take turns saying one statement with a green/blue circle over the head of the character who is talking. In total, ten pairs of statements are presented to the child, one sentence representing a fixed mindset and the other representing a growth mindset. For example, in a given selection task, either Buffy or Fluffy makes a fixed mindset statement "I like school because I'm really good at the things we do there", and the other makes a growth mindset statement "I like school because I learn to be better at things we do there". Then the child is prompted to answer "which one is more like you?" by clicking on either Buffy or Fluffy.

The variables that may cause bias in the study results are carefully controlled. We use gender neutral names and colors for the two identically looking characters and vary which character delivers the growth mindset statement in each turn. To control for ordering effects, the ten statements are presented in randomized order. Participants play this app as a pre/post assessment. Five of the ten statement pairs are identical in the pre/post assessments, and five are different. The app records the selections the child makes and the associated time. None of the statements used in the mindset assessment are used by the robot during the tangram interaction.

2.6 Spatial Skill Assessment App

Our spatial skill app is based on the Children's Mental Transformation Task (CMTT). The task is designed to test four types of 2-D mental transformations: 1) horizontal translation, 2) diagonal translation, 3) horizontal rotation, and 4) diagonal rotation [20, 10].

In this task, participants choose which shape would be made by moving two separate pieces together. The app instructs the children to "Look at these two pieces on the red card. Now, look at these pictures on the blue cards. If you put the two pieces on the red card together, they will make one of the pictures on the blue cards. Press the picture on the blue card made by the two pieces on the red card." (Figure 5(b)).

The spatial skill app is used as a pre/post assessment. Each time the app is played, it presents 16 items in randomized order. A different set of 16 tasks is used between the pre/post assessments. The app measures the number of correct answers (0-16) and the selection time per item.

3. EXPERIMENT DESIGN

We designed a novel experiment to investigate a set of hypotheses regarding the impact of interacting with a peer-like robot with a growth mindset on children's own expression of mindset as measured via our assessment apps.

3.1 Hypotheses

The main hypothesis is that interacting with a robot that expresses a growth mindset will have a positive impact on fostering children's growth mindset. More formally, we hypothesize two condition dependent effects:

- **H1**: Participants in the growth mindset condition (GROWTH) will score higher on the post mindset assessment app compared to the control condition, i.e., neutral mindset condition (NEUTRAL).
- **H2**: Participants performing the perseverance tangram task (i.e., the challenging puzzle with no time limit) will have condition dependent behavior, i.e., not quitting and trying harder in the GROWTH condition, compared to the NEUTRAL condition.

With respect to learning gains from this short, single-shot encounter, we anticipate seeing a small pre-to-post increase in spatial skills as measured by the child's performance on the spatial skill assessment app. However, we do not expect to see a condition dependent effect, since the impact of having a growth mindset associated on learning gains is typically a longitudinal effect.

- **H3**: A small condition independent improvement in children's spatial skills will be observed.
- **H4**: Children perceive that the GROWTH condition robot has a growth mindset.

3.2 Participants

Participants were recruited from a mailing list of local families with young children. Forty children between the ages of 5–9 years old (age $M = 6.75, SD = 1.08$; female 42.5%) participated in the study. Participants were randomly assigned and counter-balanced across conditions with respect to their age and gender: NEUTRAL condition ($N = 20$, age $M = 6.75$, $SD = 1.07$; female 45%); GROWTH condition ($N = 20$, age $M = 6.75$, $SD = 1.12$; female 40%).

3.3 Conditions

The robot's behavior differed – reacting to the child's actions and to the state of the game with different verbal phrases, facial expressions and body movements – according to either the the experimental (GROWTH) condition or the control (NEUTRAL) condition. The robot chooses its reactions from a large collection of phrases and expressions that were carefully predefined to be appropriate for each condition. For example, when the child succeeds in solving a tangram puzzle in the NEUTRAL condition, the neutral robot makes a calm, factual statement "You solved the puzzle" with a head nod. In contrast, the growth mindset robot makes an affirming statement in the GROWTH condition: "You are not afraid of a challenge. I like that!" with accompanying body language and facial expressions showing excitement.

How the robot chooses tangram puzzles to solve also differs across conditions. In the NEUTRAL condition, the robot chooses a puzzle of the same difficulty level as the child, or easier. Recall that the puzzles are spatially ordered in levels of difficulty. Hence, if the child selects a tangram puzzle in a certain position and succeeds in solving it, then the robot selects the puzzle in the same position on its turn. If the child fails on her turn, the robot chooses a puzzle one level easier (if possible). In contrast, in the GROWTH condition, the robot selects a puzzle one level of difficulty higher (if possible) when the child succeeds in solving her puzzle, or chooses one at the same level of difficulty if the child fails. In this away, the GROWTH condition robot favors more challenging puzzles relative to the child's selections.

3.4 Protocol

The experimental protocol followed three stages: 1) Welcome and pre-assessment activities, 2) Playing the tangram game with Tega, 3) post-assessment activities.

3.4.1 Playing Pre-assessment Games

At the beginning of each session, the experimenter invites the child to play several games on a tablet before playing with the robot, Tega. At the same time, the parent is asked to fill out a questionnaire. We inform the participants that they can stop at any moment, if they are bored or do not wish to continue for whatever reason. If the child agrees to play, the first game is the spatial skill app with 16 tasks requiring children to choose which shape results from moving two separate pieces together. Next, the child plays the mindset assessment app comprised of 10 pairs of statements from Buffy and Fluffy, where the child chooses which one is more like him/her.

3.4.2 Playing Tangram Puzzles with the Peer-like Robot

After playing the pre-assessment apps, the child is brought to another area where the Tega robot sits on a table with a tablet nearby. The child is invited to sit on a chair facing the robot, with the tablet between the two of them. The child is told that Tega is a "young robot who wants to play a game with you." Tega's verbal and nonverbal expressions throughout the interaction were condition dependent (see Table 1), where each of sentence was randomly selected from a pool of 6 slightly different sentences. All of Tega's sentences were followed by a gesture that expressed an appropriate nonverbal expression, e.g. engagement, interest, excitement, frustration.

When the child first sees Tega it is "asleep" with its eyes closed, making sleeping sounds. The experimenter starts the interaction by waking the robot up. Tega yawns and introduces itself "Hi, I am Tega. My friend is having a birthday party. Everything is set but the balloons. Will you help me find some balloons?". On the tablet, the child sees a robot standing in a birthday party scene but with no balloons.

Table 1: Examples of robot behavior across conditions and interaction stages

Stage	NEUTRAL	GROWTH
Tega tangram selection	"I will choose this one."	"I will choose this one because it looks challenging!"
Child tangram selection	"start by selecting a box", "which box do you want to select?"	"try hard and you will succeed", "I'm sure you can do it if you try hard"
Tega tangram solution	"there", "I will move this piece.", "it's hard."	"it's quite hard, so I will try even more.", "if I keep trying, I will succeed.", "I'll try again."
Tega win	"great, I got us another balloon for the party", "I solved the puzzle'	"that was hard, but I tried hard and nailed it", "working hard is worth it"
Child win	"good job.", "great playing.", "You seem to be on the right track."	"you worked hard and succeeded!", "Working hard is worth it.", "you are not afraid of a challenge. I like it!"
Tega lose	"that was hard", "I did not succeed", "that was difficult"	"next time I will put more effort", "I'm not afraid of a challenge. I like it!"
Child lose	"next time, friend", "better luck next time"	"you worked hard, next time you will succeed", "you tried very hard. That's what matters", "you are not afraid of a challenge"
Game end	"we had a great game together"	"we worked hard and succeeded"

To start playing the tangram game, the child clicks on the "yes" button on the screen when Tega finishes delivering its line (alternatively, the child can click the "no" option). If the child does not respond to the initial prompt, the robot will invite the child to play two more times. Otherwise the session stops.

If the child clicks the "yes" button, Tega responds with "Great, let's play. We need to go to the magic treasure room" (followed by excited expression). The tablet changes the scene to the magic treasure room, and Tega explains the task "This is the magic treasure room. It is filled with magical treasure boxes. In each treasure box you will find exactly what you seek if you can open it. The lock to each magic box is a puzzle. First we need to choose which box to try and open" (Figure 4(a)). Tega begins by playing the first round of the game, demonstrating how to select a box.

Next the tablet screen changes to the selected box (Figure 4(b)). Tega explains: "These puzzles are made of pieces of different shapes. We need to find where to put them to fill in the gray area. We have two minutes to try, until the sand in the hourglass runs out." (then the robot leans forward to look at the game). The robot tries to solve the puzzle as aforementioned in the expressive cognitive architecture section. Tega comments as it tries different moves based on the experimental condition. The first round ended with Tega successfully solving the first puzzle and earning a balloon (Figure 4(c)).

After Tega solved the first puzzle the screen changed back to the magic treasure selection room and Tega told the child: "It is your turn now" followed by a condition dependent utterance. The child and robot take turns, choosing and solving puzzles to earn balloons to decorate the party scene. Overall, they play 5 rounds of the game starting with Tega the Robot (R1) followed by the Child (C1), until the game ended with the child last turn (C5) (Figure 1(b)).

The difficulty level of the tangram puzzles changes according to the child's performance in the previous round, with the following two important exceptions. Round 3 is the **timed-challenge round**, where the game presents three difficult puzzles having more pieces. These tangrams were designed to be difficult for children to solve, allowing us to observe their behavior in the face of failure, and also enabling Tega to respond to the child's failure. Round 4 is the **perseverance round** where three challenging tangram puzzles are presented, but with no time constraint for solving. During the perseverance round it is possible to observe the level of perseverance of the child during a difficult task, whether the child keeps on trying harder or gives up over time. The final round included three doable tangram tasks, with the goal of finishing the experiment on a positive note. If at any point during this game the child appeared particularly frustrated, the experimenter reminded the child that it was OK to stop at any time.

After solving the puzzles, the game concludes at the birthday party location, where all the earned balloons decorate scene. Tega concludes the game and says goodbye based on the condition, followed by falling asleep.

3.4.3 Post-interaction assessments

After playing with the robot, the experimenter asks the child to play the three assessment apps to post-test any changes to the child's spatial skills and mindset. As discussed, both are varied from the pre-test versions. In addition, the participants were asked to answer a short questionnaire regarding their perception of Tega's mindset. In total, 10 questions were asked, among which 5 questions were growth mindset oriented and others fixed mindset oriented statements. Five-point Likert scale measured the level of participant's agreement to a given statement (always no, sometimes no, maybe, sometimes yes, always yes). The overall score was summed by assigning 0–4 points to each lowest level to highest level agreement in the growth mindset statements, and 4–0 points in the fixed mindset statements (hence the maximum one can score is 50, minimum 0).

4. RESULTS

In the following analyses, we ran Shapiro-Wilk (S-W) test to check for normality and Levene's test to check for equal variance, where applicable. We failed to reject Levene's null hypothesis at the 0.05 significance level for all dataset ($p > 0.05$), hence we conclude that there is insufficient evidence to claim that the variances are not equal. Hence, parametric (paired/unpaired t-test) and non-parametric (Wilcoxon signed-rank and Mann-Whitney's U) tests were used based on the S-W result.

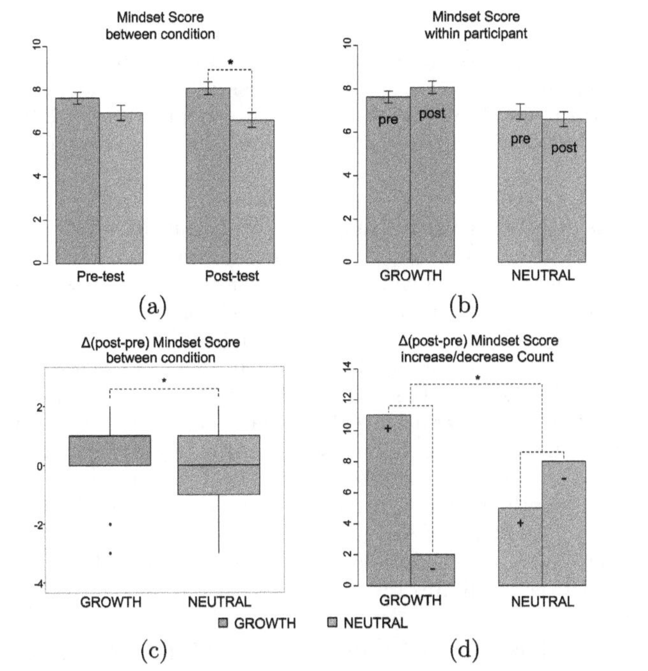

Figure 6: Analysis on children's mindset before and after interacting with the robot. Children who engaged with a growth mindset oriented robot showed an increase in self-reported growth mindset, a significant difference to the NEUTRAL group.

4.1 Mindset Assessment

In total, 33 children out of 40 completed the pre/post mindset tests. One child refused to participate in the pre-test, and six children either had to leave or refused to complete the post-test. Out of 33 children, 17 were in the NEUTRAL condition (age $M = 6.88$, $SD = 1.05$, female 41%), and 16 in the GROWTH condition (age $M = 6.69$, $SD = 1.14$, female 38%).

We summed the number of growth mindset oriented statements each participant chose among the 10 pairs of statements in the pre- and post-tests. Participants started out having a similar mindset score regardless of condition, with no significant statistical difference between conditions (NEUTRAL: $M = 6.94$, $SD = 1.78$, GROWTH: $M = 7.63$, $SD = 1.41$; t(31)= -1.22, p=0.23). However, more participants in the GROWTH condition scored higher in the post-test. We found a significant effect per condition (NEUTRAL: $M = 6.59$, $SD = 1.77$, GROWTH: $M = 8.06$, $SD = 1.48$; t(31)= -2.59, p=0.01) (Figure 6(a)). Fischer's exact test also revealed that the number of participants whose mindset score increased versus decreased significantly differed by condition (p = 0.041, odds ratio is 7.99) (Figure 6(d)). Mann-Whitney's U test showed that the amount of change pre-to-post was also significant with participants in the GROWTH condition, showing a stronger trend towards an increased growth mindset as compared to the NEUTRAL condition (Figure 6(c)). The mean ranks of the NEUTRAL and GROWTH conditions were 13.88 and 20.31, respectively; W = 83, Z = -2.00, p = 0.045, r = 0.35.

Taken together, these results suggest that there was no significant difference in mindset before the interaction with the robot. However, children's growth mindset increased after the interaction with a peer-like robot with a growth mindset. This confirms our main hypothesis **H1**.

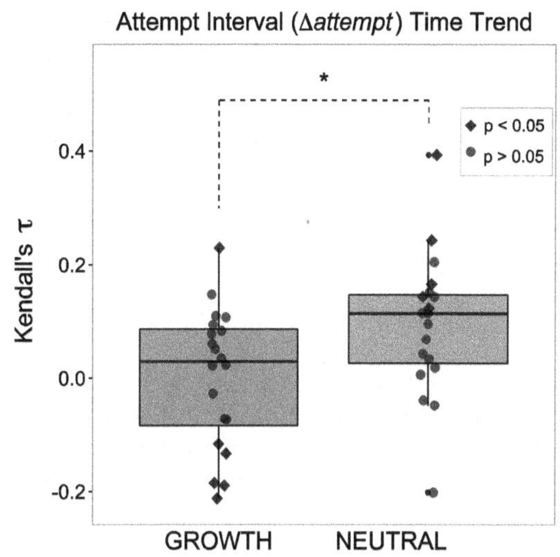

Figure 7: Time trend analysis on attempt intervals ($\Delta attempt$) was conducted in the perseverance round (C4). Result shows that children who were interacting with a growth mindset oriented robot significantly demonstrated more perseverance when confronted with a challenge. Diamond markers show trends with significance.

4.2 Perseverance Assessment

All 40 children participated in the Tangram activity with the robot. The data of one participant was corrupted due to a network problem. Among 39 children, 19 were in the NEUTRAL condition (age $M = 6.68$, $SD = 1.06$; female 47%) and 20 were in the GROWTH condition (age $M = 6.75$, $SD = 1.12$; female 40%).

We analyzed children's perseverance during round 4 (C4) by presenting a difficult puzzle with unlimited time for solving. Perseverance is a steady persistence in a course of action in spite of difficulties. As a measure of perseverance, we evaluated the trend of puzzle solving attempts a child makes over time. The app recorded the timestamps of when a puzzle piece was manipulated by the child. The time difference between two consecutive events ($\Delta attempt$) was computed to analyze the trend of attempts. If a child consistently makes more attempts over time, indicated as a decrease in $\Delta attempt$, it is regarded that the child has perseverance. On the other hand, a child who consistently attempts less over time, indicated as an increase in $\Delta attempt$, was considered as showing less perseverance. Using Mann-Kendall trend test, we analyzed each participant's significance in the $\Delta attempt$ trend (derivative of $\Delta attempt$). Kendall's correlation coefficient τ ranges from -1 (100% negative association, or perfect inversion) to $+1$ (100% positive association, or perfect agreement).

We used an unpaired t-test on Kendall's coefficients between conditions. The result revealed a significant effect between conditions (NEUTRAL $M = 0.0933$, $SD = 0.13$, GROWTH $M = 0.0016$, $SD = 0.12$; t(37) = 2.3053, p =

0.02686, Cohen's d=0.74), the GROWTH condition showing a stronger trend towards more perseverance. In Figure 7, the *tau* coefficient values for all participants are shown. The diamond markers indicate individuals with a significant trend in $\Delta attempt$. A Freeman-Halton extension of the Fisher exact probability test on the trend result summed into three categories ("significant positive", "significant negative", and "no significant change") also revealed a significant effect between conditions (p=0.022) in the trend direction. Namely, the GROWTH condition showed strong negative trend (demonstrating increasing perseverance over time) while the NEUTRAL condition showed positive trend.

In summary, children's perseverance behavior was measured by the change in the frequency of their attempts over time. Children in the GROWTH condition showed a stronger trend towards an increased frequency of attempts over time compared to the NEUTRAL condition, supporting our second hypothesis, **H2**. While most participants showed a steady frequency of attempts from beginning to end when solving a difficult puzzle, more participants who interacted with the growth mindset robot strongly demonstrated more resilience to failure over time.

4.3 Spatial Skill Assessment

In total, 36 children completed the pre- and post- spatial skill assessment app. One refused to participate in the pre-test, and three children either had to leave or refused to complete the post-test. Out of 36 children, 20 were in the NEUTRAL condition (age $M = 6.75$, $SD = 1.07$, female 45%), and 16 in the GROWTH condition (age $M = 6.69$, $SD = 1.14$, female 38%).

We summed the number of CMTT puzzles each participant answered correctly in pre- and post-tests. The medians of the pre- and post-tests were 12 and 13, respectively, showing a slight increase. Using the Wilcoxon signed-rank test, we found a significant effect on children's score before and after playing tangrams with the robot. The mean ranks of the pre- and post-tests were 31.26 and 41.74, respectively; W = 52, Z = 7.38, p < 2.2e-16, r = 1.23. All other between condition pre- and post-analyses, including Mann-Whitney's U test and Chi-square test, revealed no significant differences.

These results confirm our third hypothesis, **H3** that there was a slight increase in spatial skill score after playing with the robot, but it was not condition dependent.

4.4 Perceived Robot Mindset

All 40 children participated in the post-survey with questionnaires about Tega's mindset. The medians of the NEUTRAL and GROWTH conditions were 26.50 and 28 points, respectively. Using Mann-Whitney's U test, we found a significant effect per condition (the mean ranks of the pre- and post- tests were 16.60 and 24.40, respectively; W = 122, Z = -2.1269, p = 0.03292, r = 0.34), with the GROWTH group evaluating their robot to have a more growth-oriented mindset than the NEUTRAL group, supporting hypothesis **H4**.

5. DISCUSSION

The notion of growth mindset as formulated by Dweck [8] includes two main attributes, namely, a belief in the malleability of the brain to learn, adapt, and improve, as well as a belief in effort as a prerequisite to success. The former is highly related to the notion of curiosity, i.e. the intrinsic drive to learn [11], while the latter relates to perseverance and grit [7]. Indeed, Tega's comments and questionnaire sentences in the mindset assessment task related to the desire to learn, and the perseverance task we adopted from [22, 24] measured how children cope and continue in a challenging task.

Given the potential of social robots as peer-like companions, it behooves us to study the mechanisms by which children learn from social robots, as well as the similarities and differences between children's learning from robots as compared to human partners and other technologies. In the new paradigm explored in this work, our peer-like social robot exhibits a growth mindset in how it plays and engages with a child. The activities are also used as a probe to measure children's perseverance in the face of challenge. We examined whether young children will recognize a growth mindset of a social robot, and whether they will internalize this to influence their own. Our findings suggest a provocative new kind of relationship and interaction paradigm between children and robots, where children can identify and socially model the attributes they see in peer-like robots.

6. CONCLUSIONS AND FUTURE WORK

How children approach learning and challenge is as important as what academic skills and knowledge they acquire through education. Social robots have the potential to open new methods for how to assess and develop effective interventions that *broadly* serve children's learning skills, attitudes, and abilities.

In this work, we investigated the effects an autonomous social robot's mindset driven behavior has on a child's own mindset. Our results show that children can recognize a growth mindset exhibited by an autonomous social robot, and can socially model this in their self-reported beliefs about their own mindset, while also supporting this with consistent behaviors indicative of having perseverance.

In future work we intend to investigate the effects of long-term interaction with a growth mindset robot. We hypothesize a two-phase influence, wherein initially a growth mindset will be promoted, followed by increased learning gains. Furthermore, we intend to extend the expressive cognitive architecture of the robot to include other high-level aspects of learning, e.g., curiosity, and study the effects of such a complex architecture on children's behavior, attitudes, and learning outcomes.

7. ACKNOWLEDGMENTS

The authors would like to thank Madelyn Payne and Tonghui Zhu for assisting conducting the user study. This research was supported by the National Institute of Health (NIH), under grant 5R01HD086899-02. Any opinions, findings and conclusions, or recommendations expressed in this paper are those of the authors and do not represent the views of the grant agency.

8. REFERENCES

[1] D. H. Ackley, G. E. Hinton, and T. J. Sejnowski. A learning algorithm for boltzmann machines. *Cognitive science*, 9(1):147–169, 1985.

[2] P. Alves-Oliveira, P. Arriaga, G. Hoffman, and A. Paiva. Boosting Children's Creativity Through Creative Interactions with Social Robots. In *The Eleventh ACM/IEEE International Conference on Human Robot Interaction*, HRI '16, pages 591–592, Piscataway, NJ, USA, 2016. IEEE Press.

[3] J. Aronson, C. B. Fried, and C. Good. Reducing the Effects of Stereotype Threat on African American College Students by Shaping Theories of Intelligence. *Journal of Experimental Social Psychology*, 38(2):113–125, Mar. 2002.

[4] L. S. Blackwell, K. H. Trzesniewski, and C. S. Dweck. Implicit theories of intelligence predict achievement across an adolescent transition: A longitudinal study and an intervention. *Child development*, 78(1):246–263, 2007.

[5] G. Bohning and J. K. Althouse. Using tangrams to teach geometry to young children. *Early childhood education journal*, 24(4):239–242, 1997.

[6] C. Breazeal, P. Harris, D. DeSteno, J. Kory, L. Dickens, and S. Jeong. Young children treat robots as informants. *Topics in Cognitive Science*, page (under review), 2014.

[7] A. L. Duckworth, C. Peterson, M. D. Matthews, and D. R. Kelly. Grit: Perseverance and passion for long-term goals. *Journal of Personality and Social Psychology*, 92(6):1087–1101, 2007.

[8] C. Dweck. *Mindset: The new psychology of success*. Random House LLC, 2006.

[9] C. S. Dweck. Mindsets and human nature: promoting change in the Middle East, the schoolyard, the racial divide, and willpower. *American Psychologist*, 67(8):614, 2012.

[10] S. B. Ehrlich, S. C. Levine, and S. Goldin-Meadow. The importance of gesture in children's spatial reasoning. *Developmental psychology*, 42(6):1259, 2006.

[11] S. Engel. *The Hungry Mind: The origins of curiosity in childhood*. Harvard University Press (in press), 2015.

[12] C. Good, J. Aronson, and M. Inzlicht. Improving adolescents' standardized test performance: An intervention to reduce the effects of stereotype threat. *Journal of Applied Developmental Psychology*, 24(6):645–662, Dec. 2003.

[13] G. Gordon and C. Breazeal. Bayesian Active Learning-Based Robot Tutor for Children's Word-Reading Skills. In *AAAI*, pages 1343–1349, 2015.

[14] G. Gordon, C. Breazeal, and S. Engel. Can children catch curiosity from a social robot? In *Proceedings of the Tenth Annual ACM/IEEE International Conference on Human-Robot Interaction*, pages 91–98. ACM, 2015.

[15] G. Gordon, S. Spaulding, J. K. Westlund, J. J. Lee, L. Plummer, M. Martinez, M. Das, and C. Breazeal. Affective Personalization of a Social Robot Tutor for ChildrenâĂŹs Second Language Skills. In *Thirtieth AAAI Conference on Artificial Intelligence*, 2016.

[16] E. A. Gunderson, S. J. Gripshover, C. Romero, C. S. Dweck, S. Goldin-Meadow, and S. C. Levine. Parent Praise to 1-3 Year-Olds Predicts Children's Motivational Frameworks 5 Years Later. *Child development*, 84(5):1526–1541, Sept. 2013.

[17] G. D. Heyman and C. S. Dweck. Children's Thinking about Traits: Implications for Judgments of the Self and Others. *Child Development*, 69(2):391–403, Apr. 1998.

[18] J. Jirout. 'i try to learn as much as i can' vs. 'i try to get the best grade i can': A study of children's ideas about learning and school. In *Cognitive Development Society Meeting*, 2015.

[19] M. L. Kamins and C. S. Dweck. Person versus process praise and criticism: Implications for contingent self-worth and coping. *Developmental Psychology*, 35(3):835–847, 1999.

[20] S. C. Levine, J. Huttenlocher, A. Taylor, and A. Langrock. Early sex differences in spatial skill. *Developmental psychology*, 35(4):940, 1999.

[21] J. Movellan, M. Eckhardt, M. Virnes, and A. Rodriguez. Sociable robot improves toddler vocabulary skills. In *Proceedings of the 4th ACM/IEEE international conference on Human robot interaction*, pages 307–308, 2009.

[22] C. M. Mueller and C. S. Dweck. Praise for intelligence can undermine children's motivation and performance. *Journal of Personality and Social Psychology*, 75(1):33–52, 1998.

[23] K. Oflazer. Solving tangram puzzles: A connectionist approach. *International Journal of Intelligent Systems*, 8(5):603–616, Jan. 1993.

[24] E. O'Rourke, K. Haimovitz, C. Ballweber, C. Dweck, and Z. Popovic. Brain points: a growth mindset incentive structure boosts persistence in an educational game. pages 3339–3348. ACM Press, 2014.

[25] H. W. Park, R. A. Coogle, and A. Howard. Using a shared tablet workspace for interactive demonstrations during human-robot learning scenarios. In *2014 IEEE International Conference on Robotics and Automation (ICRA)*, pages 2713–2719. IEEE, 2014.

[26] H. W. Park and A. M. Howard. Understanding a child's play for robot interaction by sequencing play primitives using hidden markov models. In *Robotics and Automation (ICRA), 2010 IEEE International Conference on*, pages 170–177. IEEE, 2010.

[27] H. W. Park and A. M. Howard. Retrieving experience: Interactive instance-based learning methods for building robot companions. In *2015 IEEE International Conference on Robotics and Automation (ICRA)*, pages 6140–6145. IEEE, 2015.

[28] Z. Qu, C. Yu, Y. Shi, J. Huang, L. Tian, and Y. Shi. TangramTheatre: presenting children's creation on multimodal tabletops. In *CHI'14 Extended Abstracts on Human Factors in Computing Systems*, pages 2077–2082. ACM, 2014.

[29] M. Quigley, K. Conley, B. Gerkey, J. Faust, T. Foote, J. Leibs, R. Wheeler, and A. Y. Ng. Ros: an open-source robot operating system. In *ICRA workshop on open source software*, volume 3, page 5. Kobe, Japan, 2009.

[30] P. A. Smiley and C. S. Dweck. Individual differences in achievement goals among young children. *Child development*, 65(6):1723–1743, 1994.

[31] F. Tanaka and S. Matsuzoe. Children teach a care-receiving robot to promote their learning: Field experiments in a classroom for vocabulary learning. *Journal of Human-Robot Interaction*, 1(1), 2012.

[32] J. K. Westlund, J. J. Lee, L. Plummer, F. Faridi, J. Gray, M. Berlin, H. Quintus-Bosz, R. Hartmann, M. Hess, S. Dyer, and others. Tega: A Social Robot. In *2016 11th ACM/IEEE International Conference on Human-Robot Interaction (HRI)*, pages 561–561. IEEE, 2016.

[33] D. S. Yeager and C. S. Dweck. Mindsets that promote resilience: When students believe that personal characteristics can be developed. *Educational Psychologist*, 47(4):302–314, 2012.

Give Me a Break! Personalized Timing Strategies to Promote Learning in Robot-Child Tutoring

Aditi Ramachandran, Chien-Ming Huang, Brian Scassellati
Department of Computer Science
Yale University
{aditi.ramachandran, chien-ming.huang, brian.scassellati}@yale.edu

ABSTRACT

A common practice in education to accommodate the short attention spans of children during learning is to provide them with non-task breaks for cognitive rest. Holding great promise to promote learning, robots can provide these breaks at times personalized to individual children. In this work, we investigate personalized timing strategies for providing breaks to young learners during a robot tutoring interaction. We build an autonomous robot tutoring system that monitors student performance and provides break activities based on a personalized schedule according to performance. We conduct a field study to explore the effects of different strategies for providing breaks during tutoring. By comparing a fixed timing strategy with a *reward* strategy (break timing personalized to performance gains) and a *refocus* strategy (break timing personalized to performance drops), we show that the personalized strategies promote learning gains for children more effectively than the fixed strategy. Our results also reveal immediate benefits in enhancing efficiency and accuracy in completing educational problems after personalized breaks, showing the restorative effects of the breaks when administered at the right time.

Keywords

Child-robot Interaction; Personalization; Education

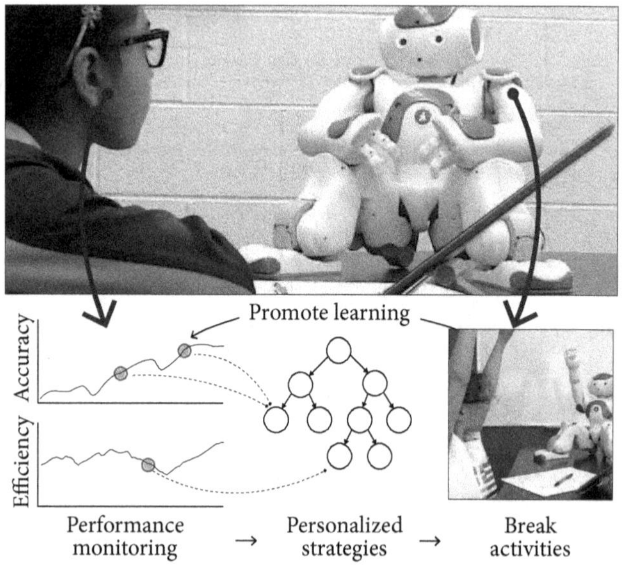

Figure 1: We studied personalized strategies for providing breaks to promote children's learning during one-on-one tutoring interactions with a robot.

1. INTRODUCTION

Among the large variety of learning technologies available, social robots have shown great promise as tutoring agents [9, 10, 29]. The advantages of physical embodiment especially help establish effective human-robot interactions [25, 33]. Prior human-robot interaction (HRI) research has also demonstrated that embodied tutoring agents can increase cognitive learning gains [15]. Moreover, robots can increase enjoyment and can provide social and emotional support [12, 22, 27] to facilitate effective learning. In addition, robots can personalize their tutoring strategies to meet various needs, such as different learning capacities and readiness levels, and can provide individualized experiences to maximize learning outcomes for students. As informed by the intelligent tutoring systems (ITS) community (e.g., [2]), prior HRI work has explored the impact of personalization on student learning and has demonstrated that personalized learning interactions can greatly benefit student learning outcomes [14, 26]. However, prior work has mainly studied content personalization, focusing on providing educational content that suits the student's ability and progress.

Aside from educational content, one crucial aspect in a learning interaction is the student's engagement and attention, particularly for younger learners who often have short attention spans. The attention spans of children can be as short as five minutes in a learning interaction [23], and the capacity for sustained attention only develops significantly between age 11 and adulthood [17]. Accommodating this need in learning interactions for young students is extremely important. Research has suggested that breaks are beneficial and provide needed cognitive rest during learning [1, 16]. Moreover, interspersing non-task breaks into an extended learning task may reduce interference and strengthen the learner's performance [3, 32]. Therefore, to effectively promote learning for younger students, robots need to intelli-

HRI '17, March 06-09, 2017, Vienna, Austria

DOI: http://dx.doi.org/10.1145/2909824.3020209

gently provide necessary breaks over the course of a learning interaction (Figure 1).

Break timing—when to provide a break—is particularly important, as it allows students to have needed cognitive rest at the right time. In a traditional learning environment, such as a classroom, breaks are usually taken at regular intervals. On the other hand, in a tutoring interaction, breaks can take place at times personalized to an individual. Breaks can be positive reinforcers for desired behavior (e.g., improved learning performance). Alternatively, breaks can be an opportunity for students to refocus after experiencing a decline in learning performance. In this work, we explore how a tutoring robot can provide breaks following a personalized schedule based on learning performance and seek to understand how such personalization might influence student learning outcomes.

2. BACKGROUND

In this section, we present literature showing that breaks can contribute to effective learning, and offer evidence about different ways to provide these breaks. We then review prior HRI work involving personalization in learning.

2.1 Non-task Breaks and Learning Gains

Breaks—pausing the current task to rest or to work on a different task—are beneficial for cognitive- and attention-loaded tasks. For example, during cognitive work involving recognition memory, breaks can foster achievement gains [32]. Furthermore, breaks of varying lengths can have restorative effects on reaction time during an auditory response task [16]. Accordingly, breaks play an important role in learning, a complex activity demanding the learner's cognitive attention. Learning can be particularly challenging for children, as their attention spans can be quite short, making them susceptible to distractions during learning [3, 23]. In support of this need, a common educational practice is to provide breaks throughout a school day at scheduled times. Primary schools in various countries that allow children to take 10- to 15-minute breaks every 40 to 45 minutes of classroom instruction report increased attentiveness after the breaks, indicating the importance of breaks during learning [20, 21]. However, limited time and resources during a school day necessitate that all children receive these breaks at the same time. Each individual has different learning needs and varied attention spans, suggesting that these non-task breaks may be most useful if provided at the "right" time.

Alternative educational practices suggest that non-task breaks could be provided in ways more personalized to each individual. For example, *success-based rewards* can enhance performance [24]. This provides evidence for one design of a personalized timing strategy for breaks in which breaks are used as success-based rewards for students demonstrating learning improvement. This strategy uses these breaks as a positive reinforcer for desired performance improvements. Another classroom practice, *positive time-out*, informs a second design of a personalized timing strategy to prevent or mitigate negative emotions. "Positive time-out" allows a child to take a brief break to avoid outbursts caused by affective reactions such as frustration [18]. Students can experience a wide variety of negative emotions during learning, often due to poor performance, and these can have a further negative impact on learning gains [19]. Thus, this strategy provides breaks during moments of potential negative emotion to enhance learning gains.

2.2 Personalized Robot Tutoring

Social robots have been shown to be a promising educational technology, largely because of their capabilities to provide personalized instruction for individual students [5]. Prior work done in this domain has focused on content-based personalization where the robot's personalized behavior directly involves the content of the learning task at hand. For example, Leyzberg et al. showed that providing personalized lessons based on an assessment of a person's skills on a cognitive task could significantly improve performance as compared to those who received non-personalized lessons or no lessons at all [14]. Westlund and Breazeal demonstrated that children showed vocabulary improvements in a story-telling task over time when the robot personalized the difficulty level of the words to match the child's ability [34]. Another relevant study by Schadenberg et al. explored the personalization of the difficulty level of a game that children played with a social robot, demonstrating that the level could be effectively adapted to each individual according to an ongoing assessment of the child's performance [28]. Different from prior studies, in this work, we explore how non-content personalization can impact learning outcomes.

Learning is a complex process involving a variety of supportive mechanisms that are often not directly related to the cognitive task at hand, such as help-seeking behavior, affective support, and rapport-building. Prior work in HRI has explored how robot tutors might personalize their behavior based on some of these supporting mechanisms. For example, Ramachandran et al. showed that a robot employing adaptive strategies that regulate a child's use of help while solving math problems can improve learning gains [26]. Gordon et al. studied a robot employing affective personalization and used reinforcement learning to discern which affective states each child preferred for the robot during a learning interaction [4]. Similarly, Henkemans et al. demonstrated the potential of a health education robot that personalized its behavior towards a child by referring to the child's name, favorite activity, and color during conversation [6]. Our work explores the personalization of the timing of when to provide breaks during tutoring to enhance learning.

The HRI community has further explored computational methods to estimate the engagement or attention of a user and has studied how robots can utilize the estimation to create effective learning. Leite et al. built data-driven classifiers to detect disengagement in groups of children versus individual children [11]. Other recent work by Lemaignan et al. defined an online method of assessing a child's attention during a learning interaction [13]. Szafir and Mutlu showed that a robot can monitor attention in real-time based on EEG sensor data and use this information adaptively to improve student recall ability [30]. Rather than elaborated estimation of attentional state, our work uses performance-based features during learning to guide tutoring interactions.

3. ROBOT TUTORING SYSTEM

In this section, we provide an overview of our design of an autonomous robot tutoring system (Figure 2). We also present the personalized strategies and support mechanisms implemented for our investigation of how the robot tutor may personalize break timing to promote learning.

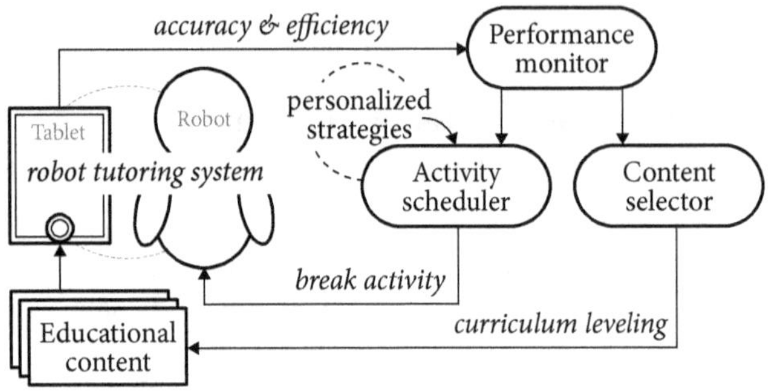

Figure 2: System architecture of our robot tutoring system.

3.1 System Overview

Our robot tutoring system consists of three main software components—*performance monitor*, *activity scheduler*, and *content selector*. The performance monitor is responsible for continuously tracking the student's learning performance, particularly his or her accuracy and efficiency at solving the educational problems presented on a tablet. The activity scheduler utilizes the collected performance information as well as personalized strategies to decide when to provide a non-task break activity during the student's learning interaction. The content selector uses the student's accuracy performance to selectively pick subsequent educational content that matches the student's mastery of the learning material. Specifically, the content selector decides the suitable difficulty level of the problems presented to the student. We use the Nao robot in our system to provide tutoring support.

3.2 Personalized Strategies

In this work, we explore three strategies for choosing when to provide a break during a tutoring interaction. The implementation of these strategies will be discussed in Section 4.2. Below, we describe the design rationale of these strategies.

Fixed strategy—This strategy provides breaks to students on a fixed schedule at regular intervals, reflecting the classroom practice that all children receive breaks at specified times rather than times particular to the individual.

Reward strategy—This strategy provides breaks as a reward after good performance as informed by the educational practice of "success-based rewards" [24]. This strategy seeks to postively reinforce desired learning improvement.

Refocus strategy—This strategy seeks to interrupt negative behaviors, such as distraction, during learning by providing a break when a drop in performance is detected. This design is informed by the educational practice of "positive time-out" [18], providing a student with the opportunity to refocus by taking a break from the task at hand.

3.3 Support Mechanisms for Tutoring

In addition to the personalized strategies, our system also implements several basic support mechanisms, including providing necessary information on the tablet application and exhibiting engaging robot behaviors, to facilitate tutoring interactions with young learners. All behaviors described in this section apply to all students regardless of the assigned conditions for the user study described in Section 4.2. At the start of a tutoring session, the robot greets each student and conducts a small, interactive lesson on an educational topic. After the lesson, the robot presents a series of questions on the taught topic for the student to practice. We carefully designed robot behaviors to give the students the impression that the robot was responsible for facilitating the learning interaction. For instance, the robot looks at the students when speaking and looks at the tablet while they work on practice questions. The robot also uses gestures throughout a session, often extending an arm towards the tablet to invite students to direct their attention towards it.

The content selector chooses each practice question from a bank of problems with multiple difficulty levels to accommodate a variety of learners. All students start with the lowest level of questions available and can only advance to subsequent levels after demonstrating a specified level of mastery. The robot provides feedback on whether an answer is correct or incorrect after each individual problem. If the answer is incorrect, the robot also provides general feedback about how to solve the problem, while the tablet displays the associated worked-out solution. Moreover, the tutoring application helps manage the flow of the tutoring interaction by providing buttons on the screen that allow the student to initiate the presentation of the next problem and disabling buttons displayed on the tablet while the robot verbally delivers tutoring information. Upon reaching the allotted time, the robot congratulates the student for completing a session.

4. METHODS

In this section, we describe a user study investigating the effects of different personalized strategies for determining break timing, as employed by the robot tutoring system described in Section 3, on students' learning outcomes.

4.1 Evaluation Context

The user study was contextualized in a tutoring interaction in which children learned about mathematical concepts and then practiced these concepts by completing problems with the robot, thereby creating a repetitive learning interaction. Students completed a 40-minute learning interaction to approximate the length of a scheduled class period during an elementary school day. We present the educational content below, and provide a description of the non-task break activities that were used across all experimental conditions.

4.1.1 Educational Content

We chose to teach two math concepts involved in "order of operations" that the students had not previously learned in their classrooms. Specifically, the students learned that multiplication comes before addition and subtraction (C_1: *multiplication*), as well as the concept that parentheses come before all other operations, including multiplication (C_2: *parentheses*). We designed practice problems for each of the two concepts for three difficulty levels; examples are provided in Table 1. Students had to complete a minimum of ten questions per difficulty level. Moreover, they needed to

Table 1: Examples of practice math problems for each of the concepts and difficulty levels given to the students.

	C_1: *Multiplication*	C_2: *Parentheses*
Level 1	$2 + 8 \times 2$	$5 \times (2 + 4)$
Level 2	$5 + 6 \times 1 + 6 \times 4$	$6 + (2 + 6) \times 7$
Level 3	$31 + 5 \times 9 - 7 \times 4$	$8 + 8 \times (1 + 5) + 3$

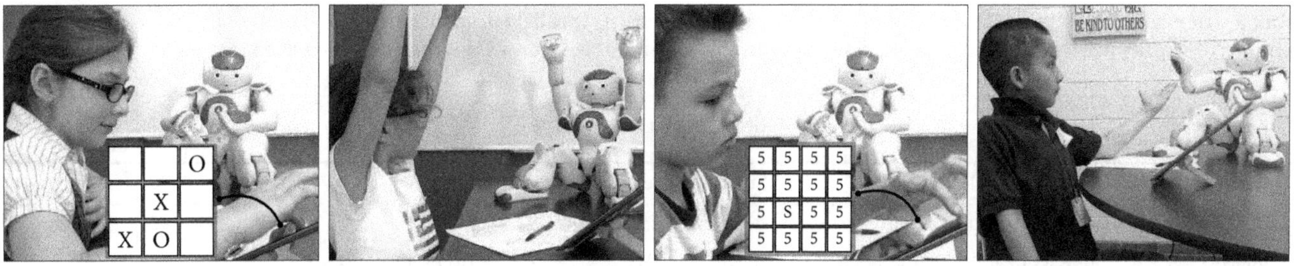

(a) Game play: tic-tac-toe (b) Physical exercise: stretch activity (c) Refocusing activity: spot-it (d) Relaxation: breathing activity

Figure 3: Four break activities that were received during the tutoring session. Each break activity lasted about two minutes.

achieve 70% accuracy to be considered to have mastery of that difficulty level before advancing to the next level.

4.1.2 Break Activities

Throughout the tutoring session, the robot provided the students with brief breaks from the learning activity. We designed four break activities that leveraged the physical and social nature of the robot, including game play, physical exercise, a refocusing activity, and relaxation, which all students could receive in the same order (Figure 3). Each activity lasted approximately two minutes and aimed to provide mental "rest" from the math-based task. The stretch and relaxation breaks were specifically designed to be two minutes long, whereas children completed as many rounds of tic-tac-toe and the visual focus activity as they could within two minutes. The robot engaged with the child during each activity; the robot played tic-tac-toe against the child, led the child in the stretch and relaxation exercises, and facilitated each round of the refocusing activity. Students were not informed in advance that they would be receiving breaks, thereby eliminating any initial expectation for breaks.

4.2 Experimental Design

We designed a between-subjects study involving three experimental conditions—*fixed*, *reward*, and *refocus*—that realized the three strategies described in Section 3.2. The only independent variable in this study was the timing of the breaks. Table 2 summarizes the implementation of the activity scheduler, listing the triggers that initiated breaks in the experimental conditions. Below, we provide detailed descriptions of the conditions and our implementation of the triggering mechanisms used in all conditions.

4.2.1 Fixed Condition

In the *fixed* condition, the robot provided a break at regular intervals for each student regardless of their real-time performance on the learning task. This design reflects the classroom practice that all students get breaks at the same time as everyone else, regardless of an individual's need for a break. Acknowledging the short attention spans of children [23], we implemented the fixed strategy by providing a break every six minutes, allowing most participating students to receive the four distinct breaks over the 40-minute session.

4.2.2 Reward Condition

The *reward* condition, as informed by the educational practice of "success-based rewards" [24], implemented the reward strategy as described in Section 3.2. In this condition, the robot provided a break to the user upon detection of substantial improvement during the session. The performance monitor measured learning performance using two quantities: the accuracy of the student in answering questions correctly, and the time it took for the student to complete each question. A local *window* of recent history (five questions) of user performance (see Figure 4) was kept for both accuracy data and timing data as the session progressed. After each question, the local window data was compared to the entire *history* of data to understand whether there had been a performance increase in accuracy and efficiency (timing). The history data was reset when the difficulty level changed.

The implementation of the reward strategy can be represented conceptually as a decision tree (Table 2). First, the strategy considered increases in accuracy (type 2). Subsequently, the strategy would consider improvements in timing (type 3). Based on whether sizable changes (20%) occurred with the local windows of accuracy and timing as compared to the whole history, a break was given to the participant. If no substantial performance changes occurred for ten consecutive questions, but the participant's overall history of accuracy remained high ($\geq$70%), the student received a break for performing consistently well (type 4).

4.2.3 Refocus Condition

The *refocus* condition, as informed by "positive time-out" [18], provided a break upon detecting performance drops. The implementation of this condition also relied on the performance monitor calculating a local window of accuracy data as well as timing data in the same way as previously described for the reward condition. The conceptual decision tree structure applies here, as well: we first considered

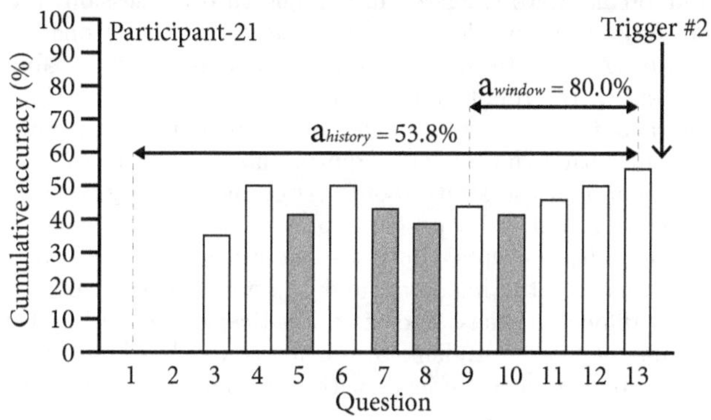

Figure 4: Sample user accuracy data showing how *window* and *history* values were calculated. The window size was five questions. Here, trigger type 2 was initiated because the percent change between $\mathbf{a}_{history}$ and $\mathbf{a}_{window}$ was greater than 20%. Gray bars represent incorrect answers.

Table 2: Break triggering mechanisms for each condition. Percent changes from history to window data for accuracy and timing are represented by $\Delta Accuracy$ and $\Delta Time$, respectively. Overall history accuracy is denoted by $\mathbf{a}_{history}$. N is the number of times each type was triggered. The conceptual decision tree shows the order in which the triggers were considered.

Condition	Trigger type	Description	Implementation	N	Conceptual decision tree
Fixed	1	Fixed schedule	Six minutes elapsed	39	N/A
Reward	2	Accuracy improvement	$\Delta Accuracy \geq 20\%$	43	
	3	Efficiency improvement	$\Delta Time \leq -20\%$, $\mathrm{a}_{history} \geq 70\%$, $\lvert\Delta Accuracy\rvert \leq 20\%$	0	
	4	Good performance over time	$\{ \lvert\Delta Accuracy\rvert , \lvert\Delta Time\rvert \} \leq 20\%$ for 10 questions, $\mathrm{a}_{history} \geq 70\%$	1	
Refocus	5	Efficiency drop	$\Delta Time \geq 20\%$, $\lvert\Delta Accuracy\rvert \leq 20\%$	14	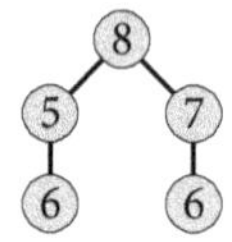
	6	Low performance over time	$\{ \lvert\Delta Accuracy\rvert , \lvert\Delta Time\rvert \} \leq 20\%$ for 10 questions, $\mathrm{a}_{history} < 70\%$	2	
	7	Timing drop, indicating guessing	$\Delta Time \leq -20\%$, $\mathrm{a}_{history} < 70\%$, $\lvert\Delta Accuracy\rvert \leq 20\%$	15	
	8	Accuracy drop	$\Delta Accuracy \leq -20\%$	13	

drops in accuracy (type 8), followed by changes in efficiency as measured by time to complete each problem (types 5 and 7). If the drop in performance between the local window and the entire history was sufficient (20%), a break was triggered. If no sizable performance drops (20%) occurred but the participant's overall history of accuracy remained low (under 70%) for ten questions in a row, the student received a break for low overall performance over time (type 6).

4.3 Experimental Procedure and Setup

Both parental and child consent for each student was obtained prior to conducting this study. Additionally, children were informed that there were no negative consequences for stopping the interaction at any time. Participating students were removed from their classrooms one at a time for the duration of approximately one hour each. Students were first asked to complete a pretest, consisting of 12 questions, to assess their knowledge of the learning concepts. Free-response questions were used to prevent students from answering correctly due to guessing. After the pretest, students engaged with the robot in a 40-minute tutoring session. This session consisted of a short lesson from the robot, followed by a series of practice problems for students to complete. According to the experimental conditions, the robot provided corresponding breaks throughout the session. If more than four breaks were triggered in a single tutoring session, the break activities would repeat starting from the first one.

During the tutoring interaction, students sat at a table in front of the robot and the tablet (Figure 1). Each child interacted exclusively with the autonomous robot tutoring system during the session, requiring no input from the experimenter in the study room. After the tutoring session, students completed a posttest to assess their knowledge of the learning concepts. Both the pretest and posttest were the same length, including four questions of each of the three difficulty levels, and were identical except the order of the questions. Students also completed a brief questionnaire about their experience with the robot. Students were given pencils and stickers after completing the entire study and returned to their classrooms.

4.4 Measures

To explore how personalized break timing may impact learning outcomes, we employ three objective measures: (1) *learning gains*, (2) *efficiency* in problem solving, and (3) *accuracy* in problem solving. We define normalized learning gain (*nlg*) that captures the normalized difference between pretest and posttest scores for each student i:

$$nlg(i) = \frac{score_{\text{post}}(i) - score_{\text{pre}}(i)}{1 - score_{\text{pre}}(i)}$$

Both the pretest and posttest scores are represented as accuracy scores calculated by dividing the number of questions answered correctly by the total number of questions. This *nlg* metric, ranging from -1.0 to 1.0, provides an index of improvement for each student, accounting for differing incoming knowledge levels.

In addition to learning gains, we seek to understand whether the break activities have any immediate effects on student performance in completing each problem. To this end, we calculate average efficiency and accuracy in solving problems, using a window of five problems, before and after each break. As breaks were initiated by different trigger types (Table 2), we assess the difference between performance before and after the breaks separately for each trigger type.

4.5 Participants

Forty students were recruited from elementary schools to participate in this study and were randomly assigned to one of three experimental conditions. Two participants were excluded from this data analysis due to non-compliance and technical problems during data collection, resulting in a total of 38 participants (13 females). Among the 38 participants, there were 12, 14, and 12 participants in the fixed, reward, and refocus conditions, respectively. The participating students were in third grade; the average age was 8.53 years old (SD=.60). The groups were gender balanced, and there were no major differences found between the three conditions regarding age. Pretest scores for the three groups were: Fixed (M = .33, SD = .33); Reward (M = .18, SD = .28); Refocus (M = .25, SD = .18). A one-way ANOVA showed no statistical differences between the three groups, $F(2, 35) = 1.04$, $p = .363$, regarding the pretest.

5. RESULTS

In this section, we first present findings characterizing how the robot tutoring system was used by students, to provide a

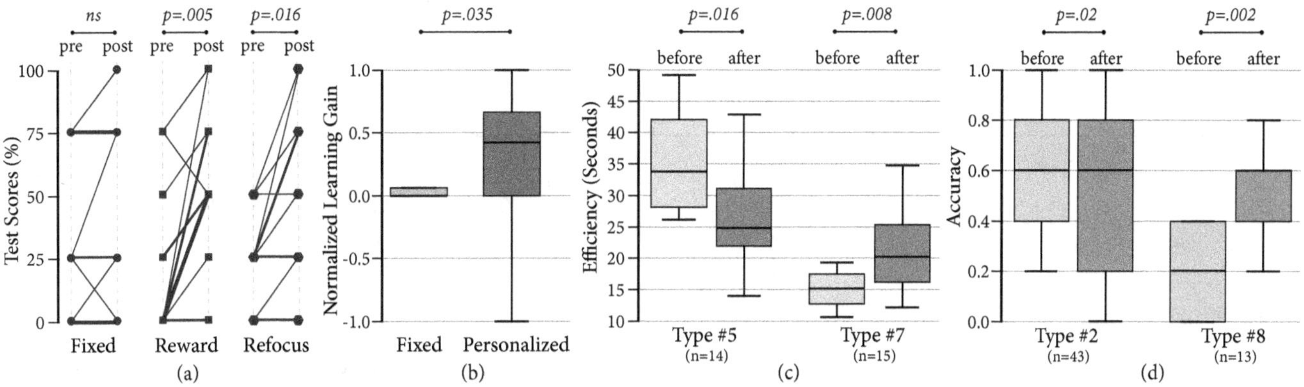

Figure 5: Results show the benefits of personalized break timing strategies: (a) Both the reward and refocus groups significantly improved in learning gains from pretest to posttest. Thicker lines indicate multiple participants with the same scores. (b) The personalization group (reward and refocus groups combined) improved significantly more than the fixed group, as measured by nlg. (c) Trigger types 5 and 7 significantly affected how much time students spent on problems before and after breaks. (d) Trigger types 2 and 8 significantly affected accuracy scores before and after breaks. For all boxplots, the darker line inside the box represents the median, and the extents of the box represent the first and third quartiles.

basis for our further data analyses. We then present results on student learning gains and performance during problem solving (summarized in Figure 5). For all the statistical tests reported below, we used an α level of .05 for significance. We used non-parametric statistical tests when appropriate according to the distribution of the analyzed data.

5.1 Characterization of Tutoring Sessions

Participating students were from differing backgrounds and were not able to make homogeneous progress throughout the sessions. Across the three conditions, 52.6% of the students remained in level one for the entire session, 26.3% progressed to level two, and 21.1% were able to progress to level three. Due to such diversity, in the following section, we focus our analyses on student performance on level one assessment questions to draw fair comparisons. While students received a varying number of break activities according to the timing strategies, the average number of breaks provided per student was 3.74, and this was not significantly different across conditions, $F(2, 35) = .749$, $p = .480$. Moreover, the number of breaks received and normalized learning gain were not correlated for participants in all groups, $r(36) = .10$, $p = .540$ (Pearson correlation). Furthermore, not all types of triggers were initiated equally during the sessions. The number of times that triggers were initiated is summarized in Table 2. In the reward condition, trigger type 2 (accuracy improvement) was initiated most frequently, whereas type 3 was never initiated and type 4 was only initiated once. In the refocus condition, trigger types 5, 7, and 8 occurred at a comparable rate, while type 6 was only observed twice. Accordingly, we considered trigger types that were initiated more than twice, namely types 1, 2, 5, 7, and 8, in our analyses of the effects of each trigger type.

5.2 Learning Gains

As less than 50% of the students advanced past the level-one difficulty, we focused our analysis on level-one questions to understand learning gains on content that all students spent time practicing with the robot. To assess whether students improved their scores from pretest to posttest, we used Wilcoxon Signed-ranks tests, treating the test score as a within-subjects measure, to assess each student's learning gains over the course of the tutoring session. Figure 5 (a) shows each student's score on the level-one difficulty questions on both the pretest and the posttest, separated according to experimental condition. Students in the fixed condition had posttest scores (Mdn = 1.0, $IQR = 3.0$) that did not differ significantly from their pretest scores (Mdn = 1.0, $IQR = 3.0$), $Z = -1.134$, $p = .257$. For students in the reward condition, posttest scores (Mdn = 2.0, $IQR = 1.25$) were significantly higher than pretest scores (Mdn = 0.0, $IQR = 1.25$), $Z = -2.829$, $p = .005$. Posttest scores (Mdn = 2.0, $IQR = 2.0$) were significantly higher than pretest scores (Mdn = 1.0, $IQR = 1.5$) for students in the refocus condition as well, $Z = -2.401$, $p = .016$. These results together show that the students who received personalized break timing strategies, either *reward* or *refocus*, significantly improved their scores, while the fixed group did not. These results provide evidence indicating that the personalization of when to provide breaks during a tutoring interaction can positively impact learning.

Next, we compared normalized learning gains, nlg, between groups using a Kruskal-Wallis test. This analysis showed marginal difference in nlg between the different conditions, $H(2) = 5.086$, $p = .079$. To further understand the potential benefits of personalized timing strategies, we created a *personalized* group by combining the reward and refocus groups. We then ran a Mann-Whitney test comparing nlg between the fixed and personalized groups (Figure 5 (b)). This comparison showed that the normalized learning gain was significantly greater for the personalized group (Mdn = .41, $IQR = .69$) than for the fixed group (Mdn = 0.0, $IQR = .19$), $U = 89.000$, $p = .035$.

5.3 Immediate Break Effects

Besides overall learning gains, we were interested in whether certain trigger types provided immediate effects on efficiency or accuracy during the tutoring interaction. Thus, we compared average performance (both efficiency and accuracy) for the window of five problems before and after each break separately for each trigger type using paired t-tests. Results for this analysis are in Table 3. These comparisons were carried out for each distinct trigger type as we sought to un-

Table 3: Results of t-tests used to assess immediate effects of breaks on accuracy and efficiency by trigger type. (*) and (**) denote $p < .050$ and $p < .010$, respectively. Significant results are shaded in green.

Trigger type	Description	N	Accuracy			Efficiency (Seconds)		
1	Fixed schedule	39	Before	After		Before	After	
			M=0.50 SD=0.27	M=0.52 SD=0.35	t(38)=-0.387 p=.701	M=45.42 SD=26.68	M=42.39 SD=26.21	t(38)=1.212 p=.233
2	Accuracy improvement	43	Before	After		Before	After	
			M=0.62 SD=0.24	M=0.50 SD=0.33	t(42)=2.412 p=.02*	M=24.92 SD=10.39	M=25.04 SD=10.79	t(42)=-0.089 p=.929
5	Efficiency drop	14	Before	After		Before	After	
			M=0.54 SD=0.28	M=0.50 SD=0.37	t(13)=0.763 p=.459	M=35.33 SD=8.10	M=26.66 SD=8.38	t(13)=2.765 p=.016*
7	Timing drop, indicating guessing	15	Before	After		Before	After	
			M=0.51 SD=0.33	M=0.39 SD=0.28	t(14)=1.890 p=.080	M=16.85 SD=6.77	M=21.65 SD=7.56	t(14)=-3.064 p=.008**
8	Accuracy drop	13	Before	After		Before	After	
			M=0.22 SD=0.17	M=0.52 SD=0.28	t(12)=-3.987 p=.002**	M=38.28 SD=20.05	M=34.96 SD=16.90	t(12)=1.307 p=.216

derstand how different timings of breaks (i.e., different types of trigger) might shape student efficiency and accuracy.

5.3.1 *Efficiency in Problem Solving*

Our analysis revealed that trigger types 5 and 7 had significant effects on how much time students spent on problems before and after breaks, as summarized in Figure 5 (c). Trigger type 5 was initiated when students' efficiency dropped while there were no sizable changes in their accuracy. Breaks triggered by type 5 improved students' efficiency significantly, as students spent significantly less time solving problems after the breaks as compared to the time they spent before the breaks. This result indicates that providing a break after this trigger may refocus the students, thus leading to improved efficiency in solving problems.

Trigger type 7 represented the situation where students' overall accuracy was not desirable, yet they spent less time on problems at hand, suggesting guessing on answers without investing time into each problem. Our analysis revealed that students spent significantly more time after breaks initiated by trigger type 7 than they did before. This increase in time spent on problems may suggest that after the breaks students were able to refocus their attention on the math task. Finally, for trigger types 1, 2, and 8, there was no significant difference in efficiency before and after the breaks.

5.3.2 *Accuracy in Problem Solving*

Results showed that trigger types 2 and 8 had significant effects on average accuracy before and after the breaks (Figure 5 (d)). Trigger type 2 was initiated upon detection of a local increase in accuracy, indicating that a student received a break based on this trigger while improving performance. The results of the t-test showed that average accuracy decreased after trigger type 2 was initiated. While the causes of this drop were not certain, we speculated that these breaks may have distracted some students in the short-term as they received them when they were in the "flow" of improving.

In the refocus condition, trigger type 8 was initiated specifically after a local performance drop was detected. Our analysis showed that students significantly improved their accuracy from before to after the breaks triggered by type 8. This improvement in accuracy following these breaks further suggests the restorative effects non-task breaks may have on performance during learning when triggered effectively. For trigger types 1, 5, and 7, there was no significant difference in accuracy before and after the breaks.

5.4 Additional Observations

In addition to the statistical analyses on student learning gains and perfomance in problem solving, we also made several observations and formed a preliminary understanding of students' experience of interacting with our tutoring system. Overall, we observed that the students were very engaged with the robot. They glanced periodically toward the robot and ocassionally touched the robot during the sessions. We also observed students enjoying interacting with the robot by expressing smiles and laughing. Additionally, most students followed the robot's instructions during breaks to stretch their bodies and participated in the relaxation activity.

Students rated their experience with the robot tutoring system positively on 5-point scales. There were no significant differences on these ratings between the study groups. In particular, students in the fixed ($M = 4.83$, $SD = 0.39$), reward ($M = 4.50$, $SD = 0.94$), and refocus ($M = 4.42$, $SD = 0.79$) groups felt refreshed after the provided breaks, $F(2, 35) = 1.028$, $p = .368$. Students also wanted to have a similar robot tutor to help with their math homework (fixed: $M = 4.42$, $SD = 1.24$; reward: $M = 4.50$, $SD = 1.02$; refocus: $M = 4.75$, $SD = 0.62$), $F(2, 35) = .368$, $p = .695$.

6. DISCUSSION

In this paper, we explore when a tutoring robot should provide a break to children to promote their learning. To this end, we developed an autonomous robot system to support tutoring interactions. We then conducted a field study to use our robot system to engage young students in learning math concepts. Our results showed that personalized timing strategies for providing breaks during learning can benefit students' learning gains. We further found that some strategies can lead to immediate performance benefits. Below, we discuss challenges in robot-child tutoring and the benefits of personalization we observed in our user study. We also discuss the limitations of this work that inform future work aiming to enable effective, personalized robot-child tutoring.

6.1 Challenges in Robot Tutoring

The major challenges in autonomous robot-child tutoring center around the vast individual differences between children during learning. In our study, less than half of the students progressed past the questions of the starting difficulty level. This observation indicates the diverse learning abilities present among children. In addition, children are likely to have differing preferences for teaching strategies of the robot and break activities they enjoy. For example, *learning by teaching* is an alternative teaching strategy that has been explored in HRI and may benefit learning for children [7, 31]. An effective robot tutor should therefore accommodate these potential differences in learners. Moreover, these robot tutors can employ nonverbal behaviors selectively to facilitate learning. For instance, Huang and Mutlu demonstrated that a robot emphasizing different types of gestures can shape how well the users remembered the information presented by the robot [8]. These challenges in diverse backgrounds and varying preferences provide rich opportunities for designing personalized interaction to promote learning.

6.2 Benefits of Personalization

Contributing to the increasing evidence showing the benefits of personalization in human-robot tutoring (e.g., [14, 26]), results of this work demonstrate the positive impact personalized break timing has on learning outcomes. While children in all conditions seemed to enjoy the breaks, only those in the personalized (reward and refocus) conditions showed significant learning gains (Figure 5 (a)). Moreover, the children with breaks on a personalized schedule outperformed those with breaks on a fixed schedule in terms of learning gains (Figure 5 (b)). These results show the importance of break timing during a learning interaction. Although we did not observe significant learning differences emerge as a result of employing different personalized strategies, our implementation of the reward and refocus strategies provide insight into how these strategies might be realized. Additional work is needed to explore alternative personalized strategies, such as a combination of the reward and refocus strategies, as well as other plausible implementation.

Our analysis also revealed that certain break triggers led to immediate changes in efficiency and accuracy during the tutoring interaction, providing design implications for robot tutoring systems. Specifically, breaks triggered based on negative performance changes led to desired immediate effects during learning, showing that performance-based metrics are useful features for providing breaks for cognitive rest. For example, after taking a break initiated by trigger type 5 (efficiency drop possibly signifying a negative affective state, such as disengagement), students improved their efficiency in problem solving, indicating a potential restorative effect following the break. Similarly, providing a break after trigger type 7 (timing drop, potentially due to guessing) prompted students to spend more time on problems, suggesting the break's potential to refocus the students on the learning task. Finally, breaks provided after trigger type 8 (drop in accuracy, possibly signifying frustration or confusion) led to an increase in accuracy following the break, again showing the potential of these breaks to refocus young learners. Together, these findings showed that the refocus strategy providing "positive time-out" had a positive impact on immediate learning performance.

However, these personalized triggers must be carefully designed, as not all of them led to positive performance changes. Initiating trigger type 2 to provide a break when students were showing improved accuracy caused accuracy to drop after the break. Interestingly, students receiving breaks as success-based rewards still benefitted over the whole session as evidenced by their improved test scores. More research is necessary to obtain a more comprehensive understanding of the broader effects of this type of trigger.

6.3 Limitations and Future Work

While showing benefits of personalized timing strategies for providing breaks, this work has limitations that inform future research. In this work, we contextualized our study in a single 40-minute one-on-one tutoring interaction. Participating students only interacted with our robot system once to learn two specific math concepts. Future research needs to consider how such tutoring systems may help children learn over several sessions and on a variety of learning topics. Moreover, we employed performance metrics of accuracy and efficiency to drive personalized strategies. While these metrics directly indicate how well the student learned, they do not capture information about visual attention, cognitive load, and other related processes involved in learning. Future work should include a variety of channels of information (e.g., EEG [30] or head pose [13]) to more accurately model user state during learning. A richer representation of user state allows a robot tutor to provide a greater personalized learning experience. In addition, the robot's social character and role can affect a child's engagement during a learning task [35]. Future work should explore how the social dynamics and the role of the robot (peer or teacher) during tutoring may influence learning outcomes. Lastly, this study focused specifically on when to provide cognitive rest during tutoring. Additional work should explore different implementations of various types of breaks.

7. CONCLUSION

In this paper, we investigated personalized timing strategies for providing non-task breaks to children during a robot tutoring interaction. We built an autonomous robot tutoring system and conducted a field study to compare the effectiveness of different break timing strategies in promoting learning. Results from our study showed that students receiving personalized strategies were able to improve their test scores from pretest to posttest significantly more than those receiving breaks on a fixed schedule. Furthermore, we found that certain types of break triggers provided immediate benefits for students to solve problems more efficiently and accurately. Results of this work have positive implications for creating effective, personalized tutoring interactions.

8. ACKNOWLEDGMENTS

This work was supported by the National Science Foundation, award #1139078 (Socially Assistive Robotics). We thank Arsalan Sufi and Kevin Jiang for helping to prepare the system and the experiment. We also thank the students and staff at the schools where data was collected.

9. REFERENCES

[1] A. Ariga and A. Lleras. Brief and rare mental "breaks" keep you focused: Deactivation and reactivation of task goals preempt vigilance decrements. *Cognition*, 118(3):439–443, 2011.

[2] D. I. Cordova and M. R. Lepper. Intrinsic motivation and the process of learning: Beneficial effects of contextualization, personalization, and choice. *Journal of educational psychology*, 88(4):715, 1996.

[3] F. N. Dempster. The rise and fall of the inhibitory mechanism: Toward a unified theory of cognitive development and aging. *Developmental review*, 12(1):45–75, 1992.

[4] G. Gordon, S. Spaulding, J. K. Westlund, J. J. Lee, L. Plummer, M. Martinez, M. Das, and C. Breazeal. Affective personalization of a social robot tutor for children's second language skills. In *Thirtieth AAAI Conference on Artificial Intelligence*, 2016.

[5] J. Greczek, E. Short, C. E. Clabaugh, K. Swift-Spong, and M. Mataric. Socially assistive robotics for personalized education for children. In *AAAI Fall Symposium on Artificial Intelligence and Human-Robot Interaction (AI-HRI)*, 2014.

[6] O. A. B. Henkemans, B. P. Bierman, J. Janssen, M. A. Neerincx, R. Looije, H. van der Bosch, and J. A. van der Giessen. Using a robot to personalise health education for children with diabetes type 1: A pilot study. *Patient education and counseling*, 92(2):174–181, 2013.

[7] D. Hood, S. Lemaignan, and P. Dillenbourg. When children teach a robot to write: An autonomous teachable humanoid which uses simulated handwriting. In *Proceedings of the Tenth Annual ACM/IEEE International Conference on Human-Robot Interaction*, pages 83–90. ACM, 2015.

[8] C.-M. Huang and B. Mutlu. Modeling and evaluating narrative gestures for humanlike robots. In *Robotics: Science and Systems*, pages 57–64, 2013.

[9] T. Kanda, T. Hirano, D. Eaton, and H. Ishiguro. Interactive robots as social partners and peer tutors for children: A field trial. *Human-computer interaction*, 19(1):61–84, 2004.

[10] J. Kennedy, P. Baxter, E. Senft, and T. Belpaeme. Higher nonverbal immediacy leads to greater learning gains in child-robot tutoring interactions. In *International Conference on Social Robotics*, pages 327–336. Springer, 2015.

[11] I. Leite, M. McCoy, D. Ullman, N. Salomons, and B. Scassellati. Comparing models of disengagement in individual and group interactions. In *Proceedings of the Tenth Annual ACM/IEEE International Conference on Human-Robot Interaction*, pages 99–105. ACM, 2015.

[12] I. Leite, A. Pereira, G. Castellano, S. Mascarenhas, C. Martinho, and A. Paiva. Modelling empathy in social robotic companions. In *International Conference on User Modeling, Adaptation, and Personalization*, pages 135–147. Springer, 2011.

[13] S. Lemaignan, F. Garcia, A. Jacq, and P. Dillenbourg. From real-time attention assessment to with-me-ness in human-robot interaction. In *The Eleventh ACM/IEEE International Conference on Human Robot Interation*, pages 157–164. IEEE Press, 2016.

[14] D. Leyzberg, S. Spaulding, and B. Scassellati. Personalizing robot tutors to individuals' learning differences. In *Proceedings of the 2014 ACM/IEEE international conference on Human-robot interaction*, pages 423–430. ACM, 2014.

[15] D. Leyzberg, S. Spaulding, M. Toneva, and B. Scassellati. The physical presence of a robot tutor increases cognitive learning gains. In *34th Annual Conference of the Cognitive Science Society (Cog. Sci.'12)*, 2012.

[16] J. Lim and K. Kwok. The effects of varying break length on attention and time on task. *Human Factors: The Journal of the Human Factors and Ergonomics Society*, page 0018720815617395, 2015.

[17] K. E. McKay, J. M. Halperin, S. T. Schwartz, and V. Sharma. Developmental analysis of three aspects of information processing: Sustained attention, selective attention, and response organization. *Developmental Neuropsychology*, 10(2):121–132, 1994.

[18] J. Nelsen. *Positive Time-out: And Over 50 Ways to Avoid Power Struggles in the Home and the Classroom.* Harmony Books, 1999.

[19] R. Pekrun, T. Götz, W. Titz, and R. P. Perry. Academic emotions in students' self-regulated learning and achievement: a program of qualitative and quantitative research. *Educational Psychologist*, 37(2):91–105, 2002.

[20] A. D. Pellegrini and C. M. Bohn. The role of recess in children's cognitive performance and school adjustment. *Educational Researcher*, 34(1):13–19, 2005.

[21] A. D. Pellegrini, P. D. Huberty, and I. Jones. The effects of recess timing on children's playground and classroom behaviors. *American Educational Research Journal*, 32(4):845–864, 1995.

[22] A. Pereira, C. Martinho, I. Leite, and A. Paiva. iCat, the chess player: the influence of embodiment in the enjoyment of a game. In *Proceedings of the 7th International Joint Conference on Autonomous Agents and Multiagent Systems-Volume 3*, pages 1253–1256. International Foundation for Autonomous Agents and Multiagent Systems, 2008.

[23] G. Petty. Teaching today: A practical guide. 2009.

[24] W. D. Pierce and J. Cameron. A summary of the effects of reward contingencies on interest and performance. *The Behavior Analyst Today*, 3(2):221, 2002.

[25] A. Powers, S. Kiesler, S. Fussell, and C. Torrey. Comparing a computer agent with a humanoid robot. In *Human-Robot Interaction (HRI), 2007 2nd ACM/IEEE International Conference on*, pages 145–152. IEEE, 2007.

[26] A. Ramachandran, A. Litoiu, and B. Scassellati. Shaping productive help-seeking behavior during robot-child tutoring interactions. In *The Eleventh ACM/IEEE International Conference on Human Robot Interation*, pages 247–254. IEEE Press, 2016.

[27] M. Saerbeck, T. Schut, C. Bartneck, and M. D. Janse. Expressive robots in education: varying the degree of social supportive behavior of a robotic tutor. In *Proceedings of the SIGCHI Conference on Human*

Factors in Computing Systems, pages 1613–1622. ACM, 2010.

[28] B. Schadenberg, M. Neerincx, F. Cnossen, and R. Looije. Personalising game difficulty to keep children motivated to play with a social robot: a bayesian approach. *Cognitive Systems Research*, 2016.

[29] E. Short, K. Swift-Spong, J. Greczek, A. Ramachandran, A. Litoiu, E. C. Grigore, D. Feil-Seifer, S. Shuster, J. J. Lee, S. Huang, et al. How to train your dragonbot: Socially assistive robots for teaching children about nutrition through play. In *The 23rd IEEE International Symposium on Robot and Human Interactive Communication*, pages 924–929. IEEE, 2014.

[30] D. Szafir and B. Mutlu. Pay attention!: designing adaptive agents that monitor and improve user engagement. In *Proceedings of the SIGCHI Conference on Human Factors in Computing Systems*, pages 11–20. ACM, 2012.

[31] F. Tanaka and S. Matsuzoe. Children teach a care-receiving robot to promote their learning: Field experiments in a classroom for vocabulary learning. *Journal of Human-Robot Interaction*, 1(1), 2012.

[32] T. C. Toppino, J. E. Kasserman, and W. A. Mracek. The effect of spacing repetitions on the recognition memory of young children and adults. *Journal of experimental child psychology*, 51(1):123–138, 1991.

[33] J. Wainer, D. J. Feil-Seifer, D. A. Shell, and M. J. Mataric. Embodiment and human-robot interaction: A task-based perspective. In *RO-MAN 2007-The 16th IEEE International Symposium on Robot and Human Interactive Communication*, pages 872–877. IEEE, 2007.

[34] J. K. Westlund and C. Breazeal. The interplay of robot language level with children's language learning during storytelling. In *Proceedings of the Tenth Annual ACM/IEEE International Conference on Human-Robot Interaction Extended Abstracts*, pages 65–66. ACM, 2015.

[35] C. Zaga, M. Lohse, K. P. Truong, and V. Evers. The effect of a robot's social character on children's task engagement: Peer versus tutor. In *International Conference on Social Robotics*, pages 704–713. Springer, 2015.

Windfield: Learning Wind Meteorology with Handheld Haptic Robots

Ayberk Özgür[1], Wafa Johal[1,2], Francesco Mondada[2] and Pierre Dillenbourg[1]
[1]CHILI, [2]LSRO, EPFL
Lausanne, Switzerland
{name.surname}@epfl.ch

ABSTRACT

This article presents a learning activity and its user study involving the *Cellulo* platform, a novel versatile robotic tool designed for education. In order to show the potential of Cellulo in the classroom as part of standard curricular activities, we designed a learning activity called *Windfield* that aims to teach the atmospheric formation mechanism of wind to early middle school children. The activity involves a didactic sequence, introducing the Cellulo robots as hot air balloons and enabling children to feel the wind force through haptic feedback. We present a user study, designed in the form of a real hour-long lesson, conducted with 24 children in 8 groups who had no prior knowledge in the subject. Collaborative metrics within groups and individual performances about the learning of key concepts were measured with only the hardware and software integrated in the platform in a completely automated manner. The results show that almost all participants showed learning of symmetric aspects of wind formation while about half showed learning of asymmetric vectorial aspects that are more complex.

Keywords

Human-Robot Interaction; Robots for Learning; Haptic Interfaces; Tangible Robots

1. INTRODUCTION

As robotics and computers became more and more present in daily activities, efforts were made in some countries during the 70's and 80's to introduce their use in school, the earliest of which was done with the Logo Turtles based on the work of Papert. Despite these institutional advances, these efforts were eventually dropped, and robots disappeared from schools for about two decades ([9]). The most prominent reason explaining this failure was that robots were expensive and unreliable, causing disinterest in educational practitioners.

One other common reason for explaining this disinterest in robotics and computer science is explained by what Gander *et al.* call the *teacher availability deadlock*: "As long as

HRI '17, March 06 - 09, 2017, Vienna, Austria

ISBN 978-1-4503-4336-7/17/03...$15.00
DOI: http://dx.doi.org/10.1145/2909824.3020231

(a) A team of 3 learners carrying out Windfield: They are probing the map with their robots (that represent hot air balloons) to feel the winds and discover the hidden atmospheric pressure points.

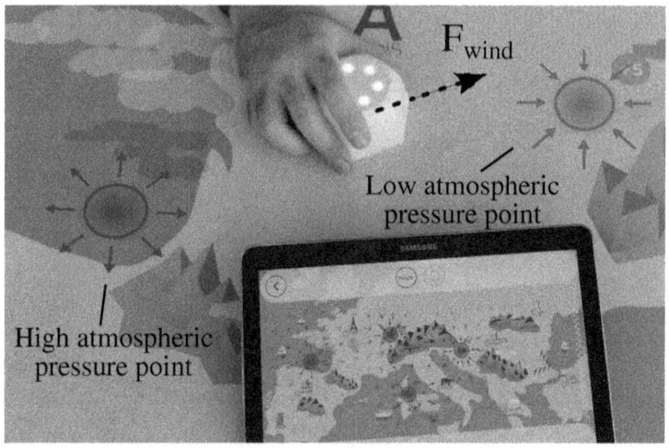

(b) *Feel the Wind* interaction. Low and high pressure points are hidden in the map (overlaid in figure but not shown on paper in reality), creating winds and pushing the grasped robots. The tablet displays the map and allows the learners to guess the positions of the pressure points by drag-and-drop (all found correctly in the above instance). Directions of winds can also be displayed (seen in this instance) if the group is observed to be stuck.

Figure 1: Windfield activity and haptic interaction.

informatics is not in the curriculum, there is little incentive to educate teachers in the subject; as long as there are no teachers, there is little incentive to introduce the subject." Since Papert, many attempts were made to introduce robots in education (with subjects well beyond programming or robotics such as language) but mainly stayed limited to extra-curricular activities. The reasons for this particular limitation can be found in several studies on school teachers' opinions on robotics (such as [38, 19, 26, 17]): Besides viewing robots as expensive, resource demanding and a potential source of distraction, teachers want the technology to adapt to their practice and not the opposite. For better acceptance, such technologies should primarily target helping them achieve their duty more efficiently.

In the *Cellulo* project, our focus is to attempt to fit the current curriculum while minimizing the financial investments for schools and maximizing the usability of the robots by teachers. Our robotic platform, designed with these constraints, aims to be versatile, ubiquitous and practical. Our robots are low-cost and carry few but powerful affordances such as planar haptic and tangible interaction. They operate on printed paper sheets and are aided by consumer-grade mobile tablets; such elements are either fully (paper) or potentially (tablet) ubiquitous in the classroom. The combination of these elements results in a platform that can be easily deployed, orchestrated and maintained. The design of learning with our platform is activity-driven, where each activity is intended to teach a singular, well-defined concept found within the curriculum. A major hypothesis in our project is that many such concepts can be mapped to efficient activities with our platform so that its usage as part of daily learning life in the classroom can be justified.

In this article, we present the first complete learning activity with Cellulo, called *Windfield* (seen in Figure 1), that aims to teach the atmospheric formation mechanism of wind (introduced as part of scientific thinking and climate knowledge in schools in the country where this study was conducted) to early middle school children. Our contributions also include the design and results of an experimental user study conducted with 24 children in the form of a real hour-long lesson. Therefore, this study marks the first step towards definitively showing the educational value of the Cellulo platform. The rest of the article is as follows: After discussing the related work in Section 2, we describe in Section 3 the robotic platform used for the Windfield experiment. Then, we present the user study on Windfield in Section 4. Section 5 presents the results and discussion on our findings. Finally, we give our outlook and future plans for Cellulo in Section 6.

2. RELATED WORK

Due to the historical evolution of educational robots, teaching programming and robotics preceded all other subjects. Later, other closely-related Science, Technology, Engineering and Mathematics (STEM) subjects were brought into focus. Educational robots conceived to teach these subjects were classically designed as facilitators in learning the subject through their related inherent qualities such as programmability and sensor/actuator hardware; in other words, they played the *tool* role identified by [26]. [38] calls this approach "robots for education", and points out that the method can potentially be used to teach subjects of any kind, while also acknowledging its clear historical focus on STEM.

[5, 16] provide reviews of studies that target such topics and the devices used for this purpose; individual programmable mobile robots (often with a differential drive for locomotion) and programmable robotic construction kits seem to be the two major choices for the tool approach. Within this approach, subjects of focus include engineering ([34, 25]), mathematics and problem solving ([37, 12]), robotics and programming ([36, 2, 40, 28, 33]), physics ([43]) and STEM in general ([4]). Our work aims to venture beyond this mostly classical approach to the tool role where the robot's inherent qualities are directly mapped to the learning scenario (*e.g.* program the existing hardware or build necessary hardware from existing components to solve a task) towards an approach where the robot's *apparent* qualities are mapped to the learning scenario, *e.g.* mapping the interaction paradigms that the robot offers to a key quantity whose behavior must be understood within a curriculum topic. We hypothesize that this approach will offer more versatility and subject coverage than what is currently found in the literature.

Later on, social robots that play the role of *tutors* that provide help to learners or *peers* that stimulate learning (identified again by [26]) were introduced. These robots are often designed to exploit social aspects of interaction, and are unsurprisingly often found in the form of humanoids (such as Nao). Although these robots are applied to the teaching of a larger variety of subjects, our approach differs from these in the sense that our robots do not possess inherent or apparent intelligence or social qualities; their behaviors are designed to be practical and only seek to spark social interaction in the form of collaboration among the learners. Therefore, this class of studies is not considered here.

From another perspective, robots that enable collaborative learning may have greater potential of adoption into the classroom. Studies that are concerned with collaborative learning aim to measure social interactions among the learners and group dynamics. Such studies are relatively new and less numerous in the domain of robots for education; examples are [24] (teaching geometry) and [7, 20, 44, 15] (teaching programming and robotics). We aim to not only improve the currently lacking subject coverage, but also equip our platform with natural collaborative aspects by designing low cost, replaceable robots that operate in large numbers. If desired, multiple learners can interact simultaneously with a collaborative activity via multiple shared robots or one/multiple personally assigned robot(s). The embedded hardware on each robot can then be used to calculate several complex metrics related to collaboration, as described in Section 4.4.

Haptics is conceptually designated to be one of the main modalities of interaction within our robot-enabled learning activities, including the one discussed in this paper that utilizes a fairly large collaborative workspace that presents a significant challenge for haptics. This challenge was partly addressed by Mobile Haptic Interfaces (such as [27, 3, 11, 30] that are human-sized platforms and [1, 35] that are relatively smaller desktop robots) that were not used in educational or collaborative computer-human interaction studies so far.

Although studies that are concerned with the use of haptics in learning are limited to traditional grounded mechanisms (often off-the-shelf devices), they still present significant motivations for us to pursue haptics as a main interaction modality with our mobile robots: [22] gives a review that exposes the potential of haptics in improving motivation and attention, in kinesthetic and embodied learning, and in the learning of invisible phenomena. Moreover, a number of successful studies that focus on teaching diverse subjects across various levels of education can be found, such as biology ([23, 14, 6]), physics ([42, 10, 18, 21]), geometry ([41]) and handwriting ([8]). Nearly half of these studies show improvement in learning with the addition of haptic feedback, reinforcing our motivation to integrate meaningful haptics in our activities.

Figure 2: Typical scene from a Cellulo activity, illustrating the three main components of the platform. (A) marks the paper playground containing printed graphics and the optical microdot pattern allowing the robots to localize globally with high accuracy and framerate. (B) marks the tablet running the activity application software and coordinating the robots connected to it via Bluetooth. (C) mark the mobile robots, each able to self-localize on the paper (with instant recovery from kidnapping), move omnidirectionally along their three DOFs (shown on one robot with (x, y, θ)) and give independent haptic feedback along the same DOFs when grasped.

3. PLATFORM DESIGN

The design of our platform was done to be practical and compatible with conditions typically found in classrooms. It is composed of three components as seen in Figure 2: Printed paper sheets that can be of quasi unlimited size, a tablet and haptic-enabled handheld mobile robots. Our robots have a plain appearance and are capable of holonomic motion, haptic feedback and absolute 3DOF global localization while on the printed paper sheets. 6 capacitive touch buttons individually illuminated with full RGB colors on the top surface provides simple in-situ input/output.

The locomotion system was designed to withstand intensive use expected in a classroom; as such, it contains measures to increase the lifetime of the components and is passively backdrivable to a degree (see [29] for details). Similar practicality concerns guided the design of the localization system, allowing each robot to self-localize with sub-mm accuracy at about 93Hz framerate while on the printed microdot pattern via a downward-facing camera found underneath the robots (see [13] for details). This design further allows the robots to recover instantly from kidnapping when returned to paper, and thus be used as active tangible items.

Each robot is connected to the consumer-grade tablet through Bluetooth 2.1 serial ports and acts as a peripheral, reporting all events (*e.g.* pose changed) and receiving commands (*e.g.* track pose goal) to/from the tablet. A cross-platform *QtQuick* application runs on the tablet to coordinate the robots and provide a graphical user interface. Latency-critical or high-bandwidth software components are built within the robots' firmware (*e.g.* motion controller, localization) while components that require high computational/memory resources or need to change depending on the activity are offloaded to the per-activity QtQuick applications that run on the tablet.

Considering these resource requirements, a classroom is required to obtain the necessary number of robots (that cost about €125 each at the prototype stage), acquire the necessary number of mobile tablets (that are becoming more and more affordable and are likely already available within the school) and have the poster-sized activity sheets produced in common printing houses. At this point, launching the desired educational activity on demand is as effortless as running the mobile application on the tablets, unrolling the activity sheets and associating the necessary number of robots (that are identical and exchangeable) with the application by releasing them on the activity sheets.

4. WINDFIELD EXPERIMENT

4.1 Activity Design

Windfield is designed as a semi-gamified activity where learners are taught how atmospheric pressure results in winds through a robotic simulation of "hot air balloons" over Europe. Wind meteorology was carefully selected from an early middle-school curriculum as a subject that is not particularly taught in detail, as a means to better demonstrate the additional value that Cellulo brings.

An overview of the activity can be seen in Figure 1. There are high and low pressure points of various intensities that create outwards and inwards winds respectively at a distance; the strength of these wind forces are decayed with squared distance. The wind force at any given point on the map is then calculated as the vectorial sum of the wind forces created by all pressure points. Other factors that affect realistic winds such as the Coriolis effect are not considered for simplicity of the taught concept. There are two distinct phases to the activity that both take place on the same 0.76m × 1.7m activity sheet partially seen in Figure 1a, hereafter called the *playground*.

Feel the Wind is the first phase where pressure points are hidden and the robots (*i.e.* hot air balloons) are used as tangible haptic devices (interaction scheme seen in Figure 1b) to probe desired points on the playground to feel the wind and discover the hidden pressure points. Learners are allocated one robot each and place their guesses as a team on the tablet's graphical display where the entire playground and each robot's hot air balloon are displayed in real time. The robots (*i.e.* tangibles) are intended to be visually mapped by the learners onto their hot air balloon counterparts on the tablet display via graphical landmarks found on the playground (*e.g.* cities, mountain ranges, clouds, boats, flock of birds, dolphins). This allows reasoning as to whether the particular forces applied to the robots are meaningful upon placing pressure point guesses on the display, since they are visible on the tablet but not on the paper playground.

Each robot in the activity self-localizes as soon as it is placed on the playground and sends its global position to the tablet application. Upon receiving a position, the tablet application calculates the virtual wind force at that position (depending on the configuration of pressure points) and sends back the locomotion output command to the robot (scaled to fit the robot's output limits). This output is effectuated as long as the learner's grasp is detected via the touch keys on top of the robot, resulting in force feedback that represents the wind force. Furthermore, in order to reduce the natural frictional impedance of the robot (due to partial passive backdrivability of the wheels) during external manipulation, a portion of the velocity vector (estimated by localization

	Phase	Goals	Time (min)
IN.	Introduction	Introduction to platform and lesson Assessment of pre-knowledge by discussion on weather forecast video	5
F2.	*Feel the Wind* with 2 pressure points	Exploration of wind and pressure mechanism with robots	10
IV.	Informative video	Comprehension of wind mechanism and mid-term synthesis	5
F4.	*Feel the Wind* with 4 pressure points	Application of wind mechanism knowledge	15
CW.	*Control the Wind*	Transfer of knowledge into constructive use	10-20
PT.	Closing & post-test	Measurement of knowledge gain	5
			Total: 50-60

Table 1: Didactic sequence in the Windfield lesson.

(a) Low pressure point (b) High pressure point

Figure 3: Pressure point icons used in *Feel the Wind.*

poses) is internally summed to the locomotion output. This enhances the comfort while the robot is being dragged across the playground, and is therefore called *backdrive assist.*

Control the Wind is the second phase where positions and strengths of the pressure points are under the control of learners to create the necessary winds to bring one robot (*i.e.* hot air balloon) from the start position to the finish line, stopping by as many cities as possible to collect the most points without leaving the playground. Learners place the pressure points, designate their intensities and start the simulation through the tablet. One robot (now functioning as a mobile robot and not a haptic device) enacts the simulation with a simple pose tracking motion controller whose target is commanded by the tablet application upon receiving the poses periodically sent by the robot.

This activity is a second revision over our previous work where only *Feel the Wind* was present with a simple velocity controller that provided the haptic feedback and grasp detection that relied on high-level key presses. This first revision was improved with a more advanced haptics controller, better grasp detection and backdrive assist as described above. For performance reasons, the simplified Finite Element Analysis method previously used for simulating the wind forces was replaced with analytic calculation. *Control the Wind* was added to give the didactic flow to the activity that lets the learners discover the effects of atmospheric pressure points at their discretion and then lets them transfer this knowledge and use it constructively in a game.

4.2 Lesson Design

A lesson taking between 50 and 60 minutes was designed with the above activity components; its didactic sequence can be seen in Table 1. During the lesson, the experimenters act only as observers and facilitators; the learners are left to interact with the system by themselves during each phase involving the Cellulo platform, with the tablet providing enough information for them to be autonomous. All phases in the lesson are explained below.

Figure 4: Screenshot from F2 (*Feel the Wind* with 2 pressure points). Visuals in F4 look similar. The low pressure point is found; the high pressure point is yet to be discovered. Vector field representation of wind intensities and directions are not normally shown to the group unless they are observed to be stuck or are nearing the time limit.

4.2.1 *Introduction* (IN)

The group of 3 learners are first greeted and shown a 1 minute video clip of a TV news weather broadcast where the meteorology reporter gives the current atmospheric pressure status. They are asked whether they are already familiar with the concepts used in the broadcast to verify the absence of pre-knowledge on the subject. They are then explained the subject of the lesson they are about to experience and how it is connected to this everyday occurrence whose underlying principle possibly evades their attention. They are explained that the high and low pressure points blow air outwards and absorb air inwards respectively and that they have effects at a distance that diminish when moved away. These facts are explained in the presence of brief slides that show the same icons used in the activity for high and low pressure points for easier retention; these are shown in Figure 3.

4.2.2 *Feel the Wind with 2 pressure points* (F2)

The learners are then invited over to the activity sheet and are given one robot each. They are told to put the robots on the map to feel the wind at desired locations; they are made aware of the depictions of hot air balloons that are continuously displayed on the tablet screen. They are also shown how to drag and drop the pressure points on the tablet to make guesses. At this point, the experimenters completely stop interacting with the group and let them do the activity on their own until the time limit. A sample screenshot displaying this task is seen in Figure 4.

One high pressure and one low pressure point (same intensity and opposite directionality) are hidden at random positions that are at least 200mm apart from each other. They are not given more information unless they are observed to be stuck or are nearing the 10 minutes limit. At this point, they are shown the wind directions and strengths on the entire map in the form of a vector field display on the tablet. If the pressure points are found with the help of this display, the learners are invited to nevertheless feel around the pressure point with their robots.

4.2.3 *Informative video* (IV)

After the brief introduction to the activity, the learners are shown a 5 minutes informative video from a TV show called *C'est pas Sorcier*[1] aimed at explaining scientific phenomena to young children. The short clip explains how hot and cold air loses and gains density and therefore pressure with respect to its surroundings. It continues to explain how masses of air displace between these areas, resulting in winds. In the video, the same colors are used to depict high/low pressure points as in our activity.

4.2.4 *Feel the Wind with 4 pressure points* (F4)

After **IV**, the learners are invited to discover 2 high and 2 low pressure points (all having the same intensity) positioned randomly that are again at least 200mm apart from each other. If they are observed to be stuck nearing the 15 minute limit, they are again shown the wind vector field all over the playground on the tablet.

4.2.5 *Control the Wind* (CW)

The learners are explained that in this next task, they are supposed to position 3 low and 3 high pressure points themselves in order to move one balloon across the playground and collect points by visiting cities. Points associated with cities were chosen according to how difficult they are to visit, and the cities were distributed such that it is practically possible to visit only a subset of them. They are shown how to modify the intensity of the pressure points and how to start and reset the simulation and are not aided further.

They are not given the ability to modify the directionality of the pressure points in order to encourage them to use both high and low pressure dynamics in different situations. They do this task as a team as there is a single simulation to be optimized. The progress of the group is monitored and the task is allowed to continue up to 20 minutes if room for more progress is clearly observed. Otherwise, it is finished at the 10 minute limit.

4.2.6 *Closing & Post-test* (PT)

Finally, each individual member of the group is subjected to a post test composed of 4 questions (with increasing difficulty) that assess different aspects of the wind formation mechanism that should have been understood in result of the lesson. Each question displays a number of pressure points on the playground and asks the learner to draw an arrow depicting the blow of the wind in that hypothetical scenario. Screenshots depicting each question is given in Figure 5; they are the following, with the aspect that must be understood to answer correctly given in quotes:

Q1. Two p.p. – *"Wind blows from high to low pressure"*

Q2. Three p.p. – *"Identical pressures have similar effect at similar distance"*

Q3. Two p.p., wind in a specific area is asked – *"At similar distance, opposite pressures' vectoral effects combine to result in winds parallel to the line that connects them"*

Q4. Three p.p., wind in a specific area is asked – *"At dissimilar distances, pressure that is closer has a larger vectoral effect; the resulting wind is the sum of these vectors"*

Learners are prevented from sharing information during the post-test. After the post-test, the learners are asked their general opinions about the lesson and are thanked for their participation.

4.3 Participants & Data Collection

24 learners (12M, 12F, 11.9 ± 0.900 years-old, min. 10, max. 13) participated in the experiment in 8 groups of 3 learners during 2 days. It was verified through the age group selection (*i.e.* younger than when this subject is taught at school) and through the brief discussion in the **IN** phase that no formal pre-knowledge existed about the subject. The groups were formed randomly and treated separately. Each group was observed for behaviors that may explain findings later on. Poses of all robots used by all learners in all groups were recorded with maximum framerate (about 93Hz) as long as on the playground. In addition, all grasp and release events, all kidnap and return to playground events and all GUI events (such as button click, drag and drop positions *etc.*) were recorded.

4.4 Calculated Metrics

In addition to task completion times, **CW** scores and accuracy of given answers to correct answers in **PT**, a number of other more complex metrics were calculated from the robot position sequences obtained from **F4**. These are given below.

4.4.1 *Similarity of exploration across entire* F4

We build the (per learner) 2D histogram of all visited positions where each bin is 20mm×20mm and contains the total time spent by the robot at that location. Then, we calculate the *soft cosine similarity* ([39]) across all pairs of learners within groups, defined as:

$$S(t^a, t^b) = \frac{\sum_i^N \sum_j^N s_{ij} t_i^a t_j^b}{\sqrt{\sum_i^N \sum_j^N s_{ij} t_i^a t_j^a} \sqrt{\sum_i^N \sum_j^N s_{ij} t_i^b t_j^b}} \tag{1}$$

where N is the number of bins, t_i^l is the time spent at bin i by learner l and s_{ij} is the similarity index between bin i and bin j, which is calculated as:

$$s_{ij} = \begin{cases} \frac{D - d_{ij}}{D}, & \text{if } d_{ij} < D \\ 0, & \text{otherwise} \end{cases} \tag{2}$$

where d_{ij} is the physical distance between the centers of bins i and j. D is the maximum distance to be considered for

[1]English: *It's not Magic*, can be viewed at www.youtube.com/watch?v=mmenMWUKt0O with subtitles

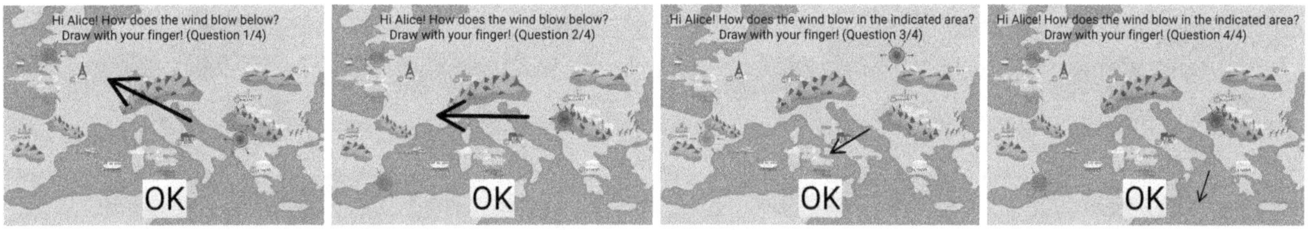

(a) **Q1:** 2 p.p. (b) **Q2:** 3 p.p. (c) **Q3:** 2 p.p.; draw in the box (d) **Q4:** 3 p.p.; draw in the box

Figure 5: Post-test questions. Roughly correct answers drawn on each question.

similarity, which is chosen as the maximum size of one robot (corner to corner, 85mm).

The similarity measure indicates the likeness of spatial coverage between two learners, and may provide insights on collaboration quality within a group. High similarity may indicate redundancy of exploration (implying low collaboration quality), but may also indicate co-exploration (and not necessarily low quality collaboration) if leader-follower effects are present. On the other hand, low similarity may indicate efficient exploration by division of labor, indicating high collaboration quality, if enough communication is present within the group.

4.4.2 *Entropy of exploration across entire* F4

With the same histograms as above, as well as with the overall histograms per group, we calculate the normalized Shannon entropy as follows:

$$H(t) = -\frac{1}{\log_2 N} \sum_i^N \hat{t_i} \log_2 \hat{t_i} \qquad (3)$$

where N is the number of bins and $\hat{t_i}$ is the time spent at bin i, normalized by the total time spent over all bins. Entropy measures the "disorder" of exploration; higher entropy corresponds to more equal distribution of time spent across the explored area (and *not* the entire playground area), while low entropy corresponds to less equal time distribution, possibly due to time spent around focal points. Therefore, lower entropy may indicate "getting stuck at" or returning to certain points rather than exploring the map without revisiting previous locations.

4.4.3 *Cross recurrence of exploration in* F4

To extract temporal information, robot positions of each learner were resampled at 1Hz (averaging all available positions closest in time) starting at the same instance to obtain synchronized positions within groups, since current robot hardware does not offer this synchronization mechanism across multiple robots. With these synchronized positions, cross recurrences between all pairs in each group were calculated (inspired by [32] in the eye tracking literature):

$$R^{ab}(t_i, t_j) = \begin{cases} 1, & \text{if } d^{ab}(t_i, t_j) < D_{\min} \\ \frac{D_{\max} - d^{ab}(t_i,t_j)}{D_{\max} - D_{\min}}, & \text{if } D_{\min} \leq d^{ab}(t_i, t_j) \leq D_{\max} \\ 0, & \text{otherwise} \end{cases} \qquad (4)$$

where $d^{ab}(t_i, t_j)$ is the distance between learner a's robot position at time t_i and learner b's robot position at time t_j, $D_{\min}$ is the distance below which there is full recurrence (chosen as one robot width, *i.e.* 85mm, since two robots

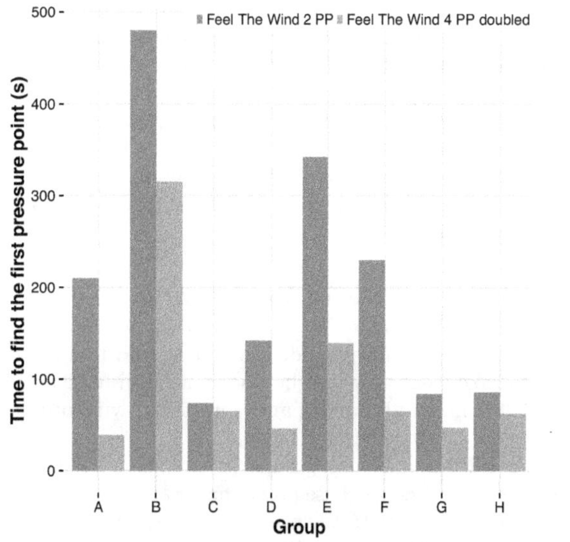

Figure 6: Time to find the first pressure point for each group in F2 (Feel the Wind 2 PP) and F4 (Feel the Wind 4 PP). F4 times are artificially doubled to acommodate twice the point density in F4.

cannot occupy the same space at the same time) and $D_{\max}$ is the maximum allowed distance for recurrence (chosen as two robot widths, *i.e.* 170mm). With this, we measure the normalized leader-follower relationship index, calculated as:

$$L^{ab} = \frac{\sum_{0 \leq t_j - t_i \leq S} R^{ab}(t_i, t_j)}{\sum_{0 \leq t_j - t_i \leq S} A^a(t_i) A^b(t_j)} \qquad (5)$$

where S is the maximum time difference to consider (chosen as 10 seconds) and $A^l(t)$ equals 1 if learner l's robot is on the playground and is being grasped at time t (*i.e.* active), and equals 0 otherwise. By definition, L^{ab} is between 0 (no leadership) and 1 (a leads b 100% of the time).

5. RESULTS & DISCUSSION

5.1 Feel the Wind

We measured the time to find the first pressure point in **F2** and **F4** (time for each group presented in Figure 6) to determine the effect of midterm synthesis with the informative video. Comparison was done after doubling the time in **F4** due to double the density of points on the playground. A paired t-test (within group) showed significant decrease

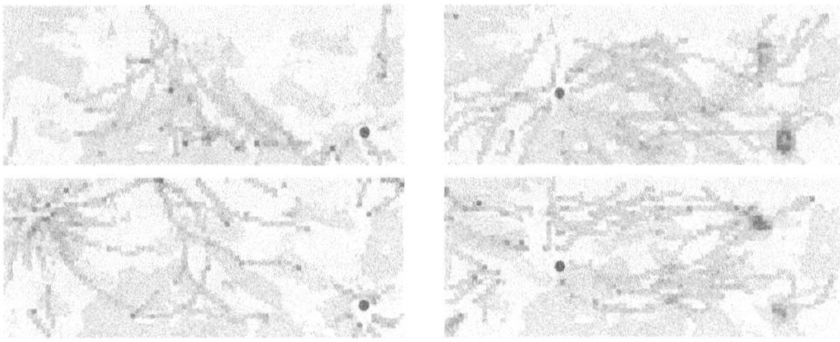

(a) Two learners in group B. Top and bottom learners approach the same point from 3 and 6 different angles respectively.

(b) Two learners in group F. Top and bottom learners approach the same point from 6 and 4 different angles respectively.

Figure 7: Similar "approach" patterns towards high pressure points (marked with blue dots) found in two different groups. Low pressure points also clearly visible in group F as the two high density areas towards the east. Some focal points and traversals are visible over Mediterranean islands and boats, assumed by learners to host pressure points.

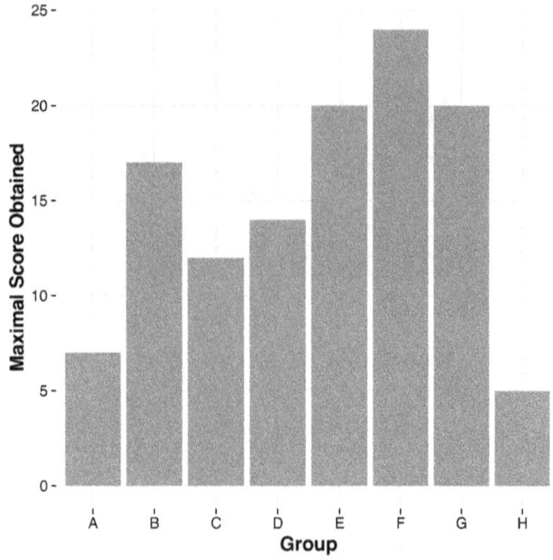

Figure 8: Maximal scores obtained by each group in CW. 31 points are available in total (intentionally made impossible to fully obtain).

($t(7) = 3.9773, p = 0.005$) from **F2** ($M = 205, SD = 144$) to **F4** ($M = 97, SD = 93$). This improvement hints at the effect of the informative video, but it should be noted that this improvement may also be due to natural habituation to the platform, as all participants interacted with our robots for the very first time in **F2**.

During **F2** and **F4**, all groups were observed to find a low pressure point first as these points naturally act as "sinkholes" and lead the robots to themselves when they are allowed to move. While this agrees with our previous findings, we are not able to prevent this degradation of haptic interaction as it requires force sensing that is not yet implemented on our robots. However, in **F4**, some groups eventually found all pressure points while the rest found at least one high pressure point before being shown the visual vector field representation of winds, at which point they found the final point within a few seconds.

Furthermore, positional densities of individual robots over the entire playground revealed certain patterns of interaction, seen in Figure 7. In certain groups, learners developed the strategy where they "approach" suspected high pressure points from different angles. In almost all groups, focal points of high density coinciding with low pressure points are observed due to the aforementioned "sinkhole" effect. More interestingly, focal points and traversals are observed over graphical items found on the playground sheet (*e.g.* boats, islands, cities) some of which can be seen in Figure 7. While not intentional by design, this phenomenon agrees with our observations of the dialogue within most groups; learners often thought that pressure points should be located on such graphics and conveyed this towards their groupmates.

From a broader perspective, the total entropies of groups were found to be correlated with their average similarities in **F4** (Pearson's $r = 0.908, n = 6, p = 0.0018$). This implies that members of groups who were spending time more uniformly in their spatial exploration (not necessarily exploring more or less area) tended to cover similar areas. This may indicate that more uniform groups scanned similar areas without staying at focal points (which typically corresponded to low pressure points because of the aforementioned "sinkhole" effect) compared to less uniform groups who covered dissimilar areas and stayed at more focal points; this can suggest a difference in collaboration quality.

5.2 Control the Wind

Figure 8 illustrates the maximal scores attained by groups during the entire **CW**. The maximal scores are observed to be widely varying across groups ($M = 14.88, SD = 6.64, \min = 5, \max = 24$), but were not found to be correlated with the number of attempts ($M = 45, SD = 36.2, \min = 17, \max = 123$). Furthermore, the scores were not found to be correlated with any metric from Feel the Wind, preventing us from drawing conclusions about the transfer of knowledge. This was likely due to the trial-and-error natured approach observed from most groups allowed by the design of the activity; this is acknowledged as a shortcoming and discussed in the following section.

5.3 Post-test

The accuracy of the answers given to the questions described in Section 4.2.6 were measured by computing the angle difference between the answer and the actual wind direction, considering answers with less than 30° difference correct. This revealed three distinct categories of answers: Correct ones, incorrect ones and ones that are exactly the opposite of correct answers. We interpreted this latter type as the learner failing to recall the correct association between push/pull and the depictions of high/low pressure points, but otherwise showing correct understanding of that particular wind formation aspect. Therefore, we labeled these answers as semi-correct (with again 30° tolerance).

Figure 9 shows the partition of each answer type for each group and each question. Scores for **Q1** (96% correct or semi-correct) and **Q2** (92% correct or semi-correct) indicate that most learners understood the directionality and symmetry of wind at central locations. Scores for **Q3** (58% correct or semi-correct) and **Q4** (42% correct) show a clear drop in performance, as these questions were more complex and required the understanding of diminishing wind intensity

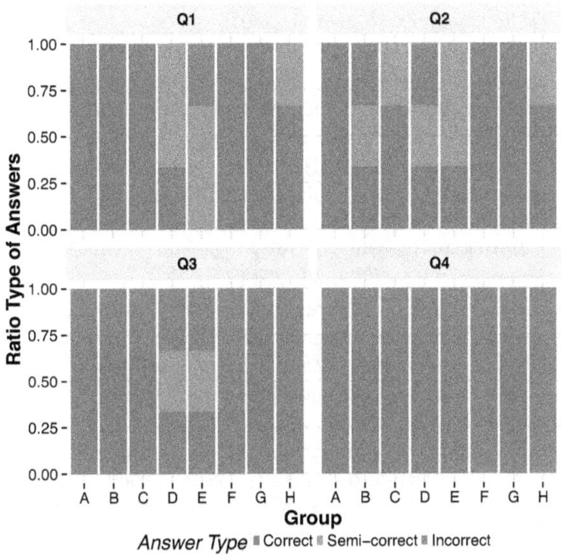

Figure 9: Ratio of type of answers for each group and post-test question. "Correct": answers with 30° accuracy. "Semi-correct": answers with 30° accuracy in the complete opposite direction. "Incorrect": any other answer.

with distance and asymmetrical vector summation. When correctness and semi-correctness of individual scores are considered among all learners, it is seen that 33% of them are 50% successful, 46% of them are 75% successful, and 21% of them are 100% successful. This implies that all learners are at least 50% correct or semi-correct.

Finally, the correlation between metrics described in the previous Section and post test scores were investigated. The absolute raw differences between correct and given angles were found to fall just short of being significantly inversely correlated with total group entropies (Pearson's $r = -0.678, n = 6, p = 0.065$); further study may indicate that learners that "do not get stuck in focal points" tend to gain more understanding of the subject phenomenon and perform better in such an activity. This is also suggested by our observations of certain groups where the "sinkhole" effect mentioned previously inadvertently pulled the robots into the (already correctly found) low pressure points and the learners visited the same location over and over again, decreasing entropy and exploration quality.

No other correlation was found between the post test scores and other measures, direct (time to find low/high pressure points, **CW** scores, number of trials in **CW**) or calculated (mean S and L within groups). This may imply that such collaboration metrics in their aggregated form may be inappropriate for predicting learning gains, or simply that there is need for more data. In any case, stronger hypotheses and data from more participants are required in the future to measure the relation between these exploration and collaboration metrics and actual learning gains.

6. CONCLUSION & FUTURE WORK

This paper introduced the first rigorously designed and studied learning activity using the Cellulo platform, the subject of which was selected from within the actual school curriculum. We presented a lesson designed with the activity and its didactic sequence to let learners explore, apply and transfer the knowledge of simple wind meteorology using handheld mobile robots. Vastly different interaction modalities that incorporate these handheld robots were used during this sequence, such as haptic and paper-based tangible interaction. These were all easily understood and effectively used: All groups found a significant portion of pressure points within time in **F2** and **F4**, most groups earned a significant portion of the total score (intentionally made impossible to fully obtain) in **CW**. Almost all learners showed learning of symmetric aspects of wind formation while about half showed learning of more complex, asymmetric vectoral aspects.

There are a number of shortcomings of the platform and the activity design. The grasp detection mechanism that uses the capacitive touch buttons does not allow closed loop control on the haptic feedback and modulating the output based on the detected grasp does not guarantee precise haptic output, allowing the learners to release the robots and follow their motion which is due to the motor outputs intended for haptic feedback. To mitigate these problems, we are investigating force/torque sensors to be installed on the outer shell of the robot; [31] is a promising candidate for this purpose. In addition, the user study was conducted with a limited number of participants, and more could allow us to obtain clearer results on learning gains.

From a didactic point of view, Feel the Wind tasks contain randomness when distributing the pressure points to cover a larger set of situations that also resulted in an undesirable chance factor in our user study. Pressure points could have been intentionally placed to induce certain situations and learners could have been encouraged to understand these specific situations. This consideration may aid in improving the learning of the subject's aforementioned asymmetric vectoral aspects by focusing on cases that involve such situations. Furthermore, Control the Wind was observed to attract trial-and-error based approaches and to be too sensitive to the position of pressure points; its design should be refined in order to negate these effects. A discretization over space for setting pressure points or a wait time (forcing predictive thinking) before the next trial may solve these issues.

During the study, a control group was not used as we do not yet claim to improve learning (compared to *e.g.* existing robotic platforms or classical teaching methods) but rather to show that Cellulo is indeed usable as a "tool" to teach an actual curricular subject. Using this study as a stepping stone, we will attempt to break the *teacher availability deadlock* by exhibiting these concrete results to educators. Therefore, in order to definitively prove the versatility and the educational potential of Cellulo, we are currently designing new activities with teachers that will soon be tested in classrooms. In the longer term, we plan to test activities with the same learner groups in the same classrooms in order to eliminate the novelty effect (that may have influenced the learners' engagement in this study) and measure the acceptance of Cellulo as a teaching tool.

7. ACKNOWLEDGMENTS

We would like to thank the Swiss National Science Foundation for supporting this project through the National Centre of Competence in Research Robotics and Dr. Kshitij Sharma for providing insights on measures used in the eye-tracking literature.

8. REFERENCES

[1] C. A. Avizzano, M. Satler, and E. Ruffaldi. Portable Haptic Interface with Omni-Directional Movement and Force Capability. *IEEE Transactions on Haptics*, 7(2):110–120, 2014.

[2] T. Balch, J. Summet, D. Blank, D. Kumar, M. Guzdial, K. O'Hara, D. Walker, M. Sweat, G. Gupta, S. Tansley, J. Jackson, M. Gupta, M. N. Muhammad, S. Prashad, N. Eilbert, and A. Gavin. Designing Personal Robots for Education: Hardware, Software, and Curriculum. *IEEE Pervasive Computing*, 7(2):5–9, 2008.

[3] F. Barbagli, A. Formaglio, M. Franzini, A. Giannitrapani, and D. Prattichizzo. An Experimental Study of the Limitations of Mobile Haptic Interfaces. In *Experimental Robotics IX: The 9th International Symposium on Experimental Robotics*, pages 533–542. 2006.

[4] B. S. Barker and J. Ansorge. Robotics as Means to Increase Achievement Scores in an Informal Learning Environment. *Journal of Research on Technology in Education*, 39(3):229–243, 2007.

[5] F. B. V. Benitti. Exploring the educational potential of robotics in schools: A systematic review. *Computers & Education*, 58(3):978–988, 2012.

[6] P. Bivall, S. Ainsworth, and L. A. E. Tibell. Do Haptic Representations Help Complex Molecular Learning? *Science Education*, 95(4):700–719, 2011.

[7] R. Burbaite, V. Stuikys, and R. Damasevicius. Educational Robots as Collaborative Learning Objects for Teaching Computer Science. In *System Science and Engineering (ICSSE), 2013 International Conference on*, pages 211–216, 2013.

[8] M. A. Eid, M. Mansour, A. H. El Saddik, and R. Iglesias. A Haptic Multimedia Handwriting Learning System. In *Proceedings of the international workshop on Educational multimedia and multimedia education*, pages 103–108, 2007.

[9] W. Gander, A. Petit, G. Berry, B. Demo, J. Vahrenhold, A. McGettrick, R. Boyle, M. Drechsler, A. Mendelson, C. Stephenson, C. Ghezzi, and B. Meyer. Informatics education: Europe cannot afford to miss the boat, Report of the joint Informatics Europe & ACM Europe Working Group on Informatics Education. Available at: http://europe.acm.org/iereport/ie.html, 2013.

[10] F. G. Hamza-Lup and I. A. Stanescu. The haptic paradigm in education: Challenges and case studies. *Internet and Higher Education*, 13(1-2):78–81, 2010.

[11] K.-L. Han, O. K. Choi, I. Lee, I. Hwang, J. S. Lee, and S. Choi. Design and Control of Omni-Directional Mobile Robot for Mobile Haptic Interface. In *Control, Automation and Systems, 2008. ICCAS 2008. International Conference on*, pages 1290–1295, 2008.

[12] K. Highfield, J. Mulligan, and J. Hedberg. Early mathematics learning through exploration with programmable toys. In *Proceedings of the Joint Meeting of PME 32 and PME-NA*, pages 169–176, 2008.

[13] L. O. Hostettler, A. Özgür, S. Lemaignan, P. Dillenbourg, and F. Mondada. Real-Time High-Accuracy 2D Localization with Structured Patterns. In *Proceedings of the 2016 IEEE International Conference on Robotics and Automation (ICRA)*, pages 4536–4543, 2016.

[14] M. G. Jones, J. Minogue, T. R. Tretter, A. Negishi, and R. Taylor. Haptic Augmentation of Science Instruction: Does Touch Matter? *Science Education*, 90(1):111–123, 2006.

[15] M. E. Jordan and R. R. McDaniel Jr. Managing uncertainty during collaborative problem solving in elementary school teams: The role of peer influence in robotics engineering activity. *Journal of the Learning Sciences*, 23(4):490–536, 2014.

[16] M. E. Karim, S. Lemaignan, and F. Mondada. A review: Can robots reshape K-12 STEM education? In *Proceedings of the 2015 IEEE International Workshop on Advanced Robotics and its Social Impacts (ARSO)*, pages 1–8, 2015.

[17] J. Kennedy, S. Lemaignan, and T. Belpaeme. The cautious attitude of teachers towards social robots in schools. In *Proceedings of the 21th IEEE International Symposium in Robot and Human Interactive Communication, Workshop on Robots for Learning*, 2016.

[18] Y. Kim, S. Park, H. Kim, H. Jeong, and J. Ryu. Effects of Different Haptic Modalities on Students' Understanding of Physical Phenomena. In *Proceedings of the 2011 IEEE World Haptics Conference (WHC)*, pages 379–384, 2011.

[19] E. Lee, Y. Lee, B. Kye, and B. Ko. Elementary and Middle School Teachers', Students' and Parents' Perception of Robot-Aided Education in Korea. In *EdMedia: World Conference on Educational Media and Technology*, pages 175–183, 2008.

[20] K. A. Mills, V. Chandra, and J. Y. Park. The architecture of children's use of language and tools when problem solving collaboratively with robotics. *The Australian Educational Researcher*, 40(3):315–337, 2013.

[21] J. Minogue and D. Borland. Investigating Students' Ideas About Buoyancy and the Influence of Haptic Feedback. *Journal of Science Education and Technology*, 25(2):187–202, 2016.

[22] J. Minogue and M. G. Jones. Haptics in Education: Exploring an Untapped Sensory Modality. *Review of Educational Research*, 76(3):317–348, 2006.

[23] J. Minogue, M. G. Jones, B. Broadwell, and T. Oppewall. The impact of haptic augmentation on middle school students' conceptions of the animal cell. *Virtual Reality*, 10(3-4):293–305, 2006.

[24] R. Mitnik, M. Nussbaum, and A. Soto. An autonomous educational mobile robot mediator. *Autonomous Robots*, 25(4):367–382, 2008.

[25] F. Mondada, M. Bonani, X. Raemy, J. Pugh, C. Cianci, A. Klaptocz, S. Magnenat, J.-C. Zufferey, D. Floreano, and A. Martinoli. The e-puck, a Robot Designed for Education in Engineering. In *Proceedings of the 9th Conference on Autonomous Robot Systems and Competitions*, volume 1, pages 59–65, 2009.

[26] O. Mubin, C. J. Stevens, S. Shahid, A. A. Mahmud, and J.-J. Dong. A review of the applicability of robots in education. *Journal of Technology in Education and Learning*, 1:209–0015, 2013.

[27] N. Nitzsche, U. D. Hanebeck, and G. Schmidt. Design

Issues of Mobile Haptic Interfaces. *Journal of Robotic Systems*, 20(9):549–556, 2003.

[28] G. Nugent, B. Barker, N. Grandgenett, and V. I. Adamchuk. Impact of Robotics and Geospatial Technology Interventions on Youth STEM Learning and Attitudes. *Journal of Research on Technology in Education*, 42(4):391–408, 2010.

[29] A. Özgür, W. Johal, and P. Dillenbourg. Permanent Magnet-Assisted Omnidirectional Ball Drive. In *Proceedings of the 2016 IEEE/RSJ International Conference on Intelligent Robots and Systems (IROS)*, 2016.

[30] A. Peer and M. Buss. A New Admittance-Type Haptic Interface for Bimanual Manipulations. *IEEE/ASME Transactions on Mechatronics*, 13(4):416–428, 2008.

[31] C. Reeks, M. G. Carmichael, D. Liu, and K. J. Waldron. Angled Sensor Configuration Capable of Measuring Tri-Axial Forces for pHRI. In *Proceedings of the 2016 IEEE International Conference on Robotics and Automation (ICRA)*, pages 3089–3094, 2016.

[32] D. C. Richardson and R. Dale. Looking To Understand: The Coupling Between Speakers' and Listeners' Eye Movements and its Relationship to Discourse Comprehension. *Cognitive Science*, 29(6):1045–1060, 2005.

[33] F. Riedo, P. Rétornaz, L. Bergeron, N. Nyffeler, and F. Mondada. A Two Years Informal Learning Experience Using the Thymio Robot. In *Advances in Autonomous Mini Robots*, pages 37–48. Springer, 2012.

[34] C. Rogers and M. Portsmore. Bringing Engineering to Elementary School. *Journal of STEM Education: Innovations and Research*, 5(3/4):17, 2004.

[35] M. Sarac, M. A. Ergin, A. Erdogan, and V. Patoglu. ASSISTON-MOBILE: A Series Elastic Holonomic Mobile Platform for Upper Extremity Rehabilitation. *Robotica*, 32(08):1433–1459, 2014.

[36] E. Schweikardt and M. D. Gross. roBlocks: A Robotic Construction Kit for Mathematics and Science Education. In *Proceedings of the 8th International Conference on Multimodal Interfaces*, pages 72–75, 2006.

[37] G. S. Shakir Hussain, Jörgen Lindh. The effect of LEGO Training on Pupils' School Performance in Mathematics, Problem Solving Ability and Attitude: Swedish Data. *Journal of Educational Technology & Society*, 9(3):182–194, 2006.

[38] N. Shin and S. Kim. Learning about, from, and with Robots: Students' Perspectives. In *Proceedings of the IEEE International Symposium on Robot and Human Interactive Communication (RO-MAN)*, 2007.

[39] G. Sidorov, A. Gelbukh, H. Gómez-Adorno, and D. Pinto. Soft Similarity and Soft Cosine Measure: Similarity of Features in Vector Space Model. *Computación y Sistemas*, 18(3):491–504, 2014.

[40] F. R. Sullivan. Robotics and science literacy: Thinking skills, science process skills and systems understanding. *Journal of Research in Science Teaching*, 45(3):373–394, 2008.

[41] J. L. Toennies, J. Burgner, T. J. Withrow, and R. J. Webster. Toward Haptic/Aural Touchscreen Display of Graphical Mathematics for the Education of Blind Students. In *Proceedings of the 2011 IEEEWorld Haptics Conference (WHC)*, pages 373–378, 2011.

[42] E. N. Wiebe, J. Minogue, M. G. Jones, J. Cowley, and D. Krebs. Haptic feedback and students' learning about levers: Unraveling the effect of simulated touch. *Computers & Education*, 53(3):667–676, 2009.

[43] D. C. Williams, Y. Ma, L. Prejean, M. J. Ford, and G. Lai. Acquisition of Physics Content Knowledge and Scientific Inquiry Skills in a Robotics Summer Camp. *Journal of Research on Technology in Education*, 40(2):201–216, 2007.

[44] T. T. Yuen, M. Boecking, E. P. Tiger, A. Gomez, A. Guillen, A. Arreguin, and J. Stone. Group Tasks, Activities, Dynamics, and Interactions in Collaborative Robotics Projects with Elementary and Middle School Children. *Journal of STEM Education: Innovations and Research*, 15(1):39, 2014.

(Ir)relevance of Gender? On the Influence of Gender Stereotypes on Learning with a Robot

Natalia Reich-Stiebert　　Friederike Eyssel

CITEC Cluster of Excellence Cognitive Interaction Technology, Bielefeld University

Inspiration 1, 33619 Bielefeld, Germany

+49 (0)521 106-12133
nreich@cit-ec.uni-bielefeld.de

+49 (0)521 106-12044
feyssel@cit-ec.uni-bielefeld.de

ABSTRACT

Education research has documented a trend that reflects gender-based differences in the choice of fields of study. This, in turn, contributes to an imbalance in the representation of men and women in particular professions: In educational contexts, female teachers predominantly teach stereotypically female areas of study like social sciences and humanities, whereas male teachers are mainly represented in stereotypically male domains like mathematics. Research further provides evidence for the fact that this gender-stereotyped division of labor in education significantly impacts students' learning and motivation. Would gender-related stereotypes also bias learning processes with robots? This is plausible in light of the fact that social robots become more and more popular in learning settings. Thus, should the next generation of educational robots be 'gendered' and what impact would robot gender have on task performance, particularly in the context of a gender-stereotypical human-robot interaction (HRI) task?

To investigate these issues, we examined the influence of robot gender on learning when completing either stereotypically female or stereotypically male learning tasks. 120 university students (60 females and 60 males) completed either stereotypically female or stereotypically male tasks with the support of a male vs. female instructor robot. The manipulation check indicated that participants recognized the robot's alleged gender correctly. Importantly, our results suggest that prevailing gender stereotypes associated with learning do not apply to robots that perform gender-stereotypical tasks. Interestingly, our findings indicated that a mismatch of robot gender and gender typicality of the respective task led to increased willingness to engage in prospective learning processes with the robot. We discuss these results with respect to future research on HRI and learning, and with regard to practical implications associated with the introduction of robots into higher education.

HRI '17, March 06-09, 2017, Vienna, Austria.

 ISBN 978-1-4503-4336-7/17/03…$15.00.

DOI: http://dx.doi.org/10.1145/2909824.3020242

Keywords

Gender stereotypes; learning; human-robot interaction; educational robots; robot evaluation.

1. INTRODUCTION

Imagine the following scenario: An educational robot helps you to complete a math task that focuses on the three classic binomial formulas. The robot provides information on the formulas and how they can be expanded. The robot gives you advice and corrects your mistakes. In a second step, please imagine that you have to learn about a range of rhetorical means used in literary studies with the help of a robot. The robot explains various rhetorical means, their use, and how to integrate them in speech. Considering both scenarios, did you imagine that one and the same robot assisted you? Or did you envision a male robot teaching you binomial formulas, whereas a female educational robot came to mind when being instructed about rhetorical means? Possibly, it might also have been the other way around. From a scientific point of view, we have to examine which combination will have the most positive impact on learning performance and intrinsic motivation. Is it the match or the mismatch between robot gender and gender typicality of a given task? Empirically, it remains to be investigated whether 'female' gendered robots might support learning in science, technology, engineering, and mathematics (STEM) disciplines more effectively, whereas 'male' gendered robots deployed in linguistics and literary studies could potentially contribute to better learning outcomes and to higher motivation in students.

These assumptions arise in light of the persisting gender-based performance gap in early education, in higher education, and in academia. Accordingly, opportunities for male and female students are not yet equal: A large body of literature indicates that stereotypes link gender to achievement in various subject areas with girls outperforming boys in the verbal domain, including linguistics and literature. Boys, on the other hand, have been shown to achieve a better performance in mathematical and scientific fields [e.g., 1-7]. Moreover, a vast amount of research highlights the impact of teacher gender on student achievement [e.g., 8-10]. For instance, [8] have investigated the impact of a same-sex professor on students' interest in a subject and found that female students who initially had women professors reported increased interest to take additional courses in geology, mathematics and statistics, whereas male students with male professors in education and social work courses reported higher interest in these domains and were much more likely to major in these areas. Likewise, [9] have examined whether college students would benefit from same-sex role models. These authors found that female students benefit more from female rather than male role models. Similarly, female students identified more strongly with female role models. Male students, in contrast, were not influenced by same-sex role models. [10] confirmed that an increased exposure to female scientists, engineers, and mathematicians promoted female students' self-concept, attitudes, and effort toward these disciplines.

Are these findings from education research also applicable to HRI and social robotics? Broadly, there is evidence that humans tend "to imbue the real or imagined behavior of nonhuman agents with humanlike characteristics, motivations, intentions or emotions" [11, p. 864], and that people are inclined to treat nonhuman entities like other humans [e.g., 12, 13]. That means, anthropomorphizing nonhuman entities serves the function of making sense of an uncertain environment, of reducing stress [14] by providing a framework of meaning by making a nonhuman agents' behavior appear more understandable and predictable [15]. In doing so, people rely on knowledge that is related to themselves or the general category of "humans" because knowledge about what is human is chronically accessible [see 11]. Thus, when people form impression of other persons (or robots), they refer back to visual cues that activate social categories such as age, race, and gender [16, 17]. Relating these findings to HRI, research has shown that people interact with robots in ways that are similar to human–human interaction [e.g., 18-20] and that they likewise apply social categorization processes to robots [19, 21]. Accepting this premise, might the gendered design of an educational robot show positive effects on human-robot learning outcomes? To shed light on this, we studied the interplay between an educational robots' gender, gender-stereotyped tasks, and participant sex and their impact on learning outcomes, learning motivation, and robot evaluation.

2. RELATED WORK

To date, the interplay between robot gender and gender typicality of tasks has received scant attention in HRI research. While extensive research has been carried out on the impact of a virtual agents' gender on students' learning, only one study has attempted to investigate the effect of an educational robots' gender on participants' learning outcomes. To illustrate, much research on virtual pedagogical agents recognizes the critical role played by agent gender in learning activities [e.g., 22-26]. For instance, [25] have investigated the differential impact of learning about electrical circuits with a female animated pedagogical agent (APA) and a male APA. Results showed that female students achieved higher learning outcomes when the APA matched their sex, whereas male students reached better outcomes when they learned with a female APA. Similarly, [26] have found that female students had increased interest, self-efficacy, and math performance after learning with a female animated virtual agent. Likewise, male students performed better when they interacted with the female agent. Thus, the female agent tended to be most effective regardless of participants' sex. In contrast, [22] have reported that a male learning companion produced the most positive impact on female students' achievement in mathematics and attitudes toward math compared to a female learning companion. The authors argued that female students transferred the persisting gender stereotypes about mathematics to the learning companion and thus, they regarded the male learning companions' information as more reliable. In a similar vein, a study by [24] has investigated participants' performance, effort, and motivation in mathematics after learning with a female versus a male virtual agent that displayed rapport behavior. The findings confirm that participants' performance and effort increased significantly when interacting with an agent of the opposite gender. Taken together, the state-of-the-art in research on gender and learning processes provides an inconsistent and even contradictory picture. However, importantly, the existing studies outline the critical role of gender in learning interactions between students and pedagogical agents.

To our knowledge, only one study has already investigated the interplay of robot and participant gender: In an experiment, [27] have examined whether the match or mismatch of a gendered HRI task and robot gender, affected participants' performance and their evaluation and anthropomorphization of the target robot. For this purpose, participants had to sort sewing equipment into a sewing box in the female-task condition and tools into a toolkit in the male-task condition. Participants were either instructed by a female or by a male robot. Results demonstrated that gender typicality of the HRI task had a significant impact on participants' task performance and their evaluation of the robot. Interestingly, participants made more errors, reported less willingness to accept help from the robot in a future task, and anthropomorphized the robot less after performing a stereotypically female task. Moreover, the female robot was evaluated as more competent within the context of the stereotypically male task, that is, when robot gender and task gender typicality were mismatched. It seems that participants ascribed more competence to the female robot when it – unexpectedly – demonstrated knowledge in a field that did not correspond with its alleged gender. This finding is surprising because previous research revealed that a match between robot gender and task gender typicality is preferred and leads to greater acceptance of the robot [21, 28]. Although the findings by [27] clearly provide a valuable contribution to research on gender in HRI, it is important to note that the HRI task that participants had to complete as part of the experiment was rather artificial and lacked external validity, as it consisted of sorting virtual objects into a toolkit or into a sewing box, respectively. Thus, it still remains unclear how robot gender affects more externally valid, common tasks or processes like acquiring knowledge. In addition, the effects of robot gender on an individual's motivational state and how people experience HRI have to be explored further. Finally, new research has to examine the conditions under which a match or mismatch of robot gender and task gender typicality might be advantageous in HRI.

Taken together, previous results highlight the fact that gender is not only an important aspect in the context of human-human learning processes [1-10], but also in the context of learning processes that are supported by virtual agents and robots. Nevertheless, little research has been undertaken to investigate the influence of a robots' gender on learning outcomes and motivation, and further, previous research has hardly considered the gender typicality of different tasks. So far, previous work has completely neglected the impact of robot gender on human-robot learning in particular *academic domains* and its influence on the evaluation of HRI and human motivation. To this end, we set out to examine the impact of gender in human-robot learning in higher education and second, we manipulated robot and task gender typicality. This way, students were given the opportunity to engage in learning processes with a female (vs. a male) robot in the context of stereotypically female (vs. stereotypically male) academic tasks.

2.1 Hypotheses

Given the inconsistent outcomes regarding interaction effects of task gender typicality and gender of a virtual or robot agent, respectively, we proposed two hypotheses: Firstly, we postulated a matching-hypothesis according to which robot gender matches the gender typicality of the task (H1). This would be the case, for instance, when a female robot would provide support in a stereotypically female task. This assumption is supported by findings from human-computer interaction: For example, [29] have shown that participants displayed gender-stereotypic responses to computers and that matching the gender between task and computer features resulted in more positive perceptions of the computer. Further evidence for the positive effect of matching the features of a nonhuman entity to its tasks comes from HRI. Precisely, it was found that matching robot appearance to tasks improved human-robot cooperation and people's acceptance of the robot [28, 30]. The matching-hypothesis read:

H1: We assumed that participants would demonstrate better objective learning outcomes, they would report higher subjective learning motivation, higher satisfaction with the learning interaction, and report stronger anthropomorphization of the robot when the robot gender *matched* the gender typicality of the task.

Alternatively, the competing mismatch-hypothesis (H2) assumed a mismatch of robot gender and the gender typicality of the task. This hypothesis is grounded, inter alia, on the findings by [24]: These authors have demonstrated that learning with an agent of the opposite gender increased participants' learning outcomes. Further, we assumed that a mismatch between robot gender and gender typicality of the task should increase people's attention toward the robot and the information provided by the robot, so that the mismatch could contribute to a better objective task performance. The mismatch-hypothesis read:

H2: We expected that participants would show better learning outcomes, higher learning motivation, higher satisfaction with the learning interaction, and higher anthropomorphization of the target robot when the robot gender *mismatched* the gender typicality of the task.

3. METHOD

3.1 Participants and Design

Participants were 120 (60 females, 60 males; M_{age} = 24.57, SD_{age} = 4.73) German university students from different majors (e.g., physics, psychology, economics, etc.) who were recruited at Bielefeld University. To measure the link between robot gender, gendered task and participant sex, we choose a 2 (*robot gender*: male vs. female) x 2 (*task gender typicality*: male vs. female) x 2 (*participant sex*: male vs. female) between-subjects factorial design. Participants were randomly assigned to each of the eight resulting experimental conditions.

Clearly, user, robot, and task characteristics need to be taken into account in HRI, to account for differences between male vs. female response patterns towards male vs. female robots helping with stereotypically male or female tasks. However, in the literature, participant *sex* is often referred to as participant *gender*, and terms are used interchangeably. Sex refers to biological and physiological features. Gender, however, is a social construction. We controlled for both aspects by including these factors in the experimental design. A person's biological sex sometimes does not correspond with the perceived gender identity. Thus, in our data, we checked whether the experimental 'assignment' to the male vs. female category coincided with participants' self-identification as male and female. For all participants, the assignment to a male vs. female sex coincided with participants' self-identified gender.

3.2 Procedure

Participants were tested individually in a laboratory at Bielefeld University. The experimenter informed them that the study concerned a HRI task and that they had to solve three brief tasks while being instructed by a robot. The experimenter explained that she would stay in the laboratory behind a partition in order to provide technical assistance in case needed. Participants were seated in front of the robot NAO (NAO Evolution, Academic Edition, blue, SoftBank Robotics, see Figure 1) and a laptop was placed to the left of the robot. During the interaction, the robot sat on the desk and performed a set of head and arm movements to support its explanations and to point to the laptop. Participants were informed that the robot would instruct them autonomously on the upcoming tasks. To convey the impression that the robot would act autonomously, we used a Wizard-of-Oz approach [31] to operate the robot in synchrony with participants' individual learning pace and ability to solve the tasks. The robot introduced participants to the upcoming learning tasks and mentioned that they would have to use the laptop or to pay attention to the robot. The robots' introductory instruction on the learning tasks read as follows:

Hello [NAO waves his arm], I'm glad that you're participating in this learning experiment. My name is Nero/ Nera and I'm going to explain you three [NAO opens his hand] different tasks. Afterwards you have to solve them. For completing the tasks, you will need this laptop [NAO points to the laptop]. I will tell you when the time comes. Otherwise please look at me and listen to me carefully. When you're ready, we can start with the first learning task.

Throughout the learning interaction the robot provided participants with the demands of each specific task, pronounced the new words in the memory tasks, and explained how to expand the binomial formulas or how to use particular rhetorical means in the practical task. Following the learning interaction, the robot asked participants to complete several questionnaires that were also computerized and included the dependent measures. Finally, participants were debriefed, reimbursed, and dismissed.

3.3 Experimental Manipulation

3.3.1 Robot Gender

Robot gender was manipulated by two aspects: the robots' name and its voice. Previous research has indicated that the name of a robot is a good indicator of its alleged gender [e.g., 19, 27]. According to [27], "Nero" and "Nera" were clearly identified as male and female robot names, respectively. Therefore, we decided to use the same names in our research to indicate robot gender. Regarding robot voice, findings suggest that a particular voice can trigger a set of expectations associated with the speaker's gender.

Figure 1. The robot provides instructions.

That is, a male voice might produce expectations and responses based on stereotypes about males, whereas a female voice generating responses based on stereotypes about females [29]. In order to manipulate the robot's voice, we used the text-to-speech Mac OS X voice application with the German voice package and selected a typically female and a male voice. The voices were played through the robots' loudspeakers to strengthen the perception that the voice belongs to the robot. We avoided to use the NAO robot voice as it is only possible to regulate the pitch of the voice into higher and lower frequencies. To assure that the voices were correctly perceived as male and female, and that both voices were regarded equally comprehensible, we conducted a pilot study with 40 participants (18 females, 22 males; M_{age} = 24.45, SD_{age} = 4.77). In this pretest, participants had to learn and solve tasks using a laptop. These tasks were intended for the application in the main study. Task instructions and explanations were provided by synthesized male versus female voices to be used in the main study. For each voice, participants had to decide whether the respective voice sounded male or female. Additionally, participants were asked to rate each voice on 7-point Likert scales (1 = *not at all*, 7 = *very much*) on how pleasant, comprehensible, dominant, friendly, warm, and competent they perceived the respective voice. This was done to avoid differences in perception of these dimensions across voice samples. Regarding gender typicality of the voice, we found that 100 % of the participants perceived the female voice as female and the male voice as male. With respect to the evaluation of the voices, as predicted, we did not obtain significant differences between the female and the male voice regarding pleasantness, comprehensibility, dominance, friendliness, warmth, and competence, all *ps* > .18.

3.3.2 Task Gender Typicality

Participants had to learn and solve one of two gendered task sets. Each task set consisted of three different tasks including two memory tasks, one auditory and one visual, and a practice task within an academic domain. Sensory preferences influence the ways in which students learn. To take into account interindividual differences in preference for information presentation mode, we relied on visual and auditory information presentation. These modes of information processing are most common in learning according to research from education and instruction psychology [e.g., 32]. The former mode emphasizes the visual presentation of information, whereas the latter mode highlights the auditory presentation of information. Both memory tasks comprised learning of fictitious words. With respect to the practice task, we chose tasks from two academic domains where participants had to apply their acquired or refreshed knowledge to a specific practical task like solving $(4 + 3)^2$, for instance. Thus, different task types were not only chosen to serve different perceptual preferences for learning, but also to investigate more complex authentic tasks from the academic field.

Task gender typicality was manipulated based on the context of the task: In the 'female-task condition', we preselected stereotypically female fields of interest like a cosmetic product, art history, and literary studies. In the 'male-task condition', participants were presented with tasks associated with stereotypically male areas of interest like a shaving product, architecture, and mathematics. In the auditory task, participants had to learn and memorize ten fictitious contents of either a cleansing lotion (female task condition) or an aftershave (male task condition). The robot spoke the words (e.g., *Fesyl, Sulfan, Kaltas*) and participants had to repeat them loudly and had to memorize them. In the visual task, participants had to learn and memorize ten fictitious geometric figures in art history (female task condition) or architecture (male task condition). The robot spoke the words (e.g., *Porim, Broler, Lisant*) and pointed to the laptop screen that displayed the figures (see Figure 2). In the following, participants had to repeat and memorize the words again. Finally, in the practice task participants had to learn three German-language rhetorical means (female task condition) or three binomial formulas in mathematics (male task condition). Afterwards they had to apply their knowledge to solve the three tasks.

To assure that the gender stereotypicality of the selected task contents would be identified correctly, we conducted a second pretest with another independent sample of 40 participants (20 females, 20 males; M_{age} = 23.44, SD_{age} = 2.92). They were asked to rate the gender stereotypicality of each task using a 7-point Likert scale from 1 (*male*) to 7 (*female*). Results revealed that the auditory and visual tasks were regarded as typically female (i.e., recalling ingredients of a cleansing lotion in the auditory task: M = 4.55, SD = 1.36, $t(19)$ = 1.81, p = .09, figures from art history in the visual task: M = 4.60, SD = 1.20, $t(19)$ = 2.45, p = .02) rather than typically male (i.e., recalling aftershave ingredients in the auditory task: M = 1.65, SD = 1.23, $t(19)$ = -8.57, p < .001, figures from architecture in the visual task: M = 3.60, SD = 0.68, $t(19)$ = -2.63, p < .02). Likewise, the practice task for the stylistic devices was identified as typically female (M = 4.60, SD = 0.75, $t(19)$ = 3.56, p = .002) while the binomial formula task was rated as typically male (M = 2.95, SD = 1.15, $t(19)$ = -4.10, p = .001). Importantly, as the two task sets were chosen to be equal regarding difficulty of the learning contents, we further assessed the number of correctly remembered contents and figures in the memory tasks and the number of correctly solved questions in the practice task, respectively. Further, we asked subjects to rate the tasks on 7-point Likert scales (1 = *not at all*, 7 = *very much*) regarding the task complexity. As predicted, task types were perceived as equally demanding, all *ps* > .06. Table 1 depicts the task characteristics based on the pretest.

3.4 Dependent Measures

3.4.1 Manipulation Checks

To check whether participants had correctly identified the male vs. female robot targets as male or female, respectively, we asked participants to indicate the robots' gender on a 7-point Likert scale (1 = *female*, 7 = *male*). Further, in order to assure that the tasks were perceived as equally complex, participants had to indicate on a 7-point Likert scale (1 = *not at all*, 7 = *very much*) task complexity as well as perceived competence and motivation during task completion.

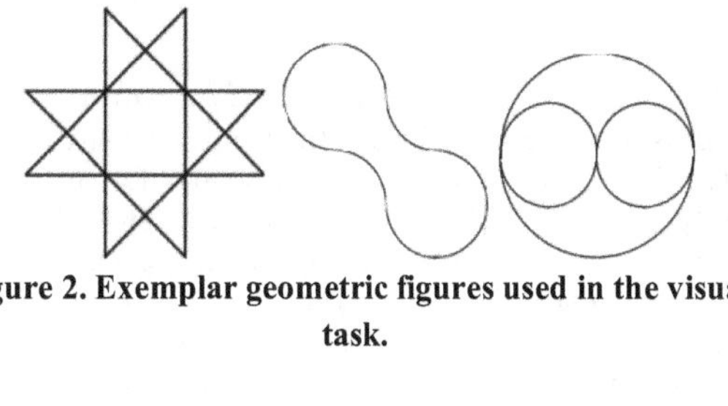

Figure 2. Exemplar geometric figures used in the visual task.

Table 1. Task difficulty ratings for female and male tasks in the pretest.

Task type	Typically male task *M* (*SD*)	Typically female task *M* (*SD*)	*t* (40)	*d*
Auditory task				
Correct answers	2.50 (2.26)	2.35 (1.84)	2.30	-0.07
Task complexity	5.80 (1.24)	6.15 (0.99)	-0.99	0.31
Visual task				
Correct answers	5.35 (2.43)	5.75 (2.79)	-0.48	0.15
Task complexity	5.35 (1.60)	4.95 (1.32)	1.94	-0.27
Practice task				
Correct answers	2.26 (1.10)	2.80 (0.52)	-1.97	0.62
Task complexity	3.50 (2.07)	3.25 (2.12)	-0.26	-0.12

3.4.2 Objective Learning Outcome

To measure objective learning outcomes, we assessed the number of correctly remembered terms in the memory tasks (auditory and visual task, each yielding a maximum of ten correct solutions) as well as the number of correct solutions in the practice task, yielding a maximum of three correct ones. As a second performance measure, we assessed the subjective evaluation of task performance by asking participants to indicate task complexity and their perceived motivation and competence during the given task on a 7-point Likert scale (1 = *not at all*, 7 = *very much*).

3.4.3 Learning Motivation during HRI

We first assessed participants' learning mood, followed by a measure of self-reported intrinsic motivation, to evaluate participants' motivational state during the interaction task, To measure participants' affective state, we used a short version form of an instrument developed by [33]. Participants had to indicate their feelings during the HRI (e.g., attentive, amused, relaxed). To assess intrinsic motivation, we administered the short German version of the Intrinsic Motivation Inventory proposed by [34]. Example items read: "I enjoyed learning with the robot.", "I am satisfied with my performance at this learning task with the robot." or "I felt pressured while learning with the robot". For both aspects of the evaluation of the subjective learning atmosphere, participants had to state their level of agreement by means of 7-point Likert scales (1 = *strongly disagree*, 7 = *strongly agree*).

3.4.4 Evaluation of HRI-Mediated Learning

To assess the user-friendliness of the educational robot, we adapted the *Usability Scale* by [35], a tool for measuring the usability of a technical system, and the *Perceived Ease of Use Scale* by [36], to investigate participants' acceptance of technical systems, to education robots. The questionnaire covered user satisfaction with the robot as learning instructor. By means of an 8-item questionnaire (e.g., "The interaction with the robot was smooth", "The robot's voice was clearly understandable" or "The robot knew exactly what I had to do during the different tasks"). Finally, three items tapped participants' willingness to engage in prospective learning interactions with the robot. We used the following items to assess such contact intentions: "I would like to work again on such a task with the robot", "I would seek the robots' help for other tasks, too" and "I would like to own the robot in order to use it frequently for learning". To collect responses, we used 7-point Likert scales ranging from 1 (*strongly disagree*) to 7 (*strongly agree*).

3.4.5 Evaluation of the Robot

Anthropomorphism encompasses the ascription of humanlike characteristics and mental states to nonhuman entities [11], and is a phenomenon that also applies to robots [e.g. 19, 37]. To assess anthropomorphic inferences of the robot, we used two measures: First, we assessed the extent to which participants attributed *agency* – the capability to plan and to act – to the robot by adapting a scale provided by [38]. The scale has been validated in the robotics context in previous research [e.g., 39-41]. Participants had to rate the robot on the subscale *agency* that included six items regarding memory and thought. Second, we measured participants' impression of the robot's *warmth*, including the robots' good intentions, and *competence*, the capability to pursue, using an adapted short version of a scale developed by [42]. These twelve items have likewise been successfully used in the context of HRI research [e.g., 19, 31]. The perception of the robot as a learning companion was assessed by means of a 12-item semantic differential on 7-point bipolar rating scales whose extremes are designated by two opposite adjectives (e.g., *comprehensible/ incomprehensible, friendly/ unfriendly, interested/ disinterested*).

3.4.6 Control Variables

We assessed *prior experience with the robot NAO* and *technology commitment* to control for undesired effects of these two variables on the evaluation of the HRI and the robot as previous research has shown that technical affinity and prior robot experience significantly influence the evaluation of robots [see 43, 44]. Prior experience with the robot NAO was captured by the item "Do you have experiences with the robot NAO?" in forced-choice format (yes vs. no). We measured participants' affinity for technology by applying a short version of the Technology Commitment Scale provided by [45]. The scale consisted of eight items that could be rated on 7-point Likert scales (1 = *strongly disagree*, 7 *strongly agree*). An example item read: "I am eager to use the latest technical gadgets".

4. RESULTS

We conducted *t*-tests to check the effectiveness of the experimental manipulation, to test whether the task complexity was perceived equally demanding, and whether participants perceived themselves equally motivated and competent to solve the tasks. Further, we conducted a MANCOVA to examine interaction effects and main effects of robot gender and task gender typicality on the dependent measures. Table 2 provides an overview of descriptive statistics and internal consistencies (Cronbach's α) of the measures.

4.1 Manipulation Check

To check the effectiveness of the experimental manipulation of robot gender, we tested whether the robot was correctly perceived as male or female, respectively. To do so, we computed a one-sample *t*-test against the neutral scale midpoint (scale value = 4 on a 7-point scale; the endpoints of the scale were 1 = *more female* vs. 7 = *more male*).

Table 2. Descriptive statistics and internal consistencies.

Measures	*M*	*SD*	Min	Max	*α*
Learning mood	5.05	0.88	2.90	6.80	.80
Intrinsic motivation	4.13	0.86	1.50	6.63	.72
Ease of use	5.84	0.94	1.17	7.00	.72
Contact intentions	4.03	1.69	1.00	7.00	.82
Agency attribution	4.29	1.10	2.00	7.00	.72
Warmth	3.57	1.09	1.33	6.33	.84
Competence	3.17	1.07	1.33	5.83	.80

Results were as predicted: In the female-robot condition, the robot was recognized as more female ($M = 3.07$, $SD = 1.54$), whereas in the male-robot condition, the robot was correctly perceived as more male ($M = 6.27$, $SD = 1.04$), $t(119) = 3.53$, $p = .001$, $d = 0.32$. To ensure that participants perceived the tasks equally demanding, and that they perceived their competence and motivation in solving the tasks equal, we further conducted *t*-tests to compare the typically female and male tasks. Table 3 provides the results that indicated that the visual and auditory tasks were perceived as equally demanding. Regarding the practice task, however, the typically male task (i.e., solving the binomial formula) was perceived more difficult than the typically female task (i.e., working on rhetorical means). Likewise, participants felt more competent in solving the typically female practice task than the male practice task.

4.2 Objective Learning Outcome

We conducted a 2 (*robot gender*: male vs. female) by 2 (*task gender typicality:* male vs. female) by 2 (*participant sex:* male vs. female) MANCOVA with the covariates *prior experience with the robot NAO*, *technical affinity*, and *field of study* (dummy coded: 1 = social sciences and humanities, 2 = STEM-related domains) to test the effects on the learning outcome. Unexpectedly, we found a significant main effect of task gender typicality on the learning outcome, $F(3, 96) = 9.92$, $p < .001$, $\eta_p^2 = .24$. In line with participants' self-reports on task complexity (see Table 3), participants provided more correct answers in the typically female practice task (rhetorical means; $M = 2.63$, $SD = 0.11$) than in the typically male practice task (binomial formulas; $M = 1.81$, $SD = 0.11$). Further, we obtained a significant *task gender typicality* by *participant sex* interaction effect, $F(3, 96) = 6.56$, $p < .001$, $\eta_p^2 = .17$. Univariate analyses showed that female participants provided more correct answers in the typically male auditory task ($M = 2.92$, $SD = 0.27$) compared to male participants ($M = 1.89$, $SD = 0.27$). Likewise, male participants provided more correct answers when solving the typically female auditory task ($M = 2.40$, $SD = 0.25$) than female participants ($M = 1.84$, $SD = 0.27$), $F(1, 98) = 10.42$, $p < .01$, $\eta_p^2 = .10$. With respect to the practice task, we found a similar pattern: Female participants reported more correct answers in the typically male practice task ($M = 2.08$, $SD = 0.17$) than male participants ($M = 1.55$, $SD = 0.17$). On the other hand, male participants provided more correct answers for the typically female practice task ($M = 2.86$, $SD = 0.16$) than female participants ($M = 2.41$, $SD = 0.17$), $F(1, 98) = 9.69$, $p < .01$, $\eta_p^2 = .09$. No other effects reached statistical significance, all *ps* > .18.

4.3 Subjective Evaluation of HRI

With respect to the evaluation of the robot and participants contact intentions to the robot, a 2 (*robot gender*: male vs. female) by 2 (*task gender typicality*: male vs. female) by 2 (*participant sex*: male vs. female) MANCOVA with the covariates *prior experience with the robot NAO*, *technical affinity*, and *field of study* (dummy coded: 1 = social sciences and humanities, 2 = STEM-related domains) revealed neither significant main effects nor significant interaction effects, all *ps* > .38. However, in the univariate analyses, we obtained a significant *robot gender* by *task gender typicality* interaction effect on contact intentions, $F(1, 101) = 4.88$, $p < .05$, $\eta_p^2 = .05$ (see Figure 3). As predicted in the mismatch-hypothesis, participants who were instructed to solve a typically female task with a male robot reported higher contact intentions ($M = 4.58$, $SD = 0.32$) compared to participants who learned a typically male task with a male robot ($M = 3.91$, $SD = 0.32$). Likewise, participants who were instructed to solve a typically male task with a female robot reported higher contact intentions ($M = 4.17$, $SD = 0.31$) than participants who solved a typically female task with the support of a female robot ($M = 3.43$, $SD = 0.33$). No other significant effects were found, all *ps* > .21.

5. DISCUSSION

In recent years, the development and application of educational robots has become an important scientific and societal issue because the use of education robots has a significant impact on people's motivation and cognition [e.g., 46-48]. In this context, the issue regarding core features that should be taken into account in educational robot design becomes more and more relevant. Particularly, does gender play a role when it comes to human-robot learning, and if yes, are prevailing gender stereotypes about teachers, learners and learning processes applicable to learning processes studied in HRI? To date, little research has been undertaken to investigate whether assigning a male or a female gender to a robot increases task performance in learning contexts, intrinsic motivation, and robot acceptance [see 27]. To further investigate this issue, we explored the influence of gender stereotypes on learning with a robot in higher education. To do so, we postulated two competing hypotheses grounded in psychological literature on the impact of gender stereotypes on learning [e.g., 1, 3-6]: The matching-hypothesis (H1) stated that participants would provide higher objective learning outcomes and evaluate the HRI and the robot better when the robot gender matched the gender typicality of the task.

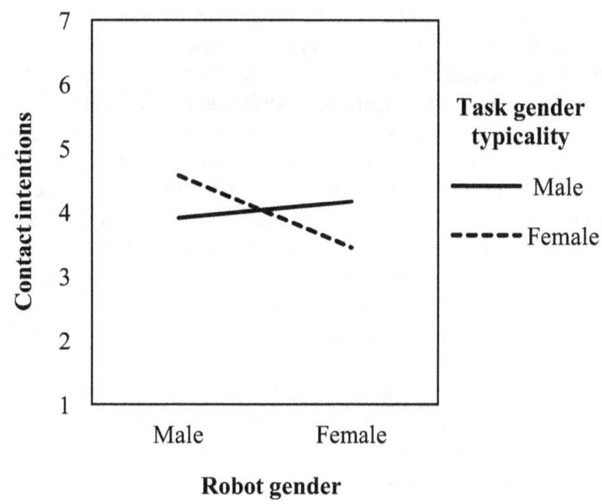

Figure 3. Robot gender by task gender typicality interaction effect on contact intentions.

Table 3. Results for perception of task difficulty in the female and male tasks.

Task type	Typically male task M (SD)	Typically female task M (SD)	t (118)	d
Auditory task				
Task complexity	5.68 (1.23)	5.82 (0.93)	-0.71	0.13
Perceived competence	2.45 (1.28)	2.58 (1.50)	-0.52	0.09
Motivation	4.98 (1.35)	4.72 (1.52)	1.02	-0.18
Visual task				
Task complexity	5.38 (1.15)	5.05 (1.63)	1.29	-0.23
Perceived competence	2.85 (1.44)	3.05 (1.41)	-0.77	0.14
Motivation	5.30 (1.17)	5.10 (1.37)	0.86	-0.16
Practice task				
Task complexity	3.05 (2.00)	2.05 (1.33)	3.23**	-0.59
Perceived competence	4.37 (2.26)	5.38 (1.81)	-2.72*	0.49
Motivation	5.27 (1.60)	5.57 (1.52)	-1.05	0.19

* $p < .01$, ** $p < .006$ (Bonferroni corrected)

In contrast, the mismatch-hypothesis (H2) presumed that the objective outcomes and the subjective evaluation would be better when the robot gender mismatched the gender typicality of the task. With our results, we extended the previous literature on gender effects in HRI with respect to the following aspects:

First, we tested the effect of gender typicality of academic learning tasks on HRI and showed that *robot gender* had no influence on participants' objective learning performance. That is, participants learning was neither positively nor negatively affected by learning with a 'male' or a 'female' robot. Despite the large sample size in the present study, further research should be carried out including even larger samples to investigate the effect of robot gender on learning performance in more detail. Moreover, in future investigations, other objective measures like response time or gaze to measure participants' attention should be taken into account. However, we found significant interaction effects of *task gender typicality* and *participant sex*: Female participants outperformed male participants in typically male tasks, whereas male participants outperformed female participants in typically female tasks. This mismatch is surprising in light of previous findings from educational research [1, 3, 6]. It seems that participants paid more attention to tasks that did not match their own sex and they gained higher learning outcomes. This mismatch might have unconsciously drawn participants' attention to the common gender stereotypes, namely, that males perform better in STEM-related domains, while females show higher performance in social sciences or linguistics, for instance. This in turn might have led females to put more effort into accomplishing the stereotypically male tasks, and males showed more effort in trying to solve the stereotypically female tasks, respectively. To rule out this possibility, it would be worth investigating how to counteract gender stereotypical expectations by using educational robots that make salient that gender-based performance discrepancies are less and less prevalent across different disciplines. For example, the robot could state that males and females perform equally in domains like literary studies, linguistics or humanities, while females are equally capable in solving STEM-related tasks like their male counterparts. Another possibility would be to apply the psychological intervention of value affirmation with educational robots, as this intervention proved to be successful in reducing the gender achievement gap in college science [49]. Value affirmation protects people from psychological threat – as it is the case with achievement gaps based on gender stereotypes – and provides them with internal resources that are necessary for coping [50]. Accordingly, robots could be used to strengthen the belief in personal values. In doing so, it could be possible to foster gender equity in academic performance in higher education using educational robots.

Second, we explored the effect of *robot gender* on participants' subjective evaluation of the HRI and the robot in more detail by assessing learning motivation and learning interaction. Unexpectedly, we found no significant main or interaction effects of robot gender and task gender typicality on our dependent measures. In our study, robot gender neither influenced participants' objective learning outcomes nor did it affect their subjective perception of the perceived quality of HRI in the learning context and their intrinsic motivation. Likewise, participants did not differentiate between gendered robot types with regard to ease of use, and attribution of agency and of warmth and competence. One factor that might have influenced the perception of the robots' gender might be the fact that in German language, the generic masculine form is used for the word 'robot'. That is, grammatically speaking, in German language, a robot has a 'male' gender. In German language, the grammatical case of articles and pronouns has a strong impact on people's perception of words, especially when grammatical cues between noun and pronoun or article mismatch [51]. This subtlety could potentially have affected the perception of the robots' gender in our experiment during which participants had to learn with the support of the robot ('male' in grammatical terms) Nera ('female' by first name and vocal cues) and listen to *her* explanations, as Nera was an ostensibly female robot with a female voice in our study. In this sense, one might argue that match versus mismatch were not optimally operationalized in the case of the female robot target. However, given that we found an analogous pattern of results for the male robot, the lack of findings regarding the evaluation of the HRI and the robot could be simply due to the fact that – at least in the context of our research – robot gender was not deemed important for human learning. To substantiate this notion, perceived subjective relevance of robot gender in education should be assessed in follow-up studies.

Above and beyond this aspect, our findings have potential positive implications for social robotics: Gender stereotypes affect various aspects of everyday life and still produce a gender-based performance imbalance in learning settings [e.g., 52-55]. Thus, the fact that robot gender did *not* play a major role in human-robot learning interactions, could be exploited to reduce these gender-related performance disparities and contribute to equal opportunities for female and male learners in higher education. For instance, educational robots could be used to support group learning (of mixed-sex groups) in stereotypically male as well as female domains without benefiting or discriminating learners of a specific sex, as it probably would be the case when a male or female teacher would instruct the group.

In partial support of the mismatch hypothesis (H2), our results indicated that a mismatch of robot gender and task gender typicality led to increased willingness for future learning with the robot. That is, participants were more inclined to engage in human-robot learning in the future when they were taught a stereotypically male task by a female robot, and a stereotypically female task by a male robot, respectively. Obviously, although a mismatch between robot gender and task gender typicality did not affect participants learning performance, it influenced how participants perceived the interaction with the robot. This may have to do with expectancy violation – namely, being confronted with a male robot that teaches a stereotypically female domain and vice versa – and the associated increased enthusiasm for using this robot for learning. This is an important issue for prospective research: Future studies should include measures that evaluate participants' *actual* enjoyment of the interaction in order to explore whether this in turn affects participants' increased contact intentions for future learning interactions. However, our results are in line with findings by [27] that documented the advantages of a mismatch during an actual HRI task on the evaluation of the robots' competence. Taken together, our findings suggest that a mismatch between robot gender and task gender typicality might be beneficial for HRI. This is, because a mismatch can increase the acceptance of robots for educational purposes. For instance, by applying female robots in STEM-related subjects to enhance students' willingness to use the support of robots for their science and technology learning. This implication is particularly interesting with respect to the general introduction of robots into university and school settings as it was found, for instance, that students and teachers were quite hesitant to use robots for their learning and teaching [44, 56-58]. Combining these findings, robots could probably make their way into learning environments easier when they are ascribed a gender that mismatches the gender typicality of their future application area.

Moreover, follow-up studies should take several methodological issues into consideration to explore open research questions further: For instance, with respect to task choice, we found significant differences in task complexity and perceived competence in solving the task for the practice tasks. Participants perceived the female practice task (i.e., rhetorical means) as easier than the male practice task (i.e., solving binomial formulas). This outcome is surprising in light of the results of our pilot study of this material. In order to avoid potential confounds, such as task complexity or task difficulty, prospective studies should administer additional practice tasks with different levels of difficulty. Ideally, these tasks should also include other domains like physics or educational sciences. In the present study, participants were instructed by the robot NAO – as it is one of the most widely used humanoid robots in the field of education and research [see 59]. In line with our pretest results, participants in the main study also recognized the robots' gender according to the gender manipulation via robot voice and robot name: Participants categorized the 'female' robot as more female and the 'male' robot as more male, respectively. Previous research [see 27, 60] further supports the fact that both, robot name and a robots' gendered voice, are sufficient to activate participants' perception of a robot as male or female. Nevertheless, future research should consider manipulating a robots' gender by taking into account other factors like clothing, movement, color, or posture, for instance. Finally, future studies should use robots that imply gendered design a priori, for example, the robot Flobi [61]. Since humanoid robots tend to be ascribed gender-specific traits that identify them as male or female [62], it is plausible that the NAO robot was perceived somewhat male, although participants correctly recognized the experimental manipulation of robot gender via name and voice. The assignment of a male or a female gender can even occur with ambiguously gendered robots [62], and it seems that this is the case with the robot NAO as NAO is referred as "he" [see 59].

6. CONCLUSION

In sum, the current study adds to a growing body of literature on the impact of gender stereotypes on learning with educational agents. Above and beyond previous findings, our results suggested that in the context of human-robot learning, robot gender does not affect participants' learning, intrinsic motivation, and the evaluation of the robot. Only participants' contact intentions were affected to some extent: Participants were more interested in future learning with a robot when the robots' gender did not match the task gender typicality of a given task. Interestingly, precisely this outcome could be vital for social robotics: Using robots in learning context could serve as an intervention to overcome persisting gender-stereotypes and to promote equal learning opportunities for male and female students. In the same vein, robotics design can increase end-users' willingness for future use of educational robots by gendering robots under consideration of future application areas. A further key strength of our study was the investigation of the influence of robot gender on human-robot learning in specific academic areas by further taking into account different learning channel preferences. Nevertheless, future research should systematically explore the effects of different types of gendered robots on human learning and their application in various domains. Further, although our sample size was fairly large for a HRI study and we counterbalanced participants' sex, future research should take into account different groups of learners in order to enhance external validity. That is, our sample included only university students from different fields of study, but it would be worthwhile to investigate the effects of gender stereotypes on learning with robots in school contexts and with school children of different ages. Precisely, it would be interesting to explore whether a male educational robot would affect elementary school students' learning as this group of students is predominantly thought by female teachers. With respect to the introduction of educational robots into school settings, another important issue that should be considered is the role that a robot should perform. Findings have shown that university students and teachers prefer to use robots as teaching assistants or tutors to support individual or group learning [44, 56]. In line with this, future approaches should take into consideration these learning requirements and explore the impact of gender stereotypes in the context of student-teacher-robot interactions. In these more applied contexts, students – but also teachers – as potential end-users of educational robots could provide additional insights into the issue whether and how robot gender influences students' learning, particularly learning of gender-stereotypic tasks.

7. ACKNOWLEDGMENTS

We thank Angie Pfaff, Jule Adriaans, and Nathalie Brock for their efforts in programming and data collection. This research has been conducted in the framework of the European Project CODEFROR (FP7 PIRSES-2013-612555) and it was supported by the Cluster of Excellence Cognitive Interaction Technology 'CITEC' (EXC 277) at Bielefeld University, which is funded by the German Research Foundation (DFG).

8. REFERENCES

[1] Brown, C. and Corcoran, M. 1997. Sex-based differences in school content and the male-female wage gap. *J. Labor. Econ.* 15, 3 (Jul. 1997), 431-465.

[2] Ceci, S. J., Williams, W. M., and Barnett, S. M. 2009. Women's underrepresentation in science: Sociocultural and biological considerations. *Psychol. Bull.* 135, 2 (Mar. 2009), 218-261.

[3] Else-Quest, N. M., Hyde, J. S., and Linn, M. C. 2010. Cross-national patterns of gender differences in mathematics: A meta-analysis. *Psychol. Bull.* 136, 1 (Jan. 2010), 103-127.

[4] Kessels, U. 2005. Fitting into the stereotype: How gender-stereotyped perceptions of prototypic peers relate to liking for school subjects. *Eur. J. Psychol. Educ.* 20, 3 (Sep. 2005), 309-323.

[5] Meece, J. L., Glienke, B. B., and Burg, S. 2006. Gender and motivation. *J. School. Psychol.* 44, 5 (Oct. 2006), 351-373.

[6] Mendez, L., Mihalas, S., and Hardesty, R. 2006. Gender differences in academic development and performance. In *Children's needs III: Development, prevention, and intervention*, G. G. Bear and K. M. Minke, Eds. National Association of School Psychologists, Washington, DC, 553-565.

[7] Su, R., Rounds, J., and Armstrong, P. 2009. Men and things, women and people: A meta-analysis of sex differences in interests. *Psychol. Bull.* 135, 6 (Nov. 2009), 859-884.

[8] Bettinger, E. P. and Long, B. T. 2005. Do faculty serve as role models? The impact of instructor gender on female students. *Am. Econ. Rev.* 95, 2 (May 2005), 152-157.

[9] Lockwood, P. 2006. "Someone like me can be successful": Do college students need same-gender role models? *Psychol. Women Quart.* 30, 1 (Mar. 2006), 36-46.

[10] Stout, J. G., Dasgupta, N., Hunsinger, M., and McManus, M. A. 2011. STEMing the tide: using ingroup experts to inoculate women's self-concept in science, technology, engineering, and mathematics (STEM). *J. Pers. Soc. Psychol.* 100, 2 (Feb. 2011) 255-70.

[11] Epley, N., Waytz, A., and Cacioppo, J. T. 2007. On seeing human: A three factor theory of anthropomorphism. *Psychol. Rev.* 114, 4 (Oct. 2007), 864-886.

[12] Nass, C., Moon, Y., Morkes, J., Kim, E. Y., and Fogg, B. 1997. Computers are social actors: A review of current research. In *Human values and the design of computer technology*, B. Friedman, Ed. CSLI Press, Stanford, CA, USA, Aug. 1997, 137-162. DOI= http://dl.acm.org/citation.cfm?id=278222.

[13] Reeves, B. and Nass, C. 1996. *The media equation: How people treat computers, television, and new media like real people and places.* Cambridge University Press, Cambridge, MA.

[14] Kuchenbrandt, D., Riether, N., and Eyssel, F. 2014. Does anthropomorphism reduce stress in HRI? In *Proceedings of the 9th ACM/IEEE International Conference on Human-Robot Interaction* (Bielefeld, Germany, March 03 - 06, 2014). HRI '14. ACM. New York, NY, 218-219. DOI = http://dl.acm.org/citation.cfm?id=2563710.

[15] Waytz, A., Morewedge, C. K., Epley, N., Monteleone, G., Gao, J. H., and Cacioppo, J. T. 2010. Making sense by making sentient: Effectance motivation increases anthropomorphism. *J. Pers. Soc. Psychol.* 99, 3 (Sep. 2010), 410-435.

[16] Fiske, S. T. and Neuberg, S. L. 1990. A continuum model of impression formation from category-based to individuating processes: Influences of information and motivation on attention and interpretation. *Adv. Exp. Soc. Psychol.* 23 (Apr. 1990), 1-74.

[17] Zebrowitz, L. 1997. *Reading faces*. Westview Press, Boulder, CO.

[18] Echterhoff, G., Bohner, G., and Siebler, F. 2006. "Social Robotics" und Mensch-Maschine-Interaktion: Aktuelle Forschung und Relevanz für die Sozialpsychologie [Social robotics and human–machine interaction: Current research and relevance for social psychology]. *Z. Sozialpsychol.* 37, 4 (Dec. 2006), 219-231.

[19] Eyssel, F. and Kuchenbrandt, D. 2012. Social categorization of social robots: Anthropomorphism as a function of robot group membership. *Brit. J. Soc. Psychol.* 51, 4 (Dec. 2012), 724-731.

[20] Salem, M., Eyssel, F., Rohlfing, K., Kopp, S., and Joublin, F. 2013. To err is human (-like): Effects of robot gesture on perceived anthropomorphism and likeability. *Int. J. Soc. Robot.* 5, 3 (Aug. 2013), 313-323.

[21] Eyssel, F. and Hegel, F. 2012. (S)he's got the look: Gender stereotyping of robots. *J. Appl. Soc. Psychol.* 42, 9 (Jul. 2012), 2213-2230.

[22] Arroyo, I., Woolf, B. P., Royer, J. M., and Tai, M. 2009. Affective gendered learning companion. In *Proceedings of the International Conference on Artificial Intelligence in Education* (Brighton, England, July 06 - 10, 2009). AIED '09. IOS Press, Amsterdam, The Netherlands, 41-48.

[23] Baylor, A. M. and Kim, Y. 2004. Pedagogical agent design: The impact of agent realism, gender, ethnicity, and instructional role. *Lect. Notes Comp. Sc.* 3220 (Sep. 2004), 592-603.

[24] Karacora, B., Dehghani, M., Krämer, N., and Gratch, J. 2012. The influence of virtual agents' gender and rapport on enhancing math performance. In *Proceedings of the 34th Annual Conference of the Cognitive Science Society* (Sapporo, Japan, August 1 - 4, 2012). CogSci '12. Curran Associates, Red Hook, New York, NY, 563-568.

[25] Ozogul, G., Johnson, A. M., Atkinson, R. K., and Reisslein, M. 2013. Investigating the impact of pedagogical agent gender matching and learner choice on learning outcomes and perceptions. *Comput. Educ.* 67 (Sep. 2013), 36-50.

[26] Plant, E. A., Baylor, A. L., Doerr, C. E., and Rosenberg-Kima, R. B. 2009. Changing middle-school students' attitudes and performance regarding engineering with computerbased social models. *Comput. Educ.* 53, 2 (Sep. 2009), 209-215.

[27] Kuchenbrandt, D., Häring, M., Eichberg, J., Eyssel, F., and André, E. 2014. Keep an eye on the task! How gender typicality of Tasks Influence human–robot interactions. *Int. J. Soc. Robot.* 6, 3 (Aug. 2014), 417-427.

[28] Goetz, J., Kiesler, S., and Powers, A. 2003. Matching robot appearance and behavior to tasks to improve human-robot

cooperation. In *Proceedings of the 12th IEEE International Workshop on Robot and Human Interactive Communication* (Millbrae, CA, USA, October 31 - November 02, 2003). RO-MAN '03. IEEE, New York, NY, 55-50.

[29] Nass, C., Moon, Y., and Green, N. 1997. Are computers gender-neutral? Gender stereotypic responses to computers. *J. Appl. Soc. Psychol.* 27, 10 (May 1997), 864-876.

[30] Powers, A., Kramer, A. D. I., Lim, S., Kuo, J., Lee, S. L., and Kiesler, S. 2005. Eliciting information from people with a gendered humanoid robot. In *Proceedings of the 14th IEEE International Symposium on Robot and Human Interactive Communication* (Nashville, TN, USA, August 13 - 15, 2005). RO-MAN '05. IEEE, New York, NY, 158-163.

[31] Kelley, J. F. 1984. An iterative design methodology for user-friendly natural-language office information applications. *ACM T. Inform. Syst.* 2, 1 (Jan. 1984), 26-41. DOI= http://dl.acm.org/citation.cfm?id=357420.

[32] Pashler, H., McDaniel, M., Rohrer, D., and Bjork, R. 2008. Learning styles. Concepts and evidence. *Psychol. Sci. Public. Interest.* 9, 3 (Dec. 2009), 105-119.

[33] Krämer, N., Simons, N., and Kopp, S. 2007. The effects of an embodied conversational agent's nonverbal behavior on user's evaluation and behavioral mimicry. *Lect. Notes Comput. Sc.* 4722 (Sep. 2007), 238-251.

[34] Deci, E. L. and Ryan, R. M. 2003. Intrinsic motivation inventory. Retrieved June 6, 2015 from http://www.selfdeterminationtheory.org/questionnaires/10-questionnaires/50.

[35] Brooke, J. 1996. SUS: A "quick and dirty" usability scale. In *Usability Evaluation in Industry*, P. W. Jordan, B. Thomas, B. A. Weerdmeester, and I. L. McClelland, Eds., Taylor & Francis, London, Sept. 1996, 189-194.

[36] Davis, F. D. 1989. Perceived usefulness, perceived ease of use, and user acceptance of information technology. *MIS. Quart.* 13, 3 (Sept. 1989), 319-340.

[37] Kamide, H., Eyssel, F., and Arai, T. 2013. Psychological anthropomorphism of robots measuring mind perception and humanity in Japanese context. *Lect. Notes Comp. Sc.* 8239 (Oct. 2013) 199-207.

[38] Gray, H. M., Gray, K., and Wegner, D. M. 2007. Dimensions of mind perception. *Science* 315, 5812 (Feb. 2007), 619.

[39] Eyssel, F., Kuchenbrandt, D., Bobinger, S., de Ruiter, L. and Hegel, F. 2012. 'If you sound like me, you must be more human': On the interplay of robot and user features on human-robot acceptance and anthropomorphism. In *Proceedings of the 7th Annual ACM/IEEE Conference on Human-Robot Interaction* (Boston, MA, USA, March 05 - 08, 2012). HRI '12. ACM. New York, NY, 125-126. DOI = http://dl.acm.org/citation.cfm?id=2157717.

[40] Eyssel, F. and Reich, N. 2013. Loneliness makes the heart grow fonder (of robots). On the effects of loneliness on psychological anthropomorphism. In *Proceedings of the 8th Annual ACM/ IEEE Conference on Human-Robot Interaction* (Tokyo, Japan, March 03 - 06, 2012). HRI '13. ACM. New York, NY, 121-122. DOI = http://dl.acm.org/citation.cfm?id=2447597.

[41] Eyssel, F. and Pfundmair, M. 2015. Predictors of psychological anthropomorphization, mind perception, and the fulfillment of social needs: A case study with a zoomorphic robot. In *Proceedings of the 24th IEEE International Symposium on Robot and Human Interactive Communication* (Kobe, Japan, August 31 - September 04, 2015). RO-MAN '15. IEEE, New York, NY, 827-832.

[42] Fiske, S. T., Cuddy, A. J. C., Glick. P., and Xu, J. 2002. A model of (often mixed) stereotype content: Competence and warmth respectively follow from perceived status and competition. *J. Pers. Soc. Psychol.* 82, 6 (Jun. 2002), 878-902.

[43] Reich, N. and Eyssel, F. 2013. Attitudes towards service robots in domestic environments: The role of personality characteristics, individual interests, and demographic variables. *J. Behav. Robot.* 4, 2 (Dec. 2013), 123-130.

[44] Reich-Stiebert, N. and Eyssel, F. 2015. Learning with educational companion robots? Toward attitudes on education robots, predictors of attitudes, and application potentials for education robots. *Int. J. Soc. Robot.* 7, 5 (Nov. 2015), 875-888.

[45] Neyer, F. J., Felber, J., and Gebhardt, C. 2012. Entwicklung und Validierung einer Kurzskala zur Erfassung von Technikbereitschaft (Technology Commitment) [Development and validation of a short technology commitment scale]. *Diagnostica* 58, 2 (Mar. 2012), 87–99.

[46] Han, J., Jo, M., Jones, V., and Jo, J. H. 2008. Comparative study on the educational use of home robots for children. *J. Inform. Process. Syst.* 4, 4 (Dec. 2008), 159-168.

[47] Riether, N., Hegel, F., Wrede, B., and Horstmann, G. 2012. Social facilitation with social robots? In *Proceedings of the 7th Annual ACM/IEEE International Conference on Human-Robot Interaction* (Boston, MA, USA, March 05 - 08, 2012). HRI '12. ACM. New York, NY, 41-48. DOI= http://dl.acm.org/citation.cfm?id=2157697.

[48] Saerbeck, M., Schut, T., Bartneck, C., and Janse, M. D. 2010. Expressive robots in education. Varying the degree of social supportive behavior of a robotic tutor. In *Proceedings of the SIGCHI Conference on Human Factors in Computing Systems* (Atlanta, GA, USA, April 10 - 15, 2010). CHI '10. ACM, New York, NY, 1613-1622. DOI= http://dl.acm.org/citation.cfm?doid=1753326.1753567.

[49] Miyake, A., Kost-Smith, L. E., Finkelstein, N. D., Pollock, S. J., Cohen, G. L., & Ito, T. A. 2010. Reducing the Gender Achievement Gap in College Science: A Classroom Study of Values Affirmation. *Science*, 330, 6008 (Nov. 2010) 1234-1237.

[50] Steele, C. M. 1988. The psychology of self-affirmation: Sustaining the integrity of the self. In *Advances in experimental social psychology,* L. Berkowitz, Ed. Academic Press, New York, 261-302.

[51] Garnham, A., Gabriel, U., Sarrasin, O., Gygax, P., and Oakhill, J. 2012. Gender representation in different languages and grammatical marking on pronouns: When beauticians, musicians, and mechanics remain men. *Discourse Process.* 49, 6 (May 2012), 481-500.

[52] Steele, C. M. 1997. A threat in the air: How stereotypes shape intellectual identity and performance. *Am. Psychol.* 52, 6 (Jun. 1997), 613-629.

[53] Leyens, J. P., Desert, M., Croizet, J. C., and Darcis, C. 2000. Stereotype threat: Are lower status and history of stigmatization preconditions of stereotype threat? *Pers. Soc. Psychol. Bull., 26*, 10 (Nov. 2000), 1189-1199.

[54] O'Brien, L. T. and Crandall, C. S. 2003. Stereotype threat and arousal: Effects on women's math performance. *Pers. Soc. Psychol. Bull.* 29, 6 (Jun. 2003), 782-789.

[55] Nguyen, H. H. D. and Ryan, A. M. 2008. Does stereotype threat affect test performance of minorities and women? A meta-analysis of experimental evidence. *J. Appl. Psychol.,* 93, 6 (Nov. 2008), 1314-1334.

[56] Reich-Stiebert, N. and Eyssel, F. (2016). Robots in the classroom: What teachers think about teaching and learning with education robots. Lecture Notes in Computer Sciene, 9979 (Oct. 2016), 671-680.

[57] Serholt, S. and Barendregt, W. 2014. Students' attitudes towards ethical dilemmas in the possible future of social robots in education. In *Proceedings of the 23rd International Symposium on Robot and Human Interactive Communication* (Edinburgh, Scotland, August 25 - 29, 2014). RO-MAN '14. IEEE. New York, NY, 955-960.

[58] Fridin, M. and Belokopytov, M. 2014. Acceptance of socially assistive humanoid robot by preschool and elementary school teachers. *Comput. Hum. Behav.* 33 (Apr. 2014), 23-31. DOI= http://dl.acm.org/citation.cfm?id=2608967.

[59] Aldebaran Soft Bank Group. NAO. Solutions for Education and Research. Retrieved September 13, 2016 from https://www.aldebaran.com/en/solutions/education-research.

[60] Siegel, M., Breazeal, C., & Norton, M. I. 2009. Persuasive Robotics: The Influence of Robot Gender on Human Bahavior. In Proceedings oft he IEEE/ RSJ International Conference on Intelligent Robots and Systems (St. Louis, USA, October 11-15, 2009). IROS '09. IEEE, New York, NY, 2563-2568.

[61] Hegel, F. 2010. *Gestalterisch-konstruktiver Entwurf eines sozialen Roboters* [Design and conception of a social robot]. Der Andere Verlag, Tönning, Germany.

[62] Marchetti-Bowick, M. 2009. Is your roomba male or female? The role of gender stereotypes and cultural norms in robot design. *Intersect* 2, 1 (Sep. 2009), 90-103.

Do Sensory Preferences of Children with Autism Impact an Imitation Task with a Robot?

Pauline Chevalier
Robotics & Computer Vision Lab, U2IS, ENSTA-ParisTech
828 boulevard des Maréchaux
Palaiseau, France
pauline.chevalier@ensta-paristech.fr

Gennaro Raiola
Robotics & Computer Vision Lab, U2IS, ENSTA-ParisTech
828 boulevard des Maréchaux
Palaiseau, France
gennaro.raiola@ensta-paristech.fr

Jean-Claude Martin
LIMSI, CNRS, Université Paris-Saclay
Bât 508, Campus Universitaire
Orsay, France
martin@limsi.fr

Brice Isableu
PSYCLE, Aix-Marseille Univ
Aix-en-Provence, France
brice.isableu@univ-amu.fr

Christophe Bazile
Groupement des Associations Partenaires de l'Action Sociale, France
cbazile@gapas.org

Adriana Tapus
Robotics & Computer Vision Lab, U2IS, ENSTA-ParisTech
828 boulevard des Maréchaux
Palaiseau, France
adriana.tapus@ensta-paristech.fr

ABSTRACT

Imitation is of major importance during social interactions, would it be between humans or between a human and a robot. This is even more true when considering users with special needs. In this paper, we describe an experimental imitation task protocol using a robot Nao that we designed to assess whether sensory profiles of children with Autistic Spectrum Disorder (ASD) influence their capabilities to imitate or to initiate gestures that are going to be imitated. We based our work on the hypothesis that children with an overreliance on proprioceptive cues and hyporeactivity to visual cues have a greater difficulty imitating and improve their skills more slowly than children with an overreliance on visual cues and hyporeactivity to proprioceptive cues. Twelve children and teenagers with ASD participated in seven imitation sessions over eight weeks. As expected, we observed that children with an overreliance on proprioceptive cues and hyporeactivity to visual cues had more difficulties imitating the robot than the other children. Moreover, the repeated sessions revealed to have positive effects on social behaviors displayed by all children (gaze to the partner, imitations) toward a human partner after the sessions with the robot. We conclude on the possible impacts of such results on the design of social human-robot interactions for users with ASD.

Keywords

Autism; Socially Assistive Robotics; Proprioception

HRI '17, March 06-09, 2017, Vienna, Austria
© 2017 ACM. ISBN 978-1-4503-4336-7/17/03...$15.00
DOI: http://dx.doi.org/10.1145/2909824.3020234

1. INTRODUCTION

Autism Spectrum Disorder (ASD) is the name for a group of developmental disorders that are characterized by deficits in communication and social skills and the presence of restricted and repetitive patterns of behaviors, interest or activities, as described in the DSM-V [1]. A great inter-individual variability is present in ASD: the symptoms of ASD fall on a continuum [1]. Some individuals can show much more severe symptoms than others. This inter-variability in ASD leads to a necessity to adapt and to personalize therapy for each individual.

Since individuals with ASD usually display a strong interest for computers, information and communication technologies have been used with participants with ASD (see [29] for a review). Research on Socially Assistive Robotics (SAR) for therapy for individuals with ASD is rapidly growing [18] and positive effects of robots on ASD participants have been observed [42, 16, 48, 41, 46, 10]. Although SAR features encouraging results for users with ASD, the individual differences are seldom considered.

We aim at investigating inter-individual differences between participants with ASD in order to design more adapted robot-based therapies for children with ASD. We consider proprioceptive and visual profiles [7] as an indicator of the social skills of our participants. We explain how we designed an experimental framework based on imitation of and by a robot. We describe the impact of our participants' individual profile on their behaviors during the imitation task. These results suggest that using an imitation task in human-robot interactions with children with ASD is especially useful for training social skills of children who have an overreliance on proprioceptive cues and hyporeactivity to visual cues. Sensory profiles could thus be used to guide the selection of social tasks that need to be trained for each individual user.

The remainder of the paper is organized as follows: Section 2 describes related work. Section 3 presents the methods used in this paper. Section 4 describes the design and the evaluation of the imitation task. Section 5 presents the results of the interaction between the robot and twelve children with ASD. Section 6 presents the paper's conclusions and a discussion of the results.

2. RELATED WORK

Motor, sensory, and visual processing impairments are present in autism and were taken into account recently with the publication of the DSM-V [1]. They have been outlined in SAR for ASD [20]. These deficits have an influence on the quality of life of individuals suffering from ASD and on their social development.

An overreliance on proprioceptive information is suggested in individuals with ASD [27, 28, 34, 24, 25, 30]. Proprioception can be defined as a person's ability to determine his/her own body segment positions (i.e., joint position sense) and detect his/her own limb movements (kinesthesia). It is derived from complex somatosensory signals provided to the brain by multiple muscle [26, 4, 44], joint [21], and skin receptors [17]. Individuals with ASD show normal to exacerbated integration of proprioceptive cues compared with typically developed (TD) individuals [27]. In [30], proprioceptive integration in ASD has been studied to gain a better knowledge of how these information influence social capacities. The authors observed that the greater the reliance on proprioception, the more children with ASD exhibited impairments in imitation and social interaction.

Moreover, individuals with ASD show impaired visual processing skills. Yet, vision is an important component of communication and social behaviors. As described in [45], the visual processing and gaze functions in individuals with ASD may lead to numerous impairments: unusual eye contact, difficulty following the gaze of others, difficulty supporting joint attention, and difficulty interpreting facial and bodily expressions of emotion.

We hypothesize that for our participants with ASD:

- (**H**) a mitigated behavioral response (i.e., hyporeactivity) to visual motion and an overreliance on proprioceptive information are linked to difficulties integrating social cues and engaging in successful interactions with a robot.

To test our hypothesis, we needed a relevant task for the children to perform with the robot. Numerous studies observed the effects of a robot partner in imitation therapy for children with ASD [42, 16, 48, 41, 46, 10]. Indeed, imitation is described as one of the precursors of social cognition [37] and the dynamics of imitation (i.e., turn taking, initiation of new behaviors, and adaptation to other's behavior) are altered in the large majority of individuals with ASD [50, 5, 39]. But there is a substantial variability in imitation deficiencies in children with ASD: some children with ASD can learn or imitate spontaneously, while others have larger impairments [6]. A positive impact of imitation-based therapies on social skills was observed in children with ASD [12, 13, 40, 36, 22]. In [38], the authors found that there was a significant correlation between the level of imitation and level of imitation recognition in children with ASD. Some children with ASD recognized they were imitated. Those children showed different strategies to test the intentionality of their partners, such as: changing the rhythm of activity, changing the object used, and stopping the current action while gazing at the partner. Some children did not test their partners, but their attention increased and they showed more positive affects towards their partner. This may indicate that the children were aware they were being imitated without understanding the intentionality of the partner. These results underline the inter-variability of the symptoms in ASD, and the need to take them in account for therapy.

In SAR, the authors in [14] suggested that a task involving imitating robots could have a positive impact on individuals with ASD compared to a task involving imitating humans. Indeed, it was observed that children with ASD had impaired detection of biological motion compared to non-biological motion [33]. The authors in [42] observed in a longitudinal study with the Robota robot that social behaviors, such as gaze, touch, and imitation increased over time in children with ASD. In [16], the authors observed that the imitation of body movements and of familiar actions was higher when the children with ASD were paired with a human partner than with a robot partner. However, children with ASD who were paired with a robot showed increased shared attention and imitated facial expressions more than the children paired with a human partner. The authors in [48] observed the social engagement of four children with ASD and investigated whether they were more engaged with a Nao robot or with a human partner. There was a high variability in the reactions to the Nao robot. The robot did not impact the social engagement of two of the children. The other two displayed more gaze and smile/laughter behaviors with the robot compared to the human. One child performed better in the imitation task with Nao robot than with the human partner.

In the above studies, the authors described that SAR for training and learning imitation with individuals with ASD had a positive impact on their social skills. Training skills across several sessions is important in order to achieve a learning effect. Indeed, individuals with ASD show difficulties to learn new skills and to generalize them to new situations and new stimuli [23]. In addition, when evaluating SAR for individuals with ASD, it is important to verify if the skills learned with the robot are also applied later when interacting with a human partner [18, 47]. However, the authors in the above studies did not take in account any inter-individual variability.

In this paper, we propose to investigate inter-individual differences between participants with ASD. When individual differences between users with autism are considered, researchers consider mainly the cognitive level of the users. Here, we propose to compare our participants on their sensory profiles. We propose an imitation task with repeated sessions in order to observe the improvement and generalization of the acquired skills. To our knowledge, this is one of the first study to investigate proprioceptive and visual profiles for SAR for children with ASD.

3. METHODS

3.1 Participants

We conduct our research in collaboration with two care facilities for people suffering from ASD: IME MAIA (France) and IME Notre Ecole (France), associations for children and teenagers with ASD. Our subject pool is composed of 12 children with ASD (11.7±2.6 years old, two female participants) from these two care facilities. For confidentiality reasons, we coded the participants' identities as follows: CH#, with # from 1 to 12. From the care-centers, we recruited only participants who had an ASD diagnosis. Unfortunately, we did not have access to diagnostic reviews as ADOS-G, ADI-R or other ASD diagnostic assessments. Informed consent for participation was obtained from the parents. The experimental protocol was approved by the EA 4532 University local ethics committee.

3.2 Proprioceptive and Visual Preferences

The first step of our work was to define the profiles of our participants. As explained in Section 2, we aimed to identify if the integration of proprioceptive and visual cues impact the social and interaction skills of an individual with ASD. We used that we have developed in the past [7] to define each participant's profile. Our method is the combination of a well-known questionnaire: the Adolescents/Adults Sensory Profile (AASP) [3], and an experimental setup.

The AASP questionnaire assesses the individual's sensory processing preferences in terms of neurological thresholds for stimulation (high-low) and self-regulation strategies (active-passive) [15]. It has been already widely used in research for individuals with ASD [32, 19, 11]. It enables to collect an individual's movement, visual, touch, and auditory sensory processing preferences. The questionnaire was filled by the caregivers. Although we could have used the Sensory Profile questionnaire [15] which is dedicated to children, we decided to use the same AASP questionnaire that we used with adult participants in another study [7]. The caregivers who worked with us on this study estimated that the AASP questionnaire would also suit the children and teenagers from their care-centers.

The experimental setup consists in the assessment with a force platform of: (1) the effect of a moving virtual visual scene on an individual's postural control and (2) the individuals' capability to use proprioceptive inputs provided in dynamics of balance to reduce visual dependency [2, 31]. To form the groups among the participants, a Clustering analysis (dendrogram, Ward method) was performed on the results of the AASP and the experimental setup data. The reader can find a full explanation of the setup in [7].

The resulting groups are as follows:

- Group G1, with the following children: CH3; CH5; CH8; CH10 and CH11; Participants in this group show an overreliance on proprioceptive cues and a hyporeactivity to visual cues;
- Group G2, with the following children: CH1; CH2; CH4; CH6; CH7; CH9; and CH12; Participants in this group show a hyporeactivity to proprioceptive cues and a overreliance on visual cues.

These two groups enabled us to analyse the imitation skills of our participants in regards to our hypothesis **H1**. Table 1 provides the participants personal information and their groups.

3.3 Current Work

In this paper, we present the design of an imitation experimental protocol for children with ASD. During the sessions, the children were instructed to imitate a partner, and were also imitated by the partner. With the imitation task, we aimed to validate the relevance of the proprioceptive and visual individual profiles we defined in the previous Section as

Table 1: Participants' personal information

G#	ID#	Gender	Age	Comments
G1	CH3	M	12	-
	CH5	F	11	Low level of cognition; Non-verbal; West Syndrome (uncommon to rare epileptic disorder).
	CH8	M	15	-
	CH10	M	10	-
	CH11	M	17	Low level of cognition
G2	CH1	M	11	-
	CH4	M	13	High level of cognition. Asked to be part of the program to meet the Nao robot.
	CH6	M	13	-
	CH9	F	12	-
	CH12	M	9	-
	CH2	M	9	Suffers of echolalia
	CH7	M	8	-

a prerequisite for maximizing the robot influence (usability) on facilitating imitation and improving social interaction. We sought to validate our hypothesis **H**. More precisely, we hypothesized that:
An individual with an overreliance on proprioceptive cues and a hyporeactivity to visual cues would:

- **(HA)** struggle more to imitate his/her partner;
- **(HB)** struggle more initiating movements for his/her partner to imitate him/her;
- **(HC)** have slower improvements in his/her imitation skills across the sessions;

than an individual with a hyporeactivity to proprioceptive cues and a overreliance on visual cues.

4. DESIGN OF THE IMITATION TASK

4.1 Content of the Interaction

With the help of the caregivers from our partner facilities, we designed an imitation task with a robot. We wanted in this experiment to observe the effect of training session on imitation skills, and the generalization on a human partner. So as, the participants interacted with a human partner and a robot (Nao, from SoftBank robotics, formally Aldebaran). The children knew the human partner but had never worked with her in therapeutic sessions. As the authors in [35] observed that children who saw the robot act in a social-communicative way were more likely to follow its gaze than those who did not, and to remove fear or reluctance towards the robot, the Nao robot was presented to the children before this experiment [7]. As all of the children met the robot before, and knew the experimenter, there were no expected novelty effects in any of the partners (human or robot). The sessions were organized identically for all participants, as described in Table 2. There was seven sessions for each participant. Each session had a code name: H# for a session with

Table 2: Planning of the experimental protocol. Sessions are coded as follow: H# for a session with a human partner, and R# for a session with Nao robot as partner, with # from 0 to 6 for each number of sessions.

Week	Session code	Session purpose	Session partner
Week 0	H0	Baseline	Human
Weeks 1	R1	Baseline	Robot
Weeks 2 to 4	Training	R1-R4	Robot
Week 5	Break	-	-
Week 6	H5	Post-test	Human
Week 7	R6	Post-test	Robot

Figure 1: Pictures of the setup with the human partner (left) and robot partner (right)

a human partner, and R# for a session with Nao as partner, with # from 0 to 6 for each number of sessions. The first and 5th sessions (H0 and H5) were with the human partner, and the other ones (R1, R2, R3, R4 and R6) with the robot partner. The sessions H0 and R1 were baseline sessions, enabling us to observe the skills of the children with both of the partner before the training sessions. Sessions R2 to R4 were the repeated sessions for training the imitation skills. After session R4, we observed a break of one week. Then, the 6th and 7th sessions (H5 and R6) were post-test sessions, enabling us to observe if there were generalization effects on the imitation skills of the participants.

The sessions were held in a reserved room in each of the care centers. The children were in front of the partner. When the session was with the robot, the robot was placed on a table, due to the small size of the Nao robot. An Xtion RGB-D camera was fixed in front of the child, and 2 cameras recorded the sessions. The child could sit or stand in front of the partner. Figure 1 shows the setup for both partners. There are two phases in each session: (a) the child imitates the partner (human/robot) and (b) the partner (human/robot) imitates the child.

4.1.1 Phase (a): the child imitates the partner

In this phase, the child has to imitate the arms movements of the partner (human or robot). Several imitation tasks have been proposed in other studies for example involving objects [37]. We decided to define a simple gesture imitation since these motor tasks may be impacted by visual and proprioceptive preferences and because of the limitations of the embodiment of the robot Nao. The protocol was design with the help of the caregivers from the care-facilities in regards of their work with the children with ASD.

To keep the attention of the participants and make the interaction meaningful, we designed it as a playful task. The partner was initiating arms movements on a song, as she/it was dancing. As we work with children with a wide range of cognition levels and motor skills, the songs lacked lyrics and the gestures were limited to the arm gestures. Each movement is a combination of the left and right arms (L and R, respectively) taking one of the following five positions: D: down; U: up; F: in front; P: in ψ; and T: in T form, see Figure 2. The movements to imitate were randomly ordered to avoid a learning effect between the repetitions. For the human partner, the movements were chosen in real time, and for the robot partner, the list of movements was computed at the beginning of a dance.

We used three songs, with the same rhythms and durations (1 min 30 s). During a session, two of the three songs were used. In this way, we hoped to keep the children interested, as well as to be able to alternate the songs between the sessions. A song is played a maximum of two times in a session. In ASD, unusual responses to sensory stimuli have been observed [43]. To prevent unexpected behaviors toward the songs, we asked to the caregiver for each child if they tolerated and liked music, and we had the possibility to lower or turn off the music if needed. Overall, the children liked the music. The child imitated the partner a maximum of four times by session (in total, six minutes of imitation). Participants were able to take short breaks, if needed, between the dances.

We wished to propose sessions that adapt to each participant, stimulating and evolving in time. To avoid boredom across the sessions, the number of arms gestures increased throughout the sessions in an adaptive manner i.e., related to 80% of gestures correctly imitated (see Table 3 to see the movements that were imitated during a specific session). The number of correct movement was annotated by the experimenter while the child was performing the imitation. The time between the movements was modulated by the performance of the child during a dance within a session. In a session, if a participant performed 80% of the movements in two consecutive dances, the time between two movements decreased in the next dance. If the child was unable to imitate 80% of the movements the time between two movements was unchanged. The time between two movements was 8 seconds and could decrease to 6, 4, and 2 seconds, depending on the participant's performance. The time between two movements were discussed with the caregivers. The first sessions started with a movement every 8 seconds, to enable the caregivers to have enough time to correct and encourage the children to imitate the partner. It was also short enough not to lose the attention of the children. The decreases were chosen to gradually increase the attention of the children towards the partner. In sessions H0 and R1, the partner produced a movement every 8 seconds. At the beginning of the R2 to R4 sessions, the time between two movements was set as the one reached at the last dance of the previous session. In the H5 and R6 sessions, the partner started the session with the frequency reached in the session R4. If a participant reached the level of a movement every 2 seconds, the first dance was reset to a movement every 4 seconds in the next session. Indeed, to follow this frequency of a movement every 2 seconds was quite demanding to maintain for 4 dances. Finally, if the participant imitated 80% of the movements, the partner cheered for the child at the end of a repetition. During this phase, the caregiver was next to the child and was asked to help him/her understand the imitation task, encourage the child to imitate the partner and correct his/her arms position, if needed.

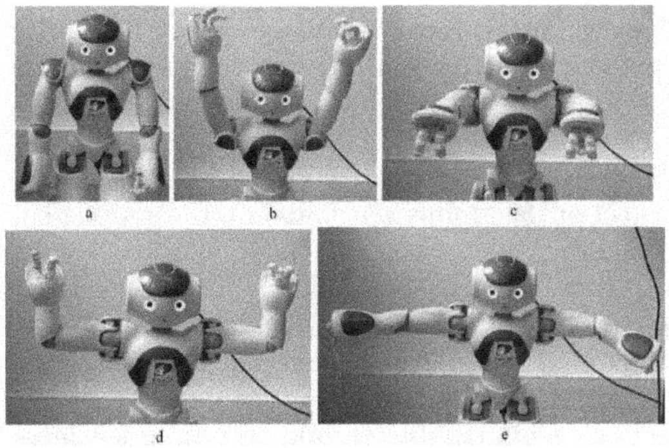

Figure 2: Example of the arm positions for Nao: a: LDRD; b: LURU; c: LFRF; d: LPRP; and e: LTRT

Table 3: Arm positions for the partner. Each movement is a combination of the left and the right arm (L and R, respectively) taking one of the following five positions: D: down; U: up; F: in front; P: in ψ; T: in T form

Session code	Movements
H0-R1	M1 = LDRD + LURU + LFRF + LPRP + LTRT
R2	M2 = M1 + LURP + LPRU + LTRF + LFRT
R3	M3 = M2 + LURD + LDRU + LTRP + LPRT
R4-H5-R6	M4 = M3 + LFRP + LPRF + LTRU + LURT

4.1.2 *Phase (b): the partner imitates the child*

In this phase, the partner imitated the gross arm movements of the child. The child was told to do slow large arms movements. A different song of 1 m 30 s was played during this phase. It permitted to link between the Phases (a) and (b). In addition, we hoped it will encourage the child to perform movements, and it gave a time limit to this task. In the care facilities we work with, the children work mostly with a timer. During this phase, the caregiver remained with the child and tried to encourage him/her to perform arms movements.

4.1.3 *Observed behaviors*

The sessions were recorded and the behavior of the participants was manually annotated. In both phases, we observed the participants' *percentages of gaze* to the human/robot and *percentages of smiles* during the interaction. In addition, in Phase (a), we observed the *imitation score* was assessed; in Phase (b), the *free initiations* were noted. Imitation scores were annotated as follows: "0" if there was no movement, if there was a movement that appeared to be random or not connected to the movement of the partner or incorrect; and "1" if the movement was correctly imitated. Then, we computed the percentage of the movement that was correctly imitated. As described in Section 4.1.1, the number of movements increased if the child correctly imitated the partner. We defined the *number of movements* the children imitated as an indicator of the improvement and success of a child to imitate the partner. Free initiation is the percentage of the time during which the child initiates movements for the partner to imitate him/her during Phase (b).

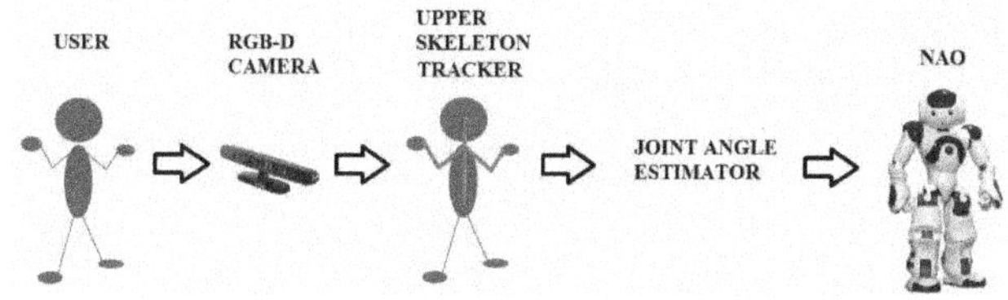

Figure 3: Schematics of the imitation system

4.2 System Design

4.2.1 *Phase (a)*

We used API Naoqi[1] provided by Softbank Robotics to program the gestures for imitating Nao. The experimenter launched the program when the child was ready and in position in front of the robot. The song and gestures started together. The experimenter could stop the song and gestures at any moment.

4.2.2 *Phase (b)*

We used a RGB-D camera (Xtion Asus[2]) and the ROS package Openni2_tracker[3] to track the participants' upper body. The tracker provides the skeleton of the user, which is a list of body joints. These joints are translated into the motor commands for the Nao robot through a joint angle estimator and Naoqi. The joint angle estimator converts the shoulder and elbow angles from the participant into scaled angles for Nao. See in Figure 3 a schematic of the system. The participants could stay seated and no calibration-pose was needed to start the imitation by the robot. A similar system has been used successfully in previous studies [48].

4.3 Data Analysis

In total, each participant performed 7 sessions of approximately 10 minutes, interacting with the partner (human and robot), resulting in 84 videos. A first coder annotated all videos and a second coder, unaware of the hypotheses of the setup, annotated 20% of the videos, which were randomly chosen. An intraclass correlation coefficient (ICC) was computed to assess the inter-coder reliability. The ICC was 0.86, which shows good inter-coder reliability. We observed the effect of the groups on the participants' gaze direction, imitation scores, free initiation, and smiles as explained in Section 4.1.3. We performed a repeated-measure ANOVA on participants' behaviors. Post-hoc analyses were performed with Tuckey's HSD test.

5. RESULTS

All 12 children performed all seven sessions of the experiment. They were enthusiastic to participate in the sessions, even the children who did not perform well on the task. A child, CH2 (G3), was very agitated and perturbed for the final four sessions (out of seven sessions) due to personal issues. We did not include him in the statistical analysis of the proprioceptive and visual profiles because his behavior

[1]http://doc.aldebaran.com/2-1/naoqi/

[2]https://www.asus.com/fr/3D-Sensor/Xtion_PRO/

[3]https://github.com/ros-drivers/openni2_tracker

changed significantly. As for all the other participants, we still describe his behavior.

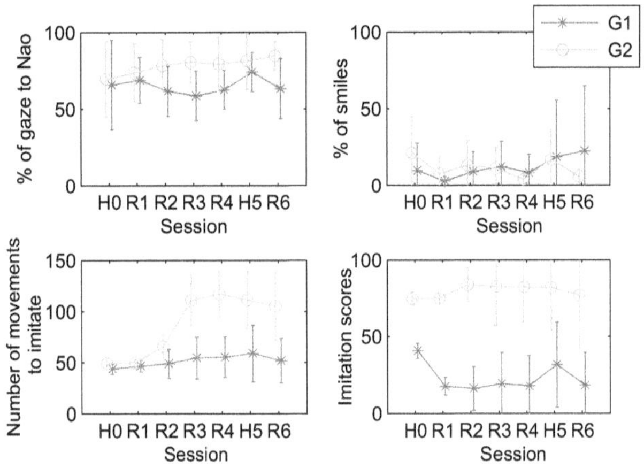

(a) Phase (a)

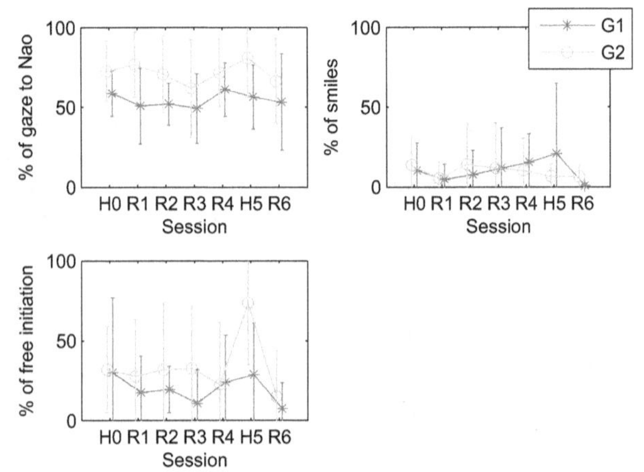

(b) Phase (b)

Figure 4: Observed behaviors by groups G1 and G2 through the sessions in Phases (a) and (b). H# for a session with a human partner, and R# for a session with Nao as partner, with # from 0 to 6 for each number of sessions.

5.1 Phase (a)

In this phase, children had to imitate the partner. Figure 4a show the observed behaviors for the G1 and G2 groups in Phase (a).

Gaze to the partner.

We observed a weak significant main effect of the groups on the gaze direction of the children during Phase (a) ($F(1,9) = 4.21$; $0.05 < p < 0.1$). Participants from G1 looked globally less to the partner than the participants from group G2 (G1: $M = 64.83$, $SD = 17.13$; G2: $M = 78.02$, $SD = 16.89$). We observe in Figure 4a an increase in the mean gaze to the partner, through the session for group G2, indicating that the repeated sessions helped the children from group G2 to look more at their partners. We do not observe an increase on the participants from group G1 (Figure 4a). However, the participants from group G1 seemed to look more at the partner in session H5 than in the other sessions, even if this result is not significant. This may indicate that the repeated sessions with the robot helped those children to look more at a human partner.

Smiles.

No effect of the groups was found on the smiling behavior of the children.

Number of movements for the children to imitate.

We found a significant main effect of the groups on the number of the imitated movements ($F(1,9) = 34.94$; $p < 0.01$). Children from group G1 produce fewer imitation movements than the children from group G2 (G1: $M = 51.34$, $SD = 17.25$; G2: $M = 87.14$, $SD = 35.04$). This indicates that children from group G2 improved faster than children from group G1. Both groups had an increase in their number of movements.

Imitation scores.

We found a significant main effect of the scores on the groups ($F(1,9) = 17.65$; $p < 0.01$). Children from group G2 were more successful than children from group G1 (G1: $M = 23.09$, $SD = 26.81$; G2: $M = 79.79$, $SD = 20.25$). In Figure 4a, even if this result is not significant, we can observe that the children from G1 seemed to have a higher score in the sessions with the human partner, which is different from the children in group G2.

5.2 Phase (b)

In this phase, the partner had to imitate the arm movements of the child. Figure 4b shows the observed behaviors for the G1 and G2 groups in Phase (b). The participants from G1 had more difficulties understanding that they had to produce movements regardless of those of the partner, and that the robot was imitating them. When the session was with the robot, they often imitated the robot instead of initiating movements. Indeed, the robot was slightly moving from the noise based on skeleton data form the RGB-D camera and some children were reproducing the slight movements of the robot.

Gaze to the partner.

We observed a weak significant effect of the groups on the gaze direction of the children during Phase (b) ($F(1,5) = 5.46$; $0.05 < p < 0.1$). Participants from G1 looked globally less often to the robot than the participants from group G2 (G1: $M = 54.46$, $SD = 4.39$; G2: $M = 71.60$, $SD = 6.31$).

Smiles.

No effect of the groups was found on the smiling behavior of children. In Figure 4b children in group G1 smiled less in the last session of the therapy than in the other sessions.

Free initiation.

Free initiation was not significantly different between the groups on the whole experiment ($F(1,5) = 0.08$; $p = ns$). In Figure 4b, we can observe that in H5, the free initiation increased in both groups G1 and G2, and more drastically in G2 than in G1.

5.3 Observed behaviors

We describe here the behaviors of the participants during the sessions.

CH3 (G1) was very enthusiastic to play with the robot and really appreciated the songs. In Phase (a), we observed an improvement of the gaze for the human partner after the sessions with the robot. He looked the human partner more successfully after the sessions with the robot. Indeed, in session H0, he gazed 80.52% of the time to the human, and 94.64% in session H5 after the four sessions with the robot partner and the week-long break. The number of movement to imitate increased with the sessions, indicating an improvement in the imitation. In Phase (b), the child was moving his arms to make the partner move, but he was not looking at the partner most of the time. Instead, he was closing his eyes or putting the head down.

CH5 (G1) had troubles understanding the tasks in Phases (a) and (b). In Phase (a), she gazed at her partner approximately 76% of the time. She imitated the human partner better than the robot partner. In Phase (b), it was very difficult to keep her focused on the task.

CH8 (G1) had difficulties understanding the imitation and initiation tasks in both Phases (a, b). However, his caregiver said he liked the sessions because he was not reluctant to come, and that he may have understood the task but was unwilling to perform the task.

CH10 (G1) performed the task but had some difficulties imitating the movement in Phase (a) (he was performing a random movement or always performing the same movement). At the end of each session with the robot, he kissed it on the head. The gaze behavior of this child did not improve with time in Phase (a); instead, it stayed stable. In Phase (b), the child initiated movements for a significant amount of time in sessions H5 and R6. He may have benefited from the repetitive sessions with the robot for this skill.

CH11 (G1) had difficulties understanding the imitation and initiation tasks. He performed evading gaze behavior. However, his gaze at the partner was higher after session H0 in Phase (a). He gazed more at the human partner after the session with the robot. In H0, he looked at the partner 14.10% of the time, which was 60.72% in H5. By contrast, in Phase (b), his gaze increased from H0 to R4 and decreased with the human partner in H5.

CH1 (G2) was very enthusiastic about participating to the sessions. He even ran to the experiment room. In Phase (a), his gaze to the partner was good and constant over the time. He always succeeded with the imitation task and was able to follow the robot movement when the gestures were every 2 seconds. The number of movement to imitate increased with the sessions, indicating an improvement in the imitation. In Phase (b), his gaze to the robot decreased in the last session. Free initiation was higher in session H5 than in the other sessions.

CH4 (G2) expressed some reluctance to participate in the sessions and most of the time he asked to perform only two to three dances with the robot. However, his gaze on the partner was good and constant over the time. He always succeeded in the imitation task and he was able to follow the robot movement when the gestures were every 2 seconds. In Phase (b), the child did not want to initiate movement with the human partner in the first session H0, but he accepted the participation conditions during the remainder of the experiment. He initiated movement with the robot and tested the behavior of the robot. During session H5, he seemed to enjoy initiating movements with the human partner, and smiled more during this session.

CH7 (G2) was enthusiastic about performing the task at the beginning of a session and then showed signs of boredom from the middle to end of sessions. We observed that this participant increased his gaze on the partner in Phase (a). The number of movement to imitate increased with the sessions, indicating an improvement in the imitation. In Phase (b), with the robot partner, he did not understand he was imitated. He was imitating the robot movement. The percentage of free initiation was higher with the human partner ($M = 67.35$; $SD = 3.51$) than with the robot partner ($M = 9.81$; $SD = 11.80$), and no improvements were visible from H0 to H5 sessions. However, the child looked more at session H5 (70.86%) than at session H0 (63.85%).

In Phase (a), CH9 (G2) showed an improvement in her gazing behavior to the partner throughout the experiment. She also improved her imitation skills by being more focused on the partner. Indeed, she looked more at her caregiver than at the partner and was not focused on the task at all. We observed that this participant increased his gaze on the partner in Phase (a). The number of movement to imitate increased with the sessions, indicating an improvement in the imitation. She succeeded in reaching the level at which were the partner was moving every 2 seconds. In Phase (b), she did not initiate the partner except in session H5. She may have benefited from the repetitive sessions with the robot for this skill.

CH12 (G2) was enthusiastic to participate in the sessions. He understood the tasks. In Phase (a), we observed that his gaze towards the partner increased through the sessions. The gaze on the human after the sessions with Nao robot was higher compared to during the first session. The number of movement to imitate increased with the sessions, indicating an improvement in the imitation. He succeeded in performing the imitation task and was able to follow the robot movement when the gestures occurred every 2 seconds. In Phase (b), except in session R1, the participant focused his attention on the partner. The gaze percentage increased over time. In session H5, he was really enthusiastic to initiate movement in the human partner and asked to repeat the task several time.

As mentioned before, CH2 (G3) was very agitated and perturbed for the last four sessions due to personal issues. From H0 to R2, the gaze to the partner of the child increased and then decreased for Phase (a). In Phase (b), he was quite agitated and it was difficult to get the robot to imitate him.

CH6 (G3) was very enthusiastic about participating in the sessions. He even ran to the experiment room and asked if he was going to see the robot when he saw the experimenter in the care center. In Phases (a) and (b), his gaze on the partner was good and constant over time. He always succeeded in performing the imitation task and was able to follow the robot movement when the gestures were every 2 seconds. The number of movement to imitate increased with the sessions, indicating an improvement in the imitation. In Phase (b), his gaze on the robot decreased in the last session. He had few difficulties understanding Phase (b) with the robot partner. He imitated the robot in the beginning, but after a few trials, he understood the task and initiated movement for the robot.

6. CONCLUSIONS AND DISCUSSION

In this paper, we explain how we developed a robot-based imitation experimental protocol for children with ASD. We aimed to validate the relevance of the proprioceptive and visual individual profiles to design robot-based therapy for individuals with ASD.

We observed that participants who had hyporeactivity to visual motion and an overreliance on proprioceptive information (children from group G1) gazed less towards their partner than participants who had an overreliance to visual motion and a hyporeactivity on proprioceptive information (children from group G2), during both phases of the sessions. Children from group G1 were less successful in imitating the partner than children from G2. Children from group G1 were less likely to initiate movement that could be imitated by the partner than children from group G2. Finally, children from group G1 had a slower improvement in their imitation skills than children from group G2.

As in the literature [42, 16, 48, 41, 46, 10], we observed positive effects of using a robot partner for individuals with ASD to improve imitation skills. We observed that children from group G2 gazed more to their partners through the sessions in Phase (a). The repeated interactions may have helped the children in both groups to look more at the human partner, and children from group G2 to improve their will to initiate movements with a human partner. However, some children did not succeed in imitating the partner across the sessions or did not seem to understand that they were being imitated. The task may have been too complicated or inadequately adapted to them, and they might have needed more sessions to display real improvements of their imitation skills. For some children, Phase (b) was difficult to set-up, because they were unwilling to stand in front of the RGB-D camera for the time when they were correctly tracked, which might have contributed to their limited understanding of this phase. Overall, the repetitive sessions seemed to have a positive impact on the children's social skills for both groups G1 and G2. In addition, children seemed to enjoy the interactions: most of them showed enthusiasm when interacting with the robot. Overall, our results are in line with other results from similar studies showing the positive impact of imitation training for participants with autism. This supports that robot-based training of social skills for autistic users should feature an imitation task.

Whereas most studies with autistic users split the participants according to their cognitive level, we have split our group of users according to their sensory preferences. Our results suggest that this new way of splitting users with autism might be relevant for defining personalized protocols for training social skills and for designing associated multimodal human-robot interaction.

A main interest in SAR is to propose more autonomous robots, that will be able to adapt to the individual needs of children over longer periods of time [49]. Our results could help to design more adapted robot-based therapy for individuals with ASD as we observed that both groups had different gazing during the experimental protocol. Using users' gaze to predict the outcome of interactions with a robot could be a successful step to make robots more autonomous.

Taken together, with earlier assessments of our ASD population in other behavioral tasks [7, 9, 8] the present findings suggest that robot's cognitive architecture should integrate a module dedicated to online detection of sensory profiles, and then afford personalized scenario e.g., based on controlling the visual complexity of communication signals for training social skills in an optimal way.

Future works should focus on the design of more adapted tasks to all participants with a more autonomous robot-based system.

7. ACKNOWLEDGMENTS

We thank the children, their families, and the care centers' teams. This work is supported by Région Ile de France.

8. REFERENCES

[1] A. P. Association et al. *Diagnostic and statistical manual of mental disorders (DSM-5®)*. American Psychiatric Pub, 2013.

[2] A. Bray, A. Subanandan, B. Isableu, T. Ohlmann, J. F. Golding, and M. A. Gresty. We are most aware of our place in the world when about to fall. *Current Biology*, 14(15):R609–R610, 2004.

[3] C. Brown and W. Dunn. *Adolescent-Adult Sensory Profile: User's Manual.* Therapy Skill Builders, 2002.

[4] D. Burke, K.-E. Hagbarth, L. Löfstedt, and B. G. Wallin. The responses of human muscle spindle endings to vibration of non-contracting muscles. *The Journal of physiology*, 261(3):673–693, 1976.

[5] M. Carpenter, M. Tomasello, and T. Striano. Role reversal imitation and language in typically developing infants and children with autism. *Infancy*, 8(3):253–278, 2005.

[6] T. Charman and S. Baron-Cohen. Another look at imitation in autism. *Development and psychopathology*, 6(03):403–413, 1994.

[7] P. Chevalier, B. Isableu, J.-C. Martin, and A. Tapus. Individuals with autism: Analysis of the first interaction with nao robot based on their proprioceptive and kinematic profiles. *Advances in Robot Design and Intelligent Control*, pages 225–233, 2015.

[8] P. Chevalier, J.-C. Martin, B. Isableu, C. Bazile, D.-O. Iacob, and A. Tapus. Joint attention using human-robot interaction: Impact of sensory preferences of children with autism, to appear. *RO-MAN 2016*, 2016.

[9] P. Chevalier, J.-C. Martin, B. Isableu, C. Bazile, and A. Tapus. Impact of sensory preferences of individuals with autism on the recognition of emotions expressed by two robots, an avatar, and a human. *Autonomous Robots*, pages 1–23, 2016.

[10] D. Conti, S. Di Nuovo, S. Buono, G. Trubia, and A. Di Nuovo. Use of robotics to stimulate imitation in children with autism spectrum disorder: A pilot study in a clinical setting. In *Robot and Human Interactive Communication (RO-MAN), 2015 24th IEEE International Symposium on*, pages 1–6. IEEE, 2015.

[11] L. Crane, L. Goddard, and L. Pring. Sensory processing in adults with autism spectrum disorders. *Autism*, 13(3):215–228, 2009.

[12] G. Dawson and A. Adams. Imitation and social responsiveness in autistic children. *Journal of abnormal child psychology*, 12(2):209–226, 1984.

[13] G. Dawson, D. Hill, A. Spencer, L. Galpert, and L. Watson. Affective exchanges between young autistic

children and their mothers. *Journal of abnormal child psychology*, 18(3):335–345, 1990.

[14] J. J. Diehl, L. M. Schmitt, M. Villano, and C. R. Crowell. The clinical use of robots for individuals with autism spectrum disorders: A critical review. *Research in autism spectrum disorders*, 6(1):249–262, 2012.

[15] W. Dunn. The sensory profile: UserâĂŹs manual (psychological corporation, san antonio, tx). 1999.

[16] A. Duquette, F. Michaud, and H. Mercier. Exploring the use of a mobile robot as an imitation agent with children with low-functioning autism. *Autonomous Robots*, 24(2):147–157, 2008.

[17] B. B. Edin. Cutaneous afferents provide information about knee joint movements in humans. *The Journal of Physiology*, 531(1):289–297, 2001.

[18] D. Feil-Seifer and M. J. Mataric. Defining socially assistive robotics. In *Rehabilitation Robotics, 2005. ICORR 2005. 9th International Conference on*, pages 465–468. IEEE, 2005.

[19] H. Ferguson, B. S. Myles, and T. Hagiwara. Using a personal digital assistant to enhance the independence of an adolescent with asperger syndrome. *Education and Training in Developmental Disabilities*, pages 60–67, 2005.

[20] E. Ferrari, B. Robins, and K. Dautenhahn. Therapeutic and educational objectives in robot assisted play for children with autism. In *RO-MAN 2009-The 18th IEEE International Symposium on Robot and Human Interactive Communication*, pages 108–114. IEEE, 2009.

[21] W. Ferrell, S. Gandevia, and D. McCloskey. The role of joint receptors in human kinaesthesia when intramuscular receptors cannot contribute. *The Journal of physiology*, 386(1):63–71, 1987.

[22] T. Field, T. Field, C. Sanders, and J. Nadel. Children with autism display more social behaviors after repeated imitation sessions. *Autism*, 5(3):317–323, 2001.

[23] A. Froehlich, J. Anderson, E. Bigler, J. Miller, N. Lange, M. DuBray, J. Cooperrider, A. Cariello, J. Nielsen, and J. E. Lainhart. Intact prototype formation but impaired generalization in autism. *Research in autism spectrum disorders*, 6(2):921–930, 2012.

[24] B. Gepner, D. Mestre, G. Masson, and S. de Schonen. Postural effects of motion vision in young autistic children. *NeuroReport*, 6(8):1211–1214, 1995.

[25] B. Gepner and D. R. Mestre. Brief report: postural reactivity to fast visual motion differentiates autistic from children with asperger syndrome. *Journal of Autism and Developmental disorders*, 32(3):231–238, 2002.

[26] G. M. Goodwin, D. I. McCloskey, and P. B. Matthews. Proprioceptive illusions induced by muscle vibration: contribution by muscle spindles to perception? *Science*, 175(4028):1382–1384, 1972.

[27] E. Gowen and A. Hamilton. Motor abilities in autism: a review using a computational context. *Journal of autism and developmental disorders*, 43(2):323–344, 2013.

[28] S. Greffou, A. Bertone, E.-M. Hahler, J.-M. Hanssens, L. Mottron, and J. Faubert. Postural hypo-reactivity in autism is contingent on development and visual environment: a fully immersive virtual reality study. *Journal of autism and developmental disorders*, 42(6):961–970, 2012.

[29] C. Grossard and O. Grynszpan. Entraînement des compétences assistées par les technologies numériques dans lâĂŹautisme: une revue. *Enfance*, 2015(01):67–85, 2015.

[30] C. C. Haswell, J. Izawa, L. R. Dowell, S. H. Mostofsky, and R. Shadmehr. Representation of internal models of action in the autistic brain. *Nature neuroscience*, 12(8):970–972, 2009.

[31] B. Isableu, B. Fourre, N. Vuillerme, G. Giraudet, and M.-A. Amorim. Differential integration of visual and kinaesthetic signals to upright stance. *Experimental brain research*, 212(1):33–46, 2011.

[32] C. R. Jones, F. Happé, G. Baird, E. Simonoff, A. J. Marsden, J. Tregay, R. J. Phillips, U. Goswami, J. M. Thomson, and T. Charman. Auditory discrimination and auditory sensory behaviours in autism spectrum disorders. *Neuropsychologia*, 47(13):2850–2858, 2009.

[33] A. Klin, D. J. Lin, P. Gorrindo, G. Ramsay, and W. Jones. Two-year-olds with autism orient to non-social contingencies rather than biological motion. *Nature*, 459(7244):257–261, 2009.

[34] R. Kohen-Raz, F. R. Volkman, and D. J. Cohen. Postural control in children with autism. *Journal of Autism and Developmental Disorders*, 22(3):419–432, 1992.

[35] A. N. Meltzoff, R. Brooks, A. P. Shon, and R. P. Rao. âĂIJsocialâĂİ robots are psychological agents for infants: A test of gaze following. *Neural Networks*, 23(8):966–972, 2010.

[36] J. Nadel. *Imitation et communication entre jeunes enfants*, volume 13. Presses Universitaires de France-PUF, 1986.

[37] J. Nadel. Imitation and imitation recognition: Functional use in preverbal infants and nonverbal children with autism. *The imitative mind: Development, evolution, and brain bases*, pages 42–62, 2002.

[38] J. Nadel. Do children with autism understand imitation as intentional interaction? *Journal of Cognitive & Behavioral Psychotherapies*, 4(2), 2004.

[39] J. Nadel and G. Butterworth. *Imitation in infancy*, volume 16. Cambridge University Press Cambridge, 1999.

[40] J. Nadel-Brulfert and P. Baudonniere. The social function of reciprocal imitation in 2-year-old peers. *International Journal of Behavioral Development*, 5(1):95–109, 1982.

[41] I. Ranatunga, M. Beltran, N. A. Torres, N. Bugnariu, R. M. Patterson, C. Garver, and D. O. Popa. Human-robot upper body gesture imitation analysis for autism spectrum disorders. In *International Conference on Social Robotics*, pages 218–228. Springer, 2013.

[42] B. Robins, P. Dickerson, P. Stribling, and K. Dautenhahn. Robot-mediated joint attention in

children with autism: A case study in robot-human interaction. *Interaction studies*, 5(2):161–198, 2004.

[43] S. J. Rogers and S. Ozonoff. Annotation: What do we know about sensory dysfunction in autism? a critical review of the empirical evidence. *Journal of Child Psychology and Psychiatry*, 46(12):1255–1268, 2005.

[44] J. Roll and J. Vedel. Kinaesthetic role of muscle afferents in man, studied by tendon vibration and microneurography. *Experimental Brain Research*, 47(2):177–190, 1982.

[45] D. R. Simmons, A. E. Robertson, L. S. McKay, E. Toal, P. McAleer, and F. E. Pollick. Vision in autism spectrum disorders. *Vision research*, 49(22):2705–2739, 2009.

[46] A. Taheri, M. Alemi, A. Meghdari, H. Pouretemad, and S. Holderread. Clinical application of humanoid robots in playing imitation games for autistic children in iran. *Procedia-Social and Behavioral Sciences*, 176:898–906, 2015.

[47] A. Tapus, M. Mataric, and B. Scassellati. Attention to facial emotion expressions in children with autism. *IEEE Robotics and Automation Magazine (RAM), Special Issue on Grand Challenges in Robotics*, 14(1), 2007.

[48] A. Tapus, A. Peca, A. Aly, C. Pop, L. Jisa, S. Pintea, A. S. Rusu, and D. O. David. Children with autism social engagement in interaction with nao, an imitative robot–a series of single case experiments. *Interaction studies*, 13(3):315–347, 2012.

[49] S. Thill, C. A. Pop, T. Belpaeme, T. Ziemke, and B. Vanderborght. Robot-assisted therapy for autism spectrum disorders with (partially) autonomous control: Challenges and outlook. *Paladyn, Journal of Behavioral Robotics*, 3(4):209–217, 2012.

[50] M. Tomasello. *The cultural origins of human cognition.* Harvard university press, 2009.

How to Open an Interaction Between Robot and Museum Visitor? Strategies to Establish a Focused Encounter in HRI

Raphaela Gehle
University of Duisburg-Essen
Universitätsstraße 12, Essen
Germany
raphaela.gehle@uni-due.de

Karola Pitsch
University of Duisburg-Essen
Universitätsstraße 12, Essen
Germany
karola.pitsch@uni-due.de

Timo Dankert
CITEC, Bielefeld University
Inspiration 1, Bielefeld,
Germany
tdankert@techfak.uni-bielefeld.de

Sebastian Wrede
CITEC, Bielefeld University
Inspiration 1, Bielefeld,
Germany
swrede@techfak.uni-bielefeld.de

ABSTRACT

On the basis of a video corpus of human-robot-interaction in a museum guide scenario, we address the challenge how a robot could determine the appropriate moment of opening an interaction with a visitor. Considering such "openings" as a stepwise coordinated process, we used a wizard-of-oz setup to investigate the wizard's timely decisions about when to look at the visitor resp. to verbally greet him/her (during early stages called "pre-beginnings"). Analysis is based on both robot internal and external data and combines qualitative sequential case analysis and quantification. Analysis reveals features for classification of two visitors types and corresponding opening strategies.

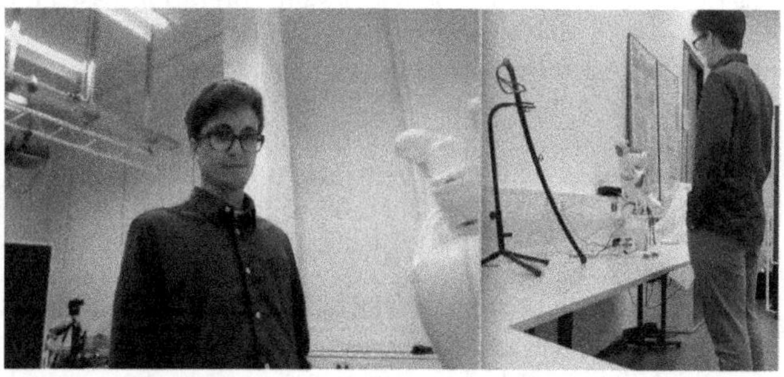

Figure 1: Robot's internal vision and external cam: Successful establishment of contact.

1. INTRODUCTION

Once a robot is deployed in real-world settings such as e.g. in the role of a museums guide, it is faced with the challenge of getting in contact with a potential interaction partner and to open a 'focused encounter' [6][15][18][21][24].

Research on *human* interaction has shown that such openings constitute a process of fine-grained coordination between co-present actors who - through their interaction - attempt to signal to each other whether they are willing to engage in a focused encounter and what the nature of their interaction might be [5][6][10][22]. Thus, the moments before the first greeting (called "pre-beginnings") are crucial as participants closely monitor each others' conduct and finely tune their own conduct with regard to the others' focus of attention, body orientation and behavior in space. In the field of *HRI*, little is known about the relevant activities involved in a stepwise process of opening an interaction including decisions over appropriate next moves with a robot's naturally limited set of interactional resources (but see [18]). Therefore, in this paper, we investigate "pre-beginnings" during openings of 1:1 human-robot-interactions in a laboratory museum guide setting using a human wizard to decide about the timing and choice of the robot's next actions. The following research questions are addressed:

(1) User behavior: How do visitors act when they enter a museum site to explore an exhibition? When and how could an interaction be initiated?

(2) Wizard decisions: How does a wizard interpret a visitor's activities to prepare for an adequate opening and which practices does the wizard apply to react to the results of his/her monitoring of the visitor's conduct?

Analysis considers the interactional negotiations between human and robot/wizard as they appear on the interactional surface. Analysis shows that it is insufficient to *design a fixed interactional conduct* to open an interaction. Instead, a robot should be equipped with a set of opening strategies to be chosen depending on its online analysis of the visitor's

HRI '17, March 06-09, 2017, Vienna, Austria

DOI: http://dx.doi.org/10.1145/2909824.3020219

conduct. To deal with the flexibility required for opening an interaction the wizard investigated in our study make creative use of the limited resources of pre-defined robot conduct.

2. OPENING A FOCUSED ENCOUNTER

2.1 HHI: Situated interactional coordination

The activity of "opening" a focused encounter has been shown - for human interaction - to be a coordinative process during which the co-present actors negotiate with each other their respective accessibility [6][9][10][12][22]. During so-called "pre-beginnings" (i.e. the moment before the actual verbal greeting) potential interaction partners permanently monitor the multimodal activities and accessibility of the other [6][9][10][12] and adjust their own conduct (head orientation, spatial behavior, body orientation) accordingly.

In this paper, we adopt an approach which closely relies on these ideas of interactional negotiation and coordination and attempt to investigate to what extent a robotic system could engage in such coordinative processes with the human user when attempting to engage in interaction with him/her. Such an endeavor is challenging as it requires precise description of user conduct, it's interpretation based on limited sensor information and models or flexible building blocks allowing for interactional coordination.

In a similar vein, Yamazaki et al. [26] investigate prior-to-request and request behavior in human interaction (health care situations in which residents attempt to actively establish contact with members of staff) to inform the design of HRI. They investigate the multimodal practices and coordination of caregivers' displays of availability and tailored initiation of clients' requests. They outline implications for (a) the development of a service robot concerning the display of *availability* towards humans that are engaged in several activities, (b) a display of *recipiency* via gaze, head and body orientation and (c) *acknowledgment* to signal that a request has been recognised.

2.2 HRI: Computational approaches

Openings in human-robot-interaction, however, have only rarely been considered as a process of interactional coordination. One line of research focuses on developing computational approaches to classify human conduct during openings.

In a museum scenario, Rashed et al. [21] focus on participants' *trajectories* and *attentional focus* and differentiate three types of walking trajectories to estimate whether a museum visitor might need guidance. As the results are based on initial observational experiments not including a robot, it remains unclear so far how to negotiate an adequate moment for offering an interaction depending on the visitor's behavior and robot conduct. Also Bohus and Horvitz [1] develop a model predicting engagement as Rashed based on trajectories and attentional focus and consider them in relation to *temporality* in two different environments. Shi et al. [24] also consider *spatial formation* and the *participation state* and point out that humans show different behavior based on their subsequent plans (with the robot showing pre-defined conduct during openings).

Another line of research focuses primarily on interactional aspects of openings. Yousuf et al. [29] develop a system which classifies whether group members look at the robot which actively moves towards visitors to open the interaction when gaze contact is established. In the reported study, the visitors where instructed in terms of specific gaze behavior and the robot 'waits' for visitors who actively signal their interest in interaction at some point.

Holthaus et al. [7] designed a model for a responsive receptionist robot drawing on interactional space to realize a distance based opening. The robot adapts its head orientation depending on the participant's distance. They found that the robot is perceived being interested in contact and available for interacting. Pitsch et al. [15][16][18] show that visitors who experience a responsive robotic system during the opening, tend to stay until the end of an interaction, whereas users who experience a non-responsive system tend to disengage [18][19]. In particular, the robot's conduct and responsiveness during the "pre-beginning" allows visitors to build hypotheses about the robot's interactional competences (which might fail later on).

In summary, research in recent computational approaches of HRI considers features like trajectories and attentional focus and temporality. But we also see technical limitations for implementing features such as detecting specific hand gestures [20] into an autonomous system to provide a basis for the robot's next actions. Yet, interactional coordination under circumstances of online monitoring and coordination to enable robots to autonomously engage in negotiation during the process of opening have only rarely been addressed in current systems.

3. DESIGN OF THE ROBOT'S OPENING STRATEGIES: LOOK VS. TALK?

To explore ways of enabling a robot system to get in contact with a user and to engage in a focused encounter based on the idea of interactional negotiation and coordination, we developed an initial model for an opening strategy focusing on the "pre-beginning" (see section 3.2) in a museum guide scenario. In particular, it includes decisions about shifts in the robot's head orientation (when to look at the user?) and the moment of verbally addressing the user (when to talk to the user?). The model was implemented as a finite state machine and linked to the robot's visual perception and thus contains the realistic choices prepared for an autonomous robot system. In the study presented in this paper, a human wizard assumes the role of deciding about the appropriate next robot move at a given point in time based on a pre-defined list of relevant choices in the initial model. This way, we will gain information to further tailor the model to be deployed by the autonomous robot in subsequent stages of the project.

3.1 Initial robot conduct: 'Look around' - perception and availability

We assume the robot to be placed in a museum site (see e.g. [4][17][18]) and to be faced with the initial challenge of both detecting an interaction partner and signaling its own availability. As some robots may have limited perceptual abilities - e.g. due to limited sensors, lighting conditions - we opted for an initial idle strategy in which the robot continuously moves its head slowly from one side of the room to the other. This way, the field of view which might be limited by the robot's sensors can be enlarged and thus the chance of detecting interaction partners should be increased.

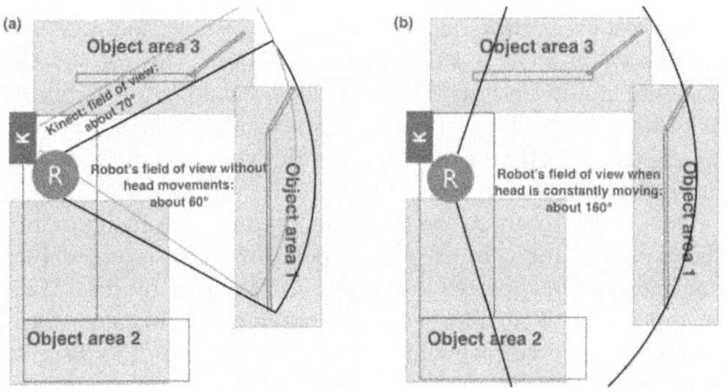

Figure 2: Field of view: (a) static gaze and kinect, (b) increased field of view due to head movements

Fig. 2 details these differences for the example of a NAO robot which is used in our project: Fig. 2 a shows the NAO's field of view using a static gaze strategy, i.e. approximately 60° with its internal camera, or about 70° with an externally attached Kinect camera (not used online in this study). Fig. 2b shows the robot's increased field of view when it continuously moves its head from one side of the room to the other, reaching at about 160°. Also, the robot thereby displays availability (e.g. [26]) and activity in an unfocused way until it autonomously detects an interaction partner or - as in this study - the wizard chooses to proceed to a next state (see Fig 3).

3.2 Interactional decisions: Look at the visitor? Talk to him/her? Look away?

Insights provided by previous studies on openings in HHI and HRI (in particular [18][26]) point to the relevance of co-participants looking at each other (and thus signal availability *and* reciprocity of perception) at relevant moments in time before they actually begin to verbally address each other. As we wanted to investigate how a robotic system could make use of these resources for opening an interaction, they were integrated as subsequent steps in a finite state approach (see Fig. 3): 'look at', 'talk to' or 'look away'.

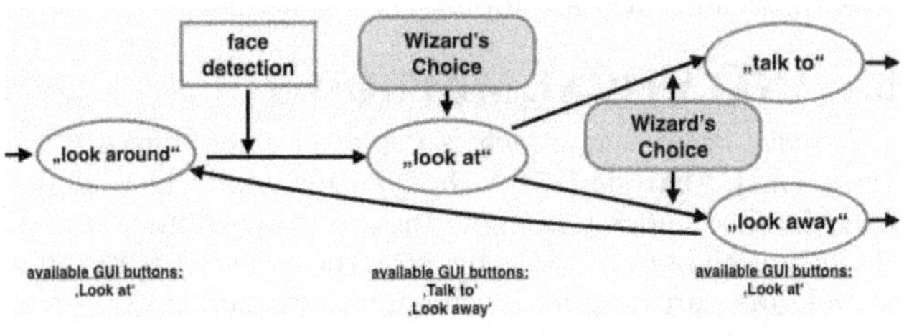

Figure 3: Opportunities to trigger robot states.

As the decision about when to assume the next step requires high interactional competences to interpret the visitors' conduct, we adopted a wizard-of-oz approach in this study as an intermediate step towards developing an autonomous robot system. The wizard assumes the role of deciding about the next robot move at a given point in time based on a pre-defined list of realistic choices prepared for the autonomous version of the system (see section 3.2).

The combination of the initial model with the wizard-of-oz approach (added to an otherwise autonomous robot system) leads to the following states and choices for performing an opening:

State 'look around'. In its idle-mode (see section 3.1) the robot is set up to (a) automatically look around and to be attentive to detect faces and (b) wait for the wizard's decision about *when* to look at the visitor.

State 'look at'. When the wizard triggers the 'look at' state the robot autonomously adjusts its head towards a detected face. Misdetections might occur and thus lead to the robot directing its head to an (interactionally) inappropriate direction.

Choice between the states 'talk to' and 'look away'. While the robot is in the state of looking at a (sometimes: presumably) detected face, the wizard has the opportunity either to make the robot start to 'talk to' the participant or to trigger a 'look away'-behavior. 'Talk to' makes the robot formulate a verbal greeting ("Hello I am NAO"), 'look away' makes the robot lower its head position. This provides for the opportunity to either further interact or disengage.

State 'talk to.' Once the robot is in the state 'look at', the wizard is able to choose the option 'talk to' the participant, which triggers the verbal greeting "Hello I am Nao". From now on the robot constantly adjusts its head to the detected face autonomously. As soon as the wizard triggers the next move, the robot continues with another verbal activity (offering information: "I could tell you something about the time of the middle-ages. Would you be interested?").

The concrete combination of these building blocks is chosen by the wizard depending on the situation. This leads not only to different practices of performing the opening but also enables us to investigate the ways in which the wizards attempt to adjust and coordinate their actions with the observed visitor conduct.

4. ROBOT SYSTEM

To explore ways of enabling a robot system to get in contact with a user and to engage in a focused encounter, the resources for opening an encounter (as detailed in section 3.2) were implemented in a small-scale humanoid robot (NAO). It was based on a set of modularized system components organized by a dedicated middleware architecture. While in previous studies this robot system was set up to run autonomously in a real-world museum site [4][17][18], for this study parts of its interactional decisions were controlled by a human wizard with the scenario being transferred to the laboratory. For the functions investigated here, the following system components are relevant:

Perception depends on NAO's internal VGA camera. The system runs autonomous face tracking (VFOA, see [14]) in order to adjust the robot's head direction to face the assumed interaction partner.

Dialogue consists of pre-configured talk and gesture. A dedicated dialogue component was used in combination with a finite state machine that includes the building blocks of our opening model.

The *coordination module* sends information to the wizard's GUI, which prompts a change into the next set of options at moments of changing states (see Fig. 3).

The sensory data was streamed via network and processed via an external computer. The robot's internal data about head location and rotation and face detection of the participant [14] was processed online and recorded for subsequent offline analysis.

5. STUDY AND DATA

A user study was conducted at Bielefeld University.

5.1 Study Setup

A NAO robot was set up to act as a museum guide offering information about three different areas of a museum exhibition, which we recreated in the laboratory. These different areas (see Fig. 4) were equipped with a wall of pictures and combined text (area 1), physical objects (area 2) and a large banner of a medieval tombstone (area 3).

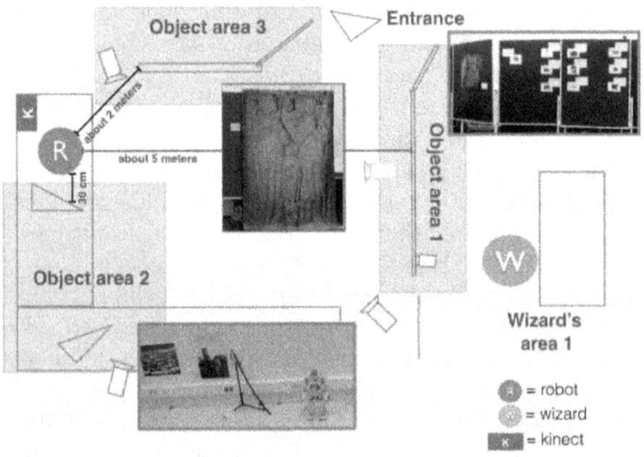

Figure 4: Setting: Museum Guide Robot.

Due to its small size (58 cm), the robot was placed on a table. The wizard was placed behind a wall in the same room. This way, the wizard would have at his/her disposal to make decisions both (i) auditory information, and (ii) the robot's internal vision of scene which was transmitted online to the wizards GUI with a delay of about 3 - 5 ms.

The interaction between human and robot was designed as a 1:1 HRI-setting and encompasses (a) an initial opening phase, (b) information about different exhibits and (c) a farewell. The average interaction lasted for about 2 - 3 minutes. In general, all participants except one individual were successfully engaged by the robot.

5.2 Visitor instructions

Participants were asked to visit the exhibition. We attempted to prevent visitors from walking straight to the robot by suggesting (yet not 'instructing') that they might orient to a specific object at the beginning:
Option 1: Maybe you'd like to start at the swords;
Option 2: Maybe you'd like to start at the tombstone;
Option 3: Maybe you'd like to start at the wall of pictures.
Thus, the laboratory setting provides for variability in the visitors' conduct during the pre-beginning which an opening model should be able to address and with which the human wizards have to deal.

Participants were informed about the nature of the study, (without being told that they would interact with a robot), that they will be video-recorded and that they could interrupt the study at any given moment. All participants gave written informed consent.

5.3 Wizard instructions

To obtain mostly spontaneous decisions about the question of when and how to open an interaction on the basis of the resources provided by the model (see section 3.2), the human wizards were instructed to assume the role of the museum guide and to decide if they would offer a guided exhibition tour. The wizard had to decide *when to open* an interaction and *when to allow for the participant to explore the exhibition on his/her own.*

During the interaction the wizard had neither insights into the system's hypotheses of the position of a detected face nor into the respective state in the dialogue model. This is important to avoid effects of a wizard waiting e.g. for a correctly detected face which would compromise the insights into the precise moment and reasons for their decision. On the wizard GUI, only the buttons for triggering next actions changed depending on the current robot state to provide the designed set of options (see Fig. 3).

5.4 Participants

Visitors: Thirty-eight persons (24 male, 14 female) were recruited to participate as visitors in the study both by leaflets and personal advertising. Their social situation ranged from being school pupils and students (from freshman to phd-students of different disciplines) over administration secretaries to senior citizens and their aged ranged from 19 to 65. This way participants with a range of different backgrounds were recruited comparable to the situation in a real-world museum.

Wizards: To secure wizard-independent decisions we asked four different persons to act as wizards. They were student assistants from the field of communication studies without, however, disposing of explicit knowledge about computer science or the field of human-robot-interaction.

5.5 Data

The study was conducted over three consecutive days during which 38 robot-to-single interactions were recorded. The data corpus is comprised of recordings from 4 external HD video cameras, the robot's internal VGA camera, logfiles of the respective dialogue states and recordings of the visitors' spatial conduct by a Kinect camera (independent of the robot system). Occurring changes in the robot's internal states and thus the wizard's timing and type of choice were automatically transferred to Elan Annotation Software [3]. In sum, we obtained a full data set for 34 trials.

6. ANALYTICAL METHOD

A multi-layered approach is deployed combining a Conversational Analysis [25] with quantification: This allows for a detailed understanding of the fine-grained interactional structures and negotiations between the co-participants and, at the same, provides for a general understanding of the frequency and relevance of the occurring phenomena (i.e. the procedures chosen by the wizards).

The first analytical step consists of detailed *qualitative micro-analysis* of two exemplary cases. In this, we aim at providing comparable interactional circumstances to analyze collections of cases and on this basis to describe alternative trajectories of interaction which take into account the emergent nature of interaction. The overall goal consists of gaining a better understanding of the range of the members' practices to inform the robot design (as opposed to transferring the wizards' decisions one by one to a robotic system). This approach enables us to investigate the sequential relationship of the visitors' multimodal actions in relationship to the robot's conduct. We mainly focus on the wizard's perception of the situation (via the robot's internal cameras). Additionally, we consider the participants' perception and understanding ('members perspective') of the robot's actions signaled via their conduct and reactions.

In a second analytical step, we undertake *quantitative evaluation* of the annotations to evaluate how results of qualitative analysis are applicable to the entire corpus.

7. QUALITATIVE CASE ANALYSIS: CREATIVE USE OF ROBOT'S RESOURCES

As the wizard is only provided with the same information also robot systems would dispose of, this creates circumstances during which a wizard has to creatively use the available interactional resources of the robotic system. The analytical focus is placed (i) on the different ways of visitors approaching the robot respectively the exhibits, and integrates (ii) misdetections occurring in the robot's visual perception.

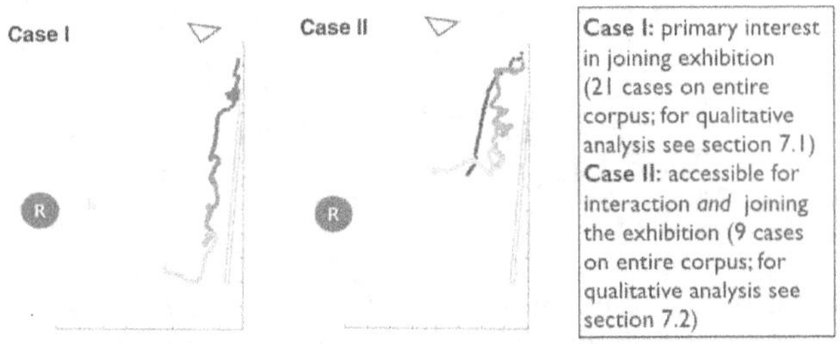

Figure 5: Trajectories for two types of visitors.

Two exemplary cases were chosen due to the tasks and requirements they set for the wizard when deciding about when and how to open the interaction. Although both participants start at the same object area (area 1) they show different displays of accessability towards the robot. This also is detectable on basis of kinect trajectories (see Fig. 5).

7.1 Case Analysis I: Engaging a participant being focused on exhibits

The first case provides an example of the wizard's procedures to engage in interaction with a participant who is primary interested in exploring the exhibition. Analysis will reconstruct different steps of their interactional negotiation:

Participant enters the room. We enter the scene when the robot is in the attentive idle mode for detecting faces. The participant (P1) enters the room (see Fig. 6a) and moves directly towards the first part of the exhibition (area 1), where he arrives after 3 seconds (see Fig. 6b, # 00.03.000). The robot's head direction and the resulting video stream allows the wizard to observe the participant's trajectory from the entrance towards the wall. The robot's internal cameras show that the participant does not orient to the robot during this initial stage (see Fig. 6a,b).

Participant begins to inspect the exhibits. P1 is engaged in looking at object area 1, which leads to him turning his back to the robot (see Fig. 6c). The robot's head orientation is shifting from left to right during this phase as suggested by the 'look around'-state. This lasts for about 3.26 minutes during which the participant slowly moves alongside the wall, not being accessible for interaction.

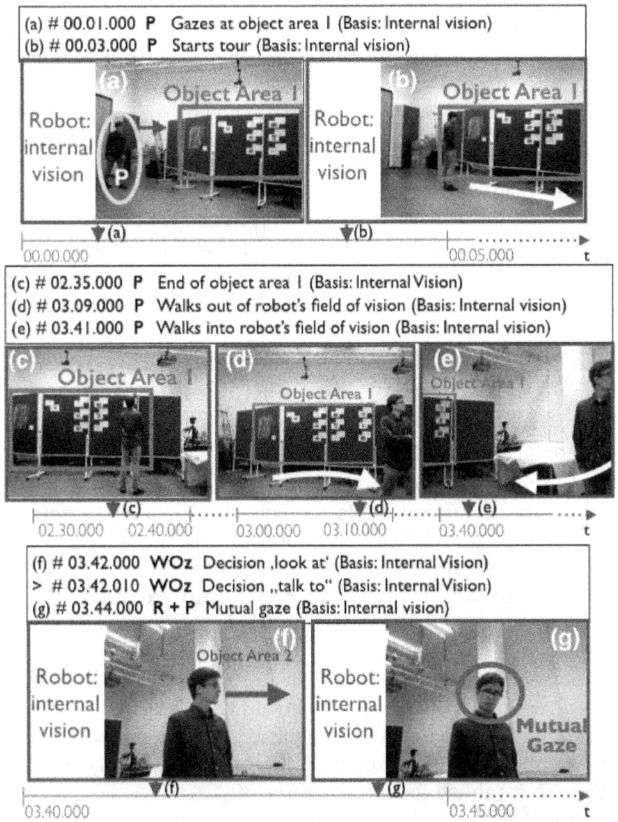

Figure 6: Case Analysis I: Opening with a visitor who is primary exhibit oriented.

Relevant moment of transition. As P1 approaches the right side of object area 1, the wizard anticipates the upcoming phase of transition (see Fig. 6c), i.e. the visitor's next move. At the moment, when the participant turns his body, the wizard triggers 'look at' (see Fig. 6c) and thus shows this moment to be adequate for getting in contact.

Robot's fallability. Following the 'look at' command, the robot attempts to direct its head to a location where it assumes to find an interaction partner. However, as the robot's VFOA component produces a misclassification the robot's head turns towards object area 1 while P walks out of the robot's field of view (# 3.09.000, see Fig. 6d).

Wizard's creative use of the robot's interactional resources. To cope with this situation, the wizard triggers the state 'look away', which was initially designed for the moments when a participant signals that he/she would not be interested in engaging. Interestingly, by using this option, the wizard shows (a) a situated interpretation of the presence and type of trouble ('robot's misdetection'), (b) his/her knowledge about the robot's resources (e.g. how does it look like to 'look away' in this situation) and (c) a spontaneous strategy of how to creatively use the robot's (limited) resources to deal with the situation in a flexible way. He spontaneously 'creates' a resource to actively manipulate the robot's field of view. As the 'look away'-state is triggered, the robot lowers its head and then automatically changes into 'look around'-state. This creates a chance to restart and to provide for a new opportunity to detect the participant's face.

Second chance. The wizard now decides to leave the robot in the 'look around'-state until the moment at which P1 reappears in the robot's field of view (see Fig. 6e). During a period of 1080ms after P1 reappears, the wizard triggers the next state ('look at') so that the robot starts to adjust its head to P1. Immediately afterwards, the wizard triggers 'talk to' and thereby the verbal opening "Hello I am Nao" gets performed. As a reaction to the robot's proactive way of opening (see Fig. 6g), this leads P1 to look at the robot and establish a situation of assumed 'reciprocal attention' which provides a relevant basis for further interaction.

7.2 Case Analysis II: Engaging a participant open to engage and exhibit oriented

The second case analysis provides an example for investigating the relationship between the wizard's decisions and the conduct of a participant who is both engaged in inspecting exhibits and accessible for engaging in an interaction. The participant offers several opportunities for gaze contact with the robot during the "pre-beginning".

Participant interested in robot and exhibit. P2 enters the room and looks at the robot at an early stage of co-presence (#00.08.000). He shows his awareness of the robot and the different object areas before beginning to inspect the exhibits in area 1. During this period, P2 stands immobile with his gaze alternating between the robot and several exhibits. He thereby offers the opportunity for the robot to establish gaze contact (cf. [9]).

Robot's limited opportunities to monitor the participants moves. Due to the circumstance that the robot continuously turns its head ('look around' state), the wizard can only monitor the participant's movements during the short period of time (1182ms) in which the participant enters the room. The next occasion at which P2 becomes visible in the robot's field of view, he has already reached object area 1 and is focussed on the exhibits.

Engaged in inspecting object area 1. By chance, the wizard is able to monitor P2's activities for about 17 seconds before loosing sight contact, because of the robot's head movement. During this period, P2 focuses on the pictures displayed in object area 1, with only minor spatial transitions between them. Thereby, P2's body orientation is not entirely turned away from the robot (cf. [9]) although the object area provides for turning the back to the robot. After P2 has inspected half of object area 1 (see Fig. 7b), he turns towards the robot (see section 7c).

Wizard triggers actions of "pre-beginning". This dual orientation exhibited by P2 provides for opportunities during which the wizard/robot could establish gaze contact. Consequently, the wizard triggers 'look at' and the robot perceivably adjusts its head towards the participant's face.

Robot's fallability. Similar to the system's performance in case analysis 1, the robot turns its head towards an area of the room different from the actual position of the visitor, again due to a perceptual misdetection. Also in this case, the wizard triggers the 'look away'-state to elicit another chance to correctly detect the participant's face.

Interpretation of the robot's supposed rejection. Due to triggering the 'look away'-state, the robot lowers its head in a situation in which P2 is looking at the robot. Immediately, also P2 also lowers his gaze (see Fig. 7d) and then starts to turn back to the wall he had been inspecting previously. He thereby shows his interpretation of the robot's move as an indication that the robot would not be available for getting in contact.

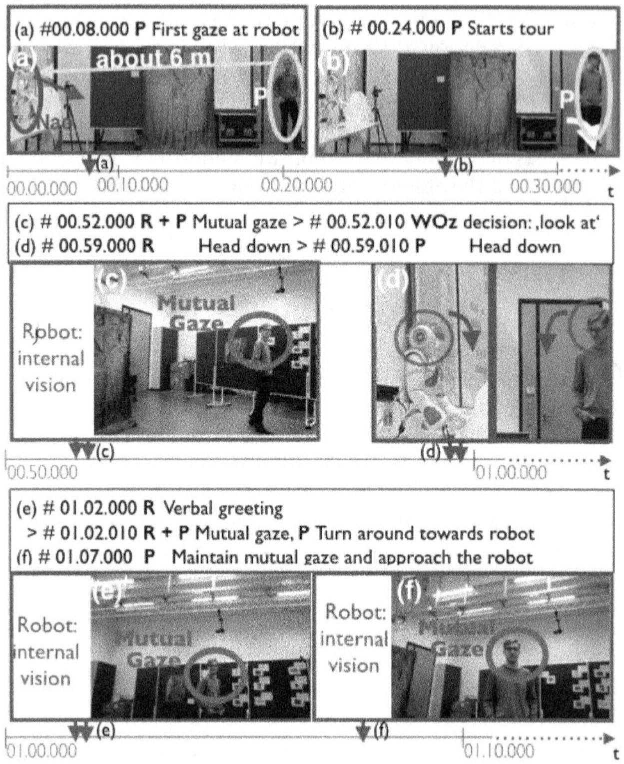

Figure 7: Case Analysis II: Opening with a visitor who is exhibit oriented *and* open for interaction at the same time.

Successful opening. At the earliest (technically) possible moment, the wizard triggers the 'look at'-state and immediately afterwards 'talk to'. Due to a correct face detection, the robot adjusts its head in a reasonable way, so that the verbal opening comes along with a reasonable head direction while addressing P2 who turns back around (see Fig. 7e) and afterwards approaches the robot (see Fig. 7f).

7.3 Case Analysis: Summary

The first cases analysis reveals the ways in which a wizard handles the challenge of a visitor that does not provide for chances to establish gaze contact until his bodily orientation shifts during a major spatial transition. Such major transitions appear - also in other cases of the corpus - to be highly relevant moments for attempts of offering to engage in an interaction. The wizard's strategies for dealing with this situation constitute of anticipating the visitors next moves and thus to pro-actively create a precisely timed opportunity for getting in contact and attempt to open an interaction. The second case analysis investigates a situation in which the participant pro-actively provides for opportunities in which contact could be established with the robot. The visitors splitted bodily orientation indicates his interest in both focussing on the exhibits and being available to engage in an interaction with the robot.

Both cases show that the wizard closely monitors the participant's actions. A moment of bodily re-orientation and gaze towards the robot leads to triggering the 'look at'-

state. This shows that the wizard uses the moment of re-orientation as an opportunity to open an interaction. Particularly relevant is also the wizard's creative use of the available resources when introducing a so far unforeseen way of manipulating the robot's head orientation and thereby its field of view after a misdetection has been produced.

In summary, both qualitative sequential analyses show that several parameters are relevant for choosing an appropriate moment to establish contact: gaze of participant, body orientation and periods of transition.

8. QUANTITATIVE EVALUATION

The analytical results provided in the preceding micro-analysis of two cases of HRI raise the question as to how these interactional procedures are transferable to other cases. Therefore, in a second analytical step we undertake a quantitative evaluation in which we abstract from single case analysis to a systematic view on the phenomena of our entire data corpus.

8.1 Methodical step: Annotation

Using information about relevant interactional parameters derived from qualitative analysis (see section 7), the data corpus was annotated using a timeline based annotation software (Elan) which provide the basis for manually generating an excel sheet to count the occurences of several procedures. The annotations include:

Robot states: automatically transfered to Elan depending on the system logs.

Participant's gaze direction: manually annotated in Elan. Categories: (a) gaze at robot (b) gaze at area 1, 2 or 3.

Participant's trajectory: plotted based on data of kinect 2 (for examples see section 7). Additionally, transitions were annotated manually ('major transition' and 'minor transition') as well as the participant's position including information about the distance to the corresponding object area.

Degree of focusing: manually annotated in Elan. Distinctions were made upon the distance to the object (< 0.5m and 1.5 - 2.0m) and body posture (i.e. leaning forward).

Moments of hesitation: annotated manually in Elan during transition from the entrance to the first exhibit.

Body posture and orientation: annotated manually using combined categories of 'leaning forward' or 'standing upright' and information about facing the robot ('facing robot', 'rotated towards robot', 'oriented towards object area').

8.2 Circumstances for 'look at'-state

As a first step, we link the moments of triggering 'look at' with classification of visitor behavior (transitions and gaze) as well as with perceptional circumstances the wizard has to deal with (absence of participant in the field of view). Triggering 'look at' might occur twice until engagement is established.

The wizard triggers the 'look at'-state during a participant's major transition in 18 cases 3 out of which occur during the transition from the entrance to the first object. This appears to be preferred in comparison to triggering 'look at' during minor transitions (4 cases, see table 1). Furthermore, in 10 cases the wizard triggers 'look at' although the visitor is engaged in looking at an object. In 17 cases 'look at' is immediately triggered after the participant reoccurs in the robot's field of view (see Fig 8). This structure is comparable to case analysis I in which the wizard had to creatively handle trouble due to the perceptional circumstances.

Moment for triggering 'look at'	Amount
During **major** transition from entrance to first object	3 cases
During **major** transition from one object area to another object area	15 cases
Minor transition (while P is engaged in looking at one object area)	4 cases
While the participant looks at an object	10 cases
Immediately (< 2.2 secs) after seeing participant again	17 cases

Table 1: Moments at which the wizard chooses to trigger the 'look at'-state

8.3 Visitor providing opportunities to get into contact.

As a second step, we show the structural relation of the two features (transitions and gaze towards the robot) between each other. In 27 instances visitors use periods of (major) transitions to offer an opportunity to enter in contact with the robot via gaze (see Fig 8). We structurally linked this information with the occurence of transition phases (see Fig. 8). In 7 cases the participant offers an opportunity for gaze contact during a minor transition (see section 7.2).

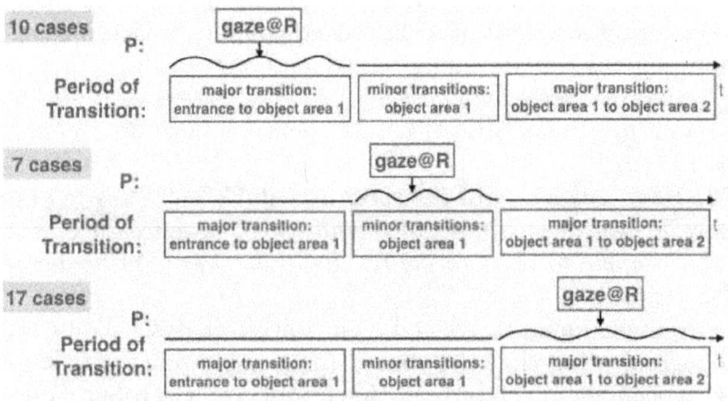

Figure 8: Participant's gaze in relation to periods of transiton during the opening.

As a third step, we structurally link the wizards' choices with the classification of visitor conduct. We see that the participants' gaze functions as a precondition for 'talk to' in 26 cases (see Fig. 9). In 10 cases 'look at' is triggered firstly. Until triggering 'talk to' the participant gazes at the robot. Nevertheless, there are also 8 cases in which the wizard triggers a sequence of 'look at' and 'talk to' without prior gaze of the visitor.

8.4 Circumstances for sequences of 'look-at' and 'talk to'-state.

Quantitative evaluation firstly suggests that despite different structural preconditions under which an opening has to be performed there are structural similarities, especially considering aspects of visitor behavior (transitions and gaze)

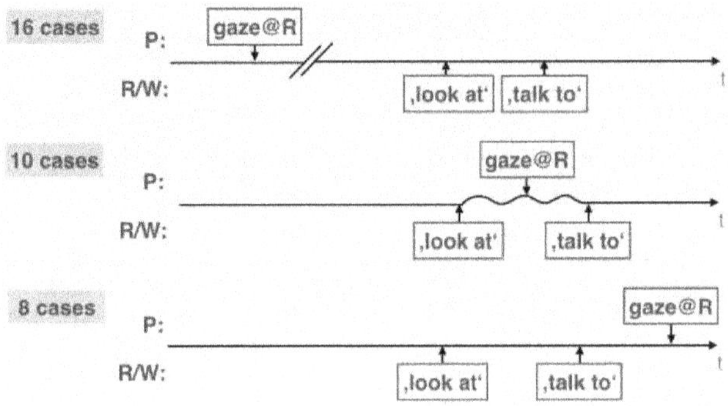

Figure 9: Sequencial structures of 'look at' and 'talk to' related to participant's gaze.

and effects from perceptional limitations. Secondly, related to these moments of possible anticipation (transitions) we find structural opportunities to establish gaze contact (see Fig. 8). Thirdly, we showed the sequential organization of building blocks of robot conduct related to visitors' behavior (gaze towards robot).

9. SUMMARY AND IMPLICATIONS

This study set out to investigate ways in which a robot system could engage in basic interactional coordination with a human user when attempting to get in contact and to engage in a focused interaction. In particular, the analytical focus was placed on the moment of "pre-beginnings" and examined on the basis of 1:1 human-robot interactions in a laboratory museum setting the following interrelated questions using a wizard-of-oz approach combined with a semi-autonomous robot system:

(1) How do visitors act when they enter a museum site to explore an exhibition? When and how could an interaction be initiated?

(2) How does a wizard interpret a visitor's activities to prepare for an adequate opening and which practices does the wizard apply to react to the results of his/her monitoring of the visitor's conduct?.

Combined qualitative and quantitative analysis shows, on a general level, that the wizard (a) needs resources to deal with occurring misinterpretations caused by the robot's perception and (b) makes creative use of the robot's resources. Thus, to develop building blocks for an autonomous robot system which should enable it to engage in a stepwise process of opening requires a flexible set of opening strategies - as opposed to a model of fixed interactional conduct as it has been suggested in the literature so far.

Towards this goal, two types of visitor conduct have been described that a robot would need to be able to detect and distinguish to use flexible opening strategies tailored to the respective visitor's conduct. Quantitative evaluation of the data corpus allows us to abstract to comparable structural embeddedness of visitor behavior and interactional sequentiality. As a starting point, our analysis points to the following set of features and robot conduct.

Features of visitor conduct

Case I: Visitor primarily focused on exhibits
Gaze direction: Visitors' gaze directed to the robot (and thus his/her availability) to be expected mainly during major transitions between different areas of an exhibition or when entering the room. No fixations towards the robot when moving alongside an object area.
Trajectory: Visitor presumably walking along the perimeter of the exhibition area.
Body orientation: Visitor's mainly body orientation to an object area. Knowledge about exhibition/object areas required to provide e.g. for major transitions should be linked with expectations about user conduct in specific areas.

Case II: Visitor open to interact and exhibit oriented
Gaze direction: Visitor exhibits alternating gaze fixations between an object area and the robot.
Trajectory: Visitor presumably walking along the perimeter of the exhibition area.
Body orientation: Visitor's movement in space presumably intermitted by rotations of the upper body to the robot.

Elements for a flexible opening strategy

Case I: Visitor primarily focused on exhibits
Step 1: Prepare for detecting gaze fixation (e.g. [23]) (or head orientation) and/or bodily orientation towards robot.
Step 2: When no gaze is detected during transition from entrance to the first object area, wait for the visitor to arrive at a relevant area for a major transition and start moving.
Step 3: When detecting gaze and/or body orientation respectively rotation towards the robot trigger 'look at'.
Step 4: Wait for a moment, where the participant looks at the robot, then immediately (< 2.2 secs) trigger a sequence of 'look at' and 'talk to'.

Case II: Visitor available for interaction while focusing on an exhibit
Step 1: Prepare for detecting gaze (cf. [23]) (or head orientation) and/or bodily orientation towards robot.
Step 2: When detecting gaze and/or bodily orientation/ rotation towards the robot trigger 'look at'. Thereby, enable gaze contact/mutual gaze (cf. [23]) and trigger 'look at' at moments of visitor's movement.
Step 3: Check whether visitor reorients the whole body towards robot and maintains gaze contact (potentially approaches).
Step 4: Trigger sequence of 'look at' and 'talk to'.

10. FUTURE WORK

At this initial stage, a special focus is placed on 'gaze' as an interactional resource, in subsequent approaches this should be enlarged towards multiple modalities. Future work will consist of further qualitative analysis to distinguish different types of visitor conduct and define features, especially concerning trajectories and bodily visitor conduct as well as further processes of abstraction from single case analysis to comparable structures on the corpus. Also further work will consist in implementation in an autonomous robot as well as testing the proposed flexible opening strategies.

ACKNOWLEDGMENT

The authors acknowlegde the financial support from 'CITEC' (EXC 277), Bielefeld University (project: 'Interactional Coordination and Incremenality in HRI') and the Volkswagen Foundation (Dilthey Fellowship 'Interaction & Space', K. Pitsch) and CoR-Lab.

11. REFERENCES

[1] D. Bohus, E. Horvitz, Learning to predict engagement with a spoken dialog system in open-world settings, Proceedings of the SIGDIAL 2009, pp. 244-252

[2] T. Dankert, M. Goerlich, S. Wrede, R. Gehle, K. Pitsch, Engagement detection during deictic references in human robot interaction. International Conference on Social Robotics (ICSR 2016), pp. 930 - 939

[3] Elan Annotation Software: https://tla.mpi.nl/tools/tla-tools/elan/

[4] R. Gehle, K. Pitsch, T. Dankert, S. Wrede, Trouble-based group dynamics in real-world HRI - Reactions on unexpected next moves of a museum guide robot. 24th International Symposium on Robot and Human Interactive Communication (Ro-MAN 2015), Kobe, Japan, pp. 407-412

[5] E. Goffman, Behavior in public places. Notes on the Social Organization of Gathering, Free Press, 1967.

[6] E. Goffman, Encounters. Two studies in the sociology of interaction, The Advanced Studies in Social Sciences, Indianapolis, 1967.

[7] P. Holthaus, K. Pitsch, S. Wachsmuth, How Can I Help? - Spatial Attention Strategies for a Receptionist Robot, International Journal of Social Robotics 3(4):383 - 393, 2012.

[8] Y. Kato, T. Kanda, H. Ishiguro, May I help you? - Design of human-like polite approaching behavior, HRI 2015, 2015, pp. 35-42.

[9] A. Kendon, Some functions of gaze direction in two-person conversations, A. Kendon (Ed), Conducting Interaction. Patterns of Behavior in Focused Encounters, 1990.

[10] L. Mondada, Emergent focused interactions in public places: A systematic analysis of the multimodal achievement of a common interactional space, Journal of Pragmatics, 2008, pp. 1977-1997.

[11] L. Mondada, R. Schmitt, Zur Multimodalität von Situationseröffnungen, in L. Mondada, R. Schmitt (Eds.) Situationseröffnungen: Zur Multimodalen Herstellung Fokussierter Interaktion, Studien zur Deutschen Sprache, 2010, pp. 7-52.

[12] K. Mortensen, S. Hazel, Moving into interaction - Social practices for initiating encounters at a help desk, Journal of Pragmatics, 2014, pp. 46-67.

[13] Nao Robot: www.aldebaran.com

[14] S. Sheiki, J.-M. Odobez, Recognizing the visual focus of attention for human robot interaction, in HBU, 2012, pp. 99-112.

[15] K. Pitsch, H. Kuzuoka, Y. Suzuki, L. Süssenbach, P. Luff, C. Heath, "The first five seconds": Contingent stepwise entry into an interaction as a means to secure sustained engagement in HRI, 18th International Symposium on Robot and Human Interactive Communication (Ro-MAN 2009), Toyama, Japan, 2009, pp. 985-991.

[16] K. Pitsch, K. S. Lohan, K. Rohlfing, J. Saunders, C. L. Nehaniv, B. Wrede, Better be reactive at the beginning. Implications of the first seconds of an encounter for the tutoring style in human-robot-interaction. 21th International Symposium on Robot and Human Interactive Communication (Ro-MAN 2012), Paris, France, pp. 974 - 981.

[17] K. Pitsch, R. Gehle, S. Wrede, Addressing multiple participants. A museum guide robot's gaze shapes visitor participation, ICSR 2013, Bristol, UK, 587-588.

[18] K. Pitsch, Ko-Konstruktion in der Mensch-Roboter-Interaktion. Kontingenz, Erwartungen und Routinen der Eröffnung, in U. Dausendschön-Gay, E. Gülich, U. Kraft (Eds.): Ko-Konstruktion als interaktive Verfahren, Bielefeld, Benjamins, 2015, pp. 229-257.

[19] K. Pitsch, Limits and Opportunities for Mathematizing Communicational Conduct for Social Robotics in the Real-World? - Towards enabling a Robot to make use of the HumanâĂŹs Competences, AI & Society, 2015, pp. 1-7.

[20] W. Quan, H. Niwa, N. Ishikawa, Y. Kobayashi, Y. Kuno, Assisted-care robot based on sociological interaction analysis. Computers in Human Behavior, 27(5), 2011, pp. 1527-1534.

[21] G. Rashed, R. Suzuki, T. Kikugawa, A. Lam, Y. Kobayashi, Y. Kuno, Network guide robot system proactively initiating interaction with humans based on their local and global behaviors, ICIC 2015, Switzerland 2015, pp. 283-294

[22] E.A. Schegloff, Sequencing in Conversational Openings, American Anthropologist, Volume 70, Issue 6, 1968, pp. 1075 - 1095

[23] L. Schillingmann and Y. Nagai, Yet another gaze detector: An embodied calibration free system for the iCub robot, RAS 2015, pp. 8-13.

[24] C. Shi, M. Shiomi, T. Kanda, H. Ishiguro, N. Hagita, Measuring communication participation to initiate conversation in human-robot interaction, Journal of Social Robotics: 7, 2015, pp. 889-910.

[25] J. Sidnell, T. Stivers, The handbook of conversation analysis, in Blackwell Handbooks of Linguistics, Wiley, 2012.

[26] K. Yamazaki, M. Kawashima, Y. Kuno, N. Akiya, M. Burdelski, A. Yamazaki, H. Kuzuoka, Prior-to-request and request behaviors within elderly day care: Implications for developing service robots for use in multiparty settings. In ECSCW 2007, pages 61âĂŞ78.

[27] A. Yamazaki, K. Yamazaki, M. Okada, Y. Kuno, Y. Kobayashi, Y. Hoshi, K. Pitsch, P. Luff, D. vom Lehn, C. Heath, Revealing Gauguin: Engaging visitors in robot guide's explanation in an art museum, CHI 2009, pp. 1437 - 1446

[28] A. Yamazaki, K. Yamazaki, T. Ohyama, Y. Kobayashi, Y. Kuno, A techno-sociological solution for designing a museum guide robot: Regarding choosing an appropriate visitor, HRI 2012, Boston, Massachusetts, USA, 2012, pp. 309-316.

[29] M.A. Yousuf, Y. Kobayashi, Y. Kuno, A. Yamazaki, K.Yamazaki, How to move towards visitors: A model for museum guide robots to initiate conversation. In RO-MAN, 2013 IEEE

Predicting and Regulating Participation Equality in Human-robot Conversations: Effects of Age and Gender

Gabriel Skantze
KTH Speech Music and Hearing
Lindstedtsv. 24
10044 Stockholm, Sweden
+46-8-7907874
skantze@kth.se

ABSTRACT
In this paper, we investigate participation equality, in terms of speaking time, between users in multi-party human-robot conversations. We analyse a dataset where pairs of users (540 in total) interact with a conversational robot exhibited at a technical museum. The data encompass a wide range of different users in terms of age (adults/children) and gender (male/female), in different combinations. Overall, the analysis indicates that demographically heterogeneous pairs are more imbalanced, especially pairs of adults and children, where children are less prone to self-select in the turn-taking. The analysis also indicates that it is possible for the robot to reduce the imbalance by addressing the least dominant user and asking directed questions. However, for children to respond, it is important to seek mutual gaze and switch addressee often. Finally, we show that it is possible to predict the imbalance at an early stage in the interaction – in order to increase the participation equality as early as possible – and that knowledge about the users' age and gender helps in this prediction.

Keywords
Human-robot interaction; Turn-taking; Speech; Multi-party interactions; Age; Gender; Children; Participation equality

1. INTRODUCTION
Conversational robots are becoming increasingly common in areas such as education and elderly care. The physical appearance of the robot allows it to not only convey both verbal and non-verbal signals (in the form of prosody, gaze and gestures), but also to take part in interactions where the physical situation is of importance, such as discussions about objects in the shared space. This also allows robots to take part in multi-party interactions with several users, something which is much harder with, for example, conversational agents on 2D displays [19]. Compared to a dyadic setting, where only one user interacts with the robot, multi-party interaction allows users to not only talk to the robot, but also to each other. In an educational setting, this could potentially increase the engagement and learning outcomes. However, multi-party interaction also allows for more imbalanced participation. If one of the interlocutors is more dominant, it is possible that the others will not have a chance to contribute as much. Therefore, it is very important for a robot in such settings to be aware of the *participation equality* between the speakers, that is, the relative amount of speaking time for the participants. If a robot is able to predict any imbalance in speaking time, and if it can take actions to regulate the turn-taking and balance the interaction, this would be an argument for involving robots in conversational settings. Unlike humans, such a robot could use a completely unbiased model, purely based on statistics, to make these decisions.

HRI '17, March 06 - 09, 2017, Vienna, Austria

ACM 978-1-4503-4336-7/17/03…$15.00
DOI: http://dx.doi.org/10.1145/2909824.3020210

In this paper, we investigate three research questions. Firstly, there are several studies that find important differences in turn-taking behaviour between adults and children [9, 16], and between males and females [1, 6, 7]. Such differences could lead to different levels of participation equality. Thus, we want to study the effects of these variables on turn-taking behaviour and participation equality in multi-party human-robot interaction. Secondly, we want to study the effects of the robot's behaviour on the users' turn-taking behaviour. To what extent can the robot regulate the turn-taking by actively selecting the next speaker? Related to this, we also want to understand whether different user groups respond differently to the robot's turn-taking regulation signals. Thirdly, we want to study whether it is possible to predict the imbalance in participation at an early stage, and whether knowledge about age and gender help in this prediction. Such a prediction could potentially allow the robot to start shaping the turn allocation as early as possible in the dialogue.

The data we analyse comes from a system that was exhibited at the Swedish National Museum of Science and Technology for nine days [26]. As illustrated in Figure 1, two visitors at a time played a collaborative game together with the robot head Furhat (see Figure 2), in a fully automated setup. On the touch table between the players, a set of cards are shown. The two visitors and the robot are given the task of sorting the cards according to some criterion. For example, the task could be to sort a set of inventions in the order they were invented, or a set of animals based on how fast they can run. This is a collaborative game, which means that the users have to discuss the solution together with the robot. However, the robot does not have perfect knowledge about the solution. Instead, the robot's arguments are motivated by a randomized belief model. This means that the users have to determine whether they should trust the robot's belief or not, just like they have to do with each other. Thus, the robot's role in the interaction is similar to that of the users – it is not intended to be perceived as a tutor. During the nine days of the exhibition, we recorded hundreds of interactions with users from the general public, including adults and children. Since the robot's turn-taking behaviour was randomly selected for each turn, it is possible to study the effects on the users' behaviours.

In a previous analysis of the recorded data [26], we have shown that the robot's verbal and non-verbal behaviours – including filled pauses, breath and gaze – affect the user's turn-taking behaviours. However, we did not analyse whether these behaviours differed between adults and children, or males and females, as done here.

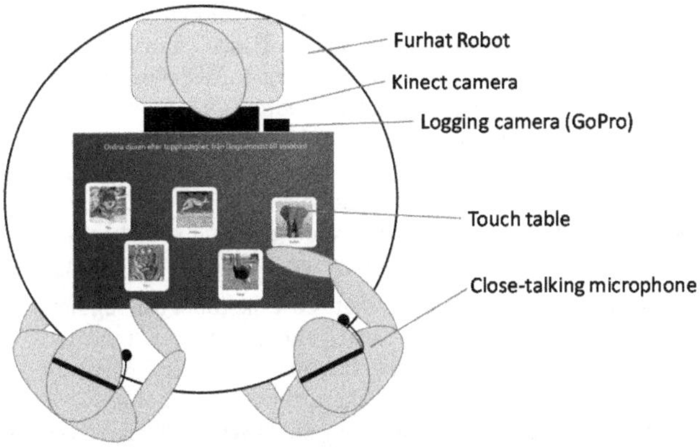

Figure 1: The setup used in the museum.

Figure 2: Left: Partial view from the logging camera. Right: The Furhat robot head.

2. BACKGROUND

In this section, we will provide a background on turn-taking in multi-party interaction, review the literature on effects of age and gender on turn-taking, and discuss related work on how to detect and regulate participation equality in human-robot interaction.

2.1 Turn-taking in Spoken Interaction

Many human social activities require some kind of turn-taking protocol, which regulates the order in which the different actions are supposed to take place, and by whom. This is obvious when, for example, playing a game of chess (where the protocol is very simple), but it also applies to spoken interaction. Since it is difficult to speak and listen at the same time, speakers in dialogue have to somehow coordinate who is currently speaking and who is listening. In a seminal article, Sacks et al. [24] described a protocol for this, which is schematically illustrated in Figure 3. In their view, speakers try to minimize the amount of gaps and overlaps between turns. At certain points in the speech, there are *Transition-Relevance Places* (TRPs), where a shift in turn could potentially take place. At these places, the current speaker may select a next speaker, who then 'has the right and is obliged' to take the next turn to speak, whereas no other participants are supposed to do so. If the current speaker does not select a next speaker, any participant has the opportunity to 'self-select', or the current speaker may continue. In a two-party (dyadic) conversation, the selection of the next speaker is trivial, but if there are several speakers (multi-party interaction), the current speaker typically gazes at the selected next speaker, or may use some other indicator, such as the person's name or a pointing gesture.

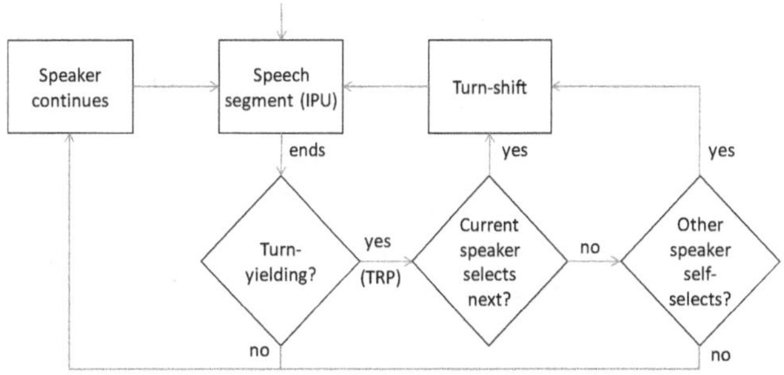

Figure 3: The 'standard model' of turn-taking as proposed by Sacks et al. (1974)

Traditionally, spoken dialogue systems have rested on a very simplistic model of turn-taking, where a certain amount of silence (say 700 ms) is used as an indicator that the user has stopped speaking, and that the turn is yielded to the system. The problem with this model is that turn-shifts are often supposed to be much more rapid than this, and that pauses within a turn may often be longer. Thus, the system will sometimes appear to give sluggish responses, and sometimes interrupt the user. A more accurate model would make a more continuous decision, trying to identify whether the user is *yielding* or *holding* the turn. Several studies have found that speakers use their voice and face to give *turn-holding* and *turn-yielding cues* [8, 11, 15]. For example, an incomplete syntactic clause or a filled pause (such as 'ehm') typically indicates that the speaker is not yielding the turn. Prosodically, a rising or falling pitch at the end of a segment tend to be turn-yielding, whereas a flat pitch is turn-holding. The intensity of the voice tends to be lower when yielding the turn, and the duration of the last phoneme tends to be shorter. Gaze has also been found to be an important cue – speakers tend to not look at the addressee during an utterance, but then shift the gaze towards the addressee when yielding the turn [14]. Studies on human-human dialogue have shown that the more turn-yielding cues are presented together, the more likely it is that the other speaker will take the turn [8, 11, 15]. Thus, one way of deciding whether the robot should take the turn or not after a speech segment, is to use machine learning to combine these different cues [12, 17].

It is important to stress that the diagram shown in Figure 3 is highly simplistic, and humans often 'violate' this schema. For example, speakers do not always take the turn even though they have been 'selected', and people may sometimes speak before the current speaker's speech segment is completed, resulting in overlapping speech. Indeed, the turn-taking model of Sacks et al. [24] has been challenged by other researchers, who argue that speakers do not always try to minimize gaps and overlaps, but that the criteria for successful interaction is highly dependent on the kind of interaction taking place [23]. In this view, overlaps can be a sign of engagement, and it is possible that conversational systems should not necessarily always avoid overlaps. Common signals, that often give rise to overlapping speech, are *backchannels* – short utterances (such as 'mhm' or 'aha'), which the listener provides to show continued attention [29].

2.2 Effects of Age and Gender on Turn-taking

Managing turn-taking is one of the first interactional skills humans have to learn. This learning begins by dyadic interaction with the caregiver, who is responsible for regulating most of the turn-taking [9]. Later on, children also learn how to claim the floor in multi-party interaction, a skill that is mastered around the age of six. Even after that, children continue to learn how to take turns, and reduce gaps and overlaps. Whereas adults often take turns with very short gaps (around 250ms), children's gaps are typically longer – in some studies average gap length has been measured at 1.5-2 seconds [9]. This gap length shortens with age, as the child learns to better pick up turn-yielding cues, project the interlocutor's turn ending, and plan their own response [9]. Researchers have also compared child-child interaction with child-adult interaction [16]. Typically, children conversing with adults allow the adult to regulate the interaction, and then pick up these regulatory behaviours and employ them when talking to other children. Thus, we can expect interaction between children to be more balanced than interaction between adults and children.

The differences between male and female turn-taking behaviours has been the subject of several studies. In same-sex settings, men tend to follow the standard model by Sacks et al. (minimizing gaps and overlaps), to a larger extent, whereas a much larger amount of overlap has been found in conversations between women [6]. These overlaps should not be regarded as competitive, as most often they are the result of women helping to complete each other's utterances and giving backchannels. The conversational style between women has therefore been characterized 'cooperative', whereas conversation between men is more 'competitive' [7]. Despite being more talkative in general, in mixed-sex settings, women have been found to talk less than men [7], and men seem to interrupt women more than the other way around [1].

Examining the interaction between age and gender, some studies have investigated the mechanisms by which linguistic gender differences develop. Studies on children have shown that young girls seem to be more talkative and fluent than boys (both to their mothers and to other children), but that boys tend to dominate mixed conversations at a relatively early age [7]. In child-adult interactions, fathers seem to interrupt children more than mothers, and both parents interrupt girls more than boys [7].

2.3 Turn Regulation and Participation Equality in Human-robot Interaction

Several previous studies have found that conversational agents can shape the turn-taking and assignment of participant roles in multi-party interaction [5, 19, 21]. The most common signal is to use gaze to actively select the next speaker. For this to work, it must be clear who the agent is looking at. A problem with animated agents on 2D displays is that it is impossible for the user to see exactly where the agent is looking, a problem typically referred to as the 'Mona Lisa effect' [19]. This is because the agent and user don't share the same physical space. Thus, in a multi-party setting, this means that the agent cannot establish exclusive mutual gaze with one of the users, and in a situated interaction the object that is the target of the gaze cannot be inferred. However, studies have shown that if an animated face is back-projected on a 3D mask, as done with the Furhat robot head used here, the turn-yielding accuracy is improved [19], and humans can utilize the robot's gaze to disambiguate references to objects to achieve joint attention [20, 25]. In a study on turn-taking in multi-party child-robot interaction, [18] examined the likelihood of children answering quiz questions, depending on where and how the robot directed its gaze. However, we are not aware of any studies that systematically compare how children and adults respond to turn-taking signals from an artificial agent in the same interactional setting.

If indeed a robot can regulate the turn-taking in multi-party interaction, this opens up the possibility of allowing the robot to balance the level of participation between the participants. One example of such an attempt is [2], where a virtual agent was used to balance the contributions from a group of children playing a game. Such balancing also requires a measure of dominance or participation equality. In [28], a model for classifying children's social dominance in group interactions is presented. Based on manual annotation of social dominance, a model was trained. The main predictor that turned out to be useful was the children's gaze towards the robot. However, it should be noted that there was no two-way spoken interaction between the robot and the children, and thus is cannot be regarded as a conversation. Another example is [22], where a dominance estimation model (based on gaze and speech) was used to decide how the robot should regulate the interaction using gaze.

In this study we will also investigate how the robot can regulate the turn-taking and balance the participation. However, this study is different from most previous studies on this subject. Firstly, the robot has a similar role as the speakers, thus it does not have a clear 'function' (i.e., acting as a tutor or quiz host). As we have seen in our previous analyses, the addressee in this kind of interaction is often not so easy to determine [26]. Many utterances in more conversational settings are not targeted towards a specific person, but rather as open statements or questions. Thus, most turn-shifts will be done using self-selection. Secondly, the discussion in our task necessarily involves references to objects in the physical surroundings. In such settings, speakers also naturally look at these objects. This has been shown to clearly affect the extent to which humans otherwise gaze at each other to yield the turn [3, 13].

In summary, several studies have examined both turn-taking regulation and participation equality in human-robot conversations, as well as gender and age effects on turn-taking. However, we are not aware of any previous studies that have systematically investigated these issues in combination.

3. HUMAN-ROBOT INTERACTION SETTING

The interactional setting that is under investigation here, and was briefly described in the Introduction, is illustrated in Figure 1. Two users are seated at a large table with a multi-touch screen, opposite the Furhat robot head (see Figure 2), which has an animated face back-projected on a translucent mask, as well as a mechanical pan-tilt neck [20]. This allows Furhat to direct the gaze using a combination of head and eye movements. The animated face allows for very accurate and expressive lip movements, facial gestures and gaze, which have been shown to be easy for users to read [20]. The synthetic voice (unit selection) is also complemented by non-verbal expressions, such as sighs, breathing, filled pauses and different types of backchannels. In our experience, Furhat does not typically give rise to an uncanny valley effect, despite the human-like appearance, possibly because of its slightly cartoonish design.

Both users were wearing unidirectional headset microphones, which allowed for the recording of two separate good quality audio streams (given the noisy setting in the museum). A Kinect camera (v2) was used to track the location and rotation of the users' heads, and a GoPro camera was used for logging.

The interaction starts when two users are seated and press a 'Start' button on the touch screen. Furhat initiates the interaction by asking them for their names. Then five cards are shown on the table and Furhat describes the sorting criterion, after which the discussion starts. When the task has been discussed for some time, a button is shown on the table that can be pressed to reveal the solution. Furhat then comments on the solution, comparing it with his own belief (admitting mistakes or pointing out that they should have listened to him). After that, the players can play another round if they wish. An example interaction is shown in Table 1[1]. After having played two rounds, the users are encouraged by Furhat to allow others to play. The system only manipulates the cards when switching between tasks – only the players can move the cards during the discussion.

Table 1: Example interaction (translated from Swedish)

U-1	I wonder which one is the fastest [looking at cards]
U-2	I think this one is fastest [touching a lion card], what do you think? [looking at robot]
R	I'm not sure about this, but I think the lion is the fastest animal [looking at cards]
U-1	Okay [moving the lion]
R	Now it looks better
U-2	Yeah... How about the zebra? [looking at robot]
R	I think the zebra is slower than the horse. What do you think? [looking at U-1]
U-1	I agree
U-2	I'm not sure, the zebra has to be fast to escape the lion...
R	mhm

The system was implemented using the open source framework IrisTK[2] [23], which provides an event-driven modularized architecture for real-time multi-modal dialog processing. The speech recognition was done with two parallel cloud-based large vocabulary speech recognition modules, which allowed Furhat to understand the users even when they were talking simultaneously. Since the speech is of a very conversational nature, the word-error-rate is typically very high (around 60%). However, our previous analysis [26] has showed that this is mainly due to errors in function words, and less due to errors in content words. In any case, given this high rate of error, modelling such dialog on a deeper semantic and pragmatic level would not be feasible. However, our main goal here is to create a believable dialog agent that can be used as a test-bed for studying turn-taking. Our approach has therefore been to exploit the redundancy offered by the multi-modal nature of the interaction, where for example the movement of the cards can be used together with the noisy speech recognition to infer which objects are being discussed. For a more detailed technical description of how this was accomplished and how the system was implemented, please refer to [26].

4. DATA PROCESSING AND ANALYSIS

Interactions were recorded during the 9 days the system was exhibited at the Swedish National Museum of Science and Technology. For this analysis, we have filtered out complete interactions where the same pairs played at least one round together, and where the logs were complete. Even though the interaction continued if one of the players was lost in the Kinect face tracking, we have only analysed instances where the Kinect tracked both players throughout the whole interaction. This selection was done partly because we base some of our analyses on the Kinect data, but also because failure in Kinect face tracking may indicate that the users were not properly seated at the table and taking part in the interaction. Since we are doing automatic analysis, we want to make sure that their speech patterns can be interpreted as reactions to the ongoing conversation and to Furhat's behaviour. This selection amounts to a total of 292 interactions (with 584 users). The average length of these interactions was 4.5 minutes. Since people freely walked up to the system and interacted with it, we were not able to collect data on actual age and gender. Therefore, we have relied on manual annotation of age and gender based on the video recordings, by an annotator experienced with children. We are of course aware of the uncertainty in this annotation, but we should stress that we have only based our analysis on the rough distinction between children and adults, and not the exact age. The result of the annotation in terms of distribution is shown in Figure 4.

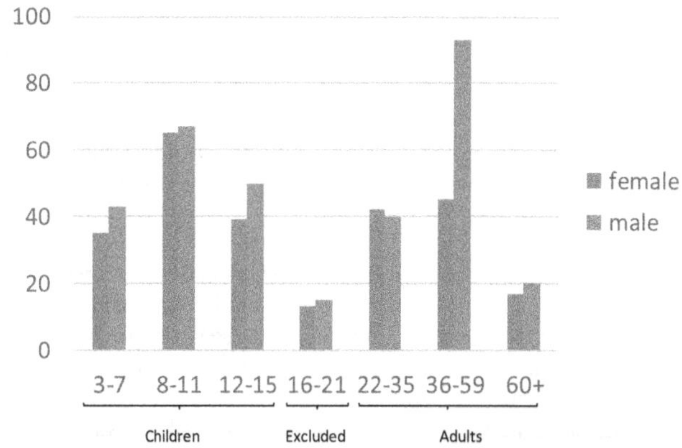

Figure 4: Number of users in different age groups.

As is evident, the distribution of gender is fairly even across age groups (overall 43.5% female), with the exception of middle aged visitors, for whom males are more common. To make the distinction between children and adults clearer, we exclude from our analysis all interactions where one of the participants was judged to be between 16 and 21 years old. The relatively few users in this range could perhaps be explained by the technical museum setting, which seems to attract adults in company with children, but perhaps fewer people in their late adolescence or early adulthood. For our analysis, we treat users below this span as children, and users above it as adults. This leaves us with 270 interactions and 540 individual users. To verify the age and gender coding, 20% of the interactions were coded by a second annotator. The agreement with the first annotator (in terms of child/adult and male/female) was 100%. The number of combinations of demographic categories in user pairs is shown in the rightmost column in Figure 5. As is evident, even though all combinations are represented, they are not evenly distributed; there are, for example, 33 pairs with two adult males, but only eight pairs with two adult females.

In this study, we have chosen to base all further analysis on completely automatic processing of the interaction logs, partly due to the large amount of annotation that would otherwise be required, but also to avoid subjective indicators and increase the reproducibility of the analysis. We mainly analyse speech activity, which is extracted by applying voice activity detection on the audio streams (with a 200 ms end-of-speech threshold). This way, we can measure which speaker responds when Furhat says something, the total speaking time and overlaps between the speakers. We measure participation equality in terms of speaking time, which we think is a

[1] A video of a complete interaction with visualization can be seen at https://www.youtube.com/watch?v=5fhjuGu3d0I and some footage of different users at https://www.youtube.com/watch?v=PtMOI0WHeE4

[2] http://www.iristk.net

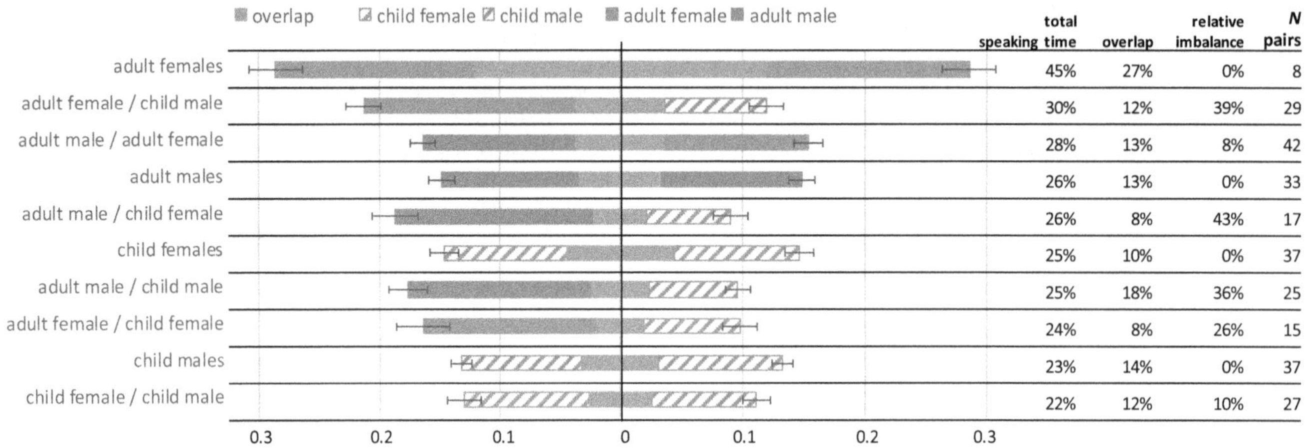

Figure 5: Average speaking time (with SE) and overlaps in different user type pairs. Total speaking time shows a proportion of the whole interaction where at least one of the users is speaking. Overlap is relative to total speaking time.

more objective measure than, for example, 'social dominance' used in similar studies [22, 28], but the reader should be aware that these are not exactly the same thing. We also analyse the users' head pose movements, which are registered by the Kinect, as a proxy for gaze. This way, we can measure whether users are looking at Furhat, given the same threshold that was used in the online system. Although this cannot be used to capture quick glances or track more precise gaze targets, previous studies have found head pose to be a fairly reliable indicator of visual focus of attention in multi-party interaction, given that the targets are clearly separated [4]. We do not analyse interruptions, even though this has been the subject of many studies (especially on gender effects), since we have not found a method for extracting these automatically and reliably. It is tempting to use overlaps as an indicator for this, but overlaps do not have to indicate interruptions (as discussed in the Background), and interruptions can occur without overlap [10]. Furthermore, when analysing the logs, it was clear that overlaps were mostly of a collaborative nature, mainly due to the nature of the task.

5. RESULTS

We report here the results from the data analysis. An alpha level of .05 was used for all statistical tests.

5.1 Speaking Time and Overlaps

We start by making a basic analysis of the total speaking time (as a proportion of the total time of the interaction), to see if there are any effects of age or gender. The average speaking time across all interactions for different user types is shown in Figure 6. As is evident, adult females speak most (M = 19.3%, SD = 9.2), followed by adult males (M = 16.2%, SD = 8.1), child females (M = 13.0%, SD = 8.8) and child males (M = 12.0%, SD = 6.9). A 2x2 ANOVA with age and gender as between-subjects factors revealed a main effect of age, $F(1, 536) = 52.85$, $p < .001$, $\eta_p^2 = 0.09$ and gender, $F(1, 536) = 8.28$, $p = .004$, $\eta_p^2 = 0.015$, but no interaction effect. Thus, on average, females speak more than males, and adults speak more than children. These results are in line with what was found in the literature (2.2).

However, this analysis only indicates the overall average. As the literature suggests, speaking time is likely to depend on the constellation of user types. The average amount of speaking time, and overlaps, for different pairs are shown in Figure 5. As is evident, the speaking time for the same user type varies a lot, depending on the pairing. Overall, children have much less speaking time when paired with an adult than when paired with another child, which is in line with what has been found in related work. Correspondingly, adults have much more speaking time when paired with a child, than when paired with another adult. From our impressions, adults in these settings often take on a protective role with the child, trying to 'explain' what is happening, regulating the interaction, and to some extent ignoring the robot. At the same time, this leads (most likely without intention) to less participation from the child.

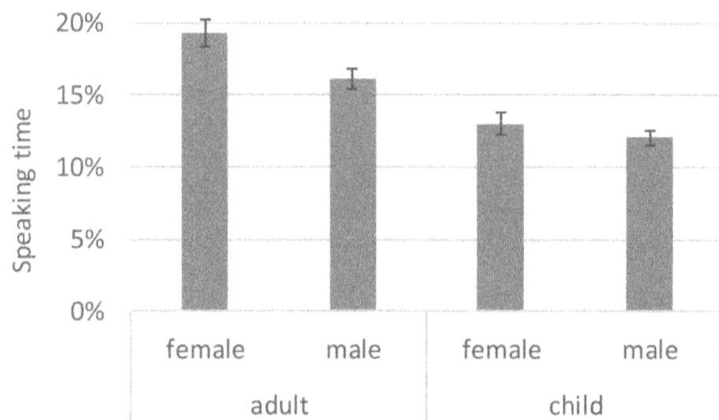

Figure 6: Average speaking time (with SE), as a proportion of the whole interaction, for different user types.

Although adult females have the overall highest speaking time in general (Figure 6), the combination of two adult females clearly reinforces this effect, and leads to a strikingly high total proportion of 45% speaking time (compared to, for example, two adult males with 26% total speaking time). They also have a very large amount of overlap (27%), which is twice as much as adult males (13%). Interestingly, this is also in line with what has been found in the literature [6].

We also investigated the amount of gazing towards Furhat, as measured by the head pose data from the Kinect. We measured both the proportion of gazing towards Furhat when he was speaking (which indicates to what extent the users attended to what Furhat said), and the amount of gazing towards Furhat when the user was speaking (which indicates to what extent the users addressed Furhat). We did not find any gender effects, but age had an effect, which is shown in Figure 7. A two-way ANOVA was conducted, with age and peer age as variables, which showed a statistically significant interaction effect on proportion of gaze towards Furhat, both while Furhat was speaking ($F(1, 536) = 8.65$, $p < .01$) and while the user was speaking ($F(1, 536) = 8.3$, $p < .01$). Thus, it seems like children attend less to the robot in general, and that adults in adult-child pairs attend more to the child. This strengthens the interpretation that adults in such settings take on a regulatory role and spend attentional resources on monitoring their children. Furthermore, since the children seem to be attending more to the cards or the human peer, they may be less receptive to turn-taking cues from the robot.

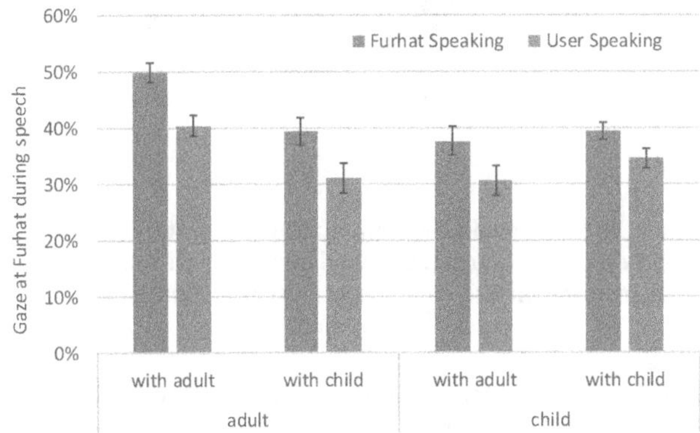

Figure 7: Average gazing towards Furhat (with SE), while user is speaking, and while Furhat is speaking.

5.2 Imbalance

It is important to note that that Figure 5 only indicates the overall imbalance between user types, which makes the homogenous pairs look perfectly balanced. In reality, these interactions are of course often imbalanced. To make a more systematic comparison of participation equality in different combinations of user types, we have defined an *Imbalance score* that was calculated for each interaction according to the following equation, where ST_{max} denotes the total speaking time for the speaker that speaks the most, and ST_{min} denotes the total speaking time for the other speaker.

$$Imbalance\ (absolute) = 1 - \frac{ST_{min}}{ST_{max}}$$

This function gives an absolute score between 0 and 1, indicating the amount of imbalance between the speakers (where 0 means perfect balance, and 0.5 that one speaker speaks twice as much as the other). The average of these scores for different pairs of user types are shown in Figure 8 as an *absolute* imbalance score. For the demographically heterogeneous pairs, we also calculated a *relative* imbalance score, which is the same as the absolute score, but with a sign (negative or positive) that indicates the direction of the imbalance between the two types of users. A one sample t-test was conducted to see which of the relative scores deviated from 0. These results are also shown in Figure 8 (where * denotes significant deviation using Bonferroni correction, $\alpha = .05 / 6 = .0083$). Note that a high absolute imbalance still allows for a relative imbalance closer to zero, if the imbalance goes in different directions between pairs and thereby cancel each other out when averaging.

As is evident from the figure, the imbalance between different user types varies a lot. Interestingly, the top and the bottom of the figure follows the patterns found in the literature review in 2.2 on turn-taking and gender. The most imbalanced pairs are child females with adult males. It is also interesting to note that while both adult males and females with child males have a high relative imbalance, there is no significant relative imbalance between adult females and child females. The most balanced pairs are adult females, which also had the most speaking time and amount of overlap (Figure 5). This might perhaps strengthen the characterization of female-female talk as 'cooperative', as argued by [7]. However, contrary to what was reported in [7], there is no significant imbalance in total speaking time between males and females when two adults or two children interact.

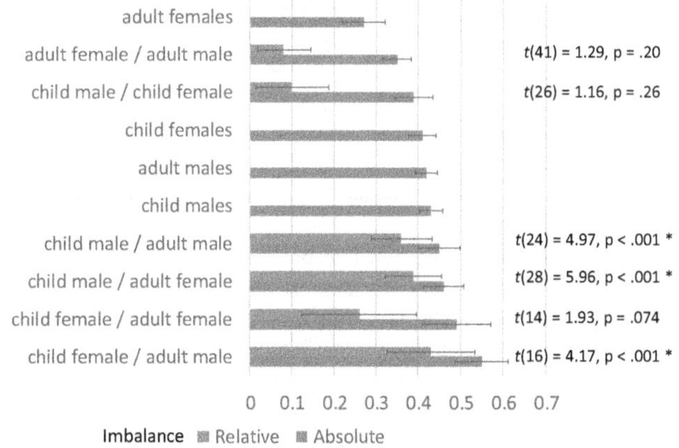

Figure 8: Average imbalance of speaking time (with SE) in different pairs of users (dominant speaker to the right). Test-statistics for relative imbalance > 0.

5.3 Regulating Turn-taking

It is important to note that there might be different causes behind the imbalances in speaking time. For example, it could be because one of the users speak in longer utterances, or it could be because one of the users is more prone to grab the turn. To address this question, we investigated the imbalance in turn-taking after the turn was yielded by the robot. This was calculated using the same formula that was used for calculating the imbalance of speaking time above, but instead we counted the number of times each speaker responded within three seconds (note that this makes it possible for none of the users, or both, to respond). Overall, this yielded a turn-taking imbalance of 0.367, which is fairly close to the overall speaking time imbalance of 0.422. Thus, the imbalance can in large part be explained by the turn-taking. To better understand the mechanisms behind the imbalance, and how it can be mitigated, we now turn to a more detailed analysis of the turn-taking behaviours of the users.

At the museum, Furhat's turn-yielding behaviour was randomly selected for each turn, both in terms of addressee and speech act (question or statement). This gives us an opportunity to study the causal effect of these behaviours on the relative imbalance in which user speaks next. For each interaction, we defined the user that ended up speaking the most as the 'dominant' user, and the other the 'non-dominant' user. In Table 2, we show the relative imbalance in four different conditions:

1. The robot asking a question to both participants, rapidly switching the gaze between them (both users may self-select).
2. The robot making a statement and looking at the cards (both users may self-select).
3. The robot looking at the dominant user, asking a question (robot selects next speaker).
4. Same as previous, but for the non-dominant user.

Table 2: Effects of different turn-regulating strategies. A positive relative imbalance indicates that the dominant user responded.

Strategy	N	Dominant responds	Non-dominant responds	Relative imbalance
1. Question, attend both	788	67.4%	51.0%	0.243
2. Statement, attend table	1092	55.8%	27.9%	0.499
3. Question, attend dominant user	313	81.5%	13.7%	0.831
4. Question, attend non-dominant user	339	28.0%	67.8%	-0.587

As is evident from Table 2, when both users can self-select, the dominant user is in general more likely to grab the turn. It is interesting to compare condition 1 and 2, since condition 1 creates a larger expectation that at least one of the users should respond, and also provides a clearer way of responding, whereas condition 2 leaves the continuation more open. As is evident from the table, the imbalance is larger for condition 2. Thus, non-dominant users seem to be less prone to self-select in these cases, and such turn-shifts are therefore more likely to increase the imbalance. Looking at condition 3 and 4, it is clear that a direct question from Furhat to one of the users will make that user much more likely to respond, even when the non-dominant user is addressed. Thus, it should be possible for the robot to decrease the imbalance by addressing this user more often.

By analysing direct questions (condition 3 and 4) in more detail, we can also gain a better understanding of how this 'next-speaker-selection accuracy' (i.e., the likelihood that the targeted user responds within 3 seconds) can be improved. First, we investigated the effect of including the addressee's name in the question (which was done randomly). For questions of the type 'What do you think (Peter)?', the accuracy increased from 66.9% to 83.9% if the addressee's name was included ($\chi^2(1) = 5.77$, $p = 0.016$). Thus, getting the users' name is valuable for improving the balance.

In previous studies we have found that when the robot keeps addressing the user who was speaking most recently, that user is less likely to respond again, compared to when the robot switches to the other user [26, 27]. Thus, by switching addressee, the next-speaker selection accuracy may increase. Since children are most often the non-dominant speaker, we also wanted to investigate whether this effect is different for children and adults. In the game, a typical example of keeping the addressee is when the robot follows up a comment by one of the users with a question like 'why do you think so?'. An alternative is to switch addressee by asking the other user 'and what do you think?'. The effect of these two strategies, split between children and adults, is shown in Figure 9. A chi-square test revealed a significant difference between keeping and switching addressee for children ($\chi^2(1) = 8.48$, $p = .0036$), but not for adults ($\chi^2(1) = 0.11$, $p = .74$). Thus, repeated questions towards children are less likely to reduce the imbalance. When a non-dominant child has not spoken recently, the robot has a better chance of reducing the imbalance by addressing that child with a question.

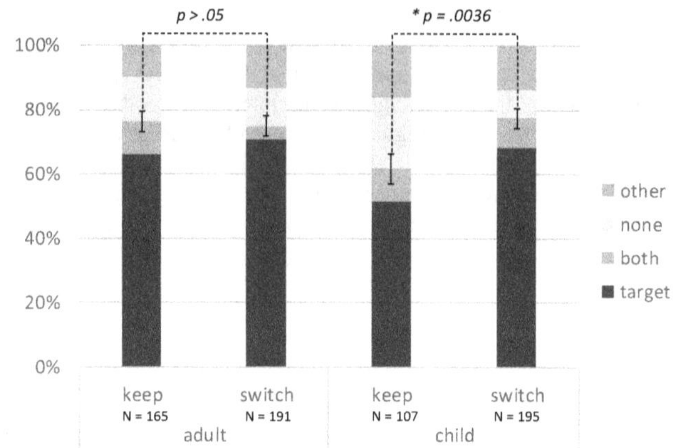

Figure 9: Next-speaker-selection accuracy (with SE) for cases where the robot targeted a particular user with a question, depending on age and whether the previous speaker is addressed.

Next, we examined the effect of mutual gaze, since we have also found this to be an important factor in previous studies [26]. Figure 10 shows the next-speaker-selection accuracy in targeted questions, depending on whether the addressee is looking back at the robot at the time the turn is yielded (as registered by the Kinect). Again, a chi-square test revealed a significant difference for children ($\chi^2(1) = 8.62$, $p = .0033$), but not for adults ($\chi^2(1) = 2.71$, $p = .10$). Thus, seeking mutual gaze is especially important when yielding the turn to children.

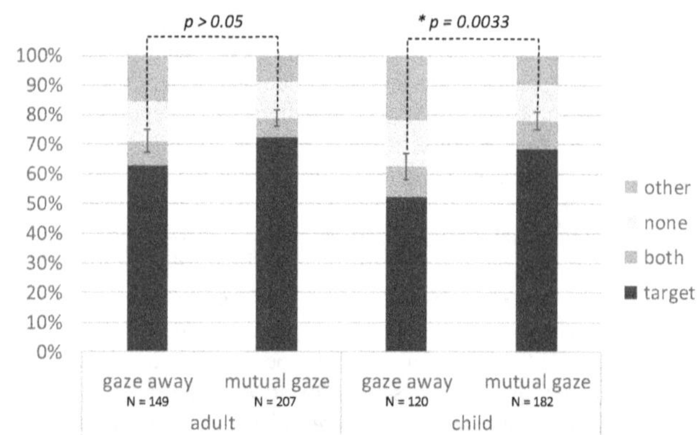

Figure 10: Next-speaker-selection accuracy (with SE) for cases where the robot targeted a particular user with a question, depending on age and mutual gaze

5.4 Predicting Imbalance

Given the possibility for the robot to regulate the turn-taking and thereby shift the balance in the interactions, an interesting question is how early on in the interaction the system could predict the participation equality. The earlier this could be done, the more proactive the robot could be. To explore this, we evaluated a multiple linear regression model for predicting the final relative imbalance. To explore how soon into the interaction the imbalance can be predicted, we evaluated the model at different time steps T, using the available features up to that point. We included the following sets of features that we deemed to be indicative:

- IMBALANCE: The current relative imbalance up to point T, as defined in 5.2.
- DEMOGRAPHICS: Information about the user types. The combination of age and gender of the two users were encoded into six dummy variables.
- GAZE: The head pose movements of the users (registered by the Kinect) as a proxy for their gaze behaviour. As discussed in Section 2.3, gaze has been shown in related studies to be highly indicative of social dominance. We measured the proportion of gaze by both users towards Furhat, (a) in total, (b) while Furhat was speaking, and (c) while the user was speaking, up to point T.

A multiple linear regression model was built at 15 seconds intervals (up to 90 seconds into the dialogue), and the correlation coefficient (R) was used for evaluation of the predictive power. The features from IMBALANCE and DEMOGRAPHICS were both useful in the prediction, as shown in Figure 11, whereas GAZE only gave a negligible improvement at 15 seconds (an increase of the R-value of 0.01, not shown in the figure). This is contrary to what has been found in related attempts at modelling social dominance [22, 28], where gaze has been an important factor.

Not surprisingly, IMBALANCE is an increasingly useful feature (since the final imbalance is the target function). However, the correlation between the current and final imbalance is not very strong early on in the dialogue. Interestingly, we can see that information about the mix of age and gender clearly improves the prediction, especially at an early stage.

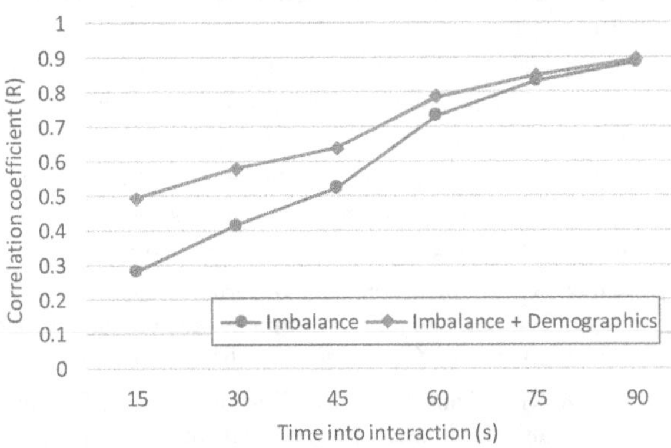

Figure 11: Prediction of imbalance at different time steps, with and without demographic information.

6. CONCLUSIONS AND DISCUSSION

Taken together, the results indicate that it is possible to predict participation imbalance at a fairly early stage, and that it is possible for the robot to reduce the imbalance, by asking directed questions to the non-dominant user. Overall, demographically heterogeneous pairs are more imbalanced in terms of participation, but it should be stressed that homogenous pairs also have a high level of imbalance and might need turn-regulation. The highest levels of imbalance are found in pairs of adults and children, where children are less prone to take the turn. By avoiding yielding the turn with open statements too often, and posing more directed questions towards the child, the balance can be improved. This effect can be reinforced further if the robot also switches addressee often, seeks mutual gaze with the addressee and, possibly, uses the name of the addressee.

We have not found any previous studies on participation equality in multi-party interaction, where all combinations of age (adult/child) and gender (male/female) have been systematically studied in the same conversational setting. Thus, we think the present study is unique in this regard. Since we have employed completely automated measures, it should be possible to replicate and verify the findings in other settings. Furthermore, using a robot in this setting adds a level of control: we can make sure the same question is executed in exactly the same way across interactions, and that the selection of turn-taking signals is chosen randomly.

Much of the findings in terms of participation equality are in line with the patterns reported in the literature: Women speak more than men [7], and adults speak more than children [9]. Children speak less when paired with an adult than with another child [16]. The most imbalanced pairs are those with adults males and child females [7]. Women have much more total speaking time, proportion of overlaps and equality in speaking time when paired with another woman, compared to when paired with a man [6, 7]. However, we have not found any significant relative imbalance when a man and a woman, or a boy and a girl, are paired. This is contrary to what is reported in the literature, in which males have been found to talk more than females in mixed-gender settings [7]. One should of course be aware that our study was performed in a Swedish context, and that the results may not necessarily be generalizable to other cultures. Furthermore, the setting is of course very specific: a technical museum where visitors play a game together with a robot.

The generally high levels of overlaps (especially in conversations involving two women) pose a challenge for current conversational systems, which most often rely on a simplified no-gap-no-overlap model of turn-taking. Furthermore, depending on the microphone setting, overlapping speech may be hard to pick up. Before these issues are solved, it would be interesting to explore how the robot could also regulate turn-taking in order to avoid overlaps.

The study we have presented here was done 'in the wild', where visitors of the museum voluntarily walked up to the robot and played the game. Although this has given us the opportunity to collect and analyse data from a diverse population, one should be aware that we did not randomly assign subjects in pairs. As such, the study constitutes a natural experiment, and we had no control over the number of subjects in each demographic group. It should also be pointed out that although the subjects to a large extent conformed to the system's turn-regulating signals on the turn-level, and each such turn should in itself reduce the imbalance, we do not know whether there are any long-lasting effects on the imbalance, i.e., whether these interventions will encourage non-dominant subjects to start self-selecting more. Therefore, we encourage future studies involving more controlled experiments that can address these questions. Finally, one should also be aware that adjusting for participation equality might not always be desirable. For example, in adult-child interactions, the adult may take on a tutoring role, which should not necessarily call for a correction of speaking time imbalance. Thus, there are other factors that should be taken into account for making this decision.

7. ACKNOWLEDGEMENTS

This work is supported by the Swedish research council (VR) project *Coordination of Attention and Turn-taking in Situated Interaction* and the EU Horizon 2020 project *BabyRobot*. Thanks to Martin Johansson and Jonas Beskow for their contributions to setting up the system, and thanks to everyone helping out with the exhibition: Saeed Dabbaghchian, Björn Granström, Joakim Gustafson, Raveesh Meena, Kalin Stefanov and Preben Wik. The author would also like to thank the anonymous reviewers for their very helpful remarks.

8. REFERENCES

[1] Anderson, K.J. and Leaper, C. 1998. Meta-analyses of gender effects on conversational interruption: Who, what, when, where, and how. *Sex Roles*. 39, 3/4 (1998), 225–252.

[2] Andrist, S., Leite, I. and Lehman, J. 2013. Fun and fair: influencing turn-taking in a multi-party game with a virtual agent. *Proceedings of the 12th International Conference on Interaction Design and Children - IDC '13*. (2013), 352–355.

[3] Argyle, M. and Graham, J.A. 1976. The central Europe experiment: Looking at persons and looking at objects. *Environmental Psychology and Nonverbal Behavior*. 1, 1 (1976), 6–16.

[4] Ba, S.O. and Odobez, J.-M. 2009. Recognizing visual focus of attention from head pose in natural meetings. *IEEE Transactions on Systems, Man, and Cybernetics, Part B: Cybernetics*. 39, 1 (2009), 16–33.

[5] Bohus, D. and Horvitz, E. 2010. Facilitating multiparty dialog with gaze, gesture, and speech. *Proceedings of ICMI* (Beijing, China, 2010).

[6] Coates, J. 1994. No Gap, Lots of Overlap; Turn-taking Patterns in the Talk of Women Friends. *Researching language and literacy in social context: A reader*. Multilingual Matters.

[7] Coates, J. 2004. *Women, Men and Language: A Sociolinguistic Account of Gender Differences in Language, 3rd edition*. Routledge.

[8] Duncan, S. 1972. Some Signals and Rules for Taking Speaking Turns in Conversations. *Journal of Personality and Social Psychology*. 23, 2 (1972), 283–292.

[9] Ervin-Tripp, S.M. 1979. Children's verbal turn-taking. *Developmental pragmatics*. E. Ochs and B. Schieffelin, eds. Academic Press. 391–414.

[10] Gravano, A. and Hirschberg, J. 2012. A Corpus-Based Study of Interruptions in Spoken Dialogue. *Interspeech-2012*. (2012).

[11] Gravano, A. and Hirschberg, J. 2011. Turn-taking cues in task-oriented dialogue. *Computer Speech & Language*. 25, 3 (2011), 601–634.

[12] Johansson, M. and Skantze, G. 2015. Opportunities and Obligations to Take Turns in Collaborative Multi-Party Human-Robot Interaction. *Proceedings of the 16th Annual Meeting of the Special Interest Group on Discourse and Dialogue (SIGDIAL)* (2015), 402.

[13] Kawahara, T., Iwatate, T. and Takanashi, K. 2012. Prediction of Turn-Taking by Combining Prosodic and Eye-Gaze Information in Poster Conversations. *Interspeech 2012* (2012).

[14] Kendon, A. 1967. Some functions of gaze direction in social interaction. *Acta Psychologica*. 26, (1967), 22–63.

[15] Koiso, H., Horiuchi, Y., Tutiya, S., Ichikawa, A. and Den, Y. 1998. An analysis of turn-taking and backchannels based on prosodic and syntactic features in Japanese Map Task dialogs. *Language and Speech*. 41, (1998), 295–321.

[16] Martinez, M.A. 1987. Dialogues among Children and between Children and Their Mothers. *Child Development*. 58, 4 (1987), 1035–1043.

[17] Meena, R., Skantze, G. and Gustafson, J. 2014. Data-driven models for timing feedback responses in a Map Task dialogue system. *Computer Speech and Language*. 28, 4 (2014), 903–922.

[18] Al Moubayed, S. and Lehman, J. 2015. Regulating Turn-Taking in Multi-child Spoken Interaction. *Intelligent Virtual Agents* (2015).

[19] Al Moubayed, S. and Skantze, G. 2011. Turn-taking Control Using Gaze in Multiparty Human-Computer Dialogue: Effects of 2D and 3D Displays. *Proceedings of the International Conference on Audio-Visual Speech Processing 2011*. (2011), 99–102.

[20] Al Moubayed, S., Skantze, G. and Beskow, J. 2013. The furhat back-projected humanoid head-lip reading, gaze and multi-party interaction. *International Journal of Humanoid Robotics*. 10, 1 (2013).

[21] Mutlu, B., Kanda, T., Forlizzi, J., Hodgins, J. and Ishiguro, H. 2012. Conversational Gaze Mechanisms for Humanlike Robots. *ACM Trans. Interact. Intell. Syst.* 1, 2 (2012), 12:1-12:33.

[22] Nakano, Y.I., Yoshino, T., Yatsushiro, M. and Takase, Y. 2015. Generating Robot Gaze on the Basis of Participation Roles and Dominance Estimation in Multiparty Interaction. *ACM Transactions on Interactive Intelligent Systems*. 5, 4 (2015), 1–23.

[23] O'Connell, D., Kowal, S. and Kaltenbacher, E. 1990. Turn-taking: A critical analysis of the research tradition. *Journal of psycholinguistic*. (1990).

[24] Sacks, H., Schegloff, E. and Jefferson, G. 1974. A simplest systematics for the organization of turn-taking for conversation. *Language*. 50, (Dec. 1974), 696–735.

[25] Skantze, G., Hjalmarsson, A. and Oertel, C. 2014. Turn-taking, feedback and joint attention in situated human-robot interaction. *Speech Communication*. 65, (2014), 50–66.

[26] Skantze, G., Johansson, M. and Beskow, J. 2015. Exploring turn-taking cues in multi-party human-robot discussions about objects. *ICMI 2015 - Proceedings of the 2015 ACM International Conference on Multimodal Interaction* (2015).

[27] Skantze, G., Moubayed, S. Al, Gustafson, J., Beskow, J. and Granström, B. 2012. Furhat at Robotville: A Robot Head Harvesting the Thoughts of the Public through Multi-party Dialogue. *Proceedings of IVA-RCVA* (Santa Cruz, CA, USA, 2012).

[28] Strohkorb, S., Leite, I., Warren, N. and Scassellati, B. 2015. Classification of Children's Social Dominance in Group Interactions with Robots. *ICMI* (2015), 227–234.

[29] Yngve, V.H. 1970. On getting a word in edgewise. *Papers from the sixth regional meeting of the Chicago Linguistic Society* (Chicago, Apr. 1970), 567–578.

Threatening Flocks and Mindful Snowflakes: How Group Entitativity Affects Perceptions of Robots

Marlena. R. Fraune[1], Yusaku Nishiwaki[2], Selma Šabanović[1], Eliot R. Smith[1], and Michio Okada[2]

[1]Indiana University
{mfraune; selmas; esmith4}@indiana.edu;

[2]Toyohashi University of Technology
y143364@edu.tut.ac.jp; okada@tut.jp

ABSTRACT

Robots are expected to become present in society in increasing numbers, yet few studies in human-robot interaction (HRI) go beyond one-to-one interaction to examine how characteristics of robot groups will affect HRI. In particular, people may show more negative or aggressive behavior toward entitative (i.e., cohesive) robot groups, like they do toward entitative human groups, compared to diverse groups. Furthermore, because people in collectivist (e.g., Japan) and individualistic (e.g., US) cultures respond to groups and to cues of entitativity differently, entitative robot groups may affect people differently across such cultures. This study examines how robot Entitativity Condition (Single Robots, Diverse Group, Entitative Group) and Country (USA, Japan) affect emotions toward, mind attributions to, and willingness to interact with robots. Results indicate that Entitative robot groups, compared to Single robots, were viewed more negatively. Entitative robots were also more threatening than Diverse robots. Diverse robot groups, compared to Single robots, were viewed as having more mind, and participants were more willing to interact with them. These findings were similar in the USA and Japan. This indicates that robot group entitativity and diversity is critical to keep in mind when designing robots.

General Terms

Experimentation, Human Factors.

Keywords

Human-robot interaction, Intergroup interactions, Group effects, Entitativity.

1. INTRODUCTION

Over 14 million home robots (e.g., Roomba vacuum cleaners) were made and distributed by the iRobot company since 2002 [1]. Just last year, 1000 humanoid Pepper robots were made and distributed in Japan [2]. In the upcoming years, it is expected that humans will view and interact with more robots of various types – and not just in one-on-one interactions, but in interactions involving groups of humans and groups of robots.

HRI'17, March 6–9, 2017, Vienna, Austria.
 ISBN 978-1-4503-4336-7/17/03...$15.00.
DOI: http://dx.doi.org/10.1145/2909824.3020248

Intergroup interaction between humans and robots is still a newly emerging topic in human-robot interaction (HRI); however, a well-developed literature in social psychology indicates many challenges in interactions among groups. Groups commonly behave more aggressively than individuals toward outgroup members [3, 4]. This aggression is expected, and in turn, those interacting with groups typically behave more aggressively towards them [3, 5-7]. This aggressive behavior becomes even more pronounced the more united, cohesive, or "entitative" the group is [8]. Because robots are often created as identical units, they have a high chance of being perceived as entitative outgroups, and thus, aggressed against. So far, the literature shows that groups of humans may behave more aggressively than individuals toward robots (e.g., [9, 10]). However, the effects of attributes of robot groups, such as their entitativity, in HRI have not yet been studied.

This paper examines (1) How intergroup HRI differs from dyadic HRI, (2) How characteristics of robot groups – in particular, robot entitativity – affect emotions toward them and perceptions of them, and (3) How these intergroup dynamics differ across countries in which group membership and ingroup entitativity have different cultural meanings. These questions were based on findings from social psychology, which we review in the Background section. The results of our study, described in detail below, suggest that robot group entitativity is a crucial factor in how people respond to robots across cultures.

2. Background

Group membership drastically changes how people interact with the world, from the emotions they feel [11, 12] to their opinions and priorities. People conform to ingroup members in their opinions, values [4, 13], and behavior toward others [4]. In sum, in intergroup situations, people often behave more like a stereotypical group member than when acting individually [14].

Adopting the group's goals and values often (but not always [15, 16]) results in more aggressive behavior against outgroup members [5-7].

In HRI, the effects of groups have received little attention, as most studies focus on dyadic interaction (i.e., one human interacting with one robot). Recent studies have found that people respond differently to an individual robot than to a group of robots. For example, when participants watched videos of robots that appeared and behaved similarly to humans, people preferred them in groups rather than individually. Conversely, robots that appeared and behaved in a machine-like manner were preferred individually rather than in groups [17]. In a field experiment, researchers found that differences in robots' behavior can make people prefer them individually or in groups. In this case, the findings were apparently opposite to the abovementioned study – that is, minimally social robots (robots with a few human-like features) that behaved interactively or "socially" (i.e., contingently responded to humans and robots) were preferred individually rather than in groups, and the reverse was true of robots that behaved purely functionally (i.e., behavior was focused on the task) [18]. These differences in responses toward groups of robots may depend on characteristics of the robot groups – in particular, how similarly they behaved, or their entitativity (discussed more below).

2.1 Entitativity

Characteristics of groups, like group entitativity (i.e., similar appearance, similar background, shared goals, and shared fate), affect group dynamics. In human interaction, aspects of entitativity increase perceived group cohesiveness [8], and through this, perceived threat from and aggression toward the group [5].

In HRI, researchers have found that some of these factors influence how people identify robots as belonging together. In one study, participants watched a video of three minimally social Keepon robots and had to choose if robot C was in a group with robot A or B. C was the same as A, B, or neither, based on appearance (color of stripes) or behavior (dance motion). When C's characteristics matched another robot's, people grouped C with that other robot more frequently, with behavior being slightly more influential than appearance [19].

In the studies [17, 18] described above, entitativity may reconcile the findings as a key factor influencing whether robots were liked in groups or not. In a video study [17], different types of robots may have been viewed as differently entitative. For example, the anthropomorphic robots' humanlike behavior was likely more familiar to participants, and people perceive familiar things to be more diverse (i.e., less entitative) [20]. In the field experiment [18], the groups of functional robots may have been liked in groups because they did not interact with each other (unlike the interactive robots), making them seem less entitative. In human-human interaction, intragroup interaction was shown to increase perceived entitativity [21], but this field experiment did not parse apart differences in effects of robot ingroup versus outgroup intragroup interaction.

Research in HRI indicates that people use robots' shared characteristics to group them together [19], but research has not yet examined if robot entitativity also increases perceived threat from and behavioral aggression toward robots groups. Because robots are often created as identical, perceived entitativity of robot groups is likely to be high, making it critical to explore how robot entitativity affects intergroup interactions.

2.1.1 Entitativity and Mind

Another finding is that high entitativity of groups relates to low perceptions of mind of the members [22]. This occurs even as the high-entitativity group is perceived as more agentic and effective [23]. Mind is often divided into two components: intelligence or uniquely human abilities (i.e., the ability to plan, to calculate) and sociality or experience (i.e., the ability to feel pain, love) [24, 25].

Denying humans these attributes of mind is called dehumanization and relates to less caring behaviors toward the individuals dehumanized [24]. Conversely, applying these attributes of mind to robots is termed anthropomorphism and relates to behaving toward them as though they are humans [26-28], often with more respect and care.

Robots are often perceived to have low mind compared to humans [29]. But a low entitative (i.e., diverse) group of robots may elicit increased perceptions of mind. This may be useful in cases in which anthropomorphizing robots enhances interactions with them.

2.2 Culture

Cultural values such as individualism and collectivism are critical in understanding the effects of intergroup interaction. People from individualistic cultures (e.g., USA) tend to have a dualistic approach during intergroup interaction. For example, people categorize a target as either an ingroup or an outgroup member. In contrast, those from collectivistic cultures (e.g., Japan) tend to view intergroup interaction in terms of relationships and networks. For example, they behave positively toward a friend of a friend instead of just ingroup members [30-32]. Other differences between these types of cultures include that people from individualistic cultures rate individuals higher than groups on entitativity [33], agency [34], and changeability [35] in comparison to people from collectivistic cultures. This suggests that across these two types of cultures, intergroup HRI will differ.

Depending on culture, people also differently perceive intergroup dynamics related to entitativity. People from individualistic cultures tend to focus on *static* or "essence" properties of entitativity, such as similar physical appearance and background. People from collectivistic cultures tend to focus on *dynamic* properties of entitativity, such as common goals and outcomes [33, 36]. These differences mean that culture affects how people interpret factors of entitativity. Thus, the same group of robots could be viewed as more or less entitative (and therefore threatening) depending on the perceiver's culture and mindset.

2.3 Present study

In the present study, we manipulated the entitativity of the robots using various factors identified in Campbell's [8] and subsequent papers (e.g., [33, 37-39]). Participants interacted with the robots that varied in Condition (Single Robots, Diverse Group, Entitative Group), then completed questionnaires about them. The study was performed in two Countries (USA, Japan).

Hypotheses:

1. **Condition**
    a. **Threat.** Interaction with Entitative Groups will increase perceived threat from a test compared to interactions with Diverse Groups and Single Robots.
    b. **Emotions.** Participants will feel more negative toward Entitative than Diverse Groups and Single Robots.
    c. **Attributions of Mind.** Diverse Groups will be rated as having more mind than Entitative Groups and Single robots.
    d. **Willingness to Interact.** Participants will be more willing to interact with Diverse Groups than Entitative Groups and Single Robots.
2. **Country**
    a. **Country and Entitativity Factors.** In the USA, ratings of static entitativity will be a stronger moderator of emotions and willingness to interact with robots, whereas in Japan, ratings of dynamic entitativity will be a stronger moderator.

3. METHOD

3.1 Design

The study manipulated robot Entitativity Condition (Single Robots, Diverse Group, Entitative Group) and Country (USA, Japan) in a between-subjects design.

3.2 Robots

This study used three different appearances of mechanomorphic robots. These robots used the iRobot Create base. This was covered by a shape cut of heavy cardboard and a cloth cover to make the robots larger and therefore more visually salient (see Figure 1). It also allowed physical appearance to be changed as part of the entitativity manipulation. Robots were decorated with WebCams to give the appearance that they could perceive the world. In actuality, all their motions and their "answers" on the task (described below) were preprogrammed.

3.2.1 Entitativity Manipulation

In this paper, we manipulate entitativity in four ways: robot appearance, motion, decisions, and proximity. It is important to manipulate entitativity in multiple ways because entitativity is a multifaceted concept. As such, we chose several key components of entitativity to represent the group's entitativity. If we had chosen only one component, we would not be measuring the effects of entitativity overall, rather we would be measuring the effects of robot similarity in appearance or in decision-making. Manipulating multiple components simultaneously also made entitativity more salient and noticeable to participants.

In the Group conditions, robot appearance, motion, and decisions were changed for the overall manipulation of entitativity (see Tables 1 and 2 for details). In the Diverse Group condition, the experiment used three robots of three different types (see Table 1 for details). Characteristics were counterbalanced across robots across participants (e.g., for one participant, Toby was a green hemisphere that moved slowly and got 60% of the answers correct, and for another, Toby was a red cylinder with ears that moved quickly and got 80% of the answers correct). In the Entitative Group or Single conditions, one type of robot was used (see Table 2 for an example) with similarly counterbalanced characteristics.

In regard to robot placement and motion, Diverse Robots were placed separately from each other and moved independently of each other (see Figure 2). Entitative Robots were placed beside each other and performed the same motions at the same time (see Figure 3). Single Robots were placed in the same location and orientation as one of the robots in the other two conditions (counterbalanced across participants).

Figure 1. Three types of robots

Table 1. Differences in robot characteristics – example of a Diverse Group

Name	Appearance	Motion	Decisions
Toby	Green hemisphere	Slow, moves little	60% correct*
Erin	Red cylinder with ears	Slow, moves more	80% correct*
Zee	Silver cylinder	Quick	90% correct*

Table 2. Similarities in robot characteristics – example of an Entitative Group

Name	Appearance	Motion	Decisions
Zee 2	Green hemisphere	Slow, moves little	80% correct*
Zee 3	Green hemisphere	Slow, moves little	80% correct*
Zee 6	Green hemisphere	Slow, moves little	80% correct*

* "Correct" here refers to giving the same answers as the participant.

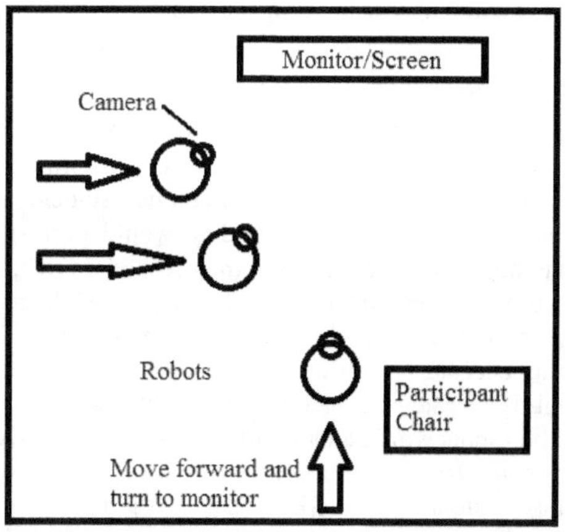

Figure 2. Study room layout in the Diverse condition

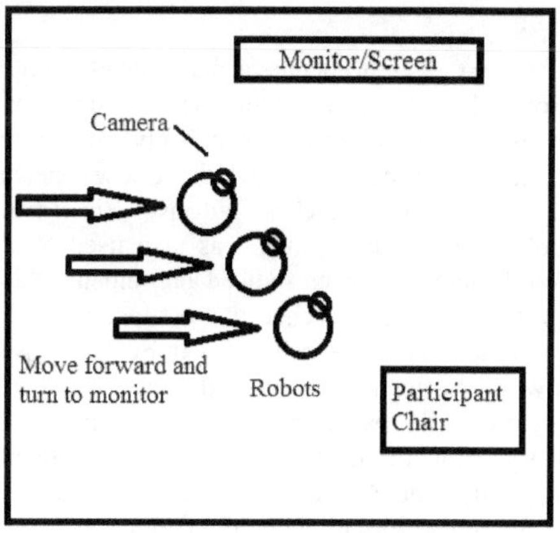

Figure 3. Study room layout in the Entitative condition

3.2.2 Robots' Control

The robots were controlled using the Wizard of Oz (WoZ) technique. A Raspberry Pi and Arduino linked the iCreate robots to a server and to a tablet from which the robots were controlled using https://robotmoose.com/. Each robot was preprogrammed to perform two types of general behavior:

- Approach – at the start of the task, robots approached the computer monitor. This involved driving forwards and turning to face the monitor.

- Task Behavior – while participants completed the task, robots occasionally shifted their positions. This involved moving forward, backward, or left and right for approximately one second. This occurred about once every 30 seconds to remind participants of the robots' presence and ingrain perceptions of entitativity.

These two behaviors were labeled as buttons on the experimenter's tablet. During the study, when the experimenter pressed the buttons, the robots would delay for about 20 seconds (so participants would not catch on to what the experimenter was doing) and then perform the behaviors.

3.3 Procedure

In both the United States and Japan, the robots were in their own room so participants did not see them before interaction. For the task humans performed with the robots, participants entered the robots' room individually so they would have no distractions. In the United States, the experiment took place in the R-House laboratory's living environment, a home-like setting. In Japan, an exact equivalent could not be used. Instead, the commons area near the cafeteria was used with partitions set up to create the robots' room. The experiment was performed between 1 PM and 5 PM, to avoid busy times around lunch and dinner.

Participants entered the experiment location and signed the informed consent forms. Participants were informed that the purpose of this study was to examine student cognitive performance. They were told that they would perform a short object-matching task, and that from their responses (e.g., response time, accuracy), the robots would categorize them as low, medium, or high ability. This manipulation was used to induce mild threat because group effects are more salient and visible under slightly threatening than neutral conditions. They were also told that the robots would attempt the task simultaneously because they were being trained to recognize images as well as to classify participants autonomously (i.e., not with the help of the computer). This allowed participants to view robots' answers (which are the same or different) as part of the Entitativity manipulation.

Participants were given a document that trained them in the task (see Section 3.4 – Object-Matching Task for details). Next, the researcher escorted participants individually into the room with the robots and the computer on which the task was performed (see Figures 2 and 3). The researcher read instructions from a tablet (which, unknown to participants, was also used to control the robots). While the researcher showed participants the computer and set up, the robots approached the test location and turned to face the monitor. The researcher stood by and answered any questions while participants completed three trial runs. Then, the researcher left while participants completed the 27 test runs. During this portion of the trial, the robots periodically shifted position so participants would not forget the robots' presence and to further ingrain the Entitativity manipulation.

After completing the task, participants were led out of the room. They were told that the robots would assess their skill level, and that in the meantime, they should take a survey about their experience so far. When the survey was complete, participants were told that the experiment was actually finished. They were given the debriefing form and were free to go.

3.4 Object-Matching Task

Robots and participants sat in front of a monitor that showed them three different objects at a time (e.g., A – table, B – truck, C – goldfish). Then, they were shown a fourth object (e.g., D – fish). Their goal was to choose which object D was most similar to (see Figure 4). All agents give their answers privately. Then, when participants pressed the "Next" button, their answers appeared below their names. Agents were allowed to review this for five seconds before the program progressed to the next trial.

On one third of the trials, the answer was obvious, as in the example in Figure 4. On the other two thirds of the trials, the answer was ambiguous (e.g., matching a fancy cake to wine, an onion, or a brain). This was done so that participants would not be certain of how well they were performing.

Robots gave the same answer as participants 60-90% of the time whether the answer is obvious or ambiguous (see Table 1). The other 10-40%, they chose a random alternative answer. Diverse robots chose answers independently of each other. Entitative robots always chose the same answers.

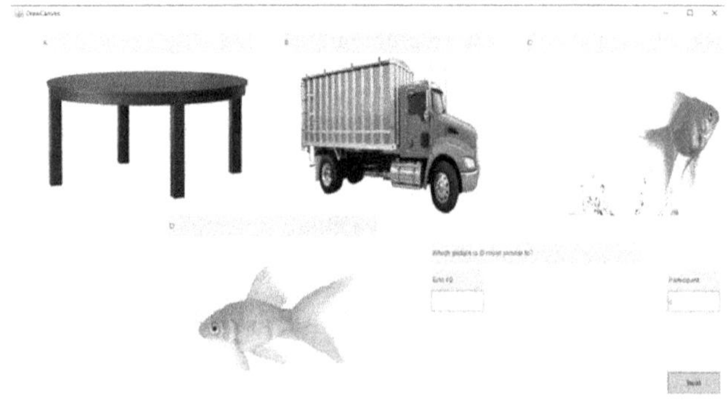

Figure 4. Screenshot from the object matching task (Single Robot condition).

3.5 Measures

Participants answered questions about robots on seven point Likert scales from 1 (Strongly Disagree) to 7 (Strongly Agree).

Entitativity Manipulation Check. Entitativity of robots was measured using a combination of questions from several different scales [33, 36, 38-43]. Questions were combined to create measures of overall entitativity (e.g., "This group of robots should be thought of as a whole").

Threat. We measured how much threat participants felt from the test by examining their perceived Fairness (e.g., "Do you think the robots will judge your skill fairly/appropriately?"). Responding that the robots would judge less fairly indicates that participants felt threatened by the robot's potentially unfair judgment in the situation. This measure was created specifically for the study.

Emotions. A direct measure of emotion toward robots was used (e.g., "I fear robots;" "I respect robots") [44].

Attributions of Mind. Participants' attribution of mind to the robot was measured with Kozak, Marsh and Wegner's [25] scale. The scale is distributed into two subscales: social intelligence (e.g., these robots "have goals") and social emotion (e.g., these robots "are capable of emotion").

Willingness to Interact. Participants were asked, if they were in various contexts (e.g., "home," "factory"), how much they would want to interact with robots. This measure was taken from previous research [17].

Entitativity and Country. Questions were created from literature on general, dynamic, and static entitativity [33, 36, 38-43] to create measures of the concepts. For example: General Entitativity (e.g., "This group of robots should be thought of as a whole"), Dynamic Entitativity (e.g., "These robots are affected by behaviors of other members of this group of robots") and Static

Entitativity (e.g., "These robots have similar physical appearances").

Demographics. Demographics (age, gender, field of study, technological experience) were also recorded.

4. RESULTS

Data were analyzed using SPSS, generally with 3 (Condition) x 2 (Country) ANOVAs. Inspection of the dependent variable distributions revealed no marked departures from distributional assumptions. Bonferroni corrections were used for post hoc tests.

4.1 Participants

Participants were students in the USA (N = 88) and Japan (N = 85). In the USA, they were recruited through the psychology participant pool and were paid in one psychology credit for class. In Japan, there was no participant pool, so participants were recruited through flyers and word of mouth and were paid 500 Japanese yen.

Participants were spread approximately evenly across Condition (Single, Entitative, Diverse) in both Countries (USA: 30, 30, 28; Japan: 28, 28, 29 respectively). Participants were an average age of 20.1 in the USA and 21.6 in Japan, with 41% female in the USA and 12% female in Japan.

Because gender differed across countries but was not a factor of interest in this study, we explored if gender affected the results by performing t-tests with gender as the independent variable for each of the reported measures. One participant identified as "trans." Because we did not have enough trans participants to include this as its own group, this data was excluded from the gender t-tests (but was included in all tests in which gender was not a variable of interest). In all but two cases (i.e., positive emotion, social intelligence), gender did not significantly affect the results ($ps > .010$). We report the significant differences in the respective sections and perform follow-up 2 (Gender) x 3 (Condition) ANOVAS to determine if gender affected the results further. We did not perform 2 (Gender) x 3 (Condition) x 2 (Country) ANOVAs because the resulting groups would have been too small to reasonably interpret.

4.2 Manipulation Check

First, a manipulation check tested the effectiveness of the entitativity manipulation between the Diverse and Entitative conditions (i.e., did participants rate the entitative condition as overall more Entitative than the Diverse condition). Conditions affected perceived entitativity ($F(1, 110) = 19.93, p < .001, n_p^2 = .153$). The Entitative ($M$ =4.94, SD = 0.92) robots were rated as more entitative than the Diverse robots (M = 4.19, SD = 0.88). There was no main effect of Country ($F(1, 110) = 1.72, p = .190$) or interaction effect between Condition and Country ($F(1, 110) = 1.81, p = .182$).

4.3 Conditions

4.3.1 Threat

Test Fairness differed depending on Condition ($F(2, 162) = 3.41, p = .035, n_p^2 = .040$; see Figure 5). Participants in the Diverse condition (M = 4.38, SD = 1.01; p = .027) rated the test as more fair than those in the Entitative Condition (M = 4.13, SD = 1.07), indicating as predicted higher threat in the Entitative condition. No differences were found between the Single condition (M= 4.4, SD = 0.95) and Entitative (p = .463) or Diverse (p = .656) conditions. No effect was found for Country ($F(1, 162) = 0.083, p = .779$) or interaction between Condition and Country ($F(2,167) = 0.79, p = .458$).

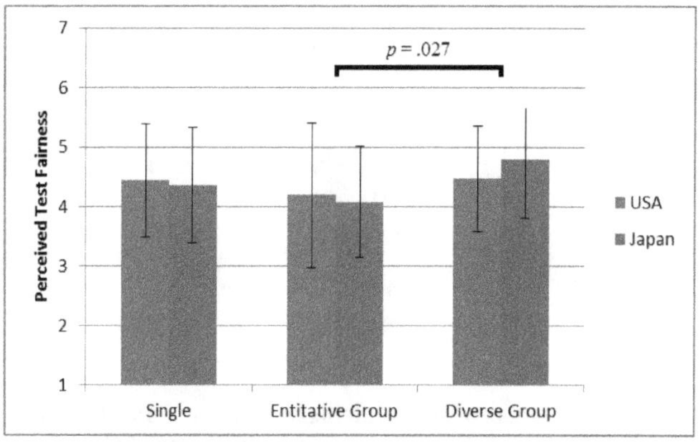

Figure 5. Ratings of test fairness (as a measure of Threat) across Condition. *Error bars denote SD

4.3.2 Emotions

First, we verified that the Emotion scale yielded a positive and a negative scale using factor analysis (with Varimax rotation with Kaiser Normalization). The analysis indicated two main factors of emotions: Positive emotions (happy, respect, security, sympathy, and excited) and Negative (disgust, fear, pity, anger, anxiety, sad, uneasy). We created one scale of positive emotions and one of negative emotions by averaging the ratings that most strongly correlated with the respective factors.

Positive emotions differed depending on country ($F(1, 167) = 43.24, p <.001, n_p^2 =.206$). USA ($M$ = 2.83, SD = 0.63) participants rated robots more positively than Japanese participants (M = 2.17, SD = 0.68). No effect of Condition ($F(1,167) = 1.53, p = .220$) or interaction between Condition and Country were found ($F(1,167) = 0.04, p = .962$).

A t-test (equal variances not assumed; p = .038) also indicated a marginal effect of gender on positive emotions ($t(97.94) = -1.98, p = .051$) with females ($M$ = 2.67, SD = 0.62) reporting higher levels of positive emotions than males (M= 2.44, SD = 0.76).

Negative emotions were rated marginally differently across Conditions ($F(1, 167) = 2.51, p = .084, n_p^2 =.029$). Robots were rated marginally less negative in the Single (M= 1.76, SD = 0.64) than Entitative (M = 2.02, SD = 0.66; p = .086) condition. There was no difference between Diverse (M = 1.84, SD = 0.62) and Single (p = .863) or Entitative (p = .370) conditions and no effect of Country ($F(1, 167) = 0.72, p = .397$) or interaction between Condition and Country ($F(1, 167) = 1.81, p = .167$).

4.3.3 Attributions of Mind

4.3.3.1 Intelligence.

Condition affected ratings of robot intelligence ($F(2, 167) = 3.27, p = .012, n_p^2 =.051$; Figure 6). Participants rated Single robots (M = 3.32, SD = 1.39) as significantly less intelligent than robots in Diverse groups (M = 3.93, SD = 1.31; p = .017) and marginally less intelligent than robots in Entitative groups (M = 3.81, SD = 1.30; p = .065). No difference was found between robots in Entitative and Diverse groups (p = 1.00).

Country also affected ratings of intelligence ($F(1, 167) = 75.37, p < .001, n_p^2 =.311$). Japanese participants rated robots as more intelligent (M = 4.44, SD = 1.13) than USA participants (M = 2.95, SD = 1.14).

A t-test (equal variances assumed; p = .921) also indicated an effect of gender on ratings of intelligence ($t(170) = 2.48, p = .014$) with females (M = 3.28, SD = 1.34) rating robot intelligence as lower than males (M= 3.85, SD = 1.33).

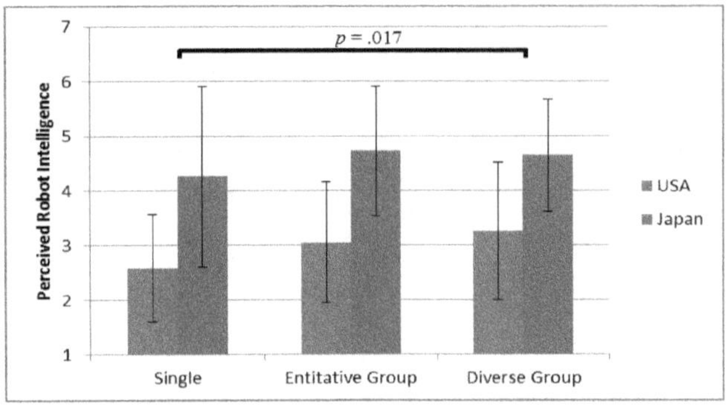

Figure 6. Ratings of robot intelligence across Condition and Country. *Error bars denote SD; main effects of Country occurred, but are not indicated in the figure.

4.3.3.2 Social Emotion.

Condition significantly affected ratings of robots' social emotion ($F(2, 167) = 4.87$, $p = .009$, $n_p^2 = .055$; Figure 7). Participants rated Diverse Groups ($M = 3.05$, $SD = 1.06$; $p = .012$) as having significantly more mind than Single Robots ($M = 2.47$, $SD = 0.96$). No differences were found between Entitative ($M = 2.86$, $SD = 1.05$) and Single ($p = .112$) or Diverse ($p = .987$) robots.

No effects of Country ($F(1, 167) = 0.67$, $p = .413$) or interaction between Condition and Country ($F(1, 167) = 0.80$, $p = .454$) were found.

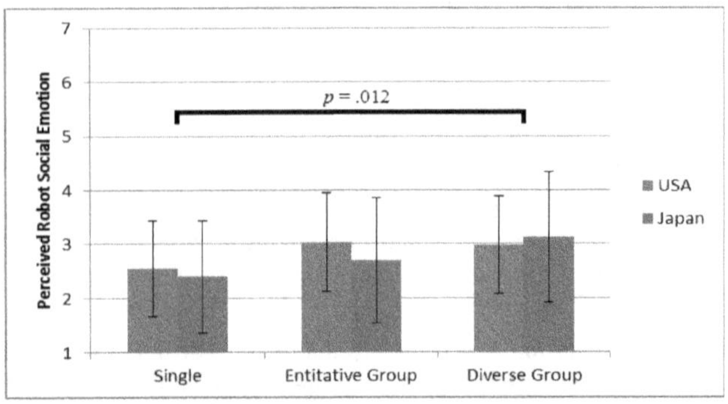

Figure 7. Ratings of robot social emotion across Condition and Country. *Error bars denote SD.

4.3.4 Willingness to Interact

Condition showed a marginal effect on willingness to work with robots ($F(2,167) = 2.40$, $p = .093$, $n_p^2 = .028$). Participants were marginally more likely to want to work with robots in the Diverse ($M = 3.56$, $SD = 0.58$) than Single ($M = 3.31$, $SD = 0.67$) condition ($p = .089$). The Entitative condition ($M = 3.45$, $SD = 0.66$) did not differ from the Single ($p = .611$) or Diverse ($p = 1.00$) conditions.

There was no effect of Country ($F(2,167) = 0.20$, $p = .658$) or interaction between Condition and Country ($F(2,167) = 1.55$, $p = .215$).

4.4 Country and Type of Entitativity

Using the three Types of Entitativity (General Entitativity, Dynamic Entitativity, Static Entitativity), a repeated measures ANOVA with each type of entitativity as the repeated measures tested if participants from different countries varied in how they rated the types of entitativity depending on robot Entitativity condition (i.e., Diverse, Entitative – this measure was not included for the Single Robot condition because entitativity was measuring the cohesiveness of groups, not of individuals). Sphericity was violated ($p = .005$) so a Greenhouse-Geisser test was performed with appropriate corrections.

Robots were rated differently across the different types of entitativity ($F(1.83, 66.02) = 5.42$, $p = .006$, $n_p^2 = .048$). General Entitativity ($M = 4.57$, $SD = .98$) was rated significantly lower than Static Entitativity ($M = 4.81$, $SD = .87$; $p = .005$) and marginally lower than Dynamic ($M = 4.70$, $SD = .93$; $p = .069$). Dynamic was marginally lower than Static Entitativity ($p = .085$).

Country and Type of Entitativity had a marginally significant interaction effect ($F(1.83, 66.02) = 3.03$, $p = .055$, $n_p^2 = .027$) with USA participants rating robots higher on General and Dynamic Entitativity, but not on Static Entitativity, than Japanese participants (See Figure 8).

There was no interaction effect of Condition and Type of Entitativity ($F(1.83, 66.02) = 0.10$, $p = .892$) or Country, Condition, and Type of Entitativity ($F(1.83, 66.02) = 2{,}08$, $p = .133$).

Linear regression found no relationship between ratings of different Types of Entitativity on Positive or Negative emotions for participants overall or for participants of one or the other country ($ps > .100$).

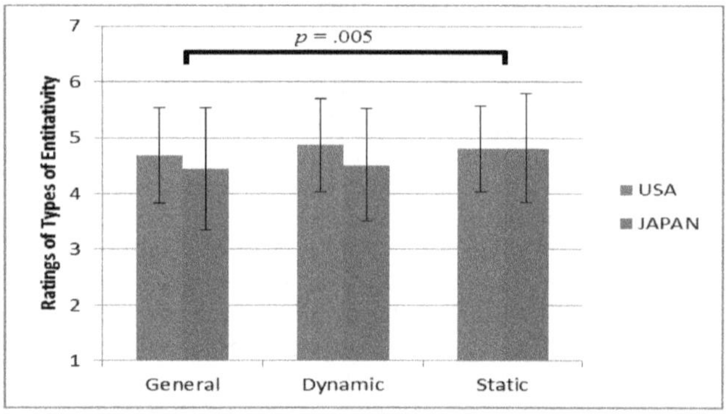

Figure 8. Ratings of different Types of Entitativity across Conditions and Country. *Error bars denote SD.

5. DISCUSSION

5.1 Manipulation Check

The manipulation check indicated that the Condition manipulation succeeded; participants perceived robots in the Entitative condition to be more entitative than robots in the Diverse condition.

5.2 Conditions

Overall, the data partially support the hypotheses – that is, the Entitative groups, compared to Diverse groups and Single robots, were seen as more threatening. Compared to Single robots, they were also seen as more negative. Diverse groups of robots, compared to Single robots, were viewed as having more mind, and participants were more willing to interact with robots in the Diverse condition. These findings are discussed in more detail below.

The sections will focus on the differences across conditions, and in the last paragraph of each section will include differences between countries.

5.2.1 Threat

Threat from the robots was measured with perceptions of how fair the test was (i.e. because responding that the robots would judge less fairly indicates that participants felt threatened by the robot's potentially unfair judgment in the situation). The data supported the hypothesis that participants would rate the test as less fair in the Entitative than Diverse condition. This suggests that participants felt more threat from the Entitative than Diverse groups of robots, paralleling research with humans [45, 46]. No other effects were found on Test Fairness.

Country. USA participants rated themselves as having performed better than Japanese participants. These results are in line with prior findings that people from Western cultures rate themselves more positively than people from Eastern cultures [47].

5.2.2 *Emotions*

As expected, the overall emotion scale yielded two factors: positive emotions and negative emotions. As in previous studies, conditions did not affect positive emotions [17, 48].

As hypothesized, conditions affected negative emotions (but only with marginal significance). In the Entitative condition, participants rated robots as more negative than in the Single condition. No other effects are found. This indicates that robots may be viewed as more negative when they are seen as threatening (see above section). Again, this parallels research on entitativity in human groups [46].

Country. USA participants rated robots more positively than Japanese participants. This is in contrast to prior work suggesting that Japanese people feel more positively toward robots than Westerners [49]. However, a test of the effects of gender on positive emotion also indicated that females reported marginally more positive emotion toward robots. The more positive results in the USA may therefore be due to greater percentage of female participants in the USA compared to Japan. Another possible explanation is that participants prefer robots that fall in line with their cultural values [50], and these robots, being built by Westerners, may inadvertently be preferred by Westerners. Because this is beyond the main topic of the paper, we will not speculate further here.

5.2.3 *Attributions of Mind*

Diverse groups of robots were viewed as more intelligent and socially capable than Single robots. As hypothesized, this suggests that having robots in diverse groups increases the perceptions of those robots' mind. This parallels findings in social psychology [22]. To create more anthropomorphic-seeming robots, designers may have them interact in diverse groups. Research has yet to show if this works only in diverse robot groups or if a robot in a group of non-robots would also be viewed as having more mind.

Country. Country also affected ratings of intelligence. Japanese participants rated robots as more intelligent than USA participants. This difference may be due to the effect of gender (i.e., male participants rating robots as more intelligent than female participants). Future studies may examine whether country or gender has a larger effect on ratings of intelligence of robots. However, these differences were not hypothesized in this study, and we will not speculate further until other studies have confirmed this difference.

We also note that overall, participants disagreed that the robots had mind (i.e., ratings of mind were very low). If the study were replicated with more humanlike robots or robots that were considered to have more mind, the findings might be more pronounced.

5.2.4 *Willingness to Interact*

As hypothesized, participants reported more willingness to interact with robots in the Diverse than Single condition (though this is only marginally significant). This indicates that making robots part of a diverse group of robots may make people more accepting of robots in general – but this should be confirmed in future studies.

Country. Country did not affect willingness to interact with robots.

5.2.5 *Overview*

Overall, these findings provide further support for differential effects between interactions with single robots and robot groups. In particular, they indicate that the entitativity or diversity of robot groups significantly affects perceptions of them and willingness to interact with them in the future. Compared to single robots, entitative groups of robots were perceived as more threatening and negative. Conversely, compared to single robots, diverse groups of robots were perceived as having more mind, and participants were more willing to interact with them.

Robot Design. These findings can be applied to the design of robots: Robots that need to be taken more seriously can be made entitative in groups, whereas robots that people are supposed to enjoy interacting with can be made diverse in groups.

Overall, Country had few effects on these major findings, and it did not interact with Condition. This indicates that these effects of entitativity and diversity extend across cultures, at least with these student samples.

5.3 Country and Type of Entitativity

We divided the entitativity measure into three Types of Entitativity (General, Dynamic, Static) to match with suggestions from previous literature that entitativity differs across cultures [33]. The results indicated that participants perceived types of entitativity differently across cultures, partially supporting the hypothesis. Specifically, USA participants rated robots higher on General and Dynamic Entitativity, but not on Static Entitativity, than Japanese participants.

Contrary to the hypothesis, this study found no effect of ratings of different Types of Entitativity on ratings of emotions toward robots (positive or negative) either overall or for participants of one or another country. This is surprising, given that previous literature typically indicates that dynamic entitativity is more salient in Eastern cultures whereas static entitativity is more salient in Western cultures [33]. It may be that specific questions included in these measures, while taken from factors of importance identified in previous literature, are not representative of general, dynamic, and static entitativity. Furthermore, the overall level of dynamic and static entitativity perceived in the robots may not have been sufficient to affect user responses. Future studies should test and identify scales that will effectively measure each type of entitativity.

5.4 Limitations and Future Studies

Our experiment found differences between group and single robots in the predicted directions at the $p < .10$ level (e.g., in perceived test fairness, negative emotions toward robots, willingness to interact with the robots). Given that the differences were in the predicted direction, and that the robots could be seen as having minimally threatening forms and behavior, we conclude that when more threatening robots (e.g., factory robots) or a more threatening context are used, the differences will be magnified. We suggest future research should extend these results to such more threatening situations to determine the extent to which the robots may affect feelings of threat and willingness to interact.

Our conclusions do, however, show that interactions with multiple robots will likely be different (e.g., more threatening) than interactions with individuals. These conclusions are important because robots will most likely be working in groups in the real world and the factors we identify could be of specific interest in those cases. When robots actually interact with participants in everyday spaces, they will likely be seen as even more threatening (e.g., "robots will take my job"). The effects of robot entitativity in these circumstances will influence people to accept or reject robots in their lives (or approach or avoid them). These results were similar across cultures, so we can expect group dynamics to be an important factor in human-robot interaction design across cultural contexts.

Future studies should also examine how entitativity and diversity of robot groups affect perceptions of robots when the robots are there to help people. In collaborative settings, people may be more trusting of entitative robots (e.g., because the robots will be perceived as coordinated and effective) [39].

Different types of robots should also be examined. It is likely that larger robots will be considered more threatening, and the effects of entitativity will be stronger with these robots, compared to robots in the present study. Depending on context, the human likeness of robots may also make the robot seem more intelligent, which may increase stress toward humans. For example, intelligent beings may be better able to judge us, or it may threaten our optimal distinctiveness (i.e., we like to think we are unique) [51]. These effects should also be tested.

The only differences this study identified between entitative and diverse groups of robots was in the threat measure; that is, participants found the entitative groups to be more threatening than the diverse groups. Other differences were not found. It may be that the threat induced by the entitativity manipulation was not enough to affect the other measures. It may also be that differences in perceptions of the robots' mind across conditions affected perceptions of threat. Future studies should use larger sample sizes or more threatening robots to determine how these types of robot groups differ from each other. They should also use different manipulations of robot entitativity.

In this study, Country did not interact with the effects of Condition. In future studies, more countries should be included to examine the universality of these findings.

To more closely examine how different types of entitativity may affect people from different countries differently, more robust scales of each type of entitativity should be created and tested. Another potential reason for not finding these differences was that university students were used in both countries. Often, university students behave differently from the remainder of the population [52]. Future studies might test differences in the effects of perceived entitativity for the broader population.

6. CONCLUSION

Robots are already being used in education, healthcare, work, and home environments, but due to negative group effects, these robots may not reach their full potential to assist humans. Furthermore, while designing robots to look and act completely the same might be more technically and economically expedient, the effects of entitativity can be negative in certain situations, requiring more diversity in robot appearance and behavior. Developing a study of intergroup interaction in HRI is critical for developing robots that reach and exceed expectations for enhancing human daily lives.

This study indicates that the entitativity and diversity of robots in groups affects how people perceive them and how willing they are to interact with them. Future studies should examine how the context relates the effects of entitativity in robot groups.

7. ACKNOWLEDGMENTS

Our thanks to Matthew Francisco, Katie Gates, Margaret Krupp, Ben C. Oistad, Christine Rheintgen, Catherine Sembroski, Jonah Simon, and Kawaguchi Yamamura for their assistance in preparing study materials and running the study. Thank you to NSF EAPSI grant number 1613902 and JSPS for funding.

8. REFERENCES

[1] "History." 2016. *iRobot.* Retrieved from http://www.irobot.com/About-iRobot/Company-Information/History.aspx

[2] "1000 'Pepper' units sell out in a minute. " 2015. *Aldebaran: SoftBank Group.* Retrieved from https://www.aldebaran.com/en/press/press-releases/1000-pepper-units-sell-out-in-a-minute

[3] Meier, B. P., and Hinsz, V. B. 2004. A comparison of human aggression committed by groups and individuals: An interindividual–intergroup discontinuity. *Journal of Experimental Social Psychology, 404*, 551-559.

[4] Wildschut, T., and Insko, C. A. 2007. Explanations of interindividual–intergroup discontinuity: A review of the evidence. *European Review of Social Psychology, 181*, 175-211.

[5] Insko, C. A., Wildschut, T., and Cohen, T. R. 2013. Interindividual–intergroup discontinuity in the prisoner's dilemma game: How common fate, proximity, and similarity affect intergroup competition. *Organizational Behavior and Human Decision Processes, 1202*, 168-180.

[6] Schopler, J., and Insko, C. A. 1992. The discontinuity effect in interpersonal and intergroup relations: Generality and mediation. *European Review of Social Psychology, 31*, 121-151.

[7] Wildschut, T., Insko, C. A., and Pinter, B. 2007. Interindividual-intergroup discontinuity as a joint function of acting as a group and interacting with a group. *European Journal of Social Psychology, 372*, 390.

[8] Campbell, D. T. 1958. Common fate, similarity, and other indices of the status of aggregates of persons as social entities. *Behavioral Science, 31*, 14-25.

[9] Brscić, D., Kidokoro, H., Suehiro, Y., and Kanda, T. 2015. Escaping from children's abuse of social robots. *Paper presented at the Proceedings of the Tenth Annual ACM/IEEE International Conference on Human-Robot Interaction.*

[10] Chang, W.-L., White, J. P., Park, J., Holm, A., and Sabanovic, S. 2012. The effect of group size on people's attitudes and cooperative behaviors toward robots in interactive gameplay. *Paper presented at the RO-MAN, 2012 IEEE.*

[11] Yzerbyt, V., Dumont, M., Wigboldus, D., and Gordijn, E. 2003. I feel for us: The impact of categorization and identification on emotions and action tendencies. *British Journal of Social Psychology, 424*, 533-549.

[12] Smith, E. R., Seger, C. R., and Mackie, D. M. 2007. Can emotions be truly group level? Evidence regarding four conceptual criteria. *Journal of Personality and Social Psychology, 933*, 431.

[13] Sechrist, G. B., and Stangor, C. 2001. Perceived consensus influences intergroup behavior and stereotype accessibility. *Journal of Personality and Social Psychology, 804*, 645.

[14] Ellemers, N., Pagliaro, S., and Barreto, M. 2013. Morality and behavioural regulation in groups: A social identity approach. *European Review of Social Psychology, 241*, 160-193.

[15] Gergen, K. J., Gergen, M. M., and Barton, W. H. 1973. Deviance in dark. *Psychology Today, 75*, 129.

[16] Johnson, R. D., and Downing, L. L. 1979. Deindividuation and valence of cues: Effects on prosocial and antisocial behavior. *Journal of Personality and Social Psychology, 379*, 1532.

[17] Fraune, M. R., Sherrin, S., Sabanovic, S., and Smith, E. R. 2015. Rabble of robots effects: Number and type of robots modulates attitudes, emotions, and stereotypes. *Human Robot Interaction*, 109-116.

[18] Fraune, M. R., Kawakami, S., Sabanovic, S., De Silva, R., and Okada, M. 2015. Three's company, or a crowd?: The effects of robot number and behavior on HRI in Japan and the USA. *Robotics: Science and Systems.*

[19] Nawroj, A. I., Toneva, M., Admoni, H., and Scassellati, B. 2014. An exploration of social grouping in robots: Effects of behavioral mimicry, appearance, and eye gaze.

[20] Linville, P. W., Fischer, G. W., and Salovey, P. 1989. Perceived distributions of the characteristics of in-group and out-group members: Empirical evidence and a computer simulation. *Journal of Personality and Social Psychology, 57*2, 165.

[21] Gaertner, L., and Schopler, J. 1998. Perceived ingroup entitativity and intergroup bias: An interconnection of self and others. *European Journal of Social Psychology, 28*6, 963-980.

[22] Morewedge, C. K., Chandler, J. J., Smith, R., Schwarz, N., and Schooler, J. 2013. Lost in the crowd: Entitative group membership reduces mind attribution. *Consciousness and Cognition, 22*4, 1195-1205.

[23] Waytz, A., and Young, L. 2012. The group-member mind trade-off attributing mind to groups versus group members. *Psychological Science, 23*1, 77-85.

[20] Haslam, N., Loughnan, S., Kashima, Y., and Bain, P. 2008. Attributing and denying humanness to others. *European Review of Social Psychology, 19*1, 55-85.

[25] Kozak, M. N., Marsh, A. A., and Wegner, D. M. 2006. What do I think you're doing? Action identification and mind attribution. *Journal of Personality and Social Psychology, 90*4, 543.

[26] Epley, N., Waytz, A., and Cacioppo, J. T. 2007. On seeing human: A three-factor theory of anthropomorphism. *Psychological Review, 114*4, 864.

[27] Gray, K., Young, L., and Waytz, A. 2012. Mind perception is the essence of morality. *Psychological Inquiry, 23*2, 101-124.

[28] Waytz, A., Gray, K., Epley, N., and Wegner, D. M. 2010. Causes and consequences of mind perception. *Trends in Cognitive Sciences, 14*8, 383-388.

[29] Gray, H. M., Gray, K., and Wegner, D. M. 2007. Dimensions of mind perception. *Science, 315*5812, 619-619.

[30] Jin, N., Yamagishi, T., and Kiyonari, T. 1996. Bilateral dependency and the minimal group paradigm. *Japanese Journal of Psychology.*

[31] Yamagishi, T., Jin, N., and Kiyonari, T. 1999. Bounded generalized reciprocity: Ingroup boasting and ingroup favoritism. *Advances in Group Processes, 16*1, 161-197.

[32] Yuki, M., Maddux, W. W., Brewer, M. B., and Takemura, K. 2005. Cross-cultural differences in relationship-and group-based trust. *Personality and Social Psychology Bulletin, 31*1, 48-62.

[33] Kurebayashi, K., Hoffman, L., Ryan, C. S., and Murayama, A. 2012. Japanese and American perceptions of group entitativity and autonomy: A multilevel analysis. *Journal of Cross-Cultural Psychology, 43*2, 349-364.

[34] Menon, T., Morris, M. W., Chiu, C.-y., and Hong, Y.-y. 1999. Culture and the construal of agency: Attribution to individual versus group dispositions. *Journal of Personality and Social Psychology, 76*5, 701.

[35] Haslam, N., Holland, E., and Karasawa, M. 2013. Essentialism and entitativity across cultures. *Culture and Group Processes*, 17-37.

[36] Yuki, M. 2003. Intergroup comparison versus intragroup relationships: A cross-cultural examination of social identity theory in North American and East Asian cultural contexts. *Social Psychology Quarterly*, 166-183.

[37] Denson, T. F., Lickel, B., Curtis, M., Stenstrom, D. M., and Ames, D. R. 2006. The roles of entitativity and essentiality in judgments of collective responsibility. *Group Processes and Intergroup Relations, 9*1, 43-61.

[38] Lickel, B., Hamilton, D. L., Wieczorkowska, G., Lewis, A., Sherman, S. J., and Uhles, A. N. 2000. Varieties of groups and the perception of group entitativity. *Journal of Personality and Social Psychology, 78*2, 223.

[39] Castano, E., Sacchi, S., and Gries, P. H. 2003. The perception of the other in international relations: Evidence for the polarizing effect of entitativity. *Political Psychology, 24*3, 449-468.

[40] Rydell, R. J., and McConnell, A. R. 2005. Perceptions of entitativity and attitude change. *Personality and Social Psychology Bulletin, 31*1, 99-110.

[41] Lickel, B., Hamilton, D. L., and Sherman, S. J. 2001. Elements of a lay theory of groups: Types of groups, relational styles, and the perception of group entitativity. *Personality and Social Psychology Review, 5*2, 129-140.

[42] Rydell, R. J., Hugenberg, K., Ray, D., and Mackie, D. M. 2007. Implicit theories about groups and stereotyping: The role of group entitativity. *Personality and Social Psychology Bulletin, 33*4, 549-558.

[43] Brewer, M. B., Hong, Y.-Y., , and Li, Q. 2004. Dynamic entitativity. *The Psychology of Group Perception*, 19.

[44] Cottrell, C. A., and Neuberg, S. L. 2005. Different emotionalreactions to different groups: a sociofunctional threat-based approach to" prejudice". *Journal of Personality and Social Psychology, 88*5, 770.

[45] Wildschut, T., Pinter, B., Vevea, J. L., Insko, C. A., and Schopler, J. 2003. Beyond the group mind: A quantitative review of the interindividual-intergroup discontinuity effect. *Psychological Bulletin, 129*5, 698.

[46] Dasgupta, N., Banaji, M. R., and Abelson, R. P. 1999. Group entitativity and group perception: Associations between physical features and psychological judgment. *Journal of Personality and Social Psychology, 77*5, 991.

[47] Heine, S. J., and Lehman, D. R. 1999. Culture, self-discrepancies, and self-satisfaction. *Personality and Social Psychology Bulletin, 25*8, 915-925.

[48] Wullenkord, R., Fraune, M. R., Eyssel, F., and Sabanovic, S. 2016. Getting in touch: How imagined, actual, and physical contact affect evaluations of robots. *RO-MAN 2016.*

[49] Kaplan, F. 2004. Who is afraid of the humanoid? Investigating cultural differences in the acceptance of robots. *International Journal of Humanoid Robotics, 1*03, 465-480.

[50] Salem, M., Ziadee, M., and Sakr, M. 2014. Marhaba, how may I help you?: Effects of politeness and culture on robot acceptance and anthropomorphization. *Paper presented at the Proceedings of the 2014 ACM/IEEE international conference on Human-robot interaction.*

[51] Brewer, M. B. 2003. Optimal distinctiveness, social identity, and the self.

[52] Henrich, J., Heine, S. J., and Norenzayan, A. 2010. The weirdest people in the world? *Behavioral and Brain Sciences, 33*2-3, 61-83.

S/he's too Warm/Agentic! The Influence of Gender on Uncanny Reactions to Robots

Jahna Otterbacher
Program in Social Information Systems
Open University of Cyprus
P.O. Box 12794
2252 Latsia CYPRUS
jahna.otterbacher@ouc.ac.cy

Michael Talias
Faculty of Economics and Management
Open University of Cyprus
P.O. Box 12794
2252 Latsia CYPRUS
michael.talias@ouc.ac.cy

ABSTRACT

Gender stereotypes are strong influences on human behavior. Given our tendency to anthropomorphize, incorporating gender cues into a robot's design can influence acceptance by humans. However, little is known about the interaction between human and robot gender. We focus on the role of gender in eliciting negative, "uncanny" reactions from observers. We create a corpus of YouTube videos featuring robots with female, male and no gender cues. Our experiment is grounded in Gray and Wegner's (2012) model, which holds that uncanny reactions are driven by the perception of robot agency (i.e., ability to plan and control) and experience (i.e., ability to feel), which in turn, is driven by robot appearance and behavior. Participants watched videos and completed questionnaires to gauge perceptions of robots as well as affective reactions. We used Structural Equation Modeling to test whether the model explains reactions of both men and women. For gender-neutral robots, it does. However, we find a salient human-robot gender interaction. Men's uncanny reactions to robots with female cues are best predicted by the perception of experience, while women's negativity toward masculine robots is driven by perceived agency. The result is interpreted in light of the "Big Two" dimensions of person perception, which underlie expectations for women to be warm and men to be agentic. When a robot meets these expectations, it increases the chances of an uncanny reaction in the other-gender observer.

Keywords

"Big Two" dimensions; Experimentation; Gender stereotypes; Measurement; Social perception; Uncanny reaction.

1. INTRODUCTION

On any given day, while going about our business in the world, we must interact with others from various walks of life. Therefore, our well-being depends on our ability to perceive others both accurately and efficiently. We make inferences about who someone is and how she or he is likely to behave towards us. To this end, social stereotypes can be interpreted as socio-cognitive heuristics that help us make sense of others [7, 19]. If we know that someone belongs to a particular social group (e.g., based on gender, age or race), we can infer additional information about him or her (e.g., expected behaviors and even character traits). This saves us time and effort in regulating our own behavior in our interactions with others [24].

Despite that social stereotypes are normative expectations that humans hold about other humans [19], there is increasing evidence that stereotypes influence human behaviors in the context of HRI. For researchers working in the CASA (Computers as Social Actors) tradition [30], this is not at all surprising. Experimental results have shown that humans instinctively apply social expectations to artificial agents, "mindlessly" attributing human characteristics to them such as gender and ethnicity [28]. It has been shown that even a single, minimalist gender cue endowed on an agent, such as a feminine or masculine voice [29], or a piece of headwear (e.g., a pink bow versus a black hat [20]), can trigger the illusion of agent gender, bringing about normative expectations surrounding its identity and behavior. We do not yet fully understand the extent to which the application of social stereotypes is under our conscious control [17]. However, many argue that stereotype effects are not only uncontrollable and automatic; they are also essential for the efficient processing of social information that enables our interactions with one another [3]. This brings serious questions to the table concerning robot design and anthropomorphism.

Recent work highlights the fact that *gender stereotyping* in HRI is common, and may result in both positive and negative consequences. Positively, Rhim and colleagues [31] found that using gender cues in a multi-task robot can be beneficial in terms of user acceptance. They altered the robot's voice and found that users were more accepting of the female cue version of the robot for social tasks (e.g., leading them in an exercise routine), whereas they preferred the male cue version for functional tasks. Eyssel and colleagues [13], again manipulating the voice of a robot to provide gender cues, found that when users inferred a robot to be of their own gender, they were more likely to feel close to it.

However, in Eyssel and Hegel's study of the effect of visual cues [12], they found that "even robots fall victim to gender stereotypes" (p. 2). They used hairstyles (long versus short) as gender cues. Participants were more likely to choose the short-haired robot for stereotypically male

HRI '17, March 06-09, 2017, Vienna, Austria
© 2017 ACM. ISBN 978-1-4503-4336-7/17/03...$15.00
DOI: http://dx.doi.org/10.1145/2909824.3020220

tasks (e.g., repairing machines) and the long-haired robot for stereotypically female tasks (e.g., elderly and childcare). Participants also applied gender-normative character traits for the robots, ascribing the short-haired robot as assertive and determined, and describing the long-haired robot as being sensitive and cooperative. Gender stereotypes can give rise to problematic behavior in the context of HRI. For instance, De Angeli and colleagues [8] note that humans are actually more prone to antisocial behaviors when interacting with machines with humanlike and engendered interfaces; in particular, agents with female gender cues are often subjected to unintended sexual attention and harassment [4].

1.1 Gender and affective reactions to robots

Incorporating gender cues into the design of a robot is clearly one way to make it more humanlike, in terms of appearance and/or behavior. But while it is known that robot gender cues play a key role in shaping HRI, few studies have considered the interaction between gender cues and the human's own gender. According to Rhim and colleagues [31], "because people use their innate cues to understand other people, participants may evaluate gendered robots differently according to his or her gender" (p. 56). In a similar vein, Duffy [11] explains that while designing robots with a humanlike form is often viewed as the "obvious strategy" in terms of gaining human acceptance, that interaction is "fundamentally observer-dependent." In other words, there is still much work to be done in terms of exploring the ways in which humans anthropomorphize machines, and how this in turn affects their acceptance of them.

In the current work, we focus on *gender differences* in humans' initial, affective reactions to robots with gender cues (female, male and no cues). Given that gender cues are very often visual and audial, we study negative affective reactions to various robots depicted in videos. Negative ("uncanny") reactions to robots have often been explained in terms of robot appearance and behaviors (i.e., "humanlikeness"); when a robot appears a little too human, this can trigger a reaction of fear or disgust [26]. More recently though, Gray and Wegner [16] put forward an explanatory model of this reaction, which holds that a humanlike appearance causes humans to attribute experience (i.e., the ability to fear and feel pain) to a robot, which is what drives the negative reaction to the robot.

We conducted an online experiment to examine the role of gender – both of the participant as well as the gender cues of the robot – in eliciting a negative reaction from the human. We found that there is a salient interaction between human and robot gender. The mechanism underlying men and women's negative affective reactions to robots without gender cues is the same; however, men and women react negatively to opposite-gender robots for different reasons. Men are likely to fear or be disgusted by female cue robots when they perceive the robots to have feelings. In contrast, women react negatively to male cue robots that they perceive as having agency (i.e., competency to plan and control).

We interpret the findings in terms of the recent research on gender stereotypes in person perception [1, 7]. While women are believed to be (and are expected to be) warm (i.e., communal, emotive), men are ascribed agentic character traits (e.g., competent, capable). When the gendered robots in our experiment elicited these social expectations from humans too well, this often resulted in uncanny reactions. Our results provide evidence that there is a salient human gender – robot gender interaction, which cannot be ignored by HRI researchers investigating the role of robot gender cues in human perception and acceptance of robots.

2. BACKGROUND

Before describing our experiment, we explain the key dimensions of person perception that are known to drive human social stereotypes. Next, we review the role of robot "humanlikeness" in human perception and acceptance of robots. Finally, we describe the model put forward by Gray and Wegner, which provides an explanation for negative reaction to humanlike robots.

2.1 The "Big Two" in person perception

Over the past decade, social psychologists have largely come to a consensus that our perceptions of others are made on the basis of two dimensions. The first, known as agency or competence, has to do with perceived status (i.e., whether or not we perceive someone as being accomplished and/or capable of achieving goals) [14]. The second, known as the warmth or communal dimension, is related to perceived competition (i.e., someone who is warm has pro-social intentions and therefore, does not pose a threat, whereas someone lacking in warmth is threatening to others). Because of our instincts for self-preservation, the second dimension is said to be the more important of the two [1].

Of particular relevance to the current work, is that social stereotypes are captured by combinations of the two dimensions. For instance, the prevailing gender stereotypes hold that women are characterized by (and should be) high warmth and low agency. On the contrary, men are characterized by agency but not warmth. Backlash effects, where stereotype-incongruent individuals – agentic women and/or warm men – suffer social and/or economic reprisals from their peers, serve as evidence of the degree of influence that gender stereotypes have on human-human interactions [27, 34]. There is also evidence that gender stereotypes have not changed much over time [9].

As mentioned, HRI researchers have found that people interpret robots with gender cues in terms of the "Big Two" dimensions, with female cue robots being characterized by warm character traits and male cue robots being described as agentic [12]. In the current work, we will show that this same stereotypic interpretation of robots can lead to a negative affective reaction, when robots are "too good" at eliciting these gender stereotypes in opposite-gender people.

2.2 Robot appearance and human reaction

Many claim that in order to achieve acceptance, a robot should look and act in a humanlike manner, as not to trouble the human or make interaction cumbersome. Some researchers argue that robot function is much more important than physical appearance [2]. However, others argue that to be able to evaluate robot behavior, its appearance should be as humanlike as possible, as not to distort the human's interpretation of its behavior [25]. Some evidence supports this second position, in that more humanlike designs are better able to elicit expected social norms of interaction with humans, as compared to less humanlike designs [23].

Mori [26] warned decades ago that when an artificial being comes too close to resembling a human, that the resulting affective reaction from humans is likely to be one of fear

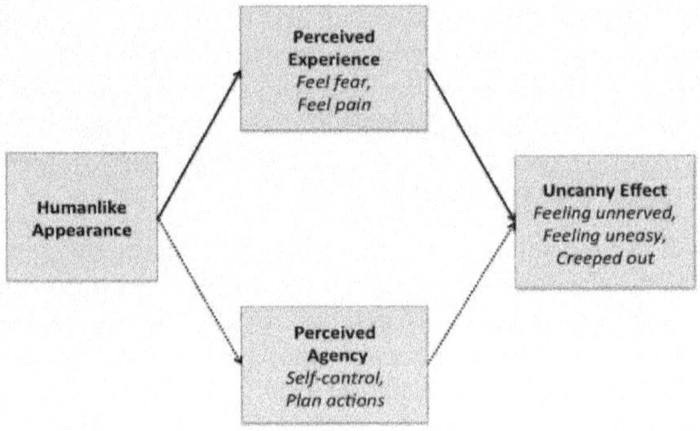

Figure 1: Uncanny reaction to robots [16].

or disgust. In his often-referenced "Uncanny Valley," he predicted that while the correlation between humanlikeness and human acceptance starts off in a positive, linear fashion, its peak is followed by a sharp dive. In other words, a being that is a bit too humanlike causes feelings of uncanniness in its human observers. However, empirical studies over the years have produced mixed results.

2.3 Explanatory model of negative reaction

Psychologists Gray and Wegner proposed a specific explanation of the uncanny reaction to robots [16]. As illustrated in Figure 1, they claim that robot appearance, when very humanlike, leads humans to ascribe experience to the machine (i.e., the capacity to feel and sense), above and beyond agency (i.e., the ability to plan and exercise self-control). It is this perception of experience that evokes a negative affective reaction. They explain that humans, and only humans, are expected to have experience and feelings. Thus, we find it unnerving when we observe other humans to lack experience (e.g., psychopaths) but not when they lack agency (e.g., people with developmental disorders) [15].

To test their theory, Gray and Wegner carried out an experiment in which they showed two videos to participants. Both depicted Kaspar the social robot[1] , however, while one showed its mechanical parts, the other showed it with humanlike facial features. The questionnaire in Table 2 was administered to participants, after viewing a video. As expected, the more humanlike Kaspar elicited more uncanny reactions than did the mechanistic Kaspar. In addition, results confirmed that when a participant found the robot to be humanlike, that he or she was more likely to report a belief that it could feel fear and pain (i.e., experience), which in turn, led to more negative reactions. However, there was little evidence that the perception of robot agency led to an increased likelihood of an uncanny response.

3. METHODOLOGY

To study the interaction between the observer's gender and the gender cues of the robot, in relation to the human's affective reaction to the robot, we needed to present multiple stimuli (i.e., robots with masculine, feminine and no gender cues) to participants. We employed a methodology that exploits social media. Our study was exempted from a full ethics review at our institution.

[1]http://www.herts.ac.uk/kaspar

Sung and colleagues [38] explained that HRI researchers have recognized the need to employ a variety of methodologies, given the limitations of laboratory experiments. They describe the potential benefits and trade-offs of alternative methods, such as ours, in which it is not possible to control all variables in the environment (e.g., all aspects of robot appearance). Previous studies have also evaluated responses to robots as depicted in videos (e.g., [21, 22, 39]) with some finding strong correlations between in-person and video reactions to a given robot [21, 39].

3.1 Robot video corpus

We used the YouTube Application Programming Interface (API) (version 3.0[2]) to create a corpus of 42 short videos featuring intelligent robots. We did not handpick the videos with respect to perceived robot gender and/or physical features and capabilities; rather, the corpus we created represents a set of robots that a YouTube user would be likely to encounter in a search for "intelligent robots." Using the API, we submitted six queries using the search.list method; retrieving the maximum number of results (50) yielded a set of 300 videos. The queries included "intelligent robot" along with the following phrases: "life like," "humanoid," "industrial," "caregiver," "social" and "advanced AI." From the 300 results, we eliminated those that 1) featured more than one robot, 2) were longer than five minutes, 3) had fewer than 100 public comments, 4) did not actually show a robot within the first minute, and 5) were slideshows or pictures rather than videos of the robot.

We then asked three independent annotators to watch each video. In order to ensure that they attuned to possible gender cues, we asked them to indicate the presence or absence of the following humanlike features [10]: eyes, eyebrows, nose, mouth, ears, torso, arms and legs. In addition, they were asked to indicate whether the robot was shown moving or talking. Finally, they were asked if gender could be attributed to the robot. In 34 cases (81%), annotators agreed on this characteristic; for the remaining eight cases, they discussed this characteristic and came to a consensus. Interestingly, the only humanlike robots causing confusion with respect to gender cues were those resembling children. NAO and Jibo also generated debate. Judges settled on a label of neutral for these robots. After the above procedures, we were left with 42 videos featuring a diverse range of robots; examples are shown in Table 1.

3.2 Online questionnaire

For each video, we recruited a gender-balanced group of 50 participants, master level MTurk workers residing in the U.S. Our participants were relatively young (mean of 35.9 years, median of 35, minimum of 18, maximum of 69), which is in line with previous studies of crowd workers [33]. Mean task completion time was five minutes and workers were paid $1 for their participation. After providing their gender and age, workers watched the video and responded to each item in Table 2, as 5-point Likert items from 1 ("not at all") to 5 ("extremely"). We subjected the responses to the first seven items in the questionnaire to a confirmatory factor analysis, using R's *Factanal* package[3] , with varimax rotation. This

[2]https://developers.google.com/youtube/v3/docs/search/list

[3]https://stat.ethz.ch/R-manual/R-devel/library/stats/html/factanal.html

Table 1: Example robots in the video corpus with YouTube ID.

Neutral	Female cues	Male cues
Honda ASIMO (1V9XUMCPGF8)	Actroid-F robot nurse (I7tYwnqot6M)	Geminoid-DK (V9figWCdq7U)
Aldebaran's Pepper (lqlyxg1-gE0)	Nexi MDS (aQS2zxmrrA)	Hanson Robotics' Joey Chaos (psAMNhMqhZA)
Aldebaran's NAO (nNbj2G3GmAo)	AIST HRP-4C (X3oH01RXZrI)	Hanson Robotics' Jules (RNKLuXUh3M4)
Jibo (3N1Q8oFpX1Y)	Geminoid F (cy7xGwYdRk0)	Hanson Robotics' Philip K. Dick (UIWWLg4wLEY)

Table 2: Measuring perceived robot experience and agency, and affective response [16]

Robot experience	To what extent do you believe the robot has the capacity to feel **pain**? To what extent do you believe the robot has the capacity to feel **fear**?
Robot agency	To what extent do you believe the robot has the capacity to **plan** actions? To what extent do you believe the robot has the capacity to exercise **self-control**?
Affective reaction	To what extent does the robot make you feel **unnerved**? To what extent does the robot make you feel **uneasy**? To what extent does the robot make you feel **"creeped out"**?
Human likeness	Overall, to what extent do you find the robot **humanlike**?

confirmed the validity of our experiment, as responses loaded onto three distinct factors, as shown in Table 3.

3.3 Statistical model and hypothesis testing

First, we used responses over all 42 robots in our corpus, in order to confirm that the model put forward by Gray and Wegner, which was developed in the context of an experiment involving one robot as depicted in two videos, explains people's affective reactions in our online experimental context, in which we have not hand-picked robots with specific features. Specifically, we generated a structural equation model (SEM) via Maximum Likelihood Estimation using R's *Lavaan* package[4]. As shown in Tables 4 and 5, our model incorporates the estimation of four latent constructs from measurements obtained via the questionnaire responses (robot's humanlike appearance, perceived experience, perceived agency, and the human affective response to the robot (i.e., the uncanny effect)), as well as the relationships between the constructs (i.e., structural model).

Table 3: Factor loadings (n = 2,100 responses).

	Factor 1: Uncanny	Factor 2: Experience	Factor 3: Agency
Creeped	0.90		
Uneasy	0.95		
Unnerved	0.92		
Fear		0.97	
Pain		0.80	
Control		0.31	0.69
Plan			0.98
Cumulative Variance	0.37	0.62	0.84

Once we confirmed the relationship between a robot's humanlike appearance, which drives the human's interpretation of its ability to experience pain and fear, which leads to a negative reaction from humans, we considered the three types of robots (those with male, female and no gender cues) separately. In particular, we fit a SEM that explains men and women's responses to each type of robot. We then compared the models in order to observe possible differences in the mechanism behind human uncanny response to robots, once both participant and perceived robot gender are taken into consideration.

Specifically, for all combinations of human gender / robot gender cues, we tested the following hypotheses:

H1: *The extent to which a robot is "humanlike" influences human perception of its capability to feel pain and fear.*
H2: *The extent to which a robot is "humanlike" influences human perception of its capacity to plan and exercise self-control.*
H3: *When humans perceive a robot to have experience, this leads to more negative affective responses to it.*
H4: *When humans perceive a robot to have agency, this leads to more negative affective responses to it.*

4. BASELINE MODEL

Here, we describe the SEM developed to explain men and women participants' affective responses in general, using data collected with respect to all 42 robots in our corpus. Table 4 details the standardized, estimated coefficient on each variable in our measurement model, as well as the appropriate tests for statistical significance. Likewise, Table 5 reports the estimated coefficients for the structural model (i.e., path analysis). Figure 2 provides a visual representation of the model. Based on the SEM, all four hypotheses are supported.

Generally speaking, our analysis supports the model put forth by Gray and Wegner. The more participants perceived a robot to have capacity for experience, the more likely they were to have a negative affective response to it (i.e.,

[4]https://cran.r-project.org/web/packages/lavaan/lavaan.pdf

Table 4: All robots – Measurement model ($^*p<.001$).

	Men Participants		Women Participants	
	Est.	*z*	*Est.*	*z*
Experience				
Fear→Experience	0.852	fixed	0.936	fixed
Pain→Experience	0.943	17.48*	0.955	11.18*
Agency				
Control→Agency	1.180	fixed	1.117	fixed
Plan→Agency	1.151	10.05*	1.028	9.82*
Uncanny				
Unnerved→Uncanny	1.229	fixed	1.208	fixed
Uneasy→Uncanny	1.302	55.90*	1.250	58.83*
Creeped→Uncanny	1.272	48.54*	1.254	52.80*

Table 5: All robots – Model path coefficients ($^*p<.001$).

	Men Participants		Women Participants	
	Std. path coefficient	*z*	*Std. path coefficient*	*z*
H1: Humanlike→ Experience	0.423	9.68*	0.187	4.49*
H2: Humanlike→ Agency	0.289	6.12*	0.343	6.87*
H3: Experience→ Uncanny	0.227	6.69*	0.148	4.48*
H4: Agency→ Uncanny	0.147	4.26*	0.103	3.12*
	RMSEA = 0.12 CFI = 0.95 Obs. = 1,037		RMSEA = 0.13 CFI = 0.95 Obs. = 1,099	

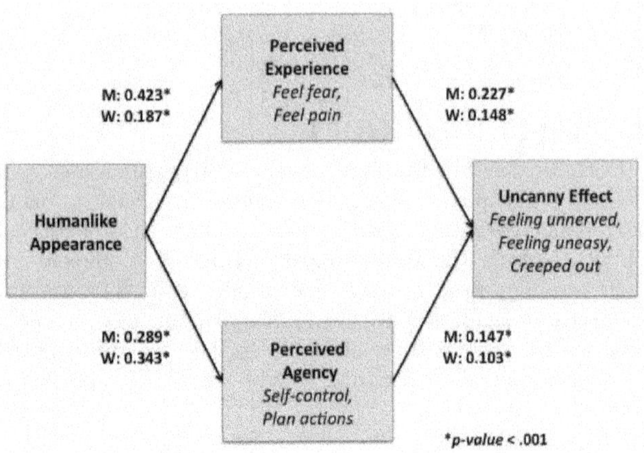

Figure 2: Uncanny reaction of men (M) and women (W) participants to all robots in the corpus.

to experience "uncanniness"). However, in contrast to Gray and Wegner, who found no significant relationship between a robot's perceived agency and the uncanny effect, we found that perceived agency also contributed positively to the likelihood of experiencing an uncanny reaction. We believe that this difference is due to the fact that we exposed participants to a wide range of robots depicted in videos. While Gray and Wegner did not describe the content of the videos of Kaspar, it can certainly be said that in our corpus, robot agency is often highlighted. For instance, the video depicting Honda's ASIMO[5] demonstrates its new "autonomous behavior control technology," which allows it to mix up a drink and serve it to an observer. Similarly, Aldebaran's Pepper[6], is shown not only dancing, but also greeting and entertaining visitors at a store. In other words, given the content of the videos in our corpus, we are not surprised to find that robot agency can also be a source of uncanniness for human observers.

Finally, while Gray and Wegner did not consider the possible influence of participant gender in their perception and response to the robot, we have shown that the explanation of human negative affective response is valid for both the men and women participants in our study. However, while the basic mechanism is the same across genders, there are interesting differences, particularly with respect to the relative importance of variables in the path model (i.e., structural relationships). The influence of a robot's humanlike appearance on the human's perception of its capability to experience and have agency is of note. For men participants, robot appearance (i.e., humanlikeness) has a stronger influence on the perception of its ability to experience, as compared to women. In contrast, for women participants, robot appearance is highly influential on their perception of robot agency, as compared to men.

5. GENDER-NEUTRAL ROBOTS

Tables 6 and 7 present the SEM when estimated on the subset of data that concerns robots without gender cues. Robots in this category include Aldebaran's NAO and Pepper, as well as Jibo, Inc.'s social robot, which are not endowed with many obvious gender cues – facial features, hairstyles or a voice that might lead humans to interpret them as being male or female.

The model provides support for all four hypotheses. However, we again find gender differences with respect to the extent of influence of robot appearance on perceived experience (with the relationship being stronger for men participants) and agency (with the relationship here being stronger for women than men participants).

6. FEMALE-CUE ROBOTS

Tables 8 and 9 present the estimated model when we consider only the nine videos that depict robots with female gender cues. The videos include robots, such as the Geminoid F[7], that have visual and voice gender cues, as well as those with fewer cues, such as the Nexi MDS[8] (i.e., female voice cue only). The basic hypothesis of Gray and Wegner still applies here; for both men and women participants,

[5]https://www.youtube.com/watch?v=1V9XUMCPGF8
[6]https://www.youtube.com/watch?v=lqlyxg1-gE0
[7]https://www.youtube.com/watch?v=cy7xGwYdRk0
[8]https://www.youtube.com/watch?v=aQS2zxmrrA

Table 6: Gender-neutral robots – Measurement model (*p<.01).

	Men Participants		Women Participants	
	Est.	*z*	*Est.*	*z*
Experience				
Fear→Experience	0.881	fixed	0.865	fixed
Pain→Experience	1.023	8.49*	0.821	8.64*
Agency				
Control→Agency	1.331	fixed	1.067	fixed
Plan→Agency	1.063	7.11*	1.088	9.95*
Uncanny				
Unnerved→Uncanny	1.242	fixed	1.178	fixed
Uneasy→Uncanny	1.300	37.54*	1.207	42.89*
Creeped→Uncanny	1.277	34.00*	1.164	36.80*

Table 7: Gender-neutral robots – Model path coefficients (*p<.01).

	Men Participants		Women Participants	
	Std. path coefficient	*z*	*Std. path coefficient*	*z*
H1: Humanlike→ Experience	0.284	4.55*	0.165	3.25*
H2: Humanlike→ Agency	0.323	4.36*	0.465	7.93*
H3: Experience→ Uncanny	0.159	3.25*	0.175	3.95*
H4: Agency→ Uncanny	0.112	2.47*	0.120	2.60*
	RMSEA = 0.14 CFI = 0.94 Obs. = 508		RMSEA = 0.12 CFI = 0.95 Obs. = 601	

Table 8: Female-cue robots – Measurement model (*p<.001).

	Men Participants		Women Participants	
	Est.	*z*	*Est.*	*z*
Experience				
Fear→Experience	0.850	fixed	1.041	fixed
Pain→Experience	0.985	12.86*	0.853	7.24*
Agency				
Control→Agency	0.982	fixed	1.141	fixed
Plan→Agency	1.197	2.70*	1.169	7.17*
Uncanny				
Unnerved→Uncanny	1.103	fixed	1.082	fixed
Uneasy→Uncanny	1.124	24.49*	1.168	23.6*
Creeped→Uncanny	1.184	22.40*	1.193	22.1*

Table 9: Female-cue robots – Model path coefficients (**p<.01,*p<.05).

	Men Participants		Women Participants	
	Std. path coefficient	*z*	*Std. path coefficient*	*z*
H1: Humanlike→ Experience	0.628	6.65**	0.169	2.05*
H2: Humanlike→ Agency	0.167	1.67	0.436	4.72**
H3: Experience→ Uncanny	0.435	5.43**	0.266	3.94**
H4: Agency→ Uncanny	0.167	1.71	0.291	3.85**
	RMSEA = 0.11 CFI = 0.97 Obs. = 163		RMSEA = 0.14 CFI = 0.94 Obs. = 225	

there is a positive relationship between the robot's humanlikeness and the human's perception of robot experience, and in turn, between the perception of robot experience and the human's negative reaction. H1 and H3 are confirmed.

However, while perceived agency drives the negative reaction amongst women participants, the same is not true for men participants. For men, the robot's humanlikeness plays no role in whether they perceive the robot as having agency; likewise, perceived agency does not bring about an uncanny reaction. In other words, hypotheses two and four are supported only when we consider women's affective reactions to the robots with female gender cues.

7. MALE-CUE ROBOTS

Tables 10 and 11 depict the model of affective reactions to the seven robots with male gender cues.

These robots include three androids by Hanson Robotics: Jules[9], the Philip K. Dick android[10], and Joey Chaos[11]. Another featured robot is the Geminoid-DK[12]. Male gender cues include short (or no) hair, masculine facial characteristics and a deep voice.

As in the case of female cue robots, the SEM fitted on our male cue robot data only partially supports Gray and Wegner's model. The hypotheses concerning the links between humanlikeness of the robot, its perceived agency, and the uncanny reaction of the human (H2, H4) are confirmed. However, H1 and H3, which concern the relationship between humanlikeness and perceived experience, and experience and uncanny reaction, are confirmed only on the data collected from men participants in our study.

More specifically, a humanlike robot with male gender

[9]https://www.youtube.com/watch?v=RNKLuXUh3M4
[10]https://www.youtube.com/watch?v=UIWWLg4wLEY
[11]https://www.youtube.com/watch?v=psAMNhMqhZA
[12]https://www.youtube.com/watch?v=V9figWCdq7U

Table 10: Male-cue robots – Measurement model ($^{*}p<.001$).

	Men Participants		Women Participants	
	Est.	*z*	*Est.*	*z*
Experience				
Fear→Experience	0.803	fixed	1.315	fixed
Pain→Experience	0.850	7.71*	0.905	3.18*
Agency				
Control→Agency	1.110	fixed	1.104	fixed
Plan→Agency	1.243	6.89*	1.094	4.90*
Uncanny				
Unnerved→Uncanny	1.169	fixed	1.242	fixed
Uneasy→Uncanny	1.283	26.74*	1.267	24.70*
Creeped→Uncanny	1.264	23.73*	1.304	21.32*

Table 11: Male-cue robots – Model path coefficients ($^{**}p<.01$,$^{*}p<.05$).

	Men Participants		Women Participants	
	Std. path coefficient	*z*	*Std. path coefficient*	*z*
H1: Humanlike→ Experience	0.357	4.16**	-0.040	-0.58
H2: Humanlike→ Agency	0.387	4.56**	0.174	2.10*
H3: Experience→ Uncanny	0.205	3.05**	0.158	2.27*
H4: Agency→ Uncanny	0.141	2.06*	0.268	3.11**
	RMSEA = 0.13 CFI = 0.95 Obs. = 259		RMSEA = 0.13 CFI = 0.95 Obs. = 178	

cues is not more likely to be perceived as having feelings by women. However, it is more likely to be perceived as having agency. Similarly, the link between perceived experience and uncanny reaction is less salient for women participants as compared to men.

8. DISCUSSION

Researchers have found that incorporating gender cues into a robot's design can have a significant effect on HRI. Even simple cues, such as a pink bow versus a black hat placed on the robot's head [20], or a short versus long hairstyle [12] are likely to lead human observers to perceive the robot as having gender. In turn, humans are likely to use such gender cues to make inferences as to the robot's character traits, as well as the tasks for which it is most suitable [6, 12, 31]. However, as discussed, endowing robots with gender is not always beneficial; gendered agents are more susceptible to abuse by humans, with female gendered robots often being the subjects of abuse and sexual harassment [4].

Currently, we set out to better understand the possible interaction between human observer gender and gender cues incorporated into a robot's design. Specifically, we sought to understand if the mechanism believed to underlie negative affective reactions to robots, the "uncanny effect," is the same for men and women observers. Because the uncanny effect is often explained in terms of robot appearance and behavior, we could evaluate human observers' initial reactions to a robot using videos as stimuli. In addition, because Gray and Wegner's model incorporates the variables of perceived robot experience and agency, which mediate the relationship between robot appearance (i.e., humanlikeness) and uncanny reaction, it served as a means to theoretically ground our examination of the role of gender and human perception of robots.

Table 12 summarizes the results of our experiment. We are able to replicate the findings of Gray and Wegner in the case of non-gendered robots. In other words, when a robot has no gender cues, the mechanism behind uncanny responses is not correlated to the observer's (i.e., participant's) gender. However, the mechanism driving an uncanny reaction is different for men and women, when the robot is endowed with gender cues.

Specifically, for female cue robots, the uncanny response in men is driven only by perceived experience, and not perceived agency. In contrast, for male cue robots, the negative response in women is driven primarily by perceived agency. As explained, person perception researchers have discovered that two key dimensions describe how we perceive and evaluate others: the extent to which one is warm / communal, and agentic / competent. Social stereotypes are captured by combinations of these two dimensions, with women largely being viewed as being (and expected to be) high in warmth, but low in agency. In contrast, the stereotypical man is characterized by high agency, and not too much warmth [1].

It is therefore interesting to observe that perceived experience, which relates to feelings, in a robot with female gender cues, is exactly what elicits an uncanny reaction from men participants (but not women). Likewise, we see that high perceived agency, which relates to competency, is key in bringing about a negative reaction from women participants. In other words, a robot that conforms too well to human social expectations and stereotypes is more likely to be perceived as uncanny.

It is not yet clear why participants of the opposite gender (with respect to the robot's perceived gender), appear to be subject to greater influence by these stereotypes as compared to same-gender participants. Eyssel and colleagues [13] have found evidence of a preference for same-gender robots, based on voiced gender cues; thus, it is possible that our participants also favor same-gender robots and are perhaps less fearful of them.

Although our work concerns gender and the uncanny reaction, we can also look to the literature concerning the role of robot gender in persuading a human interlocutor, in interpreting our findings. In general, the empirical results with respect to persuasion are mixed; in some cases researchers report that a same-gender agent is more likely to influence the human's behavior [18]. This finding is in line with the widely held result in social psychology that we are more drawn to others like us (i.e., the in-group effect). However,

Table 12: **Summary of findings.**

Participant gender / Robot gender cues	Men No cues	Women No cues	Men Female cues	Women Female cues	Men Male cues	Women Male cues
H1: Humanlike→Experience	Confirm	Confirm	Confirm	Weak Confirm	Confirm	No
H2: Humanlike→Agency	Confirm	Confirm	No	Confirm	Confirm	Weak Confirm
H3: Experience→Uncanny	Confirm	Confirm	Confirm	Confirm	Confirm	Weak Confirm
H4: Agency→Uncanny	Confirm	Confirm	No	Confirm	Weak Confirm	Confirm

other researchers have reported the opposite effect, with the other-gender agent having more influence on the human [40, 37]. Note while these studies consider virtual, non-embodied agents, Siegel et al. [37] found no evidence of a difference between their results involving a co-present robot and a situation where there was no robot co-present with the human participant.

One consistent finding across all of these studies, as well as our own, is that the cross-gender effect is more salient for men participants as compared to women. In other words, men are somehow more affected (i.e., persuaded by or "creeped out" by) the female-cue agent, than are women by the male-cue agent. In explaining this, Siegel et al. cite findings by Schermerhorn et al [35], which suggest that men are more likely than women to treat a robot as a social agent, rather than simply a machine.

In future work, we plan to revisit the YouTube videos in our corpus, in order to analyze more closely the behaviors of the female and male robots. For instance, it would be interesting to see if the female robots' appearance and behaviors are more stereotypically female, as compared to the male-cue robots. In a study of human-human communication, Carli [5] found that women are better able to influence men (rather than other women), but only when their behaviors are stereotype-congruent (e.g., when they speak demurely and tentatively rather than aggressively). On the other hand, men were found to be universally influential, regardless of their behaviors. In our corpus, if we can find examples of female-cue robots that conform more/less to the female gender stereotype, we can then observe if there are differences in people's reactions to them. This might help us better understand the cross-gender effect that we, and other researchers, have observed.

8.1 Limitations

Our corpus of YouTube videos featured a wide range of robots. For instance, some are research prototypes being developed by researchers and governments (e.g., NASA's Valkyrie, Geminoid-DK), whereas others are social robots that are currently available or are intended for eventual use by the public (e.g., Jibo, Pepper). It is possible that using the video as a stimulus triggers a response that not only depends on the robot's appearance and behavior. In other words, it could be that the robot's intended use might also cause a participant to feel a certain way (e.g., a fear of having a robot like Jibo in the home environment).

Finally, as in most online studies, our participants may not represent the public at large. Amazon Mechanical Turk workers residing in the U.S. have been reported to be relatively young (median age of 30 years old) and highly educated (63% having obtained a college degree) [33]. Therefore, we should keep in mind that our results may not extrapolate to other demographics, and in particular, to the affective reactions of elderly persons, who may be the members of the public most likely to interact on a frequent basis with social robots in the near future [32, 36].

9. CONCLUSIONS

Our work addressed the need to better understand the interaction between the human observer's own gender and the gender cues incorporated in the design of a robot. To date, several studies have shown that even subtle gender cues lead human observers to infer that robots are gendered, and in turn, apply human social expectations in interpreting robot identity and behavior. While this can have positive consequences, negative consequences, such as robot abuse, can also result when robots create the illusion of human gender too well. Future work should delve deeper into the origins of the cross-gender differences that we have documented, and if and why opposite-gender observers may be more susceptible to influence by gender stereotypes in the context of HRI, more so than same-gender observers. In sum, the study of interactions between humans and gendered robots is a ripe area for further research, which will lead to better understanding not only of enhanced robot design, but also of the nature of human socio-cognitive processes.

10. ACKNOWLEDGEMENTS

We would like to thank the three anonymous reviewers, as well as the meta-reviewers, for their constructive comments, which helped us in preparing the final version of the paper.

11. REFERENCES

[1] A. E. Abele and S. Bruckmüller. The bigger one of the "Big Two"? Preferential processing of communal information. *Journal of Experimental Social Psychology*, 47(5):935–948, 2011.

[2] K. O. Arras and D. Cerqui. Do we want to share our lives and bodies with robots? a 2000 people survey. Technical report, 2005.

[3] J. A. Bargh. The cognitive monster: The case against the controllability of automatic stereotype effects. 1999.

[4] S. Brahnam and A. De Angeli. Gender affordances of conversational agents. *Interacting with Computers*, 24(3):139–153, 2012.

[5] L. L. Carli. Gender, language, and influence. *Journal of Personality and Social Psychology*, 59(5):941, 1990.

[6] J. Carpenter, J. M. Davis, N. Erwin-Stewart, T. R. Lee, J. D. Bransford, and N. Vye. Gender representation and humanoid robots designed for domestic use. *International Journal of Social Robotics*, 1(3):261–265, 2009.

[7] A. J. Cuddy, S. T. Fiske, and P. Glick. Warmth and competence as universal dimensions of social perception: The stereotype content model and the bias map. *Advances in experimental social psychology*, 40:61–149, 2008.

[8] A. De Angeli, S. Brahnam, P. Wallis, and A. Dix. Misuse and abuse of interactive technologies. In *CHI'06 Extended Abstracts on Human Factors in Computing Systems*, pages 1647–1650. ACM, 2006.

[9] A. B. Diekman and A. H. Eagly. Stereotypes as dynamic constructs: Women and men of the past, present, and future. *Personality and social psychology bulletin*, 26(10):1171–1188, 2000.

[10] C. F. DiSalvo, F. Gemperle, J. Forlizzi, and S. Kiesler. All robots are not created equal: the design and perception of humanoid robot heads. In *Proceedings of the 4th conference on Designing interactive systems: processes, practices, methods, and techniques*, pages 321–326. ACM, 2002.

[11] B. R. Duffy. Anthropomorphism and the social robot. *Robotics and autonomous systems*, 42(3):177–190, 2003.

[12] F. Eyssel and F. Hegel. (S) he's Got the Look: Gender Stereotyping of Robots. *Journal of Applied Social Psychology*, 42(9):2213–2230, 2012.

[13] F. Eyssel, D. Kuchenbrandt, S. Bobinger, L. de Ruiter, and F. Hegel. 'If you sound like me, you must be more human': On the interplay of robot and user features on human-robot acceptance and anthropomorphism. In *Proceedings of the seventh annual ACM/IEEE international conference on Human-Robot Interaction*, pages 125–126. ACM, 2012.

[14] S. T. Fiske, A. J. Cuddy, P. Glick, and J. Xu. A model of (often mixed) stereotype content: competence and warmth respectively follow from perceived status and competition. *Journal of personality and social psychology*, 82(6):878, 2002.

[15] K. Gray, A. C. Jenkins, A. S. Heberlein, and D. M. Wegner. Distortions of mind perception in psychopathology. *Proceedings of the National Academy of Sciences*, 108(2):477–479, 2011.

[16] K. Gray and D. M. Wegner. Feeling robots and human zombies: Mind perception and the uncanny valley. *Cognition*, 125(1):125–130, 2012.

[17] A. G. Greenwald and M. R. Banaji. Implicit social cognition: attitudes, self-esteem, and stereotypes. *Psychological review*, 102(1):4, 1995.

[18] R. E. Guadagno, J. Blascovich, J. N. Bailenson, and C. Mccall. Virtual humans and persuasion: The effects of agency and behavioral realism. *Media Psychology*, 10(1):1–22, 2007.

[19] D. L. Hamilton and T. K. Trolier. Stereotypes and stereotyping: An overview of the cognitive approach. 1986.

[20] E. H. Jung, T. F. Waddell, and S. S. Sundar. Feminizing robots: User responses to gender cues on robot body and screen. In *Proceedings of the 2016 CHI Conference Extended Abstracts on Human Factors in Computing Systems*, pages 3107–3113. ACM, 2016.

[21] C. D. Kidd and C. Breazeal. Effect of a robot on user perceptions. In *Intelligent Robots and Systems, 2004.(IROS 2004). Proceedings. 2004 IEEE/RSJ International Conference on*, volume 4, pages 3559–3564. IEEE, 2004.

[22] K. F. MacDorman. Subjective ratings of robot video clips for human likeness, familiarity, and eeriness: An exploration of the uncanny valley. In *ICCS/CogSci-2006 long symposium: Toward social mechanisms of android science*, pages 26–29, 2006.

[23] K. F. MacDorman and H. Ishiguro. The uncanny advantage of using androids in cognitive and social science research. *Interaction Studies*, 7(3):297–337, 2006.

[24] C. McGarty, V. Y. Yzerbyt, and R. Spears. *Stereotypes as explanations: The formation of meaningful beliefs about social groups*. Cambridge University Press, 2002.

[25] T. Minato, M. Shimada, H. Ishiguro, and S. Itakura. Development of an android robot for studying human-robot interaction. In *International Conference on Industrial, Engineering and Other Applications of Applied Intelligent Systems*, pages 424–434. Springer, 2004.

[26] M. Mori, K. F. MacDorman, and N. Kageki. The uncanny valley [from the field]. *IEEE Robotics & Automation Magazine*, 19(2):98–100, 2012.

[27] C. A. Moss-Racusin, J. E. Phelan, and L. A. Rudman. When men break the gender rules: Status incongruity and backlash against modest men. *Psychology of Men & Masculinity*, 11(2):140, 2010.

[28] C. Nass and Y. Moon. Machines and mindlessness: Social responses to computers. *Journal of social issues*, 56(1):81–103, 2000.

[29] C. Nass, Y. Moon, and N. Green. Are Machines Gender Neutral? Gender-Stereotypic Responses to Computers With Voices. *Journal of applied social psychology*, 27(10):864–876, 1997.

[30] C. Nass, J. Steuer, and E. R. Tauber. Computers are social actors. In *Proceedings of the SIGCHI conference on Human factors in computing systems*, pages 72–78. ACM, 1994.

[31] J. Rhim, Y. Kim, M.-S. Kim, and D. Y. Yim. The effect of gender cue alterations of robot to match task attributes on user's acceptance perception. In *Proceedings of HCI Korea*, pages 51–57. Hanbit Media, Inc., 2014.

[32] L. Ring, L. Shi, K. Totzke, and T. Bickmore. Social support agents for older adults: longitudinal affective computing in the home. *Journal on Multimodal User Interfaces*, 9(1):79–88, 2015.

[33] J. Ross, L. Irani, M. Silberman, A. Zaldivar, and B. Tomlinson. Who are the crowdworkers?: shifting demographics in Mechanical Turk. In *CHI'10 extended abstracts on Human factors in computing systems*, pages 2863–2872. ACM, 2010.

[34] L. A. Rudman and J. E. Phelan. Backlash effects for disconfirming gender stereotypes in organizations. *Research in organizational behavior*, 28:61–79, 2008.

[35] P. Schermerhorn, M. Scheutz, and C. R. Crowell. Robot social presence and gender: Do females view robots differently than males? In *Proceedings of the 3rd ACM/IEEE international conference on Human robot interaction*, pages 263–270. ACM, 2008.

[36] T. Shibata and K. Wada. Robot therapy: A new approach for mental healthcare of the elderly–a mini-review. *Gerontology*, 57(4):378–386, 2010.

[37] M. Siegel, C. Breazeal, and M. I. Norton. Persuasive robotics: The influence of robot gender on human behavior. In *2009 IEEE/RSJ International Conference on Intelligent Robots and Systems*, pages 2563–2568. IEEE, 2009.

[38] J.-Y. Sung, R. E. Grinter, H. I. Christensen, and L. Guo. Housewives or technophiles?: Understanding domestic robot owners. In *Human-Robot Interaction (HRI), 2008 3rd ACM/IEEE International Conference on*, pages 129–136. IEEE, 2008.

[39] M. L. Walters, D. S. Syrdal, K. Dautenhahn, R. Te Boekhorst, and K. L. Koay. Avoiding the uncanny valley: Robot appearance, personality and consistency of behavior in an attention-seeking home scenario for a robot companion. *Autonomous Robots*, 24(2):159–178, 2008.

[40] C. Zanbaka, P. Goolkasian, and L. Hodges. Can a virtual cat persuade you?: The role of gender and realism in speaker persuasiveness. In *Proceedings of the SIGCHI conference on Human Factors in computing systems*, pages 1153–1162. ACM, 2006.

Why Do They Refuse to Use My Robot?: Reasons for Non-Use Derived from a Long-Term Home Study

Maartje de Graaf
University of Twente
Drienerlolaan 5
7522 NB Enschede, The Netherlands
m.m.a.degraaf@utwente.nl

Somaya Ben Allouch
Saxion University of Applied Sciences
M.H. Tromplaan 28
7513 AB Enschede, The Netherlands
s.benallouch@saxion.nl

Jan van Dijk
University of Twente
Drienerlolaan 5
7522 NB Enschede, The Netherlands
j.a.g.m.vandijk@utwente.nl

ABSTRACT

Research on why people refuse or abandon the use of technology in general, and robots specifically, is still scarce. Consequently, the academic understanding of people's underlying reasons for non-use remains weak. Thus, vital information about the design of these robots including their acceptance and refusal or abandonment by its users is needed. We placed 70 autonomous robots within people's homes for a period of six months and collected reasons for refusal and abandonment through questionnaires and interviews. Based on our findings, the challenge for robot designers is to create robots that are enjoyable and easy to use to capture users in the short-term, and functionally-relevant to keep those users in the longer-term. Understanding the thoughts and motives behind non-use may help to identify obstacles for acceptance, and therefore enable developers to better adapt technological designs to the benefit of the users.

Keywords

Discontinuance; Domestic environment; Domestic robots; Long-term use; Non-use; Rejection; Resistance; Technology acceptance.

1. INTRODUCTION

One overarching goal of robot researchers and developers is widespread acceptance of robots within our society. Most research in human-robot interaction that includes end users mainly focuses on the reasons why and the ways in which people use or interact with their robots. The role of users has been increasingly addressed within the technology acceptance literature, especially during the mid-1990s. Involving end-users in the early stages of development helps researchers understand the cultural and social contexts of acceptance and enables developers to apply this gained knowledge into their designs, a paradigm that has recognized that users shape technology [34], [51], [57]. Discovering people's perceptions, expectations and impressions of socially interactive technologies in their private domestic environments over a longer period of time is vital for informing the design and acceptance of these technologies. By including the user, an attempt is made to overcome problems associated with approaches that focus on the actors that produce the technologies such as scientists, engineers, politicians, financers and marketers. This paradigm of social or mutual shaping of technology has been debated for robotics similarly [47]. Research that investigates the long-term acceptance of socially interactive technology in domestic environments is necessary for a successful diffusion of these types of technology within society.

A large body of academic research over the past decades points towards the expansion of the digital divide between users and non-users of technology [10], [22], [48], [49], [58]. While most HRI studies look at adoption or acceptance, it is equally important to investigate reasons why people do not want to use or interact with a robot. Defining people only as users who (re-)shape technology confirms the "technocratic vision of the centrality and normativity of technology" ([59], p. 25). An important and understudied topic in technology acceptance research in general is about those people who refuse to use a technology or abandon it after initial adoption [48], [49]. Similarly, past research in HRI, and technology adoption in general, has highlighted that reasons for rejection often trump reason for adoption [60]. Indeed, a review on (long-term) studies on technology acceptance shows that many report high rates of people refusing or abandoning the technologies under study [55]. A similar trend can be observed for HRI research (e.g., [12], [13], [15], [23]). Following others, we argue that users need to be evaluated in relation to the more invisible group; people who refuse or abandon the use of a technology. The reasons for this refusal or abandonment could be used to inform the development of new technologies and their applications to the benefits of potential end users. Therefore, people who do not want to use our robots are just as important as those who embrace them. However, comparing these research results on non-users to studies focusing on users is challenging because each study employs different definitions, various measures, unequal devices, and have tested these within diverse populations [49]. Therefore, a solid theoretical framework of non-use of technological devices is still lacking [55], and consequently, the academic understanding of non-use of technology remains weak.

Moreover, only a minority of studies have investigated the long-term use of technological systems in home environments. Thus, the traditional technology acceptance literature lacks a profound body of long-term research, even despite its extensive history in information systems research [53]. This is not any different for the field of HRI, in which most studies are not longitudinal either. The main reason for a shortage of long-term HRI studies is that robot technologies are generally not robust enough to be studied outside the lab for extended periods of time without supervision of an expert. However, developing user experiences with a technology or gaining use skills might change the user's attitudes towards [21], [54], uses of [36], [44], or even their conceptualizations [43] of that technology. While most HRI research is mainly based on short-

HRI'17, March 6–9, 2017, Vienna, Austria.
 ISBN 978-1-4503-4336-7/17/03...$15.00
DOI: http://dx.doi.org/10.1145/2909824.3020236

term interactions or assessments of responses to written or visual stimuli, only a minority of HRI studies have paid attention to what happens with the users' behavior toward robots after these initial exposures or interactions. However, the phase after initial use trails is exactly where people decide between adopting and continuing or rejecting and discontinuing the use of a technology. Studying human-robot interaction in real-world contexts over a longer period of time offers a different opportunity to assess acceptance or non-use of robots. The few existing longitudinal HRI studies often report that their robot system failed to engage their users in the longer term (e.g., [12], [13], [15], [23]). Yet, to our knowledge, no HRI study has currently addressed people's in-depth motivations for refusing or abandoning the use of a robot system over a longer period of time.

Our current study complements earlier research by filling the gap of long-term interaction and non-use of robots by looking into the process of acceptance or non-use in people's own homes over a 6-month period. One of the goals of our long-term home study was aimed at providing more insight in the reasons why people refused or abandoned the use of a robot in domestic environments. In this paper, we will report on these findings. Refusal or abandonment, in the literature often referred to as non-use, can be divided into several subgroups [45], [49], [59]. In this paper, we follow Wyatt et al.'s [59] subgroup categories of resisters, rejecters, excluded and expelled. Resisters are those people who never used a technology simply because they did not want to. Rejecters are those people who have voluntarily stopped the use of a technology for their own reasons. Following Rogers [45], we will further split this group into rejecters and discontinuers in our study. Rejecters are those who actively reject the use of a technology before an actual adoption, and discontinuers are those who decide to stop using a technology after previous initial adoption. The excluded are those people that never used a technology because they cannot get access for a variety of reasons, and they do not have the choice to adopt or not. Finally, the expelled are those people who have had access to the technology at some point, but have involuntarily lost their access for whatever reason. The aim of this paper is to gain insight into the users' motivations for their non-use of a robot in their own homes. Gaining these insights may help to identify obstacles for acceptance that could help developers to better shape the design of domestic robots to the benefits of the potential end users.

2. METHOD

To study acceptance and non-use in a real-world context, we investigated people's interactions with the robot guided by voluntary use. Therefore, we allowed our participants to stop using the robot at any point during the study, in which case we collected their reasoning and motivations for non-use with both quantitative and qualitative methods.

2.1 Data Collection and Procedure

The study ran from October 2012 to May 2013 and consisted of six sessions of data collection ranging from two weeks before to six months after the introduction of the robot at the participants' homes. We collected reasons for refusal and abandonment through questionnaires and interviews.

To investigate what acceptance factors explain why people stopped their use of the robot, we administered a questionnaire at six points in time to 102 participants. All scales to measure the acceptance factors in this study have been validated in previous work on robot acceptance [14]. A list of these factors are presented in table 1, together with their reference and internal consistency statistics. In addition to these scale, we asked the participants at all sessions of data collection whether or not they were still using the robot. If they indicated that they had stopped using the robot, they were asked to provide a description of their motivations for non-use. SPSS 14 was used to analyze the quantitative data. Several binary logistic regression analyses were performed to determine which factors explained why the participants stopped using the robot.

Table 1. Acceptance factors used in the questionnaire

Acceptance Factor	Reference	Alpha
Usefulness	Heerink et al. [20]	.95
Ease of use	Heerink et al. [20]	.74
Adaptability	Heerink et al. [20]	.77
Intelligence	Bartneck et al. [4]	.90
Enjoyment	Heerink et al. [20]	.92
Attractiveness	McCroskey [37]	.93
Animacy	Bartneck et al. [4]	.83
Social presence	Biocca et al. [6]	.79
Sociability	Rubin & Martin [46]	.76
Companionship	McCroskey [37]	.88
Social influence	Karahanna et al. [26]	.87
Status	Moore et al. [39]	.94
Trust	McCroskey [37]	.93
Attitude tw. robots	Nomura et al. [40]	.69
Self-efficacy	Bandura [3]	.88
Anxiety tw. robots	Nomura et al. [40]	.78
Personal innovativeness	Aragwal et al. [2]	.89

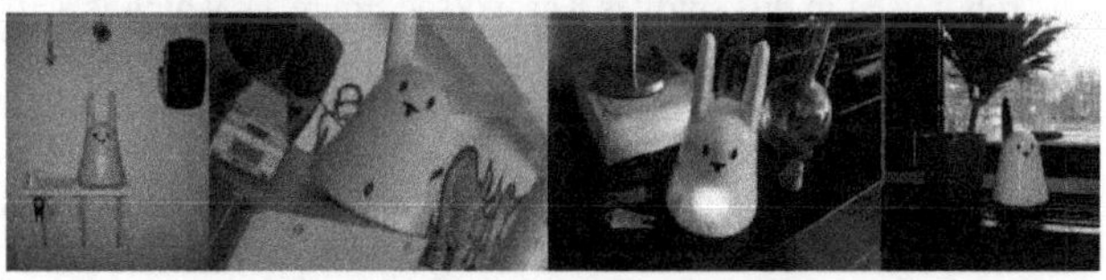

Figure 1. The Karotz robot employed in the participants' homes.

Follow-up semi-structured interviews were conducted with a subset of the participants, in their own homes to obtain more detailed information concerning user experiences with the robot. To gain additional insight into the participant's motivations for non-use, we asked questions about the evaluation of the robot (e.g., 'Can you describe some advantages / disadvantages of the robot?') and evaluation of the participant's use behavior and acceptance (e.g., 'How often have you used the robot in the last period?'; 'Do you think you will continue the use of the robot, why / why not?'), and in-depth follow-up questions were asked to unravel the underlying motivations for non-use. In total, we collected 97 interviews from 21 participants over the six points in time. Each interview was approximately of 30-45 minutes in duration, and was then audio-recorded and transcribed verbatim with each participant's permission. The participants were interviewed alone, regardless of whether the person lived alone or not, because we were interested in the participant's individual experiences with the robot within their household. Based on the transcriptions of the interviews, key concepts were identified and translated into a coding scheme by the primary coder (see table 2). At least one code from the coding scheme was applied to each interview section. The participants' descriptions of their reasons for non-use obtained from the questionnaires were coded using the same coding scheme. Approximately 33% of the data obtained from the questionnaires and interviews were double coded by a second researcher with substantial intercoder agreement (Cohen's Kappa of .73, [29]). In the results, 'striking' or 'typical' quotes [19] were selected that illustrated, confirmed or enhanced our understanding of the experiences of the participants with the robot, as explained through the emerged key concepts from the coding scheme.

Table 2. Coding Scheme

Code	Definition
Disenchantment	A state of disappointment or disillusion regarding (the use of) the robot.
End of novelty	Losing the earlier increased interest in the robot.
Lack of motivation	Lacking a driving force to use the robot.
Need not satisfied	Being displeased or feeling discontent with a sought need the robot should fulfill.
Reliance on others	The act of or the perceived need to rely on others to be able to (properly) use the robot.
Replaced by other device	The replacement of applications or the complete use of the robot with another device.
Restrictions and problems	Foreseeing or experiencing barriers to use the robot.

2.2 The Robot

The robot used in this study is Karotz (see figure 1), which is a 30-cm high internet-enabled rabbit-shaped ambient electronic device. Communication occurs via verbal communication, the LED-light in its belly, the moveable ears, and by detecting the presence of other objects nearby. As the Karotz is permanently connected to the internet, it is able to react to, transmit, or broadcast all types of content available on his network. Examples include news, messages, music, texts, alerts, and radio. The built-in webcam enables users to communicate with family members at home or to keep an eye on their homes while away. More information on the robot can be found at http://store.karotz.com/en_WW/ . In total, 70 Karotz robots were placed into people's own homes with the intention to be used for up to 6 months.

Each robot was installed with a basic set of applications, such as daily news broadcasts, daily local weather reports, favorite radio stations, personalized reminders, and randomly spoken phrases to make the robot be perceived as more autonomous and animate. This basic set of applications ensured that the user experience was somewhat similar among the participants, or at least initially as some participants chose to adjust these applications to their own needs. Besides the required applications, participants were free to install additional applications that they thought would be useful or fun for their households. Almost all participants positioned the robot somewhere in their living room.

2.3 Participants

In total, 70 robots were employed in people's own homes, which resulted in 168 people exposed to our robots. In total, 102 participants were able and willing to complete the questionnaires. There were 48 males and 54 females, and their ages ranged from 8 to 77 (M= 37.74, SD= 16.87). Each participant was categorized into a household type (largely determined by other people who also lived in the household) and a goal was to equalize the number of participants within each household type. In the end, 28 participants were single, 26 participants lived with a spouse, 23 participants were part of a young family (with children aged younger than 12), 15 participants were part of a mature family (with children aged older than 12), and 10 participants did not provide their household type. Most participants lived in the region of our university. In total, 21 participants (male= 7, female= 14) consented to being interviewed in the follow-up sessions to complement the questionnaires. The participants were allowed to keep the robot as a compensation for their participation in our study. We recruited all of our participants using various methods, such as word of mouth, advertising in public locations (e.g., libraries, leisure centers and supermarkets), and snowball sampling, by asking assigned participants for referrals to other people who might participate. During recruitment, we tried to balance out the households' demographic profiles to seek diversity. The participants who stopped using the robot were excluded from any data collection sessions after their decision to drop out of the study. Figure 2 shows the participant attrition rate for the interviews and questionnaire.

3. RESULTS

Slightly less than half of the participants (n= 47) were still using the robot at the end of the study, and intended to continue to use the

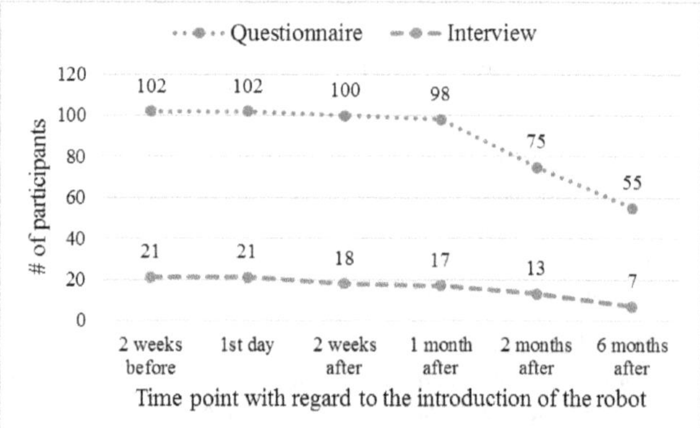

Figure 2. Attrition rate of participants included in the questionnaire and interview samples

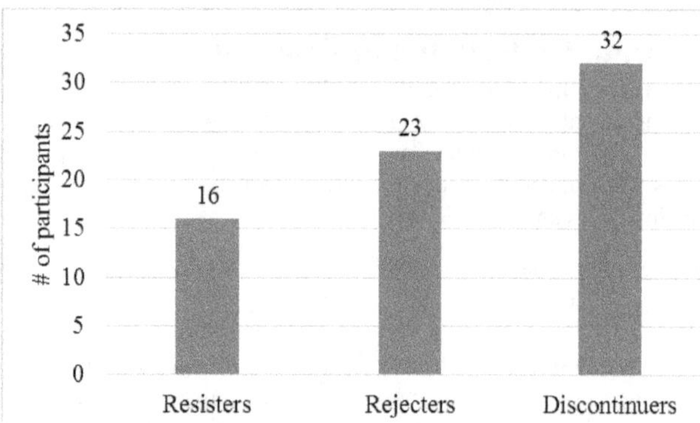

Figure 3. Spread among the different non-user groups

robot after the completion of the study. These participants were labelled as users, and results regarding these participants have been published in previous work [15]. In this paper, we focus only on the participants who stopped their participation and use of the robot, including their motivations to do so (n= 71). We have divided these participants into resisters, rejecters and discontinuers (see figure 3 on the previous page). Resisters (n= 16) were defined in our study as those participants who initially signed up for the study but withdrew before the study started. Rejecters (n= 23) were defined as those participants who stopped the use of the robot at two weeks or one month after the introduction. Discontinuers (n= 32) were defined as those participants who stopped the use of the robot at two or six months after the introduction. There were no significant differences for the demographics between these groups (i.e., users, resisters, rejecters, or discontinuers)based on gender ($\chi^2(2)$= 0.736, p= .692), age ($F(3,112)$= 2.502, p= .062), household type ($\chi^2(9)$= 12.318, p= .196), educational level ($\chi^2(4)$= 5.713, p= .222), income ($\chi^2(10)$= 12.628, p= .245), or pet ownership ($\chi^2(3)$= 0.593, p= .898). Thus, the participants in our study were equally distributed among the different groups and their demographic profiles did not have an effect on their duration of use of the robot.

However, each group of non-users provided their own unique motivations, refusal, or abandonment and different technology acceptance factors explained why they had stopped their use of the robot. The remainder of this section will report on these differences divided by each group of non-users.

3.1 Resisters

In total, 16 persons initially signed up but later withdrew from the study before the first data collection session began (see table 3). Most of the resisters did not respond to follow-up messages for participation, or did not explain why they did not want to participate anymore, i.e., '*no reason*' (n= 6). Among those resisters who did provide a reason, the primary response given was that the robot could not speak Dutch, i.e., '*language*' (n= 6). It was either the participant or their child(ren) that could not speak English or German, which resulted in their decision to not start participating in the study. Another reason for non-adoption was '*privacy concerns*' (n=2). These participants explicitly asked several questions about the embedded camera, which user data would be collected by the robot or the researchers, and expressed their discomfort about the violation of their privacy. The two remaining resisters could not participate in the study, either because of concerns that the robot would exceed the data limit of their internet connection, or because of being busy with other activities.

Table 3. Reasons for non-use for resisters

	Reported reason	
Reason for non-use	**%**	**(*n*)**
No reason given	38	(6)
Language	38	(6)
Privacy concerns	12	(2)
Other reasons	12	(2)
Total	**100**	**(16)**

3.2 Rejecters

In total, 23 participants stopped using the robot at two weeks or one month after the introduction and are categorized as rejecters.

3.2.1 *Influential factors of non-use for rejecters*

Two binary logistic regression analyses (Are you still using the robot?; Yes= 0, No= 1) were performed to determine which factors explained why rejecters had stopped their use of the robot at either two weeks and one month after its introduction. Hence, rejecters were compared to both users and discontinuers at this stage. The results of the residual Chi-square statistic (χ^2= 19.86, p < .001) suggested that the addition of one or more of the acceptance factors significantly affected the predictive power of the model (see table 4 on the next page). Two steps were needed to realize the final model and showed a negative effect for enjoyment (b= -1.44, p < .001) and a positive effect for intelligence (b= 1.13, p= .007). When the participants evaluated the robot as less enjoyable but more intelligent, they were more likely to reject the use of the robot at two weeks after introduction compared to participants who continued their use of the robot after this point. This result can be explained with some quotes from the interviews indicating that a few participants used the robot as a tool that should only perform assigned tasks: "*It seems like he leads a life of its own, as if he just does what he wants instead of what I want him to do.*" –female, 57, living alone. A few other participants indicated that they felt uncanny with the autonomous or intelligent behavior of the robot: "*A few times I was shocked or even devastated by it [...] when he suddenly started to ask questions.*" –male, 32, living alone; or even feared increasing intelligence of machines: "*Artificial intelligence, I am against that [...] it can be dangerous, when a robot is smarter than humans at a given time [...] but he still has no emotions. This could be damaging.*" –female, 22, living in student dorm. Another binary logistic regression analysis was performed for rejection one month after the introduction of the robot. The results of the residual Chi-square statistic (χ^2= 31.89, p < .001) suggested that the addition of one acceptance factor significantly affected the predictive power of the model (see table 5). One step was needed to realize the final model and showed a negative effect for usefulness (b= -2.33, p < .001). When the participants evaluated the robot as less useful, they were more likely to reject the use of the robot at one month after introduction compared to participants who continued their use of the robot after this point. Indeed, a lot of participants indicated in the interviews that the robot failed to fulfil any gratifications: "*I have switched him off, because it does not have an added value.*" – male, 30, living with spouse; and that other devices better served their needs: "*Eventually you come to the conclusion that it is more convenient to use your smartphone.*" –female, 27, living with spouse.

Table 4. Determinants of non-use for rejecters at two weeks after the introduction

Factor	***β***	**SE**	***p***	**Odds ratio**	**CI for odds ratio**
Enjoyment	-1.43	0.38	.000	0.24	0.11 – 0.50
Intelligence	1.13	0.42	.007	3.11	1.35 – 7.13

Table 5. Determinants of non-use for rejecters at one month after the introduction

Factor	***β***	**SE**	***p***	**Odds ratio**	**CI for odds ratio**
Usefulness	-2.33	0.56	.000	0.10	0.03 – 0.29

3.2.2 *Reasons for non-use for rejecters*

The quantitative results are supported by the in-depth explanations of non-use given by the participants in the interviews. By far, the two main reasons why rejecters stopped using the robot were '*disenchantment*' and '*restrictions and problems*' (see table 6). Some participants noted that they just disliked some aspect of the technology, i.e., '*disenchantment*'. Most participants who rejected the robot for this reason indicated that the robot was all but fun to use or interact with: "*[The robot] is annoying.*" –male, 29, living with spouse. Other specifications for this reason indicated that the participants did not appreciate the autonomous, unaccountable actions of the robot: "*Often acts weird. Awake when I do not want it.*" –female, 25, living with spouse. This perception of the robot was why some participants had uninstalled all the autonomous settings on the robot. The second most noted reasons for rejection were encountering '*restrictions and problems*' for the use of the robot. There are many restrictions and problems people might encounter before adopting a technology. Participants denoted they did not have enough spare time, did not want to make the effort or indicated that it was too difficult to master how to use the robot: "*I have not had the time yet.*" –female, 37, living alone, and "*Too difficult.*" –female, age unknown, living with mature family.

Fewer noted reasons to reject the robot included '*lack of motivation*', '*need not satisfied*' and '*replaced by other device*'. Regarding '*lack of motivation*', some participants who completed the questionnaires were just part of the households in which other family members had signed up for the study: "*He [the robot] is standing in the living room, but I am not doing anything with it myself.*" –female, 21, living with mature family. A few participants felt that the robot could not satisfy a certain need, i.e., '*need not satisfied*' and assessed that (the use of) the robot was irrelevant, not good enough, or that there were better alternatives: "*I think it is a combination of software and hardware. If it was just the software, then my potential killer app could become available in the future... But the hardware is also mediocre, so he [the robot] does not provide any benefits.*" –male, 38, living with young family. A few other participants had replaced (applications of) the robot by other devices, i.e., '*replaced by other device*': "*He [the robot] cannot do much and what he can do my smartphone does as well, and more.*" –female, 29, living with spouse.

Table 6. Reasons for non-use for rejecters

Reason for non-use	Reported reason %	(*n*)
Disenchantment	37	(28)
End of novelty	2	(2)
Lack of motivation	10	(7)
Need not satisfied	10	(7)
Reliance on others	2	(2)
Replaced by other device	10	(7)
Restrictions and problems	29	(22)
Total	**100**	**(51)**

3.3 Discontinuers

In total, 32 participants stopped using the robot at two months or six months after the introduction and are therefore categorized as discontinuers.

3.3.1 Influential factors of non-use for discontinuers

Two binary logistic regression analyses (Are you still using the robot?; Yes= 0, No= 1) were performed to determine which factors explained why discontinuers had stopped their use of the robot at either two or six months after its introduction. Hence, discontinuers were compared to users only at this stage. A binary logistic regression analysis was performed for discontinuance two months after introduction. Unfortunately, the Hosmer and Lemeshow test showed a significant result ($\chi^2(7)$= 52.50, $p < .001$). This means that the acceptance factors included in this study could not explain why participants discontinued the use of the robot at two months after introduction compared to participants who continued their use of the robot after this point. Another binary logistic regression analysis was performed for discontinuance six months after introduction. The results of the residual Chi-square statistic (χ^2= 19.86, $p < .001$) suggested that the addition of one or more of the acceptance factors significantly affected the predictive power of the model (see table 7). Two steps were needed to realize the final model and showed that there was a negative effect for both adaptability (b= -0.76, p= .049) and sociability (b= -1.19, p= .041). When the participants evaluated the robot as less adaptable to their needs and less sociable, they were more likely to discontinue the use of the robot at six months after introduction compared to participants who intended to continue their use of the robot after completion of our study. This result is supported by the explanation from the participants stating that they would appreciate richer social interactions with the robot: "*I would have liked him better when he was more responsive, offered more interactions. I would have used him more often, because currently he does not initiate anything on his own.*" –female, 27, living with spouse; and "*He should at least be able to detect me in the room. That's the definition of company, more interaction. Currently it is just one-way communication.*" – male, 32, living alone.

Table 7. Determinants of non-use for discontinuers at six months after the introduction

Factor	β	SE	p	Odds ratio	CI for odds ratio
Adaptability	-0.76	0.39	.049	0.47	0.22 – 0.99
Sociability	-1.19	0.58	0.41	0.30	0.10 – 0.95

3.3.2 Reasons for non-use for discontinuers

Some similar findings can be drawn from the participants' in-depth justifications for non-use shared in the interviews. By far, the two most noted reasons for discontinuance were '*need not satisfied*' and '*replaced by other device*' (see table 8). Replacement occurs when something else, such as another technology, offers a better solution or provides more satisfaction in performing the same task or fulfilling the same need(s). Most participants indicated that other devices offered a better solution or provide more satisfaction in performing the same task or fulfilling the same need: "*If I want to listen to the radio I can easily turn on internet radio or just the regular radio in the living room.*" –female, 22, living in student dorm, and "*If I had just a desktop PC than I may have used it [the robot] more often. But my laptop is always on when I am at home.*" –female, 33, living alone. According to the discontinuers, the robot offered many functionalities that other devices in their homes, such as the television, radio or smart phone, also had to offer. And most participants indicated that they preferred using these devices instead off the robot. Other participants believed that the robot was unable to satisfy their needs, i.e., '*need not satisfied*'. Based on their assessment that the robot was: irrelevant, "*We heard what we had programmed... we did not use [the robot] actively... It was standing in the way and has no added value.*" –female, 26, living with young family; did not conform to expectations, "*I cannot do anything with [the robot]... I had expected to be able to do more things with it.*" –female, 57, living alone; or that there were better alternatives, "*I have him [the robot] switched off more often, because it has no benefits for me.*" –male, 30, living with spouse. It basically came down to the robot not being able to fully adapt to the users' needs.

Much less noted reasons to discontinue the use of the robot were '*restriction and problems*', '*end of novelty*', and '*disenchantment*'. Similar to some rejecters, the a few discontinuers also indicated that they encountered some barriers that restricted their ability to embrace the use of the robot. Some experienced difficulties understanding the robot by explaining that the speech function of the robot was not always optimal: "*More understandable speech function [would be an improvement]. In that way, you could actually comprehend the news and other stuff which would make it [the robot] interesting again.*" –male, 30, living with spouse. A few participants indicated that they believed the robot sometimes failed to connect to their wireless internet connection: "*She [the robot] cannot find the internet connection despite several attempts.*" –female, 77, living alone. Another given reason to discontinue the use of the robot was that the participants were done exploring the applications of the robot and could not find a useful purpose: "*It does not intrigue me as much as it did. [...] I liked it in the beginning to discover new stuff.*" –female, 24, living with mature family. When the newness was gone, there was nothing left to explore. Some other participants disliked aspects of the robot or did not enjoy the use of it. For example, some participants no longer liked the spoken phrases of the robot: "*I did not find it funny anymore what he [the robot] said... So I removed the plug.*" –female, 38, living with mature family.

Table 8. Reasons for non-use for discontinuers

	Reported reason	
Reason for non-use	**%**	***(n)***
Disenchantment	11	(6)
End of novelty	11	(6)
Lack of motivation	5	(2)
Need not satisfied	27	(14)
Reliance on others	2	(1)
Replaced by other device	27	(14)
Restrictions and problems	16	(8)
Total	**100**	**(75)**

4. GENERAL DISCUSSION

This study aimed at gaining insight into user motivations not to use a robot in their own homes. Providing understanding of those who are non-users along with their motivations for non-use could yield important insights for policy makers and suppliers of robots. Contrary to what was expected from previous research (e.g., [45], [49], [59]), the results of our long-term home study indicated that there were no demographic differences between the user groups. One very reasonable explanation for these results is the fact that the people who responded to the call for participation of our study might have been innovators or early adopters [45] who were already interested in using a robot in their own homes in the first place.

However, the user groups each provided their own unique reasons why they dropped out of the study or stopped their use of the robot. The most common reason why resisters dropped out of our study was the unavailability of the Dutch language on the robot. This result is similar to the findings of Selwyn [49] who has reported that resisters of computer technologies are more likely to experience some type of barrier (e.g., time, age, health) or a lack of knowledge, even though they had some degree of access at some point. This language barrier can easily be fixed by making interactions with the robot possible in the user's mother tongue. However, one can imagine that, when more sophisticated robot systems will become ubiquitous in society, the lack of other digital or 21st century skills may become a barrier of use. Similar findings emerge for digital media and the need for certain digital skills necessary to make optimal use of these digital media [9]. For example, ever since the emergence of the internet, users have continuously expressed disappointment and worries concerning information retrieval, navigating the web, and keeping their personal information secure [59]. The question remains whether particular skills may exist or are needed for the optimal use of robot technologies in the future. It is widely assumed in research on the digital divide that non-users are falling into existing and deep-rooted patterns of social and economic inequalities [10], [22], [48], [49], [58]. We believe that the impact of the consequences heavily depend on who will (mostly) benefit from the robot revolution, which has similarities to the digital revolution which took place and is still taking place online on the World Wide Web [9], [11], [17]. Therefore, future research should keep track of what types of 21st Century skills are necessary to make optimal use of robot technologies and how potential divides between users and non-users of these technologies may enhance or reduce prevailing societal inequalities.

The main reasons for rejecters to abandon the use of the robot was their evaluation of the robot as less enjoyable, too intelligent or autonomous, and less useful. A negative evaluation of robots that are deemed too intelligent or autonomous has been reported before in a cross-cultural study indicating that this is a universal preference for future robots [31]. This challenges the long-term goal in robotics to develop fully autonomous machines. Some people perceive robots as tools that should only perform tasks imposed by its owner. However, it also seems that people are still unfamiliar with intelligent and autonomous behavior of machines, which could indicate that familiarization may decrease people's aversion towards artificial intelligence. Discontinuers mainly stopped using the robot because they had expected more sociable behaviors from the robot, or because they had replaced (functionalities of) the robot with another device since the robot was unable to adapt to their needs for personalization. Although robot technology is rapidly enhancing, the added value of most robot systems is still inferior compared to other domestic devices already present in the home. Thus, the challenge for robot designers is to create robots that are enjoyable and easy to use or (socially) predictable to capture users in the short-term, and functionally-relevant and possess enhanced social behaviors to keep those users in the longer-term.

Since many robot users encounter an expectation gap during initial use periods [12], [13], [15], [35], one direction for future research on acceptance and non-use of robot technologies is to integrate the expectation-confirmation model [5] into the model of the theory of planned behavior [1]. According to the theory of planned behavior, the main determinant of a behavior is a behavioral intention, which in turn is determined by the belief structures of attitude, subjective norm, and perceived behavioral control. The expectancy-confirmation model does not assume a linear relation between initial adoption and continued use as do traditional models and theories (e.g., the technology acceptance model [8], and the diffusion of innovations theory [45]). According to the expectancy-confirmation model, people decide to continue to use a technology based on the level of satisfaction and confirmation of their prior expectations. These principles of expectations versus satisfaction may be valuable for the investigation of robot acceptance. Prior expectations have been found to not only affect the evaluation of the robot system after introduction [27], [41], but also often results in a gap between people's prior expectations of a robot and its actual performance after deployment [12], [13], [15], [35]. Including the evaluation of prior expectations and how those expectations affect the evaluation of robot acceptance in the long-term may provide additional insights into who will and will not accept robots in the future. This course of action may account for the expectation gap often reported in human-robot interaction studies, and may represent possible mutual shaping effects. In this manner, actual use behavior is reconnected to the preceding belief structures inherent to the theory of planned behavior. Together, the theory of planned behavior and the expectation-confirmation model may constitute a promising research direction for providing insights into the discontinuance of technology use.

Another point of discussion is a lack of definition of what duration of the study, or how many interactions, should be considered long-term? Some researchers argue that long-term starts when sustained use is achieved, which is after the novelty effect wears off and familiarization starts [32], [52]. However, there is reason to believe that the exact timeline for this process might differ between types of technologies. Whereas some studies report an end of the novelty effect around two months of use [13], [52], other results show that sustained use already started after four weeks of use [24]. Indeed, psychology research on a wide range of behavior changes indicates that people need approximately two months (i.e., 66 days on average) to establish a new behavior, but that there was a marked variation from 18 to 254 days depending on the type of behavior that needed to be established [28]. Thus, what is long-term may depend on the type of technology or the behavioral change under investigation, and is most likely related to the frequency and intensity of the (use) behavior. Therefore, caution is needed in defining long-term as a fixed time frame.

4.1 Implications

One of the most influential explanations of the societal acceptance of technologies can be found in the diffusion of innovations [50]. The diffusion of innovations theory, which was developed by Rogers [45], points to a recurring s-curve of the expansion of technology adoption in society, from the innovators and the early adopters to the early majority and late majority and eventually to those individuals characterized as laggards. This s-curve can be interpreted as a technologically deterministic perspective that asserts that the availability of a technology inevitably leads to use, which results in a somewhat negative positioning of non-users as an impediment to the saturation of a technology in society [50]. Simply defining non-users as not yet users (e.g., [45]), as 'have-nots' (e.g., [22]) or as 'information poor' (e.g., [56]), together with concerns that focus on turning non-users into users, only provides a narrow view on the spectrum of those who do not (want to) use technologies [48], [49]. Another shortcoming in today's research on technology acceptance lies in the definition of non-users. Defining non-use by asking people whether or not they use a certain technology at a certain point in time with a yes or no question is the most straightforward method of definition, used by [42], [61] among others. Some researchers argue for a more refined definition of non-use that distinguishes between degrees of non-use (e.g., [45], [48], [59]). However, the incoherence in the definition of non-use that is currently in favor [49], [55] results in a weak academic understanding of the non-use of technology. There is a need for the development of a more dynamic and nuanced conceptual framework to characterize users and non-users, which conceptualizes users along a continuum with degrees and types of involvement that may change depending on life changes [58]. Simply because a technology is available in the house does not imply that all people in that household will actually use it.

People who refuse or abandon the use of a technology in either passive or active and deliberate ways are contributing to the debates (re)shaping cultural interpretations of that technology just as much as those who eagerly embrace our innovations, albeit in different ways [48]. The present work is the first longitudinal study within the field of HRI to offer first insights into people's reasoning and motivation why they do not want to use or interact with a robot. As shown by the results of our longitudinal study, users and the different groups of non-users have their own unique reasons for either their acceptance [15] or refusal and abandonment (this paper) of robots in their own private spaces. Thus, non-users are just as important as users for the development of future robots and their acceptance within society.

Finally, consequences related to the use and non-use of robots in our future society should be further investigated. That said, it should be noted that the participants in our long-term home study were provided with robots without any attached cost. Therefore, the motivations of non-use provided by our participants somewhat differ from the motivations of 'actual' future users who will need to buy and employ robots themselves. Especially our sample of resisters consists of a biased sample, since a more representative group would have included all the people that have read the call for participation without applying for the study. Unfortunately, we did not have access to this group nor did we observe who all these people were. This makes it difficult to draw final conclusions on this perspective at this point of robot diffusion within society. When robots become more widespread in society, future research should include both users and non-users of robot technologies to investigate people's motivations to accept, reject or abandon the use of robots. Thus, remaining questions for robotics research are whether and how prevailing phenomenon regarding non-use and the digital divide will continue for robot technologies, and what types of individual motivations and societal consequences are related to the non-use of robot technologies in the future.

4.2 Limitations

For this study, employing 70 robots in people's own homes over a longer period of time, required us to depend on a commercially available robot. To date, research robots are still not robust enough to be studied outside the lab for extended periods of time without the supervision of an expert. Because commercially available robots still have limited capacities, this might cause a gap between initial expectations and actual experiences after initial interactions with the robot [35]. Our participants also encountered such a gap [15], which for some participants mainly influenced their decision to quit using the robot. Similar results were found by Fernaeus et al. [12], who also reported that, after an initial novelty effect, people stopped using the robot due to having high expectations which the robot did not fulfill. Robot designers should try to bridge this expectation gap by identifying the most important improvements that should be made [35]. The results presented in this paper may be used as guidelines from the perspective of non-users.

Another limitation is that, for this study, we used a zoomorphic robot which offered only very simplistic interactions. Different outcomes may be concluded from studies conducted that employ other types of robots, e.g., humanoids, that also offer a richer interaction modality. Therefore, replication of our study is needed with other types of robots and more sophisticated social behaviors to ascertain whether similar motivations occur to refuse or abandon the use of robots. Yet, people experience interactions with zoomorphic robots as more satisfying than interactions with humanoid robots, because people do not expect full responsiveness from animals [25]. Thus, until robot technology is able to mimic or simulate human behavior more realistically, a zoomorphic appearance may be more appropriate for robots in which their main purpose is to be social.

4.3 Conclusion

Investigating user motivations and reasons to refuse or abandon the use of a robot provide important insights for the design and acceptance of robots in our society. Our investigation on user experiences with robots in people's private spaces over a longer period of time have identified obstacles for acceptance, and this knowledge may enable designers to better adapt robot innovations that benefits users which can increase acceptance. The results of our long-term study showed that each group of non-users provided their own unique motivations and reasons for their resistance, rejection, or discontinuance of the use of the robot within their own homes. The challenge for robot designers is to create robots that are enjoyable and easy to use, to capture users in the short-term, and that are functionally-relevant to keep those users in the longer-term. Researchers should acknowledge these different groups of non-users, and that these non-users are just as important as users for the development of future robots because they can delay the acceptance and development process of new technologies, such as robots. Understanding the thoughts and motives behind non-use may identify obstacles for acceptance, and therefore enable developers to better adapt technological designs to the benefit of the users. In this way, both users and non-users play an important role in the shaping and reshaping of future technologies.

5. ACKNOWLEDGMENTS

We would like to thank Bertram Malle and Jamy Li for their valuable comments on an earlier version of our paper.

6. REFERENCES

[1] I. Ajzen, "The theory of planned behavior," Organizational Behavior and Human Decision Processes, 50 (1991), pp. 179-221.

[2] R. Agarwal, J. Prasad, "A conceptual and operational definition of personal innovativeness in the domain of information technology," Information Systems Research, 9 (1998), pp. 204-215.

[3] A. Bandura, "Self-efficacy: Toward a unified theory of behavioral change," Psychological Review, 84 (1977), pp. 191-215.

[4] C. Bartneck, D. Kulić, E. Croft, and S. Zoghbi, "Measurement instruments for the anthropomorphism, animacy, likeability, perceived intelligence, and perceived safety of robots," International Journal of Social Robotics, 1 (2009), pp. 71-81.

[5] A. Bhattacherjee, "Understanding information systems continuance: An expectation-confirmation model," MIS Quarterly, 25 (2001), pp. 351-370.

[6] F. Biocca, C. Harms, and J.K. Burgoon, "Toward a more robust theory and measure of social presence: Review and suggested criteria," Presence, 12 (2003), pp. 456-480.

[7] S.A. Brown, and V. Venkatesh, "Model of adoption of technology in households: A baseline model test and extension incorporating household life cycle", MIS Quarterly, 29 (2005), pp. 399-426.

[8] F.D. Davis, Perceived usefulness, perceived ease of use, and user acceptance of information technology," MIS Quarterly, 13 (1989), pp. 319-340.

[9] A.J.A.M. van Deursen, and J.A.G.M. van Dijk, "Internet skill levels increase, but gaps widen: A longitudinal cross-sectional analysis (2010–2013) among the Dutch population," Information, Communication & Society, 18 (2015), pp. 782-797.

[10] J.A.G.M. van Dijk, "Digital divide research: achievements and shortcomings", Poetics, 34 (2006), pp. 221-235.

[11] P. DiMaggio, E. Hargittai, W.R. Neuman, and J.P. Robinson, "Social implications of the internet," Annual Review of Sociology, 27 (2001), pp. 307-336.

[12] Y. Fernaeus, M. Håkansson, M. Jacobsson, and S. Ljungblad, 'How do you play with a robotic toy animal?: A Long-Term Study of Pleo.' International Conference on Interaction Design and Children. (Barcelona, Spain: New York, USA, 2010).

[13] J. Fink, V. Bauwens, F. Kaplan, and P. Dillenbourg, "Living with a vacuum cleaning robot: A 6-month ethnographic study," International Journal of Social Robotics, 5 (2013), pp. 389–408.

[14] M.M.A. de Graaf, and S. Ben Allouch, "Exploring influencing variables for the acceptance of social robots", Robotics and Autonomous Systems, 16 (2013), pp. 1476–1486.

[15] M.M.A. de Graaf, S. Ben Allouch, and J.A.G.M. van Dijk, "Long-term evaluation of a social robot in real homes", Accepted for publication in Interaction Studies Special Issue: New Frontiers in Human-Robot Interaction, 17 (2016), pp. 1-25.

[16] M.M.A. de Graaf, S. Ben Allouch, and J.A.G.M. van Dijk. "A Phased Framework for Long-Term User Acceptance of Socially Interactive Technologies in Domestic Environments", New Media & Society, (unpublished), pp. 1-33.

[17] E. Hargittai, "Social implications of the internet," Annual Review of Sociology, 1 (2001), pp. 307-336.

[18] P.A. Hancock, D.R. Billings, K.E. Schaefer, J.Y.C. Chen, E.J. de Visser, and R. Parasuraman, "A meta-analysis of factors affecting trust in human-robot interaction", The Journal of the Human Factors and Ergonomics, 53 (2011), pp. 517-527.

[19] A. Hansen, S. Cottle, R. Negrine, and C. Newbold, Media audiences: Focus group interviewing. In S. Cottle, R. Negrine, C. Newbold, and J.D. Halloran (Eds.). 'Mass Communication Research Methods'. London, UK: Macmillan (1998) pp. 257-287.

[20] M. Heerink, B. Kröse, V. Evers, and B. Wielinga, "Assessing acceptance of assistive social agent technology by older

adults: The Almere model", International Journal of Social Robotics, 2 (2010), pp. 361-375.

[21] S.R. Hiltz, and K. Johnson, "Measuring acceptance of computer-mediated communication systems," Journal of the American Society for Information Science, 40 (1989), pp. 386-397.

[22] J. Howland, "The 'digital divide': Are we becoming a world of technological 'haves' and 'have-nots'?", Electronic Library, 16 (1998), pp. 287-289.

[23] T. Kanda, R. Sato, N. Saiwaki, and H. Ishiguro, "A two-month field trial in an elementary school for long-term human–robot interaction," IEEE Transactions on Robotics, 23 (2007), pp. 962-971.

[24] E. Karapanos, J. Zimmermann, J. Forlizzi, and J.B. Martens, 'User 'experience over time: An initial framework'. International Conference on Human Factors in Computing Systems. (Boston, MA, USA, 2009).

[25] P.H. Kahn, B. Friedman, D.R. Perez-Granados, and N.G. Freier, "Robotic pets in the lives of preschool children", Interaction Studies, 7 (2006), pp. 405-436.

[26] E. Karahanna, and M. Limayem, "E-mail and V-mail usage: Generalizing across technologies", Journal of Organizational Computing and Electronic Commerce, 10 (2000), pp. 49-66.

[27] T. Komatsu, R., Kurosawa, and S. Yamada, "How does the difference between users' expectations and perceptions about a robotic agent affect their behavior?" International Journal of Social Robotics, 4 (2012), pp. 109-116.

[28] P. Lally, C.H.M. van Jaarsveld, H.W.W. Potts, and J. Wardle, "How are habits formed: Modelling habit formation in the real world," European Journal of Social Psychology, 40 (2009), pp. 998–1009.

[29] J.R. Landis, and G.G. Koch, "The measurement of observer agreement for categorical data", Biometrics, 33 (1977), pp. 159-174.

[30] R. LaRose, and M.S. Eastin, "A social cognitive theory of internet uses and gratifications: Toward a new model of media attendance", Journal of Broadcasting & Electronic Media, 48 (1994), pp. 358-377.

[31] H.R. Lee, and S. Sabanovic, 'Culturally variable preferences for robot design and use in Korea, Turkey, and the US'. International Conference on Human-Robot Interaction. (Bielefeld, Germany, 2014).

[32] I. Leite, C., Martinho, and A. Paiva, "Social robots for long-term interaction: A survey," International Journal of Social Robotics, 5 (2013), pp. 291-308.

[33] D. Li, P.L.P. Rau, and Y. Li, "A cross-cultural study: Effect of robot appearance and task", International Journal of Social Robotics, 2 (2010), pp. 175-186.

[34] M. Lie, and K.H. Sorensen, Making technologies our own?: Domesticating technology into everyday life, in M. Lie, and K.H. Sorensen, (Eds.). 'Making technologies our own?: Domesticating technology into everyday life'. Scandinavian University Press: Oslo, Norway (1996) pp. 1-30.

[35] M. Lohse, 'Bridging the gap between users' expectations and system evaluations', The International Symposium on Robot and Human Interactive Communication. (Atlanta, GA, USA, 2011).

[36] A. Majchrzak, R.E. Rice, A. Malhotra, N. King, and S. Ba, "Technology adaptation: The case of computer-supported inter-organizational virtual teams," MIS Quarterly, 24 (2000), pp. 569-600.

[37] J.C. McCroskey, and J.J. Teven, "Goodwill: A reexamination of the construct and its measurement", Communication Monographs, 66 (1999), pp. 90-103.

[38] J.W. Moon, and J.G. Kim, "Extending the TAM for a world-wide-web context", Information & Management, 38 (2001), pp. 217-230.

[39] G.C. Moore, and I. Benbasat, "Development of an instrument to measure the perceptions of adopting an information technology innovation," Information Systems Research, 2 (1991), pp. 192-222.

[40] T. Nomura, T. Kanda, T. Suzuki, and K. Kato, "Prediction of human behavior in human-robot interaction using psychological scales for anxiety and negative attitudes toward robots," IEEE transactions on robotics, 24 (2008), pp. 442-451.`

[41] S. Paepcke, and L. Takayama, "Judging a bot by its cover: An experiment on expectation setting for personal robots," International Conference on Human-Robot Interaction (Osaka, Japan, 2010).

[42] B. Phillips, and H. Zhao, "Predictors of assistive technology abandonment", Assistive Technology, 5 (1993), pp. 36-45.

[43] R.E. Rice, and N. Contractor, "Conceptual effects of office information systems: A methodology and application for the study of alpha, beta, and gamma change," Decision Sciences, 21 (1990), pp. 301-317.

[44] R.E. Rice, and E.M. Rogers, "Reinvention in the innovation process," Knowledge: Creation, diffusion, utilization, 1 (1980), pp. 499-514.

[45] E.M. Rogers, 'Diffusion of innovations (5th edition)'. New York, NY, USA: The Free Press (2003).

[46] R.B. Rubin, and M.M. Martin, "Development of a measure of interpersonal communication competence," Communication Research Reports, 11 (1994), pp. 33-44.

[47] S. Šabanović, "Robots in Society, Society in Robots", International Journal of Social Robotics, 2 (2010), pp. 439-450.

[48] S. Satchell, and P. Dourish, 'Beyond the user: use and non-use in HCI'. The Annual Conference of the Australian Computer-Human Interaction (Melbourne, Australia, 2009).

[49] N. Selwyn, "Digital division or digital decision? A study of non-users and low-users of computers", Poetics, 34 (2006), pp. 273-292.

[50] N. Selwyn, "Apart from technology: understanding people's non-use of information and communication technologies in everyday life", Technology in Society, 25 (2003), pp. 99-116.

[51] R. Silverstone, E. Hirsch, and D. Morley, Information and communication technologies and moral economy of the household. In R. Silverstone, and E. Hirsch (Eds.). 'Consuming technologies: Media and information in domestic spaces'. London, UK: Routledge and Kegan Paul (1992) pp. 15-31.

[52] J.Y. Sung, R.E. Grinter, and H.I. Christensen, "Domestic robot ecology: An initial framework to unpack long-term

acceptance of robots at home," International Journal of Social Robotics, 2 (2010), pp. 417-429.

[53] S. Taylor, and P.A. Todd, Understanding information technology usage: A test of competing models," Information Systems Research, 6 (1995), pp. 144-176.

[54] V. Venkatesh, and F.D. Davis, "A theoretical extension of the technology acceptance model: Four longitudinal field studies", Management Science, 46 (2000), pp. 186-204.

[55] R. Wessels, B. Dijcks, M. Soede, G.J. Gelderblom, and L. de Witte, "Non-use of provided assistive technology devices, a literature overview", Technology and Disability, 15 (2003), pp. 231-238.

[56] A. Wilson, "The information rich and the information poor", Journal of Information Management, 39 (1986), pp. 1-6.

[57] S. Wyatt. 'Bringing users and non-users into being across methods and disciplines'. (2007) Retrieved from: http://nonuse.jedbrubaker.com/wp-content/uploads/2014/03/Wyatt_Toronto_April_2014.pdf

[58] S. Wyatt, F. Henwood, A. Hart, and J. Smith, "The digital divide, health information and everyday life", New Media & Society, 7 (2005), pp. 199-218.

[59] S. Wyatt, G. Thomas, and T. Terranova, They came, they surfed, they went back to the beach: Conceptualising use and non-use of the Internet. In S. Woolgar (Ed.). 'Virtual Society? Technology, Cyberbole, Reality'. Oxford, UK: Oxford University Press, (2002) pp. 23-40.

[60] J.E. Young, R. Hawkins, E., Sharlin, and T. Igarashi, "Towards acceptable domestic robots: Applying insights from social psychology", International Journal of Social Robotics, 1 (2009), pp. 95-108.

[61] A. Venkatesh S.A. Brown S.A., "A longitudinal investigation of personal computers in homes: adoption determinants and emerging challenges," MIS Quarterly, 25 (2001), 71-102.

[62] V. Venkatesh, and F.D. Davis, "A theoretical extension of the technology acceptance model: Four longitudinal field studies," Management Science, 46 (2000), pp. 186-204.

Marionette: Enabling On-Road Wizard-of-Oz Autonomous Driving Studies

Peter Wang, Srinath Sibi, Brian Mok, & Wendy Ju
Center for Design Research
Stanford University
{ xywang, ssibi, brianmok, wendyju }@stanford.edu

ABSTRACT

There is a growing need to study the interactions between drivers and their increasingly autonomous vehicles. This paper describes a method of using a low-cost, portable, and versatile driver interaction system in commercial passenger vehicles to enable on-road partial and fully autonomous driving interaction studies. By conducting on-road Wizard-of-Oz studies in naturalistic settings, we can explore a range of driving conditions and scenarios far beyond what can be conducted in laboratory simulator environments.

The Marionette system uses off-the-shelf components to create bidirectional communication between the driving controls of a Wizard-of-Oz vehicle operator and a driving study participant. It signals to the study participant what the car is doing and enables researchers to study participant intervention in driving activity. Marionette is designed to be easily replicated for researchers studying partially autonomous driving interaction. This paper describes the design and evaluation of this system.

CCS Concepts

•**Human-centered computing → HCI design and evaluation methods;** *Field studies;*

Keywords

Autonomous Vehicle Interfaces; Methodology; On-Road simulation; Marionette; Steering Wheel;

1. INTRODUCTION

Recent years have seen a series of rapid advances in the field of autonomous driving. [1, 26, 37] The National Highway Traffic Safety Administration (NHTSA) classifies the automated driving systems in cars into five levels: Level 0 (No automation), Level 1 (Function specific automation), Level 2 (Combined function automation), Level 3 (Limited self-driving automation), to Level 4 (Fully autonomous cars). [23] We are already seeing some cars with Level 2 automation functionality on the market. [22] Despite recent advances in autonomous driving technology, the interaction between drivers and their partial autonomous vehicles is still poorly understood. Many of the key challenges to automation lie in the area of human-machine interaction. [20] While some in the autonomous vehicle community have argued that partial automation is dangerous and can be by-passed with full automation [7], those in the human-robot interaction community recognize that these questions represent an early and high-profile case of interaction with automation, which, in any situation with people present, in or around the vehicle, cannot be resolved simply with more automation. [10, 11]

HRI '17, March 06-09, 2017, Vienna, Austria

DOI: **http://dx.doi.org/10.1145/2909824.3020256**

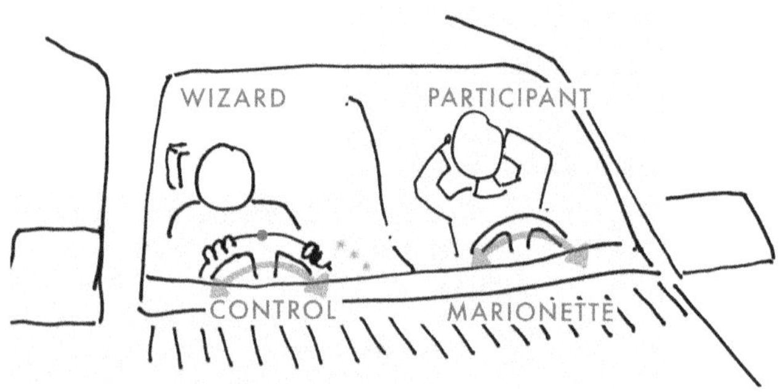

Figure 1: The Marionette Interface is asymmetrically coupled to the vehicle control to enable on-road simulation of partial automation

To ensure the safe operation and improve the design of Level 2 and Level 3 partial autonomous vehicles, more widespread design and testing of driver-vehicle interaction is necessary. We believe that low-cost research platforms that enable on-road testing of driver vehicle interactions without the need for an actual autonomous car can enable more researchers to test and develop more novel interfaces and interaction patterns for autonomous vehicles.

Marionette is a low-cost and easy-to-replicate simulated autonomous driving interface system for on-road studies. Marionette combines a Wizard-of-Oz (WOZ) protocol, a false steering wheel and driving pedal interface for study participants, and an instrumented steering wheel and display for the driving wizard to enable testing of automated driving interaction with human participants on real roads. This system was designed using inexpensive and easily accessible parts to increase the numbers of interaction researchers that can employ this system to perform a variety of autonomous vehicle interaction studies.

2. RELATED WORK

Marionette builds off of existing protocols for on-road simulation of autonomous driving [3] to enable better simulation of partial automation driving scenarios. However, this previous protocol can only simulate Level 4 autonomous vehicles due to the lack of a driver-vehicle interface. To simulate partial automation of Level 2 and 3 vehicles, we must provide a convincing simulation for the study participant to "override," or conduct a manual take-over of the simulated autonomous vehicle. The control system for our research platform must resemble the control systems of real autonomous driving vehicles from an interaction perspective.

2.1 Actual Autonomous Control

The predominant interaction paradigm for actual autonomous vehicles in the commercial and research sectors involves physical control of the steering wheel in front of the human driver by an autonomous driving system. [16, 2, 19, 4] In other words, an electric servo is integrated into the steering system in a way that allows a computer system to physically move the steering wheel during autonomous operation. The acceleration and braking of the autonomous vehicle system, in contrast, is typically decoupled from the physical acceleration and braking pedals, although any physical input to the acceleration and braking pedals would initiate the "override" of autonomous operation by the driver. Thus, any system attempting to emulate automation must be able to not only control the steering, acceleration, and braking in normal conditions, but also be receptive to manual "overrides." This presents several design challenges with respect to how to safely "override" the operation of the Wizard-of-Oz vehicle operator. The Marionette system described in this paper is the first to enable on-road Wizard-of-Oz studies for semi-autonomous and fully autonomous driver-vehicle interactions without permanent modification of the test vehicle.

2.2 Laboratory Simulation of Automation

Current driver interaction studies are primarily conducted through laboratory-based driving simulators. Such simulators have been shown to predict driver on-road performance [5] using distraction tasks [29] comparing cognitively impaired and healthy adults [12] and using informational interfaces [38]. However, it is still unclear how driving performance will correlate between in-simulation and on-road environments with automated vehicle interfaces when participants need to contend with real-world environmental variables and new maneuvers such as control-takeovers [14]. This is a concern, because, as John D. Lee and Bobbie D. Seppelt note, *"Developing automation without consideration of the human operator leads to new and more catastrophic failures."* [21]

2.3 On-road Simulation of Automation

On-road testing of driving behavior with participants is less common than laboratory simulation testing because of the inherent risks, but still, it is a critical component of the design and validation of vehicle interfaces and behaviors. [5] By running similar studies in the lab and on-the-road, we are able to determine the relative validity of simulator testing. [13, 18] In addition, on-road testing can take place in carefully controlled experiments; the alternative of allowing interfaces and interactions that have not been properly tested with real human drivers on the road is more dangerous.

While functioning autonomous and semi-autonomous vehicles are being tested on public roadways [9], it is desirable from a safety and legal perspective to decouple the research of driver-vehicle interaction behaviors from the development of the still-experimental autonomous driving system itself. "Wizard in the loop" experimental setups allow participants and experimenters more possible test scenarios than is permitted in actual functioning systems.[15, 8] Ghost Driver, developed by Rothenbucher et al., used a Wizard-of-Oz setup in order to study pedestrian-vehicle interaction with simulated autonomous driving cars. [31] The Wizard on Wheels system developed by Schmidt et al. at Volkswagen Germany enabled a wider range of automation, from manual control to complete automatic control, but required a specially modified vehicle which allowed a second driver hidden in the load compartment to take over parts of the driving task. This setup would be particularly difficult to replicate due to highly specialized vehicle setup as well as legal barriers for on-road studies due to the heavily modified nature of the experimental car. [34]

The RRADS system developed by Baltodano et al. was the first to explore autonomous driver-vehicle interaction using commercially available cars on public roads through Wizard-of-Oz methods. [3] However, in that system, study participants were not able to drive or take over control of the vehicle from the wizard operator. Thus, the RRADS protocol could only simulate fully autonomous vehicles due to the lack of a functional input interface that can facilitate communication between the participant and the Wizard operator. Despite the limitations of the RRADS platform, 25 percent of the participants thought that the car was actually driven by an autonomous system during the post-experimental interview. [3]

2.4 Wizard-of-Oz Simulation of Automation

Within the HRI community, there has long been skepticism about the use of Wizard of Oz testing. Researchers have expressed concerns about the validity of such studies [39], the use of deception [30], and the inability of solutions developed using Wizard of Oz to scale to actual robot implementations [6].

We feel, however, the need for real data and to test designs of autonomous vehicle interactions outweighs the issues posed by these study limitations. The risks and liabilities of using experimental autonomous vehicles on the road for human participants [28] outweigh the negatives of using Wizard of Oz to simulate automation for on-road studies. In fact, the use of non-employee study participants in autonomous vehicle studies is illegal on public roads in California. [36] If studies are to be done to understand how everyday drivers will respond to different interaction schemes or alerts in real-road settings while always maintaining vehicle control under a human operator, a Wizard-of-Oz protocol is required.

Within laboratory driving simulators, the development of coupled driving controllers has allowed Wizards to simulate automated steering behavior. Schieben et al. developed the "theater-system technique" to allow agile design and testing of interaction with highly automated vehicles. Participants used a pair of mechanically coupled steering wheels and pedals to drive a simulated vehicle. [33] Johns et al. used a similar coupled driving-control system to explore haptic communication from the automated driving system to the driver through the steering wheel. [17]

In these systems, the simulation environment can be used to mediate the respective control and feedback exerted on the Wizard and participant driving interfaces. However, as these experiments are conducted in a virtual simulation setting, there are no requirements on the part of the Wizard operator to maintain physical safety for the study participant. A system designed for on-road interaction studies, in contrast, must include provisions to protect participant drivers from harm. Any "override" action must be voluntarily executed by the Wizard when safe on-road condition permits these maneuvers. To our knowledge, no such system exists for public road simulation of automation.

3. DESIGN RATIONALE

To understand how drivers will behave in future autonomous driving scenarios in a wide variety of real world conditions, we created a Wizard-of-Oz on-road study protocol that can give study participants the experience of driving an autonomous car.

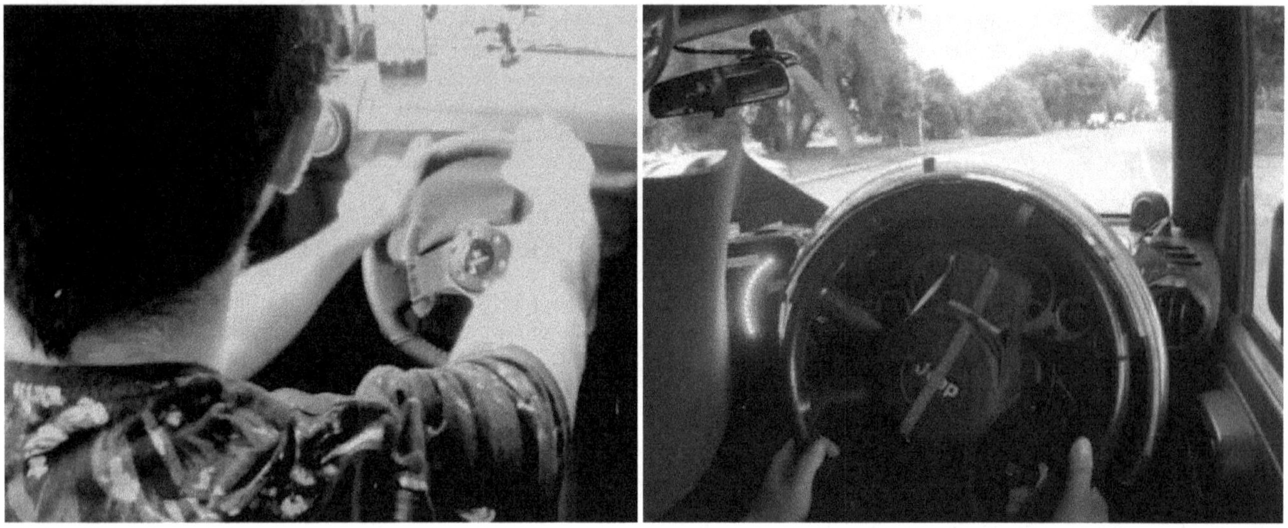

Figure 2: The Marionette Interface *(left)*: The Marionette Interface features a haptic steering wheel and a three-pedal interface for clutch, brake and throttle (not shown), The Control Interface *(right)*: The red light on the ring shows the Wizard where the participant has turned the wheel to, and the green light shows that the participant is stepping on the throttle.

3.1 Research Design Goals

For research purposes, we need participants to experience a simulation of autonomous driving. Generally, we need to be able to mirror the steering being performed on the actual steering wheel on a false steering wheel. To stage partial automation (Level 2 or Level 3) research scenarios, we need the study participants to be able to perform "override" or "manual takeover" of steering. Of course, due to safety and legal concerns of developing and executing on-the-road studies, this interface cannot actually interfere with the human driving wizard's operation of the vehicle.

Because we are interested in having a larger number of people – in particular, outside of the automotive industry – developing and experimenting with appropriate interfaces for autonomous vehicles, the replicability and ease of adoption of this system was important.

3.2 Legal and Safety Design Constraints

For our studies, we are legally required to have a licensed, trained human driver actually operating the car; all inputs and suggestions about steering, braking need to be mediated by the driver.[1] The driver needs to have an unobstructed views of the side windows, as well as of the side mirrors, and rear view mirrors.

We also have the Wizard driver test drive the vehicle several times in a closed-course environment, such as an empty parking lot, to get used to the set up, and then, when possible, have them practice the on-road course several times with experimenters as participants prior to using the system with actual study participants.

3.3 System Overview

To meet both the legal and research objectives, we devised a novel system that transmits steering wheel motion from the real steering wheel to the simulated wheel but decouples control. It signals the intended control maneuvers (steering, acceleration and braking) from the participant "driver" to the Wizard operator, who can choose to execute them if these actions will be safe. For the purposes of testing possible scenarios and prototyping possible interactions in various situations, we do not need to deceive participants, as is sometimes done in Wizard-of-Oz experiments [30], but for purposes of face and ecological validity, we need to maintain suspension of disbelief. [32]

This project utilizes parts that are inexpensive, easy to obtain, easy to assemble, and also easy to remove. We used a portable driving game controller with force feedback functionality, an external steering wheel sensor that detects position and movement of the actual steering wheel, a set of LEDs for driver communication. We built a software backbone for the project that controls and coordinates the information streams from each of the separate components. This study set-up should be simple for anyone to set up in a normal on-road passenger vehicle.

3.4 Operations Safety Testing

To make sure that the system we developed was safe to operate, we extensively test piloted the system on non-public roads using a designated Wizard driver. We made sure that the Wizard driver could easily see and react to signals from the study participant if that person turned the steering wheel or depressed the brake or throttle. However, we also made sure that the system and protocol was not so distracting that the Wizard felt they could not focus on the current driving situations taking place immediately outside the vehicle.

The Wizard operator in the Marionette system is hidden through a similar setup as the RRADS platform developed by Baltanado et al. [3]. A barrier was placed between the driver and the participant. This blocked the participant from seeing or interacting with the Wizard operator, and helped the participant to more easily maintain suspension of disbelief for the duration of the study. However, to accommodate the legal requirement that the driver must be able to see out of the side window, cutouts are placed in the barrier. The participant seat was pushed further back into the vehicle in order to accommodate the extra space needed by the Marionette Wheel. We situated the barrier so that the participant never sees the Wizard operator during the course of the driving experiment.

For our own research experiments, to facilitate the best simulated driving experience, we use a right-handed driving vehicle so that the participants can sit on the left seat. In our context, this is the normal seat drivers sit in during their normal daily drives. (The system was also tested and demonstrated in a traditional left-hand driving vehicle.) While sitting on what is the traditional driver's side

[1]California VEHICLE CODE SECTION 26700-26712

of the car does help to bolster the sense of realism in the on-road simulation, we hav found that partcipants are as responsive when the steering wheel is set up in the passenger seat. This flexibility allows researchers with non-specialized equipment to run interaction experiments in different countries.

4. IMPLEMENTATION

The Marionette prototype system consists of four hardware subcomponents: a game steering controller and pedals for the study participant ("The Marionette Interface"), an inertial-measurement sensor with an embedded controller for the driving wizard ("The Control Interface"), an LED display controlled by an embedded microcontroller to signal study participant actions to the driving wizard ("The Control Display"), and a central computer that mediates communications between the other parts. Each component is linked to the laptop computer through a USB hub. (See figure 4 The software component of the system running on the laptop is written in Node.js.

4.1 Marionette Interface

For the Marionette interface, we used the Logitech G-27 gaming wheel system, which has haptic capabilities that allowed us to steer the system without the participant's input during the autonomous portions of our study, and pedals that allow the participants to "accelerate" or "brake" during experiments.

4.2 Force-Feedback Steering Wheel

The Logitech G-27 racing wheel system was chosen as the force-feedback steering wheel. The device provides a good combination of price, functionality, and form-factor. The steering wheel is capable of up to 3.0Nm of force-feedback over 900 degrees of rotation. This matches up with the typical steering limitations of commercial passenger vehicles. [27] The steering wheel also comes in a package with a pedal assembly and a shifter assembly. The pedal system allows us to register participant "over-ride" to the acceleration and braking system, while the shifter assembly can function as a convenient remote for communication with the controller program in order to initiate a set program or change wheel functionalities. As a demonstration, we used the shifter assembly to remotely trigger a custom routine on the steering wheel as well as change the friction setting for the steering wheel.

The G-27 supports a variety of force and movement settings. This allows our system to not only mimic the real wheel operation over a variety of turning speeds, but it also allows us to dampen movements through feedback control and friction settings from the controlling computer.

The G-27 comes in a convenient size that fits inside the glove-box compartment of most cars. For our testing, we mounted the G-27 in the glove-box of the car and built a custom shell to conceal the glove-box behind a false dashboard.

4.3 The Control Interface

For the control interface used by the driving wizard, we used an Adafruit 10-DOF IMU Breakout - L3GD20H + LSM303 + BMP180 inertial measurement unit attached to an Arduino Atmega 32U4 Micro microcontroller. The IMU sensor was physically mounted together with the Arduino board to the top of the real steering wheel of the vehicle in a detachable box as seen in Figure 2.

The Arduino was loaded with a modified version of the Adafruit Simple AHRS library in order to integrate the IMU data into 3-dimensional Euler angles (pitch, roll, and yaw). The roll data was then extracted and sent over USB via serial communication to the Node program running on the controlling computer. The roll data

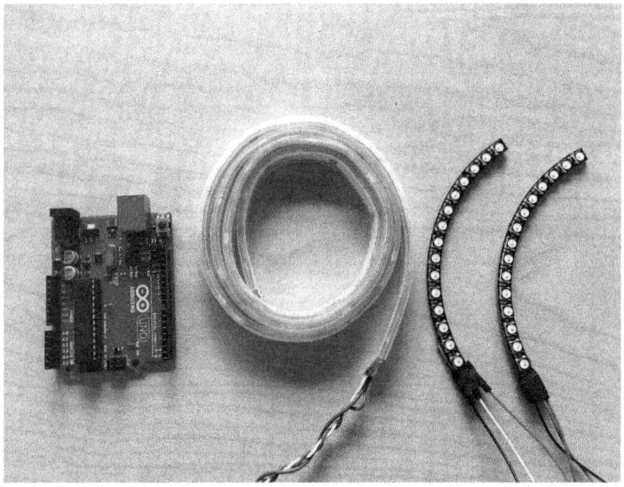

Figure 3: The Control Display Components. The Arduino Uno is shown on the left, the steering LED is shown on in the middle, and the acceleration and braking LEDs are shown on the right

contains only absolute angle data from -180 to 180 degrees, thus, by itself, it cannot track multiple wheel turns. However, because we wanted to maximize the frame-rate of the sensor reading on Arduinos with slower clock-speeds, the processing of the roll positional data into wheel turns occurs on the laptop computer in order to minimize calculation operations on the Arduino.

4.4 The Control Display

The LED display system comes in three main components as seen in Figure 3. All three LEDs are controlled through the use of a single Arduino. Firmata [35] was loaded onto the Arduino in order to facilitate the direct control of the LEDs from Node.js on the controlling computer. We used RGBW LEDs for all three displays, though single color LEDs would be sufficient for the acceleration and braking indicating LEDs. The acceleration and braking LEDs were linearly controlled by the acceleration and braking pedals of the Logitech G-27 wheel. A 50% depression on the braking pedal would light up half of the LED pixels on the braking LED string.

For the steering wheel LED, a different system of control was utilized. The LEDs were calibrated so that the lit pixel(s) corresponded to the position of the G-27 steering wheel. When the G-27 wheel travels within 5 degrees of the real wheel, the lit pixel will turn green. Thus, during free operation, the LED will follow the G-27 steering wheel and turn green when the real steering wheel matches the rotational position of the G-27 steering wheel. When the participant "overrides" the G-27 steering wheel and displaces the steering wheel from its target position, the LED will turn red and follow the operation of the G-27 wheel. The Wizard-of-Oz operator would then be able to "follow" the operation of the G-27 steering wheel if they choose.

4.4.1 *Marionette Software Controller*

The Marionette Software core of the system is built on Node.js. Node.js was chosen due to its cross-platform portability as a software runtime environment, its versatility as a language that allows for event-driven asynchronous I/O, as well as the abundance of open-source software support for Arduino and other hardware maintained by a very active community. Node combines the portability and event-driven programming capabilities of JavaScript with the full functionality of a general purpose programming/scripting language.

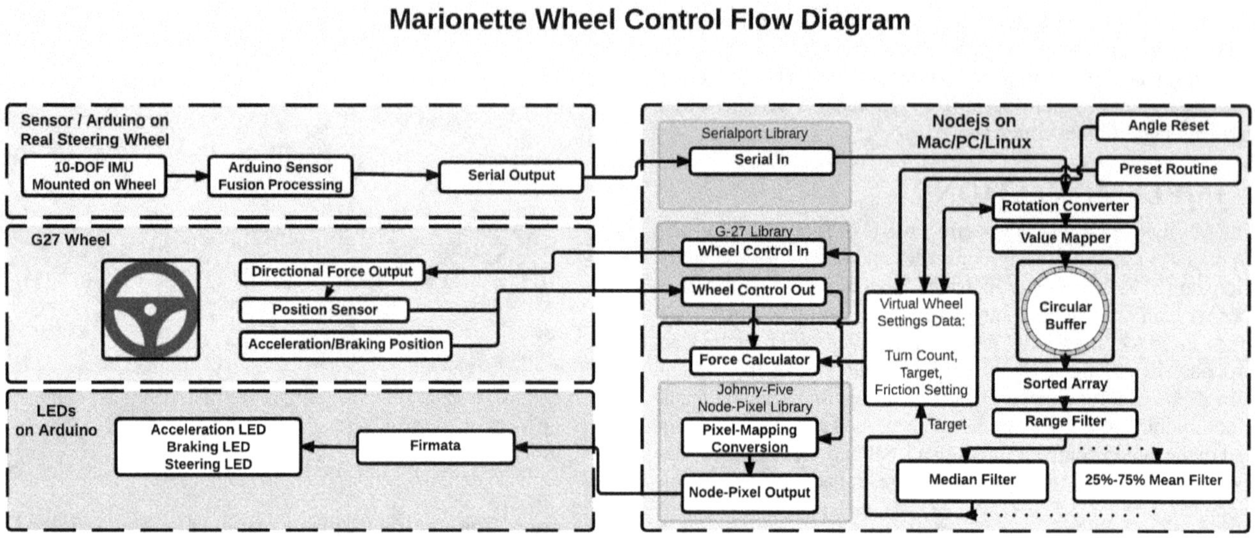

Figure 4: The Control Flow Diagram of the Marionette Software Controller. It outlines the information flow between the wheel positional sensor, the G27 gaming wheel system, the Node.js controller, and the LED display systems

The Node.js program for this system can be generally broken down into three main components: IMU interpretation, wheel control, and LED control.

4.4.2 *Software Controller IMU Interpretation*

The communication from the steering wheel position sensor is conducted by serial communication over USB. The Arduino based IMU constantly writes its roll position to serial, and that number is received by the Marionette Software Controller. The software keeps track of wheel turns based on previous rotational data. This output data is queued into a circular buffer.

Normal road conditions as well as innate vibration from the car induces a certain amount of noise to the IMU data. Therefore, two software filters are needed to reduce the noise and optimize the performance of our system. The first filter is a range filter which suspends data going to the G-27 when the buffer range exceeds a cutoff threshold. The second filter is a median filter that extracts the moving median value of the buffer. The filtered value then becomes the new target for the G-27 wheel. Due to the high frame-rate of data output from the Arduino, the delay caused by a running median filter in IMU data acquisition to G-27 target output is less than 100ms.

An additional rolling average filter was tested, but it did not perform as well as the median filter under vibrational noise.

4.4.3 *G-27 Control from Marionette Software Controller*

The Logitech G-27 was controlled through Node.js through a series of force feedback and event-driven functions. The basic functionality of G-27 wheel utilizes the open-sourced Logitech-g27 node library. The library enables friction and force control, event-based callbacks, as well as I/O functionality between the Marionette Software Controller and the G-27 wheel.

Position of the wheel was acquired through an event-callback while the steering target was adjusted by the processed IMU signal. A modified proportional control was used to adjust the force feedback of the G-27 wheel in order to use the built-in force feedback servo to drive the wheel to the desired angular position.

A producer-consumer model was used in order to coordinate the processed IMU data in conjunction with the asynchronous data from the wheel movement event-callbacks. Due to the friction settings on the wheel, a simple proportional control achieves sufficient smooth operation of the G-27 wheel. The friction setting on the G-27 wheel functions analogous to a damper. A functionality to adjust the friction setting through the shifter assembly buttons was built into Marionette Software Controller in order to enable friction setting changes during the experimentation.

The wheel position acquired through event-callbacks is also used to control the LED string around the real wheel in front of the Wizard-of-Oz vehicle operator. The values are mapped and calibrated so that the lit LED will correspond to the wheel position of the G-27 wheel. The color of the LED is dictated by the distance between the processed IMU sensor data, with the G-27 wheel position. If the difference between the two crosses a small error threshold, the LED turns red. This would indicate to the Wizard-of-Oz operator that there was a manual "over-ride" action from the participant.

The acceleration and brake pedals data is also acquired through event-based callbacks. The pedal data is then mapped linearly to the length of the acceleration and braking LEDs in order to facilitate the LED control.

5. EXAMPLE SCENARIOS

Marionette was designed to facilitate a wide variety of human interaction research. Here we present two possible use cases for our system.

5.1 Deviant Driving

The first use-case involves an on-road experimental analysis of how participants react to driving deviations. The experiment is modeled after a simulator based experiment on how drivers of partially autonomous vehicles would take control of the vehicle after deviant driving. [24] The initial setup of the scenario closely follows the protocol used in RRADS. [3] The participants were guided to the car in a manner that does not expose the Wizard Operator. Then the participant is given the instruction that they will be driving in a simulated autonomous driving system with capabilities similar to a Level 3 autonomous driving vehicle. They are also prompted on how they can take over at any time when they feel like the car is losing control or operating in an abnormal manner.

The car is then driven by the Wizard on a predetermined route. The Wizard then either drives in a normal controlled manner, or executes a series of legal but suboptimal driving maneuvers. For instance, the car might slowly drift from one side to the other within the lane. If the participant retakes control of the vehicle by "over-riding" the steering input, the Wizard operator will then stop the maneuvers and resume normal driving. Following the experiment, the participants were then interviewed, and the video footage of the drive undergoes further analysis.

This experimental setup showcases the potential for the Marionette wheel to facilitate driver behavioral studies with non-standard autonomous driving experiences as well as specific sets of maneuvering scenarios designed by the researcher.

5.2 Takeovers from Autonomous Driving

Another use-case involves the experimental analysis of how drivers can handle take-overs. The experiment is modeled after a simulator based experiment on how fast drivers can take control of the vehicle after a sudden emergency loss of automation as described in the paper by Mok et al. [25] Similar to the previous use-case, the experiment is initialized following the RRADS protocol which hides the Wizard operator from the participant. The participant is then given the same instruction that they will be driving in a simulated autonomous driving system with capabilities similar to a Level 3 autonomous driving vehicle, and again prompted that they can take over at any time.

The car is then driven by the Wizard on a predetermined route. Towards the end of the route, the Wizard will approach a round-about and trigger an auditory warning few seconds before the round-about that the automation has been turned off. The Wizard then proceeds in a circle around that round-about until the participant regains control by "over-riding" the steering wheel and turning off to the correct exit. After the exit maneuver is successful, an audio will prompt the participant that the automation has resumed and the Wizard will resume normal "autonomous driving" until the experiment is completed. The participant is then interviewed and the captured footage analyzed.

This experimental setup would showcase how this platform can be used to study various control hand-off scenarios. Depending on the specifics of the experiment, this setup can test driver hand-off behaviors ranging from distracted participants, to various audio and visual warnings for automation shutoff.

6. EVALUATION

6.1 Participants

Since the device was developed for adoption by automotive interaction researchers, we evaluated the system with automotive interaction design researchers, and asked them for their subjective feedback.

6.1.1 Population

We conducted an 8 person proof-of-concept evaluation. The participants were recruited from a workshop of HCI researchers interested in automotive interactions. Participants ranged from 25-50 years of age; there was one female participant and the rest were males. The structure of the evaluation was chosen to understand the system in a human factors experiment setting.

Figure 5: The right-hand drive Jeep was used to test the Marionette system.

6.1.2 Consent

Although this was not a full controlled experiment, but rather a proof-of-concept validation, participants signed a standard on-road study consent form, which indicates that a licensed human driver is operating the vehicle at all times, and that they can ask to stop the study at any time for any reason. The operator driving the car was visually isolated from the operator of the Marionette wheel using a partition. The same consent form also allowed participants to indicate their willingness to be videotaped.

The consent form indicated to participants that there were risks associated with the study as it takes place on the road where accidents can occur.

6.2 Wizard Training and Instructions

Prior to wizard training, a predetermined looped route was mapped out by GPS and programmed into the GPS guidance system. The vehicle was operated by a Wizard operator with experience driving the research vehicle. The Wizard practiced driving specifically with the Marionette system for two hours on a predetermined route in the days prior to the participant evaluation. The Wizard operator was instructed to use the inputs from the Marionette interface (displayed through the Control Display throttle and brake and steering wheel angle LED strips) as as a guide for driving action when it was safe to perform the indicated maneuvers. The Wizard operator was also instructed to obey all rules of the road and maintain safe driving conditions at all times. They were also instructed to drive the vehicle similar to their impression of how an autonomous vehicle would behave. For the duration of the study, the same wizard-of-oz operator performed the study in order to maintain consistency of driving styles.

6.3 Protocol

The evaluation was conducted with a Wizard operator and a study participant in a right-hand drive Jeep equipped with the Marionette system. In this evaluation, the study participants were aware such that a Wizard was driving the vehicle. The airbag on the passenger-side of the Jeep was disabled for safety.

6.3.1 Study Conditions

Traffic conditions were light to moderate with cyclists, pedestrians and a variety of traffic control mechanisms such as two and four way stop signs and roundabouts. For the entire study, the experimenter in the rear passenger seat to monitor for any interesting behavior from the participant, but otherwise, was instructed to not interact with the passenger.

6.3.2 *Pre-study Interview*

Prior to the study, we conducted a verbal pre-study interview, and recorded their gender, height or age. We asked if they were experiencing any leg or shoulder pain, which might interfere with their ability to intervene during the study. We make sure that they were licensed and had driving experience. We asked about their personal driving style preferences, and whether they tended to provide input when other people drive. We also asked about their simulator and autonomous driving experience. The interviews ranged from 7 to 13 minutes in duration.

6.3.3 *In-vehicle experiment*

Participants were first escorted to the car by a study experimenter. They were given the instructions as well as the driving route outlined on a smart phone device mounted on the dash. After participant signals that they are comfortable in the seat, they were then instructed to use the wheel to steer the car and rev the engine while the car is parked. The participant actions would be immediately relayed to the Wizard through the Marionette system and the Wizard responds by following the participant's command. This step was created to establish a cognitive association that the controls influence the cars actions, as well as functioning to make the participant comfortable in taking over the vehicle controls.

After the participant runs through the pre-drive routine, the experimenter moves to the back seat and initiates the study by playing a pre-recorded audio signaling the initiation of the automation system as well as the trip. The Wizard then initiates the drive. The participants were driven through a pre-determined course on the Stanford campus, corresponding to the map of the course shown on the smart phone. To help set participant expectations that the autonomous driving was imperfect, the Wizard deliberately drove right of center within the lane early in the drive.

After approximately 15 minutes of driving, when the vehicle approaches a round-about, a pre-recorded audio clip stated "Warning, automation failure, please take control" 2 seconds prior to entering the round-about. This would simulate a emergency control hand-off from the autonomous vehicle to the participant in a NHTSA Level 2 autonomous vehicle. If the driver did not take over control, the car would continue to drive in circles around the traffic circle. If the driver intervened, the Wizard would imitate their steering, acceleration and braking actions, given the constraint of road safety, until the vehicle was out of the circle, and then a pre-recorded audio clip would state,"Automation resumed" There-after, the Wizard resume normal control of the vehicle.

After 20 to 25 minutes of driving, the car will return to the starting point of the loop, and the participant was guided by the experimenter, who then leaves the rear seat of the car, and escorts the passenger back to the building. The escort path ensures that the passenger does not see the Wizard-of-Oz operator in the process of leaving the vehicle.

6.3.4 *Post-study interview*

A separate experimenter proceeds to conduct a post-driving interview in order to collect the participant thoughts on the overall drive. Participants are asked to recollect the drive and evaluate the experience at different portions of the drive. We also ask whether they trust the vehicle, and if there was anything unexpected or surprising about the experience.

6.4 Results

Based on video data analysis and post experiment interviews, we found that the participants were able to use the Marionette wheel system as a mode of communication to change the behavior of the "autonomous" vehicle controlled by the Wizard operator. Participants were immediately able to recognize that the device could be used as a navigational input to a self driving vehicle.

The behavior of the participants, however, greatly varied from each other while the vehicle was being operated "autonomously" by the Wizard. Some participants were extremely relaxed and sat with their hands completely off the Marionette wheel, while some other participants had a hand either close to, or hovering over the wheel. We found that generally the anxious body language greatly diminished after 5-10 minutes of on-road driving. Interestingly, because we did not limit the participant from using electronic devices, one participant almost exclusively used their smart phone during the drive. Most of the participants (except the one with the smart phone) noticed the earlier imperfections in the driving.

The behavior of the participants also varied during the emergency hand-off section of the study. Some participants responded immediately to the control hand-off and steered the car properly out of the round. Others however, did not immediately take-over control from the car. One participant allowed the car to turn two full turns in the round-about before they attempted to take control. When asked why they were so hesitant to take over control during the post-drive interview, the participant responded that, *"to me, at least, when the car is going too small into circles, the car itself should understand that something is going wrong and just stop the vehicle. It shouldn't just go around, around."* This difference in expected behavior of the vehicle could explain why there was such a large variation in emergency hand-off response between the participants.

Some of the participants indicated that their awareness that they were in a study helped to alleviate trust issues they might feel. One participant who hesitated before answering affirmatively when asked if he trusted the vehicle, stated,*"I knew there wasn't going to be any intentional screw up to cause collision because that would be bad."* Many participants were critical of the driving wizard's driving style, but the discussion of what would be better lead to very detailed descriptions of what they would like, which suggests that this type of slightly imperfect driving would be good for eliciting driver expectations.

7. LIMITATIONS AND FUTURE WORK

Fundamentally, there is a limitation on timing in our system. Because we use the Wizard operator to relay commands between the car and the participant driver, the system will never achieve synchronicity; there will always be a lag between participant driver input, and the movement of the car. As one participant pointed out during our preliminary evaluation, this might render lower level automation tests much more difficult to operate on this model due to the constant input the Wizard operator must follow from the participant driver. Additionally, because the participants inputs are interpreted by the wizard, it is difficult to truly test the participants' performance in negotiating various driving scenarios.

7.1 Wizard Feedback

One of the current limitation of the Marionette system is caused by the placement of the various components, such as the LED strip indicators for the accelerator and brake input. While they provide a easily readable interface, the indicators are located below the driver's field of vision when he or she is watching the road. This causes difficulties for the wizard operator to maintain synchronization with the participant while continuing to drive.

Currently, the use-cases limit the fidelity at which the Wizard needs to respond to the participant override. Relocating the LEDs or using Heads Up Displays (HUDs) could help resolve this issue and open up this platform to more detailed interactions between the participants and their "simulated autonomous driving system" (the Wizard operator). Similarly, the current placement of the LED display for the steering wheel position prevents the Wizard from performing ideally. Because the LED display for the steering wheel position occupies the space above the steering wheel, the wizard cannot utilize the steering wheel as effectively. For instance, when the wizard needs to make a sharp turn, it is difficult to execute the maneuver while keeping the drive smooth. By offsetting the display, the wizard will be able to perform better and drive more naturally.

The IMU sensor module is another component that can be improved to allow the wizard to perform better. In the current design, the IMU sensor module is connected to the computer through a USB cable. As the module is mounted to the steering wheel, problems may occur if the cable becomes caught in the steering wheel. This would not only hinder the wizard's driving ability, but may also disable the system if the module is disconnected. Therefore, in future designs, it is important to make sure that this component utilizes wireless communication so that it can be physically independent from the rest of the system. Additionally, the IMU is unable to accurately sense certain rapid steering wheel maneuvers. This would cause the Marionette wheel to function abnormally, which can confuse the participants. However, this can be improved by modifying parameters within the software.

Another limitation is the LED display for the position of the steering wheel. While the LED display for the accelerator and brake input can clearly and instantly provide information to the wizard, the display for the steering wheel angle has very observable latency. This is evident when the wizard is steering, as the Marionette wheel must first move according to the input provided by the IMU before the display can provide an updated position. Additionally, inherit noise from the IMU causes the display to occasionally indicate that a small correction should be made. This can be troublesome if the participant is only moving on the Marionette wheel slightly, as the wizard would not know if they need to act or not.

In the evaluation process, the wizard would sometimes need to look at what the participant is doing in order to act appropriately, which is not ideal. This can be ameliorated with the inclusion of a touch sensor indicating whether the participants are holding onto the steering wheel. This could help clarify participants' intentions.

7.2 Participant Feedback

Feedback from participants also indicated that more modes of input on the Marionette interface, such as turn indicators, would be helpful in communicating their intent to the simulated autonomous system. The Logitech steering wheel has potential for such inputs in the form of paddle shift levers and several buttons on the steering wheel. This could be incorporated into the operational protocol of the Marionette system in order to simulate high level directed commands similar to how current advanced vehicles assistance systems can conduct lane shift in autonomous mode after the user uses the turn signal.

Some participants in the pilot study also observed that the Marionette system does not have an instrument cluster indicating vital vehicular information such as speed and turn signal indicators. Such system will provide more information to the Marionette system operator in order for them to make vehicle control decisions such as ensuring that the vehicle speed is within speed limits. We hope to integrate such a display through the use of a wireless OBD port reader that can communicate with the Marionette software controller.

7.3 Future Work

There are several potential directions for the future development of this project. From a hardware perspective, we are looking to integrate a higher pixel density LED indicator for our steering indicator. Another feature that we are planning to develop is an additional trigger that can initiate haptic signals through force feedback, sounds, and/or LED cues in order to communicate takeover requests to the participant. This can be used for the critical area of on-road control hand-off studies for simulated autonomous driving situations.

With regard to software, refactoring the code into a fully functional, well documented, open-sourced package will be a priority. The ultimate goal of this project is to create a platform that other researchers can use. This package will include a series of video instructions on how to replicate this system setup for researchers with little to no previous experience in mechatronics and computer programming. A working version of the open-source code can be found here: **https://github.com/CDR-IxD/RemoteWheel**

We also plan on creating a data recording method in order to streamline the recording of participant inputs on the Marionette interface into a database during each study. This will allow us to synchronize specific on-road events with participant responses for further analysis. We plan on enabling a web-server structure so that the device can be remotely controlled through wireless 3G or 4G communication.

In terms of outcome analysis, this pilot study also illustrated how behavioral variations might fundamentally result from having different expectations of how an autonomous car should perform in certain conditions, rather than lapses in concentration or an inability to react in time.

8. CONCLUSION

We have created the first low-cost, portable, and versatile interaction research system for on-road simulated autonomous driving studies on commercial vehicles. Results of our pilot study suggests that the Marionette system facilitates the illusion of partially autonomous driving while maintaining the safety of vehicle operation for on-road studies. The Marionette system can serve as a platform method for other researchers to study on-road interactions between the driver and their simulated partially autonomous vehicle.

9. ACKNOWLEDGMENTS

This research was funded by the Center for Design Research's affiliates program. We would like to thank Sonia Baltodano, Nikolas Martelaro, and Rebecca Currano for their invaluable contribution to this endeavor. We also thank the researchers at the Center for Design Research for their feedback and experience that was vital in study design and development. We would also like to acknowledge Daniel Gagan for his development of the Logitech G27 node package.

10. REFERENCES

[1] James M Anderson, Kalra Nidhi, Karlyn D Stanley, Paul Sorensen, Constantine Samaras, and Oluwatobi A Oluwatola. 2014. *Autonomous vehicle technology: A guide for policymakers*. Rand Corporation.

[2] Thomas Bak and Hans Jakobsen. 2004. Agricultural Robotic Platform with Four Wheel Steering for Weed Detection. *Biosystems Engineering* 87, 2 (2004), 125 – 136. DOI: **http://dx.doi.org/10.1016/j.biosystemseng.2003.10.009**

[3] Sonia Baltodano, Srinath Sibi, Nikolas Martelaro, Nikhil Gowda, and Wendy Ju. 2015. RRADS: Real Road

Autonomous Driving Simulation. In *Proceedings of the Tenth Annual ACM/IEEE International Conference on Human-Robot Interaction Extended Abstracts (HRI'15 Extended Abstracts)*. ACM, New York, NY, USA, 283–283. DOI:**http://dx.doi.org/10.1145/2701973.2702099**

[4] Ralf Bergholz, Klaus Timm, and Hubert Weisser. 2000. Autonomous vehicle arrangement and method for controlling an autonomous vehicle. (Nov. 21 2000). **http://www.google.com/patents/US6151539** US Patent 6,151,539.

[5] Gerard J Blaauw. 1982. Driving experience and task demands in simulator and instrumented car: a validation study. *Human Factors: The Journal of the Human Factors and Ergonomics Society* 24, 4 (1982), 473–486.

[6] Cynthia Breazeal, Cory D Kidd, Andrea Lockerd Thomaz, Guy Hoffman, and Matt Berlin. 2005. Effects of nonverbal communication on efficiency and robustness in human-robot teamwork. In *2005 IEEE/RSJ International Conference on Intelligent Robots and Systems*. IEEE, 708–713.

[7] Stephen M Casner, Edwin L Hutchins, and Don Norman. 2016. The challenges of partially automated driving. *Commun. ACM* 59, 5 (2016), 70–77.

[8] Nils Dahlbäck, Arne Jönsson, and Lars Ahrenberg. 1993. Wizard of Oz Studies: Why and How. In *Proceedings of the 1st International Conference on Intelligent User Interfaces (IUI '93)*. ACM, New York, NY, USA, 193–200. DOI: **http://dx.doi.org/10.1145/169891.169968**

[9] Alexander Davies. 2015. I rode 500 miles in a self-driving car and saw the future. It's delightfully dull. (2015).

[10] František Duchoň, Peter Hubinský, Jaroslav Hanzel, Andrej Babinec, and Michal Tölgyessy. 2012. Intelligent vehicles as the robotic applications. *Procedia Engineering* 48 (2012), 105–114.

[11] Frank O Flemisch, Catherine A Adams, Sheila R Conway, Ken H Goodrich, Michael T Palmer, and Paul C Schutte. 2003. The H-Metaphor as a guideline for vehicle automation and interaction. (2003).

[12] Barbara Freund, Stefan Gravenstein, Rebecca Ferris, and Elias Shaheen. 2002. Evaluating Driving Performance of Cognitively Impaired and Healthy Older Adults: A Pilot Study Comparing On-Road Testing and Driving Simulation. *Journal of the American Geriatrics Society* 50, 7 (2002), 1309–1310. DOI:**http://dx.doi.org/10.1046/j.1532-5415.2002.50325.x**

[13] Stuart T Godley, Thomas J Triggs, and Brian N Fildes. 2002. Driving simulator validation for speed research. *Accident analysis & prevention* 34, 5 (2002), 589–600.

[14] Christian Gold, Daniel Damböck, Lutz Lorenz, and Klaus Bengler. 2013. "Take over!" How long does it take to get the driver back into the loop? *Proceedings of the Human Factors and Ergonomics Society Annual Meeting* 57, 1 (2013), 1938–1942. DOI: **http://dx.doi.org/10.1177/1541931213571433**

[15] Paul Green. 1985. The Wizard of Oz: a tool for rapid development of user interfaces. Final report. (1985). **http://deepblue.lib.umich.edu/handle/2027.42/174**

[16] Gabriel M Hoffmann, Claire J Tomlin, Michael Montemerlo, and Sebastian Thrun. 2007. Autonomous automobile trajectory tracking for off-road driving: Controller design, experimental validation and racing. In *Proceedings of the 26th American control Conference*. Citeseer, 2296–2301.

[17] Mishel Johns, Brian Mok, David Michael Sirkin, Nikhil Manjunath Gowda, Catherine Allison Smith, Walter J. Talamonti Jr, and Wendy Ju. 2016. Exploring Shared Control in Automated Driving. In *The Eleventh ACM/IEEE International Conference on Human Robot Interation (HRI '16)*. IEEE Press, Piscataway, NJ, USA, 91–98.

[18] Nico Kaptein, Jan Theeuwes, and Richard Van Der Horst. 1996. Driving simulator validity: Some considerations. *Transportation Research Record: Journal of the Transportation Research Board* 1550 (1996), 30–36.

[19] Krisada Kritayakirana and J. Christian Gerdes. 2012. Autonomous vehicle control at the limits of handling. *International Journal of Vehicle Autonomous Systems* 10, 4 (Jan. 2012), 271–296. DOI: **http://dx.doi.org/10.1504/IJVAS.2012.051270**

[20] Morteza Lahijanian and Marta Kwiatkowska. 2016. Social Trust: a Major Challenge for the Future of Autonomous Systems. (2016), To appear.

[21] John D. Lee and Bobbie D. Seppelt. 2009. *Springer Handbook of Automation*. Springer Berlin Heidelberg, Berlin, Heidelberg, Chapter Human Factors in Automation Design, 417–436.

[22] Todd Litman. 2014. Autonomous Vehicle Implementation Predictions. *Victoria Transport Policy Institute* 28 (2014). **http://sh.st/st/787f28ed3e745c14417e4aec27303038/http://www.vtpi.org/avip.pdf**

[23] Andrew Marinik, Richard Bishop, Vikki Fitchett, Justin F. Morgan, Tammy E. Trimble, Myra Blanco, and others. 2014. Human Factors Evaluation of Level 2 and Level 3 Automated Driving Concepts: Concepts of Operation. (2014). **https://vtechworks.lib.vt.edu/handle/10919/55082**

[24] Brian Mok, Mishel John, Nikhil Gowda, Srinath Sibi, and Wendy Ju. 2016. Take the Wheel: Effects of Available Modalities on Driver Intervention. In *IEEE Intelligent Vehicles Symposium*. IEEE.

[25] Brian Mok, Mishel Johns, Key Jung Lee, David Miller, David Sirkin, Page Ive, and Wendy Ju. 2015. Emergency, Automation Off: Unstructured Transition Timing for Distracted Drivers of Automated Vehicles. In *Intelligent Transportation Systems (ITSC), 2015 IEEE 18th International Conference on*. IEEE, 2458–2464.

[26] Michael Montemerlo, Jan Becker, Suhrid Bhat, Hendrik Dahlkamp, Dmitri Dolgov, Scott Ettinger, Dirk Haehnel, Tim Hilden, Gabe Hoffmann, Burkhard Huhnke, and others. 2008. Junior: The stanford entry in the urban challenge. *Journal of field Robotics* 25, 9 (2008), 569–597.

[27] Hans B. Pacejka. 2012. *Tire and Vehicle Dynamics*. Butterworth-Heinemann.

[28] Cyrus Pinto. 2012. How autonomous vehicle policy in California and Nevada addresses technological and non-technological liabilities. *Intersect: The Stanford Journal of Science, Technology and Society* 5 (2012).

[29] Matthew P. Reed and Paul A. Green. 1999. Comparison of driving performance on-road and in a low-cost simulator using a concurrent telephone dialling task. *Ergonomics* 42, 8 (1999), 1015–1037.

[30] Laurel D Riek. 2012. Wizard of oz studies in hri: a systematic review and new reporting guidelines. *Journal of Human-Robot Interaction* 1, 1 (2012).

[31] Dirk Rothenbücher, Jamy Li, David Sirkin, Brian Mok, and Wendy Ju. 2015. Ghost Driver: A Platform for Investigating Interactions Between Pedestrians and Driverless Vehicles. In

Adjunct Proceedings of the 7th International Conference on Automotive User Interfaces and Interactive Vehicular Applications (AutomotiveUI '15). ACM, New York, NY, USA, 44–49. DOI: **http://dx.doi.org/10.1145/2809730.2809755**

[32] Paul Saulnier, Ehud Sharlin, and Saul Greenberg. 2010. Exploring Interruption in HRI Using Wizard of Oz. In *Proceedings of the 5th ACM/IEEE International Conference on Human-robot Interaction (HRI '10)*. IEEE Press, Piscataway, NJ, USA, 125–126. **http://dl.acm.org/citation.cfm?id=1734454.1734504**

[33] Anna Schieben, Matthias Heesen, Julian Schindler, Johann Kelsch, and Frank Flemisch. 2009. The Theater-system Technique: Agile Designing and Testing of System Behavior and Interaction, Applied to Highly Automated Vehicles. In *Proceedings of the 1st International Conference on Automotive User Interfaces and Interactive Vehicular Applications (AutomotiveUI '09)*. ACM, New York, NY, USA, 43–46. DOI: **http://dx.doi.org/10.1145/1620509.1620517**

[34] G Schmidt, M Kiss, E Babbel, and A Galla. 2008. The Wizard on Wheels: Rapid Prototyping and User Testing of Future Driver Assistance Using Wizard of Oz Technique in a Vehicle. In *Proceedings of the FISITA 2008 World Automotive Congress, Munich*.

[35] Hans-Christoph Steiner. 2009. Firmata: Towards Making Microcontrollers Act Like Extensions of the Computer.. In *NIME*. 125–130.

[36] Andrew R Swanson. 2013. Somebody Grab the Wheel: State Autonomous Vehicle Legislation and the Road to a National Regime. *Marq. L. Rev.* 97 (2013), 1085.

[37] Chris Urmson, Joshua Anhalt, Drew Bagnell, Christopher Baker, Robert Bittner, MN Clark, John Dolan, Dave Duggins, Tugrul Galatali, Chris Geyer, and others. 2008. Autonomous driving in urban environments: Boss and the urban challenge. *Journal of Field Robotics* 25, 8 (2008), 425–466.

[38] Ying Wang, Bruce Mehler, Bryan Reimer, Vincent Lammers, Lisa A. D'Ambrosio, and Joseph F. Coughlin. 2010. The validity of driving simulation for assessing differences between in-vehicle informational interfaces: A comparison with field testing. *Ergonomics* 53, 3 (2010), 404–420. DOI: **http://dx.doi.org/10.1080/00140130903464358** PMID: 20191415.

[39] Astrid Weiss, Regina Bernhaupt, Daniel Schwaiger, Martin Altmaninger, Roland Buchner, and Manfred Tscheligi. 2009. User experience evaluation with a Wizard of Oz approach: Technical and methodological considerations. In *2009 9th IEEE-RAS International Conference on Humanoid Robots*. IEEE, 303–308.

Steps Toward Participatory Design of Social Robots: Mutual Learning with Older Adults with Depression

Hee Rin Lee[1], Selma Šabanović[1], Wan-Ling Chang[1], Shinichi Nagata[2], Jen Piatt[2], Casey Bennett[3], David Hakken[1]

[1]School of Informatics and Computing
Indiana University
901 E. 10th Street
Bloomington IN 47408
{hrl,selmas,wanlchan,dhakken}
@indiana.edu

[2]School of Public Health
Indiana University
1025 E. 7th Street
Bloomington, IN 47405
{snagata,jenpiatt}
@indiana.edu

[3]Faros Healthcare
44 Vantage Way, Suite 400
Nashville, TN 37228
casey.bennett@faroshealth.com

ABSTRACT

This paper presents the results of research aimed at developing a methodology for the participatory design of social robots, which are meant to be incorporated into various social contexts (e.g. home, work) and establish social relations with people. In contrast to the dominant technologically driven robot development process, we aim to develop a socially robust and responsible approach to robot design using Participatory Design (PD) methods. The PD process builds on participants' self-identified issues and concerns, and develops robot concepts according to participants' interpretations of the capabilities and potential applications of robotic technologies. We present methodological insights from an ongoing PD project aimed at designing socially assistive robots with older adults diagnosed with depression and their therapists, and identify remaining challenges in this project. We particularly focus on supporting mutual learning between researchers and participants and on promoting active participation of older adults as "designers" (rather than consumers) as foundational aspects of PD. We conclude with reflections regarding how this work can contribute to the further development of social robots and relevant PD methodologies.

Keywords

Participatory design; social robots; socially assistive robotics; older adults; depression; mental health; methodology.

1. INTRODUCTION

A growing trend in robotics is the development of robots that can function well in everyday spaces such as private homes (e.g., [1]), schools (e.g., [2]), nursing homes (e.g. [3]), hospitals (e.g., [4]), and malls (e.g., [5]). Governments and researchers in developed countries around the world, including the United States, Japan, South Korea, and the European Union, actively support the integration of such "social" robots into society [6-10]. The entry of robots into intimate places and roles, including caregiving, education, and companionship, raises concerns about the psychological well-being and development of users [11], human rights (e.g. dignity and self-determination [12,13]), and privacy [14]. The responsibility for making decisions about appropriate robot applications has so far been largely in the hands of robot designers; however, the societal significance and breadth of these concerns suggests a more inclusive, participatory process is necessary. How best to incorporate a rich understanding of the social into robot design, including an understanding of the social construction of values, meanings, and social interactions in robotics itself, and how by doing so to create more socially robust [15] and responsible social robots, remain open questions.

We see the fundamental problem facing the development of social robots as a social one: designing social environments (rather than standalone robots) with properties that foster positive human-robot interaction. The way humans design effective social environments is in itself social, so the task facing social robot development is the discovery of a social process for creating organizational environments in which humans and robots can interact regularly and, in effect, "naturally." The properties of such social environments will vary according to particular contexts, so the design challenge is to develop procedures for creating diverse and multiple appropriate social environments. We suggest prior work in Participatory Design (PD) has constructed principles and procedures for the development of information technologies and the social environments needed for their successful use in organizational settings. Our current aim is to adapt PD methodology to deliberation about and design of domestic social robots to support mental healthcare.

In this paper, we describe our experiences building up a PD methodology for developing socially robust social robots. As a case study, we explored PD methods with older adults diagnosed with depression. We decided to focus on eldercare applications because they are a major area of development for social robotics, and on depression because it is the second leading cause of disability among older adults in the US [16]. Rather than focusing on the specifics of this population, however, our aim is to provide a discussion of our process and relevant insights that can be informative for social robot design more generally. In particular, we describe how researchers and participants can be supported in an iterative practice of *mutual learning*, instead of interacting as experts and informants. The PD process showed immediate benefits for our participants, who belonged to a group of users with few prior chances to actively articulate their ideas and concerns about how robots could productively fit into their lives and whose voices were generally not seen as authoritative. In the long run, we also expect it to be useful for producing socially robust and responsible robot designs that are representative of user values and therefore more acceptable to them [17].

HRI'17, March 6–9, 2017, Vienna, Austria.
© 2017 ACM. ISBN 978-1-4503-4336-7/17/03...$15.00.
DOI: http://dx.doi.org/10.1145/2909824.3020237

2. BACKGROUND

2.1 Current Social Practices of Robot Design

As robots enter into everyday contexts, their design requirements are increasingly based not only on functional concerns, but also on subjective evaluations by users and on their fit with and effects on different contexts of use. To facilitate robot acceptance, designers and researchers have been developing social capabilities to enable humans to interact with them intuitively and naturally [18,19]. The design of robot sociality has largely been based on the idea that robots should resemble humans or other social species (e.g. animals) to trigger people to respond to them socially. With this in mind, HRI researchers have explored the anthropomorphic appearance of robots [19-21], humanlike behavior (or movement) of robots (e.g. gaze [22]), and social roles for robots (e.g. butler, maid) [23]. Kahn et al. suggested more complex design patterns for sociality [24], mimicking human modes of social interaction, such as personal introductions for a robot, or giving robots personal interests and a history to share with participants.

The efficacy of these social cues in human-robot interaction is commonly established through evaluations in laboratory experiments, or through ethnographic or user-centered studies of robots in everyday use contexts. While the former method provides generalizable but decontextualized design guidelines relating to specific design factors, the results of the second is more socially situated but difficult to apply directly to robot design. The user-centered approach retains the researcher's control of the research process. All three methods therefore fall short of actively involving users in producing the social structures necessary to enable socially robust robot use in everyday contexts, suggesting the need for alternative design methodologies for social robots.

2.1.1 Lab Experiments as a Social Context for HRI

One of the most popular methods for finding ways to engender social effects in HRI is through psychological lab experiments [24-26]. In this method, researchers design and control the social environment in which participants and robots meet: they define hypotheses to be tested, invite participants into a controlled lab context, and ask them to follow instructions to measure the effects of select social factors on HRI. This process allows researchers to isolate and statistically evaluate specific factors to find design features that contribute to robots' generalizable sociality and can be smoothly deployed as design requirements. However, lab studies have a limited ability to reflect the social context and human labor that contributes to robots' sociality in everyday use. As social critiques of robotics have mentioned, robot sociality is constructed through socially situated interactions with humans, whose actions are mutually shaped through their interactions with robots and with their broader social environment [27,28]. Robot sociality outside the lab is therefore likely to be enacted differently depending on the social situations of users. Participants in lab experiments have restricted roles and capabilities of structuring the social context, as the ideas they can express and actions they can perform are constrained by the study design. Both the limited roles of participants and the confines of the experimental environment present quite a different social context from that in which robots are eventually meant to operate.

2.1.2 Ethnographic Studies for HRI in the Wild

Ethnography has been another method used to explore robot sociality [1,4,28]. Ethnographic studies are conducted "in the wild" and focus on understanding situated uses and emergent meanings of robots in different social contexts. While lab experiments focus on certain features determined by researchers' hypotheses, ethnographic methods seek to provide a more holistic understanding of people's interactions with robots that emerge from the context under study. However, the results of ethnographic studies are often complex and locally specific, and therefore difficult to reflect back to robot design. Also, the role of participants in ethnographic studies is still constrained to providing information for researchers, rather than participating as active collaborators in setting the agenda for and making sense of the robot design process. Finally, while ethnographic studies depict the relationships and interactions between different actors and contextual factors in local cases, they do not provide a method for developing successful social relationships and uses for robots in other contexts.

2.1.3 User Centered Design

HRI researchers have also employed user centered design methods to find appropriate modes of and uses for social robots. User-centered design researchers often conduct user studies, including survey, interviews, or focus groups, to understand the needs of prospective users within specific contexts [29-31] and develop robots based on their findings. For example, in [31], researchers explored the design of a social robot delivering snacks in a workplace by conducting multiple interviews and a survey to understand workers' idea about snacking. The researchers then iteratively applied the resulting contextual understanding to the robot design. However, the researchers determined the main research directions (e.g. workers need a social robot delivering snacks) based on their assumptions. Workers had a chance to express their thoughts about snacks, but not opportunities to bring up other issues that were important to them. Participants acted as informants to the research team, rather than as collaborators actively joining in the agenda-setting and decision making process of design. Similarly to user-centered design, PD focuses on the opinions of users to identify appropriate designs and uses for social robots. However, PD also addresses the social position of participants within the research process by developing ways to empower them to make decisions and act upon their surroundings and issues they find salient.

Previous work on designing and evaluating robots has rarely allowed for the development of robots in tandem with the social structures of their use. In this paper, we propose Participatory Design (PD) as a method that can structure the relationship between the participants and researchers so that the design process produces not only specific design factors for robots, but also empowers participants, develops socially appropriate meanings for robots, and constructs sustainable social structures for using them. Rather than evaluating existing robots or contexts of use, this method aims to build the sociality of robots and the social practices of their implementation together with participants who have rich experiences and knowledge of the relevant contexts of use, as well as the needs for and potential situated meanings of robots. We suggest PD methods can facilitate the development of more nuanced and contextually meaningful robot applications that include the interpretations of users as contextual experts and the appropriate social infrastructures for the implementation of robots in daily life. In the following section, we explain how PD has been used within HRI to make robots substantively social.

2.2 Making Robots Substantively Social Through User Participation

PD posits an active role for users as direct contributors to the robot design process, who can provide contextual expertise and social know-how. This contrasts with the passive roles robotics researchers currently envision for users, as naïve lay people who evaluate robot designs based on a simplistic understanding of robots and who will hopefully develop into "sensible users" making informed decisions about robot capabilities they prefer to consume [32]. In this section, we discuss how HRI researchers have employed PD in HRI so far [33-35], particularly focusing on the roles and power relationships between participants and researchers. We show how PD creates opportunities for robotics researchers and other stakeholders to collaboratively "identify opportunities to influence technological change and its social consequences at an early stage—moments at which accountability and control could be exercised" [36,37]. With this in mind, we trace changing *participant roles* in design, from amending existing platforms, to developing robot concepts, and participating in mutual learning with researchers.

2.2.1 Participants amend existing robot platforms

Several studies have involved participants in the design of contextually appropriate behaviors for existing robotics platforms. Azenkot et al. conducted a PD study to investigate how assistive robots can guide blind people in an indoor environment [35]. Researchers employed the existing PR2 platform and participants, including both designers and non-designers with visual impairments, suggested how the robot should behave to help them navigate indoors. The Robots for Humanity project was initiated by a user with a mobility impairment and involved his wife and a robotics design team in a PD project to develop an assistive mobile manipulator using the same PR2 platform [38]. These studies employed currently available, technically highly developed robots as a given, and tried to make them more social by allowing participants to define contextually useful behaviors.

2.2.2 Participants conceptualize new robots

Caleb-Solly et al. used embodiment and scenario-focused workshops to explore older adults' ideal domestic robots without bringing in specific robot platforms [39]. In previous work, we conducted participatory studies inspired by collaborative ethnography [40] and PD [41] to develop concepts for domestic robots with participants in S. Korea based on the householders' own identification and understanding of issues they found most significant and their interpretations of home technology. We first asked householders to draw the main social actors in their home, and to describe the labor division among them. With this in mind, they then drew and described ideal domestic robots that might support their needs in the home within these social dynamics.

2.2.3 Participants and researchers as mutual learners

Green et al. [42] describe the development of CERO — a fetch and carry robot to assist physically disabled workers in the office – through a long term collaboration between two organizations, the Swedish National Labor Market Board (AMS) and the Center for Autonomous System (CAS). The researchers conducted task analysis, focus groups, and experiments with office workers. Frennert et al. [33] used a participatory approach to robot design by holding workshops with older adults to explore whether they would consider having robots in their homes, and later asking older adults to evaluate assistive robot mock-ups at home to explore the potential uses and appearance of assistive robots. This study allowed for mutual learning between researchers and participants: participants learned about technical options from researchers, and researchers learned about contextual issues from participants. The process positioned researchers and participants on more equal footing so both could address their concerns actively with each other, which is an important criterion for PD.

2.3 Empowering Users Through Mutual Learning in Participatory Design

Ever since its inception in 1960s [36,43], PD has emphasized power dynamics and social hierarchies between researchers (designers) and users as central issues in technology design. In PD, designers share decision-making with users while designing products, and users shift their roles from being informants in the traditional design process to acting as authoritative participants in co-design. Users in PD not only provide information but also learn design and technology know-how from designers, and apply it to the development of new technology concepts. Designers also learn about the values and meanings related to technology and accompanying social interactions. This process of "mutual learning" is a way for PD to address the power imbalance between researchers and users common to scientific and design research, and to empower diverse users with active knowledge about technology and allow them to take part in the conceptualization of robotic sociality. Also, mutual learning aims to cultivate critical discussions between users and researchers of the potential social applications, meanings, and consequences of robots. PD's focus on power issues differentiates PD from user-centered design studies in HRI [29-31]. Considering the importance of tackling power issues in design to PD, our project explores the mutual learning practices among our research team, older adults, and therapists while designing Socially Assistive Robots (SARs).

Users' active roles in PD also closely related to constructing ways to make robots substantively social. In our study, making robots social means finding a way to socialize them in the sociologist's sense, that is to allow for them to be socially constructed by diverse groups of people through interaction and to affect other actors and their social contexts in the process. We insist that the socially responsible design of robots requires that this socialization be explicit, open, and reflexive as to the values and priorities being inscribed into emerging robotic technologies. In trying to work out a set of PD principles on which these could be structured, we are working with a specific population, a group of older adults living in Indiana, diagnosed with depression, having additional co-occurring physical problems, and receiving social service benefits from a not-for-profit agency. As is generally the case with PD, our aim for this work is not to identify appropriate robot characteristics or ideas to stimulate designers, but rather to co-create with participants a process for integrating the social into the design of SARs in the home context.

3. A CASE STUDY OF SOCIAL ROBOT PD

Since 2014, we have been involved in a PD project with five older adults and ten clinical and caregiving staff who serve this population, recruited with the help of a local healthcare provider. The research team consists of one participatory design researcher, a health technology developer, three human-robot interaction (HRI) researchers, and two recreational therapy scholars. The project focused particularly on how Socially Assistive Robots (SARs) [44] might be used by older adults experiencing chronic depression and co-occurring physical illness while living independently in their homes. We decided to explore how to use PD in this domain because it corresponds to the robotics community's push to make robots more social and widely available, and with the turn to community-centered healthcare. We particularly chose older adults with low-income and limited education as co-designers since their knowledge has been marginalized within the assistive robot design process [17] Also, 15-20% of older adults in the US suffer from depression [45], making it a leading cause of disability.

To facilitate mutual learning as a key research aim, we iteratively developed five PD sessions (see Table 1), recognizing that merely bringing older adults together with researchers does not result in co-design, but that co-design requires methods that provide opportunities for both parties to familiarize themselves with each other's knowledge and build a relationship of trust. The PD process started with a series of semi-structured interviews carried out with five older adults in their homes, and with five non-medical, mental health therapists in their offices. Following the interviews, we held four PD workshops with our older adults and a final workshop with a second group of mental health therapists to discuss their perceptions of socially assistive robots, and how they might be used in patients' daily lives at home. Mutual learning occurred throughout the five sessions as 1) older adults were gradually exposed to existing robots and robotic sensors, and 2) researchers learned about the challenges older adults faced in addressing aging and depression. By exchanging ideas and experiences, researchers and older adults built up trust over time, making older adults feel more secure in expressing and developing their ideas with researchers, and researchers more understanding of and open to suggestions by the participants. We included clinical staff as participants to get a more multifaceted understanding of older adults' issues and the healthcare context.

All interviews and workshops were recorded and transcribed, and members of the research team coded the transcripts to identify common themes (See [34] for details on the analytical approach). The number of participants fluctuated during our study. This was due to their changing health conditions (depressive episodes, physical health issues). All participants wanted to continue the study when they were mentally and physically able.

3.1 Interviews with staff and older adults

At the beginning of the study, two members of the team, one an HRI researcher and the other a trained therapist in community mental health, visited the older adult participants in their homes to perform initial interviews. Carrying out interviews in participants' homes, researchers learned about participants' home contexts including housing arrangements (size, condition, availability of pets etc.). The contextual information provided common ground to researchers and participants when designing robots for older adults' homes in the subsequent sessions. It also helped older adults start developing a mutual trust and respect with the researchers in a space that was familiar and comfortable for them.

The interviews covered topics related to participants' everyday pursuits and activity levels, their social circle, and the realities and challenges of aging and living with depression. When interviewed, the older adults described their health problems and the courses of therapy that they would like to see, and documented their interest in participating in a project related to SARs. The patients had ideas for maintaining their psychological wellness, but they still struggled with negative emotional moments. One of the main daily life challenges they pointed out was loneliness, closely related to their physical health problems and financial issues. They all mentioned that social interaction with friends, family members, and pets made them feel better, and social isolation increased feelings of depression. Two of the five older adults had pets, but mentioned \caring for them was challenging (in later workshops, both pet owners said they had lost their pets). All five participants had been employed in the past, but only one was still working during the study. All of them used computers, but only one regularly and with enjoyment for emailing, online reading, and shopping.

Table 1 Overview of the PD process in our study, showing the mutual learning achieved by the research team and participants (Tinted rows show sessions with older adults, while the untinted rows show sessions with therapists).

Steps	Methods	Mutual learning process	
		Researchers	Participants
Step 1.a. Initial interviews with older adults	Home visit and tour	Learned about domestic environments and experiences of older adults	(participants: older adults) Met researchers, introduced to project
Step 1.b Initial interviews with therapists	Interview & presentation of existing robots	Learned how therapists interpret existing robots & see them as applying to their work	(participants: therapists) Introduced to project and capabilities of existing robots
Step 2 Workshop 1: Introducing socially Assistive Robots	Focus group: present existing robots and critique	Learned how older adults interpret existing robots, what they like & dislike about them	(participants: older adults) Learned capabilities and applications of existing robots for daily life
Step 3 Workshop 2: Designing a robot together	Focus group: discuss & visualize ideas of older adults	Learned older adults' everyday challenges, how they think robots might be used to address them	(participants: older adults) Learned how their issues could be developed into robot design possibilities
Step 4 Workshop 3: Design a robot for your everyday life	Focus group: Develop holistic robot design with older adults	Learned ways how assistive robots can be situated in older adults' domestic environments, develop full robot ideas	(participants: older adults) Learned how their ideas could be developed into robots for their homes
Step 5 Workshop 4: Robotic technology and design with robotic parts	Focus group: present robotic parts (e.g. sensors)	Learned how older adults would use different sensors in robots, also ethical concerns about data collection and use	(participants: older adults) Learned what types of robotic parts are available, discussed what kinds of uses they might have in the home to support health
Step 6 Workshop 5: Staff's perspectives of robots in patients' homes	Focus group: Present older adults' robot designs	Learned how therapists interpret older adults' design ideas, what they see as useful and problematic	(participants: therapists) Learned how older adults envision their ideal assistive robots collaboratively imagined with researchers

The therapist interviews were performed by a team member employed as a researcher in the same healthcare organization. In the interviews, the researchers learned additional information about the regular work patterns of therapists and their perspectives on the daily lives and challenges of their older adult clients. All five therapists showed interest in integrating more digital technologies, including robots, into their practice. After viewing videos of three different assistive robots (Care-O-Bot[46], GiraffPlus [47], and Paro[44], see Figure 1), therapists commented on the usability and appropriateness of such robots for their population. These robots were chosen as examples of different forms (mechanical, animal-like) and uses (domestic assistance, telepresence health, and companionship) of SARs. The therapists worried about the complexity of robots as their clients were not technically savvy and overwhelming them would not benefit their therapy. They also saw possibilities for robots to enable their clients to live on their own, particularly alleviating loneliness and providing companionship. The therapists suggested a holistic way of treating clients. They mentioned that their psychological problems cannot be separated from other factors in daily life. For example, most clients had physical health problems (e.g., diabetes, obesity) along with their mental disabilities. The client's' life issues (e.g., money management, transportation, sociality) should be treated along with their health issues to promote overall wellness and quality of life.

Following the interviews, we performed four workshops to provide older adults with information about SARs, learn how they perceived different robots, and collaboratively develop concepts and scenarios about appropriate SARs' use in older adults' homes. Through the workshops, we tried different ways to develop our understanding of older adults' needs and preferences regarding robots, and to increase their engagement as robot designers.

3.2 Workshop 1: Introducing Socially Assistive Robots

The first PD workshop included four older adult participants and three HRI researchers; an additional member of the research team helped with video recording. The researchers learned about how older adults interpret and critique existing robots from older adults' perspectives, while older adult participants learned about currently available robot technologies for people like them.

In the first hour, the participants viewed and discussed videos of four different robot systems (the three seen by therapists – Care-O-Bot, GiraffPlus, and Paro – and a fourth communication robot called Papero that could be used in the home). After showing participants each robot on video, we asked them about their initial impressions of the robot, whether and how they might use the robot in their homes, and what they would want to change about the robot. The second hour was devoted to hands-on demonstrations of four robots (Paro, Keepon, Roomba, and the programmable social robot Mugbot, See Figure 1). Participants again discussed their impressions of the robots, how useful they might be to them, and any possible changes.

In contrast to expectations that older adults might be wary of robots as advanced technologies, the participants had no hesitation about discussing robots or considering how they might fit into their homes. They described several ways in which SARs could be useful to them, commenting they would be likely to buy some of the devices we showed. Their actions and comments indicated that, of the devices described in the videos and demonstrated live, Paro was most preferred because it was easy to maintain, and could alleviate negative feelings and loneliness. Three participants wanted to take it home with them immediately. The older adults also evaluated the GiraffPlus positively, particularly commending its ability to connect them remotely with friends, family, and caregivers. In contrast, the most machine-like of the robots portrayed in the video (Care-O-Bot), and the demonstrated robot that needed active programming (MugBot), were quickly dismissed by the participants as too technical and not easy to use.

In addition to comments participants made about the robots, the discussion of robot functions reflected their everyday needs. The participants gave more details of their concerns and emphasized some topics previously mentioned in interviews. They mentioned the importance of companionship and usability in their discussions of the presented robots. In line with the therapists' interview results, participants saw ease-of-use as one of most important robot features. In this workshop, we saw that the participants attempted to connect robot "functions" to their needs and life experiences, as if they were purchasing robot functions.

Figure 1. Older adults saw videos of Giraff Plus, Care-O-Bot, Papero (left to right, upper row), and Paro (left, lower row) and interacted with another Paro, Roomba, MugBot and Keepon during the first workshop (left to right, lower row).

3.3 Workshop 2: Designing a robot together

The second PD workshop brought three of the original four older adult participants together with four researchers to develop their own designs for a social robot that could assist people like them. In this session, researchers learned about older adults' everyday issues and how the issues could be related to robotic technologies, while older adults practiced ways of translating their current life challenges into robot design possibilities. In this workshop, researchers rapidly drew sketches of participants' design ideas as a common reference point, which the group further critiqued.

We started off by asking participants to name some of the challenges they faced the last time they had felt sad or lonely. They first mentioned physical problems, like cleaning up and lifting things. Participants later brought up social challenges: distance from loved ones, lack of social activities and opportunities to volunteer in the community, and a general lack of companionship in day-to-day life. After identifying these common problems of daily living, all three participants described the appearance and functions of robots they would like to have, as the two HRI researchers visualized their descriptions through quick sketches (See Figure 2). We chose this method to lower the barrier to participation, while giving participants control over the design content and a shared representation of their ideas to further critique and develop the design as a group. The resulting designs focused on robots that could provide companionship—greet the participants in the morning, discuss the news with them, accompany them on walks—and had a humanlike presence and appearance. Participants pointed out various health-related functions robots could perform, including providing reminders and suggesting healthy things to eat, wear, and do during the day.

The main design theme in the second workshop was again social companionship, which participants mentioned 13 times while discussing daily challenges and 38 times in the stage of robot design sketching. The participants described different types of social companionship along with other functions they needed. For example, they suggested the coffee maker robot could talk to them. Participants also reframed problems related to taking the wrong medicines, accidental injuries, taking care of pets, and limitations of living spaces mentioned in workshop 1 as design requirements for a medicine taking reminder, safety guard, house chore and physical assistance, and concerns of robot size. They developed a better capability of framing their problems in relation to robot design. The need to maintain control of the robot emerged as a new topic, with participants mentioning they did not want the robot to be too smart or autonomous.

In the robot sketching stage, participants reflected more diverse needs than while reviewing life challenges, and focused on specifics more than generalities. We recognized the way participants designed the robot was connected to their association of needs to potential robot functions. Their lack of familiarity with design practices made it difficult for participants to have a more integrated concept of a robot they could use to address their needs.

Figure 2. Three drawings produced during the second workshop show different types of robotic companions.

3.4 Workshop 3: Design a robot for your everyday life

The third PD workshop allowed researchers to work with older adult participants to better ground their ideas in their domestic environments and daily practices, and to consider more general design characteristics of robots that could help people "like them." Four older adults and five researchers joined the session.

We started the session by viewing floor plans of participants' homes, which we drew based on our visits during the first interview. We then discussed how participants used different spaces in their homes, and where and how they would want robots to be present in those spaces. We had used this method in a previous study to integrate the social dynamics at home into robot design [40]. We discussed what robots should look like, and the particular functions they should have to fulfill participants' needs and the constraints of their domestic environments. Participants each had one researcher working with them to discuss their design ideas and sketch them. The resulting designs included a mechanical, zoomorphic, and humanoid robot (See Figure 3), and diverse functions (e.g. cleaning, reminders, answering door).

This workshop allowed us to see how the older adults connected their own needs and values to the design of a specific robot, as well as to identify some common themes among participants. All participants mentioned wanting to talk to the robot and using it as some form of companion (e.g. watching TV together). Two of the four participants wanted the robot to help them manage interactions with others (e.g. remind them they haven't talked to a family member for a while, tell them when a conversation was too long). All the participants modeled the robots' roles based on familiar things (e.g. pets, house helpers, the Paro robot they had seen), wanting the robot to augment these roles or replace companions that were gone (e.g. a dog that had passed away). Participants also discussed concerns about using robots in the home, such as private places they did not want the robots to go (e.g. bathroom, bedroom), and the ease of use and maintenance.

Going through participants' daily routines as part of the robot design enabled the participants to take a relatively holistic perspective to robot design compared to their designs in workshop 2. This time participants thought about the robot as an integrated application instead of as a collection of individual functions. When they discovered a need in the process of imagining using the robot in their daily routines, they spontaneously added functions and adjusted the design and scenarios of their robot prototypes. We could say participants showed their ability to envision robots relevant to their issues in more comprehensive and "designerly" ways in this workshop, thinking how different functions might interact with each other and the use context.

Figure 3. Participants designed robots with more comprehensive and holistic functions.

3.5 Workshop 4: Robotic technology and design with robotic parts

During the fourth PD workshop, we sought to involve participants more directly in the technical development of robots. Our initial plan had been to do this during the second workshop, but the participants' negative reaction to MugBot, the programmable robot we demonstrated to them, inspired us to reconsider and guide the participants into the process of technical design more gradually. In this session, researchers learned how different sensors could be used in older adults' everyday lives; older adults learned the capabilities of different robotic components, which enabled them to suggest alternative ways to construct SARs. Four researchers and four older adults participated.

We presented several robotic sensors (e.g. light sensor, microphone, natural-language processing), and gave participants time to test them out, then asked participants to imagine how they might use them in the robots they had designed in the previous session (shown in Fig. 3). We also discussed sensors that were already used in existing robots, such as Paro and a prototype robotic face, and whether participants had any concerns about using such technologies in their homes.

Participants suggested including environmental sensors (e.g., sound, dust, and humidity sensors) in their robots to examine the physical condition of their home (e.g. knowing it's time to clean). Also, participants requested a finger print sensor to manage access to collected sensor data. Regardless of the data's usefulness for clinical purposes, participants emphasized that sensor data should go to them alone, and did not want to share information collected by the robots with medical professionals. Participants also wanted to keep tight control of their robots, rather than having them act autonomously. For example, the robots would be controllable only by the owner's voice. Several themes from previous workshops were reiterated, such as robots reminding participants to take medicines and attend appointments. Participants repeated their desires to use the robots for companionship and emergency assistance in their daily lives.

In the fourth workshop, participants expressed their ideas from a design perspective more frequently than in the preceding ones, especially when they helped us figure out what to do with sensor information and how to apply it to robots. For example, one participant began asking questions about sensors in the robots that were demonstrated after the sensor training. Another participant said "What about different animals?... If you like cats, you could make one like a cat that does things that you'd want it to do." A third participant said, "But that [robot] would cost a lot more than the animal...whoops!" These examples show participants considering robot design as a more generalist enterprise, rather than a wish-list of characteristics they might prefer to buy, which requires the balancing of the preferences of different users, costs, technical capabilities, and various social values and daily needs.

3.6 Workshop 5: Staff's perspectives of robots in patients' homes

The fifth PD workshop brought our research team together with four therapists to discuss the robots that were developed by older adults in the four workshops, and how such technologies might be useful in therapeutic practice. In this session, researchers could understand older adults' needs from a therapeutic perspective; therapists learned about the needs their patients had expressed and how robotic technologies might be sued for their therapies. Four therapists and four researchers joined this session.

We first asked therapists to describe their clients' typical problems from a clinical point of view. They pointed out that lack of purpose, interest, planning skills, and insomnia during holidays are common challenges for clients with clinical depression. They explained that older clients with clinical depression were often institutionalized for long periods of time, during which they did not make decisions for themselves. They were therefore used to relying heavily on others for help with everyday life. This made their needs for assistance and social reassurance more pronounced than those of other older adults. Therapists accordingly agreed with participants that medicine and appointment reminders would be helpful functions that technology could fulfill. The therapists also suggested that recording sleep and physical activity would be helpful for clinicians.

In contrast to the potential benefits emphasized by participants, the therapists commented on several concerns. Therapists worried technical failures could cause clients serious frustration. Possible fixation to the robot could be another issue if a participant stops trying to establish relationships with other people, which might be a concern with older adults with depression who are socially isolated. Also, having a robot may bring another source of anxiety if a participant worries others could disapprove of their robot. Therapists emphasized the importance of communication; thus, they suggested that the robot asking questions or giving suggestions could be effective functions to motivate patients. They also expressed a general interest in the potential of SARs for use with older adults in domestic environments, and expressed a desire to further contribute to our studies and future projects.

4. DISCUSSION

Throughout our sessions, we examined ways to enable mutual learning between researchers and participants, aiming to facilitate a balance of power between the two groups. As a result, our research suggests the following PD principles as possible ways to position users and researchers within the robot design process.

Including users in robot design as experts on local conditions and needs.

Our work has demonstrated that our "users" (in our case those diagnosed with depression and registered for social services as such, as well as having substantial co-occurring physical problems) have ideas about how to conceptualize robots and how they might be of use to them. These ideas at a minimum can be used to provide some design inspiration to roboticists. However, we have yet to discover how to develop our users further into active participants in a SARs participatory design team and thus how to promote the likelihood that they participate actively in the design process. Our work shows that specific procedures need to and can be developed to help them move beyond framing robots as consumer items and toward thinking of them as things to be created together with other stakeholders. Some aspects of this challenge might be related to the length of time of user/participant involvement in our research. The participants opened up over time and began to think in more "designerly" (rather than consumption-oriented) ways in the last two workshops. Another challenge was possibly the social status of our participants, who had significantly lower educational and socio-economic levels than the researchers. Through the workshops, participants became more confident of their contributions. Getting more comfortable with working with the group over a longer time and gaining even more knowledge about the capabilities and functional aspects of robotics might have helped participants embrace their role as designers and decision-makers in later workshops.

Considering users' relations to other actors and institutions.

When HRI researchers investigate users, users are generally understood as individuals (and sometimes groups) interacting with a robot. However, users are also social actors who have various relationships to other social actors and institutions. To develop robots for older adults with depression, we invited not only the older adults but also their therapists and other care staff. We also developed a relationship with the non-profit health institutions that helped us coordinate our participants and are the stable bond between the older adults and therapists, and likely use contexts for future social robots. When collaborating with different social actors, we developed relationships with stakeholders considering the power relationships among them. We started our studies with older adults, since older adults normally have a limited voice and power in the healthcare context. We also acknowledged researchers might generally value therapists' ideas more than those of older adults, due to their institutional role and formal training. Although therapists' knowledge would be beneficial to develop robots, older adults are the primary users who need to be empowered in the robot design process. That is why we met with older adults more often than therapists, and why we met with them separately so both groups could express their ideas freely. A possible role for HRI researchers in PD studies would be not only finding valuable information from participants, but aggregating different stakeholders and facilitating relationships among them.

Providing benefits to participants as PD collaborators.

Our PD work with older adults of lower socio-economic status made us reflect on the relevance of such practices for the participants, not just the researchers and the future of robot design. Our participants came from a particularly vulnerable group in the general population, not just in terms of age, but in relation to their access to social, economic, and political networks through which they could make a difference in their own and other peoples' lives. We found our participants valued the workshops far beyond the monetary compensation they received for attending, as a place where they could socialize and where their voices were heard. Several times, as we were working to prepare a follow-up workshop, the participants' therapists telephoned us to ask when the next workshop would be – their clients were eager to attend. In an environment in which funding for health services is being cut to the minimum, PD research became a social and intellectual outlet for participants. In our discussions, we noticed a general lack of empowerment among our participants, who often expressed they did not have enough control over their own bodies and lives and no significant role in society. Continued work with the design team might ameliorate this, particularly as users see their ideas implemented in future robot design. While this in itself is a positive effect, it raises the question of how to make such engagement more sustainable after PD projects and attendant financial and social support are over. As collaborators, finding ways to provide direct benefits to the participants is an important part of our PD approach.

Balancing the power of researchers and users to determine the sociality of robots.

Researchers' knowledge, learned and cultivated within academic environments, has so far been essential to make robots more social. However, the HRI community may have overemphasized researchers' expertise at the expense of including more diverse perspectives of potential users and stakeholders. Researchers have their own values and assumptions when they are interpreting the responses of research participants (e.g. HRI researchers have embedded stereotyped images of older adults into assistive robot design, which prompted older adults to reject the robots despite their perceived potential usefulness [17,48].) On the other hand, users' mindsets are distinct from those of researchers. Participants evaluate and categorize robots based on how they fit within their everyday space or how the meaning of robots resonates with their values [49]. Although experiments involve users in evaluating robotic technologies, they do not allow users to express their thoughts with their own language and priorities, as the study's frame is determined by researchers. Users can only tell whether the features HRI researchers deemed important are preferable to them or not. Even with ethnographic and user-centered studies, the danger of framing users from researchers' perspectives and obscuring users' concerns persists [50]. Researchers determine the representations of users from their perspectives, which do not necessarily align with the participants' priorities and concerns. Social scientists [51,52] and anthropologists [53] have developed self-reflexive ways to examine their pre-existing assumptions and biases not only to understand participants on their own terms, but also to be aware of the power relationship between researchers and users and to reflect those in their methods of collaboration. The PD process allowed us to gradually equalize the footing of researchers and participants in robot design over several sessions, making users more confident about their ability to contribute to design and researchers more conscious of different perspectives on robot capabilities, usefulness, and challenges.

5. LIMITATIONS

We worked with a unique group of relatively isolated rural participants of lower socio-economic status, so we do not expect their designs to generalize to all older adults. Instead, we see the process of relationship building and mutual learning during social robot design as the generalizable component of our work. We also acknowledge that participants in such studies might be more positive towards robots and the design process due to their relationship with the researchers, and we strived to take this into account in our project design by covering similar issues in multiple workshops and including therapists' views as well. We hope our study contributes to methodological discussions on PD for HRI and the roles of users in the robot design process.

6. CONCLUSIONS

In recent years, the robotics community has focused on the concept of co-robotics to develop robots that can co-exist with humans in everyday contexts [54-56]. The concept of co-robotics values the possibility of robots as mutual learners, expecting more advanced sociality of robots, within various everyday use contexts. Our research seeks to make a contribution to the efforts of the HRI community to explore possibilities for the co-existence of robots in diverse human environments, and in particular to develop participatory methods for designing robots and the social contexts needed to support their successful use. It accomplishes this by bringing up foundational issues and providing a space from which to question assumptions about sociality in HRI that have been long taken for granted. It also describes several methodological steps to include participants in the design of robots in more substantial ways, and to focus the conceptualization and design of robots on a common view of the world created by designers and participants through mutual learning and collaboration.

Additionally, we explicitly reflect on the power dynamics of designing and implementing robots in eldercare. As we learned more about the lives of our patients/users/co-designers, we began to see the many ways in which their situations necessitated bending their lives to the requirements of the health-related social service system. They had learned to enter a "patient" culture, to become, among other things, patient patients. It struck us that this culture afforded many forms of dependency, and perhaps this dependency was itself a major impediment to their being able to enter more fully into the co-designer role that we encouraged them to take. Hence, it may be the case that doing PD with similar groups and individuals may require co-identification, and perhaps even co-implementation, of a more activist, anti-dependency culture. Such a process necessitates a long term commitment for researchers, participants, and the institutions they are part of, as an integral part of social robotics research and design.

7. ACKNOWLEDGMENTS

We thank our participants for their time and invaluable insights, as well as the staff of Centerstone Indiana for their help in implementing our study. We are also grateful to IUB's Center on Real Experiences with Public Health Information Technology program for funding this research.

8. REFERENCES

1. Forlizzi, J. 2007. How robotic products become social products: an ethnographic study of cleaning in the home *In Proceedings of the 2007 ACM/IEEE international conference on Human-Robot Interaction*, 129-136.
2. Tanaka, F. and Ghosh, M. 2011. The implementation of care-receiving robot at an english learning school for children. *In Proceedings of the 6th international conference on Human-Robot Interaction*, 265-266.
3. Wada, K. and Shibata, T. 2007. Living With Seal Robots—Its Sociopsychological and Physiological Influences on the Elderly at a Care House. *IEEE Transactions on Robotics* 23, 5: 972-980.
4. Mutlu, B. and Forlizzi, J. 2008. Robots in organizations: the role of workflow, social, and environmental factors in human-robot interaction. *In Proceedings of the 2008 ACM/IEEE international conference on Human-Robot Interaction*, 287-294.
5. Shiomi, M., Kanda, T., Glas, D. F., Satake, S., Ishiguro, H., and Hagita, N. 2009. Field trial of networked social robots in a shopping mall. *In 2009 IEEE/RSJ International Conference on Intelligent Robots and Systems*, 2846-2853.
6. Šabanović, S. 2014. Inventing Japan's 'robotics culture': The repeated assembly of science, technology, and culture in social robotics. *Social Studies of Science 44*, 3: 342-367.
7. Lewis, C. 2014. Japan holds first "robotics revolution" council meeting, Robohub.
8. Gates, B. 2007. A robot in every home. *Scientific American* 296, 1: 58-65.
9. 2011. National Robotics Initiative N.S. Foundation Ed.
10. Lovgren, S. 2006. A robot in every home by 2020, South
11. Heerink, M., Kröse, B., Evers, V., and Wielinga, B. 2008. The influence of social presence on acceptance of a companion robot by older people. *Journal of Physical Agents* 2, 2: 33-40.
12. Sharkey, A. and Sharkey, N. 2012. Granny and the robots: ethical issues in robot care for the elderly. *Ethics and Information Technology* 14, 1: 27-40.
13. Sparrow, R. and Sparrow, L. 2006. In the hands of machines? The future of aged care. *Minds and Machines* 16, 2: 141-161.
14. Caine, K., S, X, Abanovi, X, and Carter, M. 2012. The effect of monitoring by cameras and robots on the privacy enhancing behaviors of older adults. *In Proceedings of the 2012 ACM/IEEE international conference on Human-Robot Interaction*, 343-350.
15. Hakken, D., Teli, M., and D'andrea, V. 2010. Intercalating the social and the technical: socially robust and enduring computing. *In Proceedings of the 11th Biennial Participatory Design Conference*, 231-234.
16. Gonzalez, H. M., Tarraf, W., Whitfield, K. E., and Vega, W. A. 2010. The epidemiology of major depression and ethnicity in the United States. *J Psychiatr Res 44*, 15: 1043-1051.
17. Lee, H. R., Tan, H., and Šabanović, S. 2016. That robot is not for me: Addressing stereotypes of aging in assistive robot design. *In Proceedings of the 25st IEEE International Symposium on Robot and Human Interactive Communication(Ro-Man),*312-317.
18. Scheutz, M., Schermerhorn, P., Kramer, J., and Anderson, D. 2007. First steps toward natural human-like HRI. *Autonomous Robots* 22, 4: 411-423.
19. Breazeal, C. 2004. Social interactions in HRI: the robot view. *IEEE Transactions on Systems, Man, and Cybernetics, Part C (Applications and Reviews)* 34, 2: 181-186.
20. Bartneck, C., Kanda, T., Ishiguro, H., and Hagita, N. 2009. My Robotic Doppelgänger - a critical look at the Uncanny Valley. *In Proceedings of the 18th IEEE International Symposium on Robot and Human Interactive Communication*, 269-276.
21. Lee, H. R., Šabanović, S., and Stolterman, E. 2016. How Humanlike Should a Social Robot Be: A User-Centered Exploration. In 2016 *AAAI Spring Symposium Series.*
22. Mohammad, Y., Okada, S., and Nishida, T. 2010. Autonomous development of gaze control for natural human-robot interaction. *In Proceedings of the 2010 workshop on Eye gaze in intelligent human machine interaction*, 63-70.
23. Takayama, L., Ju, W., and Nass, C. 2008. Beyond dirty, dangerous and dull: what everyday people think robots should do. *In Proceedings of the 3rd ACM/IEEE international conference on Human Robot Interaction*, 25-32.
24. Kahn, P. H., Freier, N. G., Kanda, T., Ishiguro, H., Ruckert, J. H., Severson, R. L., and Kane, S. K. 2008. Design patterns for sociality in human-robot interaction. *In Proceedings of the 2008 ACM/IEEE international conference on Human-Robot Interaction*, 97-104.
25. Valtazanos, A. and Ramamoorthy, S. 2013. Evaluating the effects of limited perception on interactive decisions in mixed robotic domains. *In Proceedings of the 8th ACM/IEEE international conference on Human-Robot Interaction*, 9-16.
26. Nikolaidis, S. and Shah, J. 2013. Human-robot cross-training: computational formulation, modeling and evaluation of a human team training strategy. *In Proceedings of the 8th ACM/IEEE international conference on Human-Robot Interaction*, 33-40.
27. Suchman, L. 2007. *Human-machine reconfigurations: Plans and situated actions*. Cambridge University Press.
28. Chang, W.-L. and Šabanović, S. 2015. Interaction Expands Function: Social Shaping of the Therapeutic Robot PARO in a Nursing Home. *In Proceedings of the 2015 ACM/IEEE international conference on Human-Robot Interaction*, 343-350.
29. Hoffman, G., Zuckerman, O., Hirschberger, G., Luria, M., and Sherman, T. S. 2015. Design and Evaluation of a Peripheral Robotic Conversation Companion. In *Proceedings of the Proceedings of the 2015 Annual ACM/IEEE International Conference on Human-Robot Interaction*, 3-10.
30. Sirkin, D., Mok, B., Yang, S., and Ju, W. 2015. Mechanical Ottoman: How Robotic Furniture Offers and Withdraws Support. In *Proceedings of the Proceedings of the Tenth Annual ACM/IEEE International Conference on Human-Robot Interaction*, 11-18.
31. Lee, M.K., Forlizzi, J., Rybski, P. E., Crabbe, F., Chung, W., Finkle, J., Glaser, E., and Kiesler, S. 2009. The Snackbot: Documenting the design of a robot for long-term Human-Robot Interaction. *In Proceedings of the 2009 ACM/IEEE international conference on Human-Robot Interaction*, 7-14
32. Cheon, E. and Su, N. M. 2016. Integrating Roboticist Values into a Value Sensitive Design Framework for Humanoid Robots. *In Proceedings of the 2016 ACM/IEEE international conference on Alt Human-Robot Interaction*, 375-382.
33. Frennert, S., Eftring, H., and Östlund, B. 2013. Older People's Involvement in the Development of a Social Assistive Robot. *In Proceedings of the 5th International Conference of Social Robotics,* 8-18.
34. Šabanović, S., Chang, W.-L., Bennett, C. C., Piatt, J. A., and Hakken, D. 2015. A Robot of My Own: Participatory Design of Socially Assistive Robots for Independently Living Older Adults Diagnosed with Depression. *In Proceedings of the 1st International Conference, ITAP 2015*, 104-114.

35. Azenkot, S., Feng, C., and Cakmak, M. 2016. Enabling Building Service Robots to Guide Blind People: A Participatory Design Approach. *In Proceedings of the 2016 ACM/IEEE international conference on Human-Robot Interaction*, 3-10.
36. Simonsen, J. and Robertson, T. 2012. *Routledge international handbook of participatory design*. Routledge.
37. Williams, R. and Edge, D. 1996. The social shaping of technology. *Research Policy 25*, 6: 865-899.
38. Chen, T. L., Ciocarlie, M., Cousins, S., Grice, P., Hawkins, K., Hsiao, K., Kemp, C. C., King, C.-H., Lazewatsky, D. A., and Leeper, A. E. 2013. Robots for humanity: Using assistive robots to empower people with disabilities.
39. Caleb-Solly, P., Dogramadzi, S., Ellender, D., Fear, T., and Heuvel, H. V. D. 2014. A mixed-method approach to evoke creative and holistic thinking about robots in a home environment. *In Proceedings of the 2014 ACM/IEEE international conference on Human-Robot Interaction*, 374-381.
40. Lee, H. R. and Šabanović, S. 2013. Weiser's dream in the Korean home: collaborative study of domestic roles, relationships, and ideal technologies. *In Proceedings of the 2013 ACM international joint conference on Pervasive and Ubiquitous computing*, 637-646.
41. Lee, H. R., Sung, J., Šabanović, S., and Han, J. 2012. Cultural design of domestic robots: A study of user expectations in Korea and the United States. *In Proceedings of the 21st IEEE International Symposium on Robot and Human Interactive Communication (Ro-Man)*, 803-808.
42. Green, A., Huttenrauch, H., Norman, M., Oestreicher, L., and Eklundh, K. S. 2000. User centered design for intelligent service robots. *In Proceedings of the 9th IEEE International Workshop on Robot and Human Interactive Communication, 2000. RO-MAN 2000*, 161-166.
43. Gorz, A. 1967. *Strategy for labor*. Beacon Press Boston.
44. Shibata, T. 2012. Therapeutic Seal Robot as Biofeedback Medical Device: Qualitative and Quantitative Evaluations of Robot Therapy in Dementia Care. *Proceedings of the IEEE* 100, 8: 2527-2538.
45. Ciechanowski, P., Wagner, E., Schmaling, K., and Et Al. 2004. Community-integrated home-based depression treatment in older adults: A randomized controlled trial. *JAMIA* 291, 13: 1569-1577.
46. Graf, B., Hans, M., and Schraft, R. D. 2004. Care-O-bot II—Development of a Next Generation Robotic Home Assistant. *Autonomous Robots* 16, 2: 193-205.
47. Coradeschi, S., Cesta, A., Cortellessa, G., Coraci, L., Gonzalez, J., Karlsson, L., Furfari, F., Loutfi, A., Orlandini, A., Palumbo, F., Pecora, F., Rump, S. V., A, Š., Ullberg, J., and Ötslund, B. 2013. GiraffPlus: Combining social interaction and long term monitoring for promoting independent living. *In Proceedings of 6th International Conference on Human System Interactions (HSI)*, 578-585.
48. Neven, L. 2010. 'But obviously not for me': robots, laboratories and the defiant identity of elder test users. *Sociology of Health & Illness 32*, 2: 335-347.
49. Lee, H. R., Šabanović, S., and Stolterman, E. 2014. Stay on the boundary: artifact analysis exploring researcher and user framing of robot design. *In Proceedings of the SIGCHI Conference on Human Factors in Computing Systems.* 1471-1474.
50. Forsythe, D. E. 1999. "It's Just a Matter of Common Sense": Ethnography as Invisible Work. *Computer Supported Cooperative Work (CSCW) 8*, 1: 127-145.
51. Charmaz, K. 2014. *Constructing grounded theory*. Sage.
52. Clarke, A. 2005. *Situational analysis: Grounded theory after the postmodern turn*. Sage.
53. Lassiter, L. E. 2005. *The Chicago guide to collaborative ethnography*. University of Chicago Press.
54. Burrows, M. 2012. *Global Trends 2030: Alternative Worlds*. US National Intelligence Council.
55. Riek, L. D. 2014. The social co-robotics problem space: Six key challenges. *Robotics Challenges and Vision (RCV2013).*
56. Robotics, V. 2013. A Roadmap for US Robotics: From Internet to Robotics. *Robotics Virtual Organization.*

The Robotic Social Attributes Scale (RoSAS): Development and Validation

Colleen M. Carpinella
Disney Research
1401 Flower Street
Glendale, CA 91201
+1 (818) 553-6103
colleen.carpinella@disneyresearch.com

Alisa B. Wyman
Disney Research
1401 Flower Street
Glendale, CA 91201
+1(760) 716-2965
alisa.wyman@disneyresearch.com

Michael A. Perez
Disney Research
1401 Flower Street
Glendale, CA 91201
+1 (626) 378-6747
michael.perez@disneyresearch.com

Steven J. Stroessner
Disney Research
1401 Flower Street
Glendale, CA 91201
+1 (818) 553-4388
steve.stroessner@disneyresearch.com

ABSTRACT

Accurately measuring perceptions of robots has become increasingly important as technological progress permits more frequent and extensive interaction between people and robots. Across four studies, we develop and validate a scale to measure social perception of robots. Drawing from the Godspeed Scale and from the psychological literature on social perception, we develop an 18-item scale (The Robotic Social Attribute Scale; RoSAS) to measure people's judgments of the social attributes of robots. Factor analyses reveal three underlying scale dimensions—warmth, competence, and discomfort. We then validate the RoSAS and show that the discomfort dimension does not reflect a concern with unfamiliarity. Using images of robots that systematically vary in their machineness and gender-typicality, we show that the application of these social attributes to robots varies based on their appearance.

CCS Concepts

• Human-centered computing~HCI design and evaluation methods • Applied computing~Psychology • Computing methodologies~Philosophical/theoretical foundations of artificial intelligence

Keywords

Anthropomorphism; Human Factors; Human-Robot Interaction; Measurement; Perception; Personality Perception; Psychometric Scale; Robots; Robotics; Social Perception; Social Robots; Social Robotics

HRI '17, March 06 - 09, 2017, Vienna, Austria

ACM 978-1-4503-4336-7/17/03...$15.00
DOI: http://dx.doi.org/10.1145/2909824.3020208

1. INTRODUCTION

People interact with machines with ever-increasing frequency, and these exchanges also play increasingly important roles in peoples' lives. Recent research has centered on the social psychology of human-machine interactions, focusing primarily on issues of anthropomorphization and the attribution of the theory of mind to machines. Less work has systematically examined how traits and characteristics associated with robots vary based on features or perceived social category membership. To do so, a psychometrically valid, standardized measure of the social attributes that people ascribe to machines must be developed. The current research offers one such measure, the Robotic Social Attributes Scale (RoSAS). The aim of this research is to offer a means to assess the central attributes implicated in human perception of robots and, ultimately, to provide the robotic community with a tool to determine how perceived attributes affect the quality of interaction with robots.

1.1 Social Perception of People

Literature in social psychology has established two universal dimensions of person perception—warmth and competence [1]. These two central dimensions are thought to reflect questions concerning basic survival—whether another person intends to help or to harm us and if they have the ability to do so.

In general, when people are evaluated as warm and competent they are seen more favorably and experience more positive interactions. Warmth judgments are commonly rendered before competence judgments and carry more weight in interpersonal interactions. For example, when presented with faces of unknown individuals, perceivers render trustworthiness judgments before competence judgments [2]. Additionally, different combinations of warmth and competence judgments elicit distinct emotions. For instance, persons perceived as high on warmth but low on competence elicit pity or sympathy, whereas the opposite combination, (low on warmth but high on competence), elicits envy or jealousy [3]. Nevertheless, warmth and competence are the main drivers of the impression formation process in judgments of humans.

Warmth has been shown to be a focal underlying dimension of robot perception as well [4]. However, additional research is warranted to examine what attributes underlie the general perception of robot warmth and how they relate to other underlying perceptual dimensions such as competence.

1.2 Social Categorization of Robots

Existing research indicates social categorization processes underlying person perception can generalize to robots. Without being encouraged to do so, people spontaneously make social category judgments of humanoid robots' gender, race, and nationality [5]. People appear to apply gender categories and respective stereotypes to humanoid robots depending on whether their hairstyle implies a female or male gender identity [6]. In a similar study, female robots with long hair and full lips were perceived as higher on the communal dimension (e.g., friendly, polite, affectionate), whereas the male robots were perceived as more agentic (e.g., assertive, determined, authoritative) [7]. Therefore, social attributions typically applied to humans can also be applied to robots, especially if they are classified into gender categories. Moreover, the tendency to use gender stereotypes extends to other kinds of machines [8, 9].

People often anthropomorphize robots, imbuing them with human traits, goals, and motivations. The tendency to assign human characteristics to robots varies based on social contextual cues as well as people's motivations. People are more likely to anthropomorphize robots when human characteristics are accessible and applicable (e.g., when they have recently been used or when robots appear more humanlike) [10]. People are more likely to anthropomorphize a robot when the robot is perceived as an in-group member, sharing a common identity with them, compared to when the robot is perceived as an out-group member [11]. This suggests that the perceived anthropomorphic qualities of a robot are malleable based on characteristics central to the perceiver and the robot.

1.3 Measurement of Robot Characteristics

There is a wide-spread need for a standardized measurement tool in HRI research to allow comparisons across robots and across studies. The Godspeed scale [12] was developed as a way to measure human and robotic interaction, and it has become a widely used measure of human-robot interaction [13]. There are five central dimensions to the Godspeed scale: i) anthropomorphism, or the extent to which a robot appears humanlike versus machinelike [14]; ii) animacy, or how lifelike a robot seems [15, 16]; iii) likeability, or how friendly a robot seems [14]; iv) perceived intelligence of the robot [17, 18]; and v) perceived safety, or emotional state/anxiety of the perceiver [19].

Despite the widespread use of the Godspeed scale, little empirical work has examined its psychometric properties. Indeed, recent research has documented some shortcomings of the Godspeed indices [4]. Our work, presented here, and that of Ho and MacDorman [4] identifies several problematic aspects of the Godspeed scale. First, several of the scale items are confounded with positive and negative affect. Second, the items do not load as expected onto the five scale dimensions and several items do not load onto any dimensions. In other words, the items do not correspond to the underlying constructs they are meant to measure. Third, four out of the five dimensions are highly correlated, suggesting that similar rather than distinct concepts are measured. Finally, the semantic differential response format is used (i.e., the two endpoints of the scale are polar adjectives). Whereas some scale items use antonyms as endpoints, allowing a clear identification of the underlying construct being measured (unfriendly-friendly), other pairings appear to reflect more than one dimension of judgment (awful-nice). Our research uses items from the Godspeed and also insights from the psychological literature on social perception to develop and validate a more psychologically valid scale of robotic perception.

2. STUDY 1

Study 1 offers an exploratory factor analysis of responses to the Godspeed Questionnaire to assess the psychometric properties of the scale. As described earlier, the Godspeed attempts to measure five distinct dimensions: *anthropomorphism* (fake–natural, machinelike–humanlike, unconscious–conscious, artificial–lifelike, moving rigidly–moving elegantly), *animacy* (dead–alive, stagnant–lively, mechanical–organic, artificial–lifelike, inert–interactive, apathetic–responsive), *likeability* (dislike–like, unfriendly–friendly, unkind–kind, unpleasant–pleasant, awful–nice), *perceived intelligence* (incompetent–competent, ignorant–knowledgeable, irresponsible–responsible, unintelligent–intelligent, foolish–sensible), and *perceived safety* (anxious–relaxed, agitated–calm, quiescent–surprised). Using these semantic differential scale items included in the original Godspeed Scale, we tested whether the hypothesized 5-factor solution would emerge and whether items would load on the expected dimensions. Our study used 23 of the 24 Godspeed items, because artificial–lifelike appears on both the *anthropomorphism* and *animacy* subscales of the Godspeed.

2.1 Study 1 Method

2.1.1 Participants

Two hundred fifteen people (127 men, 88 women) participated via Amazon's Mechanical Turk (mTurk) in exchange for $0.60.

2.1.2 Procedure

We informed participants that we were interested in how people perceive groups in our society. Participants were told that when we encounter a name of a group, certain words might come to mind, and we were interested in measuring these associations. Participants were asked to evaluate the category 'robots' on the Godspeed items. We intentionally left the category of interest broad and did not include any images, a definition, or specification of the type of robot. We did not want the development of our scale to be tied to a specific exemplar or type of robot, so that it could serve as a general measure of robot perception.

Participants were presented with the list of attributes from the Godspeed scale in the original semantic differential format and were asked to rate the extent to which they perceived these attributes to be associated with robots. Participants were asked, "Using the scale provided, what is your impression of the category robots?" Participants responded using a 5-point likert scale for each sematic differential item. The order in which the items were presented was randomized. After providing judgments, participants were asked to fill out demographic information about themselves and thanked for their participation.

2.2 Study 1 Results

We performed an exploratory factor analysis (EFA) to assess the properties of the Godspeed scale. EFA is a statistical method used to identify conceptual variables being measured by a scale and the relationships between variables. When using EFA, you need to specify an extraction method which determines the statistical procedures that are utilized. To identify the five factors underlying the Godspeed scale items, we used principal axis factoring and designated a five factor solution [20]. Next, we needed to pick a rotation method. We chose promax rotation because there was reason to believe that the factors would be associated with one another [20].

Next, we conducted the EFA, plotted the scree plot, and examined the eigenvalues to determine the relative importance of the factors. Eigenvalues represent how much variation in scale responding can be explained by each factor; the larger the eigenvalue, the more the factor explains. [20]. The scree plot depicted in Figure 1 shows the eigenvalues (y-axis) plotted against the factor with which they are related (x-axis). We determined the importance of the factors by examining the eigenvalues. The scree plot shows a clear leveling-off point indicating that only the first three factors are important. Altogether, these three factors accounted for 46% of the overall variance in robot evaluation. Inspection of the items that loaded on each factor (factor loadings > .500) indicated that they reflected perceived anthropomorphism, perceived intelligence, and likeability. The factor loadings are depicted in Table 1, with factor loadings > .500 bolded.

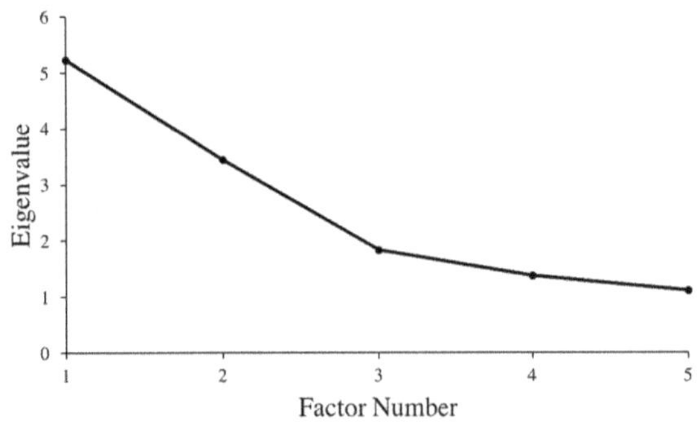

Figure 1. Scree Plot (Study 1)

The first factor reflected *anthropomorphism.* Four items comprised this factor: machinelike–humanlike, mechanical–organic, artificial–lifelike, moving rigidly–moving elegantly (α = .77). In comparing this factor against the Godspeed subscales, two items that should have loaded on this factor – fake-natural and unconscious-conscious – did not (.290 and .266, respectively), and one item that was not expected on this factor – mechanical–organic – did. While a test of the reliability for the original five items was reasonable (α = .74), it is clear that the factor that emerged here was similar to but distinct from what is reflected in the Godspeed.

The second factor reflected *perceived intelligence.* Six items comprised this factor: incompetent–competent, ignorant–knowledgeable, foolish–sensible, unintelligent–intelligent, inert–interactive, and irresponsible–responsible (α = .81). Whereas five of these items comprised the intelligence subscale of the Godspeed, one item – inert–interactive – did not. However, the reliability for the original five items was nearly identical (α = .82).

Table 1. Factor Loadings (Study 1)

Variable	Factor 1	Factor 2	Factor 3	Factor 4	Factor 5
Machinelike-Humanlike	**.846**	.071	-.094	-.108	.177
Mechanical-Organic	**.712**	-.133	-.140	.137	.137
Artificial-Lifelike	**.630**	.039	.058	.067	.009
Moving Rigidly-Moving Elegantly	**.527**	-.011	-.018	.101	-.041
Incompetent-Competent	-.035	**.796**	-.134	-.078	.088
Ignorant-Knowledgeable	-.167	**.747**	-.006	.215	.016
Foolish-Sensible	-.039	**.688**	.065	-.077	.092
Unintelligent-Intelligent	.014	**.564**	-.055	.214	.093
Inert-Interactive	.092	**.526**	.103	-.097	-.234
Irresponsible-Responsible	.075	**.517**	.062	.034	.096
Awful-Nice	-.004	-.050	**.792**	-.051	.118
Dislike-Like	-.081	.008	**.662**	-.028	.098
Unpleasant-Pleasant	.041	.094	**.606**	-.099	.051
Unkind-Kind	-.084	-.134	**.551**	.256	.088
Dead-Alive	.097	.121	-.044	**.592**	-.066
Unconscious-Conscious	.266	.166	-.038	**.571**	-.070
Anxious-Relaxed	.153	.064	.088	-.106	**.646**
Agitated-Calm	-.134	.131	.221	.085	**.543**
Unfriendly-Friendly	.361	-.010	.493	-.063	-.066
Stagnant-Lively	.356	.171	.150	.010	-.149
Quiescent-Surprised	.333	-.065	.129	.147	-.226
Fake-Natural	.290	-.207	.077	.449	.077
Apathetic-Responsive	.012	.197	.337	.062	-.191
Eigenvalue	5.224	3.440	1.830	1.378	1.109
Percent variance explained	22.71%	14.96%	7.96%	6.00%	4.82%

The scree plot suggested that Factors 4 and 5 should not be included in the scale. However, we explored these factors to determine whether they corresponded with the animacy and perceived safety components of the Godspeed. The two items that load on Factor 4 are dead–alive and unconscious–conscious. Only the first appears in the animacy subscale of the Godspeed, and the second is associated with anthropomorphism in the Godspeed. None of the other five items from the animacy subscale of the Godspeed loaded on Factor 4 (all loadings < .137). Moreover, the reliability for the original six animacy items is low (α = .57). Therefore, it appears that Factor 4 bears little resemblance to the Godspeed animacy subscale.

Factor 5 possibly reflects perceived safety as evidenced by anxious–relaxed and agitated–calm. However, the item quiescent-surprised actually loaded negatively on this factor (-.226). Moreover, the reliability for the original three perceived safety items is unacceptably low (α = .22). Therefore, based upon the scree plot and the low overlap between these results and the constructs reflected in the Godspeed, it does not appear that the proposed 5-factor solution offers a psychometrically sound characterization of scale responses.

Table 2. Factor Correlation Matrix (Study 1)

Factor	Factor 1	Factor 2	Factor 3	Factor 4
Factor 1				
Factor 2	-.01			
Factor 3	.27	.47		
Factor 4	.41	.25	.25	
Factor 5	-.09	.20	.23	.10

In examining the correlations between the factors, the first three were relatively independent with the exception of the correlations between perceived intelligence and likeability (r = .47) and anthropomorphism and Factor 4 (r = .47) (see Table 2). These results suggest that some of the Godspeed subscales might be measuring related rather than independent constructs of robot perception.

In summary, Study 1 shows that the items in the Godspeed scale load onto three unique factors— reflecting anthropomorphism, perceived intelligence, and likeability Unexpectedly, factors reflecting animacy and perceived safety did not emerge as strong constructs utilized in judging robots as a social category.

3. STUDY 2

In Study 2, we sought to complement the items from the Godspeed scale with a novel set of social attributes generated from psychological literature on social cognition. To the degree that robots are often anthropomorphized, we hypothesized that attributes central to social judgment might also play an important role in robot perception. Therefore, we aimed to develop a psychometrically valid scale to evaluate robots on social dimensions (i.e., the Robotic Social Attribute Scale; RoSAS). Participants in Study 2 were presented with the Godspeed items and a list of attributes shown to be central in social perception: The Stereotype Content Model and the Bem Sex Role Inventory [1, 21]. We sought to determine the underlying factor structure and to examine the overlap with the 3-factor solution derived from assessing responses using the Godspeed scale.

3.1 Study 2 Method

3.1.1 Participants

Two hundred ten people (105 women, 104 men, 1 unidentified) participated via mTurk in exchange for $1.25.

3.1.2 Procedure

Participants were presented with modified items from the Godspeed scale and a set of attributes from research on social cognition. To make items more comparable, we separated out the endpoints from the semantic differential Godspeed items to create unidimensional items. This generated a list of 38 unique items from the Godspeed. We then combined these items with our attributes, eliminating duplicate items, yielding a total of 83 items. Participants were asked, *"Using the scale provided, how closely are the words below associated with the category robots?"*. Participants responded using a 9-point likert scale from 1 = *definitely not associated* to 9 = *definitely associated.* The order in which the items were presented was randomized.

3.2 Study 2 Results

We performed an exploratory factor analysis on participants' responses in an attempt to develop a broader and more psychometrically valid measure of robot perception. We used principal axis factoring extraction method with a promax rotation. This factor analysis revealed three factors with eigenvalues greater than one, and the scree plot showed a clear leveling-off point after the third factor (see Figure 2). Together, these three factors accounted for 44% of the overall variance in robot evaluation. Inspection of the items that loaded on each factor (factor loadings > .500) indicated that 18 items loaded onto the three factors (see Table 3). There was no cross loading of any of the unlisted items.

We labeled the first factor *warmth.* The items that comprised this factor were: feeling, happy, organic, compassionate, social, and emotional (α = .91). The items that loaded onto the second factor related to the intelligence or ability of the robot, and we labeled this factor *competence.* The items that comprised this factor were: knowledgeable, interactive, responsive, capable, competent, and reliable (α = .84).

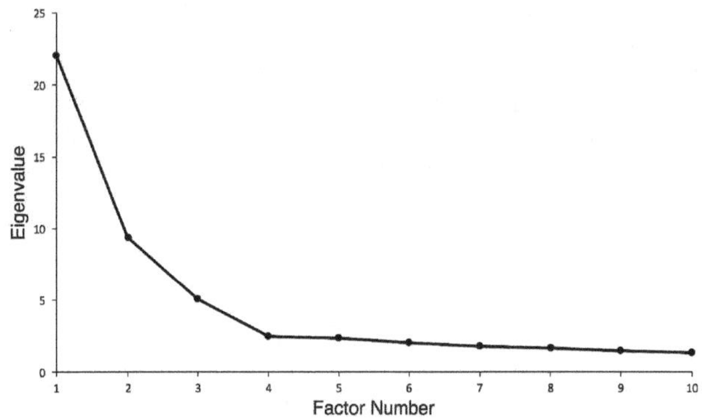

Figure 2. Scree Plot (Study 2)

Factor 3 items were related to awkwardness, and we labeled this factor *discomfort.* The items that comprised this factor were aggressive, awful, scary, awkward, dangerous, and strange (α = .82). The correlations between the factors were lower than for those between the Godspeed subscales alone (see Table 4). In examining the correlations between the factors, the factors were relatively independent (see Table 4), suggesting that the three dimensions of the RoSAS are measuring independent constructs of robot perception.

Therefore, the factor analysis for the combined Godspeed items and attributes from the social cognition literature indicates that there are three central factors underlying the evaluation of robots. The first two dimensions of warmth and competence are similar to the two trait dimensions central to person perception [1], and parallel the likeability and perceived intelligence dimensions from the Godspeed items. This attests that these are two central dimensions underlying robot evaluation. Furthermore, a third aspect of discomfort arises with the combined sets and somewhat parallels aspects of the Godspeed analysis (i.e., a thematically coherent but weak 5th factor reflecting safety concerns).

Table 3. Factor Loadings (Study 2)

Variable	Factor 1	Factor 2	Factor 3
Happy	**.831**	-.013	-.009
Feeling	**.811**	-.154	.043
Social	**.793**	.125	-.176
Organic	**.784**	-.149	-.022
Compassionate	**.778**	-.039	.030
Emotional	**.776**	-.204	.050
Capable	-.210	**.706**	-.052
Responsive	-.141	**.680**	.040
Interactive	-.225	**.652**	-.006
Reliable	-.061	**.651**	-.028
Competent	-.111	**.646**	-.040
Knowledgable	-.007	**.620**	-.021
Scary	.052	-.012	**.693**
Strange	-.053	.150	**.601**
Awkward	.049	.037	**.601**
Dangerous	-.035	.024	**.597**
Awful	.360	-.250	**.555**
Aggressive	.265	.009	**.547**
Eigenvalue	22.031	9.336	5.047
Percent variance explained	26.54%	11.25%	6.09%

The combined analysis suggests that the scale developed here has stronger psychometric properties compared to the Godspeed scale. Eigenvalues are higher (all > 5.5 vs. < 5.5, respectively) and scale reliabilities are higher (all > .82 vs. all < .82, respectively) for the combined set of attributes. Taken together, we believe that these 18 items – that we call the Robotic Social Attributes Scale (RoSAS) – offer a parsimonious and psychometrically valid scale for the social evaluation of robots.

Table 4. Factor Correlation Matrix (Study 2)

Factor	Factor 1	Factor 2
Factor 1		
Factor 2	.20	
Factor 3	.34	.18

4. STUDY 3

Study 3 focused on the unique attribute of *discomfort* that emerged in the factor analysis. This factor does not appear in measures of social perception of humans, and we considered two possible reasons why it might play a role in robot perception. One possibility is that people are concerned about feelings of discomfort that might arise in interacting with robots. A second possibility is that people might be concerned about discomfort in considering any entity that is unfamiliar. Thus, Study 3 was designed to test whether the unique third dimension of discomfort that emerged in our study of robot perception arose due to the confounding factor of unfamiliarity. In other words, perhaps the presence of a *discomfort* dimension was simply due to a lack of familiarity with robots. If so, a 3-dimension solution including a factor focusing on discomfort might emerge when people judge any unfamiliar entity. If discomfort reflects a concern with unfamiliarity, then a 3-factor solution should fit the data for novel but not for familiar entities.

4.1 Study 3 Method

4.1.1 Participants

Seventy people (36 men, 33 women, 1 unidentified) participated via mTurk in exchange for $1.20.

4.1.2 Procedure

Participants were presented with familiar and unfamiliar animal (i.e., giraffe and okapi) and human (i.e., Australian and Nauruan) linguistic categories. Participants then rated each entity on the 18-items of RoSAS. Participants were asked, "Using the scale provided, how closely are the words below associated with the category [giraffe, okapi, Australian, and Nauruan]?" Participants responded using a 9-point likert scale from 1= *definitely not associated* to 9 = *definitely associated.* The order in which the items were presented was randomized.

4.2 Study 3 Results

We performed an exploratory factor analysis on participants' responses separately for each animal and human category that was provided. We used principal axis factoring extraction method with a promax rotation.

The items for all four categories loaded onto 2 factors. For all four categories, the eigenvalues for the first two factors were above 3, while the eigenvalues for the remainder of the factors were below 2. This pattern of results held for the familiar and unfamiliar animal categories. For giraffe, the first and second factors (6.19 and 3.14) had higher eigenvalues than the third and fourth factors (1.62 and 1.26). The pattern was the same for okapi with a clear divide between the eigenvalues for the first and second (7.25 and 3.02) and the third and fourth factors (1.32 and 1.19). The familiar and unfamiliar human categories showed the same pattern. Aussie showed a clear divide between the eigenvalues for the first and second (7.38 and 3.21) and the third and fourth factors (1.13 and 1.04). For Nauruan, the first and second factors (7.97 and 3.90) had higher eigenvalues than the third and fourth factors (1.23 and 0.88). Finally, the scree plots for all four categories showed a clear leveling-off point after the second factor, indicating that for both familiar and unfamiliar entities, no discomfort dimension arises.

Therefore, the emergence of a factor focusing on discomfort in judgments of robots does not appear to arise simply due to a lack of familiarity. Studies 2 and 3 provided evidence that people spontaneously consider warmth and competence in thinking about robots, just as they do when they think about people. However, people appear to spontaneously consider discomfort when judging robots but do not do so when thinking of other unfamiliar groups. In Study 4, we sought to further validate RoSAS by testing whether the judgment of robots on these social attributes varies as a function of robot appearance.

5. STUDY 4

One implication of RoSAS is that people think about robots using dimensions of assessment that are central to judgments of human beings, specifically focusing on issues of warmth and competence. We wondered whether these attributes, which are associated with the important human social category of gender (i.e., gender stereotypes), would influence judgments of robots that had male and female features.

A second implication of RoSAS is that people focus uniquely on discomfort when thinking about robots compared with humans. We wondered whether inferences about discomfort would differentially appear for male versus female robots. We also wanted to simultaneously test how robots that varied along the humanlike-machinelike dimension would be perceived. Therefore, Study 4 tested whether robot faces that varied systematically in the gender-typicality and machine-human quality of their appearance, would be perceived differently in terms of warmth, competence, and discomfort.

5.1 Study 4 Method

5.1.1 Participants

Two hundred fifty-two people (137 women, 115 men) participated via mTurk in exchange for $1.80.

5.1.2 Stimuli and Procedure

The base faces that were used to create the robot stimuli were generated using commercial software (FaceGen Modeler) [22]. Images were Caucasian individuals manipulated to appear feminine, androgynous, or masculine. After these base faces were created, the images were edited in Photoshop to appear humanlike, human-machine blend ("blended"), or machinelike. The facial structure was kept constant, but the texture of the skin was systematically and consistently varied depending on the target type, with machinelike images constructed with a metallic skin and visible hardware. The full set of robot faces varied systematically in terms of their gender-typicality (3 feminine, 3 androgynous, 3 masculine) and their machineness (3 humanlike, 3 human-machine blend, 3 machinelike) (see Figure 3). Participants were informed that all images they were robots and in debriefing, no participants expressed concern that they were not. The gender-typicality and machineness of the images was not labeled.

Stimuli were pretested to ensure that the machineness and gender-typicality of the images was manipulated accordingly. Pretest data indicated that the machinelike stimuli were indeed rated significantly higher on machineness (M = 6.2, SD = 1.1) than blended (M = 4.9, SD = 1.3) and humanlike stimuli (M = 2.6, SD = 1.3), $F(2,122) = 238.20$, $p < .001$. Pretest data also showed that male stimuli were rated significantly higher on masculinity (M = 6.1, SD = .9) compared to the androgynous (M = 5.0, SD = 1.0) and female stimuli (M = 2.8, SD = .9), $F(2,122) = 45.20$, $p < .001$.

Participants were randomly presented with each of the nine robot images (see Figure 3). Participants completed the RoSAS for each robot face following the procedures discussed earlier. The presentation of the 18 traits was randomized across participants.

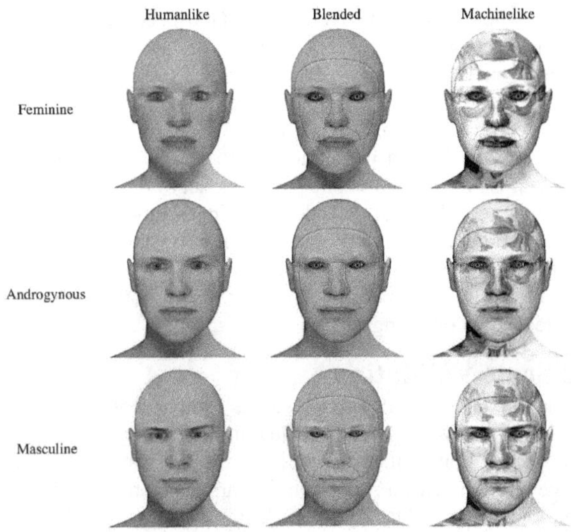

Figure 3. Robot Image Stimuli (Study 4)

5.2 Study 4 Results

5.2.1 Analytic Strategy

Image judgments were nested under participant. We therefore analyzed data using generalized estimating equations to accurately model the hierarchical nature of the data [23], specifying a normal distribution. We report unstandardized regression coefficients (B). Target Gender (1 = Female, 2 = Androgynous, 3 = Male), and Target Type were coded multicategorically (1 = Human, 2 = Human-Machine, 3 = Machine). All analyses were run in a stepwise fashion, first testing main effects and subsequently adding predicted interactions to the model. The six items comprising the warmth, competence, and discomfort dimensions were averaged. All three dimensions showed excellent reliability, $\alpha = .92$, $\alpha = .95$, and $\alpha = .90$, respectively, across all target images.

5.2.2 Warmth Judgments

Based on well-established human stereotypes, we predicted that female robots would be rated higher on warmth than male robots. To test this prediction, we regressed Warmth onto Target Gender, Target Type, and their interaction. There was a main effect of Target Gender, $\chi^2(2) = 27.80$, $p < .0001$; female robots and androgynous robots were rated as warmer than male robots, *Contrasts* = -.26 and -.20, *SEs* = .04, 95% CIs = [-.33, -.19] and [-.27, -.13]. Female robots and androgynous robots did not vary in their perceived warmth, *Contrast* = -.06, *SE* = .04, 95% CI = [-.13, .01] (see Figure 4).

We also expected that humanlike robots would be rated highest on warmth. There was a main effect of Target Type, $\chi^2(2) = 309.52$, $p < .0001$; humanlike robots were rated as significantly warmer than blended robots and machinelike robots, *Contrasts* = -.72 and -1.03, *SEs* = .04, 95% CIs = [-.80, -.65] and [-1.10, -.96]. Blended robots were seen as significantly warmer than machinelike robots, *Contrasts* = -.31, *SE* = .04, 95% CI = [-.38, -.23]. The interaction between Target Gender and Target Type was not significant, $\chi^2(4) = 5.25$, $p = .2629$. The combination of these two main effects resulted in female humanlike robots being rated the highest on warmth.

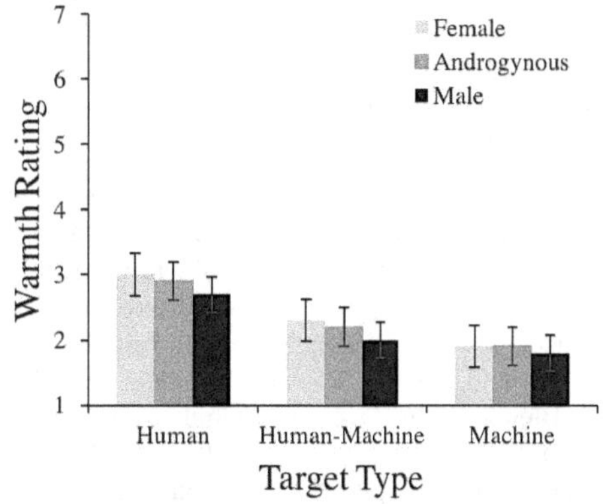

Figure 4. Warmth Judgments (Study 4)

5.2.3 Competence Judgments

Based on well-established human stereotypes, we first predicted that male robots would be rated highest on competence. To test this prediction, we regressed Competence onto Target Gender, Target Type, and their interaction. There was a main effect of Target Gender, $\chi^2(2) = 8.24$, $p = .0163$; contrary to our predictions, female robots and androgynous robots were rated as more competent than male robots, *Contrasts* = -.08 and -.14, *SEs* = .03, 95% CIs = [-.14, -.01] and [-.20, -.07]. However, female robots and androgynous robots did not vary in their perceived competence, *Contrast* = .06, *SE* = .03, 95% CI = [-.01, .12] (see Figure 5).

Next, there was a main effect of Target Type, $\chi^2(2) = 52.10$, $p < .0001$; humanlike robots were rated as significantly more competent than blended robots and machinelike robots, *Contrasts* = -.35 and -.37, *SEs* = .03, 95% CIs = [-.42, -.29] and [-44, -.31]. The perceived competence of blended and machinelike robots did not vary, *Contrast* = -.02, *SE* = .03, 95% CI = [-.09, .04].

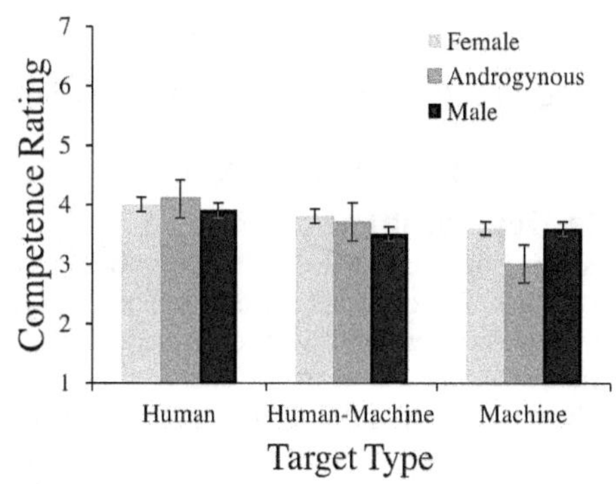

Figure 5. Competence Judgments (Study 4)

The interaction between Target Gender and Target Type was significant, $\chi^2(4) = 9.96$, $p = .0411$. In line with our predictions, robots that appeared humanlike were seen as more competent than machinelike robots. However, contrary to our predictions, female and androgynous robots were also seen as more competent.

5.2.4 Discomfort Judgments

We predicted that male robots would produce higher judgments of discomfort than female robots [5]. To test this prediction, we regressed Competence onto Target Gender, Target Type, and their interaction. There was a main effect of Target Gender, $\chi^2(2) = 24.04$, $p < .0001$; in line with our predictions, male robots and androgynous robots were rated higher on discomfort compared to female robots, *Contrasts* = .28 and .37, *SE*s = .05, 95% CIs = [.18, .37] and [.28, .47]. Male robots and androgynous robots did not vary in their perceived discomfort, *Contrast* = -.10, *SE* = .05, 95% CI = [-.19, .001] (see Figure 6).

Next, we predicted that machinelike robots would be anthropomorphized the least and therefore rated highest on discomfort. There was a main effect of Target Type, $\chi^2(2) = 283.45$, $p < .0001$; machinelike robots were rated as significantly higher on discomfort than blended robots and human robots, *Contrasts* = .49 and 1.36, *SE*s = .05, 95% CIs = [.39, .59] and [1.26, 1.46]. Blended robots were rated higher on discomfort than humanlike robots, *Contrast* = .87, *SE* = .05, 95% CI = [.77, .97]. The interaction between Target Gender and Target Type was significant, $\chi^2(4) = 11.15$, $p = .0250$. Male machinelike robots were rated the highest on discomfort.

The findings from Study 4 indicate that robots that appear female and humanlike are perceived to be warmer and more competent. Conversely, a robot appearing more male and machinelike is rated the highest on discomfort. These results show some evidence of traditional gender stereotyping and provide information about the types of robotic features that will produce more versus less discomfort.

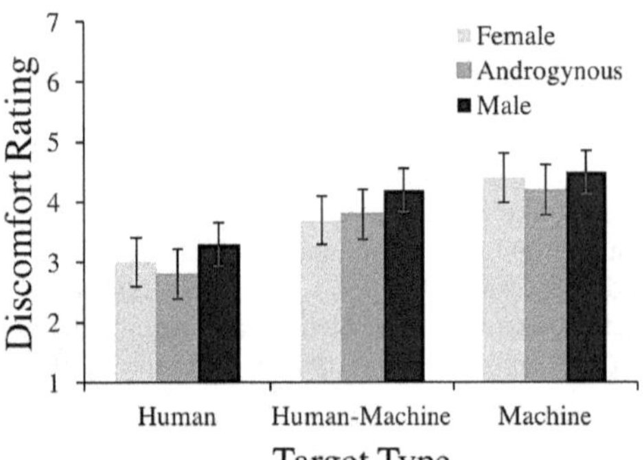

Figure 6. Discomfort Judgments (Study 4)

6. GENERAL DISCUSSION

6.1 Scale Development

Across 4 studies, we collected data with the original Godspeed items and a new set of items based on social psychological research to develop the RoSAS. We arrived at a three factor solution encompassing 18 items to characterize judgments of robots, reflecting the dimensions of warmth, competence, and discomfort. We then conceptually tested this item set with the application to familiar versus unfamiliar entities. The items loaded on only 2 factors for both familiar and unfamiliar entities, indicating that the discomfort dimension is not related to people's lack of familiarity with robots.

Although we believe the RoSAS scale is a valuable new tool for measuring HRI, we do not mean to suggest that RoSAS should completely replace existing instruments. We view the Godspeed as a complement to the RoSAS when specific constructs not well measured by the RoSAS are the focus of research. The development of the RoSAS is indebted to the Godspeed in that item variants from the Godspeed scale were used to create the RoSAS, and the Godspeed offers numerous items that that are not represented in the RoSAS. However, the current work raises questions about the psychometric properties of the Godspeed of which researchers should be aware if they use items from that instrument.

Many of the studies that have used the Godspeed scale to measure robot perception have done so with specific robots. However, the development of our scale was not tethered to specific images or videos of robots. It is precisely because the RoSAS was developed for a broad category of robots that it can serve as a standardized measurement of robot perception. We see value in developing a scale that is not normed to one particular set of robots. The type of robot that an individual considers will impact the extent to which they associate different attributes with robots; however, we aimed to identify the underlying dimensions of robot judgment. We fully expect the RoSAS ratings to differ for robots with varying features and in differing roles.

6.2 Scale Validation

Validation of RoSAS demonstrates that robots' appearance impacts perceiver's social evaluations. A robot that appears female and humanlike is perceived to be warmer and more competent; whereas, a robot that appears male and machinelike is rated highest on discomfort. Results showing that humanlike robots are evaluated more favorably in terms of their warmth and competence and lower on discomfort are not surprising given that anthropomorphic robots are viewed more positively than mechanomorphic robots [24]. Additionally, in a study examining children's perceptions of robots, they perceived humanlike robots as having feelings and being better able to understand them compared to machinelike robots [25].

These findings have implications beyond measuring responses to existing robots. We would suggest they also provide useful information about robot design and interaction. A robot that appears female and humanlike is more likely to be perceived positively (i.e., higher on warmth and competence and lower on discomfort). People may be more willing to interact with such a robot and may respond better to the robot in an interaction. Conversely, a robot intended to create fear for entertainment purposes would likely benefit from having male, machinelike features. In addition, the RoSAS can be used to determine how systematic variations in robot design might affect various aspects of experience central to human-robotic interactions.

We envision three main uses of the RoSAS. First, this scale (see Table 3 for complete set of RoSAS items) can be used as a tool to evaluate robots that have already been designed. People's perceptions of robots determine expectations that guide their robot interactions. RoSAS scores for a particular robot can inform expectations about the smoothness of social interactions. Second, the RoSAS can inform development and design of robots, especially anthropomorphic robots which mimic human appearance and behavior. For example, a goal of developing a child-friendly robot could be better achieved by testing how design choices maximize warmth and minimize discomfort. Third, the RoSAS serves as a standardized metric in HRI. Other researchers have developed a psychological scale specially for the perception of humanoid robots [26]. However, the RoSAS provides a psychometrically validated, standardized measure that can be used to measure robots developed by different people in different places for differing purposes and over time.

6.3 Limitations and Future Directions

The manner in which people evaluate robots on social dimensions presumably influences their willingness to interact with robots. However, that was not measured in these studies. Future research should examine whether there is a direct association between higher warmth and competence ratings and lower discomfort ratings and the willingness to interact with a robot. For example, questions concerning contact intention and design preference would be a valuable contribution for the design of robots that interact with humans. While the aim of our scale development was to create a scale that is generalizable to robots that vary in their appearance and role, the application of the scale to individual robots would be an additional way to utilize the RoSAS. The consequence of this application would be to smooth human-robotic interactions, especially in contexts where robots are meant to assist individuals or to provide positive interactive experiences.

One limitation of the current research is that we validated RoSAS using images of robots which did not permit any actual robot interaction. People respond differently to an embodied robot compared to a robot image projected on a screen [27]. In order to validate the scale, it remains important to move beyond images and videos by using actual robots in real-life situations.

Future research could also further examine the role of perceiver gender in robot perception. People often feel close to and more strongly anthropomorphize same-gender robots compared to opposite gender robots [7]. Although we do not find evidence in Study 4 that perceiver gender moderates any of the reported relationships, future studies should consider participant information in determining whether RoSAS evaluations hold across different demographic groups (i.e., gender and age). Further work could also be done on the specific features that trigger gender stereotyping of robots. Given that robots can display features not possible for humans, RoSAS can be a valuable tool for understanding when feature variation elicits gender stereotypes.

7. ACKNOWLEDGMENTS

We would like to thank Corey McClelland for his help in developing the robot image stimuli used in Study 4. We would also like to thank Jonathan Benitez for his feedback on prior versions of this manuscript.

8. REFERENCES

[1] Fiske, S. T., Cuddy, A. J., & Glick, P. (2007). Universal dimensions of social cognition: Warmth and competence. *Trends in Cognitive Sciences*, *11*(2), 77-83.

[2] Willis, J., & Todorov, A. (2006). First impressions making up your mind after a 100-ms exposure to a face. *Psychological Science*, *17*(7), 592-598.

[3] Fiske, S. T., Cuddy, A. J., Glick, P., & Xu, J. (2002). A model of (often mixed) stereotype content: competence and warmth respectively follow from perceived status and competition. *Journal of Personality and Social Psychology*, *82*(6), 878-902.

[4] Ho, C. C., & MacDorman, K. F. (2010). Revisiting the uncanny valley theory: Developing and validating an alternative to the Godspeed indices. *Computers in Human Behavior*, *26*(6), 1508-1518.

[5] Carpenter, J., Davis, J. M., Erwin-Stewart, N., Lee, T. R., Bransford, J. D., & Vye, N. (2009). Gender representation and humanoid robots designed for domestic use. *International Journal of Social Robotics*, 1(3), 261-265.

[6] Eyssel, F., & Kuchenbrandt, D. (2012). Social categorization of social robots: Anthropomorphism as a function of robot group membership. *British Journal of Social Psychology*, 51(4), 724-731.

[7] Eyssel, F., & Hegel, F. (2012). (S)he's Got the Look: Gender Stereotyping of Robots. *Journal of Applied Social Psychology*, 42(9), 2213-2230

[8] Nass, C., Moon, Y., & Green, N. (1997). Are Machines Gender Neutral? Gender-Stereotypic Responses to Computers with Voices. *Journal of Applied Social Psychology*, *27*(10), 864-876.

[9] Nass, C., & Moon, Y. (2000). Machines and mindlessness: Social responses to computers. *Journal of Social Issues*, *56*(1), 81-103.

[10] Epley, N., Waytz, A., & Cacioppo, J. T. (2007). On seeing human: a three-factor theory of anthropomorphism. *Psychological Review*, *114*(4), 864-886.

[11] Kuchenbrandt, D., Eyssel, F., Bobinger, S., & Neufeld, M. (2013). When a robot's group membership matters. *International Journal of Social Robotics*, *5*(3), 409-417.

[12] Bartneck, C., Kulić, D., Croft, E., & Zoghbi, S. (2009). Measurement instruments for the anthropomorphism, animacy, likeability, perceived intelligence, and perceived safety of robots. *International Journal of Social Robotics*, *1*(1), 71-81.

[13] Foster, M. E., Gaschler, A., Giuliani, M., Isard, A., Pateraki, M., & Petrick, R. (2012). Two people walk into a bar: Dynamic multi-party social interaction with a robot agent. In *Proceedings of the 14th ACM International Conference on Multimodal Interaction* (pp. 3-10).

[14] Bartneck, C., Kanda, T., Ishiguro, H., & Hagita, N. (2009, September). My robotic doppelgänger-A critical look at the uncanny valley. In *RO-MAN 2009-The 18th IEEE International Symposium on Robot and Human Interactive Communication* (pp. 269-276).

[15] Lee, K. M., Park, N., & Song, H. (2005). Can a robot be perceived as a developing creature? *Human Communication Research*, *31* (4), 538-563.

[16] Bartneck, C., Kanda, T., Mubin, O., & Al Mahmud, A. (2007, November). The perception of animacy and intelligence based on a robot's embodiment. In *2007 7th IEEE-RAS International Conference on Humanoid Robots* (pp. 300-305).

[17] Warner, R. M., & Sugarman, D. B. (1986). Attributions of personality based on physical appearance, speech, and handwriting. *Journal of Personality and Social Psychology*, *50* (4), 792-799.

[18] Parise, S., Kiesler, S., Sproull, L., & Waters, K. (1996, November). My partner is a real dog: cooperation with social

agents. In *Proceedings of the 1996 ACM conference on Computer supported cooperative work* (pp. 399-408).

[19] Kulic, D., & Croft, E. (2005, August). Anxiety detection during human-robot interaction. In *2005 IEEE/RSJ International Conference on Intelligent Robots and Systems* (pp. 616-621).

[20] Furr, M. (2011). *Scale construction and psychometrics for social and personality psychology*. SAGE Publications Ltd.

[21] Bem, S. L. (1974). The measurement of psychological androgyny. *Journal of Clinical and Consulting Psychology, 42,* 155-162.

[22] Blanz, V., & Vetter, T. (1999, July). A morphable model for the synthesis of 3D faces. In *Proceedings of the 26th annual conference on Computer graphics and interactive techniques* (pp. 187-194). ACM Press/Addison-Wesley Publishing Co.

[23] Fitzmaurice, G. M., Laird, N. M., & Ware, J. H. Applied longitudinal analysis. 2004. *Hoboken Wiley-Interscience.*

[24] Fraune, M. R., Sherrin, S., Sabanović, S., & Smith, E. R. (2015, March). Rabble of robots effects: Number and type of robots modulates attitudes, emotions, and stereotypes. In *Proceedings of the Tenth Annual ACM/IEEE International Conference on Human-Robot Interaction* (pp. 109-116).

[25] Woods, S., Dautenhahn, K., & Schulz, J. (2004). The design space of robots: Investigating children's views. In Robot and Human Interactive Communication, 2004. ROMAN 2004. 13th IEEE International Workshop, 47-52.

[26] Kamide, H., Mae, Y., Kawabe, K., Shigemi, S., & Arai, T. (2012). A psychological scale for general impressions of humanoids. In *IEEE International Conference on Robotics and Automation* (pp. 4030-4037).

[27] Kiesler, S., Powers, A., Fussell, S. R., & Torrey, C. (2008). Anthropomorphic interactions with a robot and robot-like agent. *Social Cognition,* 26(2), 169-181.

Affective Grounding in Human-Robot Interaction

Malte F. Jung
Cornell University
Department of Information Science
mjung@cornell.edu

ABSTRACT

Participating in interaction requires not only coordination on content and process, as previously proposed, but also on affect. The term *affective grounding* is introduced to refer to the coordination of affect in interaction with the purpose of building shared understanding about what behavior can be exhibited, and how behavior is interpreted emotionally and responded to. Affective Ground is achieved when interactants have reached shared understanding about how behavior should be interpreted emotionally. The paper contributes a review and critique of current perspectives on emotion in HRI. Further it outlines how research on emotion in HRI can benefit from taking an affective grounding perspective and outlines implications for the design of robots capable of participating in the coordination on affect in interaction.

Keywords

Affective grounding; emotion and emotion regulation, human robot interaction.

1. INTRODUCTION

Participating in social interaction requires the successful coordination of emotion. The kinds of emotions that are expressed by participants of an interaction over time and the ways in which they are responded shape immediate and distant outcomes of dyads, teams and larger groups. For example, the emotional interaction dynamics, the moment to moment dynamics of emotion expression and responding have been shown to be highly predictive of outcomes of married couples [39], negotiation pairs [22], engineering teams [47][48], and cancer support groups [35]. As robots increasingly participate in social interactions as direct collaborators, tools, or bystanders it is important not only to understand how robots shape the coordination of emotion in interactions but also how robots can be equipped with capabilities to actively participate in the coordination of emotion.

To date, work on emotion expression in human-robot interaction has followed the dominant paradigm of emotion as a signaling mechanism and emotion expressions are seen as signals that reveal processes and states that would otherwise be hidden. Research in HRI has focused on examining how this signaling makes people think and feel about the robot itself, often with the goal of improving communication between the person and the robot (e.g. [5]). In other words, the role of emotions and emotional expression is generally seen as a way to make robots more understandable, likable, intuitive, and predictable (or "believable") by using patterns that allow people to apply mental models and heuristics from interactions with people to infer a robot's internal states and intentions (e.g.[10][9][36][66][73]).

While this perspective takes the idea of emotion as a social signal into account, I argue that the current signaling paradigm does not successfully capture the complexity of emotion as it unfolds in interactions because it conceptualizes emotions as a phenomenon that happens within and on-top of individuals. Instead I propose that in order to the develop the understanding necessary for enabling robots to successfully participate in social interactions we need to view emotion and emotion regulation as something that takes shape in between interaction participants.

I introduce the term *affective grounding* to refer to the coordination of affect in interaction. Just as participants of interactions work together to ground the informational content of their messages (e.g. [17][16]), I propose that they need to likewise work together to build a shared understanding about the emotional meaning of each other's behavior. Emotion expression and regulation in interaction is thus conceptualized as a dynamic process by which group members collaborate to shape which emotional behaviors are exhibited, how they are interpreted and how they are responded to.

This new affective grounding perspective extends current HRI research agendas and to some degree current affective computing research in three ways. First, with the notion of affective grounding this paper contributes a perspective on emotion for HRI that conceptualizes emotion and emotion regulation as joint activities. As such it extends established literature on emotion regulation (both intra and inter-personal e.g. [40][41][70][72][95]) by positing that emotion can be seen as a form of conversation, the dynamics and flow of which are shaped through the collaborative engagement (i.e. emotion regulation) of the participants and that is to some degree independent of the participants' inner states or experiences. Second, an affective grounding perspective extends how we might study emotion in human robot interaction by focusing less on abilities to correctly identify expressions but to understand how people read emotional meaning into the behavior of robots. Third, as an interaction paradigm, an affective grounding perspective moves the focus from designing expressions for robots to make them "emotional" towards the understanding that emotion is part of any human-robot interaction and that expressions do not determine how people make sense of a robot's behavior emotionally.

HRI '17, March 06 - 09, 2017, Vienna, Austria

ACM 978-1-4503-4336-7/17/03...$15.00
DOI: http://dx.doi.org/10.1145/2909824.3020224

2. The current signaling paradigm of emotion expression in HRI and its limitations

Current approaches to emotion expression in HRI can be argued to largely fall within a signaling paradigm. According to this paradigm, emotion expressions are seen as signals that reveal processes and states that would otherwise be hidden. This signaling perspective on emotion is grounded in basic emotion theories (e.g. [26][3]), which assume the existence of a set of "basic" emotions (typically anger, sadness, fear, surprise, disgust, happiness) that are innate, each with distinct biological bases and mechanisms, and universal across cultures.

The signaling approach has its roots in Ekman's 1984 [26] proposal of a one-to-one coupling between emotions and facial expressions and the idea that a person's inner state could be reliably inferred from facial expressions. This idea of the one-to-one coupling between inter states and expressions, and the availability of detailed descriptions of facial expressions through the Facial Action Coding System [29] likely contributed to the wide adoption of this perspective among HRI researchers and the affective computing community more broadly. For example, among the eight papers that Thomaz, Hoffman and Cakmak [87] identified as computational approaches to emotion expression in HRI, seven papers rely on Ekmans six basic emotions or a subset thereof ([36][63][53][4][84][20][96]) and one paper relies on an extended set of basic emotions ([1]). The same set of basic emotions is even applied across several approaches to emotion expressions through features other than the face. For example, [56][13][57][64] all implemented basic emotions or subsets through body movements.

While classic basic emotion theories conceptualize emotion as a purely intra-personal phenomenon, the signaling perspective combines perspectives on emotions as purely intrapersonal phenomena with perspectives that acknowledge that emotions fulfill social functions. Yet the signaling perspective has relied on a narrow understanding of expressions that has centered on the physical embodiment characteristics of an expression.

2.1 Limitations of the signaling approach

The signaling perspective on emotion expression has allowed roboticists to build systems that can form emotional expressions that can be correctly labeled by people and that produce more pleasant and intuitive human-robot interactions. However, the focus on basic expressions brings with it certain limitations that are stifling efforts in HRI to build systems that are better at participating in and contributing to successful interactions. First, the signaling paradigm assumes congruence between processes that are actually distinct, second it ignores that emotional expressions are not a reliable indicator of a person's inner state, third, it ignores that the same expression can carry multiple and even emotionally opposed meanings, and finally it ignores that robots do not need to be equipped with special emotional expression capabilities to be perceived as emotionally expressive.

2.1.1 Assumption of congruence between distinct processes

The signaling approach assumes congruence between three phenomena that are actually distinct (see Figure 1): (1) Physical configuration and movement patterns (i.e. emotional expressions that people can identify as such), (2) subjective experiences, inner states and feelings, and (3) social meaning (i.e. how the expression is interpreted by participants of an interaction). However, a person's expression of a smile during an interaction and people's ability to label the expression as a smile neither necessarily means that the person is actually happy, nor does it necessarily mean that an observer interprets the smile as communicating warmth and happiness. As Hochschild's [43] work has shown, people can produce emotional expressions such smiles driven by social demands while not feeling happy at all and even robots have been shown to provide a context for social smiling [55]. Also, research by Hoque and others [45] demonstrated the flexibility in interpretation of emotional behavior when whosing that a simple smile can be interpreted in a multitude of ways. I will unpack the limitations associated with this assumption of congruency further in the following sections.

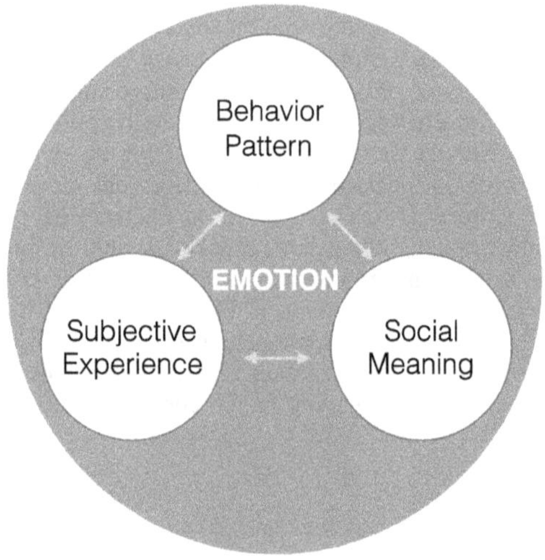

Figure 1: The dominant signaling paradigm assumes congruency between three distinct emotional phenomena that are actually largely independent of each other: The subjective experience of emotion, the behavior pattern that people label as expressing particular emotions, and the social meaning that people ascribe to behavior.

2.1.2 Emotional expressions are not a reliable indicator of a person's inner state

One limitation of the signaling approach is that it relies on the idea of congruency between expressions and inner states or that emotional expressions provide a reliable source of information about a person's inner state. However, it is often not known that Ekman later abandoned his own idea of a one-to-one coupling between emotions and expressions when evidence was accumulating that some emotions don't have distinct facial expressions (e.g. awe, guilt, shame) and that some emotions share the same expressions [77][28][74]. Other studies (e.g. [30]) have confirmed that emotion expressions do not offer a reliable source of information to infer a person's inner state, and reversely that emotion expressions can rarely be predicted based on a person's inner state, thus calling the basic premise of the signaling paradigm into question.

To illustrate this point further, consider the picture in Figure 2 on the left. Studies have shown that an expression presented in the picture can be reliably classified as a smile across cultures [27]. However, the correct classification of a facial muscle configuration, movement, or other complex body movement does not mean that the person is actually happy. This idea that our capability to reliably classify emotional expressions is distinct from a person's feelings is even more apparent when looking at the smiley image in Figure 2. The image can be clearly labeled as a smile but the smiley certainly does not feel happy.

Figure 2: People can reliable label images like the ones shown above as depicting happiness. However, the correct classification of a facial muscle configuration, movement, or other complex body movement does not mean that the entity depicted is actually happy. This disconnect between people's ability to label expressions and actual inner states is particularly apparent for the smiley image on the right.

2.1.3 Emotional expressions carry multiple meanings

Another key limitation of the signaling approach is that it relies on the idea of congruency between expressions and their emotional interpretation. However, in interactions no one-to-one relationship exists between expression and interpretation.

The very same body configuration or movement (i.e. a smile or smirk) can carry a wide array of meanings dependent on the context the interaction takes place in, the long term or immediate history of interactants, and the directionality of expressions. Dependent on the configuration of interactants the same expression can simultaneously carry multiple emotional meanings.

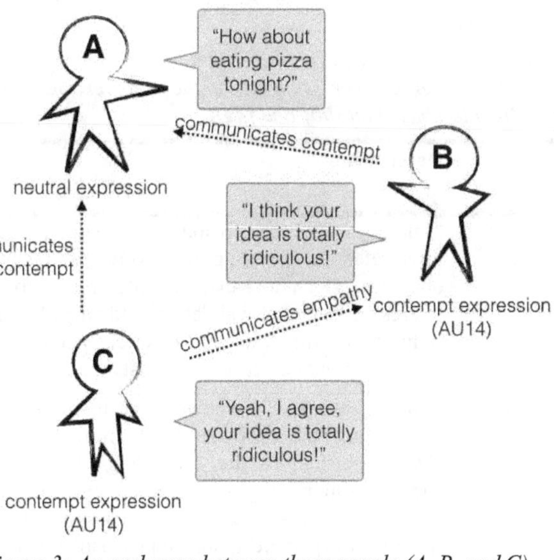

Figure 3: An exchange between three people (A, B, and C) demonstrates that the same contempt expression can be interpreted as contemptuous of empathetic at the same time, dependent on who interprets the behavior.

To illustrate this point further consider the situation depicted in Figure 3 in which person A suggests "How about eating pizza tonight" and is responded to by B who makes a smirk (categorized as Action Unit/AU 14 in the Facial Action Coding System) and says "I think your idea is totally ridiculous!". Shortly after, C also smirks and shouts "I agree, that idea is totally ridiculous!" With the same behavioral characteristics, from A's perspective, both B's and C's behaviors communicate contempt. From B's perspective, however, C's behavior communicates empathy as it is interpreted as supportive of and validating B's position.

The example above shows that the very same expression can be interpreted in two very different ways dependent on who observes the expression: contempt and empathy. One negative and hostile, one positive and warm and this emotional interpretation is independent of participant A's and C's ability to correctly label B's expression as a contempt expression.

2.1.4 There need not be an expression to communicate an emotion.

A final key limitation of the signaling approach is that it assumes that emotional expressions are required for emotion to be communicated.

In their paper about a novel approach to crowdsourcing an AI for a social robot that jointly solves tasks with human participants, Breazeal and colleagues observed a series of instances in which the robot was seen as condescending even though the robot's AI did not model emotion at all. In one such instant a participant asked the robot "Would you like me to put this item into the bucket?" upon which the robot turned around and drove away, leaving a somewhat flustered participant behind [11],p.104 (see figure 4).

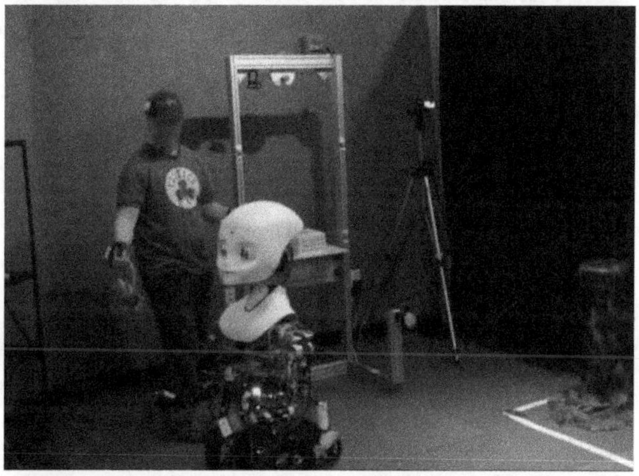

Figure 4: Interaction instance from [11] in which a participant addresses a robot with a polite question upon which the robot just turns around and drives away. While the robot's AI did not model affect and was not making specific facial or bodily expressions of emotion, the robot's behavior was perceived as ignorant.

According to the signaling paradigm there was no emotion. Neither did the robot display an emotional expression nor was the robot in any emotional internal state since emotion was not modeled as part of the robot's AI. Yet, the robot's behavior communicated condescension and lack of respect or interest towards the participant.

This exchange illustrates that the emotional interpretation of behavior is not determined by the behavior itself but by its positioning in the sequential organization of an interaction. It is jointly shaped by the participants of an interaction through the way in which a behavior is responded to. For example, a robot's behavior of turning away does not carry emotional meaning in itself, but if the behavior occurs while someone is attempting to interact with the robot, that same movement can be interpreted as disrespectful and offensive [25].

In sum, the predominant signaling perspective limits our abilities to not only understand how robots shape interactions but also how we design better systems to participate in interactions because the signaling perspective limits the focus of analysis on emotional expressions as it assumes that emotion resides in expressions, and in particular a specific set of six basic expressions. In order to understand emotion in interaction and in order to build systems that are able to shape the emotional dynamics of interactions, I argue that we need to take a new perspective on affect, and shift the focus from what is expressed towards how it is interpreted, and towards how emotional meaning is constructed out of an ongoing flow of interaction. In other words to understand and shape emotions in interactions it is less important to be able to label emotions correctly based on their physical features. Rather it is important to understand how people interpret others' behavior emotionally, how that interpretation is collaboratively established between interactants, and how behavior patterns can be produced that will communicate the intended emotional meaning to others. .

3. AFFECTIVE GROUNDING

I propose that participating in interaction not only requires coordination on content and process, as previously proposed [16], but also on affect. I use the term *affective grounding* to refer to the coordination of affect in interaction with the purpose of building shared understanding about what behavior can be exhibited, and how behavior is interpreted emotionally and responded to. Affective Ground is thus achieved when interactants have reached shared understanding about how behavior should be interpreted emotionally. Affective grounding conceptualizes emotion and emotion regulation in interaction as a collaborative activity, a phenomenon that occurs *between* interactants rather than *on top* (e.g. through facial expressions) or *within* them.

To illustrate the idea that affect is coordinated alongside content and process, consider the following example from Clark and Brennan's ([16], p.223) highly influential work on grounding:

(1) Alan: Now, - um, do you and your husband have a j- car
(2) Barbara: - have a car?
(3) Alan: Yeah
(4) Barbara: No -

From an information processing perspective [17], these messages are organized in terms of a presentation phase (1) and an acceptance phase (2-4). Barbara's utterance "have a car?" provides evidence that the content of the message has not been understood.

From an affective grounding perspective, this same sequence of utterances can also be viewed as instances of emotion and emotion regulatory moves. Alan's question "Now, - um, do you and your husband have a j- car" also expresses interest towards Barbara and sets up an emotionally relevant moment. Barbara's response, "have a car?" thus also provides emotional feedback that she is engaged in the interaction. A possible non-response from Barbara could not only mean that the question was not heard but, as I will explain in the next paragraph, even more likely would have been interpreted as disinterest and lack of respect.

This idea, that a question and answer pair can be viewed as an emotion and emotion regulatory exchange, is highlighted in Driver and Gottman's [25] research on couples. In their studies of how couples regulate emotions during everyday conversations, such as those that occur during dinner, Driver and Gottman were unable to analyze emotional interaction dynamics with traditional measures that focus on emotional expressions. Occurrences of behavior that could be classified by established emotion categorization schemes (e.g. SPAFF [19] or FACS [29]) turned out to be too scarce to provide meaningful data. Instead, Driver and Gottman found that emotion and emotion regulation was organized through bid and response pairs. A bid is defined as an attempt to interact with one another [25]. Bids can be statements (e.g., "look at that!"), questions, or even nonverbal behaviors. Once a bid is made, the subsequent responsive behavior or even the absence of responsive behavior becomes emotionally relevant. Bid and response form what Sacks and colleagues [78][80] called an adjacency pair: The emotional interpretation of the behavior following the bid is contingent upon the bid.

Responses to bid can be categorized into three basic types (see *[90] and [44]*), each carrying a different emotional meaning (see also table 1): *Turning towards* are responses that show positive engagement with the bid. Barbara's utterance, "have a car?" is an example of a turning towards response that signals listening and engagement but a simple nod would also count. *Turning away* are responses that show no engagement with the bid. An example of a turning away response would be if Barbara had not shown any responsive behavior after Allan's bid, such as not even looking or nodding at him, a response which is likely interpreted as disinterest or lack of respect. *Turning against* are responses that are actively negative or hostile, such as a belligerent "What kind of a ridiculous question is that!"

The idea of bid-response pairs highlights a perspective on affect that is independent of a person' inner states and feelings and instead as something that can be found within peoples' interactions with each other. Just as an answer needs a question to be interpretable as such, a moment of silence needs a bid to be interpretable as a turning away response from an affective perspective.

Table 1: Behavior type classification based on the relational impact an observed expression has on the observer. Behavior type classification based on [90] and [44].

Behavior Type	Description
Turning towards	"Turning towards" captures behavior that is interpreted as orienting the expresser towards the observer. Behavior that is interpreted to signal interest, excitement, validation, and empathy but also sadness and direct anger can orient people towards each other and decrease social distance.
Turning away	"Turning away" captures behavior that is interpreted as orienting the expresser away from the observer. Typical behaviors are "avoiding the interaction partner, suppressing thoughts about the situation, refusing to take action, and adopting a passive stance (p. 59)" [90] or behaviors that Coan and Gottman [19] categorized as defensive, or stonewalling and increase social distance.
Turning against	"Turning against" captures behavior that is interpreted as orienting the expresser against the observer. Behavior that is typically interpreted in this way includes what Coan and Gottman described as expressions of contempt, belligerence, criticism, or disgust [19]

3.1 Back-channel responses and repair

Two specific behaviors that have been argued to play a crucial role in the coordination of process and content [16] also play an important role in the coordination on affect: back-channel responses and repair.

Back-channels response like "mhm," for example, or nods and other forms of verbal and nonverbal acknowledgments have been argued to indicate positive evidence of understanding [16]. However the very same behaviors have been found to also signal emotional attunement toward the speaker [68][19]. As highlighted in the previous examples on bids and responses, acknowledgments can carry emotional meaning by signaling engagement and interest. Research has shown that the emotional interpretation of back-channel responses extends to robots. For example, in a study for which participants collaborated with multiple robots in solving a complex task, Jung and colleagues [49], demonstrated that robots can employ non-verbal back-channel responses to signal engagement and interest.

Similarly, the notion of "repair" not only refers to fixing misunderstandings of message content (as described in [17]) but also efforts to dampen, limit, or even eliminate the negative impact that an expression has had on the emotional progression of an interaction. For example, strong negative, rude or hostile behaviors tend to trigger negative reactions in others, sometimes initiating a downward spiral of increasing negativity [2][61][60]. To prevent a downward spiral, the impact of the initiating behavior has to be repaired through strategies such as choosing not to reciprocate a perceived violation or for the original violator to offer an apology [2]. There is also initial evidence that robots can engage in affective repair. A study that examined the collaborative efforts of three people to jointly solve a complex task with a robot found evidence that a robot's repair of a confederate's hostile remark successfully shaped interaction participants' perceptions of the interaction [50].

3.2 What implications does an affective grounding perspective have for the study of emotion in HRI?

Current analyses of emotion in human-robot interaction that follow the signaling paradigm are constrained by an analytical lens that focuses on a pre-specified set of typically six basic emotion expressions. Taking an affective grounding perspective on emotion in HRI extends current approaches to study emotional expression in human-robot interaction as it shifts the analytic focus from a phenomenon that occurs within or on top of interactants towards a phenomenon that unfolds between interactants over time as part of a joint activity. Figure 5 offers a framework to study the joint coordination of affect in human robot interaction through three key aspects: Emotion – the interpretation of behavior as emotionally relevant; Feedback – signs of trouble and confirmation about how ones own behavior gets interpreted by others; and Emotion Regulation attempts to re-adjust the emotional meaning of behavior through repair and other regulatory moves.

The notion of emotion and regulation as joint activities extends established literature on emotion and emotion regulation by adding a dynamic interactional perspective. .The majority of the literature on emotion regulation has conceptualized emotion regulation as a purely intra-personal process (see [40][41] for reviews of that work). More recent work on inter-personal emotion regulation (e.g. [70][72][95]) has acknowledged interpersonal processes to play a crucial role in how people regulate how they themselves or others feel, but this literature still conceptualizes intra-personal feelings and experiences as the object or focus of that regulation. Instead, an Affective Grounding perspective posits that emotion can be seen as a form of conversation, the dynamics and flow of which are shaped through the collaborative engagement (i.e. emotion regulation) of the participants and that is to some degree independent of the participants' inner states or experiences.

Research in the area of affective computing has begun to take interpersonal aspects into account when building emotion and emotion regulatory models for robots to improve human-robot interaction (e.g. [97]) in particular in learning (e.g. [42]) and caregiving contexts (e.g. [62]). However, this work in affective computing and HRI is consistent with the perspectives on inter-personal emotion, that focus on how people use inter-personal interactions with others to regulate intra-personal emotional experiences, states, or feelings (e.g. [70][72][95]). This paper attempts to highlight a perspective that conceptualizes emotion and emotion regulation as phenomena that unfold between people, rather than within (experience/state), or on top (emotional expression) of them and that is co-constructed by participants of an interaction over time. As such this paper also extends previous critical accounts of affective computing research that have challenged the underlying notion of emotions as objective, externally measurable units (e.g. [6][59]), towards emotion as an interactional phenomenon that can be described, studied and designed for irrespective of interactants' internal processes or states.

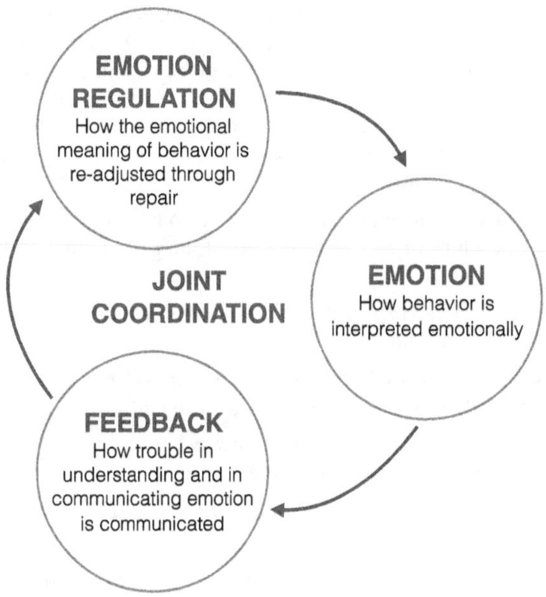

Figure 5: Framework highlighting key elements of an affective grounding perspective on emotion. The key idea here is that emotion and emotion regulation are not only internal processes but that can be seen as interpersonal processes that are jointly coordinated by participants of an interaction.

3.2.1 *Studying emotion and emotion regulation as joint activity*

Rather than starting an analysis of emotion in human-robot interaction with a predetermined set of fixed expression, an affective grounding perspective offers a lens on emotion in interaction that focuses on the question of how people orient towards emotional aspects of interactions and how emotionally relevant situations might emerge and should be responded to in interactions with robots. As argued by Goodwin and Goodwin [38]:1 "the relevant unit for the analysis of emotion is not the individual, or the semantic system of a language, but instead the sequential organization of action."

Conversation analytic approaches provide an analytic lens on emotion and emotion regulation as a joint activity and have shown successfully how the sequential organization of interactions provides the context for the emotional interpretation of behavior (see [75] for an overview). According to [75] the idea that participants of an interaction carefully coordinate "their visible emotional state in accordance with the demands (or the ongoing definition) of the situation [75]:333" can be traced back to Goffman's essay "Fun in Games [37]." For example, Jefferson, Sacks and Schegloff [46] showed that "laughter is a methodically produced activity—it is carefully coordinated with other ongoing conversational activities, such as talk or the laughter of other participants" ([75], p.334). This finding is also consistent with research in psychology by Kraut & Johnston [58], who found that people in a bowling alley upon a successful strike smiled more when facing their friends than when facing the pins. Even robots have been shown to provide a context for social smiling [55]. Further, Couper-Kuhlen [21] shows how a statement of "oh" that is expressed with a specific prosody pattern is understood as a disappointment response only when expressed in a disappointment relevant moment but the same utterance expressed in the same way takes on other meanings when placed otherwise in conversation., Research by Wilkinson and Kitzinger [92] showed how surprise is produced as an interactionally achieved performance. Finally, Perakyla & Ruusuvuori [69] demonstrate how emotion regulation in interaction can be examined from a conversation analytic perspective. This research offers a perspective on emotion expression and regulation as "outward emotive performances" [82] that are independent of internal states and instead dependent on the social dynamics of an interaction.

Studying emotion and emotion regulation as joint activity opens a space to ask a host of new questions about the role of emotion in human-robot interaction:

How do emotionally relevant situations come about in interactions with robots?

Are there differences in how we interpret a person's behavior as emotional in comparison with that of a robot?

How does the perception of a robot's behavior as emotional shape the subsequent flow of an interaction?

How do people repair emotionally taxing situations when interacting with robots?

3.2.2 Extending how to categorize expressions of emotion

Focusing on emotion and emotion regulation as a jointly coordinated activity emphasizes the role emotions play in regulating how participants of an interaction relate to each other. This interpersonal focus calls into question the usefulness of the valence and arousal model as the appropriate paradigm for categorizing emotions.

The valence and arousal model has been the dominant approach to organizing emotions in HRI. This model dates back to 1978 when Russell proposed that emotional experiences can be organized by their degrees of pleasure and displeasure as well as inactivation and activation [76]. Focusing on valence and arousal emphasizes experiential and intra-personal dimensions of emotion and ignores the interpersonal and social functions of emotion. Yet the valence arousal dimensions are the dominant framework in studying emotions expressed by robots. In part its attractiveness lies in a multitude of measures that have been developed and also in that it can be easily applied to expressive modalities other than the face. For example, both Karg and colleagues [52] as well as Sharma and colleagues [83] relied on a valence scale to measure how participants inferred a robot's inner state based on expressive movement. Focusing only on assessing users' inferences of a robot's internal state leaves important questions about what emotional meaning the behavior communicates towards others unanswered.

Emotional expressions have been shown to shape people's relational orientation towards each other in distinct ways (e.g. [54][65][89][90]). For example, an expression of joy draws others in, and an expression of hostility pushes others away. Therefore expressions can be categorized not only along a valence and arousal dimension but alternatively also along an interpersonal orientation dimension with affiliative behaviors on one end of the continuum and distancing behaviors on the other. Affiliative behaviors are those that turn people towards each other ([44]; see also [90]) and reduce interpersonal distance. Affiliative behaviors include expressions of interest, affection, humor or excitement but also more subtle, often non-verbal, signs of listening such as back-channeling through nods or "mhm" vocalizations that signal attention and engagement towards a speaker. Affiliative behaviors strengthen the relations within a group thus establishing and maintaining cooperative and harmonious interactions with other group members [32]. Distancing behaviors are those that turn people away from and even against each other ([44]; see also [90]) and increase interpersonal distance. Distancing behaviors include behaviors such as frustration, passive aggressive behavior, domineering, contempt, or belligerence. Distancing behaviors can be exhibited non-verbally for example through contemptuous eye-roll or smirk, but also through a sarcastic voice tone [19]. Distancing behaviors harm successful cooperation and harmonious interaction [32].

The difference between valence-arousal based and orientation based perspectives on affect becomes clearer when looking at behaviors that are negative from a valence perspective but positive from an affiliative-distancing perspective. Sadness, for example, while negative from a valence perspective (e.g. [76][91]), is positive from an observer perspective as it has been found to turn people towards each other, serving an affiliative function when it is interpreted as a cry for help (e.g. [18]).

Since the relational dimension of emotion is highly consequential for the progression and outcome of interactions it is important to extend our understanding of emotion in human robot interaction by including systematic analyses of how a robot's behavior orients observers of the behavior towards the robot.

3.3 What implications does an affective grounding perspective have for the development of affective capabilities in robots?

According to an extensive literature review by Thomaz, Hoffman and Cakmak [87], current computational approaches to emotion in HRI have focused on three areas:

1. Approaches to model intra-personal affective processes, for example, to drive the elicitation of expressions or to regulate attention.
2. Approaches to express emotions that can be reliably identified by humans even when expressed across various modalities.
3. Approaches for the automated detection of emotions in human interaction partners.

For robots to participate in social interactions with humans the ability to coordinate on affect is required. Building shared understanding about what behavior can be exhibited, and how behavior should be emotionally interpreted and responded to requires capabilities beyond the ones outlined above.

An important design implication of an affective grounding perspective is that it encourages designers to think of any robot as emotional even if it has no affective AI or physical architecture for "emotion expression". As such this paper reiterates Damm et al.'s [23] assertion that "in HRI one cannot be not emotional" and points designers of human robot interactions to focus on the question of *how* a robot is made "emotional" rather than *whether* it is emotional. Understanding any robot as inherently *affective* also has implications for how "emotional" or "emotionally expressive" robots should be evaluated in HRI. Current studies, that evaluate novel affective HRI systems, often compare affective with non-affective robots (e.g. [88]) in their evaluations. Observed differences are typically attributed to the presence or absence of affect rather than to a deliberate design of affective responding which misses opportunities to understand how people orient emotionally to the "un emotional" robot. In other words, HRI researchers should consider to stop thinking of the baseline condition that a novel "affective" robot is compared to as non-affective. Instead the baseline or control condition should also be understood as affective or non-deliberately affective.

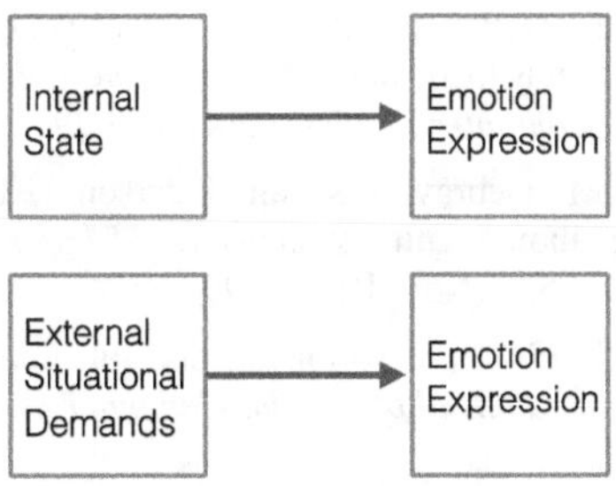

Figure 6: Extending the dominant approach that sees a robot's internal state as the key determinant of an expression towards an approach that also includes external situational demands as key determinants of a robot's .emotional expressions.

While this paper cannot provide a technical roadmap to achieving affective grounding capabilities for robots, a few starting points can be given. Most importantly, an affective grounding approach implies a shift from the current dominant approach that sees a robot's internal emotional state as the most important determinant of a robot's emotional expressions (e.g. robot made a mistake which leads to a negative affective state, and an expression of disappointment) towards an approach that includes social situational demands as important determinants of a robot's emotional expressions (e.g. a person's display of disappointment makes an empathic expression by a robot relevant, see figure 6). Thus, the trigger for a robot's appropriate emotional expression is not only an internal emotional state but a social situation that calls for an emotional expression. For example, Selting [82] showed that people have to display emotional involvement at certain specific moments while listening irrespective of their internal emotional state. Therefore robots need to learn to express emotions (e.g. show interest and engagement in the listening example) when they are socially appropriate and demanded irrespective of a robot's internal state.

Table 2: Simplified Turning System

Code	Description	Example
Bids		
Silent	Nonverbal action that the other participant can notice and acknowledge.	Pointing at an object. Handing over an object. Initialing a hand-shake or high-five.
Comment	Comment containing information exchange.	"That's a nice picture over there!"
Question	Question of general interest or information	"Do you want help with this?"
Re-bid	Repeat the same bid or similar bid after the previous one has been turned away.	
Turning Towards Responses		
Passive	It is clear that the bid has been received, but minimal effort is taken to reply.	Looks up briefly then looks away. One syllable responses.
Low Energy	Answers the bid only.	Short one-word answers and brief action.
Attentive	Welcomes the bid. Effort is made to respond.	A asks B for help (bid). B replies with a pleasant "sure!" and pours the milk.
Enthusiastic	High energy and eye contact. Effortful response.	Similar as attentive but with more enthusiasm and more signs of engagement.
Turning Away Responses		
Preoccupied	Receiver of bid is engaged in an activity and doesn't respond.	Looking out the window. Watching a screen.
Interrupt	Receiver of bid begins a new bid without acknowledging that the other participant has made a bid.	A: "Do you want me to put the ...?" B: "Grab the blue big cup there."
Disregard	Complete lack of response to the bid.	A makes a bid and B just walks away to do something else.
Turning Against Responses		
Against	Receiver of bid responds in a negative or even hostile (with contempt, criticism, domineering, belligerence or defensiveness) way	A makes a bid and B responds: "I don't give a damn!"

An crucial next step could therefore be to enable robots to become sensitive to emotionally relevant moments. That is, the sequential organization of an interaction should be taken into account as a key contextual factor in determining how a situation should be interpreted emotionally and what emotional responses need to be produced in response. While not focusing on affect, Kaindl and colleagues [51] have proposed a discourse model for HRI that draws on Sacks et al.'s [78] notion of adjacency-pairs and takes the temporal organization of discourse into account. Similarly Rich's [71] work on connection events and Chu et al's [15] work on detecting contingency point to opportunities to adapt these inference techniques to model affect in interaction and design new ways for robots to respond emotionally to demands of interactional situations.

A possible starting point could be to build on these techniques in enabling robots to recognize bids for attention that set up subsequent moments as emotionally relevant. Table 2 presents a modified version of the Turning System that was developed by Driver and Gottman [25] and that categorizes types of bid-response pairs according to their affective qualities. For example, if a person engages a robot in by making a comment about the robot's behavior and the robot does not respond at all, the interaction can be described as a comment-bid-disregard-response pair and the robot will likely be perceived as disrespectful. Alternatively, a robot that responds to such a situation with gaze and a nod (passive or low energy response) is likely perceived as attentive. The effectiveness of gaze and a nod as a one-fits-all response to a potential bid has been demonstrated by Jung and colleagues [49] in a study in which robots responded with such a behavior to any audible utterance a participant made during a joint problem solving task.

4. CONCLUSION

When people interact their behavior conveys affect alongside informational content. Because the affective dimension of messages is often unclear and open to multiple interpretations, participants of interactions whether human or robot must work to achieve affective grounding, or a mutual understanding of how behavior ought to be interpreted and responded to emotionally. Building common ground about affect is important because behavior that is interpreted in unintended ways can cause harm with potentially serious consequences for participants of an interaction, especially if the damage caused by that behavior is not repaired effectively.

For robots to participate in social interaction, they require the ability to participate in this coordination on affect because robots shape the emotional dynamics of interactions in ways that are not fully understood as they can directly induce emotions in others (e.g. [8][93]), but also indirectly by affecting related social processes such as attention (e.g [67]), and in often unintended ways (e.g. [31]). Despite a few studies that have explored the role of emotions in teamwork scenarios in which a robot collaborated directly with a human (e.g. [12][81]), not much is known about how robots affect the emotional dynamics of interactions that include them.

This paper introduced the idea of affective grounding and with that it hopefully opens new possibilities for how we can not only study emotion in human robot interaction but also build new ways for robots to engage emotionally with people. The idea that participating in interaction requires the coordination of emotion extends how we study and build emotional capabilities for robots beyond basic emotion approaches and towards approaches that view emotion and emotion regulation as joint activities.

5. ACKNOWLEDGMENTS

This paper elaborated on ideas that Susan Fussell and I developed with Ge Gao for an NSF proposal. I am grateful to Susan Fussell and Ge Gao for the invaluable discussions that led to the ideas presented here. I further want to thank Kerstin Fischer for her time and suggestions that helped me improve this paper and for the invaluable comments and suggestions I received from 6 anonymous reviewers. This material is based upon work supported by the National Science Foundation under Grant No. IIS-1421929. Any opinions, findings, conclusions, or recommendations expressed in this material are those of the authors and do not necessarily reflect the views of the National Science Foundation.

6. REFERENCES

[1] Ahn, H. S., Lee, D.-W., Choi, D., Lee, D.-Y., Hur, M., and Lee, H. (2012). Appropriate emotions for facial expressions of 33-dofs android head ever-4 h33. In RO-MAN, 2012 IEEE, pages 1115–1120. IEEE.

[2] Andersson, L. M., & Pearson, C. M. (1999). Tit for tat? The spiraling effect of incivility in the workplace. *Academy of Management Review, 24(3)*: 452–471.

[3] Barrett, L. F. (2006). Are emotions natural kinds?. *Perspectives on psychological science*, *1*(1), 28-58.

[4] Bennett, C. C. and Sˇabanovi´c, S. (2014). Deriving minimal features for human-like facial expressions in robotic faces. International Journal of Social Robotics, 6(3):367–381.

[5] Bethel,C.L., & Murphy, R. R. (2007). Non-facial/non-verbal methods of affective expression as applied to robot- assisted victim assessment. *Proceedings of HRI 2007* (287-294). NY: ACM Press

[6] Boehner, K., DePaula, R., Dourish, P., & Sengers, P. (2007). How emotion is made and measured. *International Journal of Human-Computer Studies*, *65*(4), 275-291.

[7] Bowman, M., Debray, S. K., and Peterson, L. L. 1993. Reasoning about naming systems. *ACM Trans. Program. Lang. Syst.* 15, 5 (Nov. 1993), 795-825.

[8] Breazeal, C. (2003). Emotion and sociable humanoid robots. *International Journal of Human-Computer Studies*, *59*(1), 119-155.

[9] Breazeal, C.L. (2004). *Designing sociable robots.* Cambridge: The MIT Press.

[10] Breazeal, C. and B. Scassellati. (1999). How to build robots that make friends and influence people. *Proceedings of IROS '99.*

[11] Breazeal, C., DePalma, N., Orkin, J., Chernova, S., & Jung, M. (2013). Crowdsourcing human-robot interaction: New methods and system evaluation in a public en-vironment. *Journal of Human-Robot Interaction*, *2*(1), 82-111.

[12] Breazeal, C., Kidd, C. D., Thomaz, A. L., Hoffman, G., & Berlin, M. (2005). Effects of nonverbal communication on efficiency and robustness in human-robot teamwork. *Proceedings of IROS 2005* (708-713).

[13] Bretan, M., Hoffman, G., and Weinberg, G. (2015). Emotionally expressive dynamic physical behaviors in robots. International Journal of Human-Computer Studies, 78:1–16.

[14] Brown, L. D., Hua, H., and Gao, C. 2003. A widget framework for augmented interaction in SCAPE. In *Proceedings of the 16th Annual ACM Symposium on User Interface Software and Technology* (Vancouver, Canada, November 02 - 05, 2003). UIST '03. ACM, New York, NY, 1-10.

[15] Chu, V., Bullard, K., & Thomaz, A. L. (2014, September). Multimodal real-time contingency detection for HRI. In *2014 IEEE/RSJ International Conference on Intelligent Robots and Systems* (pp. 3327-3332). IEEE.

[16] Clark, H. H. & Brennan, S. E. (1991). Grounding in communication. In L. B. Resnick, R. M. Levine, & S. D. Teasley (Eds.). *Perspectives on socially shared cognition* (pp. 127-149). Washington, DC: APA Press.

[17] Clark, H. H., & Wilkes-Gibbs, D. (1986). Referring as a collaborative process. *Cognition, 22*, 1–39.

[18] Clark, M. S., Pataki, S. P., & Carver, V. H. 1996. Some thoughts and findings on self-presentation of emotions in relationships. In G. J. O. Fletcher & J. Fitness (Eds.), *Knowledge structures in close relationships: A social psychological approach*: 247–274). Mahwah, NJ: Erlbaum.

[19] Coan, J. A., & Gottman, J. M. (2007). The specific affect coding system (SPAFF). In J. A. Coan & J. J. B. Allen (Eds.) *Handbook of Emotion Elicitation and Assessment.* (106–123). New York, NY: Oxford University Press.

[20] Costa, S., Soares, F., and Santos, C. (2013). Facial expressions and gestures to convey emotions with a humanoid robot. In Social Robotics, pages 542–551. Springer.

[21] Couper-Kuhlen, E. (2009). On combining clauses and actions in interaction. *Virittäjä, 113*(3).

[22] Curhan, J. R., & Pentland, A. (2007). Thin slices of negotiation: predicting outcomes from conversational dynamics within the first 5 minutes. Journal of Applied Psychology, 92(3), 802.Å

[23] Damm, O., Dreier, K., Hegel, F., Jaecks, P., Stenneken, P., Wrede, B., & Hielscher-Fastabend, M. (2011, January). Communicating emotions in robotics: Towards a model of emotional alignment. In *Proceedings of the workshop" Expectations in intuitive interaction" on the 6th HRI International conference on Human-Robot Interaction.*

[24] Ding, W. and Marchionini, G. 1997. *A Study on Video Browsing Strategies*. Technical Report. University of Maryland at College Park.

[25] Driver, J. L., & Gottman, J. M. 2004. Daily marital interactions and positive affect during marital conflict among newlywed couples. ***Family Processes***, 43(3): 301–314.

[26] Ekman, P. (1984). Expression and the nature of emotion. In P. Ekman & K. Scherer (Eds.), *Approaches to emotion* (pp. 319-343). Hillsdale. NJ: Erlbaum.

[27] Ekman, P., Friesen, W. V., O'Sullivan, M., Chan, A., Diacoyanni-Tarlatzis, I., Heider, K., ... & Scherer, K. (1987). Universals and cultural differences in the judgments of facial expressions of emotion. *Journal of personality and social psychology*, *53*(4), 712.

[28] Ekman. P. (1993). Facial expression and emotion. *American Psychologist, 48,* 384-392.

[29] Ekman, P., & Friesen, W. V. (1977). Facial action coding system.

[30] Fernández-Dols, J.-M., Sanchez, F. , Carrera, P., Ruiz-Belda, M.-A. (1997) Are spontaneous expressions and emotions linked? An experimental test of coherence, *Journal of Nonverbal Behavior,* vol. 31, pp. 163-177.

[31] Fincannon, T., Barnes, L. E., Murphy, R. R., & Riddle, D. L. (2004). Evidence of the need for social intelligence in rescue robots. *Proceedings of IROS 2004.* (pp. 1089-1095). IEEE/RSJ 2.

[32] Fischer, A. H., & Manstead, A. S. 2008. Social functions of emotion. In Lewis, M., Haviland-Jones, J. M., and Barrett, L. F. (Eds.), *Handbook of emotions*, (3rd ed.): 456–468. New York, NY: The Guilford Press

[33] Forman, G. 2003. An extensive empirical study of feature selection metrics for text classification. *J. Mach. Learn. Res.* 3 (Mar. 2003), 1289-1305.

[34] Fröhlich, B. and Plate, J. 2000. The cubic mouse: a new device for three-dimensional input. In *Proceedings of the SIGCHI Conference on Human Factors in Computing Systems* (The Hague, The Netherlands, April 01 - 06, 2000). CHI '00. ACM, New York, NY, 526-531.

[35] Giese-Davis, J., Spiegel, D., (2003) Emotional expression and cancer progression. *Handbook of affective sciences.* (pp. 1053-1082). New York: Oxford University Press.

[36] Gockley, R., Simmons, R., and Forlizzi, J. (2006). Modeling affect in socially interactive robots. In Robot and Human Interactive Communication, 2006. ROMAN 2006. The 15th IEEE Inter- national Symposium on, pages 558–563. IEEE.

[37] Goffman, E. (1961). Fun in games. *Encounters*, 15-81.

[38] Goodwin, M. H., & Goodwin, C. (2000). Emotion within situated activity. *Communication: An arena of development*, 33-53.

[39] Gottman, J. M., & Levenson, R. W. (1992). Marital processes predictive of later dissolution: behavior, physiology, and health. Journal of personality and social psychology, 63(2), 221.

[40] Gross, J. J. (1998). The emerging field of emotion regulation: An integrative review. *Review of General Psychology 2*, 271–299.

[41] Gross, J. J. (2013). Emotion regulation: taking stock and moving forward. *Emotion*, *13*(3), 359.

[42] Hiolle, A., Lewis, M., & Cañamero, L. (2014). Arousal regulation and affective adaptation to human responsiveness by a robot that explores and learns a novel environment. *Frontiers in neurorobotics*, *8*.

[43] Hochschild, A. R. (2003). *The managed heart: Commercialization of human feeling.* Univ of California Press.

[44] Horney, K. (1945). Our inner conflicts. New York: Norton.

[45] Hoque, M. E., McDuff, D. J., & Picard, R. W. (2012). Exploring temporal patterns in classifying frustrated and delighted smiles. *IEEE Transactions on Affective Computing*, *3*(3), 323-334.

[46] Jefferson, G.,;Sacks, H., Schegloff, E. (1987). Notes on laughter in the pursuit of intimacy. Button, G. (Ed); Lee, J.

R. E. (Ed). . Talk and social organisation., (pp. 152-205). Clevedon, England: Multilingual Matters, , 335 pp.

[47] Jung, M., Chong, J., & Leifer, L. (2012). Group hedonic balance and pair programming performance: a ective interaction dynamics as indicators of performance. In Proceedings of the SIGCHI Conference on Human Factors in Computing Systems (pp. 829-838). ACM.

[48] Jung, M. F. (2016). Coupling Interactions and Performance: Predicting Team Performance from Thin Slices of Conflict. ACM Transactions on Computer-Human Interaction (TOCHI), 23(3), 18.

[49] Jung, M. F., Lee, J. J., DePalma, N., Adalgeirsson, S. O., Hinds, P. J., & Breazeal, C. (2013, February). Engaging robots: easing complex human-robot teamwork using backchanneling. In *Proceedings of the 2013 conference on Computer supported cooperative work* (pp. 1555-1566). ACM.

[50] Jung, M. F., Martelaro, N., & Hinds, P. J. (2015). Using robots to moderate team conflict: the case of repairing violations. In *Proceedings of the Tenth Annual ACM/IEEE International Conference on Human-Robot Interaction* (pp. 229-236). ACM.

[51] Kaindl, H., Popp, R., Raneburger, D., Ertl, D., Falb, J., Szep, A., & Bogdan, C. (2011). Robot-supported cooperative work: A shared-shopping scenario. In *System Sciences (HICSS), 2011 44th Hawaii International Conference on* (pp. 1-10). IEEE.

[52] Karg, M., Schwimmbeck, M., Kuhnlenz, K., and Buss, M. (2010). Towards mapping emotive gait patterns from human to robot. In RO-MAN, 2010 IEEE, pages 258–263. IEEE.

[53] Kedzierski, J., Muszyn ́ski, R., Zoll, C., Oleksy, A., and Frontkiewicz, M. (2013). Emys—emotive head of a social robot. International Journal of Social Robotics, 5(2):237–249.

[54] Keltner, D., & Haidt, J. 1999. Social Functions of Emotions at Four Levels of Analysis. *Cognition & Emotion*, 13(5): 505–521.

[55] Kirstein, F., Fischer, K., Erkent, Ö., & Piater, J. (2015). Human smile distinguishes between collaborative and solitary tasks in human-robot interaction. In *Proceedings of HRI 2015.* (pp. 145-146). ACM.

[56] Kishi, T., Kojima, T., Endo, N., Destephe, M., Otani, T., Jamone, L., Kryczka, P., Trovato, G., Hashimoto, K., Cosentino, S., et al. (2013). Impression survey of the emotion expression hu- manoid robot with mental model based dynamic emotions. In Robotics and Automation (ICRA), 2013 IEEE International Conference on, pages 1663–1668. IEEE.

[57] Knight, H. and Simmons, R. (2014). Expressive motion with x, y and theta: Laban effort features for mobile robots. In Robot and Human Interactive Communication, 2014 RO-MAN: The 23rd IEEE International Symposium on, pages 267–273. IEEE.

[58] Kraut, R. E., & Johnston, R. E. (1979). Social and emotional messages of smiling: An ethological approach. *Journal of personality and social psychology*, *37*(9), 1539.

[59] Leahu, L., & Sengers, P. (2014, June). Freaky: performing hybrid human-machine emotion. In *Proceedings of the 2014 conference on Designing interactive systems* (pp. 607-616). ACM.

[60] Levenson, R. W., Carstensen, L. L., & Gottman, J. M. 1994. Influence of age and gender on affect, physiology, and their interrelations: A study of long-term marriages. *Journal of Personality and Social Psychology*, 67(1): 56–68.

[61] Levenson, R. W., & Gottman, J. M. 1985. Physiological and affective predictors of change in relationship satisfaction. *Journal of Personality and Social Psychology*, 49(1): 85–94.

[62] Lewis, M., & Canamero, L. (2014, August). An affective autonomous robot toddler to support the development of self-efficacy in diabetic children. In *The 23rd IEEE International Symposium on Robot and Human Interactive Communication.*

[63] Lütkebohle, I., Hegel, F., Schulz, S., Hackel, M., Wrede, B., Wachsmuth, S., and Sagerer, G. (2010). The bielefeld anthropomorphic robot head "flobi". In Robotics and Automation, 2010. ICRA 2010. Proceedings IEEE International Conference on, volume 3(7), pages 3384–3391.

[64] Masuda, M. and Kato, S. (2010). Motion rendering system for emotion expression of human form robots based on laban movement analysis. In RO-MAN, 2010 IEEE, pages 324–329. IEEE.

[65] Morris, M. W., & Keltner, D. 2000. How emotions work: The social functions of emotional expression in negotiations. *Research in Organizational Behavior*, 22: 1–50.

[66] Murphy, R. R., Lisetti, C. L., Tardif, R., Irish, L., & Gage, A. (2002). Emotion-based control of cooperating heterogeneous mobile robots. *IEEE Transactions on Robotics and Automation 18*(5), 744-757.

[67] Mutlu, B., Shiwa, T., Kanda, T., Ishiguro, H., & Hagita, N. (2009). Footing in human-robot conversations: how robots might shape participant roles using gaze cues. *Proceedings of HRI 2009* (61-68). NY: ACM Press.

[68] Pasupathi, M., Carstensen, L. L., Levenson, R. W., & Gottman, J. M. (1999). Responsive listening in long-married couples: A psycholinguistic perspective. *Journal of Nonverbal Behavior*, *23*(2), 173-193.

[69] Perakyla, A., & Ruusuvuori, J. (2012). Facial Expression and Interactional Regulation of Emotion. *Emotion in interaction, ed. A Perakyla, M Sorjonen*, 64-91.

[70] Reeck, C., Ames, D. R., & Ochsner, K. N. (2016). The social regulation of emotion: An integrative, cross-disciplinary model. *Trends in cognitive sciences*, *20*(1), 47-63.

[71] Rich, C., Ponsler, B., Holroyd, A., & Sidner, C. L. (2010, March). Recognizing engagement in human-robot interaction. In *2010 5th ACM/IEEE International Conference on Human-Robot Interaction (HRI)* (pp. 375-382). IEEE.

[72] Rimé, B. (2007). Interpersonal emotion regulation. *Handbook of emotion regulation*, *1*, 466-468.

[73] Rose, R., Scheutz, M, and Schermerhorn, P. (2008). Empirical investigations into the believability of robot affect. *Proceedings of the AAAI Spring Symposium.*

[74] Rosenberg, E. L., Ekman, P. (1994) Coherence between expressive and experiential systems in emotion," *Cognition and Emotion,* vol. 8, pp. 201-229.

[75] Ruusuvuori, J. (2013). Emotion, affect and conversation. The handbook of conversation analysis, 330-349.

[76] Russell, J. A. (1978). Evidence of convergent validity on the dimensions of affect. *Journal of personality and social psychology*, *36*(10), 1152.

[77] Russell, J. A., & Barrett, L. F. (1999). Core affect, prototypical emotional episodes, and other things called emotion: dissecting the elephant. *Journal of personality and social psychology*, *76*(5), 805.

[78] Sacks, H., Schegloff, E. A., & Jefferson, G. (1974). A simplest systematics for the organization of turn-taking for conversation. *language*, 696-735.

[79] Sannella, M. J. 1994. *Constraint Satisfaction and Debugging for Interactive User Interfaces*. Doctoral Thesis. UMI Order Number: UMI Order No. GAX95-09398., University of Washington.

[80] Schegloff, E. (2007). *Sequence organization in interaction: Volume 1: A primer in conversation analysis* (Vol. 1). Cambridge, UK: Cambridge University Press.

[81] Scheutz, M., Schermerhorn, P., & Kramer, J. (2006). The utility of affect expression in natural language interactions in joint human-robot tasks. In Proceedings of HRI 2006 (226-233). NY: ACM Press.

[82] Selting, M. (1994). Emphatic speech style mdash; with special focus on the prosodic signalling of heightened emotive involvement in conversation. *Journal of pragmatics*, *22*(3), 375-408.

[83] Sharma, M., Hildebrandt, D., Newman, G., Young, J. E., and Eskicioglu, R. (2013). Communicating affect via flight path exploring use of the laban effort system for designing affective locomotion paths. In Human-Robot Interaction (HRI), 2013 8th ACM/IEEE International Conference on, pages 293–300. IEEE.

[84] Shibata, H., Kano, M., Kato, S., and Itoh, H. (2006). A system for converting robot'emotion'into facial expressions. In Robotics and Automation, 2006. ICRA 2006. Proceedings 2006 IEEE In- ternational Conference on, pages 3660–3665. IEEE.

[85] Spector, A. Z. 1989. Achieving application requirements. In *Distributed Systems*, S. Mullender, Ed. ACM Press Frontier Series. ACM, New York, NY, 19-33. DOI= http://doi.acm.org/10.1145/90417.90738.

[86] Tavel, P. 2007. *Modeling and Simulation Design*. AK Peters Ltd., Natick, MA.

[87] Thomaz, A., Hoffman, G., Cakmak, M., (In Press) Computational Human-Robot Interaction. *Foundations and Trends in Human Computer Interaction.*

[88] Tielman, M., Neerincx, M., Meyer, J. J., & Looije, R. (2014, March). Adaptive emotional expression in robot-child interaction. In Proceedings of the 2014 ACM/IEEE international conference on Human-robot interaction (pp. 407-414). ACM.

[89] Van Kleef, G. A. (2009). How emotions regulate social life the emotions as social information (EASI) model. *Current directions in psychological science, 18*(3): 184-188.

[90] Van Kleef, G. A., De Dreu, C. K., & Manstead, A. S. (2010). An interpersonal approach to emotion in social decision making: The emotions as social information model. In Mark P. Zanna, editor: *Advances in experimental social psychology, 42, 45-96.*

[91] Watson, D., & Tellegen, A. 1985. Toward a consensual structure of mood. *Psychological Bulletin*, 98(2): 219–235.

[92] Wilkinson, S., & Kitzinger, C. (2006). Surprise as an interactional achievement: Reaction tokens in conversation. *Social psychology quarterly*, *69*(2), 150-182.

[93] Xu, J.,Broekens, J., Hindriks, K., and Neerincx, M. A. (2015). Mood contagion of robot body language in human robot interaction. *Autonomous Agents and Multi-Agent Systems* 29, 6. 1216-1248.

[94] Yu, Y. T. and Lau, M. F. 2006. A comparison of MC/DC, MUMCUT and several other coverage criteria for logical decisions. *J. Syst. Softw.* 79, 5 (May. 2006), 577-590.

[95] Zaki, J., & Williams, W. C. (2013). Interpersonal emotion regulation. *Emotion*, *13*(5), 803.

[96] Zhang, J. and Sharkey, A. J. (2011). Listening to sad music while seeing a happy robot face. In Social Robotics, pages 173–182. Springer.

[97] Ziemke, T., & Lowe, R. (2009). On the role of emotion in embodied cognitive architectures: From organisms to robots. *Cognitive computation*, *1*(1), 104-117.

It's Not What You Do, It's How You Do It: Grounding Uncertainty for a Simple Robot

Julian Hough and David Schlangen
Dialogue Systems Group // CITEC
Faculty of Linguistics and Literature
Bielefeld University
firstname.lastname@uni-bielefeld.de

ABSTRACT

For effective HRI, robots must go beyond having good legibility of their intentions shown by their actions, but also ground the degree of uncertainty they have. We show how in simple robots which have spoken language understanding capacities, uncertainty can be communicated to users by principles of grounding in dialogue interaction even without natural language generation. We present a model which makes this possible for robots with limited communication channels beyond the execution of task actions themselves. We implement our model in a pick-and-place robot, and experiment with two strategies for grounding uncertainty. In an observer study, we show that participants observing interactions with the robot run by the two different strategies were able to infer the degree of understanding the robot had internally, and in the more uncertainty-expressive system, were also able to perceive the degree of internal uncertainty the robot had reliably.

Keywords

Communicative grounding; Uncertainty; Incrementality

1. INTRODUCTION

In human-human interaction, understanding is not an all-or-nothing affair. When following a request to do something, we can act tentatively, displaying uncertainty about our understanding. In HRI, much existing work is concerned with the legibility of robot actions, under the assumption that the robot's current goal is always certain to the robot, as is the robot's basis for that goal [6, 5]. In this paper we investigate how simple robots with spoken language understanding capabilities can best communicate their internal uncertainty to users and onlookers with their non-verbal, task actions. Particularly, we investigate how the degree of a robot's uncertainty can be communicated through the manner of execution of its actions during interaction.

We take uncertainty, or the converse property, confidence, to be a first class citizen of HRI. Humans and robots generate different internal representations and use qualitatively different types of processing when interacting with each other [14], giving rise to different types and degrees of uncertainty for each agent. In an interaction with a manipulator robot which responds to a user requesting manipulation of real-world objects through speech, the types of uncertainty are on multiple levels. These levels include: uncertainty over which words are being spoken as they are recognized from an automatic speech recognizer (ASR); the current real-world location and visual properties of the objects from a computer vision processor; which target objects or locations are being referred to (language grounding, or reference resolution), and, recognition of intentions as to what to do with the objects (dialogue act and intention recognition).

In this paper we explore how simple robots can communicate their internal uncertainty to human interaction partners. After providing background on grounding uncertainty in §2, we present a grounding model for HRI which draws on dialogue systems research in §3. The model is designed to allow a robot's internal uncertainty to be communicated to users as it interprets speech, and in an online, fluid manner. In §4 we describe a proof-of-concept implementation of the model in a simple robot whose only communicative channel is the execution of its task actions, and then in §5 describe a study which proves its efficacy in communicating its uncertainty to observers of the robot's behaviour.

2. GROUNDING UNCERTAINTY IN HRI

Communicative grounding in the sense of [4, 3] is the way in which interaction participants build and align their internal representations towards shared information or "common ground". In HRI, grounding is a particular challenge, given the fundamental differences in the internal representations and processing of humans and robots [14]. Given these differences, perceived behaviour of modern robots may not reflect their internal states appropriately, as system designers may feign competences to make interaction less cumbersome, whilst obscuring the robot's real level of understanding. For robots which understand speech, the trade-off between "keeping up appearances" by displaying apparently human-like dialogue behaviour, and on the other hand grounding the robot's uncertainty, can be weighted more towards the former objective. Consequently, users may not be aware how or to what degree a robot has misunderstood them, which could have negative consequences if robots are to engage in active learning through interaction [23, 22].

In HRI, grounding research has focused on communicative problems in language grounding, for example on how per-

HRI '17, March 06 - 09, 2017, Vienna, Austria

ISBN 978-1-4503-4336-7/17/03...$15.00
DOI: http://dx.doi.org/10.1145/2909824.3020214

spective taking and frame of reference differ between robots and humans [13, 17, 16]. Also, the improvement of grounding intentions through increasing the legibility of actions has received attention– [6, 5] show the importance of legible robot motion which is more 'intent-expressive' to users.

We argue in this paper that a robot not only needs to monitor when its internal goal is becoming legible, but the robot should also be able to ground the *degree of commitment to its goal* with the user when it is uncertain, so it may get the required aid, and do so in a fluid and non-cumbersome way.

In simple robots, uncertainty can be grounded in the manner of execution of the task actions themselves, and here, our motivation is similar to [20]'s position paper on how a robot's uncertainty can be indicated through hesitation before moving. Technically, we also aim to achieve the trade-off between 'safety' and speed of movement similar to [19]'s system, however, our notion of safety here, rather than being the avoidance of physical hazards, is the state of internal certainty the robot has about the user's current intention, according to their ongoing speech. We propose this can be achieved through incorporating a fluid grounding mechanism into the robot's architecture.

3. A MODEL FOR FLUIDLY GROUNDING UNCERTAINTY FOR SIMPLE ROBOTS

We propose a communicative grounding model to make a robot's internal uncertainty common ground with the user. We draw on computational models of grounding [27, 21] and recent attempts to incrementalize grounding strategies in dialogue models [8, 7, 10], which can be purposed for simple robots with speech interfaces if certain modifications are made. The first modification is that the robot's actions have the same status as dialogue acts. The second is that commitment to goals can be real-valued rather than absolute, and this commitment can be evaluated by *strength-of-evidence functions* which monitor the degree to which each agent is showing commitment to their goal at a given point in the interaction. From the definition of these functions and the grounding model, internal measures of *understanding* and *confidence* can be calculated on-line by the robot. We explain the elements in turn below.

Statecharts with strength-of-evidence functions.

For our grounding model, we follow work using Harel statecharts [9] for dialogue control in robotic systems by [22, 26]. Fig. 1 defines the grounding state machine for a simple robot which interprets a user's speech to carry out actions. Here we characterize the user and robot as having *parallel* states, represented either side of the dotted line. This allows the robot to estimate which grounding state the robot and human are in concurrently, without having to explicitly represent the Cartesian product of all possible states.

Fig. 1 shows the states and "triggering conditions" that must be satisfied to allow state transitions (written on the arcs between state boxes, where specific conditions or "guards" are in square brackets). The main motivation of the model is to explore the criteria by which the robot judges both their own and their interaction partner's goals to have become *publicly manifest* (though not necessarily grounded) in real time, and therefore when they are showing commitment to them. To determine which grounding state each agent is in, we use evaluation functions Ev for each agent's state in the triggering conditions on the state transitions– these are *strength-of-evidence* valuation functions that return a real number value indicating the degree to which the agent has displayed their goal publicly, according to the robot's best knowledge. Goals are hidden in the case of the user state and observed in the case of the robot, yet both have to be evaluated for the degree to which they are manifest to allow appropriate interpretation of the user's speech.

$UserGoal$ is estimated as the most likely user intention in the set of possible goals $Intentions$, given the current utterance u, the robot's state $Robot$ and the current task's state $Task$, as in (1). $Intentions$ is the set of user intentions specified on a degree of abstraction deemed relevant by the system designer– for example a possible intention could be $TAKE(X)$ for a robot capable of taking object X.

$$UserGoal := \underset{i \in Intentions}{\arg\max}\ p(i \mid u, Robot, Task) \qquad (1)$$

While the estimated user's goal is continuously being updated through new evidence, this goal can only be judged to become sufficiently mutually manifest with the robot when a certain confidence criterion has been met– here we characterize this as a real-valued threshold δ. Using a real-valued threshold allows experimentation into increasing responsiveness of the robot by reducing it [10]. As Fig. 1 shows, once $Ev(UserGoal) \geq \delta$ then the state `user_showing_commitment_to_goal` can be entered. In a fully cooperative system one can assume the assignment $RobotGoal := UserGoal$ is then carried out upon entering the state (though we omit this from the core grounding model given cooperativity is not assumed).

Conversely, the Robot's view of its own grounding state uses the function $Ev(RobotGoal)$ and its own threshold ϵ. Unlike the user, the robot's goal is taken to be fully observed, however it must still estimate when $RobotGoal$ is made public by its action, and once ϵ has been reached, the robot may enter `robot_showing_commitment_to_goal`. Once in this state it is permissible for the user state to either commit to the goal and trigger grounding, else engage the robot in repair, entering `user_repairing_robot_action`. Then, as soon as is physically possible in the motor plan, the robot state will become `robot_repairing_robot_action`. The repairing state's internal processes are identical to the initial `user_uncommitted` one, except the first action upon entry is to prune $Intentions$ such that:

$$Intentions := \{i \mid p(RobotGoal \mid i) = 0\} \qquad (2)$$

(2) removes all those intentions which would eventually lead to entry to the repaired $RobotGoal$ intention. The robot will remain in this repairing state until the user's state has exited `user_repairing_robot_action`, triggering the end of the user-initiated repair interaction. Note that it is only possible for the user state to repair the $RobotGoal$, rather than $UserGoal$– the user can repair the latter through self-repair, but that is currently not represented as its own state. Repair of the robot's current action is only possible through knowing it had shown commitment to a goal which caused it (i.e. been in the state `robot_showing_commitment_to_goal`), otherwise, as per normal principles of situated dialogue, it would not be able to interpret the utterance as a repair. The strength-of-evidence function $Ev(RobotGoal)$ and the threshold ϵ are therefore of tantamount importance, as they determine when confirmations and repairs can be interpreted as

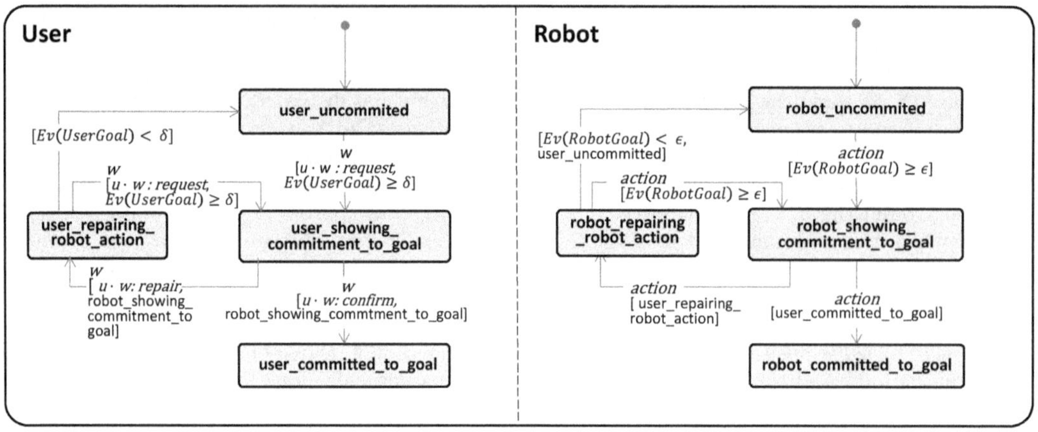

Figure 1: Interactive Statechart as modelled by the Robot. The statechart consists of two parallel, concurrent states, one for each participant. The triggering events and conditions in the transition functions (the directed edges) can reference the other state.

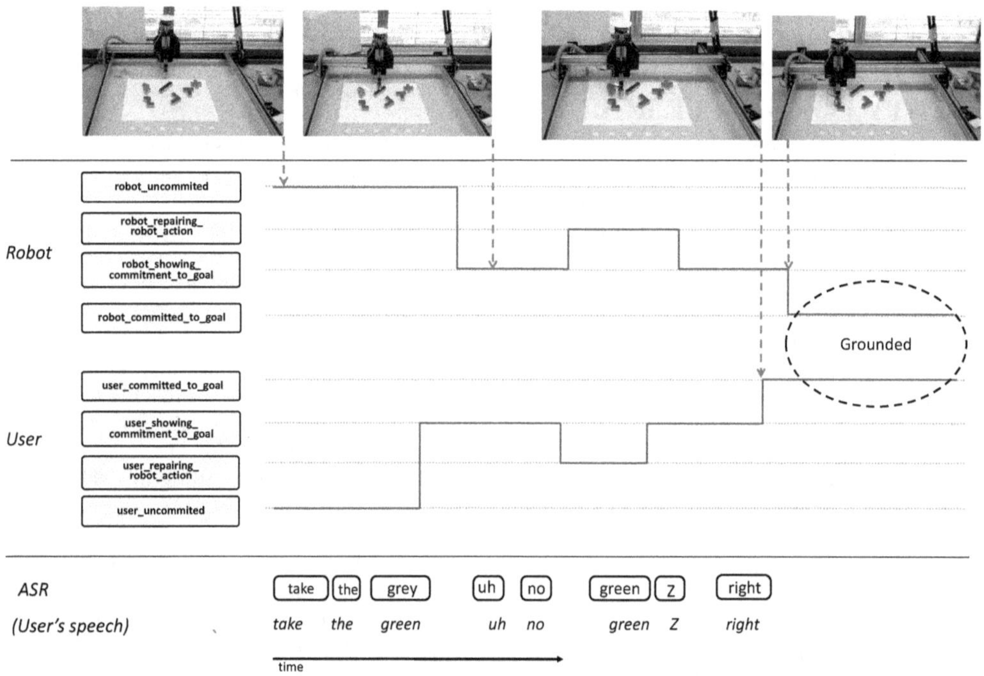

Figure 2: Concurrent User and Robot grounding states during an interaction where an initial mis-recognition of 'green' as 'grey' by the ASR, and confusion over colours in reference resolution where 'grey' gives higher probability to a blue object. The recognition of repair allows the participants to become grounded again.

such, and consequently determine the interactive dynamics of system.

Fluidity through incremental processing.

We achieve fluidity in this grounding process through incremental processing. The increment of the triggering events in the $User$ state is the latest word w in current utterance u (as opposed to the latest complete utterance). The principal Natural Language Understanding (NLU) decisions are therefore to classify incrementally which type of dialogue act u is, (e.g. u : *Confirm*), whether w begins a new dialogue act or not, and estimate $UserGoal$ from the set $Intentions$, whatever they may be in the given application. The grounding statechart is then checked to see if a transition is possible from the user's current state as each word is processed, akin to incremental dialogue state tracking [28].

For an example of the grounding model in action see Fig. 2. This shows the state dynamics for the concurrent statechart during an interaction with repair.[1] The robot's

[1]Notice how the *Robot* state mirrors, though slightly lags,

ASR error leads to it showing commitment to picking up the wrong object, where upon user-initiated repair interaction begins. From its repair state, the robot changes its goal and re-enters `robot_showing_commitment_to_goal` once its new movement has become legible. In this state, the user's confirmation "right" is interpreted as referring to the current *RobotGoal*, triggering the entry to `robot_committed_to_goal`.

In addition to the word-by-word, left-to-right incremental language understanding ability [15] describe, our system can simultaneously act after each word is processed (like [2]'s model, which is not implemented in a robot), but the novelty is that the robotic action then dynamically updates the context used to understand the following words in the utterance. This is consistent with our approach that the robot's non-verbal actions are treated with the same status as dialogue/speech acts in dialogue and speech act models.

Internal Measures of Understanding and Confidence.

With this grounding model and dialogue act and intention recognition adequate for the robot to know it is in a given grounding state, it is possible to derive measures of understanding and confidence in its own actions, in line with our motivation of making robots monitor their own uncertainty.

Unless being explicitly informed, a robot will not have direct knowledge of its own level of understanding of the user's speech. However, using our grounding model it can estimate this simply as the efficiency in transitioning within its *Robot* state machine from the initial `robot_uncommitted` state to the `robot_committed_to_goal` state for a given goal. So, the level of understanding for a given time period $t_i..t_n$ is simply as in (3), where $S(t_i..t_n)$ represents the states transitioned to over that time.

$$U(t_i...t_n) = \frac{2\times \mid \{s_j \mid s_j \in S(t_i...t_n) \wedge s_j : robot\_committed\_to\_goal\} \mid}{\mid S(t_i...t_n) \mid} \quad (3)$$

This simple measure is based on the following assumption: if the level of understanding is perfect, only two grounding state entries are required to go from being uncommitted to `robot_committed_to_goal` (see Fig .1). In the example in Fig. 2, the understanding measure for this time period would be $\frac{2}{4} = 0.5$, as the total number of state transitions is 4, and there is only one `robot_committed_to_goal` state. Understanding is therefore a measure of grounding efficiency.

Confidence, which is the inverse of uncertainty, is characterized in (4). It is simply the sum of all the strength-of-evidence measures for the user's goal which have been recorded in the state history so far, normalized by the number of state transitions. Confidence in the hypothesized *UserGoal* is the basis on which the robot's actions are made.

$$C(t_i...t_n) = \frac{\sum_j s_j.Ev(UserGoal) \in S(t_i...t_n)}{\mid S(t_i...t_n) \mid} \quad (4)$$

(4) is a summary of the evidence for the user's goal so far– simply the mean of the strength-of-evidence values that the actions were based on. If there is no uncertainty at all in the evidence about the user's goal when these actions were taken, then this measure would simply average at 1. Lower $Ev(UserGoal)$ values reduce this ongoing average confidence. We use averaging as opposed to a standard product for probability values in Markov chains as we assume confidence is additive, and the length and efficiency of the interaction is better captured by our simple understanding metric in (3).

Showing uncertainty in action execution.

When the robot repairs its action during the user's speech, this is a clear sign of unsuccessful grounding. Legible change of intent shows a lack of absolute commitment to the original goal. However, there are also ways in which simple robots can display the *degree* of uncertainty about their goal and communicate the value of $Ev(UserGoal)$ which their actions are based on. A robot can do this by waiting longer periods for confirmation before acting, as in [20], or by moving more slowly. We explore these two strategies in our experiment in §5 to communicate the robot's current internal confidence. More complex robots could display low levels of confidence through other means such as a confused facial expressions, or requesting clarification for robots with spoken language generation abilities [18].

3.1 Managing uncertainty at different levels with the Incremental Unit framework

To manage the processing in our robotic system which the grounding state machine is housed in, we use the Incremental Unit (IU) framework [25]. The input and output of each module are incremental units (IUs), which are packages of information with a pre-defined level of granularity– e.g. a *wordIU* can represent a single incremental ASR word hypothesis. IUs created in the output buffer of one module trigger downstream processing (and creation of new IUs) in other modules with access to that buffer.

IUs can be defined to be connected by directed edges, called *Grounded In* links, which in general take the semantics of "triggered by" from the source to the sink IU. Grounded In links are useful in cases where input IU hypotheses may be *revoked* (for instance, by changing ASR hypotheses), as reasoning can be triggered about how to revoke or repair actions that are Grounded In these input IUs in downstream modules– see e.g. [11].

To implement the grounding strategies above, we recast the standard Grounded In dependencies: while the output IUs are taken as Grounded In the input IUs which triggered them (from sensor modules to actuator modules), as per standard processing, in our system the reverse will also be true: consistent with the statecharts driving the behaviour, the interpretation of the user's speech is dependent on the robot's latest or currently ongoing robot action. Consequently interpretation IUs can be grounded in action IUs– see the reversed feedback arrow in Fig. 3.

To deal with concurrency issues that this closed-loop approach has, the IU modules coordinate their behaviours by sending event instances to each other, where events here are IU edit messages. The edit messages consist in *ADD*s where the IU is initially created, *COMMIT*s if there is certainty they will not change their payload, and, as mentioned above *REVOKE*s may be sent if the basis for a previously ADDed IU becomes unreliable. IUs also have different temporal statuses of being either *upcoming*, *ongoing* or *completed*, a temporal logic which allows the system to reason with the status of the actions being executed or planned by the robot.

the *User*, by virtue of the fact that it takes time to demonstrate commitment to a given goal with a sufficently strong *Ev*(*RobotGoal*) (or legibility [6]).

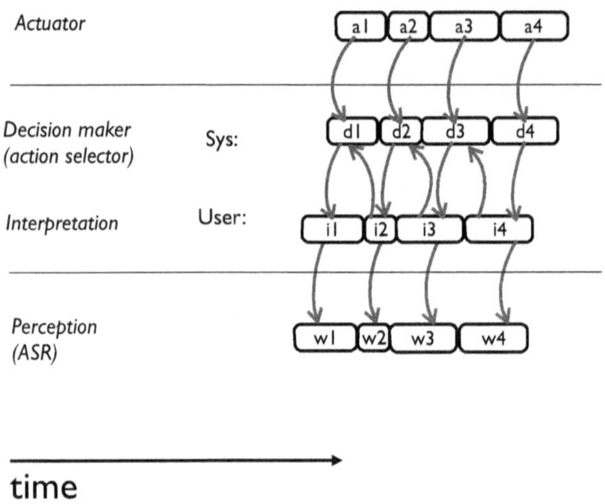

Figure 3: The addition of tight feedback over standard IU approaches helps achieve requirements of fluid interaction and situated repair interpretation. Grounded In links in blue.

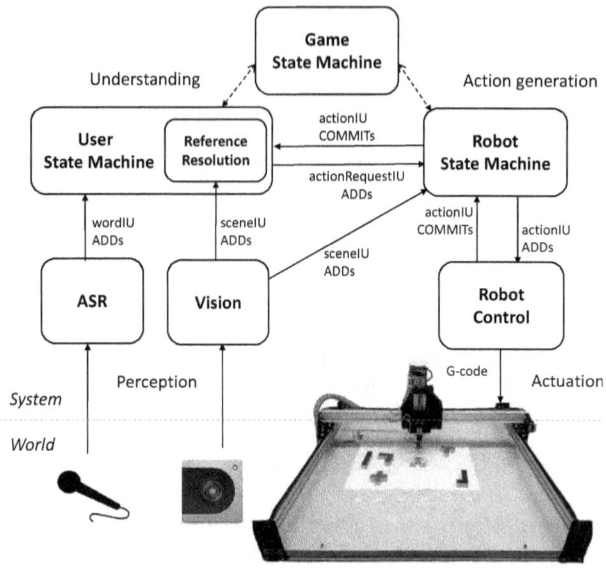

Figure 4: Robot architecture.

4. IMPLEMENTATION IN A SIMPLE PICK-AND-PLACE ROBOT

We implement the above grounding model and incremental processing in a real-world pick-and-place robot, *PentoRob* [10], the architecture of which can be seen in Fig. 4. The domain we use in this paper is grabbing and placing real-world magnetic Pentomino pieces at target locations, however the system is adaptable to novel objects and tasks.

For the robotic arm, we use the ShapeOko2,[2] a heavy-duty 3-axis CNC machine, which we modified with a rotatable electromagnet, whereby its movement and magnetic field are controlled via two Arduino boards. The sensors are a webcam and microphone.

4.1 System components

The robot was implemented in Java using the InproTK [1] dialogue systems toolkit.[3] The modules involved are described below, in terms of their input information or IUs, processing, and output IUs.

Incremental Speech Recognizer (ASR).

We use Google's web-based ASR API [24] in German mode, in line with the native language of our experimental participants. It achieves a Word Error Rate in our target domain of 20%. While it has slightly sub-optimal incremental performance, this did not incur great costs in terms of the grounding we focus on here.

Computer Vision (CV).

We utilize OpenCV in a Python module to track objects in the camera's view. This information is relayed to InproTK from Python via the Robotics Service Bus (RSB),[4] which outputs IDs and positions of objects it detects in the scene along with their low-level features (e.g., RGB/HSV values, x,y coordinates, number of edges, etc.), converting these into *sceneIUs* which the downstream reference resolution model consumes. The Robot State Machine also uses these for reasoning about positions of the objects it plans to grab.[5]

Reference resolution (WAC).

The reference resolution component consists of a Words As Classifiers (WAC) model [12]. Our robot's WAC model is trained on a corpus of Wizard-of-Oz Pentomino puzzle playing interactions. During application, as a referring expression is uttered and recognized, the classifier for each word in the expression is applied to all objects in the scene, which after normalisation, results in a probability distribution over objects. [12] report 65% accuracy on a 1-out-of-32 reference resolution task in this domain with the same features.

User State Machine.

We implement the principal NLU features within the User State Machine module, which runs the $User$ state of the interactive grounding statechart as in Fig. 1. While the statechart defines the transitions between states, their triggering criteria require the variables of the estimated current $UserGoal$ from a set *Intentions*, its strength-of-evidence function Ev and threshold δ to be defined. In our domain we characterize $UserGoal$ as simply taking or placing the most likely object in the referent set R being referred to according to WAC's output distribution given the utterance u so far (e.g. (5) and *Intentions* is simply the distribution over the possible actions of the Pentomino pieces still in play. When the action is $TAKE$, the Ev function is the probability value of the highest ranked object in WAC's distribution over its second highest rank as in (6). We experimented to find a suitable δ which (6) needs to reach as 0.05 [10].

$$UserGoal = TAKE(\arg\max_{r \in R} p(r \mid u)) \qquad (5)$$

[2]http://www.shapeoko.com/wiki/index.php/ShapeOko_2
[3]http://bitbucket.org/inpro/inprotk
[4]https://code.cor-lab.de/projects/rsb

[5]The objects' positions are calculated accurately from a single video stream using perspective projection.

$$Ev(UserGoal) = \text{Margin}(\arg\max_{r \in R} p(r \mid u)) \quad (6)$$

When the action of the goal is $PLACE$ and the system is waiting to recognize a target location as a numbered location based on the incoming *wordIU*s, we use a simpler $Ev(UserGoal)$: this remains 1.0 until 4 seconds after the last robotic action, then decays gradually to 0.05 after 10 seconds. We assigned these bounds after a short pilot study. Given the uncertainty lies in incoming wordIUs for the simple location references, a function based on the ASR confidences could be used, however for our purposes the time elapsed alone was a good enough indicator of uncertainty.

We obtain $UserGoal$ incrementally with a simple NLU method, which uses the results from the WAC reference resolution and the *Robot* and $User$'s current grounding state. Firstly, sub-utterance dialogue act (DA) classification is performed, judging the utterance to be in $\{request, confirm, repair\}$ after every word. The classifier is a simple segmenter which uses key word spotting for $confirm$ words and common $repair$ initiating words, and also classifies a $repair$ if the word changes the $UserGoal$, else outputting the default $request$. Given the DA classification, the state machine is queried to see if transitioning away from the current state is possible.

If a successful state change is achieved and $UserGoal$ has changed or been instantiated in the process, a new *ActionRequestIU* is made available in the module's right buffer, where the payload is a frame with the dialogue act type, the action type (`TAKE` or `PLACE`) and optional arguments **`target_piece`** and **`target_location`**.

Robot State Machine.

The robot state machine module partially consists of the *Robot* grounding statechart in Fig. 1, having access to triggering conditions involving the User's state through ActionRequestIUs in its input buffer. When the $User$ state is **`user_showing_commitment_to_goal`**, the *RobotGoal* is set to $UserGoal$, and through a simple planning function, ActionIUs are created to achieve it. It sends these as RSB messages to the robotic actuation module and once confirmed, also via RSB, that the action has begun, the ActionIU is *committed* and the robot's *action state*, orthogonal to its grounding state, is set to one of the following, with superstates in brackets:

```
{stationary_without_piece |
moving_without_piece |
moving_to_piece (taking) |
over_target_piece (taking) |
grabbing_piece (taking) |
stationary_with_piece(placing) |
moving_with_piece (placing) |
over_target_location (placing) |
 dropping_piece (placing)}
```

For estimation of its own grounding state, we define the robot's strength-of-evidence function as in (7):

$$Ev(RobotGoal) = \begin{cases} 1 & \text{if over\_target\_piece,} \\ 1 & \text{if over\_target\_location,} \\ 0.5 & \text{if taking} \wedge legible(RobotGoal), \\ 0.5 & \text{if placing} \wedge legible(RobotGoal), \\ 0 & \text{otherwise} \end{cases} \quad (7)$$

Here we take *legible* to be a very simple characteristic: that the elapsed time from the beginning of the current action is over 50% of the expected duration of the entire action. The simplistic function (7) embodies the assumption that there is absolute certainty that the robot's goal has been demonstrated when its arm is directly over the target pieces and locations, else if it is legibly moving to these positions, there is some evidence, else there is none. While sufficient for our purposes, more sophisticated approaches can be seen in [5]. In this paper, based on experimentation we set the threshold ϵ which (7) must reach to be 0.5 [10].

Robot actuation module.

The module controlling the robotic actuation of the ShapeOKO arm is a Python module with an Arduino board G-code interface to the arm. This sends RSB feedback messages to the robotic control module to the effect that actions have been successful or unsuccessfully started, and with their estimated finishing time.

5. EXPERIMENT: AN ONLOOKER STUDY ON INFERRING UNCERTAINTY

To test our model of grounding uncertainty in our implementation with users we carry out an onlooker experiment with two versions of our model in PentoRob. Both versions have the same model of internal uncertainty as described above, however they differ as to how they ground this uncertainty with the user in the following ways:

Uncertainty through repair only: only grounds uncertainty by allowing repairs to change its goal and therefore change its action. The maximum speed of movement is the same for every action, and it has a default waiting time over its goal pieces and locations of 1.5 seconds.

Uncertainty through movement: also allows repairs to change its goal but also exhibits its own level of confidence about its goal through its speed of movement and waiting time before acting. Its speed is proportional to its confidence about the piece or target location being referred to, according to equation (4), and its waiting time over target pieces and areas is inversely proportional to this confidence, with a maximal wait time λ seconds before taking the initiative with action a and a degradation down to 0 (no wait) according to (8) below. In this study we set λ to 3 seconds.

$$\text{WaitTime}(a) = \lambda \times (1 - Ev(UserGoal)) \quad (8)$$

The aim of the study was to evaluate our model for its ability to ground system internal measures of understanding and confidence, and whether altering simple parameters of the action execution can communicate the degree of uncertainty. Our concrete hypotheses were:

H1 Our grounding model allows observers to rate the robot's level of understanding reliably without the robot knowing whether it had successfully achieved the user's goal. Due to this measure being based on grounding efficiency in terms of number of state transitions (as in eq. (3)) there should be no difference between the two settings.

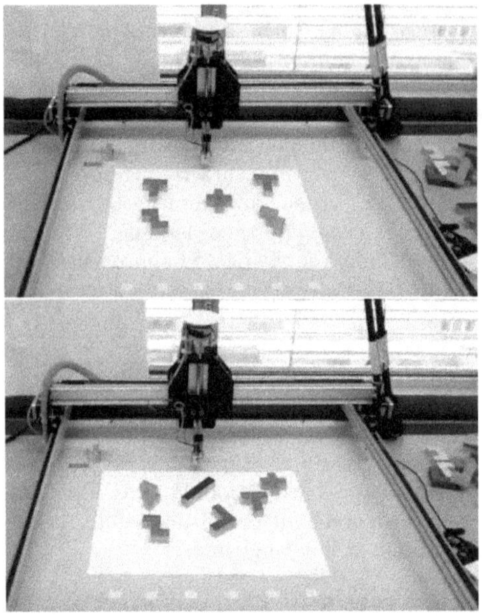

Figure 5: Setting 1 (top) and 2 (bottom).

H2 In our *uncertainty through movement* setting, users would be able to rate the robot's perceived level of confidence more closely to its internal measure of confidence (as in eq. (4)) than in the *uncertainty through repair only* setting. Given the former system maps its confidence onto parameters of its actions, this should be noticeable to users.

5.1 Method

We conducted a video observation experiment with 12 participants who were undergraduate aged students (4 male, 8 female), all of whom understood German (9 native). The participants rated videos of our robot interacting with an undergraduate aged female native German speaker. The instruction giver was not visible in the video as it was captured via a camera placed at her head level, so effected a 'point-of-view' shot where her voice could be heard – see Fig. 5. Each video showed the robot placing a number of pieces as instructed by the instruction giver. Direct interaction with the robot was not used to avoid the difficulty of giving ratings during the interaction in a way that was natural. We understood from the outset that this was not direct HRI, but believe it still has concrete implications for it.

Participants watched and rated four videos in total. The study was a within-subjects design in that participants watched videos in two halves, where they were told the first two videos showed the robot controlled by one system, and the final two showed the robot being controlled by a different system. Both pairs of videos had the same task and starting configurations for two different situations as shown in Fig 5:

1 The initial scene consists of 5 Pentomino pieces: 3 green, 2 red, where there are distractors in terms of shape, with two T-shaped pieces in each colour (introducing human-like uncertainty). The green Z and M pieces according to our computer vision module are confusable (introducing robot-specific uncertainty). All 5 pieces are to be placed in specified numbered boxes at the bottom of the screen.

2 The initial scene consists of 6 Pentomino pieces: 3 green, 3 blue. While there are no distractors in terms of shape, our computer vision module often confuses green and blue. The first 3 pieces, all green, are to be placed in the specified numbered boxes.

For all four interactions, the words recognized, dialogue acts classified, grounding state changes, robotic action requests and callbacks, understanding and confidence measures were logged by our system. These were used to test our hypotheses.

Participants watched both situations in the same order but with a randomly selected order of the system presentations. The experimenter, not co-present, paused the video after each piece was placed in its target location. During the pause, participants would rate the robot's behaviour during the clip they had just observed under two dimensions of Understanding and Confidence on a scale from 1 to 7, writing them down on a form. Before the experiment the meanings of the two ratings dimensions were explained as follows:

- Understanding- to what degree did you feel the robot understood what it had to do?
- Confidence- to what degree did you feel the robot had confidence in its decisions to act?

The purpose of the clip-by-clip rating, rather than using overall interaction-final impressions, is that we wanted to get close to the live monitoring of understanding and uncertainty required in performing joint tasks with robots, in line with our motivation in §2. We separate understanding and confidence ratings in order to see how well our model's internal measures of both dimensions correlate with the users' perceptions, emphasizing these as separate aspects, rather than conflating the ratings into one.

5.2 Results

One participant did not follow the instructions, so his results were discarded. For the remaining 11 participants, we performed Z-score normalization over their ratings, and then correlated these Z-scores with the internal understanding and confidence ratings for each of the 8 clips.

For understanding, the internal values of the system's understanding for each clip as given in (3) correlated very strongly with user ratings of perceived understanding for both systems. The *uncertainty through movement* setting correlating linearly (Pearson's R) very strongly at 0.921 ($n=88$ for this and all results below, $p<0.0001$), and in a non-parametric Spearman's rank correlating strongly at 0.832 ($p<0.0001$). Our *uncertainty through repair only* system's internal understanding for each clip also correlated strongly linearly and non-parametrically (Pearson's R= 0.841 ($p<0.0001$) and Spearman's rank = 0.765 ($p<0.0001$))– see Fig 6 (top). According to a Fisher r-to-z transformation, the two Spearman's rank correlations were not significantly different ($z=1.210$. $p=0.226$). This result gives evidence for H1 being the case in our simple domain.

For confidence, the inverse of uncertainty which we are investigating, there is a different pattern, in that while the *uncertainty through movement* setting's internal confidence correlates strongly with the observer judgements (Pearson's $R=0.726$, $p<0.0001$; Spearman's rank = 0.704, $p<0.0001$), the *uncertainty through repair only* setting only does so moderately (Pearson's $R=0.398$, $p<0.001$; Spearman's rank =

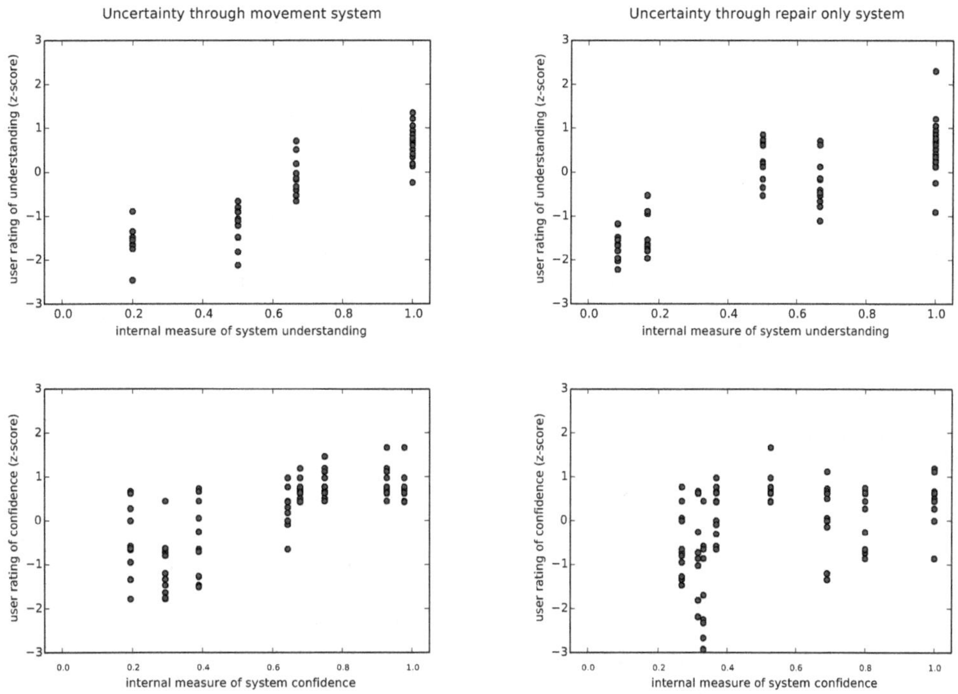

Figure 6: Top: plot of the internal understanding measures of the system (x-axis) vs. observed rated level of understanding by participants (y-axis). Bottom: internal confidence measure of the system (x) vs. observed rated confidence (y). Left-hand plots are uncertainty through movement system, right-hand repair only.

0.4018, p<0.001)– see Fig. 6 (bottom). A Fisher r-to-z transformation on the Spearman's rank coefficients shows the *uncertainty through movement*'s correlation was significantly stronger (z=2.93, p<0.01). This gives some evidence to supporting H2, that the uncertainty is more easily groundable through mapping it onto real-valued parameters in the robot's movement.

5.3 Discussion

We can tentatively conclude that uncertainty can be recognized in the *movement* system more reliably than the *repair only* system, given the stronger correlation between internal confidence values and the ratings of confidence. The correlation suggests people can not only perceive the presence of uncertainty, but its degree. Given the *repair only* system 'hides' its uncertainty in its action, this result is what we would expect, and serves as evidence that one can systematically ground levels of certainty through simple parameter changes in robotic movement alone.

There are several limitations to the study. Firstly, due to the fact video-recorded interactions were rated, one can only tentatively draw conclusions for actual HRI. It is difficult to design scenarios where users could rate the robot's levels of understanding and confidence online while they carry out a time-critical task with the robot, however other measures of uncertainty derivable from sensory information could be used. Various options such as gaze data or acoustic measures from the user's speech could be used in a further study. A future study could also be designed where uncertainty is contingent on some aspects of interactive success for the user, such as perceived rapport and trust with the robot.

Secondly, the study could be scaled to a bigger participant pool. Using crowd sourcing could potentially be useful for informing our grounding model with enough data. In spite of this limitation, from our proof-of-concept we can draw positive conclusions that on-lookers can perceive uncertainty with some reliability.

6. CONCLUSION

We have presented a grounding model for HRI and show how, when implemented in a simple robot, it can communicate a robot's levels of uncertainty, in terms of understanding and confidence, purely through the robot's task actions. While parameterization of robotic movement by confidence levels has been used in previous studies for giving extra time for sensing [19], here we do this for communicative purposes.

Our study has some pleasing potential consequences for HRI with simple robots in general. Any system with adjustable parameters in its actions could in principle adopt our grounding model. The choice of the strength-of-evidence functions and thresholds will vary with the affordances of the robot and its primary tasks. However, provided the robot has the ability to monitor the ongoing progress of its actions, and provided those actions are interruptible, our model can be adapted to novel cases.

Acknowledgments

We thank the HRI reviewers for their helpful and detailed comments. We thank Casey Kennington, Oliver Eickmeyer and Livia Dia for contributions to software and hardware and Gerdis Anderson for help running the experiments. This work was supported by the Cluster of Excellence Cognitive Interaction Technology 'CITEC' (EXC 277) at Bielefeld University, funded by the German Research Foundation (DFG), and the DFG-funded DUEL project (grant SCHL 845/5-1).

7. REFERENCES

[1] T. Baumann and D. Schlangen. The inprotk 2012 release. In *NAACL-HLT Workshop on Future Directions and Needs in the Spoken Dialog Community: Tools and Data*. ACL, 2012.

[2] T. Brick and M. Scheutz. Incremental natural language processing for hri. In *Proceedings of the ACM/IEEE international conference on Human-robot interaction*, pages 263–270. ACM, 2007.

[3] H. H. Clark. *Using language*. Cambridge university press, 1996.

[4] H. H. Clark and S. E. Brennan. Grounding in communication. *Perspectives on socially shared cognition*, 13(1991), 1991.

[5] A. D. Dragan, S. Bauman, J. Forlizzi, and S. S. Srinivasa. Effects of robot motion on human-robot collaboration. In *Proceedings of the Tenth Annual ACM/IEEE International Conference on Human-Robot Interaction*, pages 51–58. ACM, 2015.

[6] A. D. Dragan, K. C. Lee, and S. S. Srinivasa. Legibility and predictability of robot motion. In *2013 8th ACM/IEEE International Conference on Human-Robot Interaction (HRI)*, pages 301–308. IEEE, 2013.

[7] A. Eshghi, C. Howes, E. Gregoromichelaki, J. Hough, and M. Purver. Feedback in conversation as incremental semantic update. In *Proceedings of the 11th International Conference on Computational Semantics*, London, UK, 2015. ACL.

[8] J. Ginzburg, R. Fernández, and D. Schlangen. Disfluencies as intra-utterance dialogue moves. *Semantics and Pragmatics*, 7(9), 2014.

[9] D. Harel. Statecharts: A visual formalism for complex systems. *Science of computer programming*, 8(3), 1987.

[10] J. Hough and D. Schlangen. Investigating fluidity for human-robot interaction with real-time, real-world grounding strategies. In *Proceedings of the 17th Annual Meeting of the Special Interest Group on Discourse and Dialogue*, pages 288–298, Los Angeles, September 2016. Association for Computational Linguistics.

[11] C. Kennington, S. Kousidis, T. Baumann, H. Buschmeier, S. Kopp, and D. Schlangen. Better driving and recall when in-car information presentation uses situationally-aware incremental speech output generation. In *Proceedings of the 6th International Conference on Automotive User Interfaces and Interactive Vehicular Applications*. ACM, 2014.

[12] C. Kennington and D. Schlangen. Simple learning and compositional application of perceptually grounded word meanings for incremental reference resolution. Proceedings of the Conference for the Association for Computational Linguistics (ACL). ACL, 2015.

[13] T. Kollar, S. Tellex, D. Roy, and N. Roy. Toward understanding natural language directions. In *Human-Robot Interaction (HRI), 2010 5th ACM/IEEE International Conference on*. IEEE, 2010.

[14] G.-J. M. Kruijff. There is no common ground in human-robot interaction. In *Proceedings of SemDial 2012 (SeineDial): The 16th Workshop on the Semantics and Pragmatics of Dialogue*, 2012.

[15] G.-J. M. Kruijff, P. Lison, T. Benjamin, H. Jacobsson, and N. Hawes. Incremental, multi-level processing for comprehending situated dialogue in human-robot interaction. In *Symposium on Language and Robots*, 2007.

[16] C. Liu, R. Fang, and J. Y. Chai. Towards mediating shared perceptual basis in situated dialogue. In *Proceedings of the 13th Annual Meeting of the Special Interest Group on Discourse and Dialogue*. ACL, 2012.

[17] C. Liu, J. Walker, and J. Y. Chai. Ambiguities in spatial language understanding in situated human robot dialogue. In *AAAI Fall Symposium: Dialog with Robots*, 2010.

[18] M. Marge and A. I. Rudnicky. Towards overcoming miscommunication in situated dialogue by asking questions. In *AAAI Fall Symposium: Building Representations of Common Ground with Intelligent Agents*, 2011.

[19] J. Miura, Y. Negishi, and Y. Shirai. Adaptive robot speed control by considering map and motion uncertainty. *Robotics and Autonomous Systems*, 54(2):110–117, 2006.

[20] A. Moon, B. Panton, H. Van der Loos, and E. Croft. Using hesitation gestures for safe and ethical human-robot interaction. In *Proceedings of the ICRA*, pages 11–13, 2010.

[21] T. Paek and E. Horvitz. Grounding criterion: Toward a formal theory of grounding. Technical report, MSR Technical Report, 2000.

[22] J. Peltason and B. Wrede. Pamini: A framework for assembling mixed-initiative human-robot interaction from generic interaction patterns. In *Proceedings of the 11th Annual Meeting of the Special Interest Group on Discourse and Dialogue*. ACL, 2010.

[23] M. Saerbeck, T. Schut, C. Bartneck, and M. D. Janse. Expressive robots in education: varying the degree of social supportive behavior of a robotic tutor. In *Proceedings of the SIGCHI Conference on Human Factors in Computing Systems*, pages 1613–1622. ACM, 2010.

[24] J. Schalkwyk, D. Beeferman, F. Beaufays, B. Byrne, C. Chelba, M. Cohen, M. Kamvar, and B. Strope. Your Word is my Command: Google Search by Voice: A Case Study. In *Advances in Speech Recognition*. Springer, 2010.

[25] D. Schlangen and G. Skantze. A General, Abstract Model of Incremental Dialogue Processing. *Dialoge & Discourse*, 2(1), 2011.

[26] G. Skantze and S. Al Moubayed. Iristk: a statechart-based toolkit for multi-party face-to-face interaction. In *Proceedings of the 14th ACM international conference on Multimodal interaction*. ACM, 2012.

[27] D. R. Traum. A computational theory of grounding in natural language conversation. Technical report, DTIC Document, 1994.

[28] J. D. Williams. A belief tracking challenge task for spoken dialog systems. In *NAACL-HLT Workshop on Future Directions and Needs in the Spoken Dialog Community: Tools and Data*. ACL, 2012.

Implicit Communication in a Joint Action

Ross A. Knepper
Department of Computer Science
Cornell University
Ithaca, NY, USA
rak@cs.cornell.edu

Christoforos I. Mavrogiannis
Sibley School of Mechanical and Aerospace Engineering
Cornell University
Ithaca, NY, USA
cm694@cornell.edu

Julia Proft
Department of Computer Science
Cornell University
Ithaca, NY, USA
jproft@cs.cornell.edu

Claire Liang
Department of Computer Science
Cornell University
Ithaca, NY, USA
cyl48@cornell.edu

ABSTRACT

Robots must be cognizant of how their actions will be interpreted in context. Actions performed in the context of a joint activity comprise two aspects: functional and communicative. The functional component achieves the goal of the action, whereas its communicative component, when present, expresses some information to the actor's partners in the joint activity. The interpretation of such communication requires leveraging information that is public to all participants, known as common ground. Much of human communication is performed through this implicit mechanism, and humans cannot help but infer some meaning – whether or not it was intended by the actor – from most actions. We present a framework for robots to utilize this communicative channel on top of normal functional actions to work more effectively with human partners. We consider the role of the actor and the observer, both individually and jointly, in implicit communication, as well as the effects of timing. We also show how the framework maps onto various modes of action, including natural language and motion. We consider these modes of action in various human-robot interaction domains, including social navigation and collaborative assembly.

1. INTRODUCTION

An important domain for human-robot interaction involves collaboration on a joint activity, such as collaborative furniture assembly (Figure 1). A great deal of attention has been paid to what actions to perform [1, 16, 17, 27] and when to perform them [9, 13, 35] in order to complete a cooperative task. Often underappreciated, however, is the implicit communication that occurs as a result of an *action situated in context.* We call behaviors that implicitly communicate information *communicative actions.* Humans are adept at drawing inference from observed actions and common ground – in fact, they instinctively perform this inference, thus reading additional meaning about the intent of an action [8], and many people treat information gleaned implicitly through inference as though it had been stated outright. We argue that to be successful in a joint activity with humans, robots must be cognizant of implicit communication because humans will inevitably use it and expect robots to comprehend its meaning. We further argue that if a robot fails to attend to a human's interpretation of its own actions through the implicit communication mechanism, then people will perceive the robot's purely functional actions as sending random implicit signals, sowing confusion.

Figure 1: Robots that collaborate with humans, such as in an assembly task [22], must consider the correctness of both the functional and communicative aspects of their actions.

Implicit communication is identified by various terms in differing contexts. In robot motion, including reaching [10] and social navigation [29], it has been termed *legibility.* In linguistics, it has been termed *conversational implicature* [15], for which we provide a primer in Sec. 5.1.1. In natural language generation for HRI, it has been called *inverse seman-*

HRI '17, March 06 - 09, 2017, Vienna, Austria

ISBN 978-1-4503-4336-7/17/03...$15.00
DOI: http://dx.doi.org/10.1145/2909824.3020226

tics [22]. In each of these cases, the meaning is extracted by leveraging common ground. The goal of this paper is to unify these separate works by explicating a common mathematical framework that underlies all of them.

Extending an earlier workshop paper [20], we contribute:

- a unifying mathematical framework describing how and why people implicitly communicate information on top of functional behaviors,
- formal expressions for encoding and decoding communicative actions, and
- collected example applications to illustrate the theory.

2. WHY IMPLICITLY COMMUNICATE?

Humans are able to express a multitude of ideas "in code", by means other than explicit natural language statements. Motivations for implicit communication include efficiency, tact, group cohesion, and social bonding. In this section, we give examples of several categories of implicit communication. Message categories include expressing intent, coordinating plans, and conveying information. Broadly, these categories all fulfill the role of setting expectations, and we consider each separately.

Social navigation is among the most superficial forms of interaction, yet it is rife with implicit communication. In social navigation, the objective is to avoid collision with co-inhabitants of the space and reach one's destination. Combined, these objectives comprise the navigator's intent. Collision avoidance without intent expression is only the barest definition of correct navigation – it alone would not be judged as competent behavior by fellow pedestrians [31]. Competence demands that we convey our intended trajectory to nearby observers. We trust in return that they will convey their intent to us. Such intent-expressive actions minimize the global uncertainty about future motions of the agents (humans or robots) in the scene, leading to smooth and stable motion. We borrow from Barbalet [2] the definition of trust as "the confidence that another's actions will correspond with one's expectations." In the absence of social trust, people begin to behave defensively, and the efficiency of motion drops globally in response.

Coordination among team-mates engaged in a joint activity requires setting expectations of future actions. Consider the simple example of Steve and Cathy assembling furniture together, in which a number of screws must be inserted and tightened. Steve might pick up the screwdriver, which achieves the functional objective of readying Steve to tighten screws. In context, the action also implies that Cathy should gather screws for insertion in order to help. Since Steve is cooperative, Cathy knows that once she begins to insert screws, Steve will fulfill his implicit promise to tighten them.

Beyond forecasting actions, team-mates might also try to convey information about their capabilities. Human interactional expectations are broadly governed by a common set of human functional and social capabilities, whereas humans are largely uninformed about a robot's true capabilities. Therefore, robots will likely find themselves being judged according to the wrong standards. Although humans show patience for robots that fail under the right conditions, a robot that seldom works as expected will likely not remain in use, even if the failure is one of expectations rather than capabilities. Properly setting expectations allows human team-mates to avoid being disappointed by robots [5, 23, 25].

3. FRAMEWORK

In this section, we describe a framework for implicit communication, modeled as a single-shot act.

3.1 Definitions

In coordinated activities, Clark [6] distinguishes among several related concepts. A *joint activity* engages a group of two or more agents in acting together toward a common goal. Examples include a marriage ceremony, a classroom lecture, and a football game. Within the context of a joint activity, participants perform *joint actions*, which continuously unfold over some period of time. A specialization is the *joint act*, which is a one-shot joint action. For example, in the joint activity of playing golf, yelling "fore!" is a joint act by which the speaker warns any listeners of a wayward flying ball (their avoidance response, in contrast, is an individual act, performed without consideration of how it will affect the group). The fact of an act being joint or individual is purely a matter of the mental state of the involved agent(s).

Participation in a joint action may be asymmetric – for example, speech is a joint action involving a speaker and listener. Note that the listener actively participates by comprehending and back-channeling (nodding, saying "uh-huh", etc.). *Knowledge* comprises information believed by an agent to be true and is collected into a set of *facts*, each with associated confidence. Compulsory asymmetry occurs in a joint act or action when one individual, the *actor*, shares knowledge with one or more *observers*. Thus, an important aspect of the joint action is to communicate information. Frequently, an actor embeds information implicitly in an otherwise purely functional action as part of the joint activity to perform *implicit communication*.

Any communicative action will be perceived by an observer with a certain level of *surprisal*, which is an encoding of how probable the observer believes the action to be given the context. As Hohwy [19] states, surprisal is a declining function of probability: the higher an observer's surprisal, the more improbable the observer believes the action to be in the given context; the lower an observer's surprisal, the more probable the observer believes the action to be in the given context. Common-sense knowledge and a shared understanding of the context allows an actor to gauge how surprising her action will be to an observer, which in turn shapes her choice of action depending on the information she would like to convey. In the remainder of this section, we show that greater surprisal corresponds with a more strongly-conveyed message (i.e. the action is more meaningful).

3.2 Foundations

The interplay of two sets is at the core of the framework. $\mathcal{A}$ comprises all possible actions, whereas $\mathcal{M}$ is composed of all possible facts about the world.

In the course of a joint activity, an agent performs a series of actions (including single-shot acts) $a^1, a^2, \ldots, a^n \in \mathcal{A}$. Each action accomplishes both functional and communicative goals to varying degrees. Let $A_f \subseteq \mathcal{A}$ be the set of (possibly many) different ways of accomplishing the functional goal of the action. Thus, A_f can be thought of as a subgoal of the shared goal of the joint activity.

An agent $\mathcal{Q}$ performs actions in a context $M^{\mathcal{Q}}$ comprising a set of facts $m_1, m_2, \cdots \in M^{\mathcal{Q}} \subset \mathcal{M}$ that capture information about the individuals' knowledge. Only by leveraging this context can implicit communication occur. $M^{\mathcal{Q}}$ expresses $\mathcal{Q}$'s beliefs about the world, including the state history of all agents in the joint activity, the observable scene, properties of objects within it, and common-sense knowledge. An individual fact $m \in M^{\mathcal{Q}}$ can have an associated confidence, thus allowing facts in $M^{\mathcal{Q}}$ to be added, removed, or changed following the observation of an action.

$M^{\mathcal{Q}}$ is divided into several components. Knowledge that all participants in an interaction know they all share is public knowledge, M_{pub}, also called common ground. Other knowledge is not known to be public; agent $\mathcal{Q}$'s private knowledge is denoted $M^{\mathcal{Q}}_{priv}$. $\mathcal{Q}$ may be aware that a subset of the other agents know fact $m \in M^{\mathcal{Q}}_{priv}$. It is even possible that every agent in a joint activity privately knows m. In both cases, $m \notin M_{pub}$ unless all agents are all aware that m is shared by all. $\mathcal{Q}$'s total knowledge $M^{\mathcal{Q}}$ is equal to $M_{pub} \cup M^{\mathcal{Q}}_{priv}$.

Finally, the distribution $\text{P}(a|M)$ describes the likelihood that a specific agent may next perform action a in the specific context M. Even if we restrict the scope of a to actions that accomplish a particular goal, there may be a set of possible actions ($A_f \subseteq \mathcal{A}$) to choose among. Some of these actions will be preferred over others for reasons of efficiency, simplicity, or custom.

Posit that the following *common understandings* are agreed upon by all participants in the joint activity:

- the set of alternative actions A_f that would accomplish a functional goal
- the common ground context model M_{pub}
- the action distribution $\text{P}(a|M)$ (for plausible $M \subset \mathcal{M}$)

3.3 Implicit Communication Criteria

The goal of agent $\mathcal{Q}$ is to perform an action $\hat{a} \in A_f$ that satisfies functional goals while also communicating fact $\hat{m} \in M^{\mathcal{Q}}_{priv}$. However, it is not always possible to communicate an arbitrary fact $\hat{m}$ implicitly, nor is it always possible to communicate implicitly via an action $\hat{a}$.

The key idea is for the actor $\mathcal{Q}$ and observer $\mathcal{R}$ to leverage the common understandings in order to achieve implicit communication. $\mathcal{Q}$ selects an action that is surprising to $\mathcal{R}$, i.e. perceived by $\mathcal{R}$ as improbable in the given context. However, $\mathcal{R}$ does not treat the improbable $\hat{a}$ as a fluke – rather, it triggers her to seek an explanation in the form of a previously-unknown fact $\hat{m}$ that resolves the surprise. For $\mathcal{R}$ to correctly interpret $\mathcal{Q}$'s intended meaning, we propose that action $\hat{a}$ and fact $\hat{m}$ must meet four *implicit communication criteria*:

1. $\exists \hat{a}, a' \in A_f \colon \hat{a} \neq a'$
2. $\text{P}(\hat{a}|M_{pub}) < \text{P}(a'|M_{pub}) - \varepsilon$
3. $\text{P}(\hat{a}|M_{pub}) < \text{P}(\hat{a}|\hat{m}, M_{pub}) - \varepsilon$
4. $\forall m \in \mathcal{M}\backslash M_{pub} \cup \{\hat{m}\} \colon \text{P}(m|\hat{a}, M_{pub}) < \text{P}(\hat{m}|\hat{a}, M_{pub}) - \varepsilon$

The ε term incorporates variation caused by personal preference and noise. The strength of a given implicit communication is measured as the largest possible ε satisfying the criteria above. Criteria 1–2 govern the actor's generation of implicit communication, whereas criteria 3–4 govern the observer's ability to correctly interpret the intended meaning. We speak of the fact $\hat{m}$ as the *meaning* of the action because it *explains* $\mathcal{Q}$'s choice of action. We next provide additional insight into each of the criteria.

Criterion 1 requires that there must be at least two feasible, distinct actions that accomplish the functional goal, but preferably there are many more. An example of A_f that violates this criterion is placing a telephone call. Neglecting timing and caller ID, there is only one way to make somebody's telephone ring, leaving no room for a surprising choice of action.

Criterion 2 triggers the observer to search for an explanation of why the actor chose action $\hat{a}$ over the more obvious choice, a'. This criterion fails in situations where there does not exist an action $\hat{a}$ that is a priori substantially less probable than others. An example situation that violates it is one's first time visiting a clown convention, where normally-improbable actions are expected and hence unsurprising.

Criterion 3 requires that the fact $\hat{m}$ will be easy for the observer to verify as an explanation of $\hat{a}$. That is, $\hat{a}$ is unsurprising when $\hat{m}$ is known. A well-known historical violation of this criterion was John Hinckley, Jr.'s attempted assassination of President Ronald Reagan in order to gain the favor of actress Jodie Foster – it is unclear how shooting the president is intended to convey infatuation.

Criterion 4 states that no other inferred meaning m is equally or more likely than the intended explanation $\hat{m}$. There are many example violations of this criterion in the form of hand gestures that take different meanings across cultures and geographies. One case in point is a gesture that variously signifies a Satanic association, infidelity, and a college football team in Texas. All three forms have famously been used by politicians. Only by understanding each individual actor's M_{pub} at the time he made the gesture can we disambiguate among the three meanings.

3.4 Understanding and Generation

Suppose that an agent $\mathcal{Q}$ hopes to convey some information, $\hat{m} \in M^{\mathcal{Q}}_{priv}$, to agent $\mathcal{R}$ without resorting to disclosing it explicitly. $\mathcal{Q}$ selects an action $\hat{a}$ consistent with the implicit communication criteria, and $\mathcal{R}$ determines $\hat{a}$ to be an improbable action given what he knows. $\mathcal{R}$, believing $\mathcal{Q}$ to be rational, hypothesizes that there must be some unknown factor $\hat{m}$ that explains seeing $\mathcal{Q}$ perform $\hat{a}$. $\mathcal{R}$ thus searches over a set of plausible facts M and chooses $\hat{m}$ to be the fact with the highest posterior probability given $\hat{a}$ and M_{pub}. Maximizing this probability minimizes the surprisal that resulted from $\mathcal{Q}$ performing $\hat{a}$, which in turn causes $\hat{a}$ to become increasingly stronger evidence for $\mathcal{R}$'s hypothesis [19]. Hence, upon seeing $\hat{a}$, $\mathcal{R}$ proceeds to infer

$$\hat{m} \leftarrow \underset{m \in M}{\text{argmax}}\, \text{P}(m|\hat{a}, M_{pub}), \tag{1}$$

and thus $\mathcal{R}$ concludes that $\hat{m} \in M^{\mathcal{Q}}_{priv}$, i.e. $\mathcal{Q}$ believes $\hat{m}$ to be true. Using Bayes' rule, we can re-express (1) as

$$\begin{aligned}\hat{m} \leftarrow & \underset{m \in M}{\text{argmax}} \frac{\text{P}(\hat{a}|m, M_{pub})\text{P}(m|M_{pub})}{\text{P}(\hat{a}|M_{pub})} \\ = & \underset{m \in M}{\text{argmax}}\, \text{P}(\hat{a}|m, M_{pub})\text{P}(m|M_{pub}).\end{aligned}$$

Note that the prior $\text{P}(m|M_{pub})$ serves to prevent "conspiracy theories" that would otherwise result when noise gets mistakenly interpreted as signal. That is, the fact being communicated must have a reasonably likely prior probability. For example, if Bob looks up at the night sky and sees a star twinkling, he is unlikely to attribute it to a UFO, given that the prior probability of discovering intelligent extraterrestrial life is small and that there is a more plausible explanation rooted in turbulence of the atmosphere.

Next, we turn to the generation problem. The structure of the generation problem is identical to understanding, except that we now search over actions instead of facts,

$$\hat{a} \leftarrow \underset{a \in A_f}{\text{argmax}}\, \text{P}(\hat{m}|a, M_{pub}). \tag{2}$$

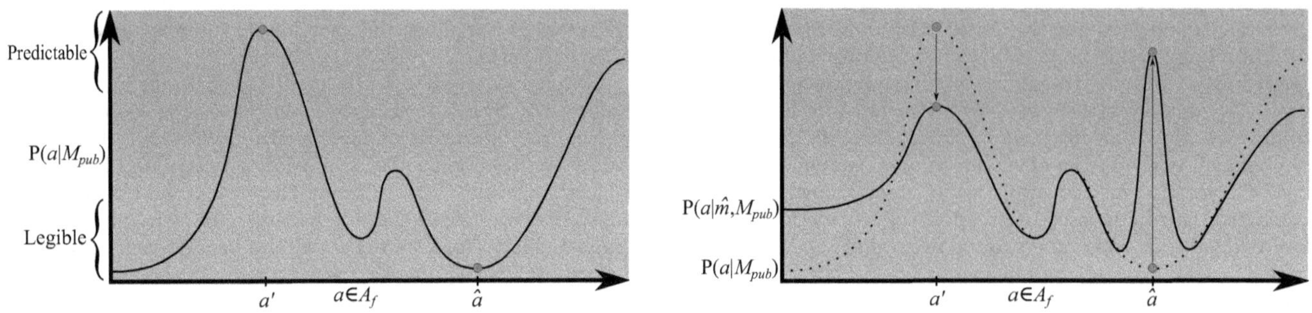

(a) A likely action such as a' is termed *predictable*, whereas we say that an unlikely action $\hat{a}$ is *legible*. See Section 5.2.1 for a full discussion of predictability and legibility. Since $\hat{a}$ is rarely observed in context M_{pub}, the observer infers that it probably was selected specifically to send a message.

(b) By performing legible action $\hat{a}$, an agent implicates the new fact $\hat{m}$ because knowledge of that fact changes the shape of the distribution, causing $\hat{a}$ to become a predictable action.

Figure 2: These plots illustrate the inference mechanism described in Section 3.4 and its effect on $\mathrm{P}(a|M_{pub})$. Among the set of actions $a \in A_f$ that accomplish a task, each can be assigned a likelihood of being observed in context. Actions with high likelihoods of $P(a|Mpub)$ are deemed *predictable*, low ones *legible*.

Applying Bayes' rule again, we can re-express (2) as

$$\hat{a} \leftarrow \underset{a \in A_f}{\operatorname{argmax}} \frac{\mathrm{P}(a|\hat{m}, M_{pub})\mathrm{P}(\hat{m}|M_{pub})}{\mathrm{P}(a|M_{pub})}$$
$$= \underset{a \in A_f}{\operatorname{argmax}} \frac{\mathrm{P}(a|\hat{m}, M_{pub})}{\mathrm{P}(a|M_{pub})}.$$

The resulting expression selects the action for which contributing $\hat{m}$ to the common ground boosts $\mathrm{P}(a|M_{pub})$ by the greatest amount. See Figure 2 for an illustration.

We expand on these ideas and provide examples in Section 5, but first we broaden our discussion to include implicit communication occurring over time and in service of joint goals.

4. ACHIEVING JOINT GOALS

In a joint activity, rational agents interact with each other and make decisions towards achieving joint goals. These goals could range from completing a collaborative assembly task to smoothly avoiding each other while navigating in a hallway. Relying only on implicit communication to achieve joint goals requires the establishment and reinforcement of trust. Implicit communication leverages trust to influence the observer's belief and converge to a consensus that is beneficial for the accomplishment of a joint goal. In this section we state our model for trust and propose an index for monitoring its evolution in order to inform decision making.

4.1 Trust

Ordinarily, participants in a joint activity act *rationally* and cooperate to achieve shared goals [18]. This policy forbids deception and supports the assumption that the common understandings (Section 3.2) are shared by all participants. Given the great diversity of knowledge and experience among people, however, this assumption is perhaps too strong to apply universally.

In particular, during interactions with strangers, we may be unfamiliar with one another's judgments regarding A_f, M_{pub}, and $\mathrm{P}(a|M_{pub})$. If we define trust as confidence in another agent's future actions [2], then it is natural for one agent to restrict their trust of another based on the limits of common understandings among the individuals, even when all agents behave rationally.

Another obstacle to trust is discrepant beliefs about facts. We allow facts about the beliefs of others to enter M_{pub}. Thus, it can simultaneously be part of the common ground that $\mathcal{G}$ believes $m^{\mathcal{G}}$ and that $\mathcal{H}$ believes $m^{\mathcal{H}}$, even if $m^{\mathcal{G}}$ and $m^{\mathcal{H}}$ conflict. $\mathcal{G}$ and $\mathcal{H}$ are then free to leverage either of these facts in the generation and understanding of implicit communications between them. Epistemic logic [11] provides tools for representing and analyzing such scenarios. Each conflicting fact introduces additional uncertainty into the communication process because the observer must infer which fact the actor premised the communication upon. Thus, trust degrades with the number of discrepancies among beliefs within a joint activity. Beyond some limit, implicit communication becomes impossible.

4.2 Consensus

In a joint activity, agents take actions with functional effects (which contribute to reaching the joint goal) but also with communicative effects. One category of communication, conveying intentions, serves to convey a preference or desire regarding a joint strategy S for accomplishing the goal. The joint strategy can be thought of as the sequence of subgoals of the joint activity, $A_f^0, A_f^1, \ldots, A_f^n$, and is drawn from the set of all possible strategies $\mathcal{S}$.

A consensus for each subgoal in the joint strategy may unfold gradually or abruptly during the course of the joint activity. As the agents act, the public knowledge M_{pub} is updated along with the agents' beliefs regarding the emerging strategy $\mathrm{P}(S|M_{pub})$. Under the assumption of rationality, as formulated in our trust model (Section 4.1), a group of competent agents taking actions bearing implicit communication signals will be able to achieve consensus over the joint strategy S. This essentially means that $\mathrm{P}(S|M_{pub})$ (which we assume is shared by all agents) will converge to a distribution that clearly indicates the emerging joint strategy. The entropy of this distribution is a measure of that convergence.

4.3 Receptivity

In many joint activities, time and timing are critical attributes of an action. Timing itself often conveys meaning, which we therefore consider as an attribute of an action $\hat{a} \in A_f$. Another important aspect of timing is its role in choosing whether (and when) to implicitly communicate. Participants in a joint activity are not equally receptive at all times to certain forms of implicit communication, particularly with regard to consensus over the joint strategy.

When participants in a joint activity lack consensus about a joint strategy, they cannot coordinate effectively to achieve shared goals. Rational agents therefore strive to reach consensus as early in a joint activity as possible in order to maximize coordination efficiency. Consequently, the bulk of implicit communication for consensus should occur towards the beginning of the joint activity. As a joint strategy S^* emerges and consensus is reached, the agents might favor more predictable, less communicative actions, or they might utilize the implicit communication channel for other purposes. More generally, the implicit consensus formation aspect of joint actions may wax and wane according to the group need. Consequently, there arises the need for monitoring (1) the state of consensus $P(S|M_{pub})$ and also (2) how receptive the group of agents is to the communicative signals being transmitted.

We formalize this monitoring process by introducing a *Receptivity* score, as

$$Receptivity = -\sum_{S \in \mathcal{S}} P(S|M_{pub}) \log(P(S|M_{pub})) \qquad (3)$$

which is the information entropy of the distribution over joint strategies, given the common ground, $P(S|M_{pub})$. Recall that common ground includes the action history within a joint activity. Intuitively, receptivity measures the willingness of individuals in a group to update their beliefs about the joint strategy, inversely proportionate with clarity. Since M_{pub} is sequentially updated over time, receptivity reflects the way the agents incorporate observed communicative signals into their own actions. The lower a receptivity score gets, the closer the agents are to a consensus over a joint strategy S^*. To avoid second-guessing a settled joint strategy, an observer suppresses strategy changes of a larger magnitude than the current receptivity level.

A consequence of a decline in receptivity is that agents can be less expressive when it drops, since other agents will likely ignore the inputs. In a scene with engaged competent agents, receptivity is expected to decrease rapidly, signifying a consensus in the joint activity. This decrease will influence the balance between the functional and communicative aspect of actions taken, shifting the focus of decision making towards the functional component. Beyond some threshold drop in receptivity, agents have become sufficiently certain about the consensus strategy S^* that they may even ignore their partners using *civil inattention* [21] to reinforce the previously agreed strategy. This behavior involves physically looking away, "so as to express that [one] does not constitute a target of special curiosity or design" [12]. At this point, only a major modification in the strategy will penetrate an agent's civil inattention.

5. CASE STUDIES

In lieu of generating new experimental results, which would apply to a single domain and communication modality, we present examples of how implicit communication has been modeled and enforced by several communities in various collaborative contexts and discuss how their frameworks align with our unifying framework for implicit communication.

5.1 Implicit Communication through Natural Language

Speech acts are among the richest functional actions in which to embed implicit communication.

5.1.1 Implicature

In this section, we give a brief background on *conversational implicature*. We seek to draw parallels between implicature and other methods of implicit communication of interest in robotics. Implicature comes from pragmatics, the linguistics subfield that studies the usage of language in context. Basic meaning that is expressed and understood by a speech act is achieved by *entailment* – that is, ideas that logically and unavoidably follow from the words chosen by a speaker.

With implicature, in contrast, the speaker *implicates* (i.e. implies or suggests) an idea without explicitly stating it. It is a frequent phenomenon in English, first described by Grice [15]. Consider this example from Lappin and Fox [24]:

> Ann: Do you sell paste?
> Bill: I sell rubber cement. ($\hat{a}$)
> *implicature: Bill does not sell paste.* ($\hat{m}$)

A test for conversational implicature in particular is whether it is *cancelable* – that is, does there exist some phrase that, when appended to the sentence, cancels the meaning of the implicature? From the above example, a phrase that cancels Bill's implicature is "I sell rubber cement, which is what you really need for your application." An implicature, once canceled, implicitly communicates nothing. The added phrase explains the initial phrase, thus increasing $P(a|M_{pub})$ and violating implicit communication criterion 2.

When it comes to dialog, people have varied and complex motives for implicating meaning rather than entailing it, including politeness, sophistication, succinctness, and social group cohesion. A detailed consideration of these objectives is beyond the scope of this paper.

Grice's *cooperative principle* states, "Make your conversational contribution such as is required, at the stage at which it occurs, by the accepted purpose or direction of the talk exchange in which you are engaged" [15]. Indeed, the cooperative principle bears more than a passing similarity to the *pedestrian bargain* of Wolfinger [36], which entreats one to behave competently and also to trust others to behave competently. These principles are both forms of the rational actor assumption [18].

A vital component of conversational implicature is provided by the four Gricean Maxims, which describe speech that obeys the cooperative principle. The four maxims are

1. Maxim of Quantity: Make your contribution as informative as is required (but not more so).
2. Maxim of Quality: Make your contribution one that is true.
3. Maxim of Relation: Be relevant.
4. Maxim of Manner: Be perspicuous. Avoid obscurity or ambiguity; be brief and orderly.

Other maxims have also been proposed, such as "Be polite." Because adherence to the cooperative principle is assumed, utterances can be interpreted in light of these maxims. A speaker can therefore deliberately flout one of the maxims (an improbable action, $\hat{a}$) in order to convey that he is employing implicature. Returning to the previous example, Ann must apply the following inference steps to conclude that Bill does not carry paste.

(a) *Contextual premise*: it is mutual, public knowledge that Bill has complete knowledge of the items he sells.
(b) *Contextual premise*: there is no contextual relationship linking sales of paste and rubber cement (inclusive or exclusive).
(c) Assume Bill follows the cooperative principle and maxims.
(d) By (a), Bill can fully resolve Ann's question, and by (c), he will.
(e) Only the propositions that Bill does or does not sell paste can completely resolve the question.
(f) By (b), there is no way to infer from Bill's answer the proposition that he does sell paste. The cooperative principle forbids obfuscation. Thus, Bill has flouted the maxim of relevance.
(g) Therefore, we conclude that Bill does not sell paste.

Lines (d)–(g) comprise the narrowing down and resolution of the search for meaning in Equation (1).

Conversational implicature is absent when all the maxims are satisfied. One indicates the use of implicature by selecting an action to deliberately flout one of the maxims – in our example, Bill flouts the maxim of Relation.

Sometimes, two maxims conflict and cannot both be satisfied with a single utterance, in which case flouting one or the other maxim is forced. An example of the latter occurs in the following exchange:

> Mark: Where is the cat?
> Sue: The cat is in the hamper or under the bed. ($\hat{a}$)
> *implicature: Sue does not know where the cat is.* ($\hat{m}$)

Because Sue does not know where the cat is, providing either location alone would violate the maxim of Quality. However, providing both locations conflicts with the maxim of Quantity because the cat is in at most one of the stated locations. Flouting the maxim of Quality would violate implicit communication criterion 2 because either location alone is plausible. Thus, Sue chooses to flout the maxim of Quantity in order to trigger Mark to search for an explanation.

5.1.2 Inverse Semantics

Though more direct than conversational implicature, the simpler speech act of entailment is fundamentally described by the same mathematics. Knepper et al. [22] present the *inverse semantics* framework for robots generating natural language help requests. Like most robot speech systems, the framework strives for extremely literal communication. However, it faces a problem of finding pithy, unambiguous means of communicating its needs in an automated assembly scene cluttered with parts that lack unique names. Since words are complex and imperfect containers for meaning, the careful selection of clear language to achieve entailment follows the same rules of generation as described in Section 3.4.

The core of inverse semantics is a forward semantics mechanism for understanding natural language, the Generalized Grounding Graph (G^3) [32]. This structure takes in natural language expressions λ as inputs and returns their meanings or groundings γ as outputs.

The inverse semantics framework inverts G^3 to perform generation by searching over the space of possible English sentences, sorted from shortest to longest, and inputting each to G^3. Inverse semantics compares the output of G^3 with the target grounding needed by the help request. The search halts with the first sentence that attains over a threshold confidence match between the two groundings. The expression given for generation,

$$\underset{\lambda}{\text{argmax}}\, P(\gamma|\lambda, \phi, M), \tag{4}$$

strongly resembles our own framework's Equation (2). Here, ϕ is a correspondence variable used to indicate the semantic likelihood of a match between λ and γ. Like our model, M symbolizes the context model in which the meaning is interpreted.

5.2 Communicative Motion

Besides natural language usage, the robotics community has studied other types of actions. An especially expressive action class for implicit communication is motion.

5.2.1 Legibility

Let us consider again the joint assembly activity in which Steve and Cathy cooperate to build furniture. Many forms of communicative action arise. One class of actions studied recently by Dragan, Lee, and Srinivasa [10] involves reaching motions. Among parts cluttering a table, Steve has to pick up a particular one. The shape of his reaching trajectory may or may not inform Cathy about Steve's intent. A direct reaching motion is predictable (high probability $P(a|M_{pub})$) and therefore not communicative. A curved trajectory, in contrast, helps Cathy to identify the target of Steve's reach before he gets there.

In general, assume that an actor $\mathcal{Q}$ is aiming at reaching a goal $G^{\mathcal{Q}}$ from a set of goals $\mathcal{G}$ in front of an observer $\mathcal{R}$. The agents share a model $P(G|\xi)$ that probabilistically attributes a goal $G \in \mathcal{G}$ to an observed trajectory ξ. The actor can leverage this knowledge to design his trajectory in a way that indicates his intended goal to the observer. Following the insights of Csibra and Gergely [8] regarding the tendency of humans to interpret observed actions as goal-directed (teleological reasoning), Dragan, Lee, and Srinivasa [10] introduced the *Legibility* score to quantify the intent-expressiveness of a trajectory ξ with respect to a goal $G^{\mathcal{Q}}$:

$$\textit{Legibility}(\xi) = \frac{\int_0^T P(G^{\mathcal{Q}}|\xi_{0\to t}) f(t) dt}{\int_0^T f(t) dt} \tag{5}$$

where T is the duration of the trajectory and $f(t)$ is a function that weights partial trajectories $\xi_{0\to t}$ higher in the beginning and lower later. It should be noted that $f(t)$ is a proxy for the role of the observer in reducing her receptivity (see Section 4.3) as $\mathcal{Q}$'s intended goal $G^{\mathcal{Q}}$ becomes more certain to her. The model $P(G|\xi)$ scores goals higher if they can be achieved efficiently (with a low energy trajectory ξ) and scores goals lower if they require higher energy.

The legibility score is essentially a weighted sum of the probabilities that the observers assign to the actor's intended goal $G^{\mathcal{Q}}$ throughout the whole trajectory ξ. Trajectories of higher legibility tend to be more curved towards the intended goal $G^{\mathcal{Q}}$, biasing the observers towards predicting the actor's actual goal, while biasing them against predicting other goals. Note that a more curved trajectory is less probable out of context due to the extra energy it expends. As a result, it might be perceived as surprising. This surprise would trigger a search for an explanation, which, in the perceived context, would lead to the conclusion that the actor $\mathcal{Q}$ is aiming at reaching the goal $G^{\mathcal{Q}}$.

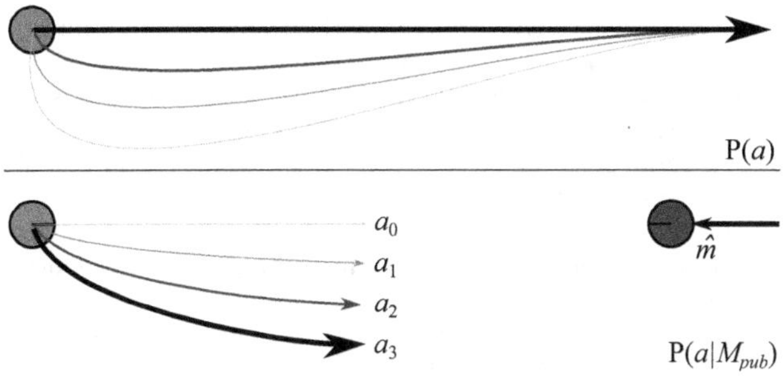

Figure 3: The red, navigating agent (human or robot) selects an action $\hat{a}$. Out of context (top), the red agent (human or robot) is not avoiding an obstacle, and so the probability of expending needless extra energy is low. In the case of an oncoming blue agent ($\hat{m}$), the likelihood of the oblivious action $P(a_0|M_{pub})$ is low due to social norms, despite being low energy. Conversely, the normally-improbable act of spending extra energy becomes probable in this context. An observer who sees only the red agent's motion can infer $\hat{m}$ from observing a_3.

5.2.2 *Dynamic Legibility*

Consider now the case of a dynamic environment, where the agents are not explicitly collaborating but since the decisions they make are coupled, it is beneficial for everyone to mutually agree on a joint strategy. Assuming again no explicit communication, the only way agents are able to agree on a strategy is to encode their understanding and preferences into their actions.

Social navigation constitutes a representative example of this class of scenarios. Although humans might not often realize that navigation in crowded environments is a collaborative activity, according to sociology studies [36], it is established on implicit cooperation. Pedestrians follow and reinforce the *pedestrian bargain*, a social convention comprising two foundational rules: (1) "pedestrians must behave like competent pedestrians" and (2) "pedestrians must trust that co-present others behave like competent pedestrians". Since the pedestrian bargain serves as a cooperative principle for social navigation, we may formulate a set of maxims for motion that echo the Gricean Maxims of conversational implicature,

1. Maxim of Efficiency: Be parsimonious.
2. Maxim of Motion: Do not collide with objects or obstruct another agent's motion.
3. Maxim of Manner: Be perspicuous and orderly.

These maxims readily come into conflict where multiple agents are present. Much as in the case of implicature, the actor will choose to deliberately flout one of the maxims – typically the maxim of Efficiency – in order to obey the cooperative principle. It is only by considering the collision-avoidance context that an observer is able to appreciate that by taking an exaggerated trajectory such as a_3 in Figure 3, the global welfare is improved, as measured by increased energy efficiency and decreased uncertainty.

Enforcing the pedestrian bargain leads to a consensus over a mutually beneficial joint strategy that allows everyone to comfortably reach their destinations. The agents continuously monitor the progress toward consensus and adjust their decision-making accordingly. Once consensus appears to have been reached, receptivity drops to zero as pedestrians initiate *civil inattention* [12, 21]. Following this mode switch, agents look away from one another as a signal that they have stopped actively avoiding each other and will instead follow their previous planned collision-free path.

Mavrogiannis and Knepper [28, 29] present a recent navigation framework that reproduces the implicit communication of social navigation. They model consensus S as a topological joint strategy using braids [3], and they develop a game-theoretic decision making policy corresponding to a utility function that compromises between efficiency and implicit communication. This utility function is defined as:

$$u(a) = \lambda E(a) - (1 - \lambda)H(a) \tag{6}$$

where λ is a weighting factor, E represents the efficiency of an action a and H is the entropy of the agents' belief regarding the emerging strategy S:

$$H(a) = -\sum_{S \in \mathcal{S}} P(S|Z^+, M) \log P(S|Z^+, M) \tag{7}$$

with Z^+ comprising Z (the state history of all agents so far), augmented with the action in consideration a and M being the context.

Picking actions that maximize the utility leads to a quick decrease in the uncertainty regarding the global joint strategy (i.e., how each agent will avoid each other), while ensuring progress towards the agent's destination. The selection of actions with a strong communicative component, especially in the beginning, was shown to reduce the likelihood of livelocks or deadlocks.

6. OTHER EXAMPLES

Teams exchange implicit information in cooperative games when the rules forbid free exchange of information. For example, the bidding conventions of contract bridge allow partners to exchange information about the respective strengths of their hands and arrive at an appropriate contract.

Finally, among married couples, this type of implicit communication eases over time across all modalities (speech, gesture, gaze, etc.) because spouses develop extremely sensitive models of $P(a|M_{pub})$, due to familiarity. Remarkably sophisticated notions can be conveyed between spouses by careful action selection in almost any context. We have considerable work remaining before robots can achieve a similar level of understanding of people.

6.1 Tact

Implicit communication is also the primary tool of tactful communication, as it alleviates the risk of awkwardness due to misunderstandings about what facts the observer already knows. Reflecting on the implicit communication criteria given in Section 3.3, an attempted implicit communication of a fact that the observer already knows does not even seem like implicit communication – it would come across as a predictable, functional action. In this case, criterion 3 is clearly violated because $\hat{m} \in M_{pub}$, and criterion 2 is probably also violated because $\hat{a}$ would seem likely.

To offer a concrete example of how speakers leverage implicit communication to achieve tact, consider a married couple discussing dinner plans:

> Jack: Remember, my friend Irving is coming for dinner.
> *implicatures: Irving is vegetarian; Irving needs*

to be served a vegetarian meal.
Kate: Let's make my mother's lasagna recipe.
implicatures: Kate knows that Irving is vegetarian; Kate's mother's lasagna recipe is vegetarian; the recipe satisfies Irving's need for a vegetarian meal.

Observe that this exchange can be read at two levels. If both parties are oblivious to the implicature because the sentences are judged predictable, then it is a simple, matter-of-fact dialog.

The statements can also be read as implicature. In both cases, the implicated statements are things that the listener should have already known. Only in the context of the couple's normal conversation can we judge how unusual it is for Jack to remind Kate about a guest (a fact she may be unlikely to forget), or for Kate to make her mother's lasagna recipe.

Only if these events are atypical can they truly be regarded as implicit communication. However, they also serve a tactful reminder function, in case Kate forgot about the guest or Jack forgot that Kate's mother's lasagna is vegetarian. A failing memory may therefore cause an action to be judged as unusual, in which case the reminder acts as an implicature. Thus, a related virtue of implicit communication is that it allows the observer to maintain the pretense of having already known a fact that they forgot.

7. PRACTICAL IMPLEMENTATION

Inference, both generation and understanding, is implemented as a search over actions and facts, respectively. Techniques are needed to streamline both search problems, due to the intractability of the literal brute force search implied by argmax in (1)–(2). Existing implementations of instances of implicit communication employ AI search-pruning techniques [22, 34] or restrict the action space A_f in order to narrow the set of options under consideration [10, 29]. In practical terms, the set of feasible actions A_f is typically hard-coded for a domain, raising the possibility that it mismatches with some human's expectation. Two people may similarly encounter a mismatch in expectation about A_f. Interestingly, the machinery described in this paper could be used by a robot to infer that an observed human action is intended to accomplish a (surprising) functional goal by leveraging the context, leading to extension of A_f.

Another challenge is to build M_{pub}, the common ground model among agents. A complete model is often both unnecessary (since many facts in the agents' shared knowledge are irrelevant for the joint activity at hand) and infeasible (since the task of modeling the full common ground presents a high cognitive burden). As a result, M_{pub} need only consist of the facts that are pertinent to the success of the joint activity. For example, in the social navigation of Mavrogiannis and Knepper [29], M_{pub} might contain an updated belief regarding the destinations and intentions of observed agents. M_{pub} is therefore instantiated as the mutual understanding that the agents involved intend to participate in the joint activity along with shared knowledge about the kinds of actions that agents will likely take to contribute to the activity [4].

For humans, M_{pub} does not necessarily include all task-relevant facts at the start of the activity. It is frequently less costly to repair a misunderstanding that results from not sharing a piece of information than to expend the effort required to ground that piece of information through the principle of least collaborative effort [7, 30]. M_{pub} is then updated interactively throughout the course of the joint activity, either when new information about the intents of the agents becomes publicly available or when the agents issue a repair that helps align their own mental models of the situation (and in doing so adds to the common ground) [26]. Machine-interpretable ontologies using tools like RDF and OWL address the general problem of managing and searching M_{pub}, as exemplified by the KnowRob project of Tenorth and Beetz [33].

Finally, the distribution $P(a|M)$ is generally best modeled through machine learning. The particular context in which one takes an action affects the probabilities of observing various possible actions, often in complex ways. For example, Knepper et al. [22] employ Tellex's generalized grounding graph (G^3) [32]. Based on a conditional random field, G^3 employs a set of *correspondence variables* to valuate the correspondence probability of a given language phrase and grounding concept. These learned relationships capture concepts including objects, actions, and spatial relations.

8. DISCUSSION

Conversational implicature and legibility, though originating in different domains, are connected by techniques of encoding and decoding meaning using teleological inference [8]. These methods rely heavily on common ground to provide clues about when a message is encoded on an action and what information the message contains. The inference process can be quite complex in real-life situations. Particularly in the case of implicature, many rules must be brought to bear in order to correctly interpret what is being implicated. Several authors [14, 34] show promising early results in modeling a simple form of implicature and performing inference by model inversion.

8.1 A Call to Action

In the coming years, modeling of implied meaning, including through implicature and legible motion, will become an increasing focus within robotics – not least because humans already use these forms of implicit communication on robots today. Humans are also already interpreting robots' actions through the lens of implicit communication. Since few robots are cognizant of the implicit meaning of their actions, today's robots send random signals to humans. By and large, humans are unable to interpret robot actions in the purely functional manner that they are intended. Thus, the robotics research community must find techniques to efficiently generate and understand implicit communication.

This direction will drive the need for improved modeling of common ground. A major hurdle to performing these inferences on robots in real-world situations is salience; today, the robot must perform a fairly undirected, brute-force search in order to discover which elements of the context are applicable. Humans, in contrast, seem to learn filters and partially pre-compute functions to expedite real-time inference in ambiguous situations. These processes are not yet understood in humans, but they will need to be deployed on robots in order to promote responsive behavior and avoid major misunderstandings.

Acknowledgments

This material is based upon research supported by the Office of Naval Research under Award Number N00014-16-1-2080 and by the National Science Foundation under Grant No. 1526035. We are grateful for this support.

References

[1] R. Alami, A. Clodic, V. Montreuil, E. A. Sisbot, and R. Chatila. "Task planning for human-robot interaction". In: *Proceedings of the 2005 joint conference on Smart objects and ambient intelligence: innovative context-aware services: usages and technologies*. ACM. 2005, pp. 81–85.

[2] J. M. Barbalet. "Social emotions: confidence, trust and loyalty". In: *International Journal of Sociology and Social Policy* 16.9/10 (1996), pp. 75–96.

[3] J. S. Birman. *Braids Links And Mapping Class Groups*. Princeton University Press, 1975.

[4] M. E. Bratman. "Shared cooperative activity". In: *The philosophical review* 101.2 (1992), pp. 327–341.

[5] E. Cha, A. D. Dragan, and S. S. Srinivasa. "Perceived robot capability". In: *Robot and Human Interactive Communication (RO-MAN), 2015 24th IEEE International Symposium on*. IEEE. 2015, pp. 541–548.

[6] H. H. Clark. *Using Language*. Cambridge University Press, May 1996.

[7] H. H. Clark and D. Wilkes-Gibbs. "Referring as a collaborative process". In: *Cognition* 22.1 (1986), pp. 1–39.

[8] G. Csibra and G. Gergely. "'Obsessed with goals': Functions and mechanisms of teleological interpretation of actions in humans". In: *Acta Psychologica* 124.1 (Jan. 2007), pp. 60–78.

[9] M. B. Do and S. Kambhampati. "Planning Graph-based Heuristics for Cost-sensitive Temporal Planning." In: *AIPS*. 2002, pp. 3–12.

[10] A. D. Dragan, K. C. Lee, and S. S. Srinivasa. "Legibility and predictability of robot motion". In: *Proceedings of the ACM/IEEE International Conference on Human-Robot Interaction*. IEEE. 2013, pp. 301–308.

[11] R. Fagin, J. Y. Halpern, Y. Moses, and M. Vardi. *Reasoning about knowledge*. MIT press, 2004.

[12] E. Goffman. *Relations in Public*. Penguin, 2009.

[13] M. C. Gombolay, R. Wilcox, and J. A. Shah. "Fast Scheduling of Multi-Robot Teams with Temporospatial Constraints." In: *Proceedings of the Robotics Science and Systems Conference*. 2013.

[14] N. D. Goodman and A. Stuhlmüller. "Knowledge and implicature: Modeling language understanding as social cognition". In: *Topics in cognitive science* 5.1 (2013), pp. 173–184.

[15] H. P. Grice. "Logic and conversation". In: *Syntax and Semantics* (1975), pp. 41–58.

[16] B. Hayes and B. Scassellati. "Discovering task constraints through observation and active learning". In: *Proceedings of the IEEE International Conference on Intelligent Robots and Systems*. IEEE. 2014, pp. 4442–4449.

[17] B. Hayes and B. Scassellati. "Effective Robot Teammate Behaviors for Supporting Sequential Manipulation Tasks". In: *Proceedings of the IEEE International Conference on Intelligent Robots and Systems*. 2015.

[18] P. Hedström and C. Stern. "Rational choice and sociology". In: *The new Palgrave dictionary of economics* (2008), pp. 872–877.

[19] J. Hohwy. *The Predictive Mind*. Oxford University Press, 2013.

[20] R. A. Knepper. "On the Communicative Aspect of Human-Robot Joint Action". In: *the IEEE International Symposium on Robot and Human Interactive Communication Workshop: Toward a Framework for Joint Action, What about Common Ground?* New York, USA, Aug. 2016.

[21] R. A. Knepper and D. Rus. "Pedestrian-Inspired Sampling-Based Multi-Robot Collision Avoidance". In: *Proceedings of the IEEE International Symposium on Robot and Human Interactive Communication*. Paris, France, Sept. 2012.

[22] R. A. Knepper, S. Tellex, A. Li, N. Roy, and D. Rus. "Recovering from Failure by Asking for Help". In: *Autonomous Robots* 39.3 (Oct. 2015), pp. 347–362.

[23] M. Kwon, M. F. Jung, and R. A. Knepper. "Human Expectations of Social Robots". In: *Late Breaking Report at the ACM/IEEE International Conference on Human-Robot Interaction*. Christchurch, New Zealand, Mar. 2016.

[24] S. Lappin and C. Fox. *The handbook of contemporary semantic theory*. John Wiley & Sons, 2015.

[25] M. K. Lee, S. Kiesler, J. Forlizzi, S. Srinivasa, and P. Rybski. "Gracefully mitigating breakdowns in robotic services". In: *Proceedings of the ACM/IEEE International Conference on Human-Robot Interaction*. IEEE. 2010, pp. 203–210.

[26] S. Lemaignan and P. Dillenbourg. "Mutual modelling in robotics: Inspirations for the next steps". In: *Proceedings of the ACM/IEEE International Conference on Human-Robot Interaction*. ACM. 2015, pp. 303–310.

[27] J. Mainprice and D. Berenson. "Human-robot collaborative manipulation planning using early prediction of human motion". In: *Proceedings of the IEEE International Conference on Intelligent Robots and Systems*. IEEE/RSJ. 2013, pp. 299–306.

[28] C. I. Mavrogiannis and R. A. Knepper. "Decentralized Multi-Agent Navigation Planning with Braids". In: *Proceedings of the Workshop on the Algorithmic Foundations of Robotics*. San Francisco, USA, Dec. 2016.

[29] C. I. Mavrogiannis and R. A. Knepper. "Towards Socially Competent Navigation of Pedestrian Environments". In: *Robotics: Science and Systems 2016 Workshop on Social Trust in Autonomous Robots*. Ann Arbor, USA, June 2016.

[30] M. J. Pickering and S. Garrod. "Toward a mechanistic psychology of dialogue". In: *Behavioral and brain sciences* 27.02 (2004), pp. 169–190.

[31] E. A. Sisbot, L. F. Marin-Urias, R. Alami, and T. Siméon. "A Human Aware Mobile Robot Motion Planner". In: *IEEE Transactions on Robotics* 23.5 (2007), pp. 874–883.

[32] S. A. Tellex et al. "Understanding natural language commands for robotic navigation and mobile manipulation". In: *AAAI Conference on Artificial Intelligence*. AAAI Publications, 2011.

[33] M. Tenorth and M. Beetz. "KnowRob: A knowledge processing infrastructure for cognition-enabled robots". In: *The International Journal of Robotics Research* 32.5 (2013), pp. 566–590.

[34] A. Vogel, C. Potts, and D. Jurafsky. "Implicatures and Nested Beliefs in Approximate Decentralized-POMDPs." In: *ACL (2)*. Citeseer. 2013, pp. 74–80.

[35] R. Wilcox, S. Nikolaidis, and J. Shah. "Optimization of temporal dynamics for adaptive human-robot interaction in assembly manufacturing". In: *Robotics Science and Systems VIII* (2012), pp. 441–448.

[36] N. H. Wolfinger. "Passing moments: Some social dynamics of pedestrian interaction". In: *Journal of Contemporary Ethnography* 24.3 (1995), pp. 323–340.

Acting, Interacting, Collaborative Robots

Danica Kragic
Royal Institute of Technology (KTH)
Centre for Autonomous Systems, Stockholm,
Sweden
dani@kth.se

ABSTRACT
The current trend in computer vision is development of data-driven approaches where the use of large amounts of data tries to compensate for the complexity of the world captured by cameras. Are these approaches also viable solutions in robotics? Apart from 'seeing', a robot is capable of acting, thus purposively change what and how it sees the world around it. There is a need for an interplay between processes such as attention, segmentation, object detection, recognition and categorization in order to interact with the environment. In addition, the parameterization of these is inevitably guided by the task or the goal a robot is supposed to achieve. In this talk, I will present the current state of the art in the area of robot vision and discuss open problems in the area. I will also show how visual input can be integrated with proprioception, tactile and force-torque feedback in order to plan, guide and assess robot's action and interaction with the environment.

Interaction between two agents builds on the ability to engage in mutual prediction and signaling. Thus, human-robot interaction requires a system that can interpret and make use of human signaling strategies in a social context. Our work in this area focuses on developing a framework for human motion prediction in the context of joint action in HRI. We base this framework on the idea that social interaction is highly influences by sensorimotor contingencies (SMCs). Instead of constructing explicit cognitive models, we rely on the interaction between actions the perceptual change that they induce in both the human and the robot. This approach allows us to employ a single model for motion prediction and goal inference and to seamlessly integrate the human actions into the environment and task context.

We employ a deep generative model that makes inferences over future human motion trajectories given the intention of the human and the history as well as the task setting of the interaction. With help predictions drawn from the model, we can determine the most likely future motion trajectory and make inferences over intentions and objects of interest.

HRI '17, March 06-09, 2017, Vienna, Austria
ACM 978-1-4503-4336-7/17/03.
http://dx.doi.org/10.1145/2909824.3020260

CCS Concepts/ACM Classifiers
Robotics, Active learning, Artificial Intelligence, Computer vision

Author Keywords
Robotics; Human-robot collaboration; Grasping;

BIOGRAPHY
Danica Kragic is a Professor at the School of Computer Science and Communication at the Royal Institute of Technology, KTH. She received MSc in Mechanical Engineering from the Technical University of Rijeka, Croatia in 1995 and PhD in Computer Science from KTH in 2001. She has been a visiting researcher at Columbia University, Johns Hopkins University and INRIA Rennes. She is the Director of the Centre for Autonomous Systems. Danica received the 2007 IEEE Robotics and Automation Society Early Academic Career Award. She is a member of the Royal Swedish Academy of Sciences, Royal Swedish Academy of Engineering Sciences and Young Academy of Sweden. She holds a Honorary Doctorate from the Lappeenranta University of Technology. She chaired IEEE RAS Technical Committee on Computer and Robot Vision and served as an IEEE RAS AdCom member. Her research is in the area of robotics, computer vision and machine learning. In 2012, she received an ERC Starting Grant. Her research is supported by the EU, Knut and Alice Wallenberg Foundation, Swedish Foundation for Strategic Research and Swedish Research Council. She is an IEEE Fellow.

Human-Robot Mutual Adaptation in Shared Autonomy

Stefanos Nikolaidis
Carnegie Mellon University
snikolai@cmu.edu

Yu Xiang Zhu
Carnegie Mellon University
yuxiangz@cmu.edu

David Hsu
National University of Singapore
dyhsu@comp.nus.edu.sg

Siddhartha Srinivasa
Carnegie Mellon University
siddh@cmu.edu

ABSTRACT

Shared autonomy integrates user input with robot autonomy in order to control a robot and help the user to complete a task. Our work aims to improve the performance of such a human-robot team: the robot tries to guide the human towards an effective strategy, sometimes against the human's own preference, while still retaining his trust. We achieve this through a principled human-robot mutual adaptation formalism. We integrate a bounded-memory adaptation model of the human into a partially observable stochastic decision model, which enables the robot to adapt to an adaptable human. When the human is adaptable, the robot guides the human towards a good strategy, maybe unknown to the human in advance. When the human is stubborn and not adaptable, the robot complies with the human's preference in order to retain their trust. In the shared autonomy setting, unlike many other common human-robot collaboration settings, only the robot actions can change the physical state of the world, and the human and robot goals are not fully observable. We address these challenges and show in a human subject experiment that the proposed mutual adaptation formalism improves human-robot team performance, while retaining a high level of user trust in the robot, compared to the common approach of having the robot strictly following participants' preference.

1. INTRODUCTION

Assistive robot arms show great promise in increasing the independence of people with upper extremity disabilities [1–3]. However, when a user teleoperates directly a robotic arm via an interface such as a joystick, the limitation of the interface, combined with the increased capability and complexity of robot arms, often makes it difficult or tedious to accomplish complex tasks.

Shared autonomy alleviates this issue by combining direct teleoperation with autonomous assistance [4–8]. In recent work by Javdani et al., the robot estimates a distribution of

HRI '17, March 06-09, 2017, Vienna, Austria

 ISBN 978-1-4503-4336-7/17/03. . . $15.00
DOI: http://dx.doi.org/10.1145/2909824.3020252

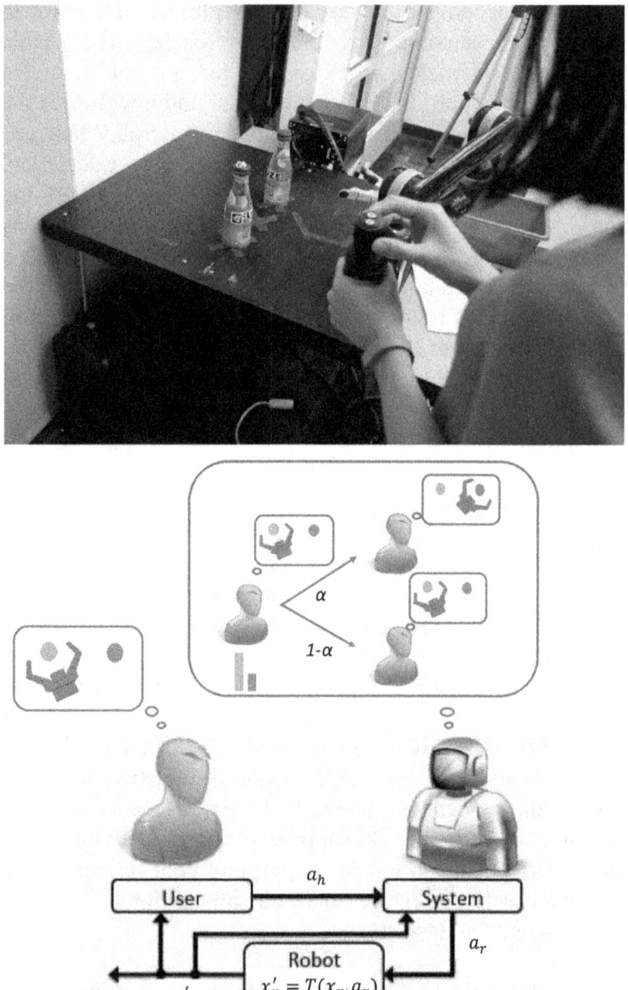

Figure 1: Table clearing task in a shared autonomy setting. The user operates the robot using a joystick interface and moves the robot towards the left bottle, which is a suboptimal goal. The robot plans its actions based on its estimate of the current human goal and the probability α of the human switching towards a new goal indicated by the robot.

user goals based on the history of user inputs, and assists the user for that distribution [9]. The user is assumed to be

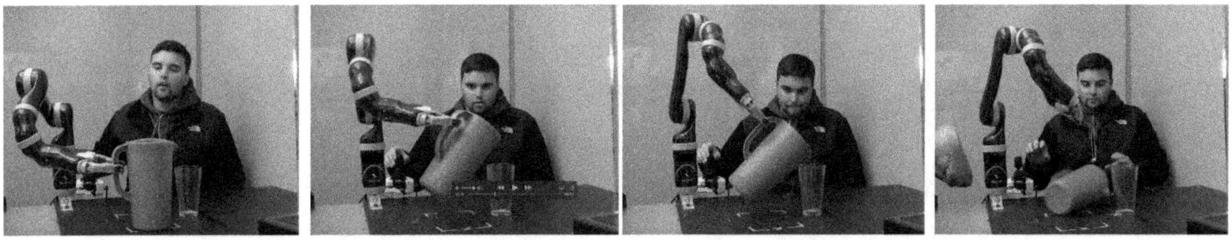

Figure 2: The user guides the robot towards an unstable grasp, resulting in task failure.

always right about their goal choice. Therefore, if the assistance strategy knows the user's goal, it will select actions to minimize the cost-to-go to that goal. This assumption is often not true, however. For instance, a user may choose an unstable grasp when picking up an object (Fig. 2), or they may arrange items in the wrong order by stacking a heavy item on top of a fragile one. Fig. 1 shows a shared autonomy scenario, where the user teleoperates the robot towards the left bottle. We assume that the robot *knows the optimal goal for the task*: picking up the right bottle is a better choice, for instance because the left bottle is too heavy, or because the robot has less uncertainty about the right bottle's location. Intuitively, if the human insists on the left bottle, the robot should comply; failing to do so can have a negative effect on the user's trust in the robot, which may lead to disuse of the system [10–12]. If the human is willing to adapt by aligning its actions with the robot, which has been observed in adaptation between humans and artifacts [13,14], the robot should insist towards the optimal goal. The human-robot team then exhibits *a mutually adaptive behavior, where the robot adapts its own actions by reasoning over the adaptability of the human teammate.*

Nikolaidis et al. [15] proposed a mutual adaptation formalism in collaborative tasks, e.g., when a human and a robot work together to carry a table out of the room. The robot builds a Bounded-memory Adaptation Model (BAM) of the human teammate, and it integrates the model into a partially observable stochastic process, which enables robot adaptation to the human: If the user is adaptable, the robot will disagree with them, expecting them to switch towards the optimal goal. Otherwise, the robot will align its actions with the user policy, thus retaining their trust.

A characteristic of many collaborative settings is that human and robot both affect the world state, and that disagreement between the human and the robot impedes task completion. For instance, in the table-carrying example, if human and robot attempt to move the table in opposing directions with equal force, the table will not move and the task will not progress. Therefore, a robot that optimizes the task completion time will account for the human adaptability implicitly in its optimization process: if the human is non-adaptable, the only way for the robot to complete the task is to follow the human goal. This is not the case in a shared-autonomy setting, since the human actions do not affect the state of the task. Therefore, a robot that solely maximizes task performance in that setting will always move towards the optimal goal, ignoring human inputs altogether.

In this work, *we propose a generalized human-robot mutual adaptation formalism*, and we formulate mutual adaptation in the collaboration and shared-autonomy settings as instances of this formalism.

We identify that in the shared-autonomy setting (1) tasks may typically exhibit less structure than in the collaboration domain, which limits the observability of the user's intent, and (2) only robot actions directly affect task progress. We address the first challenge by including the operator goal as an additional latent variable in a mixed-observability Markov decision process (MOMDP) [16]. This allows the robot to maintain a probability distribution over the user goals based on the history of operator inputs. We also take into account the uncertainty that the human has on the robot goal by modeling the human as having a probability distribution over the robot goals (Sec. 3). We address the second challenge by proposing an explicit penalty for disagreement in the reward function that the robot is maximizing (Sec. 4). This allows the robot to infer simultaneously the human goal and the human adaptability, reason over how likely the human is to switch their goal based on the robot actions, and guide the human towards the optimal goal while retaining their trust.

We conducted a human subject experiment ($n = 51$) with an assistive robotic arm on a table-clearing task. Results show that the proposed formalism significantly improved human-robot team performance, compared to the robot following participants' preference, while retaining a high level of human trust in the robot.

2. PROBLEM SETTING

A human-robot team can be treated as a multi-agent system, with world state $x_{world} \in X_{world}$, robot action $a_r \in A_r$, and human action $a_h \in A_h$. The system evolves according to a stochastic state transition function $T \colon X_{world} \times A_r \times A_h \rightarrow \Pi(X_{world})$. Additionally, we model the user as having a goal, among a discrete set of goals $g \in G$. We assume access to a stochastic joint policy for each goal, which we call *modal policy*, or *mode* $m \in M$. We call m_h the modal policy that the human is following at a given time-step, and m_r the robot mode, which is the [perceived by the human] robot policy towards a goal. The human mode, $m_h \in M$ is not fully observable. Instead, the robot has uncertainty over the user's policy, that can modeled as a Partially Observable Markov Decision Process (POMDP). Observations in the POMDP correspond to human actions $a_h \in A_h$. Given a sequence of human inputs, we infer a distribution over user modal policies using an observation function $O(a_h|x_{world}, m_h)$.

Contrary to previous work in modeling human intention [17] and in shared autonomy [9], the user goal is not static. Instead, we define a transition function $T_{m_h} \colon M \times H_t \times X_{world} \times A_r \rightarrow \Pi(M)$, where h_t is the history of states, robot and human actions $(x^0_{world}, a^0_r, a^0_h, \ldots, x^{t-1}_{world}, a^{t-1}_r, a^{t-1}_h)$. The function models how the human mode may change over time. At each time step, the human-robot team receives a real-valued reward that in the general case also depends on the human mode m_h and history h_t: $R(m_h, h_t, x_{world}, a_r, a_h)$. The reward captures both the relative cost of each goal $g \in G$, as well as the cost of disagreement between the human and the robot. The robot goal is then to maximize the expected total reward over time: $\sum_{t=0}^{\infty} \gamma^t R(t)$, where the discount factor $\gamma \in [0, 1)$ gives higher weight to immediate rewards than future ones.

Computing the maximization is hard: Both T_{m_h} and R depend on the whole history of states, robot and human actions h_t. We use the Bounded-memory Adaptation Model [15] to simplify the problem.

2.1 Bounded-Memory Adaptation Model

Nikolaidis et al. [15] proposed the Bounded-memory Adaptation Model (BAM). The model is based on the assumption of "bounded rationality" was proposed first by Herbert Simon: people often do not have the time and cognitive capabilities to make perfectly rational decisions [18]. In game theory, bounded rationality has been modeled by assuming that players have a "bounded memory" or "bounded recall" and base their decisions on recent observations [19–21].

The BAM model allows us to simplify the problem, by modeling the human as making decisions not on the whole history of interactions, but on the last k interactions with the robot. This allows us to simplify the transition function T_{m_h} and reward function R defined in the previous section, so that they depend on the history of the last k time-steps only. Additionally, BAM provides a parameterization of the transition function T_{m_h}, based on the parameter $\alpha \in \mathcal{A}$, which is the human *adaptability*. The adaptability represents one's inclination to adapt to the robot. With the BAM assumptions, we have $T_{m_h} : M \times \mathcal{A} \times H_k \times X_{world} \times A_r \rightarrow \Pi(M)$ and $R : M \times H_k \times X_{world} \times A_r \times A_h \rightarrow \mathbb{R}$. We describe the implementation of T_{m_h} in Sec. 3 and of R in Sec. 4.

2.2 Shared Autonomy

The shared autonomy setting allows us to further simplify the general problem: the world state consists only of the robot configuration $x_r \in X_r$, so that $x_r \equiv x_{world}$. A robot action induces a deterministic change in the robot configuration. The human actions $a_h \in A_h$ are inputs through a joystick interface and do not affect the world state. Therefore, the transition function of the system is deterministic and can be defined as: $T\colon X_r \times A_r \rightarrow X_r$.

2.3 Collaboration

We include the collaboration setting formalism for completeness. Contrary to the shared-autonomy setting, both human and robot actions affect the world state, and the transition function can be deterministic or stochastic. In the deterministic case, it is $T : X_{world} \times A_r \times A_h \rightarrow X_{world}$. Additionally, the reward function does not require a penalty for disagreement between the human and robot modes; instead, it can depend only on the relative cost for each goal, so that $R : X_{world} \rightarrow \mathbb{R}$. Finally, if the task exhibits considerable structure, the modes may be directly observed from the human and robot actions. In that case, the robot does not maintain a distribution over modal policies.

3. HUMAN AND ROBOT MODE INFERENCE

When the human provides an input through a joystick interface, the robot makes an inference on the human mode. In the example table-clearing task of Fig. 1, if the robot moves to the right, the human will infer that the robot follows a modal policy towards the right bottle. Similarly, if the human moves the joystick to the left, the robot will consider more likely that the human follows a modal policy towards the left bottle. In this section, we formalize the inference that human and robot make on each other's goals.

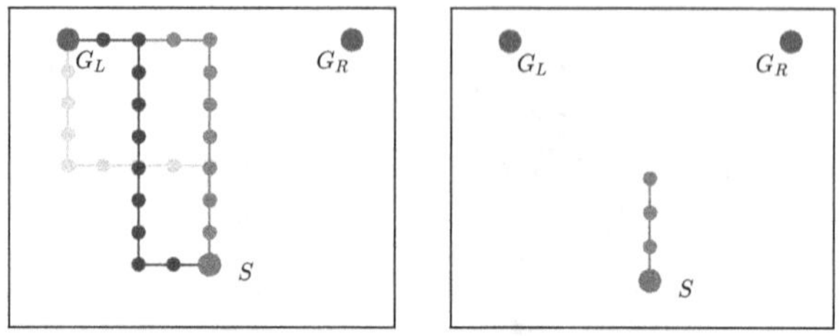

Figure 3: (left) Paths corresponding to three different modal policies that lead to the same goal G_L. We use a stochastic modal policy m_L to compactly represent all feasible paths from S to G_L. (right) The robot moving upwards from point S could be moving towards either G_L or G_R.

3.1 Stochastic Modal Policies

In the shared autonomy setting, there can be a very large number of modal policies that lead to the same goal. We use as example the table-clearing task of Fig. 1. We let G_L represent the left bottle, G_R the right bottle, and S the starting end-effector position of the robot. Fig. 3-left shows paths from three different modal policies that lead to the same goal G_L. Accounting for a large set of modes can increase the computational cost, in particular if we assume that the human mode is partially observable (Section 5).

Therefore, we define a modal policy as a stochastic joint-policy over human and robot actions, so that $m\colon X_r \times H_t \rightarrow \Pi(A_r) \times \Pi(A_h)$. A stochastic modal policy compactly represents a probability distribution over paths and allows us to reason probabilistically about the future actions of an agent that does not move in a perfectly predictable manner. For instance, we can use the principle of maximum entropy to create a probability distribution over all paths from start to the goal [22, 23]. While a stochastic modal policy represents the uncertainty of the observer over paths, we do not require the agent to actually follow a stochastic policy.

3.2 Full Observability Assumption

While m_r, m_h can be assumed to be observable for a variety of structured tasks in the collaboration domain [15], this is not the case for the shared autonomy setting because of the following factors:

Different policies invoke the same action. Assume two modal policies in Fig. 3, one for the left goal shown in red in Fig. 3-left, and a symmetric policy for the right goal (not shown). An agent moving upwards (Figure 3-right) could be following either of the two with equal probability. In that case, inference of the exact modal policy without any prior information is impossible, and the observer needs to maintain a uniform belief over the two policies.

Human inputs are noisy. The user provides its inputs to the system through a joystick interface. These inputs are noisy: the user may "overshoot" an intended path and correct their input, or move the joystick in the wrong direction. In the fully observable case, this would result in an incorrect inference of the human mode. Maintaining a belief over modal policies allows robustness to human mistakes.

This leads us to assume that modal policies are *partially observable*. We model how the human infers the robot mode, as well as how the robot infers the human mode, in the following sections.

3.3 Robot Mode Inference

The bounded-memory assumption dictates that the human does not recall the whole history of states and actions, but only a recent history of the last k time-steps. The human attributes the robot actions to a robot mode m_r.

$$\begin{aligned} P(m_r|h_k, x_r^t, a_r^t) &= P(m_r|x_r^{t-k+1}, a_r^{t-k+1}, ..., x_r^t, a_r^t) \\ &= \eta\ P(a_r^{t-k+1}, ..., a_r^t|m_r, x_r^{t-k+1}, ..., x_r^t) \end{aligned} \quad (1)$$

In this work, we consider modal policies that generate actions based only on the current world state, so that $M : X_r \rightarrow \Pi(A_h) \times \Pi(A_r)$.

Therefore Eq. 1 can be simplified as follows, where $m_r(x_r^t, a_r^t)$ denotes the probability of the robot taking action a_r at time t, if it follows modal policy m_r:

$$P(m_r|h_k, x_r^t, a_r^t) = \eta\ m_r(x_r^{t-k+1}, a_r^{t-k+1}) ... m_r(x_r^t, a_r^t) \quad (2)$$

$P(m_r|h_k, x_r^t, a_r^t)$ is the [estimated by the robot] human belief on the robot mode m_r.

3.4 Human Mode Inference

To infer the human mode, we need to implement the dynamics model T_{m_h} that describes how the human mode evolves over time, and the observation function O that allows the robot to update its belief on the human mode from the human actions.

In Sec. 2 we defined a transition function T_{m_h}, that indicates the probability of the human switching from mode m_h to a new mode m'_h, given a history h_k and their adaptability α. We simplify the notation, so that $x_r \equiv x_r^t$, $a_r \equiv a_r^t$ and $x \equiv (h_k, x_r)$:

$$\begin{aligned} & T_{m_h}(x, \alpha, m_h, a_r, m'_h) = P(m'_h|x, \alpha, m_h, a_r) \\ &= \sum_{m_r} P(m'_h, m_r|x, \alpha, m_h, a_r) \\ &= \sum_{m_r} P(m'_h|x, \alpha, m_h, a_r, m_r) \times P(m_r|x, \alpha, m_h, a_r) \\ &= \sum_{m_r} P(m'_h|\alpha, m_h, m_r) \times P(m_r|x, a_r) \end{aligned} \quad (3)$$

The first term gives the probability of the human switching to a new mode m'_h, if the human mode is m_h and the robot mode is m_r. Based on the BAM model [15], the human switches to m_r, with probability α and stays at m_h with probability $1 - \alpha$. Nikolaidis et al. [15] define α as the human adaptability, which represents their inclination to adapt to the robot. If $\alpha = 1$, the human switches to m_r with certainty. If $\alpha = 0$, the human insists on their mode m_h and does not adapt. Therefore:

$$P(m'_h|\alpha, m_h, m_r) = \begin{cases} \alpha & m'_h \equiv m_r \\ 1-\alpha & m'_h \equiv m_h \\ 0 & \text{otherwise} \end{cases} \quad (4)$$

The second term in Eq. 3 is computed using Eq. 2, and it is the [estimated by the human] robot mode.

Eq. 3 describes that the probability of the human switching to a new robot mode m_r depends on the human adaptability α, as well as on the uncertainty that the human has about the robot following m_r. This allows the robot to compute the probability of the human switching to the robot mode, given each robot action.

The observation function $O\colon X_r \times M \rightarrow \Pi(A_h)$ defines a probability distribution over human actions a_h. This distribution is specified by the stochastic modal policy $m_h \in M$. Given the above, the human mode m_h can be estimated by a Bayes filter, with $b(m_h)$ the robot's previous belief on m_h:

$$b'(m'_h) = \eta\ O(m'_h, x'_r, a_h) \sum_{m_h \in M} T_{m_h}(x, \alpha, m_h, a_r, m'_h) b(m_h) \quad (5)$$

In this section, we assumed that α is known to the robot. In practice, the robot needs to estimate both m_h and α. We formulate this in Sec. 5.

4. DISAGREEMENT BETWEEN MODES

In the previous section we formalized the inference that human and robot make on each other's goals. Based on that, the robot can infer the human goal and it can reason over how likely the human is to switch goals given a robot action.

Intuitively, if the human insists on their goal, the robot should follow the human goal, even if it is suboptimal, in order to retain human trust. If the human is willing to change goals, the robot should move towards the optimal goal. We enable this behavior by proposing in the robot's reward function a penalty for disagreement between human and robot modes. The intuition is that if the human is non-adaptable, they will insist on their own mode throughout the task, therefore the expected accumulated cost of disagreeing with the human will outweigh the reward of the optimal goal. In that case, the robot will follow the human preference. If the human is adaptable, the robot will move towards the optimal goal, since it will expect the human to change modes.

We formulate the reward function that the robot is maximizing, so that there is a penalty for following a mode that is perceived to be different than the human's mode.

$$R(x, m_h, a_r) = \begin{cases} R_{goal} & : x_r \in G \\ R_{other} & : x_r \notin G \end{cases} \quad (6)$$

If the robot is at a goal state $x_r \in G$, a positive reward associated with that goal is returned, regardless of the human mode m_h and robot mode m_r. Otherwise, there is a penalty $C < 0$ for disagreement between m_h and m_r, induced in R_{other}. The human does not observe m_r directly, but estimates it from the recent history of robot states and actions (Sec. 3.3). Therefore, R_{other} is computed so that the penalty for disagreement is weighted by the [estimated by the human] probability of the robot actually following m_r:

$$R_{other} = \sum_{m_r} R_m(m_h, m_r) P(m_r|x, a_r) \quad (7)$$

$$\text{where } R_m(m_h, m_r) = \begin{cases} 0 & : m_h \equiv m_r \\ C & : m_h \neq m_r \end{cases} \quad (8)$$

5. HUMAN-ROBOT MUTUAL ADAPTATION FORMALISM

5.1 MOMDP Formulation

In Section 3.4, we showed how the robot estimates the human mode, and how it computes the probability of the human switching to the robot mode based on the human adaptability. In Section 4, we defined a reward function that the robot is maximizing, which captures the trade-off between going to the optimal goal and following the human mode. Both the human adaptability and the human mode are not directly observable. Therefore, the robot needs to estimate them through interaction, while performing the task. This leads us to formulate this problem as a mixed-observability Markov Decision Process (MOMDP) [16]. This formulation allows us to compute an optimal policy for the robot that will maximize the expected reward that the human-robot team will receive, given the robot's estimates of the human adaptability and of the human mode. We define a MOMDP as a tuple $\{X, Y, A_r, \mathcal{T}_x, \mathcal{T}_\alpha, \mathcal{T}_{m_h}, R, \Omega, O\}$:

- $X : X_r \times A_r^k$ is the set of observable variables. These are the current robot configuration x_r, as well as the history h_k. Since x_r transitions deterministically, we only need to register the current robot state and robot actions $a_r^{t-k+1}, ..., a_r^t$.
- $Y : \mathcal{A} \times M$ is the set of partially observable variables. These are the human adaptability $\alpha \in A$, and the human mode $m_h \in M$.
- A_r is a finite set of robot actions. We model actions as transitions between discrete robot configurations.
- $\mathcal{T}_x : X \times A_r \longrightarrow X$ is a deterministic mapping from a robot configuration x_r, history h_k and action a_r, to a subsequent configuration x'_r and history h'_k.
- $\mathcal{T}_\alpha : \mathcal{A} \times A_r \longrightarrow \Pi(\mathcal{A})$ is the probability of the human adaptability being α' at the next time step, if the adaptability of the human at time t is α and the robot takes action a_r. We assume the human adaptability to be fixed throughout the task.
- $\mathcal{T}_{m_h} : X \times \mathcal{A} \times M \times A_r \longrightarrow \Pi(M)$ is the probability of the human switching from mode m_h to a new mode m'_h, given a history h_k, robot state x_r, human adaptability α and robot action a_r. It is computed using Eq. 3, Sec. 3.4.
- $R : X \times M \times A_r \longrightarrow \mathbb{R}$ is a reward function that gives an immediate reward for the robot taking action a_r given a history h_k, human mode m_h and robot state x_r. It is defined in Eq. 6, Sec. 4.
- Ω is the set of observations that the robot receives. An observation is a human input $a_h \in A_h$ ($\Omega \equiv A_h$).
- $O : M \times X_r \longrightarrow \Pi(\Omega)$ is the observation function, which gives a probability distribution over human actions for a mode m_h at state x_r. This distribution is specified by the stochastic modal policy $m_h \in M$.

5.2 Belief Update

Based on the above, the belief update for the MOMDP is [16]:

$$b'(\alpha', m'_h) = \eta O(m'_h, x'_r, a_h) \sum_{\alpha \in \mathcal{A}} \sum_{m_h \in M} \mathcal{T}_x(x, a_r, x') \\ \mathcal{T}_\alpha(\alpha, a_r, \alpha') \mathcal{T}_{m_h}(x, \alpha, m_h, a_r, m'_h) b(\alpha, m_h) \quad (9)$$

We note that since the MOMDP has two partially observable variables, α and m_h, the robot maintains a joint probability distribution over both variables.

5.3 Robot Policy

We solve the MOMDP for a robot policy $\pi_r^*(b)$ that is optimal with respect to the robot's expected total reward.

The stochastic modal policies may assign multiple actions at a given state. Therefore, even if $m_h \equiv m_r$, a_r may not match the human input a_h. Such disagreements are unnecessary when human and robot modes are the same. Therefore, we let the robot actions match the human inputs, if the robot has enough confidence that robot and human modes (computed using Eq. 2, 5) are identical in the current time-step. Otherwise, the robot executes the action specified by the MOMDP optimal policy. We leave for future work adding a penalty for disagreement between actions, which we hypothesize it would result in similar behavior.

5.4 Simulations

Fig. 4 shows the robot behavior for two simulated users, one with low adaptability (User 1, $\alpha = 0.0$), and one with high adaptability (User 2, $\alpha = 0.75$) for a shared autonomy scenario with two goals, G_L and G_R, corresponding to modal policies m_L and m_R respectively. Both users start with modal policy m_L (left goal). The robot uses the human input to estimate both m_h and α. We set a bounded-memory of $k = 1$ time-step. If human and robot disagree and the human insists on their modal policy, then the MOMDP belief is updated so that smaller values of adaptability α have higher probability (lower adaptability). It the human aligns its inputs to the robot mode, larger values become more likely. If the robot infers the human to be adaptable, it moves towards the optimal goal. Otherwise, it complies with the human, thus retaining their trust.

Fig. 5 shows the team-performance over α, averaged over 1000 runs with simulated users. We evaluate performance by the reward of the goal achieved, where R_{opt} is the reward for the optimal and R_{sub} for the sub-optimal goal. We see that the more adaptable the user, the more often the robot will reach the optimal goal. Additionally, we observe that for $\alpha = 0.0$, the performance is higher than R_{sub}. This is because the simulated user may choose to move forward in the first time-steps; when the robot infers that they are stubborn, it is already close to the optimal goal and continues moving to that goal.

6. HUMAN SUBJECT EXPERIMENT

We conduct a human subject experiment ($n = 51$) in a shared autonomy setting. We are interested in showing that the human-robot mutual adaptation formalism can improve the performance of human-robot teams, while retaining high levels of perceived collaboration and trust in the robot in the shared autonomy domain.

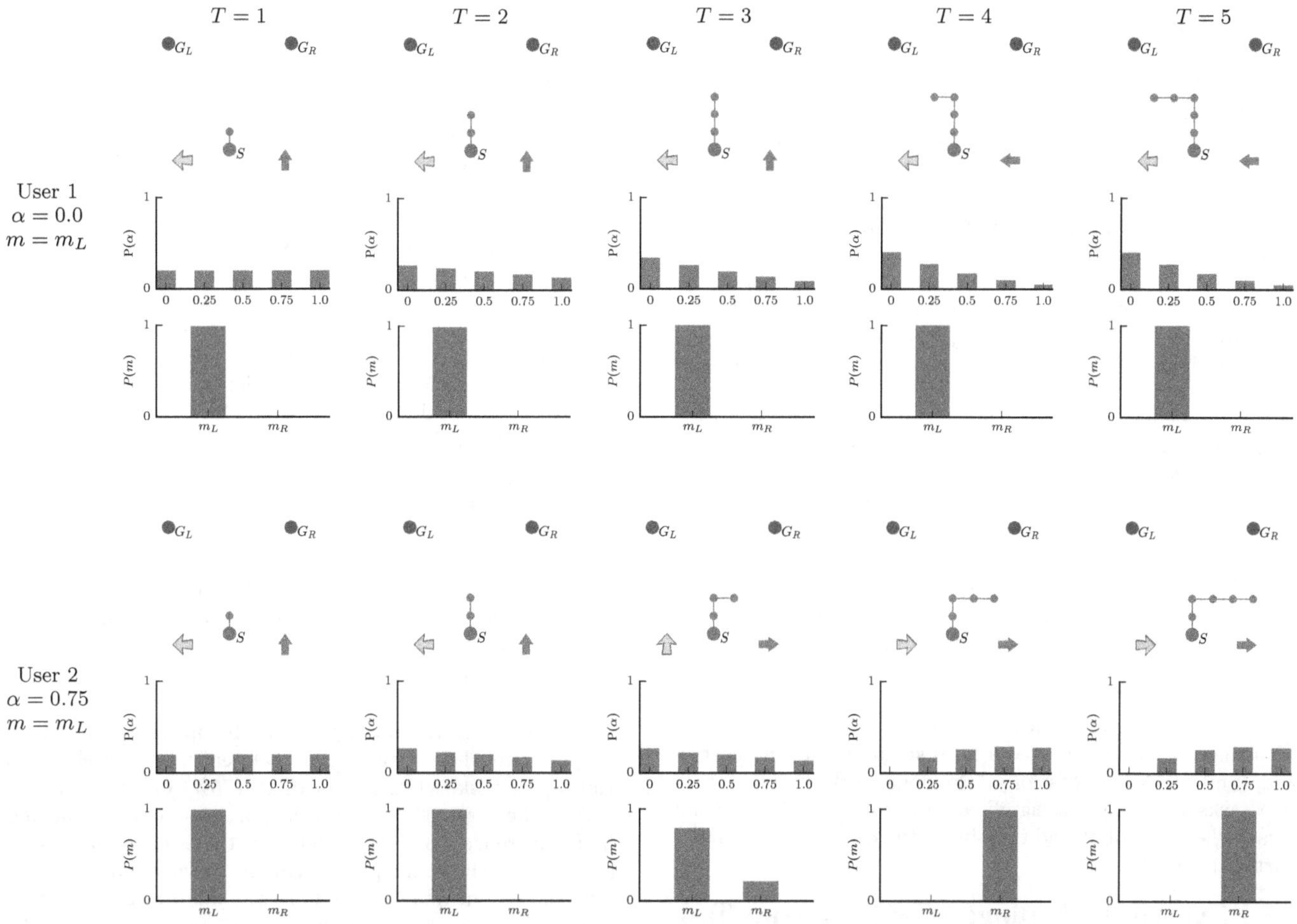

Figure 4: Sample runs on a shared autonomy scenario with two goals G_L, G_R and two simulated humans of adaptability level $\alpha = 0$ and 0.75. Both users start with modal policy m_L (associated with the left goal). The human and robot actions are {move-left, move-right, move-forward}. For both users, the upper row plots the robot trajectory (red dots), the human input (green arrow) and the robot action (gray arrow) over time. The middle row plots the estimate of α over time, where $\alpha \in \{0, 0.25, 0.5, 0.75, 1\}$. Each graph plots α versus the probability of α. The lower row plots $m \in \{m_L, m_R\}$ versus the probability of m. Columns indicate successive time-steps. User 1 insists on their initial strategy throughout the task and the robot complies, whereas User 2 adapts to the robot and ends up following m_R.

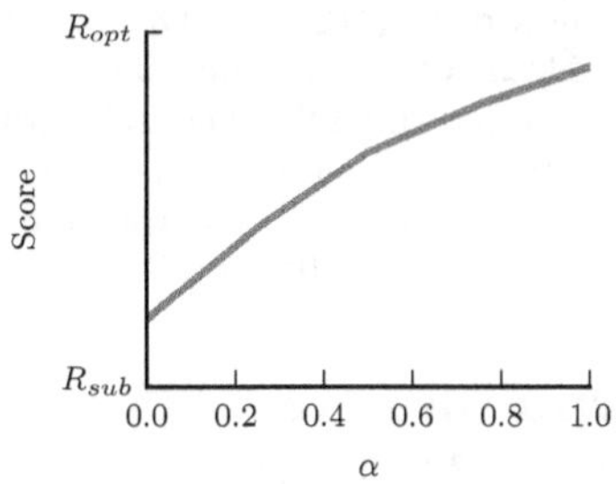

Figure 5: Mean performance for simulated users of different adaptability α.

On one extreme, we "fix" the robot policy, so that the robot always moves towards the optimal goal, ignoring human adaptability. We hypothesize that this will have a negative effect on human trust and perceived robot performance as a teammate. On the other extreme, we have the robot assist the human in achieving their desired goal.

We show that the proposed formalism achieves a trade-off between the two: when the human is non-adaptable, the robot follows the human preference. Otherwise, the robot insists on the optimal way of completing the task, leading to significantly better policies, compared to following the human preference, while achieving a high level of trust.

6.1 Independent Variables

No-adaptation session. The robot executes a fixed policy, always acting towards the optimal goal.

Mutual-adaptation session. The robot executes the MOMDP policy of Sec. 5.3.

One-way adaptation session. The robot estimates a distribution over user goals, and adapts to the user following their preference, assisting them for that distribution [9]. We compute the robot policy in that condition by fixing the adaptability value to 0 in our model and assigning equal reward to both goals.

6.2 Hypotheses

H1 *The performance of teams in the No-adaptation condition will be better than of teams in the Mutual-adaptation condition, which will in turn be better than of teams in the One-way adaptation condition.* We expected teams in the No-adaptation condition to outperform the teams in the other conditions, since the robot will always go to the optimal goal. In the Mutual-adaptation condition, we expected a significant number of users to adapt to the robot and switch their strategy towards the optimal goal. Therefore, we posited that this would result in an overall higher reward, compared to the reward resulting from the robot following the participants' preference throughout the task (One-way adaptation).

H2 *Participants that work with the robot in the One-way adaptation condition will rate higher their trust in the robot, as well as their perceived collaboration with the robot, compared to working with the robot in the Mutual-adaptation condition,. Additionally, participants in the Mutual-adaptation condition will give higher ratings, compared to working with the robot in the No-adaptation condition.* We expected users to trust the robot more in the One-way adaptation condition than in the other conditions, since in that condition the robot will always follow their preference. In the Mutual-adaptation condition, we expected users to trust the robot more and perceive it as a better teammate, compared with the robot that executed a fixed strategy ignoring users' adaptability (No-adaptation). Previous work in collaborative tasks has shown a significant improvement in human trust, when the robot had the ability to adapt to the human parter [15, 24, 25]

6.3 Experiment Setting: A Table Clearing Task

Participants were asked to clear a table off two bottles placed symmetrically, by providing inputs to a robotic arm through a joystick interface (Fig. 1). They controlled the robot in Cartesian space by moving it in three different directions: left, forward and right. We first instructed them in the task, and asked them to do two training sessions, where they practiced controlling the robot with the joystick. We then asked them to choose which of the two bottles they would like the robot to grab first, and we set the robot policy, so that the other bottle was the optimal goal. This emulates a scenario where, for instance, the robot would be unable to grasp one bottle without dropping the other, or where one bottle would be heavier than the other and should be placed in the bin first. In the one-way and mutual adaptation conditions, we told them that "the robot has a mind of its own, and it may choose not to follow your inputs." Participants then did the task three times in all conditions, and then answered a post-experimental questionnaire that used a five-point Likert scale to assess their responses to working with the robot. Additionally, in a video-taped interview at the end of the task, we asked participants that had changed strategy during the task to justify their action.

6.4 Subject Allocation

We recruited 51 participants from the local community, and chose a between-subjects design in order to not bias the users with policies from previous conditions.

6.5 MOMDP Model

The size of the observable state-space X was 52 states. We empirically found that a history length of $k = 1$ in BAM was sufficient for this task, since most of the subjects that changed their preference did so reacting to the previous robot action. The human and robot actions were {move-left, move-right, move-forward}. We specified two stochastic modal policies $\{m_L, m_R\}$, one for each goal. We additionally assumed a discrete set of values of the adaptability $\alpha : \{0.0, 0.25, 0.5, 0.75, 1.0\}$. Therefore, the total size of the MOMDP state-space was $5 \times 2 \times 52 = 520$ states. We selected the reward so that $R_{opt} = 11$ for the optimal goal, $R_{sub} = 10$ for the suboptimal goal, and $C = -0.32$ for the cost of mode disagreement (Eq. 8). We computed the robot policy using the SARSOP solver [26], a point-based approximation algorithm which, combined with the MOMDP formulation, can scale up to hundreds of thousands of states [17].

7. ANALYSIS

7.1 Objective Measures

We consider hypothesis **H1**, that the performance of teams in the No-adaptation condition will be better than of teams in the Mutual-adaptation condition, which in turn will be better than of teams in the One-way adaptation condition.

Nine participants out of 16 (56%) in the Mutual-adaptation condition guided the robot towards the optimal goal, which was different than their initial preference, during the final trial of the task, while 12 out of 16 (75%) did so at one or more of the three trials. From the participants that changed their preference, only one stated that they did so for reasons irrelevant to the robot policy. On the other hand, only two participants out of 17 in the One-way adaptation condition changed goals during the task, while 15 out of 17 guided the robot towards their preferred, suboptimal goal in all trials. This indicates that the adaptation observed in the Mutual-adaptation condition was caused by the robot behavior.

We evaluate team performance by computing the mean reward over the three trials, with the reward for each trial being R_{opt} if the robot reached the optimal goal and R_{sub} if the robot reached the suboptimal goal (Fig. 6-left). As expected, a Kruskal-Wallis H test showed that there was a statistically significant difference in performance among the different conditions ($\chi^2(2) = 39.84, p < 0.001$). Pairwise two-tailed Mann-Whitney-Wilcoxon tests with Bonferroni corrections showed the difference to be statistically significant between the No-adaptation and Mutual-adaptation ($U = 28.5, p < 0.001$), and Mutual-adaptation and One-way adaptation ($U = 49.5, p = 0.001$) conditions. This supports our hypothesis.

7.2 Subjective Measures

Recall hypothesis **H2**, that participants in the Mutual-adaptation condition would rate their trust and perceived collaboration with the robot higher than in the No-adaptation condition, but lower than in the One-way adaptation condition. Table I shows the two subjective scales that we used. The *trust* scales were used as-is from [27]. We additionally chose a set of questions related to participants' *perceived collaboration* with the robot.

Both scales had good consistency. Scale items were combined into a score. Fig. 6-center shows that both participants' trust ($M = 3.94, SE = 0.18$) and perceived collaboration ($M = 3.91, SE = 0.12$) were high in the Mutual-

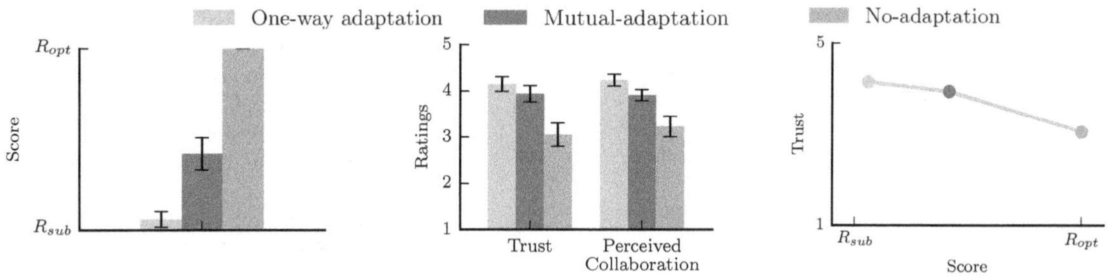

Figure 6: Findings for objective and subjective measures.

adaptation condition. One-way ANOVAs showed a statistically significant difference between the three conditions in both trust ($F(2,48) = 8.370, p = 0.001$) and perceived collaboration ($F(2,48) = 9.552, p < 0.001$). Tukey post-hoc tests revealed that participants of the Mutual-adaptation condition trusted the robot more, compared to participants that worked with the robot in the No-adaptation condition ($p = 0.010$). Additionally, they rated higher their perceived collaboration with the robot ($p = 0.017$). However, there was no significant difference in either measure between participants in the One-way adaptation and Mutual-adaptation conditions. We attribute these results to the fact that the MOMDP formulation allowed the robot to reason over its estimate of the adaptability of its teammate; if the teammate insisted towards the suboptimal goal, the robot responded to the input commands and followed the user's preference. If the participant changed their inputs based on the robot actions, the robot guided them towards the optimal goal, while retaining a high level of trust. By contrast, the robot in the No-adaptation condition always moved towards the optimal goal ignoring participants' inputs, which in turn had a negative effect on subjective measures.

TABLE I: SUBJECTIVE MEASURES

Trust $\alpha = .85$
1.I trusted the robot to do the right thing at the right time.
2.The robot was trustworthy.
Perceived Collaboration $\alpha = .81$
1.I was satisfied with ADA and my performance.
2.The robot and I worked towards mutually agreed upon goals.
3.The robot and I collaborated well together
4.The robot's actions were reasonable.
5.The robot was responsive to me.

8. DISCUSSION

In this work, we proposed a human-robot mutual adaptation formalism in a shared autonomy setting. In a human subject experiment, we compared the policy computed with our formalism, with an assistance policy, where the robot helped participants to achieve their intended goal, and with a fixed policy where the robot always went towards the optimal goal.

As Fig. 6 illustrates, participants in the one-way adaptation condition had the worst performance, since they guided the robot towards a suboptimal goal. The fixed policy achieved maximum performance, as expected. However, this came to the detriment of human trust in the robot. On the other hand, the assistance policy in the One-way adaptation condition resulted in the highest trust ratings — albeit not significantly higher than the ratings in the Mutual-adaptation condition — since the robot always followed the user preference and there was no goal disagreement between human and robot. Mutual-adaptation balanced the trade-off between optimizing performance and retaining trust: users in that condition trusted the robot more than in the No-adaptation condition, and performed better than in the One-way adaptation condition.

Fig. 6-right shows the three conditions with respect to trust and performance scores. We can make the MOMDP policy identical to either of the two policies in the end-points, by changing the MOMDP model parameters. If we fix in the model the human adaptability to 0 and assign equal costs for both goals, the robot would assist the user in their goal (One-way adaptation). If we fix adaptability to 1 in the model (or we remove the penalty for mode disagreement), the robot will always go to the optimal goal (fixed policy).

The presented table-clearing task can be generalized without significant modifications to tasks with a large number of goals, human inputs and robot actions, such as picking good grasps in manipulation tasks (Fig. 2): The state-space size increases linearly with $(1/dt)$, where dt a discrete time-step, and with the number of modal policies. On the other hand, the number of observable states is polynomial to the number of robot actions ($O(A_r^k)$), since each state includes history h_k: For tasks with large $|A_r|$ and memory length k, we could approximate h_k using feature-based representations.

Overall, we are excited to have brought about a better understanding of the relationships between adaptability, performance and trust in a shared autonomy setting. We are very interested in exploring applications of these ideas beyond assistive robotic arms, to powered wheelchairs, remote manipulators, and generally to settings where human inputs are combined with robot autonomy.

Acknowledgments

We thank Michael Koval, Shervin Javdani and Henny Admoni for the very helpful discussion and advice.

Funding

This work was funded by the DARPA SIMPLEX program through ARO contract number 67904LSDRP, National Institute of Health R01 (#R01EB019335), National Science Foundation CPS (#1544797), and the Office of Naval Research. We also acknowledge the Onassis Foundation as a sponsor.

9. REFERENCES

[1] M. Hillman, K. Hagan, S. Hagan, J. Jepson, and R. Orpwood, "The weston wheelchair mounted assistive robot the design story," *Robotica*, vol. 20, no. 02, pp. 125–132, 2002.

[2] S. D. Prior, "An electric wheelchair mounted robotic arm a survey of potential users," *Journal of medical engineering & technology*, vol. 14, no. 4, pp. 143–154, 1990.

[3] J. Sijs, F. Liefhebber, and G. W. R. Romer, "Combined position & force control for a robotic manipulator," in *2007 IEEE 10th International Conference on Rehabilitation Robotics*. IEEE, 2007, pp. 106–111.

[4] J. Kofman, X. Wu, T. J. Luu, and S. Verma, "Teleoperation of a robot manipulator using a vision-based human-robot interface," *Industrial Electronics, IEEE Transactions on*, vol. 52, no. 5, pp. 1206–1219, 2005.

[5] A. D. Dragan and S. S. Srinivasa, "A policy-blending formalism for shared control," *The International Journal of Robotics Research*, vol. 32, no. 7, pp. 790–805, 2013.

[6] W. Yu, R. Alqasemi, R. Dubey, and N. Pernalete, "Telemanipulation assistance based on motion intention recognition," in *Robotics and Automation, 2005. ICRA 2005. Proceedings of the 2005 IEEE International Conference on*. IEEE, 2005, pp. 1121–1126.

[7] P. Trautman, "Assistive planning in complex, dynamic environments: a probabilistic approach," in *Systems, Man, and Cybernetics (SMC), 2015 IEEE International Conference on*. IEEE, 2015, pp. 3072–3078.

[8] D. Gopinath, S. Jain, and B. D. Argall, "Human-in-the-loop optimization of shared autonomy in assistive robotics," *IEEE Robotics and Automation Letters*, vol. 2, no. 1, pp. 247–254, 2017.

[9] S. Javdani, S. Srinivasa, and J. A. D. Bagnell, "Shared autonomy via hindsight optimization," in *Proceedings of Robotics: Science and Systems*, Rome, Italy, July 2015.

[10] P. A. Hancock, D. R. Billings, K. E. Schaefer, J. Y. Chen, E. J. De Visser, and R. Parasuraman, "A meta-analysis of factors affecting trust in human-robot interaction," *Human Factors*, 2011.

[11] M. Salem, G. Lakatos, F. Amirabdollahian, and K. Dautenhahn, "Would you trust a (faulty) robot?: Effects of error, task type and personality on human-robot cooperation and trust," in *HRI*, 2015.

[12] J. J. Lee, W. B. Knox, J. B. Wormwood, C. Breazeal, and D. DeSteno, "Computationally modeling interpersonal trust," *Front. Psychol.*, 2013.

[13] Y. Xu, K. Ueda, T. Komatsu, T. Okadome, T. Hattori, Y. Sumi, and T. Nishida, "Woz experiments for understanding mutual adaptation," *Ai & Society*, vol. 23, no. 2, pp. 201–212, 2009.

[14] T. Komatsu, A. Ustunomiya, K. Suzuki, K. Ueda, K. Hiraki, and N. Oka, "Experiments toward a mutual adaptive speech interface that adopts the cognitive features humans use for communication and induces and exploits users' adaptations," *International Journal of Human-Computer Interaction*, vol. 18, no. 3, pp. 243–268, 2005.

[15] S. Nikolaidis, A. Kuznetsov, D. Hsu, and S. Srinivasa, "Formalizing human-robot mutual adaptation: A bounded memory model," in *The Eleventh ACM/IEEE International Conference on Human Robot Interation*. IEEE Press, 2016, pp. 75–82.

[16] S. C. Ong, S. W. Png, D. Hsu, and W. S. Lee, "Planning under uncertainty for robotic tasks with mixed observability," *IJRR*, 2010.

[17] T. Bandyopadhyay, K. S. Won, E. Frazzoli, D. Hsu, W. S. Lee, and D. Rus, "Intention-aware motion planning," in *WAFR*. Springer, 2013.

[18] H. A. Simon, "Rational decision making in business organizations," *The American economic review*, pp. 493–513, 1979.

[19] R. Powers and Y. Shoham, "Learning against opponents with bounded memory." in *IJCAI*, 2005.

[20] D. Monte, "Learning with bounded memory in games," *GEB*, 2014.

[21] R. J. Aumann and S. Sorin, "Cooperation and bounded recall," *GEB*, 1989.

[22] B. D. Ziebart, N. Ratliff, G. Gallagher, C. Mertz, K. Peterson, J. A. Bagnell, M. Hebert, A. K. Dey, and S. Srinivasa, "Planning-based prediction for pedestrians," in *IROS*, 2009.

[23] B. D. Ziebart, A. L. Maas, J. A. Bagnell, and A. K. Dey, "Maximum entropy inverse reinforcement learning." in *AAAI*, 2008, pp. 1433–1438.

[24] J. Shah, J. Wiken, B. Williams, and C. Breazeal, "Improved human-robot team performance using chaski, a human-inspired plan execution system," in *HRI*, 2011.

[25] P. A. Lasota and J. A. Shah, "Analyzing the effects of human-aware motion planning on close-proximity human–robot collaboration," *Hum. Factors*, 2015.

[26] H. Kurniawati, D. Hsu, and W. S. Lee, "Sarsop: Efficient point-based pomdp planning by approximating optimally reachable belief spaces." in *RSS*, 2008.

[27] G. Hoffman, "Evaluating fluency in human-robot collaboration," in *HRI workshop on human robot collaboration*, vol. 381, 2013, pp. 1–8.

Improving Robot Controller Transparency Through Autonomous Policy Explanation

Bradley Hayes and Julie A. Shah
Computer Science and Artificial Intelligence Lab
Massachusetts Institute of Technology
Cambridge, MA 02139
{hayesbh, julie_a_shah}@csail.mit.edu

ABSTRACT

Shared expectations and mutual understanding are critical facets of teamwork. Achieving these in human-robot collaborative contexts can be especially challenging, as humans and robots are unlikely to share a common language to convey intentions, plans, or justifications. Even in cases where human co-workers can inspect a robot's control code, and particularly when statistical methods are used to encode control policies, there is no guarantee that meaningful insights into a robot's behavior can be derived or that a human will be able to efficiently isolate the behaviors relevant to the interaction. We present a series of algorithms and an accompanying system that enables robots to autonomously synthesize policy descriptions and respond to both general and targeted queries by human collaborators. We demonstrate applicability to a variety of robot controller types including those that utilize conditional logic, tabular reinforcement learning, and deep reinforcement learning, synthesizing informative policy descriptions for collaborators and facilitating fault diagnosis by non-experts.

1. INTRODUCTION

Collaboration between humans and robots is impossible without shared expectations about teammates' behaviors and intentions [14, 28]. However, gaining insight into the processes that govern the behaviors of autonomous agents can be prohibitively difficult, requiring a worker to directly access and inspect a robot's control code — an especially challenging task if its logic is embedded in modern machine learning model-based methods.

Such control software can be complex to parse and interpret [21], particularly for modern robotics applications [20, 32]. Due to the high dimensionality of process inputs (e.g., camera images, object locations, etc.) or outputs (e.g., mechanical degrees of freedom), it can quickly become infeasible to manually encode behaviors. Methods that create robot controllers by learning behaviors from demonstration or simulation have emerged as a reasonable alternative to manual encoding [37, 1]. However, understanding controllers has become considerably more difficult as a result of incorporating these popular and effective machine learning methods, with statistical models increasingly used as drivers of control logic.

HRI '17, March 06-09, 2017, Vienna, Austria
© 2017 ACM. ISBN 978-1-4503-4336-7/17/03... $15.00
DOI: http://dx.doi.org/10.1145/2909824.3020233

As a robot's roles and responsibilities grow increasingly complex, its controller can quickly become incomprehensible through the necessary use of these methods, highlighting an implicit trade-off between capability and transparency. Providing the robot's control code or documentation to collaborators in advance is neither a viable nor scalable alternative, with misinterpretations potentially impeding team fluency or putting human workers in harm's way. Within a robot's control software, the debugging process can be expensive and time-consuming [13], with no guarantees that anomalous behavior will be identified and resolved prior to deployment. Even modern systems that provide targeted, useful information about their controllers typically require manual, task-specific annotation in order to do so [38], indicating a technical gap in general methods for automating this explanatory process.

Our aim in this work is to enable an autonomous agent to reason over and answer questions about its underlying control logic, independent of its internal representation. We demonstrate our approach's utility within three representative domains (discrete, continuous, and multi-agent) that map to three important classes of robot controllers, including hard-coded, conditional statement-driven policies, and those that rely upon trained reinforcement learning models [18] — demonstrating success with both tabular representation and neural network based Q-function approximation [26] in particular. We show that our method accurately and succinctly summarizes encoded control logic, providing a basis for establishing shared expectations between a robot and its human co-workers. The presented method also serves as a tool for debugging complex control systems, as its generated explanations can also serve to characterize undesired or mis-applied behaviors.

Our approach first involves learning a domain model of the system's operating environment from real or simulated demonstrations, using programmer specified code annotations that provide capabilities similar in spirit to a software debugger. Within this learned domain model, we use statistics computed over data extracted from continued observations of the controller's software execution traces to construct a behavioral model that effectively captures or finely approximates the agent's control logic (Section 4). We use a Boolean algebra over planning predicates [11] as a basis for grounding state regions in natural language (Section 5). Leveraging these models and language groundings, we introduce a series of algorithms that enables an agent to answer behavior-related questions (Section 6), allowing for indication of environmental conditions under which certain robot behaviors will occur ("When do you do _?"), identification of which robot behaviors will occur under a specified set of environmental conditions ("What do you do when _?"), or an explanation for why a particular behavior did not occur ("Why didn't you do _?"). In doing so, we provide workers with the capability to develop and refine their expectations concerning the behaviors of otherwise-opaque autonomous agents through direct inquiry. This interactive, targeted expectation calibration is an important initial step toward understanding and debugging robot behaviors, as it facilitates the precise identification of the ways in which expected and realized actions do not align.

2. BACKGROUND AND RELATED WORK

Traditional methods for acquiring an understanding of control logic typically involve some form of source code inspection and documentation review [2, 13] or formal verification given proper specifications [36, 23]. In order to resolve issues stemming from logical errors, automated debugging methods have been introduced [4, 3, 34] that seek to identify faulty program statements. These approaches maintain the critical assumption that identifying a faulty statement is sufficient to allow a developer to detect, understand, and correct the issue introduced by the error [31]. In their work, Parnin and Orso elaborated that these approaches are not readily applicable to complex systems with "imperfect" knowledge, such as controllers that rely upon encoded data to make decisions (e.g., statistical models) or systems that interact with an external environment (e.g., collaborative robots).

One major limitation of code inspection tools in general is that their effective use requires that the code itself be interpretable to the user attempting to understand it. Novices in particular tend to have a difficult time both understanding the intended operation of a program and identifying connections between malformed logic and actual execution behavior [12]. Fitzgerald et al. found that beginner programmers had substantial difficulty identifying errors in the conditional logic of simple programs, with repair rates reaching only 50%. In robotics domains, where such logic is often implicitly embedded in high-dimensional statistical or graphical models, classical, code inspection-based debugging approaches are largely inapplicable. Given the potential physical consequences of model-borne bugs in robot controllers and the remote likelihood of a novice interpreting such representations via inspection, it is imperative to introduce tools that do not rely upon comprehension of source code.

Verbal statements have been shown in prior work to be a preferred mechanism for summarizing and conveying information related to control logic and decision making [44, 46]. Automated methods utilizing natural language-based explanations (rather than source code analysis) have been effective for instilling appropriate levels of understanding and confidence regarding expected robot behavior [22]. Study results have indicated that achieving comprehension of control logic leads to improved team performance [46, 28, 39] and prevention of automation abuse [30]. Even in situations in which robots' explanations are neither exhaustive nor precise, the corresponding increase in transparency can improve the decision-making capabilities of collaborators [45, 29, 47].

Strategies for verbal human-robot communication that involve conveying intention and resolving ambiguity have yielded effective collaborations. Tellex et al. [42] investigated scenarios in which a human was relied upon to debug a robot's behaviors during live task execution, and contributed an algorithm enabling the robot to identify parts or obstacles that had to be manipulated in order to allow nominal operation to continue. In their work, varying levels of specificity within verbal communication were investigated for reducing collaborator uncertainty about the robot's needs when assistance was required, indicating that targeted, unambiguous requests for help were far more effective than imprecise requests. Devin et al. [9] incorporated a theory of mind that reasons about a partner's knowledge to guide a robot's behaviors and information-sharing activities, and reported an increase in collaboration efficiency when appropriate knowledge was communicated. Both works support the premise that robots capable of identifying and communicating relevant details about their operation are better teammates that are more useful and are more capable than robots lacking this capability.

Complementing human-robot interaction literature focused on generating content and determining the relevance of information to communicate, prior work in the expert systems community has investigated and characterized the principal components of effective explanations [41]: constructing an expository story relating internal knowledge to general facts, plans, and goals in a comprehensible manner. Explanation-based approaches that justify their decisions have proven capable of increasing user acceptance of and confidence in autonomous systems [48]. As ideal model summaries are precise, concise, and interpretable [24, 35], the quality of a given response is measured by its accuracy (faithfulness to the underlying model), succinctness (minimization of information transferred), and legibility (ability to be interpreted by a human). While these works provide guidance toward a necessary capability, its realization is an ongoing effort, due in part to the difficulty of generating relevant and meaningful summaries of complex controllers.

Researchers have identified Markov decision processes [33] as a promising basis for the design and implementation of these desired diagnostic and explanatory capabilities. Elizalde et al. [10] detailed a system for articulating the primary decision factors of a program, helping to direct an operator's attention to minimize failures or surprises. They accomplished this through an analysis of the principal variables composing the model's state space, simultaneously evaluating both a variable's impact on the utility function that the program is attempting to maximize and its impact on action selection at a given state. Khan et al. [19] introduce the notion of a minimally sufficient explanation for action selection at a given world state, using the fewest possible terms. Results from a human-subjects study confirmed that operators of their system utilized the advice and the minimally sufficient explanation it provided, resulting in positive subjective measures scores for the interaction. St. Clair and Matarić [38] investigated communication during a collaborative task in which a human and robot were in close proximity to one another, using pre-scripted self-narrative ("I'll do X"), role-allocative ("You do X"), and empathetic ("Oh no..." or "Great!") feedback. They found that feedback contributed to a significant decrease in task completion time, as well as more favorable subjective responses related to performing the collaborative task.

While these existing works enable certain classes of robot controller to describe or justify individual decisions from the perspective of a single state, techniques enabling general behavior summarization across state regions, independent of task or internal representation, are notably absent. Our work provides a mechanism that generalizes across application domains and controller implementations for modeling, summarizing, and communicating relevant behavioral information from robots to humans.

3. POLICY EXPLANATION

In collaborative settings, it is imperative for teammates to have compatible mental models of their task and the way in which it will be performed [28, 15, 5]. Particularly in scenarios in which humans and robots share a common environment, divergence in understanding can lead to unexpected behaviors, increasing injury risks and reducing team fluency. However, as a robot's behaviors become more complex, the ability to communicate its control logic becomes increasingly challenging. This work introduces a framework that can be used by robot programmers to provide the required level of transparency, enabling co-workers to synchronize their expectations and identify faulty behavior in robot controllers.

Given software control logic L (e.g., executable program code), a natural language inquiry Q, and a natural language response R, policy explanation requires a function $f : Q \times L \rightarrow R$. We constrain the space of these variables in our implementation for practical purposes, limiting the domain and range to values relevant to the task at hand. As further described in Section 4.2, code annotations are used as heuristics for specifying the program variables and functions to be incorporated into f, constraining the space of L to only include variables containing useful state information and functions that represent actions. Q is limited to the scope of the questions described in Section 6 regarding when behaviors will occur, which behaviors will occur in specified situations, and why certain behaviors did not occur. Finally, R is constrained to a template-based approach, explained in Section 5.

4. APPROACH

We frame our approach to policy explanation in a manner that facilitates the four operational goals outlined in Vessey's study on debugging processes [43]: problem identification, familiarity acquisition, program structure exploration, and error repair. Our proposed solution frames f as a composition of functions — a process summarized in Figure 1. With L, Q, and R as defined above, we introduce a set of question templates T (e.g., "When do you do {action}?") and binary classifiers to characterize aspects of the world state, known as predicates [11], C (e.g., "*Robot* is in *Loading Dock*"). We compute f through functions that: identify the question being posed and its arguments ($Identify\_question : Q \rightarrow T$), resolve the question template to a relevant set of program states ($Resolve\_states : T \times L \rightarrow \hat{L}, \hat{L} \subseteq L$), summarize the relevant attributes of these states into a concise representation ($Summarize\_attributes : T \times L \rightarrow C^n$), and, finally, compose these summaries into a natural language form that can be expressed to the inquiring human ($Compose\_summary : C^n \rightarrow R$). Thus, we define the following:

$$f = Compose\_summary \circ Summarize\_attributes \circ Resolve\_states \circ Identify\_question \quad (1)$$

4.1 Behavioral Modeling

We formulate a general diagnostic approach to behavior explanation that involves simultaneously learning a model of the environment (domain model) and the robot's underlying control logic (its policy). These models are learned from demonstration, during which observations are derived from information gained through inspection of running code (much like a software debugger). These observations are composed of annotations derived from the logging of function calls and their parameterizations alongside the current values of state variables at run-time. We compile the logged observations — both the domain and action models — into a single graphical model, capturing the important relational information between states and actions.

Given a unified domain and policy model, we frame the problem of behavior explanation as a four step process. First, a given query must be mapped to a *context*, or relevant set of states. This corresponds to the *Identify_question* and *Resolve_states* functions, where the input text is mapped to a query template and the query template is resolved to a set of states. Next, the relevant attributes of these states must be summarized and converted into a form interpretable by the interaction partner, corresponding to *Summarize_attributes* and *Compose_summary*. To make this natural language generation and interpretation tractable, we employ *communicable predicates*: Boolean classifiers similar to traditional STRIPS-style [11] planning predicates with associated natural language descriptions. It is through communicable predicates that our method is able to convert attributes from sets of states into natural language and vice versa.

We use the Markov decision process (MDP) framework as a basis for constructing the domain and policy models of the control software, described by the 4-tuple $(\mathbb{S}, \mathbb{A}, T, R)$ [40]. Within this framework, a domain is specified as a set of environment states $\mathbb{S}$. The actions available to an agent are specified in a set, $\mathbb{A}$. An agent in a state $s \in \mathbb{S}$ can select an action $a \in \mathbb{A}$, after which the agent transitions to another state $s' \in \mathbb{S}$ according to a probability distribution given by the transition function $T(s, a, s') = [0, 1]$. This transition results in a reward given by the reward function $R(s, a)$. A decision rule for selecting actions as a function of state is termed a policy $\pi : \mathbb{S} \times \mathbb{A} \longrightarrow [0, 1]$. An optimal policy, π^*, is the policy which maximizes total reward from every state of the MDP.

A state $s \in \mathbb{S}$ is a vector containing values for internal variables in the controller's logic. To mitigate an unnecessary, tremendous increase in state dimensionality, we describe a process for limiting the scope of $\mathbb{S}$ in Section 4.2. An action $a \in \mathbb{A}$ represents a parameterized function call from within the robot controller software, such as $move(\text{"}north\text{"}, 10)$. The transition dynamics T are learned from experience, connecting function calls (actions) with changes in the environment (program state).

4.2 Heuristics for Model Generation

The state space of program variables is likely to be too large to practically model purely through observation on any reasonable timescale. In order to accelerate our model learning, we introduce a set of heuristics that can be incorporated directly into the controller code without affecting its execution. We identify and introduce two important heuristics to accelerate model learning: one to provide a mechanism for specifying which variables should be tracked, and one to specify which functions are relevant actions. These heuristics take the form of self-modifying code added within the robot controller to track important variables and function calls. In keeping with the software debugger analogy for monitoring the robot controller's execution, these code-level modifications can intuitively be thought of as similar to function monitors or setting a variable watch, as they do not interfere with the code's normal function, but provide important usage information.

Reducing the dimensionality of the state space $\mathbb{S}$ is critical for minimizing model complexity. Toward this end, the first code-level heuristic we introduce reduces the amount of unnecessary program variables included. To accomplish this, we provide a wrapper for important program state variables. These variables are captured at each state snapshot taken during the modeling process (pre- and post-function call) and constitute the elements of the feature vectors represented as vertices in the generated MDP.

The second code-level heuristic is implemented as a series of function decorators[1], a form of metaprogramming that modifies functions at definition time, used to indicate important functions to be considered as actions within $\mathbb{A}$ (Figure 2). These indicators minimize the amount of noise in the learned transition function, allowing for more rapid convergence to a feasible domain and policy model. This decorator is intended for use on robot control functions that correspond to actions or effects in the physical world. Within our Python implementation, decorated functions are dynamically re-written at runtime to provide detailed execution logs, capturing the program state before and after function calls. Settable flags on the function decorators indicate whether to also capture the parameter set or any return values from the function call. In order

[1] https://en.wikipedia.org/wiki/Python_syntax_and_semantics

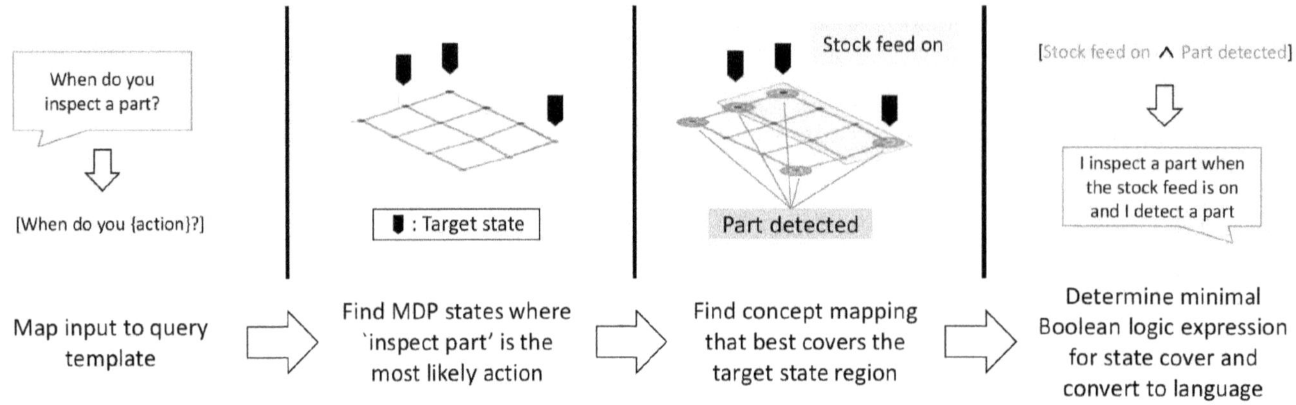

Figure 1: An illustration of our approach for mapping an action query to a policy explanation. First, the input query language is matched against pre-defined query templates. Then, a graph-search algorithm is run to find state regions fulfilling the query criteria. A set cover is found using logical combinations of communicable predicates. Finally, the cover is minimized and converted back to language via template.

```
@action(description="inspect the part",log_params=False,log_return=True)
def inspect_part(ptype,x,y,z,r,p,y):
    grasp = plan_grasp(ptype,x,y,z,r,p,y)
```

Figure 2: A snippet of code showing an example of a function decorator for the inspection task, annotating the inspect_part function in the robot's Python control program as a high level action.

to facilitate references to and from these functions that are more natural than the function names themselves, our implementation incorporates an optional parameter to specify a natural-language description to use instead.

As the control program executes, state information is recorded from the annotated variables before and after annotated function calls occur. Each time an annotated function is called, T is modified to reflect the observed (*state,action,state*) tuple. Actions are recorded as a combination of function name, serialized parameters, and serialized return value, depending on the parameters the decorator was initialized with, as seen in Figure 2. This process constructs an MDP from the observed code execution paths. To extend this observation-based model to work with previously unseen states, a simulator is required.

5. LANGUAGE GROUNDING

In order to provide interpretable explanations of an agent's needs, behaviors, or intentions, it is necessary to have a framework that can ground its output in terms that the system's interaction partners can understand. We use collections of boolean classifiers that we term *communicable predicates* to provide a meaningful abstraction over low-level information, such as feature vectors. These classifiers, when paired with string templates describing the meaning of true or false classifications, offer a means of translating internal knowledge into natural-language responses.

We identify three primary predicate types that may be necessary for expressing knowledge related to behavioral inquiries: general, robot-specific, and domain-specific. One example of a general, scenario-agnostic predicate that spans many application domains is a classifier that articulates a spatial relation — for example, the predicate "nearby(A,B)," which returns true when entity A is near to entity B and false otherwise, can be used across a variety of tasks or situations. Robot-specific predicates, such as 'isPowered(component)', which would return true if *component* were powered and false otherwise, may be required to allow an agent to communicate details about itself. Finally, there may be domain-specific characteristics that are not covered by general spatial relations or robot attributes — such as "isWidgetStockFeedOn()", which may relay information about a particular component of the robot's specialized environment. Importantly, the predicates that are used neither need to exist within the robot's code nor rely on input from the robot's sensors, as they are only used for grounding world state information in language.

5.1 Grounding State Regions

We approached the challenge of succinctly describing state regions as a minimal set cover problem, seeking the smallest logical expression of communicable predicates that precisely cover the target states. Algorithm 1 provides such a solution, resolving an arbitrary set of states into a natural language description by using a Boolean algebra over the space of defined predicates. States are projected onto the corners of the unit hypercube defined by the vector comprising predicate classification values (Algorithm 1, lines 7-8, 13-14). The resultant hypercube vertices are equivalent to disjunctive normal form (DNF) clauses, with predicate value assignments as literals.

DNF formulae are an ideal representation for describing combinations of predicates, providing a product-of-sums logical expression satisfying a state region descriptor function $f(s \in \mathbb{S}) \rightarrow \{0,1\}$. $f(s)$ is equal to 1 when predicate values for s fulfill the Boolean logic encoded in f and is 0 otherwise. Thus, each target state's hypercube projection is added as a minterm in f, causing the function to return 1 when tested on any state in the target region. For example, given the communicable predicate set $\mathbb{C} = \{C_1, C_2\}$, a formula that describes a region containing a state s_0 for which $\{C_1(s_0)$=True, $C_2(s_0)$=False$\}$ and a state s_1 for which $\{C_1(s_1)$=False, $C_2(s_1)$=False$\}$, the resulting f is specified as follows:

$$f(s) = (C_1 \neg C_2) + (\neg C_1 \neg C_2)$$

Once the region is expressed as a logical formula, our approach calls for application of the Quine-McCluskey algorithm [25, 17] (Algorithm 1, line 16) to perform Boolean logic minimization on the collection of minterms in f. Continuing the previous example, the resulting formula becomes the following:

$$f(s) = \neg C_2$$

As the Quine-McCluskey algorithm has memory and runtime requirements that are exponential according to the size of the predicate set, an approximate algorithm, such as ESPRESSO or its variants [8], can be used instead for large collections of predicates.

Algorithm 1: Convert State Region to Language

```
Input: Target state set S, Non-target state set S̄,
       Communicable predicate set C
Output: String representations for clauses in DNF Formula of
        S grounded in elements of C
assert S ∩ S̄ = ∅;
include_list ← { };
exclude_list ← { };
foreach s ∈ S do
    state_val = 0;
    i = 0;
    foreach c ∈ C do
        state_val |= (c(s) == True) << i++;
    end
    include_list ← include_list ∪ state_val;
end
foreach s ∈ S̄ do
    state_val = 0;
    i = 0;
    foreach c ∈ C do
        state_val |= (c(s) == True) << i++;
    end
    exclude_list ← exclude_list ∪ state_val;
end
qm_minimization ← Quine_McCluskey(ones=include_list,
  zeros=exclude_list);
clauses ← [];
foreach minterm ∈ qm_minimization do
    str ← '';
    foreach literal ∈ minterm do
        if literal is False then str += c.negative_string;
        else str += c.positive_string;
        str += ' and ';
    end
    clauses.append(str);
end
return 'or '.join(clauses);
```

With a minimized logical form, our algorithm generates explanations through application of predicate-specific string templates to each element of the formula. Consider two predicates, X and Y, representing whether a robot is active or idle and whether the factory line is running or not, respectively. Given the logical product-of-sums output $X * \neg Y + \neg X$ or equivalent logical expression $(X \wedge \neg Y) \vee (\neg X)$ representing conditions under which a robot performs a critical behavior, natural-language templates allow our algorithm to verbalize these outputs, producing outputs like "*The robot is idle* and *the widget is not present* or *the robot is active*."

Our formulation also affords the ability to quantify linguistic overstatement and understatement, mapping to false positive and false negative rates, respectively. A robot can use this information to modulate its interaction partners' confidence in its output, as overstatements and understatements provide upper and lower bounds on the conditions being approximated by the generated logical expression of predicates.

6. QUERIES FOR POLICY ANALYSIS

We focused on a set of question types derived from a survey of literature related to human-computer interaction and software debugging, fulfilling expert-derived debugging criteria [43]. These

Figure 3: Visualization of an inspection task for a robot on an assembly line, used as a representative example for motivating our selected query types. When a part is loaded onto the conveyor belt, the robot receives a stock feed signal and must locate and pick the part before it is out of range, inspect it, and place it back on the conveyor.

questions allow for insight into when a robot will perform a behavior, identification of a robot's behaviors under specified conditions, and explanation of the differences between a robot's demonstrated behavior and its expected behavior. We identified a query template, representative use case, and response resolution algorithm for each question type. In order to build intuition about situations in which our selected queries are useful, we grounded our examples in a scenario in which an industrial robot is tasked with inspecting parts on a conveyor belt cued by a stock feed signal (Figure 3).

6.1 Identifying Conditions for Actions

We utilized the template "When [do | will] you {action}?" to identify queries related to specifying conditions under which a particular action would be executed. Once the relevant regions of state space are identified, Algorithm 1 can summarize them using natural language (for example, "When will you pick up the widget?"). Given a reasonable specification of language templates for robot actions (e.g., *pick(x)* → "pick up x"), we can functionally resolve the intention of the query to "Describe the states where the most likely action is *pick('widget')*." Algorithm 2 describes the process for identifying the relevant state region to be described in the query response. Our algorithm, given an appropriate library of communicable predicates, produces the response, "I *get the widget* when *the stock feed signal is on and my camera has detected a widget and the widget is within reach*."

Once a state region is identified[1], it can be summarized via Algorithm 1 and inserted into the following template: "I perform {action} in {region}." Explanation size can be bounded by imposing a threshold on the number of descriptive clauses returned by Algorithm 1 (as in Algorithm 4 lines 6-7), with the queried agent providing a default response indicating the infeasibility of answering the question (e.g., "I perform {action} in too many contexts to succinctly describe.").

6.2 Explaining Differences in Expectation

We utilized the template "Why (didn't | aren't) you {action}?" to identify queries related to divergence in expected and observed behaviors. For example, if the robot in Figure 3 fails to pick a part up off the conveyor belt, a collaborator may ask "Why didn't

[1]For domains involving large state spaces where full enumeration is infeasible, sampling based approaches can provide substitutions for V in our query algorithms.

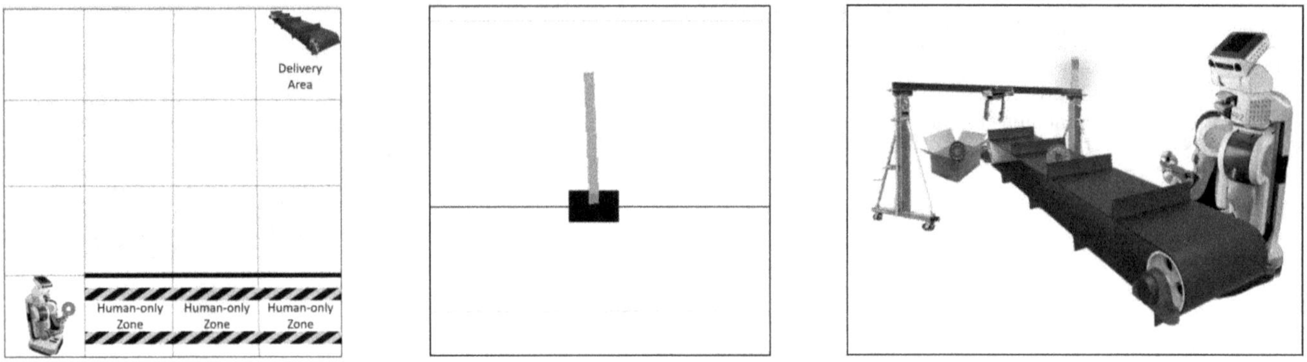

Figure 4: Visualizations of each application domain evaluated in Table 1. Left: A GridWorld-style parts delivery task, in which a robot must pick and deliver parts whilst avoiding human-only areas. Middle: The CartPole stabilization task [7], wherein a robot must attempt to balance and stabilize a pole placed on the middle of a mobile cart. Right: A parts inspection task, in which an inspection robot cued by a stock feed signal must locate and inspect parts placed by a separate loading robot.

Algorithm 2: Identify Dominant-action State Region

Input: Behavioral Model $G = \{V, E\}$, Target Action a
Output: Set of target states S_{π^a} where a_t is the dominant action, Set of non-target states $S_{\pi^* \setminus a}$
$S_{\pi^a} \leftarrow \{\}$;
$S_{\pi^* \setminus a} \leftarrow \{\}$;
foreach $s \in V$ **do**
  $a^* \leftarrow$ most frequent action executed from s;
  if $a^* == a$ **then** $S_{\pi^a} \leftarrow S_{\pi^a} \cup s$;
  else $S_{\pi^* \setminus a} \leftarrow S_{\pi^* \setminus a} \cup s$;
end
return $S_{\pi^a}, S_{\pi^* \setminus a}$;

Algorithm 3: Identify Behavioral Divergences

Input: Behavioral Model $G = \{V, E\}$, Target Action a, Previous state s_p, Distance threshold D_{const}
Output: Explanation of difference between current state and state region where a_t is performed, explanation of where a_t is performed locally.
$S_{\pi^a} \leftarrow \{\}$;
$S_{\pi^* \setminus a} \leftarrow \{\}$;
foreach $D \in \{1, ..., D_{const}\}$ **do**
  foreach $s \in \{v \in V \mid distance(v, s_p) \leq D\}$ **do**
    $a^* \leftarrow$ most frequent action executed from s;
    if $a^* == a$ **then** $S_{\pi^a} \leftarrow S_{\pi^a} \cup s$;
    else $S_{\pi^* \setminus a} \leftarrow S_{\pi^* \setminus a} \cup s$;
  end
end
expected_region $\leftarrow$ describe($S_{\pi^a}, S_{\pi^* \setminus a}, C$);
current_region $\leftarrow$ describe($\{s_p\}, S_{\pi^a}, C$);
return diff(expected_region, current_region), expected_region;

you inspect the part?" In this case, an explanation is desired that characterizes the difference between the current state and nearby states where the indicated action is performed. In Algorithm 3, pseudocode is provided to extract and characterize the difference between the current state and state regions where the desired behavior occurs. The *describe* function is specified in Algorithm 1.

Algorithm 3 outputs a list of predicate values that differ between the robot's previous state and nearby states where the desired behavior occurs. In our implementation, we utilized the template "I didn't {action} because {difference between current state and states where action is executed}. I {action} when {action region description}." to communicate these differences. For example, consider the case of a stock feed signal malfunction during the part inspection scenario (Figure 3), wherein a part is both present on the conveyor belt and detected by the robot, but the stock feed signal is off. Using the predicates defined in Section 7.3, this query type produces the following output: "I didn't *inspect the part* because *the stock feed signal is off*. I *inspect the part* when *the stock feed signal is on and I have detected a part and the part is within reach*." facilitating rapid fault diagnosis.

6.3 Understanding Situational Behavior

While the previous query type produces explanations for behavior that does not match expectations, a more proactive approach would involve communicating policy details in advance. The third and final query type we addressed is the inverse of the first: a means of summarizing how a robot will behave under specific circumstances. We used the template "What will you do when {DNF state region description}?" to designate these queries. This allows a collaborator to ask a variety of safety- and productivity-critical questions, such as "What will you do when *a human is near you*?" or "What will you do when *the stock feed signal is on and a part is detected*?" Algorithm 4 provides a description for each action type typically performed within the provided state region description. These descriptions are then individually applied to the template, "I {action} when {state region description}."

With respect to the first example inquiring about a nearby human, given a "humans nearby" predicate, if Algorithm 4 returns an empty set ($descriptions = \emptyset$) our system would generate a standard response, "I perform no action under those conditions," helping to confirm the safety of a human entering its work cell. For the second example, assuming the robot had the ability to signal its human co-workers for assistance, our approach may return, "I will *inspect the part* when *the part is within reach*. I will *contact an associate for assistance* when *the widget is not within reach*."

7. CASE STUDIES

We report results for three representative application domains that cover three different types of robot controller. For each domain, we provide a description of the environment, the controller implementation (and corresponding state space), and the predicate library we defined. We report algorithm output for each descriptive query type, providing autonomously generated policy summaries

Algorithm 4: Characterize Situational Behavior

Input: Behavioral Model $G = \{V, E\}$, Communicable Predicate Library C, State region description d, Max action threshold $cluster\_max$

Output: Explanation of policy behavior in d per action and its accompanying state region

```
S ← dict();
descriptions ← dict();
DNF_description ← convert_to_DNF_formula(d, C);
foreach s ∈ {v ∈ V | test_dnf(v,DNF_description) is True }
do
    S[π(s)] ← S[π(s)] ∪ s;
    if |S| > cluster_max then
        return too_many_actions_error
    end
end
foreach a ∈ S do
    descriptions[a] ← describe(S[a], V \ S[a], C);
end
return descriptions;
```

for each controller. We report results for a parts delivery task (GridWorld [40]) to show application to general planning tasks with discrete state spaces, a stabilization task (CartPole [6]) to show application to control policies with continuous state spaces, and a multi-agent parts inspection task in which agents did not communicate to showcase application within a complex dynamic environment.

For each domain, we detail the training process for the robot's controller. Once a final controller was obtained, we froze the operating parameters and began logging any annotated function calls that occurred, building our external graphical model for querying. We show that, for each application domain, our approach was able to capture and explain the robot's policy, allowing collaborators to extract relevant behavior summaries. To generate the summaries in Table 1, we concatenate results from queries of "When do you {action}?" for each action in the domain.

7.1 Delivery Task

During the parts delivery task (Figure 4-left), the robot began in the bottom-left position of a 4x4 GridWorld and was required to pick up a part at that location, navigate to the delivery area, and place the part on the conveyor belt, while avoiding any zones designated "human-only." The world reset and a negative reward was applied if the robot delivered the part anywhere other than the delivery area, or if an episode extended beyond 15 actions. A negative reward was also applied to any actions inside a human-only zone, but the world did not reset. Positive rewards were applied if the robot successfully delivered the part, and the world was then reset. Invalid actions, such as navigating into a wall, resulted in no state change.

The delivery task's state space included the robot's position on the grid and whether it was carrying a part. The robot had six available actions, each implemented as a separate function (for ease of code annotation) in the controller program: "pick," "place," "north," "south," "east," and "west." We used nine predicates, encoded as binary classifiers over the state space: "near human zone," "at human zone," "near delivery area," "at delivery area," "north of goal," "south of goal," "east of goal," "west of goal," and "has part."

Reinforcement learning was used to train a tabular agent policy with $\epsilon-$greedy exploration ($\epsilon = .75$). Once the agent could successfully complete the task more than 90% of the time, we ceased further training and froze the model parameters. With a mathematical model governing the robot's action decisions, we applied our code-level annotations and built our queryable model of the robot over the course of 250 action observations.

7.2 Stabilization Task

During the stabilization task (Figure 4-middle), an agent operating in a continuous state space attempted to balance a pole on a moving base. The task state was represented using a 4-tuple encoding cart position, cart velocity, pole angle, and pole angular velocity. The agent had two available actions — move left or move right — which affected the momentum of both the cart and pole. Each episode began with a random initialization of the cart and pole positions, with zero initial velocity. We trained a 2-layer, fully connected neural network with a rectified linear activation function to approximate the Q-function, producing a difficult-to-interpret controller capable of solving the CartPole domain. Each episode lasted up to 200 steps or until the pole fell.

We defined 10 predicates to describe states in this domain: "pole falling left/right," "pole stabilizing left/right," "pole standing up," "cart moving left/right," "cart positioned far left/right," and "cart near middle." The predicates describing a pole falling indicate that the pole is off-center and has a velocity driving it away from an upright position. Predicates describing the pole as stabilizing indicate an off-center pole moving toward an upright position.

Our method was able to summarize a successful policy that was approximated with initially random parameters, despite the occasional presence of incorrect actions taken by the controller, producing approximately correct explanations with overstatement and understatement. The description provided was close to the expert description of a successful task strategy (Table 1).

7.3 Inspection Task

We implemented the inspection task used as the running example in Section 6 to motivate our query types, depicted in Figures 3 and 4-right. The state space for this task included the part's 2D position on the conveyor belt when in sight of the robot (otherwise, a default value of -1,-1 was reported), the robot's head orientation (an angle between -60 and -20 degrees from the robot's axial plane), and a Boolean stock feed variable that indicated whether the robot should expect a part to be in sight. The head orientation of the robot was divided into three ranges (low, middle, and high), and dictated whether a part was detected based on its position on the conveyor belt. Any orientation in the "high" position ($(-30, -20]$) allowed detection for parts in the top 20% of the belt, the "middle" position ($[-50, -30]$) enabled detection for the middle 60% of the belt, and the "low" position ($[-60, 50)$) enabled detection for parts in the bottom 20% of the belt. The robot's starting head orientation was -40. The true position of the part was a hidden variable, dictated by its placement by another robot in the environment. Once a part was placed on the conveyor belt, the stock feed signal was activated. The part was not detectable to the inspection robot for a random duration between 1 and 3 timesteps after it was placed. Due to the conveyor belt moving the part down the line, the inspection robot had a window of four timesteps (plus the 1-3 timestep delay) to detect and inspect a part once the stock feed signal was activated before the part would advance beyond the robot's reach, causing task failure. Once a part was inspected, the stock feed signal was deactivated.

The robot had four actions it could take: "inspect part," "look high," "look middle," and "look low." The "inspect part" action failed if it was taken when the part was not detected (e.g., at position -1,-1) or if it was out of reach, which only occurred if it was

Domain	Expert Description	Autonomous Description
Delivery	Move north when south of a delivery area and holding the part. Move east when west of a delivery area and not near a human zone. Move west when in a human zone. Pick the part when near a human zone and west of a delivery area and south of the delivery area. Place the part when at a delivery zone.	I move north when I am south of a delivery area and have the part. I move east when I am west of a delivery area and have the part and not near a human zone. I move west when I am at a human zone. I do not perform move south. I pick the part when I am near a human zone and west of the delivery area and south of the delivery area. I place the part when I am at the delivery zone.
Stabilization	Move left when the pole is falling left and the pole is not stabilizing right. Move right when the pole is falling right and the pole is not stabilizing left.	I move left when the cart is not at the far left and the pole is falling left. I move right when the cart is at the far left or when the cart is in the middle and the pole is falling right or when the cart is in the far right and the pole is stabilizing left.
Inspection	Inspect the part when the stock feed is on and a part is detected and the part is reachable. Look low when looking in the middle and the stock feed is on and a part is not detected. Look high when looking low and the stock feed is on and a part is not detected. Look in the middle when the stock feed is off.	I inspect the part when the stock feed is on and I can reach the part. I look low when the stock feed is on and I have not detected a part and I am looking in the middle. I look in the middle when the stock feed is off or when the stock feed is on and I have not detected a part and I am looking high. I look high when the stock feed is on and I have not detected a part and I am looking low.

Table 1: Autonomously generated policy summaries learned from the three application domains, presented alongside expert summaries of successful solutions given in terms of the available predicates for each domain.

placed in the top 10% of the conveyor belt. The "look high", "look middle", and "look low" actions rotated the robot's head to pre-set positions of $-20, -40, and -60$ degrees respectively. We implemented six predicates for abstracting over the state space: "stock feed on," "part detected," "part reachable," "looking high," "looking middle," and "looking low." The robot controller for this task was manually coded with standard conditional logic, employing a middle/low/high scanning pattern when searching for parts to inspect after the stock feed signal was activated. Our method accurately summarized the behavior of the policy defined by the Python program that controlled the inspection robot (Table 1).

Given that this domain contained a potential failure case that was outside the inspection robot's control, we additionally probed why an action did not occur in order to gain insight into unexpected behavior. We introduced a fault into the controller of robot loading the conveyor belt, such that it placed its parts only in the top 10% of the belt, out of reach of the inspection robot. At the time step after the robot detected the part but did not inspect it, we queried our model with the following: "Why didn't you inspect the part?" Using Algorithm 3, the model was able to identify the issue, responding with the following: "*I did not inspect the part because I cannot reach the part. I inspect the part when the stock feed is on and I have detected a part and I can reach the part.*" This ability to actively probe the robot's controller facilitates the isolation of factors contributing to task failures.

8. CONCLUSIONS AND FUTURE WORK

In this work, we have presented a novel mechanism for modeling and explaining robot control policies. Our methods allow non-experts to gain insights into the operation of autonomous agents and to better calibrate their expectations of the agents' behaviors, making robot controllers more transparent. The approach we present generalizes to arbitrary control logic, allowing for wide application across a variety of contexts.

By introducing an abstraction over the state space with communicable predicates, we present a novel framing of the explanation process as a minimal set cover and subsequent Boolean logic minimization problem. As a result of this, we are able to produce succinct behavioral explanations grounded in language that humans can understand. The algorithms we introduce allow collaborators to extract useful pieces of information without requiring a full understanding of an agent's logic, as well as facilitate the debugging of aberrant behaviors by providing a mechanism to explain differences between the conditions under which particular actions occur. We demonstrated the applicability of our method within three representative robotics domains using three different types of controllers: a tabular Q-Learner, a neural network based Q-Learner, and a controller based on hard-coded conditional logic.

A natural extension to the method we describe is to perform guided policy learning, using parsed natural language descriptions of valid task strategies to map advice down to state regions (as rewards or penalties) for biasing exploration during policy learning. Autonomous symbol abstraction techniques [16, 27] may also be applied to the learned domain MDPs, reducing the programmer's workload with respect to annotating actions within the control software. We also see applications of this work to human behavior explanation, as inverse reinforcement learning can be used to learn a policy which can then be explained with our technique.

9. REFERENCES

[1] P. Abbeel and A. Y. Ng. Apprenticeship learning via inverse reinforcement learning. In *Proceedings of the twenty-first international conference on Machine learning*, page 1. ACM, 2004.

[2] G. Antoniol, G. Canfora, G. Casazza, A. De Lucia, and E. Merlo. Recovering traceability links between code and documentation. *Software Engineering, IEEE Transactions on*, 28(10):970–983, 2002.

[3] T. Ball, M. Naik, and S. K. Rajamani. From symptom to cause: localizing errors in counterexample traces. In *ACM SIGPLAN Notices*, volume 38, pages 97–105. ACM, 2003.

[4] T. Ball and S. K. Rajamani. The slam project: debugging system software via static analysis. In *ACM SIGPLAN Notices*, volume 37, pages 1–3. ACM, 2002.

[5] J. Baraglia, M. Cakmak, Y. Nagai, R. Rao, and M. Asada. Initiative in robot assistance during collaborative task

execution. In *2016 11th ACM/IEEE International Conference on Human-Robot Interaction (HRI)*, pages 67–74. IEEE, 2016.

[6] A. G. Barto, R. S. Sutton, and C. W. Anderson. Neuronlike adaptive elements that can solve difficult learning control problems. *IEEE transactions on systems, man, and cybernetics*, (5):834–846, 1983.

[7] G. Brockman, V. Cheung, L. Pettersson, J. Schneider, J. Schulman, J. Tang, and W. Zaremba. Openai gym, 2016.

[8] O. Coudert. Two-level logic minimization: an overview. *Integration, the VLSI journal*, 17(2):97–140, 1994.

[9] S. Devin and R. Alami. An implemented theory of mind to improve human-robot shared plans execution. In *The Eleventh ACM/IEEE International Conference on Human Robot Interation*, pages 319–326. IEEE Press, 2016.

[10] F. Elizalde, L. E. Sucar, M. Luque, J. Diez, and A. Reyes. Policy explanation in factored markov decision processes. In *Proceedings of the 4th European Workshop on Probabilistic Graphical Models (PGM 2008)*, pages 97–104, 2008.

[11] R. E. Fikes and N. J. Nilsson. Strips: A new approach to the application of theorem proving to problem solving. *Artificial intelligence*, 2(3-4):189–208, 1971.

[12] S. Fitzgerald, G. Lewandowski, R. McCauley, L. Murphy, B. Simon, L. Thomas, and C. Zander. Debugging: finding, fixing and flailing, a multi-institutional study of novice debuggers. *Computer Science Education*, 18(2):93–116, 2008.

[13] B. Hailpern and P. Santhanam. Software debugging, testing, and verification. *IBM Systems Journal*, 41(1):4–12, 2002.

[14] B. Hayes and B. Scassellati. Challenges in shared-environment human-robot collaboration. In *Collaborative Manipulation Workshop at the 8th ACM/IEEE International Conference on Human-Robot Interaction.*, volume 8, page 8, 2013.

[15] B. Hayes and B. Scassellati. Effective robot teammate behaviors for supporting sequential manipulation tasks. In *IEEE/RSJ International Conference on Intelligent Robots and Systems (IROS)*, 2015.

[16] B. Hayes and B. Scassellati. Autonomously constructing hierarchical task networks for planning and human-robot collaboration. In *International Conference on Robotics and Automation (ICRA)*. IEEE, 2016.

[17] T. K. Jain, D. S. Kushwaha, and A. K. Misra. Optimization of the quine-mccluskey method for the minimization of the boolean expressions. In *Autonomic and Autonomous Systems, 2008. ICAS 2008. Fourth International Conference on*, pages 165–168. IEEE, 2008.

[18] L. P. Kaelbling, M. L. Littman, and A. W. Moore. Reinforcement learning: A survey. *Journal of artificial intelligence research*, 4:237–285, 1996.

[19] O. Z. Khan, P. Poupart, and J. P. Black. Minimal sufficient explanations for factored markov decision processes. In *ICAPS*, 2009.

[20] J. Kober, J. A. Bagnell, and J. Peters. Reinforcement learning in robotics: A survey. *The International Journal of Robotics Research*, page 0278364913495721, 2013.

[21] P. Koopman. A case study of toyota unintended acceleration and software safety. 2014.

[22] J. D. Lee and K. A. See. Trust in automation: Designing for appropriate reliance. *Human Factors: The Journal of the Human Factors and Ergonomics Society*, 46(1):50–80, 2004.

[23] X. Leroy. Formal verification of a realistic compiler. *Communications of the ACM*, 52(7):107–115, 2009.

[24] Z. C. Lipton, D. C. Kale, C. Elkan, R. Wetzell, S. Vikram, J. McAuley, R. C. Wetzell, Z. Ji, B. Narayaswamy, C.-I. Wang, et al. The mythos of model interpretability. *IEEE Spectrum*, 2016.

[25] E. J. McCluskey. Minimization of boolean functions. *Bell system technical Journal*, 35(6):1417–1444, 1956.

[26] V. Mnih, K. Kavukcuoglu, D. Silver, A. A. Rusu, J. Veness, M. G. Bellemare, A. Graves, M. Riedmiller, A. K. Fidjeland, G. Ostrovski, et al. Human-level control through deep reinforcement learning. *Nature*, 518(7540):529–533, 2015.

[27] A. Mohseni-Kabir, C. Rich, S. Chernova, C. L. Sidner, and D. Miller. Interactive hierarchical task learning from a single demonstration. In *Proceedings of the Tenth Annual ACM/IEEE International Conference on Human-Robot Interaction*, pages 205–212. ACM, 2015.

[28] S. Nikolaidis and J. Shah. Human-robot cross-training: computational formulation, modeling and evaluation of a human team training strategy. In *Proceedings of the 8th ACM/IEEE international conference on Human-robot interaction*, pages 33–40. IEEE Press, 2013.

[29] M. Oudah, V. Babushkin, T. Chenlinangjia, and J. W. Crandall. Learning to interact with a human partner. In *Proceedings of the Tenth Annual ACM/IEEE International Conference on Human-Robot Interaction*, pages 311–318. ACM, 2015.

[30] R. Parasuraman and V. Riley. Humans and automation: Use, misuse, disuse, abuse. *Human Factors: The Journal of the Human Factors and Ergonomics Society*, 39(2):230–253, 1997.

[31] C. Parnin and A. Orso. Are automated debugging techniques actually helping programmers? In *Proceedings of the 2011 International Symposium on Software Testing and Analysis*, pages 199–209. ACM, 2011.

[32] L. Perlmutter, E. Kernfeld, and M. Cakmak. Situated language understanding with human-like and visualization-based transparency. In *Robotics: Science and Systems (RSS)*, 2016.

[33] M. L. Puterman. *Markov decision processes: discrete stochastic dynamic programming*. John Wiley & Sons, 2014.

[34] M. Renieres and S. P. Reiss. Fault localization with nearest neighbor queries. In *Automated Software Engineering, 2003. Proceedings. 18th IEEE International Conference on*, pages 30–39. IEEE, 2003.

[35] M. T. Ribeiro, S. Singh, and C. Guestrin. " why should i trust you?": Explaining the predictions of any classifier. *arXiv preprint arXiv:1602.04938*, 2016.

[36] V. D. Silva, D. Kroening, and G. Weissenbacher. A survey of automated techniques for formal software verification. *Computer-Aided Design of Integrated Circuits and Systems, IEEE Transactions on*, 27(7):1165–1178, 2008.

[37] W. D. Smart and L. P. Kaelbling. Effective reinforcement learning for mobile robots. In *Robotics and Automation, 2002. Proceedings. ICRA'02. IEEE International Conference on*, volume 4, pages 3404–3410. IEEE, 2002.

[38] A. St Clair and M. Mataric. How robot verbal feedback can improve team performance in human-robot task collaborations. In *Proceedings of the Tenth Annual ACM/IEEE International Conference on Human-Robot Interaction*, pages 213–220. ACM, 2015.

[39] K. Stubbs, P. J. Hinds, and D. Wettergreen. Autonomy and common ground in human-robot interaction: A field study. *IEEE Intelligent Systems*, 22(2):42–50, 2007.

[40] R. S. Sutton and A. G. Barto. *Reinforcement Learning: An Introduction*. The MIT Press, 1998.

[41] W. R. Swartout and J. D. Moore. Explanation in second generation expert systems. In *Second generation expert systems*, pages 543–585. Springer, 1993.

[42] S. Tellex, R. Knepper, A. Li, D. Rus, and N. Roy. Asking for help using inverse semantics. In *Robotics: Science and systems*, volume 2, page 3, 2014.

[43] I. Vessey. Expertise in debugging computer programs: A process analysis. *International Journal of Man-Machine Studies*, 23(5):459–494, 1985.

[44] V. H. Visschers, R. M. Meertens, W. W. Passchier, and N. N. De Vries. Probability information in risk communication: a review of the research literature. *Risk Analysis*, 29(2):267–287, 2009.

[45] N. Wang, D. V. Pynadath, and S. G. Hill. The impact of pomdp-generated explanations on trust and performance in human-robot teams. In *Proceedings of the 2016 International Conference on Autonomous Agents & Multiagent Systems*, pages 997–1005. International Foundation for Autonomous Agents and Multiagent Systems, 2016.

[46] E. A. Waters, N. D. Weinstein, G. A. Colditz, and K. Emmons. Formats for improving risk communication in medical tradeoff decisions. *Journal of health communication*, 11(2):167–182, 2006.

[47] K. W. Wong and H. Kress-Gazit. Let's talk: Autonomous conflict resolution for robots carrying out individual high-level tasks in a shared workspace. In *Robotics and Automation (ICRA), 2015 IEEE International Conference on*, pages 339–345. IEEE, 2015.

[48] L. R. Ye and P. E. Johnson. The impact of explanation facilities on user acceptance of expert systems advice. *Mis Quarterly*, pages 157–172, 1995.

Is a Robot a Better Walking Partner If It Associates Utterances with Visual Scenes?

Ryusuke Totsuka[1,2] Satoru Satake[1] Takayuki Kanda[1] Michita Imai[1,2]

[1]ATR Intelligent Robotics and Communication Laboratories
2-2-2 Hikaridai, Seika-cho, Souraku-gun, Kyoto, Japan

[2]Keio University
3-14-1 Hiyoshi, Kouhoku-ku, Yokohama, Kanagawa, Japan

{totsuka, satoru, kanda, michita}@atr.jp

ABSTRACT

We aim to develop a walking partner robot with the capability to select small-talk topics that are associative to visual scenes. We first collected video sequences from five different locations and prepared a dataset about small-talk topics associated to visual scenes. Then we developed a technique to associate the visual scenes with the small-talk topics. We converted visual scenes into lists of words using an off-the-shelf vision library and formed a topic space with a Latent Dirichlet Allocation (LDA) method in which a list of words is transformed to a topic vector. Finally, the system selects the most similar utterance in the topic vectors. We tested our developed technique with a dataset, which successfully selected 72% appropriate utterances, and conducted a user study outdoors where participants took a walk with a small robot on their shoulder and engaged in small talk. We confirmed that the participants more highly perceived the robot with our developed technique because it selected appropriate utterances than a robot that randomly selected utterances. Further, they also felt that the former type of robot is a better walking partner.

CCS Concepts

•Human-centered computing → Empirical studies in interaction design •Computing methodologies → Robotic planning

Keywords

Association of utterance and visual scene, walking partner robot

1. INTRODUCTION

Walking is a common human activity, sometimes alone, but often with others. Future social robots are expected to serve as companions and partners, hence we expect that people will walk with robots in the future. In fact, in many scenes people are already walking with robots. For instance, walking with a robot can function as rehabilitation [1] and physical therapy [2]. Robots move with people as museum guides [3-5], shopping guides [6], tour guides [7], passenger guides [8], shopping assistants [9, 10], and helpers in nursing home [11].

While walking, we often engage in small talk. We might walk around different locations, such as a park, an office building, or a shopping mall. If a robot walks with a person, does it matter where they talk? Does it matter what they see?

HRI '17, March 06-09, 2017, Vienna, Austria.
© 2017 ACM. ISBN 978-1-4503-4336-7/17/03...$15.00
DOI: http://dx.doi.org/10.1145/2909824.3020212

Figure 1. Small talk while walking with a robot

Conversation topics are often *associative* to visual scenes. For instance, in a shopping mall, we might engage in conversation about items that we might buy or relate recent good/bad shopping experiences: "When there are many shops, I'm tempted to do more shopping." We discuss such topics because we know these utterances are relevant to the current scenes.

However, what if a robot tried to engage in such small talk? Without an appropriate capability to *associate* topics with scenes, it would engage in bizarre conversations. For instance, when we go hiking in a beautiful nature spot, if a robot talks about shopping (Figure 1), "What are your favorite shops?" or "I like shopping because I'm excited to see new items," we might feel discouraged.

We believe that where they talk and what they see is relevant. This belief motivates us to develop a technique that *associates* visual scenes with the topics of small talk. In this study, we answer the following research questions:

- How can we build a robot that selects topics that are *associative* to the current visual scene?
- While walking with a robot, do we perceive whether a topic selected by a robot with the above capability is *appropriate* for the current scene?
- Does this capability make the robot a *better walking partner*?

2. RELATED WORKS

2.1 Interaction While Walking

Many HRI studies have addressed interaction when either a person or a robot moves, such as spatial formation and proximity [12-15], passing behavior [16, 17], and approaching behavior [18-20]. Some studies addressed the interaction while people are walking, although they focused on navigation algorithms as a natural way to follow people [21], adjusting a robot's speed [22], and the establishment of walking formations [23]. In some of the above studies, the robots talked to their users, although the conversation contents were pre-scripted and chosen independently of the scene or the robot's location.

Garden Harbor Shopping mall Parking lot Corridor

Figure 2. Examples of visual scenes from five locations in dataset

In other robot applications, a location-based approach is used for topic selection. Of course, the conversation topic is altered depending on the location. Museum guide robots ([3-5]) offered explanations about exhibits. A shopping guide robot explained targeted shop items [6], and a shopping assistant chatted about items near it [10]. Common to these applications, the contents were pre-scripted and associated with the locations; however, such an approach is only applicable when a robot is always operated in a limited space.

If robots are used anywhere in the future, applying such a location-association approach will be difficult. Instead, we develop a mechanism where a topic is selected based on visual scenes. With this approach, users will probably use their robots at various locations, including parks and walkways nearby their houses. In the past, few studies have been conducted on the mechanism that allows a robot to choose a conversation topic based on visual scenes.

2.2 Chatting with Robots

Chatting with robots has often been considered in the literature. A series of studies used non-verbal factors. For instance, gaze is crucial for natural interaction [24], improves performance [25], denotes an establishment of engagements [26], establishes comfortable turn-taking [27], and controls participation roles [28].

Other studies have addressed topic selection for robots or agents. Chatting and topic selection is well studied in linguistic research, with experiments ranging from early seminal works [29] to some more advanced studies that use topic models [30]. It is known to be important for robots to change explanations that depend on the user's knowledge [31]. Small talk [32] is critical for building relations with agents as well as understanding past interactions [33] and empathetic utterances [34]. Maas et al. developed a robot that tracks conversation topics from multimodal input and is aware of the current topic and can respond to changes [35]. Even though such studies suggest the importance of monitoring and selecting appropriate conversation topics, few studies have incorporated visual scenes into topic selection.

Although not focused on visual scenes, location-aware systems in which coordinates in the real world obtained by GPS or other positioning devices are used for information-providing (e.g., Siri). Robots can also chose topics with a location-based approach (e.g., [3-6, 10], discussed in Section 2.1). However, since such an approach requires that contents be pre-defined for the coordinates of specific locations, applying it to partner robots is difficult because they need to go to any anonymous location with users.

3. DATASET

We assume that a robot will learn from small-talk contents by observing human conversations. To imitate such situations, we collected videos from a person's view while walking and prepared small-talk contents that might be broached on such walks.

3.1 Method

We collected various scenes and targeted daily anonymous locations where people might walk with others. To visually cover different spots, we chose five locations: a garden, a harbor, a shopping mall, a parking lot, and an indoor corridor. Figure 2 shows an example of the view from each of these locations. For each one, we took videos for five minutes while walking. The camera direction was fixed in the walking direction.

Then we created small-talk contents for the video images. We used the first half of each video for this and kept the latter half to evaluate the performance (Section 4.6). For each six seconds of the segment (a sufficient duration for making one utterance), we prepared one sentence to be spoken while someone walked in the segment. For each segment, we retrieved three images and associated a sentence to them to make the association robust to the deviations in the visual scenes. We retrieved 75 images from each video (one image every two seconds) and prepared 25 sentences. We prepared 125 sentences for 375 images from the five videos.

As we prepared the sentences, we were careful about three issues. First, we prepared sentences that fit the visual scenes. Second, we prepared each sentence to be independent from previous sentences because we planned to use them independently later. Third, because we planned to use them in the experiment, we made sentences that had similar quality to avoid sentences that were either too fun or too boring. To accomplish this, we conducted a preliminary evaluation, in which text contents were displayed to human participants and compared across five different locations to confirm that they had similar levels of enjoyableness.

3.2 Examples of Contents in Dataset

Figure 3 shows an example of the sequences of the images and the associated utterances included in our dataset. The images are from the video of the garden. For every three images, one utterance is associated. Note that the utterances were prepared in Japanese. We used an off-the-shelf translation engine to convert them into English for subsequent processing. However, because such machine translation often yielded confusing sentences, we modified the translated sentences for our paper.

4. SYSTEM

4.1 Choice of Algorithms

Various approaches implement the association of ideas. One approach is keyword matching, which is widely used for search engines. For instance, when a scene has trees, we can search for utterances that include the term 'tree.' However, we often talk about topics that are associative without being directly mapped. For instance, we might ask, "Have you gone hiking recently?" in a visual scene with trees (Figure. 3, for example). We aim to achieve such associations.

Of course, associations are not random. A tendency exists where some utterances co-occur with some visual scenes. The question is how to learn such bias in co-occurrence from the data. Because there are established methods for text-text association, which

Image			...
Utterance	Surrounded by many trees, I feel cool and comfortable.	Have you gone hiking recently?	...

Figure 3. Examples of associations (associated images and utterances) in dataset

learns from such bias in co-occurrence, we converted images into text and applied a text-based method that computes associations.

We chose the Latent Dirichlet Allocation (LDA) method [36], which is a generative statistical model for natural language documents. It assumes that each document is formed from a mixture of *topics*, allowing comparisons across documents in terms of *topic* similarity. This algorithm performs well and achieves associations in a human-readable way that yields topics representing hidden tendencies in co-occurrence.

4.2 System Overview

Figure 4 illustrates our system architecture. The input to the system is the visual scenes captured by the robot's camera. The captured images are sent to a *vision module* and converted into a list of words. The system's main routine is the *association module*. The *vision module* output is sent to the *association module*, where utterance contents are stored in the database in advance. When there is input from the *vision module*, it computes the similarity between the input and the stored utterances and selects the most similar utterance. Finally, the selected utterance is sent to the robot, which says it in a synthesized voice.

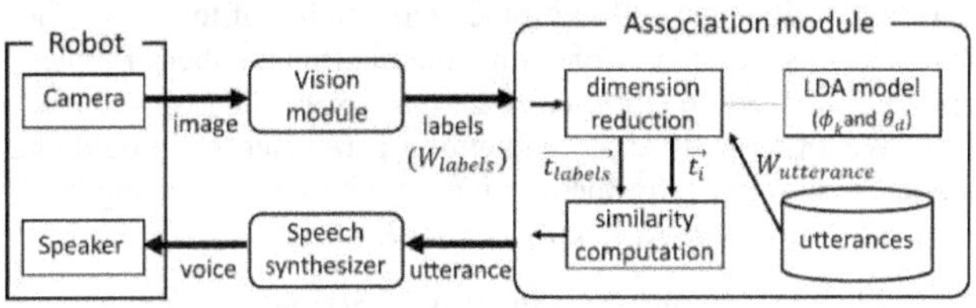

Figure 4. System architecture

4.3 Vision Module

The vision module converts images into a list of words. We used the label-detection capability of Google Cloud Vision [37], which is a web API provided by Google Inc. Figure 5 shows examples of the label-detection result. The image at the top was analyzed by the API, and the bottom is the resulting text where the text on the left side is the detected labels, and the value on the right side represents the confidence of each label; to keep the computation simple, we only used the labels, not the confidence values.

property	0.82306892	transport	0.8908574
lawn	0.64235741	waterway	0.84038585
cottage	0.609711	shore	0.82845044
pasture	0.5881415	sea	0.80729067
area	0.57691193	river	0.78013432
farm	0.56997228	walkway	0.71582484
hacienda	0.52595049	reservoir	0.61026609
ranch	0.511426		

Figure 5. Label-detection example with Google Cloud Vision

For instance, the vision module detects a *lawn* in the image from the garden and a scene about *transportation* and *sea* from the harbor image. Some labels do not accurately represent the scene, including *farm*, *hacienda*, and *ranch* in the garden image. Typically, we detected 5-13 labels for the images in our dataset. Very rarely, no label was detected; in such cases we retrieved the image again until it gained some labels.

In addition, to stabilize the result, we used three image frames. The obtained labels from the three images are concatenated into one list, which was used as the output from the vision module. A label with such multiple words as public transport and real estate was processed as a single word by simply connecting the words with underscores: public_transport and real_estate).

4.4 Association Module

The association module computes the similarity between a list of words from the *vision module* and the small-talk utterances stored in the database.

4.4.1 Data Representation

Denote an utterance (a sentence with several words) as:

$$W_{utterance} = \{word_1, word_2, word_3, \cdots\} \quad (1)$$

An image is sent to the *vision module* and converted into a list of labels. Here, denote the list of labels obtained from the *vision module* as:

$$W_{labels} = \{label_1, label_2, label_3, \cdots\} \quad (2)$$

In each $W_{utterance}$ and W_{labels}, the data are represented as a bag-of-words, meaning that the order of the words is ignored; we only count the number of times each word appears.

The data prepared in the dataset in Section 3 are represented as a set of associations of an image and an utterance. We combine the elements in each association as one bag-of-words representation:

$$W_{association} = W_{utterance} + W_{labels} \quad (3)$$

We denote the set of all the associations in the dataset as corpus *C*. Note that this association corresponds with the document in LDA.

For the later process, we removed the stop words from $W_{association}$. Such words as 'I' and 'is' appear commonly regardless of the nature of the sentences or the documents. Thus, counting these words does not help us compute similarity across *associations*, but it actually distorts the computation. We typically assume that these words are stop words and remove them from the computation. We also removed them from all the *associations* using a standard stop-word list. Since some labels from the vision module were too common across scenes from different locations, we removed them from our dataset: floor, flooring, and property.

4.4.2 Latent Dirichlet Allocation (LDA)

Next we briefly explain how LDA computes the similarity between contents. The bag-of-words representation of each bit of data can be transformed as a *word vector* with a huge dimension where each dimension corresponds to the number of times each appears. As a simple example, assume that the space of the *word vectors* only has three terms: apple, orange, and tea; assume the following sentence, "I bought an apple and an orange and made an apple pie." Because 'apple' appears twice and 'orange' appears once, the *word vector* representation would be $(2, 1, 0)$. If we compare such vector representations, we can compute the similarity across *word vectors*.

However, computing similarity with these *word vectors* is not useful in reality. If we denote the number of unique terms in the corpus as V, then *word vectors* form a V-dimensional space. Even with the small amount of data reported in Section 3, there were 401 terms included in corpus C, and thus the dimension of the *word vector* in our case was V=401. LDA is typically applied for a corpus with a large number of documents, and thus word vectors are sparse with very high dimensionality (often, $V > 10^7$).

The key idea for using the LDA method is dimension reduction. Although the dimensions of *word vectors* are huge, we can represent the information in a vector with much lower dimensions. There are biases in the co-occurrences of terms, i.e., some terms co-occur more frequently than others. For instance, we expect that 'sea' and 'swim' often appear together. LDA represents each group of terms that often co-occurs together as a *topic* and transforms the *word vectors* with high dimensionality into *topic vectors* with low dimensionality.

To scrutinize the dimension reduction process, because LDA is a generative statistical scheme, it models all the generations of words in a document as a probabilistic process and assumes K potential topics. Then across the whole corpus, a topic(s) is generated based on topic distribution θ_d, and each word in a document (in our case, *association*) is generated from topic k (k=1, ..., K), where the generation of a word from topic k is modeled based on word distribution $\phi_k = \{\pi_{k,1}, \pi_{k,2}, \dots, \pi_{k,V}\}$, where ϕ_k and θ_d follow a Dirichlet distribution (a continuous multivariate probability distribution), and $\pi_{k,i}$ represents the normalized probability of the occurrence of word w_i generated from topic k.

Based on this generative modeling, given number of topics K, it infers word distributions ϕ_k for all topics k (k=1, ..., K) and topic distribution θ_d that are most likely to fit corpus C. There are a couple of approaches that infer the parameters that define these probability distributions, among which we used an online variational Bayes algorithm [38]. More details of the LDA method can be found in the literature (e.g., [36]). We used a library called *gensim* [39] for implementing the LDA method.

Given the parameters for probability distribution functions ϕ_k and θ_d, we can compute *topic vector* $\vec{t}$ from *word vector* $\vec{w}$. ϕ_k forms the basis vectors for the *topic vector* space. Here, since the high dimensional space of the *word vectors* is projected into a K-dimensional *topic vector* space, which is a much lower dimension than the original V-dimensional space. With the LDA method, a document is allocated to a *topic vector* space.

Finally, the similarity between two *topic vectors*, $\vec{t_i}$ and $\vec{t_j}$, is computed as a cosine similarity:

$$similarity(\vec{t_i}, \vec{t_j}) = \cos(\vec{t_i}, \vec{t_j}) \quad (4)$$

4.4.3 Selecting Utterances from Visual Scenes

Our algorithm selects utterances that are expected to be associative to the current visual scene. The basic idea allocates the visual scenes and utterances into the same topic space using the LDA method. Then when we select an utterance and retrieve those that are most similar to the current visual scene in the *topic vector* space formed with the LDA method.

As explained in Section 4.3.1, we concatenated the list of words (labels) given by the vision module and the sentence for an utterance into one *association* represented as bag-of-word ($W_{association}$). Then with corpus C that is formed from all the *associations*, we trained the LDA model, meaning that we inferred the parameters for distributions ϕ_k and θ_d.

With this training, we expect that a *topic vector* space will be formed in a way to allow it to associate visual scenes and utterances. We expect to have co-occurrence of the words in utterances and labels from the *vision modules* that are used in similar contexts. For instance, the term 'insects' is sometimes used in a garden where vision modules often output the label 'grass,' and the terms 'insects' and label 'grass' are likely to be associated to the same topic and considered similar in the topic space. Thus, we expect that a *word vector* $\overrightarrow{w_{labels}}$, formed from an image from the *vision module*, will be allocated to a *topic vector* that shows similarity to the *topic vectors* of the utterances that were associated to similar visual scenes.

Based on the above assumption, our algorithm selects an associative utterance for *word vector* $\overrightarrow{w_{labels}}$ (labels computed from visual scenes in the *vision module*) as:

$$selected\_utterance = \underset{i}{\operatorname{argmax}}(similarity(\overrightarrow{t_{labels}}, \vec{t_i})) \quad (5)$$

where $\vec{t_i}$ is the *topic vector* for utterance i in the database and $\overrightarrow{t_{labels}}$ is the *topic vector* computed from $\overrightarrow{w_{labels}}$. We excluded utterances that were used once from later selections for the same user.

4.5 Training

We prepared 375 *associations* (combinations of images and utterances) as corpus C, as described in Section 3, and trained the LDA model using the corpus with the method reported in Section 4.3.2 for which we need to provide the number of topics K. There is no established theory for estimating the true number of topics K, and thus we need to empirically set it at a value that isn't too large [40]. We empirically explored the best parameter that would yield a good performance for the training set without over-fitting it with an excessively large K. Finally, we set K to 14.

Table 1. Training result for word distributions for topics

$\phi_{shop-like}$		$\phi_{car-like}$		$\phi_{nature-like}$		...
pedestrian	.062	parking	.065	ecosystem	.042	
shopping	.053	car	.051	land_lot	.038	
road	.045	lane	.050	grass	.035	
city	.042	road	.050	woodland	.035	
crowd	.040	vehicle	.043	tree	.035	
street	.037	pedestrian_crossing	.035	plant	.032	...
shopping_mall	.030	pedestrian	.031	meadow	.029	
retail_store	.027	lot	.026	pasture	.026	
downtown	.024	asphalt	.023	yard	.026	
transport	.020	zebra_crossing	.023	woody_plant	.026	
⋮	⋮	⋮	⋮	⋮	⋮	

Table 1 shows examples of word distributions ϕ_k for three of topics named shop-like, car-like, and nature-like topics. For each word distribution, the left side terms represent the terms loaded for this topic, and the right side values represent the probability of generating each term on the left side. The terms are arranged in descending order by probability. Terms with larger probabilities are more likely to appear. For instance, in shop-like topics, the term 'pedestrian' is on the top with a value of .062, meaning that it is more likely to appear than other terms lower in the column. The probability value can be interpreted in a generative-model way, where in a document with a shop-like topic, the term 'pedestrian' is generated with a probability of .062 for each chance of generating a word.

4.6 System Behavior Examples

Next we explain how the system behaves with an example with two utterances (U1 and U2) and two photos (P1 and P2) from the dataset when two new photos (P3 and P4), which are not in the dataset, were taken from the street. They have slightly different visual scenes. Our system computes the similarity and selects the target utterance for these new photos.

Figure 6-a illustrates the allocations of these utterances and photos to the *topic vector* space. For simplicity, we only illustrate them and explain their behavior on a plane with two dimensions (car-like and shop-like) of *topic vectors*. Utterance U1 ("Are you good at driving a car?") has term 'car' that has a rather high probability of .051 in $\phi_{car-like}$. The terms in U2 ("Do you enjoy just looking around shops?") has some probabilities in $\phi_{shop-like}$ ('shops' is .014, 'looking' is .007, and 'enjoy' is .007). Their *topic vectors* in this plane were computed as $\overrightarrow{t_{U1}}$ = (0.03, 0.62) and $\overrightarrow{t_{U2}}$ =(0.70, 0.02). (Computation for *topic vectors* from sentences follows the same procedure used in the modeling: given the distributions ϕ_k, it infers topic distribution θ_d that is most likely to fit the words probability in the word vector.) The *vision module* yields labels for P1 as W_{P1} = {lane, road, automobile, vehicle, traffic, sport_utility_vehicle, street, parking, pedestrian, compact_car}. The terms 'lane,' 'road,' 'vehicle,' 'parking lot,' and 'pedestrian' are in $\phi_{car-like}$ with high probability. They were allocated to the *topic vector* of $\overrightarrow{t_{P1}}$ = (0.01, 0.89). W_{P2} ={crowd, transport, city, shopping_mall, retail_store, bazaar, pedestrian, public_transport, shopping, market}, which was allocated to $\overrightarrow{t_{P2}}$ = (0.89, 0.01).

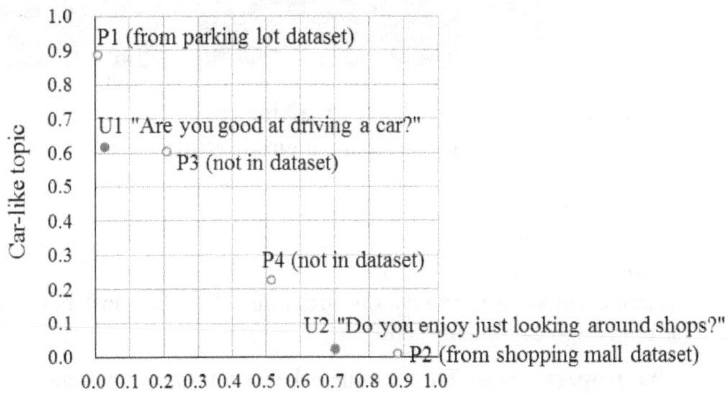

(a) Illustration of *topic vector* space

(b) P1 (from parking lot dataset)

(c) P2 (from shopping mall dataset)

(d) P3 (not in dataset)

(e) P4 (not in dataset)

Figure 6. Utterances and photos allocated in *topic vector* space

The system computes P4 as rather similar to U2, while P3 resembles U1. In P3, there are few pedestrians (no crowd) and one car. W_{P3} ={mode_of_transport, vehicle, lane, pedestrian, traffic}.

Table 2. Confusion matrix for evaluation with the dataset

		Selected				
		Garden	Harbor	Mall	Parking lot	Corridor
Actual	Garden	60	12	0	3	0
	Harbor	4	30	4	3	34
	Mall	1	0	67	5	2
	Parking lot	3	2	1	69	0
	Corridor	7	15	6	5	42

Here, the terms 'vehicle,' 'lane,' and 'pedestrian' are in $\phi_{car-like}$, but 'pedestrian' also has a high probability in $\phi_{shop-like}$. The computation resulted in $\overrightarrow{t_{P3}}$ = (0.21, 0.60). If the system selects an utterance from candidates U1 and U2, the cosine similarity computed from Eq. 5 is 0.79 for U1 and 0.32 for U2, and hence the system chooses U1.

In contrast, in P4, there is a crowd of people, and the system computes it as rather similar to U2. W_{P4} ={road, street, lane, pedestrian, crowd, transport, city, urban_area, neighborhood, human_settlement}. Some of the terms in W_{P4} are included in $\phi_{shop-like}$ and $\phi_{car-like}$, although terms like 'pedestrian' and 'crowd' have high probability in $\phi_{shop-like}$. The computation resulted in $\overrightarrow{t_{P4}}$ = (0.52, 0.22). Since the cosine similarity is 0.39 for U1 and 0.67 for U2, the system chooses U2.

4.7 Performance Evaluation

We evaluated the proposed method using the dataset from Section 3. Videos were taken from five locations. The first half of each one was used for training. We used the second half for our evaluation. As in the preparation for the training data, we retrieved 75 images from each video (one image every two seconds). Overall, 375 images were retrieved. Then each image was sent to the *vision module*, where it is converted to a *word vector* $\overrightarrow{w_{labels}}$, which was projected to the *topic vector* $\overrightarrow{t_{labels}}$ using the trained LDA model. The system selected the utterance that is most similar to this image input using Eq. 5.

For simplicity, we evaluated whether the system selects an utterance that is from the same type of location (i.e., a garden, a harbor, a shopping mall, a parking lot, or an indoor corridor) with the image. For instance, if the system selects an utterance prepared for a garden for an image from a garden, it is evaluated as 'appropriate.' Perhaps some such 'appropriate' images are not completely appropriate. A system may select something about tree because it was trained for a visual scene in a garden with trees, but the tested image might not have a tree in it. Nevertheless, this simplified definition of appropriateness helps us understand the rough performance of our proposed system.

Table 2 shows the confusion matrix for the evaluation. Overall, it selects appropriate utterances with 72% success. If the selection is randomly done, its success is 20%. Our proposed method selected appropriate utterances reasonably well.

The system selects appropriate topics for garden, mall, and parking lot. In contrast, it is less robust for images from the harbor. In some images from harbor, the labels from the *vision module* included 'transport' and 'infrastructure' that can also be seen in the corridor image (such labels as public_transport and metro_station are shown in the corridor images, so the indoor corridor seems to resemble a public transportation space). As a result, sometimes utterances from the corridor are chosen as images from the harbor.

5. EXPERIMENT

5.1 Hypothesis and Prediction

People would generally have a good sense of judging whether small-talk topics are relevant to the current visual scene. If our system works as designed, it should appropriately select a topic that is associative to the current visual scene, and participants should be able to differentiate between the selections done by this system and those done by from other systems. For comparison, we used a random selection. A better method might exist than random selection, like the location-based approach discussed in Section 2.1. However, although we could use such positioning devices as a GPS to locate the current coordinates, since we are developing a technique for daily anonymous locations, it is difficult to assume that the contents are already associated to such anonymous locations. Based on this idea, we made the following prediction:

> **Prediction 1**: Participants will perceive that the robot with the *proposed method* discussed topics that are more appropriate for the scenes than a robot with *random selection.*

We speculated that it may be necessary for our walking partners to be able to associate visual scenes with small-talk topics. Based on such a capability, the agents must understand the surrounding environments. Like empathy discussed in the literature [32, 34], this understanding leads to the ability to share feelings related to visual scenes. It might lead us to feel that such an agent resembles us, because similarity is considered a key feature for empathy [41]. Utterances based on sharing sensory perceptions encourage immersive interaction [42]. Thus, it might matter whether the robot can select topics that are associative to visual scenes. Based on the above speculation, we made this prediction:

> **Prediction 2**: A robot with the *proposed method* will be perceived as a better walking partner than a robot with *random selection.*

As discussed in Section 2.2, many approaches make a robot that is a better partner. We believe that future walking partner robots will combine such approaches with this association capability; nevertheless, in this study, we focus on comparisons of association capability.

5.2 Method

5.2.1 *Participants*

Fifteen Japanese people (10 males and 5 females, average age, 25.8 years) were paid for their participation.

5.2.2 *Robot*

We used the robot (Figure 7-a), TEROOS-M [43], which was originally designed for a telepresence application, sat on a person's shoulder (Figure 8). It has a human-like face, stands 22-cm high, is 9-cm wide, 25-cm deep, and weighs 650 g. The robot has a camera, a microphone, and a speaker. We used the camera as input to the system and the speaker for conversation. We used speech synthesis software, Open JTalk [44], for generating utterances. It has two degrees of freedom for controlling its face and camera directions, but for this study since we processed the visual information from the walking direction, we did not control it. It is linked to a cellular network for a connection to Google Cloud Vision.

5.2.3 *Conditions*

We compared two conditions:

> ***Proposed method:*** The robot selected a topic using the system described in Section 4.

> ***Random selection:*** The robot randomly selected an utterance from the same utterance database as in the *proposed* condition. As in the proposed method, an utterance that was once used was not used again.

The study had a within-participant design, and the order of the conditions was counter-balanced.

5.2.4 *Procedure*

The experiment was conducted outside on a walking course in a garden, which was in the dataset, and a parking lot, which was different from the one in the dataset (Figure. 7-b). We conducted our experiments on sunny days without rain. First, we explained the situation to the participants. They had to take a walk for their health. The robot talked to them by selecting conversation topics that corresponded to the scenes. We asked them to respond to the robot, even though it did not respond to what they said. Then we described the walking course to them.

They walked with the robot on their shoulder for five minutes. While they were walking, the robot talked about every 15 seconds. This timing was adjusted based on preliminary trials to avoid being too long or too short. Finally, the robot said, "thank you for the walk," and the session ended. After a 15-minute break, they continued the second session with another condition with the same procedure as in the first session. The experimental protocol were approved by our IRB.

(a) Robot (b) Walking course

Figure 7. Experimental setup

5.2.5 *Measurement*

After each session, the participants filled out a questionnaire for the following questions on a 1-to-7 point Likert scale where 1 is the most negative (strongly disagree) and 7 is the most positive (strongly agree) for each sentence:

- **Appropriateness**: Three items asked about appropriateness of utterances for locations/scenes: "how much the robot utterance felt out-of-place" (reversed item), "how well the robot utterances matched the locations", and "how well the robot seemed to talk with looking at scenes". Because there is no existing measures, we developed these items through our own preliminary trials – so it should be noted that these items have not been tested in any other studies. The average scores from the three items in the scale resulted in a Cronbach's $\alpha = .755$.
- **Evaluation as a walking partner**: A single item asked about how well the robot acted as a walking partner.

After they finished both sessions, we conducted interviews.

5.3 Result

5.3.1 *Observation*

The participants strolled with the robot as if on a normal daily walk (Figure 8). When the robot did not talk, they walked silently, and when the robot talked, they responded. They sometimes only provided a short backchannel, like "yes" or "no." They sometimes replied by repeating part of the phrase the robot said. For instance, when a robot said, "I don't like weeds because they have too many bugs," one answered, "I agree, I don't like bugs, either."

Some participants engaged in more dialogs with the robot and behaved as if they were talking with people. They sometimes replied with their own words when the robot talked. Some participants sometimes briefly mentioned their own experiences. For instance, when the robot asked, "Have you ever blown a puff of dandelion seeds into the air?" the participant smiled and said, "Yes, I often did that when I was a child." When the robot said, "In a big parking lot, sometimes I forget where I parked," one participant said, "Yes, me too. I've done that before." Some looked at the robot's face or nodded when they replied.

Figure 8. Experiment scene

In contrast, when the robot mentioned a topic that did not match the scene, the participants often responded with wry smiles or confusion. For instance, when the robot talked about a rat when they were in the parking lot, she said, "What? A Rat?" While they were walking in a garden, the robot said to another person, "Did anybody ever damage your car while it was parked?" she replied "No, . . . What?" expressing surprise about the topic. To another participant in a garden, the robot said, "It's hot in the parking lot without any shade." The participant paused and impatiently asked, "What?" The robot broached a couple of topics that did not match the visual scenes, and he continued to make a wry smile.

5.3.2 Verification of Predictions

Figure 9-a shows the *appropriateness* result. We conducted a one-way repeated-measure analysis of variance (ANOVA), which revealed significant differences ($F(1, 14) = 38.057$, $p < .001$, $\eta_p^2=.731$). Thus, as predicted, the *appropriateness* scores in the proposed model were significantly better than the scores in the *random selection* condition. Prediction 1 was supported.

Figure 9-b shows the result for the *evaluation as a walking partner*. We conducted a one-way repeated-measure analysis of variance (ANOVA), which revealed significant differences ($F(1, 14) = 7.996$, $p = .013$, $\eta_p^2=.364$). Thus, as predicted, the *evaluation as a walking partner* scores in the proposed model were significantly better than the *random selection* condition scores. Prediction 2 was supported. In addition, Poisson correlation from two measurements is .652, and R^2 from regression analysis is .425. Hence, a considerable portion of the *evaluation as a walking partner* score can be explained by the *appropriateness score*.

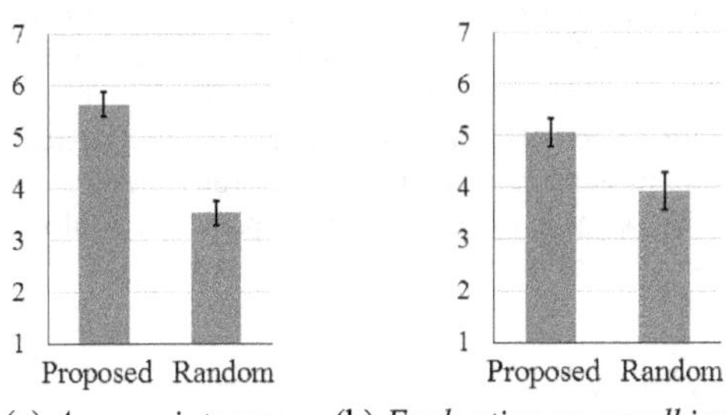

(a) *Appropriateness* (b) *Evaluation as a walking partner*

Figure 9. Experiment results

5.3.3 Analysis of System Behavior

Next we evaluated our system's performance during the experiment. The walking course had a segment in the middle that does not match either a garden or a parking lot (during this segment, the visual scene contains road, buildings, and nature. Based on this input, the robot would often choose sentences from the garden and parking lot dataset, but sometimes it would choose sentences from another), so we only evaluated the segments that belonged to either the garden or the parking lot. Like in Section 4.6, we defined each utterance selection as appropriate if it is from the same location category. For instance, if an utterance from the garden dataset is selected in the garden, it is deemed appropriate.

Based on the above criteria, the selections with the proposed method were judged to be appropriate for 75.38% (s.d. 8.58) of the utterances, while the random selection was 25.32% (s.d. 10.88). The performance in the experiment with a real robot resembled the one reported in Section 4.6. The performance in the random condition was slightly better than the expected chance ratio of 20%. Under some conditions, the performance in the experiment was lower. For instance, after rain there were puddles in the garden, and then the labels provided by the vision module included the term 'waterway,' which usually appears in the harbor images in our dataset. So sometimes the proposed method selected utterances from the harbor dataset.

As an additional analysis, we evaluated the frequency of topic switching. Various topics are included in each dataset; for instance, utterances from the garden dataset includes topics such as glasses, trees, barbecue, picnic, and bugs. Topic switching occurred on average 17.1 times per experiment in the proposed condition and 19.2 times in the random selection condition.

5.3.4 Interview Results

In the interviews, we first asked about their impression of walking with a robot. All of the participants responded positively. The most frequent comment (mentioned by five participants) was like "It was more fun than walking alone." Three participants addressed similar issues: "It could be a conversation partner (thus, better than walking alone)." Other comments were provided: "The walk felt shorter when I was walking with the robot" and "because it was not a person, I could just be myself." Some participants further speculated about future uses for it as, "It might prevent dementia in elderly people" and "It could reduce accidents at pedestrian crossings."

Next, we asked what they perceived as the differences in the two robots. 14 out of 15 participants reported that the robot in our proposed model engaged in appropriate conversations for locations/scenes better than other one. Some commented that the robot in the random selection condition sometimes discussed rather difficult topics. One participant mentioned that when she walked with the robot with the proposed model, her attention was more focused on the scenery, so she felt that she was walking more slowly by looking around at the visual scenes. Another person felt distant from the robot in the random condition because it seemed to be desperately forcing topics.

Then we asked how such a difference between the two robots influenced their evaluations of it as a walking partner. 11 participants who preferred the robot in the proposed method provided such comments as "I was able to have a meaningful conversation," "Replying was easier," "I felt I was sharing the scene with the robot, so I was able to enjoy the conversation," and "talking is natural if it fits the visual scenes." One participant preferred the robot in the random method. She perceived that the robot in it was better at selecting appropriate topics for visual scenes. Although for her, the robot chose appropriate topics in 71% of the cases in the proposed condition and 29% in the random condition. Three participants expressed no preference between the two robots: "I enjoyed talking with the robot regardless whether the utterances matched the visual scenes," and "It is sometimes good to talk about things that match the scene, but it isn't always necessary."

Finally, we solicited their opinions about how to improve the robot to make it a better walking partner. Regarding its conversation capability, a majority described the one-way dialog as a problem and complained that it did not respond: "The robot didn't adapt to personal information like age, gender, and personal interests," "I wanted the robot to talk about the scenes," and "In addition to the scenes, I wanted it to talk about the weather." Other comments addressed its weight and that its synthesized voice was sometimes not very intelligible.

6. Discussion

6.1 Walking with Robot on user's Shoulder?

Having a robot on a shoulder might be controversial. Perhaps a partner robot should move or walk by itself. Perhaps a similar service could be provided by a virtual agent in a smartphone. We believe that such alternative options might realize a walking partner. We expect that one would argue that it is not natural for people to engage in conversations with an entity on their shoulder.

To counter such arguments, we point out that all of our participants expressed positive opinions about their experience with the robot on their shoulder. Other successful uses of robots and telepresence devices on user shoulders have been reported [43, 45, 46]. Walking with a robot on a shoulder is one option for achieving a partner robot for walking. A strength of this approach is that it can provide great freedom in the areas in which it operates. It can go anywhere people can go, which is often very difficult with mobile robots under the limitations of today's techniques. We believe that a real-world embodiment is beneficial for allowing users to engage in interaction, even though we acknowledge that a similar level of engagement might be realized using computer-based agents.

We believe that similar phenomena could occur with different robots (e.g., mobile robots) or agents if they are perceived as a kind of human-like friendly entity to which people wish to engage in conversation. For any such entity, our system could be easily connected. It just requires a camera that is oriented in a walking direction and a computation resource with a connection to the Internet for Google Cloud Vision.

6.2 Improvements for Walking Partner Robot

We only developed a system within a scope to experiment with a robot's capability to associate utterances to scenes, and thus much more work is required to prepare our system to be a walking partner. First, since we did not fully connect our system to a dialog system, it lacks a mechanism to let the robot respond to its user. 11 out of 15 participants complained because the robot lacked such a feature. This could probably be implemented with available automatic speech recognition (ASR) techniques.

Second, the robot does not necessarily always talk about the visual scenes. As discussed in Section 2.2, there are strategies for building relations between robots and users (e.g., [32-34]). Likewise, while walking, perhaps the robot should adapt itself better to the users, e.g., talking about their personal interests. We believe that in reality the ideal robot will sometimes respond to landscapes, but it will also usually broach other issues. For instance, it is perfectly acceptable if a dialog starts from visual scenes and moves to other topics and finally engages in a dialog about topics that users are greatly interested in. Our findings will probably contribute to creating such a robot system, although apparently it remains an open question how to integrate them into a larger dialog system. Our future work will address such issues.

6.3 Applicability of Proposed Mechanism

We have not yet tested our system beyond the images from the five locations in the dataset. Although from our experience with this dataset, the system is applicable for different locations if a vision module provides distinctive labels. If the images from new locations yield similar labels with existing locations, but they are in fact similar (e.g., images from parking lots and sidewalks both yield labels like 'car' and 'driving,' where we also discuss topics about driving), then the system will probably find topic spaces so that the contents (shared in both locations) are more likely to be used in such locations that visually resemble each other. Certainly, the performance is bounded by the algorithm in the vision module (in our case, the Google Cloud Vision API). If the label detection's performance were improved, our system could separate the topics more specifically. Currently the vision module does not distinguish between types of trees and weeds, but if such distinctions were possible, a robot system could provide many more details about plants.

We believe that our system is scalable for an increase of corpus size. Admittedly our dataset is rather small, if compared with a typical use of LDA, e.g., analyzing entire pages of Wikipedia. If a larger corpus were used, we expect that the topic space could be more precisely separated into higher dimensional spaces.

6.4 Limitations

Since our study was only conducted in such specific contexts as visual scenes, people, and culture with the current experimental result, generalizing our findings is difficult. Further studies are necessary with people from different cultures. Perhaps the expected associative ways are different depending on locations or situations. In such natural locations as parks, forests, mountains, and the sea, the situation might somewhat resemble our experiment, and thus our approach might also similarly work. In contrast, if people are window-shopping, they might expect a more specific conversation about items they can see, including clothes, accessories, home appliances, and food. In such situations, perhaps more direct mapping is required between what is seen and what is to be discussed; if a person is window-shopping and looking at a specific item, talking about it is more natural than shop-type topics.

7. CONCLUSION

We realized a walking partner robot and developed a robot system that selects associative utterances to current visual scenes. Using a dataset of images from five different locations, our developed system worked reasonably well in an experiment where participants walked with a small robot and engaged in small talk. We confirmed that the participants noticed that the robot appropriately selected topics associated with the visual scenes, and they preferred such a walking partner robot more than a robot that randomly selects topic. Our participants were also positive about walking with such a partner robot because it provided enjoyment that was better than being alone.

8. ACKNOWLEDGMENTS

This work was supported in part by the Tateishi Science and Technology Foundation, and in part by JST, CREST.

9. REFERENCES

[1] H.-M. Gross, et al., Roreas: Robot Coach for Walking and Orientation Training in Clinical Post-Stroke Rehabilitation—Prototype Implementation and Evaluation in Field Trials, *Autonomous Robots*, pp. 1-20, 2016.

[2] D. Hebesberger, C. Dondrup, T. Koertner, C. Gisinger and J. Pripfl, Lessons Learned from the Deployment of a Long-Term Autonomous Robot as Companion in Physical Therapy for Older Adults with Dementia: A Mixed Methods Study, *The Eleventh ACM/IEEE International Conference on Human Robot Interation*, pp. 27-34, 2016.

[3] W. Burgard, et al., The Interactive Museum Tour-Guide Robot, *National Conf. on Artificial Intelligence (AAAI1998)*, pp. 11-18, 1998.

[4] R. Siegwart, et al., Robox at Expo.02: A Large Scale Installation of Personal Robots, *Robotics and Autonomous Systems*, vol. 42, pp. 203-222, 2003.

[5] M. Shiomi, T. Kanda, H. Ishiguro and N. Hagita, Interactive Humanoid Robots for a Science Museum, *IEEE Intelligent Systems*, vol. 22, pp. 25-32, 2007.

[6] H.-M. Gross, et al., Toomas: Interactive Shopping Guide Robots in Everyday Use - Final Implementation and Experiences from Long-Term Field Trials, *IEEE/RSJ Int. Conf. on Intelligent Robots and Systems (IROS2009)*, pp. 2005-2012, 2009.

[7] D. Karreman, G. Ludden and V. Evers, Visiting Cultural Heritage with a Tour Guide Robot: A User Evaluation Study in-the-Wild, *International Conference on Social Robotics*, pp. 317-326, 2015.

[8] R. Triebel, et al., Spencer: A Socially Aware Service Robot for Passenger Guidance and Help in Busy Airports, *Field and Service Robotics*, pp. 607-622, 2016.

[9] E. W. Y. Kwong, C. K. Y. Lai, E. Spicciolato and M. C. M. Wong, Views of Adults on Shopping Trolleys: Implications for the Development of a Shopping Trolley, *The Ergonomics Open Journal*, vol. 3, pp. 32-37, 2010.

[10] Y. Iwamura, M. Shiomi, T. Kanda, H. Ishiguro and N. Hagita, Do Elderly People Prefer a Conversational Humanoid as a Shopping Assistant Partner in Supermarkets?, *ACM/IEEE Int. Conf. on Human-Robot Interaction (HRI2011)*, pp. 449-456, 2011.

[11] J. Pineau, M. Montemerlo, M. Pollack, N. Roy and S. Thrun, Towards Robotic Assistants in Nursing Homes: Challenges and Results, *Robotics and Autonomous Systems*, vol. 42, pp. 271-281, 2003.

[12] K. Dautenhahn, et al., How May I Serve You? A Robot Companion Approaching a Seated Person in a Helping Context, *ACM/IEEE Int. Conf. on Human-Robot Interaction (HRI2006)*, pp. 172-179, 2006.

[13] H. Kuzuoka, Y. Suzuki, J. Yamashita and K. Yamazaki, Reconfiguring Spatial Formation Arrangement by Robot Body Orientation, *ACM/IEEE Int. Conf. on Human-Robot Interaction (HRI2010)*, pp. 285-292, 2010.

[14] J. Mumm and B. Mutlu, Human-Robot Proxemics: Physical and Psychological Distancing in Human-Robot Interaction, *ACM/IEEE Int. Conf. on Human-Robot Interaction (HRI2011)*, pp. 331-338, 2011.

[15] D. Feil-Seifer and M. Mataric', Distance-Based Computational Models for Facilitating Robot Interaction with Children, *Journal of Human-Robot Interaction*, vol. 1, pp. 55-77, 2012.

[16] E. Pacchierotti, H. I. Christensen and P. Jensfelt, Evaluation of Passing Distance for Social Robots, *IEEE Int. Symposium on Robot and Human Interactive Communication (RO-MAN2006)*, pp. 315-320, 2006.

[17] E. A. Sisbot, L. F. Marin-Urias, R. Alami and T. Simeon, A Human Aware Mobile Robot Motion Planner, *IEEE Transactions on Robotics*, vol. 23, pp. 874-883, 2007.

[18] R. Kelley, et al., Understanding Human Intentions Via Hidden Markov Models in Autonomous Mobile Robots, *Proceedings of the 3rd ACM/IEEE international conference on Human robot interaction*, pp. 367-374, 2008.

[19] S. Satake, et al., How to Approach Humans?: Strategies for Social Robots to Initiate Interaction, *ACM/IEEE Int. Conf. on Human-Robot Interaction (HRI2009)*, pp. 109-116, 2009.

[20] M. A. Yousuf, Y. Kobayashi, Y. Kuno, A. Yamazaki and K. Yamazaki, How to Move Towards Visitors: A Model for Museum Guide Robots to Initiate Conversation, *IEEE Int. Symposium on Robot and Human Interactive Communication (RO-MAN2013)*, pp. 587-592, 2013.

[21] R. Gockley, J. Forlizzi and R. Simmons, Natural Person-Following Behavior for Social Robots, *ACM/IEEE Int. Conf. on Human-Robot Interaction (HRI2007)*, pp. 17-24, 2007.

[22] E. Sviestins, N. Mitsunaga and T. Kanda, Speed Adaptation for a Robot Walking with a Human, *ACM/IEEE Int. Conf. on Human-Robot Interaction (HRI2007)*, pp. 349-356, 2007.

[23] Y. Kobayashi, et al., Robotic Wheelchair Moving with Caregiver Collaboratively Depending on Circumstances, *Extended Abstracts on ACM Conference on Human Factors in Computing Systems (CHI2011)*, 2011.

[24] C. L. Sidner, C. Lee and N. Lesh, Engagement by Looking: Behaviors for Robots When Collaborating with People, *Seventh Workshop on the Semantics and Pragmatics of Dialogue, Kruiff-Korbayova and Kosny*, pp. 123-130, 2003.

[25] B. Mutlu, J. Forlizzi and J. Hodgins, A Storytelling Robot: Modeling and Evaluation of Human-Like Gaze Behavior, *IEEE-RAS Int. Conf. on Humanoid Robots (Humanoids'06)*, pp. 518-523, 2006.

[26] C. Rich, B. Ponsler, A. Holroyd and C. L. Sidner, Recognizing Engagement in Human-Robot Interaction, *ACM/IEEE Int. Conf. on Human-Robot Interaction (HRI2010)*, pp. 375-382, 2010.

[27] Y. Kobayashi, et al., Choosing Answerers by Observing Gaze Responses for Museum Guide Robots, *ACM/IEEE Int. Conf. on Human-Robot Interaction (HRI2010)*, pp. 109-110, 2010.

[28] B. Mutlu, T. Shiwa, T. Kanda, H. Ishiguro and N. Hagita, Footing in Human-Robot Conversations: How Robots Might Shape Participant Roles Using Gaze Cues, *ACM/IEEE Int. Conf. on Human-Robot Interaction (HRI2009)*, pp. 61-68, 2009.

[29] J. Weizenbaum, ELIZA—A Computer Program For the Study of Natural Language Communication Between Man and Machine, Communications of the ACM, 9.1: 36-45, 1966.

[30] S. Matsumoto and M. Araki, Scoring of response based on suitability of dialogue-act and content similarity, Proceedings of the 12th NTCIR Conference on Evaluation of Information Access Technologies, 2016.

[31] C. Torrey, S. R. Fussell and S. Kiesler, How a Robot Should Give Advice, *ACM/IEEE Int. Conf. on Human-Robot Interaction (HRI2013)*, pp. 275-282, 2013.

[32] T. W. Bickmore and R. W. Picard, Establishing and Maintaining Long-Term Human-Computer Relationships, *ACM Transactions on Computer-Human Interaction (TOCHI2005)*, vol. 12, pp. 293-327, 2005.

[33] M. K. Lee, et al., Personalization in Hri: A Longitudinal Field Experiment, *ACM/IEEE Int. Conf. on Human-Robot Interaction (HRI2012)*, pp. 319-326, 2012.

[34] I. Leite, G. Castellano, A. Pereira, C. Martinho and A. Paiva, Empathic Robots for Long-Term Interaction: Evaluating Social Presence, Engagement and Perceived Support in Children, *International Journal of Social Robotics*, vol. 6, pp. 329-341, 2014.

[35] J. F. Maas, T. Spexard, J. Fritsch, B. Wrede and G. Sagerer, Biron, What's the Topic? A Multi-Modal Topic Tracker for Improved Human-Robot Interaction, *ROMAN 2006-The 15th IEEE International Symposium on Robot and Human Interactive Communication*, pp. 26-32, 2006.

[36] D. M. Blei, A. Y. Ng and M. I. Jordan, Latent Dirichlet Allocation, *Journal of Machine Learning Research*, vol. 3, pp. 993-1022, 2003.

[37] *Google Cloud Vision Api*, https://cloud.google.com/vision/.

[38] M. Hoffman, F. R. Bach and D. M. Blei, Online Learning for Latent Dirichlet Allocation, *Advances in Neural Information Processing Systems*, pp. 856-864, 2010.

[39] R. Rehurek and P. Sojka, Software Framework for Topic Modelling with Large Corpora, *Proceedings of the LREC 2010 Workshop on New Challenges for NLP Frameworks*, pp. 45-50, 2010.

[40] J. Tang, Z. Meng, X. Nguyen, Q. Mei and M. Zhang, Understanding the Limiting Factors of Topic Modeling Via Posterior Contraction Analysis, *International Conference on Machine Learning (ICML)*, pp. 190-198, 2014.

[41] L. D. Riek, T.-C. Rabinowitch, B. Chakrabarti and P. Robinson, How Anthropomorphism Affects Empathy toward Robots, *Proceedings of the 4th ACM/IEEE International Conference on Human-Robot Interaction*, pp. 245-246, 2009.

[42] M. Imai and M. Narumi, Robot Behavior for Encouraging Immersion in Interaction, *Proceedings of Complex Systems Intelligence and Modern Technological Applications (CSIMTA 2004)*, pp. 591-598, 2004.

[43] T. Kashiwabara, H. Osawa, K. Shinozawa and M. Imai, Teroos: A Wearable Avatar to Enhance Joint Activities, *Proceedings of the SIGCHI Conference on Human Factors in Computing Systems*, pp. 2001-2004, 2012.

[44] *Open Jtalk*, http://open-jtalk.sourceforge.net/.

[45] N. Sakata, T. Kurata, T. Kato, M. Kourogi and H. Kuzuoka, Wacl: Supporting Telecommunications Using Wearable Active Camera with Laser Pointer, *Seventh IEEE International Symposium on Wearable Computers (ISWC)*, pp. 53-56, 2003.

[46] S. Kratz, D. Kimber, W. Su, G. Gordon and D. Severns, Polly: Being There through the Parrot and a Guide, *Proceedings of the 16th International Conference on Human-Computer Interaction with Mobile Devices & Services*, pp. 625-630, 2014.

Game-Theoretic Modeling of Human Adaptation in Human-Robot Collaboration

Stefanos Nikolaidis*, Swaprava Nath†, Ariel D. Procaccia†, and Siddhartha Srinivasa*
{*Robotics Institute, †Computer Science Department}, Carnegie Mellon University
snikolai@cmu.edu, {swapravn, arielpro}@cs.cmu.edu, siddh@cmu.edu

ABSTRACT

In human-robot teams, humans often start with an inaccurate model of the robot capabilities. As they interact with the robot, they infer the robot's capabilities and *partially adapt* to the robot, i.e., they might change their actions based on the observed outcomes and the robot's actions, without replicating the robot's policy. We present a *game-theoretic model* of human partial adaptation to the robot, where the human responds to the robot's actions by maximizing a reward function that changes stochastically over time, capturing the evolution of their expectations of the robot's capabilities. The robot can then use this model to decide optimally between taking actions that reveal its capabilities to the human and taking the best action given the information that the human currently has. We prove that under certain observability assumptions, the optimal policy can be computed efficiently. We demonstrate through a human subject experiment that the proposed model significantly improves human-robot team performance, compared to policies that assume complete adaptation of the human to the robot.

1. INTRODUCTION

A lot of work in robotics has focused on enabling robots to perform useful tasks for and with people. One of the main goals has been to make robots part of our everyday life, helping people as effective members of human-robot teams. In order to leverage recent advances in robot capabilities, human teammates should know what the robot can and cannot do: the robot's perceived capability should match its true capability.

Prior work has shown that there is often a disconnect between users' perceptions and a robot's true capability, mainly due to lack of experience with working with robots and to the influence of popular culture [8, 12, 28]. This gap in expectation can significantly reduce human-robot team performance [15].

For example, we consider the table-clearing task illustrated in Fig. 1. The user and the robot are tasked with clearing the table by placing items in the bins. The clearing task is repeated a number of times. We call each repetition a *round.* The user lacks the following information about the robot:

- The robot does not know where the green bin is. If the robot moves, it may collide with the green bin, inadvertently pushing the adjacent blue bin off the table.
- The robot cannot lift the bottle that is farthest away from its base: the bottle is filled with water and the torques required for a lifting motion exceed the robot's motor torque limits. If the robot attempts to lift the bottle, the robot's control software will abort and the robot will stop moving.

Nikolaidis et al. [25] proposed a human-robot mutual adaptation formalism, where the robot builds a model of human adaptation to guide the user towards an optimal — with re-

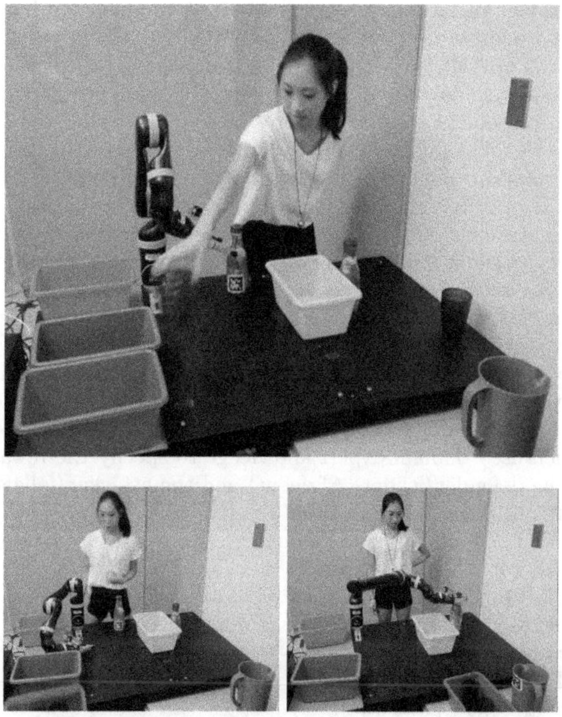

Figure 1: Top: User performs a repeated table-clearing task with the robot. The robot fails intentionally in the beginning of the task, in order to reveal its capabilities to the human teammate. Bottom-left: The robot drops the blue bin off the table while moving towards the left bottle. Bottom-right: The torques applied exceed their limits when the robot attempts a grasp at an extended configuration, and the robot stops moving.

HRI '17 March 06-09, 2017, Vienna, Austria

DOI: http://dx.doi.org/10.1145/2909824.3020253

spect to some objective performance metric — way of completing the task. Every time the human and the robot take an action, the user was modeled as either *completely adopting the robot policy as her[1] own* with some probability, or keeping her current policy. This probability was defined as the user's adaptability, which indicated her willingness to adapt to the robot. The formalism allowed the robot to infer the adaptability of its teammate through interaction, and guide the user towards an optimal policy unknown to them in advance.

While in [25], the human was modeled as completely adopting the robot's optimal policy with some probability, in many collaborative settings human adaptation can be more subtle. We use the table-clearing task described above as an example, and we let the robot attempt to grasp the bottle that is closest to its base, dropping the blue bin in the process. This will likely cause the human teammate to change her actions: in the next round, she will move the green or blue bin out of the robot's way. However, without observing the robot fail in lifting the other bottle, she still has no information about which action to take (i.e. emptying the bottle of water), if the robot attempts to lift the bottle.

This is an example, where *the human may change their actions based on the robot actions, while not completely adopting the robot's optimal policy.*

In this paper, we propose a game-theoretic model of human partial adaptation to the robot. We assume that the robot knows a "true" objective metric of team performance in the form of a reward matrix. We base this assumption on insights from early work on Stackelberg security games, which used domain expert knowledge to specify the reward of the defender/leader (AI agent) and the attacker/follower (human), showing remarkable results [32].

We model the human as following a best-response strategy to the robot action, based on their own, possibly distorted, reward function. The human reward function changes over time, as the human observes the outcomes of the robot and her own actions.

The model allows the robot to *reason over how the human expectations of the robot capabilities will change based on its own actions.* The robot uses this model to compute an optimal policy, which enables it to decide optimally between *revealing information* to the human and *choosing the best action given the information that the human currently has.*

We prove that, if the robot can observe whether the user has learned at each round, the computation of the optimal policy is simple (Lemmas 1 and 2), and can be done in time polynomial in the number of robot actions and the number of rounds (Theorem 1).

We show through a human subject experiment in a table-clearing task that the proposed model significantly improves human-robot team performance, compared to policies that assume complete human adaptation to the robot. Additionally, we show through simulations that the proposed model performs well for a variety of randomly generated tasks. This is the first step towards modeling the change of human expectations of the robot capabilities through interaction, and integrating the model into robot decision making in a principled way.

[1]We use the female pronoun for the human, and the neuter pronoun for the robot.

2. RELEVANT WORK

A lot of research in robotics has focused on one-way robot adaptation to the human, where the robot learns a human skill or preference [1–4, 9, 24, 27]. Other approaches enable robots to reduce the uncertainty over human intention through information-seeking actions [6, 7, 20, 22, 26], through negotiation with the human [19], or through decomposition of a complex task into subtasks [23]. There has also been work in human adaptation to the robot in social [13,14,18,29], and physical human-robot interaction [17].

Li et al. [21] suggest that the human-robot collaboration problem in physical human-robot interaction can be modeled as a two-player game. They assume that the human partner exerts a force by optimizing an unknown cost function; the robot's cost-function is then updated based on the gradient of the error between the actual force applied by the human and the force predicted by the robot's cost function, until an equilibrium is achieved. Menell et al. [16] define a cooperative inverse reinforcement learning (CIRL) problem as a partial information two-player game, where the robot maximizes the unknown human reward in a cooperative setting. They show that solving the game results in active teaching and active learning behaviors. The framework has yet to be evaluated in a human subject experiment. In contrast to both papers, in our work the roles are reversed, since the human learns the robot reward through interaction. In a repeated collaborative task with different actions, human adaptation can be more subtle than in a force exchange scenario. Additionally, the learner (human) does not run an inverse reinforcement learning algorithm. Instead, we model the human as learning with some probability the best-response to the robot action observed. This captures how human actions change over time based on their updated expectations of the robot capabilities, and it enables the robot to decide optimally between communicating the true rewards to the human and maximizing the immediate reward given the current human strategy.

There is also relevant work in the social navigation domain: In the manuscript by Trautman et al. [33], human and robot trajectories are jointly planned as the optimum of a reward function that combines goal completion and collision avoidance. Sadigh et al. [31] model the interaction of a human driver with an autonomous car as a dynamical system, where the human follows a best-response strategy to the robot actions. By contrast, we focus on a repeated task in a collaborative setting where the human reward function may change over time, as the human observes the outcomes of the robot and her own actions.

We draw upon insights from previous work on a particular class of Stackelberg games [10], the *repeated Stackelberg security games* [5]. In this setting, the follower observes the leader's possibly randomized strategy, and chooses a best-response. We extend this model to a human-robot collaboration setting, where the leader is the robot and the follower is the human, and we model human adaptation by having the follower's reward stochastically changing over time.

3. FORMAL MODEL

Consider a two-player game represented by the player set $N = \{\mathrm{R}, \mathrm{H}\}$, where player R is the `Robot` and player H is the `Human`. Each of them has a *finite* set of actions denoted by $A^{\mathrm{R}} = \{a_1^{\mathrm{R}}, \ldots, a_m^{\mathrm{R}}\}$ and $A^{\mathrm{H}} = \{a_1^{\mathrm{H}}, \ldots, a_n^{\mathrm{H}}\}$ respectively. The payoff associated with each pair of actions is uniquely identified by a matrix $R = [r_{i,j}], (i,j) \in [m] \times [n]$, where the entry $r_{i,j}$ denotes the reward[2] for the action pair $(a_i^{\mathrm{R}}, a_j^{\mathrm{H}})$ chosen by these two players. We denote the reward vector corresponding to row i by r_i, i.e., $r_i = (r_{i,1}, \ldots, r_{i,n})$. Importantly, the *same reward* is experienced together by both players. Therefore this is an *identical payoff* game where the goal is to maximize the total reward obtained in T (finite) rounds of playing this repeated game. If the reward matrix was perfectly known to both the agents, they would have played the action pair that gives the maximum reward in each round.

However, we assume that in the beginning of the game, the robot has perfect information about the reward matrix, whereas the human has possibly incorrect information (captured by a reward matrix R^H which the human *believes* to be the true reward matrix). In different rounds of the game, the human probabilistically learns different entries of this matrix and picks action accordingly. We will assume that the human is capable of taking the optimal action given her knowledge of the payoffs, e.g., if a specific row of this matrix is completely known to the human and the robot plays the action corresponding to this row,[3] the human will pick the action that maximizes the reward in this row. However, if the entries of a row are yet to be learned by the human, the human picks an action according to arg max r_i^H, where r_i^H is the i-th row of R^H.

The only aspect of this game that may change over time is the state of the human, which we denote by $x_t, t \in [T]$. Therefore, the state of the game is simply the state of the human agent. We denote the state space of the game as $\mathcal{X}$; it will be instantiated below in different models of information dissemination.

A policy $\pi = (\pi_1, \ldots, \pi_T)$ is a sequence of robot action functions $\pi_t : \mathcal{X} \to A^{\mathrm{R}}$, $t \in [T]$. The decision problem of the robot is to find the optimal policy $\pi^* = (\pi_1^*, \ldots, \pi_T^*)$ that maximizes the expected payoff U_1 starting from round 1, defined as follows. Denoting the strategy of the human by $s^{\mathrm{H}} : A^{\mathrm{R}} \times \mathcal{X} \to A^{\mathrm{H}}$.

$$U_1(\pi|x_1) \triangleq \mathbb{E}\left[\sum_{t=1}^{T} R(\pi_t(x_t), s^{\mathrm{H}}(\pi_t(x_t), x_t)) \middle| x_1\right] \qquad (1)$$
$$\pi^* \in \operatorname*{argmax}_{\pi} U_1(\pi|x_1)$$

4. APPROACH

We consider a setting where, in each round, the robot plays first by choosing a row. We model the strategy of the human $s^{\mathrm{H}} : A^{\mathrm{R}} \times \mathcal{X} \to A^{\mathrm{H}}$ as maximizing a human reward function R^{H}. In other words, the human *best responds* to the robot action, according to the (possibly erroneous) way she currently perceives the payoffs. The human reward matrix R^{H} evolves over time, as the human learns the "true" reward R through interaction with the robot. We propose a model of human *partial adaptation*, where the human learns with probability α the entries of row r_i that correspond to the robot action a_i^{R} played, and with probability $(1-\alpha)$ none of the entries. We consider the following models, based on when the human learning occurs, and on whether the robot directly observes if the human has learned.

[2]We will use the terms 'reward' and 'payoff' interchangeably.
[3]We will refer to this robot action as *playing a row*.

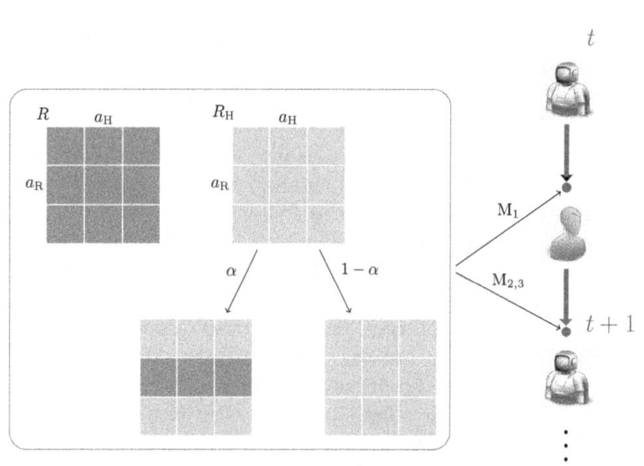

Figure 2: Models of human partial adaptation, described in Sec. 4. The human learns with probability α the entries of row r_i that correspond to the robot action a_i^{R} played, and with probability $1-\alpha$ none of the entries. The learning occurs before her action (*learning from robot action* – $\mathbf{M_1}$), or after her action (*learning from experience* – full observability ($\mathbf{M_2}$) or partial observability ($\mathbf{M_3}$)).

$\mathbf{M_1}$. The human learns the payoffs immediately after the robot plays a row, and before she takes her own action. The robot can infer whether the human has learned the row, by observing the reward after the human has played in the same round. We call this *learning from robot action*, where the robot has *full observability* of the human internal state. This model is studied in Sec. 6.1.

$\mathbf{M_2}$. The human learns the payoffs associated with a row after she plays in response to the robot's action. The robot can observe whether the human has learned before the start of the next round, for instance by directly asking the human, or by interpreting human facial expressions and head gestures [11]. We call this model *learning from experience*, where the robot has *full observability* of the human internal state. This model is studied in Sec. 6.2.

$\mathbf{M_3}$. Identically to model $\mathbf{M_2}$, the human learns a row after her action in response to the robot action. However, the robot does not immediately observe whether the human has learned, rather infers it through the observation of human actions in subsequent rounds of the game. This is a case of *learning from experience, partial observability.*

We note that we do not define a model for *learning from robot action, partial observability* case, since the robot can always directly observe whether the human has learned, based on the reward resulting from the human action in the same round.

Figure 2 shows the different models. In Section 5, we discuss the general case of partial observability (Model $\mathbf{M_3}$) and formulate the problem as a Markov Decision Process [30]. Computing the optimal policy in this case is exponential in the number of robot actions m. However, when the robot has full observability of the human state (Models $\mathbf{M_1}, \mathbf{M_2}$), the optimal policy has a special structure and can be computed in time polynomial in m and T (Section 6).

5. THEORY: PARTIAL OBSERVABILITY

In this section we examine the hardest case, where the human learns the payoffs associated with the row after their choice of actions, and the robot cannot directly observe whether the human has learned the payoffs (model $\mathbf{M_3}$). Instead, the robot infers whether the human has learned the row by observing the human response in subsequent rounds of the game.

While the human state is partially observable, we can exploit the structure of the problem and reduce it to a Markov Decision Process based on the following observation: the probability of the human having learned a row is either 0 when it is played for the first time; α after it is played by the robot and the human responds sub-optimally; and 1 after the the human has played the actual best-response strategy (according to R) for that row (which means she has learned the true rewards in the previous round).

We define a Markov decision process in this setting as a tuple $\{\mathcal{X}, A^{\mathrm{R}}, P, R, T\}$, where:

- $\mathcal{X} \in \{0, \psi, 1\}^m$ is a finite set of human states. A state x is represented by a vector $(x_1, x_2, ..., x_m)$, where $x_i \in \{0, \psi, 1\}$ and i is the corresponding row in the matrix. The starting state is $x_i = 0$ for each row i. $x_i = \psi$ indicates that the robot does not know whether human has learned row i or not. In this state, the human plays the best response in that row with probability α, or an action defined by the strategy s^{H} of the human with probability $(1-\alpha)$. If the human plays best-response, then the robot knows that human has learned row i, thus the entry for that row is $x_i = 1$.
- $A^{\mathrm{R}} = \{a_1^{\mathrm{R}}, \ldots, a_m^{\mathrm{R}}\}$ is a finite set of robot actions.
- $P : \mathcal{X} \times A^{\mathrm{R}} \longrightarrow \Pi(\mathcal{X})$ is the state transition function, indicating the probability of reaching a new state x' from state x and action a_i^{R}. State x transitions to a new state x' with all vector entries identical, apart from the element x_i corresponding to the row played. If the robot plays i for the first time ($x_i = 0$), the corresponding entry in the next state x' deterministically becomes $x'_i = \psi$, since the robot no longer knows whether the human has learned the payoffs for that row. If $x_i = \psi$, the human may have learned that row in the past and play the best-response strategy, leading to a transition to $x'_i = 1$ with probability α. If the human does not play the best-response strategy, the robot still does not know whether they will have learned the payoffs after the current round, thus $x'_i = \psi$ with probability $(1-\alpha)$. If $x_i = 1$, the corresponding entry in all subsequent states will be $x'_i = 1$, i.e., if the human learns a row, we assume that she remembers the row in the future.
- $R : A^{\mathrm{R}} \times A^{\mathrm{H}} \longrightarrow \mathbb{R}$ is the reward function, giving the immediate reward gained by performing a human and robot action. Note that if action i is played and the state has $x_i = \psi$, the reward will be based on the best response in row i of R with probability α, and on row i of R^{H} with probability $(1-\alpha)$ — we consider the *expected* reward.
- T is the number of rounds.

The robot's decision problem is to find the optimal policy $\pi^* = (\pi_1^*, \ldots, \pi_T^*)$ to maximize the expected payoff U_1 as defined in Eq. 1.

We observe that in the current formalism, the size of the state-space is $|\mathcal{X}| = 3^m$, where m is the number of robot actions. Therefore, the computation of the optimal policy requires time exponential in m. In Section 6, we show that for the case where the robot can observe whether the human has learned the payoffs, the optimal policy can be computed in time polynomial in m and T.

6. THEORY: FULL OBSERVABILITY

In this section, we assume that the robot can observe whether the human has learned the payoffs. We instantiate state x_t as a vector $(x_{t,1}, x_{t,2}, \ldots, x_{t,m})$, where each $x_{t,i}$ is now a binary variable in $\{0, 1\}$ denoting the robot's knowledge in round t of whether row i is learned by the human. In contrast to Sec. 5, there is no uncertainty about whether the human has learned or not (therefore no ψ state).

6.1 Learning from Robot Action

This is the scenario where the human might learn the payoffs immediately after the robot plays a row, and before she takes her own action (Model $\mathbf{M_1}$ in Sec. 4). Clearly, the robot can figure out if the human learned the row by observing the reward for that round. Our algorithmic results in this model strongly rely on the following lemma.

LEMMA 1. *In model $\mathbf{M_1}$, if, under the optimal policy π^*, there exists $\tau \in \{2, \ldots, T\}$ and $i \in [m]$ such that $x_{\tau,i} = 1$ and $\max r_i \geqslant \max r_j$ for all j such that $x_{\tau,j} = 1$, then $\pi_t^*(x_t) = a_i^{\mathrm{R}}$ for all $\tau \leqslant t \leqslant T$ and for all $x_t = x_\tau$.*

This lemma says that the optimal policy for the robot is to pick the action a_i^{R} when i is the row that yields the maximum reward among the rows already learned by the human. As we will show in detail later, this directly leads to a computationally efficient algorithm, via the following insight: *if the robot plays a row and this row is successfully revealed to the human, the optimal policy for the robot is to keep playing that row until the end of the game.*

The main idea behind the proof below is: if at round $t-1$ the optimal policy plays row 2, and that row is revealed, then it will not explore the unrevealed (higher rewarding) row 1 afterwards. The reason is that if the optimal policy chose to explore row 1 at some time in the future — which is a contradiction to the lemma — then playing row 1 at round $t-1$ would have been optimal, therefore an optimal policy would not have played row 2 at round $t-1$.

PROOF OF LEMMA 1. Assume for contradiction that the lemma does not hold, and let t be the *last* round in which the optimal policy violates the lemma, i.e., the last round in which there are $i, j \in [m]$ such that $x_{t,i} = 0$ and $x_{t,j} = 1$, but the optimal policy plays row i. Without loss of generality assume that these i and j are rows 1 and 2, respectively. For all rounds from $t+1$ to T, it holds (by the choice of t) that if row i is revealed to the human, the optimal policy will continue playing a_i^{R} (if there are multiple such rows, it plays the one with highest reward).

Let the maximum rewards corresponding to rows 1 and 2 be R_1 and R_2, respectively, i.e., $R_k = \max r_k$. We assume w.l.o.g. that row 2 has the highest maximum reward among all revealed rows. We can also assume that $R_1 > R_2$, since a policy that moves away from a row that is simultaneously known and more rewarding is clearly suboptimal.

If a row is not learned, the reward associated with actions a_1^{R} and a_2^{R} are C_1 and C_2, where $C_k = r_k[\operatorname{argmax} r_k^H]$. Clearly, $C_1 \leqslant R_1$ and $C_2 \leqslant R_2$. Since the optimal policy chose a_1^{R} in round t over a_2^{R}, the expected payoff of choosing a_1^{R} in round t must be larger than that of a_2^{R}, i.e.,

$$\alpha(R_1 + U_{t+1}(\pi^*|(1,1,\ldots))) + (1-\alpha)\cdot(C_1 + U_{t+1}(\pi^*|(0,1,\ldots))) > R_2 + U_{t+1}(\pi^*|(0,1,\ldots)),$$

where the first term on the LHS shows the expected payoff if row 1 is learned in round t, and the second term shows the payoff when it is not. It follows that

$$\alpha(R_1 + R_1 \cdot (T-t-1)) + (1-\alpha)\cdot(C_1 + R_2 \cdot (T-t-1)) > R_2 + R_2 \cdot (T-t-1). \quad (2)$$

The implication holds because from round $t+1$, we assume (by the choice of t) that the optimal policy continues playing the best action among the revealed rows. We make the above inequality into an equality by adding a slack variable $\epsilon > 0$ as follows.

$$\alpha R_1 \cdot (T-t) + (1-\alpha)(C_1 + R_2 \cdot (T-t-1)) = R_2 + R_2 \cdot (T-t-1) + \epsilon. \quad (3)$$

Denote the LHS of the above equality as ρ_1. Note that this is the assumed optimal value of the objective function at round t when the state x_t is $(0,1,\ldots)$, i.e., $U_t(\pi^*|(0,1,\ldots)) = \rho_1$. Rearranging the expressions above, we get,

$$\alpha R_1 \cdot (T-t) + (1-\alpha)C_1 = R_2 + \alpha R_2 \cdot (T-t-1) + \epsilon. \quad (4)$$

We claim that if the optimal policy chooses the action a_1^{R} at round t, then the expected payoff in round $t-1$ from choosing the action a_1^{R} would have been larger than that of the action a_2^{R}. If our claim is true, then the current policy, which chose a_2^{R} at $t-1$, cannot be optimal, and we reach a contradiction. To analyze the decision problem in round $t-1$, we need to consider two possible states of the game in this round.

Case 1: $x_{t-1} = (0,0,\ldots)$. In this state, playing a_1^{R} gives an expected payoff of

$$\alpha(R_1 + U_t(\pi^*|(1,0,\ldots))) + (1-\alpha)(C_1 + U_t(\pi^*|(0,0,\ldots))) \geqslant \alpha(R_1 + R_1(T-t)) + (1-\alpha)(C_1 + U_t(\pi^*|(0,0,\ldots))). \quad (5)$$

The inequality holds because in state $(1,0,\ldots)$, playing a_1^{R} yields at least R_1 in every subsequent round. Playing a_2^{R} in round $t-1$ yields,

$$\alpha(R_2 + \rho_1) + (1-\alpha)(C_2 + U_t(\pi^*|(0,0,\ldots))). \quad (6)$$

This expression is similar to the RHS of Equation (5), except that the expected payoff at $x_t = (0,1,\ldots)$ is assumed to be ρ_1. We claim that the expression on the RHS of Eq. (5) is larger than the expression in Eq. (6), for which we need to show that

$$\begin{aligned} &\alpha(R_1 + R_1(T-t)) + (1-\alpha)C_1 \\ &\quad > \alpha(R_2 + \rho_1) + (1-\alpha)C_2 \\ \iff &\alpha R_1 + R_2 + \alpha R_2 \cdot (T-t-1) + \epsilon \\ &\quad > \alpha(R_2 + R_2 + R_2 \cdot (T-t-1) + \epsilon) + (1-\alpha)C_2 \\ \iff &\alpha R_1 + R_2 + \epsilon > \alpha R_2 + \alpha R_2 + (1-\alpha)C_2 + \alpha\epsilon. \end{aligned}$$

In the first equivalence, we substitute the expression from Eq. (4) on the LHS and the expression of ρ_1 from Eq. (3) on the RHS. The second equivalence holds by canceling out one term. We see that the final inequality is true since $R_2 \geqslant C_2, R_1 > R_2$, and $0 < \alpha < 1$.[4]

Case 2: $x_{t-1} = (0,1,\ldots)$, in this state playing the action a_1^{R} gives an expected payoff of at least

$$\alpha(R_1 + R_1 \cdot (T-t)) + (1-\alpha)(C_1 + U_t(\pi^*|(0,1,\ldots))) = \alpha(R_1 + R_1 \cdot (T-t)) + (1-\alpha)(C_1 + \rho_1). \quad (7)$$

This is similar to the RHS of Eq. (5) except that now we can replace $U_t(\pi^*|(0,1,\ldots))$ with ρ_1. On the other hand, the expected payoff of the action a_2^{R} in round $t-1$ is given by $R_2+\rho_1$ — because at state $(0,1,\ldots)$ in round $t-1$, action a_2^{R} gives R_2 deterministically, since the human knows row 2. The state remains the same even after reaching round t. The expected payoff at this round for this state is assumed to be ρ_1. Now to show that the expression in Eq. (7) is larger than $R_2 + \rho_1$, we need to show that

$$\begin{aligned} &\alpha(R_1 + R_1 \cdot (T-t)) + (1-\alpha)(C_1 + \rho_1) > R_2 + \rho_1 \\ \iff &\alpha R_1 + \alpha R_1 \cdot (T-t) + (1-\alpha)C_1 > R_2 + \alpha\rho_1 \\ \iff &\alpha R_1 + R_2 + \alpha R_2 \cdot (T-t-1) + \epsilon \\ &\quad > R_2 + \alpha R_2 + \alpha R_2 \cdot (T-t-1) + \alpha\epsilon \\ \iff &\alpha R_1 + \epsilon > \alpha R_2 + \alpha\epsilon \end{aligned}$$

The first equivalence comes from reorganizing the inequality. The second equivalence is obtained through substitution using Eqs. (3) and (4). The third equivalence follows by canceling out two terms. The last inequality is true since $R_1 > R_2$ and $0 < \alpha < 1$.

To summarize, we have reached a contradiction in both cases, which are exhaustive. This proves the lemma. □

6.2 Learning from Experience

Recall that in model $\mathbf{M_2}$, the human learns with probability α all payoffs associated with a row *after* she plays her action in response to the robot playing an unrevealed row. She does not learn with probability $1-\alpha$. This model is the same as model $\mathbf{M_3}$ of Sec. 5, with an additional assumption: before the robot takes its next action, it can observe the current state.

We show that in this setting too, the optimal policy has a special structure similar to that under model $\mathbf{M_1}$ (Sec. 6.1), which can be computed in time polynomial in m and T.

LEMMA 2. *In model* $\mathbf{M_2}$, *if, under the optimal policy* π^*, *there are* $\tau \in \{2,\ldots,T\}$ *and* $i \in [m]$ *such that* $x_{\tau,i} = 1$ *and* $\max r_i \geqslant \max r_j$ *for all* j *such that* $x_{\tau,j} = 1$, *then* $\pi_t^*(x_t) = a_i^{\mathrm{R}}$ *for all* $\tau \leqslant t \leqslant T$ *and for all* $x_t = x_\tau$.

The proof is similar to the proof of Lemma 1. However, the expected payoffs and the corresponding inequalities are different. Therefore, we provide a proof sketch that identifies the differences from the previous proof.

PROOF OF LEMMA 2 (SKETCH). As before, the idea of the proof is to show that if the optimal policy changes its action from playing the revealed row that yields maximum reward, a_2^{R}, to playing an unrevealed row of higher maximum reward, a_1^{R}, for the last time in round t, then it must have done so in its previous round, leading to a contradiction. In model $\mathbf{M_2}$, the human does not observe the payoffs of the row played by the robot before she plays her own action. Therefore, we can assume w.l.o.g. that when an unrevealed row is played, its reward is no larger than the maximum reward of that row, e.g., $C_1 \leqslant R_1$ if row 1 is played. Hence, if the optimal policy changes its action from a_2^{R} to a_1^{R} in round t when $x_t = (0,1,\ldots)$, the inequality equivalent to Eq. (2) must be

$$C_1 + \alpha R_1 \cdot (T-t-1) + (1-\alpha)R_2 \cdot (T-t-1) > R_2 + R_2 \cdot (T-t-1). \quad (8)$$

[4]If $\alpha = 1$, playing the row $\arg\max R_i$ is optimal and the lemma holds trivially. For $\alpha = 0$, the lemma is vacuously true. So, we assume $0 < \alpha < 1$ w.l.o.g.

After adding the slack variable, we get,

$$\begin{aligned}\rho_1 &\triangleq C_1 + \alpha R_1 \cdot (T-t-1) + (1-\alpha) R_2 \cdot (T-t-1) \\ &= R_2 + R_2 \cdot (T-t-1) + \epsilon \\ \Longrightarrow & C_1 + \alpha R_1 \cdot (T-t-1) = R_2 + \alpha R_2 \cdot (T-t-1) + \epsilon.\end{aligned}$$

In *Case 1*, the expected payoff of playing a_1^{R} is at least: $C_1 + \alpha R_1 \cdot (T-t) + (1-\alpha) U_t(\pi^* | (0, 0, \ldots))$. The expected payoff of playing a_2^{R} is: $C_2 + \alpha \rho_1 + (1-\alpha) U_t(\pi^* | (0, 0, \ldots))$. We show that the first expression is larger than the second, i.e.,

$$\begin{aligned}& C_1 + \alpha R_1 \cdot (T-t) > C_2 + \alpha \rho_1 \\ \Longleftrightarrow\ & \alpha R_1 + R_2 + \alpha R_2 \cdot (T-t-1) + \epsilon \\ & \quad > C_2 + \alpha R_2 + \alpha R_2 \cdot (T-t-1) + \alpha \epsilon \\ \Longleftrightarrow\ & \alpha R_1 + R_2 + \epsilon > C_2 + \alpha R_2 + \alpha \epsilon.\end{aligned}$$

The final inequality holds since $R_1 > R_2 \geqslant C_2$ and $0 < \alpha < 1$.

Similarly for *Case 2*, the expected payoff of playing a_1^{R} is at least:

$$\begin{aligned}& C_1 + \alpha R_1 \cdot (T-t) + (1-\alpha) U_t(\pi^* | (0, 1, \ldots)) \\ & \quad \geqslant C_1 + \alpha R_1 \cdot (T-t) + (1-\alpha) R_2 \cdot (T-t).\end{aligned}$$

On the other hand, the expected payoff of playing a_2^{R} is $R_2 + \rho_1$. We again show that the RHS of the first expression is larger than the second, i.e.,

$$\begin{aligned}& C_1 + \alpha R_1 \cdot (T-t) + (1-\alpha) R_2 \cdot (T-t) > R_2 + \rho_1 \\ \Longleftrightarrow\ & C_1 + \alpha R_1 \cdot (T-t-1) + \alpha R_1 + (1-\alpha) R_2 \cdot (T-t-1) \\ & \quad + (1-\alpha) R_2 > R_2 + R_2 + R_2 \cdot (T-t-1) + \epsilon \\ \Longleftrightarrow\ & R_2 + R_2 \cdot (T-t-1) + \epsilon + \alpha R_1 + (1-\alpha) R_2 \\ & \quad > R_2 + R_2 + R_2 \cdot (T-t-1) + \epsilon \\ \Longleftrightarrow\ & \alpha R_1 > \alpha R_2,\end{aligned}$$

which holds since $R_1 > R_2$ and $0 < \alpha < 1$. □

Algorithm 1 Optimal Policy: Full Observability

Input: matrix R, time horizon T, parameter α
Output: optimal action a_t^* in each round t
$U_t(x_t), a_t^*(x_t) = \texttt{OptPolicy}(x_t, t)$
procedure $\texttt{OptPolicy}(x_t, t)$
  if $t > T$ **then**
    return (0, None)
  else
    if x_t has at least one 1 **then**
      find a row k^* s.t. $k^* \in \operatorname{argmax}_{k: x_{t,k}=1} \max r_k$
      return $(\max r_{k^*} \times (T-t), k^*)$
    else
      find a row
      $i^* \in \operatorname{argmax}_{k \in [m]} [\alpha(R_k + U_{t+1}(\mathbf{e}_k)) + (1-\alpha)(C_k + U_{t+1}(\mathbf{0}))]$
      and its value u_{i^*} (*for model* $\mathbf{M_1}$)
      OR
      find a row
      $i^* \in \operatorname{argmax}_{k \in [m]} [C_k + \alpha U_{t+1}(\mathbf{e}_k) + (1-\alpha) U_{t+1}(\mathbf{0})]$
      and its value u_{i^*} (*for model* $\mathbf{M_2}$)
      return (u_{i^*}, i^*)

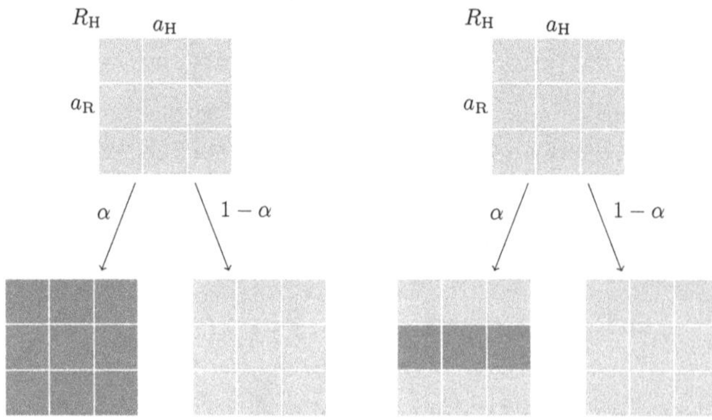

(a) (b)

Figure 3: The robot reward matrix R is in dark shade and the human reward matrix R^{H} in light shade. (a) The robot reveals its whole reward matrix with probability α. (b) The robot reveals the row played (in this example row 2) with probability α.

6.3 Design of an efficient algorithm

As advertised, using Lemmas 1 and 2, we can easily prove the following theorem.

THEOREM 1. *In models* $\mathbf{M_1}$ *and* $\mathbf{M_2}$, *an optimal policy can be computed in polynomial time.*

Indeed, the algorithm is specified as Algorithm 1. Here $\mathbf{e}_k$ denotes the m-dimensional standard unit vector in direction k. This algorithm runs in time polynomial in m and T since the inner `else` condition does not branch into two independent computations. This is because when at least one coordinate of x_t is 1, the inner `if` condition is met and the expected payoff in that case is computed without recursion. Therefore, in every round the number of computations is $O(m)$, and the algorithm has complexity $O(mT)$.

7. FROM THEORY TO USERS

We conduct a human subject experiment to evaluate the proposed model in a table-clearing task (Fig. 1). We focus on the case where the human *learns from experience* (Models $\mathbf{M_2}, \mathbf{M_3}$). We are interested in showing that the policies computed using the partial adaptation model will result in better performance than policies that model the human as completely adapting to the robot, which is an assumption used in previous work on human-robot mutual adaptation [25].

7.1 Manipulated Variables

Observability. We used two settings — one where the robot does not directly observe whether the human has learned (Sec. 5), and one where the robot observes directly whether the human has learned (Sec. 6.2).
Adaptation. We compared the proposed partial adaptation model with a model of complete adaptation, where the robot models the human as learning all rows of the payoff matrix with probability α after a row is played, instead of learning only the row played (Fig. 3a).

7.2 Hypothesis

We hypothesize that the robot policies that model the human as partially adapting to the robot will perform better than the policies that assume complete adaptation of the human to the robot.

7.3 Experiment Setting

Table-clearing task. We test the hypothesis in the table-clearing task of Fig. 1, where a human and a robot collaborate to clear the table from objects. In this task, the human can take any of the following actions: {pick up any of the blue cups and place them on the blue bin, change the location of any of the bins, empty any of the bottles of water}. The robot can either remain idle or pick up any of the bottles from the table and move them to the red bin. The goal is to maximize the number of objects placed in the bins.

The human does not have in advance the following information about the robot: (1) the robot does not know the location of the green bin. Therefore, when the robot attempts to grab one of the bottles, it may push the green bin, dropping the blue bin off the table. (2) The robot will fail if it picks up the bottle that is farthest away from it, if that bottle has water in it. This is because of its motor torque limits.

Model parameters. This information is represented in the form of a payoff matrix R. The entries correspond to the number of objects in the bins after each human and robot action. Table 1 shows part of R; it includes only the subset of human actions that affect the outcome. For instance, if the robot starts moving towards the bottle that is closest to it (action 'Pick up closest') and the human does not move the green or blue bin out of the way, the robot will drop the blue bin off the table, together with any blue cups that the human has placed. Therefore, at the end of the task only the bottle will be cleared from the table, resulting in a reward of 1. If the robot attempts to pick up both bottles (action "pick up both") and the human does not empty the bottle of water before the robot grasps it, the robot will fail, resulting in a reward of 0. If the human has emptied the bottle and moved the blue bin (action "Clear cups & move bin & empty bottle"), the robot will successfully clear both bottles without dropping the bin, resulting in a reward of 4 (2 bottles in the red bin and 2 cups in the blue bin).

In the beginning of the task, we assume that the human response to all robot actions will be "Clear cups"; since the human has not observed the robot dropping the bin or failing to pick up the bottle, she has no reason to move the bin or empty the bottle of water. We also assume that she does not learn any payoffs if the robot remains idle ("Noop" action). We set the probability of learning $\alpha = 0.9$, since we expected most participants to learn the best-response to the robot actions after observing the outcome of their actions.

Procedure. The experimenter first explained the task to the participants and informed them about the actions that they could take, as well as about the robot actions. Participants were told that the goal was to maximize the number of objects placed in the bins at each round. They performed the task three times ($T = 3$). In the full observability setting, the experimenter asked the participants after each round, what would their action be if the robot did the same action in the next round. The experimenter then inputted their response (learned or not learned) into the program that executed the policy. When the robot failed to pick up the bottle, the experimenter informed them that the robot had failed. Participants were told that the error message displayed in the terminal was: "The torque of the robot motors exceeded their limits." This is the generic output of our ROS-based hardware interface, when the measured torques exceed the manufacturer limits. We added a short, general explanation about how torque is related to distance and applied force. At the end, participants answered open-ended questions about their experience in the form of a video-taped interview.

	Clear cups	Clear cups & move bin	Clear cups & move bin & empty bottle
Noop	2	2	2
Pick up closest	1	3	3
Pick up both	0	0	4

Table 1: Part of payoff matrix R for table-clearing task. The table includes only the subset of human actions that affect performance.

7.4 Subject Allocation

We recruited 60 participants from a university campus. We chose a between-subjects design in order to avoid biasing users towards policies from previous conditions.

8. RESULTS AND DISCUSSION

Analysis. We evaluate team performance by the accumulated reward over the three rounds of the task (Fig. 4-left). We observe that the mean reward in the partial adaptation policy was 42% higher than that of the complete adaptation policy in the partial observability setting, and 52% higher than that of the complete adaptation policy in the full observability setting. A factorial ANOVA showed no significant interaction effects between the observability and adaptation factors. The test showed a statistically significant main effect of adaptation ($F(1, 56) = 18.58, p < 0.001$), and no significant main effect of observability. These results support our hypothesis.

The difference in performance occurred because in the complete adaptation model the robot erroneously assumed that the human had learned the best-response to the "Pick up both" action, after the robot played the row "Pick up closest". In this section, we examine the partial and complete adaptation policies in the *partial-observability* setting. The interpretation of the robot actions in the *full-observability* setting is similar, and we omit it because of space limitations. The robot chooses the action "Pick up both" for round $T = 1$ (as well as for $T = 2, 3$) in the partial adaptation condition[5], since the loss of receiving zero reward at $T = 1$ is outweighed by the rewards of 4 in subsequent rounds, if the human learns the best-response to that action, which occurs with high probability ($\alpha = 0.9$). On the other hand, the robot in the complete adaptation condition takes the action "Pick up closest" at $T = 1$ and "Pick up both" at $T = 2$ and $T = 3$. This is because the model assumes that the human

[5]Unless specified otherwise, for the rest of this section we refer to the partial observability level of the observability factor.

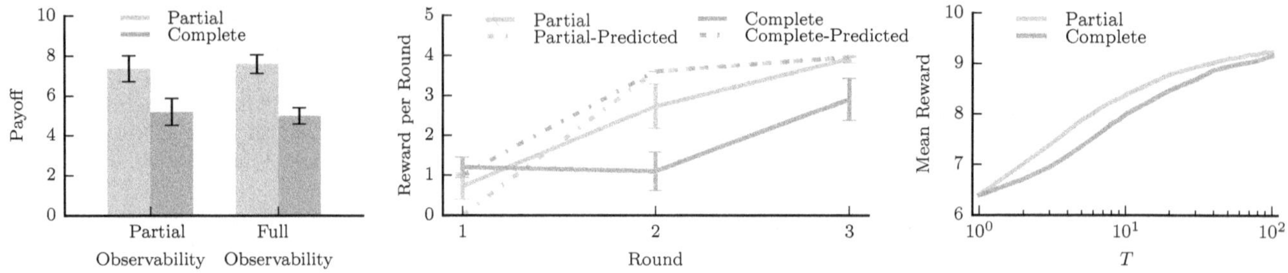

Figure 4: Left: Accumulated reward over 3 trials of the table-clearing task for all four conditions. Center: Predicted and actual reward by the partial and complete adaptation policies in the partial observability setting. Right: Mean reward over time horizon T for simulated runs of the complete and partial adaptation policies in the partial observability setting. The gain in performance from the partial adaptation model decreases for large values of T. The x-axis is in logarithmic scale.

will learn the best-response for all robot actions if the robot plays either "Pick up closest" or "Pick up both", and the predicted reward of 1 for the action "Pick up closest" is higher than the reward of 0 for "Pick up both" at $T = 1$.

Fig. 4 (center) shows the expected immediate reward predicted by the partial and complete adaptation model for each round in the partial observability setting, and the actual reward that participants received. We see that the immediate reward in the complete adaptation condition at $T = 2$ was significantly lower than the predicted one. The reason is that six participants out of 10 in that condition did not infer at $T = 1$ that the robot was unable to pick up the second bottle and did not empty the bottle at $T = 2$, which was the best-response action. From the four participants that emptied the bottle, two of them justified their action by stating that "there was enough time to empty the bottle" before the robot would grab it. The same justification was given by three participants out of eleven in the partial adaptation condition, who emptied the bottle at $T = 1$ without knowing that this was required for the robot to be able to pick it up. This caused the actual reward to be higher than its predicted value of 0. Additionally, the actual reward at $T = 2$ was lower than the predicted value. We attribute this to the fact that 73% of participants learned the best-response for the robot action (emptying the bottle that was farthest away) in that round, whereas the predicted value assumed a probability of learning $\alpha = 0.9$. In $T = 3$, the actual reward matched the prediction closely, since all participants eventually learned that they should empty the bottle.

Generalizability of the results. The results discussed above are compelling in that they arise from an actual human-subject experiment, but they are limited to one task. We are interested in showing — via simulations — that the proposed model performs well for a variety of tasks. We randomly generated instances of the reward matrix R and α values and simulated runs of the partial and complete adaptation policies for increasing time horizons T. The simulated humans partially adapted to the robot, and the robot did not observe whether they learned. For each value of T, we randomly sampled 1000 reward matrices R and simulated 100 policy runs for each sampled instance of R. Fig. 4 (right) shows the reward averaged over the number of rounds T, policy runs and instances of R. For $T = 1$, the mean reward is the same for both models, since there is no adaptation. The partial adaptation policies consistently outperform the complete adaptation ones for a large range of T. For large values of T the performance difference decreases. This is because the human eventually learns the true payoffs and the gain from playing the true best response outweighs the initial loss caused by the complete adaptation model.

Selection of α. We note that the α value, which represents the probability that the human learns the true robot capabilities, is task and population-dependent. In our experiment, participants were recruited from a university campus, and most of them were able to infer that they should empty the bottle, after observing the robot failing and being notified that "the robot exceeded its torque limits." Different participant groups may require a different α value. The value of α could also vary for different robot actions; we conjecture that our theoretical results hold also when there is a different adaptation probability α_i for each row i of the payoff matrix, which we leave as future work.

9. CONCLUSION

We presented a game-theoretic model of human partial adaptation to the robot. The robot used this model to decide optimally between taking actions that reveal its capabilities to the human and taking the best action given the information that the human currently has. We proved that under certain observability assumptions, the optimal policy can be computed efficiently. Through a human subject experiment, we demonstrated that policies computed with the proposed model significantly improved human-robot team performance, compared to policies that assume complete adaptation of the human to the robot.

While our model assumes that the human may learn only the entries of the row played by the robot, there are cases where a robot action may affect entries that are associated with other actions, as well. For instance, Cha et al. [8] have shown that conversational speech can affect human perception of robot capability in physical tasks. We are excited to explore the structure of probabilistic graphical models of human adaptation, and use the theoretical insights from this work to develop efficient algorithms for the robot.

Acknowledgments

This work is funded by the DARPA SIMPLEX program through ARO contract number 67904LSDRP, the National Institutes of Health (#R01EB019335), the National Science Foundation (CPS-1544797, CCF-1215883, IIS-1350598, CCF-1525932), the Office of Naval Research (N00014-16-1-3075), a Fulbright-Nehru postdoctoral fellowship, and a Sloan Research Fellowship. We also acknowledge the Onassis Foundation as a sponsor.

10. REFERENCES

[1] P. Abbeel and A. Y. Ng. Apprenticeship learning via inverse reinforcement learning. In *ICML*, 2004.

[2] B. Akgun, M. Cakmak, J. W. Yoo, and A. L. Thomaz. Trajectories and keyframes for kinesthetic teaching: a human-robot interaction perspective. In *HRI*, 2012.

[3] B. D. Argall, S. Chernova, M. Veloso, and B. Browning. A survey of robot learning from demonstration. *Robot. Auton. Syst.*, 2009.

[4] C. G. Atkeson and S. Schaal. Robot learning from demonstration. In *ICML*, 1997.

[5] M.-F. Balcan, A. Blum, N. Haghtalab, and A. D. Procaccia. Commitment without regrets: Online learning in stackelberg security games. In *Proceedings of the Sixteenth ACM Conference on Economics and Computation*, pages 61–78. ACM, 2015.

[6] T. Bandyopadhyay, K. S. Won, E. Frazzoli, D. Hsu, W. S. Lee, and D. Rus. Intention-aware motion planning. In *WAFR*. Springer, 2013.

[7] F. Broz, I. Nourbakhsh, and R. Simmons. Designing pomdp models of socially situated tasks. In *RO-MAN*, 2011.

[8] E. Cha, A. D. Dragan, and S. S. Srinivasa. Perceived robot capability. In *Robot and Human Interactive Communication (RO-MAN), 2015 24th IEEE International Symposium on*, pages 541–548. IEEE, 2015.

[9] S. Chernova and M. Veloso. Teaching multi-robot coordination using demonstration of communication and state sharing. In *AAMAS*, 2008.

[10] V. Conitzer and T. Sandholm. Computing the optimal strategy to commit to. In *Proceedings of the 7th ACM conference on Electronic commerce*, pages 82–90. ACM, 2006.

[11] R. El Kaliouby and P. Robinson. Real-time inference of complex mental states from facial expressions and head gestures. In *Real-time vision for human-computer interaction*, pages 181–200. Springer, 2005.

[12] J. Forlizzi. How robotic products become social products: an ethnographic study of cleaning in the home. In *Proceedings of the ACM/IEEE international conference on Human-robot interaction*, pages 129–136. ACM, 2007.

[13] M. A. Goodrich and A. C. Schultz. Human-robot interaction: a survey. *Foundations and trends in human-computer interaction*, 2007.

[14] A. Green and H. Huttenrauch. Making a case for spatial prompting in human-robot communication, in multimodal corpora: From multimodal behaviour theories to usable models. In *workshop at LREC*, 2006.

[15] V. Groom and C. Nass. Can robots be teammates?: Benchmarks in human–robot teams. *Interaction Studies*, 8(3):483–500, 2007.

[16] D. Hadfield-Menell, A. Dragan, P. Abbeel, and S. Russell. Cooperative inverse reinforcement learning, 2016.

[17] S. Ikemoto, H. B. Amor, T. Minato, B. Jung, and H. Ishiguro. Physical human-robot interaction: Mutual learning and adaptation. *IEEE Robot. Autom. Mag.*, 2012.

[18] T. Kanda, T. Hirano, D. Eaton, and H. Ishiguro. Interactive robots as social partners and peer tutors for children: A field trial. *Human-computer interaction*, 2004.

[19] E. Karpas, S. J. Levine, P. Yu, and B. C. Williams. Robust execution of plans for human-robot teams. In *ICAPS*, 2015.

[20] O. Lemon and O. Pietquin. *Data-Driven Methods for Adaptive Spoken Dialogue Systems: Computational Learning for Conversational Interfaces*. Springer Publishing Company, Incorporated, 2012.

[21] Y. Li, K. P. Tee, W. L. Chan, R. Yan, Y. Chua, and D. K. Limbu. Role adaptation of human and robot in collaborative tasks. In *2015 IEEE International Conference on Robotics and Automation (ICRA)*, pages 5602–5607. IEEE, 2015.

[22] O. Macindoe, L. P. Kaelbling, and T. Lozano-Pérez. Pomcop: Belief space planning for sidekicks in cooperative games. In *AIIDE*, 2012.

[23] T.-H. D. Nguyen, D. Hsu, W. S. Lee, T.-Y. Leong, L. P. Kaelbling, T. Lozano-Perez, and A. H. Grant. Capir: Collaborative action planning with intention recognition. In *AIIDE*, 2011.

[24] M. N. Nicolescu and M. J. Mataric. Natural methods for robot task learning: Instructive demonstrations, generalization and practice. In *AAMAS*, 2003.

[25] S. Nikolaidis, A. Kuznetsov, D. Hsu, and S. Srinivasa. Formalizing human-robot mutual adaptation: A bounded memory model. In *The Eleventh ACM/IEEE International Conference on Human Robot Interation*, pages 75–82. IEEE Press, 2016.

[26] S. Nikolaidis, R. Ramakrishnan, K. Gu, and J. Shah. Efficient model learning from joint-action demonstrations for human-robot collaborative tasks. In *HRI*, 2015.

[27] S. Nikolaidis and J. Shah. Human-robot cross-training: computational formulation, modeling and evaluation of a human team training strategy. In *HRI*, 2013.

[28] A. Powers and S. Kiesler. The advisor robot: tracing people's mental model from a robot's physical attributes. In *Proceedings of the 1st ACM SIGCHI/SIGART conference on Human-robot interaction*, pages 218–225. ACM, 2006.

[29] B. Robins, K. Dautenhahn, R. Te Boekhorst, and A. Billard. Effects of repeated exposure to a humanoid robot on children with autism. In *Designing a more inclusive world*. 2004.

[30] S. J. Russell and P. Norvig. *Artificial Intelligence: A Modern Approach*. Pearson Education, 2003.

[31] D. Sadigh, S. Sastry, S. A. Seshia, and A. D. Dragan. Planning for autonomous cars that leverages effects on human actions. In *Proceedings of the Robotics: Science and Systems Conference (RSS)*, 2016.

[32] M. Tambe. *Security and game theory: algorithms, deployed systems, lessons learned*. Cambridge University Press, 2011.

[33] P. Trautman and A. Krause. Unfreezing the robot: Navigation in dense, interacting crowds. In *Intelligent Robots and Systems (IROS), 2010 IEEE/RSJ International Conference on*, pages 797–803. IEEE, 2010.

Towards Adaptive Social Behavior Generation for Assistive Robots Using Reinforcement Learning

Jacqueline Hemminghaus
CITEC, Bielefeld University
33619 Bielefeld, Germany
jhemming@techfak.uni-bielefeld.de

Stefan Kopp
CITEC, Bielefeld University
33619 Bielefeld, Germany
skopp@techfak.uni-bielefeld.de

ABSTRACT

In this paper we explore whether a social robot can learn, in and from a task-oriented interaction with a human user, how to employ different social behaviors to achieve interactional goals under specific situational circumstances. We present a multimodal behavior generation architecture that maps high-level interactional functions and behaviors onto low-level behaviors executable by a robot. While high-level behaviors are selected based on the state of the user as well as the interaction, reinforcement learning is used within each behavior to optimize its local mapping onto lower-level behaviors. The approach is implemented and applied in a scenario in which a social robot (Furhat) assists a human player in solving a Memory game by guiding the attention of the user to target objects. Results of an evaluation study demonstrate that participants are able to solve the Memory faster with the adaptive, assistive robot.

CCS Concepts

•Computing methodologies → Cognitive robotics; Sequential decision making; •Applied computing → Interactive learning environments; •Human-centered computing → *Empirical studies in HCI;*

Keywords

Reinforcement Learning; Assistive Robotics; Multimodal Behavior Generation; Human-Robot Interaction

1. INTRODUCTION

Social robots are increasingly applied in assistive settings where they interact with human users to support, e.g. language learning [24], well-being and healthy living [4], or daily activities [36]. In all of these scenarios, abilities for robust and reliable social interaction are mandatory. However, while there is growing empirical evidence suggesting how robots should be designed or how they should behave suitably in interactive contexts, there are still many open challenges when it comes to building robots that interact autonomously with their human users. These challenges arise, first, from the mere difficulty and complexity of task-oriented communication and social interaction that is often envisioned to comprise spoken language commands and non-verbal behaviors to attain mutual understanding, engagement or assistance in the human-robot interaction. In addition, different users (or user groups) exhibit considerable inter-individual differences with respect to their preferences, skills or limitations for a task-oriented human-robot interaction. This makes it hard to develop reliable technical approaches that scale well across situations and users. This problem is amplified by the fact that robots are increasingly applied to interact with special user groups, from children to elderly users, and from typically developing users to those with impairments (e.g. autistic children, cognitively impaired users). Further, we now have a variety of robot platforms which differ with respect to their communicative affordances (see Figure 1). Behavior generation approaches are thus always tailored to the specific robot being employed.

HRI '17, March 06 - 09, 2017, Vienna, Austria

ISBN 978-1-4503-4336-7/17/03...$15.00

DOI: http://dx.doi.org/10.1145/2909824.3020217

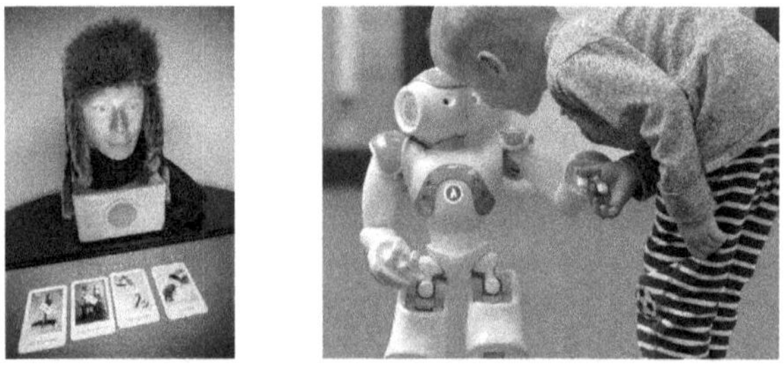

Figure 1: Interactive robots with different communicative affordances (left: *Furhat*; right: *Nao*).

In this paper we present first steps towards an approach to generate the social behavior of an assistive robot in an adaptive way. Our goal is to explore whether a social robot can learn - in and from a task-oriented interaction with the human user - how to employ certain social behaviors to achieve given interactional goals in specific situational circumstances. Specifically, we investigate the use of reinforcement learning [43] for this purpose. We focus on the important assistive function of guiding the attention of the user towards specific objects in a shared spatial environment. That is, we ask whether a social assistive robot can learn when and how to guide the attention of its user in specific situational contexts.

In Section 2 we first discuss related work on assistive robots and adaptive social behavior in human-robot interaction. Section 3 introduces our overall concept of social behavior generation, which decomposes the overall planning and execution problem into a hierarchy of higher-lever functions (e.g. grab-attention, guide-attention, motivate, etc.) and lower-level executable behaviors that can fulfill these functions. Section 4 presents where and how reinforcement learning can be applied within this behavior hierarchy, to enable adaptive behavior generation at the lower ("execution") level. We then describe an evaluation study in Section 5 for which this approach was implemented into an autonomous robot, Furhat [1], and tested in a game interaction (play of Memory) in which the robot could learn to utilize spatial referencing and attention guidance to provide assistance. Finally the results are presented in Section 6 and discussed in Section 7.

2. RELATED WORK

Assistive robotics is a growing research field with many potential applications. Especially the development of educational robots have been of interest and recent results increasingly suggest the potential of robots in educational scenarios [24]. For example, the mere social presence of an interactive robot is found to support second language learning [34]. Generally, such tutoring systems are expected to adapt to the students' input and their needs, and to provide help in form of hints or tailored instructions as a human teacher would do [10, 18, 40]. However, this adaption mainly refers to the particular exercises or tutoring acts issued [20], but not the generated social behavior of the robot.

While many social robots, especially in therapeutic scenarios, are controlled through predefined behaviors by a Wizard-of-Oz interface [42] or a remote control [27], there already exist approaches to autonomous behavior generation. Most often, the displayed behaviors are determined through a control architecture that rests on predefined interaction patterns, behavior primitives or motor programs [7, 11, 15]. This is sufficient for narrow task domains and very specific user interactions, but it is limited in terms of flexibility and adaptivity to different users, interaction contexts, or robot platforms.

These limitations can be compensated by using adaptive algorithms for the behavior development, like reinforcement learning, where the robot learns through experience from interacting with its environment: the robot receives either a positive or negative reward for its actions, which results in a heuristic process where the robot tries to maximize its future rewards. This is equivalent to developing an optimal policy for action selection. There are three main methods to solve reinforcement learning problems [43]: dynamic programming, Monte Carlo and temporal difference methods. For the present scenario, dynamic programming is not suitable because it needs a full model of the environment, which cannot be established due to unpredictability of the interaction with the user. Monte Carlo methods are completely model-free but they work with episodes and not in an incremental way. This makes it difficult to implement online versions of them. In contrast, temporal difference methods are suitable as they are model-free, as the Monte Carlo methods, and work online using step-by-step computation.

Additionally, reinforcement learning algorithms can be split in three different categories based on how the optimal policy is obtained [6]. Value iteration algorithms obtain the optimal policy by finding an optimal value function. In policy iteration algorithms an optimal value function is found by evaluating policies and employing these functions for achieving a new improved policy. In both categories, algorithms can be either model-free or model-based, but for policy iteration an initial policy is needed. In continuous state spaces, policy search algorithms directly search for an optimal policy with optimization techniques (e.g. gradient-based). For example, [38] adjusts a robot's interaction distance, gaze, motion, speech and timing depending on the user's body signal, with a policy gradient reinforcement learning approach. A different approach is to consider the decision-making process as driven by the fulfillment of goals and needs. In this view, the robot has to learn which behavior out of its repertory fulfills certain goals or needs [35]. Other recent approaches use reinforcement learning to minimize human effort and to optimize an industrial robot's dynamics to the operator skills in order to minimize tracking errors [39], or to increase the efficiency of task completion and user adaption through socially inspired rewards for the reinforcement process [16].

In the field of virtual agents, there are elaborated behavior generation approaches that encompass content planning, behavior planning and behavior execution [28, 44]. These approaches have been proposed for various social behaviors, e.g. turn-taking, co-verbal hand gestures, head gestures, body posture, expressive eye gaze or facial expression [cf. 21]. The underlying approaches are either model-based, i.e. predefined, based on heuristic decision rules derived from empirical data [8, 9, 33], or data-based, i.e. directly extracted from empirical data using machine learning techniques [12, 32]. However, none of them has looked at an online adaptation of behavior generation and how it can be based on social feedback or interactional outcomes in online interaction.

3. OVERALL APPROACH

In order to frame the behavior generation problem, we adopt a classical hierarchical approach [13, 19, 22, 23], in which high-level behaviors are mapped onto low-level behaviors that are directly executable by the robot. High-level behaviors directly correspond to interactional functions like guiding attention, motivating, or providing positive feedback, while low-level behaviors pertain to concrete social acts such as directed gaze, specific gestures, or verbal utterances. Low-level behaviors allow for parameterization in accord with the desired high-level function (e.g. a target location for directed gaze or a specific referring expression embedded in a verbal utterance).

The behavior generation architecture (Figure 2) starts after a simple control module has interpreted the user's behavior for cues of her attentive and affective state, and has chosen a high-level function to achieve an intended goal in the current situation. Generation starts with planning, which maps the selected high-level behavior onto low-level behaviors (so-called primitives). Then, these primitives choose one or more available actions and synchronizes them (control step). These new multimodal actions are structured over time to create either nested or sequentially arranged action commands that are sent to the connected robot control layer or, to allow for connection to any kind of robot, issue abstract commands in BML [29] that need to be in-

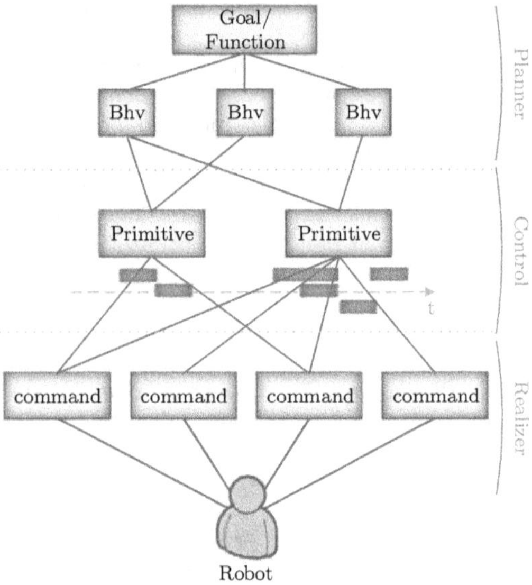

Figure 2: General structure of the behavior planning and realization process. Depending on a given goal or function, corresponding behaviors (Bhv) are chosen and split into sub-behaviors. Eventually, primitives (lowest-level behaviors) create sequential or parallel actions and send direct or abstract control commands to the robot control layer.

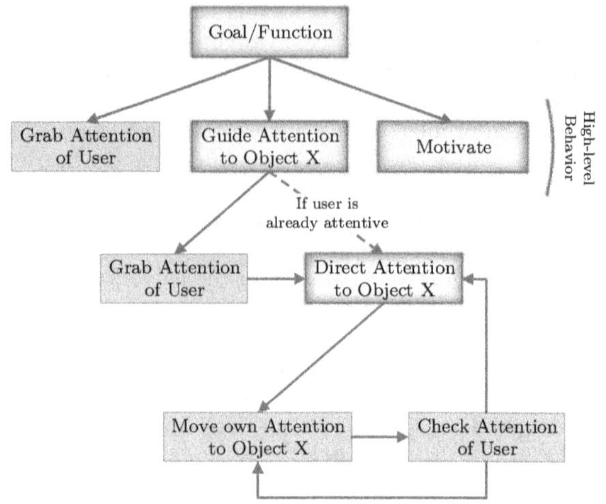

Figure 3: Exemplary behaviors that are hierarchically ordered and executable by the control module. Arrows represent the flow of the execution process. Highlighted behaviors indicate primitives that send either direct control or abstract commands including one or a combination of basic actions executable by the robot. For example, the guide-attention behavior is decomposed into sub-behaviors to control different phases. Note that behaviors are reusable (e.g. the grab-attention behavior is used twice).

terpreted and executed by a realization tool, e.g. the Asap Realizer [30], which is connected to the corresponding robot engine.

As shown in Figure 3, each behavior can delegate subgoals to sub-behaviors, which can further delegate subgoals to other behaviors, and so on. The corresponding structure by splitting high-level behaviors and delegating subgoals results in a hierarchical tree, which can be interpreted as reusable behavior patterns or templates. Importantly, each behavior decides by itself which action or sub-behavior is the most appropriate one. The goal of the present work, then, is to enable the robot to learn which behavior (or behavior combination) to pick in order to best realize a given high-level behavior.

4. ADAPTIVE BEHAVIOR GENERATION

The previously described behavior generation process can potentially be made adaptive in various ways. To start with, we focused on the decision process at the middle layer of the behavior hierarchy, i.e. regarding the choices how a given high-level behavior (e.g. directing attention) is realized through low-level behaviors. Because the robot should learn through its experience while interacting with its environment and its interaction partner, each low-level behavior has been equipped with a temporal difference reinforcement learning algorithm that can be implemented to adapt online and is model independent [26, 43]. One of the most generic temporal difference methods is Q-Learning [45], which has formed the basis for many specialized methods, like least square policy iteration [31] or batch mode fitted Q-iteration scheme [14]. As a starting point, and to evaluate the general appropriateness of temporal difference methods in the proposed scenario, we adopted Q-Learning (see the last section for a discussion on this).

In Q-Learning, the policy is formulated as a $Q(\vec{s}, \vec{a})$ matrix, where $\vec{s}$ describes the current state of the environment and $\vec{a}$ the action the robot uses to manipulate or interact with the environment. In the selected scenario, we formulate the policy as a $Q_p(\vec{s_u}, \vec{a_b})$ matrix, where $\vec{s_u}$ represents the user's current state, e.g. consisting of her behavior, attentive and affective state, whereas $\vec{a_b}$ represents the response of the robot. The Q-Learning approach is suitable because, even if it needs time to converge to an optimal policy, it is possible to choose actions before the optimal policy is reached. As treatment for the exploitation-exploration dilemma, we implemented the ϵ-greedy algorithm.

The action space A_b of the robot encompasses all possible actions of the robot. Here, an action $\vec{a_b} \in A_b$ can be any combination of behavioral modalities the robot provides, e.g. pointing, speaking, gazing, etc. or any combination of those. As state space S_u any values describing the user's state are possible. Currently, we model the user's communicative intent as well as her attentive and affective states. Right now the latter is derived indirectly from the gaze and speech behavior of the user, but an extension to more elaborated schemes using emotional valence and engagement is planned [20].

Adaption takes place anytime when the Q-matrix is updated. This happens when the goal of a behavior is reached or when a behavior is unsuccessfully stopped, in both of these cases the corresponding value in the Q-matrix is updated as follows:

$$Q_p(\vec{s_u}, \vec{a_b}) = (1-\alpha) \cdot Q_p(\vec{s_u}, \vec{a_b}) + \alpha \cdot (r + \gamma \cdot max\ Q_p(\vec{s_u'})) \quad (1)$$

	gaze	facial expression	head gesture	speech
costs	1	3	3	5

Table 1: Execution costs for each modality used by the robot head Furhat.

where $\vec{s_u'}$ is the new observed users state after the action was executed, α the learning rate and γ a discounting factor. The reward r depends on the success of the chosen action to fulfill the goal of the behavior, r_{pos}. Each time an action has no effect, it receives a negative reward r_{neg}. Additionally the given reward is weighted with the costs c of the chosen action. Table 1 shows the costs for each modality used in the proposed study. For combined actions the costs of all corresponding modalities are summed up.

$$r = \begin{cases} \text{success}, & r_{pos} - c \\ \text{no effect}, & c \cdot r_{neg} \end{cases} \tag{2}$$

As shown by [25], it is possible to distract the user from the task through social behavior of the robot because more attention is paid to the robot's behavior due to its novelty, or the behavior increases the cognitive load of users inhibiting their capacity to process task related information. In order to prevent a permanent distraction, the robot should strive to execute "minimal but sufficient" behaviors for the goal at hand, or sometimes even no behavior at all. As the likelihood to be distracted again may differ across users, the decision process of whether to generate a behavior or not needs to be adapted to each user, too. In our approach, this adaptation is realized via another policy based on a $Q_i(\vec{s_u}, a_h)$ matrix, where $\vec{s_u}$ is the user state as used in the behavior action selection. The corresponding action space A_h simply consists of two actions which can be interpreted as Boolean, where true equals the robot executes the behavior and false corresponds to no behavior.

$$a_h \in A_h,\ mit\ A_h = [true, false] \tag{3}$$

5. PROTOTYPE IMPLEMENTATION AND EVALUATION STUDY

To apply and test the proposed approach, we focused on the attention-guiding behavior. The refined behavior structure can be seen in Figure 3. As evaluation scenario we chose a Memory game that participants had to solve together with the robot head Furhat [1] (see Figure 4).

5.1 Scenario: Memory Game Assistance

The Memory game consists of eighteen cards containing nine pairs of pictures with contours of leafs on them (see Figure 5). During the game, the robot can autonomously decide to assist the participants in the game, e.g. if explicitly asked for or by analyzing the user's gaze behavior and speech. We selected this scenario for the following reasons: (1) the participants have an explicit task which they can solve on their own or with the help of the robot; (2) guiding attention to static spatial locations (cards) is a major assistive function; (3) task difficulty can be manipulated by choosing difficult images (similar images, few identifying characteristics), by increasing the number of pairs or by establishing a maximum time allowed for solving the game; (4) the robot can adapt its behavior to improve its helpfulness over multiple runs.

Figure 4: Experimental setup with the participant solving the Memory game on a touchscreen in front of the robot head Furhat.

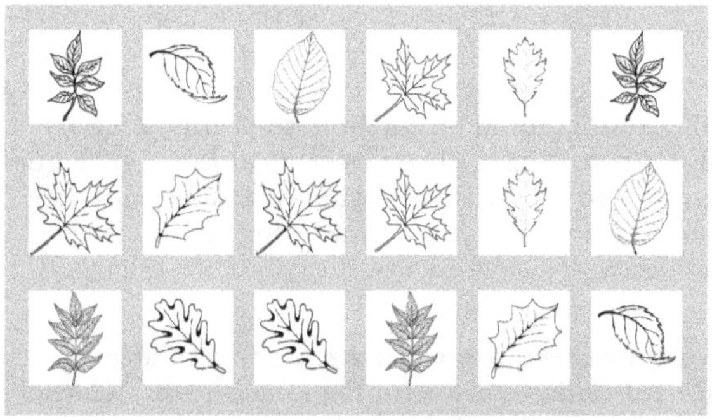

Figure 5: Card set used in the study.

During the study, the robot interprets the multimodal input of the participants, in particular their gaze and speech behavior. To not impose any constraints on how participants can ask for help, we employed a Wizard-of-Oz approach in which a human helped to categorize any requests for help (as an explicit request for help, an indirect request, or a general request for Furhat to engage). Table 2 shows how the different combinations of user input events (speech input, gaze behavior) are interpreted. For simplicity, we map any combination of input events onto a discrete three-value scale ('++', '+', '-') indicating the probability that the user requires help.

Once the user state is interpreted, it is combined with the current task demands to determine a probability for the robot to provide assistance. In the Memory game, the current situation is characterized by the game state given by the number of pairs that remain to be found. Currently we differentiate between three different game states (9-7, 6-4, or 3-1 pairs remaining, respectively). Table 3 shows how the different user states are combined with the game states to yield a discretized probability of robot assistance.

In addition, the different user input events together with the game state define the state vector $\vec{s_u}$, according to which the robot will have to determine the quality of its possible assistive actions:

$$\vec{s_u} \in \begin{pmatrix} user\_gaze \\ user\_speech \\ game\_state \end{pmatrix} \tag{4}$$

However, for the behavior selection we only used the game state as the robot already decided to help based on the com-

	S: -	S: furhat	S: help request	S: indirect request	S: furhat request
G: -	-	+	++	+	+
G: furhat	-	+	++	++	+
G: object	-	+	++	+	-
G: search	++	++	++	++	+
G: world	+	++	++	++	+

Table 2: Interpreted user state for different combinations of user input events: 'G:' denotes gaze behavior, 'S:' denotes speech input as categorized by a human wizard. The values in the table indicate the interpreted user state, as probability of the user requiring assistance.

	GS: 9-7	GS: 6-4	GS: 3-1
US: -	-	-	-
US: +	++	+	-
US: ++	++	++	+

Table 3: Combination of the interpreted user state ('US'; determined according to Table 2) with the game state ('GS'; given by the number of remaining pairs in the Memory game); values indicate the probability of the robot providing help.

bined state describing the users state and the game situation. This reduces the resulting Q-matrix for behavior selection down to 9 x 15 (state, behavior)-pairs, as shown in Figure 10. To achieve a good action selection within the study setting we used a fixed $\epsilon = 0.4$ for the ϵ-greedy algorithm and also a fixed, but relatively low learning rate $\alpha = 0.2$ to balance the learning effect.

5.2 Realization

We employ the talking robot head Furhat [1] (see Figure 1, left), which consists of a mask bot projected with an animated graphical face from within. The head is mounted on a 2-DOF neck joint enabling pitch and yaw rotations, i.e. head nodding and shaking. The robot is equipped with a loudspeaker and a microphone for speech-based or otherwise acoustic interaction. Through a connected Kinect [37] the robot is able to recognize different users and their positions in the environment.

As our current assistance use case is guiding attention, we include the following modalities on this robot platform: facial expression, head nod, gaze and speech. These modalities represent all affordances the robot head Furhat provides. At the same time, they have an important role in face-to-face interaction and are already well applied in related systems [2, 3, 17, 41]. Additionally, they are used by humans to guide the attention of others to points of interest. For example, [5] analyzed the behavioral hints and cues of mothers who directed their children's attention to specific objects. The annotated cues were classified as deictic, locating, naming, describing or background information. For our action selection, we draw on their findings regarding deictic and locating cues, which may be expressed non-verbally by nodding, pointing or directed gaze as well as verbal referring expressions. Cues of the other categories are not applied to the chosen scenario, because we have no distinct naming for each card nor do we include background information to enable an easier finding of the card [5].

In the present scenario, we implemented the following actions for Furhat: a sad frown, potentially indicating that there is something Furhat wants to do, but does not know how to; directed gaze at the correct second card; nodding to potentially convey agreement; referring expressions to identify the correct second card, e.g. 'Look in the second row, third column'. Note that any combination of theses actions is included as well. Furhat's referring actions like gaze and speech always referred to the correct solution (second card).

5.3 Evaluation Study

We conducted an evaluation study in the Memory game scenario, to investigate the effects of the robot's learning behavior and its adaption to the user. We defined two experimental conditions:

1. In the *learning condition* the robot decides if the participant needs support depending on state $\vec{s_u}$ as shown in Table 3. This state also determines the reward or punishment for supporting the participant, allowing us to investigate whether the robot learns when help is really necessary. Further, once the robot decided to support the participant, it randomly chooses either the action with the maximal Q-value out of all possible combinations of actions and modalities (60% probability) or explores other action combinations (40% probability). If the action helps the user in finding a correct pair, the robot will be rewarded, otherwise punished.

2. In the *random condition* the robot ignores the input of the user. Instead, it first randomly decides, with a probability of 50%, whether to help or not, and then randomly chooses an action to execute.

In a sense, the random condition is a minimal control condition. We adopted it in order to gain initial findings on what the potential positive and negative effects of the robot's behavior may be. Nevertheless, both conditions can be compared, because both draw from the very same pool of behaviors and, at the beginning, the learning condition chooses randomly, too. Additionally, even when the algorithm gathered some knowledge about the behaviors' helpfulness, there is still a chance of 40% that the algorithm chooses a behavior randomly for exploration.

Given the Memory game assistance as task for the evaluation, the number of attempts the participants needed to complete the game provides a direct measure of the assistance provide by the robot. We thus expect that participants in the learning condition solve the Memory faster than the ones in the random condition.

Participants 26 students (of Bielefeld University and the University of Applied Science at Bielefeld) of age between 19 and 33 participated in the study. One participant was excluded due to technical issues during the study. Half of the participants had no or little experience with humanoid robots.

Experimental Setup The experimental setup is visualized in Figure 4 with one participant sitting in front of the robot head Furhat solving a Memory game. Above the robot head we mounted a Kinect v2 [37], which enables recognition of the participant and the playing field between the robot and the participant. To visualize the Memory game we used a 27 inch touchscreen on which we displayed 18 cards, 6 in a row and 3 in column, containing 9 image pairs. As images we used sketches of different leafs, some more similar than the others (see Figure 5). The wizard was seated behind the robot outside the interaction space, so that he did not disturb the interaction. An additional camera was mounted next to the participants recording the whole interaction.

Procedure At the beginning, each participant was assigned to one of the two conditions (between-subjects design) and was instructed to solve 5 Memory games, each with as few moves as possible but with as much time needed. They were informed that they could ask Furhat for help if they are stuck. Each Memory game is started by clicking on a start button and all 18 cards are displayed. Depending on the condition, the timing of the procedure differs (Figure 6): In the adaptive condition, after the first card is turned, the participants could ask for help or look for the second card by themselves. While looking for the other card the Wizard interprets the users behavior for cues of uncertainty or helplessness and informs the adaptive algorithm, which increases the probability that Furhat helps without being asked. In the random condition, after the first card of a pair is turned, Furhat decides randomly if it should help. If yes, it waits for another 2 seconds before choosing again randomly a particular action and executing it. Once all cards are turned, the game resets and displays the start button again until a number of 5 Memory games have been solved.

6. RESULTS

In this section we present the results of the conducted study regarding (1) how fast or more precisely with how many moves the participants were able to solve the task in each condition (as a measure of the robot's overall assistance) and (2) how the robot learned which of his behaviors are the most supportive ones for assisting a user.

6.1 Overall Game Assistance

As shown in Figure 7, the participants in the random condition needed on average more card turns to complete the game than in the learning condition. An independent-samples t-test was conducted to compare random and help conditions. Participants in the random condition turned significantly more card pairs on average about 19.73 cards ($\sigma^2 = 4.08$), whereas participants in the learning condition needed on average 15.25 moves ($\sigma^2 = 2.96$), $t(23) = 4.54, p < 0.001, r = 0.69$. The average length of the game stays around 20 moves in the random condition, except for the third run where it decreases to around 18.58 moves. On the contrary, in the learning condition, the average game length slightly increases until the fourth run and then drops to only 13,61 ($\sigma^2 = 2.43$) for solving the last Memory game, which is only around five moves more than the optimum of 9 moves.

6.2 Learning of Assistive Behavior

The second question of interest is whether the robot in the learning condition has acquired knowledge regarding which one of its behaviors helps best to assist its user in a particular interaction. Figure 10 shows the average of all Q-matrices that were learned at the end of the study. As can be seen, in each game state one or two actions received a high value which represents the assumption of how successful the action was and in further situations might be. In every game state with more than 3 remaining pairs, an action containing either gaze or speech is the most successful one. Especially in the game state 9-7 even both speech and gesture, combined with head gesture and facial expression were necessary.

To analyze how the robot adapts to different interactions and users, we compare the Q-values of three different (game state, behavior)-pairs as they were learned in two interactions with different participants. Figure 8 shows the corresponding values. In the interaction shown in the top diagram, the values of the action *ghs* in the game state 8 has high Q-values which decrease over repeated runs, while action $gfhs$ in game state 4 or action *gh* in state 5 remain at relatively low values. In contrast, the bottom diagram shows an interaction in which the action *gh* has a high Q-value in game state 5. Likewise, 8 : *ghs* and 4 : $gfhs$ have relatively high Q-values with this participant, where $4 : gfhs$ is decreasing over the course of the interaction.

7. DISCUSSION AND CONCLUSION

In this paper we presented first steps towards an adaptive behavior generation for assistive robots. In the current approach, high-level behaviors are predefined and mapped onto lower-level behaviors that represent the set of communicative affordances of the robot. Q-learning is used to adapt and optimize this mapping based on the direct reward the robot experiences, both within and across interactions with the user. In an evaluation with the robot head Furhat that assists in Memory games, we compared this learning-based behavior generation to a random behavior condition.

The analysis of the results of the evaluation study show that the behavior of the robot in the learning condition achieved a better task assistance than the behavior in the random condition, even though the participants in the learning condition did not ask for help as much as in the random condition (mostly around maximal 6 requests during the whole study, see Figure 9).

Yet, due to the relatively small number of interactions with one particular user, the robot could not always fully explore its behavioral possibilities to adapt to the user. This leads to situations, in which the user asked the robot for help but the robot executed a behavior that in the current situation was not that as helpful as expected. While this can be expected to improve with further interactions, we are exploring in ongoing work how faster reinforcement learning schemes (such as LSPI [31]) can help to mitigate this problem. Another limitation is that action selection is based on the game state, which so far only accounts for the number of remaining pairs and not, e.g. their spatial arrangement.

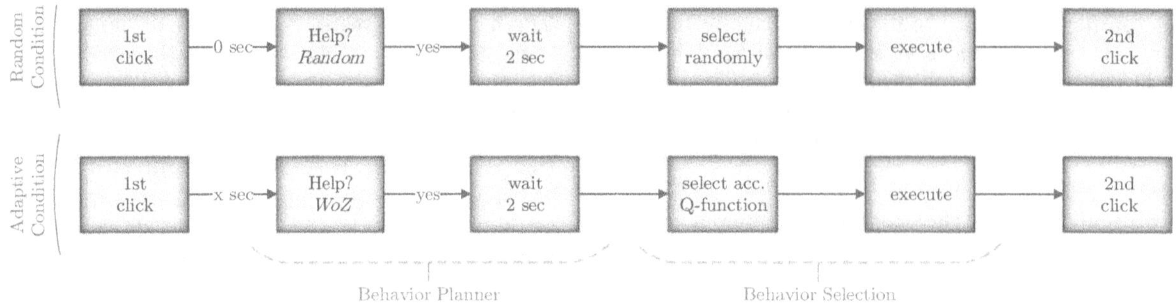

Figure 6: Temporal structure of the procedure according to which each behavior is planned and selected after the first card of a move is turned.

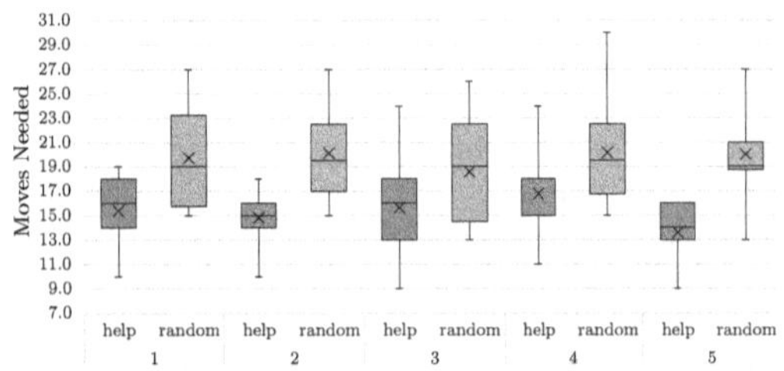

Figure 7: Number of moves needed to solve the Memory game over all participants in each run played and in each condition. The cross indicates the mean value in the given condition and run.

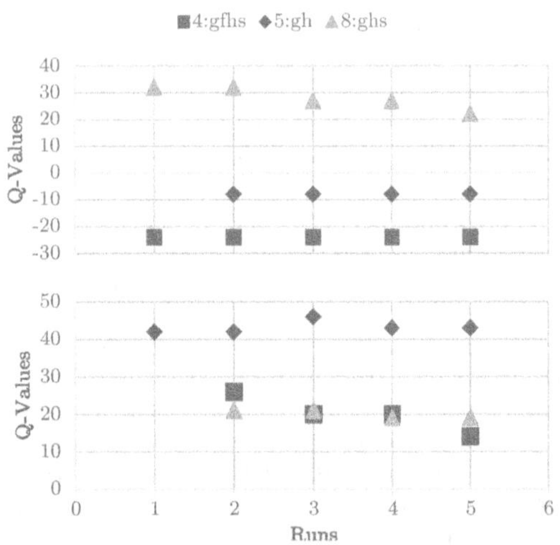

Figure 8: Excerpt of Q-values from the Q-matrix of two participants displaying the personalization of the robot in the same (game state, action)-pairs.

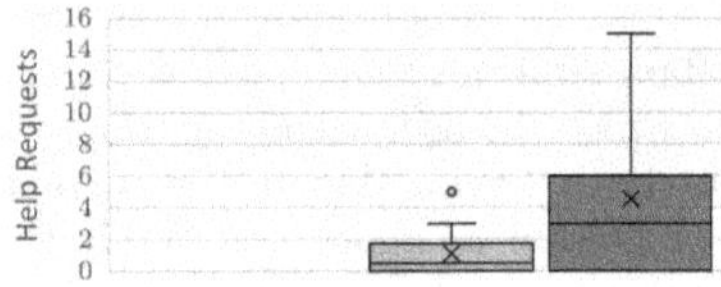

Figure 9: Distribution of help requests of participants in the different conditions (light blue: random; dark orange: learning). The cross indicates the mean value in the given condition.

Several points can be taken away from the learned Q-values. First, and interestingly, the robot did adapt differently to different users which, for some part, can be seen as a basis for achieving the overall better assistance in the learning condition. Second, when averaging over all learning episodes with different users, we can make several interesting observations. Actions with a head gesture and facial expression ended up being rated higher in easier game states than speech or gaze actions. While this seems reasonable, as users in easy situations may not need overly explicit assistance, another explanation may be the recognition of the robot by the users: When there are only three or less pairs left, users did not recognize the robot wanted to help them because they were focused on the game. Additionally, the probability of finding the correct pair was very high and hence the robot got rewarded for almost any action. Likewise, the low values for gaze behavior without speech may be due to participants not recognizing the robot behavior while focusing on the display. And, even when they did recognize the behavior they may have either interpreted the action as help refusal or had problems identifying the correct card and swapped a wrong one, which led to a negative reward for the action. The latter also indicates an adaption to the setting, because actions without speech were rated lower in higher game states, but in lower ones they lead to correct card pairs.

Additionally, misinterpretation happened with actions including speech, when participants did not (or, at least, not immediately) correctly understand the instruction. This again led to a punishment of the chosen action, for which the probability of being explored again stays relatively low (as can be seen in the top graph of Figure 8). While this problem should be mitigated over time, when the robot tests actions more often, it hints to a general problem when relying on social reward. A possible solution to this is to have the robot repeat its intent a second time or, ultimately, to incorporate notions of grounding to ensure the users understand all hints properly.

Another interesting finding was made at the end of the study when the participants commented on the study. Even if most of the participants thanked Furhat after receiving a helpful hint, participants of the learning condition characterized the robot as helpful, courteous and attentive. In contrast, in the random condition, the robot was perceived as more annoying, because it interrupted the concentration of the participants, in their opinion helped too early or did not help after all.

Gamestate	s	h	hs	f	fs	fh	fhs	g	gs	gh	ghs	gf	gfs	gfh	gfhs
9	0.0	25.7	11.5	0.0	0.0	0.0	18.0	53.0	27.0	0.0	20.3	20.0	0.0	28.5	65.0
8	38.3	33.0	25.3	24.0	31.0	0.0	6.0	34.0	0.0	0.0	20.5	17.0	10.5	32.7	15.3
7	28.0	45.0	30.0	26.0	22.0	45.0	15.0	48.0	31.0	24.0	0.0	36.0	32.0	17.3	25.3
6	0.0	2.0	34.0	35.0	34.0	0.0	0.0	82.0	0.0	19.0	0.0	15.0	31.0	16.0	0.0
5	33.7	0.0	0.0	0.0	5.0	20.0	13.0	24.0	58.0	43.0	18.0	76.5	27.0	23.0	13.5
4	0.0	48.5	18.0	0.0	0.0	0.0	2.0	63.0	0.0	0.0	32.0	0.0	23.0	63.0	12.0
3	0.0	53.5	0.0	76.0	0.0	0.0	0.0	53.0	0.0	0.0	69.0	47.0	27.0	0.0	0.0
2	39.0	44.0	28.5	0.0	0.0	0.0	0.0	0.0	0.0	36.5	0.0	42.0	22.0	36.0	0.0

Figure 10: Average Q-Matrix of behavior selection after 5 rounds of solving the Memory game averaged over all participants in the learning condition. Rows represent the different game states (number of pairs of cards remaining) and columns represent the different behavior combinations (abbreviated as follows: s = speech, h = head gesture, f = facial expression, g = gaze).

Overall, even with this first approach and the relatively small study, our findings provide evidence pointing towards the potential feasibility and benefits of using reinforcement learning for adapting the social behavior of assistive robots in a comprehensive and flexible way to their individual users, to the specific interactional contexts, as well as to the affordances of a specific robot platform.

8. ACKNOWLEDGMENTS

This work was supported by the BabyRobot project supported by the EU Horizon 2020 Program, grant number: 687831, and by the Cluster of Excellence Cognitive Interaction Technology 'CITEC' (EXC 277) at Bielefeld University, funded by the German Research Foundation (DFG).

9. REFERENCES

[1] S. Al Moubayed, J. Beskow, G. Skantze, and B. Granström. Furhat: A back-rojected human-like robot head for multiparty human-machine interaction. In *Cognitive Behavioural Systems*, pages 114–130. Springer Berlin Heidelberg, 2012.

[2] S. Andrist, X. Z. Tan, M. Gleicher, and B. Mutlu. Conversational gaze aversion for humanlike robots. *ACM/IEEE International Conference on Human-Robot Interaction*, pages 25–32, 2014.

[3] G. Bailly, S. Raidt, and F. Elisei. Gaze, conversational agents and face-to-face communication. *Speech Communication*, 52(6):598–612, 2010.

[4] T. Belpaeme, P. E. Baxter, R. Read, R. Wood, H. Cuayáhuitl, B. Kiefer, S. Racioppa, I. Kruijff-Korbayová, G. Athanasopoulos, V. Enescu, et al. Multimodal child-robot interaction: Building social bonds. *Journal of Human-Robot Interaction*, 1(2):33–53, 2012.

[5] A. Bridges. Directing two-year-old's attention; some clues to understanding. *Journal of Child Language*, 6(02):211–226, 1979.

[6] L. Busoniu, R. Babuska, B. De Schutter, and D. Ernst. *Reinforcement learning and dynamic programming using function approximators*, volume 39. CRC press, 2010.

[7] M. Cakmak, C. Chao, and A. L. Thomaz. Designing interactions for robot active learners. *IEEE Transactions on Autonomous Mental Development*, 2(2):108–118, 2010.

[8] J. Cassell, Y. Nakano, T. Bickmore, C. Sidner, and C. Rich. Annotating and generating posture from discourse structure in embodied conversational agents. In *Workshop on representing, annotating, and evaluating non-verbal and verbal communicative acts to achieve contextual embodied agents*, 2001.

[9] J. Cassell, H. H. Vilhjálmsson, and T. Bickmore. Beat: the behavior expression animation toolkit. In *Life-Like Characters*, pages 163–185. Springer, 2004.

[10] C.-W. Chang, J.-H. Lee, P.-Y. Chao, C.-Y. Wang, and G.-D. Chen. Exploring the possibility of using humanoid robots as instructional tools for teaching a second language in primary school. *Educational Technology & Society*, 13(2):13–24, 2010.

[11] C. Chao and A. L. Thomaz. Controlling social dynamics with a parametrized model of floor regulation. *Journal of Human-Robot Interaction*, 1(1):78–95, 2012.

[12] C.-C. Chiu and S. Marsella. How to train your avatar: A data driven approach to gesture generation. In *International Workshop on Intelligent Virtual Agents*, pages 127–140. Springer, 2011.

[13] R. Cooper and T. Shallice. Contention scheduling and the control of routine activities. *Cognitive Neuropsychology*, 17(4):297–338, 2000.

[14] D. Ernst, P. Geurts, and L. Wehenkel. Tree-based batch mode reinforcement learning. *Journal of Machine Learning Research*, 6(Apr):503–556, 2005.

[15] D. Feil-Seifer and M. J. Mataric. B 3 ia: A control architecture for autonomous robot-assisted behavior intervention for children with autism spectrum disorders. *RO-MAN 2008-The 17th IEEE International Symposium on Robot and Human Interactive Communication*, pages 328–333, 2008.

[16] E. Ferreira and F. Lefevre. Reinforcement-learning based dialogue system for human–robot interactions with socially-inspired rewards. *Computer Speech & Language*, 34(1):256–274, 2015.

[17] S. M. Fiore, T. J. Wiltshire, E. J. Lobato, F. G. Jentsch, W. H. Huang, and B. Axelrod. Toward understanding social cues and signals in human–robot interaction: effects of robot gaze and proxemic behavior. *Frontiers in psychology*, 4:859, 2013.

[18] M. Fridin. Storytelling by a kindergarten social assistive robot: A tool for constructive learning in

preschool education. *Computers & education*, 70:53–64, 2014.

[19] M. Fujita, Y. Kuroki, T. Ishida, and T. T. Doi. Autonomous behavior control architecture of entertainment humanoid robot sdr-4x. *IEEE International Conference on Intelligent Robots and Systems*, 1:960–967, 2003.

[20] G. Gordon, S. Spaulding, J. K. Westlund, J. J. Lee, L. Plummer, M. Martinez, M. Das, and C. Breazeal. Affective personalization of a social robot tutor for children's second language skills. In *30th AAAI Conference on Artificial Intelligence*, 2016.

[21] J. Gratch, J. Rickel, E. André, J. Cassell, E. Petajan, and N. Badler. Creating interactive virtual humans: Some assembly required. *IEEE Intelligent Systems*, 17(4):54–63, 2002.

[22] Y. Hoshino, T. Takagi, U. Di Profio, and M. Fujita. Behavior description and control using behavior module for personal robot. *IEEE International Conference on Robotics and Automation*, 4:4165–4171, 2004.

[23] D. Hu, Y. Gong, B. Hannaford, and E. J. Seibel. Semi-autonomous simulated brain tumor ablation with ravenii surgical robot using behavior tree. *IEEE International Conference on Robotics and Automation*, pages 3868–3875, 2015.

[24] T. Kanda, T. Hirano, D. Eaton, and H. Ishiguro. Interactive robots as social partners and peer tutors for children: A field trial. *Human-Computer interaction*, 19(1):61–84, 2004.

[25] J. Kennedy, P. Baxter, and T. Belpaeme. The robot who tried too hard: Social behaviour of a robot tutor can negatively affect child learning. *Human Robot Interaction*, pages 67–74, 2015.

[26] S. G. Khan, G. Herrmann, F. L. Lewis, T. Pipe, and C. Melhuish. Reinforcement learning and optimal adaptive control: An overview and implementation examples. *Annual Reviews in Control*, 36(1):42–59, 2012.

[27] E. S. Kim, L. D. Berkovits, E. P. Bernier, D. Leyzberg, F. Shic, R. Paul, and B. Scassellati. Social robots as embedded reinforcers of social behavior in children with autism. *Journal of Autism and Developmental Disorders*, 43(5):1038–1049, 2013.

[28] S. Kopp, C. Becker, and I. Wachsmuth. The virtual human max-modeling embodied conversation. *Artificial Intelligence Group, University of Bielefeld, PO Box*, 2006.

[29] S. Kopp, B. Krenn, S. Marsella, A. N. Marshall, C. Pelachaud, H. Pirker, K. R. Thórisson, and H. Vilhjálmsson. Towards a common framework for multimodal generation: The behavior markup language. In *Intelligent Virtual Agents*, pages 205–217. Springer, 2006.

[30] S. Kopp, H. van Welbergen, R. Yaghoubzadeh, and H. Buschmeier. An architecture for fluid real-time conversational agents: Integrating incremental output generation and input processing. *Journal on Multimodal User Interfaces*, 8(1):97–108, 2014.

[31] M. G. Lagoudakis and R. Parr. Least-squares policy iteration. *Journal of Machine Learning Research*, 4(Dec):1107–1149, 2003.

[32] B. Lance and S. Marsella. The expressive gaze model: Using gaze to express emotion. *IEEE Computer Graphics and Applications*, 30(4):62–73, 2010.

[33] J. Lee and S. Marsella. Nonverbal behavior generator for embodied conversational agents. In *International Workshop on Intelligent Virtual Agents*, pages 243–255. Springer, 2006.

[34] D. Leyzberg, S. Spaulding, M. Toneva, and B. Scassellati. The physical presence of a robot tutor increases cognitive learning gains. *Proceedings of the 34th Annual Conference of the Cognitive Science Society*, 2012.

[35] M. Malfaz, Á. Castro-González, R. Barber, and M. A. Salichs. A biologically inspired architecture for an autonomous and social robot. *IEEE Transactions on Autonomous Mental Development*, 3(3):232–246, 2011.

[36] S. Meyer zu Borgen, T. Korthals, L. Ziegler, and S. Wachsmuth. ToBI-team of bielefeld the human-robot interaction system for RoboCup@Home 2015. 2015.

[37] Microsoft Corporation. Kinect for windows, 2016.

[38] N. Mitsunaga, C. Smith, T. Kanda, H. Ishiguro, and N. Hagita. Robot behavior adaptation for human-robot interaction based on policy gradient reinforcement learning. In *2005 IEEE/RSJ International Conference on Intelligent Robots and Systems*, pages 218–225. IEEE, 2005.

[39] H. Modares, I. Ranatunga, F. L. Lewis, and D. O. Popa. Optimized assistive human–robot interaction using reinforcement learning. *IEEE transactions on cybernetics*, 46(3):655–667, 2016.

[40] J. Movellan, M. Eckhardt, M. Virnes, and A. Rodriguez. Sociable robot improves toddler vocabulary skills. In *Proceedings of the 4th ACM/IEEE international conference on Human robot interaction*, pages 307–308. ACM, 2009.

[41] R. W. Picard and R. Picard. *Affective computing*, volume 252. MIT press Cambridge, 1997.

[42] B. Robins, K. Dautenhahn, R. T. Boekhorst, and A. Billard. Robotic assistants in therapy and education of children with autism: can a small humanoid robot help encourage social interaction skills? *Universal Access in the Information Society*, 4(2):105–120, 2005.

[43] R. S. Sutton and A. G. Barto. *Reinforcement learning: An introduction*, volume 1. MIT press Cambridge, 1998.

[44] M. Thiebaux, S. Marsella, A. N. Marshall, and M. Kallmann. Smartbody: Behavior realization for embodied conversational agents. In *Proceedings of the 7th international joint conference on Autonomous agents and multiagent systems-Volume 1*, pages 151–158. International Foundation for Autonomous Agents and Multiagent Systems, 2008.

[45] C. J. C. H. Watkins. *Learning from delayed rewards*. PhD thesis, University of Cambridge England, 1989.

The When, Where, and How: An Adaptive Robotic Info-Terminal for Care Home Residents – A long-term Study

Marc Hanheide
University of Lincoln
Brayford Pool
Lincoln, LN6 7TS, UK
mhanheide@lincoln.ac.uk

Denise Hebesberger
Akademie für Altersforschung
Seeböckgasse 30A
1160 Vienna, Austria
denise.hebesberger@gmx.at

Tomáš Krajník
University of Lincoln
Brayford Pool
Lincoln, LN6 7TS, UK
tkrajnik@lincoln.ac.uk

ABSTRACT

Adapting to users' intentions is a key requirement for autonomous robots in general, and in care settings in particular. In this paper, a comprehensive long-term study of a mobile robot providing information services to residents, visitors, and staff of a care home is presented, with a focus on adapting to the *when* and *where* the robot should be offering its services to best accommodate the users' needs. Rather than providing a fixed schedule, the presented system takes the opportunity of long-term deployment to explore the space of possibilities of interaction while concurrently exploiting the model learned to provide better services. But in order to provide effective services to users in a care home, not only then *when* and *where* are relevant, but also the way *how* the information is provided and accessed. Hence, also the usability of the deployed system is studied specifically, in order to provide a most comprehensive overall assessment of a robotic info-terminal implementation in a care setting. Our results back our hypotheses, (i) that learning a spatio-temporal model of users' intentions improves efficiency and usefulness of the system, and (ii) that the specific information sought after is indeed dependent on the location the info-terminal is offered.

Keywords

Machine Learning (primary keyword); Older Adults; Interaction Design; User Interface Design; Field Study; Usability Study

1. INTRODUCTION

Care is considered one of the application domains that service robots will have significant positive impact in. Recent advances have seen several robotic systems being designed for care task, e.g., [19, 3]. Among the many areas of application a robot can fulfill in care homes these days is liaising with residents and visitor alike and providing them with information. In contrast to fixed information terminals, however, it is in their nature that they can offer requested information where and when it is needed. A robot can move around an environment and be available where required. Ideally, in order to maximise its utility, an autonomous robot should anticipate what information is needed and at what time and what place it is requested. This schedule, while it can principally be designed by an expert, should adhere to the users' needs, and we suggest that it can best be learned from past experience in an autonomous manner. Hence, in the work presented in this paper, we precisely follow this aim, namely to investigate how the delivery of information to residents, staff, and visitors – in short, the users – in a care home can be optimised and improved. This question is studied by means of an autonomous system, deployed over several weeks in a real-world care home, featuring an *info-terminal* as an implementation designed to allow users to access information relevant to them at most appropriate times and locations. Fig. 1 depicts some impressions from the deployment of the robot in said residential care setting.

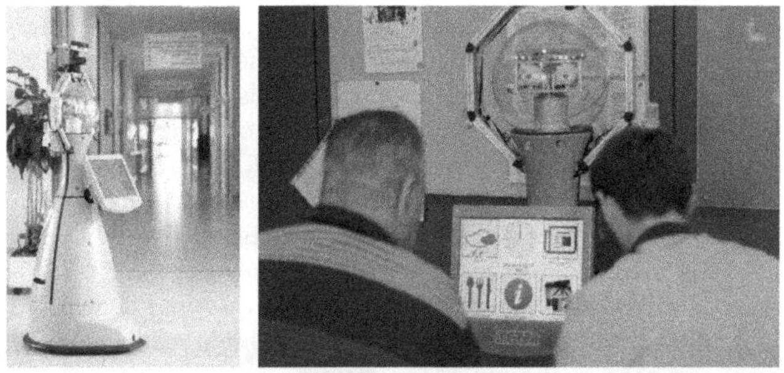

(a) Robotic platform. (b) Subject using the developed info-terminal using touch-screen interaction.

Figure 1: Robot in the care environment.

In particular, we are looking at two complementary key aspects towards the general aim of providing a usable info-terminal to residents, visitors, and staff alike:

a) **Interface:** *How* can information be presented and accessed by the users of a mobile robot, taking into account requirements of the environment and respecting demands and abilities of the user base? We have developed a touch-screen based interaction on a mobile

HRI '17, March 06–09, 2017, Vienna, Austria
© 2017 ACM. ISBN 978-1-4503-4336-7/17/03...$15.00
DOI: http://dx.doi.org/10.1145/2909824.3020228

robotic platform, displaying a carefully selected set of information from different domains (see Sec. 2). The work presented in this paper assessed usability aspects of the interface itself in a dedicated user study, and also analysed which information users request at the various places the info-terminal is provided as part of the long-term study. The outcomes of this analysis yield findings which will inform further development of the robotic system. Most importantly, the user study is required to assess if older adults with cognitive impairments are indeed able to use the info-terminal, hence forms a prerequisite for the validity of the subsequent analysis of usage patterns.

b) **Adaptive Scheduling:** *When* and *Where* should the robot make itself available to be used by the users? In a mobile autonomous robot like the one presented here, this is a question of scheduling, not only the time, but also deciding on the place where to make itself available. However, with the needs of the users not fully known upfront, the system should *explore* on its own where and when it is needed, and then *exploit* this knowledge to deliver a better service. This paper presents an analysis of the long-term adaptation by means of autonomously *exploring* the space of possibilities and, at the same time, *exploiting* a learned spatio-temporal model to yield a higher success and use rate in the long-term study.

The system presented in this paper is the third iteration of ongoing iterative development of a mobile robotic system in a care home developed collaboratively by 6 research groups. The overall focus is to learn about long-term changes and dynamics and exploit these to improve the service quality and usability of deployed robots [6]. The robot is autonomous and usually operated without any engineers or researchers present on site. The system developed provides a unique opportunity to study interaction with fully autonomous systems deployed for long periods of time. It serves the users through a number of different tasks. These specific tasks, including the info-terminal, implemented on the robot have been chosen from the list of tasks relevant to users in a care setting as identified in [8]. They have highlighted an info-terminal as one of the most relevant tasks for a mobile robot in a care home. Other services implemented on the robot include an application in occupational therapy [7, 5], and guiding visitors to specific rooms.

Every year, the system is deployed at the same care home for increasingly longer periods where it runs completely autonomously and offers its services. For the study presented in this paper, stemming from the third iteration of deployment, we assume that most users are generally familiar with the robot on-site and that there is only a limited novelty effect to be observed in general. The results presented in this paper originate from this deployment of the fully autonomous robot (no technicians or maintainers at site) for 63 days, covering a period from mid March to mid May 2016. Following the SiNA (Systematic Interaction Analysis) paradigm [15] for task-focused, interacting robotic systems, each annual iteration comprises a systematic analysis of user behaviour and task accomplishment, linked with detailed analysis of system logs to identify patterns of significant deviation from intended or expected interaction to derive improvements and modifications for the next implementation cycle. The work presented in this paper hence is a contribution to the most recent evaluation-implementation cycle in this model. Consequently, the paper comprises three core contributions, namely

(i) as a technical contribution it proposes a computational model to adapt to users regarding the spatio-temporal characteristics (the *when* and *where*) of the provision of info-terminal services. This contribution is presented in Sec. 3 and proven to yield improved performance over time in the long-term study in Sec. 5.2;

(ii) a dedicated user study of the usability of the implemented info-terminal and its interface with a focus on older adults (see Sec. 5.1), to verify suitability of the approach and confirm general usability as a prerequisite for the adaptation outlined above; and finally

(iii) an analysis of the information actually requested by the users during the long-term deployment in dependence of the different location the info-terminal was offered, presented in Sec. 5.3, yielding insights into the location-dependence of information and suggested further improvements of the info-terminal implementation for future deployments.

Hence, the paper specifically aims to verify the hypotheses that *(H1)* adapting to user needs over space and time in long-term deployment yields more use of the info-terminal, and *(H2)* the information requested by users is dependent on the location the info-terminal is provided.

2. THE MOBILE INFO-TERMINAL

The *info-terminal* focused on in this paper is only one of a number of different services the robot engages in during its long-term deployment. An info-terminal is a touch-screen based implementation of a mobile information point, allowing users to request information or be entertained on the screen of the mobile platform. Hence, the system is similar to static information points often available in care homes but with the added ability to provide the information at varying places in the overall environment.

2.1 Robotic Platform and System

For the development of the autonomous system a 1.76m tall SCITOS G5 mobile robotic platform is employed. The system allows autonomous, uninterrupted operation for up to 7 hours without recharge. It has a cone shaped, green hull that is mounted by a plexiglas head with two actuated blue eyes that can blink (cf. Fig. 1(a) to appraise the robot's appearance). On top of the head a Kinect camera is held in place by an aluminium frame surrounding the head for people and obstacle perception. The robot moves at a maximum speed of 0.55m/s. Safe navigation is further facilitated by a SICK s300 laser range finder used for obstacle avoidance and localisation. A touch screen on the back of the robot is the focal point for human interaction and employed for the info-terminal. A more comprehensive description of the system as a whole is presented in [6] and it is released as a whole as open source based on ROS[1].

2.2 Info-Terminal Interface and Operation

The info-terminal interface is designed with it main users (older adults) in mind. Physically, it consists of the touch-screen mounted on the back of the robot, accessible to

[1]https://github.com/strands-project-releases/strands-releases/wiki

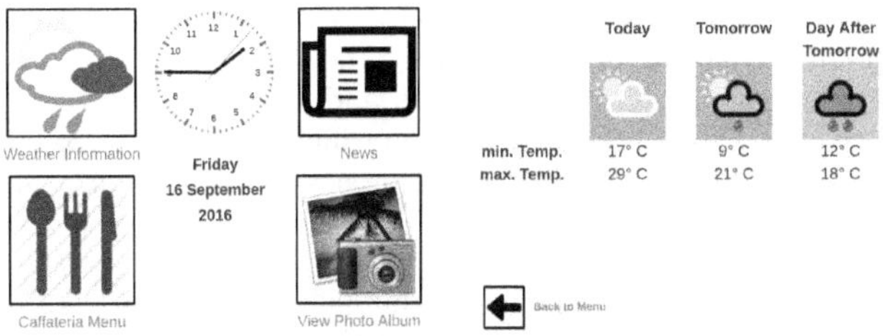

(a) Home screen (b) Weather

Figure 2: Exemplary interface designs for the touch-screen based info-terminal.

wheelchair users and walking people alike. In particular design recommendations for such touch-based interfaces for older adults have been considered regarding button and font sizes [9] and general human factors [4, 2]. Fig. 2 shows two exemplary information screens implemented in the info-terminal interface. The information screens accessible through touch ("click") interaction from the main menu screen (Fig. 2(a)) are:

Weather Shows the local weather forecast for today and two successive days (see Fig. 2(b)).

News Shows both national and local news from the care home, automatically updated from a national TV station news feed and the institutions facebook feed, respectively.

Restaurant Menus Displays today's menus of the local cafeteria and the residents' choices for lunch. The second (residents menu) can be accessed through a further click from the local cafeteria menu in a separate tab to avoid overloading the screen with information.

Photo Album This entertainment element feature an edited collection of photographs, mostly of natural environments, but also featuring photos of the care home itself.

From each these information screen, users can navigate back to the main menu via a "back" button. The interface is implemented in HTML5 and JavaScript and served via a web browser operating in full-screen mode.

During the autonomous deployment, the robot would schedule, using a robot task scheduler [18], info-terminal tasks to be executed at chosen locations. The decision which location to offer the service at is to be taken by the approach to be presented in Sec. 3. At the scheduled time, the robot would make its way to the chosen location, position itself so its touch screen is easily accessible by users, and display the main menu of the info-terminal, ready for any user to interact with it. The default duration to wait for users to interact with he system is 10 minutes, however, to ensure the robot drives not off in the middle of an interaction, this duration is prolonged by a minute if an interaction is still ongoing at the end of the default duration.

3. SCHEDULING THE WHEN AND WHERE

The efficiency of the info-terminal service is dependent on the robot's ability to provide the service at the right locations and times. These need to be selected with respect to the behavioural habits of the people at the deployment facility and with the robot's need to recharge its batteries. For example, since the area around a cafeteria might be busy during noon, the robot should offer the info-terminal service there during the midday and visit its charging station during night-time, when the chances of meeting people are low.

While the selection of the right locations and times could follow a fixed schedule created by a human expert, this kind of solution would be impractical for the following reasons: First, a good schedule requires that the expert is familiar with the behaviours and activities of the people at the deployment facility and can use this knowledge to assess the likelihood of people interacting with the robot at given areas and times. Second, even if the expert had such detailed knowledge, the behavioural patterns of the people might change over time, which would cause any fixed-schedule-based system to gradually lose efficiency. Finally, manual creation of a detailed schedule that reflects the daily and weekly patterns of human activity is a time-consuming task.

Thus, instead of using a fixed schedule, we only provide our robot with a set of candidate locations to offer the service and let it decide where and when it should provide the info-terminal by itself. This requires the robot to build and maintain a spatio-temporal model that can predict the chance of obtaining an interaction at a given location and time and use the model's predictive capabilities to construct a schedule that maximises the number of potential interactions. In other words, the robot needs not only to explore the environment to understand which areas are busy and which not, but also to exploit the obtained knowledge and provide the info-terminal service at the relevant locations during the busy times. These two contradictory requirements constitute a classic explore/exploit dilemma [22].

3.1 Spatio-temporal modelling

Given that the robot offers the info-terminal at k different locations, our spatio-temporal model consists of k functions $p_l(t)$, which represent the probability $p_l(t)$ of an interaction at a location l and time t. The spatio-temporal modelling method has to create and refine these functions from sparse and irregular data about the interaction success which are obtained during routine robot operation.

A typical spatio-temporal model used in similar scenarios is based on Gaussian Processes, which allow the robot to learn the dynamics of the environment and decide which path to take in order to refine its model efficiently [21, 16, 17]. However, the works of [13, 1, 10], which compared several types of temporal models that characterise the presence and activities of people in domestic and office environments, concluded that the Gaussian Processes were outperformed by the concept of Frequency Map Enhancement [12].

3.1.1 Frequency Map Enhancement - (FreMEn)

The FreMEn method assumes that the probabilities of the modelled phenomena are influenced by hidden processes which might be periodic. Through the use of frequency transforms, the FreMEn can efficiently identify the periodicity and influence of multiple hidden processes that affect the observed phenomena and use the extracted knowledge for long-term predictions. This reflects the fact that probabilities of interactions are subject to daily and weekly routines performed by people at the deployment area.

During out robot operation, each candidate info-terminal location is tied to a FreMEn model that maintains the number of performed interaction attempts n, mean probability μ, and two sets $\mathcal{A}$, $\mathcal{B}$ of complex numbers α_k and β_k that correspond to the set Ω of potential periodicities ω_k of the hidden processes that affect the chance of successful interaction (i.e. the chance that the info-terminal is used). To initiate an interaction, the robot positions itself at a given location, records the current time t, displays the info-terminal interface and waits for a predefined amount of time. If the info-terminal interface is used by anyone during the given time period, the robot sets the interaction flag $a(t)$ to 1, otherwise it keeps $a(t)$ equal to 0. After the time period elapses, the FreMEn model of the given location is updated as follows:

$$\begin{array}{lcll} \mu & \leftarrow & \frac{1}{n+1}\left(n\mu + a(t)\right), & \\ \alpha_k & \leftarrow & \frac{1}{n+1}\left(n\alpha_k + a(t)\,e^{-jt\omega_k}\right) & \forall\,\omega_k \in \Omega, \\ \beta_k & \leftarrow & \frac{1}{n+1}\left(n\beta_k + \mu\,e^{-jt\omega_k}\right) & \forall\,\omega_k \in \Omega, \\ n & \leftarrow & n+1, & \end{array} \tag{1}$$

where μ represents the mean, time-independent probability of interaction, n is the number of interaction attempts performed, and α_k, β_k represent the frequency spectrum of the history of past interactions $a(t)$. While the absolute value of each α_k corresponds to the influence of a hidden process with the frequency ω_k on the probability of interaction $p(t)$, the β_k serve as corrections that prevent the model overfitting during the early stages of model construction.

To predict the probability of interaction at a given time t, we first construct a set $\mathcal{C}$ consisting of complex numbers $\gamma_k = \alpha_k - \beta_k$, which are ordered reverse to their absolute values. Then, we select the first m elements γ_j along with their corresponding frequencies ω_j. The elements γ_j and ω_j, which correspond to the influence and periodicity of the hidden processes that affect the interaction probability are then used to estimate the interaction probability at a given location and time by:

$$p(t) = \varsigma(\mu + \sum_{j=1}^{m} |\gamma_j| cos(\omega_j t + \mathtt{arg}(\gamma_j))), \tag{2}$$

where the function $\varsigma(.)$ ensures that $p(t) \in [0,1]$. Since we assumed that the interaction probabilities will be influenced mainly by daily and weekly routines, we set the constant m to the value of 2. An overview and additional details of the FreMEn concept are provided in [11].

3.2 Model exploration and exploitation

However, the spatio-temporal modelling method is not sufficient by itself. First, in order to create the model and keep it up to date, the robot must be able to provide the model with useful data. Second, one has to determine how to use the predictions to guide the robot in order to maximise the number of interactions. Both of these aims have to take into account the limitations of the robot, especially the energy-based constraint that requires the robot to recharge its batteries at least 50% of its operational time.

The first part of the problem, called life-long spatio-temporal exploration, was studied in [13, 20]. In here, the authors evaluated several spatio-temporal models and exploration strategies to be able to predict people occurrence in office and domestic environments. The paper [13, 20] concluded that the best model is based on the FreMEn concept and the best exploration strategy, i.e. a process that determines which locations to visit and when to visit them, is based on a Monte-Carlo scheme which takes into account the information gain obtainable by a visit to a given location. In the work presented in [13], the robot would establish a new schedule each midnight, ensuring that at least 50% of the time is spend on the charging station. The schedule would then be followed throughout the day, with occasional modifications imposed by unexpected events.

Unlike in [13, 20], which aim to create an accurate spatio-temporal model, but do not need to exploit the information the model provides, we need an accurate model only because its predictions are essential to create a schedule for the info-terminal service. Thus, our strategy needs to take into account both information gain that keeps the model up-to-date and the probability of obtaining an actual interaction. To construct the schedule for the next day, the robot partitions the following day to slots of identical duration and calculates the utility of visiting each location as

$$u_l(t) = \epsilon\, h(p_l(t)) + (1-\epsilon)\, p_l(t), \tag{3}$$

where ϵ represents the exploration/exploitation ratio and $h(p)$ is the information gain calculated by

$$h(p) = -p \ln_2 p - (1-p)\ln_2(1-p). \tag{4}$$

After calculating the utility function for all possible times and locations, a schedule is generated by a Monte Carlo scheme, which prefers locations and times according to the utility function $u_l(t)$. The exploration/exploitation ratio ϵ determines how much emphasis is given to the model building compared to the model exploitation. An ϵ equal to 1 would result in a system that builds the best model possible, while not using it to obtain many interactions. Setting ϵ to 0 will cause the system to try to get many interactions, but risking that the robot will miss some good locations and times. For details on the Monte-Carlo based schedule creation, see the paper [13].

4. STUDIES DESIGN

During each year of the project the robot is deployed at the same long-term care provider. Key target groups are older adults with progressed dementia, severe multi-morbidity or physical deficiencies. Furthermore the care home features units for persons with vigil coma or advanced multiple sclerosis. In total 350 beds are provided for permanent residency and there is a staff of approximately 465 employees. The robot is deployed only at the ground floor of the care facility, traversing corridors that link the administrative wing, with different offices, with a reception hall and a therapy wing with an ambulance area for acute medical aid. Hence, the potential user group is very heterogeneous, ranging from residents with cognitive decline, their visitors, to employees from different professions. Corridors are often crowded with by-passers, either on foot or with the help of different walking aids, wheelchairs or bedridden persons.

It is within this environment the robot has been deployed for a total of 63 days, providing a number of services (see Section 1) among which is the info-terminal. Two dedicated studies are presented in this context: (i) a post-hoc analysis of logged data from the 63 days duration of the long-term deployment of the info-terminal robot, called "Long-term

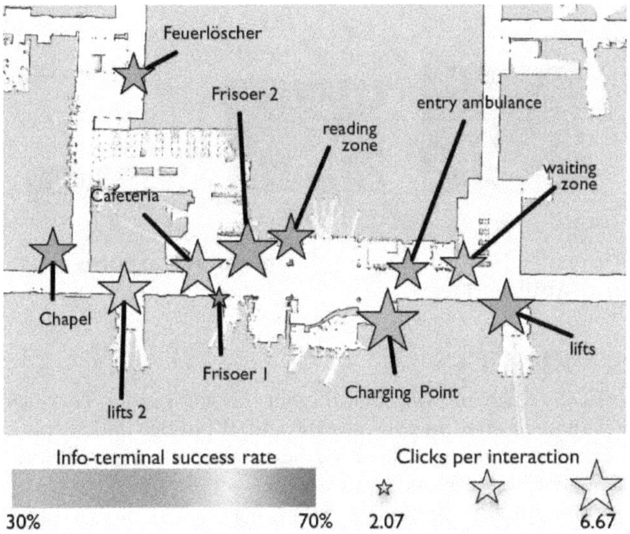

Figure 3: Partial map of info-terminal locations indicating overall success rates for specific locations and how many clicks per task were recorded. The locations "Kindergarten", "Infoboard", and "Lift 3" are off this map for readability.

Study" (Sec. 4.1), and (ii) a focused evaluation of the perceived usability of the info-terminal with a sample of older residents ("Usability Evaluation", Sec. 4.2).

4.1 Long-term Study of Info-Terminal

The info-terminal is embedded into the general 63 days of robot deployment. During this deployment, the adaptive scheduling outlined in Sec. 3 has been employed in order to determine where the robot would go at a specific moment in time. As described earlier, the info-terminal is just one of a number of tasks implemented on the robot. However, the info-terminal constitutes the task that is running the most by far, roughly being active more than 90% of the active operational time of the robot. In this paper, we focus the analysis solely on this info-terminal task.

While the other tasks are either pre-scheduled for specific time slots or requested by staff on-site spontaneously, the info-terminal has been set up to work opportunistically, i.e., it will schedule info-terminal tasks as long as it is not requested to engage in any of the other tasks. Hence, the robot, if not engaged in any other task, every ten minutes went to one of the 14 designated info-terminal locations (see Fig. 3 for a partial map of most of the locations, one location is off the map, omitted for readability), chosen according to the Monte-Carlo sampling outlined in Sec. 3. It shall be noted that the specific location to offer the info-terminal service is chosen entirely autonomously at any given time, based on the successively refined spatio-temporal models. To achieve this adaptation, the robot learned which of the designated 14 locations and times are the most suitable ones to offer the info-terminal service. As mentioned in Sec. 3, each of these locations l was associated to a temporal model $p_l(t)$, which represents the probability of successful interaction at time t. During the deployment, the robot had to establish temporal models that can predict the probability of interaction for any time t despite the fact, that it can operate only during working hours on weekdays.

The robot operated every weekday between mid March and mid May from 9am until 6pm for a total span of 63 days. A total of 20 days were excluded from the study because these were either public holidays or weekends for which no permission to run the robot had been given, or they were due to technical problems (e.g. two days were excluded because a power board had to be replaced). As a result, 43 days have been subjected to further analysis.

During the entire deployment, the system captured for each attempted info-terminal task the following information:

1. location where the info-terminal is run,
2. date and time when it was started,
3. information screens users chose to look at (either "weather", "news", "restaurant menu", or "photos"),
4. number of clicks ("interactions") on the touch screen.

This information was both used to adapt the spatio-temporal model in Sec. 3, as well as to analyse the system performance in relation to hypotheses *H1* and *H2*, which were specified in the last paragraph of Section 1. Overall, an info-terminal task was assumed as successful if at least some user interacted with the system during the 10 minute period of the individual task, i.e., the user chose to request at least one of the information screens.

4.2 Usability Evaluation

In order to complement the long-term study in a more controlled setting and to specifically assess the implementation of the info-terminal itself, a complementing usability evaluation study has been conducted in the course of the third deployment of the robot in 2016. Its main purpose was to gain further insights into perceived usability of this task in general and the design of the screen in particular. This study was embedded in the overall context of the long-term study, but with explicitly selected participants in a set location. This allowed to eradicate any location-specific effects. In the context of the overall deployment, these specific appointments of subjects with a facilitator were scheduled in the system as special info-terminal tasks with a priority overriding the usual info-terminal routines.

4.2.1 Sample

13 older adults, all residents of the care home participated in the study. They were all recruited by members of care staff. The criteria for inclusion of participants were: age 65 or older; living in the care home for more than three months; able to autonomously move in the care home; no diagnosis of severe dementia (this was important to gain valid feedback for using the info-terminal). Furthermore we tried to balance for gender. The participants were aged between 66 and 94 years ($M = 80.77$). Seven participants were male and six participants were female. None of them had a diagnosis of severe dementia. Eight persons stated that they had never used the robot before. Of the five participants using the robot, one used it once a week, three used it once a day and one person made use of the robot several times per day. Regarding technical experience only two participants told us that they possessed a laptop and a smartphone. 11 participants said they had no experience with computers. One participant possesses a laptop, two a smartphone, eight own a key-operated phone.

4.2.2 *Procedure*

We arranged fixed single appointments with each participant. At the set times the participant was invited into the reception area, where the robot was positioned in its docking station, presenting the screen towards the open space. A facilitator introduced the participant to the project, the aim of the evaluation study, and to the robots touch-screen (an initial demo-task – accessing the news menu – was conducted by the participant together with the facilitator). After signing an informed consent, socio-demographic data were collected and subjects were asked if they already had used the robot. Thereafter the facilitator asked the participant to complete a series of pre-defined tasks that increased in difficulty, as they required the user to enter the info-terminal menu by an additional layer. These tasks were:

1. **Time**: Participants first were asked to find out what time it is on the robots screen (clock is situated directly on the overall screen, cf. Fig. 2(a)).
2. **Weather**: Participants were asked to tell the interviewer the weather forecast for the next day. The task consisted of only one step: clicking on the weather icon and reading the forecast for the next day (user had to enter one layer of the menu, cf. Fig. 2(b)).
3. **Resident-Menu of the day**: Participants were asked to tell the interviewer the menu of the day for residents. This task consisted of three steps: Return to the main menu of the robot's interface by first clicking on the return arrow on the left lower corner of the weather screen. Second, access the "menu of the day"-screen, by clicking on the button "menu of the day" and third access the "residents menu of the day"-screen, by clicking on the button "to the residents menu" (two layers of the menu structure had to be entered).

Cut-off times for completing those tasks were also defined. For task 1 the time out was 30 seconds, for task 2 it was 60 seconds and for task 3 90 seconds were chosen. This should help to compare performances between participants and also prevent them to become too frustrated if not able to complete the task. An observer was present to document the performance of the participants on an observation form. He noted down if the user was able to solve the task within the cut off time, the number of errors and what kind of errors occurred (pressing the icons too long or too short, pressing a wrong icon, person did not find the correct icon to press) and number and form of hints (help to press the icon, verbal hints, both) needed to complete the task. After the three usability-tests, participants took part in a short semi-structured interview to gain further insight into usability issues and their perception of and attitude toward the robot. They were asked about their technical pre-experience and their experience with the robot (frequency of use prior to study), their opinion about the optical design and comprehensibility of the menu, the readability of the readability of the contents on the screen, how difficult it was to click on the screen, if they had to think a lot when using the screen (the last five questions were to be answered on a 5-point Likert scale (not at all, rather not, don't know, rather, very much). The whole procedure took approximately 30 minutes per participant. The robot was not moving at any time during this interaction.

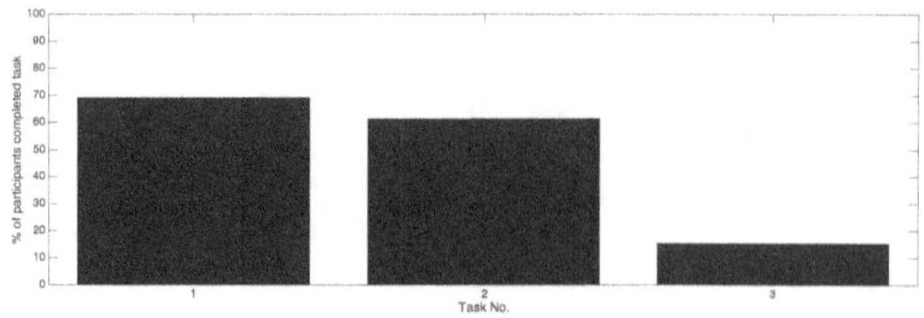

Figure 4: Rates of accomplishment of the three tasks in usability study.

5. RESULTS

In the following, we shall present our key results, addressing the two main hypotheses *H1* and *H2* in Sec. 5.2 and 5.3, respectively. Before this analysis of the long-term interaction, findings originating from the focused usability study are presented in the following Sec. 5.1.

5.1 Usability Evaluation

The focused usability evaluation was to assess the perceived Usability by older adults and to identify the key issues of the current interface implementation. Chi-square analysis of the quantitative data and non-parametric tests did not yield any significant results. Thus we will report descriptive findings of our info-terminal evaluation.

5.1.1 *Task performance*

The three tasks were increasingly difficult for the participants, reflected in differing accomplishment rates shown in Fig. 4. While task 1 was solved by 69.2% (one person needed verbal hints to solve task 1), and task 2 by 61.5% (no help required), only 15.4% (2 persons) of the sample could complete the 3rd task within pre-defined cut-off times for each task, one needing verbal help and another solved task 3 independently. Frequently noted problems in using the touch screen were: pressing icons too long (11 times) and not finding or noticing icons (8 times), clicking the wrong icon (7 times) or clicking icons to short (2 times) - error rates are given over all three task for all 13 participants.

5.1.2 *Observation*

As the majority of participants never used a computer before they did not have a concept of a typical menu structure. Furthermore the meaning of some interface icons was not clear for the residents of the care home. E.g. the icon leading to the photo gallery was misinterpreted as access to a photo camera. Due to the photos-icon, some thought that they could take pictures with the robot. Furthermore the info-icon and its label were not clear to some. 4 out of 13 participants had difficulties to access the time via the clock on the screen. The clock was too small, misinterpreted as an icon or not readable. Some participants missed feedback when using the robot, e.g. when the loading of contents took longer, they did not know if the touch screen had registered their action.

5.1.3 *Questionnaire*

Descriptive statistics showed that the optical design was liked by most participants (38.5% very much, 38.5% rather). 7.7% stated to not like the design at all. Most participants also rated the interface as understandable (69.2% very much, 23.1% rather; 7.7% not at all). 69.2% of participants stated that the texts were very much readably, 15.4% stated that they rather were and 15.3% stated that it was (rather) not readable. In terms of ease of use 61.6% of the older adults stated that they had rather or no difficulties at all. 38.5% found it rather or very much difficult to use the screen. In terms of cognitive effort of using the screen 46.2% mentioned that it was no effort at all and 38.5% mentioned that it was rather no effort. No participant stated that it was very much an effort to use the screen, 15.4% meant that it rather was an effort.

5.2 Adaptive Scheduling

The main goal of the adaptive scheduling described in Sec. 3 is to learn about the best locations and times to offer the info-terminal service, and to verify our hypothesis *H1* which stated that adapting to user needs over space and time in long-term deployment yields more use of the info-terminal. Over the 43 days where the info-terminal was run, the robot offered its service to its users a total of 1770 times. In 760 of these occasions (42.9%), the users actually used the info-terminal, indicated by clicking on the screen. Fig. 3 presents the locations at which the info-terminal was offered, the respective success rates of the provision of the info-terminal, and the number of clicks recorded for each task at a location. As described in 3, each of these locations l was associated with a temporal model $p_l(t)$, which represents the probability of successful interaction at time t. Thus, one of the results obtained are the temporal models for the individual locations. Examples of five temporal models learned during the actual deployment are shown in Figure 5, which indicates that despite of the fact that the temporal modelling method could not obtain data from nights (operations times were restricted to 9am-6pm), it predicted that during night, the probability of interaction is very low.

This result was obtained trough interpolation from the observation that early morning and late evening interactions are less probable than interactions during mid-day. These models also exhibit both daily and weekly periodicities: one can see that in some areas, obtaining an interaction on Friday afternoon is slightly less probable than during the other days. In the case of the Cafeteria temporal model, the interpolation into the night time is actually misleading – here, the robot observed that the info-terminal at the Cafeteria is mainly used during four peak times that might correspond to breakfast, lunch, afternoon tea and dinner. Thus, having no data from night, the robot simply assumed that the Cafeteria is busy every 2-3 hours.

However, the temporal model serves only as a means to construct a meaningful schedule that improves the chances that the visitors and staff of the facility use the info-terminal service. During the initial stages of the deployment, the robot visited all locations with the same frequency, because initially, all $p_l(t)$ were equal to 0.5. As the robot learned the model, it started to prefer visiting certain locations at certain times, which resulted in increased chances of obtaining an interaction. Figure 6 shows the success rates of interactions over time along with a linear regression model. The p value of the linear model F-statistics versus a constant model is $6.74 . 10^{-4}$, which indicates that the increase of the interaction success rate is statistically significant with $p < 0.001$. Thus, we can say with certainty that during the deployment, the robot gradually increased the chance of the info-terminal usage by the visitors and clients of the facility.

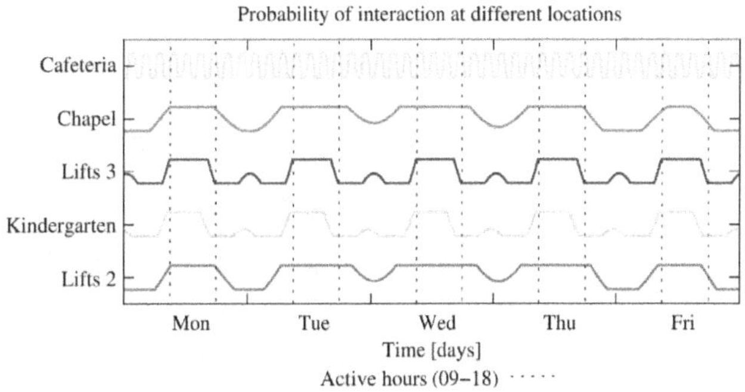

Figure 5: Examples of temporal models of selected locations.

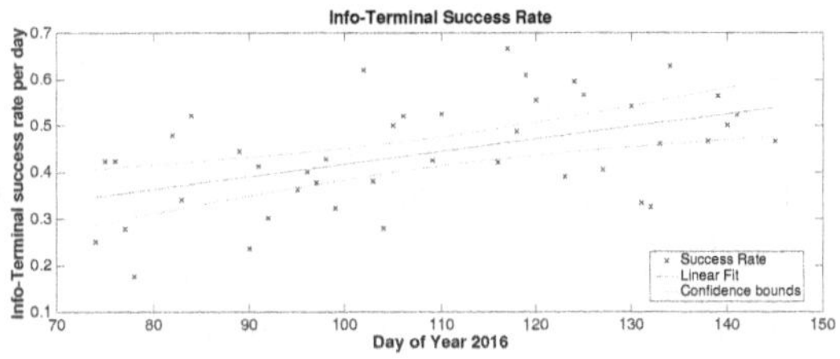

Figure 6: Interaction success rate over time.

5.3 Where information is requested

In order to analyse which information user chose to look at at the various location the info-terminal was offered, a contingency table of the frequencies of specific information screen being requested has been computed from the logs of interactions, shown in table 1. In this table, all locations but the "ChargingPoint" that offered info-terminal tasks are included. "ChargingPoint" has been omitted, as it is a special case where info-terminal was offered all the time when charging and not specifically scheduled for in most cases. Here, we counted all interactions (clicks on the screen) that led to the display of the specific information screen, as described in Sec. 2.2. Over all the 760 instances users interacted with the info-terminal, they displayed clicked to see different information screens a total of 2513 times (just above 3.3 interactions per successful task on average). Multiple clicks per task execution can be a result of several users interacting during the 10 minute window or one user looking at different information screens in one session. The data does not allow to discriminate between these two conditions. However, for the analysis at hand, this discrimination is irrelevant anyway, as we are interested to identify only if the information requested by users is dependent on the location (*H2*).

Overall, the χ^2 statistics for this contingency table indicate a very significant rejection of the null hypothesis ($df = 33, p < 0.001$, overall $\chi^2 = 107.8$) that the information requested is independent of the location the robot is offering the info-terminal service. Consequently, we can assume that indeed the kind of information requested is depending on the location where it is requested, confirming hypothesis *H2*. Likewise does table 1 highlight once again the variance in usage of the info-terminal at the different locations, exploited in the adaptation of the info-terminal scheduling.

	Kinderg.	Ambul.	Feuerl.	Wait. Z.	Lifts 1	Cafet.	Read. Z.	Chapel	Lifts 2	Lifts 3	Infob.	Frisoer 1	Frisoer 2	SUM
Menu	25	61	23	34	43	48	34	36	69	49	23	37	7	489
Weather	29	37	28	34	35	44	36	28	45	33	10	20	7	386
News	21	33	24	34	31	29	14	22	36	29	13	41	3	330
Photo	165	127	96	128	79	110	111	110	170	62	71	69	10	1308
SUM	240	258	171	230	188	231	195	196	320	173	117	167	27	2513

Table 1: Contingency Table of information screens requested in dependency of the 13 locations chosen for this analysis. The names of the locations (in columns) correspond to the ones in Fig. 3. "ChargingPoint" has been omitted from this study.

6. DISCUSSION

Info-terminal scheduling. While *H1* is confirmed and the robot gradually learned the spatio-temporal dynamics of people's usage patterns and adjusted its schedule to improve the usage of the info-terminal, the schedule building strategy was rather simple. First, the strategy ignored travelling times between the individual locations, so the schedule sometimes produced sequences of location visits, where the robot spend more time navigating than offering the info-terminal service. Second, the exploration/exploitation dilemma was addressed not by using two different strategies, but simply by combining the exploration and exploitation utility in a single function (3) with an arbitrarily chosen exploration/exploitation ratio ϵ. Since there are multiple options how to address the service scheduling problem and verification of each option would take at least 4 weeks, we already used the temporal models learned by the robot in the deployment to create a dynamic simulation of the deployment environment. Using this simulator, we tested over 50 different scheduling strategies, service utility functions and path planning policies and we found out that a more complex utility function in combination with distance-aware path planning can double the number of potential interactions [14]. Thus, for the next deployment of the robot, implemented these improvements and we will compare them to the original scheduling method.

Usage Patterns. As can also be seen in Fig. 3 there is not only a dynamic model, but also a static trend indicating that some locations are more popular than others. Of course, this static trend is also represented in the spatio-temporal model as μ for each location (see eq. 1), but looking at it a bit closer can give us some indication of the general use of the info-terminal. The most successful location (in terms of number of info-terminal provisions that lead to actual interactions with users) is "lifts" with 68.2% successful tasks. One can hypothesise that this is due to people regularly waiting close to that location and therefore opportunistically using the robot. The most clicks per task were recorded for location "Kindergarten", which indeed is a close to an on-site Kindergarten, probably explained by children being particularly engaged with the robot. It is subject to future research to look at particular user groups, an aspect currently not possible to investigate to due ethical guidelines prohibiting the recording of individual interactions. The confirmation of hypothesis *H2* in Sec. 5.3 leads to another suggested improvement for the next iteration of the system. As it is clear that users are preferring certain types of information at certain places (and possibly even at certain times), a redesigned interface with an always visible menu-bar will allow to start an info-terminal task with the most likely sought after information screen already visible.

Usability. The usability study showed that while users are capable of interacting successfully with the system, also indicated by the number of successful info-terminal tasks identified in the long-term deployment logs, there is also strong evidence that the interface needs to undergo further improvement as part of the evaluation-implementation cycle. Admittedly, these findings are rather specific to the presented system and mostly hint suggested improvements from users and the facilitator: For instance, there ought to be an appropriate form of feedback that the click of the user was registered and the new page is already loading. And due to the generally low complexity of the info-terminal GUI, its interface should be redesigned in a way that makes it possible to provide support for GUI navigation. Environmental support in form of an additional menu bar reduces demands on working memory and facilitates recognition (instead of recall) [2]. These insights will inform the next iteration of the system development.

7. CONCLUSION

This paper presented a spatio-temporal model in order to model the *when* and *where* of interactions in order to improve the service provisioning of a mobile robotic info-terminal. The info-terminal system has been assess as usable by older adults, however, additional insights into how users use the system and what they struggle with in the current implementation have been presented in a focused usability study. We concluded that while the system is sufficiently usable to render the long-term findings valid, the interface itself indeed needs to more even more simplified, reducing memorisation requirements of the users. The presented longer-term study of 63 day autonomous robot deployment in a real-world care environment itself has statistically confirmed the two hypotheses that (i) modelling the spatio-temporal dynamics in usage pattern of the info-terminal yields are more efficient use over time, and that (ii) the specific information sought after is indeed dependent on the location the info-terminal is offered. Furthermore, insights into how users use the system and what they struggle with in the current implementation have been presented in a focused usability study,

Acknowledgements

The work is supported by the European Community's Seventh Framework Programme under grant agreement 600623 'STRANDS' and the CSF project No. 17-27006Y.

8. REFERENCES

[1] Coppola, C., Krajník, T., Bellotto, N., and Duckett, T. Learning temporal context for activity recognition. In *Proceedings of the European Conference on Artificial Intelligence (ECAI)* (Sep 2016).

[2] Farage, M. A., Miller, K. W., Ajayi, F., and Hutchins, D. Design principles to accommodate older adults. *Global journal of health science 4*, 2 (2012), 2–25.

[3] Fischinger, D., Einramhof, P., Papoutsakis, K., Wohlkinger, W., Mayer, P., Panek, P., Hofmann, S., Koertner, T., Weiss, A., Argyros, A., and Vincze, M. Hobbit, a care robot supporting independent living at home: First prototype and lessons learned. *Robotics and Autonomous Systems 75* (2016), 60–78.

[4] Fisk, A. D., Rogers, W. A., Charness, N., Czaja, S. J., and Sharit, J. *Designing for older adults: Principles and creative human factors approaches.* CRC press, 2009.

[5] Gerling, K., Hebesberger, D., Dondrup, C., Körtner, T., Hanheide, M., and Linder, T. Robot Deployment in Long-Term Care: A Case Study of a Mobile Robot in Physical Therapy. *Zeitschrift für Geriatrie und Gerontologie* (2016).

[6] Hawes, N., Burbridge, C., Jovan, F., Kunze, L., Lacerda, B., Mudrová, L., Young, J., Wyatt, J., Hebesberger, D., Körtner, T., Ambrus, R., Bore, N., Folkesson, J., Jensfelt, P., Beyer, L., Hermans, A., Leibe, B., Aldoma, A., Fäulhammer, T., Zillich, M., Vincze, M., Al-Omari, M., Chinellato, E., Duckworth, P., Gatsoulis, Y., Hogg, D. C., Cohn, A. G., Dondrup, C., Fentanes, J. P., Krajník, T., ao M. Santos, J., Duckett, T., and Hanheide, M. The STRANDS project: Long-term autonomy in everyday environments. *IEEE Robotics and Automation Magazine* (2016). to appear.

[7] Hebesberger, D., Koertner, T., Gisinger, C., Pripfl, J., and Dondrup, C. Lessons learned from the deployment of a long-term autonomous robot as companion in physical therapy for older adults with dementia – a mixed methods study. In *Proceedings of the Eleventh ACM/IEEE International Conference on Human Robot Interaction (HRI)*, HRI '16, IEEE (Christchurch, New Zealand, Mar 2016), 27–34.

[8] Hebesberger, D., Körtner, T., Pripfl, J., Gisinger, C., and Hanheide, M. What do staff in eldercare want a robot for? An assessment of potential tasks and user requirements for a long-term deployment. In *Proceedings of the IROS Workshop on "Bridging user needs to deployed applications of service robots"* (Hamburg, Sep 2015).

[9] Jin, Z. X., Plocher, T., and Kiff, L. Touch Screen User Interfaces for Older Adults: Button Size and Spacing. In *Universal Access in Human Computer Interaction. Coping with Diversity (UAHCI)*, C. Stephanidis, Ed. Springer Berlin Heidelberg, Beijing, China, Jul 2007, 933–941.

[10] Jovan, F., Wyatt, J., Hawes, N., and Krajník, T. A poisson-spectral model for modelling the spatio-temporal patterns in human data observed by a robot. In *Proceedings of the IEEE/RSJ International Conference on Intelligent Robots and Systems (IROS)* (Daejeon, South Korea, Oct 2016).

[11] Krajník, T. Frequency map enhancement (FreMEn), Aug 2016. http://www.fremen.uk.

[12] Krajník, T., Fentanes, J. P., Cielniak, G., Dondrup, C., and Duckett, T. Spectral analysis for long-term robotic mapping. In *Proceedings of IEEE International Conference on Robotics and Automation (ICRA)* (HongKong, China, May 2014).

[13] Krajník, T., Santos, J., and Duckett, T. Life-long spatio-temporal exploration of dynamic environments. In *Proceedings of the European Conference on Mobile Robots (ECMR)* (Lincoln, United Kingdom, Sept 2015), 1–8.

[14] Kulich, M., Krajník, T., Přeučil, L., and Duckett, T. To explore or to exploit? learning humans' behaviour to maximize interactions with them. In *Proceedings of the Workshop on Modelling and Simulation for Autonomous Systems (MESAS)* (Rome, Italy, Jun 2016).

[15] Lohse, M., Hanheide, M., Pitsch, K., Rohlfing, K. J., and Sagerer, G. Improving HRI design by applying Systemic Interaction Analysis (SInA). *Interaction Studies, Special Issue: Robots in the Wild: Exploring HRI in naturalistic environments 10*, 3 (dec 2009), 298–323.

[16] Marchant, R., and Ramos, F. Bayesian optimisation for intelligent environmental monitoring. In *Proceedings of the IEEE/RSJ International Conference on Intelligent Robots and Systems (IROS)* (Oct 2012), 2242–2249.

[17] Marchant, R., and Ramos, F. Bayesian optimisation for informative continuous path planning. In *Proceedings of the IEEE International Conference on Robotics and Automation (ICRA)* (HongKong, China, May 2014), 6136–6143.

[18] Mudrova, L., and Hawes, N. Task scheduling for mobile robots using interval algebra. In *Proceedings of the IEEE International Conference on Robotics and Automation (ICRA)* (Seattle, USA, May 2015), 383–388.

[19] Park, C., Kang, S., Kim, J., and Oh, J. A study on service robot system for elder care. In *Proceedings of the 9th International Conference on Ubiquitous Robots and Ambient Intelligence (URAI)* (2012), 546–547.

[20] Santos, J. M., Krajník, T., and Duckett, T. Spatio-temporal exploration strategies for long-term autonomy of mobile robots. *Robotics and Autonomous Systems* (2016).

[21] Singh, A., Ramos, F., Whyte, H. D., and Kaiser, W. J. Modeling and decision making in spatio-temporal processes for environmental surveillance. In *Proceedings of the IEEE International Conference on Robotics and Automation (ICRA)* (Anchorage, USA, May 2010).

[22] Sutton, R. S., and Barto, A. G. *Reinforcement learning: An introduction.* MIT press Cambridge, 1998.

Of Space and Smell: The Strange Evolution of the Human Nose

Lucia F. Jacobs
University of California, Berkeley
Berkeley, California
jacobs@berkeley.edu

ABSTRACT

We humans are the Cyrano de Bergerac's of the primate world, with conspicuously large external noses compared to other great apes. To understand why our nose evolved we must first understand the function of olfaction. To do this requires traveling back in time to the evolution of the first brain. I will describe the hypothesis that the sense of smell evolved as a sense of direction, playing a critical role in navigation and that this function explains why olfactory systems are so plastic and variable in size across animals. The navigation function of olfaction in humans has been largely neglected and I will describe studies showing that humans can orient accurately to odors in real world and virtual reality environments. But why such a nose? To understand this, I return to an evolutionary framework to describe how the first nose, a structure used both for respiration and olfaction, appeared in air-breathing fish. I describe a new hypothesis (PROUST: perceiving and representing odor utility in space and time) to explain how the evolution of air-breathing could have forced vertebrates to segregate olfactory mapping of space to the main olfactory system and the mapping of odors across time to the newly evolved second (vomeronasal) olfactory system. This dichotomy of function and the subsequent conflict between mapping time versus space using odors, could have led to a number of novel vertebrate solutions to sample odors, including the forked tongue of the snake and the human external nose. I will end by proposing that this perspective on the evolution and function of human olfaction could enhance current paradigms in human-robot communication and decision making.

CCS Concepts/ACM Classifiers

• Hardware~Biology-related information processing • Hardware~Neural systems

Author Keywords

Navigation; sensory evolution; olfaction

BIOGRAPHY

Professor Jacobs heads the Cognitive Biology Lab in the Department of Psychology and the Helen Wills Institute of Neuroscience at the University of California, Berkeley. After training in animal behavior (1978 B.S., Cornell), ecology and evolutionary biology (1987 Ph.D., Princeton) and postdoctoral fellowships in neuroscience (Universities of Toronto, Pittsburgh and Utah), she joined the Berkeley faculty in 1993. Her group focuses on the ecology and evolution of navigating choices: how animals make choices about what and where to eat, how to navigate and map new terrains and how generally to integrate diverse sources of information to make adaptive decisions in uncertain environments. Animal species include humans, search dogs and rodents (domestic and wild). Her theoretical work on navigation focuses on the evolution of limbic structures (hippocampus, olfactory systems) and their integrated role in spatial navigation. She is the recipient of a NSF CAREER award, Hellman Junior Faculty Award, Prytanean Faculty Award, Mary Rennie Epilepsy Award and a 2015 NSF Ideas Lab Collaborative Grant for olfactory navigation. She has published over 50 papers in the fields of animal behavior, animal cognition, behavioral neuroscience and brain and behavioral evolution.

HRI'17, March 6–9, 2017, Vienna, Austria.
ACM ISBN 978-1-4503-4336-7/17/03.
http://dx.doi.org/10.1145/2909824.3020259

REFERENCES

1. Jacobs, L. F. (2012). From chemotaxis to the cognitive map: the function of olfaction. Proceedings of the National Academy of Sciences of the United States of America, 109, 10693–10700. http://doi.org/10.1073/pnas.1201880109
2. Jacobs, L. F., Arter, J., Cook, A., & Sulloway, F. J. (2015). Olfactory orientation and navigation in humans. *PLoS ONE*, *10*(6), e0129387. http://doi.org/10.1371/journal.pone.0129387.s001

Probing the Design Space of a Telepresence Robot Gesture Arm with Low Fidelity Prototypes

Patrik Björnfot
Department of Informatics
Umeå University
901 87 Umeå, Sweden
patrik.bjornfot@umu.se

Victor Kaptelinin
Department of Informatics
Umeå University
901 87 Umeå, Sweden
victor.kaptelinin@umu.se

ABSTRACT

The general problem addressed in this paper is supporting a more efficient communication between remote users, who control telepresence robots, and people in the local setting. The design of most telepresence robots does not allow them to perform gestures. Given the key role of pointing in human communication, exploring design solutions for providing telepresence robots with deictic gesturing capabilities is, arguably, a timely research issue for Human-Robot Interaction. To address this issue, we conducted an empirical study, in which a set of low fidelity prototypes, illustrating various designs of a robot's gesture arm, were assessed by the participants (N=18). The study employed a mixed-method approach, a combination of a controlled experiment, elicitation study, and design provocation. The evidence collected in the study reveals participants' assessment of the designs, used in the study, and provides insights into participants' attitudes and expectations regarding gestural communication with telepresence robots in general.

Keywords

Telepresence robots; mobile remote presence; referential gestures; pointing; interaction design; low fidelity prototypes.

1. INTRODUCTION

Telepresence robots, also known as Mobile Remote Presence (MRP) systems, are a technology, which is increasingly common in many everyday settings, such as offices, classrooms, and healthcare environments [13] [16]. A telepresence robot is a device, which is remotely controlled by a person, often referred to as a "pilot", and serves as a physical avatar of the person, his or her embodied social proxy in a local setting.

A diversity of telepresence robots is currently available on the market [16]. The general outline of a telepresence robot is often similar to the general outline of a human body. A typical telepresence robot comprises a wheeled base ("feet") and a camera/ display unit ("head"), connected to one another by a vertical pole.

HRI '17, March 06-09, 2017, Vienna, Austria

DOI: http://dx.doi.org/10.1145/2909824.3020223

Recently Mobile Remote Presence has become a topic of active research in Human-Robot Interaction (HRI) and Human-Computer Interaction (HCI) [2] [13] [26] [33]. In particular, studies have shown that telepresence robots can significantly improve the quality of interaction between a remote communication participant and local people. It was found that the use of telepresence robots supports ad hoc conversations (e.g., impromptu hallway discussions), makes the social presence of a remote person at the workplace more visible and appreciated by their colleagues (e.g., [31] [34]), and in other ways helps to compensate for negative aspects of working from a distance.

At the same time, the use of telepresence robots is associated with a number of problems, and further work is needed to find solutions to these problems. One of the problems, discussed in this paper, is a lack of gestural capabilities, typical of most telepresence robots. While, as mentioned, many robots look, very roughly, like humans, a noticeable difference is that robots typically do not have arms. There are some notable exceptions: for instance, a pioneering example of an experimental telepresence robot, named PRoP [24], was equipped with a pointing device resembling a human arm. However, the vast majority of popular telepresence robot models currently do not feature arm-like components.

The absence of arms means that robots cannot perform gestures, which is, arguably, an important limitation. Most telepresence robots are, in fact, *social* telepresence devices. Their primary, or often even sole, purpose is to support more flexible, physically situated, and embodied communication between remote pilots and local people. Given that gestures play a key role in interpersonal communication, it can be concluded that it is essential for robots to have gestural capabilities in order to fulfill their purpose.

The study reported in this paper aims to contribute to the development of gestural capabilities of telepresence robots by exploring the design space (or, rather, sub-space) of robot arms from an HCI perspective. The study focuses on "pointer arms", that is, arms, which are specifically intended to make it possible for the robot to perform deictic gestures.

The remainder of the paper is organized as follows. In the next section we present an overview of existing relevant research, clarify our intended contribution, and explain the rationale behind the choice of the methods used in our study. In the sections that follow we present, respectively, the methods used in the study, the results, and a discussion of our findings. We conclude with general reflections on the study and an outline of issues for future research.

2. BACKGROUND

2.1 Telepresence robots as a communication technology: The importance of gestures

Telepresence robots in most everyday settings, such as offices, are almost exclusively used for communication. By making it possible for remote participants to actively choose their locations and perspectives, approach other people, e.g., to initiate an ad hoc conversation, and by increasing the visibility of a person in a setting, telepresence robots take a step beyond fixed-location videoconference systems. Arguably, a key direction of further development of telepresence robots should be making the robots a more effective and efficient communication technology. The aim of this paper is to explore one particular strategy of making telepresence robots a more powerful communication technology, namely, enhancing gestural capabilities of such robots.

Various strands of research in psychology, linguistics, ethology, and so forth, indicate that gestures play a fundamental role in human communication and cognition. For instance, Tomasello [32] argues that pointing and pantomiming were the first uniquely human forms of communication. McNeil [19] provides a thorough analysis of different types of gestures – iconic, deictic, beat, and metaphoric - and their integration with speech. A number of studies show that acquisition and mastering gestures is an essential aspect of human cognitive development, and that gestures not only express one's thoughts, but also can be considered a factor that influences the development of thinking itself [11]. However, as discussed below, so far the effort to support telepresence robots' gestural capabilities has been rather limited.

2.2 Related research: Gestures in HRI

Early in the development of telerobotic systems, both in academia and industry, there has been considerable interest in supporting gesture-based communication. A pioneering MRP system PRoP (Personal Roving Presence) featured an arm-like pointing device, which was considered an essential component of the overall design of the system [24]. Another relatively early system, PEBBLES [16] [33] had a rudimentary hand, which could be used for simple gestures, such as indicating a pupil's willingness to answer a teacher's question. The design of bidirectional communication robots CALLY and CALLO [36] employed a different approach, namely, using two identical robots in two different locations and making it possible for the user to control the remote robot by controlling the co-located robot, and vice-versa. An HRI-coaching system supporting full-body robot control is presented in [3]. Probably, the most advanced gesturing capabilities are implemented in the design of GestureMan, a special purpose telepresence robot (or rather several generations of robots), which is intended to support remote instruction on physical tasks [17] .

Recently, however, a common approach has been to develop "armless" robots. Some robots, such as QB and MantaroBot [16] are equipped with laser pointers, but such devices only make it possible to highlight objects rather than perform pointing gestures, and the majority of systems do not feature any pointing devices at all.

At the same time, researchers in human-robot interaction and interaction design repeatedly emphasize the need for supporting gestural interaction. For instance, Tsui and Yanco [33] observe:

> "As social interaction is the primary goal of social telepresence robots, failure to design for eye gaze, facial expressions, and nonverbal gestures will result in systems that hinder the ability to achieve telepresence for the user and/or the interactant".

The BEAMING project [7] emphasizes the need to support communicational and deictic gestures. Kaptelinin [15] argues that MRP systems should provide support for pointing, and outlines a set of requirements a pointing device for an MRP system should meet.

Therefore, enhanced gesture support can be considered a timely task in telepresence robotics research and development, a task, which is almost universally considered important but has not been sufficiently addressed so far.

There are two main streams of related research in gestures and robotics, firstly, the one related to how human gestures are interpreted by robots, e.g. [21][22] [30], and, secondly, the one related to gestures performed by robots when interacting with humans, e.g. [14]. This paper places itself in a third stream; we seek to find out how gestures can be mediated via robots in human-human interaction, with added challenges of making sure the gestures conform to social conventions.

The focus on performing deictic gestures (that is, pointing) via robot arms, which is somewhat similar to the focus of our study, characterizes some research dealing with assembly line arms, especially in scenarios where human intervention is needed [8], [9], [12], [29]. This research has produced some relevant findings: for instance, it was shown that gestures performed by robot arms should have good visibility and clarity. However, these analyses typically do not take into account social aspects of human-robot interaction, which aspects are central for our research.

2.3 Research methods: Experiment, gesture elicitation, and design provocation

A wide range of methods for user research, design, and evaluation have been developed in HCI and interaction design [27]. The present study employs low fidelity prototypes in combination with three empirical user research methods: controlled experiments, gesture elicitation, and design provocations. The choice of these methods is determined by the specific aims of our study and reflects the state of the art in HCI research methodology.

Low fidelity ("lo-fi") prototypes, as opposed to high fidelity ("hi-fi") prototypes, do not have the "look and feel" of the finished product. The value of sketches and lo-fi prototypes in design is often underestimated [5] and they can be considered "not serious enough". However, experience shows that lo-fi prototypes have a number of advantages, especially when engaging potential users early in the lifecycle of a design project. In particular, when working with lo-fi prototypes the participants are more inclined to suggest substantial changes to the designs they assess and focus on the underlying concept rather than the appearance of a prototype [27].

Controlled experiments, essentially modeled after the experimental method in psychology, have a long history in HCI [4]. Currently controlled experiments are, probably, less popular in HCI than studies conducted in natural setting, but they continue to play an important role in the field.

Gesture elicitation studies are intended to identify the most natural gestures, for different types of interaction between people and technology, by asking the participants to actually perform the gestures (e.g., [6]). As discussed below, the variant of the method used in our study was different from more traditional variants. Instead of asking people to show the gestures they themselves would perform by using *their own arms and hands*, we asked the participants to show what gestures they would expect a robot to perform, by physically adjusting the position *of the robot's arm.*

People who do not have prior experience with a novel technology can find it difficult to articulate a concrete opinion about the technology. Design provocations address this issue by presenting the participants with concrete designs, which designs can be (and often deliberately are) not optimal, to facilitate critical comments and suggestion improvements, and thus reveal participants' underlying assumptions and criteria for assessing the technology in question. Design provocations established themselves in HCI and interaction design as a part of wider user research and design methodologies, such as cultural probes [10], critical design [1][25], and reflective design [28].

The combination of methods used in the study was intended to provide different perspectives on the same object of analysis. This approach follows the general idea of "method triangulation", which is considered an important strategy for increasing the external validity of a study [23].

3. METHOD

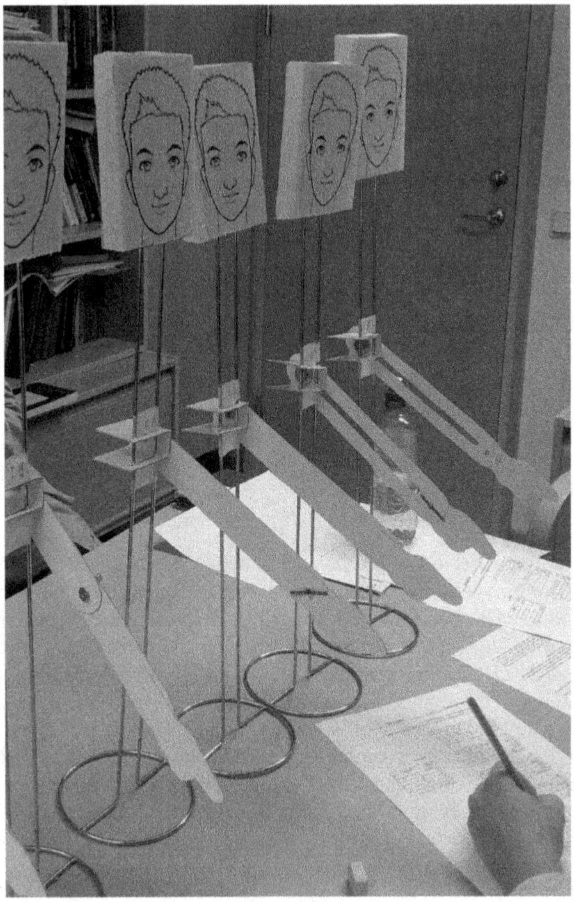

Figure 1. Experimental setting.

3.1 Participants

Eighteen participants, from 21 to 30 years of age (average age: 25 y. o.), 10 males and 8 females, took part of the study. Most of the participants were students at a Swedish university.

3.2 Materials

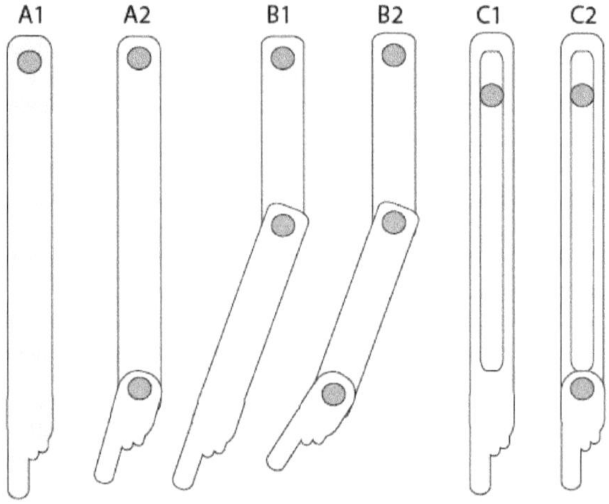

Figure 2. The arm designs used in the study.

3.2.1 Prototypes

The experiment employed low fidelity prototypes (Figure 1) implementing six different designs of a robot arm (Figure 2). The designs were selected because they are characterized by low complexity and therefore represent a natural starting point for exploring robot arms' gestural expressivity. The designs were produced by combining two factors: (a) the construction of the arm ("Arm Type"), and (b) whether or not the "hand" was a fixed part of the arm or could be moved independently ("Independent Hand").

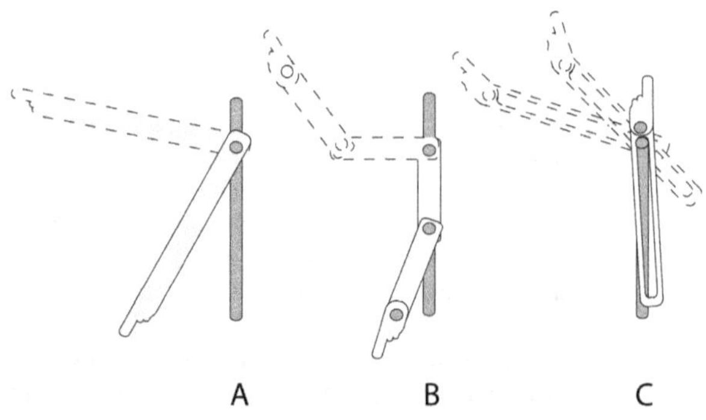

Figure 3. Arm Types: Fixed Attachment Stick (A), Elbow Joint (B), and Sliding Attachment Stick (C).

There were three levels of the Arm Type factor, which corresponded to the following variants of arm construction: a one-piece arm with a fixed connection to the robot body ("Fixed Attachment Stick", Figure 3A), a two-piece arm having an equivalent of an elbow joint in the middle ("Elbow Joint", Figure 3B), and a one-piece stick with a sliding connection to robot's body ("Sliding Attachment Stick", Figure 3C). The Independent Hand factor had two levels, Yes or No (see Figure 4).

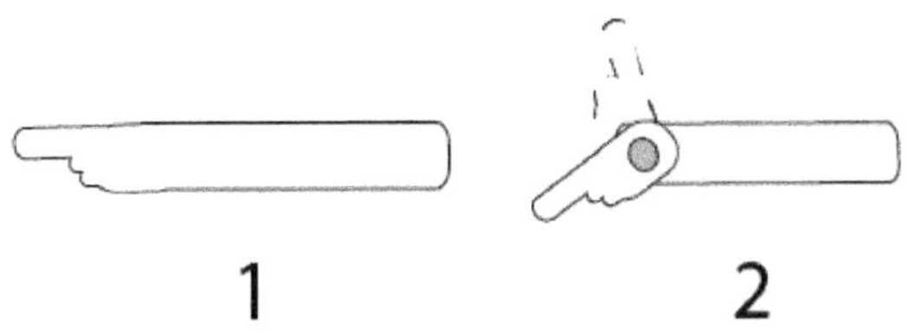

Figure 4. Independent Hand Factor levels: No Independent Hand (1), Independent Hand (2).

In the discussion below the six prototypes are coded using letters and numbers. The letters, A-C, signify three different arm types: Fixed Attachment Stick (A), Elbow Joint (B), and Sliding Attachment Stick (C). The numbers, 1 and 2, signify two levels of the Independent Hand factor: absence (1) or presence (2) of an independent hand. For instance, C1 means "Sliding Attachment Stick without an independent hand".

All six low fidelity prototypes were implemented using identical wireframe stands, 67 cm high, and identical "head parts" made of polystyrene foam. The arms were made of durable glossy cardboard; wing nuts were used to conveniently adjust the connection between different parts of an arm (Figure 1).

3.2.2 Imaginary use scenarios

Three different use scenarios of a telepresence robot performing a pointing gesture were presented to the participants. The first scenario ("Can I talk to you?") described a robot approaching a group of people and indicating an intention to talk to one person from the group. The second scenario ("Look at this!") described a robot referring to an object in the local environment, a gadget lying on a desk, during a conversation with a local person. The third one ("Mind the door") described a robot approaching a door and indicating the intention to "touchlessly" open it (as if using a "remote control"). The scenarios did not specify the pilot's user interface.

The choice of the scenarios was informed by empirical and conceptual analyses of telepresence robots [16][33], which identify a number of issues, common for various use contexts. Three such issues, reflected in the experimental scenarios, were: (a) addressing a specific person, (b) referring to an object in the local setting, and (c) dealing with obstacles while navigating a telepresence unit.

3.3 Experiment design

The experiment employed a two-factor within-subject experimental design. Six experimental factors corresponded to the six robot arm designs described in section 3.2.1; they were produced by combining three levels of the Arm Type factor and two levels of the Independent Hand factor. To minimize potential order effects, a Latin Square plan was used to determine the sequence of conditions for individual participants.

3.4 Procedure

Each of the participants was tested individually by a team of experimenters, each team comprising 3-4 persons. The experimenters were master's level students taking a course in user research; running an experimental study was a course assignment. The experimenters received a training on how to conduct the study; the training included one of the researchers going through a complete trial experimental session with each of the experimenter teams.

Each experimental session comprised three parts, corresponding to the three scenarios described in section 3.2.2. In each of these parts the participants were first required to read a scenario description. The descriptions were provided as printed documents to avoid potential researchers' biases. Then the participants were asked to explore the six prototypes (by following a predefined order), fill in a form, adjust the position of each of the prototype arms to show what the participant thought was the most natural gesture for the prototype, and take part in a brief interview. The total time for each individual session was about 40 min.

3.5 Types of empirical data collected in the study

3.5.1 Assessment with numerical scores

For each of the three imaginary use scenarios the participants were asked to provide two different types of scores. First, they was supposed to assign ranks to the six designs, ranging from "1", which indicated the best design overall, to "6", indicting the worst design. Second, after demonstrating the most appropriate gestures for each of the six prototypes, the participants were asked to use four seven-point Likert scales to assess the gestures according to the criteria of clarity, confusability, politeness, and perceived safety. The scales' values were ranging from "-3" to "+3", with more positive scores corresponding to more positive assessments. The selection of the criteria was informed by a previous study by Kaptelinin [16].

3.5.2 Elicited gestures

Each of the participants was required to physically manipulate the prototypes to show what gestures they thought were the most appropriate ones for each of the three scenarios. In total, the participants produced 324 gestures, which were photographed by the experimenters.

3.5.3 Interviews

In addition to providing numerical scores and producing gestures, the participants were required to explain the reasons for their ranking, assessments, and the choice of gestures. The participants were also encouraged to express their opinions about the designs, suggest improvements, and share their general reflections about gesture-based interaction with telepresence robots.

4. RESULTS

4.1 Numerical scores

4.1.1 Overall ranking

Figure 5 provides an overview of how the participants ranked the six prototypes used in the study, separately for each of the three scenarios. The figure shows that the most highly rated design was the most human-like one, B2 ("Elbow Joint with an independent hand"). Seven participants ranked B2 the highest in all three scenarios. The lowest ranks were given to A1 ("Fixed Attachment Stick without an independent hand"). The ranks of other prototypes were distributed between these two extremes.

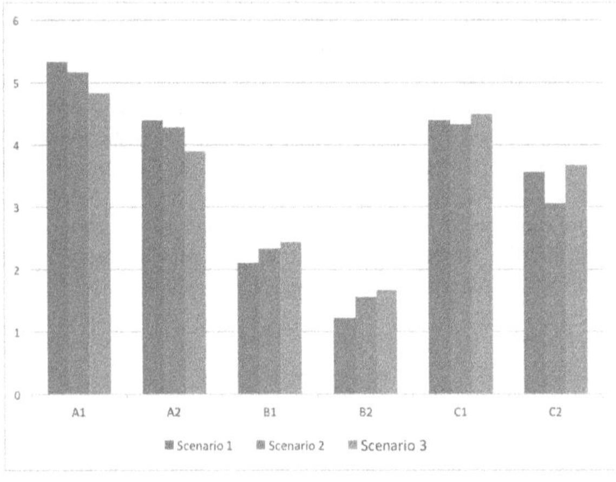

Figure 5. Mean ranks of the prototypes, separately for each of the three scenarios (shorter bars correspond to higher ranks).

Three patterns in the overall ranking results deserve special attention. First, the order of prototypes, from best to worst, was the same in all three scenarios: B2, B1, C2, A2, C1, A1. Second, within all arm types (A, B, and C) the prototype with an independent hand received a higher average rank than the prototype without an independent hand. Third, the results suggest that there are individual differences in the ranking: while B2 was ranked as one of the top two (#1 or #2) most often (48 times), other prototypes also received top ranks: B1 (41 times), C2 (10 times), C1 (6 times), A1 (3 times), and A2 (1 time).

4.1.2 Assessment of visibility, clarity, politeness, and perceived safety

The results of the assessment of the prototypes, in each of the scenarios, according to their visibility clarity, politeness, and perceived safety, are consistent with the data from overall ranking. The Arm Type B ("Elbow Joint") received highest mean ranks, and was followed by C and A, according to both overall ranking and scale-based assessment (see Table 1). The mean ranking is consistent across all scenarios.

Table 1. Mean four-scale scores and mean ranks for three Arm Types.

Model	Visibi-lity	Cla-rity	Polite-ness	Feels Safe	Total Value	Rank
A	2,2	1,6	0,3	0,6	4,7	4,6
B	2,4	2,2	1,7	1,8	8,0	1,9
C	2,0	1,6	0,6	0,8	5,0	3,9

The arms with independent hands were rated higher than arms without independent hands, again according to both overall ranking and scale-based assessment (see Table 2). The ranking is consistent across all scenarios.

Table 2. Mean four-scale scores and mean ranks for two levels of the Independent Hand factor.

Independ-ent hand	Visibi-lity	Cla-rity	Polite-ness	Feels Safe	Total Value	Rank
No	2,2	1,7	0,7	1,0	5,5	3,9
Yes	2,2	1,9	1,0	1,1	6,3	3,0

The total sum value of a condition for all four criteria correlates with the mean rank of the condition.

4.2 Elicited gestures

4.2.1 Scenario 1 ("Can I talk to you?")

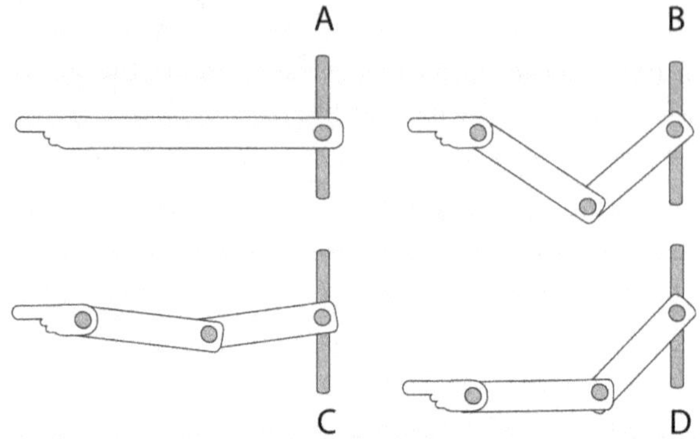

Figure 6. Gestures produced by the participants in Scenario 1.

The most common gesture elicited in Scenario 1 was a straightforward pointing (see Figure 6A). It was suggested in 25% of the cases. Similar to this gesture was a slightly downwards pointing gesture, suggested in 8% of the cases. These two gestures have a mean ranking of, respectively, 4,4 and 4,7 (where 1 is best, and 6 is worst).

When producing gestures with Arm Type B ("Elbow Joint") prototypes, 77% of the participants used the shoulder joint to move the arm down, while the "forearm" and hand were still pointing forward. These gestures generally had a better ranking. Eight percent of the gestures included the "upper arm" directed down at 45°, the "forearm" raising up at 45°, and the hand pointing straight ahead (Figure 6B). In 6.5% of the cases the whole arm basically pointed straight ahead, with just a slight bent of the elbow (Figure 6 C). In additional 6% of the gestures the upper arm was directed down at 45°, while the forearm and hand were pointing straight ahead (Figure 6D).

Seven of the participants commented that it was impolite to point at someone, and three of these participants did not even want to point. The participants thought that it was more polite to point with a non-straight arm, and all of these seven participants used the elbow joint on B-prototypes to bend the arm.

4.2.2 Scenario 2 ("Look at this!")

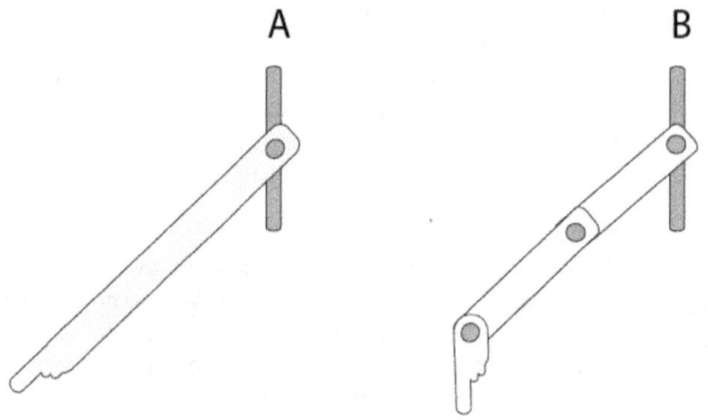

Figure 7. Gestures in Scenario 2.

Gestures elicited in Scenario 2 were rather homogeneous. In 56.4% of the cases the proposed gesture was the one shown in Figure 7A: the arm and hand were pointing down at 45°. In 9% of the cases the arm was pointing at 45° down, and the hand was pointing straight down (Figure 7B). The mean rankings of both of these gestures where close to average (3,72 and 2,9, while the average was 3).

Half of the participants indicated in their comments that a key factor when performing the ranking of the prototypes was the flexibility of the arms (5 additional participants mentioned it in relation to other scenarios). For instance, one of the participants, who had all prototypes do exactly the same gesture, stated that they rated the arms only on the basis of their flexibility, and therefore rated the B2 the highest, followed by B1.

4.2.3 Scenario 3 ("Mind the door")

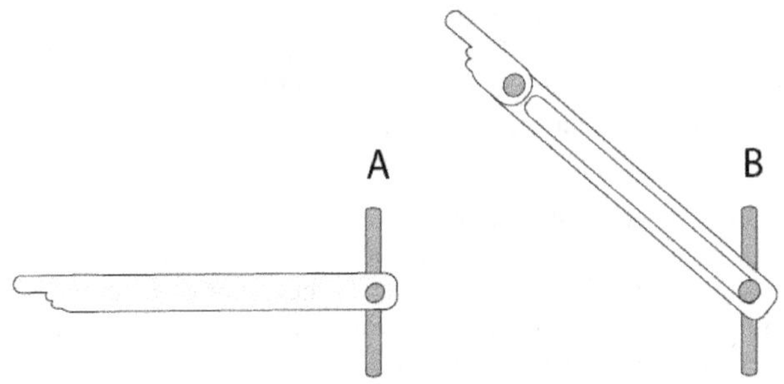

Figure 8. Gestures in Scenario 3.

In this scenario 38% of the gestures were simply pointing straight ahead (the mean ranking was 5,17), see Figure 8A. In 14% cases the arm was pointing up at 45 degrees (the mean ranking was 3), see Figure 8B.

A concern raised by three of the participants was that it was hard to make a gesture that signals "the door is about to open" and not "I need help to open the door".

4.3 Suggestions for improvement

In addition to ranking, scale-based assessment, and gesture elicitation the participants, in each of the three scenarios, were also encouraged to critically evaluate the proposed designs and suggest possible ways of improving them. The suggestions for improvement are summarized below and listed in Table 1.

In Scenario 1 ("Can I talk to you?") the majority of suggestions were related to politeness. The suggested improvements were: (a) providing a more complex hand, which would comprise more than just an index finger, (b) making it possible for the robot to rotate the hand about the arm's axis, (c) provide fully flexible ball bearing joints (1 participant), and (d) support pointing with face recognition.

By proposing an increased flexibility of the arm the participants tried to avoid what was considered a "rude pointing". One participant noted that "It is difficult to be polite when you point with a finger", and suggested that this issue can be addressed by supporting either the use of an open hand or subtle movements of the pointing finger.

The reason for suggesting face recognition functionality was to simplify pilot's task of pointing to a particular person.

Most of the suggestions in Scenario 2 ("Look at this!") were dealing with clarity, visibility, and solving the problem of precision. The suggested improvements were: (a) using a LED/Laser pointer, (b) making the shoulder height adjustable, (c) holding a remote in robot's hand, (d) including lights that would visually highlight the arm, (e) when pointing, using the entire hand instead of a finger. The LED/Laser pointer was supposed to increase the accuracy of pointing, and adjustable shoulder height was meant to increase the flexibility of pointing to meet the requirements of different tasks and environments. To point with a full hand instead of a finger was the only suggestion that reduced the precision of pointing.

Improvement suggestions in Scenario 3 ("Mind the door") mostly focused on visibility. They included: (a) horizontal (e.g., left to right) movement of the arm, e.g., to signal that the local user should move out of the way, (b) rotation of the hand about the arm's axis, and (c) using robot's "head screen" for displaying animation. In addition, two participants highlighted the need for supporting repetitive movements.

As a general suggestion, two participants proposed using LED lights on the robot as "warning signals" of different types of actions.

Table 3. Summary of improvement suggestions.

Name	# of Participants	Scenario
Providing a more advanced hand, not just a finger	6	1 & 3
A two DoF hand (combining vertical and horizontal movements)	5	1 & 3
Fully flexible, three DoF ball joints	1	1
Supporting pointing with face recognition	1	1
Employing a LED/Laser pointer	3	2
Making the shoulder joint height adjustable	1	2
Placing a remote control in robot's hand	1	2
Pointing with a hand instead of finger	1	2
Lighting up the arm	1	2
Horizontal arm movement	4	3
Using robot's screen for animations displaying intended actions	1	3
Using LED light to signal events	2	Other

4.4 Other comments of the participants

4.4.1 Human likeness

In their general comments and reflections, most participants (14 out of 18) expressed their positive assessment of human likeness of telepresence robots. As one participant observed: "The more human the better". This notion is supported by the fact that Arm Type B ("Elbow Joint") prototypes, which were described by the participants as "human-like", were also ranked and assessed most positively. In a similar vein, one participant suggested that Arm Type C prototypes ("Sliding Attachment Stick") should have a shoulder in order to "look more human".

4.4.2 Participants role in the scenarios

It is evident that even though the participants were instructed to take the role of the local user, they provided comments and reflections from the pilot's side, as well. Most notable was the suggestion to use face-recognition for a more efficient detection of potential communication partners.

5. DISCUSSION

5.1 Design provocation

The scenarios used in the study made the participants question the proper way to interact via an MRP system. Participants' comments highlighted the importance of cultural norms (e.g., "It is impolite to point to a person" or "I would not point at people at all"), and, at the same time, the participants demonstrated and explained how to increase politeness (e.g., by using an open hand, avoiding direct pointing, waving, etc.). Arm Type A ("Fixed Attachment Stick") designs in Scenario 1 served as designed provocations: they made the participants realize that a straight arm can be considered "authoritarian", "commanding" and "rude". However, even though the expressive capabilities of Arm Type A designs were mostly considered essentially inadequate, the participants had no choice but use them to produce "the best possible" gestures because it was required by the instructions. Included in the ranking, the gestures provide a baseline for comparison for gestures produced with other designs.

When encountering problems caused by the limitations of the arm designs used in the study, the participants suggested a number of improvements. Several of such improvements were in line with making robot arms more human-like. However, there were also other types of suggested improvements, which had no references to the human body. For example, different types of lights and lasers, as well as various ways of utilizing the robot´s "head" screen, were proposed. These types of improvements, which did not imply human likeness, would not be proposed if MRP systems were assumed to have the same capabilities as human beings. It appears that the suggestions, instead, reflect an assumption that regarding nonverbal communication capabilities telepresence robots may have specific advantages to be exploited, not limited to just replicating human capabilities.

5.2 Flexibility and human-likeness

Flexibility was a key theme in participants' comments related to Scenario 2, even in cases when this capability was not actually used. The most plausible explanation appears to be that the participants were thinking about similar scenarios, in which extended flexibility would have been needed. One could argue that the rating forced the participant to go beyond the context of the scenario at hand in order to make a more general comparison between the designs to establish the "winner". This explanation is currently just a hypothesis, which needs to be investigated empirically. It should be mentioned that several of the participants provided improvement suggestions that intend to increase arm's flexibility, such as a rotating hand, horizontal movement, or adjustable shoulder height.

Another desirable attribute of telepresence robots that was commonly mentioned by the participants was "human-likeness", mainly in relation to politeness, but also in relation to forming gestures in general.

Judging from participants' comments, the results can be interpreted as an indication that human-likeness and flexibility were considered desirable qualities, which positively affected the rating regardless of whether the capabilities were actually used in gesture elicitation. The arm type that was most human-like, B2, had more joints than other arm types, and was therefore also the most flexible one. An interesting issue to explore would be a comparison of B2 with other designs, featuring more joints (and thus being less human-like), in order to separate human-likeness from flexibility.

5.3 Is human-likeness optimal?

It is natural that the human body provides a basic point of reference when looking at social communication via MRP systems. After all, as humans, we are mostly used to socially interacting with other humans.

The comment "the more human the better", expressed by some participants, is an important indication; it shows that the participants think that achieving human-likeness is a key direction of further improvement of telepresence robots. However, striving for human-likeness faces two significant challenges: first, the need to explain the phenomenon of Uncanny Valley and, second, deal with the issue of "false expectations".

The Uncanny Valley phenomenon means that if a robot resembling a human still lacks some human traits, it can elicit negative feelings in people who perceive it [20]. It also means that when striving for human likeness robot designers run a very real risk of making people feel uncomfortable.

The other factor that needs to be taken into account when considering human-likeness as a design objective is that technology, in this case, the "arm", may imply more human capabilities that it actually has, which may give rise to false expectations. For example, the suggestion that the arm should feature a "full hand", if implemented, can make local people interacting with a telepresence robot think that the arm has the capability of picking up things, even if the arm can only be used for gestures.

In light of the above arguments, it can be concluded that the role and effect of human-likeness in mobile remote presence needs to be studied more thoroughly, for instance by exploring robot arm designs, which have identical functional capabilities but differ in "human likeness".

5.4 Gestures and culture

Our study suggests that people use their cultural norms and expectations, such as those related to "politeness", when imagining and modeling robot arm gestures. However, the study does not present any concluding evidence regarding the specific relationship between culture and gesture-based communication. It was not an object of analysis in our study, and further research is needed to explore this issue.

In particular, the cultural background of the participants was rather homogeneous; the majority of them were students at a Swedish university. In future studies involving participants with more diverse cultural backgrounds can be a way to better understand the role of culture in mobile remote presence.

An important issue for further research is also the dynamics of cultural expectations and norms over time. Studies have shown that such expectations and norms develop when telepresence robots are introduced to real-life settings and activities [18], and one can expect similar phenomena to take place when/if gesture-based communication with telepresence robots becomes a common aspect of everyday contexts. Emerging social practices are likely to be reflected in new or modified norms, e.g., regarding what is considered polite.

6. CONCLUSION

The underlying idea of the study reported in this paper is that designing gesture arms for telepresence robots is an important issue for Human-Robot Interaction, and addressing this issue requires a systematic exploration of the entire design space of such gesture arms. Some findings of our study, e.g., that the participants preferred a human-like arm with an elbow joint and that designs with an independent hand systematically showed an advantage (if a modest one) over designs without such hand, can be of certain interest to the designers of robot arms. Admittedly, the study explores only a small subset of relevant design issues, and further work is needed to provide a more substantial guidance for design. However, the intended contribution of our study extends beyond an assessment of concrete design solutions.

The evidence collected in the study allows us to make a general assessment of the research strategy we adopted, that is, the use of low fidelity prototypes. The evidence suggests that low fidelity prototypes – which can be produced quickly and are inexpensive – can facilitate participants' engagement and constructive critical assessment of design solutions. The unfinished nature of the prototypes stimulates imagination, and physical embodiments of design concepts support the participants in making specific critical comments and suggestions for improvement.

At the same time, our evidence suggests that low-fidelity prototypes have some substantial limitations. In particular, while the prototypes were effective in bringing in the issue of politeness, the issue of safety, which is arguably no less important, was not a prominent theme in the discussion. A possible explanation is that the small form factor of the prototypes did not make it possible for the participants to *experience* telepresence robots as a source of potential danger.

In sum, our study suggests that design explorations of telepresence robot arms, based on low-fidelity prototypes, can be a useful strategy. Using such prototypes as a first step when exploring a novel design space is a fast and cheap way to define the direction of research and design. It makes it possible to freely and efficiently, if tentatively, explore a wide range of issues, identify some of the key ones, facilitate participants' feedback, and stimulate the search for new alternatives. At the same time, studies employing low fidelity prototypes cannot be expected to provide definitive answers to research and design questions. They need to be complemented with more advanced prototypes and products, which would make it possible to extend the scope of analysis to include more developed technological solutions and more realistic user experiences, actions, and contexts.

7. ACKNOWLEDGMENTS

We want to thank Umeå University students taking the "User Research for Interaction Design" course (Fall 2016) for running the experiments and four anonymous reviewers for their valuable comments. The work reported in this paper was funded by The Swedish Research Council (Vetenskapsrådet), grant 2015-05316.

8. REFERENCES

[1] Bardzell, J., and Bardzell, S. 2013. What is "critical" about critical design? Proceedings of CHI '13. ACM New York, 3297-3306 DOI= http://dx.doi.org/10.1145/2470654.2466451

[2] Beer, J. M. and Takayama, L. 2011. Mobile remote presence systems for older adults: Acceptance, benefits, and concerns. *Proceedings of HRI 2011*. NJ: IEEE. DOI= http://dx.doi.org/10.1145/1957656.1957665

[3] Bogdanovych, A., Stanton, C., Wang, X., and Williams, M.-A. 2012. Real-time human-robot interactive coaching system with full-body control interface. In *Robot Soccer World Cup XV*. Lecture Notes in Artificial Intelligence. Springer, Berlin, 562-573.

[4] Blandford, A., Cox, A. L., and Cairns, P. A. 2008. Controlled Experiments. In Cairns, P.A., & Cox, A.L. (eds.). *Research Methods for Human Computer Interaction.* CUP.

[5] Buxton, B. 2007. *Sketching User Experience: Getting the Design Right and the Right Design.* Morgan Kaufmann, SF.

[6] Chan, E., Seyed, T., Stuerzlinger, W., Yang, X.-D., and Maurer, F. 2016. User Elicitation on Single-hand Microgestures. Proceedings CHI 2016. DOI= http://dx.doi.org/10.1145/2858036.2858589

[7] Cohen, B., Lanir, J., Stone, R., and Gurevich, P. 2011. Requirements and design considerations for a fully immersive robotic telepresence system. In *Proceedings of HRI 2011 Workshop on Social Robotic Telepresence* (pp. 16-22).

[8] Ende, T., Haddadin, S., Parusel, S., Wüsthoff, T., Hassenzahl, M., and Albu-Schäffer, A. (2011, September). A human-centered approach to robot gesture based communication within collaborative working processes. In *2011 IEEE/RSJ International Conference on Intelligent Robots and Systems* (pp. 3367-3374). IEEE. DOI= http://dx.doi.org/10.1109/IROS.2011.6094592

[9] Gleeson, B., MacLean, K., Haddadi, A., Croft, E., and Alcazar, J. (2013, March). Gestures for industry: intuitive human-robot communication from human observation. In *Proceedings of the 8th ACM/IEEE international conference on Human-robot interaction* (pp. 349-356). IEEE Press.

[10] Gaver, B., Dunne, T., and Pacenti, E. (1999). Cultural probes. interactions 6 (1), Jan./Feb.,21– 29.

[11] Goldin-Meadow, S. 2015. Gesture and cognitive development. In Handbook of Child Psychology and Developmental Science. V. 2. Wiley.

[12] Haddadi, A., Croft, E. A., Gleeson, B. T., MacLean, K., and Alcazar, J. (2013, May). Analysis of task-based gestures in human-robot interaction. In *Robotics and Automation (ICRA), 2013 IEEE International Conference on* (pp. 2146-2152). IEEE. DOI= http://dx.doi.org/10.1109/ICRA.2013.6630865

[13] Herring, S.C., Fussell, S. R., Kristoffersson, A., Mutlu, B., Neustaedter, C., and Tsui, K. 2016. The Future of Robotic Telepresence: Visions, Opportunities and Challenges. Proceeding of CHI EA '16. NY: ACM Press, 1038-1042. DOI= http://dx.doi.org/10.1145/2851581.2886423

[14] Huang, C.-M., and Mutlu, B. "Modeling and Evaluating Narrative Gestures for Humanlike Robots." *Robotics: Science and Systems*. 2013.

[15] Kaptelinin, V. 2016. Supporting Referential Gestures in Mobile Remote Presence: A Preliminary Exploration. In Inclusive Smart Cities and Digital Health. LNCS, v. 9677, Springer International Publishing, 262-267. DOI= http://dx.doi.org/10.1007/978-3-319-39601-9_23.

[16] Kristoffersson, A., Coradeschi, S., and Loutfi, A. 2013. A review of mobile robotic telepresence. *Advances in Human-Computer Interaction* 2013, 3, nnn-nnn.

[17] Kuzuoka, H. Oyama, S., Yamazaki, K., Suzuki, K., and Mitsuishi, M. 2000. GestureMan: A Mobile Robot that

Embodies a Remote Instructor's Actions. *Proceedings CSCW'00*, December 2-6, 2000, Philadelphia, PA. 155-162. DOI= http://dx.doi.org/10.1145/358916.358986

[18] Lee, M. K. and Takayama, L. 2011. "Now, I have a body": uses and social norms for mobile remote presence in the workplace. *Proceedings CHI 2011*. DOI= http://dx.doi.org/10.1145/1978942.1978950

[19] McNeill, D.D. 1992. *Hand and mind: What gestures reveal about thought.* University of Chicago press.

[20] Mori, M., MacDorman, K. F., and Kageki, N. (2012). The uncanny valley [from the field]. *IEEE Robotics & Automation Magazine*, *19*(2), 98-100.

[21] Nehaniv, C L., Dautenhahn, K., Kubacki, J., Haegele, M., Parlitz, C., and Alami, R. A methodological approach relating the classification of gesture to identification of human intent in the context of human-robot interaction." *ROMAN 2005. IEEE International Workshop on Robot and Human Interactive Communication, 2005*. IEEE, 2005.

[22] Obaid, M., Kistler, F., Häring, M., Bühling, R., and André, E. (2014). A framework for user-defined body gestures to control a humanoid robot. *International Journal of Social Robotics*, *6*(3), 383-396. Doi > 10.1007/s12369-014-0233-3

[23] Oulasvirta, A. 2009. Field experiments in HCI: Promises and challenges. In P. Saariluoma, H. Isomaki (Eds.), *Future Interaction Design II*. Springer. DOI= 10.1007/978-1-84800-385-9_5

[24] Paulos, E. and Canny, J. 1998. PRoP: Personal Roving Presence. Proceedings CHI 98. DOI= http://dx.doi.org/10.1145/259081.25919

[25] Pierce, J., Sengers, S., Hirsch , T., Jenkins, T., Gaver, W., and DiSalvo, C. 2015. Expanding and Refining Design and Criticality in HCI. *Proceedings of CHI 15*. 20183-2092. DOI= http://dx.doi.org/10.1145/2702123.2702438

[26] Rae, I., Mitlu, B., and Takayama, L. Bodies in motion: Mobility, presence, and task awareness in telepresence. Proceedings of CHI'14. ACM Press, NY (2014). DOI= http://dx.doi.org/10.1145/2556288.2557047

[27] Rogers, Y., Sharp, H., and Preece, J. 2015. *Interaction Design: Beyond Human-Computer Interaction*. 4th edition. Wiley.

[28] Sengers, P., Boehner K., David S., and Kaye J. 2005. Reflective design. Proceeding CC '05 Proceedings of the 4th decennial conference on Critical computing: between sense and sensibility. ACM. New York, 49-58.

[29] Sheikholeslami, S., Moon, J., and Croft, E.A. 2015. "Exploring the effect of robot hand configurations in directional gestures for human-robot interaction. "Intelligent Robots and Systems (IROS), 2015 IEEE/RSJ International Conference on. IEEE, 2015. DOI= http://dx.doi.org/10.1109/IROS.2015.7353879

[30] Stanton, Christopher, Anton Bogdanovych, and Edward Ratanasena. "Teleoperation of a humanoid robot using full-body motion capture, example movements, and machine learning." *Proc. Australasian Conference on Robotics and Automation*. 2012.

[31] Takayama, L. and Go, J. (2012). Mixing metaphors in mobile remote presence. *Proceedings of CSCW '12*. NY: ACM Press. DOI= http://dx.doi.org/10.1145/2145204.2145281

[32] Tomasello, M. *Origins of Human Communication*. MIT Press, Cambridge, Mass. (2008)

[33] Tsui, K.K. M. and Yanco, H. A. 2013. Design challenges and guidelines for social interaction using mobile telepresence robots. *Reviews of Human Factors and Ergonomics* 9, 1, 227-301. DOI= http://dx.doi.org/10.1109/ROMAN.2004.1374827

[34] Venolia, G., Tang, J., Cervantes, R., Bly, S., Robertson, G. G., Lee, B., and Inkpen, K. 2010. Embodied social proxy: Mediating interpersonal connection in hub-and-satellite teams. *Proceedings of CHI '10*. NY: ACM Press, 1049-1058. DOI= http://dx.doi.org/10.1145/1753326.1753482

[35] Yim, J.-D., and Shaw, C. D. (2011). Design considerations of expressive bidirectional telepresence robots. *Proceeding of CHI 2011, Extended Abstracts*. NY: ACM Press, 781-790. DOI= http://dx.doi.org/10.1145/1979742.197963

A Motion Retargeting Method for Effective Mimicry-based Teleoperation of Robot Arms

Daniel Rakita, Bilge Mutlu, Michael Gleicher
Department of Computer Sciences, University of Wisconsin–Madison
1210 West Dayton Street, Madison, WI 53706 USA
{rakita, bilge, gleicher}@cs.wisc.edu

ABSTRACT

In this paper, we introduce a novel interface that allows novice users to effectively and intuitively tele-operate robot manipulators. The premise of our method is that an interface that allows its user to direct a robot arm using the natural 6-DOF space of his/her hand would afford effective direct control of the robot; however, a direct mapping between the user's hand and the robot's end effector is impractical because the robot has different kinematic and speed capabilities than the human arm. Our key technical idea that by *relaxing* the constraint of the direct mapping between hand position and orientation and end effector configuration, a system can provide the user with the feel of direct control, while still achieving the practical requirements for telemanipulation, such as motion smoothness and singularity avoidance. We present methods for implementing a motion retargeting solution that achieves this relaxed control using constrained optimization and describe a system that utilizes it to provide real-time control of a robot arm. We demonstrate the effectiveness of our approach in a user study that shows novice users can complete a range of tasks more efficiently and enjoyably using our relaxed-mimicry based interface compared to standard interfaces.

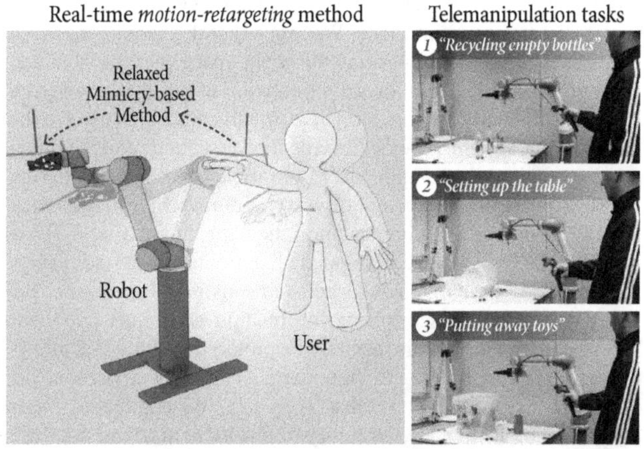

Figure 1: We propose a mimicry-based telemanipulation method that uses relaxed constraints on the mapping between a user and a robot arm as an effective real-time control mechanism and evaluate it in three telemanipulation tasks that follow a home care scenario.

1. INTRODUCTION

Telemanipulation systems, where a human user controls a robot arm from a distance, are valuable in scenarios where automation is impractical, where human judgment is essential, or where having the user engaged in the task is desirable [25]. However, controlling a robot arm from a distance introduces a number of challenges, including limitations in the capabilities of human operators and technical challenges in effectively translating human operator commands into robot actions. While shared control strategies are often used to improve performance by providing higher-level control through automation, such strategies have limited applicability, as they require prior knowledge of user goals, target object locations, and feasible robot trajectories [29, 35, 24, 6, 1, 36, 8]. Therefore, many applications involving telemanipulation must rely on direct control of robot arms. While successful real-world applications of direct control exists, such as tele-surgery, these interfaces are designed for expert users with substantial skill and training. Broadening applications and the potential users of telemanipulation, such as family members providing remote home care for an elder parent, requires interfaces that are intuitive and effective to novice users.

HRI '17, March 06-09, 2017, Vienna, Austria
 ISBN 978-1-4503-4336-7/17/03...$15.00
DOI: http://dx.doi.org/10.1145/2909824.3020254

Our goal is to provide a direct control interface that will allow novice users to effectively teleoperate robot arms and will support applications such as remote home-care or tele-nursing that require considerable human judgment and involvement without the opportunity for extensive training in system operation [18, 14]. We posit that enabling users to work in the "natural" space of their arms will allow them to draw on their inherent kinesthetic sense and ability to perform tasks in controlling a robot. That is, mapping the movement of the user's arm, particularly the position and orientation of their hand, to the movement of the robot can allow intuitive and effective control of the robot without significant training. Capturing arm motion has become practical with the recent emergence of a variety of technologies, including visual tracking (e.g., the Microsoft Kinect[1]) and wireless controllers (such as the HTC Vive[2] shown in Figure 1). However, translating captured motion into robot movements in a manner that successfully meets the demands of robot control remains a key challenge. Furthermore, because we lack satisfactory solutions to this challenge, the premise that such a mapping between human and robot arms serves as effective interface for direct control has not been validated.

The key technical challenge stems from differences in the characteristics and capabilities of robot and human arms, making a direct

[1]Microsoft Kinect: https://dev.windows.com/en-us/kinect
[2]HTC Vive: http://www.vive.com/us/

mapping unworkable for a number of reasons. First, kinematic differences between the arms mean that small movements of the human arm may require large, abrupt movements of the robot arm. Second, joint and velocity limits make smooth tracking of the user's movement difficult, leading to robot arm motion that is less predictable and harder to control. Finally, because the physiology of the user's arm may differ greatly from that of the robot arm, and the user has no kinesthetic sense of the configuration of the robot's arm, the user may inadvertently guide the robot into kinematic singularity. A practical telemanipulation system must not only mimic the user's movements well enough that they have the feeling of direct control, but it must also generate smooth, continuous robot motions that avoid singularity.

In this paper, we present a telemanipulation method that addresses this challenge to provide novice users with an easy-to-learn and easy-to-use direct control interface. We argue that the benefits of using the user's natural arm space as the input space may be obtained without considering position and orientation of the user's hand as a hard constraint. By appropriately *relaxing* the mapping between the human input and the robot's movement, we can approximate direct control solutions that support an easy-to-use interface while offering the flexibility to achieve motion with minimized joint velocities, smooth positional tracking, and no kinematic singularities. To accomplish these goals, we developed an optimization-based inverse kinematic solver that allows for relaxed constraints that can be adjusted dynamically based on what information is currently important. We have implemented this method in a prototype system that allows naïve users to control a UR5[3] robot arm using input devices including a wireless 6-DOF controller (Figure 1). We conducted a user study to demonstrate the feasibility of this method and to compare its effectiveness in enabling novice users to perform manipulation tasks using a 6-DOF stylus and a touch-screen interface.

The specific contributions of our work include (1) a mimicry-based robot arm control method that serves an easy-to-learn and easy-to-use direct manipulation interface; (2) solutions to technical challenges involved in effectively mapping human and robot arm motions and their implementation into an integrated robot control system (§4 and §5); and (3) a demonstration of the feasibility, effectiveness, and user perceptions of the control method relative to alternative, commonly used control interfaces through a user study (§6).

2. RELATED WORK

In this work, we draw on prior work in the robotics literature on kinematic mapping, human-to-robot motion remapping, and control principles. We also draw on the animation literature for work exploring retargeting motion to new characters of different scales or structures.

Human-to-robot Motion Remapping — Moving robots using human motion has a long history dating back to the early turn-crank master-slave device developed by Goertz [12] (for a survey on teleoperation devices and methods, see the work by Hokayem and Spong [15]). Since then, research has explored various scenarios that involve controlling robots using human motion. Pollard et al. [27] present a method to transfer human motion data and accompanying stylistic motion qualities to a humanoid robot, despite the discrepancy between human and robot degrees of freedom, joint velocity limits, and joint rotation ranges. Suleiman et al. [32] present a robot imitation approach and show that their analytical solution to the optimization converges quickly and effectively. Our work uses an optimization framework to address degree-of-freedom and joint-velocity-limit differences, though our approach focuses on real-time robot arm control applications, as opposed to the off-line methods mentioned above.

Robot Control with Human Motion — Prior work has used human motion in various robot control settings. Dragan et al.[9] explore teleoperation with customizable interfaces, where both the task context and assistive scaffolding (e.g., input goal estimation) are identified as important factors to support teleoperation and manipulation. Human pose states are one possible way to interface with the robot and serve as a starting point for inferring user intent in this framework. A large body of work in robotic surgery investigates systems that use specialized input devices to map and scale the surgeon's motions to a robot to perform minimally invasive procedures (see the work by Lanfranco et al. [19] for an overview). While our work addresses some similar problems, such as keeping the end effector path smooth and steady when performing dexterous tasks, analogous to the work by Taylor et al. [33], overall, mapping motions in free space at the scale of the user's hand space presents separate challenges. Also, work in haptics explores methods to make telemanipuations more tangible by detecting the user's motion and applying resistive forces with a haptic feedback device to simulate where objects would be in the user's workspace. We note that our method would integrate well with such devices as they become more feasible at the human-scale (See Okamura [26] for an outline on the history of such techniques).

Direct Control — Direct control involves specifying joint values in an unambiguous fashion from input to output device. For a comprehensive overview of teleoperation classifications, Niemeyer et al. [25]. While many believe direct control to be too tedious for users to complete tasks, some prior work suggests that users prefer direct control for some tasks [17]. Our approach aims to gain benefits of both direct and shared control: we want the user to feel like he/she has control over all robot movements in a direct control manner, while the system makes automatic adjustments that adapt to the environment and achieve attractive motion qualities analogous to shared control methods. Specialized input devices such as the ROBOpuppet system by Eilering et al. [10] make direct control more efficient by specifying poses on a miniature version of the robot in order to puppet the full robot. Because of the intuitive nature of this control method, we would like to compare mimicry-based control against this puppeteering approach in future work.

Retargeting Methods in Animation — Because our goal is to map motion from a human arm to a structurally dissimilar robot arm, we turn to the animation literature, where retargeting motion between different characters is a well studied problem. Because articulated characters and robots both consist of links and joints, principles can often be adapted between the two fields. Gleicher [11] first looked at retargeting motion capture data to new characters of different sizes and geometry using "spacetime constraints." We draw on some of the optimization techniques used in this line of work to map motion between kinematically dissimilar human and robot arms. A motion retargeting technique that works in real-time was proposed by Shin et al. [30], which allows character puppetry for live performances. We expand on the idea of importance-based inverse kinematics proposed in this work in order to fade motion goals in and out based on what is currently important using dynamically relaxed constraints.

3. TECHNICAL OVERVIEW

Our goal is to give the user the feeling of direct control from the user's hand to the robot, while achieving this effect with practical robot motions. A system must, therefore, map between measured configurations of the hand to configurations of the robot in real-time

[3]UR5: https://www.universal-robots.com/products/ur5-robot/

in a manner that achieves both objectives. At each instant in time, our system estimates the hand configuration, maps its estimate to a goal configuration of the robot, and executes robot movements to move toward this goal. The middle step of performing the mapping, known as *retargeting*, is the core of our approach. We divide retargeting into two steps (Figure 2). First, we map the measured position and orientation of the hand (6-DOF) from the space of the hand into a corresponding position and orientation in the robot's workspace. Second, we compute a configuration of the robot (i.e., joint angles) that achieves the position and orientation goal for its end effector.

In our current implementation, the first step (spatial mapping) is kept simple in order to preserve the direct nature of the interface. Positions are measured relative to the starting configuration so that the initial hand position corresponds to the initial robot configuration. Orientation displacements with respect to initial frames are copied directly, so that the end effector goal matches the hand orientation. A clutching mechanism disconnects positional motions of the input device, effectively re-centering the mapping. If the workspace of the robot has a significantly different scale than that of the human arm, the positional displacement is appropriately scaled.

The mapping from end effector goals to a joint configuration is commonly known as *inverse kinematics* (IK) (see Buss [3] for a review of common IK methods). Given the constraint of an end effector goal, an IK solver determines the corresponding joint angles that achieve the goal. However, telemanipulation must consider practical goals beyond simply matching the end effector configurations. A simple approach of directly mapping the 6-DOF hand configuration to a goal for the end effector at each time step fails, as motions of the user's hand often leads to a series of configurations that do not provide a valid robot motion. The differences in kinematics between the user's arm and the robot mean that a series of hand configurations from a smooth arm motion may require complex, large, and potentially discontinuous, robot motions. We confirmed this behavior empirically in experiments with a variety of IK techniques such as Jacobian Pseudoinverse [3], DLS [3], S-DLS [4], SQP [2], and IKfast.[4] In our pilot studies, the naïve approach failed in all trials: user hand motions lead to robot motions that violated velocity limits. In contrast, we have observed no instances of this failure in trials that used our approach. While some IK methods are capable of achieving secondary goals using redundant degrees of freedom, such a strategy requires a robot with extra degrees of freedom, and also makes the other goals secondary.

Our approach considers that the practical needs of creating viable motions may be more important than achieving precise end effector goals. We therefore frame the IK problem as an optimization where each goal can be appropriately weighted and provide methods for dynamically tuning the weights during movement to emphasize different objectives. *Our key insight* is that exactly matching the end effector goal is not always required to give the feeling of direct control. For example, when the user makes a fast large-scale motion, it may be more important to have the robot move in a smooth, continuous, and singularity-avoiding manner than to exactly reproduce the trajectory. The user may not notice small deviations in end effector position or orientation when moving quickly. In fact, they may be more likely to notice a lack of smoothness, fast joint deviations (that may be required to make small end effector movements), or if the robot becomes immovable due to a singularity. Therefore, our methods automatically *relaxes* the end effector goals (i.e., de-emphasizes them with respect to others), so that the robot can achieve movement-oriented goals.

[4]IKfast: http://openrave.org/docs/0.8.2/openravepy/ikfast/

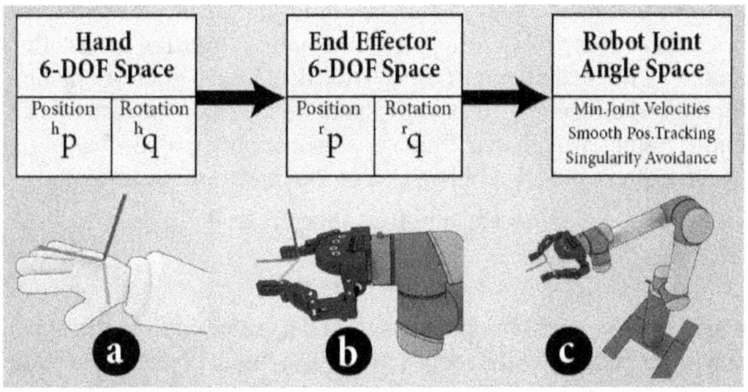

Figure 2: An overview of our method. (a) Given a goal position and orientation in the user's hand frame, (b) we map these goals to the end effector tool space of the robot, (c) and we solve for joint angles that sufficiently meet the desired end effector goals, while also achieving other attractive motion qualities.

Our inverse kinematics solver poses the computation of joint angles from a given end effector position as a constrained optimization. The hard constraints used are singularity avoidance and joint limits, while end effector position and orientation goals are treated as an objective function to be minimized. Other aspects of the robot's motion, such as smoothness in both joint and end effector space, are also used as objectives. The relative weighting of the various objectives is adjusted for each computation based on what the system determines is important at that instant.

4. RETARGETING METHOD

The core of our approach is the inverse kinematic solver that finds a goal configuration for the robot (i.e., joint angles) given information about the goal position and orientation of its end effector. At each step, our system obtains a measurement of the user's hand configuration, maps this to a position and orientation in the robot's workspace, employs the IK solver to determine the appropriate joint angles, and sends this configuration to the robot.

We denote the robot configuration as Θ, an n–vector of joint angles (where n is the number of robot joints). The robot configuration is adjusted at each system update; thus, Θ implicitly depends on a time t. We have a preset initial configuration for the robot, referred to as Θ_0. We denote the goal position for the robot's end effector by the three-vector ${}^r\mathbf{p}$ and the goal orientation for the end effector by the quaternion ${}^r\mathbf{q}$. We denote the user's hand position and orientation as ${}^h\mathbf{p}$ and ${}^h\mathbf{q}$, respectively. A subscript zero denotes an initial configuration; for example, ${}^h\mathbf{p}_0$ signifies the original position of the hand. The coordinate systems of the input device and the robot are aligned for both position and rotation.

At each step, ${}^r\mathbf{p}$ and ${}^r\mathbf{q}$ are determined based on the measured configuration of the user's hand (${}^h\mathbf{p}$,${}^h\mathbf{q}$). The end effector goal position is found by matching the displacement of the user's hand with respect to its initial position: ${}^r\mathbf{p} = {}^r\mathbf{p}_0 + s({}^h\mathbf{p} - {}^h\mathbf{p}_0)$. If the workspace of the robot is of significantly different scale than that of the human arm, the positional displacement can be appropriately scaled using the term s. The goal orientation for the end effector ${}^r\mathbf{q}$ is calculated by representing the same rotation of the hand in the robot's end effector frame. From an input stream of quaternions $\mathbf{q}$, we first capture the user's initial hand orientation and save it as ${}^h\mathbf{q}_0$. We represent each new hand orientation that comes in with respect to that initial frame by taking the quaternion displacement: ${}^h\mathbf{q} = \mathbf{q}^{-1} * {}^h\mathbf{q}_0$, where $*$ denotes quaternion multiplication. Next, we interpret the user's hand rotation in the end effector frame of the robot, seen as a part of step "b" in Figure 2. We represent the orientation of the robot using a quaternion by converting the rotation matrix of the end effector frame. We calculate the goal orientation for the end effector by rotating the hand's quaternion into the robot's initial frame through quaternion multiplication: ${}^{r}\mathbf{q} = {}^{h}\mathbf{q} * {}^{r}\mathbf{q}_0$.

We express the IK problem as a constrained optimization:

$$\begin{gathered}\Theta = \underset{\Theta}{\arg\min}\ \ \mathbf{f}(\Theta) \text{ s.t. } \mathbf{c}(\Theta) \geq \mathbf{0} \\ l_i \leq \Theta_i \leq u_i, \forall i\end{gathered} \tag{1}$$

where $\mathbf{c}(\Theta)$ is a set of constraints, l_i and u_i values define the upper and lower bounds for the robot's joints, and f is an objective function. Our challenge is to encode our goals for the mapping within the constraints and objectives. Singularity avoidance is encoded as a constraint. Other goals are encoded in the objective function.

Our objective function is the weighted sum of four terms:

$$\mathbf{f}(\Theta) = \omega_j f_j(\Theta) + \omega_e f_e(\Theta) + \omega_p f_p(\Theta) + u\omega_o f_o(\Theta) \tag{2}$$

where f_j is a joint smoothness term, f_e is an end effector smoothness term, f_p is a positional matching term, and f_o is an orientation matching term. The constants ω_i are corresponding weighting terms, and u is a scalar *importance value* that is computed to adjust the weightings between the various factors. For all experiments in this paper, we use $\omega_j = 3$, $\omega_e = 2$, $\omega_p = 10$, and $\omega_o = 5$ We discuss the various objective terms in §4.2, and the computation of u in §4.1.

4.1 Importance-Based Inverse Kinematics

Central to our objective function is the idea that we adjust the relative weights of the objective terms based on what is important at the moment. This objective is accomplished by computing the value of u in Equation 2 before the optimization begins for each step. The idea of dynamically adjusting objective weights in an IK solver based on which constraints are currently important in motion retargeting was introduced by Shin et al. [30].

The original importance-based approach determined the importance of end-effector goals based on proximity to objects; when the end-effector is close to an object, its configuration is more likely to be important because it will interact with the object. Lacking information about objects in the scene, we use a different importance measure: as the velocity of the hand increases, the precise configuration becomes less important. This measure may be seen as an approximation to the distance-based heuristic: as the user's hand approaches an object, they will naturally slow down to allow for precise manipulations of it. The velocity heuristic is also motivated by the observation that, when the hand and robot end-effector move quickly, it is less likely that orientation errors will be noticed or that precise orientation is required.

We compute the importance value based on velocity as:

$$u = \frac{v_{max} - \|\mathbf{v}_h\|}{v_{max}} \tag{3}$$

where v_{max} is a pre-calibrated maximum hand velocity per update, and $\|\mathbf{v}_h\|$ is the magnitude of the current hand velocity vector. The system described in §5 uses a v_{max} value of 0.04. As seen in Equation 2, the importance weight u only affects the orientation matching objective, not position matching.

4.2 Optimization Terms and Constraints

The following sections provide further detail on the terms used in our objective function as well as how we use the nonlinear optimization constraints and bounds to supplement our mimicry-based control approach.

Joint Velocity Minimization — Standard kinematic remapping techniques for mimicry-based control may result in motion that is too discontinuous to be used for control applications, because small positional or rotational changes in the user's hand may lead to distant configurations in the robot's joint space. Thus, we would like to favor successive solutions that provide smooth joint position changes by relaxing the constraints on end effector position and rotation goals.

To achieve smooth positional changes in real-time, we add a term in our objective function that attempts to minimize the magnitude of joint velocities:

$$f_j(\Theta) = \|\Theta'\|^2 \tag{4}$$

We approximate the joint velocity value by using backwards finite differencing.

Position Tracking — When controlling a robot with arm motion, it is important that the robot smoothly and accurately tracks the relative position of the user's hand so that the robot motion is more predictable and easier to control. Because we want users to feel like the robot is completing tasks the same way they would with their own arm, robot motion that lags behind in task space or introduces jagged end effector paths will likely break this immersive experience. However, because the robot's joint limits and velocities may differ from the user's arm, it may be difficult to smoothly track the user's relative hand path over time. We address this challenge by introducing two terms in our optimization objective function. First, we add a term that attempts to match the end effector position to the goal position ${}^{r}\mathbf{p}$. The calculation of this goal position is described at the head of §4. We take our preset initial configuration for the robot Θ_0 and calculate the original end effector position by using the forward kinematics equation of the robot, denoted here as $FK(\Theta_0)$. We formulate the following objective term to minimize the error between the goal position and current displacement of the end effector with respect to its initial position:

$$f_p(\Theta) = \|{}^{r}\mathbf{p} - FK(\Theta)\|^2. \tag{5}$$

We would also like the end effector path to be smooth in order to achieve robot motion that is more predictable and easier to track. This idea follows previous findings that smoothing in the end effector space improves user reaction times to robot arm motions [16]. Smoothing in the end effector position space has the additional benefit of filtering input signal noise in real-time, making the system sufficiently adept for dexterous adjustments. We achieve this effect in a similar fashion to Equation 4, although this calculation minimizes the end effector velocity in Cartesian space. We formulate this minimization as an optimization term as follows:

$$f_e(\Theta) = \|FK'(\Theta)\|^2. \tag{6}$$

Orientation Matching — Because the orientation of a person's hand is important in many tasks, such as pouring tea, placing a lego piece on a board, or unscrewing a light bulb, equipping the robot arm with the ability to mimic the orientation of the user's hand is critical to accomplish tasks in the same way. To achieve this goal, we must converge on the correct end effector orientation in optimization.

We denote the orientation of the robot's end effector (represented as a quaternion) as ${}^{e}\mathbf{q}$, which is computed as a function of Θ using the forward kinematics equations of the robot. We minimize the difference between this actual orientation and the goal orientation ${}^{r}\mathbf{q}$. We measure the difference between orientations as the magnitude of the rotation vector between them [21], $disp(\mathbf{q}_1, \mathbf{q}_2) = log(\mathbf{q}_1^{-1} * \mathbf{q}_2)$. The objective term is therefore:

$$f_o(\Theta) = \|disp({}^{r}\mathbf{q}, {}^{e}\mathbf{q})\|^2 \tag{7}$$

We scale the orientation term using u in the objective function as seen in Equation 3 based on our assumption that orientation is most important as users slow their motion as their hands approach an object. Thus, the importance of the end effector orientation dynamically fades in as an object is approached. Conversely, when the user is moving his/her hand quickly, the orientation goal is relaxed so that the robot has extra degrees of freedom available to smoothly track this fast moving position goal.

Kinematic Singularity Avoidance — Kinematic singularities are a well studied robotics problem [13]. These objectionable robot poses occur when the Jacobian matrix $\mathbf{J}(\Theta)$ that maps joint velocities to end effector tool velocities, i.e., $\dot{\mathbf{x}} = \mathbf{J}(\Theta)\dot{\Theta}$, loses full rank. Under these circumstances the chain may lock since an instantaneous change in one of the end effector DOFs is unattainable. When the Jacobian matrix is near singular, small changes in the end effector tool space can induce large, diverging velocities in joint angle space, which is unsafe for many applications including direct control.

Because the user's arm physiology may differ greatly from the structure of the robot arm, and the user has no kinesthetic sense of the robot's objectionable kinematic singularity poses, the user may unknowingly guide the robot into such a singularity. To reconcile this problem, we ensure that the robot automatically maintains a safe distance from such configurations. Much previous work exists on kinematic singularity avoidance for control, especially for 7-DOF redundant mechanisms [5]. Our simplified singularity avoidance technique fits conveniently as a constraint in the optimization framework and works for robot arms of various DOFs.

We use the manipulability measure proposed by Yoshikawa [34] to define how far the robot is from a singularity. Using this distance, we specify a constraint as follows:

$$\mathbf{c}(\Theta) := \sqrt{|det(\mathbf{J}(\Theta)\,\mathbf{J}(\Theta)^T)|} - s_{min} \geq 0 \tag{8}$$

Here, s_{min} signifies a lower bound for the manipulability measure. A good value for this bound may depend on the robot arm used, so some analysis of the mechanism's manipulability ellipse may be worthwhile. We have observed a value of 2^{-24} to suffice for our system described in §5.

Self Collision Avoidance and Stability — To avoid self collisions, we set the optimization bounds l_i and u_i for all joints in Θ_i in Equation 1 to values where self collisions are not likely, while still allowing maximum task flexibility. Effective values will depend on the robot platform, and we note that using joint limits as a method to avoid self collisions may not generalize to all robot geometries. Stability is a key concern for any teleoperation system (see Lawrence [20] for a more detailed discussion). The upper and lower bounds on Θ additionally ensure that the joint values can never diverge.

5. SYSTEM DETAILS

We have realized our approach in a system designed to provide sufficient performance, flexibility, and safety in order to demonstrate its value in a human participants study.

Input Device — For natural input, our system uses an HTC Vive controller, a wireless, handheld device that provides precise position and orientation information with low latency across a sufficiently large workspace. The controller also includes a trigger, which we use to operate the gripper, and a number of other buttons (one of which we use as a clutch). While other motion capture techniques, such as video tracking, may provide even more natural movement, the robustness and ease of setup of the Vive controller made it convenient for a user study, as it required no per-user calibration and did not fail during any of our experiments.

Robot Manipulator and Controller — For manipulation, our system uses a Universal Robots UR5 robot equipped with a Robotiq 85 gripper. These devices are commonly used in collaborative industrial settings. The UR5 is a 6-DOF arm with approximately the same workspace as a human arm but with very different kinematics. We operate the robot using position control, sending joint target commands directly to its controller via a network connection. The controller receives commands at up to 125 Hz, and our system sends goal targets as quickly as possible. Upon receiving a target, the robot moves its joints toward the goal as quickly as possible (given the safety speed limits). When an updated configuration is sent to the controller, the previous goal is over-written with the new target. The robot controller utilizes virtual safety planes and speed limits.

The Robotiq gripper involves a two-finger compliant design. To simplify operation, our system only sends open and close commands to the gripper, freeing the user from having to precisely control its configuration or force. The compliant design of the gripper affords some flexibility in grasping approach.

System Architecture — We have implemented our approach as a distributed system. Input devices are connected to a Windows PC, which runs an interface layer developed within the Unity game engine. This environment provides a flexible, low-latency interface to various input devices. The interface streams controller values over a socket connection to the retargeting engine. The retargeting engine runs on a second PC running the Linux operating system. It receives input device information, computes target configurations for the robot, and communicates these targets to the robot controller via a network connection. While the distributed setup across two computers may increase system latency, this architecture afforded flexibility in interfacing to different input devices and robot hardware. Each component of the system runs asynchronously, processing commands as quickly as possible.

Our retargeting engine can be connected to a simulator, rather than the actual robot, which allowed us to confirm the infeasibility of using the end effector goals directly with a standard IK solver.

Optimization Solver — Our retargeting engine is written in Python. To solve the non-linear constrained optimization, we use the `slsqp` solver included in the `scipy` package. The solver implements a variant of sequential quadratic programming. We provide it with derivatives of the constraint and objective functions computed with automatic differentiation via the `ad` package. Each step is executed as an independent optimization, although we use the results of the previous step as an initial condition. Our solver takes 8 ms per solution, and on a testbed of 20,000 trials, the solver converged 100% of the time. The average IK position and rotation deviations over five test motions are 4.3 mm and 0.012 radians respectively, with maximal deviations of 12.0 mm and 0.021 radians. Precise end effector control is considered more important when the user's hand slows down to afford dexterous maneuvers such as picking up or rotating objects, inducing average deviations of 0.9 mm and 0.007 radians when the user's hand velocity is below 0.1 m/s.

While local minima are a risk in our approach, we have not observed it to be a problem in practice. Because each optimization search starts at the previous solution, a local minimum will likely still be a good solution in the neighborhood of the previous configuration, meaning that the system will not be greatly disturbed.

Latency Measurement — A drawback of our architecture is that its distributed setup may lead to latency. While each component is efficient, the total system latency aggregates between parts. Rather than reporting component performance, we have measured the end-to-end system latency as a measure of the latency experienced by users. For this measurement, we recorded a high speed (240 Hz) video of the controller and the robot, starting with both at a complete stop. We marked the frames where movement in each was first visible. While this approach has some subjectivity in identifying the frames with first movement, it does include the entire system latency including the robot's inertia. We were able to reliably measure 130-140 ms.

Latency is known to degrade the effectiveness of teleoperation systems [25]. Previous work suggests that latency does not become a factor until it becomes much worse than our system's performance (Rayman et al. [28] suggest 400 ms, while Lum et al. [23] suggest 250 ms). However, as these guidelines are based on tele-surgery applications, the effects of latency on novice users are still unknown. In future work, we will explore ways to further reduce our latency.

6. USER STUDY

In order to show that a teleoperation interface using the natural space of the human hand can facilitate novice users' control of a robot arm, we developed a set of physical tasks and conducted a human-participants study to compare user performance and experience with our system against various input devices. For input type, we selected an appropriate implementation.

6.1 Hypothesis

Our principle hypothesis is that *relaxed mimicry control* will outperform alternative, commonly used control methods on task performance and user experience for novice users due to its effectiveness, intuitiveness, and learnability.

6.2 Experimental Design, Tasks, & Procedure

To test our hypothesis, we designed a 3 × 1 within-participants experiment in which naïve participants used three control paradigms (relaxed mimicry, Geomagic Touch,[5] and the UR5 native touch-screen interface) in a random order to complete three physical tasks.

Control Methods — We compare the relaxed mimicry control to a Geomagic Touch *6-DOF stylus* and the native *touchscreen interface* of the UR5. The Geomagic Touch device is a 6-DOF stylus device commonly used for robot control, 3D sculpting, or surgery simulation. In fact, prior work suggests that highly complex operations, such as simulated surgery, can be completed with such stylus devices by trained experts [31]. However, we note that our goal is not to test expert use of this input method, but chose the 6-DOF stylus as a comparison baseline, because it is a commonly used method to achieve Cartesian control of a robot's end effector. Additionally, it allows for fluid manipulation of all 6-DOFs, thus serving as an apt comparison to test our hypothesis that the input space of the user's hand is effective and intuitive for robot control.

Users controlled the robot with the Geomagic 6-DOF stylus device by moving and rotating the stylus attached to the device base, which the robot automatically matched through its relative position and orientation. We used the same optimization-based IK solver to drive the robot using the 6-DOF stylus; however, we tuned the weights and motion scaling to tailor the solver to be compatible with this device. The weights were chosen to provide sufficient relaxation required to avoid invalid motions from reasonable inputs.

The touchscreen controller was the native on-screen interface on the UR5 teach pendant. Using this method, participants controlled the robot by holding down arrow symbols on the screen using a stylus that each corresponded to one of the six 6-DOFs of the end effector. We included this control method as a comparison baseline, because a touchscreen interface is supplied with many popular robot platforms. We do note that the most common use case for such interfaces is to pose the robot for teaching waypoints as opposed to real-time control. The three methods can be seen in Figure 3.

Tasks — To ensure the applicability and generalizability of our findings to wide range of physical manipulation tasks, we developed three tasks that followed a home-care scenario (Figure 3), as a setting that involves a novice user in an unstructured environment, both key motivations for our work. Participants were presented with

[5]Geomagic Touch: http://www.geomagic.com/en/

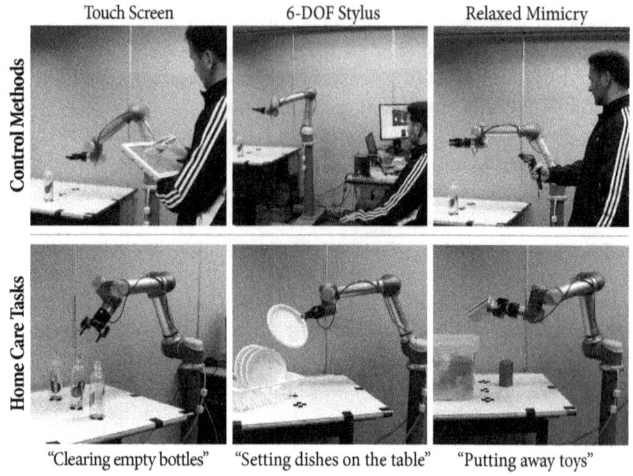

Figure 3: The three control methods (top row) and three home-care tasks (bottom row) used in our user study.

the story of logging in to the robotic teleoperation system to care for a friend or family member by clearing off a table by disposing trash or putting away unused objects and setting the table up for dinner. In the first task, which served as a simple pick-and-place task, the participant picks up three empty disposable water bottles and dropped them into a recycling bin. Our second task involved taking two plates from a dish rack and placing them on the table. Because the plates start vertically, the task tests the rotational usability of the input modalities by requiring a rotation to set the plates correctly on the table. In the third task, the participant picked up two LEGO Quatro towers and dropped them in a toy bin, as a pick-and-place task with increased complexity. Because the square pieces only fit within the fingers of the gripper if the grasp is orthogonal to the end effector facing vector, this task further constrained the orientation of the end effector compared to grasping cylindrical bottles.

Procedure — Following informed consent, participants were provided with detail on the study goals and tasks. Before using each control method, participants viewed a short training video. The videos outlined how to use the control method and specified important safety guidelines. The video-based introduction was used to standardize how participants were trained on each control method. After expressing readiness, participants were presented with a training task of picking up a single water bottle and dropping it in a recycling bin in order to get accustomed to the control method. This training task was selected due to its simplicity and the preparation it offered for the first study task. Each participant performed the training task a minimum of three times and had the option of performing it up to two additional times. If the participant task times did not decrease or become stable by the third trial, the experimenter suggested that the participant performed one or two additional trials.

After the training, participants performed tasks in the order, *three bottles*, *plates*, then *legos*, for each control method. This order ensured that task difficulty increased through the experiment. After each task, the experimenter reset the robot to the same initial configuration to standardize the starting point. After completing the training and experimental tasks using a control method, participants filled out a questionnaire pertaining to that method.

To ensure physical safety, participants stood out of the envelope of the robot at all times. Additionally, four virtual safety planes surrounding the robot were defined in the robot's low-level controller, which prompted it to halt if its end effector reached any of the planes. The training videos advised the participants to stay away

Table 1: Descriptive statistics for all measures.

	Touch Screen		6-DOF Stylus		Mimicry	
Measure	M	SD	M	SD	M	SD
Aggregate (s)	433.79	102.5	296.38	145.68	124.75	47.98
Bottles (s)	160.75	36.04	110.20	63.34	53.33	22.97
Plates (s)	133.46	45.60	68.41	50.10	27.67	13.31
Legos (s)	139.58	45.47	117.75	72.56	43.75	21.71
Ease of Use	5.63	1.41	4.51	1.23	5.67	0.95
Satisfaction	5.96	1.10	5.97	0.84	6.52	0.53
Enjoyment	4.81	1.50	5.13	1.45	5.99	1.09

Table 2: Inferential statistics for all measures. T, S, and M denote *Touch Screen*, *6-DOF Stylus*, and *Mimicry*, respectively.

					Pairwise Comparisons		
Measure	DF	R^2	f	p	M-S	M-T	S-T
Aggregate (s)	2	.99	80.4	<.0001	<.0001	<.0001	<.0001
Bottles (s)	2	.99	53.5	<.0001	<.0001	<.0001	<.0001
Plates (s)	2	.99	55.9	<.0001	.0006	<.0001	<.0001
Legos (s)	2	.99	27.7	<.0001	<.0001	<.0001	.2300
Ease of Use	2	.97	8.84	.0006	.0019	.9900	.0021
Satisfaction	2	.99	3.40	.0420	.0700	.0700	1.000
Enjoyment	2	.89	7.40	.0018	.0250	.0020	.5700

from the safety planes during the trials. If a safety plane was reached, the robot returned to its initial configuration, which required the participant to restart the task.

6.3 Measures & Analyses

To assess participants' task performance, we measured *task time* for each task and an aggregate time representing the total time it took participants to complete all tasks. Participants were given unbounded time to complete each task.

To measure participants' perception of the different control methods, we administered a questionnaire based on prior research on measuring user preferences [7, 22], including scales to measure *satisfaction*, *ease-of-use*, and *enjoyment*. Each scale included three items measured on a seven-point rating scale (1 = strongly disagree; 7 = strongly agree). Ease of use was measured using items "The control method made it easy to accomplish the task," "I felt confident controlling the robot," and "I could accurately control the robot" (Cronbach's $\alpha = 0.76$). The satisfaction scale included items "Controlling the robot was easy to understand," "I would like to control a robot like this in the future," and "I found the control method useful" (Cronbach's $\alpha = 0.74$). Finally, enjoyment was measured using items "Controlling the robot was fun," "I felt satisfied while controlling the robot," and "I felt happy while controlling the robot" (Cronbach's $\alpha = 0.75$).

We analyzed data from all measures using one-way repeated measures analyses of variance (ANOVA), including control method, *relaxed mimicry*, *6-DOF stylus*, or *touchscreen*, as a within-participants variable. All pairwise comparisons used Tukey's HSD test to control for Type I error in multiple comparisons.

6.4 Participants

We recruited 24 participants (11 male, 13 female) from the University of Wisconsin–Madison campus with ages 18–46 ($M = 22.875$, $SD = 6.05$). Participants reported low-to-moderate familiarity with robots ($M = 2.92$, $SD = 1.61$, measured on a seven-point scale). Eleven participants reported participating in prior robotics research studies. The study took 60 minutes, and each participant received $10 for their time.

6.5 Results

We outline the results from the analyses of our data, comparing our relaxed-mimicry-based control method to baseline control paradigms over numerous tasks. To facilitate readability, a textual description of the results are provided below, and all statistical details are given in Tables 1–2 and Figures 4–5.

Objective Measures — The analysis showed full support for our hypothesis with respect to objective measures (Figure 4). Relaxed mimicry control significantly outperformed both the geomagic touch and touch screen interface control methods on all tasks for all pairwise comparisons. Controlling a robot using the natural arm space afforded improved task performance on all tasks. On average, the aggregate task was completed three minutes faster than the 6-DOF stylus device and five minutes faster than the touch screen.

As illustrated in the far right graph in Figure 4, learning times from the first three trials of the training task show much steeper learning curves for the 6-DOF stylus and touch screen, suggesting that more learning was required to reach competency with these input methods. Even at the end of training, participants do not get as proficient as they do immediately with our mimicry-based method.

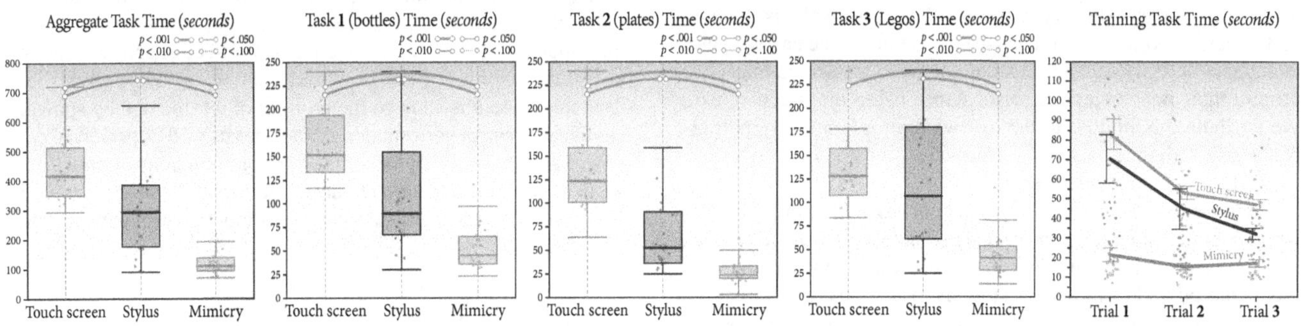

Figure 4: Tukey boxplots of data from the performance measures for each control method across tasks. Far left: aggregate task time derived by adding times from the bottles, plates, and legos tasks. Far right: learning curves for each control method. The extents of the box represent the the first and third quartiles. The line inside the box represents the second quartile (the median). The difference between the first and third quartiles is the interquartile range (IQR). Arc thickness denotes the significance level at $p < .001$, $< .010$, $< .050$, and $p < .100$ in comparisons.

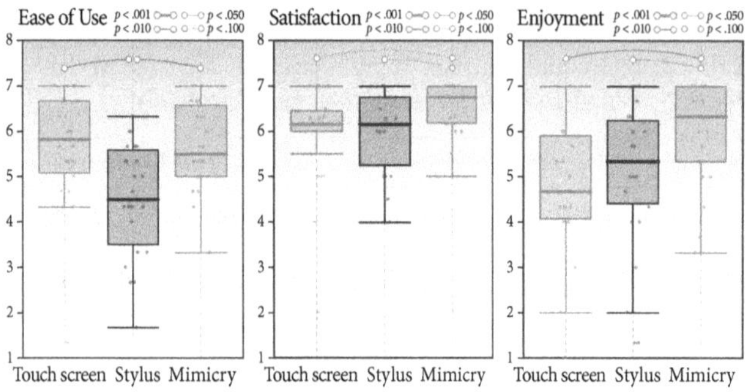

Figure 5: Tukey boxplots of data from subjective measures of *ease of use*, *satisfaction*, and *enjoyment*.

Subjective Measures — Our hypothesis was partially supported by data from subjective measures (Figure 5). Participants found the mimicry-based method to be significantly easier to use than the 6-DOF stylus device, but the touch screen was found to be equally easy to use. The mimicry method was marginally more satisfactory over the 6-DOF stylus device and touch screen. Finally, data from the enjoyment measure fully supported our hypothesis, participants finding the mimicry-based method to be more enjoyable than the 6-DOF stylus and touch screen.

7. DISCUSSION

In this paper, we proposed a method for direct tele-control of a robot arm with natural arm movements as an effective telemanipulation interface for novice users. We have addressed the key technical challenge of creating an appropriate mapping from the user's arm motions to the robot that provides users with a feeling of direct control while producing acceptable robot motions by relaxing optimization end-effector goals. We have implemented the method into a system that uses a commodity 6-DOF input device to control a robot arm and conducted a user study that demonstrates the effectiveness of the system for novice users.

The results from our user study support the premise that controlling a robot using the natural free space of the arm as an input space has usability advantages for novice users. Our results show the effectiveness of the relaxed mimicry-based control over alternative, commonly used control methods, including touch-screen and 6-DOF stylus interfaces, across three different tasks. The results are consistent across objective and subjective measures. The mimicry-based control method was found to be more enjoyable and marginally more satisfactory than these alternative methods. Finally, participants reported the mimicry-based method to be easier to use than the 6-DOF stylus controller but not the touch-screen interface, despite their poor objective performance using the touch-screen. We attribute this finding to the overwhelming familiarity participants have with touch-screen interfaces from their day-to-day use of computers and mobile devices.

Limitations — While the results from our study show that mimicry-based control is a feasible and promising method to provide a direct interface for telemanipulation, the limitations of the present implementation and testing suggest many extensions. Although our present implementation enables a sufficient demonstration of the effectiveness of the method, we have not determined the relative contribution to performance caused by each method component. While our initial simulation-based testing indicated that *some* method was necessary to address practical concerns of movement quality, such as avoiding unwanted rapid movements of the robot or getting stuck in singularities, we have not established whether or not the methods we employed offer the best solutions.

Another limitation of the our work is that the current implementation considers only the 6-DOF rigid configuration of the hand. It does not provide for control over the rest of the arm, or fine control over the robot hand. Such additional control may be important to avoid collisions in more cluttered environments and specify more dexterous manipulations. In the future, we will extend our approach with sensing of the user's arm and hand as well as integrating some degree of shared control for collision avoidance and grasp planning. Our current work considers simple environments; extending to complex and cluttered environments offers a number of challenges beyond collision and manipulation, such as operator visibility.

Our current implementation requires the user to hold a 6-DOF controller and use a button to open and close the gripper. While this input device is reliable and accurate, it may not be as natural as directly measuring the hand using, e.g., motion capture or computer vision technology. In future work, we would like to understand whether these alternative devices provide naturalness that affords an even more effective interface and whether the practical issues in using direct measurement (e.g., noise and accuracy) can be addressed. More generally, while our relaxed mimicry approach may be applied to almost any input device, it will require adaptation and experimentation to understand the user control scenarios in which it can, and should, be applied. Similarly, our present experiments do not consider haptic or tactile feedback. Integrating such feedback into our approach may provide the advantages of both.

Our focus on novice users may over-emphasize the initial learning time. While Figure 4 (far right) suggests that users may learn other methods quickly, the advantages of mimicry persist on the final task of the experiment. Further experimentation would be required to determine at what point novice performance converges to that of an expert and what designs might be most effective for experts.

8. CONCLUSION

In this paper, we present a mimicry-based telemanipulation interface that maps the movements of the user's hand in its natural space to control a robot arm. The premise of the interface is that allowing users to direct a robot using the natural space of his/her own hand would afford intuitive control for novice users. To realize the interface, we developed an IK solver that addresses the issues in mapping human arm motions to robot control. Our solver makes mimicry control feasible in practice by relaxing the mapping from the user's hand to the robot end effector, allowing it to achieve motion goals such as minimized joint velocities, smooth positional tracking, and kinematic singularity avoidance. We created a prototype system that instantiated our mimicry method that was effective and safe enough to test the premise of our proposed interface as a hypothesis in a user study. Results showed the promise of our method by showing significant control performance advantages as well as perceived ease of use and enjoyability benefits over common control paradigms. We will continue to improve our mimicry-based control method in future work and will compare it against more control alternatives.

9. ACKNOWLEDGEMENTS

This research was supported by National Science Foundation award 1208632. We would like to thank Christopher Bodden for contributing to early iterations of this work, as well as Alper Sarikaya, Tomislav Pejsa, Sean Andrist, and Catherine Steffel for valuable feedback.

References

[1] D. Aarno, S. Ekvall, and D. Kragic. Adaptive virtual fixtures for machine-assisted teleoperation tasks. In *Proceedings of the 2005 IEEE International Conference on Robotics and Automation*, pages 1139–1144. IEEE, 2005.

[2] P. Beeson and B. Ames. Trac-ik: An open-source library for improved solving of generic inverse kinematics. In *2015 IEEE-RAS 15th International Conference on Humanoid Robots (Humanoids)*, pages 928–935. IEEE, 2015.

[3] S. R. Buss. Introduction to inverse kinematics with jacobian transpose, pseudoinverse and damped least squares methods. *IEEE Journal of Robotics and Automation*, 17(1-19):16, 2004.

[4] S. R. Buss and J.-S. Kim. Selectively damped least squares for inverse kinematics. *Journal of Graphics, GPU, and Game Tools*, 10(3):37–49, 2005.

[5] S. Chiaverini. Singularity-robust task-priority redundancy resolution for real-time kinematic control of robot manipulators. *IEEE Transactions on Robotics and Automation*, 13(3):398–410, 1997.

[6] J. W. Crandall and M. A. Goodrich. Characterizing efficiency of human robot interaction: A case study of shared-control teleoperation. In *2002 IEEE/RSJ International Conference on Intelligent Robots and Systems*, volume 2, pages 1290–1295. IEEE, 2002.

[7] F. D. Davis. Perceived usefulness, perceived ease of use, and user acceptance of information technology. *MIS Q.*, 13(3):319–340, 1989.

[8] A. D. Dragan and S. S. Srinivasa. A policy-blending formalism for shared control. *The International Journal of Robotics Research*, 32(7):790–805, 2013.

[9] A. D. Dragan, S. S. Srinivasa, and K. C. Lee. Teleoperation with intelligent and customizable interfaces. *Journal of Human-Robot Interaction*, 2(2):33–57, 2013.

[10] A. Eilering, G. Franchi, and K. Hauser. Robopuppet: Low-cost, 3d printed miniatures for teleoperating full-size robots. In *2014 IEEE/RSJ International Conference on Intelligent Robots and Systems (IROS 2014)*, pages 1248–1254. IEEE, 2014.

[11] M. Gleicher. Retargetting motion to new characters. In *Proceedings of the 25th annual conference on Computer graphics and interactive techniques*, pages 33–42. ACM, 1998.

[12] R. C. Goertz, R. A. Olsen, and W. M. Thompson. Electronic master slave manipulator, Aug. 5 1958. US Patent 2,846,084.

[13] C. Gosselin and J. Angeles. Singularity analysis of closed-loop kinematic chains. *IEEE Transactions on Robotics and Automation*, 6(3):281–290, 1990.

[14] K. Hauser. Recognition, prediction, and planning for assisted teleoperation of freeform tasks. *Autonomous Robots*, 35(4):241–254, 2013.

[15] P. F. Hokayem and M. W. Spong. Bilateral teleoperation: An historical survey. *Automatica*, 42(12):2035–2057, 2006.

[16] M. Huber, C. Lenz, M. Rickert, A. Knoll, T. Brandt, and S. Glasauer. Human preferences in industrial human-robot interactions. In *Proceedings of the International Workshop on Cognition for Technical Systems*, pages 4749–4754, 2008.

[17] D.-J. Kim, R. Hazlett-Knudsen, H. Culver-Godfrey, G. Rucks, T. Cunningham, D. Portee, J. Bricout, Z. Wang, and A. Behal. How autonomy impacts performance and satisfaction: Results from a study with spinal cord injured subjects using an assistive robot. *IEEE Transactions on Systems, Man, and Cybernetics-Part A: Systems and Humans*, 42(1):2–14, 2012.

[18] D. Labonte, P. Boissy, and F. Michaud. Comparative analysis of 3-d robot teleoperation interfaces with novice users. *IEEE Transactions on Systems, Man, and Cybernetics, Part B: Cybernetics*, 40(5):1331–1342, 2010.

[19] A. R. Lanfranco, A. E. Castellanos, J. P. Desai, and W. C. Meyers. Robotic surgery: a current perspective. *Annals of surgery*, 239(1):14–21, 2004.

[20] D. A. Lawrence. Stability and transparency in bilateral teleoperation. *IEEE Transactions on Robotics and Automation*, 9(5):624–637, 1993.

[21] J. Lee. Representing rotations and orientations in geometric computing. *IEEE Computer Graphics and Applications*, 28(2):75–83, 2008.

[22] A. Lin, S. Gregor, and M. Ewing. Developing a scale to measure the enjoyment of web experiences. *Journal of Interactive Marketing*, 22(4):40–57, 2008.

[23] M. J. Lum, J. Rosen, H. King, D. C. Friedman, T. S. Lendvay, A. S. Wright, M. N. Sinanan, and B. Hannaford. Teleoperation in surgical robotics–network latency effects on surgical performance. In *2009 Annual International Conference of the IEEE Engineering in Medicine and Biology Society*, pages 6860–6863. IEEE, 2009.

[24] K. Muelling, A. Venkatraman, J.-S. Valois, J. Downey, J. Weiss, S. Javdani, M. Hebert, A. B. Schwartz, J. L. Collinger, and J. A. Bagnell. Autonomy infused teleoperation with application to BCI manipulation. *arXiv preprint arXiv:1503.05451*, 2015.

[25] G. Niemeyer, C. Preusche, and G. Hirzinger. Telerobotics. In *Springer Handbook of Robotics*, pages 741–757. Springer, 2008.

[26] A. M. Okamura. Methods for haptic feedback in teleoperated robot-assisted surgery. *Industrial Robot: An International Journal*, 31(6):499–508, 2004.

[27] N. S. Pollard, J. K. Hodgins, M. J. Riley, and C. G. Atkeson. Adapting human motion for the control of a humanoid robot. In *IEEE International Conference on Robotics and Automation, 2002. Proceedings. ICRA'02.*, volume 2, pages 1390–1397. IEEE, 2002.

[28] R. Rayman, S. Primak, R. Patel, M. Moallem, R. Morady, M. Tavakoli, V. Subotic, N. Galbraith, A. van Wynsberghe, and K. Croome. Effects of latency on telesurgery: an experimental study. In *International Conference on Medical Image Computing and Computer-Assisted Intervention*, pages 57–64. Springer, 2005.

[29] L. B. Rosenberg. Virtual fixtures: Perceptual tools for telerobotic manipulation. In *Virtual Reality Annual International Symposium, 1993 IEEE*, pages 76–82. IEEE, 1993.

[30] H. J. Shin, J. Lee, S. Y. Shin, and M. Gleicher. Computer puppetry: An importance-based approach. *ACM Transactions on Graphics (TOG)*, 20(2):67–94, 2001.

[31] M. S. Sorensen, J. Mosegaard, and P. Trier. The visible ear simulator: a public pc application for gpu-accelerated haptic 3d simulation of ear surgery based on the visible ear data. *Otology & Neurotology*, 30(4):484–487, 2009.

[32] W. Suleiman, E. Yoshida, F. Kanehiro, J.-P. Laumond, and A. Monin. On human motion imitation by humanoid robot. In *International Conference on Robotics and Automation, 2008. ICRA 2008. IEEE*, pages 2697–2704. IEEE, 2008.

[33] R. Taylor, P. Jensen, L. Whitcomb, A. Barnes, R. Kumar, D. Stoianovici, P. Gupta, Z. Wang, E. Dejuan, and L. Kavoussi. A steady-hand robotic system for microsurgical augmentation. *The International Journal of Robotics Research*, 18(12):1201–1210, 1999.

[34] T. Yoshikawa. Manipulability of robotic mechanisms. *The International Journal of Robotics Research*, 4(2):3–9, 1985.

[35] E. You and K. Hauser. Assisted teleoperation strategies for aggressively controlling a robot arm with 2d input. In *Robotics: Science and Systems*, volume 7, page 354, 2012.

[36] W. Yu, R. Alqasemi, R. Dubey, and N. Pernalete. Telemanipulation assistance based on motion intention recognition. In *Proceedings of the 2005 IEEE International Conference on Robotics and Automation*, pages 1121–1126. IEEE, 2005.

A Comparison of Remote Robot Teleoperation Interfaces for General Object Manipulation

David Kent
Georgia Institute of Technology
Atlanta, Georgia 30332
dekent@gatech.edu

Carl Saldanha
Georgia Institute of Technology
Atlanta, Georgia 30332
csaldanha3@gatech.edu

Sonia Chernova
Georgia Institute of Technology
Atlanta, Georgia 30332
chernova@cc.gatech.edu

ABSTRACT

Robust remote teleoperation of high-DOF manipulators is of critical importance across a wide range of robotics applications. Contemporary robot manipulation interfaces primarily utilize a free-positioning pose specification approach to independently control each axis of translation and orientation in free space. In this work, we present two novel interfaces, *constrained positioning* and *point-and-click*, which incorporate scene information, including points-of-interest and local surface geometry, into the grasp specification process. We also present results of a user study evaluation comparing the effects of increased use of scene information in grasp pose specification algorithms for general object manipulation. The results of our study show that constrained positioning and point-and-click significantly outperform the widely used free positioning approach by significantly reducing the number of grasping errors and the number of user interactions required to specify poses. Furthermore, the point-and-click interface significantly increased the number of tasks users were able to complete.

Keywords

Robot Teleoperation; User Interface Design; Usability Study

1. INTRODUCTION

Robust remote teleoperation of high-DOF manipulators is of critical importance across a wide range of applications, including assistive robotics, space exploration, search-and-rescue, and web-based robot control. As use cases for remote teleoperation expand beyond pick-and-place to more complex manipulation tasks, there is a growing need to develop effective user interfaces that minimize operator error and improve task efficiency.

Most mouse-and-keyboard robot manipulation interfaces currently utilize a 6-DOF ring-and-arrow marker for independently controlling each axis of rotation and translation. The marker can be used to directly move an end-effector or set pose goals to which the robot can autonomously plan and move. Leeper et al. [13] evaluated multiple interfaces based on the ring-and-arrow marker design, showing that increasing robot autonomy results in better performance in object picking tasks.

In this work, we view interfaces for remote robot control as falling on a spectrum of reliance on scene information. The ring-and-arrow marker makes no use of scene information, giving robot operators complete control over the pose of their robot's end-effector in free space. While this degree of flexibility gives users the maximum level of control, the size of the workspace can become a burden that can increase the likelihood of operator error. Our work compares the ring-and-arrow marker to alternate approaches for human-in-the-loop robot manipulation that leverage depth information. We focus specifically on mouse-and-keyboard approaches, as these input devices are readily available to most of the population. We introduce two alternate approaches to the ring-and-arrow marker – one that uses depth information at a single point in the environment, and another that proposes grasp poses based on local 3D scene geometry – to explore the trade-offs inherent to scene information use in a general robot manipulation context. The presented techniques do not use scene or object recognition; as a result, despite using scene information, they can be immediately deployed in new environments without training. We evaluate all three interaction approaches over a variety of manipulation tasks, from pick-and-place to more complex tasks including opening containers and pouring.

This paper makes three contributions to teleoperation for manipulation. The first is a novel interaction method for positioning a 6-DOF end-effector that we call *constrained positioning*. We designed this method to incorporate a small amount of scene information into an approach that provides users with fine-grained control over grasp pose specification. The result is a constrained step-by-step approach that allows users to set a grasp point, approach angle, and grasp depth with a reduced number of mental transformations.

The second contribution is an extension to the AGILE grasp approach [22] for general object manipulation. We present a heuristic-based approach that replaces AGILE's classification step, resulting in an autonomous grasp calculator better suited to manipulating man-made objects during human-in-the-loop operation. We leverage the resulting approach, which we call *point-and-click*, to create an interaction method that incorporates a large amount of scene information, requiring only supervisory control from a user.

Our final contribution is a usability comparison of the

HRI '17, March 06-09, 2017, Vienna, Austria

DOI: http://dx.doi.org/10.1145/2909824.3020249

above human-in-the-loop object manipulation approaches. We present the results of a remote manipulation user study that compare the efficiency and effectiveness of the *constrained positioning* and *point-and-click* approaches with the ring-and-arrow marker approach. Our results show with statistical significance that *constrained positioning* and *point-and-click* outperform the widely used ring-and-arrow marker approach. Both approaches significantly reduce the number of grasping errors and the number of interactions required by the user. Furthermore, *point-and-click* significantly increases the number of tasks completed and significantly decreases average task completion time.

2. RELATED WORK

Unconstrained methods allowing individual control of task space translation and rotation are widely used in robotics. Leeper et al. present and evaluate an interactive marker composed of rings and arrows (Figure 1) for just such a purpose [13], which can be rendered in a 3D scene such as rviz [19] or online via Robot Web Tools' ros3djs [24]. The marker can be used at varying levels of robot autonomy, including (in order of increasing robot autonomy) a) real-time arm position control, b) setting waypoints executed through linear interpolation, c) setting pose goals followed by autonomous trajectory execution with obstacle avoidance, and d) adjusting autonomously calculated grasp poses for fully autonomous grasp execution. Leeper et al. found the ring-and-arrow marker to be an effective tool for an object picking task, noting that users of the interface made fewer mistakes as the autonomy of the robot increased. Ciocarlie et al. showed the same marker could be used for general mobile manipulation in household environments [2]. The Robots for Humanity project [1] also uses these 6-DOF markers for teleoperating a robot to perform everyday tasks. Many teams competing in the DARPA Robotics Challenge used this same marker for multiple purposes, including positioning key points of a humanoid robot for balance or manipulation [26, 12, 3], positioning 3D object templates over sensor data [12], and correcting point cloud alignment [18]. The ring-and-arrow marker has also found use in web interfaces. In previous work, we used the marker in an interface for crowdsourcing object recognition and picking [11]. More recently, Grice and Kemp showed similar controls superimposed on a camera stream displayed in a web interface, rather than rendering them in a 3D environment [10].

Figure 1: 6-DOF positioning ring-and-arrow marker

Despite its widespread use, the ring-and-arrow approach requires the user to perform many mental 3D rotations, which Zhai and Milgram show to be mentally taxing [25]. When the marker is rendered in a 3D environment, the user has to control both the transformation of the camera within the 3D environment and the transformation of the 6-DOF marker itself. When projected onto a 2D camera feed, manipulating the marker causes it to become unaligned with the user's viewing angle, which Parsons identifies as a particularly difficult case requiring complex mental transformations [17]. There are two approaches to alleviate this difficulty: isolate transformations where possible (e.g. separating rotation and translation) [16], or reduce the number of transformations that the user is required to make [4]. Both of these approaches can be accomplished by incorporating more scene information into grasp pose specification methods, and as such they inspire the *constrained positioning* and *point-and-click* methods contributed in our work.

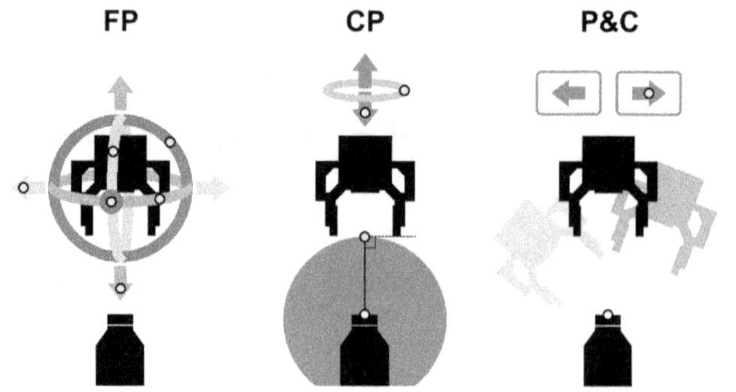

Figure 2: Interaction approaches arranged by number of major interaction points. Yellow points represent setting initial grasp poses; blue points represent pose refinement

Alternative control methods for 6-DOF object positioning have been studied primarily outside the field of robotics. By using a smartphone as an input device, researchers have shown multiple interfaces for controlling objects in 3D video games [9] and editing meshes in 3D space [7]. These approaches typically involve separating translations and rotations by assigning them to either the touch screen or the motion of the phone itself. Navidget, a tool for free-space camera positioning developed specifically for 2D input devices, provides another method of 6-DOF control. It separates translations and rotations into a multi-step process, while additionally reducing the total number of positioning operations by fixing the interaction to a local area and a selected approach angle [5].

Another approach to grasp pose specification is to completely remove the requirement for transformations by autonomously calculating grasp poses. This is a difficult problem for novel and unrecognized objects, particularly because point cloud data provides only partial object shape information. Hsiao et al. present a heuristic-based approach, biasing grasps to orthogonal overhead or side poses [8]. Other work uses classifiers with hand-specified features. One example uses contacts, symmetry, and force-closure as features[20], used to classify grasp stability. Another example is the AGILE grasp approach [22], which classifies antipodal grasps. Other work detects grasping affordances to identify handle-like geometry [23]. Deep learning provides another classification approach which learns the grasp features [15, 14].

3. INTERACTION APPROACHES

In this work, instead of focusing on a single interface, we examine a spectrum of grasp pose specification approaches for remote manipulation interfaces. Based on our literature review, we identified three interaction approaches for specifying 6-DOF end-effector poses[1]. The first approach, *free positioning* (*FP*), leverages the ring-and-arrow marker frequently used in manipulation teleoperation. The approach

[1]A video of our three approaches can be found here: https://youtu.be/ySgwyTsOkkY

uses no scene information, instead providing the user with full control over transformations about every Cartesian axis. The second approach, *constrained positioning* (*CP*), leverages a point-of-interest in the scene to constrain the pose specification process. Our third method, *point-and-click* (*P&C*), enables the robot to autonomously calculate and propose grasp poses by incorporating a local surface extracted from the scene.

The relationship between the three approaches is shown in Figure 2. We selected these three techniques to incorporate increasing use of scene information into the grasp specification process. We hypothesize that incorporating more scene information into the pose specification algorithms will reduce user effort by reducing the number of interactions and the time required to specify a grasp pose, as well as lower the required situational awareness of the user by offloading some of the decisions onto the algorithm.

After pose specification, the three approaches handle grasp execution in the same manner. Once the user confirms the pose, the robot uses the same motion planning algorithm and execution control loop to move to the specified location. All three approaches require at most a point cloud as input, and do not rely on object recognition. As such they can be used in novel environments with no need for training time on new objects.

3.1 Free Positioning

Our first approach allows the user to position the robot's end-effector into any pose. We use the standard ring-and-arrow marker and base the approach on the Grasp Execution strategy described by Leeper et al. [13], rendered in a 3D viewer. As such, the user first sets a pose by clicking and dragging on any of the three arrows or rings corresponding to the three Cartesian axes of translation and rotation, respectively. Once the grasp pose is set, the arm autonomously plans and executes an obstacle-avoiding trajectory resulting in a grasp at the specified pose.

We chose this supervisory autonomous planning and execution approach over direct control for two reasons. First, Leeper et al. showed approaches in which the robot performs more autonomous trajectory planning and execution result in better performance (i.e. more successful grasps and fewer collisions). Second, since our system is targeting remote teleoperation, latency is an important concern. Direct control is highly sensitive to latency as it requires real-time visual feedback from the robot's sensors, whereas supervisory methods are virtually invariant to latency, since all of the execution is performed on-board [21]. All ring-and-arrow interactions are performed client-side, so they are not limited by latency.

3.2 Constrained Positioning

Our second approach seeks to separate the required positioning transformations in an intuitive manner, as well as to reduce the number of transformations wherever possible. We base our approach on the Navidget interaction technique [5] designed for 3D camera positioning. Camera positioning is a useful analogy for end-effector positioning, as both involve specifying a 3D transformation using 2D inputs. Extending a Navidget-like approach to robot grasping results in a novel interaction method for constrained end-effector positioning. The constrained positioning approach is a 3-step process, visualized in Figure 3 and explained below.

1. *Select a grasp point.* The user first specifies a point-of-interest, in this case a grasp point, by clicking on a camera stream. This constrains the final grasp pose to one that must pass through the selected point.

2. *Set an approach angle.* Once the grasp point is selected, *constrained positioning* renders a sphere around the point-of-interest. The user can then set an approach angle with a single click on the sphere's surface. The approach angle is determined by calculating a pitch and yaw angle that create an orthogonal vector to the surface of the sphere. In this way, the user can specify two degrees of rotation in a single action.

3. *Adjust the roll and grasp depth.* Navidget does not include a method for controlling the camera's roll, and while it does include a method for setting the depth of the camera, it does not translate well to robot grasping. As such, we include a single ring and arrow marker so that the user can adjust the wrist roll and the depth of the grasp by clicking and dragging the ring and arrow, respectively.

By using a small amount of scene information (the selected point-of-interest), we are able to base the approach around a grasp point and an approach angle, reducing the number of transformations the user is required to input from 6 degrees of freedom (3 rotations and 3 translations) to 4 degrees of freedom (3 rotations and a single translation). Furthermore, the sphere metaphor allows us to group 2 rotations into a single action with an intuitive visual-spatial representation. Since Navidget was designed with 2D input in mind, the entire process naturally lends itself to superimposition over a camera stream. As such, we treat this method as an Augmented Reality (AR) approach that does not require a separately rendered 3D scene. By eliminating the 3D rendered scene, we save screen real estate, reduce the amount of context-switching required by the user, and reduce latency by eliminating the need to stream point clouds.

3.3 Point-and-Click

Our third approach autonomously calculates grasp poses based only on a single mouse click. We base the grasp calculation on the AGILE grasp method [22]. The original AGILE algorithm has two steps. First, it samples a set of antipodal gripper hypotheses from a point cloud within a given workspace. The sampling algorithm samples the space around the point cloud to find gripper poses that do not intersect the point cloud, but do contain a subset of points between the gripper's fingers. Since these gripper poses are calculated from a point cloud, the algorithm assumes some shape information is missing due to occlusion. To address this, the second step of the algorithm is to classify the gripper pose hypotheses as antipodal or not, using a HOG descriptor to encode the points contained within each gripper pose hypothesis.

Our extension to AGILE replaces the antipodal gripper pose classifier with a heuristic-based approach. We found that the antipodal classifier was too conservative for our general manipulation tasks, frequently resulting in only one or zero grasps. Since we designed a human-in-the-loop system, we require an autonomous grasp calculator that provides more grasp options for the user to choose from. With that in mind, we designed a set of heuristics that result in

(a) Original image stream (b) Clicking the mug handle selects it as the grasp point (c) Clicking on the sphere sets an approach angle (d) Ring and arrow markers can be used to adjust wrist roll and grasp depth (e) The robot executes the final grasp

Figure 3: Constrained positioning steps

Algorithm 1 Autonomous Grasp Planning and Ranking

```
Require: Point pointOfInterest, PointCloud cloud
 1: Workspace w = createWorkspace(pointOfInterest);
 2: List<Pose> hands = findGraspsAGILE(cloud, w);
 3: List<Pose> grasps = cluster(hands);
 4: PointCloud pc = crop(cloud, w);
 5: Plane p = planeSegmentation(pc);
 6: Orientation n = surfaceNormal(p)
 7: List<PointCloud> clusters = cluster(pc);
 8: PriorityQueue<Pose> rankedGrasps;
 9: for all g in grasps do
10:     PointCloud c = nearestCluster(clusters, g);
11:     h_n = n_n*distance(g.orientation, n);
12:     h_o = n_o*dstToOrthogonal(g.orientation, PCA(c));
13:     h_p = n_p*distance(g.position, pointOfInterest);
14:     graspRating = α * h_n + β * h_o + (1 − (α + β)) * h_p
15:     rankedGrasps.push(g, graspRating);
16: end for
17: return rankedGrasps;
```

approximately 5 to 20 potentially effective grasps for the objects used in our general manipulation tasks. We introduce three metrics:

- h_n minimizes the distance between the orientation of the grasp's approach angle and the orientation of the dominant plane's surface normal. Most manipulation features, such as handles and knobs, are situated such that perpendicular grasp poses are more effective.
- h_o represents whether the grasp's orientation is orthogonal to the principal direction (computed with Principal Component Analysis) of the local geometry around the grasp point. This comes from our observation that most man-made objects are designed to be grasped with poses orthogonal to their principal direction, i.e. poses that are "aligned" with the object.
- h_p minimizes the proximity of the grasp point to the algorithm's input point. Since the user specifies a grasp area by inputting an initial grasp point, the third heuristic prioritizes grasps that are closest to the user input.

Each heuristic is multiplied by a normalizing constant (n_n, n_o, and n_p) to place them on a [0,1] scale.

The full algorithm for leveraging the above grasp pose estimates and heuristics is shown in Algorithm 1. The grasp planner takes as input a point-of-interest and a point cloud. All calculations occur within a local workspace (in our case, a 10 cubic centimeter volume) situated around the point-of-interest. The algorithm first uses AGILE grasp to compute a set of hand hypotheses, which we then cluster by position and orientation into a set of unranked grasps (lines 2-3). Note that the hand hypotheses from the AGILE grasp pipeline are not classified by the AGILE classifier. Next, the algorithm performs a few calculations required to compute the heuristics, including cropping the point cloud to the workspace, segmenting the dominant plane, computing its surface normal, and separating the cropped point cloud into local geometry clusters based on Euclidean distance (lines 4-7). For each grasp, the algorithm computes a ranking based on our three heuristics (lines 10-14). The final ranking is determined from a linear combination of the three heuristics, which can be assigned different priority by adjusting the constants α and β (line 14). The ranked grasps are then returned in a priority queue where lower rankings are preferred. For our experiments, we used experimentally determined values of $\alpha = 0.6$ and $\beta = 0.25$, which prioritize perpendicular grasps most, and user input least.

We leverage the above algorithm to create a point-and-click user interface. The user first inputs the point-of-interest by clicking on a point within a camera stream. Algorithm 1 then autonomously calculates a ranked list of grasp points within the local area around the clicked point. The ranked list is presented to the user, who then selects a final grasp to execute. As with *constrained positioning*, even though the algorithm relies on 3D data, we can show only the 2D camera stream to the user as the input to the interface requires only a single click.

4. EVALUATION STUDY DESIGN

We performed an evaluation study in order to compare the effectiveness of the three interaction approaches identified in the previous section. Our system is designed for collecting robot demonstrations from remote users. The robot itself consists of a Kinova JACO2 arm with a Robotiq-85 2-finger gripper and two Asus Xtion PRO LIVE 3D cameras mounted to a workbench. The user interfaces are implemented using Robot Web Tools [24] so that they can be displayed in a web browser.

4.1 Procedure

We recruited 45 participants from a college campus to take part in a between-subjects study. Participants ranged in age from 20-39, with 30 males and 15 females. Each participant received \$10 as compensation. Participants were asked to rate their experience on a 1 (no experience) to 5 (very experienced) scale with robotics (2.8±1.2), video games (3.4±1.3),

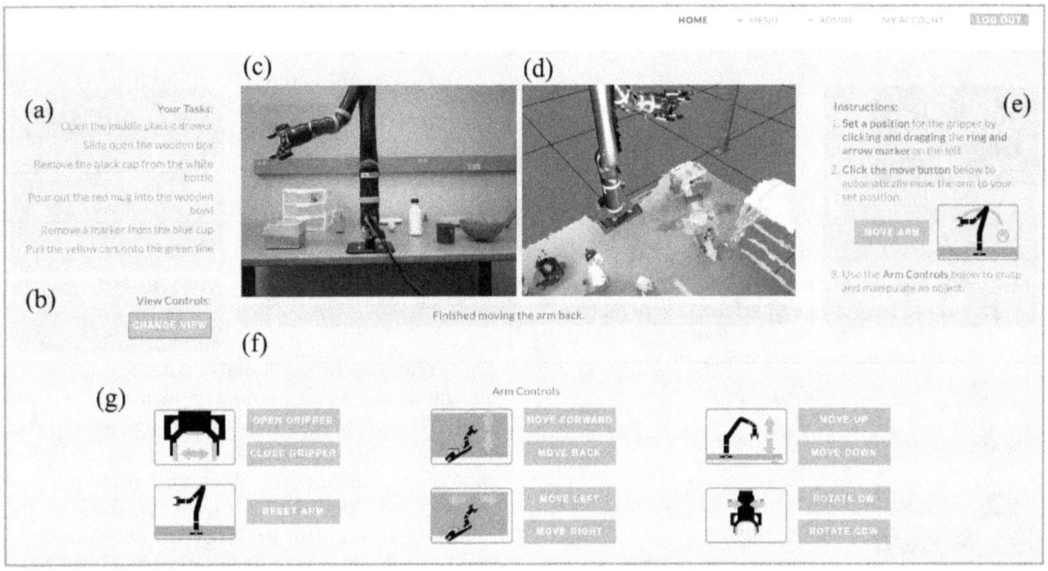

Figure 4: Complete study interface showing elements for the *free positioning* condition. (a) List of tasks (b) Controls to cycle through the top and side camera streams (c) Live camera stream with AR overlay; AR overlay contents and interactivity depend on the condition (d) Rendered 3D viewer, only used in *free positioning* (e) Manipulation instructions specific to the interface condition (f) Feedback bar displaying the current action being executed, successful execution of an action, or failed execution of an action with suggestions for improvement (g) Primitive actions for controlling the arm and gripper

and 3D software (3.0 ± 1.3). Participants were then assigned to one of three conditions, with 15 participants per condition, balanced by gender and level of robotics experience.

Upon arriving, participants were brought to a computer out of sight and sound of the lab where the robot was operating. After completing the demographics and experience survey, participants were given up to 10 minutes to complete two training tasks using the interface to which they were assigned. During training, they could ask the researchers questions about using the interface. Once training was complete and participants had no further questions, they were instructed to complete as many tasks as possible within a 30 minute time period. Upon completion of the tasks or at the end of the allotted time, participants completed a NASA TLX [6] exit survey to evaluate workload while using their respective interfaces.

Each participant was given the same list of tasks to complete during the study. They could complete the tasks in any order, and skip or return to previously attempted tasks at any time. The tasks were as follows:

- *(Training) Move the lemon onto the white plate.* A simple pick-and-place task.
- *(Training) Reset the arm when you're finished.* An introduction to the reset primitive action, which moves the arm to a preset position that does not occlude the objects in either camera view. This also ensured the main part of the experiment would begin with the arm in a consistent starting pose.
- *Open the middle plastic drawer.* A task to grasp the correct handle in a set of stacked drawers.
- *Slide open the wooden box.* Manipulation of an uncommon object that typically required some exploration.
- *Remove the black cap from the white bottle.* A precision task requiring rotation and translation.
- *Pour out the red mug into the wooden bowl.* A task that could only be completed by performing an appropriate grasp for pouring on the mug's handle.
- *Remove a marker from the blue cup.* A cluttered-environment manipulation.
- *Pull the yellow cart onto the green line.* A task involving manipulating an object by pulling a string.

4.2 Conditions and Interfaces

The interface used for the study can be seen in Figure 4. In every condition, the interface included the same presentation of the tasks, a camera stream that can be switched between the top and side camera, a text-based feedback bar, and a set of primitive actions. The content of the AR camera stream overlay (c), inclusion of the 3D viewer (d), and the set of manipulation instructions (e) varied among the conditions.

The primitive actions included generally useful actions such as fully opening or closing the gripper and resetting the arm to a position that did not occlude the workspace from either camera view. The remaining actions were selected as the minimum set of primitive actions required to complete any task after performing a grasp. This included fixed-distance 10 centimeter translations in each Cartesian direction (with respect to a coordinate frame aligned with the cameras) and 90 degree clockwise and counter-clockwise gripper rotation with respect to the JACO's wrist. We specifically chose these actions and fixed distances so that the tasks could be completed, thus evaluating the quality of the grasps for each task, while also making it virtually impossible to skip the initial grasp specification by using only the primitive actions to complete a task. In this way we

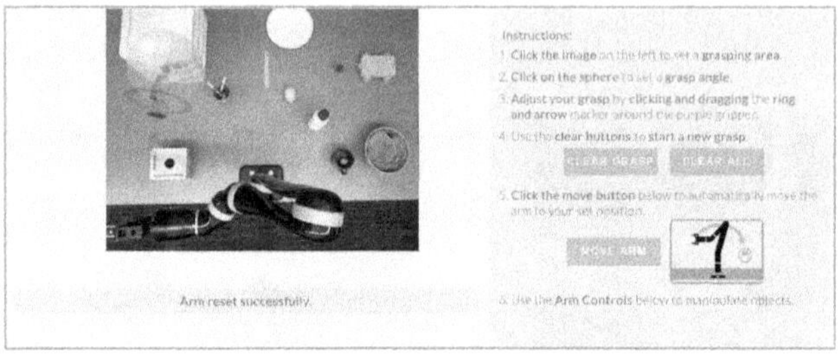

(a) Camera stream with AR overlay and manipulation instructions used for the *constrained positioning* interface. These replace elements *c*, *d*, and *e* in Figure 4. This example shows a grasp being specified on the drawers using the top camera view

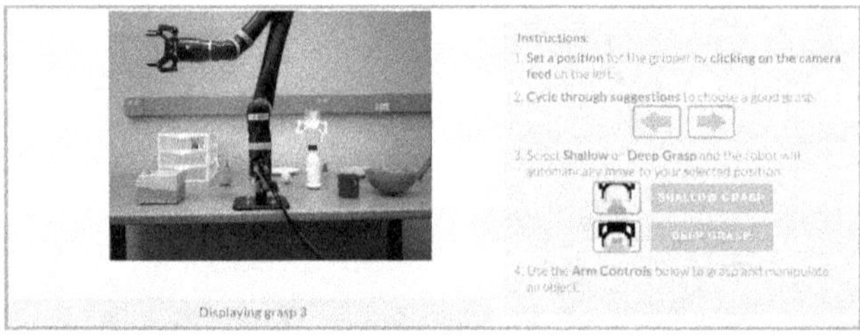

(b) Camera stream with AR overlay and manipulation instructions used for the *point-and-click* interface. These replace elements *c*, *d*, and *e* in Figure 4. This example shows a grasp calculated for the bottle cap displayed on the side camera view

Figure 5: Differences between the three interface conditions

could ensure the users would need to use the interface elements specific to their condition, which were the main focus of our evaluation.

4.2.1 Free Positioning Interface

The first condition uses the *free positioning* approach, described in Section 3.1. As such, it is very similar to our previous remote pick-and-place interface [11], containing a 3D viewer side-by-side with the camera stream. Along with the ring-and-arrow marker, the 3D viewer includes renderings of point clouds from the two depth cameras and a model of the robot in its current pose, to provide context and increase the user's situational awareness. The user can adjust the viewpoint of the 3D viewer by rotation, translation, and zoom. The AR overlay also displays a rendering of the pose goal with respect to the currently selected camera view, but all of the interaction occurs within the 3D viewer.

4.2.2 Constrained Positioning Interface

The second condition corresponds to the *constrained positioning* approach, described in Section 3.2. Since this method is designed specifically for 2D inputs, it does not require a 3D viewer, and so the user is provided with only the switchable camera stream and an AR overlay. The unique components of the *constrained positioning* interface are shown in Figure 5a, replacing elements (c), (d), and (e) in Figure 4. The initial grasp point is set by clicking directly on a point in the camera stream, and the interaction then follows the step-by-step process outlined in 3.2, with all interactions occurring within the AR overlay.

4.2.3 Point-and-Click Interface

The third condition corresponds to the *point-and-click* approach described in Section 3.3. The user inputs a point-of-interest by clicking on the camera stream. The autonomous grasp planner then calculates a set of suggested grasps based on the local scene geometry around the point-of-interest. The AR overlay displays one suggested grasp at a time, starting with the best ranked grasp, which the user can change by clicking the next and previous arrows. If they see a grasp they like, the user can initiate grasp execution by selecting a preset grasp depth of "shallow" or "deep", depending on the task. If they do not find a suitable grasp, the user can click on another point at any time to calculate and rank a new set of grasps. Since the only interaction comes from clicking on a point in the camera streams, this condition does not require a 3D viewer. The unique components of the *point-and-click* interface are shown in Figure 5b, replacing elements (c), (d), and (e) in Figure 4.

Table 1: Measures and descriptions

tasks completed	$number\ of\ completed\ tasks$
task success rate	$\frac{completed\ tasks}{attempted\ tasks}$
time per completed tasks	$\frac{\sum elapsedTime(completed\ tasks)}{completed\ tasks}$
errors per task	$\frac{misses+bad\ grasps}{attempted\ tasks}$
interactions per task	$\frac{interactions}{attempted\ tasks}$

4.3 Measures

We used multiple measures to evaluate users' performance, efficiency, and workload between the three interfaces.

4.3.1 Observed Measures

We identify a set of observable measures intended to measure each participant's performance (*tasks completed, task success rate, errors per task*) and efficiency (*time per completed tasks, interactions per task*). These measures are all calculated from values logged during the main portion of the study, after the training period concluded. Definitions of the measures are listed in Table 1.

We define a *completed task* as any task in which the goal was met at some point within the 30 minute time period, a *failed task* as any task which was rendered impossible to complete (e.g. pouring out the mug somewhere other than the bowl), and an *attempted task* as any task the user devoted time towards completing. We define a *miss* as an attempted grasp that does not contact an object or the environment, and a *bad grasp* as any grasp that does make contact but cannot be used to complete the task. We define an *interaction* as any mouse button press that involves specifying or executing a grasp. This includes dragging a ring-and-arrow marker (*free positioning* and *constrained positioning*), setting or clearing a grasp point or approach angle (*constrained positioning*), calculating a new set of grasps or viewing a different calculated grasp (*point-and-click*), executing a grasp (all conditions), repositioning the virtual camera in the 3D viewer (*free positioning*), and changing camera streams (all).

4.3.2 Self-Reported Measures

Each participant completed a NASA TLX form upon completion of the study, to measure workload for each of the interfaces, including *mental demand, physical demand, temporal demand, performance, effort*, and *frustration*.

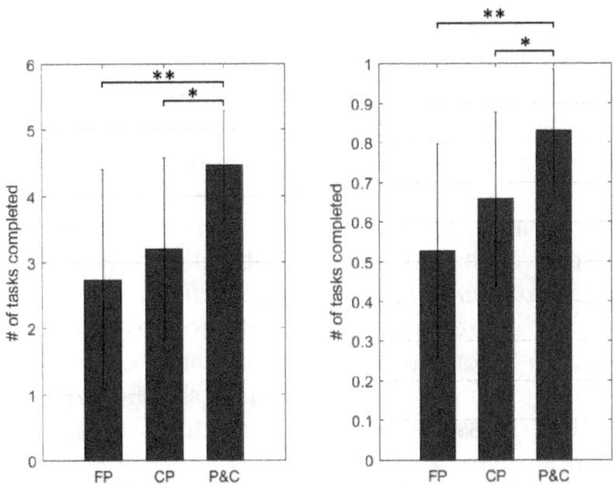

(a) Mean number of tasks completed (±1 SD)

(b) Mean task success rate (*tasks completed / tasks attempted*, ±1 SD)

Figure 6: Task completion measures

5. RESULTS

For each of our performance and efficiency measures described in Section 4.3.1, we conducted a one-way between subjects Analysis of Variance (ANOVA) to compare the effects of user control level on each measure. If a significant effect was found, we performed a Tukey HSD post test to determine which conditions significantly differed. We present the results for the set of observed measures below.

We first present task completion measures, shown in Figure 6. ANOVA showed a significant effect of scene information incorporation for both *tasks completed* ($F(2, 42) = 6.75, p = 0.0029$) and *task success rate* ($F(2, 42) = 7.20, p = 0.0021$) for the three conditions. *Point-and-click* significantly outperformed both *free positioning* ($p = 0.0027$) and *constrained positioning* ($p = 0.034$) in number of tasks completed. We note a similar result with task success rate, where users of the *point-and-click* interface had significantly higher completion rates over their attempted tasks than users of the *free positioning* interface ($p = 0.0014$), and the same trend appears between *point-and-click* and *constrained positioning* ($p = 0.09$). Taken together, we observe that incorporating more scene information into the grasp pose specification algorithm results in both a greater quantity of tasks being completed with a greater quality of attempt than algorithms incorporating little to no scene information. We found no significant difference between *free positioning* and *constrained positioning*, although we note that they have comparatively high variance (see Section 6).

Number of errors made, including a breakdown of errors into misses and bad grasps, is shown in Figure 7. Our analysis showed a significant effect of scene information incorporation on number of errors for the three conditions ($F(2, 42) = 18.39, p < 0.001$). Both *constrained positioning* and *point-and-click* differed significantly from *free positioning* ($p < 0.001$ in both cases), although there was no significant difference between the two. The same relationship can be seen when accounting for time, shown in Table 2. As such, we observe that grasp specification algorithms that do not use any scene information introduce a risk of increased operator error.

The average time per completed task was 5.04 ± 2.19 min, 4.41 ± 2.03 min, and 3.17 ± 1.16 min for *free positioning*, *constrained positioning*, and *point-and-click*, respectively. We

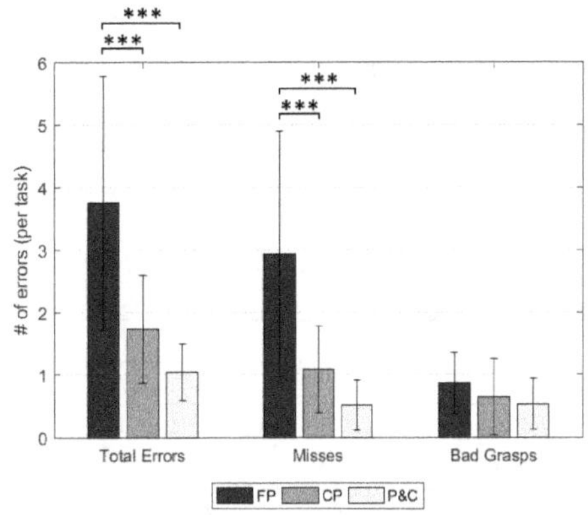

Figure 7: Breakdown of mean errors (±1 SD)

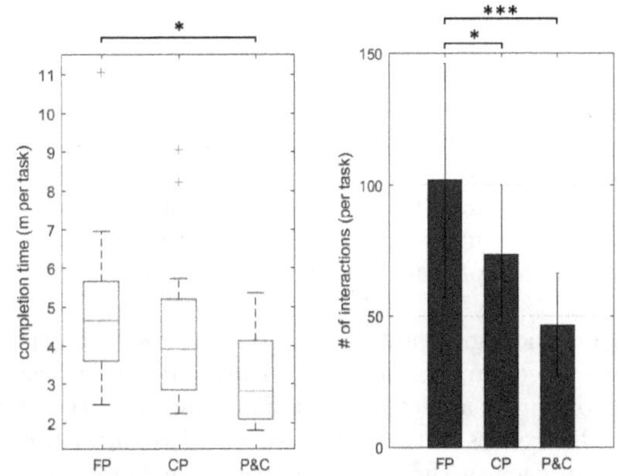

(a) Mean time per task (±1 SD)

(b) Mean number of interactions (±1 SD)

Figure 8: Efficiency measures

note that for the *free positioning interface*, two users were unable to complete any tasks, and so their data is omitted from the completion time analysis. Our analysis showed a significant effect of scene information incorporation on completion time ($F(2, 40) = 3.87, p = 0.029$) for the three conditions. *Point-and-click* users completed tasks significantly faster than *free positioning* users ($p = 0.026$). Similar to the task completion measures, *free positioning* and *constrained positioning* had higher variance in task completion time, resulting in more outliers than *point-and-click* (Figure 8a).

Our analysis showed scene information incorporation had a significant effect on the number of interactions ($F(2, 42) = 11.31, p < 0.001$) for the three conditions, shown in Figure 8b. *Free positioning* significantly differed from *constrained positioning* ($p = 0.049$) as well as *point-and-click* ($p < 0.001$). *Constrained positioning* and *point-and-click* exhibit the same trend ($p = 0.065$), favoring greater use of scene information. *Interactions per minute* are shown in Table 2. We observe a direct relationship where incorporating more scene information into grasp specification algorithms reduces the number of interactions required by the user, resulting in interfaces that are more efficient to use.

Based on all of the results, it is apparent that both of the novel conditions outperform the commonly used *free positioning* condition. *Constrained positioning* and *point-and-click* significantly reduced the number of grasping errors per task, and they require significantly fewer interactions per

Table 2: Time-controlled measures

measure	FP	CP	P&C
errors/min	0.58 ± 0.19	0.33 ± 0.14	0.28 ± 0.19
interact./min	15.1 ± 4.6	11.5 ± 3.3	10.1 ± 4.8

Table 3: NASA TLX Results

measure	FP	CP	P&C
total workload	64.5 ± 10.9	64.1 ± 14.1	57.5 ± 10.6
mental demand	12.9 ± 8.4	11.9 ± 9.1	12.1 ± 8.4
phys. demand	4.5 ± 6.6	2.5 ± 5.1	0.9 ± 2.7
temp. demand	9.1 ± 7.7	9.2 ± 7.4	8.2 ± 6.9
performance	10.5 ± 6.9	11.8 ± 8.5	13.1 ± 8.5
effort	13.3 ± 5.4	12.6 ± 5.3	11.9 ± 4.7
frustration	14.2 ± 10.6	16.0 ± 11.4	11.2 ± 10.5

task. Between *constrained positioning* and *point-and-click*, the *point-and-click* interface has the advantage. Along with a reduction in errors and interactions, *point-and-click* also results in a significantly better task completion rate, a significantly higher number of tasks completed, and a significantly lower completion time per task as compared to *free positioning*.

We found no significant correlations between robotics experience, video game experience, or 3D software experience and any of our measures. We also found no statistically significant differences between the workload reported by participants in each of the three conditions, or between any of the individual components contributing to workload. The results of the NASA TLX are reported in Table 3.

6. DISCUSSION AND FUTURE WORK

Our results consistently show that interaction approaches with greater incorporation of scene information result in improved performance for manipulation tasks across all of our objective measures. In particular, the *point-and-click* interface allowed users to complete a greater number of tasks more quickly, complete tasks more consistently, and make fewer mistakes than users with the *free positioning* and *controlled positioning* interfaces, all while performing fewer interactions.

The *point-and-click* condition had notably smaller variance than the other two conditions. The cause of the large variance in the *free positioning* and *constrained positioning* conditions comes from the potentially high number of errors. The full 6-DOF control of *free positioning*, and to a lesser extent the 4-DOF control of *constrained positioning*, create such a large workspace of possible grasp poses that non-carefully-planned movements will usually result in a failed grasp. The outliers in the *free positioning* and *constrained positioning* conditions spent the majority of their time attempting a single task, moving the gripper around the object without successfully grasping it. For the *point-and-click* interface, however, simply clicking on the object to be manipulated often resulted in a successful grasp, thus lowering the variance among non-expert users. Non-expert user variance is an important concern when designing interfaces meant to be deployed to the wider population. We leave identification of the causes of the non-expert user performance variance to future work.

While *point-and-click* had the clearest advantages over the other interfaces, *constrained positioning* does have a significant advantage over *free positioning* in reducing the number of errors made by users. The most frequent type of error was missing a grasp, in which the gripper failed to make contact with any part of the environment, object or otherwise. Both *constrained positioning* and *point-and-click* require the user to focus their end-effector positioning around a point cloud by clicking on a point to initiate the interaction. Constraining the interaction to a physical surface significantly reduces the number of missed grasps, resulting in more efficient use of the arm.

Dependency on a point cloud does create limitations for the new interaction approaches, however. *Point-and-click* requires an accurate point cloud. For difficult to detect objects, such as highly specular objects, it will not be able to calculate a good set of grasps. For objects undetectable by depth cameras, such as transparent objects, neither *constrained positioning* nor *point-and-click* will work, since the initial point of interest cannot be selected. An ideal interface would include an option to switch to *free positioning* for redundency in these cases.

A final interesting point comes from the NASA TLX data. While there are clear advantages to incorporating more scene information in manipulation interfaces (including a significant reduction in number of interactions), users do not appear to feel any reduction in workload. To further explore this, we suggest conducting a within-subjects evaluation study so that more subjective measures about preferred interaction methods can be collected.

7. CONCLUSION

This work introduces alternative 6-DOF end-effector positioning approaches to the widely used ring-and-arrow marker for remote object manipulation, by incorporating scene information into the grasp specification algorithms. The results are a constrained positioning approach which reduces pose specification to a 4-DOF process performed in 3 steps, and a point-and-click approach which leverages autonomous grasp planning to simplify pose specification to a single click.

The results of our evaluation study show that the common ring-and-arrow marker free positioning approach is significantly less effective than our novel approaches. Our constrained positioning and point-and-click approaches translate to more efficient user interfaces, resulting in significantly fewer errors and requiring significantly fewer interactions than the free positioning interface. Further, the point-and-click interface allowed users to complete a significantly greater number of general manipulation tasks with a significantly higher success rate per attempted tasks than the common ring-and-arrow approach. Despite measurable improvements in performance, however, users did not report a reduction in workload for either the constrained positioning or point-and-click approaches.

8. ACKNOWLEDGMENT

This work was supported in part by the National Science Foundation award number IIS 13-17775 and the Office of Naval Research award number N000141410795.

9. REFERENCES

[1] T. L. Chen, M. Ciocarlie, S. Cousins, P. M. Grice, K. Hawkins, K. Hsiao, C. C. Kemp, C.-H. King, D. A. Lazewatsky, H. Nguyen, et al. Robots for humanity: A case study in assistive mobile manipulation. 2013.

[2] M. Ciocarlie, K. Hsiao, A. Leeper, and D. Gossow. Mobile manipulation through an assistive home robot. In *2012 IEEE/RSJ International Conference on Intelligent Robots and Systems*, pages 5313–5320, Oct 2012.

[3] M. DeDonato, V. Dimitrov, R. Du, R. Giovacchini, K. Knoedler, X. Long, F. Polido, M. A. Gennert, T. Padır, S. Feng, et al. Human-in-the-loop control of a humanoid robot for disaster response: A report from the darpa robotics challenge trials. *Journal of Field Robotics*, 32(2):275–292, 2015.

[4] B. P. DeJong, J. E. Colgate, and M. A. Peshkin. Improving teleoperation: reducing mental rotations and translations. In *Robotics and Automation, 2004. Proceedings. ICRA'04. 2004 IEEE International Conference on*, volume 4, pages 3708–3714. IEEE, 2004.

[5] M. Hachet, F. Decle, S. Knodel, and P. Guitton. Navidget for easy 3d camera positioning from 2d inputs. In *Proceedings of the 2008 IEEE Symposium on 3D User Interfaces*, 3DUI '08, pages 83–89, Washington, DC, USA, 2008. IEEE Computer Society.

[6] S. G. Hart and L. E. Staveland. Development of nasa-tlx (task load index): Results of empirical and theoretical research. *Advances in psychology*, 52:139–183, 1988.

[7] A. Henrysson and M. Billinghurst. Using a mobile phone for 6 dof mesh editing. In *Proceedings of the 8th ACM SIGCHI New Zealand chapter's international conference on Computer-human interaction: design centered HCI*, pages 9–16. ACM, 2007.

[8] K. Hsiao, S. Chitta, M. Ciocarlie, and E. G. Jones. Contact-reactive grasping of objects with partial shape information. In *Intelligent Robots and Systems (IROS), 2010 IEEE/RSJ International Conference on*, pages 1228–1235. IEEE, 2010.

[9] N. Katzakis, M. Hori, K. Kiyokawa, and H. Takemura. Smartphone game controller. In *Proceedings of the 74th HIS SigVR Workshop*. Citeseer, 2011.

[10] C. C. Kemp and P. M. Grice. Assistive mobile manipulation: Designing for operators with motor impairments. In *RSS 2016 Workshop on Socially and Physically Assistive Robotics for Humanity*, 2016.

[11] D. Kent, M. Behrooz, and S. Chernova. Construction of a 3d object recognition and manipulation database from grasp demonstrations. *Autonomous Robots*, 40(1):175–192, 2016.

[12] S. Kohlbrecher, A. Romay, A. Stumpf, A. Gupta, O. Von Stryk, F. Bacim, D. A. Bowman, A. Goins, R. Balasubramanian, and D. C. Conner. Human-robot teaming for rescue missions: Team vigir's approach to the 2013 darpa robotics challenge trials. *Journal of Field Robotics*, 32(3):352–377, 2015.

[13] A. Leeper, K. Hsiao, M. Ciocarlie, L. Takayama, and D. Gossow. Strategies for human-in-the-loop robotic grasping. In *Human-Robot Interaction (HRI), 2012 7th ACM/IEEE International Conference on*, pages 1–8, March 2012.

[14] I. Lenz, H. Lee, and A. Saxena. Deep learning for detecting robotic grasps. *The International Journal of Robotics Research*, 34(4-5):705–724, 2015.

[15] S. Levine, P. Pastor, A. Krizhevsky, and D. Quillen. Learning hand-eye coordination for robotic grasping with deep learning and large-scale data collection. *arXiv preprint arXiv:1603.02199*, 2016.

[16] M. R. Masliah and P. Milgram. Measuring the allocation of control in a 6 degree-of-freedom docking experiment. In *Proceedings of the SIGCHI conference on Human Factors in Computing Systems*, pages 25–32. ACM, 2000.

[17] L. M. Parsons. Inability to reason about an object's orientation using an axis and angle of rotation. *Journal of experimental psychology: Human perception and performance*, 21(6):1259, 1995.

[18] C. Phillips-Grafflin, N. Alunni, H. B. Suay, J. Mainprice, D. Lofaro, D. Berenson, S. Chernova, R. W. Lindeman, and P. Oh. Toward a user-guided manipulation framework for high-dof robots with limited communication. *Intelligent Service Robotics*, 7(3):121–131, 2014.

[19] M. Quigley, K. Conley, B. Gerkey, J. Faust, T. Foote, J. Leibs, R. Wheeler, and A. Y. Ng. Ros: an open-source robot operating system. In *ICRA workshop on open source software*, volume 3, page 5. Kobe, Japan, 2009.

[20] A. Saxena, L. L. Wong, and A. Y. Ng. Learning grasp strategies with partial shape information. In *AAAI*, volume 3, pages 1491–1494, 2008.

[21] T. B. Sheridan. Space teleoperation through time delay: review and prognosis. *IEEE Transactions on robotics and Automation*, 9(5):592–606, 1993.

[22] A. ten Pas and R. Platt. Using geometry to detect grasp poses in 3d point clouds. In *IntâĂŹl Symp. on Robotics Research*, 2015.

[23] A. Ten Pas and R. Platt. Localizing handle-like grasp affordances in 3d point clouds. In *Experimental Robotics*, pages 623–638. Springer, 2016.

[24] R. Toris, J. Kammerl, D. V. Lu, J. Lee, O. C. Jenkins, S. Osentoski, M. Wills, and S. Chernova. Robot web tools: Efficient messaging for cloud robotics. In *Intelligent Robots and Systems (IROS), 2015 IEEE/RSJ International Conference on*, pages 4530–4537. IEEE, 2015.

[25] S. Zhai and P. Milgram. Quantifying coordination in multiple dof movement and its application to evaluating 6 dof input devices. In *Proceedings of the SIGCHI conference on Human factors in computing systems*, pages 320–327. ACM Press/Addison-Wesley Publishing Co., 1998.

[26] M. Zucker, S. Joo, M. X. Grey, C. Rasmussen, E. Huang, M. Stilman, and A. Bobick. A general-purpose system for teleoperation of the drc-hubo humanoid robot. *Journal of Field Robotics*, 32(3):336–351, 2015.

Haptic Shape-Based Management of Robot Teams in Cordon and Patrol

Samuel J. McDonald and Mark B. Colton
Department of Mechanical Engineering
Brigham Young University
Provo, Utah 84602

C. Kristopher Alder and
Michael A. Goodrich
Department of Computer Science
Brigham Young University
Provo, Utah 84602

ABSTRACT

There is a growing need to develop effective interaction methods that enable a single operator to manage a team of multiple robots. This paper presents a novel approach that involves treating the team as a moldable volume, in which deformations of the volume correspond to changes in team shape. The team possesses a level of autonomy that allows the team to travel to and surround buildings of interest in a patrol and cordon scenario. During *surround* mode, the operator explores or manipulates the team shape to create desired formations around a building. A spacing interaction method also allows the operator to adjust how robots are spaced within the current shape. Separate haptic feedback is developed for each method to allow the operator to "feel" the shape or spacing manipulation. During *travel* mode, the operator chooses desired travel locations and receives feedback to help identify how and where the team travels. Results from a user study suggest that haptic feedback significantly improves operator performance in a reconnaissance task when task demand is higher, but may slightly increase operator workload. In the context of the experimental setup, these results suggest that haptic feedback may contribute to heads-up control of a team of autonomous robots. There were no significant differences in levels of situation awareness due to haptic feedback in this study.

Keywords

human-swarm interaction; haptic feedback; situation awareness

1. INTRODUCTION

There are many current and future scenarios in which a human must manage a team of robots. Potential scenarios include wilderness search-and-rescue [9], rescue operations in buildings damaged by fire or earthquake [1, 13], searching buildings by law enforcement agencies [10], pollution monitoring and clean-up [11], and military patrol and cordon operations in an urban environment [17]. In each scenario, the robot team serves as an extension of the operator's ability to gather information in complex and often dangerous environments. Enabling the human operator to manage the robot team in an intuitive, effective, and time-efficient manner is therefore critical to the success of operations involving robot teams.

A common approach in controlling autonomous robots (in use by current military, law enforcement, and search-and-rescue agencies) is for a single robot to be controlled and monitored by one or many human operators (see, for example, [20]). This interaction model is clearly not ideal if the objective of employing autonomous robots is to augment the capabilities of humans and maximize the information-gathering capabilities of the team [8, 26]. A preferable interaction model is for a single human operator to control multiple autonomous robots [12, 16, 19]. The effectiveness of such an approach is limited by the operator's ability to command the actions of multiple agents and receive information about the state of the robot team, while accomplishing a primary task, whether it be search-and-rescue, surveillance, etc.

When the robot team possesses appropriate autonomy for the given scenario, the problem becomes one of "team management" rather than "robot control," enabling the operator to focus on task objectives and interpretation of gathered data, rather than on the robots. With the proper management interface, the operator is able to devote more attention and resources to a primary task and remain "heads-up" while managing the team. In this paper, "heads-up" refers to having a sufficient level of competency in a single task to focus visual attention elsewhere on other important tasks. An operator who is "heads-down" tends to focus solely on a single task and may experience difficulty in responding quickly or accurately to additional tasks that require visual attention. In a human-robot interaction scenario, this could occur when an operator is so focused on a graphical user interface that awareness of surroundings or response to incoming commands is degraded. While considering a single-operator-multiple-robot interaction, enabling the operator to achieve heads-up control is challenging.

In general, when multiple tasks demand attention from the same sensory channel, interference can degrade performance or possibly result in task overload [27]. The operator's ability to multi-task can improve with the use of a multimodal interface, using both visual and haptic feedback. Haptic feedback has been shown to reduce collisions when piloting individual robotic vehicles [5, 23], and provide a sense

HRI '17, March 06-09, 2017, Vienna, Austria

DOI: http://dx.doi.org/10.1145/2909824.3020243

of team-level properties when managing multiple robots [21, 22, 24, 25]. There are, however, possible drawbacks to using haptic feedback, as it has been shown to increase operator workload in some studies [14, 15].

The objective of the present work is to investigate the effects of haptic feedback on heads-up control, situation awareness (SA), and workload while managing a small team of robots in reconnaissance and surveillance tasks. A user study was conducted to verify the effectiveness of this approach in completion of a primary task, and quantify its effects on operator workload, situation awareness, and other measures.

2. ROBOT BEHAVIORS

In this work, a simulated team of robots is managed in a military patrol and cordon exercise, in which the robot team must autonomously travel between specified locations (patrol) and surround buildings (cordon), although the interaction approach will be generalizable to other scenarios that require a human operator to control the movement and distribution of autonomous robots. The individual and team behaviors of the robots in this work were developed in [2, 3]; an overview of those behaviors are given in this section. In this scenario, the operator uses the team to search around buildings of interest in an urban environment. Only the exterior regions of the building are considered while searching. The robots are modeled as autonomous, omni-directional agents, and for simplicity, their movement is planar in x and y.

There are two modes available to the team, *travel* and *surround*. Graphs are used to describe the relationships between robots, with each robot corresponding to a node in the graph. An example formation for each mode is shown in Figure 1.

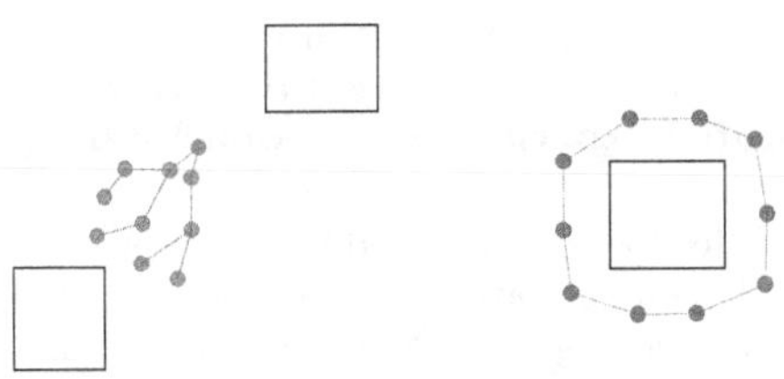

Figure 1: *Travel* (left) and *surround* (right) modes. Individual circles are graph nodes (robots), and colored lines are graph connections. *Travel* mode is represented by a tree formation. *Surround* mode is represented as a spanning ring formation around one building.

A *travel* is used when the team is traveling between buildings, and represents the patrol action. In *travel* mode, the team formation is governed by the graph connections, where each robot follows another lead robot. This allows the robots to obey forces that repel them from the current building and travel to a new one. The resulting swarm behavior is that of a spanning forest, where the graph connections can be traced to one or two robots that lead the team in the direction of travel. The robots attempt to stay close together until a nearby building is identified, at which point the *surround* mode is enabled.

A *surround* is used when the team is surrounding a building, and represents the cordon action. In *surround* mode, the model determines a surrounding shape and the team forms a spanning ring around a building. The team can successfully surround buildings of convex or concave geometry. Transitions between these two modes are handled by the robot behaviors model. In either mode, robots are attracted to nearby buildings, but repelled by building boundaries to prevent the team from passing through buildings.

3. HUMAN-TEAM INTERACTION

Several interaction methods were developed to allow a single operator to manage a team of robots. Some methods are enabled by default and others are enabled by engaging buttons on a haptic interface. The physics of each interaction method are explained in detail to provide insight into the underlying haptic sensations, thereby giving greater substance to the corresponding human interaction.

3.1 Modeling Clay: A Haptic Metaphor

In a brainstorming breakout session at the 2012 AAAI Fall Symposium on Human Control of Biological Swarms, a breakout group developed the idea of using a deformable medium, such as modeling clay, as a "joystick" to command the distribution of large-scale swarm-like teams of homogeneous vehicles. Diana *et al.* [7] demonstrated a molding scheme in which an operator formed modeling clay into various shapes in the view of an overhead camera and a team of robots replicated the formation commanded by the shaped clay. We modify the modeling clay metaphor so that a human can shape the distribution of robot teams by manipulating a *virtual* deformable volume through stretching, pulling and other operations. The modeling clay metaphor forms the basis for the haptic sensations that the user feels while distributing the robot team. Note that, unlike the work in [7], physical modeling clay is not used in our method; the concept and physics of modeling clay are used to generate the visual and haptic representation of the robot team.

3.2 Force Node Network

In surround mode, virtual modeling clay is modeled discretely by placing potential force field spheres at the location of each robot in the spanning ring and at multiple points between robots. In essence, these potential spheres form the nodes of a "force graph" on which the haptic interaction forces and graphical representation of the deformable volume are based. An example of how the force nodes span between robots is shown in Figure 2. Notice that some force nodes are specifically assigned to a robot location. A virtual haptic cursor is also displayed to the operator that maps to physical haptic device movement.

To provide a dynamic system that the operator can manipulate, the potential spheres also form the mass nodes of a virtual mass-spring-damper network. Virtual frictional forces are also used to model plastic deformation of the volume. Each force node in the network is positioned a distance $\delta_{spacing} = r_n/4$ from neighboring nodes, where r_n is the node radius. In other words, nodes are placed close enough together to cause eight consecutive nodes to overlap. This provides sufficient node density for compelling haptic interaction and responsive team interaction. Parameter values for mass, spring, and damping constants were subjectively chosen to allow each node to maintain sufficient distance relative to neighboring nodes, stabilize the network, and create a distinguishable volume with which to interact. Each

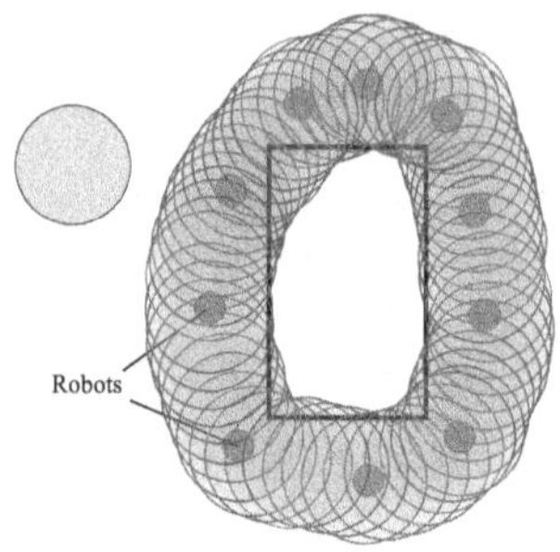

Figure 2: Force nodes (light blue) form a spanning ring shape after the team (dark blue) has surrounded a building. The haptic cursor (gray) is controlled by the operator.

node has a z-position of zero, such that one hemisphere is above the ground surface, and the other hemisphere is below the surface. The deformable ring naturally maps to the spanning ring in surround mode, and can be mapped to the spanning forest in travel mode; see sections 3.3 and 3.4. The deformable ring forms the basis for computing the haptic feedback force felt by the operator.

3.3 Surround Interaction

In *surround* mode, there are three types of interaction modes with corresponding force feedback algorithms. They are shape exploration, shape manipulation, and spacing manipulation. Each mode is designed to encourage collective, team-level control, rather than micromanagement of each robot.

3.3.1 Shape Exploration

This mode allows the user to explore the shape of the robot team without influencing it. The force nodes are fixed and the operator cannot cause them to move during contact, but force feedback is still provided. The force feedback is computed as a function of penetration distance on each of the nodes with which there is contact. Thus, the nodal force feedback during this mode is given by

$$\mathbf{f}_n = -\sum_{n=1}^{N} k_n \mathbf{e}_n, \tag{1}$$

where k_n is the node stiffness coefficient and $\mathbf{e}_n$ is the penetration vector for the n-th contacted node. Contact between the haptic cursor and virtual ground surface results in a ground feedback force, $\mathbf{f}_g$. The total haptic feedback force in shape exploration is then

$$\mathbf{F}_{sh} = \mathbf{f}_g + \mathbf{f}_n. \tag{2}$$

The nodal force $\mathbf{f}_n$ allows the user to feel the team distribution. The ground-plane force $\mathbf{f}_g$ provides a virtual fixture that enables the user to easily keep the haptic cursor in the same plane as the robot team, making exploration of the team's shape more convenient. A visualization of the feedback produced by coming in contact with a set of fixed force nodes is shown in Figure 3.

3.3.2 Shape Manipulation

During shape manipulation, the network nodes are allowed to move in response to contact from the haptic cursor,

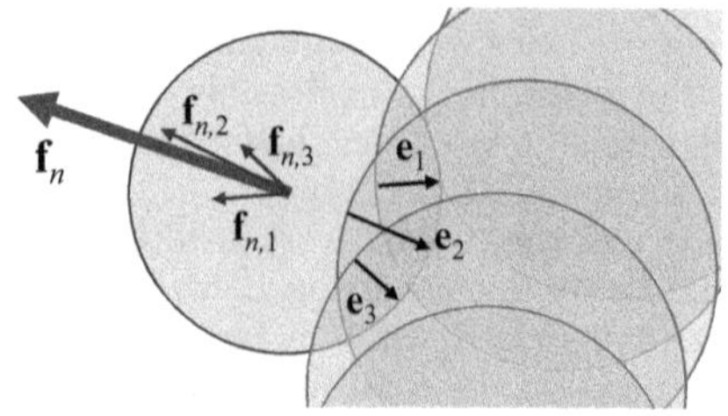

Figure 3: The haptic feedback force, $\mathbf{f}_n$, is produced due to interaction between the haptic cursor and several force nodes.

as shown in Figure 4. The motion of the nodes is calculated from the governing equations of a mass-spring-damper network. The robot positions are updated from the adjusted robot node positions. This method allows the operator to quickly adjust the shape of the robot team without needing to interact with each robot individually.

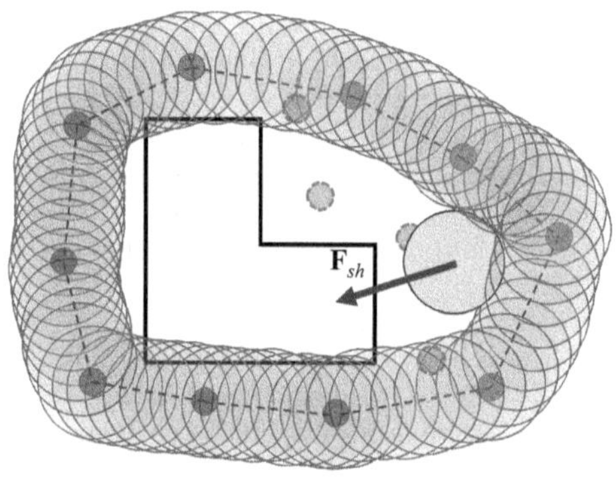

Figure 4: Adjusted team shape, showing previous (orange) and current (dark blue) robot positions. The operator experiences a feedback force, $\mathbf{F}_{sh}$.

The force feedback is governed by the same equations presented in shape exploration. In the case of shape manipulation, equal and opposite forces are exerted on the nodal network, resulting in motion and deformation of the network. The feedback is designed to provide forces similar to what one would feel while plastically deforming physical modeling clay. The operator must use the haptic cursor to interact with the shape and exert forces on the network that exceed the frictional forces, which are included to simulate plastic deformation, in which the force nodes remain in a location even when the haptic cursor is no longer exerting a force on the network.

3.3.3 Spacing Manipulation

The autonomous behavior of the team creates an initially uniform distribution, meaning that each robot maintains an equal distance from neighboring robots throughout the spanning ring shape. Spacing manipulation mode allows the operator to adjust inter-robot distances, moving them closer together in some portions of the shape and farther away from each other in others. The method allows the operator to simply gesture toward a set of robots in the team with the haptic cursor, causing robots to concentrate more (decrease spacing) in the direction of cursor movement relative to the team's center. An example of spacing manipulation is shown in Figure 5.

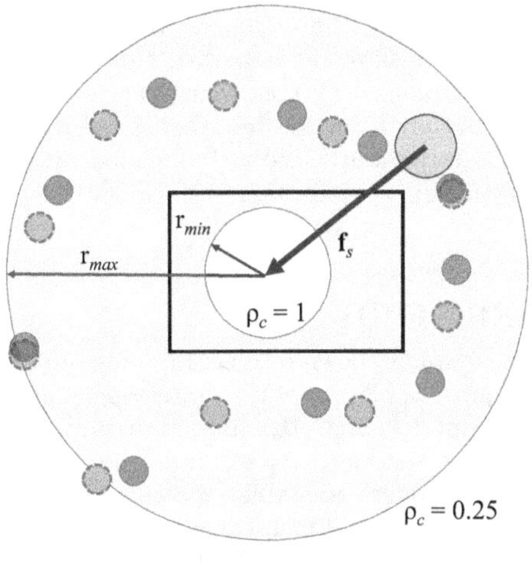

Figure 5: Adjusted team spacing, showing previous (orange) and current (dark blue) robot positions as a result of moving the haptic cursor away from the center of the formation. The robot spacing is a function of the location of the haptic cursor within the manipulation boundary (green).

Since each robot is assigned a node in the network, neighboring nodes act as potential new locations for each robot. The robot spacing within the shape is modeled as a set of equilibrium distances, L_i, that act in the discrete space of the nodal network. Given a team of M robots, the equilibrium distance L_i is assigned to the space between the i-th and the $i+1$-th robots, and the M-th and 1st robots share L_M. These distances determine how the robots are distributed within the shape, irrespective of the dynamics that govern the shape in a more continuous environmental space. Nodal network properties such as total perimeter, P_n, and center of mass, $\mathbf{C}_n$ are used to adjust these distances based on cursor location. The initial equilibrium distance is $L_O = P_n/M$ and each equilibrium distance is governed by the relationship $L_i = \rho_i L_O$, where ρ_i is an equilibrium distance factor.

As the cursor moves a distance r away from $\mathbf{C}_n$, the robot with closest proximity to the cursor is denoted robot c. The equilibrium distance factor for this robot is set first and is given by

$$\rho_c = \begin{cases} 1 & r < r_{min} \\ 1 - 0.75\frac{r - r_{min}}{r_{max} - r_{min}} & r_{min} \leq r \leq r_{max}, \\ 0.25 & r > r_{max} \end{cases}$$

where r_{max} is the distance from $\mathbf{C}_n$ to robot furthest away from $\mathbf{C}_n$ and $r_{min} = 0.25r_{max}$. From there, other factors are calculated as

$$\rho_i = \rho_c + \frac{4(1-\rho_c)}{M}n, \quad (3)$$

where n is the minimum number of robot nodes aways from robot c. Equation (3) ensures that $\sum_{i=1}^{M} L_i = P_n$, which is to be expected.

The total distance between robot nodes, d_i, is the sum of the distances between neighboring nodes that connect one robot node to another. Robot nodes transfer to neighboring nodes in order to maintain $|L_i - d_i| \leq 0.25L_i$. This tolerance allows for a range of distances to acquire equilibrium and prevent desired robot positions from switching unnecessarily between neighboring nodes. Due to the finite amount of nodes in the network, robot node positions simply establish the desired positions of robots. The continuous dynamic motion is handled separately by applying forces to the robots and guiding them directly to these positions.

When this type of manipulation is enabled, a force, $\mathbf{f}_s$, is produced that is directed toward $\mathbf{C}_n$, proportional to the cursor's distance away from $\mathbf{C}_n$, such that

$$\mathbf{f}_s = k_s(\mathbf{C}_n - \mathbf{p}_{cursor}) - b_s\mathbf{v}_{cursor}, \quad (4)$$

where k_s is the spacing force stiffness coefficient, b_s is the spacing damping coefficient, and $\mathbf{p}_{cursor}$ and $\mathbf{v}_{cursor}$ are the position and velocity of the haptic cursor, respectively. This feedback is designed to give the operator a sense of the gesture direction relative to the team by modeling the force as a virtual spring that connects the cursor to the team's center-of-mass. The magnitude also informs the operator of the strength of the spacing adjustment in that direction. As the operator may be quickly gesturing toward various sections of the team shape, a damping force is provided to prevent the device motions from being too abrupt. This damping effect also helps the device feel more like a grounded joystick rather than a free-moving cursor. The ground force feedback is also active in this mode, so the total feedback force felt by the operator will then be

$$\mathbf{F}_s = \mathbf{f}_g + \mathbf{f}_s. \quad (5)$$

3.4 Travel Interaction

Travel interaction allows the operator to move the team from one building to another. The haptic feedback is divided into relative travel and shape exploration forces, which are explained in the following sections.

3.4.1 *Relative Travel*

The relative travel force occurs while the team is traveling between buildings. It activates once the travel position is being chosen, and deactivates once the team has switched to *surround* mode. The relative travel force is

$$\mathbf{f}_r = k_r(\mathbf{C}_n - \mathbf{p}_{cursor}) - b_r\mathbf{v}_{cursor}, \quad (6)$$

where k_r is the relative travel stiffness coefficient and b_r is the relative travel damping coefficient. Similarly to the feedback force provided during a spacing manipulation, a small level of damping is used to stabilize the cursor motion while choosing a travel position. The total haptic feedback force felt by the operator during relative travel is then

$$\mathbf{F}_r = \mathbf{f}_g + \mathbf{f}_r. \quad (7)$$

This force is designed to help the operator gain a sense for the relative distance between the cursor and the team. The force is strong enough to guide the device toward the team location, but not strong enough to prevent the operator from moving the device as desired. With training, the operator may interpret these forces to gain a better sense for where and how the team is traveling. Figure 6 shows the process of sending a travel command to the team. The user selects a location by pressing a travel button on the haptic interface. The team moves to that location and the

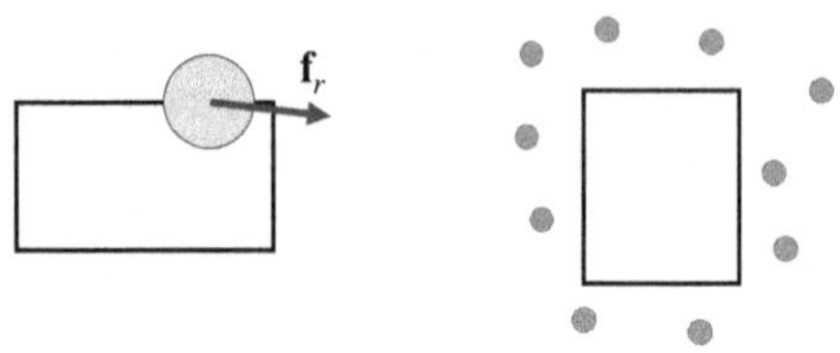

(a) Travel command in process

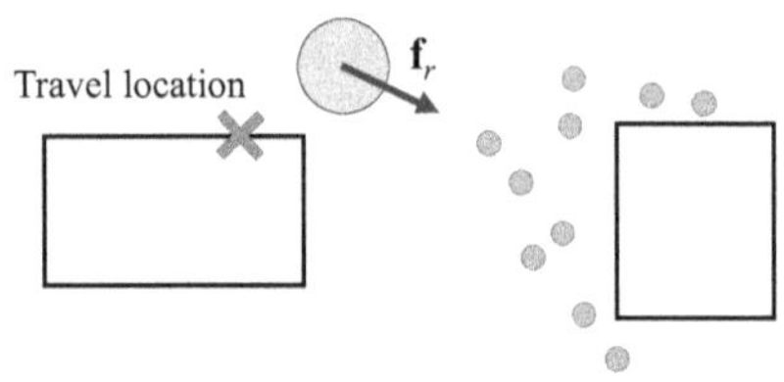

(b) Travel command is applied

Figure 6: This figure shows the travel command process and the direction of the relative force feedback, $\mathbf{f}_r$. In (a), the team is still in *surround* mode and the travel location has been determined, but not applied. In (b), the team begins its motion toward the selected travel location (marked with a red X).

operator experiences the relative travel force from the device as the team travels. This discrete command process is used rather than continuously "dragging" the team via velocity commands so that the operator can use the time on more urgent tasks while relying on the autonomous behavior of the team to complete the travel motion.

3.4.2 *Shape Exploration*

During *travel* mode, the operator may explore the overall shape of the team by coming in contact with the traveling force nodes. The nodal network is created similar to *surround* mode, except, in *travel* mode, a convex hull [6] is formed around the team and forms an outer boundary that represents the overall team shape.

Since robots are also positioned within the nodal network, a virtual surface is needed to enclose the shape formed by the nodal network. This virtual surface lies tangent with the top of the nodes and within the convex hull. When the cursor comes into contact with this surface, an additional force is produced to simulate an enclosed volume. To help visualize this force, a side-view of the nodal network is shown in Figure 7.

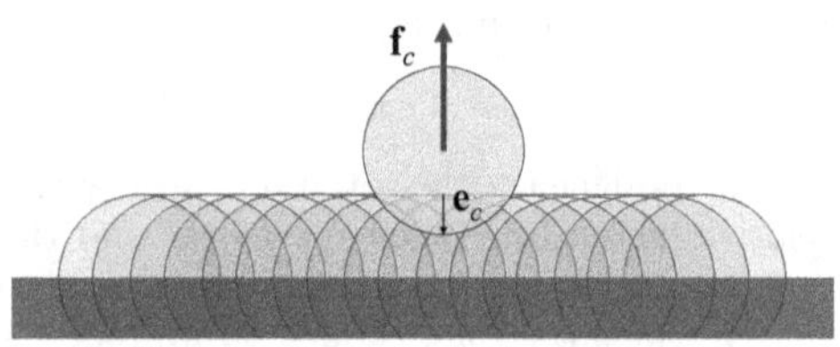

Figure 7: Side-view of interaction with convex hull surface during travel mode.

Similar to the ground force, the convex hull surface is modeled as a flat, stiff surface. The force produced when the haptic cursor comes into contact with this surface is

$$\mathbf{f}_c = -k_c \mathbf{e}_c, \tag{8}$$

where k_c is the convex hull stiffness coefficient and $\mathbf{e}_c$ is the penetration vector into the bounding surface.

The force produced by contacting the force nodes, $\mathbf{f}_n$ is given in Equation 1 and the relative travel force is also in effect, so the total haptic feedback force felt by the operator during travel shape exploration is

$$\mathbf{F}_t = \mathbf{F}_r + \mathbf{f}_n + \mathbf{f}_c. \tag{9}$$

4. USER STUDY

Past research has shown interest in military-based scenarios that require a single operator to teleoperate one or more robots while performing other mission-related tasks [4]. A user study was conducted to examine the effects of haptic feedback on an operator's ability to manage a robot team while performing several tasks. The study primarily focuses on how the presence of haptic feedback affects operator performance, whether the operator uses some or all interaction methods available.

4.1 Experimental Apparatus

A simulation system was designed as a means to experimentally determine how well an operator can manage a team of robots while being required to perform additional mission-related tasks and switch attention between multiple displays. Each participant used a dual-monitor, multimodal workstation as shown in Figure 8. The Novint Falcon desktop haptic device was placed to the right of the monitors and is the primary controller used during the simulation. The operator uses a dominant hand to control the Falcon and a non-dominant hand to enter keyboard input.

Figure 8: Dual-monitor, multimodal workstation with Novint Falcon desktop haptic device.

4.1.1 *Task Description*

The operator has two main tasks, which are: (1) Continuously search for and find as many hotspots as possible and (2) Respond to and follow incoming messages. The primary task involves manipulating team shape and spacing in order to maximize the number of hotspots being uncovered. Hotspots are points of interest in the environment, used to simulate a simple reconnaissance task. The operator is only concerned with locating and uncovering hidden hotspots and not in interpreting their meaning. Past research has used hidden points in an environment as a means of measuring team coverage [21]. The operator is provided a sensor reading for each robot. The strength and location of the sensor readings in the environment are used to locate hotspots. Hotspots are hidden in groups of one, two or three, which all need to be detected within a short window of time for the group to be counted as found. This requires the operator to make a specific formation in order to detect and find all the hotspots in each group. For each environment, the percentage of hotspots found is used as the main measure for primary task performance.

Hotspots are detected by means of a sensor attached to each robot. Each sensor reading is binary, in that it has only two possible outcomes, detection or no detection. A true positive detection occurs when a reading is obtained while a hotspot is within sensor range. The true positive rate, p_t, is modeled probabilistically with a Gaussian distribution from the location of the sensor, given by

$$p_t = p_{min} + (p_{max} - p_{min})e^{-d^2/\sigma^2}, \qquad (10)$$

where p_{min} is a minimum true positive rate, p_{max} is a maximum true positive rate, d is the euclidean distance from the sensor and σ is the standard deviation of the Gaussian curve. With r_{sensor} being the range of the sensor, the standard deviation was chose to be $\sigma = r_{sensor}/3$. Sensor readings are not always indicative of nearby hotspots. A false positive detection occurs when a reading is obtained while no hotspots are in range. The false positive rate, p_f, is another predetermined constant. Values given to the mentioned constants are $p_{min} = 0.50$, $p_{max} = 0.80$, and $p_f = 0.10$.

The secondary task involves an incoming message feed, which has been preprogrammed to display messages that are timed with the simulation. The operator is asked to respond to incoming messages, which include relocation instructions, search suggestions and probing SA questions to measure the operator's level of SA. The operator responds to relocation instructions and search suggestions by managing the team accordingly. A typed numerical response is required to respond to SA questions.

4.1.2 Multitasking and Heads-up Awareness

Given a single viewpoint of an environment, while it is most convenient and realistic to concentrate all visual information on a single display, our simulator splits information across multiple displays in order to simulate a less than ideal case. For example, robot state information is shown on the main team display, but sensor readings are shown on a second display. Although the user may desire those two pieces of information to be visually displayed on the same screen, they are separated to simulate a situation in which the operator needs to be aware of surroundings rather than being heads-down in the team display. In a practical scenario, unlike this experimental scenario, additional events that may require the operator's attention may include video surveillance, mission planning, mission-related discussions with other people or interruptions due to emergency. Since many of these more realistic scenarios require additional training, a simple division of information was preferred and remains ecologically viable.

It has been posited that the presence of haptic feedback will have a positive effect on an operator's performance while placed in this multitasking scenario. Therefore, experimental comparisons need to be made to test this claim. In situations where task demand is low, it is expected to see little difference between measurements between the presence and absence of haptic feedback. When more task demand is placed on the operator, it is expected that task performance will decrease, SA may decrease and workload may increase as compared to when task demand is lower. If haptic feedback has an influence on the experimental measures, there should be a noticeable difference between the presence and absence of haptic feedback while observing results from environments with high or low task demand.

4.2 Experimental Design

The user study was designed as a full two-factorial experiment with factors being haptic feedback (no haptics/haptics) and world difficulty (easy/hard). Two easy worlds and two hard worlds were developed to accommodate all the combinations of factors and levels. A pilot study was performed to tune the difficulty of the hard worlds until a noticeable difference was seen in task performance between easy and hard worlds. The hard worlds were more difficult in that they required the operator to find more hotspots in the same amount of time. The combinations of factors and levels were balanced by each world type of equal difficulty to prevent one world type from being paired with haptics or no haptics. Results from the pilot study validate this approach.

The experiment was held in the MAGICC Lab on Brigham Young University (BYU) campus and there were a total of 19 participants in the study, of which three were female. The ages of participants ranged from 21 to 30, with an average age of 25. Prior to participation in the study, each participant was given enough time to review and sign a consent form. The purpose of the study was explained in general terms and participants were ensured that they were not required to have any previously knowledge of human-robot interaction to successfully complete the study. Each participant was seated in front of the multimodal workstation shown in Figure 8. The participant took about thirty minutes to complete a tutorial and two practice sessions with and without haptic feedback. Up to that point, the participant could ask any questions about the haptic controller, the simulator or the task description.

The remaining four sessions were each six minutes long and were used to collect experimental data. A psuedo-random ordering of the combinations of factors and levels were used to eliminate the effects of ordering in the data. During each session, the participant managed a team of 10 robots to perform the required tasks. Upon completion of each session, the participant reported NASA TLX workload ratings. Workload weightings were reported after all sessions had been completed. Immediately following the last session, each participant also completed an exit questionnaire to document a preference toward haptic feedback. Each participant was asked to rate their preference between 1 (not preferred) and 5 (preferred) on the use of haptic feedback while adjusting shape, adjusting spacing, traveling and overall preference.

5. RESULTS

This section details key results from the user study. A more comprehensive list of results and analysis can be found in [18]. A mixed models analysis of variance (ANOVA) with blocking on subject was used to determine significant effects on several measures of interest using a significance level of 0.05. Interactions between factors and levels were considered first, and then general effects were considered second if no interactions were significant. Combinations of factors are listed as "NE" for no haptics (No) in an easy world, "YE" for haptics (Yes) in an easy world, "NH" for no haptics in a hard world, and "YH" for haptics in a hard world.

5.1 Task Performance

There was a significant interaction between haptic feedback and world difficulty for percent hotspots found ($F(1, 18)$ = 4.94, p = 0.039). There was no significant difference in interaction between haptic feedback and no haptic feedback in the easy world, but haptic feedback did improve performance overall (NE-YE mean = -4.805). This suggests that haptic feedback provides a relatively small advantage in finding hotspots when task demand is low.

When comparing haptic feedback with no haptic feedback in the hard world, the presence of haptic feedback significantly improved the operator's ability to find hotspots, as shown in Figure 9. Additional measures also showed that the operator was more effective at finding hotspots with shape manipulation than spacing manipulation. Shape manipulation was also most effective with haptic feedback. Results from the post-experiment questionnaire showed that on average, participants preferred the use of haptic feedback overall (rating of 3.7 on a scale from 1 to 5), which is consistent with statistical results.

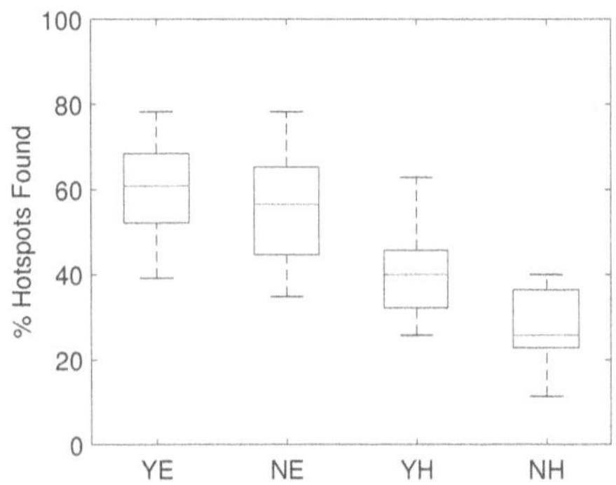

Figure 9: Boxplots for percent hotspots found, showing median values (red) and interquartile ranges (blue).

Measures such as reaction time and response accuracy were used to determine how well the operator responded to incoming messages that defined the secondary task. There were no significant effects due to haptic feedback or world difficulty on secondary task performance. This is not a surprising result because haptic feedback did not directly benefit the operator in responding to incoming messages. It was, however, hoped that there would be some significant difference overall when participants were provided haptic feedback.

5.2 Situation Awareness

There was a significant difference to SA accuracy score due to world difficulty, but not due to haptic feedback. When having the operator give responses to questions of equal difficulty between easy and hard worlds, there was a significantly higher score in the easy world than compared to the hard world. This suggests that the operator had greater task awareness in the easy world because those responses were more accurate, as shown in Figure 10.

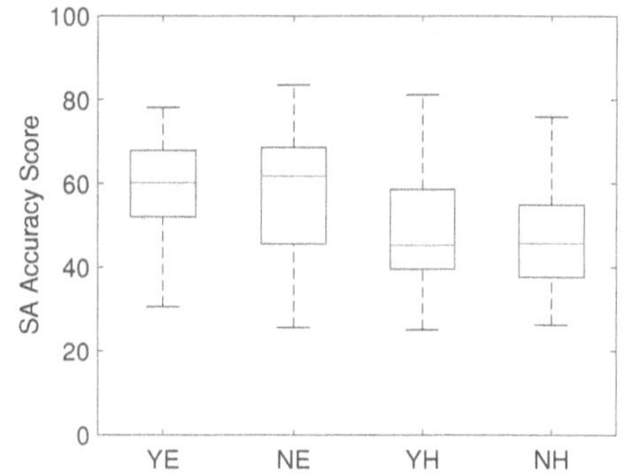

Figure 10: Boxplots for SA accuracy score, showing median values (red) and interquartile ranges (blue).

The SA accuracy score is averaged with the SA response time score to produce the total SA score. Based on these results, the SA accuracy score is useful in measuring key aspects of SA that are not covered by the SA response time measure. There is a slight trend that suggests that haptic feedback may increase SA (N-Y mean = -2.501), but is not significant enough to draw conclusions. These results do suggest, however, that haptic feedback does not have a negative effect on the operator's SA accuracy, which is an advantage of its incorporation with the presented interaction methods.

5.3 NASA TLX Workload

The NASA TLX workload measure returned with significant interaction between haptic feedback and world difficulty ($F(1, 18) = 5.19$, $p = 0.035$). Only one significant difference was found between haptics in the easy world and haptics in the hard world, which can be seen in Figure 11. This suggests that workload increases when managing the team in a harder world, which is to be expected due to a higher task demand. When task demand is kept low, as is the case in an easy world, the operator workload is lower and the presence of haptic feedback has little effect.

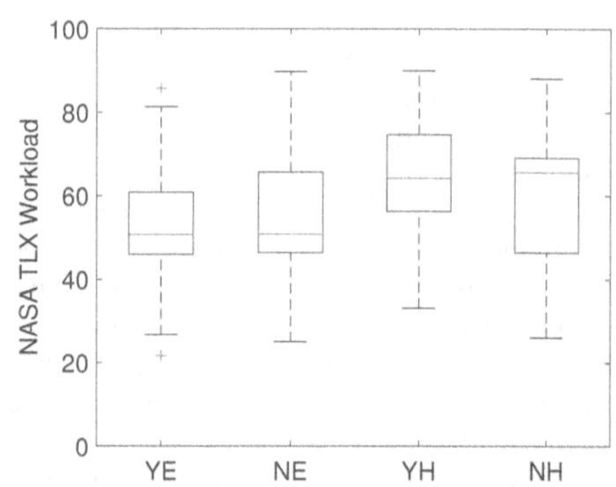

Figure 11: Boxplots for NASA TLX workload, showing median values (red), interquartile ranges (blue) and outliers (red).

There is a slight increase in workload when comparing haptics to no haptics in the hard world (NH-YH mean = -4.757). This difference, however, is not statistically significant and may even be caused by inconsistency of ratings between sessions or a misinterpretation of subscale definitions by participants.

6. DEMONSTRATION MINI-STUDY

Due to the significance of the results from the user study, a short experiment was also conducted to investigate the effects of visual feedback on operator performance with haptic feedback enabled. The aim was to investigate differences in task performance when the operator has obscured vision of the team. The experimental design is identical to the previous experiment, except only the team display is used and sensor readings are shown with team positions. Only 7 individuals were used in this experiment and no statistical analysis was performed.

Results show that with haptic feedback, the operator is able to manage the team and achieve close to the same level of performance without visual feedback of robot positions. As shown in Figure 12, participants performed better with visual feedback enabled. Without visual feedback, haptic feedback still provided enough information for participants to score within 2% in the easy world and 6% in the hard world on average. Workload scores only increased by 1.7% in the easy world and 5% in the hard world without visual feedback. These results complement those of the previous experiment in that haptic feedback does help to improve the operator's heads-up awareness.

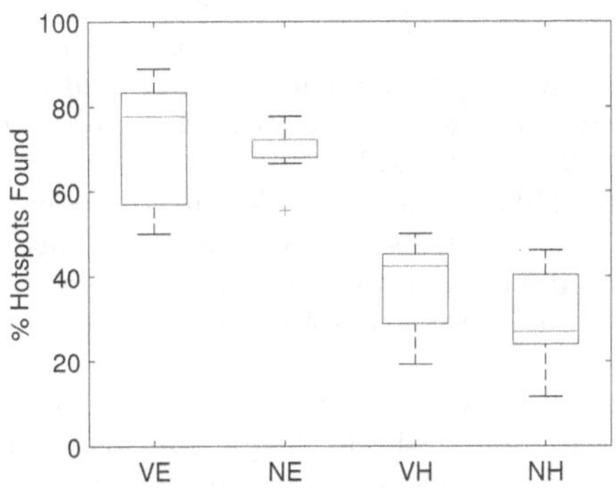

Figure 12: Boxplots for percent hotspots found, showing median values (red), interquartile ranges (blue) and a single outlier (red).

7. CONCLUSIONS

This work presents novel team interaction methods that are based on a modeling clay metaphor. The proposed methods allow a single operator to make intentional, global adjustments to the robot team by treating it as virtual clay. This was made possible by the high level of autonomy that the robots possess. The haptic channel was utilized to improve the virtual clay sensation as perceived by the operator and reduce the amount of information that needed to be visually processed.

A multimodal simulation system was developed as an experimental test bed to investigate the effects of haptic feedback on operator performance, SA and workload. Overall, the results show that haptic feedback significantly improves the operator's ability to find hotspots when task demand is higher. The operator may have used the haptic feedback to more quickly orient the haptic cursor relative to the team in preparation for the next manipulation. Since haptic feedback allows the operator to feel the shape instead of just see it, the operator could look at the sensor readings on the secondary display without even looking at the primary display for periods of time. Observations of the participants' performance throughout the experiment also validate these conclusions. It is clear that haptic feedback did improve performance, and since haptic feedback provides operators with team information without binding them to a visual display, this encourages a more heads-up approach. This improved performance shows that heads-up control of the team can be more easily achieved with haptic feedback than without it.

In the current setup, there were no significant benefits to using haptic feedback during spacing manipulation or travel mode. Haptic feedback likely made no difference in travel mode due to the simplicity of the travel objective. Ultimately, the results from the experiment show that under a higher task demand, haptic feedback made it easier for the operator to maintain heads-up control and achieve a greater level of performance as defined by this specific experimental simulation. Results from the mini-study also suggest that heads-up control can be achieved by means of haptic feedback even without visual feedback. Treating the team as virtual clay shows promise as an interaction model and may be suitable for many other human-swarm interaction scenarios. It is not presumed that this will always be the case, but it is hoped that these results will be useful in the development of future interfaces.

Although there were some improvements in SA score with haptic feedback, they were not significant. The only significant differences to SA score were due to world difficulty level. This does, however, suggest that the chosen SA measurement technique produces SA scores that reflect the expected trend for an operator's SA. The results also show a slight increase in operator workload with haptic feedback, using the NASA TLX measure, but the results were not statistically significant. Given the significant improvement in task performance, however, this trade-off may still be acceptable. With training, haptic feedback can be used to improve operator performance, especially when coupled with an intuitive interaction model such as the proposed virtual clay model.

Future work may include comparing the proposed interaction methods to existing methods to determine whether benefits of haptic feedback can be generalized to all types of interaction. Work could also be done to adjust interaction methods and feedback parameters to optimize user experience and provide more effective feedback. The modeling clay metaphor was used in this work to represent team shape in either surround or travel modes. In developing additional interaction methods, one might consider using this metaphor in other ways such as making topological changes or managing multiple teams at once.

8. ACKNOWLEDGMENTS

This work was funded by the United States Army Research Laboratory through contract W911NF-14-1-0633.

9. REFERENCES

[1] L. Alboul, J. Saez-Pons, and J. Penders. Mixed human-robot team navigation in the GUARDIANS project. In *Proceedings of the International Conference on Safety, Security, and Rescue Robotics*, Sendei, Japan, October 2008.

[2] C. K. Alder. A distributed control algorithm for small swarms in cordon and patrol. Master's thesis, Brigham Young University, 2016.

[3] C. K. Alder, S. J. McDonald, M. B. Colton, and M. A. Goodrich. Toward haptic-based management of small swarms in cordon and patrol. *2015 Swarm/Human Blended Intelligence Workshop (SHBI)*, pages 1–8, 2015.

[4] M. Barnes, F. Jentsch, J. Y. C. Chen, E. Haas, and K. Cosenzo. Soldier-robot teams: Six years of research. *Proceedings of the Human Factors and Ergonomics Society Annual Meeting*, 54(19):1493–1497, sep 2010.

[5] A. M. Brandt and M. B. Colton. Haptic collision avoidance for a remotely operated quadrotor UAV in indoor environments. *Proceedings of IEEE International Conference on Systems, Man and Cybernetics*, pages 2724–2731, 2010.

[6] M. de Berg, M. van Kreveld, M. Overmars, and O. Schwarzkopf. *Computational Geometry: Algorithms and Applications*. Springer, 2000.

[7] M. Diana, J. P. De La Croix, and M. Egerstedt. Deformable-medium affordances for interacting with multi-robot systems. *IEEE International Conference on Intelligent Robots and Systems*, pages 5252–5257, 2013.

[8] M. A. Goodrich. On maximizing fan-out: Towards controlling multiple unmanned vehicles. In M. Barnes and F. Jentsch, editors, *Human-Robot Interactions in Future Military Operations*. Ashgate Publishing, Surrey, England, 2010.

[9] M. A. Goodrich, B. S. Morse, D. Gerhardt, J. L. Cooper, M. Quigley, J. A. Adams, and C. Humphrey. Supporting wilderness search and rescue using a camera-equipped mini UAV. *Journal of Field Robotics*, 25(1-2):89–110, 2008.

[10] H. Jones and P. Hinds. Extreme work teams: Using SWAT teams as a model for coordinating distributed robots. In *Proceedings of the 2002 ACM Conference on Computer Supported Cooperative Work*, CSCW '02, pages 372–381, New York, NY, USA, 2002. ACM.

[11] S. Jung and M. A. Goodrich. Shaping couzin-like torus swarms through coordinated mediation. In *IEEE International Conference on Systems, Man, and Cybernetics (SMC)*, pages 1834–1839. IEEE, 2013.

[12] A. Kolling, P. Walker, S. Member, N. Chakraborty, K. Sycara, and M. Lewis. Human interaction with robot swarms : A survey. *IEEE Transactions on Human-Machine Systems*, 46(1):1–18, 2015.

[13] V. Kumar, D. Rus, and S. Singh. Robot and sensor networks for first responders. *Pervasive Computing, IEEE*, 3(4):24–33, Oct 2004.

[14] T. Lam, H. Boschloo, M. Mulder, M. van Paassen, and F. van der Helm. Effect of haptic feedback in a trajectory following task with an unmanned aerial vehicle. In *Proceedings of IEEE International Conference on Systems, Man and Cybernetics*, volume 3, pages 2500–2506. IEEE, 2004.

[15] T. M. Lam, M. Mulder, and M. M. van Paassen. Haptic interface in UAV tele-operation using force-stiffness feedback. In *Proceedings of IEEE International Conference on Systems, Man and Cybernetics (SMC)*, pages 835–840, 2009.

[16] M. Lewis. Human interaction with multiple remote robots. *Reviews of Human Factors and Ergonomics*, 9:131–174, 2013.

[17] P. Maxwell, A. A. Maciejewski, H. J. Siegel, J. Potter, and J. E. Smith. A mathematical model of robust military village searches for decision making purposes. In *IKE*, pages 311–316, 2009.

[18] S. J. McDonald. Haptic shape-based management of robot teams in cordon and patrol. Master's thesis, Brigham Young University, 2016.

[19] M. J. Micire. *Multi-Touch Interaction for Robot Command and Control*. PhD thesis, University of Massachusetts Lowell, 2010.

[20] R. R. Murphy and J. L. Burke. The safe human-robot ratio. In M. Barnes and F. Jentsch, editors, *Human-Robot Interaction in Future Military Operations*, chapter 3, pages 31–49. Ashgate Publishing, 2010.

[21] S. Nunnally, P. Walker, N. Chakraborty, M. Lewis, and K. Sycara. Using coverage for measuring the effect of haptic feedback in human robotic swarm interaction. *IEEE International Conference on Systems, Man, and Cybernetics*, pages 516–521, 2013.

[22] S. Nunnally, P. Walker, M. Lewis, N. Chakraborty, and K. Sycara. Using haptic feedback in human robotic swarms interaction. *Proceedings of the Human Factors and Ergonomics Society Annual Meeting*, 57(1):1047–1051, 2013.

[23] R. M. Philbrick and M. B. Colton. Effects of haptic and 3D audio feedback on operator performance and workload for quadrotor UAVs in indoor environments. *Journal of Robotics and Mechatronics*, 26(5):580–591, 2014.

[24] T. Setter, H. Kawashima, and M. Egerstedt. Team-level properties for haptic human-swarm interactions. *American Control Conference*, 2015.

[25] D. Sieber, S. Musić, and S. Hirche. Multi-robot manipulation controlled by a human with haptic feedback. *IEEE International Conference on Intelligent Robots and Systems*, 2015-December:2440–2446, 2015.

[26] J. M. Whetten, M. A. Goodrich, and Y. Guo. Beyond robot fan-out: Towards multi-operator supervisory control. In *Proceedings of IEEE International Conference on Systems, Man, and Cybernetics*, Istanbul, 2010.

[27] C. D. Wickens. Multiple resources and performance prediction. *Theoretical Issues in Ergonomics Science*, 3(2):159–177, 2002.

Design and Evaluation of Adverb Palette: A GUI for Selecting Tradeoffs in Multi-objective Optimization Problems

Meher T. Shaikh
Brigham Young University
meherts@byu.edu

Michael A. Goodrich
Brigham Young University
mike@cs.byu.edu

ABSTRACT

An important part of expressing human intent is identifying acceptable tradeoffs among competing performance objectives. We present and evaluate a set of graphical user interfaces (GUIs), that are designed to allow a human to express intent by expressing desirable tradeoffs. The GUIs require an algorithm that identifies the set of Pareto optimal solutions to the multi-objective decision problem, which means that all the solutions are equally good in the sense that there are no other solutions better for every objective. Given the Pareto set, the GUIs provide different ways for a human to express intent by exploring tradeoffs between objectives; once a tradeoff is selected, the solution is chosen. The GUI designs are applied to interactive human-robot path-selection for a robot in an urban environment, but they can be applied to other tradeoff problems. A user study evaluates GUI designs by requiring users to select a tradeoff that satisfies a specified mission intent. Results of the user study suggest that GUIs designed to support an artist's palette-metaphor can be used to express intent without incurring unacceptable levels of human workload.

Keywords

Keywords: human-robot interaction, multi-objective decision making, user interface design, robot path-planning

1. INTRODUCTION

An important part of specifying human intent is identifying acceptable tradeoffs among competing performance objectives. In a multi-objective problem with conflicting performance objectives, the set of Pareto optimal solutions is precisely the set of all possible solutions that satisfactorily tradeoff between the different objectives. Recall that a solution is Pareto optimal if, roughly speaking, there is no other solution that is better for every objective. Since each Pareto solution represents a potentially acceptable tradeoff, specifying intent is roughly equivalent to selecting a desirable Pareto optimal solution.

When a human selects a single solution, making tradeoffs between the objectives creates the need for a robust and intuitive interface that allows a user to select a satisfactory tradeoff without imposing high workload. In a supervisory control problem, given a scenario of (a) what needs to be done — the strategic intent to be accomplished — and (b) a set of ways that a task can be performed, the human (c) determines "how" the task will be done using a GUI.

This paper presents three possible GUI designs that provide a medium to explicitly express human intent for how a task will be done given a set of objectives expressed as adverbs; the adverbs convey what could be important in how the task can be done. The GUI designs allow the human to evaluate different solutions and select one that best matches strategic objectives of the problem. The work in this paper builds from prior work on using Pareto Analysis for exploring tradeoffs [20], which defines the problem as follows:

> The solution points [in] the Pareto [Set] are mathematically indifferent with respect to each other, and thus the selection phase ... is subjectively driven by the human decision maker. This process involves exploration of the [Set], and eventually, the challenge in selecting a solution is to account for gains and losses while adhering to personal preferences.

We discuss different GUI designs and a user study that compares these designs. Generally speaking, the GUI designs are based on the metaphor of an artist's palette, where an artist mixes different colors to produce a desired hue. The adverbs correspond to different objectives to be accomplished; each adverb is a different color, and the mixes of colors represent different tradeoffs between objectives. For example, in a robot path-planning application, consider a command for a robot to "Go quickly and safely from point A to point B." The adverbs associated with these objectives are "quickly" and "safely". Like an artist, the operator can mix the adverbs on the interface such that a *single* path is selected that is both quick and safe from a set of available paths. Results of a user study demonstrate that this

HRI '17, March 6–9, 2017, Vienna, Austria.

ISBN 978-1-4503-4336-7/17/03...$15.00

DOI: http://dx.doi.org/10.1145/2909824.3020225

metaphor can be very useful for helping a human find acceptable tradeoffs between competing objectives.

Figure 1 shows an example Pareto-optimal set for a two-objective problem. Each point in the curve represents a solution and its associated pay-offs for *objective 1* and *objective 2*. The upper left dot represents a solution that has maximum pay-off for *objective 2* at the expense of *objective 1*, and lower right dot represents a solution that has maximum pay-off for *objective 1*. Dots between the extremes represent tradeoffs between the objectives.

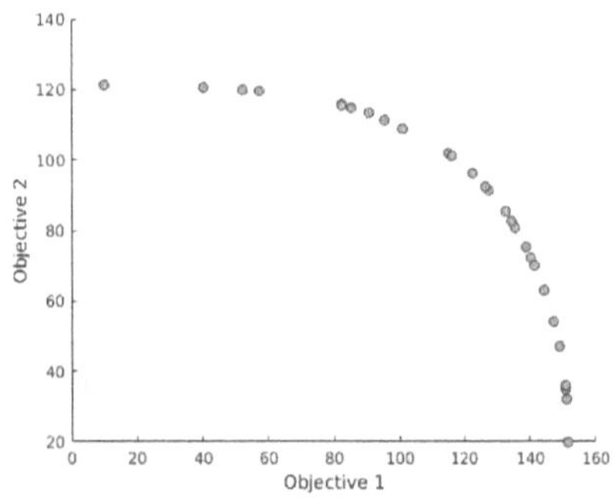

Figure 1: Path Planning with MORRF* for two objectives.

The paper presents GUI designs, *palette*, *sliders*, and *prism*, that are based on the color-blending metaphor and that can be generalized to many problems that require tradeoffs. A fourth GUI design, *waypoints*, is specific to path-planning. The three color-blending designs are described later in the paper.

We apply the GUIs to a robot path-planning problem where multiple performance objectives need to be satisfied. Although there exist many algorithms for multi-objective optimization (see, for example, [16, 6, 7, 25, 15, 2]), we use the MORRF* algorithm [25] because it efficiently generates Pareto optimal solutions specifically for path-planning.

Figure 2 shows an example of one of the designs in AP (the *palette* design) applied to robot path-planning. The left panel of the interface is problem-specific and shows the available alternatives/solutions for the problem. The right panel allows the human to express intent; it is the area where the human can explore many tradeoffs. Based on the human-actions on the right, the left panel updates to show the result/solution. For example, the left side of Figure 2 depicts a map that shows in gray Pareto optimal paths that a robot can take, and the right side of the interface provides an area that can be used by the human to find tradeoffs among the paths. Based on the command issued on right side panel, one of the gray paths gets highlighted on the left panel.

2. RELATED WORK

Making tradeoffs in decision-making is also known as multiple criterion decision-making [24] and multiple attribute decision-making [13]. The goal is to select a decision over available alternatives in a way that balances or trades off between the objectives, i.e, to choose from among a finite set of discrete alternatives [10, 20]. This paper uses three objectives: minimizing distance from the robot's start location to a goal location, avoiding exposure of the robot to one or more enemies, and avoiding collisions with obstacles.

The literature on designing user interfaces for human-machine interaction is vast (see [12, 14, 8, 4, 1] for some examples). There are indeed many graphical interfaces for managing robots in HRI [11, 18, 17, 21]. The interface in the paper differs from these other interfaces in that it is intended to enable interactive decision-making in selecting a solution that satisfies a decision tradeoff. The interfaces in this paper is more similar to decision-support systems than to traditional supervisory control interfaces.

The GUIs presented in this paper are perhaps best classified as ecological interfaces [23, 5] because they seek to enable decision-making easier and more intuitive for a human using a natural metaphor, in this case, a color palette. The metaphor is designed to help a human create a mental model of the tradeoffs and how changing from one solution to another alters how tradeoffs are balanced [22]. The three objectives that we consider are represented by the colors red, green and blue respectively, and the problem domain is supervisory control of a remote robot. Designing interfaces for supervisory control is an important part human-robot interaction (*HRI*), and designing intuitive and efficient interfaces has been a challenging issue in HRI [9, 11].

3. ADVERB PALETTE

The *Adverb Palette (AP)* designs are mouse-based interactive GUIs designed to help a human express intent over Pareto optimal tradeoffs. AP interfaces help a user to trade off among objectives in a way a painter selects colors from a given set of colors. A blend/mixture of colors corresponds to a single tradeoff from the available Pareto optimal tradeoffs. The AP designs are general enough to work for many problems with tradeoffs, and the designs and evaluation are applied to robot path-planning.

The path planning problem is for a robot to go from a start location x_{init} to a goal location x_{goal} within a configuration space (in this paper, a 2-D world). Each GUI has two parts: the *map* in the left panel, which is a task-specific interface that aids visualization of paths, and the *command interface (CI)* in the right panel, which is a general-purpose interface that a user can use to balance different adverbs. The command area allows a user to express intent by balancing tradeoffs, and the map gets updated to show task-specific details by highlighting the corresponding path.

Consider three adverbs, Quickly, Stealthily, and Safely, symbolized by colors *red*, *green* and *blue*, respectively.

- Quickly: prefer shorter paths.
- Stealthily: avoid being viewed by enemies.
- Safely: stay away from obstacles.

Given the Pareto optimal solution set, the goal is to enable a user to find a tradeoff that best expresses his or her intent. Expressing intent has two subproblems to be solved:

1. express a desired tradeoff, and
2. map the tradeoff to a Pareto optimal solution.

We focus on the aspect of human intent that requires satisfactory tradeoffs between competing objectives.

All interfaces include a task-specific map that shows all the routes (paths) in gray. Before tradeoffs are explored, a highlighted path is displayed that gives equal preference to all the adverbs. This paper refines intial *palette*, *sliders*, and *waypoints* from prior work [19] and introduces the *prism* design. This paper also discusses the mapping from intent to solution, and evaluates the designs through a user study. We begin by discussing how to condition the objectives so that they can be expressed using the color-blending metaphor.

3.1 Conditioning Objectives

Objectives may be expressed in incommensurable units, and this causes problems for using the palette metaphor. We perform an affine transformation and normalize objectives so that the multiple objective criterion can be reasonably compared.

Let S denote the set of Pareto optimal solutions, and let the costs associated with a particular solution $s_j \in S$ and objective $k \in \{1, \ldots, K\}$ be denoted by $c_k(s_j)$. (Please check our prior work [19] for cost functions computations applied to robotic path planning).

For each solution, we convert the solution costs to solution pay-offs by multiplying by -1 yielding pay-offs for each objective $p_k(s_j) = (-1)c_k(s_j)$ and then normalize them to $[0, 1]$

$$\hat{p}_k(s_j) = \frac{p_k(s_j) - \min_{s_\ell \in S}\{p_k(s_\ell)\}}{\max_{s_\ell \in S}\{p_k(s_\ell)\} - \min_{s_\ell \in S}\{p_k(s_\ell)\}}.$$

The corresponding normalized vector $\boldsymbol{p}(s_j) \in [0, 1]^K$ for a solution is thus given by

$$\boldsymbol{p}(s_j) = [\hat{p}_1(s_j), \hat{p}_2(s_j), \cdots, \hat{p}_K(s_j)]^T. \tag{1}$$

3.2 Palette

The *palette* displays three initial circles called the "primary dabs," one for each adverb (objective). The user expresses intent by clicking on one of the primary dabs (e.g., take the shortest path) or creates tradeoffs by dragging and dropping adverbs color dabs into the white area of the *CI* to create smaller circles called "paint dab" that blend colors. By creating different paint dabs and then exploring how each dab corresponds to a different path, a user can visualize the consequences of different commands. Line segments connect either the primary dabs and paint dabs or paint dabs to other paint dabs, producing a tree structure that allows the human to see the proportions of each objective.

Figure 2 shows an example command where the user desires a path that is quick and safe but does not care about being seen by enemies, which is represented numerically as " 50% quickly, 0% stealthily, 50% safely ". The pie graph on the lower left area in the *CI* shows the proportion of each objective in a particular paint dab. Blending in multiple adverbs (colors) is thus equivalent to making tradeoffs with multiple objectives. The default magenta paint dab in Figure 2 is an equal mixture "33.33% quickly, 33.33% stealthily, 33.33% safely".

Let dab_d represent any paint dab on *CI*. Let n_i be the number of times the user has dragged adverb i on dab_d, where $0 > i \leq K$. The total number of drags a user makes for dab_d is $n = \sum_{i=1}^{K} n_i$. The *user's intent* from the palette is the vector $\vec{h}^{\text{pal}}$

$$\vec{h}^{\text{pal}} = \left[\frac{n_1}{n}, \frac{n_2}{n}, \ldots, \frac{n_K}{n}\right]^T. \tag{2}$$

3.3 Sliders

Figure 3 shows the *sliders* interface. The user adjusts the trackbars to get to a desired mixture, and the corresponding solution/path from the left panel is selected. The three sliders represent the three adverbs. The user can issue any of the three primary commands to the robot (e.g., take the shortest path) by sliding the corresponding slider (e.g., red) to the maximum units. The sum of the units on the sliders does not exceed 100 units, so if the *red*, *green*, or *blue* sliders are at say $33, 33, 34$ units respectively, then moving the *blue* slider to 60 units will cause a change to the slider units to $20, 20, 60$ units respectively. Unlike the palette, the user can explore different tradeoffs while moving a slider, and settle down to a certain position if she desires it. As the user moves one slider the other two sliders move automatically to maintain the sum to 100 units, and the corresponding solution/path gets shown on the map.

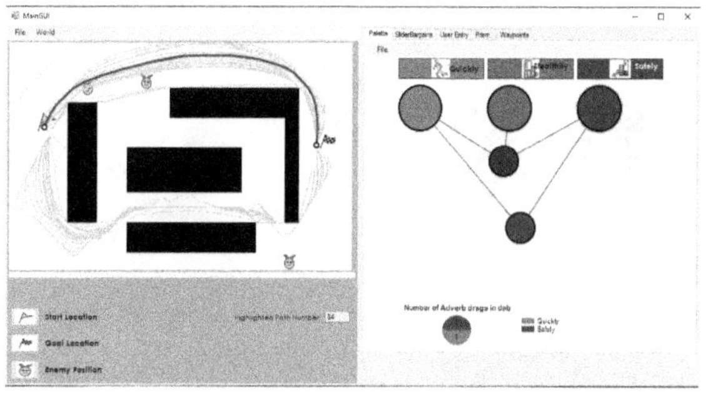

Figure 2: Quick and safe command in lowermost dab: map shows the corresponding highlighted path.

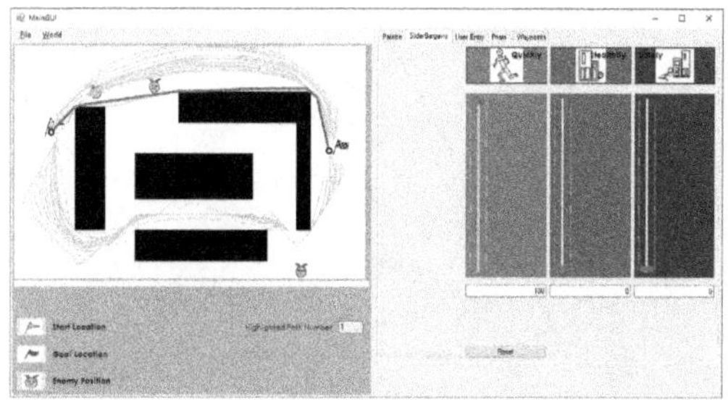

Figure 3: Adverb Palette: Slider interface.

Let s_i is the score specified by slider i. The maximum unit on a slider corresponds to the cheapest solution for that objective and the minimum unit corresponds to the most expensive solution. The *human intent* can be represented as a vector $\vec{h}^{\text{sli}}$ as:

$$\vec{h}^{\text{sli}} = \left[\frac{s_1}{100}, \frac{s_2}{100}, \cdots, \frac{s_K}{100}\right]^T. \tag{3}$$

3.4 Prism

Figure 4 shows the *prism* interface. Here the user can move the mouse over different areas of *prism* and discover its associated paths. Each point on the prism is a color corresponding to a certain proportion of adverbial objectives, expressed using a *barycentric coordinate system.*

As a review of barycentric coordinates, consider a triangle defined by three vertices, R, G, and B. Any point P inside or on the triangle can be written as a unique convex combination of the three vertices. Figure 5 illustrates the concept. The dots on the edges and those inside the triangle are example points that P may take. For a point P there is a unique sequence of three numbers such that the sum of these three numbers is 1. The three numbers, denoted by α, β, and γ

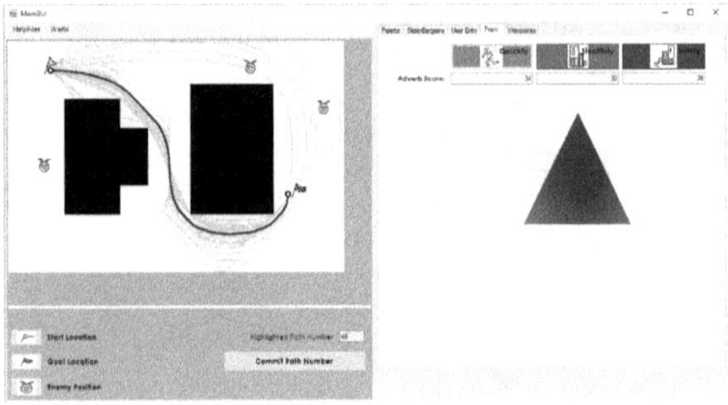

Figure 4: Adverb Palette: Prism interface.

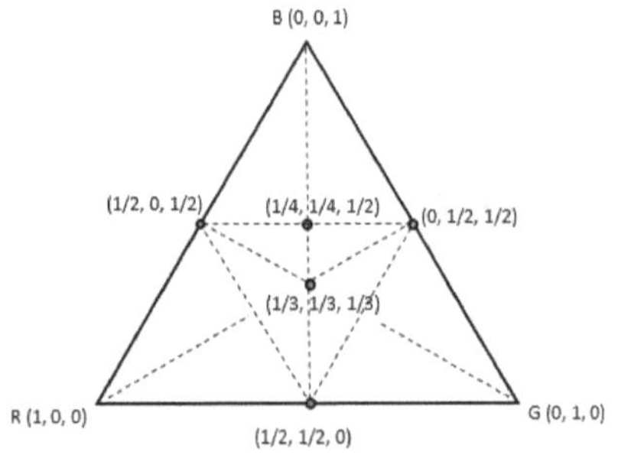

Figure 5: Barycentric coordinates on an equilateral triangle.

indicate the *barycentric* coordinates of point P with respect to the triangle. In the prism interface, α, β, and γ represent the proportion of *quickly*, *stealthily*, and *safely*, respectively. Intent for the prism is represented as

$$\vec{h}^{\text{pri}} = [\alpha, \beta, \gamma]^T. \tag{4}$$

The prism interface only works with three coordinates, and is therefore limited to three objectives.

3.5 Waypoints

The *waypoints* interface is path-planning specific while the other three interfaces are generic AP designs. The *waypoints* interface assists a user to construct her own path on the map by allowing her to provide location guidelines that the robot should visit while taking a path. Unlike the other three interfaces, the user here does not make a tradeoff among the available paths from the algorithm but instead makes her own path on the map. She can however compare her path with the best or worst with respect to an adverb based on the Pareto optimal paths' best and worst for that particular adverb. Figure 6 shows a path constructed using the waypoints interface. The graphs on the right panel show how well the user-created path compares to the best and worst objective scores from the solutions in the Pareto set.

4. MAPPING BETWEEN STRATEGIC INTENT AND PAY-OFFS

The *palette* and *sliders* interfaces produce a human intent vector denoted by $\vec{h}^{\text{pal}} = [h_1, h_2, ..., h_K]^T$ and $\vec{h}^{\text{sli}} = [s_1, s_2, ..., s_K]^T$, respectively. The *prism* interface produces the intent $\vec{h}^{\text{pri}} = [\alpha, \beta, \gamma]^T$. We can interpret this tradeoff in a vector space by associating intent with an orientation/direction with respect to some reference frame. More

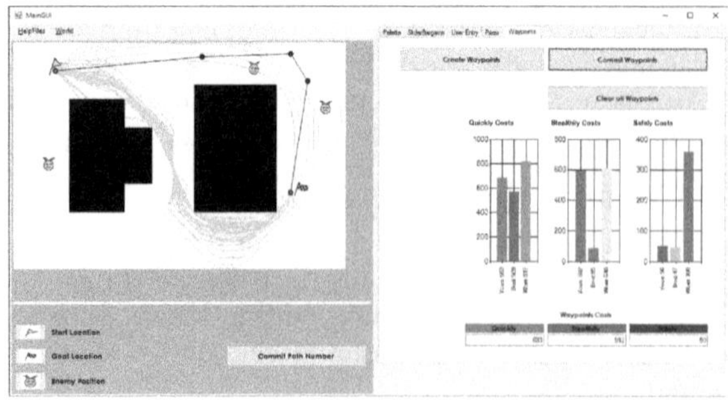

Figure 6: Waypoints interface.

precisely, we operationally define intent as a vector $\vec{h}$ that represents an ideal tradeoff, that is the balance between competing objectives that the human wants to achieve.

The multi-objective optimization algorithm gives a pool of possible solutions. Since each Pareto optimal solution has pay-off values associated with it, it can also be represented as a payoff vector using Eq. (1). Thus we have two vector representations, a human intent vector and the Pareto-optimal solution expressed as a payoff vector.

Given the human intent $\vec{h}$ and the payoff vector for every Pareto optimal solution, we need a mechanism to match the intent to one of the solutions. Intuitively for $\vec{h}$, the solution that has each of the individual pay-off values most closely matching to the corresponding individual intent values would be the one that would be finally selected. The mapping between the tradeoff point and the solutions would then be defined as closeness of the intent to the Pareto optimal solution.

We subjectively evaluated four different mapping strategies. Two of these strategies, WPM and TOPSIS are detailed in [3]. The others that we considered are the popular methods *euclidean distance* and *cosine similarity* for finding similar or matching entities. TOPSIS, WPM, and cosine similarity all gave the same results for mapping. Cosine similarity is the most simple, and subjectively produced better results than euclidean distance.

The cosine similarity between a path vector, $\boldsymbol{p}(s_j)$ and the human intent vector is $\boldsymbol{h}$ is $\frac{\boldsymbol{h}\cdot\boldsymbol{p}(s_j)}{\|\boldsymbol{h}\|\|\boldsymbol{p}(s_j)\|}$. For the given $\boldsymbol{h}$, if the solution $\boldsymbol{p}(s_j)$ ends up with the same orientation, then they have the cosine similarity of 1, and if they are at, say, 90° apart then they end up with the cosine similarity of 0 indicating that they have nothing in common.

Consider Figure 7. The triangle represents the set of possible tradeoffs. Each of the dots on the triangle represents a human intent, and each of the dots to the upper right of the triangle represents a Pareto optimal solution. The dark vectors represent the objective forming the space, stealth, safety, and quickness. The other vectors represent intent and solution vectors. θ_i represents the cosine similarities between the intent vector $\boldsymbol{h}_{\text{ex}}$ and the solution vector $\boldsymbol{p}(s_i)$

5. OBJECTIVE FUNCTIONS

Solving multi-objective optimization problems require computing costs or pay-offs for the involved objectives. Since here we apply AP to robot path-planning, we briefly describe in the following paragraphs the costs computed for a

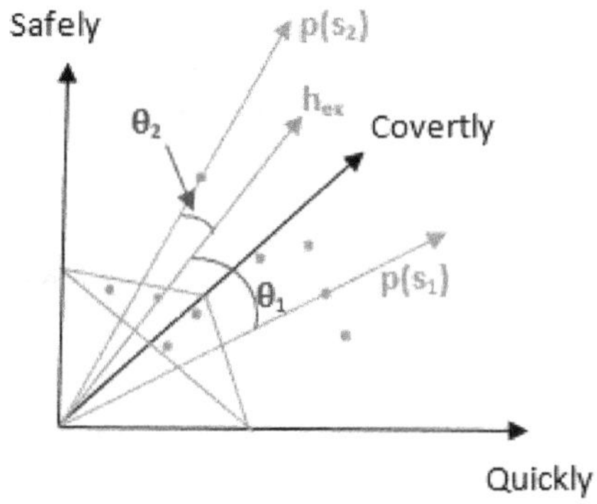

Figure 7: Path Comparison w.r.t example human intent vector $\boldsymbol{h}_{\text{ex}}$.

particular robotic-path. Recall that for this application we consider three costs; *quickly*, *stealthily* and *safely*.

A safe path is a collision free path. Hence, the safety cost of a robot location in a configuration space is encoded as a function of inverse distance between the robot position and the nearest obstacle in that space. The cost can be computed for every possible point in the configuration space. Therefore, the safety cost of a particular robotic path is the accumulation of the safety cost of individual points that make the path; see Figure 8a for an example safety cost for the polygonal obstacles – darker colors are safer.

(a) Safety cost for every robot location.

(b) Stealth function with three enemies.

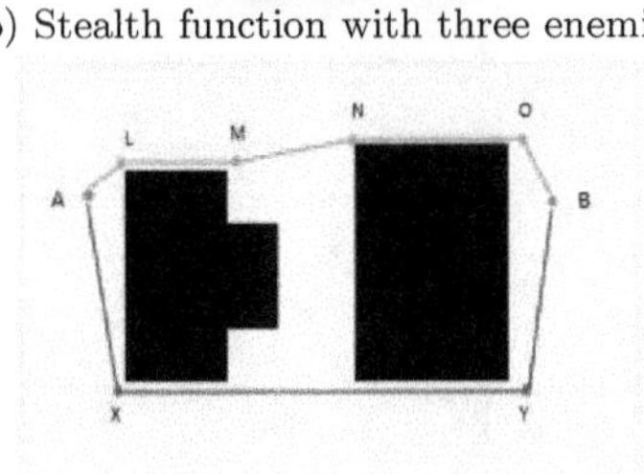

(c) Path **ALMNOB** is quicker than the path **AXYB**.

Figure 8: Objective functions.

A stealthy path is less likely to be detected or seen by enemies in the world. The stealth cost function is expressed in terms of the probability of the path being seen by the enemy, and is computed as a function of two factors: the distance of the robot from each of the enemies and the visibility of the robot from the enemies. The resulting effect yields detection likelihood of the robot from the enemies. The stealth cost can thus be determined for every possible point of the robot location in the configuration space. Therefore, the stealthy cost of a path (starting from the initial state to the goal state) can be determined as the sum of the stealthy costs of individual points constituting the path. Figure 8b illustrates a world with three enemies and its corresponding stealthily objective function. If the robot has to travel from the top left corner to the bottom right corner of the configuration space, a path that goes between the obstacles and lower part of the space is more stealthy than a path that goes through the left side of the left obstacle in the space.

A quick path minimizes path length (assuming constant robot speed). The 'quickly' cost is the euclidean distance between the start and the goal position such that the obstacles do not intercept the path. Figure 8c shows two path options going from start location **A** to goal location **B**. The path distance of the path formed by points **ALMNOB** is less than the path distance for **AXYB**, hence the orange path is comparatively quicker than the blue path.

6. USER STUDY

Following a pilot study among university students to refine the AP designs, we conducted an IRB-approved user study to evaluate the four GUI principal designs. The aim was to discover how successful would be the user in finding tradeoffs among the given solutions using the GUI designs.

Participants were invited for a one-hour study through an advertisement posted in various departments of the university. 24 people participated, 17 males and 7 females, with a mean age of 24.8. All but one participant was a university student. The participants belonged to diverse majors including food, film, elementary education, nursing, and computer science. Each participant received \$15 as compensation. All participants completed all the tasks assigned for the study.

6.1 User Study Procedure

After completing the informed consent process, each participant completed a short demographic questionnaire that included questions on familiarity with using a mouse, exposure to video games, age, and education. The participant then watched a 19 minute video tutorial that described the four GUI designs and showed how to use them in response to a particular scenario or task. Participants were issued a command in written English for the robot to perform such as:

> It is critical to the commander that the robot takes a quick and safe path. Enter the highlighted path number as per this command.

Following the training, participants executed four sets of practice tasks, one for each interface. The practice tasks and the world on which practice tasks were carried out were identical for each interface. Each practice task had an ideal path indicated by a path number, and the task was designed in a way that the user could easily figure out this path on the map in response to the command. The user was allowed three practice attempts to choose the correct path.

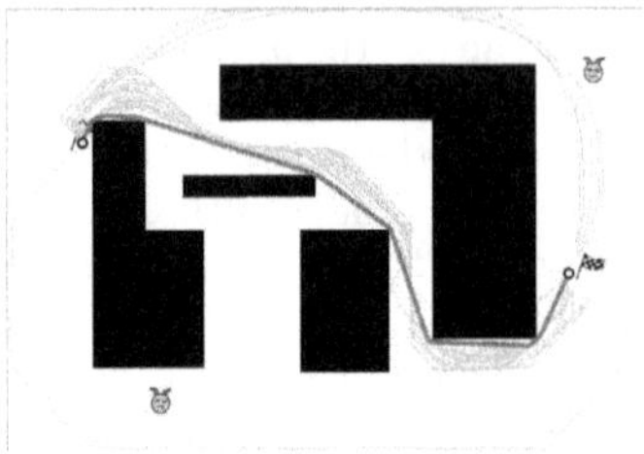

(a) Easy world/command: "Issue a command that makes the robot reach its goal as quickly as possible. Enter path number below."

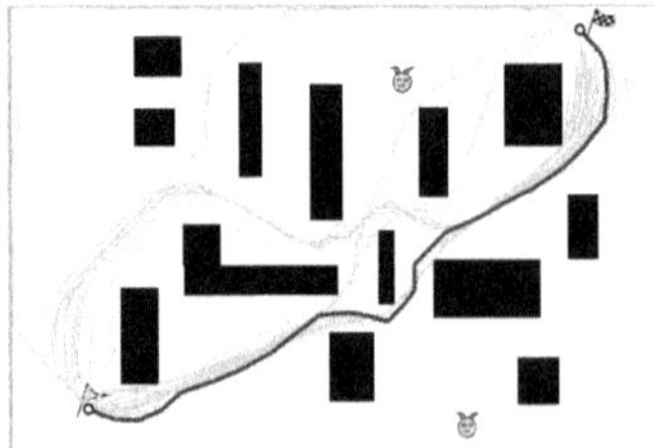

(b) Hard world/command: "It is critical to the commander that the robot takes a path that hides the robot from enemy and that does not come close to buildings. The commander doesn't care if the distance from the start to the goal is big. Enter path number below."

Figure 9: Difficulty level: (a) Easy and (b) Hard.

The experiment was a two-factorial experiment with factors being interface type (palette, sliders, prism, waypoints) and difficulty level (easy, hard). The *difficulty level* is a function of two components: The first component is fairly general, namely, choosing a tradeoff is harder if it has to deal with more objectives/adverbs. The second component is task specific, namely the number of obstacles in the worlds. Hard tasks demand tradeoffs that involve multiple objectives (more than one) and have more obstacles, and easy tasks demand tradeoffs on at the most only two objectives and have fewer obstacles. Four sets of easy tasks and four sets of hard tasks were designed (two tasks in each set), allowing unique pairings of interfaces and worlds. Figure 9(a) and (b) show an example of an easy and hard task, respectively.

Subjective Workload: NASA TLX Scores. Each participant evaluated tasks using all six categories of the NASA TLX questionnaire: *mental demand*, *physical demand*, *temporal demand*, *performance*, *effort* and *frustration*.

Interface Appeal. After completing all tasks, participants ranked the interfaces that reflected their preference for three categories, ranked from most preferred to least preferred. The categories are how appealing the interface is, how easy the interface is to use, and how time-consuming the interface is to use.

Objective Metrics. In addition to subjective workload and user preferences, we evaluated the AP designs using three objective metrics. In each task, a command was given to the participant via the user interface; the command was constructed to describe an ideal path. The first metric evaluates how well participants could express tradeoffs, and the other metrics included both expressing tradeoffs and selecting paths.

- *Accuracy* quantifies the degree to which the tradeoff/solution selected by the user matches the intended tradeoff. Accuracy is measured as the cosine similarity between the intended tradeoff vector and the user-selected tradeoff vector.
- *Interface time* is the time spent performing all tasks required in a particular interface and world.
- *Answer time* is the time spent executing the tasks. For each individual task, answer time is captured from the first click or drag made on the GUI interface to the last click or drag made on the interface. It excludes the time spent to type in the answer for a task. The answer times for each individual tasks are then added to get the total answer times for all tasks on an interface for a particular world.

Participants were not given feedback on whether they executed the tasks correctly or not, and the order of interface/difficulty level was counterbalanced.

6.2 Hypothesis testing

We evaluated the following hypothesis:

1. *Hypothesis 1*: Each AP interface design can be used to successfully complete all assigned tasks.
2. *Hypothesis 2*: Hard tasks have longer completion times and higher subjective workload than easy tasks.
3. *Hypothesis 3*: The interfaces *palette* and *prism* would produce the lowest workload and shortest completion times.

7. RESULTS

Hypotheses were tested using SAS with *Restricted Maximum Likelihood Estimation* for a mixed-design ANOVA using Tukey-Kramer adjustment on subjects.

7.1 F statistics

Table 1 shows the effect of interface, difficulty level, and the combined effect of interface and difficulty on different measures/metrics of user's interaction. The asterisk $*$ denotes significant differences. There were significant differences in interface design and difficulty, but there were few differences for interface plus difficulty level.

7.1.1 Accuracy

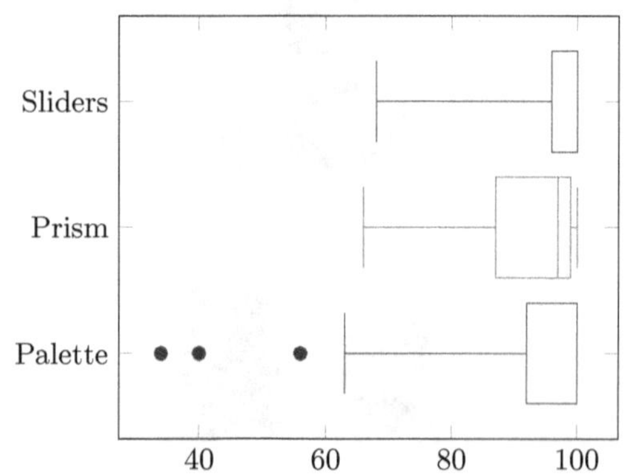

Figure 10: Accuracy of different interfaces.

The waypoints interface was statistically less accurate than all other interfaces, and the other three interfaces had no statistically significant differences; see Figure 10. Difficulty level had no effect on accuracy.

Metrics	Interface (I/F)		Difficulty (DL)		I/F × DL	
	F Value	Pr > F	F Value	Pr > F	F Value	Pr > F
Accuracy	4.28	0.006*	0.02	0.885	3.42	0.018*
Answer Time	44.24	< 0.001*	2.32	0.13	0.16	0.93
Interface Time	98.20	< 0.001*	6.39	0.013*	0.10	0.962
Mental	27.02	< 0.001*	2.33	0.129	0.29	0.832
Physical	8.77	< 0.001*	0.07	0.788	0.16	0.923
Temporal	12.08	< 0.001*	1.25	0.266	0.39	0.762
Performance	17.33	< 0.001*	11.47	< 0.001*	0.32	0.81
Effort	26.05	< 0.001*	5.66	0.0185*	0.21	0.887
Frustation	13.39	< 0.001*	0.87	0.352	0.27	0.846

Table 1: Effect of interface, difficulty level, and interaction of interface and difficulty level on various measures.

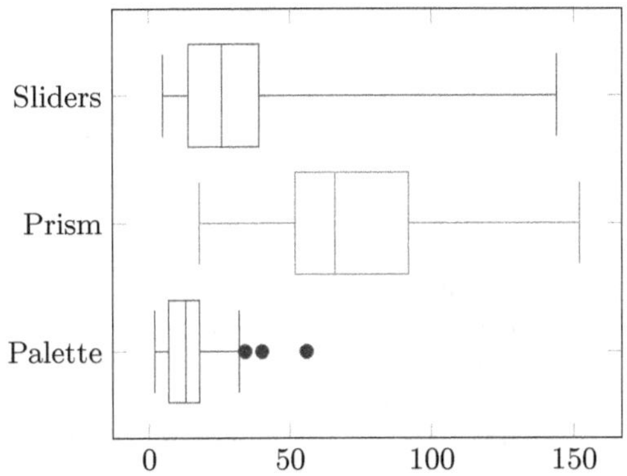

Figure 11: Answer Time in seconds on different interfaces.

Interface	Interface	t value	p
Palette	Prism	-4.31	< 0.001*
Palette	Sliders	-1.43	0.482
Palette	Waypoints	-10.65	< 0.001*
Prism	Sliders	2.88	0.023*
Prism	Waypoints	-6.34	< 0.001*
Sliders	Waypoints	-9.22	< 0.001*

Table 2: Pairwise differences in answer time.

7.1.2 *Answer Time*

Table 2 shows p values for pairwise differences between interfaces for answer time (negative t value indicates that the answer time on *prism* is higher than on *palette*). *Palette* and *sliders* are similar, *prism* is statistically slower than *palette* and *sliders*, and *waypoints* is statistically slower than them all. Figure 11 illustrates the differences for *palette*, *prism*, and *sliders*. Difficulty level has no impact on answer time.

7.1.3 *Interface Time*

Interface	Interface	t value	p
Palette	Prism	-2.48	0.066
Palette	Sliders	-0.79	0.86
Palette	Waypoints	-15.07	< 0.001*
Prism	Sliders	1.69	0.331
Prism	Waypoints	-12.59	< 0.001*
Sliders	Waypoints	-14.28	< 0.001*

Table 3: Pairwise differences of Interface Time.

Except for *waypoints*, which was signficantly slower, interface type did not affect interface time. *Palette*, *sliders* and *prism* were not significantly different (see Table 3).

Task difficulty did have an effect on interface time. *Interface Time* for hard tasks was higher than for easy tasks ($t = -2.55, p = 0.0117$). Table 4 shows the statistics as a function of individual interfaces.

I/F	Task	Interface time	
		t value	p
Palette	E vs H	-3.03	0.006*
Prism	E vs H	-2.92	0.008*
Sliders	E vs H	-2.8	0.01*
Waypoints	0.689	-0.53	0.603

Table 4: Interface Time on different interfaces. t value computed as E minus H.

7.1.4 *Subjective Workload*

We used a 20-point scale/score for each of the NASA-TLX question. Except for the performance scale, a value of one corresponds to least workload factor and the score of 20 suggests highest workload. For the *performance* NASA TLX factor, the highest value is the best. Table 5 shows the values obtained from the mixed-design ANOVA on the partcipant's NASA TLX scores. It is seen that the interface type affects workload. The *palette* and *sliders* have similar workload profiles. Furthermore, *waypoints* deviates from every other interface, and *prism* deviates from *palette* and *sliders*. Summarizing, the workload increased roughly in the following order palette $\prec$ sliders $\prec$ prism $\prec$ waypoints.

Difficulty level impacted two NASA TLX scores. Performance is significantly worse on hard tasks ($t = 3.41, p < 0.001$). Effort was also significantly worse on hard tasks ($t = 2.40, p = 0.018$).

7.2 User Preference

Participants ranked the four interfaces with respect to *appeal*, *ease of use*, and *time consuming* on an integer scale of 1 to 4, where 1 is best 4 is worst. Results showed that all interfaces show significant differences.

Table 6 suggests that the most appealing interface to the users was the *palette* and the least appealing was the *waypoints*. The suggested order of appeal is palette $\succ$ sliders $\succ$ prism $\succ$ waypoints.

Each interface differed significantly from the others in terms of ease of use, with *palette* being the easiest to use and *waypoints* being the hardest. Furthermore, *sliders* was

I/F	I/F	Mental	Physical	Temporal	Performance	Effort	Frustration
Palette	Prism	0.022*	0.02*	0.089	0.009*	0.009*	< 0.001*
Palette	Sliders	1	1	0.93	1	0.97	0.98
Palette	Waypoints	< 0.001*	< 0.001*	< 0.001*	< .001*	< 0.001*	< 0.001*
Prism	Sliders	0.015*	0.02*	0.018*	0.021*	0.034*	0.002*
Prism	Waypoints	< 0.001*	0.596	0.073	0.011*	< 0.001*	0.648
Sliders	Waypoints	< 0.001*	< 0.001*	< 0.001*	< 0.001*	< 0.001*	< 0.001*

Table 5: Pairwise differences for subjective workload computed using NASA TLX. I/F = Interface.

I/F	I/F	Appeal		Ease ofUse		Time Cons	
		t value	p	t value	p	t value	p
Palette	Prism	-6.65	< 0.001*	-11.4	< 0.001*	-13.79	< 0.001*
Palette	Sliders	-2.52	0.06	-5.87	< 0.001*	-9.19	< 0.001*
Palette	Waypoints	-10.08	< 0.001*	-20.23	< 0.001*	-25.66	< 0.001*
Prism	Sliders	4.12	< 0.001*	5.55	< 0.001*	4.6	< 0.001*
Prism	Waypoints	-3.44	0.004*	-8.81	< 0.001*	-11.87	< 0.001*
Sliders	Waypoints	-7.56	< 0.001*	-14.36	< 0.001*	-16.47	< 0.001*

Table 6: Pairwise differences between interfaces for appeal variables.

easier than *prism*, with both lying between the two extremes of *palette* and *waypoints*.

The *time-consuming* variable for interfaces was very similar to *ease of use*. The p-values suggest that each of the interfaces differed significantly from each other with *palette* being the least time-consuming and *waypoints* being the most time-consuming. Furthermore, *sliders* took less time than *prism*, with both lying between the two extremes of *palette* and *waypoints*.

Thus, all the interfaces were different from each other for the appeal variables, where in each case *palette* was preferred to the interfaces with *sliders* second.

7.3 Discussion

Results indicate that *waypoints* interface is significantly worse than the other three. This is not surprising since the waypoints interface requires participants to both plan a path and explore tradeoffs. It takes more time, induces higher subjective workload, and produces paths that differ significantly from the path intended in the command. We ignore this interface and discuss the others.

Hypothesis 1. Results of accuracy showed that there were no significant differences between *palette*, *sliders*, and *prism*, meaning that the users were able to find an acceptabe tradeoff using each interface. Each interface produced at least 90% accuracy, and difficulty level had no impact on accuracy. We fail to reject hypothesis 1, which suggests that each user can use each of the interfaces successfully.

Hypothesis 2. Difficult tasks took more time and subjective workload than easy tasks. We therefore find support for hypothesis 2.

Hypothesis 3. Both *palette* and *sliders* produced similar interface times, but *prism* required more time to answer the tasks, thereby making it significantly less effective. Similarly, both *palette* and *sliders* produced similar subjective workload, and *prism* had significantly higher subjective workload. The results of users' preferences demonstrated that users preferred *palette* to find tradeoffs among the Pareto optimal solutions. The interface *sliders* followed suit, and then *prism*. Hence, we reject hypothesis 3. Instead *palette* and *sliders* were similarly usable, and *prism* was significantly more challenging.

We hypothesize that participants found it hard to comprehend the mixing of adverbs through *prism*. Note that *prism* used the same optimal solutions that the palette and the sliders used, but participants found it hard to know where to click on the prism to get the solution for a task.

8. SUMMARY AND FUTURE WORK

We have presented four interactive GUI designs for selecting tradeoffs from among Pareto optimal solutions to a multi-objective optimization problem. The AP interface designs provide a novel way of blending objectives and enables users to find and express tradeoffs. The user study indicated that the *palette* and *sliders* designs were usable and relatively easy to use because of its metaphor of mixing colors in an artist's way. A rough aggregation of all measures suggests a slight superiority for the *palette* over *sliders*, and both were superior to the *prism* design, presumably because participants had a hard time understanding this interface.

The results from the *waypoints* interface design suggest that providing an interface that explicitly enables a participant to express tradeoffs is useful. Since expressing tradeoffs are an important part of expressing human intent, an interface that helps a user to understand and express tradeoffs may be useful for many problems.

Some of the participants explicitly disliked *prism*. Future work should be performed on *prism* such as naming or scaling the boundaries of the interface so that people can more easily understand how *prism* works.

Since the GUI designs presented here only consider three adverbs, future work should make GUI designs generic so that they can be applied to a variable number of objectives. It is possible that mixing more colors will make the interface less intuitive, so future work should explore the limitations on the interface as a function of more colors. Also, the current application was robotic-path planning. Future work should explore whether the GUI for other applications that require tradeoffs, such as a social robot that must find a path so that it balances proxemic concerns with energy or safety concerns. Finally, future work should explore palette-based designs that do not rely exclusively on color, adding redundant cues to aid easier human perception.

9. ACKNOWLEDGMENTS

This work was funded by the United States Army Research Laboratory through contract W911NF-14-1-0633. All results, findings, and conclusions are the responsibility of the authors and do not necessarily reflect the opinions of the funding organization.

10. REFERENCES

[1] J. A. Adams. Critical considerations for human-robot interface development. In *Proceedings of 2002 AAAI Fall Symposium*, pages 1–8, 2002.

[2] F. Ahmed and K. Deb. Multi-objective optimal path planning using elitist non-dominated sorting genetic algorithms. *Soft Computing*, 17(7):1283–1299, 2013.

[3] F. S. Azar. Multiattribute decision-making: use of three scoring methods to compare the performance of imaging techniques for breast cancer detection. 2000.

[4] M. Baker, R. Casey, B. Keyes, and H. A. Yanco. Improved interfaces for human-robot interaction in urban search and rescue. In *SMC (3)*, pages 2960–2965. Citeseer, 2004.

[5] K. B. Bennett, S. M. Posey, and L. G. Shattuck. Ecological interface design for military command and control. *Journal of Cognitive Engineering and Decision Making*, 2(4):349–385, 2008.

[6] J. Bruce and M. Veloso. Real-time randomized path planning for robot navigation. In *Intelligent Robots and Systems, 2002. IEEE/RSJ International Conference*, volume 3, pages 2383–2388. IEEE, 2002.

[7] A. Bry and N. Roy. Rapidly-exploring random belief trees for motion planning under uncertainty. In *Robotics and Automation (ICRA), 2011 IEEE International Conference*, pages 723–730. IEEE, 2011.

[8] J. Y. Chen, E. C. Haas, and M. J. Barnes. Human performance issues and user interface design for teleoperated robots. *Systems, Man, and Cybernetics, Part C: Applications and Reviews, IEEE Transactions on*, 37(6):1231–1245, 2007.

[9] F. Driewer, M. Sauer, and K. Schilling. Discussion of challenges for user interfaces in human-robot teams. In *EMCR*. Citeseer, 2007.

[10] T. Gal, T. Stewart, and T. Hanne. *Multicriteria decision making: Advances in MCDM models, algorithms, theory, and applications*, volume 21. Springer Science & Business Media, 2013.

[11] M. A. Goodrich and A. C. Schultz. Human-robot interaction: A survey. *Foundations and trends in human-computer interaction*, 1(3):203–275, 2007.

[12] D. S. Hall, L. G. Shattuck, and K. B. Bennett. Evaluation of an ecological interface design for military command and control. *Journal of Cognitive Engineering and Decision Making*, 6(2):165–193, 2012.

[13] C.-L. Hwang and K. Yoon. *Multiple attribute decision making: Methods and applications a state-of-the-art survey*, volume 186. Springer Science & Business Media, 2012.

[14] M. W. Kadous, R. K.-M. Sheh, and C. Sammut. Effective user interface design for rescue robotics. In *Proceedings of the 1st ACM SIGCHI/SIGART Conference on Human-robot interaction*, pages 250–257. ACM, 2006.

[15] L. E. Kavraki, P. Švestka, J.-C. Latombe, and M. H. Overmars. Probabilistic roadmaps for path planning in high-dimensional configuration spaces. *Robotics and Automation, IEEE Transactions on*, 12(4):566–580, 1996.

[16] S. M. LaValle. Rapidly-exploring random trees: A new tool for path planning. 1998.

[17] K. Liu, D. Sakamoto, M. Inami, and T. Igarashi. Roboshop: multi-layered sketching interface for robot housework assignment and management. In *Proceedings of the SIGCHI Conference on Human Factors in Computing Systems*, pages 647–656. ACM, 2011.

[18] D. Sakamoto, Y. Sugiura, M. Inami, and T. Igarashi. Graphical instruction for home robots. *Computer*, 49(7):20–25, 2016.

[19] M. T. Shaikh, M. A. Goodrich, D. Yi, and J. Hoehne. Interactive multi-objective path planning through a palette-based user interface. In *SPIE Defense+ Security*, pages 98370K–98370K. International Society for Optics and Photonics, 2016.

[20] O. M. Shir, S. Chen, D. Amid, D. Boaz, A. Anaby-Tavor, and D. Moor. Pareto optimization and tradeoff analysis applied to meta-learning of multiple simulation criteria. In *Proceedings of the 2013 Winter Simulation Conference: Simulation: Making Decisions in a Complex World*, pages 89–100. IEEE Press, 2013.

[21] Y. Sugiura, D. Sakamoto, A. Withana, M. Inami, and T. Igarashi. Cooking with robots: designing a household system working in open environments. In *Proceedings of the SIGCHI Conference on Human Factors in Computing Systems*, pages 2427–2430. ACM, 2010.

[22] A. B. Talone, E. Phillips, S. Ososky, and F. Jentsch. An evaluation of human mental models of tactical robot movement. In *Proceedings of the Human Factors and Ergonomics Society Annual Meeting*, volume 59, pages 1558–1562. SAGE Publications, 2015.

[23] K. J. Vicente and J. Rasmussen. Ecological interface design: Theoretical foundations. *Systems, Man and Cybernetics, IEEE Transactions on*, 22(4):589–606, 1992.

[24] J. Wallenius and S. Zionts. *Multiple criteria decision making: From early history to the 21st century.* World Scientific, 2011.

[25] D. Yi, M. A. Goodrich, and K. D. Seppi. MORRF*: Sampling-based multi-objective motion planning. In *Proceedings of the 24th International Conference on Artificial Intelligence*, pages 1733–1739. AAAI Press, 2015.

Movers, Shakers, and Those Who Stand Still: Visual Attention-grabbing Techniques in Robot Teleoperation

Daniel J. Rea, Stela H. Seo, Neil Bruce, James E. Young
University of Manitoba
{daniel.rea, stela.seo, bruce, young}@cs.umanitoba.ca

ABSTRACT

We designed and evaluated a series of teleoperation interface techniques that aim to draw operator attention while mitigating negative effects of interruption. Monitoring live teleoperation video feeds, for example to search for survivors in search and rescue, can be cognitively taxing, particularly for operators driving multiple robots or monitoring multiple cameras. To reduce workload, emerging computer vision techniques can automatically identify and indicate (cue) salient points of potential interest for the operator. However, it is not clear *how* to cue such points to a preoccupied operator – whether cues would be distracting and a hindrance to operators – and how the design of the cue may impact operator cognitive load, attention drawn, and primary task performance. In this paper, we detail our iterative design process for creating a range of visual attention-grabbing cues that are grounded in psychological literature on human attention, and two formal evaluations that measure attention-grabbing capability and impact on operator performance. Our results show that visually cueing on-screen points of interest does not distract operators, that operators perform poorly without the cues, and detail how particular cue design parameters impact operator cognitive load and task performance. Specifically, full-screen cues can lower cognitive load, but can increase response time; animated cues may improve accuracy, but increase cognitive load. Finally, from this design process we provide tested, and theoretically grounded cues for attention drawing in teleoperation.

CCS Concepts

• **Human-centered computing → Interaction design → Interaction design process and methods → User interface design**

Keywords

Human-robot interaction; multi-robot teleoperation; attention;

1. INTRODUCTION

Improved robot teleoperation interfaces for applications including the military [38], industrial [42], or domestic tasks [27,29], remains an ongoing research challenge. To improve operator efficiency, a goal of teleoperation is to enable fewer people to control or monitor more robots, increasing the human-robot ratio [31,53], and getting more work done faster. Unfortunately, increasing the information given to operators, such as simultaneous video feeds from separate cameras or robots, results in higher cognitive load and operator error (e.g., [12,35,36,42]). As such, a primary goal of teleoperation usability research is to improve overall operator effectiveness: provide them with the tools and information they need to perform their

HRI '17, March 06-09, 2017, Vienna, Austria
© 2017 ACM. ISBN 978-1-4503-4336-7/17/03...$15.00
DOI: http://dx.doi.org/10.1145/2909824.3020246

Figure 1. Visually cueing a point of interest on a tiled camera feed, e.g., by using a bouncing circle that draws attention to a point of interest (green light, red lines indicate circle movement, and are not shown in the interface).

tasks, without overloading them mentally. We follow this theme, exploring tools to increase performance on visual search tasks.

Emerging computer vision techniques (e.g. [7,47]) can help operators in visual search tasks by automatically identifying potential points of interest, and indicating (*cueing*) the points for inspection. However, it is not yet clear how this information should be cued to an operator to effectively gain their attention, without distracting from the primary task. This balance is not obvious: cues cannot be too subtle, as while attention is focused (e.g., on a search task) people may not notice events outside their immediate focus [50]. Cues that are too intrusive can be annoying, frustrating, and distracting to the point of negatively impacting the primary search task [46].

Drawing from psychology literature on human attention, we conducted an iterative design exploration of using visual cues in a multi-robot search and rescue context. We iteratively designed, implemented, and evaluated cue variants based on cue proximity (at a target point or full-screen) and cue motion (moving or static), while measuring operator visual-search accuracy, response time, and cognitive load. Results indicate that moving cues can help operators find more lights than static cues. Further, cues located at a light, particularly when moving, can be the quickest for operators to assess, but also increase cognitive demand. Well-designed full-screen cues can achieve similar task effectiveness while simultaneously lowering the cognitive load required on operators. In addition to our study results and reflection on these parameters, we present a set of tested, iteratively designed cues that aide operators in visual search tasks without negatively impacting the impact on cognitive load.

2. RELATED WORK

Supporting teleoperation (aiming to increase performance and lower cognitive demands) by modifying how video feeds are presented is an active research area [12,17,27,38]. Much of this has revolved around camera location and viewpoint choice, for example, egocentric views enable an operator to see the world from the robot's perspective [12,26,27], environmental views provide robot-in-context information [17], while bird's-eye and third-person views provide this context calibrated around the robot as it moves [14,39,40]. When multiple feeds are displayed, research has explored layout options, such as displaying all screens in a tiled fashion to maximize available information [44], or using picture-in-picture techniques to prioritize screen real-estate toward more important views [24]. Feeds can be hidden until requested [15], with operators perhaps rotating through them [3] – reducing information load and saving screen space [15]. Rather than projecting views or representing camera placement, we aim to support teleoperation by providing task-specific help: drawing operator attention to points of interest while mitigating the negative effects of the interruption.

The video feed itself is commonly augmented with graphics to represent relevant information, such as sensor data [22,38], or task information as with ecological design [17,29,42], including notifications [9]. We expand on this work, by investigating how to notify users of potential points of interest within a video feed.

In computer vision, saliency detection refers to the problem of detecting image regions that are likely to be salient to a human viewer. This is a complex problem which considers physiology of vision as well as psychology. Saliency detection has been used successfully to shift [52] and predict [7,49] gaze, improve visibility in augmented reality [21], and model analysis of context [10]. It has also been used to modify video scenes, and to draw human attention toward objects (e.g. [52]); in this case, the changes were subtle and the goal was for impacting viewer tendency to look at areas, not direct attention to immediate concerns. For teleoperation, saliency detection has been applied only rarely, to inform interface design of sensor readouts [9], or to minimize transmission bandwidth [47]; here, low-saliency regions use lower resolution, effectively blurring them. We extend this work by investigating how visual cues can be designed to appropriately draw operator attention to such points identified through saliency detection, while aiming to lower operator distraction that may impact task performance.

Human visual attention, particularly for visual search, has a rich history in psychology. Studies frequently focus on static abstract images [10,23,25,48], or abstract videos with colors or shapes changing and moving against solid backgrounds [1,3,8,21–23]. Studies with natural scenes tend to use static images [10,49,50]. Some video work in natural scenes focuses on closed-circuit television monitors [3,11,20,43]. Robots, unlike CCTV cameras, move throughout their environment freely, presenting highly dynamic and noisy camera views from constantly shifting perspectives; further, increasingly dynamic environments tax users' attention resources [32,45]. As such, prior attention results must be specifically evaluated in the unique, high-demand teleoperation context.

Notification work for general desktop applications has focused on *when* to draw attention [4,18,19,30], which does not apply to our task, where operators must be immediately notified and respond in a short time (before a target leaves the screen). Work on *how* to draw attention is much more limited. Some has highlighted how interruptions can be distracting or annoying, and has investigated how to minimize these problems [52], while (recently) noting the lack of solutions to this problem [46]. Further, heavy use of interruptions can lead to users ignoring them [8]. These results, primarily from web and desktop applications, motivate the need for our research in the visually-intense and noisy teleoperation task, exploring attention-drawing cue design that balances being attention-grabbing while not being distracting or being ignored due to fatigue.

3. ATTENTION AND PERCEPTION

Human visual attention – how people choose what to focus their vision resources on – is a well-studied topic in biology, neurology, psychology, etc. Attention can be defined as an enhanced response to stimuli at an attended location and, as a result, reduced response to stimuli elsewhere [50]. Thus, we can expect people to have increased focus on some task elements (e.g., during searching, driving, reading), and, inversely, difficulty noticing things outside of their focus [37], even highly-salient points of interest – this is called inattentional blindness [28]. This is especially difficult during noisy dynamic tasks, such as teleoperation [41]. We aim to work within human patterns of attention to devise visual mechanisms to help gain people's attention and direct it to points of interest, with minimal overall hindrance or additional strain on cognitive resources.

One technique for focusing attention, called goal-based attention, cognitively directs attention to known criteria or stimuli, such as a known suspect on CCTV [20]. Goal-based attention is relevant to teleoperation as operators often have specific, if broadly defined, tasks that drive visual search and cognition such as "find and rescue all victims in a disaster." Complicated search goals (multiple criteria, complex shapes) and environments, such as disaster environments, reduce the effectiveness of goal-based attention [20,37,51]. Increasing the number of cameras will also reduce the effectiveness of goal-based attention due to the increased search area [43]. Goal-based attention quickly reaches limitations in complicated tasks and environments that may be present in tele-robotic search and rescue.

Alternatively, stimulus-driven attention draws a person's attention to salient stimuli, such as bright lights, motion, or high contrast graphics. Interfaces could have objects appearing [13], elements starting to move [1,2], or motion perpendicular to other motion in the visual field [13]; not all changes are similarly salient, for example, color shift, or motion types such as receding motion or movement parallel to other ongoing motions, have been found to be less effective at drawing attention [1,13]. Stimulus-driven design suffers less from fatigue in comparison to goal-based attention, and further suffers less from inattentional blindness, important for long-term attention (vigilance) [11]. As such, we design cues leveraging stimulus-based attention to mitigate some of the limitations incurred by the operator's goal-driven attention.

4. CUE DESIGN PROCESS

Our investigation into how cue design impacts teleoperator performance employed an iterative design process: we drew from perception and attention literature to inform design, devised a mock urban search and rescue task for evaluation, implemented our cues into the mock task, and conducted formal experiments to learn of the impact of our cue designs. Our results informed the design of new cues and conducted more experiments, for a total of one pilot (9 participants) and two formal studies (with 20 participants each).

4.1 Cue Evaluation Test Bed

We developed a test bed that engages participants in mock urban search and rescue, performing visual search on teleoperation feeds, enabling us to test the impact of our cues on visual search.

4.1.1 Task

Participants monitored a collage of four tiled video feeds from teleoperated robots exploring a mock-disaster environment (Figure 1), and were asked to search for stimuli that represented points of interest (e.g. potential victims, dangerous equipment). Participants tapped the screen near the stimuli to show they had identified it.

For our stimulus, we aimed for an abstract stimulus that would more readily generalize to a broad range of tele-operation tasks. As such, we avoided being domain-specific, and potentially confounding variables such as shape or pattern. Our design goal was for an abstract, generalizable stimulus which is unambiguous once found, yet still difficult to find. We chose green point lights as our target. Further, we aimed to increase visual search validity by using a visually noisy scene with realistic robot movement and video quality, building on existing fully abstract perception work by investigating attention in a more representative visual environment.

4.1.2 Teleoperation Videos

We pre-recorded our robot teleoperation videos for consistency across participants. As participants only monitored the feeds, and did not actually see the teleoperators, this is equivalent to live operation for our evaluation purposes.

We arranged a room to have furniture, electronics, and debris scattered around (Figure 1), and remotely controlled a NAO H25 robot over Wi-Fi traversing the space. The video was recorded from the robot's head camera (640x480 at 17 FPS).

We recorded five videos, each having a unique room and debris arrangement, while maintaining similar visual clutter, layout, lighting conditions, and robot movement properties (speed, frequent turns, minimal stopping). We compiled five different (but comparable in character) four-tile collages for a repeated-measures study design. We modified the video selection and position in the collage using incomplete Latin Squares to minimize learning effects. Each video and collage lasted six minutes and four seconds long.

4.1.3 Stimuli (light) Placement and Timing

We placed several centrally-controlled green LED lights throughout the mock environment to serve as our stimuli. Light timing and placement posed several challenges. First, only one light at a time should be illuminated in the entire collage, to avoid confusion over which stimulus a participant noticed. As such, lights could not simply be left on, and had to be triggered as needed. Second, lights should not turn on or off in-scene, as this change itself is a confounding stimulus [13], and should change off-camera. Third, there should be a consistent minimum delay between the stimuli (but not fixed, to avoid predictability), to avoid confusion over which light a participant responds to (we used one second). Finally, light occurrence between the videos in a collage should be evenly balanced.

The coordination of lights turning on and off within a video, and between videos, was non-trivial, particularly given how videos would be combined into various collage configurations. We employed a master schedule that dictated light timing, and made minor imperceptible changes to video speed to ensure all constraints were met. Each video was over six minutes and four seconds long and had exactly 12 light stimuli. Thus, each collage had exactly 48 light stimuli, which showed up on average every 8 seconds. As each video had a unique stimuli timing, the relative timing between the stimuli changed in each collage due to our Latin Square balancing.

4.1.4 Cue Integration into Video

All visual cues were created using post-processing in Adobe Premiere and After Effects. For each experiment, a full set of collage videos were made for each cue (each collage had a version with one cue type applied) to allow for within-participant counterbalancing.

Rather than simply attaching cues to all lights in a video collage, for improved ecological validity we also included false-positive cues (cue without stimuli), false-negative cues (stimuli but no cue), and cue misses (a stimulus, but cue at an incorrect location). These not only simulate the realities of imperfect saliency-detection systems [5], but were designed to imbue a sense of diligence in participants, as they could not completely trust the cueing system.

Further, introducing cueing errors into a system, while realistic, can have overall detrimental effects on performance: operators can lose trust in unreliable cues and overcompensate with increased attention, introducing additional error [2,13,33,34], potentially more than an un-cued case. As such, these standard errors must be part of a test bed for comparing cues to an un-cued base case.

In our case, each collage contained 52 cue instances: 40 correct true-positive cues (77%), 4 false-positive cues, 4 false-negatives (no cue), and an additional 4 cue misses, for a total of 23% error cases. False cue rates were based on prior attention work [33].

4.1.5 Instruments

Participant taps (indicating they saw a light) produced a short beep to indicate it was registered, and were recorded and automatically processed for response time and accuracy. Accuracy was further broken down into correct identification of a light, tapping with no light or cue, and tapping the cue and not the light in the mis-cue case (cue in wrong location). A tap was correct if it occurred in the correct feed within 2 seconds of the light disappearing (a generous upper limit based on an expected maximum .5s reaction time [34]).

After each task (i.e., with one cue), participants filled out a short questionnaire to measure subjective cognitive load (NASA TLX [16]), and custom 20-point Likert-like items (mimicking the appearance of the TLX scales) for nausea, trust in the interface, enjoyability, and self-perception of speed at the task.

At the end of the experiment, participants answered a free-form short answer section on pros and cons of each cue, as well as any comments on any motion sickness, or other comments.

Participants sat in front of a Microsoft Surface 2 tablet, with the video collage displayed in full-screen and at max brightness, with the minimum tilt setting. Participants were not allowed to pick up the tablet or change the tilt. The desk, chair, and tablet displaying the collages that participants used were placed at fixed initial positions, though participants could adjust the chair to be comfortable.

4.1.6 Procedure

Before beginning the experiment, participants are briefed on the task before reading and signing an informed consent form. They were then given a 30-second practice collage to watch, and shown how to indicate where in the collage a light appeared (by tapping). They were told that the videos were pre-recorded using real robot, and were informed of, with examples, of how the cueing system sometimes made mistakes (false cues).

Before starting the tasks, participants are shown example collages containing all visual cues in the order they would appear in the experiment. Participants were told (and reminded before each task) to act as quickly as possible as time was being recorded.

The experiments used within-participants design, with participants completing the task with all cue designs; cue orders and cue-collage mapping were counterbalanced using incomplete Latin Squares.

Before each task we displayed the cue to refresh the participant's memory, and the task started when the participant touched the screen). Between tasks, before moving on to a new que, there was a mandatory three-minute break to mitigate the impact of fatigue; during this time, participants filled out the post-task questionnaire.

After all tasks were complete, participants completed the post-experiment questionnaire, and were debriefed on the experiment.

4.2 Cue Design

Our cue-design methodology was based on our background exploration in human attention literature, as summarized in Section 3. As motion is highly effective at drawing attention [1,2], it is a strong candidate for cue design. However, motion can be distracting [46], and may have a negative impact on primary task performance. Further, in our search and rescue application, the visual field is already noisy: constantly changing as the robot navigates; we need to investigate if motion cueing is still effective in this scenario, or, if the combined motion of the cue and robot becomes even more distracting. We investigate cue motion as a design variable: cues that move (*moving* cues), and cues that do not move (*static* cues). As the light is always moving in the visual field of the robots, we defined static cues to be fixed relative to the moving light.

On-screen cue location is important as it impacts the cue visibility: an operator may be focusing elsewhere when a light appears. Cues located near a light encode the location of the light and thus reduces the search space once noticed [43]. Therefore, we may expect these cues to elicit fast response times, as once a cue is seen, an operator does not need to search for the light. However, due to inattentional blindness, operators may not notice even highly salient cues outside their current attention [41], and so we examine full-screen cues (visible everywhere at once). These should be easy to notice, no matter where an operator is focusing, which indicates to the operator that a target is currently on screen. Therefore, we investigate the cue proximity as our second design variable: cues at the light (*at-light* cues) and cues over the entire visual field (*full-screen* cues).

We use these two design variables, cue motion and cue proximity, to drive our cue design as well as evaluation.

5. INITIAL CUE DESIGN AND PILOT

We conducted an initial pilot study as a broad exploration into cue design for supporting teleoperation visual search, using our two design variables: cue motion, and cue proximity. In the pilot, our full protocol was not followed: we only measured accuracy, and we used an earlier and rougher video collage that was longer, had less rigorous light spacing, and had all cue types intermixed.

5.1 Initial Cue Design

We designed and implemented an initial set of nine cues based on our perception literature exploration and our two design variables.

Our initial at-light (cue proximity variable) cues were *red circle* and *grey circle*, simple outlines, and *exposure*, a disc of increased exposure, over the stimulus. These were chosen to explore the impact of visual contrast, a known factor in salience [11,20].

For investigating movement, we animated the grey circle to bounce one cue radius either left to right (*vertical* cue) or top to bottom (*horizontal* cue). Motion direction, either parallel to or orthogonal to visual flow, can impact salience [1,13]; given that our robots turn often but do not look up or down frequently (except when they fall), *horizontal* is parallel and *vertical* is orthogonal.

For the full-screen component of cue proximity, we aimed to impact the whole visual field, to be difficult to ignore, while simultaneously trying to indicate where the light is. We tried blurring (*blur* cue) or darkening (exposure reduction) the entire screen except for a disc around the light. Both changes in clarity and exposure have been shown to be salient [6,52]. These cues cannot trivially be made dynamic, as simply animating them would not be effective as both the blur and darken effects would not show change as they move.

For our full-screen, moving cue, we drew from video-game design and implemented a common targeting animation: *target* was a circle approximately the size of the screen that appeared and rapidly shrank towards the target. While the shrinking motion should attract attention, particularly as a shrinking circle has orthogonal motion to all visual flow directions [1,13], a risk is that it may appear as a receding motion, which has been shown to be less salient [1].

For all moving cues, the animation lasted for 1 second for consistency across cues; horizontal and vertical bounce cues and target cues all became static grey circles until the light left the screen.

5.2 Pilot Study

Our primary focus of the pilot study was to direct our exploration for more formal study by evaluating our test bed, testing our design variables, and obtaining an initial sense of our cue design successes and failures. As such, we ran our pilot with all eight initial cues (red circle, grey circle, exposure, horizontal bounce, vertical bounce, blur, darken, and target) and compared their impact on how many lights participants correctly identified (accuracy). While we compare data across all cues, of particular interest to us was which cues performed best in each design configurations: at-light static, at-light moving, full-screen static, and full-screen moving.

In addition, we added a case with no cueing (just the light stimuli): this was to measure the overall impact of cueing (e.g., can possibly make performance worse), as well as to test the task itself, to ensure that it was sufficiently difficult to benefit from cues.

5.2.1 Results

We conducted our pilot with nine participants recruited from our general university population. A one-way repeated measures ANOVA showed an effect of cue type on accuracy ($F_{8,64}$=5.71, η^2=0.42, p<.001, Figure 2). Post-hoc comparisons (with Bonferroni correction) comparing all cues to each other revealed the best performing cue for each design parameter set. While Target was the only full-screen moving cue, it was validated by performing statistically better than four other cues. If there was not a clear winner, we simply picked the cue with the highest mean.

In the no-cue case, operators found on average 66% of lights (std. dev 17%). This was comparable to some of the worse cues (exposure, horizontal bounce). This indicates that our test bed and visual-search task are sufficiently difficult, where the addition of cues can potentially improve on the success rate. However, some cues seem to perform at least as badly as having no cue at all (Figure 2).

6. FIRST DESIGN ITERATION

The results of our pilot study gave us initial representative candidates for each design parameter combination: grey circle performed best as our at-light, static cue, the full-screen dark effect as our full-screen, static cue, the vertical bouncing circle as our at-light moving cue, and the video-game inspired targeting as our full-screen

Table 1. Representative cues for testing our cue proximity and movement design parameters.

		cue proximity	
		at-light	full-screen
cue movement	static	circle	dark
	moving	bounce	target

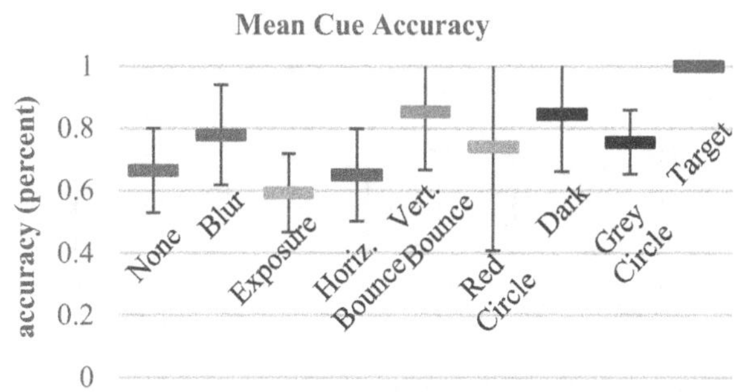

Figure 2. Mean accuracy of our initial cues. Error bars show 95% confidence intervals.

moving cue. We refer to these as *circle, dark, bounce*, and *target*, respectfully, as summarized in Table 1 and shown in Figure 3.

We employed the full test-bed protocol as a within-participants experiment: each participant completed the task with each of the four interfaces. We counterbalanced cue and collage order.

The purpose of this iteration was to more formally and rigorously test our design variables, cue proximity and movement, using our candidate representative cues developed through the exploratory pilot study. We again included the no-cue case to more rigorously test the overall impact of cueing in comparison to the un-cued base case (e.g., cueing may possibly hinder performance).

6.1 Results

We recruited 20 participants (8 female) from the local university population. The mode age (collected in ranges) was 26-30, at 35%.

Repeated-measures ANOVA comparing all cue against the no-cue case) showed an effect of cue type on response time (Figure 4b, $F_{2.8,52.3}$=41.9, η^2=.69, p<.001, Greenhouse-Geisser correction), accuracy (Figure 4c, $F_{2.0,38.3}$=30.8, η^2=.62, p<.001, Greenhouse-Geisser correction), and cognitive load (Figure 4a, $F_{2.2,41.8}$=6.5, η^2=.26, *p*=.003, Greenhouse-Geisser correction). Planned contrasts against no cue showed all others to be more accurate and to have lower cognitive load (*p*<.002), while circle, bounce, and dark had faster response time; no response-time difference was found against target (*p*<.01). While Figure 4 shows overall means and confidence intervals, the within-participants statistics uses relational scores.

We performed 2-way repeated-measures ANOVAs (cue proximity X motion) on operator accuracy, response time, and cognitive load (Figure 5). Bonferroni-corrected post-hoc tests were performed (with main effects) to investigate the effect for each of the levels.

We found a main effect of cue proximity on operator response time: at-light was faster than full-screen (Figure 5b, $F_{1,19}$=107.3, η^2=.85, *p*<.001, 95% CI [-232ms, -154ms]). Post-hoc tests revealed that circle was faster than dark (*p*=.021, 95% CI [-153ms, -14ms]), and bounce was faster than target (*p*<.001, 95% CI [-353ms, 252ms]).

We also found a main effect of cue movement on response time revealing that static was faster than moving, (Figure 5b, $F_{1,19}$=4.9, η^2=.20, *p*=.04, 95% CI [-113ms, -3ms]). Post-hoc tests revealed that dark was faster than target, p < .002, 95% CI [-235ms, -98ms]; static circle versus moving bounce was n.s. There was an interaction effect between the two parameters ($F_{1,19}$=24.3, η^2= .56, *p*<.001).

We found a main effect of cue proximity on operator accuracy, revealing that operators found more lights with at-light cues than with full-screen cues (Figure 5c, $F_{1,19}$=4.4, η^2=.19, *p*<.05, 95% CI [0 lights, 1.15 lights]). Post-hoc tests showed circle to have better accuracy than dark (*p*=.42, 95% CI, CI [-.23, -2.8 lights found]).

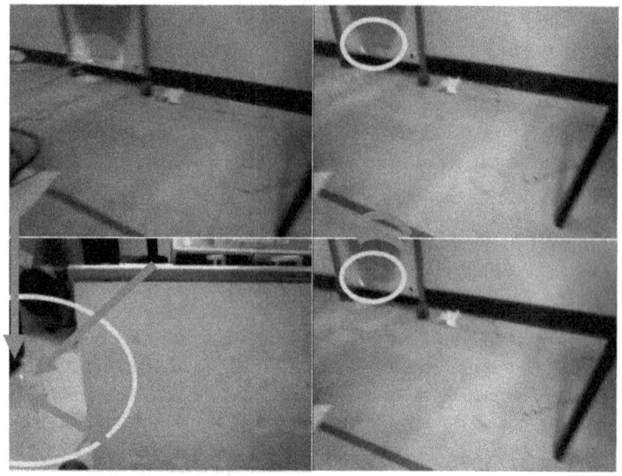

Figure 3. Our four interfaces for the first design iteration: dark (top-left), circle (top-right), target (bottom-left), bounce (bottom-right). Red markup indicates motion and are not shown in the interface.

We also found a main effect of cue motion on operator accuracy: operators found more lights with moving cues ($F_{1,19}$=6.5, η^2=.26, *p*<.05, 95% CI [-1.773, -.177 lights]). Post-hoc tests were all n.s.

We found a main effect of cue proximity on cognitive load, revealing that participants rated full-screen cues as demanding lower cognitive load (Figure 5a, *p*<.01, $F_{1,19}$=8.4, η^2= .31, 95% CI [-9.087, -1.463] NASA TLX points). Tests for main effect for cue movement, and interaction effects were all non-significant.

In summary, the 2x2 ANOVAs indicated that participants were faster and found more lights with at-light cues than full-screen cues, although the full-screen cues demanded lower cognitive load. Participants further were faster with static cues than moving cues, although they found more lights with moving cues.

No effects were found on nausea, trust in the interface, cue enjoyability, preference, or self-perception of task speed. Further, data on miscues and misclicks (when no light was present) were all n.s.

6.2 Analysis of Participant Feedback

To gain insight into strengths, weaknesses, and differences between cues, we performed open coding on short-answer feedback.

Motion cues (bounce and target) were seen by some as attention-grabbing (positive, 16 participants for bounce, two for target), while distracting by others (11 for bounce, seven for target), describing them as being "tiresome," and "stressful to eye," (bounce) or "breaking visual concentration," and "very distracting" (target). Some participants simultaneously praised the attention-grabbing

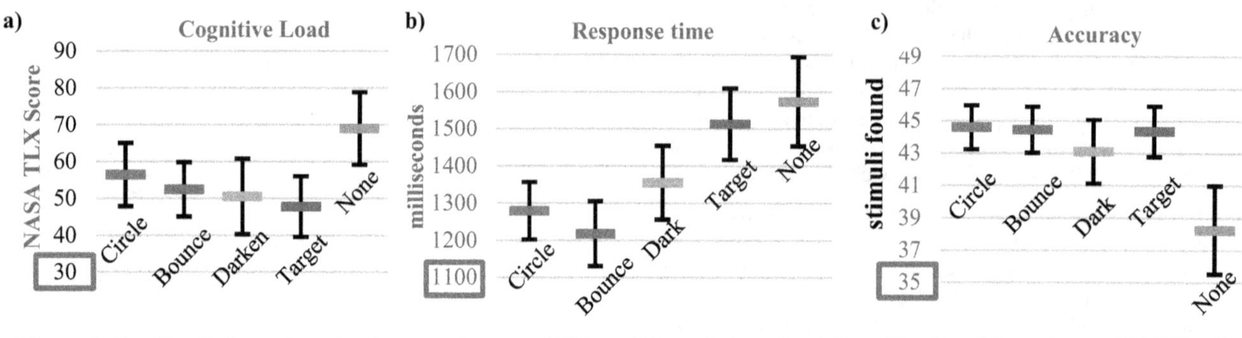

Figure 4. Results of planned contrasts, error bars are 95% confidence intervals. a) Cognitive Load Sum (range [5,120]): all cues performed better than no cue (*p*< .002). b) Response time: Only target was not better than no cues (*p*< .001). c) Mean Accuracy (range [0,52]): all cues performed better than no cues (*p*< .001).

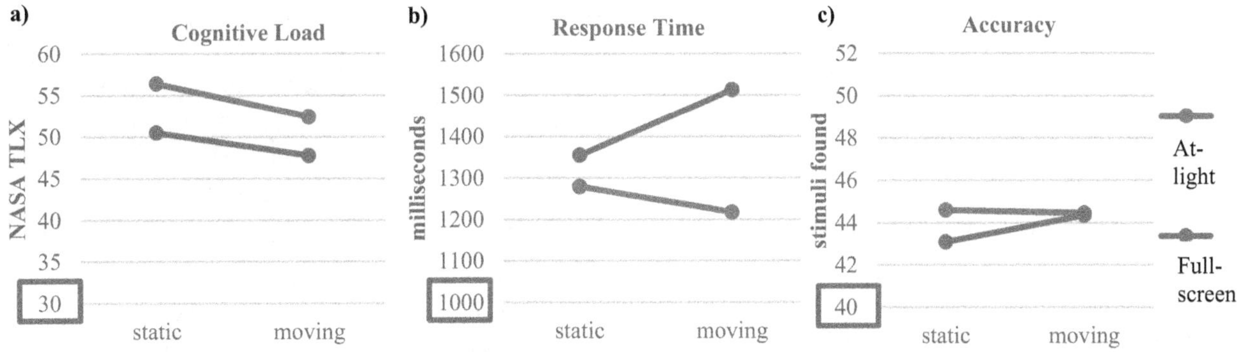

Figure 5. 2x2 (cue proximity X movement) results. a) Cognitive load (range [5, 120]): at-light cues had higher cognitive loads (p=.009). b) Response time (in milliseconds): at-light cues were faster (p< .001), and moving cues were faster (p=.04). An interaction effect is clear (p<.001). c) Accuracy (range [0,52]): at-light (p=.05) and moving (p= .019) had a higher accuracy.

properties of Bounce while commenting that it was too distracting. Static cues had fewer comments on distraction: four participants made comments such as the dark cue being "somewhat distracting," but seven noted that it was "minimally distracting." 11 participants noted that circle was "not easy to locate," and "not very distracting."

Participants commented that full-screen cues positively affected their comfort. Eight participants mentioned that the dark cue was "very relaxing," induced "less dizziness," and was "easy to visualize," and target cue had five comments about reduced stress "it highlights and easy to see. Less effort." Circle had six comments note it was "calm with a smooth motion" and that "appearing without a sense of movement diminished the urgency." No similar comments were given for bounce, but 11 participants complained it was tiring: "made me feel dizzy," "have to cautiously monitor four screens. Stressful" and, "heightened the sense of urgency."

Unique to the target cue, participants complained about its speed: five participants mentioned frustration: it was "too slow to capture the light," and "took focus off other screens for extended periods." No other cue had comments about speed.

Some participants noted the light-position information encoded in the full-screen cues. 10 mentioned that the target cue "helps you to target your focus on one [robot's video]" and that it "can tell me directly where the green light is when it's shrinking." While four people mentioned that with the dark cue the "increase light-to-background contrast made it easier to detect," eight participants conversely mentioned that it only "darkens the whole screen to let you know something has been captured" and required participants to "waste time by locating the image that is less darkened." There were no such comments found for the at-light cues.

Related to comfort, 14 participants complained about some level of nausea from the study. This was not linked to a specific interface, but was attributed by the participants to the simultaneous and often not coordinated movements of the robots.

6.3 Discussion

As with the pilot, our results confirm the validity of our test bed, as well as our cueing technique: all cues increased accuracy and lowered cognitive load, and all but the target cue increased response time (though Target was not found to be worse), when compared with no cue. Therefore, at the least, cueing may be useful to help participants in urban search and rescue tasks. Further, the benefits of our cues, for the results we measured, offset any detrimental effects that may be introduced, such as too much distraction [46].

The analysis of our two design parameters detailed important tradeoffs between design choices. Full-screen cue proximity appeared to demand lower cognitive load than at-light cues. It is not entirely clear why this may be, but participant feedback indicates that some found full screen cues more comfortable and readable, with target specifically being helpful for directing attention to a light. As well, bounce's motion (quick bounces up and down) is different from target's (smooth shrinking) which may also be a factor. Further, full-screen cues may reduce stress of potentially missing a cue, as they are much more difficult to miss.

At-light cue proximity resulted in operators finding more lights, and more quickly, than full-screen cues, despite the increased cognitive load. This can be explained in part by how at-light cues effectively make the stimulus larger. Further, at-light cues immediately indicate where the light is (once the cue is noticed). This can be contrasted with dark where participants complained they had to take time to search for it, or target, where they complained of the slow speed of our moving full-screen target cue which took an entire second to home in on the light.

Note that moving cues had slower response time. This is supported by our planned contrasts on response time: all interfaces except for Target were faster than None. Further, Figure 4b and Figure 5b suggests Target is the driving force behind the response times, performing worse than other cues, except for the no cue case.

For the cue motion design parameter, participants found a few more lights with moving cues in general, and overall were finding the lights faster than with static cues, although the specific results were mixed (the static dark was faster than the moving target). Participant feedback indicated that the moving cues were more salient, which explains the improved accuracy. The attitudes were again mixed, however, with some framing this positively as attention-grabbing or negatively as distracting, although the negative component was not reflected in performance or cognitive load scores.

Static cues were in general the poorest performers, with higher cognitive demands, and slower response times, and some participants noting that they were not easy to locate. This implies that Dark was specifically worse in Accuracy. Participants commented that they could easily see the Dark cue, but had to quickly look for the light itself: there was no position information encoded in the cue. This can be compared to Target which directly led the viewer to the light by the end of the animation.

6.3.1 First Iteration Summary

While the circle cue was better than no cue, and helped operators find the most lights, it appears to have one of the highest cognitive load demands, and did not perform well in response time (except or being faster than target) or accuracy. The dark cue similarly only performed well for speed in comparison to target, and had the lowest accuracy. Bounce was one of the strongest performers, with one of the fastest response times and best accuracies, but had complaints about distraction and fatigue, with improvements to be made in cognitive load. Target, while having speed issues, had one of the stronger cognitive load scores and was comparable on accuracy.

One important component of our analysis was the interaction effect found on response time (Figure 5b), which appears to be driven by the slow target cue. Target's poor speed was also reflected in it being the only cue that did not perform faster than no cue. Thus, we need to be careful about interpreting the response time main effects, as the specific target cue may need design improvements.

7. SECOND DESIGN ITERATION

We draw on our study results to develop a new set of cues to be tested. Some of these are iterations on our previous designs, while others are new designs based on our results from the first iteration. Our main goal in the second iteration was to develop hybrid cues with both static and moving elements, as well as full-screen and at-light elements to see if combining our cue design parameters could improve operator performance.

While the bounce cue was a strong performer, the weak point was the fatigue and cognitive load. We iterate on bounce by adding a full-screen element to try and mitigate these issues, to embed the comfort and cognitive load gains associated with our other full-screen cues. Specifically, we add a border to the video feeds for the duration of the cue, without changing the bounce itself (Figure 6). We hypothesize that this *framed bounce* will have improved cognitive load scores over the previous bounce, without negatively impacting response times or accuracy.

Participants commented on the benefits of full-screen cues encoding the location of the stimulus as well as providing an alert. We designed a new full-screen cue that statically encodes the light position; we hypothesize that avoiding moving elements can reduce frustration (and help with cognitive load), while maintaining the accuracy and cognitive load benefits of the full-screen design. Specifically, we used a greyscale radial gradient (linear, dark at edges, light at center) centered over a light (Figure 6). We anticipate that eyes can quickly follow the gradient from anywhere on screen toward the light as if looking through a tunnel. This encodes location similar to the target cue, but without the time constraint. We hypothesize that this *tunnel* cue will improve the cognitive load and accuracy over bounce, while achieving similar with response time.

As a secondary agenda, we directly iterate on our target cue. We believe that the animation that target uses to shrink toward the stimulus could be much faster, and still maintain its positive character-

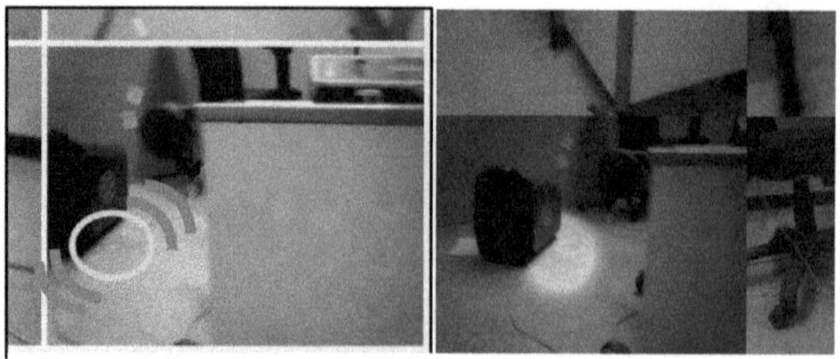

Figure 6. Our two new cues (from the left) framed bounce, and tunnel. Red lines indicate the animation

istics (low cognitive load and strong accuracy). As such, we developed a *fast target* variant which animated three times faster (0.33s instead of 1s). We hypothesize that this improved target cue will maintain the accuracy and cognitive load of target (not do worse), while improving on the response time.

We conducted our full protocol using five cues: framed bounce, fast target, tunnel, regular target (to compare against fast target), and regular bounce (to compare against framed bounce, and tunnel). We keep target and bounce in the procedure to re-test for consistency and improved comparability with within-participants.

7.1 Results and Discussion

We recruited 20 people from around the university campus. Participant ages were collected in ranges; the mode was the 18-20 range, at 55%. We analyzed our data using t-tests given our targeted hypotheses, and did not use more exploratory methods. We summarize these results in Figure 7.

When comparing framed bounce to bounce, we found a trend for framed bounce to improve cognitive load (t=1.6, p=.064, 95% CI [-1.582, 11.682], one tailed). While no difference was detected between response times (t=-1.7,p=.11,[-96ms, 10ms]), framed bounce had better accuracy (t=-2.5, p=.021, 95% CI [-2.290, -.210 stimuli]).

Comparing tunnel to bounce, we found a trend for tunnel to improve cognitive load (t=1.5, p=.08, 95% CI [-1.771, 9.971], one tailed), with no difference found on accuracy (t=1.0, p=.16, 95% CI [-.725, 2.125 stimuli], one tailed). We found tunnel to be slower than bounce (t=-3.6, p=.001, 95% CI [-162ms, -43ms]).

We found that participants had a faster response time with our fast target, than regular target (t=7.6, p<.001, 95% CI [205ms 361ms], one tailed). We did not find difference for accuracy (t=0, p=1.0) or cognitive load (t=-0.9, p=.19, 95% CI [-8.503, 3.303]).

In this study, we successfully demonstrated how hybrid cues can be developed to integrate benefits of cues throughout our design space. Our full-screen plus at-light framed bounce cue had better accuracy

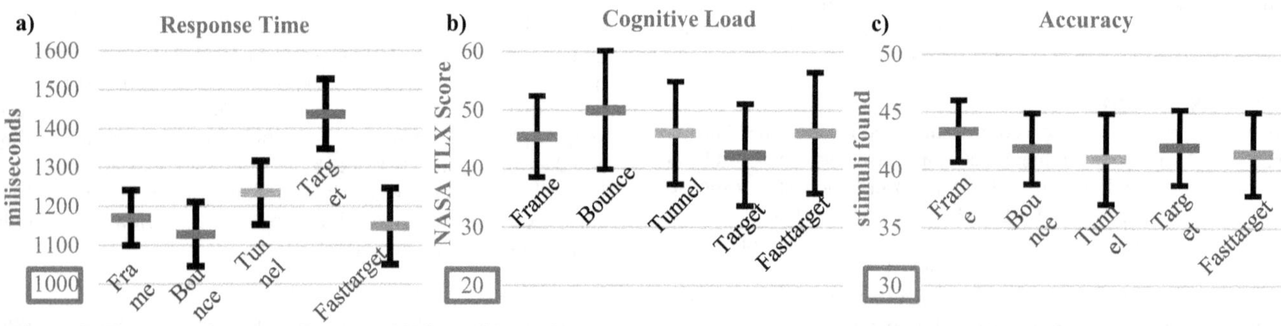

Figure 7. T-test results, error bars are 95% confidence intervals. a) Response time: Fast target was faster than target, bounce was faster than tunnel (p< .001). b) Cognitive Load (range [5,120]): there were trends for framed bounce (p=.064) and tunnel (p=.08) to incur less load than bounce. c) Mean Accuracy (range [0,48]): framed bounce helped more than bounce (p< .021).

than the regular bounce, comparable response times, and potentially improved cognitive load (a trend, requiring further study). At the same time, the failure of the tunnel cue, which may slightly improve cognitive load but harms response time, highlights the non-trivial nature of designing effective cues. It is likely our position encoding failed somehow, as it is a core concept in target, which performs well. Finally, we have demonstrated how our target cue can be improved simply by making it faster, negating many of the problems encountered with this cue in earlier study though our data points to a potential small effect of increased cognitive load.

8. Discussion

Looking across both studies (Table 2), motion and full-screen cues seem to be effective at improving accuracy, response time, and cognitive load. We also made at-light with good accuracy and response time, implying that, at least in our experiment scenario, people are good at searching for local cues as long as they stand out in some way e.g. animation. In both studies, there were still moving (original target) or full-screen cues (dark, tunnel) that did not perform well, which hints at the complexity of the design space; we cannot blindly trust a single or pair of our design variables. We did not see any cue perform worse than no cue, implying that adding visual cues to teleoperation poses little risk, and can add many benefits.

Our process, choosing design parameters and iteratively exploring implementations through performance and user feedback helped us design our best visual cues (fast target, and framed bounce). This is to say, iterative design processes applied to two parameters yielded useful results. Further, studying multiple parameters at once (our 2x2 design) also revealed interaction effects due to design parameters we did not explicitly study (speed). This leads us to recommend avoiding classic single-variable studies, as much richer results can be achieved in a complicated scenario such as teleoperation.

Our work used a scenario that was close to a complicated, real-world task. While the lights our scenario could even be considered more obvious than other urban search and rescue search targets, the no-cue case proved difficult and the results from the perception literature was still effective. The experiment procedure was also a success as the video monitoring method removed the experimental complications involved with controlling multiple robots, while enabling us to easily swap different scenarios (videos) or trying new cue types. We stress, however, our belief that using real robots to record the video is an important ecological consideration. While our study was still "in-lab," we believe our results further validates the attention literature in "messier" ecological scenarios.

False cues were a core component of our scenario design, mimicking previous work, as well as more realistically portraying how real cues in search and rescue would work. A large risk we anticipated was that false cues would undermine trust in the interfaces, and affect performance. Nowhere, however, did we see the false cue rate impact performance enough to counteract the benefit from cueing. Further, no-cue accuracies were low (66-80%) even in our controlled scenario with spaced-out stimuli. This should embolden robot designers to use modern computer vision algorithms to augment their interfaces even if they are moderately unreliable. This technology can improve robotic teleoperation *right now*.

Table 2. Summary of design parameter effects.

Cue Property	Benefits	Drawbacks
Motion	Higher accuracy	Distracting
Static	-	Poor accuracy, response time, cognitive load
Full-screen	Lower cognitive load	Careful design required for good accuracy and response time
At-light	High accuracy, response time	Increased cognitive load

9. Limitations and Future Work

While we demonstrated that changing our two design parameters could affect operator performance, we did not explore the full continuum of these dimensions. For example, our motion cues were only animated for a short time. Similarly, target was a full-screen cue, but after converging on the light, it was an at-light cue. It may be that different positions on the dimensions of cue-proximity and motion, may have different results and complex interactions. Exploring these and other design cues in the context of urban search and rescue, such as color, animation speed, length, and even non-visual cues such as sound, will help future interfaces for teleoperation.

We introduced miscues into our data, but no statistical results were found. We believe this is due to low numbers (20% of our stimuli were miscues). In response-critical situations where operators must correctly identify regions of interest that need additional resources (e.g. life-saving medical personnel), missing or mistakenly seeing a stimulus may incur great cost. While we focused on performance measures, future research could target these miscues specifically by longer experiments or greater participant numbers that allow greater data to be collected, extending the existing visual attention research on miscues to teleoperation.

Another theme that emerged was that cues that grabbed attention could be perceived as either helpful or distracting, similar to previous work [46]. Our experiment hinted that the positive or negative association may be linked to cognitive load – not task performance – and how a cue could be ignored after it was noticed. This is an important balance to achieve with multiple stimuli on-screen at once (a more realistic scenario than ours), as a cue may be so distracting it distracts from other cued stimuli. Investigating performance with multiple concurrent stimuli and stimuli densities would better illuminate how cues can draw attention away from multiple video feeds.

Finally, this research was in the context of teleoperation, but no robots were actually controlled. Single robot teleoperation remains a challenging open problem that will take much of an operator's cognitive resources, so exploring visual attention while actually controlling a robot is important future work. Moving away from teleoperation, our work may be further generalized by comparing visual search with a still camera and moving target as opposed to our moving camera with still targets.

10. Conclusion

In this paper, we introduced our investigation of the effectiveness of visual attention drawing cues in multi-robot control context. To explore cue proximity and cue motion, we designed and evaluated seven different visual cues through an iterative design process. In our mock-disaster scenario, participants found our search task difficult and our cues useful. Our design parameters had tradeoffs in performance and cognitive load, and our results indicated that full-screen and animated cues can improve accuracy, response time, and cognitive load if they are designed well. Our research provides a baseline for more research to understand cueing visual attention in teleoperation.

11. REFERENCES

1. Richard A. Abrams and Shawn E. Christ. 2003. Motion onset captures attention. *Psychological Science* 14, 5: 427–432. http://doi.org/10.1111/1467-9280.01458

2. Richard A. Abrams and Shawn E. Christ. 2006. Motion onset captures attention : A rejoinder to Franconeri and Simons (2005). *Perception & Psychophysics* 63130, 1: 114–117.

3. Pradeep K. Atrey, M. Anwar Hossain, and Abdulmotaleb El Saddik. 2008. Automatic scheduling of CCTV camera views using a human-centric approach. *IEEE International Conference on Multimedia and Expo*, IEEE, 325–328. http://doi.org/10.1109/ICME.2008.4607437

4. Brian P. Bailey and Shamsi T. Iqbal. 2008. Understanding changes in mental workload during execution of goal-directed tasks and its application for interruption management. *ACM Transactions on Computer-Human Interaction* 14, 4: 1–28. http://doi.org/10.1145/1314683.1314689

5. Ali Borji, Ming-Ming Cheng, Huaizu Jiang, and Jia Li. 2015. Salient Object Detection: A Benchmark. *IEEE Transactions on Image Processing* 24, 12: 5706–5722. http://doi.org/10.1109/TIP.2015.2487833

6. B. Bridgeman, D. Hendry, and L. Stark. 1975. Failure to detect displacement of the visual world during saccadic eye movements. *Vision Research* 15, 6: 719–722. http://doi.org/10.1016/0042-6989(75)90290-4

7. Neil D B Bruce, Christopher Catton, and Sasa Janjic. 2016. A Deeper Look at Saliency: Feature Contrast, Semantics, and Beyond. *The IEEE Conference on Computer Vision and Pattern Recognition (CVPR)*. http://doi.org/10.1109/CVPR.2016.62

8. Moira Burke, Anthony Hornof, Erik Nilsen, and Nicholas Gorman. 2005. High-Cost Banner Blindness : Ads Increase Perceived Workload , Hinder Visual Search , and Are Forgotten. *ACM Transactions on Computer-Human Interaction* 12, 4: 423–445. http://doi.org/10.1145/1121112.1121116

9. Jessie Y C Chen, Michael J. Barnes, and Michelle Harper-Sciarini. 2011. Supervisory control of multiple robots: Human-performance issues and user-interface design. *IEEE Transactions on Systems, Man and Cybernetics Part C: Applications and Reviews* 41, 4: 435–454. http://doi.org/10.1109/TSMCC.2010.2056682

10. Marvin M. Chun. 2000. Contextual cueing of visual attention. *Trends in Cognitive Sciences* 4, 5: 170–178. http://doi.org/10.1016/S1364-6613(00)01476-5

11. Fiona Donald, Craig Donald, and Andrew Thatcher. 2015. Work exposure and vigilance decrements in closed circuit television surveillance. *Applied ergonomics* 47, January 2016: 220–8. http://doi.org/10.1016/j.apergo.2014.10.001

12. J.L. Drury, J. Scholtz, and H.a. Yanco. 2003. Awareness in human-robot interactions. *IEEE International Conference on Systems, Man and Cybernetics.* 1, October. http://doi.org/10.1109/ICSMC.2003.1243931

13. Steven L Franconeri and Daniel J Simons. 2005. The dynamic events that capture visual attention: A reply to Abrams and Christ (2005). *Perception & psychophysics* 67, 6: 962–6. http://doi.org/Doi 10.3758/Bf03193623

14. Shinji Fukatsu, Yoshifumi Kitamura, Toshihiro Masaki, and Fumio Kishino. 1998. Intuitive control of "bird's eye" overview images for navigation in an enormous virtual environment. *ACM Virtual Reality Software and Technology*, 67–76. http://doi.org/10.1145/293701.293710

15. Dylan F. Glas, Takayuki Kanda, Hiroshi Ishiguro, and Norihiro Hagita. 2012. Teleoperation of multiple social robots. *IEEE Transactions on Systems, Man, and Cybernetics* 42, 3: 530–544. http://doi.org/10.1109/TSMCA.2011.2164243

16. Sandra G. Hart and Lowell E. Staveland. 1988. Development of NASA-TLX (Task Load Index): Results of Empirical and Theoretical Research. In *Human Mental Worload.* 139–183. http://doi.org/10.1016/S0166-4115(08)62386-9

17. Sunao Hashimoto, Akihiko Ishida, Masahiko Inami, and Takeo Igarash. 2011. TouchMe: An Augmented Reality Based Remote Robot Manipulation. *International Conference on Artificial Reality and Telexistence*: 1–6.

18. Eric Horvitz, Andy Jacobs, and David Hovel. 1999. Attention-sensitive alerting. *Uncertainty in artificial intelligence*, 305–313.

19. Eric Horvitz, Carl Kadie, Tim Paek, and David Hovel. 2003. Models of attention in computing and communication. *Communications of the ACM* 46, 3: 52. http://doi.org/10.1145/636772.636798

20. Christina J Howard, Tomasz Troscianko, Iain D Gilchrist, Ardhendu Behera, and David C Hogg. 2009. Searching for threat : factors determining performance during CCTV monitoring. *Security*: 1–7.

21. Denis Kalkofen, Eduardo Veas, Stefanie Zollmann, Markus Steinberger, and Dieter Schmalstieg. 2013. Adaptive ghosted views for Augmented Reality. *IEEE International Symposium on Mixed and Augmented Reality*, October: 1–9. http://doi.org/10.1109/ISMAR.2013.6671758

22. Brenden Keyes, Robert Casey, Holly a Yanco, Bruce a Maxwell, and Yavor Georgiev. 2006. Camera placement and multi-camera fusion for remote robot operation. *Proceedings of the IEEE International Workshop on Safety, Security and Rescue Robotics*: 22–24.

23. Raymond M Klein, W Joseph Macinnes, Raymond M Klein, and W Joseph Macinnes. 1999. Inhibition of Return Is a Foraging Facilitator. 346–352. http://doi.org/10.1111/1467-9280.00166

24. Tomáš Krajník, Vojtěch Vonásek, Daniel Fišer, and Jan Faigl. 2011. AR-Drone as a Platform for Robotic Research and Education. . 172–186. http://doi.org/10.1007/978-3-642-21975-7_16

25. Árni Kristjánsson, Ómar I. Jóhannesson, and Ian M. Thornton. 2014. Common Attentional Constraints in Visual Foraging. *PLoS ONE* 9, 6: e100752. http://doi.org/10.1371/journal.pone.0100752

26. Annica Kristoffersson, Silvia Coradeschi, and Amy Loutfi. 2013. A review of mobile robotic telepresence. *Advances in Human-Computer Interaction* 2013. http://doi.org/10.1155/2013/902316

27. Daniel Labonte, Patrick Boissy, and François Michaud. 2010. Comparative analysis of 3-D robot teleoperation interfaces with novice users. *IEEE Transactions on Systems, Man, and Cybernetics, Part B: Cybernetics* 40, 5: 1331–1342. http://doi.org/10.1109/TSMCB.2009.2038357

28. Arien Mack and Irvine Rock. 1999. Inattentional Blindness. *Trends in Cognitive Sciences* 3, 1: 39. http://doi.org/10.1016/S1364-6613(98)01244-3

29. Marcus Mast, Zdeněk Materna, Michal Španěl, et al. 2015. Semi-Autonomous Domestic Service Robots: Evaluation of a

User Interface for Remote Manipulation and Navigation With Focus on Effects of Stereoscopic Display. *International Journal of Social Robotics* 7, 2: 183–202. http://doi.org/10.1007/s12369-014-0266-7

30. D. Scott McCrickard and C.M. Chewar. 2003. Attuning Notification Design to User Goals and Attention Costs. *Communications of the ACM* 46, 3: 67–72.
31. Dan R. Olsen and Stephen Bart Wood. 2004. Fan-out: measuring human control of multiple robots. *Human factors in computing systems*, ACM Press, 231–238. http://doi.org/10.1145/985692.985722
32. Jason Pascoe, Nick Ryan, and David Morse. 2000. Using While Moving: HCI Issues in Fieldwork Environments. *Transactions on Computer-Human Interaction (TOCHI) - Special Issue on Human-Computer Interaction with Mobile Systems* 7, 3: 417–437. http://doi.org/10.1145/355324.355329
33. M. I. Posner, M. J. Nissen, and W. C. Ogden. 1978. Attended and unattended processing modes: The role of set for spatial location. In *Modes of Perceiving and Processing Information.* Psychology Press.
34. Michael I. Posner. 1980. Orienting of attention. *Q.J Exp.Psychol.* 32, 1: 3–25. http://doi.org/10.1080/00335558008248231
35. Z. W. Pylyshyn and R. W. Storm. 1988. Tracking multiple independent targets: evidence for a parallel tracking mechanism. *Spatial vision* 3, 3: 179–197. http://doi.org/10.1163/156856888X00122
36. Sina Radmard, Ajung Moon, and Elizabeth A Croft. 2015. Interface Design and Usability Analysis for a Robotic Telepresence Platform. *Ro-Man 2015*, 6.
37. R. A. Rensink, J. K. O'Regan, and J. J. Clark. 1996. To see or not to see: The need for attention to perceive changes in scenes. *Investigative Ophthalmology and Visual Science* 37, 3: 1–6. http://doi.org/10.1111/j.1467-9280.1997.tb00427.x
38. J. Richer and J.L. Drury. 2006. A video game-based framework for analyzing human-robot interaction: characterizing interface design in real-time interactive multimedia applications. *ACM SIGCHI/SIGART conference on human-robot interaction*: 266–273. Retrieved from http://portal.acm.org/citation.cfm?id=1121287
39. Daniel Saakes, Vipul Choudhary, Daisuke Sakamoto, Masahiko Inami, and Takeo Igarashi. 2013. A teleoperating interface for ground vehicles using autonomous flying cameras. *International Conference on Artificial Reality and Telexistence (ICAT)*, IEEE, 13–19. http://doi.org/10.1109/ICAT.2013.6728900
40. Daisuke Sakamoto, Koichiro Honda, Masahiko Inami, and Takeo Igarashi. 2009. Sketch and run: a stroke-based interface for home robots. *Conference on Human Factors in Computing Systems*: 197–200. http://doi.org/10.1145/1518701.1518733
41. Daniel J. Simons and Christopher F. Chabris. 1999. Gorillas in Our Midst: Sustained Inattentional Blindness for Dynamic Events. *Perception* 28, 9: 1059–1074. http://doi.org/10.1068/p281059
42. Ashish Singh, Stela H. Seo, Yasmeen Hashish, Masayuki Nakane, James E. Young, and Andrea Bunt. 2013. An interface for remote robotic manipulator control that reduces task load and fatigue. *IEEE ROMAN*: 738–743. http://doi.org/10.1109/ROMAN.2013.6628401
43. Matthew J. Stainer, Kenneth C. Scott-Brown, and Benjamin W. Tatler. 2013. Looking for trouble: a description of oculomotor search strategies during live CCTV operation. *Frontiers in human neuroscience* 7, September: 615. http://doi.org/10.3389/fnhum.2013.00615
44. Adrian Stoica, Federico Salvioli, and Caitlin Flowers. 2014. Remote control of quadrotor teams, using hand gestures. *ACM/IEEE international conference on Human-robot interaction*, ACM Press, 296–297. http://doi.org/10.1145/2559636.2559853
45. Peter Tarasewich. 2003. Designing mobile commerce applications. *Communications of the ACM* 46, 12: 57. http://doi.org/10.1145/953460.953489
46. Dan Tasse, Anupriya Ankolekar, and Joshua Hailpern. 2016. Getting Users' Attention in Web Apps in Likable, Minimally Annoying Ways. *Conference on Human Factors in Computing Systems*: 3324–3334. http://doi.org/10.1145/2858036.2858174
47. Wei Chung Teng, Yi Ching Kuo, and Rayi Yanu Tara. 2013. A teleoperation system utilizing saliency-based visual attention. *IEEE International Conference on Systems, Man, and Cybernetics*: 139–144. http://doi.org/10.1109/SMC.2013.31
48. Ian M. Thornton, Heinrich H. Bülthoff, Todd S. Horowitz, Aksel Rynning, and Seong-Whan Lee. 2014. Interactive Multiple Object Tracking (iMOT). *PLoS ONE* 9, 2: e86974. http://doi.org/10.1371/journal.pone.0086974
49. Antonio Torralba, Aude Oliva, Monica S Castelhano, and John M Henderson. 2006. Contextual guidance of eye movements and attention in real-world scenes: the role of global features in object search. *Psychological Review* 113, 4: 766–786. http://doi.org/10.1037/0033-295X.113.4.766
50. S. Treue and J. C. Martínez Trujillo. 1999. Feature-based attention influences motion processing gain in macaque visual cortex. *Nature* 399, 6736: 575–579. http://doi.org/10.1038/21176
51. K. VanMarle and B. J. Scholl. 2003. Attentive Tracking of Objects Versus Substances. *Psychological Science* 14, 5: 498–504. http://doi.org/10.1111/1467-9280.03451
52. Eduardo Veas, Erick Mendez, Steven Feiner, et al. 2010. Directing Attention and Influencing Memory with Visual Saliency Modulation. *ACM Conference on Human Factors in Computing Systems*: 1471–1480.
53. Holly A. Yanco and Jill Drury. 2004. Classifying human-robot interaction: An updated taxonomy. *IEEE International Conference on Systems, Man and Cybernetics* 3: 2841–2846. http://doi.org/10.1109/ICSMC.2004.1400763

Evaluating Effects of User Experience and System Transparency on Trust in Automation

X. Jessie Yang
University of Michigan
500 S State St
Ann Arbor, MI, USA
xijyang@umich.edu

Vaibhav V. Unhelkar
Massachusetts Institute of Technology
77 Massachusetts Avenue
Cambridge, MA, USA
unhelkar@mit.edu

Kevin Li
Massachusetts Institute of Technology
77 Massachusetts Avenue
Cambridge, MA, USA
kmli@mit.edu

Julie A. Shah
Massachusetts Institute of Technology
77 Massachusetts Avenue
Cambridge, MA, USA
julie_a_shah@csail.mit.edu

ABSTRACT
Existing research assessing human operators' trust in automation and robots has primarily examined trust as a steady-state variable, with little emphasis on the evolution of trust over time. With the goal of addressing this research gap, we present a study exploring the dynamic nature of trust. We defined *trust of entirety* as a measure that accounts for trust across a human's entire interactive experience with automation, and first identified alternatives to quantify it using real-time measurements of trust. Second, we provided a novel model that attempts to explain how *trust of entirety* evolves as a user interacts repeatedly with automation. Lastly, we investigated the effects of automation transparency on momentary changes of trust. Our results indicated that *trust of entirety* is better quantified by the average measure of "area under the trust curve" than the traditional post-experiment trust measure. In addition, we found that *trust of entirety* evolves and eventually stabilizes as an operator repeatedly interacts with a technology. Finally, we observed that a higher level of automation transparency may mitigate the "cry wolf" effect — wherein human operators begin to reject an automated system due to repeated false alarms.

Keywords
Supervisory Control; Trust in Automation; Long-term Interactions; Automation Transparency.

1. INTRODUCTION
The use of robots to assist humans during task performance is growing rapidly. Robots have been deployed for applications such as urban search and rescue (USAR) [1], border patrol [2], forest fire monitoring [3] and military service operations [4, 5], among others. During these tasks, robots are considered an extension of their operators, providing an on-site presence while protecting human users from potential harm [1]. Although teleoperation has been the primary mode of interaction between human operators and remote robots in several applications, increasingly autonomous capabilities including control, navigation, planning and perception [4-7] are being incorporated into robots, with the aim of reducing human operators' workload and stress levels.

HRI '17, March 06-09, 2017, Vienna, Austria
© 2017 ACM. ISBN 978-1-4503-4336-7/17/03$15.00
DOI: http://dx.doi.org/10.1145/2909824.3020230

One major design challenge for such human-robot partnerships is related to human operators' degree of trust in automated/robotic technology. Trust in automation is defined as "the attitude that an agent will help achieve an individual's goals in a situation characterized by uncertainty and vulnerability [8]". Research has indicated that the calibration between operators' trust and an automated/robotic technology's actual ability is often imperfect [9, 10]. Incidents due to over- or under-trust have been well documented [11, 12]. In order to facilitate proper trust-reliability calibration, extensive amounts of research have been conducted examining the factors influencing human operators' trust in automation [9, 10]. However, most existing research has examined trust as a steady-state variable instead of a time-variant variable, with only few exceptions [13-17].

We, thus, were interested in investigating the dynamic nature of trust. We defined *trust of entirety* as a trust measure that accounts for a human's entire interactive experience with automation. To quantify *trust of entirety*, we investigated a more fundamental research question: is the trust rating reported by a human user at time t evaluated on the basis of the user's entire interactive experience with an automated/robotic technology retrospectively from time 0, or of his or her momentary interaction with the technology? Furthermore, we examined how *trust of entirety* evolves and stabilizes over time, and how moment-to-moment trust in automation changes upon automation success or failure.

We conducted a human-subject experiment involving 91 participants performing a simulated military reconnaissance task with the help of an imperfect automation. The participants' subjective trust in automation and behavioral responses were collected and analyzed. Our results indicated that *trust of entirety* is better quantified by the average measure of "area under the trust curve [17]" instead of the traditional post-experiment trust measure. In addition, using a first-order linear time invariant (LTI) dynamical system, we found that *trust of entirety* evolves and eventually stabilizes as a human operator undergoes repeated interactions with automation. Finally, we also observed differences in moment-to-moment trust changes when human users worked with automation of varying degrees of transparency.

2. PRIOR ART AND RESEARCH AIMS

Human trust in automated/robotic technology (henceforth, referred to as trust in automation) is critical to seamless adaptation of technology, and has consequently been of interest to HRI researchers since as early as the 1980s [18]. Issues of trust-reliability mis-calibration continue to be active areas of research related to human-robot teaming in its various forms [12, 19-21]. Existing research, however, has primarily examined trust as a steady-state measure, typically evaluated through questionnaires administered to human operators at the end of their interaction with automation. Assuming that a human interacts with automation for T time units during an experiment, we denote this post-experiment measure as *Trust (T)*. In several studies [13-17], researchers have viewed trust as a time-variant measure and elicited human operators' trust in "real time" — i.e., during the interaction. Assuming that this real-time measure of trust is elicited during the interaction at time unit t ($< T$), we denote it as *Trust (t)*.

Using a simulated pasteurization task, Lee and Moray [13, 14] proposed a time-series model of automation trust. In this task, participants controlled two pumps and one heater, each of which could be set to automatic or manual control. A pump fault was introduced in the task, at which point the pump failed to respond accurately to either manual or automatic control. Based on the simulation, the dynamic variation was analyzed and *Trust (t)* was modeled as a function of *Trust (t-1)* and the automatic control's performance. Similarly, using a memory-recognition task, Yang, Wickens and Holtta-Otto [15] reported moment-to-moment, incremental improvement to trust upon automation success, and moment-to-moment, incremental decline in trust upon automation failure. Moreover, automation failure was found to have a greater influence on trust than success. The results from these studies suggest that human operators' trust calibration is a dynamic process that is sensitive to automation performance.

More recently, several studies examined how the timing of automation failures affects an operator's trust in automation. Sanchez [22] manipulated the distribution of automation failures to be concentrated at either the first or second half of a computer-based simulation task. In this study, participants completed 240 trials of a collision avoidance task in which they were required to avoid hitting obstacles while driving an agricultural vehicle with the aid of an imperfect automation. Trust in automation was reported at the end of the 240 trials, with the results indicating a significant recency effect: participants' trust in automation was significantly lower if automation failures were concentrated in the second half of the experiment.

Desai et al. [23] explored the influence of the timing of robot failures on participants' trust during a robot-controlling task. In their experiment, participants maneuvered a robot along a specified path, searched for victims, avoided obstacles and performed a secondary monitoring task. Participants could drive the robot manually or use an imperfect autonomous driving mode, which was designed to malfunction at the beginning, middle or end of the specified path. Participants reported their degree of trust at the end of experiment; the results indicated that robot failures occurring toward the end of the interaction had a more detrimental effect on trust than failures occurring at the beginning or middle of the interaction. Empirical evidence from both studies [22, 23] supported the detrimental recency effect on post-interaction trust.

In a follow-up study, Desai et al. [17] explored the effect of robot failures on real-time trust. The participants performed the same task as in the prior study, but reported their degree of trust in the robot every 25 seconds. The "area under the trust curve" was used to quantify a participant's trust in automation. Intriguingly, the results from this study showed an opposite trend as compared to the previous studies [22, 23]: robot failures at the beginning of interaction had a more detrimental effect on trust.

Our first objective for the present study is to reconcile these seemingly contradictory findings by answering a more fundamental question: Does the real-time trust rating reported by the users at time t account for the entire interaction (beginning at time 0), or only the momentary interaction? We define *trust of entirety* as a trust measure that accounts for one's entire interactive experience with automation, and postulate that if trust at time t is evaluated retrospectively, a post-interaction trust rating would be a reliable measure for *trust of entirety*. Alternatively, if trust at time t is evaluated on the basis of the momentary interaction, average measure of "area under the trust curve" would be a more appropriate measure.

Second, we examine how *trust of entirety* evolves as a human gains more experience interacting with automation. As discussed earlier, prior research has examined how the timing of automation failures affects trust in automation [17]. Here, we focus on a complementary question: how does trust, specifically *trust of entirety*, evolve as a human undergoes repeated interactions with a system with fixed reliability? During long-term interactions with a robot, while a designer may be unable to control when failures occur, he or she can design for a desired level of reliability. By studying the effect of repeated interactions on trust, we seek to glean insights into estimating human trust in automation over long-term interactions. We posit that a user, upon repeated interactions with a system, eventually achieves a stable value of *trust of entirety*. We denote this final, stable trust value as *Trust* (∞).

Third, we aim to investigate the effect of automation transparency on moment-to-moment changes to trust (i.e., *Trust (t) – Trust (t-1)*). Automation transparency has been defined as "the quality of an interface pertaining to its ability to afford an operator's comprehension about an intelligent agent's intent, performance, future plans and reasoning process [24]". Previously, Wang, Pynadath, and Hill [19] examined the effect of automatically generated explanations on trust. In their simulation, participants worked with a robot during reconnaissance missions. The robot scanned a city and informed its human teammate of potential danger. Two independent variables were manipulated in this study: robot ability (high- and low-ability conditions) and explanation (low-, confidence-level-, and observation-explanation conditions). The robot scanned eight buildings and made eight decisions per mission. Participants' trust in the robot was measured post-mission. The results indicated a higher degree of trust for high-ability robots and for robots that offered explanations for their decisions. This study shed light on the influence of automation transparency on human operators' trust in automation. Nevertheless, due to the experimental setting, their study did not explore moment-to-moment changes to trust as participants experienced automation successes and failures.

In the present experiment, we manipulated automation transparency through either binary or likelihood alarms. Compared with traditional binary alarms, likelihood alarms provide additional information about the confidence and urgency level of an alerted event [25]. We hypothesize that a high-confidence alert would engender a greater increase in trust upon automation success and a greater decline in trust upon automation failure.

3. METHODOLOGY

We conducted a human-subject experiment to answer the three questions posed in Section 2. Inspired by prior research [4, 5, 26], a military reconnaissance scenario was simulated wherein a human operator supervisory controlled a team of remote robots to gather intelligence with the help of an automated threat detector. Human

Figure 1. Dual-task environment in the simulation testbed. The two images show displays from the simulation testbed for the tracking (top) and detection (bottom) tasks respectively. Participants could access only one of the two displays at a time, and could switch between them.

participants performed 100 repeated interactions with the threat detector. Trust and behavioral responses were collected throughout the experiment. In this section, we detail the experiment setup, design, evaluation and procedure.

3.1 Simulation Testbed

Robots and automation are increasingly being used to support humans during reconnaissance operations. A key function of robots in such applications is to assist humans by gathering information about a remote environment and convey it to the operator. We created an analogue simulation testbed, depicted in Figure 1 that simulates a military reconnaissance scenario.

During the simulation, the human operator was responsible for performing a compensatory tracking task while simultaneously monitoring for potential threats in images of a city provided by a team of four drones. To assist in threat detection, alerts from an automated threat detector were also made available to the human. The participant had the option to trust and thereby accept the decisions of the threat detector as-is, or to personally inspect the images and make his or her own decisions. In this dual-task paradigm, the objective of the human operator was to maximize his or her score, which was a combination of tracking and threat detection performance. We next describe these two tasks in detail.

3.1.1 Tracking Task

A first-order, two-axis compensatory tracking task was programmed based on the PEBL's compensatory tracker task (http://pebl.sourceforge.net/battery.html). Participants using a joystick, moved a green circle to a crosshair located at the center of the display — i.e., minimize the distance between the green circle and the crosshair as shown in Figure 1.

3.1.2 Detection Task

Along with the tracking task, participants were also responsible for monitoring the environment for potential threats.

In each trial, participants received a set of four images from the simulated drones and inspected the presence or absence of threats, with the help of an automated threat detector. We incorporated two types of threat detectors as a between-subject factor, and the reliability of the threat detector was configured according to the signal detection theory (see Section 3.2 for details). An alert was triggered in both visual and auditory modalities.

Participants were asked to report the presence of one or more threats by pushing the "Report" button on the joystick as accurately and as quickly as possible. Along with the detector's alert, the participants had the option of personally inspecting the images. They were allowed to access only one of the two displays — tracking or detection — at a time, and could switch between them using a "Switch" button on the joystick. The participants could perform the tracking task using the joystick throughout the trial, even though they were allowed access to only one display at a time.

During the experiment, participants performed 100 trials of this dual-tasking military reconnaissance mission. Each trial initiated on the tracking display and lasted 10 seconds. The type and performance of the alarm, which varied between the participants, is detailed below.

3.2 Alarm Configuration

We used two types of automated threat detector during the experiment: binary and likelihood. The binary alarm provided one of two alert messages — "Danger" or "Clear" — based on whether it identified the presence of a threat. The likelihood alarm provided a more granular alert: Along with "Danger" or "Clear," it provided two additional alert messages — "Warning" or "Possibly Clear" — implying a lower level of confidence in the detector's decision.

The performance of the automated threat detector was configured based on the framework of signal detection theory (SDT). SDT models the relationship between signals and noises, as well as the threat detector's ability to detect signals among noises [27]. The state of the world is characterized by either "signal present" or "signal absent," which may or may not be identified correctly by the threat detector. The combination of the state of the world and the threat detector's alert results in four possible states: "hit," "miss," "false alarm" and "correct rejection".

Within the context of SDT, two important parameters must be set: the sensitivity (d') of the system when discriminating events rom non-events, and the criterion of the system (c_i) for determining the threshold of an alarm. These parameters are represented in Figure 2. In the present study, the quality of both types of automated threat detector was modeled by manipulating the sensitivity d', which was increased from 0.5 to 3.0 to present an increasing level of automation performance. The first threshold (c_1) was set at 1.0 and was common to both the binary alarm and the likelihood alarm. For the likelihood alarm, along with the first threshold, two additional thresholds were required: c_2, the threshold differentiating dark green ("Clear") and light green ("Possibly Clear") alerts; and c_3, the threshold differentiating red ("Danger") and amber ("Warning") alerts. The values of c_2 and c_3 were set at 0.5 and 3.0, respectively. Benchmarking previous studies [28], the base event rate was set at 30%, indicating that potential threats were present in 30 out of the 100 trials.

3.3 Design

The experiment was carried out according to a repeated-measures, between-subjects design. This design involved two independent variables: alarm type and alarm reliability. The value of alarm reliability was achieved by manipulating alarm sensitivity (d'). Two conditions were present for alarm type (binary and likelihood) and three for alarm reliability (70%, 80% and 90%), resulting in six treatment conditions, apart from a control condition. For each of these conditions, based on the associated values of d',

Table 1. Four possible states according to SDT

		State of the world	
		Signal	**No Signal**
Threat detector decision	**Signal**	Hit	False alarm
	No Signal	Miss	Correct rejection

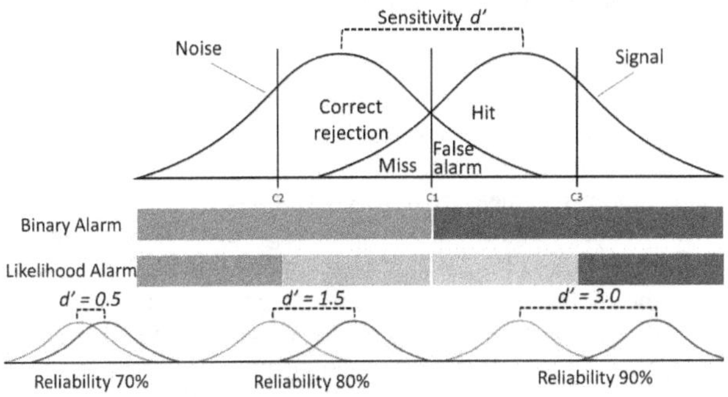

Figure 2. Demonstration of the binary and likelihood alarms, with increasing sensitivity

$c1$, $c2$ and $c3$, the corresponding occurrences of hits, misses, false alarms and correct rejections were computed (Table 2).

A total of 91 participants (average age = 24.3 years, SD = 5.0) with normal or corrected-to-normal vision and without reported color vision deficiency participated in the experiment. They were assigned to one of seven experimental conditions, including six treatment conditions and one control condition. Randomization when assigning experimental conditions was stratified according to participants' self-reported experience playing flight simulation games and first-person shooting games, in order to minimize potential confounding effects.

3.4 Dependent Measures

The dependent variables of interest for the present paper were participants' subjective trust in automation and objective measures of their display-switching behaviors. Working with the same detector, participants completed reconnaissance tasks for 100 sites (100 trials). After each site, participants indicated their subjective trust in the automated threat detector, denoted as *Trust (t)*, using a visual analog scale, with the leftmost anchor indicating "I don't trust the threat detector at all" and the rightmost anchor indicating "I trust the threat detector completely." The visual analog scale was later converted to a 0-100 scale. In addition, for each trial, whether participants switched, and the time at which participants switched their display from tracking to detection were recorded. We used these measures to compute participants' trusting behaviors, which will be discussed in Section 4.1.

3.5 Procedure

Participants signed an informed consent form and provided demographic information. They then received the following description and instructions:

"A group of potential threats has taken over a city, and we are sending you in together with four drones to find out where the threats are before a reinforcement team comes. As a soldier, you have two tasks at the same time: First, you have to make sure that the drones are maintaining level flight. Due to external turbulences, the drones (indicated as the green circle) will be unstable and the green circle will move away from the center (indicated as the crosshair sign). You will control the joystick and move the green circle back to the center as close as possible. At the same time, the four drones will navigate in the city and take surveillance pictures every 10 seconds. The pictures will be sent back to you for threat detection. You need to report to your commander if you identify a potential threat as accurately and as fast as possible by pressing the "Report" button. Due to resource limitations, you can only access one display at a time and you need to press the "Switch" button to switch between the tracking and the detection display. There is an automated threat detector to help you with the task."

If a participant was assigned to a binary alarm condition, they were told the following: "If the detector identifies a threat at a site, the red light in the detector will be on and you will also hear the sound 'Danger.' If the detector identifies there is no threat, the green light will be on and you will hear the sound 'Clear.'

If a participant was assigned to a likelihood alarm condition, they were told the following: "If the detector identifies a threat at a site, either the red light or the amber light will be on, and you will also hear the sound 'Danger' or 'Warning,' respectively. The red light and the 'Danger' sound indicate a higher level of confidence and the amber light and 'Warning' sound indicates a lower level of confidence. If the detector identifies no threat, either the dark green or the light green light will be on, and you will hear the sound 'Clear' or 'Possibly Clear.' The dark green light and the 'Clear' sound indicate a higher level of confidence that the site is safe. The light green light and the 'Possibly clear' sound mean a lower level of confidence that the site is safe.''

Table 2. Alarm configurations and corresponding numbers of hits, misses, false alarms and correct rejections

Reliability = 70%					
Binary alarm			Likelihood alarm		
Alert	Threat	Clear	Alert	Threat	Clear
Danger	9	11	Danger	5	5
			Warning	4	6
Clear	21	59	Possibly clear	6	11
			Clear	15	48
Reliability = 80%					
Binary alarm			Likelihood alarm		
Alert	Threat	Clear	Alert	Threat	Clear
Danger	21	11	Danger	15	5
			Warning	6	6
Clear	9	59	Possibly clear	4	11
			Clear	5	48
Reliability = 90%					
Binary alarm			Likelihood alarm		
Alert	Threat	Clear	Alert	Threat	Clear
Danger	29	11	Danger	28	5
			Warning	1	6
Clear	1	59	Possibly clear	1	11
			Clear	0	48

After the introduction, participants completed a practice session consisting of a 30-trial block of the tracking task only, followed by an eight-trial block including both the tracking task and the detection task. Hits, misses, false alarms and correct rejections were illustrated during the eight practice trials of combined tasks. The participants were told that the alerts from the automated threat detector may or may not be correct. The subsequent experimental block consisted of 100 trials, lasting approximately 60 minutes with a 5-minute break at the halfway point. Each participant received compensation consisting of a $10 base plus a bonus up to $5. The compensation scheme was determined through a pilot study, incentivizing participants to perform well on both tasks.

4. ANALYSIS AND RESULTS

In this section, we discuss the observations, data and results from our experiment. We first examine which user-reported trust measures are good indicators of *trust of entirety*. Next, we present a novel model to explain the evolution of *trust of entirety* over time. Finally, we present our findings on the relationship between automation transparency and moment-to-moment trust changes. Data from participants in the control group was excluded from the subsequent analysis, as they did not receive any automation aid and did not report subjective trust.

4.1 Indicators of Trust of Entirety

In prior literature, two measures of trust have been used to quantify *trust of entirety*: $Trust_{end}$, the trust rating elicited after the terminal trial T, and $Trust_{AUTC}$, the area under the trust curve. For our experiment, we computed these quantities as follows (note that the computation of $Trust_{AUTC}$ included averaging of trust across number of interactions):

$$Trust_{end} = Trust_T$$

$$Trust_{AUTC} = \frac{1}{T}\sum_1^T Trust_t, \text{ where T = number of interactions}$$

To examine whether $Trust_{end}$ or $Trust_{AUTC}$ corresponds to *trust of entirety* more appropriately, we calculated the correlation between the two subjective trust measures and the participants' trusting behaviors including their reliance and compliance behaviors. Reliance has been defined in prior literature as the human operator's cognitive state when automation indicates no signal (no threat); compliance represents the human operator's cognitive state when automation indicates a signal (threat) [29].

In the present study, we measured both response rate (RR) and response time (RT). Reliance is characterized by trusting the automation to indicate "Clear" or "Possibly Clear" in the absence of a threat, and thus no switch or a slower switch from the tracking task to the detection task. Compliance is characterized by trusting the automation to signal "Danger" or "Warning" in the presence of one or more threats, and thus reporting threats blindly with no switch to the detection task, or a rapid switch from the tracking task to the detection task. Further, we calculated the difference between reliance RT and compliance RT. This measure eliminates potential confounding effects due to participants' intrinsic characteristics of switching behaviors (i.e., participants may switch more quickly or slowly regardless of the alerts [22]).

$Compliance_{RR}(C_{RR}) =$
$Prob(report\ without\ switch\ |danger\ or\ warning\ alerts)$

$Reliance_{RR}(R_{RR}) =$
$Prob(not\ report\ without\ switch\ |\ clear\ or\ possibly\ clear\ alerts)$

$Compliance_{RT}(C_{RT}) =$
$Time\ (first\ switch\ |danger\ or\ caution\ alerts)$

$Reliance_{RT}(R_{RT}) =$
$Time\ (first\ switch|clear\ or\ possibly\ clear\ alerts)$

Table 3. Pearson correlation coefficient between trust measures and participants' trusting behavior ($^*p < .05$; $^{**}p < .01$)

	C_{RR}	C_{RT}	R_{RR}	R_{RT}	R_{RT} - C_{RT}
$Trust_{end}$	n.s.	n.s.	n.s.	n.s.	n.s.
$Trust_{AUTC}$	.31**	n.s.	.31**	n.s.	.26*

Table 3 summarizes results from Pearson's correlation analysis. $Trust_{AUTC}$ was significantly correlated with C_{RR}, R_{RR}, *and* (R_{RT} - C_{RT}), while $Trust_{end}$ was not significantly correlated with any of the behavioral measures. These results indicate that a user's degree of trust reported at time t is more influenced by their momentary interaction with automation. Therefore, we claim that $Trust_{AUTC}$ is a more appropriate measure of *trust of entirety*.

This finding could explain the seemingly contradictory findings in previous studies [17, 22, 23]: when automation failures occurred toward the end of an experiment, it resulted in a momentary decline in trust. As $Trust_{end}$ was used in these studies to quantify participants' entire interactive experience with automation, it was more severely affected as compared with a condition under which automation failures occurred at the beginning of the interactive process.

For clarification, from this point onward we use $Trust_e$ to denote *trust of entirety*. Further, in subsequent analysis $Trust_{AUTC}$ is used as an indicator for trust of entirety, $Trust_e$.

4.2 Effect of Experience on Trust$_e$-Reliability Calibration

Issues due to over- and under-trust have been a challenge for the adoption of automation, highlighting the need to investigate not only trust-reliability calibration but also how it evolves with experience. Using repeated measurements of self-reported trust, we assessed how $Trust_e$ -reliability calibration varied across trials.

A trust-reliability calibration curve depicts the correspondence between trust and reliability over a wide spectrum of automation reliability [11]. To plot the $Trust_e$-reliability calibration curve, $Trust_e$ was regressed against automation reliability. Figure 3 depicts the slope variation for the $Trust_e$-reliability calibration curve with respect to automation experience (trial number) and Figures 4 and 5 show the calibration curves for the 1st, 50th, and 100th trial, respectively, with the black line indicating the regression line, the blue lines the 95% confidence interval and the red lines the 95% predictive band. Figures 3-5 indicate that the calibration curves change with automation experience for both alarm types. In addition, for both alarm types, the calibration curve became steeper as human operators gained more experience with the threat detector. Further, the slope of the likelihood alarm curve increased more rapidly than that of the binary alarm curve.

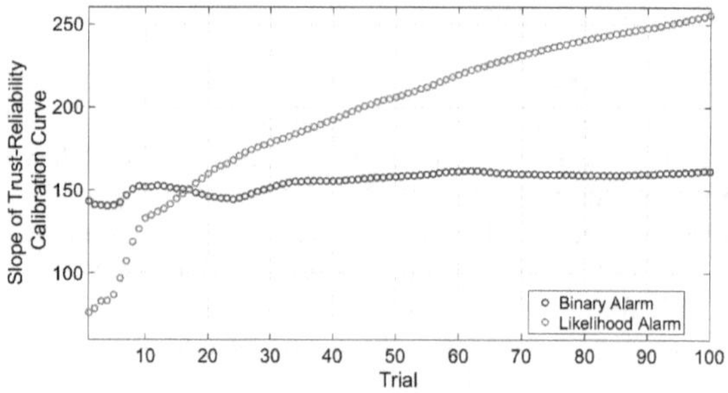

Figure 3. Variation of the slope of the $Trust_e$-calibration curve with automation experience

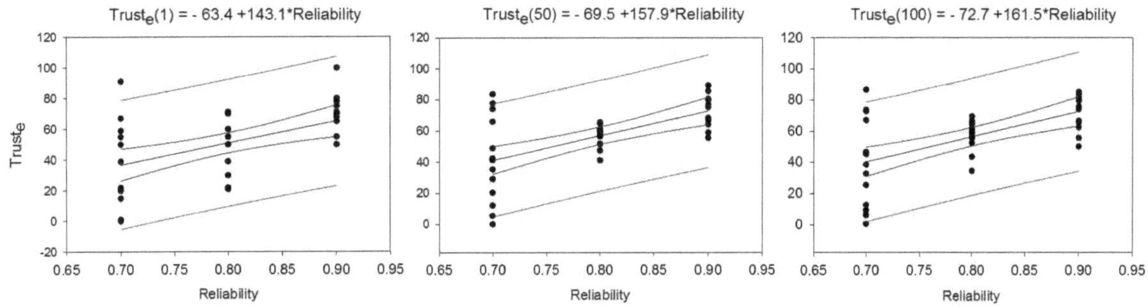

Figure 4. Variation of *Trust$_e$*-reliability calibration with automation experience for binary alarm

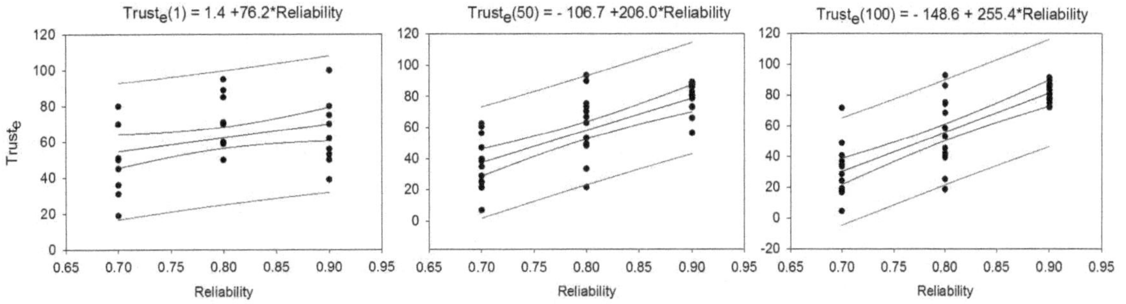

Figure 5. Variation of *Trust$_e$*-reliability calibration with automation experience for likelihood alarm

4.3 Effect of Experience on Trust$_e$

To further understand how trust evolves with experience, we analyzed *Trust$_e$* with respect to automation experience (trial number) for each of the six treatment conditions. We found that users' trust in automation evolved over time, and that change in trust, averaged across all users, exhibited an asymptotic stabilizing trend for each condition. To explain this trend, we propose a model for the evolution of trust over time. This model is inspired by the theory of dynamical systems, which has previously been used for modeling cognitive processes such as the forgetting curve [30].

We hypothesized that for a robot or automation system that does not involve a learning or adaptive component — i.e., a system with fixed performance/reliability over time — the trust of the *average user* converges to a value *Trust (∞)* as he or she gains experience with the system. Further, the evolution of trust over time can be modeled as the response of a first-order linear time invariant (LTI) dynamical system to a constant (step) input signal.

The proposed model is described mathematically as follows:

$$\frac{d\,Trust_e}{dt} + \frac{Trust_e}{\tau} = G\,u(t)$$

t corresponds to time (experience with automation), τ corresponds to the 'time constant' of the system, G corresponds to the system gain and $u(t)$ corresponds to unit step input. In the context of our experiment, these quantities further relate as follows: t represents the trial number; τ represents a quantity proportional to the number of trials needed for trust to reach its final, stable value; and the constant (step) input corresponds to a system with fixed reliability.

Upon solving the above first-order differential equation, the evolution of trust with experience can be represented as follows:

$$w = \exp(-t/\tau)$$

$$Trust_e(t) = Trust_e(final) * [1 - w] + Trust_e(initial) * [w]$$

$$Trust_e\ Change\ (t) = Trust_e\ Change(final)[1 - w]$$

We fitted the above equation to the trust measurements recorded during our experiment. The data was fit to the mean value of trust for different instances of automation — i.e., different reliability condition for each alarm type. We used Matlab's nonlinear least squares method for curve fitting, and estimated the initial trust using the mean trust level during the first interaction. The resulting plots are depicted in Figures 6 and 7 for the binary and likelihood alarm, respectively. The plots include a scatter plot of the data and the fitted curve along with its 95% confidence interval. Goodnesss of fit for each curve is quantified using "adjusted R-squared" and is listed in Table 4, which also includes the estimated value of the time constant and the estimated asymptotic value of trust.

The adjusted R-squared values indicate that the proposed first-order dynamical systems is a good fit for the empirically observed data. The goodness of fit is higher for the likelihood alarm. Further, the estimated final values of trust as determined by our first-order model vary proportionally with system reliability. Additionally, we observed two interesting patterns. First, the time constant is greater for the likelihood alarm; this implies that users require more interaction with in order to arrive at a stable trust value for the likelihood alarm. This may be due to the greater number of alternatives associated with the likelihood alarm compared with the

Table 4. Results from the first-order model of Trust

Alarm type	Reliability	Adjusted R-squared	Estimated Time Constant	Estimated *Trust(∞)*
Binary	70%	0.662	11.48	40.81
	80%	0.963	19.23	57.24
	90%	0.896	20.50	72.83
Likeli-hood	70%	0.962	35.77	30.69
	80%	0.994	49.68	53.48
	90%	0.995	41.72	83.15

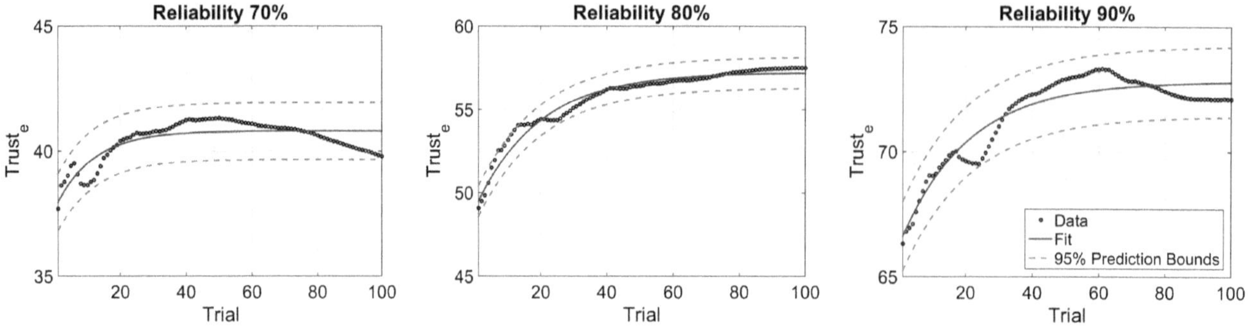

Figure 6: Variation of *Trust*$_e$ (averaged across participants) with automation experience for binary alarm.

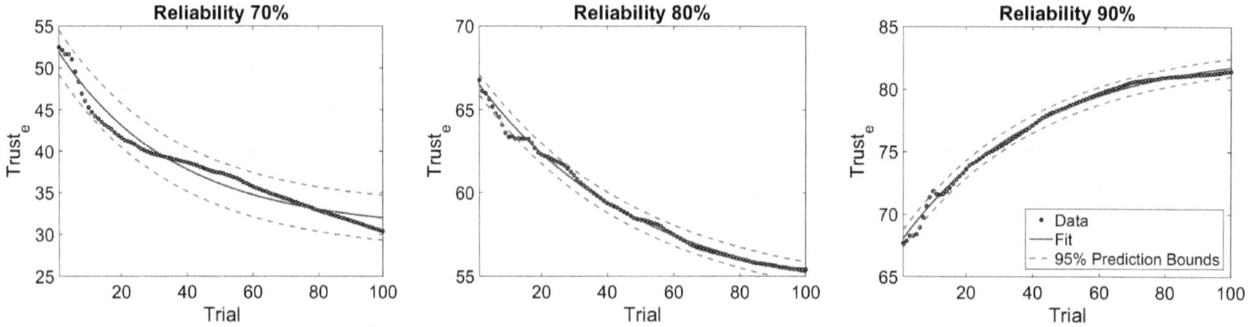

Figure 7. Variation of *Trust*$_e$ (averaged across participants) with automation experience for likelihood alarm. Notice the change in the magnitude of *Trust*$_e$ (y-axis) across the three plots for both the binary (Fig. 6) and likelihood (Fig. 7) alarm. We observe that higher automation reliability results in higher value of trust.

binary alarm, resulting in users requiring more time to create a stable, mental model of the likelihood alarm.

Second, we observed that while using binary alarms, participants' *Trust*$_e$ increased with repeated interactions with automation for all three automation reliability levels, whereas when using likelihood alarms, *Trust*$_e$ decreased over time at reliability of 70% and 80% and increased at reliability of 90%. This variation in *Trust*$_e$ evolution patterns may be explained by the interplay between operators' initial expectation of automation and their subsequent observation of automation's performance [9]. Studies have shown that people have higher initial expectation and trust when automation is portrayed as an "expert" system [31, 32]. Likelihood alarms may be perceived more "intelligent" compared to binary alarms of the same reliability and engender higher initial trust. As participants interacted with the threat detector, they adjusted their trust to reflect automation's true performance. Trust decrement may reflect participants' initial over-expectation and subsequent decrement of trust, whereas trust increment reflects initial under-expectation and subsequent increment of trust.

Note that caution is warranted when interpreting the estimates of the LTI model described above. The model is obtained using the average measurements of trust across participants; thus, it allows for estimation of the degree of trust likely to be exhibited by the average user. For instance, the final value of trust obtained by the empirical fit provides the average degree of trust that might be observed across users. Although the model does not allow for predictions regarding the evolution of trust for a single user, its utility lies in estimating the average value of trust in a system across multiple users. Further, we claim the applicability of this model only for systems with fixed reliability/performance; this may or may not extend to systems that adapt or learn during interaction.

4.4 Effect of automation transparency on momentary trust change

In order to examine the effect of automation transparency on the change of moment-to-moment trust, $Trust_t - Trust_{t-1}$, we conducted the following tests: (i) paired sample t-tests to compare the differences between high- and low-likelihood alerts, (ii) independent sample t-tests to compare the differences between binary and high-likelihood alerts, and between binary and low-likelihood alerts. Note that paired-sample t-tests have greater statistical power than independent sample t-tests.

Figures 8-11 depict momentary change of $Trust_t$ for hits, false alarms, correct rejections and misses. When the threat detector's decisions were hits, there was a marginally significant difference between high- and low-likelihood alerts (1.22 vs. 0.71, paired sample $t(38) = 1.946$, $p = .06$), indicating that a correct alert of threat presence with high confidence led to a greater increase to $Trust_t$ in comparison with $Trust_{t-1}$. When the threat detector gave false alarms, $Trust_t$ decreased. Further, the comparisons indicated a significant difference between high- and low-likelihood alerts (-4.95 vs -1.49, paired sample $t(38) = -3.11$, $p < .01$) and between binary alerts and low-likelihood alerts (-3.31 vs -1.49, independent $t(76) = -2.37$, $p = .02$).

$Trust_t$ increased when the threat detector correctly identified the absence of threats. Moreover, we observed a significantly greater improvement to $Trust_t$ for high-likelihood alerts compared with low-likelihood alerts (0.72 vs 0.40, paired sample $t(38) = 2.085$, $p = .04$), and a marginally significantly greater improvement for binary alerts compared with low-likelihood alerts (0.76 vs 0.40, independent $t(76) = 1.848$, $p = .07$). When the threat detector missed potential threat, there was a decrease in $Trust_t$, with no statistically significant differences between high- and low-likelihood alerts, between binary and high-likelihood alerts or between binary and low-likelihood alerts.

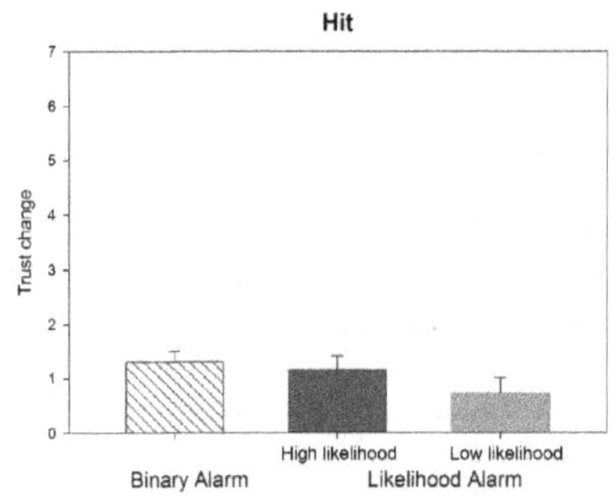

Figure 8. Momentary change of *Trust$_t$* for hits

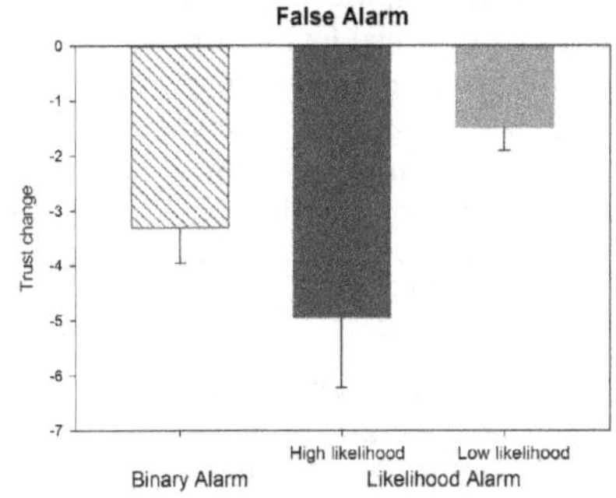

Figure 9. Momentary change of *Trust$_t$* for false alarms

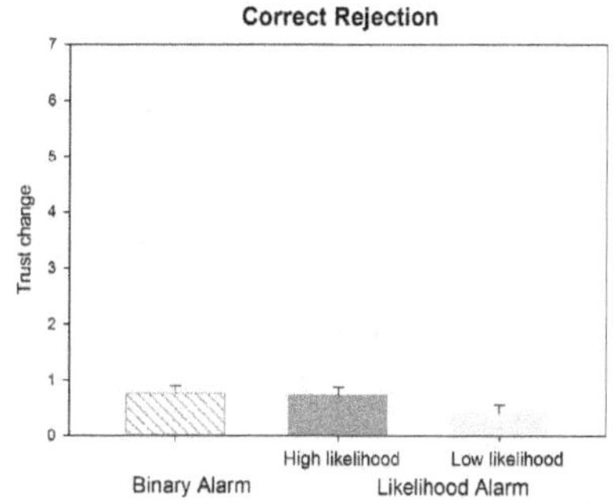

Figure 10. Momentary change of *Trust$_t$* for correct rejections

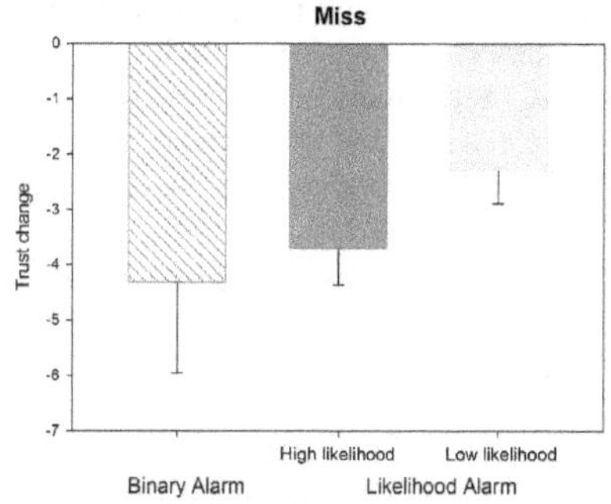

Figure 11. Momentary change of *Trust$_t$* for misses

5. DISCUSSIONS

Our first objective was to determine whether a human operator's trust rating at time *t* is evaluated on the basis of his or her entire interactive experience or according to the momentary interaction with automation. Our results indicated that trust at time *t* was evaluated according to the momentary interaction, and that *trust of entirety* was better quantified by *Trust$_{AUTC}$* compared with *Trust$_{end}$*. This finding has important implications for trust measurement during human-automation/robot interaction — specifically, merely administering a trust survey at the end of an experiment is inadequate if the intent is to measure human participants' degree of trust in an automated/robotic technology over the course of the entire interactive process. Continuous trust measure in real time is necessary to achieve this goal.

The second objective of the present study was to explore how *trust of entirety* evolves as a human gains more experience interacting with automation. Our proposed first-order LTI model suggested that *trust of entirety* evolved and stabilized as an operator interacted more with the automated system. Interestingly, we observed a larger time constant for the likelihood alarm, suggesting that human operators require longer interaction with this type of alarm in order to arrive at a stable value of trust. This finding is potentially attributable to the high- and low-likelihood information associated with the alarm, which may require additional trust calibration before a steady state is reached. Additionally, we observed variations in patterns of trust evolution, which could be explained by the interplay between human participants' initial expectation of automation and their subsequent adjustment of trust in automation.

Our third objective was to investigate the influence of automation transparency on human operators' moment-to-moment trust changes. Increasing automation transparency has been proposed as a method of increasing a human operator's trust in automation [22]. Findings from this study confirm that high-likelihood alerts engender a greater increase to momentary trust upon automation success, as well as a greater decline in momentary trust upon automation failure. Our results also shed light upon the underlying reason for the benefits of increasing automation transparency: higher automation transparency may mitigate the "cry wolf" effect.

The "cry wolf" effect is a phenomenon commonly observed in high-risk industries in which the threshold to trigger an alarm is often set very low in order to capture every critical event [9]. This low threshold, however, inevitably results in false alarms, which can cause human operators to question or even abandon the automated technology. The significant difference we observed in the response to low-likelihood and binary alerts suggests that human participants were still able to retain their trust in automation if the false alarm was provided through low-likelihood alerts. It is possible that users are less inclined to interpret these false alarms as false since the low-likelihood alerts merely suggest that a threat may exist, rather than explicitly confirm the presence of a threat.

6. CONCLUSION

Existing research examining human trust in automation and robots has primarily examined trust as a steady-state variable, with little emphasis on the evolution of trust over time. The present study explored the dynamic nature of trust.

We defined *trust of entirety* as a trust measure that accounts for a human's entire interactive experience with automation. Using a simulated reconnaissance task, we conducted a human-subject experiment (N=91) and found that *Trust$_{AUTC}$* is a more appropriate measure for *trust of entirety*. The present study also showed that *trust of entirety* evolves and stabilizes over time, and demonstrated that a higher level of automation transparency may mitigate the "cry wolf" effect.

7. ACKNOWLEDGEMENTS

This work is supported by the SUTD-MIT postdoctoral fellows program.

8. REFERENCES

[1] Murphy, R. R. 2004. Human-robot interaction in rescue robotics. *IEEE Transactions on Systems, Man, and Cybernetics,* 34, 2, 138-153.

[2] Girard, A. R., Howell A. S., and Hedrick, J. K. 2004. Border patrol and surveillance missions using multiple unmanned air vehicles. *The 43rd IEEE Conference on Decision and Control,* 620-625.

[3] Casbeer, D. W., Kingston, D. B., Beard, R. W. and McLain, T. W. 2006. Cooperative forest fire surveillance using a team of small unmanned air vehicles. *International Journal of Systems Science*, 37, 6, 351-360.

[4] Chen, J. Y. C. 2010. Robotics operator performance in a multi-tasking environment: Human-Robot Interactions in Future Military Operations. Ashgate Publishing, 294-314.

[5] Chen, J. Y. C. and Barnes, M. J. 2008. Robotics operator performance in a military multi-tasking environment. *The 3rd ACM/IEEE International Conference on Human-Robot Interaction (HRI '08)*, 279-286.

[6] Talamadupula, K., Briggs, G. Chakraborti, T. Scheutz M. and Kambhampati, S. 2014. Coordination in human-robot teams using mental modeling and plan recognition, *2014 IEEE/RSJ International Conference on Intelligent Robots and Systems (IROS)*, 2957-2962.

[7] Pratt, G. and Manzo, J. 2013. The DARPA Robotics Challenge [Competition]. *IEEE Robotics & Automation Magazine*, 20, 2, 10-12.

[8] Lee, J. D. and See, K. A. 2004. Trust in technology: Designing for appropriate reliance. *Human Factors*, 46, 1, 50-80.

[9] Hoff, K. A. and Bashir, M. 2015. Trust in Automation: Integrating Empirical Evidence on Factors That Influence Trust. *Human Factors*, 57, 3, 407-434.

[10] Hancock, P. A., Billings, D. R., Schaefer, K. E., Chen, J. Y. C., de Visser, E. J. and Parasuraman, R. 2016. A Meta-Analysis of Factors Affecting Trust in Human-Robot Interaction. *Human Factors*, 53, 5, 517-527.

[11] Wickens, C. D., Hollands, J. G., Banbury, S. and Parasuraman, R. 2013. *Engineering Psychology & Human Performance*. Pearson Education.

[12] Robinette, P., Li, W., Allen, R., Howard, A. M. and Wagner, A. R. 2016. Overtrust of Robots in Emergency Evacuation Scenarios. *The 11th ACM/IEEE International Conference on Human Robot Interaction (HRI '16)*, 101-108.

[13] Lee, J. D. and Moray, N. 1992. Trust, control strategies and allocation of function in human-machine systems. *Ergonomics*, 35, 10, 1243-1270.

[14] Lee, J. D. and Moray, N. 1994. Trust, self-confidence, and operators' adaptation to automation. *International Journal of Human Computer Studies*, 40, 1, 153-184.

[15] Yang, X. J., Wickens, C. D. and Hölttä-Otto, K. 2016. How users adjust trust in automation: Contrast effect and hindsight bias. *Proceedings of the Human Factors and Ergonomics Society Annual Meeting*, 60, 1, 196-200.

[16] Manzey, D., Reichenbach, J. and Onnasch, L. 2012. Human Performance Consequences of Automated Decision Aids: The Impact of Degree of Automation and System Experience. *Journal of Cognitive Engineering and Decision Making*, 6, 1, 57-87.

[17] Desai, M., Kaniarasu, P., Medvedev, M., Steinfeld, A. and Yanco, H. 2013. Impact of robot failures and feedback on real-time trust. *The 8th ACM/IEEE international conference on Human-robot interaction (HRI '13)*, 251-258.

[18] Muir, B. M. 1987. Trust between humans and machines, and the design of decision aids. *International Journal of Man-Machine Studies*, 27, 5, 527-539.

[19] Wang, N., Pynadath, D. V. and Hill, S. G. 2016. Trust Calibration within a Human-Robot Team: Comparing Automatically Generated Explanations. *The 11th ACM/IEEE International Conference on Human Robot Interaction (HRI '16),* 109-116.

[20] Lohani, M., Stokes, C., McCoy, M., Bailey, C. A. and Rivers, S. E. 2016. Social Interaction Moderates Human-Robot Trust-Reliance Relationship and Improves Stress Coping. *The 11th ACM/IEEE International Conference on Human Robot Interaction (HRI '16)*, 471-472.

[21] Bartlett, C. E. and Cooke, N. J. 2015. Human-Robot Teaming in Urban Search and Rescue. *Proceedings of the Human Factors and Ergonomics Society Annual Meeting*, 59, 1, 250-254.

[22] Sanchez, J. 2006. *Factors that affect trust and reliance on an automated aid.* Georgia Insititue of Technology.

[23] Desai, M., Medvedev, M., Vázquez, M., McSheehy, S., Gadea-Omelchenko, S., Bruggeman, C., Steinfeld, A. and Yanco, H. 2012. Effects of changing reliability on trust of robot systems. *The 7th annual ACM/IEEE international conference on Human-Robot Interaction (HRI '12)*, 73-80.

[24] Mercado, J. E., Rupp, M. A., Chen, J. Y. C., Barnes, M. J., Barber, D. and Procci, K. 2016. Intelligent Agent Transparency in Human–Agent Teaming for Multi-UxV Management. *Human Factors*, 58, 3, 401-415.

[25] Sorkin, R., Kantowitz, B. H. and Kantowitz, S. C. Likelihood alarm displays. 1988 *Human Factors*, 30, 4, 445-459.

[26] Wickens, C. D., Levinthal, B. and Rice, S. 2010. Imperfect reliability in ummaned air vehicle supervison and control: Human-Robot Interactions in Future Military Operations. Ashgate Publishing, 193-210

[27] Tanner, W. P. J. and Swets, J. A. 1954. A decision-making theory of visual detection. *Psychological Review*, 61, 6, 401-409.

[28] Wiczorek, R. and Manzey, D. 2014 Supporting attention allocation in multitask environments: Effects of likelihood alarm systems on trust, behavior and performance. *Human Factors*, 56, 7, 1209-1221.

[29] Dixon, S., Wickens, C. D. and McCarley, J. M. 2007 On the independence of reliance and compliance: Are false alarms worse than misses? *Human Factors*, 49, 4, 564-572.

[30] Ebbinghaus, H. 1913. *Memory: A Contribution to Experimental Psychology*. Columbia University, New York City.

[31] Madhavan, P., & Wiegmann, D. A. 2007. Effects of information source, pedigree, and reliability on operator interaction with decision support systems. *Human Factors*, 49, 5, 773–785

[32] de Vries, P., & Midden, C. 2008. Effect of indirect information on system trust and control allocation. *Behaviour & Information Technology,* 27, 1, 17–29.

Do You Want Your Autonomous Car To Drive Like You?

Chandrayee Basu
UC Merced
cbasu2@ucmerced.edu

Qian Yang
Carnegie Mellon University
qyang1@cs.cmu.edu

David Hungerman
UC Merced
dmhungerman@ucmerced.edu

Mukesh Singhal
UC Merced
msinghal@ucmerced.edu

Anca D. Dragan
UC Berkeley
anca@berkeley.edu

ABSTRACT

With progress in enabling autonomous cars to drive safely on the road, it is time to start asking *how* they should be driving. A common answer is that they should be adopting their users' driving style. This makes the assumption that users want their autonomous cars to drive like they drive – aggressive drivers want aggressive cars, defensive drivers want defensive cars. In this paper, we put that assumption to the test. We find that users tend to prefer a significantly more defensive driving style than their own. Interestingly, they prefer the style they *think* is their own, even though their actual driving style tends to be more aggressive. We also find that preferences do depend on the specific driving scenario, opening the door for new ways of learning driving style preference.

Keywords

autonomous cars; driving preferences; driving style

1. INTRODUCTION

In the age of autonomous driving, researchers and companies are getting ever-so-close to enabling cars to generate driving behavior that includes reaching the destination while satisfying safety constraints, like not colliding with other cars or pedestrians.

Once autonomous cars attain that level of capability, initially, they might be able to generate, for each driving situation, only one solution trajectory (or behavior) that satisfies these safety and feasibility constraints. But really, many solutions exist – there are many ways to drive. This depend on the individual trade-offs that each driver makes. We have an existence proof for that. Some of us are more *aggressive* drivers, valuing efficiency and being comfortable getting close to other cars on the road. Others are more *defensive*, a bit more conservative when it comes to safety, leaving a large distance to the next car for example, or quickly braking when someone attempts to merge in front.

HRI '17, March 06-09, 2017, Vienna, Austria

DOI: http://dx.doi.org/10.1145/2909824.3020250

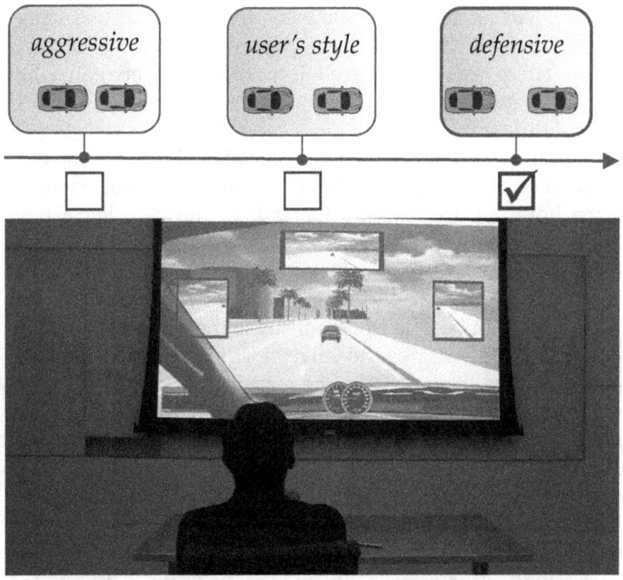

Figure 1: We first get data from user driving in different scenarios, and in a second session ask them to compare their own style (without knowing it is theirs), a more defensive style, and a more aggressive style. Participants tended to prefer a more defensive style than their own, but mistakenly thought they were actually picking their own.

Soon after we are able to generate *one* feasible behavior, we will be asking ourselves *which* behavior we should try to generate: what driving *style* should an autonomous car have? There is a natural answer to this question: cars should do what users want them to [9, 6, 22]. If the user drives aggressively, so should the car. The car should borrow the user's driving style (though not the imperfections). This is very apparent from the expression "back seat driving", which suggests that people want the driver to do what they would do.

Prior work has focused on identifying the user's driving style, via Inverse Reinforcement Learning [9, 14, 10]. In all of them, the underlying assumption is that we want cars to match our driving style: that we want them to drive like us.

In this paper, we challenge this assumption, and hypothesize that users want a driving style that is different from their own. We design and conduct a user study to start analyzing the potential differences between how users drive and how they want to be driven. Our study, conducted in a driving simulator, has two parts: first, the users come in and demonstrate their driving in different environments; second, at a later date, the same users come in and test four driving styles: their own (though they do not know it is their own), an aggressive style, a defensive style, and another user's style. We measure their preference for these styles, as well as the perceived similarity to their own style.

Our results suggest that there is truth to both sides:

> Users do not actually want the car to drive like they drive. Instead, they want the car to drive like they *think* they drive.

We found a significant difference in user's own style and preferred style, with users typically preferring more defensive driving when they are passengers. However, we also found a strong correlation between the style that users preferred, and the style that users perceived as closest to their own. There was little correlation, however, between what they thought was their own style and what *actually* was their own style.

Overall, our work does not contradict the need for customization, but suggests that it might not be sufficient to learn how the user drives. Instead, we need to learn how the user actually wants to be driven. This raises challenges for learning, because we can no longer rely on demonstrations – users can easily demonstrate how they drive, but they might not be able to demonstrate the driving style they want. Instead, we need to rely on different kinds of input and guidance from users in the learning process.

Furthermore, there is a tension between what users think they want (their style) and what they actually want (a more defensive style). On the brighter side, our results suggest that the learned output should be easily accepted by users: when the car drives in the preferred style, chances are users will perceive it as their own style anyway!

We define *driving style*, informed by prior work, in Related Work, followed by our statement of hypothesis, description of the manipulated variables, the simulation environment, the user studies and the confounds in the Methods section. Here, we also present a quantitative measure of driving style in terms of driving features derived from prior research. The rest of paper is organized into Results and Discussion.

2. RELATED WORK

The typical behavioral patterns of a driver are usually referred to by the term *driving style*. This includes the choice of driving speed, headway, overtaking of other vehicles, or the tendency to commit traffic violations [20].

Defensiveness-aggressiveness is the most commonly used metric for defining driving style. Prior work refers to drivers as aggressive/assertive versus defensive [22]; or mild versus moderate versus aggressive [21]. In the Multidimensional Driving Style Inventory (MDSI), Taubman-Ben-Ari *et al.* identified four broad driving styles: (1) reckless and careless driving, characterized by, for example, higher speed; (2) anxious driving; (3) angry and hostile driving, characterized by more use of the horn and flash functionality; and (4) patient and careful driving [18]. Similarly, Huysduynen categorized driving style as angry driving, anxious driving, dissociative driving, distress-reduction driving and careful driving style [20]. Horswill *et al.* provided a valuable distinction between skill and style in the context of driving behaviors [8]. Hong *et al.* [7] differentiated styles in terms of defensiveness, as well as by propensity for violation of rules. Scherer defined driving style in terms of comfort [16]. Lee *et al.* [11] analyzed lane changes as a function of its severity (degree to which the vehicle in the destination lane was cut off), urgency (how soon the lane change was needed), and type classification for the full population of 8,667 lane changes.

We focus on driving style based on degree of defensiveness.

Driving style is a "humanized driving" quality [6]. Hence, most of the driving style literature relates to understanding and modeling human driver behavior, in very specific traffic situations or contexts, like lane changing [11, 15, 12], intersection crossing [7, 3, 5], car following [4], and in terms of driving actions specific to those contexts (e.g., throttle and braking level, turning) and features thereof (e.g. rate of acceleration, rate of deceleration, maximum speed in a time window). *We define driving defensiveness in our work as an aggregate of driving features in various driving scenarios.* Therefore, in our study, we present a combination of all of the aforementioned traffic conditions and scenarios to our participants.

Research on driving styles has been extended to autonomous cars in two forms. One body of work includes exploratory studies on understanding how explicitly-defined driving styles relate to comfort [16]. The second body of work encompasses research on ways to teach an autonomous car how to drive from human demonstrations [1, 23, 9, 17]. Both these groups assume that an autonomous car should learn their own user's driving style or driving behavior.

3. METHODS

3.1 Hypothesis

Because being a passenger is a different experience than being a driver, we hypothesize that:

H. *Users of autonomous cars prefer a driving style that is significantly different than their own.*

3.2 Study Design

In order to test our hypothesis, we leverage a driving simulator, and let users experience and evaluate autonomous cars with different driving styles, including their own style (without their knowledge).

We conducted a study in two parts. In the first part we collected driving data of participants in a simulation environment, so that we could let them experience their own style in the second part of the study.

3.3 Manipulated Variables

We manipulated the driving styles of autonomous cars at four levels of defensiveness: ***aggressive*, *defensive*, *own style***, and a ***distractor style*** (a different participant's style). Users did not know if any of the styles were their own. Likewise, we also consciously avoided the use of the phrase "driving style" anytime during the studies, as well as, in the pre-study screening.

We define the *defensiveness* of the style objectively, as a function of several driving features (e.g., distance to other cars – the larger the distance, the more defensive the driving). We use features informed by existing literature. We describe them in Sec. 3.6.

We created the aggressive and the defensive styles of driving by demonstration, and then validated these styles using our driving features (see our Manipulation Check Sec. 3.7).

3.4 Simulator and Driving Tasks

We conducted both parts of the study in a simulation environment. Our simulation environment consisted of a standard classroom projection screen and table in front of the screen fitted with Logitech G920 steering wheel, brake, and gas pedal. We used the OpenDS driving simulation software [13] for running each of the driving simulations. The simulation platform was set up on a standard PC augmented with NVIDIA GeForce GTX 1070 and was hidden from the participants' view.

In the first part, the participants drove on a 9.6 mile long test track that consisted of 14 different driving tasks designed using the City Engine software (Fig.2).

We define a *driving task* as a sequence of driving maneuvers in response to specific traffic conditions. For each task there are two to three simulated traffic conditions that resemble everyday traffic, so as to elicit natural driving behavior from the participant.

In the second part of the study, the participants experienced 6 of these 14 tasks, each performed by autonomous cars of four different styles.

3.5 Procedure

Before the driving session in part one of the study, we familiarized participants to the driving simulator. We asked each participant to practice on two different test tracks until they felt that they were driving as they would in their everyday driving. The first track had several traffic signals and turns, and second one was on congested city roads with several traffic cars. Their driving was assisted by a voice navigation. There were road signs for speed change zone, speed limit, sharp turns, entry to expressway and exit from expressway. We instructed the participants to drive as they would on actual roads and to treat the speed limits the way they would in their usual driving. This practice session lasted 5-10 minutes for each participant.

Participants then began the first part of the study, which consisted of 15-20 minutes of driving along the 14 tasks-test track, followed by a 10 minute interview.

In the second part of the study, the autonomous cars performed six tasks (combined into four test tasks) from this list with the participant as a passenger, shown in bold letters on the list in Fig.2. To simplify, we combined the second and the third tasks in the list, i.e., lead car slows down forcing lane change and merge back to right lane into a single test task, which we refer to as Task 1 in the rest of the paper. Likewise, we combined the sixth and the seventh tasks into a single test task, called Task 2 in the rest of the paper. Thus, each autonomous car performed four test tasks in total. Two of the test tasks were on the expressway and lasted approximately 4 minutes for each style and the other two tasks on the inner city roads were shorter than 2 minutes.

After the participants had driven in an autonomous car of each driving style for each of the test tasks, we conducted a short interview-based survey with each participant.

3.6 Dependent Measures

Perceived similarity to real driving. In the first part of the study we conducted a post-driving open-ended interview with the participants to understand whether the manual driving in the simulation environment resembled their everyday driving. We asked three questions in this interview, each followed by a request for more elaboration. We asked the following questions in the interview:

1. Did you enjoy the drive?
2. Are there any positive or negative aspects of the simulation environment, the driving controls and the traffic conditions that you would like to mention?
3. On a scale of +3 to -3 [2], please rate how similar or different is this experience from your daily driving?

Open-ended responses. In the second part we asked each participant to think aloud about their emotions and feelings as they were experiencing autonomous driving.

Main subjective measures: Preference and perceived similarity to own style. After a participant had experienced each autonomous style for a given task, we conducted an interview-based survey. We asked the participants to rate each style of driving for *comfort, safety, preference for everyday use,* and *similarity with their own driving* on 7 point Likert scale.

Main objective measures: Driving style features and overall defensiveness. We measured the user's style quantitatively using task specific driving features, derived from existing literature. We carefully considered the contexts and subject demographics of each of these existing studies to ensure as much similarity in the context as possible with our study.

For car following, lane changing, and return to preferred lane, we selected the features described by Lee *et al.* in "A Comprehensive Examination of Naturalistic Lane-Changes" [11]. This study analyzed the largest naturalistic lane change dataset and specifically labelled lane change data resulting from the slowing down of the leading car. The speed range of 45 mph to 55 mph matches our driving conditions. Their dataset consisted 8667 lane changes over 23,949 miles of driving from 16 commuters of age group 20 to 60. They studied car following, lane changing, and return of preferred lane in terms of distance, time to collision, and relative speed classified by severity and urgency of lane change.

The features for tasks like turning at the intersection with a green light or stop light were derived from our preliminary interview with the participants and from Hong *et al.* [7] and Banovic *et al.* [3].

Table 1 summarizes all the features for the four driving test tasks. We used *mean distance to lead car, mean time headway, time headway during lane change,* and *distance headway during lane change* as features for Task 1 and Task 2. Task 1 had an extra feature *distance headway merge back* for scoring the merge back behavior to the right lane.

Task 3 consisted of two sub-tasks (approaching intersection at a stop light and then making a left turn at green ball). We characterized this task with 5 features: *Braking Distance from the intersection, Average speed for 20 meters before intersection, Time To Stop, Speed at the intersection,* and *Maximum turn speed.*

Task 4 constituted approaching intersection at green ball and then turning right without stopping. The features for this tasks are *Speed at the intersection* and *Maximum Turn Speed.*

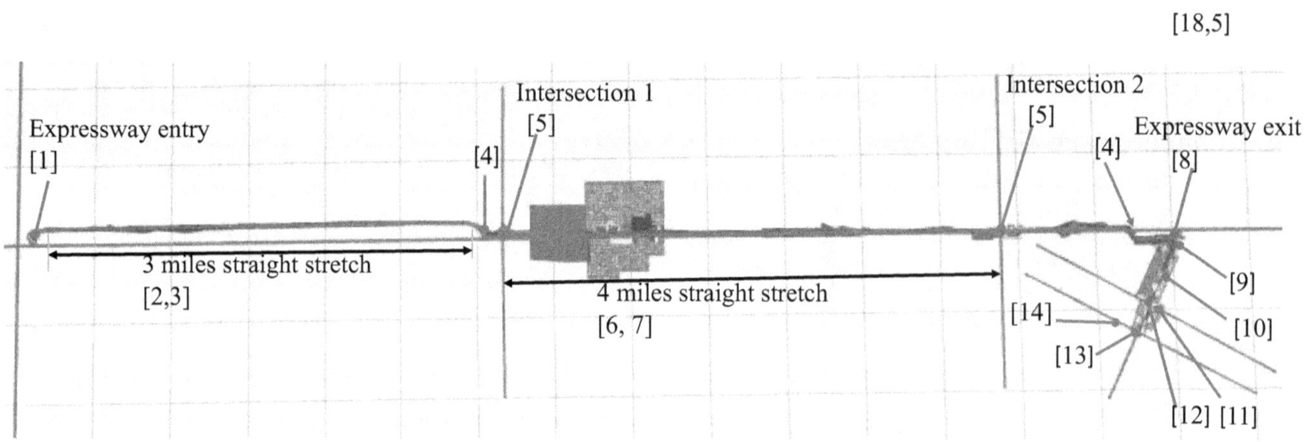

1. Merge onto expressway between two cars
2. **Lead car slow down forcing lane change**
3. **Merge back to right lane**
4. < 90 degrees Turn negotiation on expressway
5. Stop light at intersection on expressway
6. **Slow lead car in right lane forcing lane change when another car is approaching fast in the destination lane**
7. **Merge back into right lane with a continuous traffic moving at constant gap and constant speed**
8. Expressway exit
9. Sharp right turn no signal
10. Left turn on green light
11. Right turn at stop light
12. **Left turn at stoplight and yield at green**
13. **Right turn on green light**
14. Park along curb

Figure 2: Designed track: Tasks (shown in the list below the figure) are indicated in square brackets. Total road stretch is 9.6 miles.

We objectively measured a participant's overall driving style in terms of a ***Defensiveness Score***. We first normalized the feature values across participants for each feature irrespective of the task. We calculated a *Defensiveness Score* for each participant and for each task as the average over all the normalized feature values for that participant and task. We then computed an *Aggregate Defensiveness Score* for each participant by averaging their scores across the four test tasks.

3.7 Manipulation Check

We performed a manipulation check on our aggressive and defensive driving styles. We measured the aggregate defensiveness score for each style, plotted on the bottom right of Fig.3. We found that indeed, the aggressive style was less defensive than the defensive style (lower defensiveness score). We found that 86.67 % of the users' styles scored higher than the aggressive style, and lower than the defensive style. This suggests that the two reference driving styles created by demonstrations resulted in meaningful representations of aggressive and defensive driving.

3.8 Participants

Subject Allocation. We opted for a within-subjects allocation because the participants needed to choose a preferred style out of the set of available ones. We randomized the order of the conditions.

Demographics. We recruited 15 participants consisting of a mix of graduate students and undergraduate students. Before the study we sent out a screening form to each participant in order to ensure a wide distribution of demographics, driving experience and perceived driving behaviors of the participants. We also checked for a valid driving license. 3 of our participants were 30 to 31 years old, the rest of the participants were 18-24 years old.

The mean driving experience of the participants was 5.46 years with a standard deviation of 4.5 years. Participants had driven an average 214 miles with a standard deviation of 188 miles on the week before they filled out the screening form.

We asked the participants to give us some information about their perceived driving behavior using the following questions: 1. Please rate if you consider yourself a conservative or an adventurous driver on a 7-point scale, 1 being *conservative* and 7 being *adventurous*. 2. Please rate on a 7-point scale what you like about driving, 1 being *joy of motion* (like feeling the force as you accelerate) and 7 being *comfort of steadiness*. You may like some of both. 3. Rate on a 7-point scale if you think you vary your driving by road conditions, traffic and time availability, 1 being *vary always* and 7 being *I don't vary at all*. 4. Please rate your driving experience from somewhat experienced to very skillful. The purpose of these questions was to acquire some information about the participants' driving styles without explicitly using the term style or in other words give away the original goal of the study.

Approximately 46 % of the participants considered themselves well experienced in driving, and 20 % considered themselves experienced. The rest were equally distributed between somewhat experienced to very skillful. The mean score for perceived conservative-adventurous driving behavior was 3.6. Most of the participants considered themselves to be in the middle of the spectrum. Only one participant considered himself to be conservative. More participants preferred comfort and steadiness over joy of driving, the average rating being 4.46. The mean rating for variation of driving style in response to environment and traffic was 3, which means most participants believed that they alter their driving behavior according to traffic.

3.9 External Validity and Controlling for Confounds

Driving environment. We used a simulator and not real autonomous cars. However, we designed a simulation track and traffic conditions so as to elicit natural driving responses.

Features	Definitions
Mean Distance to Lead car	During car following (with 200 meters distance) the average distance between middle of the driver car and the lead car.
Mean Time Headway	During car following (with 200 meters distance) average time headway, defined as ratio of Distance headway and speed of the driver car.
Time Headway during Lane change	Distance headway divided by the speed of the driver car during lane change.
Distance Headway during Lane change	Distance between the middle of the driver car and the lead car during lane change
Distance Headway Merge Back	This is the same as Distance Headway during lane change except measured in between driver car and the following car in the destination lane.
Braking Distance from the Intersection	The distance from the intersection at which a person starts applying brakes.
Time To Stop	Braking distance divided by the speed of the car right before brake is applied.
Maximum Turn Speed	Maximum speed of the driver car over a time window during a left turn or a right turn.
Speed at the Intersection	Instantaneous speed at the intersection.
Average Speed for 20 meters before Intersection	This is the speed of the driver car averaged over a distance range of 20 meters from the intersection.

Table 1: Features for style classification

We also collected participant feedback in the first part of the study on the simulation environment and how their driving behavior in the simulated track related to their actual driving behavior.

Masking own style. One of the major challenges of this work was to ensure that a participant could not recognize his or her driving style from simulation peculiarities like scenes, traffic and controls. We wanted the participants to only recognize their driving style based on their traffic maneuvers and actions. We took several steps to camouflage the driving data of a participant in the second part of the study:

- We retained the traffic conditions and route from the first part of the study while changing the surrounding scenes and traffic cars, such that we can replicate the user's driving while removing the bias of familiar environment.
- We let the participant perform approximately 14 driving actions in the first part of the study and picked only some of these tasks for the second part of the study.
- During the second part of the study we presented the tasks in an order different from how they occurred in the manual mode. For example: In the first part, the participants first entered the expressway and performed some driving actions on the expressway and then exited the expressway and performed some more driving maneuvers on the city roads. During the second part, we presented one city road task and one expressway task in an alternate order.
- We presented the four styles for each of the test driving tasks in a randomized order, which made it more difficult to consistently recognize one style.
- We post-processed the users' driving to remove peculiarities, which we explain below.

During our pilot studies we found that due to some peculiarities of simulation environment (over-sensitive steering, less sensitive braking) and the resultant jitter in the driving data, some participants were able to recognize their own driving. For example, a participant mentioned: *"This looks like how I was driving. I had to stop at the intersection because I pressed the brake too early. The brake was tight."* Idiosyncrasies of the simulator led pilot participants to identify their driving behavior in the second part of the study. In order to eliminate these peculiarities of the simulation environment, we changed the brake stiffness and steering sensitivity and presented participants with smoothed version of their data in the second part of the study.

3.10 Trajectory Smoothing

We filtered the driving trajectories to eliminate idiosyncrasies that make the trajectory instantly recognizable.

We applied a Bilateral Filter [19] to reduce the lateral variance (or equivalently, the variance of the lateral displacements from the center of the lane) of the trajectories. By affecting only the lateral components of the trajectory, this filtering preserves distance between the cars. We applied filtering only to the stretches of the trajectory on the expressway.

Fig.4 shows a smoothed trajectory for one participant. It has 15 % lower lateral variance than the original trajectory.

4. RESULTS

4.1 Simulation Realism

In the first part of the study, in addition to collecting user driving data, we also wanted to ensure that this driving data corresponded to participants' everyday driving as much as possible. We conducted a post-driving interview, as described in the Dependent Measures subsection (Sec. 3.6). Here we present the results of the interview.

The rating mode for similarity between driving on road and driving in our study simulator was +1 on -3 to +3 scale.

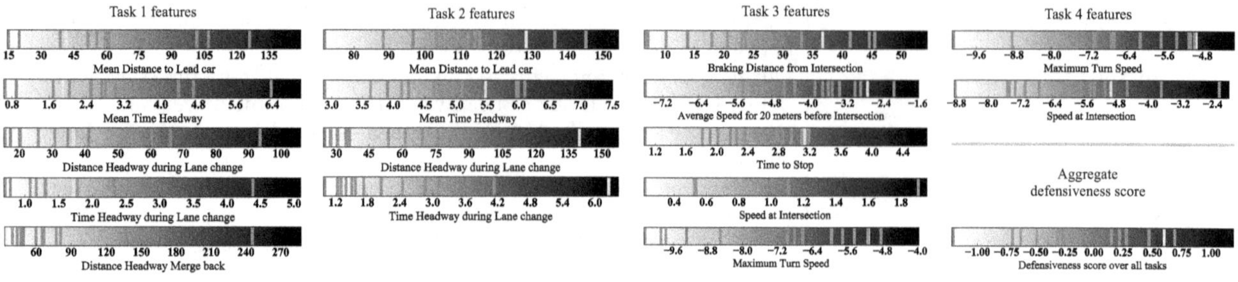

Figure 3: Participants' feature distribution

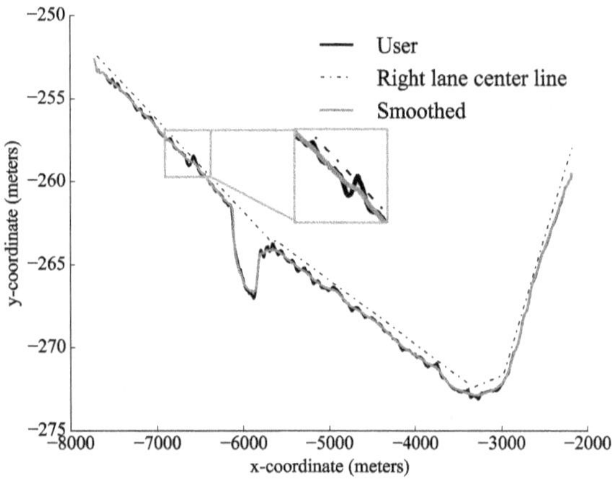

Figure 4: Smoothed trajectory compared to original trajectory of task 1 of one participant at 15 % smoothing

Four participants gave a rating of +2. Some of their positive comments were: "Not considering the room environment and just looking at the simulation graphics and the car it was pretty much the same environment as real. I would give +3 for surrounding traffic conditions". Other participants said that they felt relaxed in the simulator environment and that they could drive cautiously as they would in real traffic.

One participant who rated the driving experience similarity -2 complained about the lack of motion feedback in the system. This is the same participant who gave high rating for *joy of motion* in the screening question. However, no other participant had the same concern and got well-adjusted to the simulation environment.

Most of the participants who rated +1 to -1 found steering re-centering or brake insensitivity difficult. We also received quite opposite feedback from two participants when they compared their everyday driving to the simulator driving. For example, one participant mentioned "It felt real. It was something I could get used to after driving a while. The gas and brakes were more sensitive than my car". Another participant felt that the brakes were excellent, different from regular car.

One participant reported that she was so immersed after driving for a while, that she caught herself turning her head back to check for oncoming traffic in the destination lane. We found that participants with one or less years of driving experience could not use the simulation environment properly. Overall, the ratings and the comments supported that the simulator conditions are not *too* far from real conditions.

4.2 Feature Distribution for Participant Styles

We define driving style in terms of features mentioned in the Sec. 3.

Fig.3 shows, for each task, feature, and participant, what the participant's feature value was for that task (blue marks). The figure also shows the aggressive style values in red and defensive style values in green.

Higher negative values correspond to more aggressive behavior. All the feature values are arranged from aggressive on the left to defensive on the right. However, for features like speed where lower values mean more defensive we show and use the negation of these features.

The bottommost plot to the right shows the aggregate defensiveness score. This score is derived from the normalized feature values. 60 % of the participants are within 0.75 standard deviation aggressive and 40 % within 0.75 standard deviation defensive. Only two of the participants were more defensive than the autonomous defensive car, one of them being very close to the defensive car in the score.

> *When looking at the aggregate defensiveness, most participants lie between the aggressive and defensive styles.*

There are, however, exceptions, but for particular features in particular tasks. For task 1, several participants were more defensive than the defensive autonomous car. For the last feature of task 1, Distance Headway Merge Back, the aggressive car was not as aggressive as several participants and even our defensive car. In task 2, the aggressive and the defensive autonomous cars enclosed a middle section of the spectrum for Mean Distance Headway and Mean Time Headway. In other words, several participants were more aggressive and more defensive than the aggressive and defensive autonomous cars respectively. This is because these features were measured during car following over a long time span and are expected to have wider distributions than features characterizing instantaneous actions.

4.3 Preferred Style in Relation to Own Style

We asked participants to rate how much they would prefer driving with each style, for each task. We refer to the highest rated style(s) as the participant's preferred style(s).

Our main finding is that overall, users preferred a different style than their own. A total of 9 out of 15 participants preferred a different style than their own on at least one of the tasks. A matched pairs t-test comparing actual and preferred defensiveness score showed a significant difference ($t(1, 60) = -2.58$, $p = .0121$), supporting our hy-

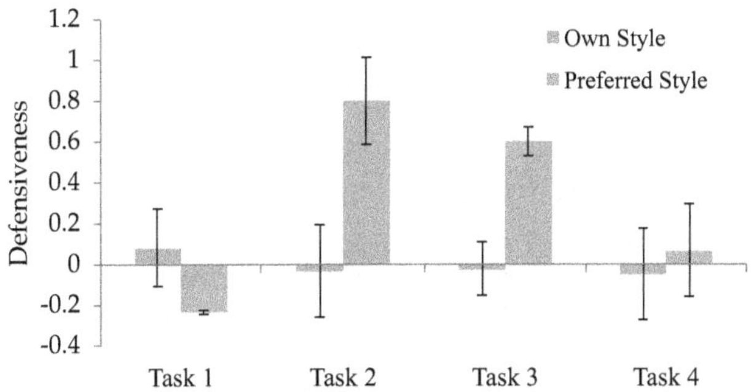

Figure 5: Mean Defensiveness Score Across Participants. The corresponding scores of aggressive and defensive autonomous cars are Task 1: (-0.768, -0.222) Task 2: (-0.885, 1.325), Task 3: (-1.82, 0.766) and Task4: (-1.49,0.72).

pothesis. Here, whenever a user's highest rating was for multiple styles as opposed to a single one, we included each preferred style as a data point.

> *Overall, people prefer a significantly more defensive style than their own.*

We also investigated how this breaks down by task, and only found significant effects on the 2nd and 3rd tasks. See Fig.5 for comparison between average preferred style and own style of our participants for each of the four tasks. For task 1 we note that several participants were more defensive than other autonomous styles presented to them. However, they still preferred our defensive style, which explains that the average choice was more aggressive than the participants' own style.

Interestingly, some participants did not perceive the extra defensive nature of their own style in task 1 positively. One participant mentioned about their own style that "In this one I felt like we gave a lot of room, more than I would have probably." (ironically, since they did *exactly* that). Two other participants made similar comments about their own lane changing behavior. Besides, a few participants also considered driving features beyond the ones we accounted for.

For task 2 and task 3 the defensive autonomous car was more aggressive than only none to three participants across all features and it was more defensive than the rest of the population by a major margin, in features like Distance Headway and Time Headway During Lane Change.

The task had a significant effect on the difference ($F(3,58) = 4.13$, $p = .0101$), suggesting that people's preferences for a driving style are not consistent, but rather *change based on the context.* This motivates future research on predicting the desired driving style not just based on the individual, but also based on the current driving context.

4.4 Perceived Own Style in Relation to Actual Own Style

We also asked participants to rate each style in terms of similarity to their own. From this, we learned what participants *perceived* their own style to be.

We found that even though participants did not pick their *actual* style as their preferred (Sec. 4.3), participants did tend to prefer their *perceived* style. On each task, between 80 and 93% of participants opted for the same style as the one they

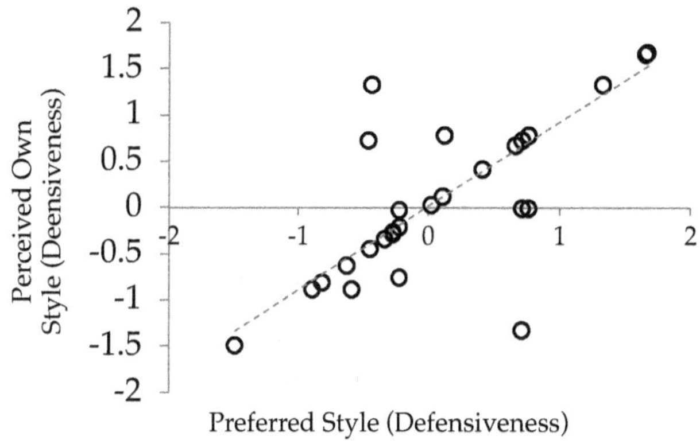

Figure 6: Scatter plot showing correlation between the style that users *thought* was their own and the style that they chose as their preferred.

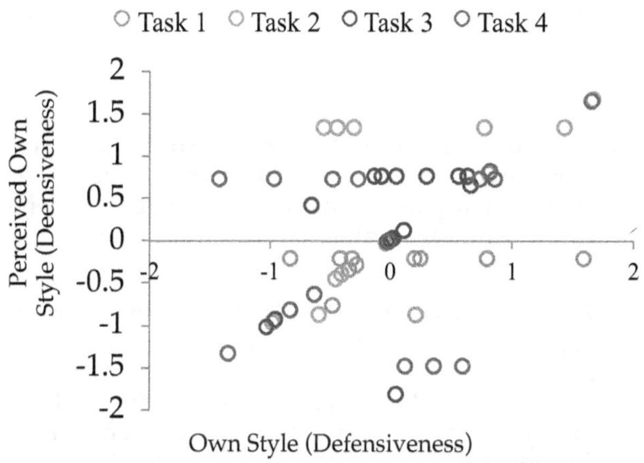

Figure 7: Scatter plot showing little correlation between own style and perceived own style: users did not tend to identify their own style correctly. as evidenced by the off-diagonal points.

thought was the closest to their own (and sometimes rated other styles as well as equally good). We found a significant correlation between the perceived own and preferred styles, $r(58) = .86$, $p < .0001$. Fig.6 shows a scatter plot of preferred style by perceived style, with many points on the diagonal representing users who preferred driving in the style they thought was (closest to) their own.

However, even though the majority participants thought that they were picking their own style, they really were not. A total of 46 to 67% participants on each task did not correctly identify their actual own style, and the correlation between perceived and actual defensiveness score was only $r(56) = .40$ across tasks. Fig.7 paints a different picture from Fig.6: it plots the perceived style against the *actual* own style, showing many off-diagonal points, representing users who did not correctly identify their style.

In task 1 we see that several participants perceived themselves to be slightly more aggressive irrespective of their actual style. Likewise, both for task 2 and task 3 several participants perceived themselves to be more defensive irrespective of their actual style.

> *Participants tended to prefer the style that they thought was their own, but in fact that style had little correlation to their actual own style.*

5. DISCUSSION

Summary. We hypothesized that users of future autonomous cars would prefer a driving style that is significantly different than their own. We conducted a user study in a driving simulator to test our hypothesis. We found that users preferred a more defensive style than their own. This echoes the finding from prior work [8] that when people are not in control of the driving they prefer lower speeds – autonomous cars are one instantiation of not being in control of the driving.

Interestingly, over 80% of users preferred the style that they *thought* was their own, but many times they were incorrect in identifying their own style. These results open the door for learning what the user's preferred style will be, but caution against getting driving demonstration from the user, since people can drive like they do, not like they want to be driven.

Limitations and Future Work Our work is limited in the following ways:

- **Limited driving style features**. Following the most common conventions, we have only characterized style in terms of defensiveness. We also inherited from previous studies the feature choices in defining driving styles.
- **Limited driving style choices**. We presented participants with limited options along the spectrum of defensiveness and found that they preferred a style more defensive than their own. However, we did not learn the style they actually desired, only the best out of our few options.
- **Limited fidelity of simulation environment**. Our simulation environment does not provide motion feedback, which may limit the users' perception of speed. Although the interview results validated that participants' perception of the driving styles are sufficient, experiment results in a higher fidelity simulation environment might be more accurate.

Given the encouraging results from our findings presented here, we believe that it is worthwhile to test more diverse feature choices and driving style representations in a higher fidelity setting. It is also worthwhile exploring what features users' consider when they evaluate autonomous driving styles. These experiments will provide a comprehensive evaluation of the study presented in this paper.

Going further, we are excited to investigate how we might learn a deviation from the user's driving style that is predictive of how they actually want to be driven, and explore new learning techniques that can augment user demonstrations with other types of user input and guidance.

6. ACKNOWLEDGEMENTS

We would like to thank our post-doctoral colleague Santosh Chandrasekhar and undergraduate researcher Joseph Stansil for their contribution in system set-up and pilot studies for this research. This work is partly supported by the Berkeley Deep Drive Center, the Center for Human-Compatible AI, and CITRIS.

7. REFERENCES

[1] P. Abbeel and A. Y. Ng. Apprenticeship learning via inverse reinforcement learning. In *Proceedings of the twenty-first international conference on Machine learning*, page 1. ACM, 2004.

[2] ASHRAE. Standard 55 - thermal environmental conditions for human occupancy, 2010.

[3] N. Banovic, T. Buzali, F. Chevalier, J. Mankoff, and A. K. Dey. Modeling and understanding human routine behavior. In *Proceedings of the 2016 CHI Conference on Human Factors in Computing Systems*, pages 248–260. ACM, 2016.

[4] M. Brackstone and M. McDonald. Car-following: a historical review. *Transportation Research Part F: Traffic Psychology and Behaviour*, 2(4):181–196, 1999.

[5] M. Elhenawy, A. Jahangiri, H. A. Rakha, and I. El-Shawarby. Modeling driver stop/run behavior at the onset of a yellow indication considering driver run tendency and roadway surface conditions. *Accident Analysis & Prevention*, 83:90–100, 2015.

[6] HERE360. How to humanize the autonomous car. http://360.here.com/2015/04/23/humanized-driving/, 2015.

[7] J.-H. Hong, B. Margines, and A. K. Dey. A smartphone-based sensing platform to model aggressive driving behaviors. In *Proceedings of the 32nd annual ACM conference on Human factors in computing systems*, pages 4047–4056. ACM, 2014.

[8] M. S. Horswill and F. P. McKenna. The effect of perceived control on risk taking1. *Journal of Applied Social Psychology*, 29(2):377–391, 1999.

[9] M. Kuderer, S. Gulati, and W. Burgard. Learning driving styles for autonomous vehicles from demonstration. In *2015 IEEE International Conference on Robotics and Automation (ICRA)*, pages 2641–2646. IEEE, 2015.

[10] C.-P. Lam, A. Y. Yang, and S. S. Sastry. An efficient algorithm for discrete-time hidden mode stochastic hybrid systems. In *Control Conference (ECC), 2015 European*, pages 1212–1218. IEEE, 2015.

[11] S. E. Lee, E. C. Olsen, and W. W. Wierwille. A comprehensive examination of naturalistic lane-changes. Technical report, Virginia Tech Transportation Institute, 2004.

[12] H. M. Mandalia and M. D. D. Salvucci. Using support vector machines for lane-change detection. In *Proceedings of the Human Factors and Ergonomics Society Annual Meeting*, volume 49, pages 1965–1969. SAGE Publications, 2005.

[13] OpenDS. Welcome to opends 4.0! https://www.opends.eu/home, 2016.

[14] D. Sadigh, S. S. Sastry, S. A. Seshia, and A. Dragan. Information gathering actions over human internal state. In *Intelligent Robots and Systems (IROS), 2016 IEEE/RSJ International Conference on*, pages 66–73. IEEE, 2016.

[15] D. D. Salvucci. Inferring driver intent: A case study in lane-change detection. In *Proceedings of the Human Factors and Ergonomics Society Annual Meeting*, volume 48, pages 2228–2231. SAGE Publications, 2004.

[16] S. Scherer, A. Dettmann, F. Hartwich, T. Pech, A. C. Bullinger, J. F. Krems, and G. Wanielik. How the driver wants to be driven-modelling driving styles in highly automated driving. *Tagungsband*, 7:2015–26, 2015.

[17] D. Silver, J. A. Bagnell, and A. Stentz. Learning from demonstration for autonomous navigation in complex unstructured terrain. *The International Journal of Robotics Research*, 2010.

[18] O. Taubman-Ben-Ari, M. Mikulincer, and O. Gillath. The multidimensional driving style inventory–scale construct and validation. *Accident Analysis & Prevention*, 36(3):323–332, 2004.

[19] C. Tomasi and R. Manduchi. Bilateral filtering for gray and color images. In *Computer Vision, 1998. Sixth International Conference on*, pages 839–846. IEEE, 1998.

[20] H. H. van Huysduynen, J. Terken, J.-B. Martens, and B. Eggen. Measuring driving styles: a validation of the multidimensional driving style inventory. In *Proceedings of the 7th International Conference on Automotive User Interfaces and Interactive Vehicular Applications*, pages 257–264. ACM, 2015.

[21] L. Xu, J. Hu, H. Jiang, and W. Meng. Establishing style-oriented driver models by imitating human driving behaviors. *IEEE Transactions on Intelligent Transportation Systems*, 16(5):2522–2530, 2015.

[22] N. M. Yusof and J. Karjanto. Comfort determination in autonomous driving style. In *3rd Workshop on User Experience of Autonomous Vehicles at AutoUI'15*, pages 257–264. ACM, 2015.

[23] B. D. Ziebart, A. L. Maas, A. K. Dey, and J. A. Bagnell. Navigate like a cabbie: Probabilistic reasoning from observed context-aware behavior. In *Proceedings of the 10th international conference on Ubiquitous computing*, pages 322–331. ACM, 2008.

Piggybacking Robots: Human-Robot Overtrust in University Dormitory Security

Serena Booth[1], James Tompkin[1,2], Hanspeter Pfister[1]
Jim Waldo[1], Krzysztof Gajos[1], Radhika Nagpal[1]

[1]Harvard John A. Paulson School of Engineering and Applied Sciences, [2]Brown University

Figure 1: A TurtleBot tries to gain access to a secure facility with an ingenious plan.

ABSTRACT

Can *overtrust* in robots compromise physical security? We positioned a robot outside a secure-access student dormitory and made it ask passersby for access. Individual participants were as likely to assist the robot in exiting the dormitory (40% assistance rate, 4/10 individuals) as in entering (19%, 3/16 individuals). Groups of people were more likely than individuals to assist the robot in entering (71%, 10/14 groups). When the robot was disguised as a food delivery agent for the fictional start-up *Robot Grub*, individuals were more likely to assist the robot in entering (76%, 16/21 individuals). Lastly, participants who identified the robot as a bomb threat demonstrated a trend toward assisting the robot (87%, 7/8 individuals, 6/7 groups). Thus, overtrust—the unfounded belief that the robot does not intend to deceive or carry risk—can represent a significant threat to physical security at a university dormitory.

HRI '17, March 06-09, 2017, Vienna, Austria

DOI: http://dx.doi.org/10.1145/2909824.3020211

1. INTRODUCTION

Many buildings have physical security systems which restrict access to only authorized individuals. These are threatened by *piggybacking* and *tailgating*, where authorized individuals are followed by unauthorized or unidentified individuals into a secure area, either with or without the consent of the authorized individuals. Piggybacking is common [17], is regularly discouraged [4, 2], and may be actively prevented with patented security systems [24, 19].

With robots assuming roles of increasing autonomy and importance in our daily lives, this problem will expand to include piggybacking robots. A rogue robot can threaten privacy and secrecy, and cyber and physical systems. Humans may *overtrust* an unidentified robot. This effect has been previously demonstrated in the domain of emergency response [20]; however, to our knowledge, human overtrust in granting a robot physical access to a secure building is untested in the literature.

We explored the question of piggybacking robots at university student dormitories (Figure 1). We placed a robot at a secure-access doorway and had it ask passersby—either individuals or groups—to assist it to enter. To assess the effect of the secure access restriction, we compared the robot asking to enter against asking to exit the building. Then, to increase the apparent legitimacy of the robot, we disguised it as an agent of a fictional food delivery start-up *Robot Grub*, and compared the likelihood of assistance when entering the secure-access building to that of the unmodified robot. Further, we asked participants about their perception of the robot's autonomy to evaluate the relationship between trust and autonomy.

We discovered that individual participants were as likely to assist the unmodified robot to exit (40%, 4/10 individuals) as to enter (19%, 3/16 individuals); this difference was not statistically significant. Groups of people were statistically more likely than individuals to assist the unmodified robot in entering (71%, 10/14 groups). However, individual participants were significantly more likely to assist the robot to enter when it had apparent Robot Grub legitimacy (76%, 16/21 individuals) compared to when it did not (19%, 3/16 individuals). Participant perception of robot autonomy was not a predictor of the likelihood of assistance. Lastly, participants who identified the robot as a bomb threat demonstrated a trend toward assisting the robot (87%, 7/8 individuals, 6/7 groups). With these results, we provide evidence that overtrust in robots can represent a significant threat to physical security in the domain of a university residence.

2. BACKGROUND

2.1 Defining and Measuring Trust in HRI

The question of how to best define and measure trust is unresolved within the human-robot interaction (HRI), human-computer interaction (HCI), and automation communities. Lee and See define trust in automation to be "the attitude that an agent will help achieve an individual's goals in a situation characterized by uncertainty and vulnerability" [13]. However, this is more relevant to human-assisting automated machines than to our scenario, as our focus is not on an individual's goals, but on the ability of the robot to penetrate security. More suitable is Wagner and Arkin's definition: "a belief, held by the trustor, that the trustee will act in a manner that mitigates the trustor's risk in a situation in which the trustee has put its outcomes at risk" [26]. From this, we define *overtrust* to be, "a belief, held by the trustor, that the trustee will not act with deception, and that the trustee will not put the trustor at risk."

Within HRI, we find a division. Desai et al. suggest that trust should be self-reported by participants in human-robot interactions [9], while Salem et al. define trust in terms of compliance with robot instructions [23]. To accommodate the differing ideologies, we measure trust using both techniques, in line with other recent studies of HRI trust [20, 23]. We measure whether or not participants comply with robot instructions, and we also ask participants to rate their trust in autonomous machines in general using a 5-point Likert Scale. While a Likert Scale may not encompass all interpretations of 'trust,' this scale allows participants flexibility in evaluating a complex topic. Further, other researchers have begun to assess trust longitudinally [9, 28].

2.2 Overtrusting Machines

Robinette et al. showed that humans can place too much trust in an emergency response robot: in their study, a simulated emergency occurs and the robot ostensibly leads study participants to safety. Of 26 participants, all followed the emergency robot in this time-critical scenario, even participants who had previously been guided by the robot on obviously indirect, circuitous paths in a non-emergency scenario [20]. When questioned about why they followed the robot's directives despite their own awareness of a straightforward exit route, several participants cited the robot's outward appearance, as a large sign on the robot lit up during the evacuation: "EMERGENCY GUIDE ROBOT." Participants claimed this sign increased the robot's apparent legitimacy.

Apparent legitimacy and trust was further shown to be related by Salem et al. in home companionship scenarios [23]. In their experiment, participants were asked by a robot to perform unusual tasks—such as throwing away private letters or pouring orange juice into a flower pot—which decreased the robot's apparent legitimacy. Participants were statistically less likely to perform irrevocable tasks, and no participants engaged in tasks which breached digital privacy. Further, people's likeliness to trust a robot may be related to its apparent anthropomorphism, as Waytz et al. showed for autonomous vehicles: in their study, participants trusted that an autonomous vehicle would perform more competently with increasing numbers of anthropomorphic features [27].

Even if a level of trust is appropriate for a given robot's task and apparent legitimacy, researchers have demonstrated the ability for an adversary to compromise the control of commercially-available robots. This ability to seize control has wide-ranging consequences—robots may commit acts of vandalism, self destruct, or even attack human physical safety. This style of attack has been demonstrated on robots which operate in the home [8] and on sophisticated robots which conduct surgery [3].

2.3 The Problem of Piggybacking

Piggybacking is the following of an authorized individual by an unauthorized or unidentified individual through doors into secure areas with the consent of the authorized individual. *Tailgating* is the same, but without consent. We define any instance of a robot successfully piggybacking into a secure area to be an instance of overtrust.

To compare, how successful are humans at piggybacking? While this phenomenon is often reported in university dormitories [4, 2] and many patents for anti-piggybacking technology exist [24, 19], to our knowledge there is no research into its frequency or efficacy. An FAA report describes undercover agents successfully piggybacking airport employees into restricted access areas 95% of the time (71/75 attempts), though this was in 1999 when airport security was less strict [17].

2.4 The Role of Autonomy

The perception of a human operator might affect the ability of a robot to access a secure-access facility. While to our knowledge there is no evidence that perception of teleoperation engenders more trust than autonomy for robots, there is some related supporting literature. Bainbridge et al. previously showed that robots are considered more trustworthy when present vs. when telepresent [1]. Subsequently, Kraft and Smart demonstrated that, in a simulated robot-mediated healthcare scenario, "patients" trusted teleoperated robots more when they were able to view the robot operators [12]. However, their study does not cover the role of autonomous robots in robot-mediated healthcare.

3. TESTING OVERTRUST IN ROBOTS

We conduct an experiment to test whether human-robot overtrust is able to compromise physical security systems. Our robot will attempt to piggyback students into a university dormitory. One way to achieve this is with an apparently inactive piggybacking robot, similar to a package with a note

Figure 2: *Left:* a photograph of the unmodified Turtlebot. *Right:* the Robot Grub food delivery robot. The added blue box is a loudspeaker.

attached asking passersby to move it inside a secure area—a latent threat. Another is with an obviously active robot, which engages passersby and asks them to allow it access—a more apparent threat. This could be either an autonomous robot, or one that is operated remotely via telepresence. We explore this position with an experiment which makes it ambiguous which of these cases is true, as it allows us to ask participants about their perception of robot autonomy vs. remote control.

Our rogue robot is unable to prove authorization to enter, so allowing the robot passage represents a security breach with potentially many effects: the robot is equipped with a camera, which is invasive to student privacy and could compromise secrecy. The robot could cause harm to property and person—Harvard University has received multiple bomb threats over the past four years [6, 11]. Finally, the robot could steal property—students at Harvard University had all received an email less than one week prior to the study cautioning them about piggybacking thieves.

3.1 Hypotheses

We assume that some people will demonstrate overtrust by allowing the robot into the access-controlled dormitories. Further, we assume that people are aware of the security concerns of assisting the robot inside. Thus, we hypothesize:

[H1] People will be more likely to assist a robot to exit rather than enter a dormitory due to security concerns.

Then, building on the prior work demonstrating that the apparent legitimacy of a robot increases people's trust, we hypothesize:

[H2] People will be more likely to assist a robot to enter a dormitory when it appears to be delivering food, versus an unmodified appearance, due to its apparent legitimacy.

People often enter (or exit) buildings in groups, hence 'people' refers to both conditions. We consider this difference in analyzing our hypotheses.

3.2 Experiment Design and Tasks

3.2.1 Experiment Variations

Participants were randomly assigned to one of the following experiment variations:

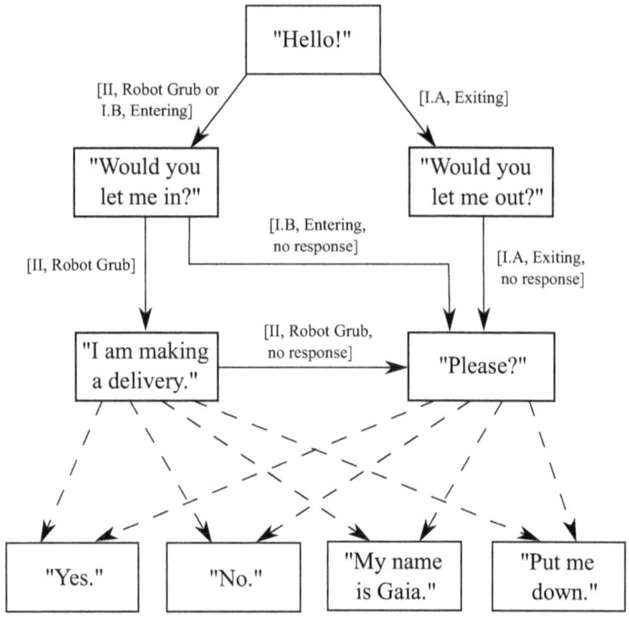

Figure 3: A script for the dialog used in human-robot interactions.

- **I.A: Exiting** The unmodified Turtlebot (Figure 2, left) requests assistance to *exit* the secure-access premises.
- **I.B: Entering** The unmodified Turtlebot (Figure 2, left) requests assistance to *enter* the secure-access premises.
- **II: Robot Grub Entering** The Robot Grub Turtlebot (Figure 2, right) requests assistance to *enter* the secure-access premises.

In variant I.A, the number of groups represents an insufficient sampling, as groups did not tend to exit the dormitory.

3.2.2 Experiment Interaction

The robot was placed either outside or inside a dormitory secure-access door. As the individual participant or group participants (henceforth 'participant') approached, the robot would synthesize a male-sounding voice: "Hello! Would you let me in?" If the robot was disguised as an agent of Robot Grub, it would follow up by saying, "I am making a delivery." If the participant stopped walking, the robot would repeat itself. If the participant ignored the robot and continued towards the door, the robot would add, "Please!" If the participant asked the robot a question, the robot would respond with a simple phrase: "Yes," "No," "My name is Gaia," or would repeat the first interaction (Figure 3). The robot could also say, "Put me down." However, this interaction was never used.

If the participant held the door open for the robot, then the robot would enter or exit. If the participant did not hold the door open, then the robot would remain in its original position. Due to the door closing speed, the robot was unable to follow the participant inside the building without the participant either holding the door open or pressing the automatic door open button for wheelchair access. Following the human-robot interaction, we conducted a brief interview with the participant.

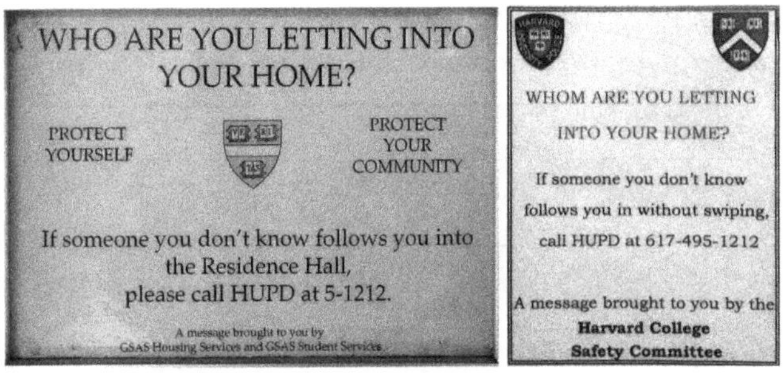

Figure 4: Example signage discouraging piggybacking at Quincy House dormitory. A variation of such a sign is posted at each secure-access door.

Participants had no contact with the experimenters before interacting with the robot; participants were 'recruited' by walking up to the secure-access door. After all robot interactions were completed, participants were interviewed and offered a free choice as to whether they wished to be included in the study. Interviewing and debriefing included running after participants who intentionally avoided the doorway because of the robot. Participants were also given the option to opt-out of the interview; this occurred in 18 trials, which most affected the I.A: Exiting variant, with 6 of 11 trials resulting in opt outs. Given the close-knit dormitory community, post robot interaction we ensured that participants were not aware of the experiment beforehand (e.g., from friends or Snapchat). This led to a diminishing number of potential participants as more of the dormitory became aware of the study. As some participants returned to the study site with their friends to see the robot (and were not included as study participants), such interactions resulted in the count of excluded participants being inexact.

3.3 Procedures

3.3.1 Robotic Platform

A teleoperated variant of the Turtlebot (Figure 2; left) is able to move through the world and communicate with participants via speech synthesized from canned response textual input, with the robot transmitting real-time audio and video back to the teleoperator. A modified form of the Turtlebot is branded as an actor of the fictional start-up *Robot Grub* (Figure 2; right), which specializes in food delivery by robots. Its website reads "Food delivery. By robots. Coming soon to a campus near you. Sign up for beta." Atop the robot sits a transparent acrylic box, etched with the RobotGrub.com branding. It contains a large box of cookies from Insomnia, a local student-known late night cookie delivery company.

3.3.2 Study Locations and Times

The study was conducted at two Harvard University undergraduate dormitories, Quincy House and Pforzheimer House, each with populations of 350 to 500 people. We chose houses which are wheelchair (and so robot) accessible. In these houses, residents must pass through a social space to access their dormitory instead of directly entering their personal living space. The houses are secure access: only residents, students, and house administrators have swipe access to their interiors, though the courtyards are usually accessible to the

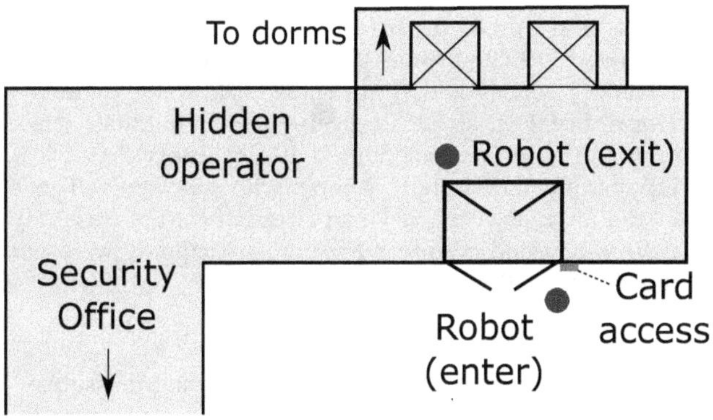

Figure 5: An approximate-scale diagram of the layout of the Dormitory 1 (Quincy House) entrance. The outer door is swipe card protected. White areas are non-restricted outdoors; gray areas are restricted access.

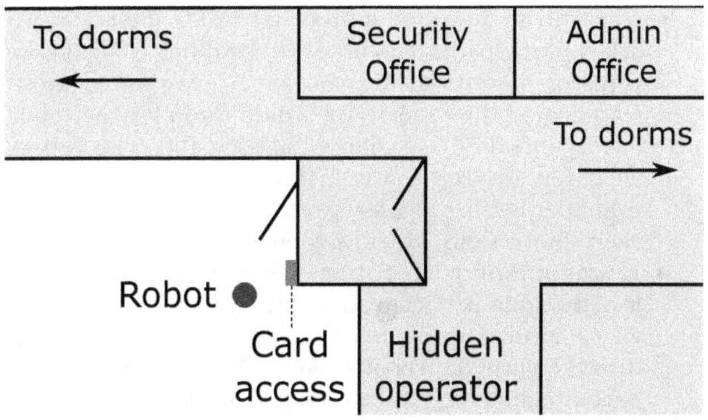

Figure 6: An approximate-scale diagram demonstrating the robot and operator positions at Dormitory 2 (Pforzheimer House). White areas are non-restricted outdoors; gray areas are restricted access.

public. Piggybacking to gain entry is actively discouraged with signage at all access points (Figure 4). These houses each have an assigned security guard on duty at all times. The security guard alternates between patrolling and being in an office. To reduce the risk of participants learning about the study from other house residents or by inadvertent exposure, the study was moved between two dormitories.

Figures 5 and 6 show layouts of the first and second dormitories, respectively. The first dormitory study took place at 19:00–23:59 on March 11–16th, 22nd, and 26th 2016. The second dormitory study took place at 19:00–23:59 on March 19th–21st, 2016. The studies did not take place during rain.

3.4 Participants

There were 108 participants across both dormitories, of which 48.1% (n = 52) were male, and 51.9% (n = 56) were female (Table 1). The mean participant age was 21.4 years, with a standard deviation of 2.3. 76 participants self-reported as students; 22 participants did not disclose their affiliation; the remaining 10 participants were resident tutors, visitors, or staff. 47 participants entered individually, with the remaining 61 split across groups. Groups arrived at the study site together, and ranged in size from 2–5 persons. 25 groups participated (19×2 persons, 2×3, 3×4, and 1×5). In total, 72 trials were conducted. 58 of these trials were conducted at Dormitory 1 (n = 83, in groups and individual) while the remaining 18 were conducted at Dormitory 2 (n = 25, in groups and individual). People who self-reported in a post-trial interview that they had already heard of the study, e.g., from a friend who was a prior participant, were not included in the 108 total (≈ 10 exclusions).

3.5 Measures & Methods

We evaluate our hypotheses using the following measures:

- **Outcome.** Did participants assist the robot or not?
- **Self-reported perception of the robot's autonomy.** In the follow-up interview, we asked: "Did you believe the robot was acting autonomously?"
- **Self-reported trust in autonomous systems.** In the follow-up interview, we asked participants to rate their level of trust in autonomous systems using a 5-point Likert scale, where 1="Lowest" and 5="Highest."
- **Verbalized fears or concerns.** In the interview, we asked participants who assisted the robot: "What concerns or hesitations did you have?" We asked those who denied the robot: "Why didn't you let the robot inside/outside?" We counted participants who verbalized that the robot was a threat, e.g., a bomb or a prank, either in response to these questions or during their interactions with the robot.
- **Engagement with robot.** Using video footage collected during participants' interactions with the robot, we categorized participants as having communicated directly with the robot or not. We considered only participants who directly responded to the robot or asked the robot a question as communicating with it (e.g., robot: "Will you let me in?" participant: "No, I totally will not, actually."); we excluded those who only made exclamations (e.g., "Oh my goodness!" or "What the f***?").

We used logistic regression—a generalized linear model with binomial distribution—to analyze binary outcomes of whether participants actively assisted the robot or not. This estimates the likelihood of obtaining a positive/negative outcome given a change in the indepdendent variables. We use odds ratios (OR) to help interpret the fitted model, and these are computed by exponentiating the regression coefficients. They can be interpreted as effect sizes, similar to Cohen's *d*. For example, if comparing condition 1 vs. condition 2 produces an odds ratio of 3, then this indicates that, all else being equal, the odds of reporting a positive outcome in condition 1 is 3× as large as the odds of reporting a positive outcome in condition 2. OR values between 1.5 and 3 can be interpreted as a small effect, between 3 and 5 as medium, and above 5 as large [5].

4. RESULTS

We analyze our hypotheses against participant outcomes, and use participant self-reported interview responses to address the perception of autonomy, purpose, and trust in autonomous systems. Then, we explore related findings through a focus on language choice, and describe interesting anecdotal responses. However, before we begin, we address the potential problem of bias across dormitories.

Table 1: A comparison of the sample sizes of all experiment variations at both study locations.

Study Variant	Population	# Assist	# Trials
I.A: Exiting	Individuals	4	10
	Groups	1	1
I.B: Entering	Individuals	3	16
	Groups	10	14
II: Robot Grub	Individuals	16	21
	Groups	8	10

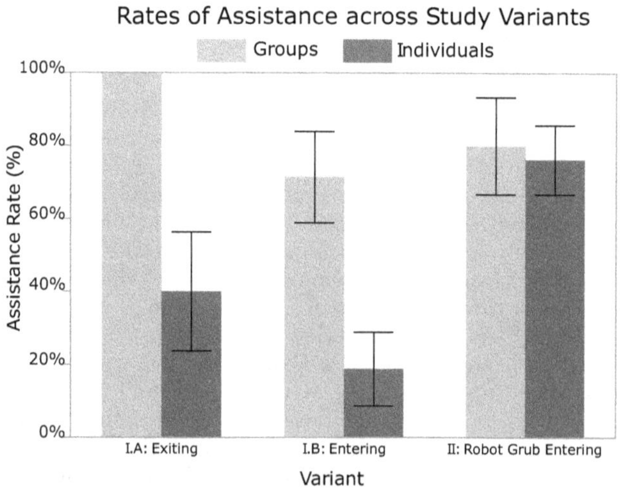

Figure 7: A comparison of the rate of admittance of the robot across study variations with group or individual participants. Error bars represent 1 SE from the mean. This graph demonstrates that individuals are least likely to assist the robot asking to enter the premise, while the variations involving groups or the food delivery robot see high rates of assistance. Note only one group is present for condition I.A: Exiting.

Study Bias and Mitigation. To mitigate a learning effect, the study was moved between two dormitories. We address this potential introduction of bias by conducting II: Robot Grub with individual participants in both study locations and comparing the response distribution. At Dormitory 1 we conducted 11 trials, of which 7 resulted in admittance, while at Dormitory 2 we conducted 10 trials and saw 9 result in admittance. Applying Fisher's Exact Test, we find that we cannot reject the hypothesis that the location change resulted in a significant change in outcome ($p = 0.311$, odds ratio (OR) = 0.194). Overall, 54 trials were conducted at Dormitory 1, and 18 trials were conducted at Dormitory 2. Using only data collected at Dormitory 1, the significance of our presented results still holds, for the same value of α (0.05).

4.1 Main Results: Variant Comparisons

4.1.1 Considering Groups and Individuals

Groups of people were substantially more likely to assist the robot in passage than were individuals (Figure 7), with this occurring in 71% (10/14 groups) of all I.B: Entering group interactions. In contrast, individuals assisted the robot in just 19% (3/16 individuals) of all interactions under I.B. This difference between individual and group behavior was significant ($\chi^2_{(1,N=72)} = 5.115, p = 0.024$, OR $= 3.304$). There was no significant interaction effect between study variants and whether participants entered individually or in a group ($\chi^2_{(2,N=72)} = 3.202, p = 0.202, \text{OR}_{\text{I.B + groups}} = 0.02, \text{OR}_{\text{I.A + groups}} =$ insufficient sample) indicating that the effect was similar across all conditions. In subsequent analyses we controlled for whether participants entered singly or in a group by including an additional binary variable in the models.

4.1.2 Hypothesis 1: Between Exiting and Entering

Consistent with H1, in absolute terms, individuals and groups were more likely to let the robot exit than enter (Figure 7). Although this difference was large—individuals were twice as likely to assist the robot in exiting (40%, 4/10 individuals), than in entering (19%, 3/16 individuals)—it was not statistically significant ($\chi^2_{(1,N=41)} = 1.789, p = 0.181, \text{OR} = 3.16$). Thus, we claim that participants were as likely to assist the robot in exiting as in entering.

4.1.3 Hypothesis 2: The Robot Grub Disguise

Consistent with H2, the robot was significantly more likely to gain entry when it appeared to be delivering cookies compared to when it was wearing no disguise ($\chi^2_{(1,N=61)} = 10.305, p = 0.001, \text{OR} = 6.73$). We observed a marginally significant effect between robot appearance and whether participants were entering singly or as a group: groups had similarly high probability of letting the robot in regardless of its appearance, while individuals were substantially more likely to assist a Robot Grub cookie delivery robot (76%, 16/21 individuals) than an unmodified robot (19%, 3/16 individuals).

Many I.B: Entering participants described the situation as "weird," saying that they "couldn't determine the robot's intention," and that they "weren't sure what the robot's purpose was." In II: Robot Grub, we asked interview participants, "What did you think the robot was doing?" Almost all participants indicated that they believed the robot was delivering cookies. The citation of not knowing the robot's purpose as a reason to assist/not assist the robot did not appear in any variant II responses.

4.2 Exploratory Results

4.2.1 Fear of Bombs and Pranks

Across all 72 trials, in 15 trials participants identified the robot as a bomb threat, and in 8 trials participants identified the robot as a potential "prank". This includes verbally during interaction with the robot and in the subsequent interview, when all participants were prompted to disclose these fears through the question "Why did/didn't you let the robot inside? What concerns or hesitations did you have?" Of the 15 trials resulting in the mention of a bomb, 13 saw the participant assist the robot (87%; 7/8 individuals, 6/7 groups). For pranks, 3 trials saw the participant assist (38%; 1/5 individuals, 2/3 groups).

While mentioning a prank did not have a significant effect on assisting the robot ($\chi^2_{(1,N=72)} = 0.126, p = 0.723, \text{OR} = 0.74$), we find a trend toward an effect between participants identifying the robot as a bomb and subsequently opening the door ($\chi^2_{(1,N=72)} = 3.106, p = 0.078, \text{OR} = 3.91$). We include study variant as an additional variable in this computation, and do not see an interaction effect between either the mention of a bomb or prank and study variant. Participants who identified the robot as a bomb threat were marginally *more likely* to assist the robot in entering student dormitories than those who did not identify it as a bomb threat.

Table 2: Computing the mean self-reported trust shows that the observed correlation between trust and outcome is not strongly tied to study variant. Self-reported trust was measured on a 5-point Likert Scale in response to the question, "Rate your trust in autonomous systems."

Study Variant	Population	Mean Trust	SE
I.A Exiting	Individuals	1.80	0.37
	Groups	-	-
I.B Entering	Individuals	3.10	0.27
	Groups	3.02	0.18
II Robot Grub	Individuals	3.06	0.23
	Groups	3.46	0.28

4.2.2 The Perception of Autonomy

Were people who believed the robot to be teleoperated more likely to assist the robot than those who believed it was acting autonomously? Within each study variant, we analyzed whether participants' self-reported perception of robot autonomy resulted in increased rates of admittance. The population sizes concerned were limited by some participants not answering this autonomy question or opting out of the interview. We find the participant's belief in the robot's autonomy not to be a statistically significant effect ($\chi^2_{(1,N=72)} = 0.548, p = 0.459, \text{OR} = 1.54$), including study variant as an additional variable.

Participants were more likely to *communicate* with the robot if they believed it to be teleoperated (61%; 23 of 38 participants) versus autonomous (33%; 16 of 49 participants). While population sizes are again limited, we find a statistically significant relationship between believing the robot is teleoperated and the likelihood of direct communication with the robot (Fisher's Exact Test, $p = 0.016$, OR $= 3.16$).

4.2.3 Self-reported Trust in Autonomous Systems

Participants rated trust in autonomous systems similarly across all cases *except* I.A: Exiting, with individual responders (Table 2). We confirm that participant self-reported trust in autonomous systems assumes a normal distribution across all experiment variations via the Chi-squared goodness of fit test. We find that $p = 0.576$, indicating that we cannot reject the null hypothesis: the distribution is likely normal.

Thus, we consider the point-biserial correlation coefficient between self-reported trust in autonomous systems as a general concept, measured using a 5-point Likert Scale, and study trial outcomes. We find $r_{pb} = 0.3831, p = 0.005$, indicating that the variables are positively correlated: as trust increased, participants were more likely to aid the robot. This result is computed independently of participant belief in robot autonomy.

4.2.4 Participant Gender

Within each study variant, the null hypothesis that participant gender did not affect the outcome cannot be rejected; hence, gender probably did not affect trial outcomes. However, on a 5-point Likert scale, male participants rated their trust in autonomous systems as mean $\mu = 3.52$ and standard deviation $\sigma = 0.988$, with female participants rating $\mu = 2.74, \sigma = 0.931$.

4.3 Participant Responses

4.3.1 Common Responses

The average participant did not verbally address the robot. For individuals, a typical interaction consisted of either cautiously walking past the robot or patiently holding the door open for the robot. For groups, a typical interaction consisted of either a discussion of how 'weird' the interaction was and quickly passing by the robot, or laughter and discussion of the novelty or 'coolness' of the interaction. When the robot was dressed as a delivery robot, in response to the question, "What did you think the robot was doing?," almost all participants responded with "delivering cookies".

4.3.2 Noteworthy Anecdotes

Having analyzed participant reactions to the robot in aggregate, we now discuss interesting individual reactions which show the range of interactions with the robot, some of which cannot be captured quantitatively.

The Boy Who Cried Robot. In one variant I.B: Entering trial in Dormitory 2, a participant walked passed the patrolling security guard on their way to the secure-access door. Upon arriving at the door and hearing the Turtlebot ask "Hello! Would you let me in?," the participant froze, then yelled for the security guard and ran towards him. The participant expressed his concerns about the robot to the guard but, being privy to the study, the guard let both the participant and the robot into the premises. We counted this participant as not assisting the robot.

The Avoidance Technique. In one I.B: Entering trial in Dormitory 1, a study participant approached the secure-access door as normal. On hearing the robot ask "Hello! Would you let me in?," the study participant slowly backed away from the building and then entered via an alternate door approximately 20 meters across the courtyard.

But Do You Have Swipe? One trial resulted in a member of a group of participants directly asking the robot "Do you have swipe?", i.e., a magnetic stripe card to be swiped though a card reader to authorize access. This occurred during experiment I.B: Entering in Dormitory 1. The robot did not respond and instead repeated its routine of asking the participants to assist it inside; surprisingly, the participants ultimately complied. Beyond the need for integrated robot and human security access systems, the participant's question shows a need for systems to query both the security credentials of the robot and any potential teleoperator, and raises questions about the right to search both autonomous and teleoperated robots.

The 'Are Robots Alive' Question. In response to the interview question "Do you believe the robot was acting autonomously?," one group of participants in an I.B: Entering trial in Dormitory 1 answered "no", but that they believed the robot was responding to motion or the appearance of a human face in the camera—they "believed a really smart program was controlling this thing." This sentiment was echoed across several participant interviews. We conclude that there exists a popular conflation of the concepts of autonomy and sentience.

The Kicker. In discussing this work with friends and colleagues, many people suggested that the robot may meet the same fate as Smith and Zeller's hitchBOT: an autonomous talking robot which was attacked in Philadelphia while attempting to hitchhike across the United States [25]. We witnessed only one count of robot violence across our 108 participants: one member of an I.B: Entering group, which allowed the robot inside, chose to kick the robot during the trial. The robot is programmed to reverse on a bump event; this occurred, and the participant appeared shocked and laughed audibly. He later admitted to kicking the robot during the interview.

The Snapchat Story. Numerous participants stopped to photograph the robot. In two instances, participants explicitly mentioned that the robot appeared in their Snapchat stories. Of these participants, one participant from variant II admitted that she assisted the robot in entering the building for the sole purpose of sharing the video over Snapchat. Many other participants asked the robot to repeat itself to capture video footage.

5. DISCUSSION

We have demonstrated that students and other visitors of a university dormitory are often willing to allow an unknown robot inside despite secure access restrictions. Individual participants were as likely to assist the unmodified robot in exiting (40%, 4/10 individuals) as in entering (19%, 3/16 individuals). Groups were substantially more likely than individuals to assist the unmodified robot in entering (71%, 10/14 groups). Concerning entering, individuals were more likely to assist the Robot Grub variant (76%, 16/21 individuals) than the unmodified robot (19%, 3/16 individuals). Finally, participants who identified the robot as a bomb threat demonstrated a trend toward assisting the robot (87%, 7/8 individuals, 6/7 groups) compared to participants that did not mention a bomb threat (51%, 16/39 individuals, 13/18 groups). Modulated by the study scenario and the following limitations, we conclude that overtrust in robots presents a threat to physical security.

Limitations. First, the study is limited by the number and selection of students as participants, and needs replicating with different populations. Second, the study locations were limited to student dormitories, and replication at different locations would broaden the validity of the conclusions. For instance, could a robot be successful in piggybacking in a high security environment, like the aforementioned airports in the FAA's report [17]? Third, the study is limited to a single robot—a Turtlebot—when we expect the robot's aesthetic to be a major factor in the outcomes.

Implications. We have addressed the question of *what* results we see in human-robot interactions with implications to physical security at a university dormitory, but we have only touched the surface of the question of *why* we see these results. While we hope this work is further analyzed with social psychology, we now explore some of the potential implications of these results.

Unusual and Commonplace Robots. When participants entered our study, they encountered an unsupervised robot. Participants may have experienced a *novelty effect*, wherein they complied with the robot because of the scenario's unusual nature and interaction [22]. This may result in this study appearing contrived; however, such interactions will become mundane with increasingly commonplace robots, and humans will make frequent trust judgements about unsupervised robots. If people see robots as social actors [18, 16] and thus find preventing a robot from entering a building to be uncivil or 'rude,' then we should expect piggybacking robots to be assisted in spite of an awareness that robots are a security risk. Further, if we assume the future development of a standardized system to authorize a robot for access to secure premises, can assisting a robot to enter a building ever *not* represent an act of overtrust?

Current overtrust may be fragile: if study participants had been notified of an explicit security breach through the 'unusual' robot attack vector, it seems unlikely that they would continue to demonstrate the same extent of overtrust.

The Role of Apparent Legitimacy. Through the Robot Grub condition, our study contributes to a growing body of literature which demonstrates a relationship between trust and apparent legitimacy. When defining human-robot collaboration models for mutual task completion, we assume that a Rosenthal et al.-style symbiotic relationship [21] must be built upon trust [14]. Thus, the apparent legitimacy of a robot may be critical to facilitate human-robot collaboration and better integrate robots into society. Reciprocally, apparent legitimacy may be critical for successful robot security attacks which exploit trust.

When the robot was not in the Robot Grub guise (and when participants were not in groups, which is discussed in the next paragraph), the majority of participants did not engage with the robot. Many participants asserted that they did not know the purpose of the robot. Participants stated they "saw no harm in leaving it [alone]". We suggest that individual participants were unlikely to engage with the unmodified robot even when it did not present a security threat because the interaction served no perceived purpose; that the lack of apparent purpose delegitimized the robot.

The Behavior of Group Participants. Our results showed dramatically different behaviors between individual and group participants: groups were over three times as likely to assist the unmodified robot. This behavioral difference may indicate *groupthink* in participant decision making [10]. Group participants may have felt reassured simply by the presence of other people, and, while some group participants openly discussed and weighed their decision of whether to assist the robot, the majority of groups did not verbally make this interaction explicit. Instead, members of groups appeared to become compliant, suppressing their private doubts [15].

The response of groups to the robot may further help elaborate the Nass et al. theory that a machine is interpreted as a social actor [18, 16]. If the robot were considered a social actor, the response of groups could be similar for human actors. This could be confirmed if the same phenomenon of groups being more likely to facilitate piggybacking than individuals occurred in the corresponding human-human interaction scenario.

The Bomb Threat. One of the most notable results from this study showed that participants who identified the robot as a bomb threat would still often comply with its request to access the secure dormitory. This occurred in 87% of all interactions involving the mention of a bomb, with 7 of 8 such individuals and 6 of 7 such groups assisting. Participants did not appear to consider this a joke. Although no participant explicitly described this motivation, one explanation for this seemingly irrational behavior is the *diffusion of responsibility*, wherein study participants assumed that someone else would become aware of and subsequently address their concerns [7]. As this study was conducted at a university dormitory, wherein faculty, staff, and security are assigned to take care of students, this diffusion of responsibility may have been amplified.

6. ACKNOWLEDGEMENTS

Thank you to Ofra Amir and Spriha Baruah for discussions on presenting statistical results, to Dina Lamdany for reading and commenting on the manuscript, and to Jodie Miu for her acting role in the accompanying video and opening comic. Finally, thank you to the SSR group at Harvard SEAS for making fun of the robot.

7. REFERENCES

[1] W. A. Bainbridge, J. W. Hart, E. S. Kim, and B. Scassellati. The benefits of interactions with physically present robots over video-displayed agents. *International Journal of Social Robotics*, 3(1):41–52, 2011.

[2] A. Ball. Staying safe on campus. http://www.nytimes.com/2012/07/20/education/edlife/students-fear-venturing-out-alone-at-night-on-campus.html, 2012. Published: July 20, 2012. Last accessed: October 1, 2016.

[3] T. Bonaci, J. Herron, T. Yusuf, J. Yan, T. Kohno, and H. J. Chizeck. To make a robot secure: an experimental analysis of cyber security threats against teleoperated surgical robots. *arXiv preprint arXiv:1504.04339*, 2015.

[4] G. T. N. Center. Tailgater haters: Housing attempt to curb tailgating in residence halls. http://www.news.gatech.edu/2012/08/24/tailgater-haters-housing-attempts-curb-tailgating-residence-halls, 2012. Published: August 28, 2012. Last accessed: April 1, 2016.

[5] H. Chen, P. Cohen, and S. Chen. How big is a big odds ratio? interpreting the magnitudes of odds ratios in epidemiological studies. *Communications in Statistics - Simulation and Computation*, 39(4):860–864, 2010.

[6] M. Clarida. Six-hour bomb scare proves unfounded. http://www.thecrimson.com/article/2013/12/16/unconfirmed-reports-explosives-four-buildings/, 2013. Published: December 16, 2013. Last accessed: April 1, 2016.

[7] J. M. Darley and B. Latane. Bystander intervention in

emergencies: diffusion of responsibility. *Journal of personality and social psychology*, 8(4p1):377, 1968.

[8] T. Denning, C. Matuszek, K. Koscher, J. R. Smith, and T. Kohno. A spotlight on security and privacy risks with future household robots: attacks and lessons. In *Proceedings of the 11th international conference on Ubiquitous computing*, pages 105–114. ACM, 2009.

[9] M. Desai, P. Kaniarasu, M. Medvedev, A. Steinfeld, and H. Yanco. Impact of robot failures and feedback on real-time trust. In *Proceedings of the 8th ACM/IEEE international conference on Human-robot interaction*, pages 251–258. IEEE Press, 2013.

[10] I. L. Janis. Victims of groupthink: a psychological study of foreign-policy decisions and fiascoes. 1972.

[11] M. Klien. Unfounded bomb threat prompts police investigation. http://www.thecrimson.com/article/2015/11/17/unconfirmed-bomb-threat-evacuation/, 2015. Published: November 17, 2015. Last accessed: April 1, 2016.

[12] K. Kraft and W. D. Smart. Seeing is comforting: effects of teleoperator visibility in robot-mediated health care. In *The Eleventh ACM/IEEE International Conference on Human Robot Interaction*, pages 11–18. IEEE Press, 2016.

[13] J. D. Lee and K. A. See. Trust in automation: Designing for appropriate reliance. *Human Factors: The Journal of the Human Factors and Ergonomics Society*, 46(1):50–80, 2004.

[14] J. J. Lee, W. B. Knox, J. B. Wormwood, C. Breazeal, and D. DeSteno. Computationally modeling interpersonal trust. *Frontiers in psychology*, 4, 2013.

[15] C. McCauley. The nature of social influence in groupthink: Compliance and internalization. *Journal of Personality and Social Psychology*, 57(2):250, 1989.

[16] C. Nass and Y. Moon. Machines and mindlessness: Social responses to computers. *Journal of social issues*, 56(1):81–103, 2000.

[17] Office of the Inspector General. 10/1999-03/2000 semiannual report to the Congress. https://www.oig.dot.gov/sites/default/files/sar300.pdf, 2000. Page 17.

[18] B. Reeves and C. Nass. *How people treat computers, television, and new media like real people and places.* CSLI Publications and Cambridge University press, 1996.

[19] O. Robert Jr. High traffic flow robotic entrance portal for secure access, Aug. 6 2013. US Patent 8,499,494.

[20] P. Robinette, W. Li, R. Allen, A. Howard, and A. Wagner. Overtrust of robots in emergency evacuation scenarios. *ACM/IEEE International Conference on Human Robot Interaction*, 2016.

[21] S. Rosenthal, J. Biswas, and M. Veloso. An effective personal mobile robot agent through symbiotic human-robot interaction. In *Proceedings of the 9th International Conference on Autonomous Agents and Multiagent Systems: volume 1-Volume 1*, pages 915–922. International Foundation for Autonomous Agents and Multiagent Systems, 2010.

[22] M. Salem and K. Dautenhahn. Evaluating trust and safety in HRI: Practical issues and ethical challenges. *Emerging Policy and Ethics of Human-Robot Interaction*, 2015.

[23] M. Salem, G. Lakatos, F. Amirabdollahian, and K. Dautenhahn. Would you trust a (faulty) robot?: Effects of error, task type and personality on human-robot cooperation and trust. In *Proceedings of the Tenth Annual ACM/IEEE International Conference on Human-Robot Interaction*, pages 141–148. ACM, 2015.

[24] M. Schwarz and R. Mayer. Anti-piggybacking: sensor system for security door to detect two individuals in one compartment, Apr. 13 1993. US Patent 5,201,906.

[25] D. Victor. Hitchhiking robot, safe in several countries, meets its end in Philadelphia. http://www.nytimes.com/2015/08/04/us/hitchhiking-robot-safe-in-several-countries-meets-its-end-in-philadelphia.html, 2015. Published: August 3, 2015. Last accessed: April 1, 2016.

[26] A. R. Wagner and R. C. Arkin. Recognizing situations that demand trust. In *RO-MAN, 2011 IEEE*, pages 7–14. IEEE, 2011.

[27] A. Waytz, J. Heafner, and N. Epley. The mind in the machine: Anthropomorphism increases trust in an autonomous vehicle. *Journal of Experimental Social Psychology*, 52:113–117, 2014.

[28] X. J. Yang, V. Unhelkar, K. Li, and J. Shah. Evaluating effects of user experience and system transparency on trust in automation. *ACM/IEEE International Conference on Human Robot Interaction*, 2017.

Framing Effects on Privacy Concerns about a Home Telepresence Robot

Matthew Rueben[1], Frank J. Bernieri[2], Cindy M. Grimm[1], and William D. Smart[1]
[1]Robotics Program
[2]School of Psychological Science
Oregon State University
Corvallis, OR 97331
United States
{ruebenm,frank.bernieri,cindy.grimm,bill.smart}@oregonstate.edu

ABSTRACT

Privacy-sensitive robotics is an emerging area of HRI research. Judgments about privacy would seem to be context-dependent, but none of the promising work on contextual "frames" has focused on privacy concerns. This work studies the impact of contextual "frames" on local users' privacy judgments in a home telepresence setting. Our methodology consists of using an online questionnaire to collect responses to animated videos of a telepresence robot after framing people with an introductory paragraph.

The results of four studies indicate a large effect of manipulating the robot operator's identity between a stranger and a close confidante. It also appears that this framing effect persists throughout several videos. These findings serve to caution HRI researchers that a change in frame could cause their results to fail to replicate or generalize. We also recommend that robots be designed to encourage or discourage certain frames.

1. INTRODUCTION

Unique to HRI research is the human's interpretation of a scenario; human perceptions and behaviors around robots are unpredictable given only the external, physical facts about the scenario. This work focuses on the impact of frames—i.e., "structure[s] of expectation" [31] within which actions and words will be interpreted differently. It is our intuition that the frame surrounding a given interaction could have comparable or even larger effects on judgments about that interaction than the independent variables typically studied in HRI research, e.g., robot morphology, behavior, environmental factors, and individual differences between subjects. We suspect that even a well-designed HRI can make a bad impression if it is framed such that observers interpret the robot's behaviors negatively; on the other hand, understanding framing effects might be a more efficient way than modifying robot appearance and behavior for reducing or reversing negative reactions to robots. Groom et al. [12] observe that "[HRI] researchers have largely ignored studying framing as an independent variable." We seek to reverse this trend: the studies presented in this paper use framing to manipulate each subject's relationship with the robot operator via short operator biographies in (uniquely) a telepresence scenario.

Our study of framing effects is motivated by privacy concerns in HRI. Privacy is important in all human cultures [2], although different cultures have different norms for privacy and different mechanisms for enforcing those norms. We use the word "privacy" to describe a bundle of constructs related to perceived control over informational, physical, psychological, and social aspects of one's life [27]. It seems clear that telepresence robots, like autonomous robots, cause concerns about privacy. Telepresence robots are essentially video media spaces, which have a slew of privacy problems themselves (see Boyle et al. [7] for a review), but also mobile, which adds new privacy concerns. Telepresence robots can be driven into private spaces, or used to look around at things against the will of the local user(s). Our broad research focus is on how privacy judgments work in robot-mediated communication; we suspect that framing is among the main factors.

The goal of our research is to answer the question, "how does framing impact privacy judgments?" We have run four human-subjects experiments in rapid succession to gather the first measurements of these effects. Our approach is to use some text to frame a scenario presented via an animated video, to which subjects respond via a questionnaire. We recruit subjects using Amazon Mechanical Turk for quick development and turnaround, beginning with simpler scenarios and variables and then progressing to the privacy concerns that motivate our research.

Each study builds on the previous ones. *Study 1* tests whether we can measure a framing effect with our approach. *Study 2* expands upon the first one to include the effect of re-framing people partway through the study. *Study 3* tests whether our findings generalize to a new video and whether different demographic subgroups are differentially affected by framing. *Study 4* uses a suite of high-fidelity animations specifically designed to evoke privacy concerns and is our first direct measurement of privacy constructs.

This is the first study we know of about framing effects on privacy judgments in a HRI. Just a few studies have been

HRI '17, March 06-09, 2017, Vienna, Austria
© 2017 ACM. ISBN 978-1-4503-4336-7/17/03...$15.00
DOI: http://dx.doi.org/10.1145/2909824.3020218

done in privacy-sensitive robotics; although two [8, 15] focus explicitly on remotely-operated robots, none focuses on the effects of framing or on the way the robot's actions appear from a third-person perspective instead of from its video feed. Past studies of framing in human-robot interactions focus on, e.g., user perceptions of the robot's social role and degree of anthropomorphism, but not privacy, and we are unaware of any framing studies of telepresence robots.

2. RELATED WORK

2.1 Privacy

Privacy is important in all human cultures [2], although different cultures have different norms for privacy and different mechanisms for enforcing those norms. Prominent theories that describe privacy include Altman's [1] and Nissenbaum's [22]. We use a privacy taxonomy compiled from the literature [27] to divide "privacy" into component ideas: (1) Informational privacy, over personal information, includes (a) Invasion, (b) Collection, (c) Processing, and (d) Dissemination; (2) Physical privacy, over personal space or territory, includes (a) Personal Space, (b) Territoriality, and (c) Modesty; (3) Psychological privacy, over thoughts and values, includes (a) Interrogation and (b) Psychological Distance; (4) Social privacy, over interactions with others and influence from them, includes (a) Association, (b) Crowding/Isolation, (c) Surveillance, (d) Solitude, (e) Intimacy, (f) Anonymity, and (g) Reserve. We used this taxonomy to define the extents of the idea of privacy so we can work towards covering it all in our research program (i.e., towards *content validity*). The small amount of work so far on "privacy-sensitive robotics" includes Hubers et al. [15], Butler et al. [8], and Rueben et al. [28].

2.2 Privacy Concerns about Telepresence Systems

Robot-mediated communication has become possible for doctors, workers, bosses, and visitors to older adults [19]. These telepresence robots create interactions that differ both from face-to-face interactions [7] and from purely virtual systems like avatar-based telepresence [e.g., 5, 6, 18]. Even video media spaces change the privacy situation because the remote operator's actions are seen outside his/her context and dissociated from his/her identity [7]. Giving the remote user a physical (robot) body raises additional normative questions, like whether it is acceptable to rest one's feet on the robot's base [18]. Several studies on telepresence robots for older adults have identified privacy concerns [4] and behavior changes due to feeling watched by the robot [9]. The paradigm shift expected from the advent of telepresence robots may even prompt changes to U.S. privacy law [17]. This appears the be the first study that focuses on both privacy concerns and telepresence robots (in Section 7).

2.3 Animations for Studying HRI

Several studies have compared human-robot interactions over video to live ones. Woods et al. [33] have shown a strong agreement in general between being approached by a real robot and by a robot in a video. The same authors also cite findings by developmental psychologists, however, that "while babies happily interact with their mothers via live video, they get highly distressed when watching pre-recorded or replayed videos of their mothers (as it lacks the contingency between mother's and baby's behaviour)" [32]. We were careful not to use our videos to study scenarios that normally require interaction.

Powers et al. [25] compared interactions with an animated computer agent against interactions with a real robot over a video feed. They found that engagement was higher and positive personality traits were more strongly associated with the real robot, but also that people remembered what the agent said better than what the robot said. Also, McDonnell et al. [21] compared emotive actions performed by a human actor to the same actions mapped onto animated bodies. They found that the perception of emotions in the actions was mostly the same across body conditions.

Our methodology resembles the one used by Takayama et al. [30], which prototypes robot behaviors as animations and shows the videos to a large sample of people online. We use Amazon Mechanical Turk (MTurk) to recruit our subjects—consult Mason and Suri [20] for some studies that compare MTurk users to laboratory subjects. Performing a study with animated robot behaviors allowed us to provide consistent experiences for each of the study participants, to test a variety of task domains, and to engage a geographically diverse set of study participants. In terms of design research, using animations allowed us to test the behaviors we would like to build before locking in the design a robot would need to physically perform the behaviors.

2.4 Framing

A frame is a "structure of expectation" [31] within which actions and words will be interpreted differently. Framing language is metacommunicative; it tells one the frame in which to interpret subsequent communications [3]. Bateson [3] gives the example of monkeys engaged in a playful fight; the monkeys know that the bite that would normally be aggressive is fun in this context. Here the frame is "play", and "this is 'play'" would be framing language. Tannen [31] reviews the idea of a "frame" as well as the related terms "schema" and "script" across disciplines.

Groom et al. [12] cite some studies of existing expectations about robots, but observe that "researchers have largely ignored studying framing as an independent variable." Their study manipulates the role of a robot, an instance of framing, in a search and rescue context. Howley et al. [14] also manipulate the robot's social role, whereas Fischer et al. [11] have a robot issue a greeting to frame the interaction as social. Paepcke and Takayama [24] manipulate user expectations about the robot's capabilities, a framing that is very relevant to the concerns of Richards and Smart [26]. Darling [10] uses a narrative about the robot to manipulate how much users anthropomorphize it. We consider all these studies to use framing. The studies presented in this paper use framing to manipulate the familiarity of the robot operator to the participant via short operator biographies in (uniquely) a telepresence scenario.

3. APPROACH

We use the same five-part methodology for each of the four studies reported here.

(1) We *frame* our participants by having them read a paragraph of text. This text describes the occasion of the interaction and introduces the robot operator, whose identity we manipulate in our experiments. Our goal was to provide

Figure 1: Representative thumbnails from the animated videos used for the studies presented in this paper. See Sections 4–7 for video descriptions.

enough context for the video to make sense but leaving the robot's actions ambiguous enough to require interpretation.

(2) Next, we present our main *stimulus*, which is an animated video of a PR2 robot performing some actions inside a home (see Figure 1). We chose the PR2 because it has a mobile base and two arms for performing human-like manipulation tasks as well as a head and obvious eyes so users can follow its gaze, but lacks a screen for showing imagery of the remote operator—something that would introduce many variables we don't want to deal with yet. The animated videos were made in Blender. We chose to use animation so we could specify the layout and appearance of the home, and also so that the robot could perform natural-looking actions that are not only beyond the state-of-the-art for autonomy but also difficult to do using teleoperation.

(3) *Responses* are gathered using a questionnaire. We expect subjects to interpret the videos from within the contextual frame we've given them and respond accordingly.

(4) We *interpret* what is being measured by the survey responses using principal component analysis (PCA).

(5) We *iterate* on this process by using the results from one study to re-design our survey for the next study. Successive studies can act as (at least partial) replications that contribute to a meta-analysis. Iterating is made easy by the response speed on Amazon Mechanical Turk; our studies typically complete within a few hours of being launched. Also, all the elements of our studies are easy to change quickly: a paragraph for framing, an animated video for the main stimulus, and a questionnaire for the response.

4. STUDY 1: OPENING THE FRIDGE

Our first study tested whether the framing effect is measurable, and if so how large it is (RQ1-A). In all four studies our two frames manipulate the subject's familiarity with the robot operator within the hypothetical scenario.

4.1 Methods

Frame. This study used a between-groups design with 2 framing conditions. The manipulated variable was the familiarity of the respondent's relationship with the robot operator in the hypothetical scenario. The operator was "your sister" in one framing and "a home appraiser" whom "you have spoken with... once over the phone, but have never met... before in person" in the other. In both cases we used the name Lisa. A general motivation was provided for each character so the scenario was not confusing: the sister is seeing your remodeled kitchen for the first time, whereas the home appraiser is checking that it's up to code.

Main Stimulus. The video (16s long) shows an animated PR2 robot in the kitchen. The robot opens the refrigerator, looks inside, and closes it again. The camera perspective is from the next room over, the living room.

Survey Items. We created 7 items about trust, comfort, and acceptability to measure respondents' concerns about each scenario. They all used a 7-pt Likert-type response format. Two open-ended questions checked for attention and understanding of the two scenarios. No demographic information was collected in the survey.

We recruited 64 people total—31 saw the "sister" condition and 33 the "stranger" (i.e., home appraiser) condition. Subjects in each of the 4 studies were paid approximately \$10 per hour (\$1.50 per HIT for this study based on a predicted duration of about 9 minutes) and we always ensured that nobody took the same survey twice.

4.2 Results

Data reduction via principal component analysis (PCA) yielded 2 dependent variables: 6 items were combined whereas 1 remained separate, namely, "I think it's important for me to be at home while this is happening." The 6-item composite we named Comfort (α = .95); the other item we will call ShouldBeHome for short. Correlation between these two dependent variables was $r(62)$ = -.37.

Respondents were more comfortable and felt less need to stay home in the "sister" condition (RQ1-A). Two-sample t-tests showed these framing effects to be statistically significant with medium-high effect sizes (on Comfort: $t(62)$ = 3.39, d = 0.847, p = 0.00123; on ShouldBeHome: $t(62)$ = -3.16, d = -0.790, p = 0.00245).

Many people described the home appraiser's behavior as "nosy" in the open-ended responses. We decided to use this word in future versions of the survey because it fits the sorts of concerns we tried to evoke in our scenario; apparently many respondents also found it apt.

4.3 Discussion

These initial results show that the framing effect is present, sizable, and able to be detected via an online survey with text prompts and an animated video. The next 2 studies measure additional variables while replicating and generalizing the framing effect.

5. STUDY 2: FRIDGE (W/IN SUBJECTS)

The second study aimed to test what happens when a person switches between interpretive frames. We did this by re-framing our subjects in the middle of the experiment, resulting in a repeated measures design. First, we sought to replicate the framing effect we detected in Study 1 (RQ2-A). Second, we wondered whether showing both frames in series would reveal any carry-over effects, such as a halo effect that would make judgments more similar or a contrast effect that would make them more different (RQ2-B).

5.1 Methods

In this study, each subject saw both framing conditions. The framings and video were the same as for Study 1 except that the home appraiser is now a home "inspector" named "Alice" (your sister is still named "Lisa"). The order of conditions was counterbalanced. In between the two conditions we showed a text note that told respondents that an entirely new scenario will now be presented, but with the same video.

Survey Items. We used the same questions as in Study 1 with some minor wording changes as well as the addition of two new questions about whether Lisa was being "nosy" or "rude," inspired by some open-ended responses in Study 1. We also moved the open-ended items from the end of the questionnaire to its beginning to encourage respondents to think about what they saw before responding to the other items. We added a more explicit manipulation check after both conditions—"In one sentence, describe the difference between the two scenarios"—to make sure respondents read and understood the framings.

We analyzed responses from 41 people after omitting 5 for failing the manipulation checks—of the 41, 22 saw "sister" first and 19 saw "stranger" first. Eight had also participated in Study 1.

5.2 Results

Unlike for Study 1, data reduction here yielded a single dependent variable (α = .95). We named this single, 9-item dependent variable Comfort, but it consisted of different items than in Study 1. This data reduction remained stable even when responses were split by condition or order except for one interesting exception: ShouldBeHome was more strongly correlated with BeingRude and BeingNosy in the "stranger" condition than in the "sister" condition.

Respondents were more comfortable with the "sister" condition (RQ2-A). According to an ANOVA, this within-subjects framing effect on Comfort was statistically significant with a large effect size ($F(1,40)$ = 18.4, η_p^2 = .315, $p <$ .001). We also checked for an order effect on Comfort, but it was not statistically significant and was much smaller in magnitude ($F(1,40)$ = 1.34, η_p^2 = .033, *n.s.*).

Regarding the carry-over effect, subjects' Comfort ratings were more sensitive to framing when the "sister" condition was viewed first (RQ2-B). A two-sample t-test on the differences in means between the two framing conditions, however, revealed that this effect was not statistically significant (mean difference in Comfort for "sister" first: 1.73, for "stranger" first: 0.98, $t(39)$ = 1.16, p = .253).

5.3 Discussion

This study successfully replicated the large framing effect from Study 1. The effect size may be different depending on which condition comes first, but more evidence is needed to confirm this. We continue counterbalancing the order of conditions in our subsequent studies to prevent order from confounding our framing manipulation, as well as to continue measuring any difference in effect size based on which frame is presented first.

6. STUDY 3: PLAYING CHESS

We next test whether the framing effect generalizes to a different video and scenario description (RQ3-A). We also conduct a second test of whether the framing effect is moderated by which frame comes first (RQ3-B) and a first test of whether the name of the operator matters (RQ3-C). Finally, we report on the range of subjects' sensitivity to the change in frames (RQ3-D) and test whether some basic demographics are correlated with our dependent variables (RQ3-E),

6.1 Methods

Main Stimulus. The video we used for this study shows a new scenario. The PR2 is now with the observer in the living room; it drives around a chess board to face the observer, looks down at a chess board, and makes a move.

Frame. The framing paragraphs that precede the video were rewritten to fit the new scenario, but still manipulated subjects' hypothetical familiarity with the operator: the operator is either a friend you play chess with frequently or a stranger you've only met on a chess website. Also, we counterbalanced the assignment of the operator's name (Lisa or Alice) to each framing condition (sister and stranger).

Survey Items. After each showing of the video, 17 items with Likert-type response formats were presented (paraphrased in Figure 2). Of these, 7 were adapted from the

9 items in Study 2; 10 were new, many of which were tailored to this scenario (e.g., "I think using a robot like this is a good idea for improving the online chess experience."). Here we began using a 9-pt response format instead of a 7-pt one to combat floor and ceiling effects.

Next we asked 20 demographics questions. These included general information such as age, sex, and education level as well as items about experience with robots and living situation (e.g., "I am used to sharing my living space with other people such as friends, family, roommates, and guests.").

The 14 NARS items by Nomura et al. [23] were presented next, but they were adapted to be about telepresence robots (e.g., "If robots had emotions, I would be able to make friends with them" became "If robots could express emotions for someone far away, I feel I could become friends with that person") and we clarified some wordings to address the comments by Syrdal et al. [29]. We will refer to these items with "NATS", which stands for "Negative Attitudes about Telepresence (robots) Scale".

We analyzed 61 out of the 66 responses after excluding 5 people for failing our manipulation checks.

6.2 Results

This sample was comprised of 38 men, 22 women, and 1 person who left that question blank. Most respondents (72%) were white. Mean age was 32.5 years (SD: 9.2 years). Everyone had completed high school and only 4 were unemployed or unable to work. 89% had at least seen a video of a robot before, and 43% had driven a remote controlled vehicle. 75% reported that they use social media daily and 85% that they use a smartphone. Only 36% live alone and only 16% live with children.

We chose to reduce our 17-item video response survey into 3 dependent variables named PositivePresence (7 items, $\alpha = .92$), WasNotTooFast (5 items, $\alpha = .86$), and PilotEtiquette (9 items, $\alpha = .94$). Figure 2 shows the items included in each variable and their factor loadings. Correlations between these variables range from $r(120) = +.69$ to $+.84$.

All three variables were higher in the "friend" condition than in the "stranger" condition (RQ3-A). An ANOVA revealed that these framing effects were large and statistically significant (PositivePresence: $F(1,57) = 88.2$, $\eta_p^2 = .607$, $p < .001$; WasNotTooFast: $F(1,57) = 79.9$, $\eta_p^2 = .584$, $p < .001$; PilotEtiquette: $F(1,57) = 86.8$, $\eta_p^2 = .604$, $p < .001$).

As in Study 2, the framing effect was larger when the "friend" (previously "sister") framing came before the "stranger" framing (RQ3-B). Yet again, however, this effect was not statistically significant (it was largest for WasNotTooFast: difference in means for "friend" first = 1.58, for "stranger" first = 1.07, $t(59) = 1.47$, $p = .146$).

Statistically significant name effects were found for PilotEtiquette ($F(1,57) = 5.82$, $\eta_p^2 = .093$, $p = .019$) and almost for WasNotTooFast ($F(1,57) = 3.54$, $\eta_p^2 = .058$, $p = .065$), but these turned out to be due to a breakdown of random assignment[1] (RQ3-C). None of the three order effects was

ActedAppropriately	-0.25	0.16	**0.89**
BeingRude	0.13	-0.23	**-0.85**
GoodManners	-0.41	0.07	**0.78**
CameTooClose	0.27	-0.46	**-0.65**
GoodIntentions	**-0.55**	0.28	**0.58**
WorriedSneaky	0.33	**-0.53**	**-0.57**
AfraidForSafety	0.20	**-0.54**	**-0.55**
ComfyDistance	-0.50	0.35	**0.51**
FeelGood	**-0.80**	0.23	0.42
GoodForChess	**-0.79**	0.24	0.23
FeltSheWasPresent	**-0.79**	-0.08	0.04
FineWithLogin	**-0.72**	0.32	0.42
TrustToOperate	**-0.62**	0.39	**0.52**
OKtoLoginLater	**0.53**	-0.38	-0.28
ArmsSlowerPlease	0.16	**-0.83**	-0.15
DriveSlowerPlease	0.12	**-0.82**	-0.24
SelfConscious	0.41	**-0.63**	-0.21

Figure 2: Table of factor loadings for data reduction of 17-item video response survey in Study 3. From left to right, we named these PositivePresence, WasNotTooFast, and PilotEtiquette. Items placed in each composite are underlined.

statistically significant (all ps > .1) and observed effect sizes were relatively small (all η_p^2s < .04).

There were notable individual differences in sensitivity to the framing manipulation (RQ3-D). For example, PositivePresence ratings changed by a mean of 1.53 points between framing conditions, but a few respondents changed not at all or in the opposite direction. Upon inspection, it looks like many of these people did not demonstrate their understanding of the conditions very well in the open-ended questions. Manipulation checks like these are crucial for gauging experimental validity in online surveys. Most people were affected by the framing in the expected way, however; the 95% confidence interval for the mean sensitivity of PositivePresence only spans from 1.20 to 1.86 points.

We kept 13 of the 14 items in the NATS and call it the NATS-13 ($\alpha = .91$). The last item in the scale, which reads, "I feel that in the future society will be dominated by robots", only correlated at $r(59) = .19$ with the rest of the scale. Since it seems to measure a belief that could be relevant to judgments about our scenario, however, we chose to keep it as a single-item variable called SocietyWillBeDominated.

The NATS-13 was especially strongly correlated with our three dependent variables (PositivePresence $r(59) = -.71$, $r^2 = .50$; WasNotTooFast $r(59) = -.73$, $r^2 = .53$; PilotEtiquette $r(59) = -.71$, $r^2 = .50$), accounting for half of their variance (RQ3-E). Actually, this was a stronger effect than the framing manipulation itself; moving up one point on the NATS-13 was about equivalent to switching the frame from "friend" to "stranger". These correlations were statistically significant even after a conservative Bonferroni correction to account for the heightened risk of Type I error from check-

[1]Subjects assigned to the group with Lisa as the friend responded more affirmatively to the item, "I really dislike it when people enter my bedroom without my permission." This imbalance mattered because subjects who responded more affirmatively to that item were also more sensitive to the framing manipulation. Thus, part of the framing effect appeared to be a naming effect. Adding that demographic variable to the ANOVA caused all naming effects to lose statistical significance.

ing the correlations between 17 of our demographic variables and each of the 3 dependent variables.

Many of our other demographic variables besides the NATS-13 were also correlated with ratings of PositivePresence, WasNotTooFast, and PilotEtiquette (e.g., "In general, I enjoy having guests over to where I live") (RQ3-E). A few were correlated with sensitivity to the framing manipulation (e.g., "I really dislike it when people enter my bedroom without my permission"). It is interesting that these two things don't always occur together (e.g., the "enjoy having guests" example above was not strongly correlated with sensitivity to the framing manipulation).

6.3 Discussion

Our results support the conclusion that the framing effect generalizes to the chess scenario. This study has also yielded much more information than the first two did, including demographic profiles of participants, correlations between demographics and our dependent variables, and first looks at sensitivity and effects of operator name. We now turn to our constructs of interest in the realm of privacy.

7. STUDY 4: TOUR BEFORE A PARTY

This study uses four videos made to evoke different privacy concerns on our taxonomy [27] as well as survey items to measure these privacy concerns. Our main research question is whether the framing effect replicates in this domain (RQ4-A). We are also interested in several types of order effects. First, do respondents get used to seeing a robot poking around their house after watching the four videos, causing privacy concerns to be lower in the next condition (RQ4-B)? Second, is the framing effect moderated by which frame comes first (RQ4-C)? Third, does a frame wear off as respondents watch the videos (RQ4-D)? After all, the videos do not show the operator's face or any other explicit cues that he is telepresent.

We will also take another look at whether the demographics we have targeted are correlated with any of our privacy variables (RQ4-E), as well as at how sensitive these new variables are to the framing manipulation (RQ4-F). Also, we want to know how much of the framing effect is attributable to changes in trust of the operator (RQ4-G). Finally, we look at which of the four videos is most (or least) concerning with respect to privacy (RQ4-H).

7.1 Methods

Frame. The scenario is that you have invited some people to a party in your home, but one person can't attend except by logging into the robot. That person is either a close friend whom you see weekly or a stranger whom you met for the first time today. We used male names this time: Will and Chris.

Main Stimulus. The main stimulus for this study was divided into four new animated videos with survey items presented after each video. This way, participants could answer questions directly after watching a certain part of the scenario. The videos were more photorealistic than those used in the previous three studies (see Figure 1). They range from 21–34s long. Each is designed to evoke certain privacy constructs in order to cover as much of the taxonomy [27] as possible: e.g., Surveillance and Psychological Distance in the "gaze" video (the robot makes eye contact with you), Invasion and Territoriality in the "desk" video (looks in your desk drawer), Anonymity in the "photo" video (picks up a family photo), and Modesty in the "bedroom" video (sees your messy bedroom, including some women's underwear).

Survey Items. We used all new items for the video response survey. These were designed to target the privacy constructs evoked by the videos, as well as ask some more general questions. All 22 items are paraphrased in Figure 3. They all use a 9-pt Likert-type response format. Note that these items, as in the other studies, are context-sensitive; they might tap different constructs if we used them in a different scenario.

Immediately after reading each framing paragraph, participants took a 7-item trust questionnaire. Six items were adapted from the Specific Interpersonal Trust Scales (SITS-M and SITS-F) [16] and one item, shown last, we created: "I trust [Will/Chris]".

The demographics questions were the same as in Study 3 except that the NATS was modified slightly and reduced to 8 items for brevity.

At the very end of the survey we asked our respondents to rank our four videos by how concerning they were with respect to privacy.

This study was counterbalanced for the order of the two framings, for the order of the four videos according to a Latin Square design, and for which name was assigned to which framing as in Study 3. We analyzed 65 responses after discarding one that failed the manipulation check.

7.2 Results

Of the 65 responses we analyzed, 40 were males and 25 were females. 62% marked "white" as their ethnicity. The mean age was 32.0 years (SD: 8.8 years). All our respondents indicated that they had graduated high school, and all but 18% are (self-)employed. 49% had at least driven a remote-controlled vehicle before. 63% use social media every day, and all but 1 owned a smartphone. Only 29% live alone; another 29% live with children at least sometimes.

Data reduction was performed on all 22 video response questions at once to look at how the different privacy constructs might relate. Using a PCA we chose 4 composite variables for reporting (Figure 3). Each composite variable combines items that were meant to tap different privacy constructs, indicating either that those constructs overlapped in our respondents' minds or that our items failed to discriminate between them. WorriedAboutLikenesses (7 items; $\alpha = .89$) includes items about dissemination of personal information, anonymity, and psychological distance; DontMessWithMyStuff (5 items; $\alpha = .87$) includes items about invasion of personal information and territory; EmbarrassedByMess (5 items; $\alpha = .90$) includes items about collection and processing of information, namely a messy room that could cause someone to judge you; HardToBeAlone (3 items; $\alpha = .91$) includes items about solitude, intimacy, and surveillance. Intercorrelations between composites ranged between $r(128) = +.60$ and $+.73$.

Two items, one designed to tap surveillance and one for modesty, didn't correlate much with any of the others (all $|r(128)| < .22$). After analysis, we believe that they were not good measures of any relevant constructs to this study, so we do not report on them further here[2].

[2]Neither item had any statistically significant framing effects, which were very large for the rest of our dependent variables, or any statistically significant correlations with

GAZE_put_it_online	**0.66**	0.15	0.37	0.35
GAZE_eye_contact_discomfort	**0.66**	0.18	0.18	0.35
GAZE_ok_getting_ready	(omitted from PCA)			
GAZE_hard_to_be_alone	0.25	0.23	0.21	**0.85**
GAZE_hard_to_talk_privately	0.28	0.32	0.18	**0.82**
GAZE_filter_myself	0.48	0.20	0.38	**0.60**
DESK_no_drawer_sans_permission	0.05	**0.86**	0.24	0.07
DESK_worried_saw_info	0.43	0.52	**0.57**	0.18
DESK_ok_if_sees_screen	**-0.55**	-0.38	-0.28	-0.13
DESK_not_ok_because_mine	0.14	**0.89**	0.18	0.19
DESK_filter_things	0.38	**0.63**	0.39	0.29
PHOTO_ok_to_see_photo	**-0.76**	-0.09	-0.01	-0.02
PHOTO_worried_will_drop	0.28	**0.59**	-0.05	0.22
PHOTO_concerned_can_recognize	**0.76**	0.03	0.22	0.13
PHOTO_filter_things	**0.70**	0.30	0.02	0.32
BEDROOM_embarrassed_saw_mess	0.23	0.21	**0.86**	0.09
BEDROOM_would_have_cleaned	0.05	0.12	**0.85**	0.25
BEDROOM_worry_will_judge	0.46	0.24	**0.66**	0.15
BEDROOM_worried_will_put_online	**0.72**	0.20	0.34	0.28
BEDROOM_tshirts_over_underwear	(omitted from PCA)			
BEDROOM_bad_to_look_unpermitted	0.09	**0.59**	0.46	0.35
BEDROOM_filter_things	0.32	0.46	**0.51**	0.47

Figure 3: Table of factor loadings for data reduction of 22-item video response survey in Study 4. From left to right, we named these WorriedAboutLikenesses, DontMessWithMyStuff, EmbarrassedByMess, and HardToBeAlone. Items placed in each composite are underlined.

The framing manipulation effect was always in the predicted direction for our four privacy variables: higher privacy concerns for a stranger than for a friend (RQ4-A). An ANOVA revealed that these effects were all large and statistically significant (WorriedAboutLikenesses: $F(1,49) = 91.8$, $\eta_p^2 = .652$, $p < .001$; DontMessWithMyStuff: $F(1,49) = 45.5$, $\eta_p^2 = .481$, $p < .001$; EmbarrassedByMess: $F(1,49) = 79.4$, $\eta_p^2 = .618$, $p < .001$; HardToBeAlone: $F(1,49) = 38.9$, $\eta_p^2 = .443$, $p < .001$).

The effect of acclimatization (i.e., first condition vs. second condition) was only statistically significant for DontMessWithMyStuff ($F(1,49) = 4.71$, $\eta_p^2 = .088$, $p = .035$) and almost for HardToBeAlone ($F(1,49) = 3.04$, $\eta_p^2 = .058$, $p = .088$). These were both in the expected direction as well: concerns about the operator messing with your stuff or making it hard for you to be alone were lower in the second condition, suggesting that respondents became complacent as they got used to the scenarios (RQ4-B). The name (Will or Chris) of the operator was also included in the model, but was not found to have any statistically significant effects.

Just like in Studies 2 and 3 we checked whether sensitivity to framing was moderated by which frame came first. There was a consistent effect: the relationship effect was larger on all 4 composites when the respondent saw the "stranger" frame first (RQ4-C). This is in the opposite direction, however, as it was in Studies 2 and 3. To test for statistical significance, we ran two-sample t-tests for each of the 4 composites between two groups: those who saw "friend" first (n = 31) and those who saw "stranger" first (n = 34). This difference was only statistically significant for DontMessWithMyStuff (mean sensitivity for "friend" first = -0.77, for "stranger" first = -1.56, $t(63) = 2.41$, $d = 0.601$, $p = .019$).

In this study we tested whether the effects of a frame wear off as the respondents watch the four videos. For each video (e.g., "desk") within each frame (e.g., "friend") we ran a MANOVA (8 total) that tested whether that video's position in the order of videos (e.g., 3rd of 4) predicts the responses to the items that go with that video. None of these 8 tests was statistically significant; it appears that our two frames remained active for the extent of each condition, and perhaps could have for much longer, or until a significant distraction occurred (RQ4-D).

We chose 5 out of the 8 NATS items (the "NATS-5"; $\alpha = .81$) for a measure of negative emotions about telepresence systems. The remaining three we kept as single-item variables. The first was "If robots could express emotions for someone far away, I feel I could become friends with that person" (correlations with the other 3 variables were all $|r(63)| < .43$). The other two were written to figure out why the item that said "I feel that in the future society will be dominated by robots" didn't fit into the rest of the scale in Study 3; one reads, "I feel that in the future robots will be everywhere in our society", and the other reads, "I feel that in the future society will be controlled by robots." The "society will be controlled" item appears to be the misfit: it was not correlated with the NATS-5 ($r(63) = -.04$). The "robots will be everywhere" item was negatively correlated ($r(63) = -.46$) with the NATS-5, so it appears that discomfort with telepresence was linked in our sample with a belief that robots will not become ubiquitous anytime soon.

Some of our demographic variables were correlated with our privacy DVs (RQ4-E). The largest correlation was $r(128) = +.40$ between a composite of CleanUpBeforeGuests and CloseDoorsBeforeGuests ($\alpha = .49$) and EmbarrassedByMess. Also, the NATS-5 was correlated with WorriedAboutLikenesses at $r(128) = +.36$ and also the other 3 main composites, but those correlations—and, in fact, all other IV-DV correlations—were not statistically significant when we protect for Type I error from checking all possible correlations. Note that the NATS items account for much less variance here than in Study 3, wherein the 13-item NATS composite accounted for half of the variance of the dependent variables.

We also looked at how sensitive our respondents' privacy concerns were to the relationship manipulation (RQ4-F). In this study, the variable with the most individual differences in sensitivity was HardToBeAlone—its 95% confidence interval spanned from a sensitivity of -1.99 to -1.02. None of the confidence intervals for our 4 composite privacy variables crossed zero. There were also some sizable correlations between demographic variables and these sensitivities, especially with the living situation and NATS variables, but none reached statistical significance after protecting for Type I error.

According to a PCA, the 7-item scale about trusting the operator measured a single dimension, which we called "Trust" ($\alpha = .95$). It is interesting to note that although the

our demographic variables. The item texts were "I would feel comfortable doing some small tasks to prepare for the party knowing that Will could drive by and look at me like this" ("gaze" video) and "I wouldn't be as upset if the clothes basket contained t-shirts instead of underwear" ("bedroom" video).

SITS [16] from which we drew all but 1 of the items claims to measure multiple dimensions of trust, with slightly different dimensions between men and women, our items only appear to have measured one construct for both sexes in this study. We propose that this is because the respondents do not know much about the robot operator in either framing condition, so their judgments about him are not as complex as they might be for, e.g., a close friend in real life.

We can validate our composite measure of Trust by testing whether it is manipulated by the difference in frames ("friend" vs. "stranger") and not by the difference in names ("Will" vs. "Chris"). Matched-pair t-tests supported the validity of our Trust measure (relationship effect: $t(64) = 13.2$, $d = 3.31$, $p < .0001$; name effect: $t(64) = 0.349$, $d = 0.871$, $p = 0.729$).

Higher Trust ratings do appear linked to decreased privacy concerns (RQ4-G). Correlations are statistically significant with WorriedAboutLikenesses ($r(128) = -.50$) and HardToBeAlone ($r(128) = -.35$). So Trust is a significant mediator of the effect of hypothetical familiarity on privacy concerns, but there are probably other significant ones to be discovered: at most Trust accounts for 25% of the variance (WorriedAboutLikenesses) or at least a mere 7.5% (DontMessWithMyStuff and EmbarrassedByMess).

Respondents ranked the "desk" video as most concerning (votes: most 45—12—6—2 least), followed by "bedroom" (most 14—43—6—2 least), then "photo" (most 4—4—33—24 least), then "gaze" (most 2—6—20—37 least) (RQ4-H). It makes sense with our gut intuition because "desk" and "bedroom" are more invasive, we think, than mere "gaze" or touching a "photo".

8. DISCUSSION

8.1 Implications for Design

All four studies show a large effect of framing the relationship of the local user with the robot operator. This suggests that robot designers should think about how frames like these could be encouraged via robot appearance, what the robot says, and how the robot is advertised. Designers should also consider how different contexts and cultural factors, like the popular media and even other people, could impose unwanted frames over a user's interaction with a robot.

We are beginning to understand some details of how framing works. We see, starting in Study 2, that people can be prompted to switch between interpretive frames relatively easily. Some frames may "stick" better than others, though, even changing the way framing information is interpreted. Study 4 suggests that certain privacy concerns decrease as time passes or as people experience different frames. We believe people simply get used to the concerning behaviors and lower their guards, although an alternative explanation is that experimental realism begins to decrease with the second framing. An understanding of how privacy concerns about robots change with long-term usage is crucial; if concerns wear off or change in type after a few hours or days then robots will need to transition smoothly between these two phases.

8.2 On Methodology

It is surprising that the framing effect was large even with *no* signs of the operator's presence beyond the framing text. It was even present (and large) between subjects, when there were no hints about a contrast between the two frames. We would hypothesize that adding signs of the operator's presence would prolong or even increase framing effects as long as they agree with the frame. On the other hand, we are interested in what happens when conflicting information about the frame is presented to an observer, e.g., if the observer is told the robot is being used to inspect a leaky pipe but instead starts picking up your personal items.

We chose a methodology that uses animated video stimuli, quantitative data, and quick, online recruitment. We believe the animated videos are useful for studying experiences that are difficult to produce in the laboratory, which includes anything from natural robot gestures to scenarios in outer space! Also, shorter studies can operate like pilot studies when aspects of the methodology are not well-established, helping you fix problems before wasting months on a large, one-off experiment. Similarly, taking quantitative data yields early effect size estimates so we can choose proper sample sizes.

Some qualitative methods can also be short and easy to iterate on, such as focus groups. Showing our framings and videos to a focus group would be another way to explore which variables are important. Although we would not get effect size estimates or the type of insight into relationships between variables offered by PCA, a focus group conversation could explore a much broader selection of concerns and use nuanced follow-up questions to greatly increase our confidence that participants' responses mean what we think they mean.

8.3 Future Work

Future work should concentrate on which frames have the largest effect sizes on privacy concerns. We have only looked at the difference between a familiar person and a stranger operating the robot in these first 4 studies. Here are some other aspects of the frame one could manipulate: the level of control the operator has over the robot's action (full teleoperation vs. supervision); how invasive the operator's actions are expected to be based on his/her role (police officer vs. tourist); morphology of the robot; robot nonverbal behavior (e.g., smoothness of movements, posture); or the operator's social presence (via a face on a screen or operator name tag). Knowing which aspects of the context most influence user perception of privacy risks [as in 13] will help researchers and robot manufacturers know what to focus on.

The framing effect itself should also be studied. How is the frame encoded and then used to interpret subsequent information? How much longer does it last beyond the four videos and 22 survey items in Study 4? What happens, exactly, when people switch framings? Also, studying the individual differences (e.g., personality traits) that moderate framing effects would help identify groups that are especially sensitive.

We are motivated by privacy. Understanding framing will help us avoid privacy violations. More research could help us discover how privacy judgments are different in HRI; we want to identify what type(s) of privacy exactly will be problematic and which people to target with our solutions.

References

[1] I. Altman. *The Environment and Social Behavior: Privacy, Personal Space, Territory, and Crowding.* Brooks/Cole Publishing Company, Monterey, CA, 1975.

[2] I. Altman. Privacy Regulation: Culturally Universal or Culturally Specific? *Journal of Social Issues*, 33(3): 66–84, 1977.

[3] G. Bateson. A theory of play and fantasy. *Psychiatric research reports*, 1955.

[4] J. M. Beer and L. Takayama. Mobile Remote Presence Systems for Older Adults: Acceptance, Benefits, and Concerns. In *Proceedings of the 6th International Conference on Human-robot Interaction*, HRI '11, pages 19–26, New York, NY, USA, 2011. ACM. .

[5] G. Bente, S. Rüggenberg, and N. C. Krämer. Social presence and interpersonal trust in avatar-based, collaborative net-communications. In *7th Annual International Workshop on Presence*, 2004.

[6] G. Bente, F. Eschenburg, and L. Aelker. Effects of simulated gaze on social presence, person perception and personality attribution in avatar-mediated communication. In *Presence 2007: Proceedings of the 10th Annual International Workshop on Presence, October 25-27, 2007, Barcelona, Spain*, pages 207–14, 2007.

[7] M. Boyle, C. Neustaedter, and S. Greenberg. Privacy factors in video-based media spaces. In *Media Space 20+ Years of Mediated Life*, pages 97–122. Springer, 2009.

[8] D. Butler, J. Huang, F. Roesner, and M. Cakmak. The Privacy-Utility Tradeoff for Remotely Teleoperated Robots. In *Proceedings of the 10th ACM/IEEE International Conference on Human-Robot Interaction (HRI)*, Portland, OR, 2015.

[9] K. Caine, S. Sabanovic, and M. Carter. The Effect of Monitoring by Cameras and Robots on the Privacy Enhancing Behaviors of Older Adults. In *Proceedings of the Seventh Annual ACM/IEEE International Conference on Human-Robot Interaction*, HRI '12, pages 343–350, New York, NY, USA, 2012. ACM. .

[10] K. Darling. "Who's Johnny?" Anthropomorphic Framing in Human-Robot Interaction, Integration, and Policy. SSRN Scholarly Paper, Social Science Research Network, Rochester, NY, Mar. 2015.

[11] K. Fischer, B. Soto, C. Pantofaru, and L. Takayama. Initiating interactions in order to get help: Effects of social framing on people's responses to robots' requests for assistance. In *2014 RO-MAN: The 23rd IEEE International Symposium on Robot and Human Interactive Communication*, pages 999–1005, Aug. 2014.

[12] V. Groom, V. Srinivasan, C. L. Bethel, R. Murphy, L. Dole, and C. Nass. Responses to robot social roles and social role framing. In *Collaboration Technologies and Systems (CTS), 2011 International Conference on*, pages 194–203. IEEE, 2011.

[13] P. A. Hancock, D. R. Billings, K. E. Schaefer, J. Y. Chen, E. J. De Visser, and R. Parasuraman. A meta-analysis of factors affecting trust in human-robot interaction. *Human Factors: The Journal of the Human Factors and Ergonomics Society*, 53(5): 517–527, 2011.

[14] I. Howley, T. Kanda, K. Hayashi, and C. Rosé. Effects of Social Presence and Social Role on Help-seeking and Learning. In *Proceedings of the 2014 ACM/IEEE International Conference on Human-robot Interaction*, HRI '14, pages 415–422, New York, NY, USA, 2014. ACM.

[15] A. Hubers, E. Andrulis, T. Stirrat, D. Tran, R. Zhang, R. Sowell, C. M. Grimm, and W. D. Smart. Video Manipulation Techniques for the Protection of Privacy in Remote Presence Systems. In *HRI 2015 Extended Abstracts*, Portland, OR, Mar. 2015.

[16] C. Johnson-George and W. C. Swap. Measurement of specific interpersonal trust: Construction and validation of a scale to assess trust in a specific other. *Journal of personality and social psychology*, 43(6): 1306, 1982.

[17] M. E. Kaminski. Robots in the Home: What Will We Have Agreed To? 2015.

[18] M. K. Lee and L. Takayama. "Now, I Have a Body": Uses and Social Norms for Mobile Remote Presence in the Workplace. In *Proceedings of the SIGCHI Conference on Human Factors in Computing Systems*, CHI '11, pages 33–42, New York, NY, USA, 2011. ACM.

[19] J. Markoff. The Boss Is Robotic, and Rolling Up Behind You. *The New York Times*, Sept. 2010.

[20] W. Mason and S. Suri. Conducting behavioral research on Amazon's Mechanical Turk. *Behavior research methods*, 44(1):1–23, 2012.

[21] R. McDonnell, S. Jörg, J. McHugh, F. Newell, and C. O'Sullivan. Evaluating the emotional content of human motions on real and virtual characters. In *Proceedings of the 5th symposium on Applied perception in graphics and visualization*, pages 67–74. ACM, 2008.

[22] H. Nissenbaum. Privacy as contextual integrity. *Wash. L. Rev.*, 79:119, 2004.

[23] T. Nomura, T. Kanda, and T. Suzuki. Experimental investigation into influence of negative attitudes toward robots on human-robot interaction. *AI & Society*, 20(2):138–150, 2006.

[24] S. Paepcke and L. Takayama. Judging a bot by its cover: an experiment on expectation setting for personal robots. In *5th ACM/IEEE International Conference on Human-Robot Interaction (HRI)*, pages 45–52. IEEE, 2010.

[25] A. Powers, S. Kiesler, S. Fussell, and C. Torrey. Comparing a computer agent with a humanoid robot. In *2007 2nd ACM/IEEE International Conference on Human-Robot Interaction (HRI)*, pages 145–152, Mar. 2007.

[26] N. M. Richards and W. D. Smart. How Should the Law Think About Robots? In *Proceedings of "We Robot": The Inaugural Conference on Legal and Policy Issues Relating to Robotics*, Coral Gables, FL, 2012.

[27] M. Rueben, C. M. Grimm, F. J. Bernieri, and W. D. Smart. A taxonomy of privacy constructs for privacy-sensitive robotics. arXiv:1701.00841v1 [cs.CY].

[28] M. Rueben, F. J. Bernieri, C. M. Grimm, and W. D. Smart. Evaluation of physical marker interfaces for protecting visual privacy from mobile robots. In *Proceedings of the 25th IEEE International Symposium on Robot and Human Interactive Communication (RO-MAN 2016)*, pages 787–794. IEEE, 2016.

[29] D. S. Syrdal, K. Dautenhahn, K. L. Koay, and M. L. Walters. The negative attitudes towards robots scale and reactions to robot behaviour in a live human-robot interaction study. *Adaptive and Emergent Behaviour and Complex Systems*, 2009.

[30] L. Takayama, D. Dooley, and W. Ju. Expressing thought: improving robot readability with animation principles. In *Proceedings of the 6th international conference on Human-robot interaction*, pages 69–76. ACM, 2011.

[31] D. Tannen. What's in a frame? Surface evidence for underlying expectations. *Framing in discourse*, 14:56, 1993.

[32] S. Woods, M. Walters, K. L. Koay, and K. Dautenhahn. Comparing human robot interaction scenarios using live and video based methods: towards a novel methodological approach. In *9th IEEE International Workshop on Advanced Motion Control*, pages 750–755. IEEE, 2006.

[33] S. N. Woods, M. L. Walters, K. L. Koay, and K. Dautenhahn. Methodological issues in HRI: A comparison of live and video-based methods in robot to human approach direction trials. In *The 15th IEEE International Symposium on Robot and Human Interactive Communication (ROMAN)*, pages 51–58. IEEE, 2006.

Beyond Moral Dilemmas: Exploring the Ethical Landscape in HRI

Thomas Arnold
Human-Robot Interaction Laboratory
Tufts University, Medford, MA 02155, USA
thomas.arnold@tufts.edu

Matthias Scheutz
Human-Robot Interaction Laboratory
Tufts University, Medford, MA 02155, USA
matthias.scheutz@tufts.edu

ABSTRACT

HRI research has yielded intriguing empirical results connected to ethics and how we act in social contexts with robots, even though much of this work has focused on task-based, one-on-one interaction. In this paper, we point to the need to investigate a wider range of ethically relevant dynamics that interaction with robots carries with it – individually and in groups, with a single robot or more. We specifically examine three areas: 1) the primacy and implicit dynamics of bodily perception, 2) the competing interests at work in a single robot-human interaction, and 3) the social intricacy of multiple agents – robots and humans – communicating and making decisions. While these areas are not exhaustive by any means, we find they yield concrete directions for how HRI can contribute to a widening, intensifying set of ethical debates with critical empirical insight, starting to explore more of the ethical landscape in HRI.

Keywords

Ethics in HRI

1. INTRODUCTION AND MOTIVATION

Ethics in HRI is expanding with no less complexity than the field of HRI itself. As robots are becoming more autonomous and are being endowed with ever increasing decision-making capabilities, important societal questions about the legal nature and ethical status of robot actions and robot behavior are rising to the surface. They appear not only in mere philosophical debates about agency but also in technical discussions about autonomy and legal conversations about liability, as well as reflections about the very purpose of HRI research.

As multiple disciplines and domains for robotic application have prompted researchers to propose a number of distinct ethical approaches, researchers in robotics and HRI are themselves starting to recognize the need for a systematic overview of their practice, including themselves as practitioners, in the form of a code of ethics [27].

HRI '17, March 06-09, 2017, Vienna, Austria

 ISBN 978-1-4503-4336-7/17/03...$15.00
DOI: http://dx.doi.org/10.1145/2909824.3020255

From the standpoint of public policy and societal deliberation we can investigate how robots entering the social sphere may affect labor markets, healthcare, cybersecurity, and education (to name just a few area). While some single out particular roles for ethical perusal, for example nannying or healthcare [32], from the perspective of designing autonomous robots in general HRI has drawn upon landmark attempts to square computational approaches with the best of ethical theory. Researching "machine morality" or robot ethics has illuminated many challenges and opportunities to how autonomous systems could and should decide and act in the world [38].

Another source of HRI insight is discovering how human beings' own reactions to and performance with robots can shape ethical evaluation of their social collaboration. Through realistic and morally charged scenarios, HRI research has examined how humans interpret and evaluate robot behavior, even to the point of applying different moral standards to human vs. robot actions [24]. HRI ethics has also opened out onto dimensions of teamwork and group dynamics, where the impact of the robot is not just through a discrete physical task but in dynamic relationships with people in a certain setting [41]. A common thread in all these aspects of HRI and ethics is the fact that human interests, debates, dilemmas, and conflicts permeate the question "what a robot should do," and that determining good answers is not a technical puzzle but an ongoing, adaptive project. Peering into the ethical landscape of HRI requires a keen eye for overarching themes, from unidirectional emotional bonding to locating responsibility [22, 30, 10].

Not surprisingly, it has been real life applications like self-driving cars, not just the prodding of science fiction, that ultimately have brought home certain ethical quandaries, including how ethical considerations can come regrettably late in the design and implementation process. Teslas have already been operating on the road, without any kind of ethical provision that would facilitate decision-making in critical situations to minimize harm. It is heavily debated whether their introduction on the road was prudent, safe, and sufficiently transparent to the driving public.

Similarly, domestic robots are being advertised for purchase while leaving in their wake concerns about their purpose and function for users. For example, is the recently released Barbie chatbot version really intended for meaningless dialogues, or is there an intent to steer the target population – small kids – in particular directions [37]?

It is clear that ethical reflection about the design and use of robots and their possible interactions with humans must get out in front enough to address these questions as promptly and sagely as possible, lending anticipatory, not belated, insights for public deliberation. These anticipations should not be the nightmares of civilization's takeover via wild projections of human vices and desires onto AI and robotics, but a more distributed, less dramatic, but absolutely crucial set of dynamics that social robotics will plausibly generate.

HRI research has yielded intriguing empirical results connected to ethics and how humans tend to react in social contexts with robots. Still, much of this work has focused on short-term, task-oriented, one-on-one interaction, whether it be what happens when a robot is reprimanded or deemed accountable [17], or when a robot objects to a command [5], a robot cheats [33], or how honest we might be with a robot nearby [15]. As critical as it is to keep studying these phenomena, the ethics of HRI spans spatially and temporally well beyond many of those experimental settings, raising questions in dire need of answers: What are the longer-term effects that social interactions with robots – individually and in groups, with a single robot or more – will have on our everyday lives [9]? How will we recognize and evaluate which interactions are most worthwhile, and toward what kind of life and society they should contribute? And how do we ensure that robots will be genuine helpers contributing to social strengths, rather than exploiting social vulnerabilities (e.g., with people more interested in interacting with their individual companion robot than with other humans)?

To begin mapping that terrain of questions, we will examine three areas of ethical significance in HRI: 1) the primacy and implicit dynamics of bodily perception, 2) the competing interests at work in a single robot-human interaction, and 3) the social intricacy of multiple agents – robots and human beings – communicating and making decisions. These areas are not exhaustive by any means and do not occlude the many established ways in which HRI has tackled ethics so far. Still, we find that they yield concrete directions for how HRI can contribute to a widening, intensifying set of ethical debates with empirical insight. By providing concrete suggestions for empirical studies to investigate the themes underwriting the three ares we hope that HRI research will begin to broaden enough to address issues that will sooner than later have a big impact on societal ways of life.

2. THE PRIMAL, FUNDAMENTAL CHANNELS OF EMBODIED PRESENCE

The functionality of robots often and understandably centers on their perceptual, manipular, and action capabilities, maybe augmented by natural language recognition/production, and other cognitive functions such as planning and problem solving. For social robots, however, their very physical appearance and presence comes to the fore, and the particular manner of executing behaviors starts to matter: not only does robot appearance cause humans to make automatic inferences about robot properties (e.g., whether the robot is likeable, smart, etc.), but robot motion is similarly viewed as a cue to the inner life of the machine (e.g., whether it has a goal and started moving in a particular direction for that reason, or whether it is looking for something the observer does not know). When moving in delicate environments, for example, robot physical presence becomes a dimension of safety and effectiveness – how can the robot accomplish a task while not risking others in its ambit? As the implications of robotic presence are observed, especially with an array of different roles imagined for them, a different foundation of somatic factors is coming into view.

Recent developments in soft robotics as well as compliant control enable new types of physical interactions that were not possible before. General proximal presence and particularly touch – which might be called *interactive proprioception* – point to the manifold of physical interactions of human and robots that might be largely submerged from conscious articulation, yet require explicit accounting and investigation. For the role of touch is critically involved in forming attachments and social bonding in primates [12], and physical interactions with robots, especially soft robots, might have similar effects, regardless of their designers' intentions [2].

One obvious avenue through which the market for robots is playing up the importance of physicality is seen in the looming emergence of sex robots. With first prototypes already on the market, the HRI community is off to a late start investigating the implications of sex robots for human societies, including issues around physicality, privacy, and intimacy [31]. Though it is certainly important to weigh the abuse and exploitation sex robots might exacerbate [26], cordoning off "sex robots" as a distinct type of interaction is a difficult task. It is no less bodily than many other interactions of intimate care and co-presence assistive robots, for example, are being imagined to conduct. Bathing, or helping someone after a fall, or sitting while one sleeps, or watching a movie on a couch, each have rich implications for what a human being is expecting, relying upon, and projecting for the robot with whom they are sharing space. The trust and vulnerability can be conscious or not, and even simple gestures and acts of touch usher in research from psychology.

Recent work by Li suggests that physical and tactile presence may elicit more from us than we might imagine, and for reasons we have yet to explain. Robots were found more persuasive and engaging when physically present than onscreen, though virtual agents and physical robots were regarded similarly when both onscreen– not physical form, but presence, seemed to make the difference [20]. Subjects touching robots were found to be aroused in ways they may not have expected or even perceived themselves [21]. HRI research needs to address how a robot's presence and touch – with all the different forms, textures, and sounds that can come with it – affect how human beings regard and evaluate a robot's function. How do the many tactile features of robots, for example, serve as anchors and cues not just for "likeability" or positivity (categories largely used in HRI work thus far) but more targeted attributions and investments (smart about finances or wise about relationships)?

Though the popular press continues to center on sex robots when it comes to tactile relationships, the intimacy of physical movement and contact is charged on more than sexual lines. Its cultural and emotional resonances, which a robot succeeds or fails to hit upon, bear heavily on what kind of familiarity the robot can generate, what expectations a subject might be lured into forming. Psychologists have shown how seemingly insignificant aspects of one's environment can affect feelings and behavior – a warm coffee cup can facilitate feelings of trust, a trash can with eyes painted on it serve to limit littering [4, 40].

It is not difficult to transfer those lessons to the ways robots' shapes, movements, and function can command powerful reactions. The intense and poignant impact of IED (improvised explosive devices) detecting robot "dogs" on soldiers has an immediate intuitive sense – seeing these robots destroyed or disfigured is a difficult isomorphism to suppress, especially in the grueling, intense environment of a battlefield. But a whole host of less gripping, yet still somatically robust, interactions will present HRI researchers with opportunities for ethical foresight. Subtle configurations of care – what a robot does for a person, how well it performs social rituals and tasks, and what it forces the person to do for it – can have immediate effects and engender longer-term patterns of behavior [35].

The primacy of bodily interaction, with many channels of tactile or proprioceptive feedback the robot may give and receive, may not rise to the level of an urgent ban or utopian promise of a particular role for a robot. As Turkle has recently pointed out with respect to conversation, it can be more subtle and gradual transfigurations in the use of technology that gain more permanent purchase on culture [36]. How will forms of human-robot interaction in sensitive areas – especially with children and elderly people – alter expectations of personal space and safety? What forms of information can the robot gather, and what forms can it solicit, through its whole repertoire of sensory outreach? A verbal response of sympathy has certain rules and conventions according to subject matter. But how does that change when a reassuring, or off-putting, back pat is at issue? The many concerns about abuse and lack of consent that eldercare facilities face already presage the complex negotiations of what touch, personal space, and consent could and will mean for robots in that domain. Some of these considerations may seem to invite technical advances of precision. How do we get the robot to deliver the tea more smoothly, for example? But the ethics involved remain thorny. Consider the following scenario as one point of departure.

SCENARIO 1.

A domestic robot operates in the living room, where family members spend most of their time. The robot maneuvers around people who are on the floor, but has various points of the room where it stays still. The robot has a repertoire of gestures when engaged with a person, including a shoulder pat for assurance and a high five for fun. The robot also has accompanying sounds it can play, including one of the company's jingle that designers had play during high fives or when someone touched the robot and looked happy. The robot and child play a hand-clapping game, but as it gets faster the child makes a mistake. The child pushes the robot in frustration and the parent yanks the child away angrily. The robot recognizes the child's distress and puts a game up on its chest screen for distraction, then motions for the child to sit in its warm lap to watch.

This scenario hints at the ways tactile, mobile interactions could have physical and relational ramifications, both immediate and possibly longer-term. What relationships between child, parent, robot and living space will develop, and how can that be evaluated? In what types of related situations would a robot's action violate norms of intimacy, family bonds, consent, or dignity, or at least wear away at common means of establishing good relationships between people? What is the line between a manufacturer designing multiple physical means for engagement, and manipulating users' vulnerabilities? HRI research has long recognized different aspects of fluency and disfluency in how a robot is perceived, whether through language, form, and gesture [29], but must probe into even more constellations of features that could be shaping an interaction: subtle movements, postures, orientations, temperature, surface texture, etc., including the psychological effects (whether positive or exploitative, upbuilding or dignity-depriving) of a robot changing some of its features in response to a person's affect.

For the above scenario in particular, we see the research challenge of getting beyond the "one-shot lab visit", although even a short interaction could elicit visceral reactions (such arousal as in the above-mentioned study) and thus hint at a potentially larger aspect in need of further investigation. To whatever degree actual homes are viable exercises of testing robots "in the wild," or researchers can manage the careful and responsible use of public space, recognizing the richness of physical contexts will be key to tracking the means by which such physical interaction is defined [25, 28]. Through a repertoire of physical cues one could test how to distract a child, or alternatively test how best to facilitate the child's contact with other people in the room. The ways in which a robot's presence can anchor a social context will require sustained fine-grained variations of setups and a multi-modal means of observation, with attention to the different practitioners who inhabit the interaction's intended context [8]. Finally, discerning whole-body interaction will also require capturing longer-term dynamics of relationships. Drawing conclusions in HRI about the dynamics of trust, intimacy, and isolation between and among people and robots clearly calls for more longitudinal strategies in the research.

3. COMPETING INTERESTS OF INTERACTION – WHAT INTERESTS INTERSECT IN ONE-ON-ONE INTERACTION?

Given the intimate nature of many service contexts envisioned for robots (whether in medical, educational, or domestic settings), HRI work has identified many communicative challenges a social robot should meet, including how fully a user's responses should be anticipated. Across different tasks and interaction contexts, the robot's general goal is to understand the intention of the person and to communicate in a clear, accountable way about how it will act. This coordination usually applies to a task or problem that the person and robot can face together. In the past several years, there has been more thorough acknowledgement of how social and institutional backdrops complicate what "accountable" communication actually comprises. Is the robot working at the behest of the individual interactant, or, say, a medical provider (or loved ones) who bought the robot, or the larger community? Whose interests are being served and accounted for in how the robot represents and performs its actions? And what kinds of information, including ways of gaining it, does a robot have to share with an interactant?

From the other direction, what projections or attributions will a person have toward a robot that disrupt ordinary ethical associations with interaction (e.g., politeness, trust, cooperation)? How will people represent their own interests to a robot, and when will they pursue their interests warily and in more adversarial fashion? Can they, or should they, keep a secret [18]? Do they consider the robot a witness, with some degree of moral authority? Or is a robot viewed as a suspect tool of more distant authorities "behind the code?"

As robots have presented progress in their ability to process feedback from a person – intention, emotional state, physical condition, and so on – possible therapeutic and social roles have appeared more vividly in the public's imagination. The movie *Robot and Frank* shows a robot dutifully serving an elderly man as a vigilant attendant in terms of diet and health, but having no clue as to what societal norms it might violate as Frank's willing companion. While the movie puts those violations in criminal (and cinematically entertaining) forms, there is a more fundamental, expansive question of which this is only one variation: which interests of a human-robot interaction define its one-on-one space, and which ones take precedence?

When the question "What should be done?" is aimed at common-sense tasks and conversational patterns, this question seems to be a technical question of getting from input to generally agreed-upon and straightforward output (e.g., fetching the right object). But companionship through a social robot, again, entangles itself with moral norms about confidentiality, trust, and transparency. What kinds of information should a person expect a robot companion to answer about itself, and what should a robot be expected to do with the information the person shares with it? Making interests explicit – whether personal health, or public safety, or remedying loneliness – can abstractly identify a robot's chief purpose.

The more realistic ethical problem to work out, however, is how multiple interests will be prioritized. The way therapists and caregivers develop professional boundaries provides some insight about how interactions can convey and defend those priorities, yet for a robot there is not the same personal/professional divide to settle. Indeed, robotic abilities (of unseen surveillance, of extraordinary perception, of networked communication) and voids (of emotional and physical pain) may adversely affect a user's expectations of what different interests a robot could represent.

In certain therapeutic contexts the coordination of multiple interests can come together in innovative ways. Demiris's work with occupational therapists and their patients shows how an autonomous system can incorporate therapists' interest to thwart a patient's immediate interest (having a vehicle automatically keep them from hitting an obstacle) in the service of the patient's longer-term, developmental interest (improving in their ability to steer the vehicle themselves) [11] . The transparency is not essentially deceptive – the child patient could understand how the system was designed and still work with it just as, if not more, effectively. But in cases where a user or patient (and their status can be important to specify) contends with interests in tension, or is in conflict with others around them, it is much less clear what "the right thing to say and do" would be on the part of the robot. There may be a therapeutic interest in getting the person to decide to do one thing or another, followed by an explicit response from the robot explaining why it will agree to perform accordingly. But it may be that the robot more properly has to pull back entirely from the one-on-one nature of the exchange, instead of acting in the stead of people or institutions that may need to represent their interests directly. The prospect of more social police robots, where the question of authority takes on intricate, life-and-death forms, brings this vividly into view [16].

Important to note about interests, especially for HRI, is their temporal character. Just within a single interaction, at one point in time, interests can mesh and conflict. But interests, especially longer-term ones, may be seen to develop through interaction over time. While there may be no hard and fast line between those two type of interest intersections, in this paper we would emphasize the importance of a single interaction having interests in play.

The following scenario presents the challenge of negotiating different interests in a concrete social context.

SCENARIO 2.

A robot attendant works in a senior center common area, most often providing companionship and performing basic tasks of bringing food, books, blankets, etc. to residents. There is a particular resident who has started talking to the robot at length about their life and their feelings, and the staff has noticed an improvement in the resident's mood since these conversations began. The resident relies on the robot to remember previous conversations, including meaningful personal experiences they recounted. Senior center staff depend on the robot to notice and report certain obvious symptoms of physical distress or erratic behavior, and the robot is designed to enforce the center's rules in the common area. Recently this resident has brought high-sugar foods to eat in this common area, food that medical providers and the resident's family have asked not be available to them. Other residents have taken note of this food as well as the resident's frequent conversations, and staff have been asked by other residents to get more time with the robot. One evening, the resident asks the robot to stay beyond usual common area hours, to discuss a "private" matter they want the robot to keep confidential. They say it concerns their physical health and their treatment, and they feel only the robot, not the family or doctors, will listen and perhaps give good advice.

This scenario points to the difficulty of restricting the conception of human-robot dialogue to a task-specific or problem-specific framework. The one-on-one conversation proposed at the scenario's end is enough to expose a knot of ethical questions about what is best for all those with something at stake in the interaction. Even without forecasting extended interactions between the resident and robot, one can evaluate how this interaction could defend and threaten different interests. The idea of a solution seems less applicable than a negotiation, where possibly no one interest will be perfectly upheld. Personal information from the resident, who perhaps will complain, confess, conspire, or some combination thereof, will tax any simple role of companionship. This will not just be a case of individual vs. society, though it may be that too – it will involve how the individual's different interests themselves (including relationships they may, in a more secure and reflective mood, want to strengthen) will be met. Nor will HRI measures like "rapport" be goals in and of themselves – depending on the interests involved, an interaction may need to be more adversarial than cooperative. It may be better to have the robot state the limits of its confidentiality and perhaps disappoint the resident than to avoid necessary conflict because of an imagined bonding that is impossible. This latter point applies as much to those who design and deploy the social robot as to those who interact with it.

The overall research upshot for HRI is the imperative of testing how interests extend the scope of interaction beyond a single identified task or purpose, as well as how they redefine what "successful" communication and work may need to look like. Even when limited to a one-on-one interaction, HRI research can look more acutely into how interactions proceed when challenges or appeals to different interests (both those of a subject and broader social ones) are introduced, and how people's reflection on interest may affect their attributions and expectations toward robots. This can help a more robust and grounded HRI ethics weigh in on why, and in what contexts, a robot needs to act on personal disclosures, and when to occupy a stance of confidentiality. This may inform design choices about modes of reception, for example retentive listening (for one-on-one recounting) vs. mere receptive listening (in case the person wants no memory of their words on record). While it will be challenging to craft personal interactions that do not make subjects themselves vulnerable, it will be increasingly critical to track how different interests, not just measures like rapport, agency, or likeability, reveal the dynamics that human-robot interaction contains.

One major challenge in this context will be the development of experimental paradigms that are informative and rigorous while not endangering vulnerable populations. For it would be an ethical violation to experiment with the very group of people robots are supposed to support. Rather, experimental designs need to be targeted at key aspects of one-to-one interaction that can be probed with other subject populations within and outside carefully crafted social contexts (e.g., setting up social situations where subjects feel compelled to voluntarily disclose information to the robot that they do not want to share with others).

4. SYSTEMS AND GROUPS

The ethical reflection on a human-robot interaction tends to broaden the intuitive boundaries of that interaction – there are always wider environments and yet more principles and consequences to fold into one's account. As the social complexity of robotic work in various fields has emerged, the idea of teamwork has naturally drawn research interest. The organizational and computational tasks of coordinating a robot's role with multiple human colleagues (if not also multiple robots alongside them) demand several priorities to be made explicit. How does robot participation maximize efficiency? What are the most effective ways for robots to give and receive information in such a multi-agent context? How can robots enable the team and its human teammates to perform better?

While the literature on human-robot teams is breaking interesting ground across a variety of application domains, some of the morally-ambiguous dynamics of group decision-making have only begun to surface [1]. On one level, there are the wrinkles of resolving different perspectives and contributions in the course of deciding on a plan of action. There is a process/product distinction that ethical evaluation must recognize: what is the best decision for the team right now vs. what is the best method in general for reaching good team decisions going forward. And how does the robot communicate productively while navigating the authoritative rules of whose ultimate view holds sway? Within those questions lie matters of social status, authority, knowledge, trust, camaraderie, and integrity, some of which clearly would not apply to decision support systems, but they do apply to robots perceived as *agents.*

Increasingly robust settings have been found for social robots to provide organizational help, for instance a Nao robot assisting with scheduling at a busy medical practice [14]. There is a general recognition by the people interacting with the robot in such a case about what kind of information the Nao can deliver (though its performance may still surprise and impress). In other cases on the horizon, however, a robot may face unexpected negotiations amid conflict. What happens, for example, when multiple incompatible commands or requests are given to the robot by different people? There may be stock answers available, such as "This is who I am authorized to follow on this issue;" some research has looked at verbal feedback and improved performance [34]. But the exchange of reasons, enhanced when robots (and there may well be many on a team) exclusively possess information needed for deliberation, runs against the grain of pure obedience. Nor will reason-giving operate the same way in every context – there may be judgment calls to make when more evidence is practically beside the point. Relational communication and decision-making form part of this horizon not because of incorrect interpretation or incongruent purposes among the interactants, but because robots might be observing, mediating, and participating in the midst of human relationships. The status of robots, instead of a metaphysical context-free question, becomes one of social performance within a context, with their actions having indirect impact on behavior between people, not just attitudes toward the robots themselves [6]. Systematic indices of performance, therefore, must not focus on what people do with robots to the exclusion what they subsequently do with each other. We can consider the following scenario to draw out the issues further.

SCENARIO 3.

A rescue team – with a few members of the National Guard along with civilian volunteers, with the permission of National Guard command center – is patrolling neighborhoods after a flood. Due to the severity of the disaster the team will be working together for days if not weeks. A robot is brought along, with natural language capability, networked communication, and versatile mobility in water or on land. At various points team members will yell to the others that they have come upon a stranded pet, person, or structure under threat (with likely people inside). While one member of the National Guard is the designated leader, even the leader needs the rest of the team to update her in order to make a plan. The robot can often receive evidence or information that contradicts that of team members, including which area needs attention first. The team also faces deliberations about how best, given the state of the area, to triage for the needs that the team perceives around it.

This scenario encompasses some of the issues raised above about sizing up different interests, while illustrating additional complexities in terms of decision-making and collaboration. Unlike most discussions about the ethics of self-driving cars, treating this scenario means factoring in actual ethical reasoning and debate as part of a robot's participation (or least environment in which they participate). How does a robot negotiate the many consequences for following one direction over another, especially given information it alone might have? How can the robot best enable strong teamwork and better group deliberations, or at least not impede them? At what point does a robot assert its authoritative information into a debate, even though it has no formal social status? And will such insertions result in the robot's obtaining authoritative status among the team members? Unforeseen and severe circumstances will bring these questions all the more to the fore given life-and-death stakes under time pressure. The interlocking of social forms with approaches to ethical reasoning could get quite convoluted without focused empirical work.

HRI research has certainly broached some issues of communication and cooperation, tackling important questions of culture and multiple ways of measuring performance [3, 39, 13]. Still, many of the measures in this work boil down to basic attributions: trusting/not trusting, ingroup/outgroup, in favor/against, etc. But part of a true evaluative trajectory must address both process and product, and do so over enough time to capture how the human-robot work can reliably develop over many crucial situations. A one-shot achievement of teamwork is hard to imagine, much less stipulate, and the ethical stakes of the group work will include both task-specific and relational dimensions – including, crucially, relationships between people working with or among robots. The challenge for empirical testing, then, is to configure group settings and complex tasks wherein varied interactions, human-robot and human-human, can be observed and tracked along practical lines. Tracking in these setting could be more than simple attributions from team members, but objective events in how the team deliberates, decides, and discovers ways to work. One way to do this may be complex puzzle situations for groups to tackle (similar perhaps to the interactive game *Escape the Room*), where certain relational goods and team goals ("cooperate," "get to know one another") accompany a main task (e.g., "get across the ravine together"). Without some kind of more organizationally robust measures, the important ethical determination of how robots and humans can work, and in what domains, will have much less of an empirical foundation. There will be much less substance available, in sum, to flesh out what a "morally competent" robot even means [23].

5. RESEARCH CHALLENGES AND MOVING BEYOND REPLACEMENT

The horizons for HRI ethics we have described are not easily reached from where we stand today, though the sophistication of social robots they assume will also not arrive promptly tomorrow. Meeting the next level of ethical challenges will require imaginative, rigorous efforts to enable solid empirical footing for society's next steps with technology. It is worth identifying some common characteristics for research that delves into the three areas we have described, as a way not only to contribute to HRI ethics, but also to support its distinctive contributions to society's wider discussions of technology.

To begin with, studying fully embodied interaction, interest-laden communication, and group performance suggests rethinking the time frame for an interaction and its effects. Physical presence with a robot, especially the social setting that may evoke multiple interests, may be briefer or longer than a standard task-based period (e.g. 30 minutes) in order to register the types of dynamics we have discussed. In addition, however long laboratory or in-the-wild interactions are, the effects of interaction may need to be followed for longer periods than a typical lab visit. Unquestionably the longitudinal approach poses practical and logistical obstacles, just as it does with other forms of scientific research. But HRI work has broken ground in this area, for example on the habituation effect [19]. More to the point, as public debates about robots heat up, anecdotes or personal speculation will not buttress reliable conclusions about what robots are doing, nor where they should be doing it. HRI can expand the public's ethical lens to more subtle, yet also more empirically based interactive elements.

Another key feature of HRI research for the issues we raise is re-examining the implicit premises of a one-on-one human-robot interaction. While a good deal of HRI research already extends beyond dyadic interactions, changing the number of people or robots does not always provide enough contrast to that model. As we have discussed with respect to interests, a one-on-one interaction may be a crossroads for broader conflicts rather than a self-contained exercise; making some of these conflicts and consideration more explicit can test how contrived our previous models of interaction have been. In addition, if human beings are interacting on so many physical and affective levels with robots, other forms of technology (smartphones, computer, TV, game consoles) seem all the more called-for as controls for direct interactants, or at least part of the setting in which to test human-robot interaction. A recent article about the iPal robot has been met with some alarm in terms of childcare, but what if the operative contrast is not with a babysitter but a tablet [42]?

Even as they expose new depths to one-on-one interaction, these areas should allow robotic work to be viewed as more than a one-to-one replacement for a human being's role. Navigating the complex currents of embodied interaction, cross-cutting interests, and interpersonal conflict may mean reshaping how robots have been envisioned to share space and work. Auxillary or peripheral functions for social robotic work, from physical presence and movement to higher-level communication, can open up application domains to richer models of robots complementing people's efforts in service to people's needs. By contrast, testing those different positions can show where independence and contention, perhaps to correct a group's belief, can best contribute in collaborative efforts. Robots do not have to be teammates to work with a team, especially given the ethical and empirical question of how the whole range of physical presence with a robot can affect others. Keeping account of such interactive layers will help determine, in turn, when a robot can effectively share, solicit, or exchange reasons amid different sensory environments, especially within conflicted and ethically charged situations.

All in all, these research dimensions help to demonstrate HRI's distinct contributions to larger ethical discussions. While some public narratives, fed by Terminator photo-topped articles, might grab attention through familiar futurist projections, this distracts from the concrete contexts where practitioners and engineers are plying their efforts. Instead of taking common stories from movies and literature and slapping them onto present-day work, the sober challenge is to recognize the ordinary struggles and stakes that accompany proximal applications. As HRI research will be able to better demonstrate 1) how many modes of bodily presence exert a mix of influences cognitively, emotionally, physiologically, and perceptually, 2) how a direct dialogue is a node in a wider network of interests, and 3) how communal and socially spontaneous decision-making can be, we can start to more comprehensively assess what application domains are permissible or preferable for social robots. Instead of repeating the foreboding headline "The __ robots are here" and assuming a loss of a human occupation or role – whether as teacher, tutor, therapist, lover, or companion – we can more carefully sort through physical, communicative, and assistive roles in relation to human dignity and needs. As AI ethics struggles to connect to people's experience in face of inaccessible algorithms and disembodied systems, HRI will have even more reason to bear witness to the embodied, culturally embedded, and communicatively dense conditions in which social robots operate.

This is both an opportunity and challenge at the same time, for social robots will, by way of their physical bodies, have the advantage of being able to communicate and interact in ways that look natural and familiar to us (assuming these interactions are done right), while disembodied AI systems have to overcome the perceptual hiatus of lacking bodily communication. Yet, while for us the bodily presence of robots is immediately readable, it can also be misread. The job for HRI ethics is exactly to stake out the territory of influence where physical presence and physical interactions, one-on-one or in groups, in organized teams or loose clusters of people, can affect humans psychologically, both in the short and the long term.

6. CONCLUSIONS

HRI ethics will continue to convene inquiries that draw on law, policy, economics, psychology, medicine, education, and popular culture. Sizing up the effects of HRI and its prospects for increased application demand that ethical reflection stay conversant and vigilant across disciplines. Ethics must also be institutionally permeative, integral from the beginning of design processes and in the mix of academic and non-academic treatments.

In this paper we have explicated three challenging dimensions that pose increasingly significant sets of questions for social robotics. They are practically compelling all the more for not being intuitively attention-grabbing: concrete subtleties of embodiment, competing interests, and decision-making in groups may seem too ordinary in the face of science-fiction's modes of heroic or apocalyptic transcendence. But the varied social contexts into which robots may enter suggest that overly individualized scenarios, with thin articulations of embodiment and social interests, are not sufficient guides for the ethical issues that will develop. Products that grab headlines according to familiar roles (i.e., an adorable domestic companion) can still usher in physical and interpersonal subtleties whose effects reverberate beyond the marketed use (much as smartphones did not foreshadow car drivers using them compulsively). Different from disembodied AI's presentation in public discussion, HRI research is poised to amplify its ethical voice, witnessing to the multi-layered physicality and expressiveness – part of its deep-seated "social valence" – to show how we can situate robots in the world [7]. Through research reaching further into those depths, HRI work can continue to illuminate and enact humanity, for the sake society's best interests and needs.

7. ACKNOWLEDGMENTS

This work was in part funded by grant N00014-14-1-0144 from the US Office of Naval Research and grant IIS 1316809 from the US National Science Foundation.

8. REFERENCES

[1] R. C. Arkin, P. Ulam, and A. R. Wagner. Moral decision making in autonomous systems: Enforcement, moral emotions, dignity, trust, and deception. *Proceedings of the IEEE*, 100(3):571–589, 2012.

[2] T. Arnold and M. Scheutz. The tactile ethics of soft robotics: Designing wisely for human-robot interaction. *Soft Robotics*, forthcoming.

[3] C. Bartneck, D. Kulić, E. Croft, and S. Zoghbi. Measurement instruments for the anthropomorphism, animacy, likeability, perceived intelligence, and perceived safety of robots. *International journal of social robotics*, 1(1):71–81, 2009.

[4] M. Bateson, D. Nettle, and G. Roberts. Cues of being watched enhance cooperation in a real-world setting. *Biology letters*, 2(3):412–414, 2006.

[5] G. Briggs and M. Scheutz. How robots can affect human behavior: Investigating the effects of robotic displays of protest and distress. *International Journal of Social Robotics*, 6, 2014.

[6] K. Caine, S. Šabanović, and M. Carter. The effect of monitoring by cameras and robots on the privacy enhancing behaviors of older adults. In *Human-Robot Interaction (HRI), 2012 7th ACM/IEEE International Conference on*, pages 343–350. IEEE, 2012.

[7] R. Calo. Robotics and the lessons of cyberlaw. *Cal. L. Rev.*, 103:513, 2015.

[8] W.-L. Chang and S. Šabanović. Studying socially assistive robots in their organizational context: Studies with paro in a nursing home. In *Proceedings of the Tenth Annual ACM/IEEE International Conference on Human-Robot Interaction Extended Abstracts*, pages 227–228. ACM, 2015.

[9] E. Datteri. Predicting the long-term effects of human-robot interaction: A reflection on responsibility in medical robotics. *Science and engineering ethics*, 19(1):139–160, 2013.

[10] M. M. de Graaf. An ethical evaluation of human–robot relationships. *International Journal of Social Robotics*, 8(4):589–598, 2016.

[11] Y. Demiris. Knowing when to assist: Developmental issues in lifelong assistive robotics. In *2009 Annual International Conference of the IEEE Engineering in Medicine and Biology Society*, pages 3357–3360. IEEE, 2009.

[12] R. I. Dunbar. The social role of touch in humans and primates: behavioural function and neurobiological mechanisms. *Neuroscience & Biobehavioral Reviews*, 34(2):260–268, 2010.

[13] V. Evers, H. Maldonado, T. Brodecki, and P. Hinds. Relational vs. group self-construal: untangling the role of national culture in hri. In *Human-Robot Interaction (HRI), 2008 3rd ACM/IEEE International Conference on*, pages 255–262. IEEE, 2008.

[14] M. C. Gombolay. Apprenticeship scheduling for human-robot teams. In *Thirtieth AAAI Conference on Artificial Intelligence*, 2016.

[15] G. Hoffman, J. Forlizzi, S. Ayal, A. Steinfeld, J. Antanitis, G. Hochman, E. Hochendoner, and J. Finkenaur. Robot presence and human honesty: Experimental evidence. In *Proceedings of the Tenth Annual ACM/IEEE International Conference on Human-Robot Interaction*, pages 181–188. ACM, 2015.

[16] E. E. Joh. Policing police robots. *UCLA L. Rev. Discourse (2016), Forthcoming*, 2016.

[17] P. H. Kahn Jr, T. Kanda, H. Ishiguro, B. T. Gill, J. H. Ruckert, S. Shen, H. E. Gary, A. L. Reichert, N. G. Freier, and R. L. Severson. Do people hold a humanoid robot morally accountable for the harm it causes? In *Proceedings of the seventh annual ACM/IEEE international conference on Human-Robot Interaction*, pages 33–40. ACM, 2012.

[18] P. H. Kahn Jr, T. Kanda, H. Ishiguro, B. T. Gill, S. Shen, H. E. Gary, and J. H. Ruckert. Will people keep the secret of a humanoid robot?: Psychological intimacy in hri. In *Proceedings of the Tenth Annual ACM/IEEE International Conference on Human-Robot Interaction*, pages 173–180. ACM, 2015.

[19] K. L. Koay, D. S. Syrdal, M. L. Walters, and K. Dautenhahn. Living with robots: Investigating the habituation effect in participants' preferences during a longitudinal human-robot interaction study. In *RO-MAN 2007-The 16th IEEE International Symposium on Robot and Human Interactive Communication*, pages 564–569. IEEE, 2007.

[20] J. Li. The benefit of being physically present: A survey of experimental works comparing copresent robots, telepresent robots and virtual agents. *International Journal of Human-Computer Studies*, 77:23–37, 2015.

[21] J. Li, W. Ju, and B. Reeves. Touching a mechanical body: Tactile contact with intimate parts of a humanoid robot is physiologically arousing. 2016.

[22] P. Lichocki, A. Billard, and P. H. Kahn. The ethical landscape of robotics. *IEEE Robotics & Automation Magazine*, 18(1):39–50, 2011.

[23] B. Malle and M. Scheutz. When will people regard robots as morally competent social partners? In *Proceedings of Ro-Man.* 2015.

[24] B. F. Malle, M. Scheutz, T. Arnold, J. Voiklis, and C. Cusimano. Sacrifice one for the good of many?: People apply different moral norms to human and robot agents. In *Proceedings of the tenth annual ACM/IEEE international conference on human-robot interaction*, pages 117–124. ACM, 2015.

[25] N. Mirnig, E. Strasser, A. Weiss, and M. Tscheligi. Studies in public places as a means to positively influence people?s attitude towards robots. In *International Conference on Social Robotics*, pages 209–218. Springer, 2012.

[26] K. Richardson. The asymmetrical'relationship': parallels between prostitution and the development of sex robots. *ACM SIGCAS Computers and Society*, 45(3):290–293, 2016.

[27] L. D. Riek and D. Howard. A code of ethics for the human-robot interaction profession. *Proceedings of We Robot*, 2014.

[28] S. Sabanovic, M. P. Michalowski, and R. Simmons. Robots in the wild: Observing human-robot social interaction outside the lab. In *9th IEEE International Workshop on Advanced Motion Control, 2006.*, pages 596–601. IEEE, 2006.

[29] M. Salem, K. Rohlfing, S. Kopp, and F. Joublin. A friendly gesture: Investigating the effect of multimodal robot behavior in human-robot interaction. In *2011 RO-MAN*, pages 247–252. IEEE, 2011.

[30] M. Scheutz. The inherent dangers of unidirectional emotional bonds between humans and social robots. In P. Lin, G. Bekey, and K. Abney, editors, *Anthology on Robo-Ethics.* MIT Press, 2011.

[31] M. Scheutz and T. Arnold. Are we ready for sex robots? In *The Eleventh ACM/IEEE International Conference on Human Robot Interation*, pages 351–358. IEEE Press, 2016.

[32] N. Sharkey and A. Sharkey. The crying shame of robot nannies: an ethical appraisal. *Interaction Studies*, 11(2):161–190, 2010.

[33] E. Short, J. Hart, M. Vu, and B. Scassellati. No fair!! an interaction with a cheating robot. In *2010 5th ACM/IEEE International Conference on Human-Robot Interaction (HRI)*, pages 219–226. IEEE, 2010.

[34] A. St Clair and M. Mataric. How robot verbal feedback can improve team performance in human-robot task collaborations. In *Proceedings of the Tenth Annual ACM/IEEE International Conference on Human-Robot Interaction*, pages 213–220. ACM, 2015.

[35] L. Suchman. Reconfiguring human-robot relations. In *ROMAN 2006-The 15th IEEE International Symposium on Robot and Human Interactive Communication*, pages 652–654. IEEE, 2006.

[36] S. Turkle. *Reclaiming conversation: The power of talk in a digital age.* Penguin Press HC, 2015.

[37] J. Vlahos. Barbie wants to get to know your child. *The New York Times. Retrieved from http://www.nytimes.com/2015/09/20/magazine/barbie-wants-to-get-to-know-your-child.html?_r=2*, 2015.

[38] W. Wallach, C. Allen, and I. Smit. Machine morality: bottom-up and top-down approaches for modelling human moral faculties. *Ai & Society*, 22(4):565–582, 2008.

[39] L. Wang, P.-L. P. Rau, V. Evers, B. K. Robinson, and P. Hinds. When in rome: the role of culture & context in adherence to robot recommendations. In *Proceedings of the 5th ACM/IEEE international conference on Human-robot interaction*, pages 359–366. IEEE Press, 2010.

[40] L. E. Williams and J. A. Bargh. Experiencing physical warmth promotes interpersonal warmth. *Science*, 322(5901):606–607, 2008.

[41] J. R. Wilson, T. Arnold, and M. Scheutz. Relational enhancement: A framework for evaluating and designing human-robot relationships. In *Proceedings of the AAAI Workshop on AI, Ethics, and Society*, 2016.

[42] J. Wong. 'this is awful': robot can keep children occupied for hours without supervision, 2016.

Code3: A System for End-to-End Programming of Mobile Manipulator Robots for Novices and Experts

Justin Huang and Maya Cakmak
Computer Science & Engineering, University of Washington
Seattle, WA 98195
{jstn,mcakmak}@cs.washington.edu

ABSTRACT

This paper introduces *Code3*, a system for user-friendly, rapid programming of mobile manipulator robots. The system is designed to let non-roboticists and roboticists alike program end-to-end manipulation tasks. To accomplish this, *Code3* provides three integrated components for perception, manipulation, and high-level programming. The perception component helps users define a library of object and scene parts that the robot can later detect. The manipulation component lets users define actions for manipulating objects or scene parts through programming by demonstration. Finally, the high-level programming component provides a drag-and-drop interface with which users can program the logic and control flow to accomplish a task using their previously specified perception and manipulation capabilities. We present findings from an observational user study with non-roboticist programmers (N=10) that demonstrate their ability to quickly learn *Code3* and program a PR2 robot to do manipulation tasks. We also demonstrate how the system is expressive enough for an expert to rapidly program highly complex manipulation tasks like playing tic-tac-toe and reconfiguring an object to be graspable.

Keywords

Programming by demonstration; Programming tools; End-user programming; Mobile Manipulation

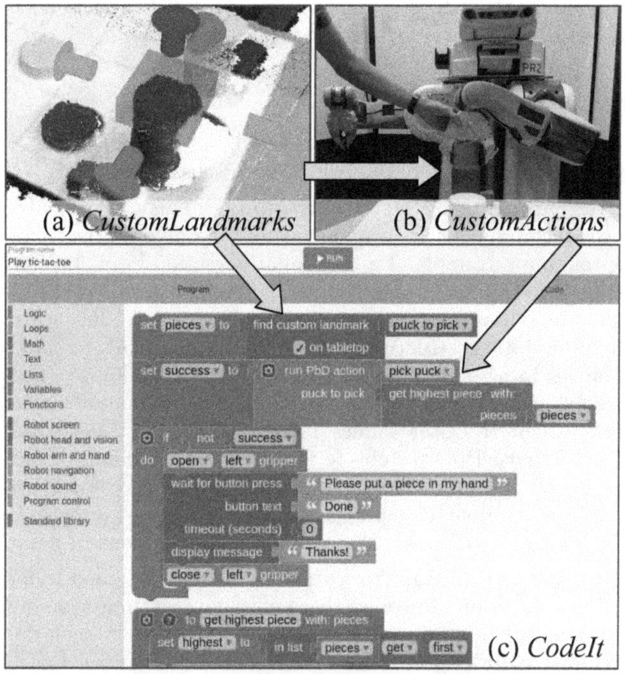

Figure 1: Overview of the *Code3* system.

1. INTRODUCTION

Programming mobile manipulator robots such as the PR2 or Fetch robots can be challenging to learn and take a long time, even for expert roboticists. Not only does it require learning a robot programming system such as ROS [33], it also requires specialized knowledge of robot perception and manipulation. These factors make robot programming inaccessible to general programmers who do not have specific skills in robotics, potentially slowing progress in the field of mobile manipulators. As an example of how long it can take, one course teaching senior computer science undergraduate students to program the PR2 with ROS required over 17 hours of lab time spread across 10 weeks [11]. Even a group of professional robotics engineers had to spend five days to program the PR2 to fetch beers from a kitchen refrigerator [1]. And, several teams of roboticists took months programming the PR2 to pick items from warehouse shelves for the Amazon Picking Challenge [15]. Our goal is to make programming mobile manipulators to do similar tasks easy for general programmers while still allowing experienced users to program more complex tasks.

This paper introduces *Code3*, a robot programming system that integrates three core components that are necessary for end-to-end programming of mobile manipulation tasks. The first, *CustomLandmarks*, lets users create a library of perceptual landmarks (objects or scene elements) by annotating the robot's sensor stream, which the robot can detect in new scenes. The second, *CustomActions*, is a kinesthetic programming by demonstration (PbD) system that lets users create a library of manipulation actions. The third component, *CodeIt*, is a drag-and-drop programming interface that lets users define control flow logic for their task

HRI '17, March 06 - 09, 2017, Vienna, Austria

ISBN 978-1-4503-4336-7/17/03...$15.00

DOI: http://dx.doi.org/10.1145/2909824.3020215

using the perception and action capabilities they developed with the other two components.

Through a user study with 10 participants, we demonstrate that non-roboticist programmers, who were novices to *Code3*, were able to program useful manipulation tasks on the PR2 robot in under an hour, after only 90 minutes of training. To achieve this rapid training and implementation time, we did not have to trade off expressivity by making *Code3* overly simplistic. In contrast, we illustrate how we can use *Code3* to program complex manipulation tasks like playing tic-tac-toe with a human player and reconfiguring an object to make it graspable. Ultimately, we envision non-roboticist programmers of all skill levels using *Code3* to rapidly prototype and program task behaviors for mobile manipulators in semi-structured environments such as retail stores, warehouses, and office buildings.

2. RELATED WORK

Code3 builds upon previous research in PbD and end-user programming for robotics, which we discuss below.

Programming by Demonstration: PbD is a commonly-used technique for programming robots by guiding the robot through an example of a manipulation action [5, 9, 14, 27]. Researchers have studied many different aspects of PbD, including how to represent actions [2, 13, 30, 36], learn high-level task structures [17, 28, 31], use PbD to train policies in a reinforcement learning framework [6, 35], and resolve design issues when interacting with human teachers [12, 24, 37]. User studies have shown that end-users can learn and use PbD systems to program various manipulation actions [2, 3]. Our system adds more flexible perception capabilities compared to previous PbD systems and integrates with a coding interface that enables logic and control flow.

User programming for robots: *Code3* is designed to let a broader group of people (those with general programming experience) program robots. Other systems have been developed with similar goals. The code interface for *Code3* is based on the *CustomPrograms* [23] system. *CustomPrograms* enables programmers to rapidly write programs for a mobile delivery robot using a visual programming interface. However, their system does not address the challenge of programming perception capabilities or manipulation actions.

Two related systems include ROS Commander [29] and RoboFlow [4], which integrate robot actions, including those programmed by demonstration, with a visual programming language using a data flow model [21]. Interaction Composer [19, 20] is a system that also combines robot actions (coded in C++) with a flow-based interface. The authors of [4, 20] point out that, in some cases, flow-based interfaces do not scale well, especially when the state space is large. In contrast, our system uses a general-purpose language for developing control flow, which roboticists and programming language experts interviewed in [4] said they would prefer to use over a data flow model.

Others have designed robot programming interfaces for creating social interactions. These include the TiViPE [25, 26], Choregraphe [32], and Interaction Blocks [34] interfaces for programming the Nao robot. They combine flow-based programming interfaces with support for timing, social dialogue, and libraries of gestures. RoboStudio [16] is a system for authoring UI and control flow for healthcare robots. Although *Code3* has some human interaction features, it focuses on programming manipulation tasks, such as fetching and carrying, delivering objects, and manipulating the environment.

3. SYSTEM DESCRIPTION

Code3 allows end-to-end programming of mobile manipulation tasks through three components: (1) *CustomLandmarks* for developing perceptual capabilities, (2) *CustomActions* for programming manipulation actions, and (3) *CodeIt* for combining the two in a high-level program that captures task requirements. This section describes these components and how they are integrated together. Our system was implemented on a PR2 robot; however, all components are easily portable to a different robot.

3.1 CustomLandmarks

Many robot programs involve detecting and locating objects. However, developing these capabilities requires expertise in robot perception or requires using automatic systems that recognize a limited set of objects. *CustomLandmarks* is a system that lets users create partial 3D models of task-relevant objects or scene parts, called *landmarks*, which the robot can locate in new scenes. This section describes how landmarks are created, represented, and searched for in new scenes. Internal evaluations, pseudocode, and other details of *CustomLandmarks* are provided in [22].

3.1.1 Landmark representation

To create a custom landmark, the user positions the robot in the task scene and points its RGBD sensor (*e.g.,* a Kinect) at the landmark of interest. The user views a 3D visualization of the data and segments the landmark by setting a 3D box around the landmark, shown in Figure 1(a). The user then gives the landmark a name, and the system records the RGBD point cloud inside the box as well as the box's position and dimensions to a database.

Custom landmarks are represented with the point cloud and the box used to segment it from the scene. The system uses the box to explictly model regions of empty space around the landmark. This adds specificity to the representation. For example, the point cloud of the corner of a tabletop does not look different from an empty patch in the middle of the table: both landmarks are flat and rectangular. By modeling empty space, the user can create a landmark that explicitly represents the corner of the table as opposed to any part of the table. Such a landmark could be used to place or align items with the corner.

This representation is flexible and allows users to create a variety of landmarks. Examples include simple objects (*e.g.,* a cup on a table), parts of objects (*e.g.,* the handle of a Tide bottle), or arbitrary parts of a task scene (*e.g.,* the front left corner of a laundry machine).

3.1.2 Search algorithm

CustomLandmarks implements an algorithm to locate a landmark in a scene. The algorithm takes a custom landmark and a point cloud representation of a scene as input, and it returns a list of locations where the landmark was found. If the algorithm does not find the landmark in the scene, it returns an empty list.

The algorithm first randomly samples points in the scene. For each sampled point, it attempts to align the landmark to the scene geometry at that point using the Iterative Closest

Point algorithm [8]. It then computes an error score for the alignment by summing two sources of error. Informally, the first source of error measures how well the shape of the landmark matches with the shape of the scene, while the second measures how much the scene intrudes on the empty space of the landmark. More formally, the first source of error is the sum of the distances between the points in the landmark's point cloud and each of their nearest points in the scene. The second is the sum of the distances between the scene points inside the landmark's box and their nearest points on the landmark. The errors are averaged to provide a single error score for the alignment. If the error score is below a certain threshold, the location of the alignment gets added to the output list. Note that the error metric does not use color information, although doing so is an area for future work.

3.1.3 Limitations

Because the landmark's shape is captured from a single RGBD point cloud, *CustomLandmarks* is sensitive to viewpoint differences, such as when an asymmetric landmark is rotated 90 degrees. To avoid this issue, users can create additional landmarks for rotated versions of the same object and search for all of those landmarks. We envision using *CustomLandmarks* (and *Code3* more generally) in semi-structured environments in which objects have known locations and a finite set of orientations.

3.2 CustomActions

Programming robot manipulation actions can also be challenging for developers, because it involves modeling the spatial positions of objects, planning arm motions, and adjusting these motions depending on the location of objects. As discussed in Section 2, PbD is a technique for defining manipulation actions that is accessible to novice users. *CustomActions* is a PbD system that builds upon the work of [3]. The main difference between the two systems is that the system of [3] uses a tabletop segmentation system to detect objects, while *CustomActions* uses *CustomLandmarks*.

Although it sounds like a minor change, using *CustomLandmarks* instead of tabletop segmentation allows users to create a much wider variety of manipulation actions than before. Tabletop segmentation searches for a nearby tabletop using the RANSAC algorithm [18]. Clusters of RGBD data points above the table are then considered to be objects. This only works in tabletop scenes and assumes that objects on the table are the only perceptual landmarks that need to be located. In contrast, using *CustomLandmarks* lets *CustomActions* locate non-tabletop objects like doorknobs and non-objects like the corner of a table.

Below, we describe the workflow for creating, representing, and executing PbD actions.

3.2.1 Action representation

Actions are represented as a sequence of poses for the robot's end-effector(s). The system also stores whether the end-effector is open or closed at each pose (for a gripper). The locations of the poses can be defined relative to either the base of the robot or to a landmark. If the user defines an end-effector pose relative to a landmark, then the system will adjust the end-effector pose whenever it detects that the pose of the landmark has changed. A simple example of an action is to pick up an object, whose position could vary, and put it into a box at a fixed position relative to the robot. The user would first create a custom landmark of the object. Then, the user would demonstrate grasping the object, moving the end-effector over the box, and letting go of the object. The end-effector poses involved in grasping the object would be defined relative to the location of the object, while the poses to drop the object in the box would be relative to the robot's base.

3.2.2 Programming an action

To specify an action, users first use the *CustomLandmarks* box interface to define the landmarks that will be involved in the action. They then hold the robot's arms and move them to the desired poses. Users save the poses by using voice commands or by clicking a button in a GUI. In the GUI, pictured in Figure 4, users can define some poses to be relative to one of the landmarks they defined earlier. When done, users give the action a name, which *CodeIt* uses later.

3.2.3 Action execution

To execute an action, the robot first points its head to locate each of the landmarks referenced in the action. Because the landmarks are not necessarily on a tabletop, *CustomActions* looks for each landmark near the location where it was last found. If the landmark has never been located before, the robot looks where the landmark was during the action demonstration. If the system locates more than one instance of a landmark, it uses the one that was detected with the lowest error score. Next, the system adjusts any poses that were defined relative to those landmarks. Finally, the robot moves its arms through the poses, opening or closing its grippers as programmed.

3.3 CodeIt

CustomActions helps users specify simple actions, but it is not expressive enough to represent complex task structure and logic like looping or branching. Our system uses *CodeIt* (an open-source and extended version of the system introduced in [23]) to enable programming of such high-level task structures. *CodeIt* implements a visual programming interface that lets users write code by connecting puzzle shaped blocks instead of typing (Fig. 1(c)). The interface provides general-purpose programming language features, including loops, conditionals, string manipulation, lists, functions, and variables. To control the robot, *CodeIt* makes calls to a high-level API that operates the robot. An example of an API method, which we call a *primitive*, is to move the robot's head to a certain pose. System developers must design and implement this API for their robot before using *CodeIt*.

The *CodeIt* interface is implemented in a web browser, enabling users to start programming the robot without having to set up a development environment. After writing a program, users click a "Run" button to execute their program on the robot. Once the program is running, the "Run" button turns into a "Stop" button that halts the program.

3.3.1 Integration of Code3 components

CodeIt provides APIs to use *CustomLandmarks* and *CustomActions*. The integration of *CodeIt* and *CustomLandmarks* occurs via a primitive that searches for a landmark in the current scene: `findCustomLandmark(landmarkName)`. The argument of this primitive is the name of a previously created custom landmark. When called, the robot searches for the landmark in the current scene and returns a (possibly empty) list of locations where the landmark was found. The user's program can examine the length of the list and iterate through it. *CodeIt* also allows users to read the x, y, and z positions of the detected landmarks, in the coordinate frame of the robot's base.

The integration of *CustomActions* with *CodeIt* occurs via a primitive that executes a previously programmed action: `runPbdAction(actionName)`. The argument of this primitive is the name of the action to run. The primitive returns true if the action executes successfully and false otherwise. An action fails if a needed landmark cannot be found in the scene or if an arm pose relative to a landmark is unreachable.

CodeIt also implements a feature that we call *preregistration*. Suppose there are three identical cans in the scene and the user has created a custom action to pick up a can and put it in a box. As described earlier, *CustomActions* will execute the action with the can that was detected with the lowest error score, which can be an arbitrary choice in practice. Preregistration allows users to specify a particular landmark to execute an action with in this situation. First, users call `findCustomLandmark` in their *CodeIt* program, which returns a list of detected landmark locations. Then, users can iterate through the list of locations and select whichever one their task needs. Finally, the landmark location can be passed as an optional argument to the `runPbdAction` primitive. This causes the robot to execute the action using the landmark that was passed in. In the above example, the user could use preregistration to have the robot put the three cans into the box in right to left order. In Section 5, we describe how we used preregistration to pick a game piece from the top of a stack. Fig. 1(c) illustrates how preregistration looks in *CodeIt*. The first block finds a custom landmark of a game piece. The user iterates through the list of game pieces and selects the highest one through a function called "get highest piece." Finally, that piece is passed into a custom action to pick a game piece.

3.3.2 Other primitives for the PR2

The work described in [23] was designed for the Savioke Relay, a mobile robot with no arms. We designed and implemented a new API to support the manipulation capabilities of the PR2 robot. We also added a touchscreen tablet to the PR2, so that the robot could display messages and receive touch input. Below, we briefly list the primitives we added to the PR2.

- Tablet interaction: `displayMessage(text)`, `askMultipleChoice(question, choiceList)`
- Head control: `lookAt(upDegrees, leftDegrees)`
- Gripper control: `setGripper(leftOrRight, openOrClosed)`, `isGripper(leftOrRight, openOrClosed)`
- Pre-programmed tucking or deploying of arms: `tuckOrDeployArms(leftAction, rightAction)`
- Pausing: `waitFor(numSeconds)`
- Text-to-speech: `say(text)`

Although we could have easily implemented the ability to autonomously navigate to named locations—as with the `goTo` primitive in [23]—our PR2 was immobile due to hardware issues.

3.4 Open-source code

We implemented *Code3* for the PR2 and Turtlebot robots. Open-source code and documentation for using *Code3* can be found at https://github.com/hcrlab/code3.

4. NOVICE USER PROGRAMMING

This section describes an observational user study of *Code3* that we conducted. Our goal was to assess the system's learnability and usability for programmers with little or no robotics experience. To study this, we trained users to program the PR2 using *Code3* and asked them to program manipulation tasks.

4.1 Procedure

The study consisted of a 60-minute training session and a 90-minute programming session. The sessions could be scheduled back-to-back or up to 3 days apart. At the beginning of the training session, users were told to imagine starting a new job at a company that programmed the PR2 robot. An experimenter read from a script to train participants on: (a) how to create actions in *CustomActions*, (b) how to use *CustomLandmarks*, and (c) how to use *CodeIt*, including how to run custom actions from code. Users were not trained on preregistration because the user study tasks did not require it.

During the first 30 minutes of the programming session, participants worked on a familiarization task, with proactive guidance from the experimenter when needed. Next, participants received a description of the program that they would be asked to create. We assigned participants to program one of two tasks (described below in Sec. 4.1.1). We alternated the order in which we assigned tasks to participants. They filled out a pre-task questionnaire, which asked users to describe the actions and landmarks that would be needed and to outline the overall program. This was included to help participants organize their thoughts.

Participants were given 50 minutes to program the task. They could test their programs on the robot at any time. We considered a task finished once the robot was able to successfully execute the task. If a participant finished their task before the end of the study, they were asked to program the other task as well. Once the user finished or ran out of time, they were asked to stop working and fill out a final questionnaire.

The experiment took place in a laboratory setting with a PR2 robot and a nearby desktop computer. *Code3* interfaces were pre-loaded on the computer. Participants used a wireless microphone to send voice commands to the PR2 when using *CustomActions*. The experimenter was located in the same room near the robot and was available to answer questions. We established the following guidelines for when the experimenter could proactively help the participant. For technical issues with the robot or the system, including issues with the voice recognition system mishearing participants, the experimenter helped right away. For other issues, when the experimenter suspected the participant was going down an unproductive path, the experimenter took note of the time and intervened after a one-minute wait. We felt these were reasonable expectations for a programmer's first day on the job. We took note of the questions asked by participants and the interventions performed by the experimenter.

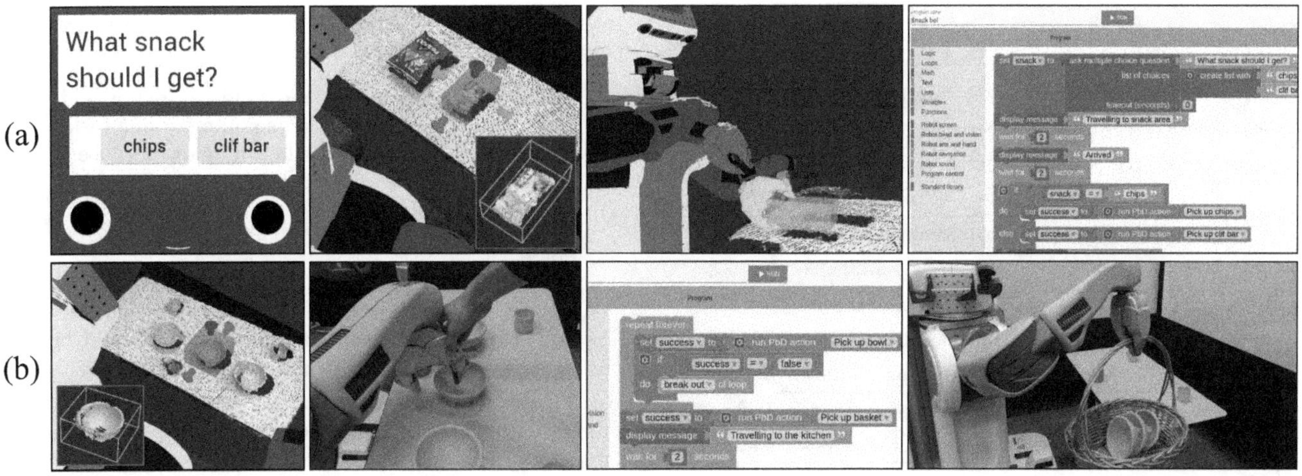

Figure 2: (a) In the *snack-bot* program, the robot fetches a user-requested snack. Users made landmarks using *CustomLandmarks* (second image, saved landmark shown inset), then demonstrated actions to pick the snacks. The third image shows the *CustomActions* GUI and the last image shows a user program made with *CodeIt*. (b) In the *waiter-bot* program, the robot places bowls into a basket and picks up the basket.

Participants were recruited from computer science mailing lists at the authors' university. They could not be robotics researchers and needed to have two or more years of programming experience. They were offered a \$30 gift card for participating and a \$5 bonus for each completed task.

4.1.1 Tasks

Familiarization task - Grocery-bot: Users were asked to program the robot to put all cans found on a table into a box. The positions and the number of cans could vary, but the box was in a fixed location on the table. To accomplish this task, users needed to create a custom landmark of a can and program an action to pick it up and drop it into the box. They also needed to write a *CodeIt* program that repeated the action until the the robot put all the cans away.

Snack-bot: In this task, the robot had to ask the user which of two snacks to retrieve: an energy bar or a bag of chips. The robot would then travel[1] to a snack area and pick up the appropriate snack. The exact positions of the snacks could vary. The robot would then travel back to the user and wait for the user to press a button on the tablet before opening its gripper. This required the user to program two actions with different custom landmarks (one for each snack) and choose which to execute. The snacks were elevated off the table with small pedestals to make them easier to grasp.

Waiter-bot: In this task, the robot started at a table with plastic bowls and cups on it. Users had to program the robot to remove all the bowls from the table and put them in a basket on the floor. Once all the bowls were in the basket, the robot had to pick up the basket and "travel" to the kitchen to deliver the bowls. As in the familiarization task, the exact number and position of the bowls could vary. This task required users to repeat an action until there were no more bowls. It also required users to program an action to pick up the basket before the robot traveled to the kitchen.

[1] Because our robot was immobile at the time of the study, users were told to simulate traveling by displaying a message on the touchscreen interface and waiting for a few seconds.

4.2 Measures

During the study, the experimenter recorded data on what questions participants asked and what help was given. Additionally, we recorded data on when participants used the *CustomLandmarks*, *CustomActions*, and *CodeIt* interfaces. We also gathered video data and screen recordings.

In our final questionnaire, we first administered the System Usability Scale (SUS) survey [10]. This widely used survey asks a series of ten 5-point Likert scale questions with alternating polarities, such as "I think that I would like to use this system frequently" and "I found the system unnecessarily complex." Scores from the SUS survey can range from 0 (worst) to 100 (best); a meta-study of 2,324 SUS surveys administered in published research found that the average score was 70.14 with a standard deviation of 21.71 [7]. Our questionnaire also asked users to qualitatively describe what was difficult about using *CustomLandmarks*, *CustomActions*, *CodeIt*, and the *Code3* system as a whole.

Finally, we asked users to specify their age and gender and to rate, on a 5-point Likert scale, their prior programming experience in general and with the programming of robots.

4.3 Results

Ten users participated in the study, 6 male and 4 female. Their ages ranged between 19-37, with an average of 26.6 (SD=6.2). On a 5-point Likert scale, users gave their prior programming experience a mean rating of 3.9 (SD=0.74, min=3, max=5) but only 1.6 (SD=0.84, min=1, max=3) in terms of prior experience with programming robots.

4.3.1 Task performance

In the 50 minutes given to them, all 10 users successfully completed at least one task, and 3 users completed both tasks. Seven participants completed the *snack-bot* task, and 6 completed the *waiter-bot* task. On average, participants spent 31:38 minutes programming a task (SD=13:40 minutes, min=15:40, max=50:50). They asked 1.38 questions (SD=1.56) and were proactively helped by an experimenter 1.92 times (SD=1.93) per task.

Measure	Result
# participants who completed exactly 1 task	7/10
# participants who completed 2 tasks	3/10
Mean general programming experience rating (1-5)	3.9
Mean robot programming experience rating (1-5)	1.6
Mean SUS score	66.75
Mean task completion time	31m 38s
Mean time spent in *CustomActions*	7m 56s
Mean time spent in *CustomLandmarks*	3m 41s
Mean time spent in *CodeIt*	5m 31s
Mean time spent testing solution	5m 29s
Mean questions asked per task	1.38
Mean instances of proactive help given	1.92

Table 1: High-level summary of user study results.

4.3.2 *Perceived usability and usefulness*

On the System Usability Survey, users scored the system an average of 66.75, with a low of 35, a high of 87.5, and a standard deviation of 16.95. This is below average compared to other systems evaluated with the SUS, and some researchers would interpret this to mean that the system's usability is "marginally acceptable" [7].

4.3.3 *Characterization of system usage*

Across all tasks, users spent an average of 3:41 minutes using the *CustomLandmarks* interface, 7:56 minutes using *CustomActions*, and 5:31 minutes using *CodeIt*. Additionally, they spent an average of 5:29 minutes testing their solutions. Fig. 3 presents a visualization of which components were in use by the users for each task. The visualization shows that generally, users created custom landmarks and actions first, then built their *CodeIt* programs, and then tested their solutions last. We found that users switched between using *CustomActions* and *CustomLandmarks* frequently. This is because the workflow for creating a custom landmark is embedded in the *CustomActions* workflow. However, some users sketched out their *CodeIt* programs earlier or conducted small scale tests of custom actions. We also note that users used *CustomActions* many times even though both tasks only required 2 actions each. This reflects the fact that users edited or remade actions after testing or after receiving experimenter guidance.

4.3.4 *Challenges in system usage*

We assessed challenges participants had using the system through survey questions, questions users asked, and proactive guidance provided by the experimenter. Below, we describe the main challenges users experienced.

***CustomLandmarks / CustomActions* integration:** Two conceptual issues came up regarding the integration of *CustomLandmarks* in the *CustomActions* system. First, many users assumed that they needed to create custom landmarks for all objects in the scene, even when the objects were in a fixed position or were not going to be manipulated. The second issue arose from the fact that creating custom landmarks was embedded in the workflow of creating a custom action. There was no way to create a landmark and use it across multiple actions or to create a landmark and retroactively apply it to an action. Users told us that the system's behavior was unexpected in this respect:

> *User 10:* I placed all the landmarks I would need for all actions at the beginning of one task, and had to place one landmark again because I needed it for a separate action.
> *User 3:* It would have been nice if I could have created a landmark after I already did the actions.

We could resolve these issues by having a separate workflow for creating a custom landmark, which could be imported into *CustomActions* through its GUI.

Remembering the steps of the workflow: Five users said that they had difficulty recalling the steps for programming an action. However, three users also said that it became easier to remember with greater experience:

> *User 5:* Getting accustomed to the workflow... was something to get used to, but it started coming a lot more naturally after the first couple of tasks.
> *User 9:* [What was difficult about *CustomActions* was] making sure not to skip any steps or commands.

Users also needed help with small, but important, details of the workflow. For example, one user got proactive guidance to program the arm to move to the side at the end of a custom action. This was so the arm would not block the robot's view of the workspace in subsequent tasks.

Editing and GUI interface for *CustomActions*: Two users said that the GUI interface for *CustomActions* was hard to interpret. The *CustomActions* GUI overlaid all the steps of an action in a single view while it was being created (see Fig. 4(a)). The GUI also dynamically updated to show actions that were being executed. One user suggested that there should be separate GUI modes for running vs. editing. Additionally, three users had issues with steps being accidentally added or deleted from their action due to misinterpreted voice commands.

> *User 5:* The overlapping opaque graphics made it difficult to see... what was anchored to what reference frame.
> *User 10:* I didn't realize that I had added one last action that released the basket at the end of the program.

Three users received guidance on how to use the GUI to tweak the steps of a programmed action without reprogramming from the beginning. Based on this feedback, we believe it would be valuable to have a "filmstrip" view of a PbD action, in which each step can be visualized and edited individually. Such an interface would also make it more obvious to the user if the system accidentally added or deleted a step.

***CustomLandmarks* box interface:** In the *CustomLandmarks* interface, users had to individually specify the positions of the 6 sides of the box (Fig. 1 and 2). Four of the 10 users said they had some trouble using this interface, although two of them said that it was not a major issue.

> *User 10:* Placing the box in 3D space was surprisingly difficult. I needed to move the camera around a lot before I could place it correctly.

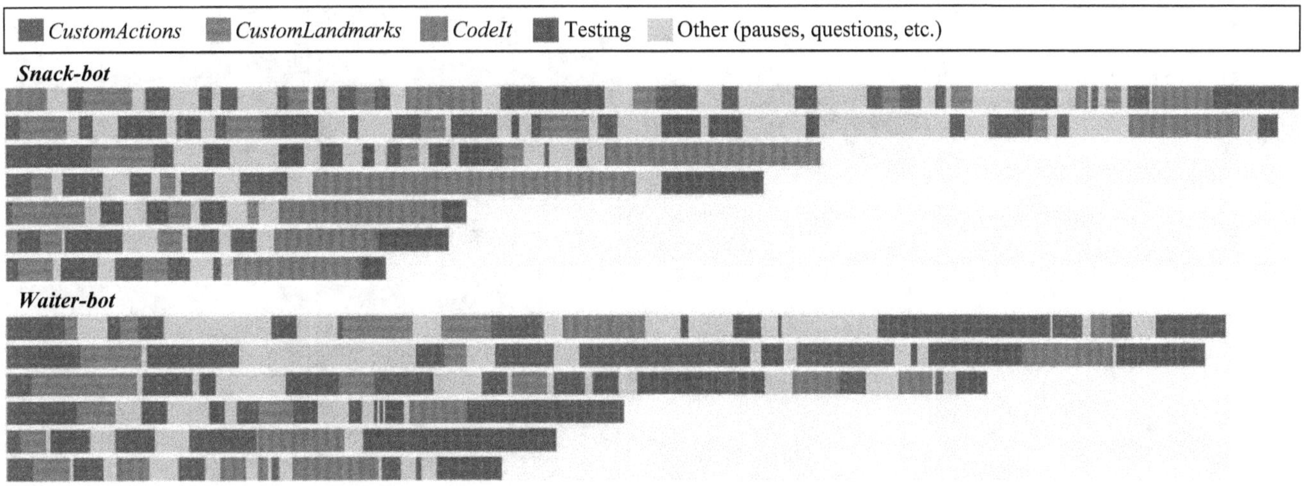

Figure 3: A visualization of which *Code3* components participants used while programming each of the user study tasks. For each row, the x-axis represents time that a participant spent working on a user study task. The color of the bars indicate which activity the user was doing; the length of the bars indicate the amount of time spent. The "Other" category includes time when users asked questions, were given help, or were paused and not using any particular interface. The length of the bars in the legend represent 1 minute of time.

> *User 9:* I wish I could just drag that box instead of having to expand the edges... Otherwise I think it was pretty simple.

4.4 Discussion

Overall, the study found that non-roboticist programmers could learn to use *Code3* to program useful tasks on the PR2. The user study tasks required perceiving and manipulating different objects, and would be, in our view, non-trivial tasks even for professional roboticists. However, all of the participants, 4 of whom were undergraduate computer science students, were able to program the robot to do at least one of the tasks in under 1 hour after just 90 minutes of training.

The study also revealed various usability issues with the current interface. The workflow of our system was optimized for users to create landmarks, actions, and *CodeIt* programs in a linear order. However, we saw that users often deviated from this workflow and needed to edit and remake custom actions and landmarks. The feedback we received suggests a need for a specialized editing GUI for *CustomActions*. This interface would need to make it easy to preview, adjust, and delete poses, and to import previously created landmarks.

5. EXPERT USER PROGRAMMING

This section describes how an expert user (the first author) used *Code3* to program two complex tasks. These tasks demonstrate the system's unique perception and flow control capabilities and show that *Code3* is not limited to programming simple manipulation tasks. Below, we describe the tasks, how we programmed them, and how they exercised the unique features of *Code3*.

5.1 Tic-tac-toe

The first task we programmed was to play a game of tic-tac-toe with a human player (Fig. 4(a)). The robot plays the game on a board with red and yellow cylindrical pieces. The robot must pick a game piece from a stack and place it on an empty square on the board. Then, the human player makes a move and presses a button on the robot's touchscreen when done. After that, the robot must examine the board and make another move. The robot must also recognize if the game is over and ask to play again.

We created a custom landmark of the game piece and programmed a custom action for the robot to pick a piece. To pick from the stack, the program used `findCustomLandmark` to locate all the pieces, then it identified the piece with the highest z position and passed it to the picking action (an example of preregistration). We created nine separate custom actions to place the piece in each of the nine squares on the board. For the robot to know the locations of the squares, we stuck a uniquely shaped foam block in the corner of the board. This foam block became a landmark; to place a piece in a particular square, the robot would position its gripper to locations relative to the block.

We took advantage of *CodeIt*'s expressivity to program the flow control logic to play the game. To read the board, the robot first searched for the custom landmark of the game piece and the custom landmark of the foam block. It then checked which squares were occupied by comparing the positions of the pieces with the position of the block. The robot used this procedure to infer which previously empty square the human player moved to on their turn. We represented the board with a list of nine strings, which were either "empty," "red," or "yellow." Because *CustomLandmarks* does not use color information, the robot tracked which pieces were red or yellow based on whose turn it was when the piece was placed on the board. The robot played to empty squares at random.

It took the author 3 hours and 23 minutes to program and test this task, with actions, landmarks, and game-playing logic created from scratch.

5.2 Picking challenge

For the second task, the author programmed the robot to pick a box of crayons from a shelf (Fig. 4(b)). The box was easy to grasp while standing upright, but impossible for the

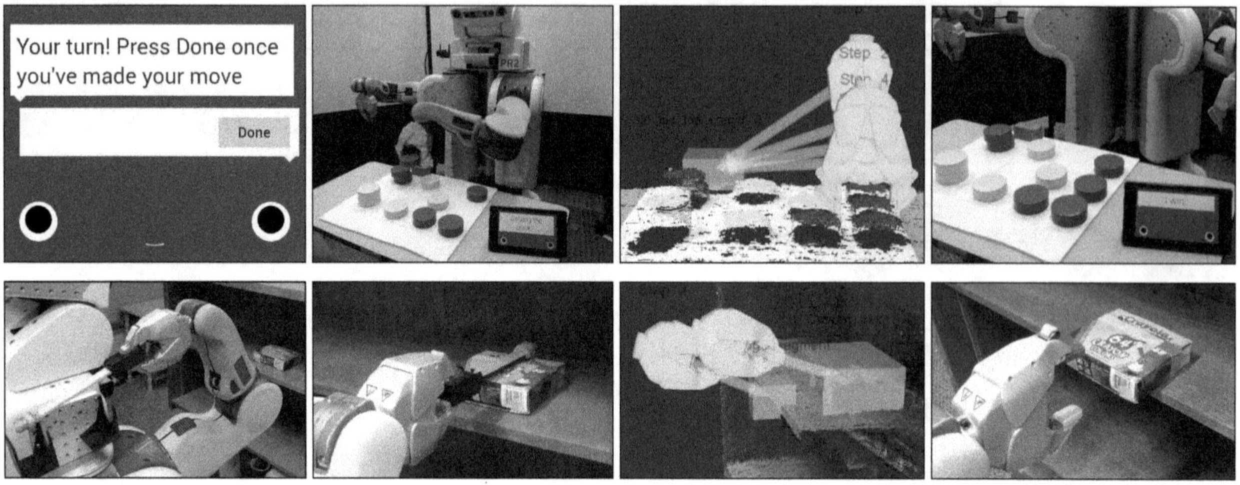

(a)

(b)

Figure 4: (a) We programmed the robot to play tic-tac-toe. The touchscreen interface facilitated turn-taking. Cell positions were known as offsets (top row, yellow arrows) from a corner landmark (green box). The robot could read the board and determine if someone had won. (b) The robot used a tool (bottom row, 1st and 2nd images) to pull a crayon box to a graspable position. The crayon box was used as a landmark to make contact with it but the edge of the shelf was used to know how far to pull (bottom row, third image).

robot to directly grasp while lying flat. We used *Code3* to program a maneuver with a tool to make the box graspable.

We built a simple tool, a 25cm wooden ruler with a handle on one end and a high-friction tip on the other, to drag the box over the edge of the shelf if the box was lying flat. We used *CustomActions* to program actions to get the tool from a shoulder holster and to place it back.

For this action to work robustly, the robot had to drag the box the right distance over the shelf edge. If dragged too far, the box would fall out of the shelf, but if not dragged far enough, the box would remain ungraspable. Pulling the box a fixed distance would not work since the box's distance from the shelf edge could vary. To address this, we created two custom landmarks: one for the box and another representing a segment of the shelf edge. We used the box landmark to know where to make contact between the tool and the box. However, when pulling the box, we used the shelf edge as the landmark so that the pulling action would end at a consistent distance to the shelf edge.

This action illustrated an interesting use of the preregistration feature. We wanted to, as much as possible, drag the box perpendicular to the shelf edge. To accomplish this, we made the landmark of the shelf edge represent a small, 6 cm segment, which *CustomLandmarks* would find at multiple locations along the shelf edge. We then iterated through the list of segment locations and selected the segment that was closest to the box's location. Dragging towards the closest shelf edge segment ensured that the box was dragged perpindicular to the shelf edge.

We programmed the robot to grasp the crayon box directly if it was standing upright. If the box was lying flat, then the robot got the tool, dragged the box as described above, replaced the tool, and finally grasped the box.

This task took us 2 hours and 28 minutes to program and test. To test the program, the robot had to successfully pick the crayon box five times in a row: twice with it standing upright and three times with it laying flat on the shelf. A first draft of the program was finished within 90 minutes, but we spent the remainder of the time testing and refining the dragging action. It took time to refine the program because for each refinement we made, we had to test the program by running it from the beginning. An improved, step-by-step editing interface for *CustomActions* could make developers more efficient for tasks like these in the future.

6. CONCLUSION

This paper introduced *Code3*, a system that enables roboticists and non-roboticist programmers alike to program a mobile manipulator to do complex tasks. We described how the system is divided into tightly integrated components for perception, manipulation, and control flow. In particular, the *CustomLandmarks* and *CustomActions* components abstract the process of programming perceptual detectors and manipulation tasks in a user-friendly way. Our user study showed that non-roboticist programmers could quickly create useful programs—such as a snack-retrieving robot or a robot that cleared a table—after just 90 minutes of training with the system. The study also revealed usability issues with our interface, which we want to improve in the future. For example, we want to improve the design of the *CustomActions* user interface to make actions easier to visualize and edit, and we want to make custom landmarks reusable across multiple actions. Finally, we showed how an expert user of *Code3* could rapidly program a PR2 to perform highly complex tasks, such as playing tic-tac-toe with a human player. In the future, we want to investigate how more advanced perception and manipulation systems can be integrated into *Code3* while remaining intuitive to use. Finally, we want to add support for more robots to our open-source release.

Acknowledgements

This work was supported by the National Science Foundation, Awards IIS-1552427 "CAREER: End-User Programming of General-Purpose Robots" and IIS-1525251 "NRI: Rich Task Perception for Programming by Demonstration."

7. REFERENCES

[1] Beer me, robot. In *Willow Garage Inc. Blog. http://www.willowgarage.com/blog/2010/07/06/beer-me-robot*, 2010.

[2] B. Akgun, M. Cakmak, J. W. Yoo, and A. L. Thomaz. Trajectories and keyframes for kinesthetic teaching: A human-robot interaction perspective. In *Proceedings of the Seventh Annual ACM/IEEE International Conference on Human-Robot Interaction*, pages 391–398, 2012.

[3] S. Alexandrova, M. Cakmak, K. Hsiao, and L. Takayama. Robot programming by demonstration with interactive action visualizations. In *Robotics: Science and Systems (RSS)*, pages 48–56, 2014.

[4] S. Alexandrova, Z. Tatlock, and M. Cakmak. RoboFlow: A flow-based visual programming language for mobile manipulation tasks. In *2015 IEEE International Conference on Robotics and Automation (ICRA)*, pages 5537–5544. IEEE, 2015.

[5] B. D. Argall, S. Chernova, M. Veloso, and B. Browning. A survey of robot learning from demonstration. *Robotics and Autonomous Systems*, 57(5):469–483, 2009.

[6] C. G. Atkeson and S. Schaal. Robot learning from demonstration. In *ICML*, volume 97, pages 12–20, 1997.

[7] A. Bangor, P. T. Kortum, and J. T. Miller. An empirical evaluation of the system usability scale. *Intl. Journal of Human–Computer Interaction*, 24(6):574–594, 2008.

[8] P. J. Besl and N. D. McKay. A method for registration of 3-D shapes. *IEEE Trans. Pattern Anal. Mach. Intell.*, 14:239–256, 1992.

[9] A. Billard, S. Calinon, R. Dillmann, and S. Schaal. Robot programming by demonstration. In *Springer Handbook of Robotics*, pages 1371–1394. Springer, 2008.

[10] J. Brooke et al. SUS-a quick and dirty usability scale. *Usability Evaluation in Industry*, 189(194):4–7, 1996.

[11] M. Cakmak. Labs. CSE 481C website. https://sites.google.com/site/cse481a/labs, 2013.

[12] M. Cakmak and A. L. Thomaz. Eliciting good teaching from humans for machine learners. *Artificial Intelligence*, 217:198–215, 2014.

[13] S. Calinon and A. Billard. Statistical learning by imitation of competing constraints in joint space and task space. *Advanced Robotics*, 23(15):2059–2076, 2009.

[14] S. Chernova and A. L. Thomaz. Robot learning from human teachers. *Synthesis Lectures on Artificial Intelligence and Machine Learning*, 8(3):1–121, 2014.

[15] N. Correll, K. E. Bekris, D. Berenson, O. Brock, A. Causo, K. Hauser, K. Okada, A. Rodriguez, J. M. Romano, and P. R. Wurman. Analysis and observations from the first Amazon Picking Challenge. *IEEE Transactions on Automation Science and Engineering*, 2016.

[16] C. Datta, C. Jayawardena, I. H. Kuo, and B. A. MacDonald. RoboStudio: A visual programming environment for rapid authoring and customization of complex services on a personal service robot. In *2012 IEEE/RSJ International Conference on Intelligent Robots and Systems*, pages 2352–2357. IEEE, 2012.

[17] S. Ekvall and D. Kragic. Robot learning from demonstration: A task-level planning approach. *International Journal of Advanced Robotic Systems*, 5(3):223–234, 2008.

[18] M. A. Fischler and R. C. Bolles. Random sample consensus: A paradigm for model fitting with applications to image analysis and automated cartography. *Communications of the ACM*, 24(6):381–395, 1981.

[19] D. Glas, S. Satake, T. Kanda, and N. Hagita. An interaction design framework for social robots. In *Robotics: Science and Systems*, volume 7, page 89, 2012.

[20] D. F. Glas, T. Kanda, and H. Ishiguro. Human-robot interaction design using Interaction Composer: Eight years of lessons learned. In *The Eleventh ACM/IEEE International Conference on Human Robot Interaction*, pages 303–310. IEEE Press, 2016.

[21] D. D. Hils. Visual languages and computing survey: Data flow visual programming languages. *Journal of Visual Languages & Computing*, 3(1):69–101, 1992.

[22] J. Huang and M. Cakmak. Programming by demonstration with user-specified perceptual landmarks. *arXiv preprint arXiv:1612.00565*, 2016.

[23] J. Huang, T. Lau, and M. Cakmak. Design and evaluation of a rapid programming system for service robots. In *2016 11th ACM/IEEE International Conference on Human-Robot Interaction (HRI)*, pages 295–302. IEEE, 2016.

[24] E. S. Kim, D. Leyzberg, K. M. Tsui, and B. Scassellati. How people talk when teaching a robot. In *Human-Robot Interaction (HRI), 2009 4th ACM/IEEE International Conference on*, pages 23–30. IEEE, 2009.

[25] T. Lourens. TiViPE-Tino's visual programming environment. In *Computer Software and Applications Conference, 2004. COMPSAC 2004. Proceedings of the 28th Annual International*, pages 10–15. IEEE, 2004.

[26] T. Lourens and E. Barakova. User-friendly robot environment for creation of social scenarios. In *International Work-Conference on the Interplay between Natural and Artificial Computation*, pages 212–221. Springer, 2011.

[27] T. Lozano-Perez. Robot programming. *Proceedings of the IEEE*, 71(7):821–841, 1983.

[28] A. Mohseni-Kabir, C. Rich, S. Chernova, C. L. Sidner, and D. Miller. Interactive hierarchical task learning from a single demonstration. In *Proceedings of the Tenth Annual ACM/IEEE International Conference on Human-Robot Interaction*, pages 205–212. ACM, 2015.

[29] H. Nguyen, M. Ciocarlie, K. Hsiao, and C. C. Kemp. ROS Commander (ROSCo): Behavior creation for home robots. In *Robotics and Automation (ICRA), 2013 IEEE International Conference on*, pages 467–474. IEEE, 2013.

[30] S. Niekum, S. Osentoski, G. Konidaris, and A. G. Barto. Learning and generalization of complex tasks from unstructured demonstrations. In *2012 IEEE/RSJ International Conference on Intelligent Robots and Systems (IROS)*, pages 5239–5246, 2012.

[31] M. Pardowitz, S. Knoop, R. Dillmann, and R. Zollner. Incremental learning of tasks from user demonstrations, past experiences, and vocal comments. *Systems, Man, and Cybernetics, Part B: Cybernetics, IEEE Transactions on*, 37(2):322–332, 2007.

[32] E. Pot, J. Monceaux, R. Gelin, and B. Maisonnier. Choregraphe: A graphical tool for humanoid robot programming. In *RO-MAN 2009-The 18th IEEE International Symposium on Robot and Human Interactive Communication*, pages 46–51. IEEE, 2009.

[33] M. Quigley, K. Conley, B. Gerkey, J. Faust, T. Foote, J. Leibs, R. Wheeler, and A. Y. Ng. ROS: an open-source robot operating system. In *ICRA Workshop on Open Source Software*, volume 3, page 5. Kobe, Japan, 2009.

[34] A. Sauppé and B. Mutlu. Design patterns for exploring and prototyping human-robot interactions. In *Proceedings of the 32nd Annual ACM Conference on Human Factors in Computing Systems*, pages 1439–1448. ACM, 2014.

[35] S. Schaal, J. Peters, J. Nakanishi, and A. Ijspeert. Learning movement primitives. In *International Symposium on Robotics Research.*, pages 561–572, 2005.

[36] H. B. Suay, R. Toris, and S. Chernova. A practical comparison of three robot learning from demonstration algorithm. *International Journal of Social Robotics*, 4(4):319–330, 2012.

[37] A. L. Thomaz and C. Breazeal. Experiments in socially guided exploration: Lessons learned in building robots that learn with and without human teachers. *Connection Science*, 20(2-3):91–110, 2008.

Simplified Programming of Re-usable Skills on a Safe Industrial Robot – Prototype and Evaluation

Maj Stenmark
Dept. of Computer Science
Lund University
Lund, Sweden
maj.stenmark@cs.lth.se

Mathias Haage
Dept. of Computer Science
Lund University
Lund, Sweden
mathias.haage@cs.lth.se

Elin Anna Topp
Dept. of Computer Science
Lund University
Lund, Sweden
elin_anna.topp@cs.lth.se

ABSTRACT

This paper presents a study on iconic programming support for mainly position-based lead-through programming of an ABB YuMi collaborative robot. A prototype tool supporting a hybrid programming and execution mode was developed and evaluated with 21 non-expert users with varying programming and robotics experience. We also present a comparison of the programming times for an expert robot programmer using traditional tools versus the new tool. The expert programmed the same tasks in 1/5 of the time compared to traditional tools and the non-experts were able to program and debug a LEGO building task using the robot within 30 minutes.

Keywords

Kinesthetic teaching, User Study, Intuitive Programming of Industrial Robots

1. INTRODUCTION

In recent years, we have had a renaissance in industrial robotics: a new segment of robot models (e.g., UR5, ABB YuMi, Rethink Robotics' Baxter and KUKA's LBR iiwa) intended for safe human–robot collaboration and simpler robot programming have emerged.

The application areas for these robot models are typically assembly of consumer electronics or repackaging of (small) products. One difference between these robots and previous models is the *lead–through* programming, or kinesthetic teaching, mode. In this mode, the user can guide the robot arm into the desired positions and thus record and replay a robot program.

Kinesthetic teaching using force-guided motions [22], gravity compensation and variable stiffness [40, 39] support also non-expert operators to program and configure tasks [31], however, dynamic environments, uncertainty and the use of noisy sensor feedback are still challenges for the operator [34], and so far, experts are still needed to program the robots on the necessary levels of robustness and precision.

HRI '17 March 06-09, 2017, Vienna, Austria

ACM ISBN 978-1-4503-4336-7/17/03.

DOI: http://dx.doi.org/10.1145/2909824.3020227

Programming by demonstration, PbD, or learning from demonstration, LfD [7], is a well-established concept in service robotics, however, these methods often require multiple demonstrations which we consider less suitable in an industrial setting where rapid instruction and evaluation is needed. The desired approach in an industrial context is rather a one–shot demonstration, from which enough parameters for an executable representation can be extracted.

Orthogonal to the PbD approach is the use of high–level instructions to simplify robot programming for industrial tasks, e.g., using natural language [33] and semantically defined parameterized motion primitives [9], often called *skills* [28, 29]. Such semantic descriptions are desirable because they enable the automatic generation of, e.g., standard PDDL[1]–descriptions for planning and scheduling of tasks or path planning and generation from virtual models [30].

We propose to aim for a middle ground by combining programming by demonstration and parametrized skill representations to simplify robot programming, i.e., *it must be possible for non-expert users to create their own skills from scratch* and specify object references that can later be used as basic building blocks in high–level approaches.

In this paper we present a prototype of a programming tool for industrial robots, which enables non–expert users to program and edit simple industrial tasks using one–shot demonstrations, i.e., kinesthetic teaching, and also reduces the programming and debugging time for an expert programmer. We extracted initial requirements regarding functionality and behavior for the design of this tool from two case studies and evaluated it in two experiments with an expert user and in a study with 21 non–experts.

The remainder of the paper is organized as follows. In Section 2 we present the background and related work for our efforts. We present the case studies for extraction of requirements in Section 3 and our resulting prototype implementation in Section 4. In Section 5 we report on the evaluation of the tool through a user study with 21 subjects and by two expert experiments. We conclude the paper in Section 6 with a discussion of our findings and suggestions for future work.

2. RELATED WORK

The research into intuitive human-robot interaction and programming is so far more active in the field of service robotics, since service robots act in dynamic non-structured environments and are intended to interact with non-expert

[1]Planning Domain Definition Language

operators. Some of the following approaches are nonetheless relevant also for work in intuitive programming of industrial robots.

For instance, robots can learn from humans by observing the human carrying out a task and extract action parameters and objects involved in this process. Billard *et al.* use objects and locations as task parameters and can extract these in a new workspace from human demonstrations [7]. Feniello *et al.* synthesize the program specification for repositioning tasks from examples, e.g., their system can learn a program sequence that sorts objects by color [10]. *Visuospatial skill learning* is also used by Ahmadzadeh *et al.* [5] to extract the geometric constraints of the objects in a task and to learn the sequence of push and pull skills in a task. Using *Gaussian mixture regression*, trajectories can be generated from the learning results [13]. From multiple demonstrations, high-level semantics such as intentions [11], transition conditions [17] and precedence constraints for sequencing of manipulation primitives [19, 21] can be extracted. Niekum *et al.* segment demonstrations automatically using (beta process autoregressive) *Hidden Markov Models*, learn the reference coordinates for each trajectory from clustering the demonstrations in different coordinate frames and iteratively refine the resulting finite state machine based on new demonstrations [25].

Low-level skills can be encoded as *dynamic movement primitives* (DMPs) [15] demonstrated using, e.g., *Imitation Learning* and further optimized using *Reinforcement Learning*. Examples of research in imitation learning methods for robot skill learning are given by Kormushev *et al.*, who combine kinesthetic learning of positional trajectories with force profiles demonstrated using a haptic input device to demonstrate ironing skills [18]. Stenmetz *et al.* use an external force/torque sensor mounted on the robot arm to record force and position simultaneously and learn the force profiles for a PID-controller. Abu-Dakka *et al.* redeploy peg-in-hole skills in new settings by adding exception strategies that randomly search for the hole to improve robustness [4]. Nemec *et al.* use a priori knowledge and reinforcement learning to reduce the number of demonstrations needed to teach a flip task to a robot [24] and Pastor *et al.* use reinforcement learning to optimize a pool strike [27]. All these methods, however, focus on one specific type of movement or task, each of which requiring a specific setup. Additionally, data driven approaches require multiple demonstrations with enough feature variation to extract task parameters and specifically for reinforcement learning based approaches it is a challenging problem to design a good cost function (which needs to be either taught or manually tuned).

Multiple demonstrations are time consuming, hence a one-shot approach is desired. Also, industrial tasks often require high precision, which can be difficult to achieve from generalizations between multiple demonstrations and the underlying representation of instructions must support adaption and debugging. Ko *et al.* list and motivate the main qualitative aspects of a programming (by demonstration) system that have to be evaluated, namely: accuracy and repeatability, adaptability and generality, learning fatigue, system complexity and production speed [16] .

Tsarouchi *et al.* identify various challenges in the human-robot interaction for industrial robots, and while e.g., multimodal communication and learning by demonstration have received significant research attention also in this field, the user interfaces are often too complex for non-expert users [38]. The learning curve can be leveled by using visual programming environments, e.g., Huang *et al.* showed that a *Scratch*-like programming language reduced the programming effort [14] and Glas *et al.* have developed *Composer* for designing social robot behavior [12]. An increasing number of industrial robots provide template skills for common applications, e.g., the UR-series from Universal Robots as well as Baxter and Sawyer from Rethink Robotics come with template pick-and-place skills, and the Franka robot from Emika lets the user download expert made *apps* (i.e., skills) and combine these into more complex task using visual programming. Apps that can be used out-of-the box with little effort make these types of robots attractive, e.g., for small companies, however, programming new re-usable skills from scratch is still a challenge, which we try to handle with the interface proposed in this paper.

In order to bootstrap the instruction process, the interaction can be improved by systems that ask leading questions [8, 23], or by using other modalities such as speech, see, e.g., Pardowitz*et al.* [26] or a graphical user interface so that the task constraints generated from a single demonstration can be understood and edited by the operators [6, 20]. We plan to enhance our system with the necessary reasoning capabilities so that such an approach to supporting the user can be integrated.

3. CASE STUDIES

We analyzed the programming process and required motion types and primitives from two rather complex applications that we had previously built for the dual-arm ABB robot YuMi. One is an emergency stop button assembly that uses force-based motions for snapping and screwing together switches and nuts [36, 2]. The second case is a position-based gift-wrapping application, which was developed as part of a commercial campaign in Sweden during the fall of 2015 and toured consumer electronic retail stores wrapping gifts all over Sweden [3, 34, 37].

Both applications rely on synchronized motion between the two arms of the ABB YuMi dual-arm robot. The robot is designed for safe human-robot collaboration and each arm has seven degrees of freedom. These features are used in the gift-wrapping application since the wrapping process uses a collaborative step and multiple contact points on the arm. Videos of both applications are available through YouTube [2, 3].

We identified several issues during the programming process, which are mostly related to the traditional programming interfaces and assumed workflow for the YuMi [34, 37]. From those issues, we derived requirements for the development of a programming interface that supports (and is supported by) our underlying architecture for skill representation and robot code generation [32].

3.1 Traditional interfaces and interaction

The ABB robot can be programmed in the ABB programming language RAPID either using an engineering tool called RobotStudio, a Windows Universal App (YuMi Online) or by using the teach pendant (an integrated joystick and touch display interface for direct robot control, a standard piece of equipment usually accompanying industrial robots, see Figure 1), directly. RobotStudio and the app can run on the same Windows device and are connected to

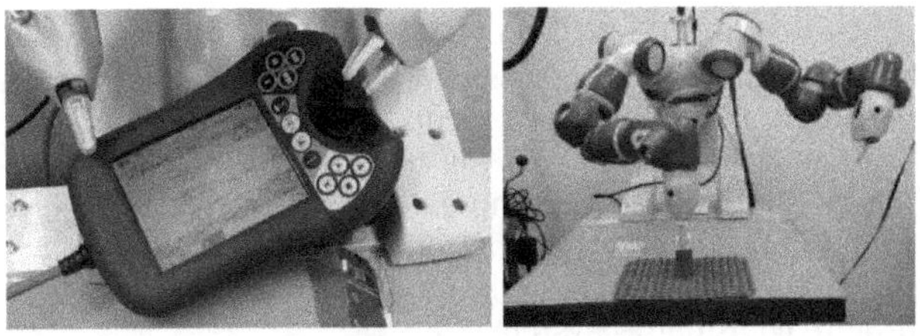

Figure 1: ABB's (YuMi's) teach pendant (left) and YuMi in the LEGO building task (right).

the robot through a local network. Each of the tools has different features. RobotStudio is intended for editing RAPID programs and for simulation. The app has an online programming interface supporting a few commands (motions and gripper actions) and has a limited debugging support. It has however a kinesthetic programming mode, lead-through, which makes it easy to teach positions in free space. Contact situations are more suitable to teach with the joystick on the teach pendant since contact forces will move the arms out of position if lead-through is enabled. The teach pendant can also be used for debugging, for example by moving the program pointer and executing instructions one-by-one.

The traditional workflow starts with offline programming and simulation before deploying a program on the physical robot. First, the program can be written and executed in the virtual environment in RobotStudio. When the user is satisfied, the program is deployed on the physical system and testing in the real environment can begin. User interaction can be added into the RAPID program by inserting dialogue prompts into the program. Then the resulting program can be deployed in the factory and the robot operator will only interact with the robot using the dialogues. All error handling procedures need to be added beforehand by the programmer.

It is not trivial to include (contact) forces and deformable material into simulations, hence, our applications required *online* programming, i.e., testing and updating using the physical robot system including the lead-through functionality for kinesthetic teaching of poses, which was non-trivial with the given interfaces due to their different features. Specifically, in the gift-wrapping application the programmers were required to sometimes circumvent the safety mechanisms originally designed for unsafe robots, but still deployed on the inherently safe YuMi.

3.2 Analysis

Our observations from programming the two applications provided an initial list of system requirements regarding which basic instructions should be possible to rapidly include and update in a program and some hypotheses about better user interaction and support, which we explain briefly in the following.

Actions: The applications required mostly motions specified through gripper target positions in Cartesian space (both relative specified objects or in world coordinated). Secondly, joint configurations were often used in the gift-wrapping application for specifying the position of other parts of the arm than the gripper. Also, both applications relied on contact motions (i.e., motions that stop when a force threshold is reached) for robust task execution. Other actions identified as common are gripper commands (open and close), movement to synchronization points for both arms, and synchronized motions of both arms.

Reuse, refinement and update: In order to be able to reuse a task, i.e., a program sequence with small changes, e.g., in object positions, it must be possible to specify work objects so that motion primitives can be programmed using relative reference coordinate systems. Also, it must be possible to easily change and adapt reference coordinate systems for existing work pieces, as it must be assumed that even expert users occasionally forget to specify the correct reference immediately.

User interaction: In the two applications, user interaction *as* part of the normal operation was limited to handling discrete events in the program flow. For stopping or pausing the execution, the operator touched the robot and simply triggered the safety system break, but that also required manual restart of the robot and required rather long cycles to update and test specific instructions. Here, we assume that a rapid cycle of stopping the execution, changing and updating instructions where necessary and testing (executing again) is desirable.

Compatibility: Since we initially assume only a subset of instructions (actions as described above) to be available in our graphical user interface, the interface should generate an editable program file that an expert user can refine further by using the traditional tools and interfaces.

Based on this list of observations and assumed requirements, we designed a prototype interface supporting users in quickly creating basic programs (skills) through kinesthetic teaching and iconic programming [35]. These skills can then later be refined and form the basis for more complex programs, which can be generated using even more high-level approaches to robot programming, as proposed earlier [33].

4. IMPLEMENTATION

In the following we describe the graphical user interface, which we developed based on the previously described findings from our case studies. The interface was also meant to be a tool for investigating, how our underlying ideas, mainly the skill representation and the reuse of skills through parameterization, would support non-expert users in programming an industrial robot.

A screen capture of the implemented programming tool is shown in Fig. 2. It is implemented as a touch-enabled Windows app running on a Surface Pro with 8 GB RAM and a wireless connection to the robot controller. The implementation is programmed in C# and uses ABB robot controller libraries for network communication and math calculations.

4.1 Features

The graphical interface divides the screen into an instruction panel to the left and a program panel to the right. In the upper left corner, the built-in basic actions are displayed in yellow, while the user-created skills (sequences and combinations of such primitives or other skills) are added to the list in purple. The default actions are the following:

`Move:` a fine-point slow move. When this instruction is added to the robot program sequence, it takes the current position of the active arm and saves it as precise goal position (trajectories between specified points are generated by the robot controller so far). The target is saved with three positions: the exact joint position for the robot arm, the Cartesian position relative to the world (or robot base) system and, if an object is selected, the position relative to the object. Thus, the user can switch coordinate systems between objects or to absolute positions, or between Cartesian and joint space motions without updating the position.

`Via:` a fast motion with zone parameter 5 mm as default, i.e., getting close to the specified pose within this zone is considered sufficient. Analogously to the fine-point move, the position is saved in absolute and relative coordinates as well as in joint space.

`Open` **and** `Close` for fully opening and closing the gripper. The gripper action will execute when added to the program.

`Contact Move:` a movement towards a contact point which will stop when detecting an estimated contact force. The current position of the robot will be used to set a contact position, but the motion will continue beyond that point.

`Sync:` adds synchronization points, i.e., points in the program sequence where both arms should reach the specified pose at the same time.

`Fingers:` an action for setting the finger positions exactly and changing the gripping force of the fingers.

`Locate objects:` will call a local procedure on the robot controller for detecting objects using the built-in cameras on the robot's hands. For the time being, the camera calibration, image settings and detection algorithms must be provided by an expert and reloaded into the controller. The detected object's reference system will, however, be updated each time the procedure is executed hence the user can use the object references to program the robot without considering the underlying code.

Under the actions, the user can add coordinate frames related to objects by pointing with the robot. These can be updated when the object is moved.

The current robot programs for respective arms are displayed to the right. Each action has a line with an individual play arrow, an editable name, a color label for the relative coordinate system, a button for updating the position, editing and a picture. The order of the sequence can be edited by dragging and dropping.

Additional buttons provide functionality for opening and closing the grippers without adding program instructions, executing, toggling the lead-through functionality of the robot and saving/loading a complete workspace consisting of skills, objects and current robot program.

4.2 Reuse of skills

Action (sub)sequences can be selected and stored as skills, these will show up in the action list as purple buttons. In the sequences the skills can be expanded and edited further.

The user can add skills with single instructions but with application-specific parameters such as speed, zone (precision parameter for movement), and object data, and thus have for example multiple types of parameterized motions. E.g., in the gift-wrapping application, the speed was different for motions manipulating the paper and pushing the box, hence, each time an instruction was added the speed parameter had to be set to the correct value.

The actions and skills are robot agnostic and can be switched between the arms. The `Sync` actions can of course cause problems if not moved in pairs. If a skill was programmed using one arm, the joint positions cannot be reused for the other arm, so the default execution will use the Cartesian positions either relative to the object or in absolute coordinates. By selecting multiple actions, the relative object can be changed and updated to another by one button click, recalculating the relative offset to the new object using the absolute coordinates system.

Once the user requests a sequence to be executed (played), the high-level representation of the program is used to generate low-level instructions (RAPID code) for the robot controller currently connected to the user interface.

Our current prototype implementation does not (yet) support more advanced (and natural) force-based motions or logging and executing trajectories, however, a respective extension is subject to ongoing work.

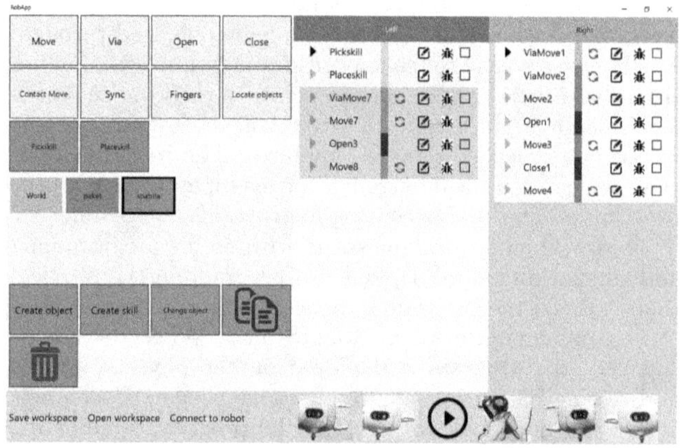

Figure 2: The graphical user interface.

4.3 User interaction and interference

The programming and debugging modes are merged into one hybrid mode, where the speed can be reduced during debugging and the safety system stops the robot in case of collisions with objects or the user, or predicted self-collisions.

The programming interface is designed to be forgiving towards the user. The user can program the entire sequence in absolute coordinates and then later add objects to the workspace and change the reference of the motion without reprogramming. The actions can be tested, refined, and updated individually, and any type of sequence can be saved as a skill.

Debugging is not a separate part of the execution process; however, the current implementation only supports running of individual actions and skills, or the entire sequence. Future work includes additional running and debugging options, e.g., running only a selected subset of actions, starting the execution at arbitrary points in the program and toggling debugging *break points*. The existing tools for jogging the robot using a joy stick or editing the generated RAPID program in a text editor are still available.

5. EVALUATION AND USER STUDY

The programming interface was evaluated by comparing programming times for one expert who programmed two robot tasks using both the new interface and traditional programming methods and through a user study with 21 non-expert, although technically or mathematically interested and experienced, users in a LEGO building task.

We see this study as an opportunity to observe potential users interacting with an industrial robot in a realistic setting, as the LEGO building task, although seemingly a child's play, has quite some challenges similar to those of assembling smaller products like, e.g., mobile phones. In the following paragraphs, we describe the study setup which had the original background of testing the effects of skill re-use and parameterization for non-expert programming of assembly tasks for industrial robots [35]. We will thus in the following explain the different conditions for testing our hypotheses on the re-use of skills and break down our results by these conditions, but we had to realize that the study turned out to be as much an evaluation of the interface's general applicability as it was a tool for testing our original hypotheses. Thus, we focus on the rather general results about the overall benefits of our approach for non-expert programming of industrial robots and on the results we could achieve in the experiments carried out by the expert.

5.1 Study setup

We recruited our subjects mainly from an undergraduate (introductory) course on robotics and through advertising at the departments of Computer Science and Automatic Control at our university to ensure a somewhat technical or software oriented background. Here, we assume that this would be the case also for prospective users (instructors) of this type of robots in industrial contexts. However, we had the subjects fill in a questionnaire to also collect data about how they ranked their own experience with programming and technical equipment, to get a more accurate understanding regarding their background.

Our subjects were asked to program one arm on a dual-arm ABB YuMi with standard grippers to assemble different types of LEGO Duplo bricks using the robot's lead-through mechanism for kinesthetic teaching of poses in combination with our graphical interface for iconic programming. Figure 1 shows the setup for the study with the robot just finishing one step of the overall task. Routines for locating two specific types of LEGO bricks with the help of the built-in camera of the robot gripper were already provided by the experiment leaders as functionalities to be invoked by inserting a respective instruction in the program sequence. This was done for convenience as the camera calibration procedure is quite tedious and time consuming and should not be part of the study. The LEGO piece localization procedures had the arm move to a predefined position, from where the pieces could be localized robustly, given that they were placed within a coarsely sketched area. This allowed to specify pick-up poses relative to the work piece. We are aware that this is quite sophisticated knowledge about robotic systems to be handled for non-experts, however, it gave us the opportunity to observe how our subjects could be supported by our interface in switching between reference coordinate frames for the different objects involved in the task.

5.1.1 Conditions and specific tasks

The overall task was carried out in two phases: The first phase was the same for all participants while the second phase divided the users evenly into three groups corresponding to the three different test conditions. During the first phase, the instructions were to program the robot arm to pick up a LEGO Duplo "2x2" piece (referred to as "small LEGO") and insert it on top of another small piece, which was already the top of a little "tower" (task step 1). This program should then be used to create a skill, i.e., a re-usable representation of a sequence of motion primitives. For the second phase, the participants were asked to program the robot arm to carry out the same task another three times, but with a "2x4" piece ("large LEGO"), which should be placed first "centered" (step 2), then "hanging over on the left" (step 3), and finally "hanging over on the right" (step 4) with respect to the "tower top". For these three steps, the different conditions defined the programming paradigm, i.e., the first group, Group A, was to re-use and refine their own previously created skills, Group B was to re-use an expert-made skill and Group C was a control group in which participants should program each step from scratch without re-use of previously created and saved skills.

The instructions were given in written form, for each phase separately. After reading the instructions for step 1 the participants were introduced to the robot and the programming interface by one of the experiment leaders for a couple of minutes and then started to work on their tasks. The experiment leader observed the process, both to be able to resolve technical problems (the robot stops and needs to be reset when it collides with any obstacle) and to assist the subjects with the handling of the programming tool in case they needed help (the tool has no built-in "help" functionality so far). Upon completion of step 1 and if the time frame allowed, the participants received the instructions for steps 2–4.

From pilot testing with involved researchers we had estimated that roughly 30 minutes for the actual programming was a suitable time limitation for each participant, however, this had the effect that in quite some cases the participants would not reach far enough into the second phase to complete all four programming steps. In this paper, we will thus focus on rather general evaluation criteria like success rate and time needed for completion in the first phase, and how many further steps the subjects managed to complete before running out of time. A more thorough analysis regarding the effect of the different methods and the subjects' individual ways of handling the task steps of the second phase is planned as future work.

After either completing all four steps or running out of time, we asked our subjects to fill in a questionnaire with both demographic questions (gender, occupation) and several five–level scale questions ranging from "not at all" to "absolutely" about their previous experiences with robots or programming, and the level of comfort they felt when handling the robot. Additionally, there was one yes/no question on whether they had ever programmed a physical robot before. We also gave them the opportunity to explain in free text what they found most difficult and what they would suggest to be changed in the programming interface.

5.1.2 Analysis

We had 21 participants (five female, 16 male), seven in each of the condition groups A, B, and C respectively. Figure 3 shows the distribution of professional background and gender as well as whether they had any previous experience of robot programming. The two participants with a non-technical professional background registered as communicator and nurse / kindergarten teacher respectively.

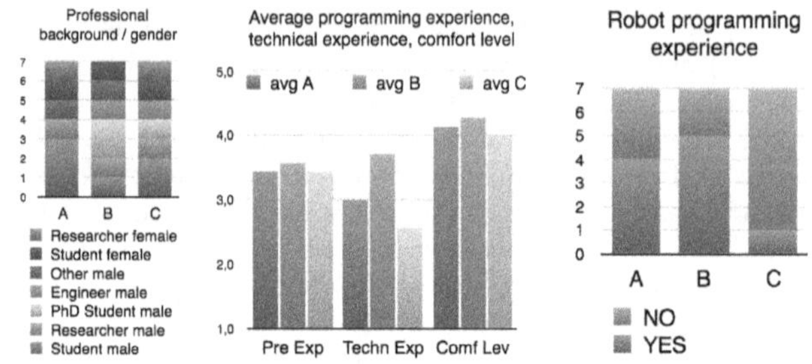

Figure 3: Participants' background and gender (left), experience and comfort level ratings (middle), and experience in programming a robot (right).

Table 1: Success (overall rating average) and time (minutes average)

	Success	Time Step 1	Time Step 2	Time Step 3	Time Step 4
All	6.0	20.6	8.1	5.0	3.5
Group A	5.0	20.4	14.5	1.5	-
Group B	9.0	18.4	3.0	5.5	2.0
Group C	4.14	22.9	9.5	9.0	8.0

We evaluated the trials for each participant according to the following criteria:

time step n**:** the time spent on completing step n after completing the previous step.

success rate: the sum of the success ratings for each step n according to the following criteria *full (3)* – the LEGO piece was fully attached on top of the "tower" robustly by the robot in step n; *partial (2)* – the LEGO piece was placed correctly but not (entirely) attached; *fail (1)* – the step was not carried out fully, i.e., the LEGO piece was not placed correctly; *n/a (0)* – the step was not carried out at all.

Table 1 summarizes the (average) results according to these criteria, broken down by the different groups, while Table 2 shows the number of subjects managing the respective step with at least partial success.

We can state that almost all participants managed to handle the first step with at least partial success. The two participants (group C) who failed completing the first step had difficulties in understanding how the robot would move (directly between specified poses) after their instructions.

One of them stated also to have felt rather uncomfortable (2) when handling the robot, despite marking rather high levels of programming (5) and technical (4) experience, and mentioned the two coordinate systems as difficult to understand. This low comfort rating was in fact the only one below the "neutral" rating of 3 for all 21 participants. Worth noting is also that all three participants reaching full success in step 4 belonged to group B, i.e., the condition with the task to re-use an expert-made skill for the last three steps. As step 2 for this group was mainly to analyze and understand the provided skill, this obviously saved them a lot of time compared to the other groups. Overall we can state, that 14 of 21 participants managed to understand the tool, the robot's movements, and the LEGO bricks' properties (including the challenge of robustly attaching them to each other) sufficiently well to complete two steps of the overall tasks within 30 minutes.

Table 2: The number of subjects reaching success rating 3-2-1 respectively in the different steps.

	Step 1 3-2-1	Step 2 3-2-1	Step 3 3-2-1	Step 4 3-2-1
All	13-6-2	11-3-0	7-2-0	3-0-1
Group A	5-2-0	3-1-0	1-1-0	0-0-0
Group B	5-2-0	6-0-0	5-1-0	3-0-0
Group C	3-2-2	2-2-0	1-0-0	0-0-1

As we noted a somewhat uneven distribution of programming and technical experiences over the different groups, we checked for correlation effects between experience ratings and success rates or time needed for the different steps respectively, but we could not find any obvious connections; programming experience, technical experience and robot programming experience had all a very low negative correlation (-0.18, -0.18, and -0.23) with time for completion of step 1 and a slightly stronger, but still very low, positive correlation (0.24, 0.22, and 0.33) with the overall success rate. Thus, we consider the different outcomes for the groups as an indication for an effect of the different conditions, i.e., being able to reuse previously programmed or even provided skill representations simplifies the programming process significantly, as the subjects in the control group (C) needed roughly the same amount of time for each step in the second phase, when programming from scratch.

In group A, who should re-use their own previously created step1 skill for the following steps, the subjects needed some time to handle the updating and parametrization of the skill in step 2, but once they had understood how to do this, the following steps were handled within rather short time frames, which were even shorter than those for group B, who otherwise had very high success rates, but had to understand and update a program that they were not familiar with from the beginning. However, sample sizes are small and became even smaller over the different steps, hence, these results should be seen with some caution and treated as trend indications rather than definite findings.

5.1.3 Specific challenges and observations

As indicated above, all participants but one felt at least neutral, if not comfortable, when handling and programming the robot. We consider this a confirmation for the overall idea of combining kinesthetic teaching with iconic programming in an interactive way, i.e., allowing for frequent switches between execution, testing / debugging and further instruction, is a good starting point for further development of the tool. However, we also have to see the comments (and observations) regarding the challenges the subjects experienced, which we summarize in the following, according to how often they were mentioned (high frequency first).

Precise positioning and fixating of the LEGO piece Many subjects mentioned the placement of the piece as a challenge. In fact, attaching two LEGO bricks to each other robustly with slippery robot grippers is tricky, and the success seems to depend a lot on whether the respective subject could determine a good strategy from the LEGO properties (the piece clicks best into place when being "folded" and then pressed, rather than through hovering over the target and moving straight down at once). The expert-made skill provided for group B followed this strategy, and worked very robustly (it merely took the expert—one of the researchers involved in the study setup—roughly two minutes to create this skill). Here, we plan to equip a future high-level interface for programming with the capability of providing suggestions based on previously known skills for similar work pieces to find the optimal strategy for a given work piece.

Different reference coordinate frames and switching between them As mentioned before, we are aware that selecting relevant coordinate frames is quite a challenge for any non-expert user, however, we can now, based on our observations of how the subjects managed to solve the problem and how exactly they could be supported, design further support based on reasoning and mixed-initiative interaction into future tools. We also observed, that many subjects simply forgot to assign the correct coordinate system, even though they understood how relative motions work. This was anticipated in the design of the tool, allowing the user to switch reference frames for an already existing movement, which made it very easy to correct the program after an issue with the reference frames was discovered.

Understanding all functionalities of the tool in the limited time frame, handling the interface This suggests that we might even have had better results, had the subjects been given more time to "play" with the tool. Some stated also informally after finishing, that "now, it would be great to start over, now I have understood this!".

Pose recording vs trajectory recording, understanding robot movement Some of the subjects, as also mentioned above, struggled to understand the concept of specifying positions to move to rather than trajectories to move along. In particular, the "contact move" posed a challenge as it results in a movement towards a virtual projection of a desired pose beyond the contact point. Further development of respective tools to include trajectory and contact force profile teaching is ongoing work.

Robustness, compensating for the LEGO piece sometimes slipping from the gripper As we did not make use of specifically designed grippers for LEGO-bricks, this was obviously a problem in some cases. It could be compensated for only through a good picking and placing strategy that would be robust to the slipping. Using more appropriate tools on the robot for grasping specific work pieces is obviously a good strategy, and is subject to investigations within the project work for the ongoing SARAFun project [1].

We see quite some of the challenges pointed out by our subjects as concrete confirmation of assumptions we had regarding obvious points to work with in the future.

In addition to not finding a strong correlation between experience and success rates, we observed that the one person with the least technical background not only felt very comfortable (4) when programming the robot, but also managed to complete all four steps of both phases within 21 minutes with full success. On the other hand, we observed highly experienced PhD students in Automatic Control struggling with the task for significantly longer periods of time and had one participant with high experience ratings failing in the first step already.

In a sideline of the study, we had one nine-year old child test the interface in the study setup. The child, while certainly an expert in LEGO building, was not a proper study participant due to a lack of English reading capabilities, but managed with only a little help regarding the switch of reference coordinate frames and the use of the contact move to program the first step (picking up and inserting the 2x2-piece on top of the "tower") within 20 minutes.

Boldly speaking, these observations seem to suggest that understanding of the task and assuming the robot to follow kinesthetic instructions as precisely as a (fellow, smaller) child, rather than assuming it being capable of understanding complex instructions, made it easier for the subjects to solve the task.

In the following we will present the evaluation of the programming tool carried out by an expert user, before drawing conclusions from our findings.

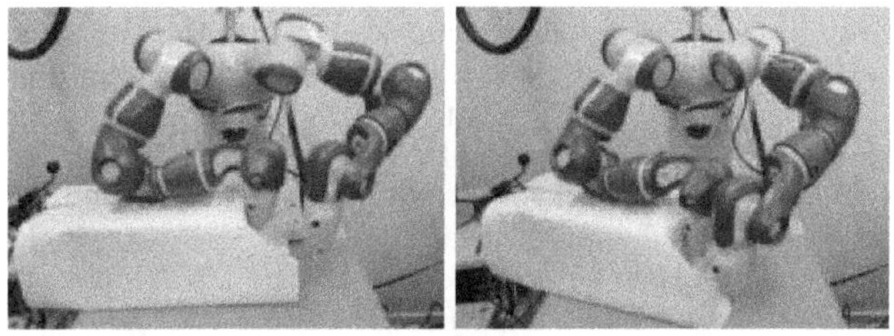

Figure 4: Paper folding (left). When rotating the box, only two positions must be updated (right).

5.2 Expert evaluation

One of the case studies we presented in section 3, the gift-wrapping task, formed the basis for the evaluation of the programming tool by an expert who is quite familiar both with programming YuMi in the traditional way using a teach pendant and coding directly in RAPID as well as with the specifics of the gift-wrapping process. For the evaluation, a folding task was chosen, where the right arm fixated a gift box with the elbow while the left straightened the corners using nine positions (fine and via), as illustrated in Figure 4. The operator used the programming tool presented in this paper to add a *packet object* to the world and programmed the actions for the left arm relative to this *packet object*. Then the box was moved to a different position and the packet and right arm positions were updated accordingly. After that the left-hand program executed without change. The entire programming, involving one test execution for each position took slightly below two minutes. The same process was then programmed using traditional tools which took slightly more than 11 minutes.

We also evaluated the interface in another context. Here, the overall task was to create two skills, one for picking a tool from a fixture and one for placing it back into the fixture. Creating a *tool object* and storing the positions for the picking and placing and saving these as skills took 70 seconds with our interface and more than 5 minutes with traditional programming methods, hence, the initial programming time was reduced by 80% using our interface compared to the traditionally provided methods. A more realistic scenario would then certainly involve multiple adjustments and parameter tuning, if required using the advanced settings in the traditional tools, however, executing and updating single instructions requires two button presses in our tool, while the traditional approach requires at least five steps, twice that if more than one coordinate system is used in the task.

We can thus state, that for an initial online programming process of applications that are difficult to test in a simulator (e.g., paper folding), our interface speeds up the programming process significantly. As it allows for debugging, executing, as well as updating and even reordering single steps in the robot program, we would expect our programming interface to be quite suitable (and faster than the traditional methods) also for more complex procedures.

6. CONCLUSION

In this paper we discussed our approach to high–level, intuitive programming of industrial robots for assembly tasks. We presented findings from an analysis of two case studies regarding the desired capabilities and functionalities of a programming interface for online programming in settings where the traditional work flow is not suitable, due to, e.g., simulation for testing not being an option. Based on these findings we developed a programming interface that supports a hybrid instruction and evaluation (execution) process and thus quick implementation and test cycles through a graphical interface for iconic programming. The interface supports also the specification of objects and their positions in the work cell of the robot, as well as updating these at any time. It is also possible to reorder instructions graphically and sequences of instructions can be saved as a skill for later re-use and refinement. We evaluated both with experts and 21 non–expert users in a user study and can state the following regarding the improvements and simplifications we assumed our tool to yield.

Already the basic support of a rapid instruction, test, and execution cycle with the possibility to reorder and update single instructions for refinement reduced the programming time for an expert by 80% compared to using the traditional programming tools and interfaces. This was specifically supported by the possibility to easily specify and refine object positions and reference frames and assigning them to certain instructions, so that re-use of program parts (skills) was enabled or even (as evaluated) a full program for one robot arm could be run without modifications, when the pose of the object the respective instructions referred to was updated. The possibility to change the frame of reference for already existing instructions is an additional convenience, as it is easy to forget to always set the correct one from the beginning, even for experts.

Our evaluation with 21 non–experts showed that the programming tool provides an interface sufficiently easy to handle, so that 19 of 21 participants could construct a satisfying solution to a LEGO–building task within 30 minutes, and 14 of them even managed to complete one or several follow–up steps. We can also state, that the reuse of previously created (own) skills and even more so of provided, expert–made skills, simplifies the programming process significantly. Our subjects struggled mainly with the precise positioning of the LEGO–bricks so that they would click into place firmly and (as we previously assumed) with the different object reference frames needed to handle picking up the pieces from arbitrary poses. For the first issue, we assume that process knowledge (how to best approach one work piece with the other to attach them correctly) was here of more significance than knowledge about the robot system, as we could not find an obvious correlation between success rate and experience. For the reference coordinate system issue we can state that although the users—even if they had understood the problem with the frames—would frequently forget to assign the correct one to their instructions, they managed to correct their mistakes quickly with the functionality for changing reference frames.

Other tools for high-level programming often assume an existing library of robot skills, e.g., tools supporting natural language instructions as for example presented by Stenmark et al. [32] need basic knowledge of objects (and their coordinate frames) and that it is possible to update and refine solutions suggested by a learning and reasoning system to industrially adequate robustness and precision. Hence, we see our interface as appropriate to support even non–expert users in handling the construction of such basic knowledge items as well as in updating and refining existing solutions.

Overall, we see our implementation as a successful prototype, which we can now use as a basis for further development and studies and software distribution within the research community. The integration of high-level (natural language) instruction capabilities with the interface as well as functionalities for teaching force profiles and trajectories as basic movement primitives, or skills are subject to ongoing work. This would presumably support the user even more in teaching contact moves and specific operations like snap–fit assembly. As the reference coordinate problem is difficult for users to both understand and then also to remember in the programming process, we plan to integrate mixed–initiative support based on reasoning about possible options regarding the assignment of reference frames to instructions.

7. ACKNOWLEDGMENTS

The research leading to these results has received funding from the European Community's Framework Programme Horizon 2020 under grant agreement No 644938 SARAFun.

8. REFERENCES

[1] H2020 sarafun - smart assembly robots with advanced functionalities - grant agreement no 644938. http://h2020sarafun.eu/. Accessed: 2016-10-03.

[2] Robotic assembly of emergency stop buttons - youtube video. https://youtu.be/7JgdbFW5mEg. Accessed: 2016-10-03.

[3] YuMi wraps Christmas gifts - youtube video. https://youtu.be/ASEtz2M1RiY. Accessed: 2016-10-03.

[4] F. J. Abu-Dakka, B. Nemec, A. Kramberger, A. G. Buch, N. Krüger, and A. Ude. Solving peg-in-hole tasks by human demonstration and exception strategies. *Industrial Robot: An International Journal*, 41(6):575–584, 2014.

[5] S. Ahmadzadeh, A. Paikan, F. Mastrogiovanni, L. Natale, P. Kormushev, and D. Caldwell. Learning symbolic representations of actions from human demonstrations. pages 3801–3808. IEEE, 2015.

[6] S. Alexandrova, M. Cakmak, K. Hsiao, and L. Takayama. Robot programming by demonstration with interactive action visualizations. In *Proceedings of Robotics: Science and Systems*, Berkeley, USA, July 2014.

[7] A. Billard, S. Calinon, and R. Dillmann. Learning from humans. In *Springer Handbook of Robotics, Chapter 74*, pages 1995–2014. Springer, 2016.

[8] M. Cakmak and A. L. Thomaz. Designing robot learners that ask good questions. In *Human-Robot Interaction (HRI), 2012 7th ACM/IEEE International Conference on*, pages 17–24, March 2012.

[9] J. Felip, J. Laaksonen, A. Morales, and V. Kyrki. Manipulation primitives: A paradigm for abstraction and execution of grasping and manipulation tasks. *Robot. Auton. Syst.*, 61(3):283–296, Mar. 2013.

[10] A. Feniello, H. Dang, and S. Birchfield. Program synthesis by examples for object repositioning tasks. In *2014 IEEE/RSJ International Conference on Intelligent Robots and Systems*, pages 4428–4435, Sept 2014.

[11] B. Fonooni, T. Hellström, and L.-E. Janlert. Priming as a means to reduce ambiguity in learning from demonstration. *International Journal of Social Robotics*, 8(1):5–19, 2016.

[12] D. F. Glas, T. Kanda, and H. Ishiguro. Human-robot interaction design using interaction composer: Eight years of lessons learned. In *The Eleventh ACM/IEEE International Conference on Human Robot Interaction*, HRI '16, pages 303–310, Piscataway, NJ, USA, 2016. IEEE Press.

[13] B. Huang, M. Li, R. L. Souza, J. J. Bryson, and A. Billard. A modular approach to learning manipulation strategies from human demonstration. *Auton. Robots*, 40(5):903–927, June 2016.

[14] J. Huang, T. Lau, and M. Cakmak. Design and evaluation of a rapid programming system for service robots. In *2016 11th ACM/IEEE International Conference on Human-Robot Interaction (HRI)*, pages 295–302, March 2016.

[15] A. J. Ijspeert, J. Nakanishi, and S. Schaal. Learning attractor landscapes for learning motor primitives. Technical report, 2002.

[16] W. K. H. Ko, Y. Wu, K. P. Tee, and J. Buchli. Towards industrial robot learning from demonstration. In *Proceedings of the 3rd International Conference on Human-Agent Interaction*, pages 235–238. ACM, 2015.

[17] J. Kober, M. Gienger, and J. J. Steil. Learning movement primitives for force interaction tasks. In *Robotics and Automation (ICRA), 2015 IEEE International Conference on*, pages 3192–3199. IEEE, 2015.

[18] P. Kormushev, S. Calinon, and D. G. Caldwell. Imitation learning of positional and force skills demonstrated via kinesthetic teaching and haptic input. *Advanced Robotics*, 25(5):581–603, 2011.

[19] A. Kramberger, R. Piltaver, B. Nemec, M. Gams, and A. Ude. Learning of assembly constraints by demonstration and active exploration. *Industrial Robot: An International Journal*, 43(5):524–534, 2016.

[20] A. Kurenkov, B. Akgun, and A. L. Thomaz. An evaluation of gui and kinesthetic teaching methods for constrained-keyframe skills. In *2015 IEEE/RSJ International Conference on Intelligent Robots and Systems (IROS)*, pages 3608–3613, Sept 2015.

[21] S. Manschitz, J. Kober, M. Gienger, and J. Peters. Learning to sequence movement primitives from demonstrations. In *2014 IEEE/RSJ International Conference on Intelligent Robots and Systems*, pages 4414–4421, Sept 2014.

[22] D. Massa, M. Callegari, and C. Cristalli. Manual guidance for industrial robot programming. *Industrial Robot: An International Journal*, 42(5):457–465, 2015.

[23] A. Mohseni-Kabir, C. Rich, S. Chernova, C. L. Sidner, and D. Miller. Interactive hierarchical task learning from a single demonstration. In *Proceedings of the Tenth Annual ACM/IEEE International Conference on Human-Robot Interaction*, HRI '15, pages 205–212, New York, NY, USA, 2015. ACM.

[24] B. Nemec, R. Vuga, and A. Ude. Efficient sensorimotor learning from multiple demonstrations. *Advanced Robotics*, 27(13):1023–1031, 2013.

[25] S. Niekum, S. Osentoski, G. Konidaris, S. Chitta, B. Marthi, and A. G. Barto. Learning grounded finite-state representations from unstructured demonstrations. *The International Journal of Robotics Research*, 34(2):131–157, 2015.

[26] M. Pardowitz, S. Knoop, R. Dillmann, and R. D. Zöllner. Incremental learning of tasks from user demonstrations, past experiences, and vocal comments. *IEEE Transactions on Systems, Man, and Cybernetics, Part B (Cybernetics)*, 37(2):322–332, April 2007.

[27] P. Pastor, M. Kalakrishnan, S. Chitta, E. Theodorou, and S. Schaal. Skill learning and task outcome prediction for manipulation. In *2011 IEEE International Conference on Robotics and Automation*, pages 3828–3834, May 2011.

[28] M. R. Pedersen, D. L. Herzog, and V. Krüger. Intuitive skill-level programming of industrial handling tasks on a mobile manipulator. In *2014 IEEE/RSJ International Conference on Intelligent Robots and Systems*, pages 4523–4530, Sept 2014.

[29] M. R. Pedersen, L. Nalpantidis, R. S. Andersen, C. Schou, S. Bøgh, V. Krüger, and O. Madsen. Robot skills for manufacturing: From concept to industrial deployment. *Robotics and Computer-Integrated Manufacturing*, 37:282 – 291, 2016.

[30] A. Perzylo, N. Somani, S. Profanter, I. Kessler, M. Rickert, and A. Knoll. Intuitive instruction of industrial robots: Semantic process descriptions for small lot production. In *IEEE/RSJ International Conference on Intelligent Robots and Systems (IROS)*, Daejeon, Republic of Korea, October 2016. https://youtu.be/bbInEMEF5zU.

[31] G. B. Rodamilans, E. Villani, L. G. Trabasso, W. R. d. Oliveira, and R. Suterio. A comparison of industrial robots interface: force guidance system and teach pendant operation. *Industrial Robot: An International Journal*, 43(5):552–562, 2016.

[32] M. Stenmark, J. Malec, and A. Stolt. From high-level task descriptions to executable robot code. In *Intelligent Systems' 2014*, pages 189–202. Springer, 2014.

[33] M. Stenmark and P. Nugues. Natural language programming of industrial robots. In *Robotics (ISR), 2013 44th International Symposium on*, pages 1–5. IEEE, 2013.

[34] M. Stenmark, A. Stolt, E. A. Topp, M. Haage, A. Robertsson, K. Nilsson, and R. Johansson. The GiftWrapper: Programming a Dual-Arm Robot With Lead-through. In *ICRA Workshop on Human-Robot Interfaces for Enhanced Physical Interactions*, 2016.

[35] M. Stenmark and E. A. Topp. From demonstrations to skills for high-level programming of industrial robots. In *AAAI Fall Symposium Series 2016, Symposium on AI for HRI*, 2016.

[36] A. Stolt, M. Linderoth, A. Robertsson, and R. Johansson. Force controlled assembly of emergency stop button. In *Robotics and Automation (ICRA), 2011 IEEE International Conference on*, pages 3751–3756. IEEE, 2011.

[37] A. Stolt, M. Stenmark, A. Robertsson, and K. Nilsson. Robotic gift wrapping or a glance at the present state in santa's workshop. In *Reglermote 2016 (Swedish meeting on automatic control 2016)*, 2016.

[38] P. Tsarouchi, S. Makris, and G. Chryssolouris. Human–robot interaction review and challenges on task planning and programming. *Int. J. Comput. Integr. Manuf.*, 29(8):916–931, Aug. 2016.

[39] M. Tykal, A. Montebelli, and V. Kyrki. Incrementally assisted kinesthetic teaching for programming by demonstration. In *2016 11th ACM/IEEE International Conference on Human-Robot Interaction (HRI)*, pages 205–212, March 2016.

[40] S. Wrede, C. Emmerich, R. Grünberg, A. Nordmann, A. Swadzba, and J. Steil. A user study on kinesthetic teaching of redundant robots in task and configuration space. *Journal of Human-Robot Interaction*, 2(1):56 – 81, 2013.

Situated Tangible Robot Programming

Yasaman S. Sefidgar, Prerna Agarwal, and Maya Cakmak
Computer Science & Engineering, University of Washington
185 Stevens Way, Seattle, WA 98195
einsian@gmail.com, prerna2@uw.edu, mcakmak@cs.washington.edu

ABSTRACT

This paper introduces *situated tangible robot programming*, whereby a robot is programmed by placing specially designed tangible "blocks" in its workspace. These blocks are used for annotating objects, locations, or regions, and specifying actions and their ordering. The robot compiles a program by detecting blocks and objects in its workspace and grouping them into instructions by solving constraints. We present a proof-of-concept implementation using blocks with unique visual markers in a pick-and-place task domain. Three user studies evaluate the intuitiveness and learnability of situated tangible programming and iterate the block design. We characterize common challenges and gather feedback on how to further improve the design of blocks. Our studies demonstrate that people can interpret, generalize, and create many different situated tangible programs with minimal instruction or with no instruction at all.

Keywords

End-User Robot Programming, Programming by Demonstration, Tangible Programming

1. INTRODUCTION

Programmability is a key advantage of industrial robots over traditional automation [16]. Robot arms, such as Universal Robot's UR5, KUKA's LWR, or ABB's YuMi, can be programmed to perform a wide variety of manipulation tasks. Indeed, these robots are currently deployed in various settings, performing tasks such as loading, unloading, sorting, kitting, packaging, assembly, or disassembly of a diverse set of items, from electronics to food. These robots are often programmed to perform their unique task in their specialized environment by highly trained experts, largely because the languages and interfaces for programming these robots are notoriously complex. For example, they usually require users to specify coordinate frames, and as UR Manaul puts it, "A problem with such frames is that a certain level of mathematical knowledge is required to be able to define such coordinate systems and also that it takes a considerable amount of time to do this, even for a person skilled in the art of robot programming and installation" [1].

HRI '17, March 06 - 09, 2017, Vienna, Austria

ISBN 978-1-4503-4336-7/17/03...$15.00
DOI: http://dx.doi.org/10.1145/2909824.3020240

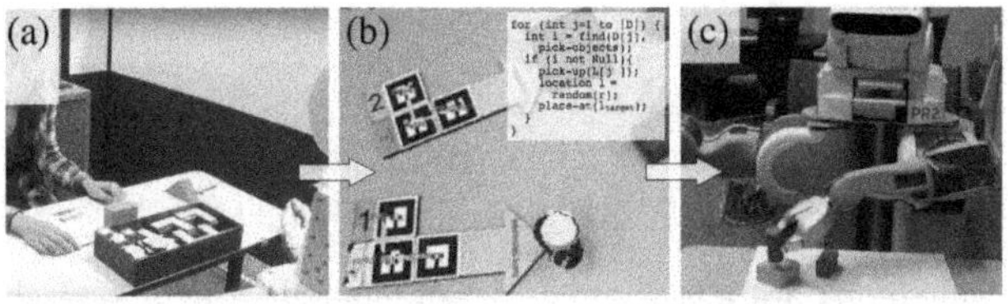

Figure 1: *(a) Situated tangible programming* involves programming a robot by combining and placing specially designed tangible blocks in the robot's workspace to select objects, locations, or regions, and to specify actions and their ordering. (b) Blocks and objects in the workspace are detected by the robot and compiled into a robot program. (c) The robot can perform the instructed task in new environments and in the absence of blocks by executing this compiled program.

The development of lower-cost and human-safe manipulators has increased the frequency of use of robotic arms by small and medium businesses in their manufacturing processes and even outside industrial contexts. As a result, robotics companies now place more emphasis on letting end-users program robots by themselves to reduce the cost of programming and eliminate down-time. For instance, ReThink's robots, Baxter and Sawyer, are advertised as being "simple to train, flexible, and re-deployable"; Franka Emika's upcoming robot, dubbed "everybody's robot," offers "visually intuitive programming."

Despite these efforts by robotics companies and decades of research on robot Programming by Demonstration, many challenges remain in enabling non-experts to program robots. Referencing objects or arbitrary parts of the environment is particularly challenging for end-users. Most industrial tools support using the robot's arm to pre-record a set of coordinate frames. As noted, this separate step complicates the programming process and requires additional skills. While the proposed "situated" techniques, such as using pointing gestures [18, 8], possibly combined with verbal descriptions [14, 19, 7, 15, 27], simplify referencing objects and locations, they are not robust enough for industrial settings.

This paper proposes a new way to program robots that takes advantage of being situated in the task context. This approach involves placing physical, tangible "blocks" in the robot's task environment to annotate objects, locations, or regions and to instruct the robot to perform actions that reference them. We first develop a programming language that supports programming of typical industrial robotic tasks and implement a proof-of-concept system with blocks that are easy to detect. We present findings from a user study (N=20) that examines the intuitiveness and learnability of situated tangible programming, and two follow-up studies, with an improved block design, that examine program interpretation (N=18) and creation (N=6) without *any* instructions. Our studies demonstrate that situated tangible programming offers a promising approach that lets novices program robots with minimal training and inform further improvements to the block design.

2. RELATED WORK

Our work contributes a new way of programming robots. Traditionally, industrial robots are programmed by saving a sequence of robot poses, assuming the position of all relevant items are known at programming time (e.g., a trash can that has a fixed position or parts that get placed at the same location and orientation by a feeder). Programming by Demonstration (PbD) extends this approach to programming capabilities that generalize to new situations. PbD has been widely researched, with work focusing on types of demonstrations [2], modalities for demonstration [29, 9], and alternative task representations [23, 21]. PbD work that focuses on manipulation tasks often involves a single object of interest in the workspace, avoiding the challenge of referencing objects. Exceptions include [3] and [24] that support limited referencing by automatically detecting objects involved in the task from a kinesthetic demonstration.

While PbD is the most popular technique in the literature, other ways in which end-users can program robots have been proposed. These include programming through natural language instructions (*e.g.*, [20, 7]) or visual programming (*e.g.*, [4, 13, 11]). Although the concept of programming manipulators with tangibles is novel, tangibles have been used for *controlling* robots, where the robot performs a task as long as the tangibles remain in its workspace. For example, Zhao *et al.* proposed placing paper tags ("Magic Cards") on the floor to task Roomba-like robots[30]. Or, Luria *et al.* introduced tangibles ("phicons") for communicating with a social robot to control smart home devices [17].

The promise of natural and direct interactions has made tangible interfaces appealing across varied application domains from music [22] and creative exploration [10] to math [26] and 3D modeling [5]. One controlled experiment with children provide evidence for benefits of tangible programming over visual programming [25]. Two different tangible programming systems developed for K-12 outreach were actually used for creating simple navigation programs for toy robots [12, 28]. Considering the situatedness inherent to many robot programming tasks, tangible programming is a promising candidate for accessible end-user programming of robot manipulators.

3. SITUATED TANGIBLE PROGRAMMING

We propose programming robots by placing tangible blocks in robot's physical workspace. To that end, we first develop the underlying programming language and design the blocks

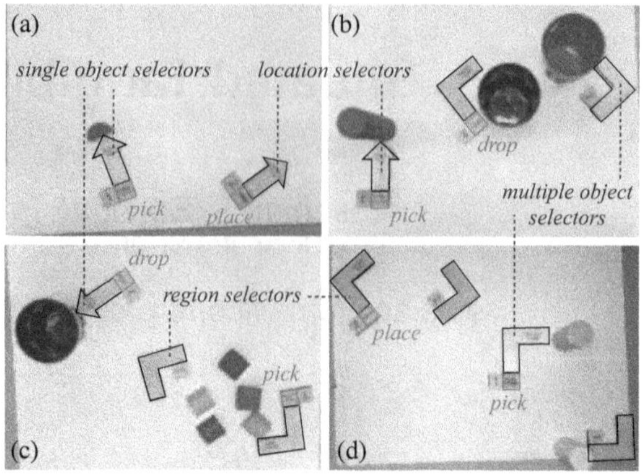

Figure 2: Example situated tangible programs in different scenes. Programs vary in the type of selection blocks used as part of the pick and place/drop instructions.

that allow creating programs in this language. Then, we present a proof-of-concept system implementation.

3.1 Domain and Programming Language

We focus on programming pick-and-place tasks in industrial settings. We assume the robot can detect the surfaces, where locations and regions of interest are defined, and the objects of interest on these surfaces (*e.g.*, parts and containers). The robot's actions are represented with four functions that can be called within a program: `pick-up-from-top`, `pick-up-from-side`, `place-at`, and `drop`. Actions take one of four types of arguments: a *location*, an *object*, a *region*, or a *list of objects*. A *location* is a 3-dimensional point on the robot's workspace and a *region* is a convex hull. Objects are represented with a *descriptor* that allows them to be localized in the robot's workspace.

In our framework, a *program* is a sequence of instructions that accomplish a certain pick-and-place task when executed by the robot. Programs can have *constants* whose values are determined at programming time. In addition each program has one *variable*, a list of all available objects, instantiated at execution time. Our language also has a number of convenience functions and control flow operators that allow looping or branching in the program.

3.2 Situated Tangible Blocks

Situated tangible programming involves creating programs in the language described in Sec. 3.1 using a set of physical *blocks*. Our design involves three categories of blocks.

Selection blocks ("selectors"). The first set of blocks allow selecting a single object, multiple objects, a location, or a region at programming time to instantiate a constant in the program. Fig. 2 shows examples of these blocks used as part of situated tangible programs. A single object is selected by an arrow placed on the surface carrying the object pointing towards it. A group of objects is selected by enclosing them between two 90° corner brackets. A location on a surface is indicated by the tip of an arrow placed on the surface. A region on a surface is indicated by two corner brackets. Note that a region specified in this way will have four corners, but is not guaranteed to be a rectangle.

Action blocks. Action blocks correspond to the robot action functions described in Sec. 3.1. To instantiate the parameter of the function, the block is attached to a selection block. Fig. 2 shows how different action blocks are attached to selection blocks as part of a program. If a `pick` or `place/drop` action block is attached to a location selector (Fig. 2(a,b)), the action is performed at that location. A pick action requires that an object be found at that location at execution time, whereas the place/drop action will adjust the height of the action depending on whether the location is empty or already has an object.

If a `pick` or `place/drop` action block is attached to a single object selector (Fig. 2(a,c)), then the descriptor of that object is added as a constant input to the program. The program will locate this object in the new scene and perform the action at its location.

If a `pick` action block is attached to a region selector (Fig. 2(c)), the robot will pick up all objects found in that region at execution time. If a `place` action block is attached to a region selector (Fig. 2(d)), the robot will place the currently held object at a random location in that region.

If a `pick` action block is attached to a multiple object selector (Fig. 2(d)), then the resulting instruction will make the robot pick all instances of objects that are the same as an object in the selected set. This creates a loop in the program. If a `place/drop` action block is attached to a multiple object selector (Fig. 2(b)), then the resulting program will find an object in the current scene that matches any of the selected objects, and will place/drop the currently held object on it.

Ordering blocks. Ordering blocks have positive integers that indicate the order of instructions in the program. To compile a complete program from a set of blocks, our system uses the ordering constraints specified by these blocks, together with the constraint that each pick action needs to be paired with a place/drop action. Fig. 2 shows how ordering blocks are attached to action blocks.

From blocks to programs. Given a scene with a set of objects and blocks, the robot needs to first group blocks and objects together (see Sec. 3.4 for implementation details). A set of blocks form a valid program if: (a) each action block has a selection block and an ordering block associated with it, (b) all pick actions have odd number orderings and all place/drop actions have even number orderings (*i.e.*, the program starts with a pick and what is picked is placed/dropped before the next pick), and (c) object selectors have objects associated with them.

Loops are created whenever a pick action is associated with a *multiple object* or *region* selector. The place/drop action that follows the pick action is considered part of the loop. Conditionals are automatically added to the program for checking membership in lists of objects, checking existence, or checking location-region relationships.

3.3 Visual Block Design

The design of the language and blocks described above are based on the requirements of the functionality that we aim to provide. While it is important for blocks to be robustly perceivable by the robot, there is flexibility in how they look. Our design goal is to maximize intuitiveness and learnability of the blocks and combined instructions for end-users. To that end, we explore the following visual and physical design elements. Our studies involved two iterations of block design, which we refer to as D1 and D2.

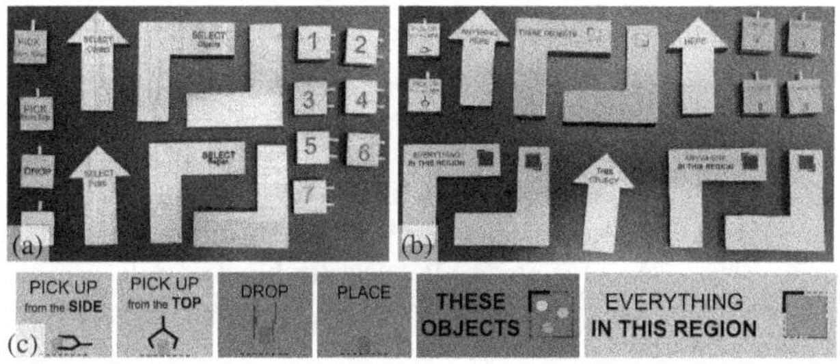

Figure 3: Situated tangible block libraries: (a) initial design (D1), (b) improved design (D2), (c) icons in D2.

Shape: Block shapes are chosen to reflect their functional category. Arrows are used for pointing to a location or to a single object to select it. Two L-shaped brackets are paired together to select an approximately rectangular region or a set of objects included in the region, analogous to using thumb and index fingers with two hands to indicate a region on a surface. Other blocks are square shaped, appropriately sized relative to the arrows and brackets, to allow combinations of blocks to look uniform.

Text and icons: Short word phrases and visual icons (D2 only) clarify the specific function of action or selection blocks. For instance, *single object* selectors and *location* selectors that have the same arrow shape, have different phrases on them. Action blocks have a verb phrase and ordering blocks have a single integer. The phrases used on D1 selectors are direct reflections of the formal terminology used here to describe different blocks. In contrast D2 uses natural language phrases. For instance, the single object selector has the phrase "select object" in D1 and "this object" in D2. Capitalization is used for emphasis as shown in Fig. 3. In D2, we also add *prepositions* to some action blocks ("place on," "drop in") and made separate location selectors for pick ("anything here") versus place ("here").

Color: Block colors (only available in D2) are also used to distinguish between block types that have the same shape. In addition, pairs of brackets were colored the same to help with association.

Peg/hole connectors: Blocks can be attached to one another through uniquely spaced peg-and-hole connectors that implicitly indicate the possibility of combining blocks while preventing false combinations.

3.4 System Implementation

We present a proof-of-concept implementation of situated tangible instructions.

Perception. Our system first detects all surfaces and objects of interest, as well as all tangible program blocks in the scene. Perception of blocks is simplified using fiducials (also known as AR Tags) incorporated into the block design. Our implementation uses the Alvar AR Tag tracking library.[1] Each type of block is given a unique identifier. Asymmetric AR Tags also allow uniquely determining the orientation of the blocks, allowing us to determine arrow and bracket orientations. Surfaces and objects are perceived using the table top segmentation functionality in the Point Cloud Library

[1]http://wiki.ros.org/ar_track_alvar

(PCL)[2]. This returns the dominant surface in the scene and a list of segmented objects on it. Objects are represented by their size, shape, and color.

Program compilation. Given a list of objects and lists of selection, action, and ordering blocks detected in the scene, our system produces a program with the following procedure. First, we iterate over all selection blocks to determine the program constants. For each *single object* selector, we iterate over the set of objects to determine which object is in the direction of the selector arrow on the surface within a certain distance. For each *multiple object* selector, we iterate over the set of objects to determine which objects are within the convex hull created by the selectors on the surface. Selected objects are saved in the program. Next, we iterate over all location and region selectors, and we save the constant location and region values as part of the program.

The next step is to iterate over all action blocks and assign them to a selector block. The peg/hole attachment mechanism on the blocks ensure that the displacement between a selection and action block follows a pattern and their orientations are aligned. These constraints allow uniquely identifying the assignment of action blocks to selection blocks. Next, we iterate over all ordering blocks and assign them to an action block. After grouping all objects and blocks, the final step is to compile the program as described in Sec. 3.2.

Actions and program execution. Our system is implemented on a PR2 robot (partially shown in Fig. 1), using the RGBD sensor mounted on the head and one of its 7 degree-of-freedom arms. The robot's actions are pre-defined as a sequence of poses relative to detected object locations. Pick actions have a pre-grasp, grasp, and lift pose determined based on the size of objects used in our evaluation and the type of pick (from top or from side). Place actions have a pre-placement, placement, and clear pose determined based on the size of objects. Drop actions have a single drop pose where the gripper is opened. All poses were pre-specified using kinesthetic demonstrations. During program execution, the robot determines the current set of objects and computes the poses for all actions that are relative to objects. The robot uses motion planning, as implemented in MoveIt![3] to move from one pose to the next.

4. EVALUATION

Following a human-centered approach, we evaluate the intuitiveness and learnability of situated tangible programming with users of varied backgrounds. We describe our evaluation spanning three studies; the first with our initial block design (D1) and the second and third with an improved design (D2) based on feedback from the first study.

4.1 Study 1: Initial Design

Programming languages and tools can be evaluated on three types of tasks: program comprehension, program creation, and debugging [6]. Our evaluation focus on the first two. To evaluate how well a program is comprehended, we employ two techniques: *demonstration* tests where we present participants with a program, situated in a scene, and ask them to demonstrate what the robot should do in that scene, and *generalization* tests in which we first show participants a program, situated in a *programming-time* scene, and next present them with robot's executions of that program in a different *execution-time* scene, and ask whether the execution is consistent with the program.

To evaluate how well people can use situated tangible blocks to create programs, we perform *program creation* tests where we describe the desired behavior of the program to be created. We provide participants with a set of objects and blocks and ask them to create a scene and a corresponding program with the described behavior.

4.1.1 Materials

Programs: Both demonstration and generalization tests involve programs with one pick and one place instruction where varied selector types are used for parametrizing the pick and place actions. Scenes and programs were prepared ahead of time and glued onto foam boards for consistency across participants. Scenes involved abstract objects varied in color, size, and shape (Fig. 2). In the demonstration test, participants are presented with different groups of four programs such that they see all selector and action types an equal number of times.

ID	Pick selector	Place/drop selector
P_1:	*location* selector	*single object* selector
P_2:	*single object* selector	*location* selector
P_3:	*location* selector	*region* selector
P_4:	*location* selector	*multiple object* selector
P_5:	*region* selector	*region* selector
P_6:	*multiple object* selector	*region* selector

Table 1: Programs used in the generalization tests. P_6 is also shown in Fig. 2(d).

Robot executions: In the generalization test, participants are presented with two executions of six different programs covering different combinations of selectors (Table 1). The executions occur in different scenes than those in which the program was presented to the participant. They differ in the objects involved in the scene and their placements. Seven out of 12 executions are fully consistent with the given program and five executions have an inconsistency (three during picking and two during placement). The executions are presented as a video of the robot manipulating objects in the scene (Fig. 4). Participants are asked to separately assess whether the pick actions and the place/drop actions in the execution are consistent with the given program, thus answering 24 yes/no questions presented randomly through a browser.

Program creation tasks: For program creation tests, participants are given a natural language description of three desired program behaviors and pictures illustrating the state of the scene before and after a sample execution of each (Fig. 5). P_A involves picking up an object placed at a particular corner of the table and placing it at the opposite corner. The intended program involves a pick and a place action, each parametrized with a *location* selector. P_B involves creating a stack of two specific objects (blue square at the bottom, red triangle on the top). The intended program involves two pick and place actions; the pick actions are parametrized with *single object* selectors and the place actions are parametrized with *location* selectors, though the placement of the second object on the first could also be

[2]http://pointclouds.org/
[3]http://moveit.ros.org/

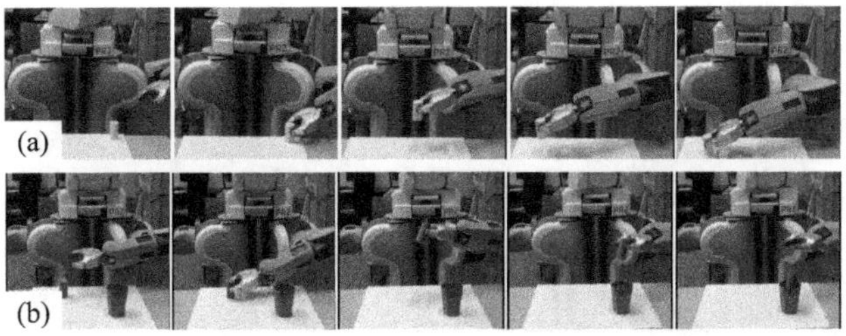

Figure 4: Filmstrips of example executions from the videos used in the generalization test. (a) A consistent execution of P_6. (b) An inconsistent execution of P_1.

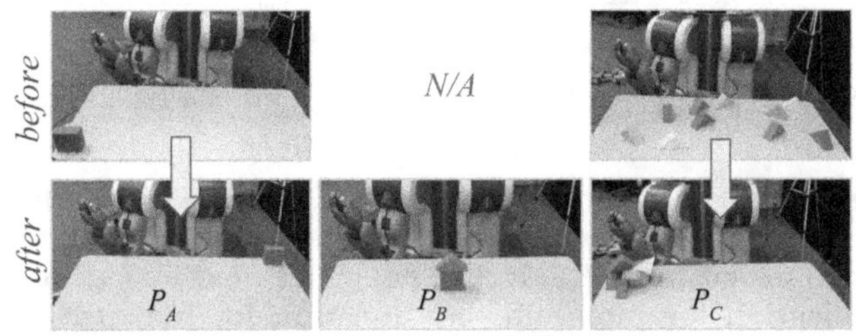

Figure 5: Before/after pictures used for describing the desired program behaviors in the program creation tests.

accomplished with a *single object* selector. P_C involves collecting triangles (of any color) and placing them near a particular corner of the table. The intended program involves a loop of pick and place actions, where the pick actions are parametrized with items from a *multiple object* selector and place actions are parametrized with a *region* selector.

4.1.2 Protocol

Our first study has three parts. In the first part, participants perform the demonstration and generalization tests without any instructions on what different blocks mean. In the second part, participants are first instructed about what each block means and how they can be combined. We then repeat the demonstration and generalization tests. In both parts we emphasize that objects are distinguished based on their shape, size, and color as the generalization test required such distinctions. Demonstration tests involve a different subset of programs, but the generalization questions are exactly the same. Order of programs in both tests are counter-balanced across participants. In the third part of the study, participants perform the program creation tasks.

4.1.3 Measurements

We record participants' demonstrations of each program in the demonstration tests, their yes/no answers and reasoning in the generalization tests, and their subjective ratings of confidence interpreting different tangible blocks in the form of 5-point Likert-style questions. In the second part, we additionally ask participants to compare their initial interpretations with our definitions and suggest alternatives that could have helped them better understand the intended meaning of each block. In the third part, we record programs created by participants and ask them to rate their experience programming with blocks.

Two authors double-coded videos of participants' demonstrations for consistency with the selection and action blocks as well as looping behavior in the program. Inconsistent demonstrations were further analyzed to identify common errors. Programs created by participants were scored for proper formation and placement of instructions and the overall program logic. Errors were noted and analyzed.

4.2 Follow-up Studies with Improved Design

Our follow up studies aim to assess the impact of the redesign on the intuitiveness of situated tangible programming without *any* instructions about the meanings of the blocks. To that end, Study 2 repeats Part 1 of Study 1 with the improved design (D2) to evaluate program comprehension. Study 3 evaluates program creation without any instruction and without having seen any example programs before. We give participants an abstract overview of situated tangible programming and then we ask them to brainstorm at least two interpretations for each block separately. Next, we ask them to connect blocks together and to brainstorm interpretations of the combinations. We do not give any feedback on their interpretations. Finally, we present them with the same program creation tests as in Study 1 in counterbalanced order.

5. FINDINGS

Participants for our studies were recruited from campus-wide mailing lists at the authors' university. Study 1 had 20 participants (12 F, 8 M); Study 2 had 18 participants (7 F, 11 M), and Study 3 had 6 participants (3 F, 3M). Study 1 took between 90 to 120 minutes, and Study 2 and 3 took 60 minutes.

We compare participants' performance on demonstration and generalization tests in two ways. First, we compare performance in Study 1, *before* and *after* being given instructions about the meanings of blocks. We refer to these two conditions as D1PRE and D1POST. Second, we compare performance before being given instructions for designs D1 (Study 1) versus D2 (Study 2). We refer to these as D1PRE and D2PRE. Note that the first comparison is within subjects and the second is between subjects. Hence, we perform paired t-tests between D1PRE and D1POST, and independent t-tests between D1PRE and D2PRE. The program creation tests in Study 1 and Study 3 are not comparable as they differ both in the design and the amount of instruction and practice provided prior to the task. We treat those conditions as observational studies.

5.1 Overall Performance

After minimal instructions, most participants were able to correctly interpret situated tangible programs for various tasks. In the D1POST condition, participants reached >90% across all metrics in the demonstration tests (Fig. 6(a)) and around 90% in the generalization tests (Fig. 6(b)). Almost all scores were significantly higher in D1POST compared to those achieved before being given instructions (D1PRE).

The redesign of the blocks (D2) significantly improved people's demonstrations in all aspects except in their interpretation of placement actions (already high with D1). Participants correctly interpreted around 80% of selection blocks attached to place/drop and above 90% of other components of programs in D2PRE. These are high scores to

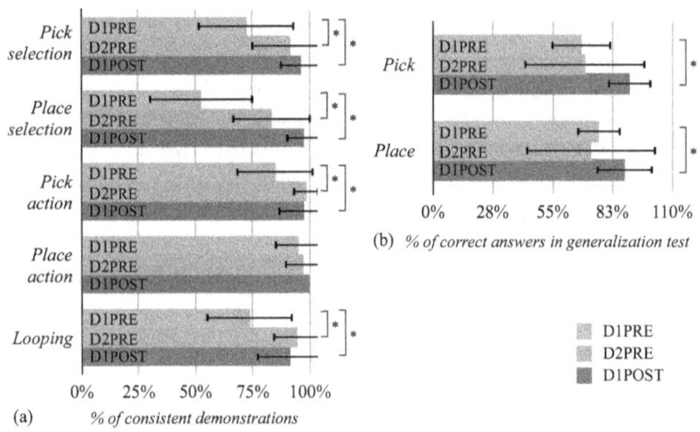

Figure 6: (a) Percentage of demonstrations (out of four) that were consistent with the program presented in the demonstration tests, in terms of interpretations of the selection and action blocks used for pick and place/drop as well as looping behavior, averaged across participants. (b) Percentage of correctly answered questions (out of 12) in the generalization test for pick and place portions of the robot's execution, averaged across participants. Statistically significant differences (p<0.05) are indicated with a *.

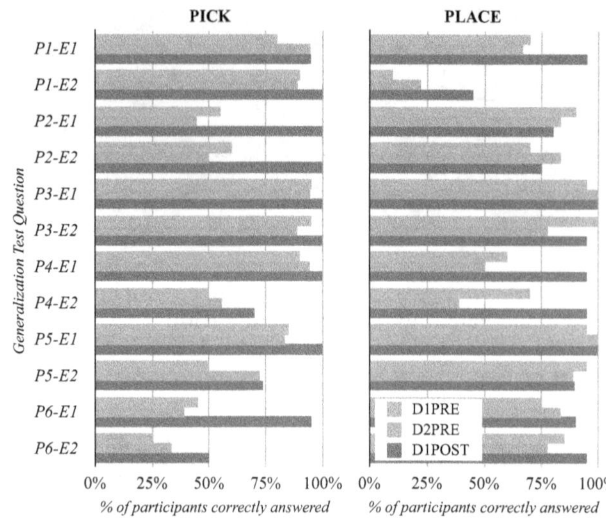

Figure 7: Percentage of participants who responded correctly to questions in the generalization test for two executions (E1, E2) of six programs (P_1-P_6); one question for pick and one question for place/drop. Three conditions are compared.

achieve without any instructions. However, people's ability to answer generalization questions did not improve with D2.

In Study 1, 70% of participants created correct programs for at least one program creation task. 40% successfully created correct programs for all three tasks. Program P_A (an abstraction of machine tending tasks) was the easiest (65% success rate), whereas P_B (an abstraction of assembly tasks) was the hardest (40% success rate). Achieving these rates with 5-minute instructions is considerable. In Study 3, in the absence of any instructions using D2, two out of six participants correctly programmed P_A and three participants correctly programmed P_B. One participant formed a valid program for P_A but the program did not satisfy the specified task (*i.e.*, it had an object selector instead of a location selector). None of the participants correctly programmed P_C; however, two had only a minor error.

5.2 Challenges with Program Comprehension

Table 2 summarizes the common challenges participants had in the demonstration tests. One of the most common challenges in D1PRE was in associating the two L-shaped brackets as parts of one selector. In D2, we tried to mitigate this issue by coloring paired brackets the same, varying the color of different bracket pairs, and including icons of a square region with opposite corners emphasized (Fig. 3). Another common issue was selecting only one object from a *multi-object* or *region* selector, rather than looping through all objects. In D2, we tried to mitigate this issue by changing the wording of the selectors to say "*everything* in this region" and "*these* objects". The other issues were due to alternative interpretations of words used on action and selection blocks (*e.g.*, "select" interpreted as an action verb), as well as their shape (*e.g.*, arrow as direction). In D2, we tried to mitigate these issues by updating the wordings; for instance, the term "select" was removed from selection blocks and replaced with referential phrases such as "this object" or "here." To further clarify the actions, we included icons of a gripper picking up an object from the side versus top.

Overall the generalization test was more challenging and it revealed additional confusions people had. To better understand challenges in the generalization test, we investigated the particular questions that participants tended to get wrong and examined the explanations of their answers. Fig. 7 shows participant's correct responses in the generalization test broken down into individual questions. The most common issue we observed was in differentiating object selectors from location/region selectors. We noted at least one instance of confusion in this regard (verified by participant's explanation) in 90%, 83.3%, and 45% of participants in D1PRE, D2PRE, and D1POST respectively.

For example, one question about P_2 (Table 1) involved the robot picking up the selected object from a different location. This is consistent with the program; however, 50% of participants in D1PRE deemed it inconsistent (Fig. 7(a), P_2-E1/E2). Further examination of their explanations revealed flawed mental models of object selectors. For example, one participant said *"The object's initial location does not seem to be at all near to the indicated point, so the robot should not grab this object."* Similarly, around 20% of participants in D1PRE thought that the robot's execution of P_1 picking a different object at the selected location was inconsistent with the program (Fig. 7(a), P_1-E1/E2); *e.g., "It violated the picking instruction because it picked up a green cylinder even though instruction #1 has an arrow with a command "pick from side" pointing to a purple cylinder."* Nonetheless, many participants gave correct answers backed by explanations that demonstrate correct mental models; *e.g., "The instruction specifies the object, which the robot finds and picks up"* (P_2, object selector) and *"Yes, the robot picks an item from the correct location"* (P_1, location selector).

Our examination of participants' responses identified additional mental model flaws that contributed to wrong answers. For example, P_1 included an object selector pointing

Error Description	D1PRE	D2PRE	D1POST
Failure to associate paired brackets as opposite corners	65%	11.1%	0%
Failure to loop over multiple objects when picking from a region or a set of objects	60%	0%	30%
Misinterpretation of "side" and "top" not in relation to objects	35%	0%	0%
Misinterpretation of the word "select" as an action	35%	NA	0%
Misinterpretation of arrow selectors as referring to a direction	10%	16.7%	0%
Misinterpretation of icons	NA	33.3%	NA
Placement on all objects for the multi-object selector with the words "these objects"	NA	16.7%	NA
Misinterpretation of "anything here" as a reference to ⩾1 object	NA	11.1%	NA

Table 2: Different user errors in the demonstration tests and percentage of participants who made the error at least once. Note that numbers in the first and third column are out of 20 (Study 1) and the second column is out of 18 (Study 2) participants.

to a purple cup, with the drop action attached to it. In an inconsistent execution, the robot dropped an object in a green cup. Only 25% of the participants in D1PRE judged this execution as inconsistent with P_1; this went up to only 33% in D2PRE. Even after being explicitly instructed about how the robot represents objects and how the object selector matches all properties of objects in D1POST, around 50% of participants still thought the robot's action was consistent with the program. The explanations of their answers revealed that even though they had a correct mental model of object selectors, they viewed the two cups as the same objects, likely because of their common affordance in the context of dropping. One participant said *"The green cup is clearly a close analogue for the purple cup, so I think dropping into the green cup is perfectly reasonable."*

Fig. 8 shows participants' responses to the Likert-scale question asking how much their initial mental model of a block matched its actual meaning after getting instructions about blocks. We see that their perceived mental model discrepancy is consistent with challenges observed prior to instructions. Actions were interpreted correctly by most participants. People's pre-instruction mental model of location selectors were more likely to be correct than those of object selectors. Also, the region and multiple object selectors were more likely to be misinterpreted.

5.3 Challenges with Program Creation

Error Description	#
Failure to distinguish between object and location selectors	5
Misuse of object selectors without the selected objects	6
Missing ordering on brackets	5
Unattached ordering blocks in attempt to reuse selection and action blocks in an earlier instruction	2

Table 3: Different user errors in the program creation test (post instructions on D1) and the number of participants (out of 20) who made that error.

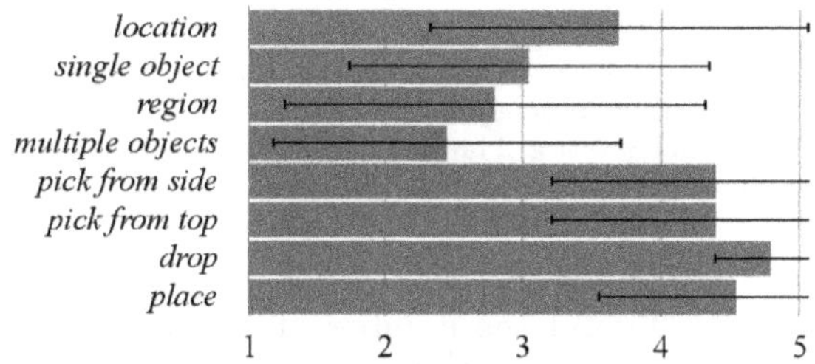

Figure 8: Responses to 5-point Likert-scale questions asking participants to rate how well their pre-instruction mental model of different block types matched their post-instruction mental model (1: very different).

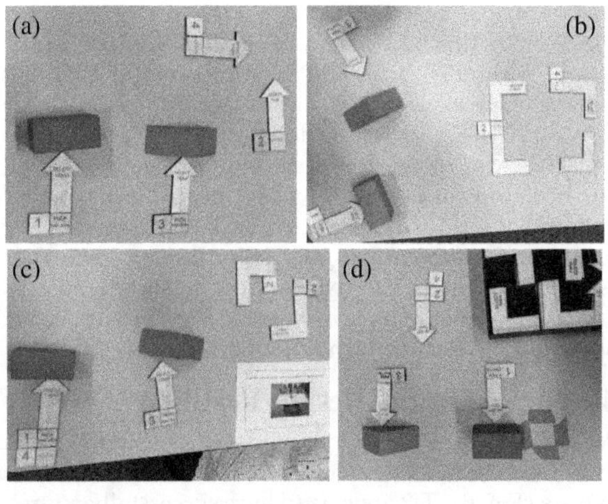

Figure 9: Alternative programs created by participants in the program creation task for P_B.

Table 3 summarizes challenges observed with program creation with D1. There were three errors that were observed in at least 5 of 20 participants. The first was improper use of object and location selectors, indicating the persistence of mental model flaws observed in demonstration and generalization tests. The second concerned improper placement of object selectors. Some of these were byproducts of the first type of error: participants who confused object and location selectors did not realize objects must be present with object selectors. Others assumed the robot could simulate the effect of pick and place actions and they used the object selector where the object should appear during the execution of the program (most common in task P_B). A program created by a participant with this error is shown in Fig. 9(a). The third common error was missing numbering on one of the brackets, which was required for distinguishing pairing of brackets when more than one pair was used in the program.

Table 4 summarizes the common errors observed in program creation test in Study 3 (using D2). We observe some of the same issues. Once again, participants did not make the distinction between object and location selectors. They commonly used "this object" interchangeably with "anything here" or "everything in this region" interchangeably with "these objects". Failing to number all brackets was also common. We additionally observed unexpected combinations of blocks. Two participants formed regions using addi-

Error Description	#
Failure to distinguish between object and location selectors	4
Missing ordering on brackets	4
Forming regions with >2 brackets (typically 4)	2
Combining arrows and bracket selectors	2

Table 4: Different errors in the program creation test using D2 and the number of participants (out of 6) who made that error.

tional brackets. Participants who incorrectly used additional brackets attributed their choice to the icons on the brackets. Two participants combined arrows with brackets to identify where the arrow is pointing. They thought that arrows indicate direction and that the bracket confines where the arrow points.

Fig. 9 shows different programs created by participants for the same task (P_B) using D1. The program in Fig. 9(a) is invalid as it places an object selector at a "future" location of the object. This error was avoided in Fig. 9(c), by attaching the place action to the object selector at the object's initial pose. Programs in Fig. 9(b) and (c) have alternative interpretations of the task description (*e.g.*, the assembly being at an exact location versus any point in a region), though these could result in the top part not being placed on the bottom part. This issue is avoided in Fig. 9(d) by using an exact location selector for placing both objects.

5.4 Impact of the Design Iteration

As mentioned in Sec. 5.1, participants performed significantly better in D2PRE compared to D1PRE in demonstration tests (Fig. 6). D2 appears to have successfully addressed issues with associating the paired brackets, misinterpretation of phrases, and looping (Table 2). However, misinterpretation of arrows as direction indicators persisted with D2. In addition, modified wordings and icons led to new confusions, albeit much less common. In their explanations during demonstrations, some participants noted matched coloring of paired brackets and the icon helped them understand that they represent a *box* together. Wordings on multi-object selectors attached to pick actions also proved helpful, as many participants commented they picked all objects in a loop because it says "everything" or "these". However, the same wording was problematic when attached to place actions. Some participants interpreted "these objects" as requiring placement on *all* objects. Despite doing better on demonstration tests, participants still had issues in generalization tests. Similar to D1, the dominant mental model flaw was treating all selectors as location selectors.

5.5 Impact of Instructions

Participants did significantly better on both demonstration and generalization tests knowing the meaning of blocks and how they form instructions. However, some issues remained even after instructions. Around 10% of participants still failed to loop over all objects when a pick action was attached to a region selector in the demonstration tests. In the generalization tests, mental model flaws associated with object versus location/region selectors were not fully addressed. In the program creation tests, instructions allowed avoiding unexpected combinations of blocks, such as using additional brackets or combining arrows and brackets.

6. DISCUSSION

Our studies demonstrate that situated tangible programming allows participants to program a robot with minimal or no instruction. We cannot draw a direct comparison with instructions given to participants for other end-user robot programming techniques in the literature; however, the ability for participants to program the robot without *any* instructions is unique.

The intuitiveness of situated tangible programming comes at the cost of expressiveness. Traditional text-based or visual programming languages allow much more complex boolean expression computations and flexible use of loops and conditionals. Programming by Demonstration allows defining new actions, whereas our approach is limited to preprogrammed actions. Nonetheless, our implementation captures many variations of pick and place tasks common in industrial settings.

The expressiveness of situated tangible programming could be increased by introducing additional blocks, such as customizable conditionals and loops. However, designing different blocks to be intuitive is challenging, as demonstrated in our studies. It is also possible to use situated tangible programming in conjunction with other end-user programming techniques. For instance, the user could define new actions with Programming by Demonstration, assign them to a block, and then use that block in a situated program.

Our studies involved programming without any system feedback or testing. Other end-user programming techniques often have *development environments* that aid the programming and debugging process. Similarly, we envision our system to provide feedback to users during programming. This could involve visualization of robot's perception, text representation of a program, and intuitive compile errors.

The most common challenge observed in our study was confusion between location and object selectors. This issue persisted across three studies with both designs in program comprehension and creation. This might have been because the shape of the block was much more salient than the color or text on it. Participants thought that the two selectors were the same because they were both arrows. This suggests semantically different blocks should have different shapes.

7. CONCLUSION

We introduce situated tangible programming: a new way of programming robots by placing tangible "blocks" in the robot's workspace. Blocks allow annotating objects, locations, or regions in the environment and specifying actions to be performed on them. We iteratively designed the blocks and introduced a proof-of-concept implementation of the system. Our evaluation shows that people can successfully comprehend and create many programs, even without any instructions. We demonstrate that design iterations can help improve intuitiveness of blocks and that people can interpret most programs correctly after minimal instructions. We identify common mental model flaws that lead to misinterpretations or creation of wrong programs, and we suggest possible improvements to address them.

Acknowledgements

This work was supported by the National Science Foundation Award IIS-1552427 "CAREER: End-User Programming of General-Purpose Robots."

8. REFERENCES

[1] Universal robots user manual. Universal robots website. https://universal-robots.com/media/8704/ur5_user_manual_gb.pdf, 2014.

[2] B. Akgun, M. Cakmak, J. W. Yoo, and A. L. Thomaz. Trajectories and keyframes for kinesthetic teaching: A human-robot interaction perspective. In *Proceedings of the seventh annual ACM/IEEE international conference on Human-Robot Interaction*, pages 391–398, 2012.

[3] S. Alexamdrova, M. Cakmak, K. Hsaio, and L. Takayama. Robot programming by demonstration with interactive action visualizations. In *Robotics: Science and Systems (RSS)*, 2014.

[4] S. Alexandrova, Z. Tatlock, and M. Cakmak. Roboflow: A flow-based visual programming language for mobile manipulation tasks. In *2015 IEEE International Conference on Robotics and Automation (ICRA)*, pages 5537–5544. IEEE, 2015.

[5] D. Anderson, J. L. Frankel, J. Marks, D. Leigh, E. Sullivan, J. Yedidia, and K. Ryall. Building virtual structures with physical blocks. In *Proceedings of the 12th annual ACM symposium on User interface software and technology*, pages 71–72. ACM, 1999.

[6] M. Burnett. Visual programming. *Wiley Encyclopedia of Electrical and Electronics Engineering*, 1999.

[7] R. Cantrell, P. Schermerhorn, and M. Scheutz. Learning actions from human-robot dialogues. In *2011 RO-MAN*, pages 125–130. IEEE, 2011.

[8] R. Fang, M. Doering, and J. Y. Chai. Embodied collaborative referring expression generation in situated human-robot interaction. In *Proceedings of the Tenth Annual ACM/IEEE International Conference on Human-Robot Interaction*, pages 271–278. ACM, 2015.

[9] K. Fischer, F. Kirstein, L. C. Jensen, N. Kr, K. Kukli, M. V. aus der Wieschen, T. R. Savarimuthu, et al. A comparison of types of robot control for programming by demonstration. In *2016 11th ACM/IEEE International Conference on Human-Robot Interaction (HRI)*, pages 213–220. IEEE, 2016.

[10] D. Gallardo, C. F. Julià, and S. Jorda. Turtan: A tangible programming language for creative exploration. In *Tabletop*, pages 89–92. Citeseer, 2008.

[11] D. F. Glas, T. Kanda, and H. Ishiguro. Human-robot interaction design using interaction composer: Eight years of lessons learned. In *The Eleventh ACM/IEEE International Conference on Human Robot Interation*, pages 303–310. IEEE Press, 2016.

[12] M. S. Horn and R. J. Jacob. Designing tangible programming languages for classroom use. In *Proceedings of the 1st international conference on Tangible and embedded interaction*, pages 159–162. ACM, 2007.

[13] J. Huang, T. Lau, and M. Cakmak. Design and evaluation of a rapid programming system for service robots. In *2016 11th ACM/IEEE International Conference on Human-Robot Interaction (HRI)*, pages 295–302. IEEE, 2016.

[14] T. Kollar, S. Tellex, D. Roy, and N. Roy. Toward understanding natural language directions. In *Human-Robot Interaction (HRI), 2010 5th ACM/IEEE International Conference on*, pages 259–266. IEEE, 2010.

[15] S. Lauria, G. Bugmann, T. Kyriacou, and E. Klein. Mobile robot programming using natural language. *Robotics and Autonomous Systems*, 38(3):171–181, 2002.

[16] T. Lozano-Perez. Robot programming. *Proceedings of the IEEE*, 71(7):821–841, 1983.

[17] M. Luria, G. Hoffman, B. Megidish, O. Zuckerman, and S. Park. Designing vyo, a robotic smart home assistant: Bridging the gap between device and social agent. In *Robot and Human Interactive Communication (RO-MAN), 2016 25th IEEE International Symposium on*, pages 1019–1025. IEEE, 2016.

[18] C. Matuszek, L. Bo, L. Zettlemoyer, and D. Fox. Learning from unscripted deictic gesture and language for human-robot interactions. In *AAAI*, pages 2556–2563, 2014.

[19] C. Matuszek, D. Fox, and K. Koscher. Following directions using statistical machine translation. In *Proceedings of the 5th ACM/IEEE international conference on Human-robot interaction*, pages 251–258. IEEE Press, 2010.

[20] S. Mohn and J. Laird. Learning goal-oriented hierarchical tasks from situated interactive instruction. In *Proceedings of the The Twenty-eighth National Conference on Artificial Intelligence (AAAI)*, 2014.

[21] A. Mohseni-Kabir, C. Rich, S. Chernova, C. L. Sidner, and D. Miller. Interactive hierarchical task learning from a single demonstration. In *Proceedings of the Tenth Annual ACM/IEEE International Conference on Human-Robot Interaction*, pages 205–212. ACM, 2015.

[22] H. Newton-Dunn, H. Nakano, and J. Gibson. Block jam: a tangible interface for interactive music. In *Proceedings of the 2003 conference on New interfaces for musical expression*, pages 170–177. National University of Singapore, 2003.

[23] S. Niekum, S. Chitta, A. Barto, B. Marthi, and S. Osentoski. Incremental semantically grounded learning from demonstration. In *Robotics: Science and Systems*, volume 9, 2013.

[24] S. Niekum, S. Osentoski, G. Konidaris, and A. G. Barto. Learning and generalization of complex tasks from unstructured demonstrations. In *2012 IEEE/RSJ International Conference on Intelligent Robots and Systems (IROS)*, pages 5239–5246, 2012.

[25] T. Sapounidis, S. Demetriadis, and I. Stamelos. Evaluating children performance with graphical and tangible robot programming tools. *Personal and Ubiquitous Computing*, 19(1):225–237, 2015.

[26] E. Schweikardt and M. D. Gross. roblocks: a robotic construction kit for mathematics and science education. In *Proceedings of the 8th international conference on Multimodal interfaces*, pages 72–75. ACM, 2006.

[27] L. She, Y. Cheng, J. Y. Chai, Y. Jia, S. Yang, and N. Xi. Teaching robots new actions through natural language instructions. In *The 23rd IEEE International Symposium on Robot and Human Interactive Communication*, pages 868–873. IEEE, 2014.

[28] A. Sipitakiat and N. Nusen. Robo-blocks: designing debugging abilities in a tangible programming system for early primary school children. In *Proceedings of the 11th International Conference on Interaction Design and Children*, pages 98–105. ACM, 2012.

[29] M. Tykal, A. Montebelli, and V. Kyrki. Incrementally assisted kinesthetic teaching for programming by demonstration. In *The Eleventh ACM/IEEE International Conference on Human Robot Interation*, pages 205–212. IEEE Press, 2016.

[30] S. Zhao, K. Nakamura, K. Ishii, and T. Igarashi. Magic cards: a paper tag interface for implicit robot control. In *Proceedings of the SIGCHI Conference on Human Factors in Computing Systems*, pages 173–182. ACM, 2009.

Not Your Cup of Tea? How Interacting With a Robot Can Increase Perceived Self-efficacy in HRI and Evaluation

Astrid M. Rosenthal-von der Pütten, Nikolai Bock & Katharina Brockmann

Social Psychology: Media and Communication, University of Duisburg Essen, Forsthausweg 2, 47057 Duisburg, Germany

a.rosenthalvdpuetten@uni-due.de; {nikolai.bock, katharina.brockmann}@stud.uni-due.de

ABSTRACT

The goal of this work is to explore the influence of do-it-yourself customization of a robot on technologically experienced students and unexperienced elderly users' perceived self-efficacy in HRI, uncertainty, and evaluation of the robot and interaction. We introduce the Self-Efficacy in HRI Scale and present two experimental studies. In study 1 (students, *n*=60) we found that any interaction with the robot increased self-efficacy, regardless of whether this interaction involves customization or not. Moreover, individual increases in self-efficacy predict more positive evaluations. In a second study with elderly users (*n*=60) we could not replicate the general positive effect of the interaction on self-efficacy. Again, we did not find the hypothesized stronger effect of customization on self-efficacy, nor did we find that relationship between self-efficacy increase and evaluation. We discuss limitations of the setting and for questionnaire design for elderly participants.

Keywords

Human-robot interaction; self-efficacy, experimental study; elderly users; robot teaching; technology acceptance; do-it-yourself

1. INTRODUCTION

The common future vision of companion robots is one of fully adaptive systems that adjust to new tasks, new situational contexts, and new user needs in real-time, using diverse resources of information. Ideally, this happens without a greater involvement of the user in the sense that he or she has to have certain skills to adjust or customize the robot to their needs. This is especially important for the predominantly targeted user group of elderly people who might not have sufficient expertise in complex technology. However, creating fully adaptive robots requires a lot of effort, is resource-intensive and poses limitations in various ways. Moreover, it is questionable whether perfect adaptivity is needed for the robot to be used efficiently and accepted by users. In contrast, adjusting and customizing a robot to one's own needs might have a positive influence, since do-it-yourself experiences (DIY) can lead to higher self-efficacy, probably creating higher acceptance and thereby possibly leading to a more constant usage of these systems. In the area of human-computer interaction (HCI) it was found that self-efficacy (the extent or strength of one's belief in one's own ability to complete tasks and reach goals, [2]), amongst other factors such as perceived ease of use and perceived usefulness, predicts usage tendencies [10]. Self-efficacy can be positively influenced by enactive attainment or in other words, the experience of mastery. This was previously used in pedagogical contexts for the transfer of technological competencies [1, 24] and could also be used to introduce socially-assistive technologies to unexperienced users. By giving the opportunity to customize systems to one's own preferences, we might increase perceived self-efficacy and thereby increase acceptance of that socially-assistive technology. Moreover, regarding different categories of products, studies have shown that consumers value those products higher that they have assembled or designed on their own compared to equivalent ready-made products, a phenomenon also known as "IKEA"-effect [29]. This phenomenon has also been found regarding the use of technologies and especially robots [17, 22]. The goal of this work is therefore, to study the influence of the adaptability or customizability of a robot through users on their self-efficacy in HRI and likewise, more positive evaluations. For this purpose, we developed a new measure, the Self-Efficacy in Human-Robot Interaction Scale (SE-HRI) which we describe in the following. Next, the questionnaire has been tested with two different samples in two experimental studies. In the first study, we tested the questionnaire and the hypotheses that a) any interaction increases self-efficacy in HRI and that b) this effect is strongest for interactions involving DIY customization of a robot. In the second study, we tested the questionnaire with a group of technologically unexperienced users of the age group 60+, because seniors are a major target group for future companion technologies. In this second study, we further explored the possible differences of what we call mediated-customization and DIY-customization.

HRI '17, March 06-09, 2017, Vienna, Austria

© 2017 ACM. ISBN 978-1-4503-4336-7/17/03…$15.00

DOI: http://dx.doi.org/10.1145/2909824.3020251

1.1 Self-Efficacy in Human-Robot Interaction

Self-efficacy has been defined by Bandura as "people's judgments of their capabilities to organize and execute courses of action required to attain designated types of performances. It is concerned not with the skills one has but with judgments of what one can do with whatever skills one possesses" [3]. Self-efficacy can be altered via various mechanisms, with enactive mastery experiences being the most effective ones since they serve as indicators of capability. Within the field of HCI, quite a number of studies have shown the influence of computer self-efficacy on diverse outcome variables such as performance [9, 15], ease of use [38], system use [9, 23], and early adoption [7]. Since self-efficacy was found to be predictive for using intentions in HCI studies, it is reasonable to assume a similar correlation in the field of human-robot interaction (HRI). Self-efficacy estimations are, however, domain specific meaning that a person can expose high self-efficacy in one domain (e.g. general computer use), but low self-efficacy in other domains (e.g. smart phone use, programming, interacting with a robot). Therefore, even users with high scores in computer self-efficacy might score low in their self-efficacy expectations regarding HRI. This might, however, not have been detected so far due to the lack of an adequate instrument capturing self-efficacy in HRI. For these reasons, we developed the Self-Efficacy in HRI Scale (SE_HRI, [31]). Self-efficacy in HRI is regarded as a state variable that can change according to the influential factors identified by Bandura [2], especially with the experience of mastery in HRI. We created a German and an English version of the scale with initially 50 items. We conducted three surveys to develop and validate the measure of Self-Efficacy in HRI. In a first study (n = 201), exploratory factor analysis revealed a two-factorial (factors perceived self-efficacy and loss of control) solution with good reliability. Confirmatory factor analysis did not confirm the two-factorial structure. Instead, it revealed a better model fit for a one-factorial solution for the German (second survey, n = 450) and the English version (third survey, n = 209) of the scale with good indices for convergent and divergent validity. The final questionnaire contains 18 items and was used in the studies presented in this paper. For a more detailed description of the scale development process we refer you to [31].

1.2 DIY and Technology Acceptance

Since socially-assistive robots are not yet market-ready, there is no information on abandonment rates for this kind of technology, nor is there reliable information on how high initial adoption rates will be. Regarding assistive technologies in general, Hurst et al. [22] discuss reasons for low acceptance rates and how they might be overcome by DIY approaches for the design of assistive technologies, since even essential devices such as hearing aids suffer a very high abandonment rate of up to 75%. Philips and Zhao identified factors for technology abandonment such as: how easy users can obtain devices, whether they were involved in the selection process, how well the device performs, and whether or not users' needs changed before or during usage [30]. It is not surprising that customized devices better meet users' needs. Previous work has discussed the need for personalization of robots to their users' needs [12], too. Lee [26] summarizes that personalization in HRI includes the customization of a robot's appearance or personality, or task preferences. Lee et al. demonstrated that a robot that offered personalized services (snack delivery) based on users' prior interactions with the robot improved rapport, cooperation, and engagement with the robot during service encounters. Saunders et al. [35] enabled participants to teach a robot human activities in a smart home and teach it to carry out behaviors in response to these activities. The authors state that "rather than passively accepting imposed solutions to a particular need, the user actively participates in formulating with the robot their own solutions and thus remains dominant of the technology and is empowered, physically, cognitively, and socially." (p.27). These are indicators that automatic personalization (robot adapts to user) has positive outcomes, but also that being actively involved in customization is can be beneficial.

Against this background, it should be our goal to take these mechanisms into account that might prevent high dropout rates of the usage of socially-assistive robot in advance and therefore screen for solutions in related fields. Hurst et al. state "that adoption rates can be improved by empowering individuals to create and modify their own Assistive Technology rather than being forced to rely on "off-the-shelf" products." (p. 11). In this regard, the researchers propose a DIY approach. It is indeed noteworthy that creating and building a device on one's own, further creates feelings of increased self-efficacy. Due to the experience of mastery when customizing, users might in consequence be more likely to adopt the technology. Hands-on experience is beneficial in many ways. In HRI it is most often used in educational contexts to increase self-efficacy when teaching students or to pre-service teachers how to program [1,25]. However, hands-on or DIY experiences also foster HRI in more social dimensions. For instance, Groom et al. [17] found that, if participants interacted with a robot they had constructed themselves, in comparison to interacting with a robot that had been built by another person, they showed greater overlap in terms of personality with the robot, they liked the robot more, and reported to be more attached to it. In this study, all participants built a robot, but only half of them interacted with this robot afterwards, while the other half interacted with another robot built by someone else. Accordingly, all participants had hands-on experience and the chance to learn about the functions of the robot. As Groom et al. conclude, this suggests that there is something fundamental about using the robot built by oneself before. Stadler et al. [36] transferred this research into a Programming by Demonstration scenario, in which participants either interacted with a robot whose behaviors were previously trained by themselves or trained by another person. Again participants rated the robot to be more similar to themselves when they interacted with a robot with behavior modules that they believed they had trained the robot themselves before. This was also superior to interacting with a robot that actually used the self-trained module but was introduced as using a module trained by a stranger. De Graf (2015) reported a longitudinal study with an entertainment robot. Participants who adopted the technology in the long run and reached the final stage in the technology adoption process were the ones who had adapted the robot to their personal needs (within the limitations given by the device [16]). Similarly, in an ethnographic study with Roombas in people's homes, Fink et al. (2013) found that "some households were not willing to engage in the effort of learning how to optimally use the robot and their process of adoption stopped in this stage" [14]. Only one of these reviewed studies reports age differences. Saunders et al. [35] found that older participants found the system more difficult to use than the younger participants, i.e. teaching the robot via the provided interface was perceived as being more complicated by older users. These users also preferred if the robot would be already set up by someone else before usage. Hence, customizing a robot on one's own is a relatively unexplored topic especially regarding different age groups. Moreover, it has not been studied how DIY customization differs from mediated customization (e.g., a service provider that sets up the robot according to the wishes of the user).

1.3 Using DIY Customization to Reduce Uncertainty in HRI

HRI is still a mystery to a lot of potential future users. On the one hand, users have a lot of expectations of what a robot can do, how it might communicate, and what actions it is able to perform. On the other hand, users are aware that their knowledge is mainly generated from science fiction [32]. Thus, especially technologically naive users experience high levels of uncertainty when confronted with the possibility to interact with a robot. Admittedly, every new encounter, also with fellow humans, is affected by uncertainty. Hence, the primary goal in initial interactions is to reduce uncertainty. According to Berger and Calabrese, this can be achieved by finding causal structures to explain the own behavior and that of others [6] and increase predictability of behaviors. Actions of oneself or others at one time are explained retroactively, i.e., based on what came before. But these actions also serve as the basis for predicting future responses. Every action and reaction is part of an information gathering process to reduce uncertainty in interaction. Attributional confidence, either in retroactive explanations of behavior or in proactive predictions of behavior, is discussed as a way of operationalizing uncertainty [8]. Indeed, it has been argued that people have "an intrinsic need to deal with the environment" ([40], p. 318), to develop an "effective familiarity" with it (p. 321), that they are motivated to master their uncertain environment by increasing its predictability and controllability. Customizing a robot and thereby understanding and also determining at least part of its behavior should increase attributional confidence and thereby decrease uncertainty. In other words, the possibility to determine the robots following behavior should give participants the sensation that they are able to predict the robot's behavior more reliably.

1.4 Research Objectives

The goal of this study is to explore the influence of (DIY) customization of a robot on technologically experienced students and unexperienced elderly users' perceived self-efficacy in HRI, uncertainty, and system evaluations. We assume that a number of different mechanisms contribute to technology acceptance. Receiving detailed information on a robot's capabilities should enable the users to better predict what to expect from the robot. Within the framework of Berger and Calabrese, this necessary information is gathered during interaction. In this regard, any interaction should reduce uncertainty. However, it seems that the amount of information or the objective quality of information does not necessarily correspond to uncertainty reduction [6]. This means that more information or objectively better information does not necessarily lead to higher uncertainty reduction. It is the perceived quality of information that contributes to uncertainty reduction. We assume that customizing the robot to one's own preferences is perceived as more valuable information (for instance, compared to an information fact sheet about the robot) because the user can at least in some part determine the behavior of the robot and has a basis to build his or her predictions on. Hence, customizing the robot should decrease uncertainty and result in higher attributional confidence and thus, also in more favorable evaluations of the robot and the interaction. Moreover, the literature suggests that hands-on experience and especially interacting with something that you constructed or customized yourself (i.e. compared to having someone customize a system for you) leads to more favorable outcomes, such as increased technology adoption and more favorable evaluations [17, 36]. In the following we present two studies to explore these assumptions.

2. STUDY 1

In the first study, student participants engaged in a social interaction with the Nao robot in a household related setting. The aim of this interaction was to create five different dishes, each based on three different ingredients, with the robot's help. Preceding this social interaction, participants either a) *trained the robot* (training interaction) which ingredients fit into which dish, b) simply *showed the robot all items* upon request in order to check whether all study materials are present (non-training interaction), or c) *read a fact sheet* about the robot's capabilities. We expected that interacting with a robot increases self-efficacy and decreases perceived loss of control. Moreover, we hypothesized that actively teaching or training the robot leads to even stronger effects. However, because of our assumption that the interaction itself, regardless of the customization, affects self-efficacy, we needed to control for the effect of the prior interaction within the training interaction group. Hence, we added the condition non-training interaction group in which participants also engage in two interactions with the robot, but with no possibility to customize the robot.

H1: Participants will report higher self-efficacy and lower loss of control at the end of the experiment compared to the baseline measure.

H2: Participants who actively trained the robot will state higher perceived self-efficacy and lower loss of control directly after the training (H2a) as well as at the end of the experiment (H2b) than participants who engaged in the interaction without training or participants who read a technical information sheet.

H3: Individual changes in self-efficacy predict evaluations of the robot. Greater increases lead to more positive evaluations.

2.1 Experimental Design and Setting

We used a 3x3 mixed design with three experimental groups (training interaction group, non-training interaction group, control group) and repeated measures on participants' self-reported self-efficacy and loss of control in HRI (baseline, after experimental treatment, after social interaction). All participants in both studies did engage with Aldebaran's Nao robot in a household related task (in the following referred to as social interaction scenario). Participants were asked to imagine they would have visitors later that day for dinner and want to find a recipe based on the foods they have in stock. The aim of the interaction was to create five different dishes, each based on three different ingredients, with the robot's help. Participants took a seat and the Nao robot and twelve different ingredients were placed on the table in front of them. As the robot had knowledge about different dishes and which ingredients fit to which dishes, it was the participants' task to show Nao three of the twelve different ingredients. The Nao would then give a recommendation for a recipe alongside pointing out what foods are possibly missing and have to be bought before preparation of the dish can begin. Preceding this social interaction scenario, participants underwent different treatments in three experimental groups.

Control group. Participants in the control group read a two-page long information sheet about the robot, its technical parameters, and social abilities.

Training interaction group. Participants in the training group trained the robot themselves to categorize foods according to their preferences. They were told to teach the robot which ingredient fits into which dish, so that the robot Nao could use this knowledge in the social interaction scenario later on. Participants were confronted with Nao (with colored dots on its hands to indicate where to touch the robot to give positive or negative reward for his answer) and twelve different ingredients in front of them on the table (cf. Figure 1). Participants showed each ingredient to the Nao at least five times. Each time Nao would ask whether the ingredient might fit into one of the five recipe categories. The participants had to provide feedback on whether Nao's suggestion has been right. They touched the robot's left or right hand in order to provide negative or positive feedback, respectively. Participants were told that Nao would use this new knowledge in the second interaction. Hence, the robot's recommendations are ostensibly based on the training, however, the robot's recommendations were based on a hardwired decision tree to guarantee the same outcome for all participants. In sum, participants could connect one ingredient to different recipe categories as well as one recipe category could contain several ingredients. We assumed that participants would take the training serious and would not intentionally compromise the learning outcome of the robot. We checked the video material and found that none of the participants trained or indicated an unexpected ingredient-category pair (e.g., chocolate-soup). Hence, their customization of the robot matched our programming.

Non-training interaction group. Participants in the non-training interaction group were asked to make sure that all ingredients needed for the following social interaction scenario were in place. During this condition, the Nao robot asked participants to show the items and then confirmed that the item was present (e.g., "We have to make sure that the pasta is here. Please show me the pasta. - participant shows pasta- Great. The pasta is here.").

Figure 1: Set-up for the training and social interaction

2.2 Participants and Procedure

Sixty (38 female, 22 male) volunteers participated in this study. All participants were university students recruited on campus. They were aged between 18 and 39 years (M=22.42, SD=4.08). All participants owned a personal computer and -with one exception-owned a smartphone. Participants had moderate experiences with robots: none of them has a robot at home, 51% had previously seen a real robot (in a museum), 48% had previously been interacting with a robot (e.g., Roomba, museum robot), and only two participants stated that they had previously programmed a robot. Upon arrival participants signed informed consent. They were seated in front of a computer and completed a web-based questionnaire consisting of demographic data, their prior knowledge of robots, and the Self-Efficacy in HRI Scale. Students completed some more questionnaires that served to validate the developed Scale and are not part of this paper. After that, depending on the respective experimental condition, participants either a) read an information sheet about the robot, b) showed the robot the different objects in order to ensure are materials are present, or c) trained the robot ingredient-recipe matches. Afterwards, they completed the Self-Efficacy in HRI Scale a second time before they interacted with Nao in the household related task described previously. At the end of the interaction, participants filled in the remaining questionnaires evaluating Nao and the interaction as well as the Self-Efficacy in HRI Scale for a third time. Participants were debriefed, compensated with €10, and thanked for participation.

2.3 Dependent Variables

The following dependent variables were consistently used in both studies and are therefore described only once. Reliability measures are presented in table 1 for Self-Efficacy in HRI and loss of control. All other reliability scores for both studies are presented in table 3.

2.3.1 Self-efficacy in HRI & Loss of Control

Participants self-efficacy was measured using the SE-HRI scale [31]. Self-efficacy in HRI is regarded as a variable that can change according to the influential factors identified by Bandura [2], especially with the experience of mastery. SE-HRI was measured at the beginning of the experiment (T1), after the experimental treatment (T2), and at the end of the experiment after the social interaction scenario (T3). The SE-HRI is a newly developed instrument. In the first phase of scale development, we identified two factors, namely *perceived self-efficacy* and *loss of control*. During the process of validation, the second factor was omitted since *loss of control* did not seem to be the negative side of self-efficacy, but a different concept closer to locus of control. Self-efficacy should be distinguished from locus of control, which refers to the belief whether outcomes are determined by one's own actions or by other forces that are outside of what one can control [4] and not to the strength of one's belief in one's own ability to complete tasks and reach goals. However, locus of control is a very interesting concept to study in context of self-efficacy expectations and we decided to include the omitted subscale in the experiments presented in this paper to explore judgements of locus of control in HRI. The SE-HRI scale comprises 18 items (e.g., I can make a robot perform a specific task; I am very confident in my abilities to control a robot; I think I could adjust a robot the way, that it could help me in my daily life). We assessed people's sense of *loss of control* with three items (e.g., I do not have any control over what a robot is doing; I do not have any influence on how a robot behaves). Items on both scales were rated on a 6-point Likert scale from strongly disagree to strongly agree.

Table 1: Reliability scores for SE-HRI & Loss of Control

	Study 1 (T1/T2/T3)			Study 2 (T1/T2/T3)		
SE-HRI	.943	.954	.965	.971	.980	.974
Loss of Control	.822	.887	.971	.811	.918	.917

2.3.2 Evaluation of the Robot and the Interaction

Evaluation of the robot. For the evaluation of the robot, we used the Godspeed Questionnaire [5], a semantic differential with 20 bi-polar items which are rated on a 5-point scale. It contains five subscales of which we used the four subscales *Anthropomorphism* (attribution of a human form, characteristics, or behavior to nonhuman things; 5 items, e.g., machinelike-humanlike, unconscious-conscious), *Animacy* (perception of lifelikeness; 5 items, e.g., mechanical-organic), *Liking* (5 items, e.g., dislike-like), and *Perceived Intelligence* (5 items, e.g. incompetent-competent).

Person perception of the robot. Participants were also asked to evaluate the robot with regard to person perception on three dimensions (*Likability, Intelligence, and Autonomy),* indicating their agreement to 22 items on a 5-point Likert scale from "I do not agree at all" to "I fully agree." While the Godspeed Questionnaire aims at technology-specific or robot-specific evaluation dimensions (e.g., animacy and anthropomorphism), the person perception scale stems from social psychology research and has been used in prior work (cf. [33, 34]). The dimension *Likability* was measured with eleven items (likable, warm, cool-, pleasant, approachable, similar to me, familiar, I can ask the robot for advice, trustworthy, I would work together with the robot). *Intelligence* was measured using five items (dumb-, intelligent, competent, incompetent-, knowledgeable). *Autonomy* contained six items (not autonomous-, self-dependent, responsible for its actions, restricted in its abilities-, free, self-determined).

Evaluation of the interaction. The general evaluation of the interaction was assessed by eight items that asked for the participants' sense of control during the interaction, the enjoyment of the interaction, and whether participants would like to use a system like this for other tasks (cf. prior work [33, 34]) with a 5-point Likert-scale.

2.3.3 Attributional Confidence

We also wanted to know how confident participants were in their belief that they were correctly attributing the robot's feelings, intentions, and values, or in other words, how well they believed they knew the robot and could make predictions of its behavior. We used the attributional confidence scale [8] consisting of seven items rated on a 6-point Likert scale from "very unsure" up to "very sure".

2.4 Results

Self-efficacy in HRI. To test whether participants do not differ in initial self-efficacy, an ANOVA with the dependent factors perceived self-efficacy and loss of control at measurement T1 was conducted and it revealed no significant differences between conditions (for means and standard deviations cf. Table 1). However, we also estimated Bayes factors using Bayesian Information Criteria [39], comparing the fit of the data under the null hypothesis and the alternative hypothesis using R and the package BayesFactor by Richard D. Morey. The estimated Bayes factor (null/alternative) suggested that the data were 2.4 times more likely to occur under a model without including an effect of experimental condition, rather than a model with this factor (***H0***).

To explore whether the training and the social interaction have a positive effect on participants' perceived self-efficacy in HRI, we conducted split-plot ANOVAs with the group factor experimental condition (non-training vs. training vs. control) and repeated measures for *perceived self-efficacy.* We did the same for *loss of control.* We found a main effect for the repeated measures on both scales indicating that self-efficacy, but also loss of control, increased over the three measuring points (***H1***) and an interaction effect of the repeated measures of both scales with the experimental condition (perceived self-efficacy: $F(38/2) = 7.32$; $p < .001$; $\eta^2 = .204$; loss of control: $F(38/2) = 2.61$; $p = .039$; $\eta^2 = .084$, ***H2***). To further explore the nature of the interaction effects we conducted three separate ANOVAS on the two scales for the three experimental conditions, respectively. While the increase in self-efficacy was not significant for participants in the control group, neither for T2 after the information material nor for T3 after the social interaction, there were significant effects for the increase of perceived self-efficacy for participants in the training and in the non-training interaction groups. Participants reported significantly greater self-efficacy after the initial interaction session (either training or non-training) compared to the baseline and significantly greater self-efficacy after the social interaction compared to the baseline (training & non-training; cf. Table 2). Contrary to our hypothesis regarding loss of control (***H1***), we found that participants in the control condition reported significantly higher loss of control at the end of the experiment compared to the baseline measure. Moreover, participants in the training group reported significantly higher loss of control directly after the training compared to the baseline measure (cf. Table 2).

Evaluation of the robot and the interaction. We conducted ANOVAs with experimental group as independent variable and subscales of the Godspeed Questionnaire (Anthropomorphism, Animacy, Perceived Intelligence, Likability) and the Person Perception Scale (Likability, Intelligence, Autonomy) and Attributional Confidence as dependent variables. The evaluation of the robot and the interaction did not differ significantly between conditions, except for the two Intelligence variables, where post hoc test showed that the non-training group rated the robot as being significantly more intelligent than the control group (Perceived Intelligence: $p = .008$; Intelligence: $p = .003$; cf. Table 3).

Influence of self-efficacy on evaluation. We assumed that changes in perceived self-efficacy predict evaluations of the robot (***H3***) with greater increases leading to more positive evaluations. To address this hypothesis, we calculated self-efficacy deltas by subtracting perceived self-efficacy scores at T1 of those scores at T3 and conducted regression analyses with the self-efficacy deltas as predictors and the following dependent variables: Godspeed Questionnaire, Person Perception Scale, Attributional Confidence, and evaluation of the interaction. We found significant regression models for evaluation of the interaction, for Anthropomorphism, Animacy, Perceived Intelligence, Likability (all Godspeed), and Intelligence and Likability (Person Perception Scale), but no models for Autonomy and Attributional Confidence (cf. Table 3).

Table 2: Repeated measures ANOVAs for experimental conditions with dependent factors perceived self-efficacy and loss of control

			T1		T2		T3						T1<T2	T2<T3	T1<T3
			μ	*SD*	μ	*SD*	μ	*SD*	*F*	η^2	*p*	*N*	*p*	*p*	*p*
Study 1 Students *n*=60	Perceived self-efficacy	total	3.02	.93	3.66	.95	3.84	1.06	36.51	.382	**<.001**	60	**<.001**	.076	**<.001**
		control	3.31	.94	3.43	1.12	3.55	1.30	1.19	.059	.299	20	.498	1.00	.725
		non-training	2.70	.83	3.79	.73	4.05	.92	32.88	.634	**<.001**	20	**<.001**	.460	**<.001**
		training	3.04	.96	3.74	.97	3.93	.89	21.06	.526	**<.001**	20	**<.001**	.074	**<.001**
	Loss of control	total	2.53	.97	2.81	1.10	2.94	1.47	3.28	.053	.052	60	.075	1.00	.112
		control	2.67	1.07	2.75	1.23	3.50	1.67	5.95	.227	**.016**	20	1.00	**.034**	.075
		non-training	2.60	1.06	2.68	1.08	2.65	1.34	.04	.002	.962	20	1.00	1.00	1.00
		training	2.33	.75	3.00	.99	2.67	1.28	3.92	.171	**.028**	20	**.005**	.589	.719
Study 2 Seniors *n*=60	Perceived self-efficacy	total	3.46	1.31	3.46	1.43	3.70	1.42	3.95	.063	**.029**	60	1.00	**.006**	.088
		control	3.58	1.19	3.63	1.61	3.98	1.46	3.72	.164	**.034**	20	1.00	**.036**	.081
		med.-custom.[a]	3.43	1.31	3.16	1.16	3.45	1.20	1.74	.084	.188	20	.530	.334	1.00
		training	3.37	1.47	3.58	1.49	3.69	1.57	1.46	.071	.242	20	.941	.744	.606
	Loss of control	total	3.07	1.31	3.09	1.35	3.09	1.63	.01	.000	.988	60	1.00	1.00	1.00
		control	3.15	1.25	2.70	1.40	2.83	1.83	1.06	.053	.357	20	.091	1.00	1.00
		med.-custom.	2.80	1.19	3.40	1.25	2.92	1.55	1.59	.077	.216	20	.274	.652	1.00
		training	3.25	1.49	3.17	1.37	3.53	1.50	.94	.094	.410	20	1.00	.636	.990

Note: all ANOVAS used Bonferroni correction for multiple comparisons; a) mediated-customization

Table 3: Repeated measures ANOVAs for experimental conditions with dependent factors Godspeed-Questionnaire, Person Perception Questionnaire, Attributional Confidence, and Evaluation of Interaction; regression analyses with self-efficacy delta as predictor

	Reliability	control		non-training		training		ANOVAs			Regression analyses				
Study 1	α	μ	SD	μ	SD	μ	SD	F	η^2	p	N	β	F	T	p
GS-Anthropomorphism	.869	2.01	.97	2.26	.97	2.01	.77	0.54	.019	.584	60	.288	2.46	2.01	**.049**
GS-Animacy	.753	3.03	.76	3.05	.72	3.10	.57	0.54	.002	.947	60	.346	2.97	2.44	**.018**
GS-Perc. Intelligence	.867	2.92	.69	3.57	.73	3.37	.79	3.94	.121	**.025**	60	.341	7.42	2.55	**.013**
GS-Likability	.916	4.06	.74	4.44	.71	4.08	.79	1.71	.057	.190	60	.289	3.53	2.05	**.045**
PP-Intelligence	.892	2.84	1.01	3.74	.92	3.36	.84	4.73	.142	**.013**	60	.285	7.36	2.14	**.036**
PP-Likability	.923	2.80	.82	3.18	.76	3.23	.98	1.50	.050	.231	60	.405	5.47	2.95	**.005**
PP-Autonomy	.789	1.90	.66	1.98	.62	2.23	.79	1.21	.041	.306	60	.163	0.66	1.10	.274
Attributional Confidence	.760	36.65	22.11	35.98	17.17	38.98	17.99	0.14	.005	.874	60	.114	0.30	0.76	.447
Evaluation of Interaction	.899	3.23	.89	3.93	.74	3.54	1.03	2.98	.095	.059	60	.448	9.62	3.47	**.001**
	Reliability	control		mediated-customization		training		ANOVAs			Regression analyses				
Study 2	α	μ	SD	μ	SD	μ	SD	F	η^2	p	N	β	F	T	p
GS-Anthropomorphism	.809	2.33	1.05	2.40	.87	2.69	.85	.845	.029	.435	60	.206	2.08	1.61	.113
GS-Animacy	.801	3.26	.99	3.10	.82	3.45	.61	.905	.031	.410	60	.108	.60	.82	.413
GS-Perc. Intelligence	.827	3.65	.78	3.59	.83	3.98	.55	1.64	.054	.203	60	-.01	.99	-.07	.943
GS-Likability	.858	4.31	.66	4.14	.69	4.48	.42	1.56	.052	.219	60	.076	.54	.58	.565
PP-Intelligence	.859	3.65	1.11	3.48	.99	4.01	.62	1.68	.056	.195	60	.176	1.67	1.36	.178
PP-Likability	.838	3.33	.72	3.23	.71	3.41	.60	.377	.013	.688	60	.061	.18	.46	.649
PP-Autonomy	.752	1.89	.91	2.09	.81	2.22	.94	.713	.024	.494	60	.003	.70	.03	.980
Attributional Confidence	.862	3.31	1.16	3.19	1.25	3.41	1.17	.184	.006	.832	60	.142	.62	1.08	.283
Evaluation of Interaction	.862	3.88	.87	4.03	.72	4.19	.88	.715	.024	.494	60	.224	2.29	1.76	.085

3. STUDY 2

For the second study with elderly users, we slightly modified the experimental design by keeping the training condition and the control fact sheet condition, but replacing the non-training condition. Instead, we added one condition to explore in more detail the effect of "mediated" versus "DIY" customization. In this additional condition, participants customized the robot with the help of a "programmer".

H4: Participants will report higher self-efficacy and lower loss of control at the end of the experiment compared to the baseline measure.

H5: Customization of any kind leads to higher perceived self-efficacy and lower loss of control.

H6: Participants who actively trained the robot will state higher perceived self-efficacy and lower loss of control directly after the training (H3a) as well as at the end of the experiment (H3b) than participants who read a technical information sheet or customized a robot with the help of a programmer.

H7: Changes in perceived self-efficacy predict evaluations of the robot. Bigger increases lead to more positive evaluations.

3.1 Experimental Design & Setting

The study setting, the study procedure and the measured used for this study were the same as for study 1. Moreover, similar to study 1, we used a 3x3 mixed design with three experimental groups and repeated measures on participants' self-reported self-efficacy and perceived loss of control in HRI (three measuring points: baseline, after experimental treatment, after social interaction). We also used the control condition (reading a fact sheet) and the training interaction condition. We replaced the non-training interaction condition with the so-called mediated-customization condition (mediated customization by the help of a "programmer").

Mediated-customization group. Participants in the mediated-customization group had to made decisions concerning the twelve ingredients. Participants were seated in front of a web-based questionnaire. Each of the twelve ingredients were represented by a picture and presented alongside the five categories of possible dishes. The twelve ingredients were: apple, cucumber, paprika, flour, chocolate, noodles, eggs, meat, broccoli, cheese, clear soup, and tomato sauce. The five categories were: soup, salad, cake, pasta, and casserole. Participants had to decide whether or not the respective food might serve as an ingredient in each of five categories of recipes. These individual sets of decisions were submitted to the experimenter and ostensibly "programmed" into the robot before the social interaction started.

3.2 Participants and Procedure

We focused on the target group of seniors and recruited participants aged 60 and above. Sixty volunteers (35 female, 25 male) participated in this study aged between 60 and 84 years (M=68.02, SD=5.38). The participants were recruited using flyers in pharmacies, bakeries, bookstores, and recreation centers for seniors. Some participants were recruited online via Facebook. Participants were randomly assigned to one of the three conditions. Eighty-eight percent of the participants owned a personal computer and 73% owned a smartphone. Participants had low experiences with robots: four of them had a robot at home (Roomba vacuum cleaning robot), 38,3% had previously seen a real robot (for instance in a museum), five participants stated that they had previously been interacting with a robot (four referring to the Roomba) and four participants stated that they had previously programmed a robot (all referring to the Roomba).

3.3 Results

Self-efficacy in HRI. Again, we tested whether participants do not differ in initial self-efficacy by means of an ANOVA with the dependent factors perceived self-efficacy and loss of control at measurement T1. Again we did not find significant differences between conditions (for means and standard deviations cf. Table 2). The estimated Bayes factor (null/alternative) suggested that the data were 7.1 times more likely to occur under a model without including an effect of experimental condition, rather than a model with this factor (***H0***). To explore whether the *mediated customization* (mediated-customization condition – help of programmer), the *DIY customization* (training condition), and/or the social interaction have a positive effect on participants' perceived self-efficacy in HRI, we conducted split-plot ANOVAs with the group factor experimental condition (control vs. mediated-customization vs. training) and repeated measures for *perceived self-efficacy*. The same tests were run for *loss of control*. We found a main effect for the repeated measures on *perceived self-efficacy* indicating that self-efficacy increased over the three measuring points (***H4***, cf. Table 2), but no effect for the experimental condition (***H5 & H6***). Consistent with the analysis of study 1, we conducted three separate ANOVAs on the two scales for the three experimental conditions, respectively. In contrast to the previous study, seniors in the control group showed a significant increase in perceived self-efficacy after T3 compared to T2, showing that the interaction with the robot led to changes in self-efficacy. However, participants in the two customization conditions (mediated-customization and training) did not report significant changes in self-efficacy, although there is a (not significant) slight upward trend of self-efficacy observable in the means in the training condition. Moreover, there were no differences regarding *loss of control* in the mediated-customization and training conditions, also contradicting ***H4*** (cf. Table 2).

Evaluation of the robot and the interaction. Similar to the previous study, there were no significant differences between conditions regarding the evaluation of the robot and the interaction (cf. Table 3).

Influence of self-efficacy on evaluation. Also for the seniors, we calculated self-efficacy deltas by subtracting perceived self-efficacy scores at T1 of those scores at T3 and conducted regression analyses with the self-efficacy deltas as predictor and the dependent variables from the Godspeed Questionnaire, Person Perception Scale, and Attributional Confidence. No significant regression models emerged (***H7***, cf. Table 3).

4. DISCUSSION

A common notion of current papers is that robots enter everyday life. We may be on the move, but still robots are -with a few exceptions like Roomba- mostly found in research labs and sometimes in small controlled field trials. Especially seniors are a major target group to use companion robots in the future, but unlike other possible user groups, they predominantly have no experiences with robots and might not know what to expect from robots. Regarding new technologies, older adults often raise concerns relating to the user-friendliness of the devices and the need for training tailored to older learners [13]. Compared to younger adults, older adults are also less likely to use new technologies in general, but this effect is mediated by self-efficacy beliefs (e.g., computer self-efficacy [11, 37]). Older adults also seem to have comparably high levels of anxieties regarding the interaction with a robot. What we observed when recruiting seniors for this experimental HRI study (for instance, for the study reported in this paper), is that people are very unsure what to expect from robots. Some mention to be afraid of not being capable of dealing with a robot, to break it, or to somehow "fail". They think they can only participate if they first acquire specific knowledge or skills. Indeed, this dimension of concerns is already reflected in some technology acceptance models regarding robots, for instance, the ALMERE Model [20] in which the construct of anxiety is represented with items such as "If I should use the robot, I would be afraid to make mistakes with it" and "If I should use the robot, I would be afraid to break something". Different studies using the model showed that older adults scored relatively high in this dimension [18, 19, 21, 27] and that age is correlated to anxiety levels [18]. Overall, it seems that a lot of seniors have quite low self-efficacy perceptions regarding HRI. This is unfortunate since HCI studies have repeatedly shown that increased computer self-efficacy leads to, for instance, better performance [9, 15] and early adoption [7]. We assumed that this correlation of self-efficacy and technology acceptance also holds true for HRI, however, there is no adequate instrument to measure self-efficacy in HRI. We introduced a new measure, the Self-Efficacy in Human-Robot Interaction Scale, that captures users' *perceived self-efficacy* in interactions with robots. The scale was then put to use in two experimental studies. The studies presented in this paper were conducted simultaneously to the process of developing the questionnaire and also served as a testbed to validate and refine the questionnaire itself. As a second goal, we wanted to investigate factors that might increase self-efficacy in HRI. Since enactive mastery is the most influential factor in increasing self-efficacy judgements, we assume that successful interactions with a robot should lead to more positive self-efficacy evaluations. Moreover, one big issue in HRI is the adaptability or customizability of socially assistive robots. Hence, somehow customizing or adapting the robot should lead to increased self-efficacy. We developed an experimental paradigm and tested this assumed influence of the adaptability or customizability of a robot through users on their perceived self-efficacy in HRI and, related to this, more positive evaluations, in two studies.

First, we tested the new questionnaire with a student sample. Students interacted with the Nao robot in a household related task (trying to find recipes for the food in stock in order to plan dishes for a dinner with invited guests). Prior to this interaction, they either a) read a fact sheet, b) engaged in an interaction in which they trained the robot relevant information for the following household related task, or c) engaged in a simple interaction without training the robot. We found the hypothesized effects: the interaction with the robot in the household-related task indeed led to increased self-efficacy (***H1***). There was an interaction effect with the experimental condition showing that a prior interaction to this social interaction scenario was significantly affecting self-efficacy. However, there was no significant difference between the non-training and the training interaction group leading to the conclusion that customizing the robot did not have the hypothesized stronger effect (***H2***). Interestingly, the interaction with the robot did not decrease perceived loss of control (***H1***). Indeed, it seems that albeit higher self-efficacy participants might not have had the feeling that they were in control of the interaction – maybe because of the interaction being very structured and the dialog being led by the robot. This is another indicator that perceived loss of control is a different concept which is more related to locus of control, just as assumed by [4] and corroborates our decision to omit the subscale of loss of control from the final scale. We also found that the individual increase in self-efficacy perceptions predicted positive evaluations of the robot and interactions (***H3***). This emphasizes the explanatory value of the SE-HRI scale as moderating or mediating variable in HRI studies. One limitation of this work is certainly the within design with three measuring points for the Self-efficacy in HRI Scale. However, if participants were trying to guess the hypothesis and answering accordingly, we should have observed similar self-efficacy increases in all conditions, since participants in the control condition received information about the robot and its capabilities and could have guessed that this was supposed to alter their ratings. This did not influence their self-efficacy statements. Hence, we do not think that our results are due to a "good subject effect" [28].

Simultaneously to the first study, a similar study was conducted with a group of technologically unexperienced users of the age group 60+. In this study we further explored the possible differences of customization with what we call *mediated-customization* and *DIY customization*. Instead of the *non-training interaction*, participants in a third experimental group customized the robot by the ostensible help of a programmer (*mediated-customization*), whom they told what knowledge they want the robot to have for the subsequent social interaction. While self-efficacy increased after the social interaction compared to the baseline (***H4***), we did not find an effect for prior interaction – regardless of the experimental treatment (*mediated-* or *DIY-customization,* ***H5***). Contrary to our hypotheses, mediated and DIY customization did not increase self-efficacy perceptions for the elderly users (***H6***) and individual increases in self-efficacy did not predict evaluations of the robot or the interaction (***H7***).

To our surprise, the findings of the first study could not be replicated. Considering the study by Saunders et al. [35], it seems that not all users (especially older users) prefer to customize a robot themselves. Some might not have the patience, regard it as inconvenient or might be unsure about their abilities to do so. It could be that these users would prefer that the robot is set up by another knowledgeable person (mediated customization). In the current work, we concentrated on the influence of different treatments on self-efficacy perceptions and not on whether and how users prefer to have a robot customized. It is also possible that older adults would benefit more from other treatments to increase self-efficacy expectations in HRI, such as social persuasion, vicarious experience (i.e. observing similar others interacting with a robot, [3]), or specialized trainings that are rather information based. However, it is also possible that the unexpected results are due to limitations of the study. We have to acknowledge that students are much more used to taking part in studies and filling in questionnaires. They know the answering schemes and how to interpret questionnaire instructions. With the senior sample we observed that participants had problems to understand the instructions. Some participants thought they should be coherent in their answers over the three measuring points. Some explicitly stated during the debriefing that they tried to remember their previous ratings and matched current ratings. In case we saw participants flipping back to previous pages (if they used a paper and pen based version), the experimenter intervened and explained the instructions again, but we certainly did not always detect if participants were biased by the same intend – to appear coherent in their answers. Moreover, some participants reported during the debriefing that they did not indicate their current self-efficacy. Instead, they believed that they would need certain skills to interact successfully with a robot. Hence, they did not regard themselves as capable of interacting with it at all and thought they needed some training. They based their assessment on this imagined training, in the sense of "If I had been trained to use a robot, then: I can make a robot perform a specific task… I am very confident in my abilities to control a robot…". In this context it is noteworthy that seniors unexpectedly rated their initial self-efficacy higher than students ($M = 3.46$ vs. $M = 3.02$). Extrapolating assumed self-efficacy after imagined training, however, is not the purpose of the questionnaire since it is meant to capture the current self-efficacy perception. Furthermore, we observed a tendency to extreme responding using predominantly the extreme values of the Likert scale (1 and 6) for a number of participants. In conclusion, the instructions should be made more explicit to the seniors: all Likert-points should be labelled (not only extremes), participants should know they have to indicate their current (not imagined) level of self-efficacy, that self-efficacy might change during the course of the experiment and hence, that they do not need to be consistent in their answers.

While some of the problems arose from the questionnaire, we think that others are due to the interactions themselves. The students had no problem to understand both tasks, to perform quite well, and also to see the goal behind the customization. They inferred that, although it is more work to train the robot now, it is beneficial for the future because the robot can make use of this knowledge in subsequent interactions and thereby suite the user's wishes. Although certainly not all, some seniors did not see the point in the training and interaction. For instance, one participant stated during the debriefing that she would have been quicker to find recipes without using the robot because she knows them all by heart. However, the robot would be more useful to men at her age because those were more unexperienced in cooking, in her view, and might need assistance of the robot. Customizing the robot to her preferences (e.g. preferred dishes for specific ingredients) seemed to be irrelevant to her. On the other hand, some older male participants were unable to cope with the task at hand. Although it seemed to be an easy task, these participants usually do not cook themselves and were not familiar with recipes and which ingredients are needed for them. Hence, the interaction might have been experienced as less successful. Altogether, we see that for different reasons this scenario was potentially not suitable for every individual in the senior study. Hence, one future goal should be to create an interaction scenario that is manageable for everyone and that is even more relevant to the users, in the sense that it touches a domain where user preferences are more diverse and crucial to be met by the robot. By this, users should be more eager to customize the robot according to their wishes.

5. CONCLUSION

We introduced the Self-Efficacy in HRI Scale and successfully applied the new measure in an experimental study with a student sample, showing that the overall experience to engage in an interaction with a robot leads to increased self-efficacy and more positive evaluations. We were not able to replicate this effect in a comparable study with a sample of elderly users. We identified a number of issues that can be addressed in the questionnaire design as well as in the design of the interaction scenario. For future directions we will work on the Self-Efficacy in HRI Scale and rework instructions and layout especially for older adults. We will design a scenario in which customization is more crucial to the user in order to make the scenario more relevant for all users.

6. ACKNOWLEDGEMENTS

This work was funded by the Science Support Center of the University of Duisburg-Essen. We want to thank the members of the Bürgerverein Ratingen Homberg e.V. for their help in the conduct of the study.

7. References

[1] Ahlgren, D. and Verner, I. 2009. Fostering Development of Students' Collective and Self-efficacy in Robotics Projects. In *Progress in Robotics*, J.-H. Kim, S. S. Ge, P. Vadakkepat, N. Jesse, A. Al Manum, S. Puthusserypady K, U. Rückert, J. Sitte, U. Witkowski, R. Nakatsu, T. Braunl, J. Baltes, J. Anderson, C.-C. Wong, I. Verner and D. Ahlgren, Eds. Communications in Computer and Information Science. Springer Berlin Heidelberg, Berlin, Heidelberg, 240–247. DOI=10.1007/978-3-642-03986-7_28.

[2] Bandura, A. 1977. Self-efficacy: Toward a unifying theory of behavioral change. *Psychological Review* 84, 2, 191–215.

[3] Bandura, A. 1986. The Explanatory and Predictive Scope of Self-Efficacy Theory. *Journal of Social and Clinical Psychology* 4, 3, 359–373.

[4] Bandura, A. 2006. Guide for constructing self-efficacy scales. *Self-efficacy beliefs of adolescents* 5, 307-337.

[5] Bartneck, C., Kulić, D., Croft, E., and Zoghbi, S. 2009. Measurement Instruments for the Anthropomorphism, Animacy, Likeability, Perceived Intelligence, and Perceived Safety of Robots. *Int J of Soc Robotics* 1, 1, 71–81.

[6] Berger, C. R. and Calabrese, R. J. 1975. Some explorations in initial interaction and beyond. Toward a developmental theory of interpersonal communication. *Human Comm Res* 1, 2, 99–112.

[7] Burkhardt, M. E. and Brass, D. J. 1990. Changing Patterns or Patterns of Change: The Effects of a Change in Technology on Social Network Structure and Power. *Administrative Science Quarterly* 35, 1, 104–127.

[8] Clatterbuck, G. W. 1979. Attributional confidence and uncertainty in initial interaction. *Human Comm Res* 5, 2, 147–157.

[9] Compeau, D. R. and Higgins, C. A. 1995. Application of Social Cognitive Theory to Training for Computer Skills. *Information Systems Research* 6, 2, 118–143.

[10] Compeau, D. R. and Higgins, C. A. 1995. Computer Self-Efficacy: Development of a Measure and Initial Test. *MIS Quarterly* 19, 2, 189–211.

[11] Czaja, S. J., Charness, N., Fisk, A. D., Hertzog, C., Nair, S. N., Rogers, W. A., and Sharit, J. 2006. Factors Predicting the Use of Technology: Findings From the Center for Research and Education on Aging and Technology Enhancement (CREATE). *Psychology and aging* 21, 2, 333–352.

[12] Dautenhahn, K. 2004. Robots We Like to Live With? - A Developmental Perspective on a Personalized, Life-Long Robot Companion. *Proceedings of the 13th IEEE International Workshop on Robot and Human Interactive Communication (RO-MAN 2004)*, 17–22.

[13] Demiris, G., Rantz, M. J., Aud, M. A., Marek, K. D., Tyrer, H. W., Skubic, M., and Hussam, A. A. 2004. Older adults' attitudes towards and perceptions of 'smart home' technologies: a pilot study. *Medical Informatics and the Internet in Medicine* 29, 2, 87–94.

[14] Fink, J., Bauwens, V., Kaplan, F., and Dillenbourg, P. 2013. Living with a Vacuum Cleaning Robot. *International Journal of Social Robotics* 5, 3, 389–408.

[15] Gist, M. E., Schwoerer, C., and Rosen, B. 1989. Effects of alternative training methods on self-efficacy and performance in computer software training. *Journal of Applied Psychology* 74, 6, 884–891.

[16] Graaf, M. de. 2015. *Living with robots: investigating the user acceptance of social robots in domestic environments*. Dissertation, Universiteit Twente.

[17] Groom, V., Takayama, L., Ochi, P., and Nass, C. 2009. I am my robot: the impact of robot-building and robot form on operators // I am my robot. In *HRI 2009. Proceedings of the Third ACM/IEEE Conference on Human-Robot Interaction*. ACM Press, New York, 31–36. DOI=10.1145/1514095.1514104.

[18] Heerink, M. 2011. Exploring the influence of age, gender, education and computer experience on robot acceptance by older adults. In *Proceedings of the 6th international conference on Human-robot interaction (HRI'11)*. ACM Press, New York, New York, USA, 147. DOI=10.1145/1957656.1957704.

[19] Heerink, M., Krose, B., Evers, V., and Wielinga, B. 2009. Measuring acceptance of an assistive social robot: a suggested toolkit. In *Proceedings of the 18th IEEE International Symposium on Robot and Human Interactive Communication (RO-MAN 2009)*, 528–533. DOI=10.1109/ROMAN.2009.5326320.

[20] Heerink, M., Kröse, B., Evers, V., and Wielinga, B. Assessing Acceptance of Assistive Social Agent Technology by Older Adults: the Almere Model. *Int J of Soc Robotics* 2, 4, 361–375. DOI=10.1007/s12369-010-0068-5.

[21] Heerink, M., Kröse, B. J., Wielinga, B. J., Evers, V., and others. 2006. Studying the acceptance of a robotic agent by elderly users. *International Journal of Assistive Robotics and Mechatronics* 7, 3, 33–43.

[22] Hurst, A., Tobias, J., McCoy, K. F., and Yesilada, Y. 2011. Empowering individuals with do-it-yourself assistive technology. In *ASSETS'11. Proceedings of the 13th International ACM SIGACCESS Conference on Computers and Accessibility, 24-26 October 2011, Dundee, Scotland*, K. F. McCoy and Y. Yesilada, Eds. ACM, New York, 11. DOI=10.1145/2049536.2049541.

[23] Igbaria, M. 1995. The effects of self-efficacy on computer usage. *Omega* 23, 6, 587–605.

[24] Liu, E. Z. F., Lin, C. H., and Chang, C. S. 2010. Student Satisfaction and Self-Efficacy in a Cooperative Robotics Course. *Soc Behav Personal* 38, 8, 1135–1146.

[25] Liu, E. Z. F., Lin, C. H., and Chang, C. S. 2010. Student Satisfaction and Self-Efficacy in a Cooperative Robotics Course. *Soc Behav Personal* 38, 8, 1135–1146.

[26] M. K. Lee, J. Forlizzi, S. Kiesler, P. Rybski, J. Antanitis, and S. Savetsila. 2012. Personalization in HRI: A longitudinal field experiment. In *7th ACM/IEEE International Conference on Human-Robot Interaction (HRI)*.

[27] McColl, D. and Nejat, G. 2014. Recognizing Emotional Body Language Displayed by a Human-like Social Robot. *Int J of Soc Robotics* 6, 2, 261–280.

[28] Nichols, A. L. and Maner, J. K. 2008. The Good-Subject Effect: Investigating Participant Demand Characteristics. *The Journal of General Psychology* 135, 2, 151–166.

[29] Norton, M. I., Mochon, D., and Ariely, D. 2011. The 'IKEA Effect'. When Labor Leads to Love. *SSRN Journal.*

[30] Phillips, B. and Zhao, H. 1993. Predictors of Assistive Technology Abandonment. *Assistive Technology* 5, 1, 36–45.

[31] Rosenthal-von der Pütten, A. M. and Bock, N. 2017. Development and Validation of the Self-Efficacy in Human-Robot-Interaction Scale (SE-HRI Scale). *Manuscript submitted for publication.*

[32] Rosenthal-von der Pütten, A. M. and Krämer, N. C. 2015. Individuals' Evaluations of and Attitudes Towards Potentially Uncanny Robots. *Int J of Soc Robotics.*

[33] Rosenthal-von der Pütten, A. M., Straßmann, C., and Krämer, N. C. 2016. Robots or Agents – Neither Helps You More or Less During Second Language Acquisition. In *Intelligent Virtual Agents. 16th International Conference, IVA 2016, Los Angeles, CA, USA, September 20-23, 2016, Proceedings*, D. Traum, W. Swartout, P. Khooshabeh, S. Kopp, S. Scherer and A. Leuski, Eds. Lecture notes in computer science Lecture notes in artificial intelligence 10011. Springer International Publishing; Imprint: Springer, Cham, Cham, 256–268. DOI=10.1007/978-3-319-47665-0_23.

[34] Rosenthal-von der Pütten, A. M. and Herrmann, J. 2016. Look Into My Blinking Red Eye! The Effects of Humanlike and Robot-Specific Nonverbal Behavior on Perception, Emotion, and Behavior. In *Paper presented at the annual meeting of the International Communication Association.*

[35] Saunders, J., Syrdal, D. S., Koay, K. L., Burke, N., and Dautenhahn, K. 2016. "Teach Me–Show Me" - End-User Personalization of a Smart Home and Companion Robot. *IEEE Trans. Human-Mach. Syst.* 46, 1, 27–40.

[36] Stadler, S., Weiss, A., and Tscheligi, M. 2014. I Trained this robot: The impact of pre-experience and execution behavior on robot teachers. In *The 23rd IEEE International Symposium on Robot and Human Interactive Communication.* [publisher not identified], [Place of publication not identified], 1030–1036. DOI=10.1109/ROMAN.2014.6926388.

[37] van Dijk, J. A. 2006. Digital divide research, achievements and shortcomings. *The digital divide in the twenty-first century* 34, 4, 221–235.

[38] Venkatesh, V. and Davis, F. D. 1996. A Model of the Antecedents of Perceived Ease of Use. Development and Test. *Decision Sciences* 27, 3, 451–481.

[39] Wagenmakers, E. J. 2007. A practical solution to the pervasive problems of p values. *Psychonomic Bulletin & Review* 14, 5, 779–804.

[40] White, R. W. 1959. Motivation reconsidered. The concept of competence. *Psychological Review* 66, 5, 297–333.

Author Index

www.ingramcontent.com/pod-product-compliance
Lightning Source LLC
LaVergne TN
LVHW082023200926
848481LV00010B/2915